PRENTICE HALL
LITERATURE
GRADE 10

COMMON CORE EDITION ©

Upper Saddle River, New Jersey

Boston, Massachusetts

Chandler, Arizona

Glenview, Illinois

PEARSON

ISBN-13: 978-0-13-319556-9
ISBN-10:   0-13-319556-2
6 7 8 9 10 V057 15 14 13 12

Master Teacher Board

Heather Barnes
Language Arts Instructor
Central Crossing High School
Grove City, Ohio

Lee Bromberger
English Department Chairperson
Mukwonago High School
Mukwonago, Wisconsin

Cathy Cassy
Communication Arts Curriculum Supervisor 6-12
St. Louis Public Schools
St. Louis, Missouri

Judy Castrogiavanni
English Teacher
Abington Heights School
Clarks Summit, Pennsylvania

Ann Catrillo
Sr. English & AP Teacher; Department Chairperson
East Stroudsburg High School South
East Stroudsburg, Pennsylvania

Susan Cisna
Instructor Middle School Education
Eastern Illinois University
Charleston, Illinois

Linda Fund
Reading Specialist
Ezra L. Nolan Middle School #40
Jersey City, New Jersey

Gail Hacker
Adjunct Professor
Springfield College School of Human Services
North Charleston, South Carolina

Patricia Matysik
English Department Chairperson
Belleville West Middle School
Belleville, Illinois

Gail Phelps
Literacy Intervention Coach
Oak Grove High School
Little Rock, Arkansas

Julie Rucker
Literacy Coach/English Teacher
Tift County High School
Tifton, Georgia

Kathy Ryan
Curriculum Coordinator
Rockwood Schools
St. Louis, Missouri

Matthew Scanlon
Vice Principal
Kinnelon High School
Kinnelon, New Jersey

Renee Trotier
Freshman Principal
Lafayette High School
Wildwood, Missouri

Carolyn Waters
Language Arts Supervisor
Cobb County Schools
Marietta, Georgia

Martha Wildman
Social Studies Teacher
Las Cruces Public Schools
Las Cruces, New Mexico

Melissa Williams
District Supervisor
Delsea Regional Schools
Franklinville, New Jersey

Charles Youngs
English Language Arts Facilitator
Bethel Park High School
Bethel Park, Pennsylvania

Contributing Authors

The contributing authors guided the direction and philosophy of Pearson Prentice Hall Literature. *Working with the development team, they helped to build the pedagogical integrity of the program and to ensure its relevance for today's teachers and students.*

Grant Wiggins, Ed.D., is the President of Authentic Education in Hopewell, New Jersey. He earned his Ed.D. from Harvard University and his B.A. from St. John's College in Annapolis. Grant consults with schools, districts, and state education departments on a variety of reform matters; organizes conferences and workshops; and develops print materials and Web resources on curricular change. He is the coauthor, with Jay McTighe, of Understanding by Design and The Understanding by Design Handbook, the award-winning and highly successful materials on curriculum published by ASCD. His work has been supported by the Pew Charitable Trusts, the Geraldine R. Dodge Foundation, and the National Science Foundation. *The Association for Supervision of Curriculum Development (ASCD), publisher of the "Understanding by Design Handbook" co-authored by Grant Wiggins and registered owner of the trademark "Understanding by Design", has not authorized, approved, or sponsored this work and is in no way affiliated with Pearson or its products.*

Jeff Anderson has worked with struggling writers and readers for almost 20 years. Anderson's specialty is the integration of grammar and editing instruction into the processes of reading and writing. He has published two books, *Mechanically Inclined: Building Grammar, Usage, and Style into Writer's Workshop* and *Everyday Editing: Inviting Students to Develop Skill and Craft in Writer's Workshop,* as well as a DVD, *The Craft of Grammar.* Anderson's work has appeared in *English Journal.* Anderson won the NCTE Paul and Kate Farmer Award for his *English Journal* article on teaching grammar in context.

Arnetha F. Ball, Ph.D., is a  Professor at Stanford University. Her areas of expertise include language and literacy studies of diverse student populations, research on writing instruction, and teacher preparation for working with diverse populations. She is the author of *African American Literacies Unleashed* with Dr. Ted Lardner, and *Multicultural Strategies for Education and Social Change.*

Sheridan Blau is Professor of Education and English at the University of California, Santa Barbara, where he directs the South Coast Writing Project and the Literature Institute for Teachers. He has served in senior advisory roles for such groups as the National Board for Professional Teaching Standards, the College Board, and the American Board for Teacher Education. Blau served for twenty years on the National Writing Project Advisory Board and Task Force, and is a former president of NCTE. Blau is the author of *The Literature Workshop: Teaching Texts and Their Readers,* which was named by the Conference on English Education as the 2004 Richard Meade Award winner for outstanding research in English education.

 William G. Brozo, Ph.D., is a Professor of Literacy at George Mason University in Fairfax, Virginia. He has taught reading and language arts in junior and senior high school and is the author of numerous texts on literacy development. Dr. Brozo's work focuses on building capacity among teacher leaders, enriching the literate culture of schools, enhancing the literate lives of boys, and making teaching more responsive to the needs of all students. His recent publications include *Bright Beginnings for Boys: Engaging Young Boys in Active Literacy* and the *Adolescent Literacy Inventory.*

Doug Buehl is a teacher, author, and  national literacy consultant. He is the author of *Classroom Strategies for Interactive Learning* and coauthor of *Reading and the High School Student: Strategies to Enhance Literacy;* and *Strategies to Enhance Literacy and Learning in Middle School Content Area Classrooms.*

Jim Cummins, Ph.D., is a professor in the Modern Language Centre at the University of Toronto. He is the author of numerous publications, including *Negotiating Identities: Education for Empowerment in a Diverse Society.* Cummins coined the acronyms BICS and CAPT to help differentiate the type of language ability students need for success.

Harvey Daniels, Ph.D., has been a classroom teacher, writing project director, author, and university professor. "Smokey" serves as an international consultant to schools, districts, and educational agencies. He is known for his work on student-led book clubs, as recounted in *Literature Circles: Voice and Choice in Book Clubs & Reading Groups* and *Mini Lessons for Literature Circles.* Recent works include *Subjects Matter: Every Teacher's Guide to Content-Area Reading* and *Content Area Writing: Every Teacher's Guide.*

Jane Feber taught language arts in  Jacksonville, Florida, for 36 years. Her innovative approach to instruction has earned her several awards, including the NMSA Distinguished Educator Award, the NCTE Edwin A. Hoey Award, the Gladys Prior Award for Teaching Excellence, and the Florida Council of Teachers of English Teacher of the Year Award. She is a National Board Certified Teacher, past president of the Florida Council of Teachers of English and is the author of *Creative Book Reports* and *Active Word Play.*

Danling Fu, Ph.D., is Professor of Language and Culture in the College of Education at the University of Florida. She researches and provides inservice to public schools nationally, focusing on literacy instruction for new immigrant students. Fu's books include *My Trouble is My English* and *An Island of English* addressing English language learners in the secondary schools. She has authored chapters in the *Handbook of Adolescent Literacy Research* and in *Adolescent Literacy: Turning Promise to Practice.*

Kelly Gallagher is a full-time English teacher at Magnolia High School in Anaheim, California. He is the former co-director of the South Basin Writing Project at California State University, Long Beach. Gallagher wrote *Reading Reasons: Motivational Mini-Lessons for the Middle and High School, Deeper Reading: Comprehending Challenging Texts 4-12,* and *Teaching Adolescent Writers.* Gallagher won the Secondary Award of Classroom Excellence from the California Association of Teachers of English—the state's top English teacher honor.

Sharroky Hollie, Ph.D., is an assistant professor at California State University, Dominguez Hills, and an urban literacy visiting professor at Webster University, St. Louis. Hollie's work focuses on professional development, African American education, and second language methodology. He is a contributing author in two texts on culturally and linguistically responsive teaching. He is the Executive Director of the Center for Culturally Responsive Teaching and Learning and the co-founding director of the Culture and Language Academy of Success, an independent charter school in Los Angeles.

Dr. Donald J. Leu, Ph.D., teaches  at the University of Connecticut and holds a joint appointment in Curriculum and Instruction and in Educational Psychology. He directs the New Literacies Research Lab and is a member of the Board of Directors of the International Reading Association. Leu studies the skills required to read, write, and learn with Internet technologies. His research has been funded by groups including the U.S. Department of Education, the National Science Foundation, and the Bill & Melinda Gates Foundation.

Jon Scieszka founded GUYS READ,  a nonprofit literacy initiative for boys, to call attention to the problem of getting boys connected with reading. In 2008, he was named the first U.S. National Ambassador for Young People's Literature by the Library of Congress. Scieszka taught from first grade to eighth grade for ten years in New York City, drawing inspiration from his students to write *The True Story of the 3 Little Pigs!, The Stinky Cheese Man,* the *Time Warp Trio* series of chapter books, and the *Trucktown* series of books for beginning readers.

Sharon Vaughn, Ph.D., teaches at the University of Texas at Austin. She is the previous Editor-in-Chief of the *Journal of Learning Disabilities* and the co-editor of *Learning Disabilities Research and Practice.* She is the recipient of the American Education Research Association SIG Award for Outstanding Researcher. Vaughn's work focuses on effective practices for enhancing reading outcomes for students with reading difficulties. She is the author of more than 100 articles, and numerous books designed to improve research-based practices in the classroom.

Karen K. Wixson is Dean of the School of Education at the University of North Carolina, Greensboro. She has published widely in the areas of literacy curriculum, instruction, and assessment. Wixson has been an advisor to the National Research Council and helped develop the National Assessment of Educational Progress (NAEP) reading tests. She is a past member of the IRA Board of Directors and co-chair of the IRA Commission on RTI. Recently, Wixson served on the English Language Arts Work Team that was part of the Common Core State Standards Initiative.

Each unit addresses a BIG Question to enrich exploration of literary concepts and reading strategies.

Introductory Unit: Common Core Student Workshops   xlviii

Building Academic Vocabulary
Writing an Objective Summary
Comprehending Complex Texts
Analyzing Arguments

Unit 1: Fiction and Nonfiction   1

Is there a difference between reality and truth?

Literary Analysis Workshop

Literary/Informational Skills:	Theme
	Central Idea
Reading Skills:	Make Predictions
	Cause and Effect
Writing Workshop:	Autobiographical Narrative
	Cause-and-Effect Essay
Vocabulary Workshop:	Using a Dictionary and Thesaurus
Communications Workshop:	Analyzing Media Messages

Unit 2: Short Stories   220

Can progress be made without conflict?

Literary Analysis Workshop

Literary Skills:	Character
	Story Structure
Reading Skills:	Make Inferences
	Draw Conclusions
Writing Workshop:	Short Story
	Problem-and-Solution Essay
Vocabulary Workshop:	Word Origins
Communications Workshop:	Viewing and Evaluating a Speech

Unit 3: Types of Nonfiction   440

What kind of knowledge changes our lives?

Literary Analysis Workshop

Informational Skills:	Author's Point of View and Purpose
	Development of Ideas
	Word Choice and Tone
Reading Skills:	Main Idea
	Evaluate Persuasion
Writing Workshop:	Letter to the Editor
	Persuasive Essay
Vocabulary Workshop:	Words With Multiple Meanings
Communications Workshop:	Delivering a Persuasive Speech

Unit 4: Poetry   624
Does all communication serve a positive purpose?

Literary Analysis Workshop

Literary Skills:	Figurative Language
	Diction and Syntax
Reading Skills:	Read Fluently
	Paraphrase
Writing Workshop:	Descriptive Essay
	Analytic Response to Literature
Vocabulary Workshop:	Connotation and Denotation
Communications Workshop:	Delivering an Oral Interpretation
	of a Literary Work

Unit 5: Drama   788
To what extent does experience determine what we perceive?

Literary Analysis Workshop

Literary Skills:	Character Development
	Conflict
	Theme
Reading Skills:	Summarize
	Reading Shakespearean Drama
Writing Workshop:	Reflective Essay
	Research Report
Vocabulary Workshop:	Borrowed and Foreign Words
Communications Workshop:	Delivering a Multimedia Presentation

Unit 6: Themes in Literature: Heroes and Dreamers   1044
Can anyone be a hero?

Literary Analysis Workshop

Literary Skills:	Theme
	Cultural Context
Reading Skills:	Analyze Cultural Context
	Compare Worldviews
Writing Workshop:	Technical Document
	Comparison-and-Contrast Essay
Vocabulary Workshop:	Idioms, Jargon, and
	Technical Terms
Communications Workshop:	Comparing Media Coverage

Resources

Glossary	R1
Literary Handbook	R15
Writing Handbook	R31
Grammar, Usage, and Mechanics Handbook	R50

? Is there a difference between *reality* and *truth?*

Introducing the Big Question			2
Ⓒ **Literary Analysis Workshop:** Fiction and Nonfiction			4
Determining Theme in Fiction		INSTRUCTIONAL ESSAY	6
Determining Central Ideas in Nonfiction		INSTRUCTIONAL ESSAY	7
Theme in Fiction	*Ray Bradbury*	***from* Fahrenheit 451** EXEMPLAR Ⓒ	FICTION	9
Theme in Fiction	*Susan Vreeland*	**Magdalena Looking**	FICTION	10
Central Idea in Nonfiction	*Anna Quindlen*	***from* A Quilt of a Country** EXEMPLAR Ⓒ	ESSAY	21
Central Idea in Nonfiction	*Susan Vreeland*	**Artful Research**	ESSAY	23

Leveled Selections

Make Predictions Plot and Foreshadowing	*W. W. Jacobs*	**The Monkey's Paw**	SHORT STORY	32
	Louise Erdrich	**The Leap**	SHORT STORY	46
	Integrated Language Skills			56

Leveled Selections

Make Predictions Author's Perspective	*Lynne Cox*	***from* Swimming to Antarctica**	AUTOBIOGRAPHY	62
	Literature in Context: Antarctica	INFORMATIONAL TEXT	69
	Maya Angelou	**Occupation: Conductorette** ***from* I Know Why the Caged Bird Sings** EXEMPLAR Ⓒ	AUTOBIOGRAPHY	78
	Literature in Context: San Francisco and the Gold Rushes	INFORMATIONAL TEXT	83
	Integrated Language Skills			86
	✓ **Test Practice: Reading** Make Predictions ▪ Writing for Assessment		88

★ INFORMATIONAL TEXT HIGHLIGHTED

Analyze Structure and Format

ⓒ **Reading for Information:** Analyzing Expository Texts   90

Ann Douglas   **Feel the City's Pulse?
It's Be-Bop, Man!**   EXPOSITORY TEXT   91

Healdsburg Jazz Festival Winter 2007   EXPOSITORY TEXT   93

Comparing Informational Texts ▪ Timed Writing   95

Comparing Style

Comparing Literary Works   96

Langston Hughes   **Marian Anderson,
Famous Concert Singer**   BIOGRAPHY   98

Sandra Cisneros   **Tepeyac**   SHORT STORY   104

Compare Styles ▪ Timed Writing   107

Writing Workshop: Narrative Text: Autobiographical Narrative   108

Writer's Toolbox: Telling the Story   109

Writer's Toolbox: Using Possessive Nouns Correctly   111

Cause and Effect
Conflict and Resolution

Leveled Selections

Jack Finney   **Contents of the Dead Man's Pocket**   SHORT STORY   118

Literature in Context: Physics   INFORMATIONAL TEXT   129

Anita Desai   **Games at Twilight**   SHORT STORY   138

Integrated Language Skills   150

Cause and Effect
Author's Purpose

Leveled Selections

Rachel Carson   **The Marginal World**   ESSAY   156

Penny Le Couteur and Jay Burreson
Making History With Vitamin C   ESSAY   168

Literature in Context: The Voyages of Captain James Cook   INFORMATIONAL TEXT   175

Integrated Language Skills   178

✓ **Test Practice: Reading** Cause and Effect ▪ Writing for Assessment   180

PHLit Online!
www.PHLitOnline.com
Interactive resources provide personalized instruction and activities online.

Evaluate Sources

© Reading for Information: Analyzing Functional and Expository Texts   182

Nigel Strudwick	**Egyptology Resources**	FUNCTIONAL TEXT	183
Renée Friedman	**Interactive Dig**	EXPOSITORY TEXT	185

Comparing Functional and Expository Texts ▪ Timed Writing   187

Comparing Irony and Paradox

Comparing Literary Works   188

R. K. Narayan	**Like the Sun**	SHORT STORY	190
Saki (H. H. Munro)	**The Open Window**	SHORT STORY	195

Comparing Irony and Paradox ▪ Timed Writing   199

Writing Workshop: Explanatory Text: Cause-and-Effect Essay   200

Jeff Anderson, M.Ed.	**What Do You Notice?** Structure and Style	200
Susan Vreeland	**Writers on Writing:** On Showing Causes and Effects	203

Writer's Toolbox: Revising Pronoun-Antecedent Agreement   205

Vocabulary Workshop: Using a Dictionary and Thesaurus   208

Communications Workshop: Analyzing Media Messages   210

© Common Core Assessment Workshop: Cumulative Review   212
© Common Core Assessment Workshop: Performance Tasks   216

© Independent Reading   218

William Golding	Lord of the Flies	FICTION
Alice Walker	Revolutionary Petunias and Other Poems EXEMPLAR ©	POETRY
O. Henry	41 Stories EXEMPLAR ©	FICTION
George Orwell	Animal Farm	FICTION
Eugene Ionesco	Rhinoceros EXEMPLAR ©	DRAMA
Wendy Thompson	The Illustrated Book of Great Composers EXEMPLAR ©	NONFICTION
Euclid	Euclid's Elements EXEMPLAR ©	NONFICTION
Charles C. Mann	Before Columbus: The Americas of 1491 EXEMPLAR ©	NONFICTION

Skills at a Glance

This page provides a quick look at the skills you will learn and practice in Unit 1.

Reading Skills

Make Predictions
  Use Your Prior Knowledge
  Ask Questions
Cause and Effect
  Reflect on Key Details
  Reread

Reading for Information

Analyze Structure and Format
Evaluate Sources

Literary Analysis

Theme
Central Idea
Plot and Foreshadowing
Author's Perspective
Comparing Styles
Conflict and Resolution
Author's Purpose
Comparing Irony and Paradox

Vocabulary

Big Question Vocabulary
Prefixes: *pro-, super-, inter-, ab-*
Roots: *-cred-, -strict-, -ver-, -ven-*
Using a Dictionary and Thesaurus
Independent Reading

Conventions

Common and Proper Nouns
Abstract and Concrete Nouns
Using Possessive Nouns Correctly
Personal Pronouns
Relative Pronouns
Revising Pronoun-Antecedent Agreement

Writing

Writing About the Big Question
Sequel
Description
Anecdote
Proposal
Timed Writing
Writing Workshop: Narrative Text: Autobiographical Narrative
Writing Workshop: Explanatory Text: Cause-and-Effect Essay

Speaking and Listening

Interview
Problem-Solving Group
Analyzing Media Messages

Research and Technology

Daily Observation Journal
Spreadsheet

 Common Core State Standards Addressed in This Unit

Reading Literature RL.9-10.2, RL.9-10.4, RL.9-10.5, RL.9-10.10

Reading Informational Text RI.9-10.2, RI.9-10.3, RI.9-10.4, RI.9-10.6, RI.9-10.8, RI.9-10.10

Writing W.9-10.2, W.9-10.2.a, W.9-10.2.b, W.9-10.2.c, W.9-10.2.d, W.9-10.2.e, W.9-10.2.f, W.9-10.3, W.9-10.3.a, W.9-10.3.c, W.9-10.3.d, W.9-10.3.e, W.9-10.5, W.9-10.9, W.9-10.9.a, W.9-10.9.b, W.9-10.10

Speaking and Listening SL.9-10.1, SL.9-10.1.a, SL.9-10.1.b, SL.9-10.1.c, SL.9-10.1.d, SL.9-10.3, SL.9-10.5

Language L.9-10.1, L.9-10.1.b, L.9-10.2, L.9-10.2.c, L.9-10.4, L.9-10.4.a, L.9-10.4.b, L.9-10.4.c, L.9-10.4.d, L.9-10.5, L.9-10.6

[For the full wording of the standards, see the standards chart in the front of your textbook.]

Can progress be made without *conflict?*

Introducing the Big Question			222
Ⓒ **Literary Analysis Workshop:** Short Stories			224
Analyzing Characters in a Short Story		INSTRUCTIONAL ESSAY	226
Analyzing Structure in a Short Story		INSTRUCTIONAL ESSAY	227
Langston Hughes	**Early Autumn**	SHORT STORY	229
C. J. Cherryh	**The Threads of Time**	SHORT STORY	231

Character
Story Structure

Make Inferences
Character and
Characterization

Leveled Selections			
William Melvin Kelley	**A Visit to Grandmother**	SHORT STORY	242
Literature in Context: The Great Migration		INFORMATIONAL TEXT	249
Anton Chekhov	**A Problem**	SHORT STORY	256
Integrated Language Skills			266

Make Inferences
Setting

Leveled Selections			
Josephina Niggli	**The Street of the Cañon**	SHORT STORY	272
Literature in Context: Spanish Vocabulary		INFORMATIONAL TEXT	274
Ray Bradbury	**There Will Come Soft Rains**	SHORT STORY	284
Integrated Language Skills			294

✓ **Test Practice: Reading** Make Inferences ▪ Writing for Assessment		296

Analyze Texts
to Extend Ideas

Ⓒ **Reading for Information:** Analyzing Expository Texts			298
Joseph D. Exline, Ed.D., *Jay M. Pasachoff, Ph.D., et al.* **Tides**		EXPOSITORY TEXT	299
NASA News	**Black Water Turns the Tide on Florida Coral**	EXPOSITORY TEXT	303
Comparing Expository Texts ▪ Timed Writing			305

★ INFORMATIONAL TEXT HIGHLIGHTED

Comparing Points of View

Comparing Literary Works 306

O. Henry **One Thousand Dollars** SHORT STORY 308

Stephen Vincent Benét **By the Waters of Babylon** SHORT STORY 314

Literature in Context: The Babylonian Captivity INFORMATIONAL TEXT 321

Compare Points of View ▪ Timed Writing 327

Writing Workshop: Narrative Text: Short Story 328

Writer's Toolbox: Using Your Imagination 329

Writer's Toolbox: Revising to Apply Consistent Verb Tense 331

Draw Conclusions Theme

Leveled Selections

Leo Tolstoy **How Much Land Does a Man Need?** SHORT STORY 338

Literature in Context: The Emancipation of the Serfs INFORMATIONAL TEXT 350

Chinua Achebe **Civil Peace** SHORT STORY 358

Literature in Context: Nigerian Civil War INFORMATIONAL TEXT 362

Integrated Language Skills 366

Draw Conclusions Symbolism and Allegory

Leveled Selections

Edgar Allan Poe **The Masque of the Red Death** SHORT STORY 372

Italo Calvino **The Garden of Stubborn Cats** SHORT STORY 384

Literature in Context: Architectural Features INFORMATIONAL TEXT 388

Integrated Language Skills 398

✓ **Test Practice: Reading** Draw Conclusions ▪ Writing for Assessment 400

Paraphrase to Connect Ideas

© **Reading for Information:** Analyzing Arguments and Expository Texts 402

The New York Times, November 10, 1999 **Editorial on the Anniversary of the Fall of the Berlin Wall** ARGUMENT 403

Marco Mielcarek **Voices from the Wall** EXPOSITORY TEXT 405

Comparing Argumentative and Expository Texts ▪ Timed Writing 407

Interactive resources provide personalized instruction and activities online.
www.PHLitOnline.com

Comparing Tone

Comparing Literary Works   408

Luisa Valenzuela	**The Censors**	SHORT STORY	410
Pat Mora	**The Leader in the Mirror**	REFLECTIVE ESSAY	414

Compare Tone ▪ Timed Writing   419

Writing Workshop: Argument: Problem-and-Solution Essay   420

Jeff Anderson, M.Ed.	**What Do You Notice?** Word Choice	420
C. J. Cherryh	**Writers on Writing:** On Revising to Tighten Sentences	423

Writer's Toolbox: Subject-Verb Agreement   425

Vocabulary Workshop: Word Origins   428

Communications Workshop: Viewing and Evaluating a Speech   430

ⓒ Common Core Assessment Workshop: Cumulative Review   432

ⓒ Common Core Assessment Workshop: Performance Tasks   436

ⓒ Independent Reading   438

Edgar Allan Poe	The Fall of the House of Usher and Other Tales	FICTION
Anton Chekhov	Anton Chekhov: Selected Stories	FICTION
Percy Bysshe Shelley	The Complete Poems of Percy Bysshe Shelley EXEMPLAR ⓒ	POETRY
Mark Twain	The Prince and the Pauper	FICTION
C. J. Cherryh	The Collected Short Fiction of C. J. Cherryh	FICTION
Jacob Bronowski and Millicent Selsam	Biography of an Atom EXEMPLAR ⓒ	NONFICTION
Booker T. Washington	Up from Slavery	NONFICTION
Peter Ackroyd	Ancient Rome: Voyages Through Time	NONFICTION

Skills at a Glance

This page provides a quick look at the skills you will learn and practice in Unit 2.

Reading Skills

Make Inferences
  Use Your Own Prior Knowledge and Experience
  Read On
Draw Conclusions
  Recognize Key Details
  Identify Patterns

Reading for Information

Analyze Text to Extend Ideas
Paraphrase to Connect Ideas

Literary Analysis

Character
Story Structure
Character and Characterization
Setting
Comparing Points of View
Theme
Symbolism and Allegory
Comparing Tones

Vocabulary

Big Question Vocabulary
Prefixes: *dis-, com-*
Suffixes: *-ence, -able, -ity, -ic, -tion, -id*
Word Origins

Conventions

The Principal Parts of Regular Verbs
Irregular Verbs
Revising to Apply Consistent Verb Tense
Action and Linking Verbs
Active and Passive Voice
Subject-Verb Agreement

Writing

Writing About the Big Question
Retelling
Letter / Book Review
Character Analysis
Narrative
Timed Writing
Writing Workshop: Narration: Short Story
Writing Workshop: Argument: Problem-
  and-Solution Essay

Speaking and Listening

Oral Reading
Group Discussion
Viewing and Evaluating a Speech

Research and Technology

Report on Sources
Research Summary

 **Common Core State Standards
Addressed in This Unit**

Reading Literature RL.9-10.1, RL.9-10.2, RL.9-10.3,
RL.9-10.4, RL.9-10.5, RL.9-10.6, RL.9-10.10
Reading Informational Text RI.9-10.4, RI.9-10.6,
RI.9-10.10
Writing W.9-10.1, W.9-10.2, W.9-10.2.a, W.9-10.2.b,
W.9-10.2.c, W.9-10.2.d, W.9-10.3, W.9-10.3.a,
W.9-10.3.b, W.9-10.3.c, W.9-10.3.d, W.9-10.3.e, W.9-10.5,
W.9-10.8, W.9-10.9.a, W.9-10.10
Speaking and Listening SL.9-10.1, SL.9-10.1.c,
SL.9-10.1.d, SL.9-10.2, SL.9-10.3, SL.9-10.6
Language L.9-10.3, L.9-10.4, L.9-10.4.b, L.9-10.4.c,
L.9-10.5, L.9-10.5.b, L.9-10.6
[For the full wording of the standards, see the standards
chart in the front of your textbook.]

What kind of *knowledge* changes our lives?

Introducing the Big Question		442
ⓒ **Literary Analysis Workshop:** Essays and Speeches		444
Analyzing the Development of Ideas	INSTRUCTIONAL ESSAY	446
Ronald Reagan · **Address to Students at Moscow State University** EXEMPLAR ⓒ	HISTORICAL ACCOUNT	449
Erik Weihenmayer · **Everest *from* Touch the Top of the World**	NARRATIVE ESSAY	452

Author's Point of View and Purpose
Development of Ideas
Word Choice and Tone

Main Idea
Expository Essay

Leveled Selections		
Alexander Petrunkevitch · **The Spider and the Wasp**	ESSAY	464
Literature in Context: Studying Animal Behavior	INFORMATIONAL TEXT	468
Dava Sobel · ***from* Longitude**	ESSAY	474
Literature in Context: Longitude and Latitude	INFORMATIONAL TEXT	478
Integrated Language Skills		484

Main Idea
Reflective Essay

Leveled Selections		
Dorothy West · **The Sun Parlor**	REFLECTIVE ESSAY	490
Rudolfo A. Anaya · ***from* In Commemoration: One Million Volumes**	REFLECTIVE ESSAY	500
Literature in Context: Mexican American Pride	INFORMATIONAL TEXT	503
Integrated Language Skills		508
✓ **Test Practice: Reading** Main Idea ▪ Writing for Assessment		510

Follow and Critique
Technical Directions

ⓒ **Reading for Information:** Analyzing Functional Texts		512
How to Use a Compass	FUNCTIONAL TEXT	513
GPS Quick-Start Guide	FUNCTIONAL TEXT	515
Comparing Functional Texts ▪ Timed Writing		517

★ INFORMATIONAL TEXT HIGHLIGHTED

Comparing Humorous Writing

Comparing Literary Works   518

Mark Twain   **A Toast to the Oldest Inhabitant:**
                    The Weather of New England   HUMOROUS SPEECH   520

James Thurber   **The Dog That Bit People**   HUMOROUS ESSAY   525

Compare Humorous Writing ▪ Timed Writing   531

Writing Workshop: Argument: Letter to the Editor   532

Writer's Toolbox: Finding Your Voice   533

Writer's Toolbox: Revising to Combine Short Sentences   535

FOCUS ON ARGUMENT

Evaluate Persuasion Persuasive Writing and Rhetorical Devices

Leveled Selections

Elie Wiesel   **Keep Memory Alive** EXEMPLAR ⓖ   SPEECH   542

Alexander Solzhenitsyn *from* **Nobel Lecture**   SPEECH   548

Literature in Context: Repression in the Soviet Union   INFORMATIONAL TEXT   550

Integrated Language Skills   554

Leveled Selections

Evaluate Persuasion Analytic and Interpretive Essays

Theodore H. White   **The American Idea**   ESSAY   560

Literature in Context: The American Revolution   INFORMATIONAL TEXT   563

Richard Mühlberger   **What Makes a Degas a Degas?**   ESSAY   568

Integrated Language Skills   574

✓ **Test Practice: Reading** Evaluate Persuasion ▪ Writing for Assessment   576

PHLit
Online!
www.PHLitOnline.com
Interactive resources provide personalized instruction and activities online.

Analyze Text Structures

ⓒ **Reading for Information:** Analyzing Expository and Functional Texts — 578

Thomas A. Hill — **The History of the Guitar** — EXPOSITORY TEXT — 579

California State University at Fullerton Course Catalog — FUNCTIONAL TEXT — 581

Comparing Expository and Functional Texts ▪ Timed Writing — 583

Comparing Authors' Purposes

Comparing Literary Works — 584

Yoshiko Uchida — ***from* Desert Exile: The Uprooting of a Japanese-American Family** — AUTOBIOGRAPHY — 586

N. Scott Momaday — ***from* The Way to Rainy Mountain** — REFLECTIVE ESSAY — 595

Compare Authors' Purposes ▪ Timed Writing — 603

Writing Workshop: Argument: Persuasive Essay — 604

Jeff Anderson, M.Ed. — **What Do You Notice?** Voice and Tone — 604

Erik Weihenmayer — **Writers on Writing:** On Persuasive Techniques — 607

Writer's Toolbox: Revising to Create Parallelism — 609

Vocabulary Workshop: Words With Multiple Meanings — 612

Communications Workshop: Delivering a Persuasive Speech — 614

ⓒ **Common Core Assessment Workshop:** Cumulative Review — 616

ⓒ **Common Core Assessment Workshop:** Performance Tasks — 620

ⓒ **Independent Reading** — 622

Elie Wiesel — Night — NONFICTION

Gordon Hutner, editor — Immigrant Voices: Twenty-Four Narratives on Becoming an American — NONFICTION

Prentice Hall — Today's Nonfiction — NONFICTION

Eric Weihenmayer — Touch the Top of the World — NONFICTION

Dee Brown — Bury My Heart at Wounded Knee EXEMPLAR ⓒ — NONFICTION

Joan Dash — The Longitude Prize EXEMPLAR ⓒ — NONFICTION

Harper Lee — To Kill a Mockingbird EXEMPLAR ⓒ — FICTION

Julia Alvarez — In the Time of the Butterflies EXEMPLAR ⓒ — FICTION

Skills at a Glance

This page provides a quick look at the skills you will learn and practice in Unit 3.

Reading Skills

Main Idea
  Summarize
Ask Questions
Evaluate Persuasion
  Persuasive Techniques
  Distinguish Between Fact and Opinion

Reading for Information

Follow and Critique Technical Directions
Analyze Text Structures

Literary Analysis

Author's Point of View and Purpose
Rhetorical Mode
Word Choice and Tone
Expository Essay
Reflective Essay
Comparing Humorous Writing
Persuasive Writing and Rhetorical Devices
Analytic and Interpretive Essays
Comparing Authors' Purposes

Vocabulary

Big Question Vocabulary
Prefixes: *suc-, para-, em-, im-*
Roots: *-tact-, -tang-, -fig-, -scend-, -jur-*
Words With Multiple Meanings

Conventions

Direct and Indirect Objects
Subject Complements
Revising to Combine Short Sentences
Degrees of Adverbs
Degrees of Adjectives
Revising to Create Parallelism

Writing

Writing About the Big Question
Business Letter
Memoir
Letter
Critique
Timed Writing
Writing Workshop: Argument: Letter to the Editor
Writing Workshop: Argument: Persuasive Essay

Speaking and Listening

Humorous Persuasive Speech
Oral Recollection
Debate
Delivering a Persuasive Speech

Research and Technology

Cover Letter and Résumé

 Common Core State Standards Addressed in This Unit

Reading Literature RL.9-10.10
Reading Informational Text RI.9-10.2, RI.9-10.3, RI.9-10.4, RI.9-10.5, RI.9-10.6, RI.9-10.7, RI.9-10.8, RI.9-10.9, RI.9-10.10
Writing W.9-10.1, W.9-10.1.a, W.9-10.1.b, W.9-10.1.c, W.9-10.1.d, W.9-10.1.e, W.9-10.2, W.9-10.2.a, W.9-10.2.d, W.9-10.2.e, W.9-10.3.a, W.9-10.3.d, W.9-10.3.e, W.9-10.4, W.9-10.5, W.9-10.7, W.9-10.9.b, W.9-10.10
Speaking and Listening SL.9-10.1, SL.9-10.1.a, SL.9-10.3, SL.9-10.4, SL.9-10.6
Language L.9-10.1, L.9-10.1.a, L.9-10.2.c, L.9-10.3, L.9-10.4, L.9-10.4.a, L.9-10.4.b, L.9-10.4.c, L.9-10.4.d, L.9-10.5, L.9-10.6
[For the full wording of the standards, see the standards chart in the front of your textbook.]

Does all *communication* serve a positive purpose?

Introducing the Big Question			626
ⓒ **Literary Analysis Workshop:** Poetry			628
Determining Meaning and Tone		INSTRUCTIONAL ESSAY	632
Jimmy Santiago Baca	**I Am Offering This Poem** EXEMPLAR ⓒ	POEM	633
Cornelius Eady	**The Poetic Interpretation of the Twist/ The Empty Dance Shoes**	POEMS	634

Figurative Language Meaning and Tone

Leveled Selections

Read Fluently The Speaker in Poetry

Poetry Collection 1

Alexander Pushkin	**The Bridegroom**	POEM	642
Federico García Lorca	**The Guitar**	POEM	649
Elizabeth Bishop	**The Fish**	POEM	650
Rudyard Kipling	**Danny Deever**	POEM	652

Poetry Collection 2

Robert Frost	**Mowing**	POEM	658
Denise Levertov	**A Tree Telling of Orpheus**	POEM	659
Naomi Shihab Nye	**Making a Fist**	POEM	664
William Carlos Williams	**Spring and All**	POEM	665
Integrated Language Skills			668

Leveled Selections

Read Fluently Poetic Forms

Poetry Collection 3

James Weldon Johnson	**My City**	POEM	677
Dylan Thomas	**Do Not Go Gentle into That Good Night**	POEM	679
Minamoto no Toshiyori	**The clustering clouds . . .**	POEM	680
Ki no Tsurayuki	**When I went to visit . . .**	POEM	680

Poetry Collection 4

Theodore Roethke	**The Waking**	POEM	685
William Shakespeare	**Sonnet 18**	POEM	687
Priest Jakuren	**One cannot ask loneliness . . .**	POEM	688
Ono Komachi	**Was it that I went to sleep . . .**	POEM	688
Integrated Language Skills			690

✓ **Test Practice: Reading** Read Fluently ▪ Writing for Assessment	692

INFORMATIONAL TEXT HIGHLIGHTED

Make Predictions: Purpose

Reading for Information: Analyzing Functional Texts 694

Folger Shakespeare Library **Library Hours and Exhibit Placards** FUNCTIONAL TEXT 695

Atlanta-Fulton Public Library System: Borrower Services FUNCTIONAL TEXT 697

Comparing Functional Texts ▪ Timed Writing 699

Comparing Tone and Mood

Comparing Literary Works 700

Gabriela Mistral **Fear** POEM 702

Gwendolyn Brooks **The Bean Eaters** POEM 703

Umberto Eco **How to React to Familiar Faces** ANALYTIC ESSAY 704

Compare Tone and Mood ▪ Timed Writing 707

Writing Workshop: Explanatory Text: Descriptive Essay 708

Writer's Toolbox: Creating a Memorable Image 709

Writer's Toolbox: Revising to Vary Sentence Patterns 711

Paraphrase Figurative Language

Leveled Selections

Poetry Collection 5

Emily Dickinson **The Wind—tapped like a tired Man** POEM 718

Yusef Komunyakaa **Glory** POEM 720

Eve Merriam **Metaphor** POEM 722

Poetry Collection 6

Edna St. Vincent Millay **Conscientious Objector** POEM 726

Dahlia Ravikovitch **Pride** POEM 727

Emily Dickinson **Tell all the Truth but tell it slant—** POEM 728

Integrated Language Skills 730

Paraphrase Sound Devices

Leveled Selections

Poetry Collection 7

Langston Hughes **The Weary Blues** POEM 736

John McCrae **In Flanders Fields** POEM 738

Carl Sandburg **Jazz Fantasia** POEM 739

Poetry Collection 8

Robert Browning **Meeting at Night** POEM 744

Alfred, Lord Tennyson **The Kraken** POEM 745

Jean Toomer	**Reapers**	POEM	746
Integrated Language Skills			748

✓ **Test Practice: Reading** Paraphrase ▪ Writing for Assessment — 750

Synthesize: Make Generalizations

ⓒ **Reading for Information:** Analyzing Functional and Expository Texts — 752

Dorling Kindersley	**Mali**	FUNCTIONAL TEXT	753
Stefan Lovgren	**Will All the Blue Men End Up in Timbuktu?**	EXPOSITORY TEXT	755
Comparing Functional and Expository Texts ▪ Timed Writing			757

Comparing Theme

Comparing Literary Works — 758

Billy Joel	**Hold Fast Your Dreams—and Trust Your Mistakes**	SPEECH	760
Bei Dao	**All**	POEM	764
Shu Ting	**Also All**	POEM	765
Compare Theme ▪ Timed Writing			767

Writing Workshop: Explanatory Text: Analytic Response to Literature — 768

Jeff Anderson, M.Ed.	**What Do You Notice?** Expressing Ideas Clearly	768
Cornelius Eady	**Writers on Writing:** On Writing Poetry About Music	771
Writer's Toolbox: Revising Common Usage Problems		773

Vocabulary Workshop: Connotation and Denotation — 776

Communications Workshop: Delivering an Oral Interpretation of a Literary Work — 778

ⓒ **Common Core Assessment Workshop:** Cumulative Review — 780

ⓒ **Common Core Assessment Workshop:** Performance Tasks — 784

ⓒ **Independent Reading** — 786

Jimmy Santiago Baca	Immigrants in Our Own Land and Selected Early Poems EXEMPLAR ⓒ	POETRY
Edgar Allan Poe	The Complete Poetry of Edgar Allan Poe EXEMPLAR ⓒ	POETRY
Willa Cather	The Song of the Lark	FICTION
Cornelius Eady	Victims of the Latest Dance Craze	POETRY
James Weldon Johnson	Lift Every Voice and Sing EXEMPLAR ⓒ	POETRY
Mark Twain	Roughing It	NONFICTION
Prentice Hall	Native American Literature	NONFICTION
E. H. Gombrich	The Story of Art EXEMPLAR ⓒ	NONFICTION

Skills at a Glance

This page provides a quick look at the skills you will learn and practice in Unit 4.

Reading Skills

Read Fluently

  Adjust Your Reading Rate

  Preview

Paraphrase

  Picture the Imagery

  Break Down Long Sentences

Reading for Information

Make Predictions: Purpose

Synthesize: Make Generalizations

Literary Analysis

Figurative Language

Meaning and Tone

The Speaker in Poetry

Poetic Forms

Comparing Tone and Mood

Figurative Language

Sound Devices

Comparing Theme

Vocabulary

Big Question Vocabulary

Prefixes: *fore-, re-*

Suffixes: *-ary, -ous, -or, -ial*

Roots: *-lun-, -temp-*

Connotation and Denotation

Conventions

Prepositions and Prepositional Phrases

Direct Objects

Revising to Vary Sentence Patterns

Prepositional Phrases

Infinitives

Revising Common Usage Problems

Writing

Writing About the Big Question

Lyric Poem

Tanka

Critical Essay

Poems

Timed Writing

Writing Workshop: Explanatory Text: Descriptive Essay

Writing Workshop: Explanatory Text: Analytic Response to Literature

Speaking and Listening

Oral Interpretation

Poetry Reading Discussion

Delivering an Oral Interpretation of a Literary Work

Research and Technology

Literary History Report

Visual Arts Presentation

 Common Core State Standards Addressed in This Unit

Reading Literature RL.9-10.1, RL.9-10.2, RL.9-10.4, RL.9-10.5, RL.9-10.10

Reading Informational Text RI.9-10.1, RI.9-10.2, RI.9-10.3, RI.9-10.4, RI.9-10.6, RI.9-10.10

Writing W.9-10.2, W.9-10.2.a, W.9-10.2.b, W.9-10.2.c, W.9-10.2.d, W.9-10.2.f, W.9-10.3.d, W.9-10.4, W.9-10.5, W.9-10.6, W.9-10.7, W.9-10.9, W.9-10.9.a

Speaking and Listening SL.9-10.1, SL.9-10.1.b, SL.9-10.6

Language L.9-10.1, L.9-10.1.b, L.9-10.3.a, L.9-10.4, L.9-10.4.b, L.9-10.4.c, L.9-10.5, L.9-10.5.a, L.9-10.5.b, L.9-10.6

[For the full wording of the standards, see the standards chart in the front of your textbook.]

? To what extent does *experience* determine what we *perceive?*

Introducing the Big Question		790
© Literary Analysis Workshop: Drama		792
Analyzing Complex Characters	INSTRUCTIONAL ESSAY	794
Henrik Ibsen **from A Doll House** EXEMPLAR©	DRAMA	797
David Henry Hwang **from Tibet Through the Red Box**	DRAMA	799

Character Development
Conflict
Theme

© Extended Study: Antigone		808
Ancient Greek Theater		810A
Aristotle and Greek Tragedy		810C
Drama Selection		
Sophocles (translated by Dudley Fitts and Robert Fitzgerald) **Antigone, Part 1**	GREEK TRAGEDY	814
Literature in Context: Greek Chorus	INFORMATIONAL TEXT	830
Integrated Language Skills		834
Sophocles (translated by Dudley Fitts and Robert Fitzgerald) **Antigone, Part 2**	GREEK TRAGEDY	839
Literature in Context: Ancient Greek Funeral Rites	INFORMATIONAL TEXT	844
Integrated Language Skills		860
✓ **Test Practice: Reading** Summarize ▪ Writing for Assessment		862

Summarize
Protagonist and
Antagonist

Summarize
Greek Tragedies

Synthesize:
Connect Ideas

© Reading for Information: Analyzing Arguments		864
Matthew Murray **Santa Claus Meets Sophocles**	ARGUMENT	865
Elyse Sommers **A "Prequel" to Antigone**	ARGUMENT	866
Comparing Arguments ▪ Timed Writing		867
Comparing Literary Works		868
Henrik Ibsen **from An Enemy of the People**	DRAMATIC SCENE	870
Comparing Universal and Culturally Specific Themes ▪ Timed Writing	INFORMATIONAL TEXT HIGHLIGHTED	877

Comparing
Universal and
Culturally Specific
Themes

Writing Workshop: Narrative Text: Reflective Essay — 878

Writer's Toolbox: Finding an Effective Idea — 879

Writer's Toolbox: Revising to Combine Sentences With Verbal Phrases — 881

Ⓒ **Extended Study:** The Tragedy of Julius Caesar — 884

Theater in Elizabethan England — 886A

Drama Selection

William Shakespeare **The Tragedy of Julius Caesar**

Act I — PLAY — 892

Literature in Context: Roman Society — INFORMATIONAL TEXT — 900

Act II — PLAY — 916

Literature in Context: Archaic Word Forms — INFORMATIONAL TEXT — 918

Literature in Context: Roman Augurs — INFORMATIONAL TEXT — 928

Literature in Context: The Roman Senate — INFORMATIONAL TEXT — 930

Act III — PLAY — 940

Literature in Context: The Roman Forum — INFORMATIONAL TEXT — 942

Act IV — PLAY — 966

Literature in Context: Stoicism — INFORMATIONAL TEXT — 976

Act V — PLAY — 986

Literature in Context: Roman Triumphs — INFORMATIONAL TEXT — 991

Integrated Language Skills — 1002

✓ **Test Practice: Reading**
Reading Shakespearean Drama ▪ Writing for Assessment — 1006

Use Text Aids
Shakespeare's Tragedies

Paraphrase
Blank Verse

Analyze Imagery
Dramatic Speeches

Read Between the Lines
External and Internal Conflict

Compare and Contrast
Characters
Tragic Heroes

PHLit Online!
www.PHLitOnline.com
Interactive resources provide personalized instruction and activities online.

Analyze
Workplace Documents

ⓒ Reading for Information: Analyzing Functional and Expository Texts — 1008

The County of Sonoma Volunteer Application — FUNCTIONAL TEXT — 1009

BLS Career Information: Urban Planner — EXPOSITORY TEXT — 1011

Comparing Functional and Expository Texts ▪ Timed Writing — 1013

Comparing
Character
Motivation

Comparing Literary Works — 1014

Lorraine Hansberry **from A Raisin in the Sun** — DRAMATIC SCENE — 1016

Compare Character Motivation ▪ Timed Writing — 1019

Writing Workshop: Informative Text: Research Report — 1020

Jeff Anderson, M.Ed. **What Do You Notice?** Controlling Idea — 1020

David Henry Hwang **Writers on Writing:** On Using Research — 1024

Writer's Toolbox: Revising to Combine Sentences Using Adverb Clauses — 1027

Vocabulary Workshop: Borrowed and Foreign Words — 1032

Communications Workshop: Delivering a Multimedia Presentation — 1034

ⓒ Common Core Assessment Workshop: Cumulative Review — 1036

ⓒ Common Core Assessment Workshop: Performance Tasks — 1040

ⓒ Independent Reading — 1042

Sophocles	Sophocles: The Theban Plays EXEMPLAR ⓒ	DRAMA
John Steinbeck	The Grapes of Wrath EXEMPLAR ⓒ	FICTION
W. H. Auden	The Collected Poetry of W. H. Auden EXEMPLAR ⓒ	POETRY
Henrik Ibsen	Ibsen: Four Major Plays EXEMPLAR ⓒ	DRAMA
Lorraine Hansberry	A Raisin in the Sun	DRAMA
Athol Fugard	"Master Harold"… and the Boys EXEMPLAR ⓒ	DRAMA
Susan Vreeland	Girl in Hyacinth Blue	FICTION
Jim Haskins	Black, Blue & Gray: African Americans in the Civil War EXEMPLAR ⓒ	NONFICTION

Skills at a Glance

This page provides a quick look at the skills you will learn and practice in Unit 5.

Reading Skills

Summarize
  Retell; Take Notes
Reading Shakespearean Drama
  Use Text Aids; Paraphrase
  Analyze Imagery; Read Between the Lines
  Compare and Contrast Characters

Reading for Information

Synthesize: Connect Ideas
Analyze Workplace Documents

Literary Analysis

Conflict
Character Development
Protagonist and Antagonist
Greek Tragedies
Comparing Universal and Culturally
  Specific Themes
Shakespeare's Tragedies
Blank Verse
Dramatic Speeches
External and Internal Conflict
Tragic Heroes
Comparing Character Motivation

Vocabulary

Big Question Vocabulary
Prefixes: *en-*
Suffixes: *-ile*
Roots: *-dict-, -fer-, -spect-, -sum-, -stru-*
Borrowed and Foreign Words

Conventions

Participles and Gerunds
Independent and Subordinate Clauses
Revising to Combine Sentences With
  Verbal Phrases
Absolutes and Absolute Phrases

Revising to Combine Sentences Using
  Adverb Clauses

Writing

Writing About the Big Question
Essay; Reflective Essay
Editorial
Obituary
Timed Writing
Writing Workshop: Narrative Text: Reflective Essay
Writing Workshop: Informative Text: Research
  Report

Speaking and Listening

Oral Report
Mock Trial
Dramatic Reading
Group Screening

Research and Technology

Women's History Report
Advertising Poster
Multimedia Presentation
Delivering a Multimedia Presentation of a
  Research Report

 **Common Core State Standards
Addressed in This Unit**

Reading Literature RL.9-10.1, RL.9-10.2, RL.9-10.3, RL.9-10.4, RL.9-10.5, RL.9-10.7, RL.9-10.10

Reading Informational Text RI.9-10.3, RI.9-10.4, RI.9-10.5 , RI.9-10.10

Writing W.9-10.1, W.9-10.1.b, W.9-10.1.e, W.9-10.2, W.9-10.2.a, W.9-10.2.b, W.9-10.2.c, W.9-10.2.d, W.9-10.3, W.9-10.3.a, W.9-10.3.c, W.9-10.3.d, W.9-10.4, W.9-10.5, W.9-10.6, W.9-10.7, W.9-10.8, W.9-10.9.a

Speaking and Listening SL.9-10.1, SL.9-10.1.b, SL.9-10.1.c, SL.9-10.1.d, SL.9-10.3, SL.9-10.4, SL.9-10.5, SL.9-10.6

Language L.9-10.1, L.9-10.1.b, L.9-10.3, L.9-10.4.a, L.9-10.4.b, L.9-10.4.c, L.9-10.5, L.9-10.6

[For the full wording of the standards, see the standards chart in the front of your textbook.]

Can anyone be a *hero?*

Introducing the Big Question   1046

© **Literary Analysis Workshop:** Themes in Literature: Heroes and
Dreamers   1048

Analyzing Theme   INSTRUCTIONAL ESSAY 1050

Chinua Achebe   ***from* Things Fall Apart** EXEMPLAR ©   FICTION 1053

John Phillip Santos   ***from* Places Left Unfinished at
                          the Time of Creation**   AUTOBIOGRAPHY 1056

Leveled Selections

Ancient Greek Myth Retold by Olivia E. Coolidge
                          Prometheus and the First People   MYTH 1066

Literature in Context: The Twelve Olympian Gods   INFORMATIONAL TEXT 1068

Native American Myth **The Orphan Boy and the Elk Dog**   MYTH 1076

Literature in Context: Traditional Great Plains Culture INFORMATIONAL TEXT 1081

Integrated Language Skills   1088

Leveled Selections

D. T. Niane   ***from* Sundiata: An Epic of Old Mali**   EPIC 1094

Literature in Context: Griot: The Mind of the People INFORMATIONAL TEXT 1103

R. K. Narayan   **Rama's Initiation *from the* Ramayana**   EPIC 1108

Integrated Language Skills   1118

✓ **Test Practice: Reading**
   Analyze Cultural Context ▪ Writing for Assessment   1120

© **Reading for Information:** Analyzing Expository Texts   1122

                        Careers in Science: Firefighter   EXPOSITORY TEXT 1123

                        **The Georgia Certified Firefighters
                        Physical Agility Test**   EXPOSITORY TEXT 1125

Comparing Expository Texts ▪ Timed Writing   1127

Theme
Cultural Context

Analyze Cultural
Context
Myths

Analyze Cultural
Context
Epic and Epic Hero

Generate Questions

INFORMATIONAL TEXT HIGHLIGHTED

Comparing Literary Works   1128

Comparing
Archetypal Narrative
Patterns

Lucius Apuleius (retold by Sally Benson)
Cupid and Psyche   MYTH   1130

Jakob and Wilhelm Grimm
Ashputtle   FAIRY TALE   1138

Compare Archetypal Narrative Patterns ▪ Timed Writing   1145

Writing Workshop: Explanatory Text: Technical Document   1146

Writer's Toolbox: Explaining the Process   1147

Writer's Toolbox: Revising to Correct Fragments and Run-on Sentences   1149

Leveled Selections

Compare Worldviews
Legends and
Legendary Heroes

T. H. White   **Arthur Becomes King of Britain**
***from* The Once and Future King**   LEGEND   1156

Literature in Context: Tournaments   INFORMATIONAL TEXT   1162

Alfred, Lord Tennyson   **Morte d'Arthur**   LEGEND   1174

Integrated Language Skills   1186

Leveled Selections

Compare Worldviews
Parody

Mark Twain   ***from* A Connecticut Yankee
in King Arthur's Court**   PARODY   1192

Literature in Context: Eclipses   INFORMATIONAL TEXT   1199

Miguel de Cervantes   ***from* Don Quixote**   PARODY   1208

Integrated Language Skills   1218

✓ **Test Practice: Reading** Compare Worldviews ▪ Writing
for Assessment   1220

Critique Generalizations and Evidence

Ⓒ Reading for Information: Analyzing Arguments — 1222

Michael Dorris	**Mothers and Daughters**	BOOK REVIEW	1223
James Berardinelli	**The Joy Luck Club**	MOVIE REVIEW	1225
Comparing Argumentative Texts ▪ Timed Writing			1227

Comparing Themes and Moral Dilemmas

Comparing Literary Works — 1228

retold by William F. Russell	**Damon and Pythias**	LEGEND	1230
Guy de Maupassant	**Two Friends**	SHORT STORY	1233
Compare Themes and Worldviews ▪ Timed Writing			1241

Writing Workshop: Informative Text: Comparison-and-Contrast Essay — 1242

Jeff Anderson, M.Ed.	**What Do You Notice?** Contrasting	1242
John Phillip Santos	**Writers on Writing:** On Making Comparisons	1245
Writer's Toolbox: Revising to Vary Sentence Structure and Length		1247

Vocabulary Workshop: Idioms, Jargon, and Technical Terms — 1250

Communications Workshop: Comparing Media Coverage — 1252

Ⓒ Common Core Assessment Workshop: Cumulative Review — 1254

Ⓒ Common Core Assessment Workshop: Performance Tasks — 1258

Ⓒ Independent Reading — 1260

Voltaire	Candide EXEMPLAR Ⓒ	FICTION
T. H. White	The Once and Future King	FICTION
Henry Louis Gates, Jr., and Nellie Y. McKay, Editors	The Norton Anthology of African American Literature EXEMPLAR Ⓒ	ANTHOLOGY
Franz Kafka	The Metamorphosis EXEMPLAR Ⓒ	FICTION
Jeffrey Gantz, Translator	Early Irish Myths and Sagas	NONFICTION
Evan S. Connell	Son of the Morning Star: Custer and the Little Bighorn EXEMPLAR Ⓒ	NONFICTION
Matthew Spalding and Patrick J. Garrity	A Sacred Union of Citizens: George Washington's Farewell Address and the American Character EXEMPLAR Ⓒ	NONFICTION

Skills at a Glance

This page provides a quick look at the skills you will learn and practice in Unit 6.

Reading Skills

Analyze Cultural Context

  Generate Questions

  Acquire Background Knowledge

Compare Worldviews

  Identify Details and Draw a Conclusion

  Compare Worldview: Compare and Contrast

Reading for Information

Generate Questions

Critique Generalizations and Evidence

Literary Analysis

Theme

Cultural Context

Myths

Epic and Epic Hero

Comparing Archetypal Narrative Patterns

Legends and Legendary Heroes

Parody

Comparing Themes and Moral Dilemmas

Vocabulary

Big Question Vocabulary

Prefixes: *multi-, ex-*

Suffixes: *-ive, -tude, -ate, -ment*

Roots: *-dur-, -fus-*

Idioms, Jargon, and Technical Terms

Conventions

Simple and Compound Sentences

Complex and Compound-Complex Sentences

Revising to Correct Fragments and
  Run-on Sentences

Commas and Dashes

Semicolons, Colons, and Ellipsis Points

Revising to Vary Sentence Structure and Length

Writing

Writing About the Big Question

Myth

Newspaper Report

Script

Parody

Timed Writing

Writing Workshop: Explanatory Text: Technical
  Document

Writing Workshop: Informative Text: Comparison-
  and-Contrast Essay

Speaking and Listening

Retelling

Improvised Dialogue

Comparing Media Coverage

Research and Technology

Influences Chart

Biographical Brochure

 **Common Core State Standards
Addressed in This Unit**

Reading Literature RL.9-10.1, RL.9-10.2, RL.9-10.3,
RL.9-10.4, RL.9-10.5, RL.9-10.6, RL.9-10.7, RL.9-10.9,
RL.9-10.10

Reading Informational Text RI.9-10.2, RI.9-10.5,
RI.9-10.7, RI.9-10.8, RI.9-10.10

Writing W.9-10.2, W.9-10.2.a, W.9-10.2.b, W.9-10.2.c,
W.9-10.2.d, W.9-10.2.e, W.9-10.3, W.9-10.3.a, W.9-10.3.b,
W.9-10.4, W.9-10.5, W.9-10.6, W.9-10.7, W.9-10.9.a

Speaking and Listening SL.9-10.1, SL.9-10.4, SL.9-10.6

Language L.9-10.1, L.9-10.1.b, L.9-10.2, L.9-10.2.a, L.9-
10.2.b, L.9-10.4, L.9-10.4.a, L.9-10.4.d, L.9-10.5, L.9-10.6

[For the full wording of the standards, see the standards
chart in the front of your textbook.]

Literature

▶ Stories

Adventure and Suspense

The Monkey's Paw
W. W. Jacobs.. 32

Contents of the Dead Man's Pocket
Jack Finney... 118

Games at Twilight
Anita Desai.. 138

One Thousand Dollars
O. Henry.. 308

Allegories

The Masque of the Red Death
Edgar Allan Poe.. 372

The Garden of Stubborn Cats
Italo Calvino.. 384

Humorous Fiction

The Open Window
Saki (H. H. Munro).. 195

from **A Connecticut Yankee in King Arthur's Court**
Mark Twain.. 1192

from **Don Quixote**
Miguel de Cervantes....................................... 1208

Myths, Folk Tales, and Legends

Things Fall Apart EXEMPLAR ©
Chinua Achebe... 1053

Prometheus and the First People
Olivia E. Coolidge.. 1066

The Orphan Boy and the Elk Dog
Native American: The Blackfeet............................ 1076

Cupid and Psyche
Lucius Apuleius... 1130

Ashputtle
Jakob and Wilhelm Grimm................................... 1138

Arthur Becomes King of Britain
from **The Once and Future King**
T. H. White... 1156

Morte d'Arthur
Alfred, Lord Tennyson..................................... 1174

Damon and Pythias
retold by William F. Russell.............................. 1230

Realistic Fiction

Magdalena Looking
Susan Vreeland... 10

The Leap
Louise Erdrich... 46

Tepeyac
Sandra Cisneros... 104

Early Autumn
Langston Hughes... 229

A Visit to Grandmother
William Melvin Kelley..................................... 242

The Street of the Cañon
Josephina Niggli.. 272

The Censors
Luisa Valenzuela.. 410

Science Fiction and Fantasy

from **Fahrenheit 451** EXEMPLAR ©
Ray Bradbury.. 5

The Threads of Time
C. J. Cherryh... 231

There Will Come Soft Rains
Ray Bradbury.. 284

By the Waters of Babylon
Stephen Vincent Benét..................................... 314

World Literature

Like the Sun
R. K. Narayan... 190

A Problem
Anton Chekhov... 256

How Much Land Does a Man Need?
Leo Tolstoy... 338

Civil Peace
Chinua Achebe... 358

Two Friends
Guy de Maupassant... 1233

▶ Drama

Plays

from **A Doll House** EXEMPLAR ©
Henrik Ibsen.. 797

from **Tibet Through the Red Box**
David Henry Hwang... 799

Antigone
Sophocles

Part 1.. 814

Part 2.. 839

from **An Enemy of the People**
Henrik Ibsen.. 870

The Tragedy of Julius Caesar
William Shakespeare
Act I..892
Act II..916
Act III...940
Act IV...966
Act V..986
from **A Raisin in the Sun**
Lorraine Hansberry 1016

▶ Poetry

Epics
from **Sundiata: An Epic of Old Mali**
D. T. Niane 1094
Rama's Initiation
from **the Ramayana**
R. K. Narayan 1108

Lyrical Poems
I Am Offering This Poem EXEMPLAR ⓒ
Jimmy Santiago Baca 633
The Poetic Interpretation of the Twist
Cornelius Eady 634
The Empty Dance Shoes
Cornelius Eady 636
The Guitar
Federico García Lorca 648
Mowing
Robert Frost 658
Spring & All
William Carlos Williams 665
Fear
Gabriela Mistral 702
The Wind—tapped like a tired Man
Emily Dickinson 718
Metaphor
Eve Merriam 722
Conscientious Objector
Edna St. Vincent Millay 726
Pride
Dahlia Ravikovitch...727
Tell all the Truth but tell it slant—
Emily Dickinson 728
The Weary Blues
Langston Hughes 736
In Flanders Fields
John McCrae 738

Jazz Fantasia
Carl Sandburg 739
All
Bei Dao 764
Also All
Shu Ting 765

Narrative and Dramatic Poems
The Bridegroom
Alexander Pushkin 642
The Fish
Elizabeth Bishop..650
Danny Deever
Rudyard Kipling...652
A Tree Telling of Orpheus
Denise Levertov 659
Making a Fist
Naomi Shihab Nye 664
The Bean Eaters
Gwendolyn Brooks 703
Glory
Yusef Komunyakaa..720
Meeting at Night
Robert Browning 744
The Kraken
Alfred, Lord Tennyson 745
Reapers
Jean Toomer 746

Sonnets and Tanka
My City
James Weldon Johnson..677
Do Not Go Gentle Into That Good Night
Dylan Thomas 679
Tanka..680
The Waking
Theodore Roethke 684
Sonnet 18
William Shakespeare 687
Tanka..688

Informational Text

▶ Arguments

Opinion Pieces

Editorial on the Anniversary of the Fall of the Berlin Wall
The New York Times 403

The American Idea
Theodore H. White 560

What Makes a Degas a Degas?
Richard Mühlberger 568

Santa Claus Meets Sophocles
Matthew Murray 865

A "Prequel" to Antigone
Elyse Sommers 866

Mothers and Daughters
Michael Dorris 1223

The Joy Luck Club
James Berardinelli 1225

Speeches

Address to Students at Moscow University EXEMPLAR©
Ronald Reagan 449

Keep Memory Alive EXEMPLAR©
Elie Wiesel 542

from Nobel Lecture
Alexander Solzhenitsyn 548

Hold Fast Your Dreams—and Trust Your Mistakes
Billy Joel 760

▶ Exposition

Content-Area Essays and Articles

A Quilt of a Country EXEMPLAR©
Anna Quindlen 21

Artful Research
Susan Vreeland 22

Feel the City's Pulse? It's Be-Bop, Man!
Ann Douglas 91

The Healdsburg Jazz Festival Winter 2007
The Grapevine Rag 93

The Marginal World
Rachel Carson 156

Making History With Vitamin C
Penny Le Couteur and Jay Burreson 168

Interactive Dig
Renée Friedman 185

Tides
Joseph D. Exline, Ed.D.; Jay M. Pasachoff, Ph.D.; et al. 299

Black Water Turns the Tide on Florida Coral
NASA News 303

The Spider and the Wasp
Alexander Petrunkevitch 464

from Longitude
Dava Sobel 474

A Toast to the Oldest Inhabitant: The Weather of New England
Mark Twain 520

The History of the Guitar
Thomas A. Hill 579

Mali
Adapted from Dorling Kindersley World Reference Atlas 753

Will All the Blue Men End Up in Timbuktu?
Stefan Lovgren 755

On Using Research
David Henry Hwang 1024

Careers in Science: Firefighter 1123

Memoirs

from Swimming to Antarctica
Lynne Cox 62

Occupation: Conductorette
Maya Angelou 78

from Places Left Unfinished at the Time of Creation
John Phillip Santos 1053

Narrative Essays

Marian Anderson, Famous Concert Singer
Langston Hughes 98

Voices from the Wall
Marco Mielcarek 405

Everest
Erik Weihenmayer 452

The Dog That Bit People
James Thurber 525

from Desert Exile: The Uprooting of a Japanese-American Family
Yoshiko Uchida 586

Personal Essays

The Leader in the Mirror
Pat Mora 414

The Sun Parlor
Dorothy West 490

from **In Commemoration: One Million Volumes**
Rudolfo A. Anaya 500

from **The Way to Rainy Mountain**
N. Scott Momaday 595

How to React to Familiar Faces
Umberto Eco 704

▶ Functional Text

Egyptology Resources
Nigel Strudwick 183
How to Use a Compass 513
GPS Quick-Start Guide 515
California State University at Fullerton Course Catalog 581
Library Hours and Exhibit Placards
Folger Shakespeare Library 695
Atlanta-Fulton Public Library System: Borrower Services 697
The County of Sonoma Volunteer Application 1009
BLS Career Information: Urban Planner
U.S. Department of Labor 1011
The Georgia Certified Firefighters Physical Agility Test
City of Perry Fire Department 1125

▶ Literature in Context—Reading in Content Areas

History Connection:
Encyclopedias and the Enlightenment (illustrated) 26

Geography Connection:
Antarctica: The Coldest Place on Earth (illustrated) 69

History Connection:
San Francisco and the Gold Rushes 83

Science Connection:
Physics 129

History Connection:
The Voyages of Captain James Cook (illustrated) 175

History Connection:
The Great Migration (illustrated) 249

Language Connection:
Spanish Vocabulary 274

History Connection:
The Babylonian Captivity 321

History Connection:
The Emancipation of the Serfs (illustrated) 350

Geography Connection:
Nigerian Civil War (illustrated) 362

Architecture Connection:
Architectural Features 388

Science Connection:
Studying Animal Behavior 468

Science Connection:
Longitude and Latitude 478

Culture Connection:
Mexican American Pride (illustrated) 503

World Events Connection:
Repression in the Soviet Union (illustrated) 550

Humanities Connection:
Greek Chorus (illustrated) 830

Culture Connection:
Ancient Greek Funeral Rites 844

History Connection:
Roman Society (illustrated) 900

Language Connection:
Archaic Word Forms 918

Culture Connection:
Roman Augurs (illustrated) 928

History Connection:
The Roman Senate (illustrated) 930

History Connection:
The Roman Forum (illustrated) 942

Humanities Connection:
Stoicism 976

History Connection:
Roman Triumphs 991

Culture Connection:
The Twelve Olympian Gods 1068

Culture Connection:
Traditional Great Plains Culture 1081

Culture Connection:
Griot: The Mind of the People 1103

History Connection:
Tournaments 1162

Science Connection:
Eclipses (illustrated) 1199

Comparing Literary Works

Comparing Style

Langston Hughes
Marian Anderson, Famous Concert Singer ..BIOGRAPHY 98

Sandra Cisneros
Tepeyac......................................SHORT STORY.......104

Comparing Irony and Paradox

R. K. Narayan
Like the Sun................................SHORT STORY.......190

Saki (H. H. Munro)
The Open Window.............................SHORT STORY.......195

Comparing Points of View

O. Henry
One Thousand Dollars..........................SHORT STORY.......308

Stephen Vincent Benét
By the Waters of Babylon.......................SHORT STORY.......314

Comparing Tone

Luisa Valenzuela
The Censors ....SHORT STORY.......410

Pat Mora
The Leader in the Mirror.................REFLECTIVE ESSAY.......414

Comparing Humorous Writing

Mark Twain
A Toast to the Oldest Inhabitant:
The Weather of New England ....HUMOROUS SPEECH 520

James Thurber
The Dog That Bit People....................HUMOROUS ESSAY.......525

Comparing Authors' Purpose

Yoshiko Uchida
from **Desert Exile: The Uprooting of a**
Japanese-American Family............................MEMOIR.......586

N. Scott Momaday
from **The Way to Rainy Mountain**......REFLECTIVE ESSAY.......542

Comparing Tone and Mood

Gabriela Mistral
Fear..POEM.......702

Gwendolyn Brooks
The Bean Eaters ....POEM.......703

Umberto Eco
How to React to Familiar Faces ....ANALYTIC ESSAY.......704

Comparing Theme

Billy Joel
Hold Fast Your Dreams—
and Trust Your Mistakes ....SPEECH.......760

Bei Dao
All ....POEM.......764

Shu Ting
Also All ....POEM.......765

Comparing Universal and Culturally Specific Themes

Henrik Ibsen
from **An Enemy of the People** ....DRAMATIC SCENE.......870

Comparing Character Motivation

Lorraine Hansberry
from **A Raisin in the Sun** ....DRAMATIC SCENE..... 1016

Comparing Archetypal Narrative Patterns

Lucius Apuleius (retold by Sally Benson)
Cupid and Psyche.................................MYTH..... 1130

Jakob and Wilhelm Grimm
Ashputtle ....FAIRY TALE..... 1138

Comparing Themes and Worldviews

retold by William F. Russell
Damon and Pythias ....LEGEND..... 1230

Guy de Maupassant
Two Friends................................SHORT STORY..... 1233

▶ Writing Workshops

Narrative Text: Autobiographical Narrative 108
Explanatory Text: Cause-and-Effect Essay 200
Narrative Text: Short Story 328
Argumentative Text: Problem-and-Solution Essay 420
Argumentative Text: Letter to the Editor 532
Argumentative Text: Persuasive Essay 604
Explanatory Text: Descriptive Essay 708
Argumentative Text: Analytic Response to Literature 768
Narrative Text: Reflective Essay 878
Informative Text: Research Report 1020
Explanatory Text: Technical Document 1146
Informative Text: Comparison-and-Contrast Essay 1242

▶ Vocabulary Workshops

Using a Dictionary and Thesaurus 208
Word Origins 428
Words With Multiple Meanings 612
Connotation and Denotation 776
Borrowed and Foreign Words 1032
Idioms, Jargon, and Technical Terms 1250

▶ Communications Workshops

Analyzing Media Messages 210
Viewing and Evaluating a Speech 430
Delivering a Persuasive Speech 614
Delivering an Oral Interpretation of a Literary Work 776
Delivering a Multimedia Presentation 1034
Comparing Media Coverage 1252

The **Common Core State Standards** will prepare you to succeed in college and your future career. They are separated into four sections—Reading (Literature and Informational Text), Writing, Speaking and Listening, and Language. Beginning each section, the College and Career Readiness Anchor Standards define what you need to achieve by the end of high school. The grade-specific standards that follow define what you need to know by the end of your current grade level.

ⓒ Common Core Reading Standards

College and Career Readiness Anchor Standards for Reading

Key Ideas and Details

1. Read closely to determine what the text says explicitly and to make logical inferences from it; cite specific textual evidence when writing or speaking to support conclusions drawn from the text.

2. Determine central ideas or themes of a text and analyze their development; summarize the key supporting details and ideas.

3. Analyze how and why individuals, events, and ideas develop and interact over the course of a text.

Craft and Structure

4. Interpret words and phrases as they are used in a text, including determining technical, connotative, and figurative meanings, and analyze how specific word choices shape meaning or tone.

5. Analyze the structure of texts, including how specific sentences, paragraphs, and larger portions of the text (e.g., a section, chapter, scene, or stanza) relate to each other and the whole.

6. Assess how point of view or purpose shapes the content and style of a text.

Integration of Knowledge and Ideas

7. Integrate and evaluate content presented in diverse formats and media, including visually and quantitatively, as well as in words.

8. Delineate and evaluate the argument and specific claims in a text, including the validity of the reasoning as well as the relevance and sufficiency of the evidence.

9. Analyze how two or more texts address similar themes or topics in order to build knowledge or to compare the approaches the authors take.

Range of Reading and Level of Text Complexity

10. Read and comprehend complex literary and informational texts independently and proficiently.

Grade 10 Reading Standards for Literature

Key Ideas and Details

1. Cite strong and thorough textual evidence to support analysis of what the text says explicitly as well as inferences drawn from the text.

2. Determine a theme or central idea of a text and analyze in detail its development over the course of the text, including how it emerges and is shaped and refined by specific details; provide an objective summary of the text.

3. Analyze how complex characters (e.g., those with multiple or conflicting motivations) develop over the course of a text, interact with other characters, and advance the plot or develop the theme.

Craft and Structure

4. Determine the meaning of words and phrases as they are used in the text, including figurative and connotative meanings; analyze the cumulative impact of specific word choices on meaning and tone (e.g., how the language evokes a sense of time and place; how it sets a formal or informal tone).

5. Analyze how an author's choices concerning how to structure a text, order events within it (e.g., parallel plots), and manipulate time (e.g., pacing, flashbacks) create such effects as mystery, tension, or surprise.

6. Analyze a particular point of view or cultural experience reflected in a work of literature from outside the United States, drawing on a wide reading of world literature.

Integration of Knowledge and Ideas

7. Analyze the representation of a subject or a key scene in two different artistic mediums, including what is emphasized or absent in each treatment (e.g., Auden's "Musée des Beaux Arts" and Breughel's *Landscape with the Fall of Icarus*).

8. (Not applicable to literature)

9. Analyze how an author draws on and transforms source material in a specific work (e.g., how Shakespeare treats a theme or topic from Ovid or the Bible or how a later author draws on a play by Shakespeare).

Range of Reading and Level of Text Complexity

10. By the end of grade 9, read and comprehend literature, including stories, dramas, and poems, in the grades 9–10 text complexity band proficiently, with scaffolding as needed at the high end of the range.

Grade 10 Reading Standards for Informational Text

Key Ideas and Details

1. Cite strong and thorough textual evidence to support analysis of what the text says explicitly as well as inferences drawn from the text.

2. Determine a central idea of a text and analyze its development over the course of the text, including how it emerges and is shaped and refined by specific details; provide an objective summary of the text.

3. Analyze how the author unfolds an analysis or series of ideas or events, including the order in which the points are made, how they are introduced and developed, and the connections that are drawn between them.

Craft and Structure

4. Determine the meaning of words and phrases as they are used in a text, including figurative, connotative, and technical meanings; analyze the cumulative impact of specific word choices on meaning and tone (e.g., how the language of a court opinion differs from that of a newspaper).

5. Analyze in detail how an author's ideas or claims are developed and refined by particular sentences, paragraphs, or larger portions of a text (e.g., a section or chapter).

6. Determine an author's point of view or purpose in a text and analyze how an author uses rhetoric to advance that point of view or purpose.

Integration of Knowledge and Ideas

7. Analyze various accounts of a subject told in different mediums (e.g., a person's life story in both print and multimedia), determining which details are emphasized in each account.

8. Delineate and evaluate the argument and specific claims in a text, assessing whether the reasoning is valid and the evidence is relevant and sufficient; identify false statements and fallacious reasoning.

9. Analyze seminal U.S. documents of historical and literary significance (e.g., Washington's Farewell Address, the Gettysburg Address, Roosevelt's Four Freedoms speech, King's "Letter from Birmingham Jail"), including how they address related themes and concepts.

Range of Reading and Level of Text Complexity

10. By the end of grade 9, read and comprehend literary nonfiction in the grades 9–10 text complexity band proficiently, with scaffolding as needed at the high end of the range.

© Common Core Writing Standards

College and Career Readiness Anchor Standards for Writing

Text Types and Purposes

1. Write arguments to support claims in an analysis of substantive topics or texts, using valid reasoning and relevant and sufficient evidence.

2. Write informative/explanatory texts to examine and convey complex ideas and information clearly and accurately through the effective selection, organization, and analysis of content.

3. Write narratives to develop real or imagined experiences or events using effective technique, well-chosen details, and well-structured event sequences.

Production and Distribution of Writing

4. Produce clear and coherent writing in which the development, organization, and style are appropriate to task, purpose, and audience.

5. Develop and strengthen writing as needed by planning, revising, editing, rewriting, or trying a new approach.

6. Use technology, including the Internet, to produce and publish writing and to interact and collaborate with others.

Research to Build and Present Knowledge

7. Conduct short as well as more sustained research projects based on focused questions, demonstrating understanding of the subject under investigation.

8. Gather relevant information from multiple print and digital sources, assess the credibility and accuracy of each source, and integrate the information while avoiding plagiarism.

9. Draw evidence from literary or informational texts to support analysis, reflection, and research.

Range of Writing

10. Write routinely over extended time frames (time for research, reflection, and revision) and shorter time frames (a single sitting or a day or two) for a range of tasks, purposes, and audiences.

Grade 10 Writing Standards

Text Types and Purposes

1. Write arguments to support claims in an analysis of substantive topics or texts, using valid reasoning and relevant and sufficient evidence.

   a. Introduce precise claim(s), distinguish the claim(s) from alternate or opposing claims, and create an organization that establishes clear relationships among claim(s), counterclaims, reasons, and evidence.

   b. Develop claim(s) and counterclaims fairly, supplying evidence for each while pointing out the strengths and limitations of both in a manner that anticipates the audience's knowledge level and concerns.

   c. Use words, phrases, and clauses to link the major sections of the text, create cohesion, and clarify the relationships between claim(s) and reasons, between reasons and evidence, and between claim(s) and counterclaims.

   d. Establish and maintain a formal style and objective tone while attending to the norms and conventions of the discipline in which they are writing.

   e. Provide a concluding statement or section that follows from and supports the argument presented.

2. Write informative/explanatory texts to examine and convey complex ideas, concepts, and information clearly and accurately through the effective selection, organization, and analysis of content.

   a. Introduce a topic; organize complex ideas, concepts, and information to make important connections and distinctions; include formatting (e.g., headings), graphics (e.g., figures, tables), and multimedia when useful to aiding comprehension.

   b. Develop the topic with well-chosen, relevant, and sufficient facts, extended definitions, concrete details, quotations, or other information and examples appropriate to the audience's knowledge of the topic.

   c. Use appropriate and varied transitions to link the major sections of the text, create cohesion, and clarify the relationships among complex ideas and concepts.

   d. Use precise language and domain-specific vocabulary to manage the complexity of the topic.

   e. Establish and maintain a formal style and objective tone while attending to the norms and conventions of the discipline in which they are writing.

   f. Provide a concluding statement or section that follows from and supports the information or explanation presented (e.g., articulating implications or the significance of the topic).

3. Write narratives to develop real or imagined experiences or events using effective technique, well-chosen details, and well-structured event sequences.

   a. Engage and orient the reader by setting out a problem, situation, or observation, establishing one or multiple point(s) of view, and introducing a narrator and/or characters; create a smooth progression of experiences or events.

b. Use narrative techniques, such as dialogue, pacing, description, reflection, and multiple plot lines, to develop experiences, events, and/or characters.

c. Use a variety of techniques to sequence events so that they build on one another to create a coherent whole.

d. Use precise words and phrases, telling details, and sensory language to convey a vivid picture of the experiences, events, setting, and/or characters.

e. Provide a conclusion that follows from and reflects on what is experienced, observed, or resolved over the course of the narrative.

Production and Distribution of Writing

4. Produce clear and coherent writing in which the development, organization, and style are appropriate to task, purpose, and audience.

5. Develop and strengthen writing as needed by planning, revising, editing, rewriting, or trying a new approach, focusing on addressing what is most significant for a specific purpose and audience.

6. Use technology, including the Internet, to produce, publish, and update individual or shared writing products, taking advantage of technology's capacity to link to other information and to display information flexibly and dynamically.

Research to Build and Present Knowledge

7. Conduct short as well as more sustained research projects to answer a question (including a self-generated question) or solve a problem; narrow or broaden the inquiry when appropriate; synthesize multiple sources on the subject, demonstrating understanding of the subject under investigation.

8. Gather relevant information from multiple authoritative print and digital sources, using advanced searches effectively; assess the usefulness of each source in answering the research question; integrate information into the text selectively to maintain the flow of ideas, avoiding plagiarism and following a standard format for citation.

9. Draw evidence from literary or informational texts to support analysis, reflection, and research.

a. Apply *grades 9–10 Reading standards* to literature (e.g., "Analyze how an author draws on and transforms source material in a specific work [e.g., how Shakespeare treats a theme or topic from Ovid or the Bible or how a later author draws on a play by Shakespeare]").

b. Apply *grades 9–10 Reading standards* to literary nonfiction (e.g., "Delineate and evaluate the argument and specific claims in a text, assessing whether the reasoning is valid and the evidence is relevant and sufficient; identify false statements and fallacious reasoning").

Range of Writing

10. Write routinely over extended time frames (time for research, reflection, and revision) and shorter time frames (a single sitting or a day or two) for a range of tasks, purposes, and audiences.

© Common Core
Speaking and Listening Standards

College and Career Readiness Anchor Standards for Speaking and Listening

Comprehension and Collaboration

1. Prepare for and participate effectively in a range of conversations and collaborations with diverse partners, building on others' ideas and expressing their own clearly and persuasively.

2. Integrate and evaluate information presented in diverse media and formats, including visually, quantitatively, and orally.

3. Evaluate a speaker's point of view, reasoning, and use of evidence and rhetoric.

Presentation of Knowledge and Ideas

4. Present information, findings, and supporting evidence such that listeners can follow the line of reasoning and the organization, development, and style are appropriate to task, purpose, and audience.

5. Make strategic use of digital media and visual displays of data to express information and enhance understanding of presentations.

6. Adapt speech to a variety of contexts and communicative tasks, demonstrating command of formal English when indicated or appropriate.

Grade 10 Speaking and Listening Standards

Comprehension and Collaboration

1. Initiate and participate effectively in a range of collaborative discussions (one-on-one, in groups, and teacher-led) with diverse partners on *grades 9–10 topics, texts, and issues,* building on others' ideas and expressing their own clearly and persuasively.

    a. Come to discussions prepared, having read and researched material under study; explicitly draw on that preparation by referring to evidence from texts and other research on the topic or issue to stimulate a thoughtful, well-reasoned exchange of ideas.

    b. Work with peers to set rules for collegial discussions and decision-making (e.g., informal consensus, taking votes on key issues, presentation of alternate views), clear goals and deadlines, and individual roles as needed.

    c. Propel conversations by posing and responding to questions that relate the current discussion to broader themes or larger ideas; actively incorporate others into the discussion; and clarify, verify, or challenge ideas and conclusions.

    d. Respond thoughtfully to diverse perspectives, summarize points of agreement and disagreement, and, when warranted, qualify or justify their own views and understanding and make new connections in light of the evidence and reasoning presented.

2. Integrate multiple sources of information presented in diverse media or formats (e.g., visually, quantitatively, orally) evaluating the credibility and accuracy of each source.

3. Evaluate a speaker's point of view, reasoning, and use of evidence and rhetoric, identifying any fallacious reasoning or exaggerated or distorted evidence.

Presentation of Knowledge and Ideas

4. Present information, findings, and supporting evidence clearly, concisely, and logically such that listeners can follow the line of reasoning and the organization, development, substance, and style are appropriate to purpose, audience, and task.

5. Make strategic use of digital media (e.g., textual, graphical, audio, visual, and interactive elements) in presentations to enhance understanding of findings, reasoning, and evidence and to add interest.

6. Adapt speech to a variety of contexts and tasks, demonstrating command of formal English when indicated or appropriate. (See grades 9–10 Language standards 1 and 3 for specific expectations.)

© Common Core Language Standards

College and Career Readiness Anchor Standards for Language

Conventions of Standard English

1. Demonstrate command of the conventions of standard English grammar and usage when writing or speaking.

2. Demonstrate command of the conventions of standard English capitalization, punctuation, and spelling when writing.

Knowledge of Language

3. Apply knowledge of language to understand how language functions in different contexts, to make effective choices for meaning or style, and to comprehend more fully when reading or listening.

Vocabulary Acquisition and Use

4. Determine or clarify the meaning of unknown and multiple-meaning words and phrases by using context clues, analyzing meaningful word parts, and consulting general and specialized reference materials, as appropriate.

5. Demonstrate understanding of figurative language, word relationships, and nuances in word meanings.

6. Acquire and use accurately a range of general academic and domain-specific words and phrases sufficient for reading, writing, speaking, and listening at the college and career readiness level; demonstrate independence in gathering vocabulary knowledge when considering a word or phrase important to comprehension or expression.

Grade 10 Language Standards

Conventions of Standard English

1. Demonstrate command of the conventions of standard English grammar and usage when writing or speaking.
   a. Use parallel structure.
   b. Use various types of phrases (noun, verb, adjectival, adverbial, participial, prepositional, absolute) and clauses (independent, dependent; noun, relative, adverbial) to convey specific meanings and add variety and interest to writing or presentations.

2. Demonstrate command of the conventions of standard English capitalization, punctuation, and spelling when writing.

   a. Use a semicolon (and perhaps a conjunctive adverb) to link two or more closely related independent clauses.

   b. Use a colon to introduce a list or quotation.

   c. Spell correctly.

Knowledge of Language

3. Apply knowledge of language to understand how language functions in different contexts, to make effective choices for meaning or style, and to comprehend more fully when reading or listening.

   a. Write and edit work so that it conforms to the guidelines in a style manual (e.g., *MLA Handbook,* Turabian's *Manual for Writers*) appropriate for the discipline and writing type.

Vocabulary Acquisition and Use

4. Determine or clarify the meaning of unknown and multiple-meaning words and phrases based on *grades 9–10 reading and content,* choosing flexibly from a range of strategies.

   a. Use context (e.g., the overall meaning of a sentence, paragraph, or text; a word's position or function in a sentence) as a clue to the meaning of a word or phrase.

   b. Identify and correctly use patterns of word changes that indicate different meanings or parts of speech (e.g., *analyze, analysis, analytical; advocate, advocacy*).

   c. Consult general and specialized reference materials (e.g., dictionaries, glossaries, thesauruses), both print and digital, to find the pronunciation of a word or determine or clarify its precise meaning, its part of speech, or its etymology.

   d. Verify the preliminary determination of the meaning of a word or phrase (e.g., by checking the inferred meaning in context or in a dictionary).

5. Demonstrate understanding of figurative language, word relationships, and nuances in word meanings.

   a. Interpret figures of speech (e.g., euphemism, oxymoron) in context and analyze their role in the text.

   b. Analyze nuances in the meaning of words with similar denotations.

6. Acquire and use accurately general academic and domain-specific words and phrases, sufficient for reading, writing, speaking, and listening at the college and career readiness level; demonstrate independence in gathering vocabulary knowledge when considering a word or phrase important to comprehension or expression.

Introductory Unit

COMMON CORE
Workshops

Building Academic Vocabulary

Writing an Objective Summary

Comprehending Complex Texts

Analyzing Arguments

Common Core
State Standards

Reading Literature 2, 10
Reading Informational Text 2, 6, 8, 9, 10
Writing 1a, 1b, 1e
Language 6

Building Academic Vocabulary

Academic vocabulary is the language you encounter in textbooks and on standardized tests and other assessments. Understanding these words and using them in your classroom discussions and writing will help you communicate your ideas clearly and effectively.

There are two basic types of academic vocabulary: general and domain-specific. **General academic vocabulary** includes words that are not specific to any single course of study. For example, the general academic vocabulary word *analyze* is used in language arts, math, social studies, art, and so on. **Domain-specific academic vocabulary** includes words that are usually encountered in the study of a specific discipline. For example, the words *factor* and *remainder* are most often used in mathematics classrooms and texts.

**Common Core
State Standards**

Language
6. Acquire and use accurately general academic and domain-specific words and phrases sufficient for reading, writing, speaking, and listening at the college and career readiness level; demonstrate independence in gathering vocabulary knowledge when considering a word or phrase important to comprehension or expression.

General Academic Vocabulary

Word	Definition	Related Words	Word in Context
adapt (uh DAPT) *v.*	change or adjust	adaptable adaptation	Remember to adapt your reading rate to the text.
anticipate (an TIHS uh payt) *v.*	look forward to	anticipation anticipatory	Look for clues that anticipate future events.
awareness (uh WAIR nuhs) *n.*	having knowledge	aware	The author has a great awareness of his readers' interests.
background (BAK grownd) *n.*	conditions that surround or come before something		An author's background shapes his or her writing.
bias (BY uhs) *n.*	point of view before the facts are known	biased	The speaker allowed his bias to show.
character (KAR ihk tuhr) *n.*	moral strength; self-discipline	characteristic characteristically	Her character was revealed in Act II.
comprehend (kom prih HEHND) *v.*	grasp mentally; understand	comprehension	The side notes will help you comprehend new vocabulary.
conduct (KON duhkt) *n.*	the way a person acts; behavior		A speaker's conduct affects how the audience views her.
confirm (kuhn FURM) *v.*	establish the truth or correctness of something	confirmation confirmatory	Confirm whether the predictions are accurate.
context (KON tehkst) *n.*	circumstances that form the setting of an event	contextual	The context of a story may be historical.

Word	Definition	Related Words	Word in Context
convey (kuhn VAY) *v.*	communicate or make known		The poet uses imagery to convey feelings.
debate (dih BAYT) *v.*	argue or discuss	debatable debater	When you debate, support your arguments.
differentiate (dihf uh REHN shee ayt) *v.*	distinguish between	differ different	When reading an essay, differentiate between fact and opinion.
discern (duh ZURN) *v.*	tell the difference between two or more things; perceive	discernable discerning	Until I reached the end of the story, I couldn't discern the character's motives.
discourse (DIHS kawrs) *n.*	ongoing communication of ideas and information	discourser	Discourse in a group is an important way to hear different opinions.
distortion (dihs TAWR shuhn) *n.*	anything that shows something in an untrue way	distort	Avoid using unreliable sources that exhibit a distortion of facts.
evaluate (ih VAL yoo ayt) *v.*	determine the worth of something	evaluation	Rubrics help students evaluate their essays.
evolve (ih VOLV) *v.*	develop through gradual changes	evolution	Dealing with conflict allows Sam to evolve and grow.
explanation (ehks pluh NAY shuhn) *n.*	clarifying statement	explain explanatory	A technical document provides an explanation.
individual (ihn duh VIHJ oo uhl) *adj.*	relating to a single person or thing	individualism individuality	Work on an individual response, and then discuss the question.
inherent (ihn HIHR uhnt) *adj.*	existing naturally in something	inherence inherently	Revising is an inherent part of the process.
insight (ihn syt) *n.*	clear idea of the nature of things	insightful	A preface provides insight into an author's purpose.
integrity (ihn TEHG ruh tee) *n.*	willingness to stand by moral principles		Heroes typically display great integrity.
interact (ihn tuhr AKT) *v.*	relate to one another; affect another	interaction interactive	The characters interact with one another in the play.
interpretation (ihn tur pruh TAY shuhn) *n.*	explanation of the meaning of something	interpret interpretive	Sonnets may have more than one interpretation.
isolation (y suh LAY shuhn) *n.*	being alone or set apart	isolate isolated	Poems address complex feelings such as isolation.
manipulate (muh NIHP yuh layt) *v.*	control by use of influence, often in an unfair way	manipulation manipulative	Some speakers use bias to manipulate their audiences.

Word	Definition	Related Words	Word in Context
meaning (MEE nihng) *n.*	significance of something	meaningful	Break down long sentences to help determine their meaning.
misinterpret (mihs ihn TUR priht) *v.*	not understand correctly	interpret misinterpretation	If you misinterpret the instructions, you will build it wrong.
modified (MOD uh fyd) *v.*	changed; altered slightly	modification modifier	The cross-outs revealed that he had modified his essay.
motive (MOH tihv) *n.*	something that causes a person to act in a certain way	motivate motivation	The character's motive was revealed in the conclusion.
objective (uhb JEHK tihv) *adj.*	not dependent on another's point of view	objectively	Critics should take an objective and unbiased stance.
oppose (uh POHZ) *v.*	set against; disagree with	opposing opposition	If you oppose another student's opinion, reply respectfully.
perspective (puhr SPEHK tihv) *n.*	the way one sees things; viewpoint		I enjoy an essay more if I understand the author's perspective.
principles (PRIHN suh puhlz) *n.*	rules for right conduct; basics	principled	The principles of spelling are simple.
radical (RAD uh kuhl) *adj.*	changed to an extreme degree	radicalism radically	Beat poetry was a radical departure from classic poetry.
resolute (REHZ uh loot) *adj.*	showing a fixed purpose	resolutely	He is resolute about being honest in his article.
resolve (rih ZOLV) *v.*	reach a conclusion or decision	resolution resolved	How do the enemies resolve their conflicts?
respond (rih SPOND) *v.*	answer; react to	respondent response	How do you respond to the suspense?
responsibility (rih spon suh BIHL uh tee) *n.*	having to answer to someone; being accountable for success or failure	responsible	It is your responsibility to cite your sources when writing a research report.
revise (rih VYZ)	modify	revision	Revise your paper by fixing any errors.
subjective (suhb JEHK tihv) *adj.*	based on or influenced by a person's feelings or point of view	subjectively subjectivity	It is difficult not to be subjective when debating.
unify (YOO nuh fy) *v.*	combine into one	unification	To unify the ideas, we should add transitions.

Ordinary Language: After reading further, I **changed** my original prediction.

Academic Language: After reading further, I **modified** my original prediction.

Ordinary Language: The author presents a unique **view** on the subject.

Academic Language: The author presents a unique **perspective** on the subject.

Practice

Examples of various kinds of domain-specific academic vocabulary appear in the charts below. On a separate piece of paper, create your own domain-specific academic vocabulary charts in which you enter new academic vocabulary words as you learn them.

Social Studies: Domain-Specific Academic Vocabulary

Word	Definition	Related Words	Word in Context
absolutism (AB suh loo tiz uhm) *n.*	the principle or the exercise of complete and unrestricted power in government	absolute	The leader's absolutism restricted the freedom of citizens.
cartography (kahr TOG ruh fee) *n.*	the design and production of maps	cartographer	The geologist studied cartography and made maps.
ideology (ahy dee OL uh jee) *n.*	the beliefs that guide individuals and groups	idea	The communist ideology took hold of eastern Europe in the twentieth century.
mercantilism (MUR kuhn ti liz uhm) *n.*	commercialism; the practice of trade and commercial activity	merchant	Mercantilism was a large factor in the exploration of new lands.
radicalism (RAD I kuh liz uhm) *n.*	the favoring of drastic political, economic, or social reforms	radical	Radicalism in certain parts of the world has led to violence.

Create a chart for these social studies academic vocabulary words: *demobilization, democratization, nomination, resettlement,* and *reunification.*

Mathematics: Domain-Specific Academic Vocabulary

Word	Definition	Related Words	Word in Context
binary system (BY nuh ree SIS tuhm) *n.*	a system of counting or measurement based on powers of two	binary digit binaries	Computers use the binary system.
derivative (dih RIV uh tiv) *n.*	the rate of change of a function at any given instant	derive derived	We are going to learn about derivatives in advanced math.
dilation (dy LEY shuhn) *n.*	the transformation that changes the size of the image in geometry	dilate	We studied the dilation of images in our geometry class.
tangent (TAN juhnt) *n.*	a line in the plane of a circle that touches the circle at only one point	tangential	We were asked to find the tangent of a circle.
vector (VEK ter) *n.*	a quantity possessing both magnitude and direction	vectors	In geometry, we learned that a vector has both magnitude and direction.

Create a chart for these mathematics academic vocabulary words: *arc, continuity, correlation, density,* and *variance.*

Science: Domain-Specific Academic Vocabulary

Word	Definition	Related Words	Word in Context
fission (FISH uhn) *n.*	splitting of the nucleus of an atom or a cell	fissure	Some organisms reproduce by fission.
fusion (FYOO zhuhn) *n.*	in physics, the joining of two nuclei to form one new nucleus	fuse	Nuclear fission and fusion are opposite processes.
genetic mutation (juh NET ik myoo TEY shuhn) *n.*	any event that changes the genetic structure of an organism	genes mutate	Some genetic mutations lead to health problems.
isotope (AHY suh tohp) *n.*	multiple forms of an element that have the same number of protons but a different number of neutrons	isotopic	There are several isotopes of hydrogen.
organelle (awr guh NEL) *n.*	a part of a cell that has a specialized function	organ organism	Cell walls and nuclei are examples of organelles.

Create a chart for these science academic vocabulary words: *catalyst, chloroplast, organic, mitochondrion,* and *semiconductor.*

Art: Domain-Specific Academic Vocabulary

Word	Definition	Related Words	Word in Context
aesthetics (es THET iks) *n.*	the study of nature, beauty, and art	aesthetic aesthetician	We studied the aesthetics of ancient Greek sculpture.
analogous colors (uh NAL uh guhs KUHL ers) *n.*	colors that are next to each other on the color wheel	analogy	The difference between analogous colors is small.
formalist (FAWR muhl ihst) *n.*	anyone who places importance on how well artists design their works	formal formalize	The critic, a formalist, liked the artists' exhibit.
imitationist (im i TEY shuhn ihst) *n.*	one who favors realism in representing art subjects	imitate imitation	Because I like realism, I call myself an imitationist.
radial balance (REY dee uhl BAL uhns) *n.*	positioning objects around a central point	balanced radius	The sun is an example of an object with radial balance.

Create a chart for these art academic vocabulary words: *asymmetrical balance, emphasis, gradation, harmony,* and *symmetrical balance.*

Technology: Domain-Specific Academic Vocabulary

Word	Definition	Related Words	Word in Context
central processing unit (SEN truhl PROS es ihng YOO nit) *n.*	component of a computer that interprets and executes programs.	CPU	The central processing unit is the "brain" of a computer.
local network system (LOH kuhl NET wurk SIS tuhm) *n.*	a system for linking computers that are close to each other	LAN	Our local network system allows us to share files.
microprocessor (MY kroh pros es er) *n.*	the part of a computer that performs logical functions	micro processing	The information was fed into the microprocessor.
peripheral device (puh RIF er uhl dih VYS) *n.*	device that attaches to a computer to perform a specific function	peripheral peripherally	This scanner is the newest peripheral device I have.
shortcut key	key or combination of keys that executes a command	cut shortcut	I used a shortcut key to run the spell checker.

Create a chart for these technology academic vocabulary words: *copyright violation, desktop publishing, Internet service provider, invasion of privacy,* and *operating system.*

Increasing Your Word Knowledge

Increase your word knowledge and chances of success by taking an active role in developing your vocabulary. Here are some tips for you.

To own a word, follow these steps:

Steps to Follow	Model
1. Learn to identify the word and its basic meaning.	The word *examine* means "to look at closely."
2. Take note of the word's spelling.	*Examine* begins and ends with an *e*.
3. Practice pronouncing the word so that you can use it in conversation.	The *e* on the end of the word *examine* is silent. Its second syllable gets the most stress.
4. Visualize the word and illustrate its key meaning.	When I think of the word *examine*, I visualize a doctor checking a patient's health.
5. Learn the various forms of the word and its related words.	*Examination* and *exam* are forms of the word *examine*.
6. Compare the word with similar words.	*Examine, peruse,* and *study* are synonyms.
7. Contrast the word with similar words.	*Examine* suggests a more detailed study than *read* or *look at*.
8. Use the word in various contexts.	"I'd like to *examine* the footprints more closely." "I will *examine* the use of imagery in this poem."

Building Your Speaking Vocabulary

Language gives us the ability to express ourselves. The more words you know, the better able you will be to get your points across. There are two main aspects of language: reading and speaking. Using the steps above will help you acquire a rich vocabulary. Follow these steps below to help you learn to use this rich vocabulary in discussions, speeches, and conversations.

Steps to Follow	Tip
1. Practice pronouncing the word.	Become familiar with pronunciation guides to allow you to sound out unfamiliar words. Listening to audio books as you read the text will help you learn pronunciations of words.
2. Learn word forms.	Dictionaries often list forms of words following the main word entry. Practice saying word families aloud: "generate," "generated," "generation," "regenerate," "generator."
3. Translate your thoughts.	Restate your own thoughts and ideas in a variety of ways, to inject formality or to change your tone, for example.
4. Hold discussions.	With a classmate, practice using academic vocabulary words in discussions about the text. Choose one term to practice at a time, and see how many statements you can create using that term.
5. Tape-record yourself.	Analyze your word choices by listening to yourself objectively. Note places your word choice could be strengthened or changed.

Writing an Objective Summary

The ability to write objective summaries is key to success in college and in many careers. Writing an effective objective summary involves recording the key ideas of a text while demonstrating your understanding.

 Common Core State Standards

Reading Literature
2. Determine a theme or central idea of a text and analyze in detail its development over the course of the text, including how it emerges and is shaped and refined by specific details; provide an objective summary of the text.

Reading Informational Text
2. Determine a central idea of a text and analyze its development over the course of the text, including how it emerges and is shaped and refined by specific details; provide an objective summary of the text.

What Is an Objective Summary?

An effective objective summary is a concise, complete, accurate, and objective overview of a text. Following are key elements of an objective summary:

- A good summary focuses on the main theme or central idea of a text and specific, relevant details that support that theme or central idea. Unnecessary supporting details are left out.
- Effective summaries are brief. However, the writer must be careful not to misrepresent the text by leaving out key elements.
- A summary should accurately capture the essence of the longer text it is describing.
- Finally, the writer must remain objective, that is, refrain from inserting his or her own opinions, reactions, or personal connections into the summary.

What to Avoid in an Objective Summary

- An objective summary is not a collection of sentences or paragraphs copied from the original source.
- It is not a long recounting of every event, detail, or point in the original text.
- Finally, a good summary does not include evaluative comments, such as the reader's overall opinion of or reaction to the piece.
- An objective summary is not the reader's interpretation or critical analysis of the work.

INFORMATIONAL TEXT

Model Objective Summary

Note the elements of an effective objective summary that are called out in the sidenotes. Then, write an objective summary of a text you have recently read. Review your summary, and delete any unnecessary details, opinions, or evaluations.

Summary of "The Gift of the Magi"

"The Gift of the Magi" by O. Henry is the ~~touching~~ story of a young couple named Jim and Della and what they give up in order to buy each other the perfect Christmas gift.

The story begins with Della counting the money she has scrimped to save. To her dismay, it only adds up to one dollar and eight-seven cents.

Della is looking around their humble flat when she comes up with an idea. Catching her reflection in the mirror, she decides that she will sell her most precious possession—her long, beautiful hair. She cries only a little before putting on her coat and going to a shop where she can sell her hair.

With the twenty dollars she receives for selling her hair and a dollar of her savings, Della buys Jim a chain to go with his most precious possession—a gold watch that had belonged to his father and to his grandfather before him.

At home, Della tries to fix her short hair by curling it and begins to prepare dinner. She prays that Jim still thinks she's pretty even without her long hair.

Jim arrives home on time, ~~right around 7 o'clock. Della notes that he is always on time.~~ He does not react in any of the ways Della thought he might. She is terrified when she can't read the peculiar expression on his face. She begins to ramble about her hair growing back and tells him that she sold it for a good reason—to buy him a gift.

Finally, Jim assures Della that her cutting off her hair does not change how he feels about her, and he hands her a package. When she opens the gift, Della understands the odd expression on his face. Jim bought her the expensive hair combs she had wanted for a very long time, only now she doesn't have the hair to put them in.

Della assures him that her hair will grow back quickly, and then she presents Jim with the watch chain she bought him. ~~Jim tumbled down on the couch and put his hands under the back of his head and smiles.~~ He tells her that he sold the watch in order to buy her the combs.

The story ends with the narrator discussing the Magi—the wise men who began the tradition of giving Christmas gifts—and challenging the reader to consider whether Jim and Della were foolish or wise in their gift-giving. ~~I think most readers will agree that their gifts to each other were wise and heartfelt.~~

A one-sentence synopsis highlighting the theme or central idea of the story can be an effective start to a summary.

An adjective describing the story indicates an opinion and should not be included in an objective summary.

Relating the development of the text in chronological order makes a summary easy to follow.

Unnecessary details should be eliminated.

This sentence should be paraphrased rather than copied exactly from the story.

Key narration at the end of the story is included in the summary.

The writer's opinions should not appear in an objective summary.

Comprehending Complex Texts

Common Core State Standards

Reading Literature
10. By the end of grade 10, read and comprehend literature, including stories, dramas, and poems, at the high end of the grades 9–10 text complexity band independently and proficiently.

Reading Informational Text
9. Analyze seminal U. S. documents of historical and literary significance (e.g., Washington's Farewell Address, the Gettysburg Address, Roosevelt's Four Freedoms speech, King's "Letter from Birmingham Jail"), including how they address related themes and concepts.

10. By the end of grade 10, read and comprehend literary nonfiction at the high end of the grades 9–10 text complexity band independently and proficiently.

Over the course of your academic years, you will be required to read increasingly complex texts as preparation for college and the workplace. A complex text is a work that contains challenging vocabulary, long, complex sentences, figurative language, multiple levels of meaning, or unfamiliar settings and situations.

The selections in this textbook provide you with a range of readings, including short stories, autobiography, poetry, drama, myths, and even science and history texts. Some of these texts will fall within your comfort zone; others will most likely be more challenging.

Strategy 1: Multi-draft Reading

Good readers develop the habit of revisiting texts in order to comprehend them completely. Get in the habit of reading a text or portions of a text two to three times in order to get the most out of your reading experience. To fully understand a text, try this multi-draft reading strategy:

1st Reading

On your first reading, read to gain the basic meaning of the text. If, for example, you are reading a story, look for the basics: who did what and to whom; what conflicts arise; how are conflicts resolved. If the text is nonfiction, look for main ideas and ways in which they are presented. If you are reading a lyric poem, identify the speaker, setting, and subject.

2nd Reading

During your second reading, focus on the artistry or effectiveness of the writing. Look for text structures and think about why the author chose those organizational patterns. Then, examine the author's creative use of language and its effects. For example, does the author employ metaphor, simile, or hyperbole? If so, what effect does that use of figurative language create?

3rd Reading

After your third reading, compare and contrast the text with others you have read that share an important feature. For example, once you have read Theodore Roosevelt's Inauguration Address (p. lix) and the excerpt from Dwight D. Eisenhower's speech (p. lxi), compare the way each speaker approaches the theme of national responsibility in a complex world. Evaluate the text's overall effectiveness and its central idea or theme.

INFORMATIONAL TEXT

Independent Practice

As you read this text, practice the multi-draft reading strategy by completing a chart like the one below.

---

from Theodore Roosevelt's Inaugural Address, March 4 1905

. . . Our relations with the other powers of the world are important; but still more important are our relations among ourselves. Such growth in wealth, in population, and in power as this nation has seen during the century and a quarter of its national life is inevitably accompanied by a like growth in the problems which are ever before every nation that rises to greatness. Power invariably means both responsibility and danger. Our forefathers faced certain perils which we have outgrown. We now face other perils, the very existence of which it was impossible that they should foresee. Modern life is both complex and intense, and the tremendous changes wrought by the extraordinary industrial development of the last half century are felt in every fiber of our social and political being. Never before have men tried so vast and formidable an experiment as that of administering the affairs of a continent under the forms of a Democratic republic. The conditions which have told for our marvelous material well-being, which have developed to a very high degree our energy, self-reliance, and individual initiative, have also brought the care and anxiety inseparable from the accumulation of great wealth in industrial centers. Upon the success of our experiment much depends, not only as regards our own welfare, but as regards the welfare of mankind. . . .

Multi-Draft Reading Chart

	My Understanding
1st Reading Look for key ideas and details that unlock basic meaning, concepts, and themes.	
2nd Reading Read for deeper meanings. Look for ways in which the author uses text structures and language to enhance meaning.	
3rd Reading Read to integrate your knowledge and ideas. Connect the text to others of its kind and to your own experience.	

Strategy 2: Close Read the Text

To comprehend a complex text, perform a close reading—a careful analysis of the words, phrases, and sentences within the text. As you close read, use the following tips to increase your understanding:

Tips for Close Reading
1. **Break down long sentences into parts.** Look for the subject of the sentence and its verb. Then, identify which parts of the sentence modify, or give more information about, its subject.
2. **Reread passages.** When reading complex texts, re-read difficult passages to make sure that you understand their meaning.

3. **Look for context clues,** such as the following:
 	
  a. Restatement of an idea. For example, in this sentence, "wasted away" restates the verb *atrophy*.
    He exercised so that his muscles would not **atrophy,** or <u>waste away</u>, because of disuse.
 	
  b. Definition of sophisticated words. In this sentence, the underlined information defines the word *monotonous*.
    The **monotonous** song was <u>dull and unvarying</u>.
 	
  c. Examples of concepts and topics. In the following passage, the underlined text provides an example of the adjective *sparse*.
    The **sparse** room <u>lacked proper furniture for guests and had no decorations on the walls</u>.
 	
  d. Contrasts of ideas and topics.
    Abandoning his usual **veracity,** Eli <u>decided to fabricate a story</u> about why he missed practice.

4. **Identify pronoun antecedents.** If long sentences or passages contain pronouns, reread the text to make sure you know to what or whom the pronouns refer. In the following passage, the underlined pronouns all have the antecedent *love*. Love has been accused of many things. *It* has caused wars, and *it* has brought peace. *It* drives people to insanity, and *it* cures disease. *It* allows the dead to live on, in the broken hearts of their survivors.
5. **Look for conjunctions,** such as *and*, *or*, and *yet*, to understand relationships between ideas.
6. **Paraphrase,** or restate in your own words, challenging passages in order to check your understanding. Remember that a paraphrase is a word-for-word rephrasing of an original text; it is not a summary.

INFORMATIONAL TEXT

Close-Read Model

As you read President Eisenhower's Address Before the General Assembly of the United Nations on December 8th, 1953, study the side notes that model ways to unlock meaning in the text.

 Common Core State Standards

Reading Informational Text 9. Analyze seminal U. S. documents of historical and literary significance (e.g., Washington's Farewell Address, the Gettysburg Address, Roosevelt's Four Freedoms speech, King's "Letter from Birmingham Jail"), including how they address related themes and concepts.

from "Atoms for Peace" by Dwight D. Eisenhower

Madame President, Members of the General Assembly:

. . .I know that the American people share my deep belief that if a danger exists in the world, it is a danger shared by all—and equally, that if hope exists in the mind of one nation, that hope should be shared by all...I feel impelled to speak today in a language that in a sense is new—one which I, who have spent so much of my life in the military profession, would have preferred never to use.

That new language is the language of atomic warfare. . .

Occasional pages of history do record the faces of the "Great Destroyers" but the whole book of history reveals mankind's never-ending quest for peace, and mankind's God-given capacity to build. It is with the book of history, and not with isolated pages, that the United States will ever wish to be identified. My country wants to be constructive, not destructive. It wants agreements, not wars, among nations. It wants itself to live in freedom, and in the confidence that the people of every other nation enjoy equally the right of choosing their own way of life.

So my country's purpose is to help us move out of the dark chamber of horrors into the light, to find a way by which the minds of men, the hopes of men, the souls of men everywhere, can move forward toward peace and happiness and well being. In this quest, I know that we must not lack patience. I know that in a world divided, such as ours today, salvation cannot be attained by one dramatic act. I know that many steps will have to be taken over many months before the world can look at itself one day and truly realize that a new climate of mutually peaceful confidence is abroad in the world. But I know, above all else, that we must start to take these steps—now.

Break down this long sentence. The speaker, *I*, is the subject, and *know* is the verb. The first phrase highlighted in green tells what the speaker knows. The last two phrases highlighted in green modify the word *belief*.

Search for context clues. The words highlighted in green can help you figure out the word highlighted in yellow.

The word "so" signals that a summarization of a key point is to come: America wants to help the world change direction.

Look for antecedents. The "we" refers to President Eisenhower and the members of the General Assembly of the United Nations.

Strategy 3: Ask Questions

Be an attentive reader by asking questions as you read. Throughout this textbook, we have provided questions for you following each selection. These questions are sorted into three basic categories that build in sophistication and lead you to a deeper understanding of the texts you read.

Here is an example from this text:

Some questions are about **Key Ideas and Details** in the text. To answer these questions, you will need to locate and cite explicit information in the text or draw inferences from what you have read.

Some questions are about **Craft and Structure** in the text. To answer these questions, you will need to analyze how the author developed and structured the text. You will also look for ways in which the author artfully used language and how those word choices impacted the meaning and tone of the work.

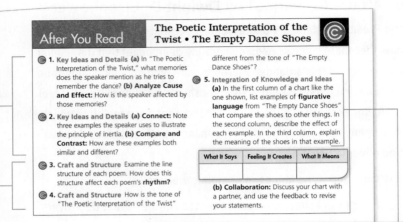

After You Read

The Poetic Interpretation of the Twist • The Empty Dance Shoes

1. **Key Ideas and Details (a)** In "The Poetic Interpretation of the Twist," what memories does the speaker mention as he tries to remember the dance? **(b) Analyze Cause and Effect:** How is the speaker affected by those memories?

2. **Key Ideas and Details (a) Connect:** Note three examples the speaker uses to illustrate the principle of inertia. **(b) Compare and Contrast:** How are these examples both similar and different?

3. **Craft and Structure** Examine the line structure of each poem. How does this structure affect each poem's **rhythm?**

4. **Craft and Structure** How is the tone of "The Poetic Interpretation of the Twist" different from the tone of "The Empty Dance Shoes"?

5. **Integration of Knowledge and Ideas (a)** In the first column of a chart like the one shown, list examples of **figurative language** from "The Empty Dance Shoes" that compare the shoes to other things. In the second column, describe the effect of each example. In the third column, explain the meaning of the shoes in that example.

What It Says	Feeling It Creates	What It Means

(b) Collaboration: Discuss your chart with a partner, and use the feedback to revise your statements.

Some questions are about the **Integration of Knowledge and Ideas** in the text. These questions ask you to evaluate a text in many different ways, such as comparing texts, analyzing arguments in the text, and using many other methods of thinking critically about a text's ideas.

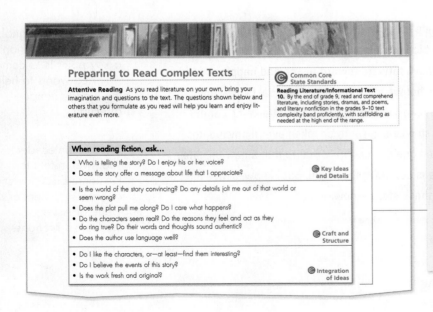

Preparing to Read Complex Texts

Attentive Reading As you read literature on your own, bring your imagination and questions to the text. The questions shown below and others that you formulate as you read will help you learn and enjoy literature even more.

Common Core State Standards

**Reading Literature/Informational Text
10.** By the end of grade 9, read and comprehend literature, including stories, dramas, and poems, and literary nonfiction in the grades 9–10 text complexity band proficiently, with scaffolding as needed at the high end of the range.

When reading fiction, ask...

- Who is telling the story? Do I enjoy his or her voice?
- Does the story offer a message about life that I appreciate?

Key Ideas and Details

- Is the world of the story convincing? Do any details jolt me out of that world or seem wrong?
- Does the plot pull me along? Do I care what happens?
- Do the characters seem real? Do the reasons they feel and act as they do ring true? Do their words and thoughts sound authentic?
- Does the author use language well?

Craft and Structure

- Do I like the characters, or—at least—find them interesting?
- Do I believe the events of this story?
- Is the work fresh and original?

Integration of Ideas

As you read independently, ask similar types of questions to ensure that you fully enjoy and comprehend texts you read for both school and pleasure. We have provided sets of questions for you on the Independent Reading pages at the end of each unit.

Ⓒ EXEMPLAR TEXT

Model

Following is an example of a complex text. The sidenotes show sample questions that an attentive reader might ask while reading.

Sample questions:

from "Classifying the Stars" by Annie J. Cannon

To the People of the State of New York:

...The very beginning of our knowledge of the nature of a star dates back to 1672, when Isaac Newton gave to the world the results of his experiments on passing sunlight through a prism. To describe the beautiful band of rainbow tints, produced when sunlight was dispersed by his three-cornered piece of glass, he took from the Latin the word *spectrum*, meaning "an appearance."

Key Ideas and Details What ideas are introduced in this paragraph? What assumptions does the author make?

...In 1814, more than a century after Newton, the spectrum of the Sun was obtained in such purity that an amazing detail was seen and studied by the German optician, Fraunhofer. He saw that the multiple spectral tings, ranging from delicate violet to deep red, were crossed by hundreds of fine dark lines. In other words, there were narrow gaps in the spectrum where certain shades were wholly blotted out.

Craft and Structure What organizational pattern does the writer use? How does the use of this pattern help to convey her ideas?

We must remember that the word spectrum is applied not only to sunlight, but also to the light of any glowing substance when its rays are sorted out by a prism or a grating.

Integration of Knowledge and Ideas In what ways does the information in this text expand on or contradict what I already know?

Ⓒ EXEMPLAR TEXT

Independent Practice

Write three to five questions you might ask yourself as you read this passage.

From "Circumference" by Nicholas Nicastro

The astrolabe ... is a manual computing and observation device with myriad uses in astronomy, time keeping, surveying, navigation, and astrology. The principles behind the most common variety, the planispheric astrolabe, were first laid down in antiquity by the Greeks, who pioneered the notion of projecting three-dimensional images on flat surfaces. The device reached a high degree of refinement in the medieval Islamic world, where it was invaluable for determining prayer times and the direction of Mecca from anywhere in the Muslim world. The astrolabe was introduced to Europe by the eleventh century, where it saw wide use until the Renaissance....

Analyzing Arguments

The ability to evaluate an argument, as well as to make one, is an important skill for success in college and in the workplace.

What Is an Argument?

In literature and writing, an *argument* is the presentation of one side of a controversial or debatable issue. Through this type of argument, the writer logically supports a particular belief, conclusion, or point of view. A good argument is supported with strong reasoning and relevant, provable evidence.

Elements of Argument

Claim (assertion)—what the writer is trying to prove
Example: Grade point averages should be weighted.

Grounds (evidence)—the support used to convince the reader
Example: Because difficult classes require much more work, the extra effort should be acknowledged.

Justification—the link between the grounds and the claim; why the grounds are credible
Example: Because GPA is an indication of a student's ability to succeed in college, students who take challenging courses should be ranked above students who take easier classes even if they earn the same grade.

Evaluating Claims

When reading or listening to an argument, critically assess the claims that are made. Analyze the argument to identify claims that are valid or can be proved true. Also evaluate evidence that supports the claims. If there is little or no reasoning or evidence provided to support the claims, the argument may not be sound. Also, be on the lookout for logical fallacies, like those listed below.

Logical Fallacies

Although they can initially seem convincing, logical fallacies do not hold up in an examination of an argument.

- **False Causality:** The invalid idea that because B occurred after A, A caused B to happen
- *Ad Hominem:* An attack on a person's character, not on the person's position on an issue
- **Red Herring:** A provocative idea that is included in an argument to distract an audience's attention from the real issue under discussion
- **Begging the Question:** The premise or assumption that the argument is true because it is said to be true
- **Overgeneralization:** A conclusion that is based on little or no evidence

 Common Core
State Standards

Reading Informational Text
6. Determine an author's point of view or purpose in a text and analyze how an author uses rhetoric to advance that point of view or purpose.
8. Delineate and evaluate the argument and specific claims in a text, assessing whether the reasoning is valid and the evidence is relevant and sufficient; identify false statements and fallacious reasoning.
Language
6. Acquire and use accurately grade-appropriate general academic and domain-specific words and phrases; gather vocabulary knowledge when considering a word or phrase important to comprehension or expression.

Model Argument

from "Thank Heaven for Little Girls" by Rich Stearns

The lyrics to Maurice Chevalier's most enduring song describe an idyllic view of little girls and the women they become. There is much in our art and literature that romanticizes girls and women and the role they play in our culture. But sadly, in our world today, being female often means being sentenced to a life of poverty, abuse, exploitation, and deprivation. Compared to her male counterpart, a girl growing up in the developing world is more likely to die before her fifth birthday and less likely to go to school. She is less likely to receive adequate food or health care, less likely to receive economic opportunities, more likely to be forced to marry before the age of 16 . . . Girls are forced to stay home from school to work. In fact, two thirds of the nearly 800 million illiterate people in the world are women. Only one in 10 women in Niger can read. Five hundred thousand women die every year from childbirth complications—that's one woman every minute . . . Women are denied property rights and inheritance in many countries. Worldwide, women own only 1 percent of the world's property. They work two-thirds of all the world's labor hours but earn just 10 percent of the world's wages. Being female, in much of our world, is not "heavenly."

And yet, in my opinion, the single-most significant thing that can be done to "cure" extreme poverty is this: protect, educate, and nurture girls and women and provide them with equal rights and opportunities—educationally, economically, and socially.

According to U.N. Secretary-General Kofi Annan: "No tool for development is more effective than the empowerment of women." This one thing can do more to address extreme poverty than food, shelter, health care, economic development, or increased foreign assistance. There is a saying in Ghana: "If you educate a man, you simply educate an individual, but if you educate a woman, you educate a nation." When a girl is educated, her income potential increases, maternal and infant mortality is reduced, her children are more likely to be immunized, the birth rate decreases, and HIV infection rates (especially in Africa) are lowered. She is more likely to acquire skills to improve her family's economic stability, and she is more likely to ensure that her daughters also receive an education. Educating girls pays dividend after dividend to the whole community. . .

The introduction explains the title and references a popular 1950s song to hook readers.

This paragraph describes the poverty and lack of freedoms that women face. Stearns will go on to argue that improving one (freedom) will improve the other (conditions of poverty).

Claim: Educating women relieves poverty.

Grounds: The claim is supported by a quotation from U.N. Secretary-General Kofi Annan and by a Ghanaian saying. Benefits from educating girls range from reducing infant mortality to improving economic stability. These benefits are assumed to address poverty and its effects.

Unstated Justification: The evidence comes from a wide range of sources: the U.N. Secretary-General, who is an authority on international issues; an African saying; and the summarized results of implied research.

A strong conclusion does more than simply restate the claim.

The Art of Argument: Rhetorical Devices and Persuasive Techniques

Rhetorical Devices

Rhetoric is the art of using language in order to make a point or to persuade listeners. Rhetorical devices such as the ones listed below are accepted elements of argument. Their use does not invalidate or weaken an argument. Rather, the use of rhetorical devices is regarded as a key part of an effective argument.

Rhetorical Device	Examples
Repetition The repeated use of certain words, phrases, or sentences	Soldiers learn **true** greatness, **true** wisdom, and **true** strength.
Parallelism The repeated use of similar grammatical structures	Sports teach **the thrill of victory** and **the agony of defeat.**
Rhetorical Question Calling attention to an issue by implying an obvious answer	Isn't freedom worth fighting for?
Sound Devices The use of alliteration, assonance, rhyme, or rhythm	There are **d**ark **d**ays that lie ahead, but we will not be **d**efeated!
Simile and Metaphor Comparing two seemingly unlike things or asserting that one thing is another	**Patriotism** spread <u>like a fire</u> through the ranks of soldiers after the General's speech.

Persuasive Techniques

Persuasive techniques are often used in advertisements and in other forms of persuasion. Although techniques like the ones below may appear in formal arguments, they are less convincing than the use of logical reasoning and authoritative evidence.

Persuasive Technique	Examples
Bandwagon Approach/Anti-Bandwagon Approach Appeals to a person's desire to belong; encourages or celebrates individuality	Come see why more people choose to shop with us.
Emotional Appeal Evokes people's fear, anger, or desire	Join the army and protect our nation from those who would destroy our way of life.
Endorsement/Testimony Employs a well-known person to promote a product or idea	"I drink Happy Throat Tea before all of my concerts."
Loaded Language The use of words that are charged with emotion	They are suffering under a brutal dictator.
"Plain Folks" Appeal Shows a connection to everyday, ordinary people	"I grew up in a working-class neighborhood, just like this one."
Hyperbole Exaggerates to make a point	We face a thousand crises everyday.

INFORMATIONAL TEXT

Model Speech

The speech excerpted below includes rhetorical devices and persuasive techniques.

from "Duty, Honor, Country" by General Douglas MacArthur

Duty, Honor, Country: Those three hallowed words reverently dictate what you ought to be, what you can be, what you will be. They are your rallying points: to build courage when courage seems to fail; to regain faith when there seems to be little cause for faith; to create hope when hope becomes forlorn. Unhappily, I possess neither that eloquence of diction, that poetry of imagination, nor that brilliance of metaphor to tell you all that they mean...

> General MacArthur uses parallelism and repetition to emphasize the ideas of *duty, honor,* and *country.*

But these are some of the things they do. They build your basic character. They mold you for your future roles as the custodians of the nation's defense. They make you strong enough to know when you are weak, and brave enough to face yourself when you are afraid. They teach you to be proud and unbending in honest failure, but humble and gentle in success; not to substitute words for actions, not to seek the path of comfort, but to face the stress and spur of difficulty and challenge;... They give you a temper of the will, a quality of the imagination, a vigor of the emotions, a freshness of the deep springs of life, a temperamental predominance of courage over timidity, of an appetite for adventure over love of ease. They create in your heart the sense of wonder, the unfailing hope of what next, and the joy and inspiration of life. They teach you in this way to be an officer and a gentleman.

> Additional instances of parallelism clarify General MacArthur's ideas and make them more emotionally engaging.

And what sort of soldiers are those you are to lead? Are they reliable? Are they brave? Are they capable of victory? Their story is known to all of you. It is the story of the American man at arms...His name and fame are the birthright of every American citizen. In his youth and strength, his love and loyalty, he gave all that mortality can give....

> Rhetorical questions call attention to a change in the topic.

From one end of the world to the other, he has drained deep the chalice of courage. As I listened to those songs of the glee club, in memory's eye I could see those staggering columns of the First World War, bending under soggy packs on many a weary march, from dripping dusk to drizzling dawn, slogging ankle deep through mire of shell-pocked roads; to form grimly for the attack, blue-lipped, covered with sludge and mud, chilled by the wind and rain, driving home to their objective, and for many, to the judgment seat of God.

> MacArthur uses alliteration, which gives his descriptions more power.

I do not know the dignity of their birth, but I do know the glory of their death. They died unquestioning, uncomplaining, with faith in their hearts, and on their lips the hope that we would go on to victory. Always for them Duty, Honor, Country.

> Parallelism makes this phrase memorable and powerful.

> Repetition of key ideas from the beginning of the speech provides a satisfying conclusion.

Composing an Argument

**Common Core
State Standards**

Writing 1.a. Introduce precise claim(s), distinguish the claim(s) from alternate or opposing claims, and create an organization that establishes clear relationships among claim(s), counterclaims, reasons, and evidence.
1.b. Develop claim(s) and counterclaims fairly, supplying evidence for each while pointing out the strengths and limitations of both in a manner that anticipates the audience's knowledge level and concerns.
1.e. Provide a concluding statement or section that follows from and supports the argument presented.

Choosing a Topic

When writing an argument, choose a topic that matters—to people in general and to you personally. Brainstorm for topics you would like to address, and then choose the one that most interests you.

Once you have chosen a topic, check to be sure you can make an arguable claim. Ask yourself:

1. What am I trying to prove? What ideas do I need to communicate?
2. Are there people who would disagree with my claim? What opinions might they have?
3. Do I have evidence to support my claim? Is my evidence sufficient and relevant?

If you are able to put into words what you want to prove and can answer "Yes" to questions 2 and 3, you have an arguable claim.

Introducing the Claim and Establishing Its Significance

Before you begin writing, think about your audience and how much they already know about your topic. Then, provide only as much background information as necessary. Remember that you are not writing a summary of the issue—you are crafting an argument.

Once you have provided context for your argument, clearly state your claim, or thesis. A written argument's claim often, but not always, appears in the first paragraph.

Developing Your Claim with Reasoning and Evidence

Now that you have stated your claim, support it with evidence, or grounds. A good argument should be supported with at least three solid pieces of evidence. Evidence can range from personal experience to researched data or expert opinion. Understanding your audience's knowledge level, concerns, values, and possible biases can help you decide which types of evidence will have the strongest impact. Make sure your evidence is current and comes from a credible source. Do not forget to credit your sources.

Work to address opposing ideas, or counterclaims, within the body of your argument. Consider points you have made or evidence you have provided that a reader might challenge. Decide how best to respond to these counterclaims.

Writing a Concluding Statement or Section

Restate your claim in the conclusion of your argument, and synthesize, or pull together, the evidence you have provided. Make your conclusion powerful and memorable so that your readers continue to think about your points.

Practice

Complete an outline like the one below to help you plan your own argument.

Brainstorming for Topics:

_____

_____

The Topic That Most Interests Me Is _____ because

_____

Arguable Claim (Thesis): _____

What I Already Know About the Issue: _____

What I Need to Find Out About the Issue:

_____

Who Is My Audience and How Much Does My Audience Know About the Issue?

_____

Possible Sources of Evidence: _____

Grounds to Support My Claim (at least three strong pieces of evidence):

1._____

2._____

3._____

Warrants for My Grounds (why my grounds are allowed to stand as evidence):

1._____

2._____

3._____

Opposing Viewpoints to Consider: _____

Media Literacy Handbook

INTRODUCTION: Today, messages are transmitted across a variety of media modes, such as film, television, radio, and the Internet. As you interact with these messages each day—in images, advertisements, movies, and an array of different contexts—it is important to consider the potential influence of the medium.

• What is the intention of the message?

• How is it communicated?

• How do specific elements of the medium—such as color, image, or font—help convey the message?

• Why might the creator of the message have selected this medium?

These are the key issues of media literacy, the study of messages in the media and their impact.

Camera Shots and Angles
Filmmakers create camera shots and sequences to help them tell stories. Some shots capture an entire scene; others zoom in on specific characters.

Special Effects

Filmmakers use special effects to create on-screen illusions that bring the imagination to life.

Questions About Film Techniques

- What effect is created by the choice of camera angle shown in the image at left? Choose another camera angle and explain how that shot might convey a different message than the one shown here.

- Study the images above. In what way does the use of special effects make the film better for viewers?

Media Literacy Handbook

Focus and Framing
A sharp focus captures all details in a photographic image. A softer focus lessens the amount of detail that can be seen. The framing of elements within a photograph directs the eye toward a portion of the image.

Lighting and Shadow
Lighting techniques are used in photography to enhance mood and direct the viewer's focus.

Special Techniques

Most images you see today have been manipulated or changed in some way. Even a small change—such as an added graphic element or a difference in shading—can alter the mood of an image.

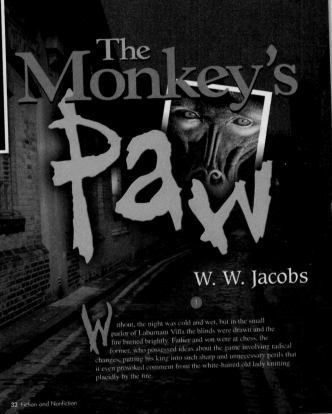

Questions About Graphics and Photos

- What would be the effect if the images at left used different focuses?

- In what way does the use of color and light create mood in the photos at left?

- What special techniques were applied to the original photographs shown above? What effect does the use of special techniques create?

Persuasive Techniques
Advertisements use carefully selected visual elements to appeal to the viewer's emotions.

Text and Graphics

Newspaper and magazine layouts are constructed to capture the eye and quickly convey the important ideas of a story. The use of type fonts, images, and page space directs the eye to portions of the printed page.

Questions About Print Media

- What image or graphic dominates the advertisement at left? How does the image make the advertisement more effective?

- Which of the above grabs your attention: the image or the text on the magazine cover? Explain.

- What do you notice first on the newspaper's front page? What overall effect does the use of type size and fonts create?

How is this book organized?

- There are six units, each focusing on a specific genre.
- Each unit has a Big Question to get you thinking about important ideas and to guide your reading.
- A Literary Analysis Workshop begins each unit, providing instruction and practice for essential skills.

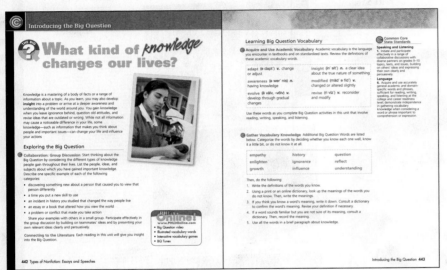

◀ At the beginning of the unit, **Introducing the Big Question** provides a reading focus for the entire unit. Use **academic vocabulary** to think, talk, and write about this question.

A **Literary Analysis Workshop** provides an overview of the unit genre, an in-depth exploration of Common Core State Standards, as well as models and practice opportunities. ▶

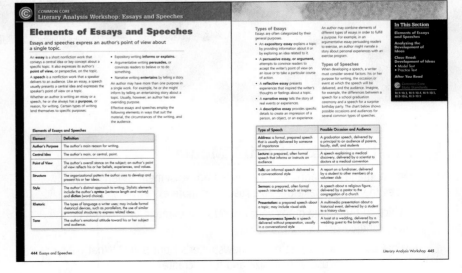

How are the literary selections organized?

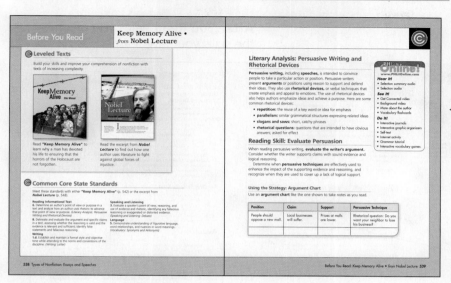

◄ **Before You Read** introduces two selection choices that both teach the same skills. Your teacher will help you choose the selection that is right for you.

Writing About the Big Question is a quick-writing activity that helps you connect the Big Question to the selection you are about to read.

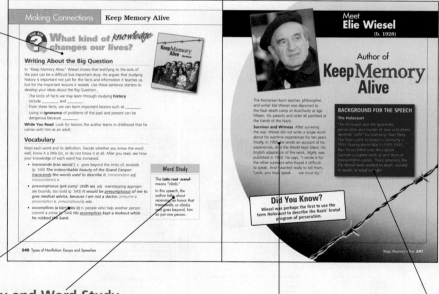

Vocabulary and Word Study introduce important selection vocabulary words and teach you about prefixes, suffixes, and roots.

Meet the Author and Background teach you about the author's life and provide information that will help you understand the selection.

How are the literary selections organized? *(continued)*

After You Read helps you practice the skills you have learned. ▼

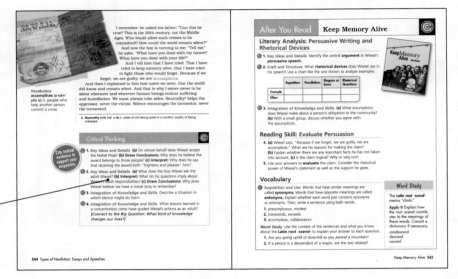

Critical Thinking questions help you reflect on what you have read and apply the Big Question to the selection.

Projects and activities help you deepen your understanding of the selection while strengthening your **writing, listening, speaking, and research skills.**

Integrated Language Skills provides instruction and practice for important grammar skills.

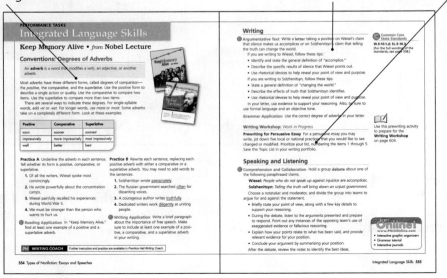

What special features will I find in this book?

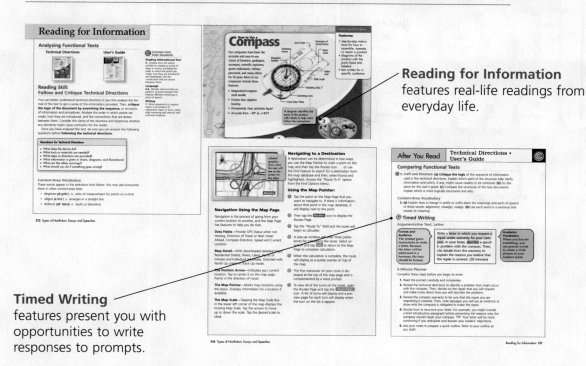

Reading for Information
features real-life readings from everyday life.

Timed Writing
features present you with opportunities to write responses to prompts.

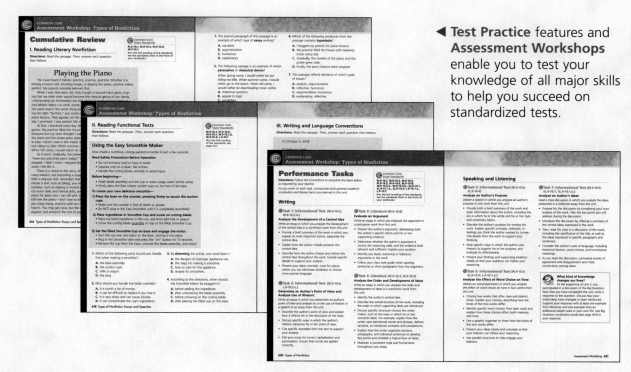

◀ **Test Practice** features and **Assessment Workshops** enable you to test your knowledge of all major skills to help you succeed on standardized tests.

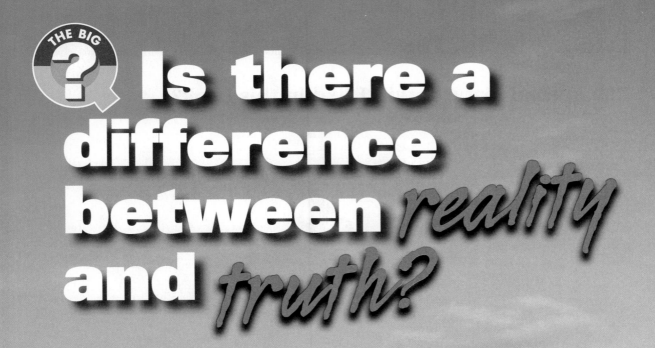

Is there a difference between *reality* and *truth?*

THE BIG
?

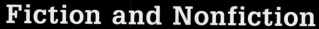

PHLit
Online!
www.PHLitOnline.com

Hear It!
- Selection summary audio
- Selection audio
- BQ Tunes

See It!
- Author videos
- Big Question video
- Get Connected videos
- Background videos
- More about the authors
- Illustrated vocabulary words
- Vocabulary flashcards

Do It!
- Interactive journals
- Interactive graphic organizers
- Grammar tutorials
- Interactive vocabulary games
- Test practice

1

Is there a difference between *reality* and *truth?*

Reality and **truth** may seem like abstract ideas, but they can influence the way you see the world. The truth is something that has been proven or that we believe is so. However, the truth can be subjective, or influenced by each person's perceptions or life experiences. In contrast, reality refers to all the things that exist in the world. Our senses, such as sight and touch, help us discern what is real. However, things that are not concrete and observable can still exist.

Two people might watch the same event, for example, but observe different things. What is true about the event to one person is not true to the other. A video might seem more objective than a diary entry about an event, but even a recording is influenced by a whole variety of subjective factors, including decisions about editing and what to include on camera. Ultimately, although it is useful to think about how people perceive reality and truth, the answer is, to some extent, as individual as people themselves.

Exploring the Big Question

Collaboration: Group Discussion Start thinking about the Big Question. With a small group, list things that are true for some but may differ from reality or from other people's perception of the truth. Describe specific examples of each of the following, building on each other's ideas.

- Something that is easy for you and difficult for a friend
- Something that you and your parents see differently
- The solution to a political issue
- A scientific theory that has some uncertainty

For each example, discuss whether truth differs from reality. State your case clearly and persuasively.

Connecting to the Literature Each reading in this unit will give you additional insight into the Big Question.

PHLit
Online!
www.PHLitOnline.com
- Big Question video
- Illustrated vocabulary words
- Interactive vocabulary games
- BQ Tunes

Learning Big Question Vocabulary

Acquire and Use Academic Vocabulary Academic vocabulary is the language you encounter in textbooks and on standardized tests. Review the definitions of these academic vocabulary words.

comprehend (käm´ prē hend´) v. understand

confirm (kən furm´) v. establish the truth or correctness of something

context (kän´ tekst´) n. circumstances that surround an event or idea and give it meaning

differentiate (dif´ ər en shē āt´) v. distinguish between

discern (di surn´, di zurn´) v. tell the difference between two or more things

evaluate (ē val´ yōō āt´) v. determine the worth of something

objective (əb jek´ tiv) adj. not dependent on a person's viewpoint

subjective (səb jek´ tiv) adj. influenced by a person's viewpoint

Use these words as you complete Big Question activities in this unit that involve reading, writing, speaking, and listening.

Gather Vocabulary Knowledge Additional Big Question words are listed below. Categorize the words by deciding whether you know each one well, know it a little bit, or do not know it at all.

concrete	perception	uncertainty
evidence	reality	verify
improbable		

Then, do the following:

1. Write the definitions of the words you know.

2. Consult a print or online dictionary to confirm the meanings you wrote down. Revise your original definitions if necessary.

3. Using the dictionary, look up the meanings of the words you do not know. Then, rewrite the definitions in your own words.

4. Use all the words in a paragraph about a situation in which it is difficult to discover the truth because people's perceptions of reality are so different.

Common Core State Standards

Speaking and Listening
1. Initiate and participate effectively in a range of collaborative discussions with diverse partners on grade 9–10 topics, texts, and issues, building on others' ideas and expressing their own clearly and persuasively.

Language
6. Acquire and use accurately general academic and domain-specific words and phrases, sufficient for reading, writing, speaking, and listening at the college and career readiness level; demonstrate independence in gathering vocabulary knowledge when considering a word or phrase important to comprehension or expression.

Elements of Fiction and Nonfiction

In **fiction,** an author tells of imaginary characters and events. In **nonfiction,** an author discusses facts or general ideas.

Fiction consists of **narratives,** or stories, that are products of an author's imagination. Not every detail in a work of fiction needs to be made up. For example, a short story may be set in a real place. Certain kinds of fiction routinely combine elements of the imaginary and the actual. In a historical novel, for example, an author may portray actual historical figures interacting with imaginary characters.

Nonfiction conveys factual information about real people, places, and events or discusses general ideas about the world. An author may describe a subject, explain how to perform a process, examine a theory, or try to convince readers to change their beliefs or take a particular course of action. Though nonfiction concerns fact, it may employ elements of fiction, such as striking language and artful pacing.

Comparison of Fiction and Nonfiction	
Fiction	**Nonfiction**
portrays imaginary people or animals, called **characters**	gives factual information about real people
describes a series of interrelated events, called the **plot**	gives factual information about real events and processes
depicts **conflicts,** or struggles between opposing forces, experienced by characters. These conflicts may be • **internal** psychological struggles, or • struggles with an **external** force.	tells of actual conflicts and real-world problems
is told from the **point of view,** or perspective, of an imaginary speaker called the **narrator.** The story may be told in the • **first-person point of view,** in which the narrator is a character in the story, or • **the third-person point of view,** in which the narrator is not a character in the story.	may be told from the point of view of the author, who is a real person, or may be written from a more **objective,** or neutral, point of view
takes place in a **setting**—a real or an imaginary time and place, including its beliefs and customs	provides factual information about real times, places, or cultures
often suggests a **theme,** or insight into life	often focuses on a **central idea,** or key concept

Major Forms of Fiction

There are three major forms of fiction.

Short stories are brief narratives. Their plots develop quickly and center around one or two main characters and a single, strong conflict and theme.

Novels are extended narratives that typically develop multiple characters, an extensive plot, and multiple conflicts. Novels often develop **subplots,** or distinct sequences of events that support or contrast with the main plot, and multiple themes.

Novellas are more concise than novels but lengthier than short stories. Novellas focus on a few main characters and a main plot, but they may develop characters and plots in more detail than a short story and may suggest more than one theme.

Major Forms of Nonfiction

Nonfiction may be divided into two large categories: functional texts and literary nonfiction.

Functional texts present facts and information intended to inform or educate the reader. Functional texts are generally objective: They do not express a particular author's point of view, and the writing style is usually clear and straightforward.

Literary nonfiction also presents facts about a subject, but it may employ literary elements such as descriptive language and dialogue to do so. As a result, it may entertain readers as well as inform them. Unlike functional texts, literary nonfiction may express the author's individual point of view.

The chart below lists and explains examples of functional texts and literary nonfiction.

In This Section

Elements of Fiction and Nonfiction

Determining Theme in Fiction

Determining Central Ideas in Nonfiction

Close Read: Theme in Fiction
- Model Text
- Practice Text

Close Read: Central Idea in Nonfiction
- Model Text
- Practice Text

After You Read

 Common Core
State Standards

RL.9-10.2; RI.9-10.2
[For the full wording of the standards, see the standards chart in the front of your textbook.]

Examples of Functional Texts	Forms of Literary Nonfiction
Reports: detailed accounts of specific topics that • synthesize, or combine, information from a variety of sources • may organize and interpret the results of studies	**Personal narratives:** true stories by real people about their own lives • The author of an **autobiography** describes major events in his or her life. • The author of a **memoir** or **journal entry** describes a particular time or experience in detail.
Newsletters: collections of brief announcements, articles, and reports published at regular intervals that • can be either formal or informal in tone • appeal to a select audience targeted by the writer	**Biographies:** true accounts of a person's life that are written by someone else and that • describe the major events of the person's life • identify why the person is interesting or significant • may include the author's opinion of the person
Online reference sources: Web sites that are set up to provide information on a topic and that • may include audio or video content • identify their source on the home page or in a link	**Essays:** short literary works that focus on developing or explaining a central idea or concept and that • may be formal or informal • express the author's point of view

Determining Theme in Fiction

Themes—insights or messages about life—are often suggested through the words, actions, and fate of a story's characters.

Common Core State Standards

Reading Literature

2. Determine a theme or central idea of a text and analyze in detail its development over the course of the text, including how it emerges and is shaped and refined by specific details; provide an objective summary of the text.

Implied Theme A **theme** is an insight into human nature that emerges over the course of a work. Though a theme may be directly stated, more often it is *implied,* or suggested through elements of the work, as in the following example:

> **Character's Actions** Main character sacrifices friendship to make her business successful.
> **Character's Experience** Although she succeeds, she is unhappy.
> **Implied Theme** Friendship is more important than success.

Each detail in a work can contribute to the development and refinement of theme, as in this example:

> **Theme** Friendship is more important than success.
> **Introduction of Theme** To succeed, the main character breaks a promise to her friend.
> **Reinforcing Detail** Another character keeps a promise to a friend, though he loses money as a result.
> **Refining Detail** The main character loses her business, showing that friendship endures while success may be fleeting.

Different Interpretations of Theme Though themes emerge from the details of a work, which are the same for everyone, people may interpret the details differently. Review this summary of Charles Dickens's classic novel *A Christmas Carol.* Draw your own conclusion about its theme. Then, compare your ideas to the statements of theme that follow.

Example

Ebenezer Scrooge is a cold and greedy business owner who cares only about acquiring wealth. He refuses to help people in need, he has no friends, and he has lost contact with his relatives. He is also uncaring toward his employee, Bob Cratchit, who cannot afford medical care for one of his children. One Christmas Eve, three spirits visit Scrooge. They make him review his past, present, and future. As a result of these visits, Scrooge realizes he has been missing out on the most important things in life. He changes his ways, befriends his employee, helps the employee's child, and seeks out his relatives.

Possible Interpretations of Theme

- Human beings have the capacity to change their lives in wondrous ways.

- Love is more important than money.

- The love of a child can melt a cold heart.

Though these interpretations are all slightly different, each reflects the events in the novel and the lesson Scrooge learns. Whatever your interpretation of a story's theme, it should emerge from the key events and details in the work and the lessons that the main characters learn from them.

Determining Central Ideas in Nonfiction

The central idea of a nonfiction work is the work's main idea, supported by its details.

**Common Core State Standards**

Reading Informational Text

2. Determine a central idea of a text and analyze its development over the course of the text, including how it emerges and is shaped and refined by specific details; provide an objective summary of the text.

Central Ideas All nonfiction texts convey one or more **central ideas**—key concepts or main points that the author wants readers to understand and remember. In some works of nonfiction, the author directly states the central idea in the introduction. For example, the author of an essay may state the central idea in a **thesis statement** in the introductory paragraph. In some works of literary nonfiction, the central idea may be *implied,* or suggested, rather than stated directly. Readers determine the central idea by analyzing details to see what general idea they combine to support.

Author's Purpose and Central Ideas The three general **purposes,** or reasons, for writing are to **inform** or explain; to **persuade,** or try to convince readers to adopt a particular opinion or take a particular action; and to **entertain**. The author's purpose and the central idea in a work are directly related.

> **Example:**
> **Subject:** mobile phones
> **General purpose:** to inform
> **Specific purpose:** to inform readers about the origins of mobile phones
> **Central idea:** In 1973, Dr. Martin Cooper realized his vision of a portable personal phone when he placed the first mobile-phone call.

> **Example:**
> **Subject:** mobile phones
> **General purpose:** to entertain
> **Specific purpose:** to entertain readers by telling amusing stories about phones, leading them to reflect on modern life
> **Central idea:** After I got my first smartphone, I no longer had a life.

Development of Central Ideas In many works of nonfiction, the author devotes the entire work to a single central idea. That central idea is supported by each paragraph in the body of the work—each paragraph explains, illustrates, proves, or comments on some aspect of the central idea.

Each paragraph, in turn, has its own main idea, which supports the central idea of the work as a whole. The main idea of a paragraph is often stated directly in a **topic sentence** at or near its beginning. The details in the paragraph support its topic sentence. The example below illustrates the relationship between a central idea, topic sentences, and supporting details.

> **Example: Central Idea and Topic Sentences**
> **Central idea in introduction:** The state's graduated driver's license program has brought many benefits.
>
> **Topic sentence, paragraph 1 of body:** The number of fatal accidents involving teenagers has dropped significantly.
>
> **Topic sentence, paragraph 2 of body:** The total number of all accidents, including fender benders, has dropped.
>
> **Topic sentence, paragraph 3 of body:** Insurance rates for teen drivers have dropped.

The following detail helps support the topic sentence of the first paragraph in the body of the work:

Since our state instituted a graduated driver's license program, we have seen a 16-percent reduction in crashes for male teen drivers between the ages of sixteen and eighteen.

Close Read: Theme in Fiction

To discover the theme of a work, examine its use of literary elements and consider the message they suggest.

As you have learned, the theme of a literary work is the insight into human nature or life that the work conveys. Often, you must infer the author's theme or analyze main literary elements and related details to reach conclusions about what the author implies, or states indirectly. By making inferences, you will find deeper meaning in a work. Keep in mind that a work may suggest more than one theme, or main message. Use the tips in the chart to guide you.

Literary Elements as Clues to Theme

Title
The **title** is the name given to an individual literary work. As you read, ask these questions:

- Do the words in the title prompt ideas or stir emotions?
- Do the words suggest any universal themes —themes related to universal human concerns such as love, friendship, nature, or time?

Statements and Observations
Comments by the narrator or the main character may suggest or give insight into the theme. As you read, ask these questions:

- What do the characters say about each other? What do their words suggest about themselves?
- Which of the narrator's statements pertain to life or human beings in general?
- What sentences stand out in your mind? Why?

Setting
The **setting** refers to the time and place in which the events of a literary work occur. Setting includes the ideas, customs, beliefs, and values of a certain time and place. As you read, ask these questions:

- When and where do the events take place?
- What details help you picture the setting?
- What perspective does the setting offer on life or the world? (For example, is life in the setting a struggle? Is it calm? Simple? Full of pretense?)

Character
The **characters** are the people or animals that take part in the action of a literary work. As you read, ask:

- What are each character's traits, or qualities?
- Does the main character change, or develop, as a result of his or her experiences?
- What lesson in life does the character learn from his or her experiences?

Symbol
A **symbol** is a character, a place, an object, or an event that represents an idea, a quality, or a theme. For example, a wedding ring represents love and fidelity. As you read, ask these questions:

- What objects or events are emphasized?
- Are any of these objects or events strongly associated with a particular idea—are they symbols? What idea do they represent?
- What deeper meaning might they suggest?

Conflict and Plot
The **plot** of a narrative is the sequence of events that it tells. **Conflict,** or a struggle between opposing forces, drives the plot. As you read, ask:

- What are the main character's struggles?
- How does the character cope with these struggles?
- What does the character learn as a result of his or her experiences?

Model

About the Text Ray Bradbury's novel *Fahrenheit 451,* a work of science fiction, was published in 1953. The novel is set in a future totalitarian society that burns books to which the government and special-interest groups object. These include classic works of literature as well as religious texts. The Fahrenheit 451 of the title is the temperature at which books will burn.

Bradbury's concerns in the novel were shaped by contemporary events. World War II had pitted the United States against Nazi Germany and Fascist Italy, where censorship was routine. After the war, fear of Communism led some Americans to scrutinize each other for dissenting political beliefs. A person suspected of disloyalty might find his or her career ruined. At the same time, television gained popularity. By 1954, over half the households in the United States had a television set. In the background of Bradbury's novel, then, is a time when ideas were considered dangerous and television was beginning to take the place of reading.

from *Fahrenheit 451* by Ray Bradbury

It was a pleasure to burn.

It was a special pleasure to see things eaten, to see things blackened and *changed*. With the brass nozzle in his fists, with this great python spitting its venomous kerosene upon the world, the blood pounded in his head, and his hands were the hands of some amazing conductor playing all the symphonies of blazing and burning to bring down the tatters and charcoal ruins of history. With his symbolic helmet numbered 451 on his stolid head, and his eyes all orange flame with the thought of what came next, he flicked the igniter and the house jumped up in a gorging fire that burned the evening sky red and yellow and black. He strode in a swarm of fireflies. He wanted above all, like the old joke, to shove a marshmallow on a stick in the furnace, while the flapping pigeon-winged books died on the porch and lawn of the house. While the books went up in sparkling whirls and blew away on a wind turned dark with burning.

Montag grinned the fierce grin of all men singed and driven back by flame.

He knew that when he returned to the firehouse, he might wink at himself, a minstrel man, burnt-corked, in the mirror. Later, going to sleep, he would feel the fiery smile still gripped by his face muscles, in the dark. It never went away, that smile, it never ever went away, as long as he remembered.

Statements Bradbury ironically compares the hands of Montag, a destroyer, to the hands of a conductor, who creates something beautiful. The passage suggests that the theme concerns both creation and destruction.

Symbol The helmet symbolizes Montag's job, to destroy books and the knowledge and dissenting opinions they contain.

Setting The action takes place on a porch and lawn, which adds horror to this scene: Montag is attacking an ordinary house.

Theme The following themes are suggested by the details in the text:

- Humankind has the drive to destroy as well as to create.
- Censorship is driven by a passion for destruction.
- Violence and ignorance go hand in hand.

Independent Practice

About the Text This selection is an excerpt from Susan Vreeland's novel *Girl in Hyacinth Blue*, a work of historical fiction. The main character is Magdalena, the fictional daughter of artist Johannes Vermeer. Vermeer himself (1632–1675) was a real person, a famous painter who lived in Delft, a city in the Netherlands, during the seventeenth century.

Title Why might the daughter of an artist, in particular, like to look at things?

Setting What does this description of the setting suggest about Magdalena's world and her feelings about it? What theme do these details introduce?

"Magdalena Looking" by Susan Vreeland

Late one afternoon when Magdalena finished the clothes washing and her mother let her go out, she ran from their house by the Nieuwe Kerk across the market square, past van Buyten's bakery, over two cobbled bridges across the canals, past the blacksmith's all the way to Kethelstraat and the town wall where she climbed up and up the ochre stone steps, each one as high as her knee, to her favorite spot in all of Delft,[1] the round sentry post. From that great height, oh, what she could see. If only she could paint it. In one direction Schiedam Gate and beyond it the twin towers of Rotterdam Gate, and ships with odd-shaped sails the color of brown eggshells coming up the great Schie River from the sea, and in another direction strips of potato fields with wooden plows casting shadows over the soil like long fingers, and orchards, rows of rounded green as ordered as Mother wished their eleven young lives to be, and the smoke of the potteries and brickeries, and beyond that, she didn't know. She didn't know.

She stood there looking, looking, and behind her she heard the creak and thrum of the south windmill turning like her heart in the sea wind, and she breathed the brine[2] that had washed here from other shores. Below her the Schie lay like a pale yellow ribbon along the town wall. The longer she looked, the more it seemed to borrow its color from the sky. In the wind, the boats along the Schie docks with their fasteners clanking and their hollow bellies nudging one another made a kind of low rattling music she loved. It wasn't just today. She loved the sentry post in every kind of weather. To see rain pocking the gray sea and shimmering the stone bridge, to feel its cold strings of water on her face and hands, filled her to bursting.

---

1. **Nieuwe Kerk** (nü´ e kärk) . . . **van Buyten's** (fän bī´ tens) . . . **Kethelstraat** (kā´ tel strät) . . . **Delft** . . . *Nieuwe Kirk* means "New Church"; Kethelstraat is a street in the city; Delft is a manufacturing city on the Schie River in the Netherlands.
2. **brine** (brīn) saltwater.

She moved to a notch in the wall and just then a gust of wind lifted her skirts. The men on the bridge waiting with their bundles to go to sea shouted something in words she did not understand. She'd never tell Mother. Mother did not want her going there. The sentry post was full of guards smoking tobacco, Mother had said. There was some dark thing in her voice, as though she thought Magdalena should be afraid, but Magdalena did not know how to feel that then, or there.

Up there, high up above the town, she had longings no one in the family knew. No one would ever know them, she thought, unless perhaps a soul would read her face or she herself would have soul enough to speak of them. Wishes had the power to knock the breath out of her. Some were large and throbbing and persistent, some mere pinpricks of golden light, short-lived as fireflies but keenly felt. She wished for her chores to be done so she'd have time to race to the town wall every day before supper, or to the Oude Kerk[3] to lift the fallen leaves from her brother's grave. She wished her baby sisters wouldn't cry so, and the boys wouldn't quarrel and wrestle underfoot or run shouting through the house. Father wished that too, she knew. She wished there were not so many bowls to wash, thirteen each meal. She wished her hair shone flaxen in the sunlight of the market square like little Geertruida's.[4] She wished she could travel in a carriage across borders to all the lands drawn on her father's map.

She wished the grocer wouldn't treat her so gruffly when he saw her hand open out to offer four guilders,[5] all that her mother gave her to pay the grocery bill that was mounting into the hundreds, as far as she could tell. She wished he wouldn't shout; it sent his garlic breath straight into her nostrils. The baker, Hendrick van Buyten, was kinder. Two times so far he let Father pay with a painting so they could start over. Sometimes he gave her a still-warm bun to eat while walking home. And sometimes he put a curl of honey on it. She wished the grocer was like him.

She wished Father would take the iceboat to the Schie more often. He'd bought a fine one with a tall ivory sail. "Eighty guilders," Mother grumbled. "Better a winter's worth of bread and meat." On winter Sundays if the weather was clear, and if he was between paintings, it whisked them skimming across the

Characters What do you learn about Magdalena in this passage, and what possible themes do her thoughts suggest?

Statements and Observations What conflict over values does the mother's statement suggest, and what light do they shed on the theme?

---

3. **Oude Kerk** (ʊuˊ de kārk)
4. **Geertruida's** (kher trīˊ das)
5. **guilders** (gilˊ dərz) *n.* The guilder is the basic unit of Dutch currency.

Practice continued

white glass of the canal. She'd never known such speed. The sharp cold air blew life and hope and excitement into her ears and open mouth.

She remembered wishing, one particular morning when Father mixed lead white with the smallest dot of lead-tin yellow[6] for the goose quill in a painting of Mother writing a letter, that she might someday have someone to write to, that she could write at the end of a letter full of love and news, "As ever, your loving Magdalena Elisabeth."

He painted Mother often, and Maria he painted once, draped her head in a golden mantle and her shoulders in a white satin shawl. She was older, fifteen, though only by eleven months. It might be fun to dress up like Maria did, and wear pearl earrings and have Father position her just so, but the only part she really wished for was that he would look and look and pay attention.

Characters What does Magdalena's greatest wish reveal about her? What does her wish add to your understanding of the theme?

More than all those wishes, she had one pulsing wish that outshone all the others. She wished to paint. Yes, me, she thought, leaning out over the stone wall. I want to paint. This and everything. The world from that vantage point stretched so grandly. Up there, beauty was more than color and shapes, but openness, light, the air itself, and because of that, it seemed untouchable. If only the act of wishing would make her able. Father only smiled queerly when she told him she wanted to paint, just as if she'd said she wanted to sail the seas, which, of course, she also wished, in order to paint what she would see. When she said so, that she wished to paint, Mother thrust into her hands the basket of mending to do.

Conflict and Plot What theme is suggested by the challenges Magdalena faces as a girl who lives in the seventeenth century?

Often from the edge of the room, she'd watch him work. Because he was always asking for quiet, with the little ones running through the room laughing or shouting, she didn't ask him many questions. He rarely answered anyway. Still, she studied how much linseed oil he used to thin the ultramarine,[7] and watched him apply it over a glassy layer of reddish brown. By magic, it made the dress he painted warmer than the blue on the palette. He would not let her go with him to the attic where he ground lead-tin yellow to powder, but he did send her to the apothecary[8] for the small bricks of it, and for linseed oil. Always there was money for that, but

---

6. **lead white . . . lead-tin yellow** references to pigments made from lead and tin and mixed with oil to produce paints of various colors.
7. **linseed oil . . . ultramarine** Linseed oil, made from the seed of the flax plant, can be used as the base for oil paint. Ultramarine is a rich blue.
8. **apothecary** (ə päth´ ə ker´ ē) *n.* historical term for a pharmacist; a dealer in medicines and various other preparations and chemicals.

she didn't know what to answer when the apothecary demanded the guilders for her brother's potions still owed after he died.

If only she could have colors of her own, and brushes. She wouldn't just paint pictures of women inside cramped little rooms. She'd paint them out in marketplaces, bending in the potato fields, talking in doorways in the sunlight, in boats on the Schie, or praying in the Oude Kerk. Or she'd paint people skating, fathers teaching their children on the frozen Schie.

Fathers teaching their children. The thought stopped her.

Looking from the sentry tower at a cloud darkening the river, she knew, just as she knew she'd always have washing and mending to do, that it would not be so. She'd worn herself out with wishing, and turned to go. She had to be home to help with supper.

On a spring day that began in no special way, except that she had climbed the town wall the afternoon before, and all over Delft lime trees lining the canals had burst into chartreuse[9] leaves, and light shone through them and made them yellower except where one leaf crossed over another and so was darker—on that spring-certain day, out of some unknown, unborn place came that scream. "I hate to mend," she shouted to the walls, to Mother, to anyone. "It's not making anything."

Father stepped into the room, looked at Mother and then scowled at Magdalena. It had been her job to keep her little brothers quiet for him, or shoo them out of doors, and here she was, the noisy one.

No one moved. Even the boys were still. At first she looked only at Father's hand smeared with ultramarine powder, not in his eyes, too surprised by the echo of her voice to fling out any additional defiance. She loved him, loved what he did with that hand, and even, she suspected, loved what he loved, though they had not spoken of it. When that thought lifted her face to his, she saw his cheeks grow softer, as if he noticed her in his house for the first time. He drew her over to the table by the window, brought the sewing basket, placed on her lap her

Characters What do Magdalena's thoughts suggest about women's lives during this time period? What theme about women is the writer suggesting?

Statements and Observations What does the author suggest is lacking in Magdalena's life? How does this suggestion reinforce your understanding of the theme?

Conflict and Plot What is the desire to "make" that leads to Magdalena's conflict with her family? How does this conflict develop the theme?

9. **chartreuse** (shär trōōz´) pale, yellowish green.

Practice continued

brother's shirt that needed buttons, adjusted the chair, opened the window, a little more, then less, and discovered that at a certain angle, it reflected her face. "If you sit here mending, I will paint you, Magdalena. But only if you stop that shouting." He positioned her shoulders, and his hands resting a moment were warm through the muslin[10] of her smock and seemed to settle her.

Mother rushed over to take away Geertruida's glass of milk.

"No, leave it, Catharina. Right there in the light."

For days she sat there, still as she could for Father, and yet sewing a few stitches every so often to satisfy Mother. In that mood of stillness, all the things within her line of vision touched her deeply. The tapestry laid across the table, the sewing basket, the same glass repoured each day to the same level, the amber-toned map of the world on the wall—it plucked a lute string in her heart that these things she'd touched, grown as familiar to her as her own skin, would be looked at, marveled at, maybe even loved by viewers of his painting.

On sunny days the panes of window glass glistened before her. Like jewels melted into flat squares, she thought. Each one was slightly different in its pale transparent color—ivory, parchment, the lightest of wines and the palest of tulips. She wondered how glass was made, but she didn't ask. It would disturb him. Outside the window the market chattered with the selling of apples and lard and brooms and wooden buckets. She liked the cheese porters in their flat-brimmed red hats and stark white clothes. Their curved yellow carrying platforms stacked neatly with cheese rounds were suspended on ropes between pairs of them, casting brown shadows on the paving stones. Two platforms diagonally placed in the midground between their carriers would make a nice composition with the repeated shapes of those bulging cheese rounds. She'd put a delivery boy wheeling his cart of silver cod in the background against the guild hall, and maybe in the foreground a couple of lavender gray pigeons pecking crumbs.

The carillon[11] from Nieuwe Kerk ringing out the hour sounded something profound in her chest. All of it is ordinary to everyone but me, she thought.

Characters What message about the power of great art do these details suggest?

Setting What details suggest that Magdalena, like her father, has an artist's eye? How do these details reinforce the theme?

---

10. **muslin** (muz´ lin) *n.* strong, plain cotton cloth.
11. **carillon** (kar´ ə län´) *n.* a set of tuned church bells.

All that month she did not speak, the occasion too momentous to dislodge it with words. He said he'd paint her as long as she didn't shout, and so she did not speak a word. Her chest ached like a dull wound when she realized that her silence did not cause him a moment's reflection or curiosity. When she looked out the corner of her eye at him, she could not tell what she meant to him. Slowly, she came to understand that he looked at her with the same interest he gave to the glass of milk.

Maybe it was because she wasn't pretty like Maria. She knew her jaws protruded and her watery, pale eyes were too widely set. She had a mole on her forehead that she always tried to hide by tugging at her cap. What if no one would want the painting? What then? It might be her fault, because she wasn't pretty. She wished he'd say something about her, but all he said, not to her directly, more to himself, was how the sunlight whitened her cap at the forehead, how the shadow at the nape of her neck reflected blue from her collar, or how the sienna of her skirt deepened to Venetian red[12] in the folds. It was never her, she cried to herself, only something surrounding her that she did not make or even contribute to knowingly. Another wish that never would come true, she saw then, even if she lived forever, was that he, that someone, would look at her not as an artistic study, but with love. If two people love the same thing, she reasoned, then they must love each other, at least a little, even if they never say it. Nevertheless, because he painted with such studied concentration, and because she held him in awe, she practiced looking calm for him as she looked out the window, but when she saw the canvas, what she intended as calm looked more like wistfulness.[13]

The painting was not bought by the brewer, Pieter Claesz van Ruijven,[14] who bought most of her father's work. He saw it, but passed over it for another. Disgrace seared her so that she could not speak that night. The painting hung without a frame in the outer kitchen where the younger children slept. Eventually the family had to give up their lodgings at Mechelen on the square, and take smaller rooms with Grandmother Maria on the Oude Langendijck.[15] Her father stopped taking the iceboat out to the Schie, sold it, in fact. He rarely

Characters What themes are reflected in Magdalena's relationship with her father?

---

12. **sienna** (sē en´ ə) . . . **Venetian** (və nē´ shən) **red** colors; sienna is a reddish or yellowish brown, and Venetian red is a brownish red.
13. **wistfulness** *n.* a mood of wishfulness or vague longing.
14. **Pieter Claesz van Ruijven** (pē ter kläs fän rī fen)
15. **Mechelen** (me´ khe len) . . . **Oude Langendijck** (ou´ de län en dīk) The Mechelen was an inn owned by the Vermeer family. The Oude Langendijck is a canal in Delft.

Practice continued

Conflict and Plot
What conflict does Magdalena have while helping to prepare her father's body for burial? What light does this conflict shed on the theme?

Characters How would you contrast Magdalena's youthful wishes and the reality of her adult life? Explain whether this contrast changes your understanding of the theme.

painted, the rooms were so cramped and dark, the younger children boisterous, and a few years later, he died.

When she washed him in his bed that last time, his fingers already cold, she had a thought, the shame of which prevented her from uttering: It would make a fine painting, a memorial, the daughter with towel and blue-figured washing bowl at bedside, her hand covering his, the wife exhausted on the Spanish chair clutching a crucifix, the father-husband, eyes glazed, looking to another landscape. While he painted everyone else, no one was there to paint him, to make him remembered. She yearned to do it, but the task was too fearsome. She lacked the skill, and the one to teach her had never offered.

Even though she asked for them, Mother sold his paints and brushes to the Guild of St. Luke. It helped to pay a debt. When Mother became sick with worry, Magdalena had the idea to take the painting to Hendrick van Buyten, the baker, because she knew he liked her. And he accepted it, along with one of a lady playing a guitar, for the debt of six hundred seventeen guilders, six stuivers,[16] more than two years' worth of bread. He smiled at her and gave her a bun.

Within a year, she married a saddlemaker named Nicolaes, the first man to notice her, a hard worker whose pores smelled of leather and grease, who taught her a pleasure not of the eyes, but, she soon realized, a man utterly without imagination. They moved to Amsterdam and she didn't see the painting again for twenty years.

In 1696, just after their only living child, Magritte, damp with fever, stopped breathing in her arms, Magdalena read in the Amsterdamsche Courant of a public auction of one hundred thirty-four paintings by various artists. "Several outstandingly artful paintings," the notice said, "including twenty-one works most powerfully and splendidly painted by the late J. Vermeer of Delft, will be auctioned May 16, 1:00, at the Oude Heeren Logement."[17] Only a week away. She thought of Hendrick. Of course he couldn't be expected to keep those paintings forever. Hers might be there. The possibility kept her awake nights.

Entering the auction gallery, she was struck again by that keenest of childhood wishes—to make a record not only of what she saw, but how. The distance

---

16. **stuivers** (stī´ fers) *n.* coins worth a fraction of a guilder; roughly, a dime.
17. **Oude Heeren Logement** (ou´ de her´ en lōzh mōn)

she'd come from that, and not even a child to show for it! She shocked herself by asking, involuntarily, what had been the point of having lived? Wishing had not been enough. Was it a mistake that she didn't beg him to teach her? Maybe not. If she'd seen that eventually, with help, she could paint, it might have made the years of birthing and dying harder. But then the birthing and dying would have been painted and the pain given. It would have served a purpose. Would that have been enough—to tell a truth in art?

She didn't know.

To see again so many of Father's paintings was like walking down an avenue of her childhood. The honey-colored window, the Spanish chair, the map she'd stared at, dreaming, hanging on the wall, Grandmother Maria's golden water pitcher, Mother's pearls and yellow satin jacket—they commanded such a reverence for her now that she felt they all had souls.

And suddenly there she was on canvas, framed. Her knees went weak.

Hendrick hadn't kept it. Even though he liked her, he hadn't kept it.

Almost a child she was, it seemed to her, gazing out the window instead of doing her mending, as if by the mere act of looking she could send her spirit out into the world. And those shoes! She had forgotten. How she loved the buckles, and thought they made her such a lady. Eventually she'd worn the soles right through, but now, brand-new, the buckles glinted on the canvas, each with a point of golden light. A bubble of joy surged upward right through her.

No, she wasn't beautiful, she owned, but there was a simplicity in her young face that she knew the years had eroded, a stilled longing in the forward lean of her body, a wishing in the intensity of her eyes. The painting showed she did not yet know that lives end abruptly, that much of living is repetition and separation, that buttons forever need resewing no matter how ferociously one works the thread, that nice things almost happen. Still a woman overcome with wishes, she wished Nicolaes would have come with her to see her in the days of her sentry post wonder when life and hope were new and full of possibility, but he had seen no reason to close up the shop on such a whim.

Character Do you think it would have been easier for Magdalena to bear her sorrows if she had been able to be an artist? Explain.

Symbol What might her father's painting of Magdalena represent?

Practice continued

Conflict and Plot
Why does Magdalena want the painting so much? In what way does her desire reinforce or add to the theme?

She stood on tiptoe and didn't breathe when her painting was announced. Her hand in her pocket closed tight around the twenty-four guilders, some of it borrowed from two neighbor women, some of it taken secretly from the box where Nicolaes kept money for leather supplies. It was all she could find, and she didn't dare ask for more. He would have thought it foolish.

"Twenty," said a man in front of her.

"Twenty-two," said another.

"Twenty-four," she said so loud and fast the auctioneer was startled. Did he see something similar in her face? He didn't call for another bid. The painting was hers!

"Twenty-five."

Her heart cracked.

The rest was a blur of sound. It finally went to a man who kept conferring with his wife, which she took as a good sign that it was going to a nice family. Forty-seven guilders. Most of the paintings sold for much more, but forty-seven was fine, she thought. In fact, it filled her momentarily with what she'd been taught was the sin of pride. Then she thought of Hendrick and a pain lashed through her. Forty-seven guilders minus the auctioneer's fee didn't come close to what her family had owed him.

She followed the couple out into the drizzle of Herengracht,[18] wanting to make herself known to them, just to have a few words, but then dropped back. She had such bad teeth now, and they were people of means. The woman wore stockings. What would she say to them? She didn't want them to think she wanted anything.

She walked away slowly along a wet stone wall that shone iridescent, and the wetness of the street reflected back the blue of her best dress. Water spots appeared fast, turning the cerulean[19] to deep ultramarine, Father's favorite blue.

---

18. **Herengracht** (her´ en khräkht) the "Gentleman's Canal"; one of the three main canals in the center of the city of Amsterdam.
19. **cerulean** (sə rōō´ lē ən) *adj.* sky-blue.

Light rain pricked the charcoal green canal water into delicate, dark lace, and she wondered if it had ever been painted just that way, or if the life of something as inconsequential as a water drop could be arrested and given to the world in a painting, or if the world would care.

She thought of all the people in all the paintings she had seen that day, not just Father's, in all the paintings of the world, in fact. Their eyes, the particular turn of a head, their loneliness or suffering or grief was borrowed by an artist to be seen by other people throughout the years who would never see them face to face. People who would be that close to her, she thought, a matter of a few arms' lengths, looking, looking, and they would never know her.

Conflict and Plot Do you think Magdalena's conflict is resolved? Explain why or why not.

Theme Consider Magdalena's wishes and conflicts as a child, as well as her experiences later in life, including her attempt to purchase her father's portrait of her. What message about unfulfilled dreams does this story convey? What other themes does the author suggest?

Close Read: Central Idea in Nonfiction

The central idea of a work of nonfiction emerges from and is supported by the details in the work.

In nonfiction works, an author often expresses the central, or main, idea in a **thesis statement.** For example, in an article about baseball, an author may state this thesis statement: Former catchers generally become good major league managers. To develop this central idea, the author might cite examples of former catchers who later excelled at managing. To further develop this idea, the author might then cite apparent exceptions to the rule and show how they actually prove it.

Sometimes, however, an author implies the central idea rather than stating it. If so, the reader must determine it by examining the supporting details in a work. For example, in an article about traffic safety, an author might describe several accidents that happened at a single intersection. These details imply the central idea that the particular intersection is dangerous.

As you read nonfiction selections, look for details that develop and support the central idea.

Clues to Central Idea	
The **title** is the name given to an individual work of nonfiction. Example: *"Perfect Pitch and Other Useful Skills for a Music Reviewer"*	A **thesis statement** is a direct statement of the central idea of a work, often found in the first paragraph. In each subsequent paragraph, a **topic sentence** generally states the central idea of the paragraph. The central idea in each paragraph helps support the central idea of the entire work. Example: *The point I want to stress is that exercise is essential to good health, as the following examples will illustrate.*

Support for Central Idea	
Statements of fact are statements that can be proven true. Example: *Water molecules consist of two atoms of hydrogen and one atom of oxygen.*	**Personal observations** are statements that an author makes based on his or her own firsthand knowledge and experiences. Example: *Having run the 20-mile marathon, I can tell you it's a tough endurance test.*
Expert opinion is information from an individual or a group that is an authority on a subject. Example: *According to the American Institute on Diet, raisins are an excellent source of potassium.*	An **anecdote** is a brief story that illustrates a point. Example: *The team was losing by 21 points, yet it managed to win the game. That shows what determination can do.*
Examples are specific illustrations of a general concept. Example: *The Community Service Club does volunteer work. For example, club members walk dogs at the town animal shelter on weekends.*	An **analogy** is a comparison of dissimilar things that focuses on an important similarity between them in order to aid understanding. Example: *Just as a single domino can topple several more, so can one revolution ignite many others.*

 **EXEMPLAR TEXT**

Model

About the Text While still in college, Anna Quindlen (b. 1953) began a career in journalism, writing for the *New York Post*. In 1986, she began writing a weekly column for *The New York Times*. In 1995, Quindlen left journalism for a time to devote herself to writing fiction and published four best-selling novels.

Quindlen's distinctive essayistic style is well suited to exploring the changes in national outlook after September 11, 2001. On that date, terrorists attacked the World Trade Center in New York City and the Pentagon in Washington, D.C. Quindlen responded in writing, mulling over the impact of the attacks on the nation's spirit. She published the following essay in *Newsweek* only weeks after the event.

from "A Quilt of a Country" by Anna Quindlen

With the end of the cold war, there was the creeping concern that without a focus for hatred and distrust, a sense of national identity would evaporate, that the left side of the hyphen—African-American, Mexican-American, Irish-American—would overwhelm the right. And slow-growing domestic traumas like economic unrest and increasing crime seemed more likely to emphasize division than community. Today the citizens of the United States have come together once more because of armed conflict and enemy attack. Terrorism has led to devastation—and unity.

Yet even in 1994, the overwhelming majority of those surveyed by the National Opinion Research Center agreed with this statement: "The U.S. is a unique country that stands for something special in the world." One of the things that it stands for is this vexing notion that a great nation can consist entirely of refugees from other nations, that people of different, even warring religions and cultures can live, if not side by side, then on either side of the country's Chester Avenues. Faced with this diversity there is little point in trying to isolate anything remotely resembling a national character, but there are two strains of behavior that, however tenuously, abet the concept of unity.

There is that Calvinist undercurrent in the American psyche that loves the difficult, the demanding, that sees mastering the impossible, whether it be prairie or subway, as a test of character, and so glories in the struggle of this fractured coalescing. And there is a grudging fairness among the citizens of the United States that eventually leads most to admit that, no matter what the

Title The title is an analogy that compares a quilt and a country. It provides a clue to the central idea of the text.

Personal Observations Based on the aftermath of the terrorist attacks, Quindlen makes the observation that the attacks unified Americans.

Facts Quindlen uses the results of a survey to support her claim that Americans are unified.

Topic Sentence This sentence states the central idea of the paragraph. The next sentence states the topic of the next paragraph, continuing to develop the central idea about American unity.

© EXEMPLAR TEXT

Model continued

Expert Opinion
Quindlen quotes the opinion of an expert to help support the idea that new immigrants are not very different from the immigrants who preceded them.

English-only advocates try to suggest, the new immigrants are not so different from our own parents or grandparents. Leonel Castillo, former director of the Immigration and Naturalization Service and himself the grandson of Mexican immigrants, once told the writer Studs Terkel proudly, "The old neighborhood Ma-Pa stores are still around. They are not Italian or Jewish or Eastern European any more. Ma and Pa are now Korean, Vietnamese, Iraqi, Jordanian, Latin American. They live in the store. They work seven days a week. Their kids are doing well in school. They're making it. Sound familiar?"

Example Quindlen uses a specific example to support the idea that the American people, regardless of their ancestry or country of birth, form a unified nation.

Tolerance is the word used most often when this kind of coexistence succeeds, but tolerance is a vanilla pudding word, standing for little more than the allowance of letting others live unremarked and unmolested. Pride seems excessive, given the American willingness to endlessly complain about them, them being whoever is new, different, unknown, or currently under suspicion. But patriotism is partly taking pride in this unlikely ability to throw all of us together in a country that across its length and breadth is as different as a dozen countries, and still be able to call it by one name. When photographs of the faces of all of those who died in the World Trade Center destruction are assembled in one place, it will be possible to trace in the skin color, the shape of the eyes and the noses, the texture of the hair, a map of the world. These are the representatives of a mongrel nation that somehow, at times like this, has one spirit. Like many improbable ideas, when it actually works, it's a wonder.

Central Idea The supporting details in the selection suggest the following central ideas:

- The unity of America as a nation is a complex and wonderful thing because the nation is founded on diversity.
- The unity of America is possible despite the diversity of American citizens because of two common attitudes: a love of struggle and a sense of fairness.

Independent Practice

About the Text In the course of writing *Girl in Hyacinth Blue*, Susan Vreeland did extensive research. In the article "Artful Research," she explains the necessity and benefits of research for writing fiction and shares some of her research methods.

"Artful Research" by Susan Vreeland

Is it possible for an ordinary person to climb over the area railings of #7 Eccles Street, either from the path or the steps, lower himself down from the lowest part of the railings till his feet are within two feet or three of the ground and drop unhurt? I saw it done myself but by a man of rather athletic build. I require this information in detail in order to determine the wording of a paragraph.

James Joyce[1] wrote this to his aunt once when he was out of Dublin. Can't you just imagine her muttering, "That boy! What will he think of next?" as she looks for her umbrella to go out in the rain and take the trolley to Eccles Street?

Excessive? Unnecessary? Stalling from the act of writing? Joyce's letter is instructive and revealing.

Similarly, I must admit that I sent my French translator on a mission to find out whether the carvings of heads on the façade of the Ministère de la Défense[2] on Boulevard Saint-Germain in Paris are repeats of the same face or different faces. Among other things, she told me I had the wrong street!

While some writers may be more cavalier, claiming that it's fiction, after all, I hold with the meticulous Joyce, not wholly out of allegiance to a recognized master, but for the sake of the richness of story that results. For me, research gives direction, depth, and authority to the writing; it doesn't just decorate a preconceived story with timely trivia.

Early research tends to be scattered, while one searches for the story, but later, usually during or after a first draft when one discovers in the work some needed information, it becomes pinpoint precise. At either time, an array of interesting material, some of it crucial, some merely useable, will emerge—and sometimes leap off the page. The results can be exciting. A single unexpected line can prompt a whole story. For example, the line in Jacob Presser's grim history, *Ashes in the Wind: The Destruction of Dutch Jewry*, indicating that in 1941, Jews were not allowed to keep pigeons, provided the genesis of my story "A Night Different from All Other Nights."

Anecdote What central idea is suggested by the anecdote about James Joyce?

Personal Observations What did Vreeland learn through her experiences with research? What central idea does she establish using her experiences?

Thesis Statement What central idea does Vreeland state here? Why might she have placed this thesis statement after her opening examples, rather than at the beginning?

Examples In what way does this example further develop Vreeland's central idea about the importance of research to fiction writing?

---

1. **James Joyce** (1882–1941) famed Irish writer noted for *Dubliners* (1914), a collection of short stories, and *Ulysses* (1922), a novel, among other works.
2. **Ministère de la Défense** (mēn i stär´ də là dā fäns´) the Ministry of Defense building in Paris, France.

Practice continued

That story is one of eight linked narratives comprising my composite novel, *Girl in Hyacinth Blue,* which traces an alleged Vermeer[3] painting in reverse chronology through the centuries, showing how defining moments in people's lives are lived under its influence. Besides the present, six time periods and numerous locales in the Netherlands are evoked: 1942 in Amsterdam; 1896 in Vreeland (yes, a real village located between Amsterdam and Utrecht); 1798 in The Hague during French rule: 1717 in Oling, Delfzijl, Westerbork, and Groningen (which I learned had been a university town since 1614, prompting my focal character to be a student); 1665 in Delft; and 1685 in Amsterdam. Naive in understanding what such a project entailed, I found that by the end, I had consulted seventy-six books.

Facts How did doing research help Vreeland shape one of her characters?

I'd been to the Netherlands only once, twenty-five years ago for three days, and I had never seen a Vermeer painting face to face. Blithely, I went ahead. I read books on Vermeer, Dutch art and social and cultural history, the Holocaust[4] as experienced in the Netherlands, the changing geography of the Netherlands as more land was reclaimed from the sea,[5] Erasmus' adages,[6] the history of costume, Passover and the practice of Jewish customs, Amsterdam's diamond trade, Dutch superstitions and treatment of witches, the French occupation, and the engineering of windmills and dikes.

Examples What central idea do these examples support?

Twenty printout pages from the Internet on the engineering of windmills (they vary regionally), on gears, wallowers, Archimedean screws, and drive shafts yielded one paragraph establishing the authority of my character the windmill engineer. More importantly, the research also suggested a metaphor appropriate for him:

I had fancied love a casual adjunct and not the central turning shaft making all parts move. I had not stood astonished at the power of its turning.

I would not have arrived at his critical self-assessment and the epiphany of the story without meandering through gears and drive shafts.

---

3. **Vermeer** (vər mir´) Jan (yän) Vermeer (1632–1675), renowned Dutch painter.
4. **the Holocaust** (häl´ ə kôst´) the persecution, imprisonment, and mass murder of Jews by Nazi Germany before and during the Second World War (1939–1945).
5. **reclaimed from the sea** Significant portions of the Netherlands were originally covered by water. To drain water from this land, the Dutch built a system of dikes (dams) and canals.
6. **Erasmus' adages** (i raz´ məs əz a´ di jez) the sayings or brief observations of Desiderius (des´ ə dir´ ē əs) Erasmus (1469–1536), an influential Dutch scholar.

Here are ten research sources and approaches, beginning with the most obvious and ending with the ultimate—travel—that I used for either *Girl in Hyacinth Blue* or my subsequent novel, *The Passion of Artemisia*, which takes place in seventeenth-century Italy.

1. **Works on history, politics, and social conditions** A couple of titles might serve to show how I approached possible narratives from different angles: on the one hand, *Daily Life in Rembrandt's Holland;* on the other, *The Embarrassment of Riches: An Interpretation of Dutch Culture in the Golden Age.* Some I used as browser books; others, for specific information. Their bibliographies proved to be good sources for characters' names.

2. **Biography, autobiography, personal narrative, and oral history** The mere memory of *Anne Frank's Diary of a Young Girl* suggested that I create a young character the antithesis of Anne in terms of self-expression, yet suffering similar revelations.

3. **Geography books** These can give information about weather, topography, crops, industry, indigenous plants, birds, and other animals.

4. **Maps** Besides those available in travel bookstores, universities often have historical map collections. This was essential for *Girl* because I had to know if certain villages and canals existed at the time of each of the stories.

5. **Travel books** Those of the descriptive sort, the older the better, provide visual and cultural detail.

6. **Novels** Novels written at the time, written about the time, or set in the same place can be helpful in revealing attitudes, concerns, expressions, syntax, and diction.

7. **Paintings** Paintings done in the same time and place as one's fiction are excellent sources of information about costume, hairstyles, jewelry, household furnishings, landscape, available foods, flowers typical of the region, even the quality of light in a region, Vermeer's "trademark."

8. **Children's and juvenile fiction and nonfiction** Works for younger readers are sufficient in some cases and have the advantages of providing evocative illustrations and simplifying complicated political histories.

Personal Observations
What is Vreeland's purpose in listing resources she used to research her novels?

Practice continued

9. **Interviews and phone calls** Don't neglect the importance of interviews and phone calls. People are intrigued by novelists and are usually delighted to be consulted. For *Girl in Hyacinth Blue,* I consulted a pigeon breeder to learn why the owning of pigeons was prohibited to Jews under the German occupation and how homing pigeons "worked."

10. **Going there!** While travel is not always practical (I wrote *Girl in Hyacinth Blue* entirely while undergoing cancer treatment and could not travel), it will yield unexpected insights.

So when does one stop researching and start writing? You write when the story comes to life, when it assumes some structure, when you can't help but start, not when you know everything you'll need to know. That's impossible to anticipate before you get into the heart of the writing. You might need to push yourself away from the safer act of research and leap into a first draft.

Don't get bogged down with fears of historical inaccuracy when writing a first draft. In one of the flood stories in *Girl in Hyacinth Blue,* the student needs to write a note. He's in a rowboat. He can't dip a pen in an inkwell. Did they have pencils in 1717? Look it up later. Keep writing. Keep the momentum going. If you don't know what they ate, leave it blank and get down the more important elements of the scene.

One caveat: Even if you put into your manuscript some fact delectable to you, recalling your delight in discovering it, if the story does not justify it, take it out. Type it up. Pin it on your wall. Use it elsewhere. But don't include it! The book is about characters, not about research.

Personal Observations
What point does Vreeland make based on her personal experiences with research? How does it further develop her central idea?

Personal Observations
How does this warning help focus Vreeland's central idea about research?

1. **Key Ideas and Details (a)** Write an **objective summary** of "Magdalena Looking." Remember that an objective summary should contain only the most important details or events. It should not contain personal opinions. **(b)** Write an objective summary of "Artful Research."

2. **Key Ideas and Details (a)** In "Magdalena Looking," what is Magdalena's "one pulsing wish"? **(b) Interpret:** What obstacles prevent her from fulfilling her wish? Use details from the selection to explain your answer.

3. **Key Ideas and Details (a)** How do the time and cultural setting of "Magdalena Looking" influence the conflict she experiences? **(b) Draw Conclusions:** Do you think she would experience similar conflicts if she lived today? Explain.

4. **Key Ideas and Details (a) Cite:** Give three details from the story that show Magdalena's character. **(b) Draw Conclusions:** Describe Magdalena's character, based on the details you have chosen.

5. **Craft and Structure (a)** From whose point of view is "Magdalena Looking" told? **(b) Analyze:** How does the point of view help you understand the character of Magdalena?

6. **Key Ideas and Details (a) Support:** Identify details in the selection suggesting that Magdalena has artistic ability. Then, identify any opposing evidence—details that suggest she does not have talent. **(b) Synthesize:** Explain why the question of Magdalena's talent is crucial to the development of the story's theme.

7. **Key Ideas and Details** What do you think was Susan Vreeland's purpose in writing "Artful Research"? Use details from the essay to support your answer.

8. **Key Ideas and Details (a) Cite:** Give two examples that Vreeland uses in the essay to show the importance of research. **(b) Evaluate:** How convincing do you find each? Explain.

9. **Integration of Knowledge and Ideas (a) Apply:** In "Artful Research," Vreeland writes, "For me, research gives direction, depth, and authority to the writing. . . ." On a chart like the one below, note three passages from "Magdalena Looking" that may reflect what Vreeland means, and explain your choices. **(b) Collaboration:** Compare your chart with a classmate's, and discuss each passage chosen.

How Research Helps in Fiction

Passage	Why You Chose it

Leveled Texts

Build your skills and improve your comprehension of fiction with texts of increasing complexity.

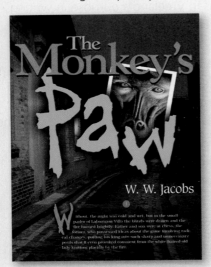

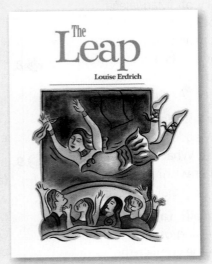

Read **"The Monkey's Paw"** to see how a mysterious object changes the lives of those who possess it.

Read **"The Leap"** to find out how a mother draws on her past as a circus performer to help her daughter.

Common Core State Standards

Meet these standards with either **"The Monkey's Paw"** (p. 32) or **"The Leap"** (p. 46).

Reading Literature
5. Analyze how an author's choices concerning how to structure a text, order events within it, and manipulate time create such effects as mystery, tension, or surprise. *(Literary Analysis: Plot and Foreshadowing)*

Spiral Review: RL.9-10.2

Writing
3. Write narratives to develop real or imagined experiences or events using effective technique, well-chosen details, and well-structured event sequences. **3.c.** Use a variety of techniques to sequence events so that they build on one another to create a coherent whole. *(Writing: Sequel)*

Speaking and Listening
1.a. Come to discussions prepared, having read and researched material under study; explicitly draw on that preparation by referring to evidence from texts and other research on the topic to stimulate a thoughtful, well-reasoned exchange of ideas. *(Speaking and Listening: Interview)*

1.b. Work with peers to set rules for collegial discussions and decision-making, clear goals and deadlines, and individual roles as needed. *(Speaking and Listening: Interview)*

Language
2. Demonstrate command of the conventions of standard English capitalization, punctuation, and spelling when writing. *(Conventions: Common and Proper Nouns)*

5. Demonstrate understanding of figurative language, word relationships, and nuances in word meanings. *(Vocabulary: Analogies)*

Literary Analysis: Plot and Foreshadowing

A **plot** is the sequence of related events in a story. A typical plot revolves around a **conflict**—a struggle between opposing forces—and follows a structure, or pattern, like the one shown in the diagram below:

- **Exposition:** background on the characters and situation
- **Rising action:** events that intensify the conflict
- **Climax:** highest point of story tension at which outcome of conflict is revealed
- **Falling action:** events following climax
- **Resolution:** remaining issues resolved; conclusions or insights revealed by narrator

Writers use various techniques to add tension to a story. One technique is **foreshadowing**—giving details that hint at upcoming events.

To provide background on characters and their experiences, some authors choose to switch from present time to past time by using **flashback.** That is an interruption in the plot to describe an action of the past. After the flashback, the story returns to the present time of the action.

Using the Strategy: Plot Diagram

Use a diagram like the one here to help you track the plot of the story.

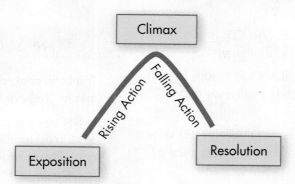

Reading Skill: Make Predictions

A **prediction** is a logical idea about what will happen. To make predictions, pay attention to story details and **use your prior knowledge.**

- Use knowledge of stories with similar plots to help you predict events.
- Use knowledge of human nature to help you predict how characters will act.

Is there a difference between *reality* and *truth?*

Writing About the Big Question

In "The Monkey's Paw," a family learns the truth behind a mysterious monkey's paw. Use this sentence starter to help you develop your ideas about the Big Question:

People may try to **verify** the truth by _____.

While You Read Look for explanations the characters offer to explain the truth behind the events in "The Monkey's Paw."

Vocabulary

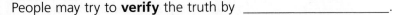

Read each word and its definition. Decide whether you know the word well, know it a little bit, or do not know it at all. After you read, see how your knowledge of each word has increased.

- **grave** (grāv) *adj.* very serious and worrying (p. 35) *The doctor had a grave expression on her face when she gave John's family the bad news.* gravely *adv.* gravity *n.*

- **maligned** (mə līnd´) *adj.* spoken ill of (p. 36) *The CD, maligned by critics, was still a tremendous hit.* malign *v.* malignant *adj.*

- **credulity** (krə doo´ lə tē) *n.* tendency to believe too readily (p. 36) *Due to his credulity, Tim was unaware that the news report was fake.* credulous *adj.* incredulous *adj.*

- **furtively** (fur´ tiv lē) *adv.* secretively; sneakily; stealthily (p. 38) *When no one was looking, she reached furtively for the last slice of pie.* furtive *adj.*

- **apathy** (ap´ ə thē) *n.* lack of interest or emotion (p. 39) *The bored audience looked at the speaker with apathy.* apathetic *adj.* apathetically *adv.*

- **oppressive** (ə pres´ iv) *adj.* causing great discomfort; distressing (p. 41) *The heat was so oppressive that they finally opened a window.* oppress *v.* oppression *n.*

> ### Word Study
>
> The **Latin root -cred-** means "believe."
>
> In this story, a character must monitor his **credulity,** or readiness to believe, as he hears a wild story about a supernatural object.

Meet
W. W. Jacobs
(1863–1943)

Author of

The Monkey's Paw

As a boy, William Wymark Jacobs traveled far and wide in his imagination. He lived in London, England, in a house near the docks, and he listened eagerly to the tales of adventure told by sailors whom he met there. These tales shaped the stories he wrote as an adult—stories in which everyday life is disrupted by strange and fantastic events. "The Monkey's Paw" is his most famous tale of the supernatural.

More Than Horror Although today W. W. Jacobs is best known for this tale of suspense, in his own lifetime he was famous as a humorist. In fact, he wrote works of various kinds, and he wrote them in quantity. When a collection of his works was published in 1931, it contained seventeen books!

BACKGROUND FOR THE STORY
The British View of India

"The Monkey's Paw" tells of an eerie object that arrives in England from India. From the late 1700s until 1947, India was a British colony. In letters and visits back home, British soldiers passed on information and misinformation about India's culture. Before long, India came to represent the mysterious and supernatural, as this story shows.

DID YOU KNOW?

Moviemakers have told the strange tale of "The Monkey's Paw" eight times! The first film version of the story was made in 1915. More recent remakes came out in 1996 and 2003.

The Monkey's Paw

W. W. Jacobs

I

Without, the night was cold and wet, but in the small parlor of Laburnam Villa the blinds were drawn and the fire burned brightly. Father and son were at chess, the former, who possessed ideas about the game involving radical changes, putting his king into such sharp and unnecessary perils that it even provoked comment from the white-haired old lady knitting placidly by the fire.

"Hark at the wind," said Mr. White, who, having seen a fatal mistake after it was too late, was amiably desirous of preventing his son from seeing it.

"I'm listening," said the latter, grimly surveying the board as he stretched out his hand. "Check."

"I should hardly think that he'd come tonight," said his father, with his hand poised over the board.

"Mate,"[1] replied the son.

"That's the worst of living so far out," bawled Mr. White, with sudden and unlooked-for violence; "of all the beastly, slushy, out-of-the-way places to live in, this is the worst. Pathway's a bog, and the road's a torrent. I don't know what people are thinking about. I suppose because only two houses on the road are let, they think it doesn't matter."

"Never mind, dear," said his wife, soothingly; "perhaps you'll win the next one."

Mr. White looked up sharply, just in time to intercept a knowing glance between mother and son. The words died away on his lips, and he hid a guilty grin in his thin gray beard.

"There he is," said Herbert White, as the gate banged to loudly and heavy footsteps came toward the door.

The old man rose with hospitable haste, and opening the door, was heard condoling with the new arrival. The new arrival also condoled with himself, so that Mrs. White said, "Tut, tut!" and coughed gently as her husband entered the room, followed by a tall, burly man, beady of eye and rubicund of visage.[2]

"Sergeant Major Morris," he said, introducing him.

The sergeant major shook hands, and taking the proffered seat by the fire, watched contentedly while his host got out tumblers and stood a small copper kettle on the fire.

At the third glass his eyes got brighter, and he began to talk, the little family circle regarding with eager interest this visitor from distant parts, as he squared his broad shoulders in the chair and spoke of wild scenes and doughty[3] deeds; of wars and plagues and strange peoples.

"Twenty-one years of it," said Mr. White, nodding at his wife and son. "When he went away he was a slip of a youth in the warehouse. Now look at him."

"He don't look to have taken much harm," said Mrs. White, politely.

---

1. mate *n.* checkmate, a chess move that prevents the opponent's king from escaping capture and so ends the game.
2. rubicund (rōō′ bə kund′) **of visage** (viz′ ij) having a red face.
3. doughty (dout′ ē) *adj.* brave.

Reading Check
Who has arrived at the White's house?

"I'd like to go to India myself," said the old man, "just to look round a bit, you know."

"Better where you are," said the sergeant major, shaking his head. He put down the empty glass, and sighing softly, shook it again.

"I should like to see those old temples and fakirs and jugglers," said the old man. "What was that you started telling me the other day about a monkey's paw or something, Morris?"

"Nothing," said the soldier, hastily. "Leastways nothing worth hearing."

"Monkey's paw?" said Mrs. White, curiously.

"Well, it's just a bit of what you might call magic, perhaps," said the sergeant major, offhandedly.

His three listeners leaned forward eagerly. The visitor absent-mindedly put his empty glass to his lips and then set it down again. His host filled it for him.

"To look at," said the sergeant major, fumbling in his pocket, "it's just an ordinary little paw, dried to a mummy."

He took something out of his pocket and proffered it. Mrs. White drew back with a grimace, but her son, taking it, examined it curiously.

"And what is there special about it?" inquired Mr. White as he took it from his son, and having examined it, placed it upon the table.

"It had a spell put on it by an old fakir," said the sergeant major, "a very holy man. He wanted to show that fate ruled people's lives, and that those who interfered with it did so to their sorrow. He put a spell on it so that three separate men could each have three wishes from it."

His manner was so impressive that his hearers were conscious that their light laughter jarred somewhat.

"Well, why don't you have three, sir?" said Herbert White, cleverly.

The soldier regarded him in the way that middle age is wont to regard presumptuous youth. "I have," he said, quietly, and his blotchy face whitened.

"And did you really have the three wishes granted?" asked Mrs. White.

"I did," said the sergeant major, and his glass tapped against his strong teeth.

"And has anybody else wished?" persisted the old lady.

"The first man had his three wishes, yes," was the reply; "I don't know what the first

▼ **Critical Viewing**
What details of this man's appearance might make you think that he is "a very holy man"? **[Support]**

two were, but the third was for death. That's how I got the paw."

His tones were so *grave* that a hush fell upon the group.

"If you've had your three wishes, it's no good to you now, then, Morris," said the old man at last. "What do you keep it for?"

The soldier shook his head. "Fancy, I suppose," he said, slowly. "I did have some idea of selling it, but I don't think I will. It has caused enough mischief already. Besides, people won't buy. They think it's a fairy tale, some of them, and those who do think anything of it want to try it first and pay me afterward."

"If you could have another three wishes," said the old man, eyeing him keenly, "would you have them?"

"I don't know," said the other. "I don't know."

He took the paw, and dangling it between his forefinger and thumb, suddenly threw it upon the fire. White, with a slight cry, stooped down and snatched it off.

"Better let it burn," said the soldier, solemnly.

"If you don't want it, Morris," said the other, "give it to me."

"I won't," said his friend doggedly. "I threw it on the fire. If you keep it, don't blame me for what happens. Pitch it on the fire again, like a sensible man."

The other shook his head and examined his new possession closely. "How do you do it?" he inquired.

"Hold it up in your right hand and wish aloud," said the sergeant major, "but I warn you of the consequences."

"Sounds like the *Arabian Nights*,"[4] said Mrs. White, as she rose and began to set the supper. "Don't you think you might wish for four pairs of hands for me?"

Her husband drew the talisman from his pocket, and then all three burst into laughter as the sergeant major, with a look of alarm on his face, caught him by the arm. "If you must wish," he said, gruffly, "wish for something sensible."

Mr. White dropped it back in his pocket, and placing chairs, motioned his friend to the table. In the business of supper the talisman was partly forgotten, and afterward the three sat listening in an enthralled fashion to a second installment of the soldier's adventures in India.

"If the tale about the monkey's paw is not more truthful than those he has been telling us," said Herbert, as the door closed behind their guest, just in time for him to catch the last train, "we shan't make much out of it."

"Did you give him anything for it, Father?" inquired Mrs. White,

---

4. ***Arabian Nights*** collection of stories from the ancient Near East telling of fantastical adventures and supernatural beings.

Spiral Review
Theme What theme does Morris's story suggest to readers that the characters do not seem to perceive?

Vocabulary
grave (grāv) *adj.* very serious and worrying

Literary Analysis
Plot How does the information about the previous wishers fore-shadow danger for the Whites?

Reading Check
According to the sergeant major, what is special about the monkey's paw?

Vocabulary
maligned (mə līnd´)
adj. spoken ill of

credulity (krə doo´
lə tē) *n.* tendency to
believe too readily

regarding her husband closely.

"A trifle," said he, coloring slightly. "He didn't want it, but I made him take it. And he pressed me again to throw it away."

"Likely," said Herbert, with pretended horror. "Why, we're going to be rich, and famous and happy. Wish to be an emperor, Father, to begin with; then you can't be bossed around."

He darted round the table, pursued by the maligned Mrs. White armed with an antimacassar.[5]

Mr. White took the paw from his pocket and eyed it dubiously. "I don't know what to wish for, and that's a fact," he said, slowly. "It seems to me I've got all I want."

"If you only cleared the house, you'd be quite happy, wouldn't you?" said Herbert, with his hand on his shoulder. "Well, wish for two hundred pounds,[6] then; that'll just do it."

His father, smiling shamefacedly at his own credulity, held up the talisman, as his son, with a solemn face somewhat marred by a wink at his mother, sat down at the piano and struck a few impressive chords.

"I wish for two hundred pounds," said the old man distinctly.

A fine crash from the piano greeted the words, interrupted by a shuddering cry from the old man. His wife and son ran toward him.

"It moved," he cried, with a glance of disgust at the object as it lay on the floor. "As I wished it twisted in my hand like a snake."

"Well, I don't see the money," said his son as he picked it up and placed it on the table, "and I bet I never shall."

"It must have been your fancy, Father," said his wife, regarding him anxiously.

He shook his head. "Never mind, though; there's no harm done, but it gave me a shock all the same."

They sat down by the fire again while the two men finished their pipes. Outside, the wind was higher than ever, and the old man started nervously at the sound of a door banging upstairs. A silence unusual and depressing settled upon all three, which lasted until the old couple rose to retire for the night.

"I expect you'll find the cash tied up in a big bag in the middle of your bed," said Herbert, as he bade them good night, "and something horrible squatting up on top of the wardrobe watching you as you pocket your ill-gotten gains."

Herbert sat alone in the darkness, gazing at the dying fire, and seeing faces in it. The last face was so horrible and so simian[7] that he gazed at it in amazement. It got so vivid that, with a little uneasy

Reading Skill
Make Predictions
What do characters in stories about wishes usually learn? Predict the results of Mr. White's wish.

---

5. **antimacassar** (an´ ti mə kas´ ər) *n.* small cover for the arms or back of a chair or sofa.
6. **pounds** *n.* units of English currency, roughly comparable to dollars.
7. **simian** (sim´ ē ən) *adj.* monkeylike.

laugh, he felt on the table for a glass containing a little water to throw over it. His hand grasped the monkey's paw, and with a little shiver he wiped his hand on his coat and went up to bed.

In the brightness of the wintry sun next morning as it streamed over the breakfast table Herbert laughed at his fears. There was an air of prosaic wholesomeness about the room which it had lacked on the previous night, and the dirty, shriveled little paw was pitched on the sideboard with a carelessness which betokened no great belief in its virtues.

"I suppose all old soldiers are the same," said Mrs. White. "The idea of our listening to such nonsense! How could wishes be granted in these days? And if they could, how could two hundred pounds hurt you, Father?"

"Might drop on his head from the sky," said the frivolous Herbert.

"Morris said the things happened so naturally," said his father, "that you might if you so wished attribute it to coincidence."

"Well, don't break into the money before I come back," said Herbert, as he rose from the table. "I'm afraid it'll turn you into a mean, avaricious[8] man, and we shall have to disown you."

His mother laughed, and following him to the door, watched him down the road, and, returning to the breakfast table, was very happy at the expense of her husband's credulity. All of which did not prevent her from scurrying to the door at the postman's knock, nor prevent her from referring somewhat shortly to retired sergeant majors of bibulous habits when she found that the post brought a tailor's bill.

"Herbert will have some more of his funny remarks, I expect, when he comes home," she said, as they sat at dinner.

"I dare say," said Mr. White, "but for all that, the thing moved in my hand; that I'll swear to."

"You thought it did," said the old lady soothingly.

"I say it did," replied the other. "There was no thought about it; I had just—What's the matter?"

His wife made no reply. She was watching the mysterious movements of a man outside, who, peering in an undecided fashion at the house, appeared to be trying to make up his mind to enter. In mental connection with the two hundred pounds, she noticed that the stranger was well dressed, and wore a silk hat of glossy newness. Three times he paused at the gate, and then walked on

Literary Analysis
Plot How does the conversation about the money foreshadow a problem?

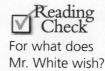

Reading Check
For what does Mr. White wish?

---

8. avaricious (av´ ə rish´ əs) *adj.* greedy for wealth.

again. The fourth time he stood with his hand upon it, and then with sudden resolution flung it open and walked up the path. Mrs. White at the same moment placed her hands behind her, and hurriedly unfastening the strings of her apron, put that useful article of apparel beneath the cushion of her chair.

She brought the stranger, who seemed ill at ease, into the room. He gazed at her furtively, and listened in a preoccupied fashion as the old lady apologized for the appearance of the room, and her husband's coat, a garment which he usually reserved for the garden. She then waited patiently for him to broach his business, but he was at first strangely silent.

"I—was asked to call," he said at last, and stooped and picked a piece of cotton from his trousers. "I come from 'Maw and Meggins.'"

The old lady started. "Is anything the matter?" she asked, breathlessly. "Has anything happened to Herbert? What is it? What is it?"

Her husband interposed. "There, there, mother," he said, hastily. "Sit down, and don't jump to conclusions. You've not brought bad news, I'm sure, sir," and he eyed the other wistfully.

"I'm sorry—" began the visitor.

"Is he hurt?" demanded the mother, wildly.

The visitor bowed in assent. "Badly hurt," he said quietly, "but he is not in any pain."

"Oh, thank God!" said the old woman, clasping her hands. "Thank God for that! Thank—"

She broke off suddenly as the sinister meaning of the assurance dawned upon her and she saw the awful confirmation of her fears in the other's averted face. She caught her breath, and turning to her husband, laid her trembling old hand upon his. There was a long silence.

"He was caught in the machinery," said the visitor at length, in a low voice.

"Caught in the machinery," repeated Mr. White, in a dazed fashion, "yes."

He sat staring blankly out at the window, and taking his wife's hand between his own, pressed it as he had been wont to do in their old courting days nearly forty years before.

"He was the only one left to us," he said, turning gently to the visitor. "It is hard."

The other coughed, and, rising, walked slowly to the window. "The firm wished me to convey their sincere sympathy with you in your great loss," he said, without looking round. "I beg that you will understand I am only their servant and merely obeying orders."

Vocabulary
furtively (fur´ tiv lē) *adv.* secretively; sneakily; stealthily

Literary Analysis
Plot In what way does the stranger's answer increase the tension of the rising action?

There was no reply; the old woman's face was white, her eyes staring, and her breath inaudible; on the husband's face was a look such as his friend the sergeant might have carried into his first action.

"I was to say that Maw and Meggins disclaim all responsibility," continued the other. "They admit no liability at all, but in consideration of your son's services they wish to present you with a certain sum as compensation."

Mr. White dropped his wife's hand, and rising to his feet, gazed with a look of horror at his visitor. His dry lips shaped the words, "How much?"

"Two hundred pounds," was the answer.

Unconscious of his wife's shriek, the old man smiled faintly, put out his hands like a sightless man, and dropped, a senseless heap, to the floor. •

In the huge new cemetery, some two miles distant, the old people buried their dead, and came back to a house steeped in shadow and silence. It was all over so quickly that at first they could hardly realize it, and remained in a state of expectation as though of something else to happen—something else which was to lighten this load, too heavy for old hearts to bear.

But the days passed, and expectation gave place to resignation— the hopeless resignation of the old, sometimes miscalled apathy. Sometimes they hardly exchanged a word, for now they had nothing to talk about, and their days were long to weariness.

It was about a week after that the old man, waking suddenly in the night, stretched out his hand and found himself alone. The room was in darkness, and the sound of subdued weeping came from the window. He raised himself in bed and listened.

"Come back," he said, tenderly. "You will be cold."

"It is colder for my son," said the old woman, and wept afresh.

The sound of her sobs died away on his ears. The bed was warm, and his eyes heavy with sleep. He dozed fitfully, and then slept until a sudden wild cry from his wife awoke him with a start.

"*The paw!*" she cried wildly. "The monkey's paw!"

He started up in alarm. "Where? Where is it? What's the matter?"

She came stumbling across the room toward him. "I want it," she said quietly. "You've not destroyed it?"

"It's in the parlor, on the bracket," he replied, marveling. "Why?"

She cried and laughed together, and bending over, kissed his cheek.

Reading Skill
Make Predictions
Do you think the Whites will make another wish? Why or why not?

Vocabulary
apathy (ap´ə the) *n.* lack of interest or emotion

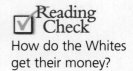
Reading
Check
How do the Whites get their money?

"I only just thought of it," she said hysterically. "Why didn't I think of it before? Why didn't *you* think of it?"

"Think of what?" he questioned.

"The other two wishes," she replied rapidly. "We've only had one."

"Was not that enough?" he demanded, fiercely.

"No," she cried triumphantly; "we'll have one more. Go down and get it quickly, and wish our boy alive again."

The man sat up in bed and flung the bedclothes from his quaking limbs. "You are mad!" he cried, aghast.

"Get it," she panted; "get it quickly, and wish—Oh, my boy, my boy!"

Her husband struck a match and lit the candle. "Get back to bed," he said unsteadily. "You don't know what you are saying."

"We had the first wish granted," said the old woman feverishly; "why not the second?"

"A coincidence," stammered the old man.

"Go and get it and wish," cried his wife, quivering with excitement.

The old man turned and regarded her, and his voice shook. "He has been dead ten days, and besides he—I would not tell you else, but—I could only recognize him by his clothing. If he was too terrible for you to see then, how now?"

"Bring him back," cried the old woman, and dragged him toward the door. "Do you think I fear the child I have nursed?"

He went down in the darkness, and felt his way to the parlor, and then to the mantelpiece. The talisman was in its place, and a horrible fear that the unspoken wish might bring his mutilated son before him ere he could escape from the room seized upon him, and he caught his breath as he found that he had lost the direction of the door. His brow cold with sweat, he felt his way round the table, and groped along the wall until he found himself in the small passage with the unwholesome thing in his hand.

Even his wife's face seemed changed as he entered the room. It was white and expectant, and to his fears seemed to have an unnatural look upon it. He was afraid of her.

"*Wish!*" she cried, in a strong voice.

"It is foolish and wicked," he faltered.

"*Wish!*" repeated his wife.

He raised his hand. "I wish my son alive again."

The talisman fell to the floor, and he regarded it fearfully. Then he sank trembling into a chair as the old woman, with burning eyes, walked to the window and raised the blind.

He sat until he was chilled with the cold, glancing occasionally

"The other two wishes," she replied rapidly. "We've only had one."

Literary Analysis
Plot In what way does this new wish increase the tension of the story?

at the figure of the old woman peering through the window. The candle-end, which had burned below the rim of the china candlestick, was throwing pulsating shadows on the ceiling and walls, until, with a flicker larger than the rest, it expired. The old man, with an unspeakable sense of relief at the failure of the talisman, crept back to his bed, and a minute or two afterward the old woman came silently and apathetically beside him.

Neither spoke, but lay silently listening to the ticking of the clock. A stair creaked, and a squeaky mouse scurried noisily through the wall. The darkness was oppressive, and after lying for some time screwing up his courage, he took the box of matches, and striking one, went downstairs for a candle.

At the foot of the stairs the match went out, and he paused to strike another; and at the same moment a knock, so quiet and stealthy as to be scarcely audible, sounded on the front door.

The matches fell from his hand and spilled in the passage. He stood motionless, his breath suspended until the knock was repeated. Then he turned and fled swiftly back to his room, and closed the door behind him. A third knock sounded through the house.

"*What's that?*" cried the old woman, starting up.

"A rat," said the old man in shaking tones—"a rat. It passed me on the stairs."

His wife sat up in bed listening. A loud knock resounded through the house.

"It's Herbert!" she screamed. "It's Herbert!"

She ran to the door, but her husband was before her, and catching her by the arm, held her tightly.

"What are you going to do?" he whispered hoarsely.

"It's my boy; it's Herbert!" she cried, struggling mechanically. "I forgot it was two miles away. What are you holding me for? Let go. I must open the door."

"Don't let it in," cried the old man, trembling.

"You're afraid of your own son," she cried, struggling. "Let me go. I'm coming, Herbert, I'm coming."

There was another knock, and another. The old woman with a sudden wrench broke free and ran from the room. Her husband followed to the landing, and called after her appealingly as she hurried downstairs. He heard the chain rattle back and the bottom bolt drawn slowly and stiffly from the socket. Then the old woman's voice, strained and panting.

"The bolt," she cried, loudly. "Come down. I can't reach it."

But her husband was on his hands and knees groping wildly on

Vocabulary

oppressive (ə pres´ iv) *adj.* causing great discomfort; distressing

Why is Mr. White afraid?

**Literary Analysis
Plot** How does the difference between what Mr. and Mrs. White are trying to do bring events to a climax?

the floor in search of the paw. If he could only find it before the thing outside got in. A perfect fusillade[9] of knocks reverberated through the house, and he heard the scraping of a chair as his wife put it down in the passage against the door. He heard the creaking of the bolt as it came slowly back, and at the same moment he found the monkey's paw, and frantically breathed his third and last wish.

The knocking ceased suddenly, although the echoes of it were still in the house. He heard the chair drawn back and the door opened. A cold wind rushed up the staircase, and a long loud wail of disappointment and misery from his wife gave him courage to run down to her side, and then to the gate beyond. The street lamp flickering opposite shone on a quiet and deserted road.

9. fusillade (fyŏŏ′ sə lād′) *n.* rapid firing, as of gunshots.

Critical Thinking

Cite textual evidence to support your responses.

1. **Key Ideas and Details** **(a)** How does each of the Whites react when first hearing the legend of the monkey's paw? **(b) Contrast:** How do the reactions of the mother and the father change?

2. **Key Ideas and Details** **(a)** What lesson does the fakir want to teach? **(b)** Does he succeed? Explain.

3. **Craft and Structure** **(a)** How does Mr. White word his first wish? **(b) Discuss:** In a group, discuss the strengths and weaknesses of other ways the wish could have been worded. Decide whether any version is foolproof. Share your decision with the class.

4. **Integration of Knowledge and Ideas** **(a)** Do the Whites begin to think that the legend of the monkey's paw is true? **(b)** How can you tell? *[Connect to the Big Question: Is there a difference between reality and truth?]*

Literary Analysis: Plot and Foreshadowing

1. Craft and Structure What information about the paw is given in the **exposition?**

2. Craft and Structure **(a)** Describe three events in the **rising action. (b)** Where does the story reach its **climax?**

3. Craft and Structure Identify two details that **foreshadow** the tragic outcome of the first wish.

Reading Skill: Make Predictions

4. (a) Using a chart like the one shown, indicate how you used your prior knowledge to **make a prediction** about one of the wishes.

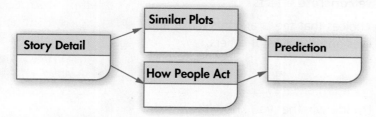

(b) Was your prediction close to the actual outcome? Explain.

Vocabulary

Acquisition and Use An **analogy** shows the relationship between pairs of words. Use a word from the vocabulary list for "The Monkey's Paw" on page 30 to complete each analogy. Your choice should create a word pair that matches the relationship between the first two words given. Explain the relationship in each analogy.

1. ran : rapidly :: crept : _____

2. kindness : cruelty :: passion : _____

3. nourished : starved :: praised : _____

4. lighthearted : cheerful :: serious : _____

5. happiness : sadness :: doubt : _____

6. cautious : reckless :: unburdened : _____

Word Study Use the context of the sentences and what you know about the **Latin root -cred-** to explain your answer to each question.

1. Would you believe an *incredible* rumor?

2. Does someone who tells lies have *credibility?*

Word Study

The **Latin root -cred-** means "believe."

Apply It Explain how the root -cred- contributes to the meanings of these words. Consult a dictionary if necessary.

credence
credo
discredit

Is there a difference between *reality* and *truth?*

Writing About the Big Question

In "The Leap," a daughter thinks about the truth of her life by contemplating how much she owes her mother. Use these sentence starters to develop your ideas about the Big Question.

Decisions that people make can affect the **reality** of their lives by _____.
The choices people make can have **concrete** effects on _____.

While You Read Think about the choices that the characters make and how their choices affect their own lives and the lives of others.

Vocabulary

Read each word and its definition. Decide whether you know the word well, know it a little bit, or do not know it at all. After you read, see how your knowledge of each word has increased.

- **encroaching** (en krōch´ iŋ) *adj.* intruding on, especially in a gradual way (p. 47) *Toward afternoon, the __encroaching__ clouds dimmed the sun.* encroach *v.* encroachment *n.*

- **commemorates** (kə mem´ ə rāts´) *v.* honors a memory (p. 47) *The memorial __commemorates__ the soldiers who died defending their country.* commemoration *n.* memorial *n.* memory *n.*

- **extricating** (eks´ tri kāt´ iŋ) *n.* setting free; removing from a difficult situation (p. 50) *__Extricating__ the kite from the tree proved to be very difficult.* extricate *v.* extrication *n.*

- **constricting** (kən strikt´ iŋ) *adj.* preventing freedom of movement; limiting (p. 51) *He found the sweater to be too __constricting__, so he bought a larger size.* constrict *v.* constriction *n.*

- **perpetually** (pər pech´ ō͞o əl lē) *adv.* continuing forever; constantly (p. 52) *He was fired for being __perpetually__ late to work.* perpetual *adj.* perpetuate *v.*

- **tentative** (ten´ tə tiv) *adj.* hesitant; not confident (p. 53) *I took a __tentative__ bite of the odd dessert.* tentatively *adv.*

Word Study

The **Latin root -*strict*-** means "confine" or "squeeze."

In this story, a character thinks living in a small town can be **constricting**, because his experiences are confined within the boundaries of this small area.

©Thomas Victor

Meet
Louise Erdrich
(b. 1954)

Author of

The Leap

Louise Erdrich's fiction and poetry celebrate life's richness. Born to a German American father and a French-Native American mother, Erdrich writes from the complex perspective of two distinct cultures.

A Family Tradition Erdrich grew up in North Dakota, where she often visited with her relatives in the Turtle Mountain Band of Chippewa, a Native American people. With little exposure to television or movies, Erdrich became fascinated by the storytelling tradition that surrounded her. "The people in our families made everything into a story," she explains. Her first published book, *Love Medicine*, a group of interrelated stories, brought Erdrich national acclaim.

BACKGROUND FOR THE STORY

Circus Families

Circus families often develop their own acts. They pass the specific skills involved, such as acrobatics or juggling, from one generation to the next. Many young circus performers, like the mother in "The Leap," bypass traditional schooling to develop the remarkable physical talents that they display to amazed audiences.

DID YOU KNOW?

Love Medicine was rejected by the first twenty-eight publishers to whom Erdrich sent it. When finally published, the book won rave reviews and the National Book Critics Circle Award.

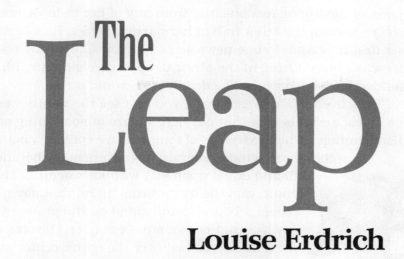

The Leap

Louise Erdrich

My mother is the surviving half of a blindfold trapeze act, not a fact I think about much even now that she is sightless, the result of encroaching and stubborn cataracts.

She walks slowly through her house here in New Hampshire, lightly touching her way along walls and running her hands over knickknacks, books, the drift of a grown child's belongings and castoffs. She has never upset an object or as much as brushed a magazine onto the floor. She has never lost her balance or bumped into a closet door left carelessly open.

It has occurred to me that the catlike precision of her movements in old age might be the result of her early training, but she shows so little of the drama or flair one might expect from a performer that I tend to forget the Flying Avalons. She has kept no sequined costume, no photographs, no fliers or posters from that part of her youth. I would, in fact, tend to think that all memory of double somersaults and heart-stopping catches had left her arms and legs were it not for the fact that sometimes, as I sit sewing in the room of the rebuilt house in which I slept as a child, I hear the crackle, catch a whiff of smoke from the stove downstairs, and suddenly the room goes dark, the stitches burn beneath my fingers, and I am sewing with a needle of hot silver, a thread of fire.

I owe her my existence three times. The first was when she saved herself. In the town square a replica tent pole, cracked and splintered, now stands cast in concrete. It commemorates the disaster that put our town smack on the front page of the Boston and New York tabloids. It is from those old newspapers, now

Reading Check

What was the narrator's mother's profession?

historical records, that I get my information. Not from my mother, Anna of the Flying Avalons, nor from any of her in-laws, nor certainly from the other half of her particular act, Harold Avalon, her first husband. In one news account it says, "The day was mildly overcast, but nothing in the air or temperature gave any hint of the sudden force with which the deadly gale would strike."

I have lived in the West, where you can see the weather coming for miles, and it is true that out here we are at something of a disadvantage. When extremes of temperature collide, a hot and cold front, winds generate instantaneously behind a hill and crash upon you without warning. That, I think, was the likely situation on that day in June. People probably commented on the pleasant air, grateful that no hot sun beat upon the striped tent that stretched over the entire center green.

They bought their tickets and surrendered them in anticipation. They sat. They ate caramelized popcorn and roasted peanuts. There was time, before the storm, for three acts. The White Arabians[1] of Ali-Khazar rose on their hind legs and waltzed. The Mysterious Bernie folded himself into a painted cracker tin, and the Lady of the Mists made herself appear and disappear in surprising places. As the clouds gathered outside, unnoticed, the ringmaster cracked his whip, shouted his introduction, and pointed to the ceiling of the tent, where the Flying Avalons were perched.

They loved to drop gracefully from nowhere, like two sparkling birds, and blow kisses as they threw off their plumed helmets and high-collared capes. They laughed and flirted openly as they beat their way up again on the trapeze bars. In the final vignette of their act, they actually would kiss in midair, pausing, almost hovering as they swooped past one another. On the ground, between bows, Harry Avalon would skip quickly to the front rows and point out the smear of my mother's lipstick, just off the edge of his mouth. They made a romantic pair all right, especially in the blindfold sequence.

That afternoon, as the anticipation increased, as Mr. and Mrs. Avalon tied sparkling strips of cloth onto each other's face and as they puckered their lips in mock kisses, lips destined "never again to meet," as one long breathless article put it, the wind rose, miles off, wrapped itself into a cone, and howled. There came a rumble of electrical energy, drowned out by the sudden roll of drums.

---

1. **Arabians** horses of the Arabian breed.

Reading Skill
Make Predictions
What details help you predict that something will go wrong?

One detail not mentioned by the press, perhaps unknown—Anna was pregnant at the time, seven months and hardly showing, her stomach muscles were that strong. It seems incredible that she would work high above the ground when any fall could be so dangerous, but the explanation—I know from watching her go blind—is that my mother lives comfortably in extreme elements. She is one with the constant dark now, just as the air was her home, familiar to her, safe, before the storm that afternoon.

From opposite ends of the tent they waved, blind and smiling, to the crowd below. The ringmaster removed his hat and called for silence, so that the two above could concentrate. They rubbed their hands in chalky powder, then Harry launched himself and swung, once, twice, in huge calibrated beats across space. He hung from his knees and on the third swing stretched wide his arms, held his hands out to receive his pregnant wife as she dove from her shining bar.

It was while the two were in midair, their hands about to meet, that lightning struck the main pole and sizzled down the guy wires, filling the air with a blue radiance that Harry Avalon must certainly have seen through the cloth of his blindfold as the tent buckled and the edifice[2] toppled him forward, the swing continuing and not returning in its sweep, and Harry going down, down into the crowd with his last thought, perhaps, just a prickle of surprise at his empty hands.

My mother once said that I'd be amazed at how many things a person can do within the act of falling. Perhaps, at the time, she

---

2. **edifice** (ed´ i fis) *n.* large structure or building.

▲ Critical Viewing
What feelings might a scene like this inspire in an onlooker? **[Infer]**

Literary Analysis
Plot In what way do these descriptions of events increase the tension in the rising action?

Reading Check
What happens to Harry on the day of the gale?

was teaching me to dive off a board at the town pool, for I associate the idea with midair somersaults. But I also think she meant that even in that awful doomed second one could think, for she certainly did. When her hands did not meet her husband's, my mother tore her blindfold away. As he swept past her on the wrong side, she could have grasped his ankle, the toe-end of his tights, and gone down clutching him. Instead, she changed direction. Her body twisted toward a heavy wire and she managed to hang on to the braided metal, still hot from the lightning strike. Her palms were burned so terribly that once healed they bore no lines, only the blank scar tissue of a quieter future. She was lowered, gently, to the sawdust ring just underneath the dome of the canvas roof, which did not entirely settle but was held up on one end and jabbed through, torn, and still on fire in places from the giant spark, though rain and men's jackets soon put that out.

Three people died, but except for her hands my mother was not seriously harmed until an overeager rescuer broke her arm in extricating her and also, in the process, collapsed a portion of the tent bearing a huge buckle that knocked her unconscious. She was taken to the town hospital, and there she must have hemorrhaged,[3] for they kept her, confined to her bed, a month and a half before her baby was born without life.

Harry Avalon had wanted to be buried in the circus cemetery next to the original Avalon, his uncle, so she sent him back with his brothers. The child, however, is buried around the corner, beyond this house and just down the highway. Sometimes I used to walk there just to sit. She was a girl, but I rarely thought of her as a sister or even as a separate person really. I suppose you could call it the egocentrism[4] of a child, of all young children, but I considered her a less finished version of myself.

When the snow falls, throwing shadows among the stones, I can easily pick hers out from the road, for it is bigger than the others and in the shape of a lamb at rest, its legs curled beneath. The carved lamb looms larger as the years pass, though it is probably only my eyes, the vision shifting, as what is close to me blurs and distances sharpen. In odd moments, I think it is the edge drawing near, the edge of everything, the unseen horizon we do not really speak of in the eastern woods. And it also seems to me, although this is probably an idle fantasy, that the statue is growing more sharply etched, as if, instead of weathering itself into a porous mass, it is hardening on the hillside with each snowfall, perfecting itself. ●

Vocabulary
extricating (eks´ tri kāt´ iŋ) *n.* setting free; removing from a difficult situation

---

3. **hemorrhaged** (hem´ ər ij'd´) *v.* bled heavily.
4. **egocentrism** (ē´ gō sen´ triz əm) *n.* self-centeredness; inability to distinguish one's own needs and interests from those of others.

It was during her confinement in the hospital that my mother met my father. He was called in to look at the set of her arm, which was complicated. He stayed, sitting at her bedside, for he was something of an armchair traveler and had spent his war quietly, at an air force training grounds, where he became a specialist in arms and legs broken during parachute training exercises. Anna Avalon had been to many of the places he longed to visit—Venice, Rome, Mexico, all through France and Spain. She had no family of her own and was taken in by the Avalons, trained to perform from a very young age. They toured Europe before the war, then based themselves in New York. She was illiterate.

Literary Analysis
Plot Which details in this paragraph provide additional exposition?

It was in the hospital that she finally learned to read and write, as a way of overcoming the boredom and depression of those weeks, and it was my father who insisted on teaching her. In return for stories of her adventures, he graded her first exercises. He bought her her first book, and over her bold letters, which the pale guides of the penmanship pads could not contain, they fell in love.

I wonder if my father calculated the exchange he offered: one form of flight for another. For after that, and for as long as I can remember, my mother has never been without a book. Until now, that is, and it remains the greatest difficulty of her blindness. Since my father's recent death, there is no one to read to her, which is why I returned, in fact, from my failed life where the land is flat. I came home to read to my mother, to read out loud, to read long into the dark if I must, to read all night.

Once my father and mother married, they moved onto the old farm he had inherited but didn't care much for. Though he'd been thinking of moving to a larger city, he settled down and broadened his practice in this valley. It still seems odd to me, when they could have gone anywhere else, that they chose to stay in the town where the disaster had occurred, and which my father in the first place had found so constricting. It was my mother who insisted upon it, after her child did not survive. And then, too, she loved the sagging

Vocabulary
constricting (kən strikt´ iŋ) *adj.* preventing freedom of movement; limiting

Reading Check

How do the narrator's mother and father first meet?

The Leap **51**

farmhouse with its scrap of what was left of a vast acreage of woods and hidden hay fields that stretched to the game park.

I owe my existence, the second time then, to the two of them and the hospital that brought them together. That is the debt we take for granted since none of us asks for life. It is only once we have it that we hang on so dearly. ●

I was seven the year the house caught fire, probably from standing ash. It can rekindle, and my father, forgetful around the house and **perpetually** exhausted from night hours on call, often emptied what he thought were ashes from cold stoves into wooden or cardboard containers. The fire could have started from a flaming box, or perhaps a buildup of creosote inside the chimney was the culprit. It started right around the stove, and the heart of the house was gutted. The baby-sitter, fallen asleep in my father's den on the first floor, woke to find the stairway to my upstairs room cut off by flames. She used the phone, then ran outside to stand beneath my window.

When my parents arrived, the town volunteers had drawn water from the fire pond and were spraying the outside of the house, preparing to go inside after me, not knowing at the time that there was only one staircase and that it was lost. On the other side of the house, the superannuated[5] extension ladder broke in half. Perhaps the clatter of it falling against the walls woke me, for I'd been asleep up to that point.

As soon as I awakened, in the small room that I now use for sewing, I smelled the smoke. I followed things by the letter then, was good at memorizing instructions, and so I did exactly what was taught in the second-grade home fire drill. I got up, I touched the back of my door before opening it. Finding it hot, I left it closed and stuffed my rolled-up rug beneath the crack. I did not hide under my bed or crawl into my closet. I put on my flannel robe, and then I sat down to wait.

Outside, my mother stood below my dark window and saw clearly that there was no rescue. Flames had pierced one side wall, and the glare of the fire lighted the massive limbs and trunk of the vigorous old elm that had probably been planted the year the house was built, a hundred years ago at least. No leaf touched the wall, and just one thin branch scraped the roof. From below, it looked as though even a squirrel would have had trouble jumping from the tree onto the house, for the breadth of that small branch was no bigger than my mother's wrist.

Standing there, beside Father, who was preparing to rush back around to the front of the house, my mother asked him to unzip her dress. When he wouldn't be bothered, she made him understand.

Vocabulary
perpetually (pər pech´ o͞o əl lē) adv. continuing forever; constantly

Reading Skill
Make Preditions Based on facts in the story about Anna's past, what do you predict she will do next?

---

5. **superannuated** (so͞o´ pər an´ yo͞o āt´ əd) adj. too old to be usable.

He couldn't make his hands work, so she finally tore it off and stood there in her pearls and stockings. She directed one of the men to lean the broken half of the extension ladder up against the trunk of the tree. In surprise, he complied. She ascended. She vanished. Then she could be seen among the leafless branches of late November as she made her way up and, along her stomach, inched the length of a bough that curved above the branch that brushed the roof.

Once there, swaying, she stood and balanced. There were plenty of people in the crowd and many who still remember, or think they do, my mother's leap through the ice-dark air toward that thinnest extension, and how she broke the branch falling so that it cracked in her hands, cracked louder than the flames as she vaulted with it toward the edge of the roof, and how it hurtled down end over end without her, and their eyes went up, again, to see where she had flown.

I didn't see her leap through air, only heard the sudden thump and looked out my window. She was hanging by the backs of her heels from the new gutter we had put in that year, and she was smiling. I was not surprised to see her, she was so matter-of-fact. She tapped on the window. I remember how she did it, too. It was the friendliest tap, a bit tentative, as if she was afraid she had arrived too early at a friend's house. Then she gestured at the latch, and when I opened the window she told me to

Vocabulary
tentative (ten´ tə tiv) *adj.* hesitant; not confident

Reading Check
What steps does the narrator take when she realizes that there is a fire?

The Leap 53

raise it wider and prop it up with the stick so it wouldn't crush her fingers. She swung down, caught the ledge, and crawled through the opening. Once she was in my room, I realized she had on only underclothing, a bra of the heavy stitched cotton women used to wear and step-in, lace-trimmed drawers. I remember feeling light-headed, of course, terribly relieved, and then embarrassed for her to be seen by the crowd undressed.

I was still embarrassed as we flew out the window, toward earth, me in her lap, her toes pointed as we skimmed toward the painted target of the fire fighter's net.

I know that she's right. I knew it even then. As you fall there is time to think. Curled as I was, against her stomach, I was not startled by the cries of the crowd or the looming faces. The wind roared and beat its hot breath at our back, the flames whistled. I slowly wondered what would happen if we missed the circle or bounced out of it. Then I wrapped my hands around my mother's hands. I felt the brush of her lips and heard the beat of her heart in my ears, loud as thunder, long as the roll of drums.

Spiral Review
Theme How does the mother turn a fall into a leap? What theme do her actions suggest?

Literary Analysis
Plot How is the conflict resolved?

Critical Thinking

Cite textual evidence to support your responses.

1. **Key Ideas and Details** **(a)** What does Anna decide to do when the circus tent pole is struck by lightning? **(b) Interpret:** In what sense does the narrator owe her life to her mother's decision?

2. **Key Ideas and Details** **(a)** Using details from the story, identify the two other ways in which the narrator owes her life to her mother. **(b) Compare and Contrast:** Compare the three ways in which the mother somehow saves the daughter's life. Note one difference and one similarity among them.

3. **Key Ideas and Details** **(a) Summarize:** Describe the scene at the end in which the mother leaps. **(b) Infer:** Why does the mother make the leap? **(c) Discuss:** In a group, discuss the qualities or ideas that the leap might represent. Choose one idea to share with the class.

4. **Integration of Knowledge and Ideas** In what ways is the narrator's view of reality shaped by the choices her mother has made? *[Connect to the Big Question: Is there a difference between reality and truth?]*

Literary Analysis: Plot and Foreshadowing

1. Craft and Structure What information about the mother is given in the **exposition**?

2. Craft and Structure **(a)** Describe three events in the **rising action.** **(b)** Where does the story reach its **climax**? Explain.

3. Craft and Structure What insight about the relationship between mother and daughter is presented in the **resolution** of the story?

4. Craft and Structure Give two examples of **foreshadowing** in the story. Give one example of a **flashback.**

Reading Skill: Make Predictions

5. (a) Using a chart like the one shown, indicate how you used prior knowledge to **make a prediction** about the outcome of the story.

(b) How closely did you predict the outcome of the story? Explain.

Vocabulary

Acquisition and Use An **analogy** shows the relationship between pairs of words. Use a word from the vocabulary list for "The Leap," on page 44, to complete each analogy. For each item, the new word pair should share the same relationship as the first two words. Explain the relationship in each analogy.

1. happiness : cheerful :: insecurity : _____

2. knowledge : teaching :: freedom : _____

3. receiving : giving :: retreating : _____

4. helps : aids :: honors : _____

5. towering : small :: expansive : _____

6. quickly : rapidly :: constantly : _____

Word Study Use the context of the sentences and what you know about the **Latin root -strict-** to explain your answer to each question.

1. Would a *strict* parent have many or few rules?

2. How would a *constrictor* snake kill its prey?

Word Study

The **Latin root -strict-** means "confine" or "squeeze."

Apply It Explain how the root -strict- contributes to the meanings of these words. Consult a dictionary if necessary.

district
restrict
stricture

Integrated Language Skills

The Monkey's Paw • The Leap

Conventions:
Common Nouns and Proper Nouns

A **noun** is a word that names a person, a place, or a thing. A **common noun** refers to any one of a certain kind of person, place, or thing. A **proper noun** names a specific person, place, or thing. Proper nouns always begin with capital letters. Look at these examples:

Common Nouns	Proper Nouns
writer	Louise Erdrich, W. W. Jacobs
city	St. Louis, Nairobi
athlete	Derek Jeter, Venus Williams

Practice A Identify the nouns in each sentence, and indicate whether they are common nouns or proper nouns.

1. Morris kept the withered paw of a monkey in his pocket.
2. Mr. White believes the legend and wishes for money.
3. When Herbert is killed at his job, his parents receive money from his employers.
4. Mrs. White tries to bring Herbert back to life using magic.

Ⓒ **Reading Application** In "The Monkey's Paw," find three common nouns and three proper nouns.

Practice B Underline the common nouns in the following sentences. Then, substitute a proper noun, if possible, to make the sentence more precise.

1. The narrator's mother was part of the trapeze act.
2. The mother had traveled to many countries.
3. The storm that caused the circus tent to collapse occurred in the summer.
4. The narrator moved back to her hometown.

Ⓒ **Writing Application** Use this model sentence to write two sentences with both common and proper nouns: *Anna's New Hampshire home contains few mementos of her life in the circus.*

PH **WRITING COACH** Further instruction and practice are available in *Prentice Hall Writing Coach*.

Writing

© Narrative Text Write a brief **sequel** to the story you read. For example, if you read "The Monkey's Paw," tell what happens when someone else finds the paw. If you read "The Leap," describe the mother's next daring rescue.

- Use a plot outline to plan your story so that events build on one another and create a satisfying whole.
- Try to capture the author's writing style. Use vivid details to describe events and create an appropriate tone.
- Use foreshadowing to build suspense.
- Add a flashback to help explain the characters' present actions.

Grammar Application Be sure to capitalize proper nouns correctly.

Writing Workshop: *Work in Progress*

Prewriting for Autobiographical Narrative For a narrative you may write, list places you have visited. Next to each, write words you associate with the place. Keep this Place List in your writing portfolio for later use.

Speaking and Listening

© Comprehension and Collaboration In a small group, conduct an **interview** between a journalist and characters in the story you read.

- If you read "The Monkey's Paw," plan an exchange of ideas between a journalist and the Whites after the tragedy. Prepare questions that will focus the Whites' retelling of the story.
- If you read "The Leap," plan an exchange of ideas between a journalist who is writing about circus families and the narrator. Prepare questions that will help the narrator retell the main events of the story.

Follow these steps to plan and role-play the interview:

- Choose roles and set rules about how to ask and respond to questions appropriately.
- Demonstrate a knowledge of the subject through the questions asked and the responses given.

After the interview, evaluate the presentation. Discuss which questions and responses were most effective, using language that conveys maturity and respect. Summarize points of agreement and disagreement. Then, compile your responses in a brief report.

© Common Core State Standards

L.9-10.2; W.9-10.3, W.9-10.3.c; SL.9-10.1.a, SL.9-10.1.b
[For the full wording of the standards, see page 28.]

Use this prewriting activity to prepare for the **Writing Workshop** on page 108.

PHLit Online!
www.PHLitOnline.com

- Interactive graphic organizers
- Grammar tutorial
- Interactive journals

Before You Read

© Leveled Texts

Build your skills and improve your comprehension of nonfiction with texts
of increasing complexity.

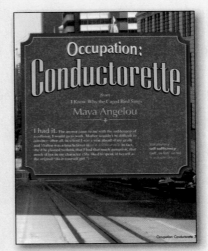

Read the excerpt from **Swimming
to Antarctica** to find out how one
woman's fierce determination helps
her complete a dangerous swim.

Read **"Occupation:
Conductorette"** to see how
a young girl's persistence helps
her when she is faced with
discrimination.

© Common Core State Standards

Meet these standards with either the excerpt from **Swimming to Antarctica** (p. 62) or **"Occupation:
Conductorette"** (p. 78).

Reading Informational Text
6. Determine an author's point of view or purpose in a
text and analyze how an author uses rhetoric to advance
that point of view or purpose. *(Literary Analysis: Author's
Perspective)*

Writing
2.b. Develop the topic with well-chosen, relevant, and
sufficient facts, extended definitions, concrete details,
quotations, or other information and examples appropriate
to the audience's knowledge of the topic. *(Writing:
Description)*

Speaking and Listening
5. Make strategic use of digital media in presentations to
enhance understanding of findings, reasoning, and
evidence and to add interest. *(Speaking and Listening:
Daily Observation Journal)*

Language
4.a. Use context as a clue to the meaning of a word or
phrase. *(Vocabulary: Word Study)*
4.d. Verify the preliminary determination of the meaning
of a word or phrase. *(Vocabulary: Word Study)*

Literary Analysis: Author's Perspective

The **author's perspective,** or point of view, in a literary work includes the judgments, attitudes, and experiences he or she brings to the subject. An author's perspective determines which details he or she includes, as in these examples:

- A writer with firsthand experience of an event might report his or her own reactions as well as generally known facts.
- A writer with a positive view of a subject might emphasize its benefits.

A work may combine several perspectives. For example, a writer might tell what it felt like to live through an event. In addition, the writer might express his or her present views of the experience. As you read, look for details, including specific words and phrases, that suggest the author's perspective.

Reading Skill: Make Predictions

As you read, **make predictions,** or develop ideas, about what will happen next. These predictions can be based on details in the text combined with your own background and experiences. You can check your predictions as you read.

- **Revise,** or adjust, your predictions as you gather more information.
- **Verify,** or confirm, predictions by comparing the outcome you predicted to the actual outcome.

To help you make, verify, and revise predictions, **ask questions** such as "Why did that happen?" and "What will be the result?"

Using the Strategy: Prediction Chart

Record your questions on a **prediction chart** like this one.

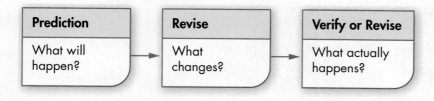

Is there a difference between *reality* and *truth?*

Writing About the Big Question

In the excerpt from *Swimming to Antarctica,* a swimmer discovers how hard she can push her body to achieve a remarkable goal. Use this sentence starter to develop your ideas abut the Big Question.

Facing **uncertainty** about your ability to accomplish a difficult task is an opportunity to _____.

While You Read Look for details that reveal the realities Cox faces during her swim.

Vocabulary

Read each word and its definition. Decide whether you know the word well, know it a little bit, or do not know it at all. After you read, see how your knowledge of each word has increased.

- **venturing** (ven´ chər iŋ) *v.* attempting to do something that involves taking risks (p. 63) *The astronauts will be venturing into space next Tuesday. adventure n. venture n. venturesome adj.*

- **prolonged** (prō lôŋd´) *adj.* extended; lengthy (p. 65) *His prolonged absence is due to serious illness. prolong v.*

- **equilibrium** (ē´ kwi lib´ rē əm) *n.* a state of balance (p. 68) *See how well she keeps her equilibrium while walking on the balance beam! equilibrate v.*

- **abruptly** (ə brupt´ lē) *adv. happening suddenly; unexpectedly (p. 68) The diner abruptly stood up and ran from the restaurant. abrupt adj. abruptness n.*

- **gauge** (gāj) *v.* measure something's size, amount, extent or capacity (p. 70) *Use the map to gauge the distance between the two museums. gauge n.*

- **buffer** (buf´ ər) *v.* lessen a shock; cushion (p. 73) *A helmet helps buffer the impact of a fall. buffer n.*

Word Study

The **Latin prefix pro-** means "forth" or "forward."

In this story, the narrator endures **prolonged** exposure, or an extended amount of time, to water that is freezing.

Author of

Swimming to Antarctica

BACKGROUND FOR THE AUTOBIOGRAPHY

Cold-Water Swimming

Swimming in frigid water, as Lynne Cox does, puts great stress on the body. The body's core—the heart, lungs, and brain—must stay warm or normal muscle and brain function will be impaired, a condition called *hypothermia*. Water temperatures as "warm" as forty-four degrees Fahrenheit would kill most swimmers.

Raised in California, Lynne Cox got started breaking records when she was young. At age fourteen, she swam twenty-six miles from Catalina Island to the California coast. The next year, she broke the men's and the women's records swimming the English Channel.

Made to Swim Cox has a high percentage of body fat, evenly distributed around her body. This fat helps her float and provides insulation. Her unique body has allowed her to swim in waters ranging from the Bering Strait to Antarctica. Today, Lynne Cox stands as the most successful cold-water long-distance swimmer ever.

DID YOU KNOW?

During her swim around the Cape of Good Hope, Cox was chased by a shark.

In 2002, swimmer Lynne Cox attempted an ambitious feat—swimming a mile in the frigid waters of Antarctica. Cox sailed on the ship Orlova with a team of seven friends, including team leader Barry Binder and her physicians, Susan Sklar, Gabriella Miotta, and Laura King. Bob Griffith and Martha Kaplan, Cox's agent, would scout for danger as Cox swam, while Dan Cohen stood by as a rescue swimmer. Scott Pelley, a television producer, also came. The ship's crew included Dr. Anthony Block and expedition leader Susan Adie. Before attempting a mile, Cox tested her reactions on a shorter swim.

from

Swimming to Antarctica

Lynne Cox

When I returned to my cabin, I thought for a long time about what I was about to attempt.

I had **mixed feelings** about the test swim. In some ways, it had given me **confidence**; I now **knew that I could** swim for twenty-two minutes in thirty-three-degree water. But it had also made me feel **uncertain**. It had been the most difficult and probably the most dangerous swim I had ever done. Part of me wanted to be **satisfied** with it. Part of me didn't want to attempt the mile. I was **afraid**.

The water temperature on the big swim would be a degree colder. Thirty-two degrees. That was a magic number, the temperature at which freshwater froze. I wondered if in thirty-two-degree water the water in my cells would freeze, if my body's tissues would become permanently damaged. I wondered if my mind would function better this time, if I would be able to be more aware of what was happening, or if it would be further dulled by the cold. Would my core temperature drop faster, more quickly than I could recognize? Would I be able to tell if I needed to get out? Did I really want to risk my life for this? Or did I want to risk failure?

The other part of me wanted to try, wanted to do what I had trained for, wanted to explore and reach beyond what I had done. That part of me was excited about venturing into the unknown. That part of me knew I would have felt a tremendous letdown if I didn't get a chance to try. I wanted to do it now.

The next morning, on December 15, 2002, Susan called me up to the bridge. She pointed out Water Boat Point. The tiny gray beach between steep glaciers was completely blocked by icebergs and brash ice.[1] There was no place to land.

We continued sailing south through the Gerlache Strait, past mountain-high glaciers and by ship-sized icebergs ranging in shades of blue from juniper berry to robin's-egg to light powder blue. In the protection of the Antarctic Peninsula, the wind dropped off and the sea grew calmer. When we reached Neko Harbor, about an hour later, Susan called me up to the bridge. She was excited. The beach was free of icebergs and brash ice. A landing was possible.

Now I would have a chance to swim the first Antarctic mile. I was thrilled and scared, but I tried to remain calm; I knew that the weather could suddenly change and the swim would be off. I met with Barry Binder, who said, "I'll get the crew into the Zodiacs[2] and come and get you when everything's set."

I walked to the ship's library, drank four eight-ounce cups of hot water, and ate two small croissants for breakfast—they were high in fat and carbohydrates, two sources of energy I would need for the swim. Then I started through the hallway to my cabin, where many of the *Orlova's* passengers were waiting, eager to find out if I was going to swim. They wished me luck and said they would wait for me at the finish. I stopped by Dan's cabin to ask him if he would jump into the water with me at the end of the swim. He was already in his dry suit, prepared to go. Everyone was doing what we had practiced. All I could do was to go back to my room and wait. Gabriella came in to take a core temperature; it was up to 100.4 degrees. Knowing I was venturing into unknown waters, I must have psyched myself

---

1. **brash ice** *n.* floating fragments of ice.
2. **Zodiacs** *n.* speedboats.

Literary Analysis
Author's Perspective
What do the opening sentences indicate about the author's attitude toward her swim?

Vocabulary
venturing (ven´ chər iŋ)
v. attempting to do something that involves taking risks

Reading Skill
Make Predictions
Use details from the narrative to predict whether Cox will succeed or fail.

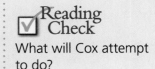
Reading Check
What will Cox attempt to do?

up so much that I increased my body temperature. Gabriella left me alone while I put on my swimsuit and sweats. I rubbed sunscreen on my face, but not on my arms or legs; it could make my skin slippery, and if my crew needed me to get out of the water quickly, that would create a problem. The night before, three of the crew had spotted a pod of eight killer whales swimming into the Gerlache Strait. They hadn't been moving fast. I hoped they were still north of us.

I stared out the window at the brown crescent-shaped beach. There were snow-covered hills directly above the beach, and massive glaciers on either side. I picked out landmarks, places I could aim for, so I'd know if I was on or off course.

Literary Analysis
Author's Perspective
What details indicate that the writer feels fear and doubt before the swim?

Dr. Block caught me at the top of the stairs, just before we stepped out the door and onto the ramp, and asked if I would sit down on a step so he could trace two veins on my hands with a blue Magic Marker. It was just a precaution, he said, in case I needed emergency assistance; this way he would easily be able to find a vein to start an IV. I gave him my right hand and watched him draw the blue lines for the television camera. It gave me the creeps. Why did he have to do this now, right before I swam? Didn't he realize this kind of stuff psychs people out? *I know the swim is dangerous, but he could have done this hours ago, not just before I swam. Get over it,* I told myself. *Shake it off. Take a deep breath. Refocus. Take another breath. Good. Now think about the swim.* I smiled. *I'm so ready for this.*

Walking to the door, I peeked out and felt a blast of icy wind hit my face from the northwest. It was blowing in off the glaciers in gusts to twenty-five knots,[3] and the air temperature was thirty-two degrees. I felt the hair rising on my arms and my jaw tighten to suppress a shiver. I was much more nervous than I had been during my first swim. I had greater expectations of myself now. I wanted to swim the first Antarctic mile, and I knew I would be very disappointed if I didn't succeed.

I stared across the icy water at Neko Harbor's beach and felt excitement building within me. Quickly, before I could lose my chance, I pulled off my sweat suit and shoes and stuck them in a corner of the ship, climbed down the gangway, sat on the platform,

Why did he have to do this now, right before I swam?

---

3. knots (näts) *n.* a rate of speed. One knot equals one nautical mile (6,076.12 feet) per hour.

and dangled my feet in the water. Surprisingly, it didn't feel any colder than it had two days before. I didn't realize then that the nerves on my skin's surface had been damaged from the first swim. I didn't know that the nerves that signaled danger weren't firing. I wasn't aware that my first line of defense was gone. I had no idea that prolonged exposure in thirty-two-degree water could cause permanent nerve and muscle damage. And I didn't know then that when an untrained person is immersed in water colder than forty degrees, their nerves are cooled down so they can't fire at the neuromuscular level. After only seven or eight minutes the person's body seizes up and [he or she] can't move. It was a good thing I didn't know any of this. All I knew was that I was ready. I took a deep breath, leaned back, and threw myself forward into the thirty-two-degree water. •

When I hit the water, I went all the way under. I hadn't intended to do that; I hadn't wanted to immerse my head, which could over-stimulate my vagus nerve[4] and cause my heart to stop beating. Dog-paddling as quickly as I could, I popped up in the water, gasping for air. I couldn't catch my breath. I was swimming with my head up, hyperventilating.[5] I kept spinning my arms, trying to get warm, but I couldn't get enough air. I felt like I had a corset tightening around my chest. I told myself to relax, take a deep breath, but I couldn't slow my breath. And I couldn't get enough air in. I tried again. My body wanted air, and it wanted it now. I had to override that reaction of hyperventilating. I had to concentrate on my breath, to press my chest out against the cold water and draw the icy air into my lungs.

My body resisted it. The air was too cold. My body didn't want to draw the cold air deep into my lungs and cool myself from the inside. It wanted to take short breaths so the cold air would be warmed in my mouth before it reached my lungs. I was fighting against myself.

I noticed my arms. They were bright red, and I felt like I was swimming through slush. My arms were thirty-two degrees, as cold as the sea. They were going numb, and so were my legs. I pulled my hands right under my chest so that I was swimming on the upper inches of the sea, trying to minimize my contact with the water. I was swimming fast and it was hard to get enough air. I began to notice that the cold was pressurizing my body like a giant tourniquet. It was squeezing the blood from the exterior part of my body and pushing it into the core. Everything felt tight. *Focus on your breath*, I told myself. *Slow it down. Let it fill your lungs. You're*

Vocabulary
prolonged (prō lôŋd´)
adj. extended; lengthy

Literary Analysis
Author's Perspective
How does this passage reflect both how it felt to live through the event and how it feels to look back on it?

Reading Skill
Make Predictions
Do these details verify your original prediction or lead you to revise it?

Reading Check
List two dangers Cox faces on her swim.

---

4. **vagus** (vāg´ əs) **nerve** *n.* either of a pair of nerves running from the brain to the heart that regulate the heartbeat.
5. **hyperventilating** *v.* breathing so rapidly or deeply as to cause dizziness or fainting.

not going to be able to make it if you keep going at this rate.

It wasn't working. I was laboring for breath harder than on the test swim. I was in oxygen debt,[6] panting, gasping. My breath was inefficient, and the oxygen debt was compounding. In an attempt to create heat, I was spinning my arms wildly, faster than I'd ever turned them over before. Laura later told me that I was swimming at a rate of ninety strokes per minute, thirty strokes per minute quicker than my normal rate. My body was demanding more oxygen, but I couldn't slow down. Not for a nanosecond. Or I would freeze up and the swim would be over.

An icy wave slapped my face: I choked and felt a wave of panic rise within me. My throat tightened. I tried to clear my throat and breathe. My breath didn't come out. I couldn't get enough air in to clear my throat. I glanced at the crew. They couldn't tell I was in trouble. If I stopped, Dan would jump in and pull me out. I still couldn't get a good breath. I thought of rolling on my back to give myself time to breathe, but I couldn't. It was too cold. I closed my mouth, overrode everything my body was telling me to do, held my breath, and gasped, coughed, cleared my windpipe, and relaxed just a little, just enough to let my guard down and catch another wave in the face. I choked again. I put my face down into the water, hoping this time I could slow my heart rate down. I held my face in the water for two strokes and told myself, *Relax, just turn your head and breathe.* •

6. **oxygen debt** *n.* an increased need for oxygen in the body brought on by intensive activity.

I choked and felt a wave of panic rise within me... I glanced at the crew. They couldn't tell I was in trouble.

It was easier to breathe in a more horizontal position. I thought it might be helping. I drew in a deep breath and put my face down again. I knew I couldn't do this for long. I was losing too much heat through my face. The intensity of the cold was as sharp as broken glass. I'd thought that swimming across the Bering Strait[7] in thirty-eight-degree water had been tough, but there was a world of difference between thirty-eight degrees and thirty-two. In a few seconds, the cold pierced my skin and penetrated into my muscles. It felt like freezer burn, like touching wet fingers to frozen metal.

Finally I was able to gain control of my breath. I was inhaling and exhaling so deeply I could hear the breath moving in and out of my mouth even though I was wearing earplugs. I kept thinking about breathing, working on keeping it deep and even; that way I didn't have time to think about the cold.

My brain wasn't working as it normally did. It wasn't flowing freely from one idea to another—it was moving mechanically, as if my awareness came from somewhere deep inside my brain. Maybe it was because my body was being assaulted with so many sensations, too different and too complex to recognize. Or maybe it was because my blood and oxygen were going out to the working muscles. I didn't know.

For the next five or six minutes, I continued swimming, telling myself that I was doing well, telling myself that this was what I

---

7. **Bering Strait** (ber´ iŋ strāt) *n.* the body of water between Russia and Alaska, joining the Pacific and Arctic oceans.

Literary Analysis
Author's Perspective
Name one way in which the details in this paragraph might be different if presented by a crew member on the boat.

Reading
Check
List two effects of the cold water on Cox's mind and body.

Vocabulary
equilibrium (ē′
kwi lib′ rē əm) *n. a*
state of balance

had trained for. Then something clicked, as if my body had gained
equilibrium. It had fully closed down the blood flow in my skin and
fingers and toes. My arms and legs were as cold as the water, but
I could feel the heat radiating deep within my torso and head, and
this gave me confidence. I knew that my body was protecting my
brain and vital organs. Staring through the clear, silver-blue water, I
examined my fingers; they were red and swollen. They were different
than when I'd been swimming in the Bering Strait, when they'd
looked like the fingers of a dead person. They looked healthy, and I
thought their swollenness would give me more surface area, more
to pull with.

I smiled and looked up at the crew, who were in the Zodiacs
on either side of me. Each of them was leaning forward, willing
me ahead. Their faces were filled with tension. Gabriella, Barry,
Dan, and Scott were leaning so far over the Zodiac's pontoon I
felt as if they were swimming right beside me. I was sprinting
faster than I ever had before, moving faster than the
Zodiac, and I was getting fatigued quickly. The
water was thicker than on the test swim, and it
took more force to pull through on each stroke.
My arms ached. I didn't feel right; I couldn't
seem to get into any kind of a rhythm. Then I
sensed that something was wrong.

We were heading to the left, toward some
glaciers. This didn't make sense; we couldn't
land there. It was too dangerous. The glaciers
could calve[8] and kill us.

"Barry, where are we going?" I shouted, using
air I needed for breathing.

He pointed out our direction—right toward

Reading Skill
Make Predictions
Do the details in this
paragraph verify or lead
you to revise your prediction about whether Cox
will succeed?

the glaciers. I didn't understand. I didn't want to go that way. I
wanted to aim for the beach. I was confused. I was moving my arms
as fast as they would go, and it was taking all I had. From each
moment to the next, I had to tell myself to keep going. The water felt
so much colder than on the test swim. It had already worked its way
deep into my muscles. My arms and legs were stiff. My strokes were
short and choppy. But I kept going, telling myself to trust the crew
and focus on the glaciers to watch the outcropping of rocks that was
growing larger. I couldn't get into any kind of pace.

Abruptly the Zodiacs zagged to the right. I looked up and
thought, *Wow, okay; we're heading for the beach now.* For a moment,
I started to feel better. I was able to extend my reach farther, and I

Vocabulary
abruptly (ə brupt′ lē)
adv. happening sud-
denly; unexpectedly

---

8. calve (käv) *v.* to give birth to young; used here to refer to the "birth" of a new ice mass
when a piece of a glacier splits off.

- Antarctica is an ice-covered continent that covers the South Pole.
- Antarctica is the coldest place on Earth. Temperatures have reached a record 120° F below zero in the winter.
- Antarctica has no native population.
- The Antarctic icecap is the largest reserve of freshwater or snow in the world.

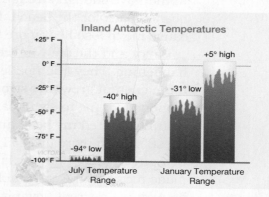

Inland Antarctic Temperatures

July Temperature Range: -94° low, -40° high
January Temperature Range: -31° low, +5° high

Connect to the Literature

What does this information suggest about the significance of Cox's endeavor?

could see passengers from the *Orlova* walking along the snowbanks. In the distance, their clothes lost their color and they looked black, like giant penguins. I saw smaller black figures, too—real penguins nesting near the edge of the shore. For a few moments, I felt like I was going to be okay, like I was going to make it in to shore, but then the Zodiacs abruptly turned farther to the right, and we were headed past the beach for another range of glaciers.

Finally, it occurred to me that the *Orlova* had anchored too close to shore for me to swim a mile, so Barry was adding distance by altering the course. And the ship's captain was on the bridge monitoring our course on his GPS[9] and radioing our Zodiacs, updating them on the distance we had traveled. One of the passengers, Mrs. Stokie, who was on the bridge with him, told me later, "The captain was watching you and he was shaking his head. He was an older man, and he had experienced everything. And now he was seeing something new. It was good for him. Still, I think he couldn't believe it."

We continued on right past the beach, toward more glaciers.

"How long have I been swimming?" I asked.

"Fifteen minutes," Barry said.

---

9. GPS "Global Positioning System," referring here to a portable device that provides information about the bearer's location and speed.

Literary Analysis
Author's Perspective
Identify one detail in this paragraph that shows Cox's past perspective and one that comes from her present perspective.

Reading
Check

What new obstacle does Cox face on her swim?

I had swum a little more than half a mile. I looked up at the shore. If I turned left, I could make it in. I could reach the shore. This struggle could be over. But I wouldn't complete the mile. I had swum farther two days before. But I was tired now, and this was so much harder. I just didn't feel right. I couldn't figure out what the problem was. I kept talking to myself, coaching myself to keep going. Then I felt it; it was the water pressure, and it was increasing on my back. It meant there was a strong current behind me. I looked at the glaciers onshore, using the fixed points to gauge how fast the current was flowing. It was flowing at over a knot. I wondered if I would have enough strength to fight it when we turned around and headed back for the beach. It would cut my speed by half and could cause me to lose heat more rapidly.

Barry and the crew in the Zodiacs couldn't feel what was happening. They had no idea we were moving into a risky area. If the current grew any stronger, it could cost us the swim. Barry motioned for me to swim past a peninsula and across a narrow channel. I lifted my head and pulled my hands directly under my chest, to gain more lift, so I could look across the bay and see if we had any other options for landing. There were no alternatives. This made me very uncomfortable. Chances were good that there would be a strong current flowing into or out of the narrow bay. And if we got caught in that current, all would be lost.

We started across the inlet, and within a moment I could feel that second current, slamming into our right side at two knots, pushing us into the inlet. Without any explanation, I spun around, put my head down, dug my arms into the water, and crabbed[10] into the current. I focused on repositioning myself so I

And if
we got caught
in that current, all
would be lost.

could parallel shore again and head toward Neko Harbor. Barry knew I knew what I was doing. But the abrupt course change caught the Zodiac drivers by surprise. They scattered in different directions, trying to avoid ramming into each other and trying to catch up with me. The motor on the lead Zodiac on my left sputtered and stopped. The second Zodiac immediately pulled up beside me. I sprinted against the current.

"How long have I been swimming?"

"Twenty-one minutes," Barry said. He and all the crew were watching me intently, their faces filled with tension and concern.

I put my head down, and something suddenly clicked. Maybe it was because I knew shore was within reach, or maybe because I got a second wind; I don't know. But I was finally swimming strongly, stretching out and moving fluidly. My arms and legs were as cold as the sea, but I felt the heat within my head and contained in my torso and I thrilled to it, knowing my body had carried me to places no one else had been in only a bathing suit. I looked down into the water; it was a bright blue-gray and so clear that it appeared as if I were swimming through air. The viscosity of the water was different, too; it was thicker than any I had ever swum in. It felt like I was swimming through gelato. And I got more push out of each arm stroke than I ever had before. I looked at the crew. They were leaning so far over the pontoons, as if they were right there with me. I needed to let them know I was okay.

I lifted my head, took a big breath, and shouted, "Barry, I'm swimming to Antarctica!"

I saw the smiles, heard the cheers and laughs, and I felt their energy lift me. They were as thrilled as I was. I swam faster, extending my arms, pulling more strongly, reaching for the shores of Antarctica. Now I knew we were almost there.

The crew was shouting warnings about ice. I swerved around two icebergs. Some chunks looked sharp, but I was too tired to care. I swam into whatever was in my path. It hurt, but all I wanted now was to finish.

As we neared shore, I lifted my head and saw the other passengers from the *Orlova*, in their bright red and yellow hats and parkas, tromping down the snowbanks, spreading their feet and arms wide for balance, racing to the water's edge to meet us. I lifted my foot and waved and saw my crew break into bigger smiles.

I'm almost done, I thought. *I feel okay. I feel strong. I feel warm inside. My arms and legs are thirty-two degrees. But I feel good. I can stretch out my strokes and put my face in the water. Maybe I can go a little farther. Maybe I can see what more I can do. Maybe I can swim five or ten more minutes. Or maybe I should be happy with what I've*

10. **crabbed** *v.* moved sideways or diagonally.

Literary Analysis
Author's Perspective
What information here reveals the writer's swimming expertise?

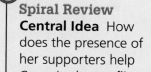

Spiral Review
Central Idea How does the presence of her supporters help Cox win the conflict between her body and her mind?

Reading Check
What changes for Cox after she shifts her course?

done. My skin is so cold I can't feel it, and when I stop swimming, I don't know how far my temperature's going to drop. I looked at my watch. Twenty-three minutes. I'd been in a minute longer than two days before. *How much difference would a minute make? I asked myself.*

How much difference is there between thirty-two-degree and thirty-three-degree water? Remember what Dr. Keatinge[11] said: once your temperature starts to drop, it will drop very fast. If you continue swimming, you're going to cool down even more. Remember how hard you shivered last time? Remember how much work it was? Remember how uncomfortable you were? This is the place where people make mistakes, when they're tired and cold and they push too far into the unknown.

You could really hurt yourself. Finish now. You've done a good job. Be satisfied with what you've done. Go celebrate with your friends. ●

Turning in toward shore, I again lifted my foot and waved it, and my friends waved back and cheered. One hundred yards from shore, I saw chinstrap penguins sliding headfirst, like tiny black toboggans, down a steep snowbank. When they reached the base of the hill, they used their bristly tails like brakes, sticking them into the snow to stop their momentum. They waddled across the beach at full tilt, holding their wings out at their sides for balance. Reaching the water, they dove in headfirst, then porpoised across it, clearing it by one or two feet with each surface dive. They tucked their wings back by their sides so they would be more aerodynamic. When they neared the Zodiacs, they dove and flapped their wings under the water as if they were flying through air. It was amazing to think this was the only place they would fly. They zoomed under me in bursts of speed, and their bubbles exploded like white fireworks. More penguins joined in. One cannonballed off a ledge, another slipped on some ice and belly flopped, and three penguins swam within inches of my hands. I reached out to touch one, but he swerved and flapped his wings, so he moved just beyond my fingertips. I had no idea why they were swimming with me, but I knew it was a good sign; it meant there were no killer whales or leopard seals in the area.

---

11. Dr. Keatinge Cox's doctor on her swim across the Bering Strait.

**Literary Analysis
Author's Perspective**
Explain in what way the author's perspective on her swim changes as she nears the shore.

**Reading Skill
Make Predictions**
How does this outcome match up with your predictions?

When I reached knee-deep water, Dan jumped in, ran through the water, looped his arm through mine, and helped me stand. "Are you okay?" he asked.

"Yes. We made it!" I said.

Everyone around me was crying. Susan Adie helped Dan pull me up the incline. Martha wrapped a towel around my shoulders. Barry hugged me tightly. Laura and Susan began drying me off. I was so cold I was already starting to shiver hard. My legs were stiffer than after the other swim. The crew helped me into the Zodiac and I flopped onto the floor. Laura and Susan piled on top of me to protect me from the wind, and we pounded across the water, my head slamming into the Zodiac's floor. I managed to lift my head so that someone could place a hand under it to buffer the impact. I was so cold and stiff and shaking harder than before.

When we reached the Orlova, it took me a minute to stand, to gain my balance, and as I climbed the ramp's steps I clung to the railing and pulled myself up, shaking hard. By the time I reached the top of the ramp, my teeth were chattering and I was breathing harder and faster than when I had been swimming. I didn't like being so cold. I didn't like my body having to work so hard. My temperature had dropped to 95.5 degrees, and I couldn't control my shaking. I just let go, and my body bounced up and down with shakes and shivers.

Quickly Martha and Dan and the three doctors huddled around me like emperor penguins, and their combined comfort and body heat began to warm me. It seemed as if I would never stop shaking,

▲ **Critical Viewing**
Does this image of chinstrap penguins match what you imagined based on Cox's descriptions? Explain. **[Connect]**

Vocabulary
buffer (buf´ ər) *v.* lessen a shock; cushion

Reading Check
What is the outcome of Cox's attempt to swim a mile?

and I was completely exhausted. Within half an hour my shivering had subsided to small body shudders. Once I was able to stand and maintain my balance, the doctors helped me pull on a special top and pants that had been designed by a friend. She had sewn pockets under the arms, in the groin area, and into a scarf and had placed chemical packs that emitted heat inside the pockets. Their placement in the clothing warmed the major blood-flow areas of my body so that I was heated from the inside out. It was effective, and within an hour my temperature was back to normal.

That night we celebrated with everyone aboard the Orlova. I had swum the first Antarctic mile—a distance of 1.06 miles, in fact—in thirty-two-degree water in twenty-five minutes. I had been able to do what had seemed impossible because I'd had a crew who believed in me and in what we as human beings were capable of. It was a great dream, swimming to Antarctica.

Literary Analysis
Author's Perspective
Which details show the difference between Cox's perspective before and after her swim?

Critical Thinking

Cite textual evidence to support your responses.

1. **Key Ideas and Details (a)** Using details from the selection, list three ways in which Cox prepares for her swim. **(b) Analyze Causes and Effects:** For each method of preparation, explain the effect it has or is intended to have.

2. **Key Ideas and Details (a)** What physical challenge causes Cox to struggle at the start of her swim? **(b) Analyze:** What does Cox's ability to overcome this challenge reveal about her?

3. **Key Ideas and Details (a)** Identify two instances in which Cox gives herself a pep talk. **(b) Summarize:** What is the main point Cox makes in each pep talk? **(c) Analyze:** Is each pep talk effective? Why?

4. **Key Ideas and Details (a) Speculate:** Identify two reasons Cox may have had for making the swim. **(b) Summarize:** List two of the dangers that Cox faced. **(c) Evaluate:** Explain whether the swim was worth the effort.

5. **Integration of Knowledge and Ideas (a)** What makes Cox able to push herself harder than she thought she could? **(b)** How does the reality of Cox's Antarctic swim differ from what she predicted it would be like? *[Connect to the Big Question: Is there a difference between reality and truth?]*

Literary Analysis: Author's Perspective

© **1. Key Ideas and Details** **(a)** Using a chart like the one shown, analyze the **author's perspective** in the selection.

Author's Perspective	
Types of Details Included	**Examples of Each**
☐ researched facts ☐ personal experiences ☐ opinions ☐ attitudes	_____ _____ _____ _____

(b) Referring to your chart, briefly describe Cox's perspective.

© **2. Craft and Structure** **(a)** List two ways in which Cox's story would be different if told by a news reporter. **(b)** Do you think Cox's firsthand point of view adds to the story's drama? Explain.

Reading Skill: Make Predictions

3. Identify details in the selection that you used to **verify a prediction.**

4. (a) Identify one prediction you **revised** as you read. **(b)** In a small group, discuss your predictions and explain why you revised them.

Vocabulary

© **Acquisition and Use** Explain whether each sentence makes sense given the meaning of the underlined word. If a sentence does not make sense, revise it using the word correctly.

1. After <u>prolonged</u> workouts at the gym, he is finally back in shape.

2. The best tightrope walkers have no sense of <u>equilibrium</u>.

3. Open the windows; I need to <u>buffer</u> myself from the outside noise.

4. <u>Venturing</u> into the forest without a map is not a good idea.

5. After it is defrosted, <u>abruptly</u> cook the turkey for three hours.

6. An odometer helps you <u>gauge</u> how many miles you drive.

Word Study Use the context of the sentences and what you know about the **Latin prefix pro-** to explain your answer to each question.

1. If a runner *proceeds* to the finish line, has she finished the race?

2. Would a *progressive* idea look toward the future or the past?

Word Study

The **Latin prefix pro-** means "forth" or "forward."

Apply It Explain how the prefix *pro-* contributes to the meanings of these words. Consult a dictionary if necessary.

projectile
propeller
proficient

Is there a difference between *reality* and *truth*?

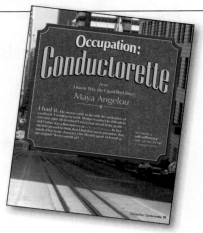

Writing About the Big Question

In "Occupation: Conductorette," a young girl experiences the harsh reality of prejudice. Use this sentence starter to develop your ideas about the Big Question.

People who are able to **comprehend** the truth behind problems in society must decide whether to _____ or

_____ .

While You Read Look for the ways the author challenges reality to fight for the job of streetcar conductor.

Vocabulary

Read each word and its definition. Decide whether you know the word well, know it a little bit, or do not know it at all. After you read, see how your knowledge of each word has increased.

- **self-sufficiency** (self´ sə fish´ ən sē) *n.* independence (p. 79) *His self-sufficiency helped him survive in the woods.* sufficient *adj.*

- **indignation** (in´ dig nā´ shən) *n.* anger that is a reaction to injustice or meanness (p. 80) *The indignation she felt towards the thief who stole her wallet was hard to put into words.* indignant *adj.*

- **dingy** (din´ jē) *adj.* dirty-looking; shabby (p. 81) *The dark walls made the room look dingy.* dingily *adv.* dinginess *n.*

- **supercilious** (so͞oʹpər silʹ ē əs) *adj.* expressing an attitude of superiority; contemptuous (p. 81) *The queen gave the peasant a supercilious smile.* superciliously *adv.* superciliousness *n.*

- **hypocrisy** (hi päk´ rə sē) *n.* the act of saying one thing but doing another (p. 81) *The environmentalist's hypocrisy was revealed when he littered.* hypocrite *n.* hypocritical *adj.*

- **dexterous** (deks´ tər əs) *adj.* having or showing mental skill (p. 83) *She showed how dexterous she was by quickly answering all the questions with ease.* dexterity *n.*

Word Study

The **Latin prefix** *super-* means "above."

In this excerpt, a young Maya Angelou tries to project confidence and show that she is above others by speaking in a **supercilious** manner, but she is really quite nervous.

Author of
Occupation: Conductorette

Maya Angelou was born Marguerite Johnson in St. Louis, Missouri. *I Know Why the Caged Bird Sings,* the work from which this selection comes, is the first part of her autobiography.

Up From Hard Times Some of the communities in which Angelou grew up were segregated— African Americans were excluded from facilities, including schools, used by whites. Yet, Angelou rejects bitterness, saying, "The honorary duty of a human being is to love."

Angelou has had diverse experiences in life. She worked with Dr. Martin Luther King, Jr., in the civil rights movement. Afterward, she moved to Africa, where she lived from 1961 to 1966. Her literary success came in the 1970s.

BACKGROUND FOR THE AUTOBIOGRAPHY

Jobs and World War II

During the 1940s, the time Maya Angelou recalls, millions of American men went overseas to fight World War II. Their absence created new opportunities at home. Six million women went to work in industry to aid the war effort, taking jobs newly open to them. Although African Americans still faced prejudice, some found—or made—new opportunities for themselves.

DID YOU KNOW?
Angelou read one of her poems at President William Jefferson Clinton's inauguration in 1993.

The young Angelou has just returned to San Francisco after an adventure-filled trip. Things are changing at home, she discovers, and her brother moves out soon after her return. Restless, and discontent, Angelou ponders her next step.

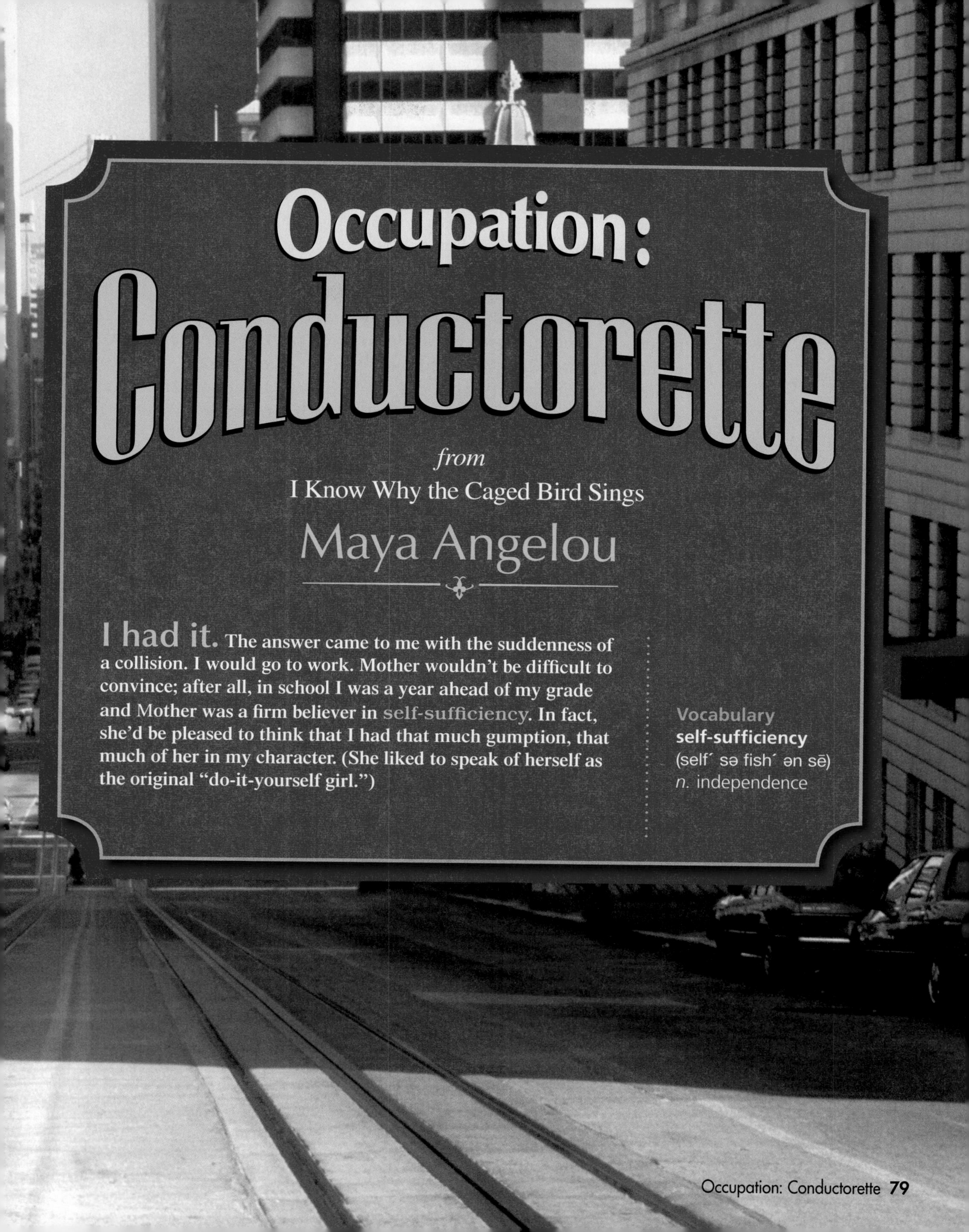

Occupation: Conductorette

from

I Know Why the Caged Bird Sings

Maya Angelou

I had it. The answer came to me with the suddenness of a collision. I would go to work. Mother wouldn't be difficult to convince; after all, in school I was a year ahead of my grade and Mother was a firm believer in self-sufficiency. In fact, she'd be pleased to think that I had that much gumption, that much of her in my character. (She liked to speak of herself as the original "do-it-yourself girl.")

Vocabulary
self-sufficiency
(self´ sə fish´ ən sē)
n. independence

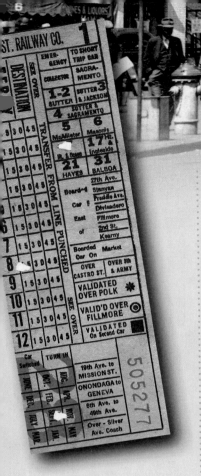

Once I had settled on getting a job, all that remained was to decide which kind of job I was most fitted for. My intellectual pride had kept me from selecting typing, shorthand or filing as subjects in school, so office work was ruled out. War plants and shipyards demanded birth certificates, and mine would reveal me to be fifteen, and ineligible for work. So the well-paying defense jobs were also out. Women had replaced men on the streetcars as conductors and motormen, and the thought of sailing up and down the hills of San Francisco in a dark-blue uniform, with a money changer at my belt, caught my fancy.

Mother was as easy as I had anticipated. The world was moving so fast, so much money was being made, so many people were dying in Guam, and Germany,[1] that hordes of strangers became good friends overnight. Life was cheap and death entirely free. How could she have the time to think about my academic career?

To her question of what I planned to do, I replied that I would get a job on the streetcars. She rejected the proposal with: "They don't accept colored people on the streetcars."

I would like to claim an immediate fury which was followed by the noble determination to break the restricting tradition. But the truth is, my first reaction was one of disappointment. I'd pictured myself, dressed in a neat blue serge suit, my money changer swinging jauntily at my waist, and a cheery smile for the passengers which would make their own work day brighter.

From disappointment, I gradually ascended the emotional ladder to haughty indignation, and finally to that state of stubbornness where the mind is locked like the jaws of an enraged bulldog.

I would go to work on the streetcars and wear a blue serge suit. Mother gave me her support with one of her usual terse asides, "That's what you want to do? Then nothing beats a trial but a failure. Give it everything you've got. I've told you many times, 'Can't do is like Don't Care.' Neither of them have a home."

Translated, that meant there was nothing a person can't do, and there should be nothing a human being didn't care about. It was the most positive encouragement I could have hoped for.

---

1. **Guam** (gwäm), **and Germany** places where World War II (1939–1945) was fought. Guam is an island in the Pacific Ocean.

▲ **Critical Viewing** Based on this ticket, what do you think might be one of the tasks of a conductorette? Explain. **[Infer]**

Vocabulary

indignation (in´ dig nā´ shən) *n.* anger that is a reaction to injustice or meanness

Literary Analysis
Author's Perspective Which details show Angelou's teenage personality? Which show her attitude as an adult?

In the offices of the Market Street Railway Company, the receptionist seemed as surprised to see me there as I was surprised to find the interior dingy and the décor drab. Somehow I had expected waxed surfaces and carpeted floors. If I had met no resistance, I might have decided against working for such a poor-mouth-looking concern. As it was, I explained that I had come to see about a job. She asked, was I sent by an agency, and when I replied that I was not, she told me they were only accepting applicants from agencies.

The classified pages of the morning papers had listed advertisements for motorettes and conductorettes and I reminded her of that. She gave me a face full of astonishment that my suspicious nature would not accept.

"I am applying for the job listed in this morning's *Chronicle* and I'd like to be presented to your personnel manager." While I spoke in supercilious accents, and looked at the room as if I had an oil well in my own backyard, my armpits were being pricked by millions of hot pointed needles. She saw her escape and dived into it.

"He's out. He's out for the day. You might call tomorrow and if he's in, I'm sure you can see him." Then she swiveled her chair around on its rusty screws and with that I was supposed to be dismissed.

"May I ask his name?"

She half turned, acting surprised to find me still there.

"His name? Whose name?"

"Your personnel manager."

We were firmly joined in the hypocrisy to play out the scene.

"The personnel manager? Oh, he's Mr. Cooper, but I'm not sure you'll find him here tomorrow. He's . . . Oh, but you can try."

"Thank you."

"You're welcome."

And I was out of the musty room and into the even mustier lobby. In the street I saw the receptionist and myself going faithfully through paces that were stale with familiarity, although I had never encountered that kind of situation before and, probably, neither had she. We were like actors who, knowing the play by heart, were still able to cry afresh over the old tragedies and laugh spontaneously at the comic situations.

The miserable little encounter had nothing to do with me, the me

Reading Check

What major obstacle does Angelou face in her job quest?

of me, any more than it had to do with that silly clerk. The incident was a recurring dream, concocted years before by stupid whites and it eternally came back to haunt us all. The secretary and I were like Hamlet and Laertes[2] in the final scene, where, because of harm done by one ancestor to another, we were bound to duel to the death. Also because the play must end somewhere.

I went further than forgiving the clerk, I accepted her as a fellow victim of the same puppeteer.

On the streetcar, I put my fare into the box and the conductorette looked at me with the usual hard eyes of white contempt. "Move into the car, please move on in the car." She patted her money changer.

Her Southern nasal accent sliced my meditation and I looked deep into my thoughts. All lies, all comfortable lies. The receptionist was not innocent and neither was I. The whole charade we had played out in that crummy waiting room had directly to do with me, Black, and her, white.

I wouldn't move into the streetcar but stood on the ledge over the conductor, glaring. My mind shouted so energetically that the announcement made my veins stand out, and my mouth tighten into a prune.

I WOULD HAVE THE JOB. I WOULD BE A CONDUCTORETTE AND SLING A FULL MONEY CHANGER FROM MY BELT. I WOULD.

The next three weeks were a honeycomb[3] of determination with apertures for the days to go in and out. The Negro organizations to whom I appealed for support bounced me back and forth like a shuttlecock on a badminton court. Why did I insist on that particular job? Openings were going begging that paid nearly twice the money. The minor officials with whom I was able to win an audience thought me mad. Possibly I was.

Downtown San Francisco became alien and cold, and the streets I had loved in a personal familiarity were unknown lanes that twisted with malicious intent. Old buildings, whose gray rococo façades[4] housed my memories of the Forty-Niners, and Diamond Lil, Robert Service, Sutter and Jack London, were then imposing structures viciously joined to keep me out. My trips to the streetcar office were of the frequency of a person on salary. The struggle expanded. I was no longer in conflict only with the Market Street Railway

---

2. **Hamlet and Laertes** (lā ʉr′ tēz) characters in William Shakespeare's tragedy *Hamlet* who duel at the end of the play.
3. **honeycomb** (hun′ ē kōm′) *n.* wax structure, filled with holes, that bees build to store honey.
4. **rococo façades** (rə kō′ kō fə sädz′) elaborately designed building fonts.

but with the marble lobby of the building which housed its offices, and elevators and their operators.

During this period of strain Mother and I began our first steps on the long path toward mutual adult admiration. She never asked for reports and I didn't offer any details. But every morning she made breakfast, gave me carfare and lunch money, as if I were going to work. She comprehended the perversity of life, that in the struggle lies the joy. That I was no glory seeker was obvious to her, and that I had to exhaust every possibility before giving in was also clear.

On my way out of the house one morning she said, "Life is going to give you just what you put in it. Put your whole heart in everything you do, and pray, then you can wait." Another time she reminded me that "God helps those who help themselves." She had a store of aphorisms which she dished out as the occasion demanded. Strangely, as bored as I was with clichés, her inflection gave them something new, and set me thinking for a little while at least. Later when asked how I got my job, I was never able to say exactly. I only knew that one day, which was tiresomely like all the others before it, I sat in the Railway office, ostensibly waiting to be interviewed. The receptionist called me to her desk and shuffled a bundle of papers to me. They were job application forms. She said they had to be filled in triplicate. I had little time to wonder if I had won or not, for the standard questions reminded me of the necessity for dexterous lying. How old was I? List my previous jobs, starting from the last held and go backward to the first. How much money did I earn, and why did I leave the position? Give two references (not relatives).

Sitting at a side table my mind and I wove a cat's ladder of near truths and total lies. I kept my face blank (an old art) and wrote quickly the fable of Marguerite Johnson, aged nineteen, former companion and driver for Mrs. Annie Henderson (a White Lady) in Stamps, Arkansas.

I was given blood tests, aptitude tests, physical coordination tests, and Rorschachs,[5] then on a blissful day I was hired as the first Negro on the San Francisco streetcars.

Mother gave me the money to have my blue serge suit tailored, and I learned to fill out work cards, operate the money changer and punch transfers. The time crowded together and at an End of Days I was swinging on the back of the rackety trolley, smiling sweetly and persuading my charges to "step forward in the car, please."

---

5. **Rorschachs** (rôr´ shäks´) The Rorschach test is a method of analyzing an individual's personality using abstract images.

For one whole semester the street cars and I shimmied up and scooted down the sheer hills of San Francisco. I lost some of my need for the Black ghetto's shielding-sponge quality, as I clanged and cleared my way down Market Street, with its honky-tonk homes for homeless sailors, past the quiet retreat of Golden Gate Park and along closed undwelled-in-looking dwellings of the Sunset District.

My work shifts were split so haphazardly that it was easy to believe that my superiors had chosen them maliciously. Upon mentioning my suspicions to Mother, she said, "Don't worry about it. You ask for what you want, and you pay for what you get. And I'm going to show you that it ain't no trouble when you pack double."

She stayed awake to drive me out to the car barn at four thirty in the mornings, or to pick me up when I was relieved just before dawn. Her awareness of life's perils convinced her that while I would be safe on the public conveyances, she "wasn't about to trust a taxi driver with her baby."

When the spring classes began, I resumed my commitment with formal education. I was so much wiser and older, so much more independent, with a bank account and clothes that I had bought for myself, that I was sure that I had learned and earned the magic formula which would make me a part of the gay life my contemporaries led.

> # You ask for what you want, and you pay for what you get.

Critical Thinking

Cite textual evidence to support your responses.

1. **Key Ideas and Details** **(a)** To what does Angelou compare her first encounter with the secretary at the railway company? **(b) Analyze Cause and Effect:** Explain how the streetcar conductorette's greeting changes Angelou's view of the meeting.

2. **Key Ideas and Details** Using details from the selection, explain why Angelou insists on becoming a conductorette.

3. **Key Ideas and Details** **(a) Interpret:** Find two passages in which Angelou's mother reacts to her quest, and explain what each shows about her mother's view of life. **(b) Draw Conclusions:** In what ways does her mother contribute to Angelou's success?

4. **Key Ideas and Details** **Summarize:** In a few sentences, objectively report what happens in the selection.

5. **Integration of Knowledge and Ideas** In what ways does Angelou challenge the accepted reality for African Americans in San Francisco? *[Connect to the Big Question: Is there a difference between reality and truth?]*

Occupation: Conductorette

Literary Analysis: Author's Perspective

1. Key Ideas and Details (a) Using a chart like the one shown, analyze the **author's perspective** in the selection.

Author's Perspective	
Types of Details Included	**Examples of Each**
❑ researched facts ❑ personal experiences ❑ opinions ❑ attitudes	_____ _____ _____ _____

(b) Use your chart to briefly describe Angelou's point of view.

2. Key Ideas and Details What is Angelou's present attitude toward her younger self? Consider her use of phrases such as "haughty indignation" to describe her reactions at the time.

Reading Skill: Make Predictions

3. Identify details in the selection that you used to **verify a prediction.**

4. (a) Identify one prediction you **revised** as you read. **(b)** In a small group, discuss your predictions and explain why you revised them.

Vocabulary

Acquisition and Use Explain whether each sentence makes sense given the meaning of the underlined word. If a sentence does not make sense, revise it using the word correctly.

1. She whines until her little brother makes her lunch for her—a clear sign of her <u>self-sufficiency</u>.

2. I painted the room a bright white to add to its <u>dingy</u> feeling.

3. When you ask him for help, give him a <u>supercilious</u> look.

4. Reading the thank-you letter gave him a great sense of <u>indignation</u>.

5. Known for his <u>hypocrisy</u>, he always said exactly what he felt.

6. Pat is such a <u>dexterous</u> thinker that she is never at a loss for words.

Word Study Use the context of the sentences and what you know about the **Latin prefix super-** to explain your answer to each question.

1. If a pet requires *supervision,* should it be left alone?

2. Does a *supervisor* generally give or receive orders?

Word Study

The **Latin prefix *super-*** means "above."

Apply It Explain how the prefix *super-* contributes to the meanings of these words. Consult a dictionary if necessary.

superimpose
superintendent
supersonic

Integrated Language Skills

from **Swimming to Antarctica •**
Occupation: Conductorette

Conventions: Abstract and Concrete Nouns

A **noun** is a word that names a person, a place, or a thing.

Concrete nouns name specific things that can be directly experienced or perceived by the senses. The word *airplane* is a concrete noun because it names something you can see, feel, and hear.

Abstract nouns name ideas or concepts that cannot be seen, heard, felt, tasted, smelled, or directly experienced. *Justice* is an abstract noun because it is a concept that cannot be directly perceived by the senses.

Concrete Nouns	Abstract Nouns
The *pancakes* are still hot.	*Honesty* is an important *trait* for everyone.
My *sister* wanted a small *dog* with soft, fluffy *fur* and a wet *nose*.	Her greatest *wish* was for *peace* around the world.
The *car* was so loud I could not hear what my *mother* was saying.	*Democracy* is an important *tradition* in the United States.

Practice A Identify the noun or nouns in each sentence, and indicate whether they are concrete or abstract nouns. There are eleven in all.

1. To swim in cold water takes much endurance.
2. Lynne Cox needed a team to help her reach her goal.
3. A cold-water swimmer usually wears a wet-suit or a drysuit.
4. Cox relied on faith and determination.

Practice B Label each noun as concrete or abstract. Then, use each word in a sentence.

1. gumption
2. streetcar
3. commitment
4. building
5. determination

Ⓒ **Reading Application** Find three concrete nouns and three abstract nouns in the excerpt from *Swimming to Antarctica*.

Ⓒ **Writing Application** Using this sentence as a model, write two sentences with both concrete and abstract nouns: *Today is a basket of joy.*

PH **WRITING COACH** Further instruction and practice are available in *Prentice Hall Writing Coach.*

Writing

Common Core State Standards

W.9-10.2.b; SL.9-10.5
[For the full wording of the standards, see page 58.]

Explanatory Text Each selection provides information to help readers imagine an important scene. Write a brief **description** of either a scene in Antarctica or a 1940s streetcar ride.

- Use your prior knowledge and the information you learned from reading Cox's or Angelou's work to help you write your description.
- Consider your purpose and audience. Then, identify the mood, or atmosphere, you want to create, such as danger, beauty, or frustration.
- Carefully select details from the selection that fit the mood you want to create.
- Use precise words and sensory details to capture the scene and to develop your ideas. Organize details logically.

Grammar Application To make your description vivid, use specific concrete nouns more frequently than abstract nouns.

Writing Workshop: *Work in Progress*

Prewriting for Autobiographical Narrative Review the Place List in your writing portfolio. Use your notes to write a few lines about each item. Choose the one that is most meaningful to you and explain why. Save this Place Description in your writing portfolio for later use.

Use this prewriting activity to prepare for the **Writing Workshop** on page 108.

Research and Technology

Presentation of Knowledge and Ideas Keep a **daily observation journal** and use it to chart one of the following situations.

- If you read the excerpt from *Swimming to Antarctica*, keep a daily observation journal charting your speed or achievements in some activity, such as how many miles you run per day or how many words you type per minute.
- If you read "Occupation: Conductorette," observe someone who has a job you might want some day. Keep a journal to chart the person's work, recording important daily tasks and the time each one takes.

Follow these steps to complete the assignment:

- Using computer software, create a graph or chart that maps the information you discover in a clear and easily understood format. Then, write a summary of your findings.
- Present your findings, graphics, and summary orally in class. Consider your audience and purpose, and convey your ideas clearly and concisely.

PHLit Online!
www.PHLitOnline.com
- Interactive graphic organizers
- Grammar tutorial
- Interactive journals

Test Practice: Reading

Make Predictions

Fiction Selection

Directions: *Read the selection. Then, answer the questions.*

The day had been sunny, but as Jack was leaving his house, he noticed the sky was rapidly darkening. He heard his father calling.

"What's up, Dad?"

"Hurry," his father said. "To the cellar. A tornado is headed this way."

"Cool!" Jack responded.

"Not cool, Jack." Jack's father glanced outside. "Look—you can see it now!" Jack followed his father's gaze. A funnel-shaped cloud was swirling along the ground, twisting and pushing forward, absorbing debris as it moved. Jack and his father bolted to the cellar and huddled in a storage room. The wind howled overhead. When the roaring passed, Jack and his father peeked outside.

They were shocked to see that the house next door was missing its roof. Cars lay upside down in the street. When Jack and his father inspected their home, the only damage was a broken window. Jack looked at his father. "We're very lucky, aren't we?"

1. What information leads you to predict that a storm is coming?

   A. The sky was rapidly darkening.
   B. Jack heard his father calling.
   C. Debris was swirling in the funnel cloud.
   D. The roar of the tornado passed quickly.

2. What prior knowledge do you need to have to predict that Jack and his father will escape harm from the tornado?

   A. knowing how fast tornadoes can move
   B. knowing that the cellar is the safest place to be during a tornado
   C. knowing how tornadoes are formed
   D. knowing the damage tornadoes can cause

3. Which infomation does *not* help you predict that the tornado will cause damage?

   A. prior knowledge about tornadoes
   B. the description of the funnel cloud
   C. the description of the wind howling
   D. Jack's comment about being lucky

4. Based on the passage, you can predict that Jack—

   A. will never fear tornadoes.
   B. will not go outside if he sees a tornado.
   C. will rebuild his neighbor's roof.
   D. will study tornadoes to learn more.

Writing for Assessment

What do you predict Jack and his father will do immediately after the tornado? Write a short paragraph explaining your prediction.

Nonfiction Selection

Directions: *Read the selection. Then, answer the questions.*

A tornado, or twister, is a very violent type of storm. When it touches down on the ground, it can cause terrible devastation. A tornado's rotational, or twisting, speed is usually estimated at about 300 miles per hour but can reach nearly 500 miles per hour. A tornado can be recognized by its funnel cloud, which dips downward from the clouds of a strong thunderstorm. The funnel becomes darker as it touches the earth because of the debris it has sucked up.

A tornado moves forward at about 30 to 40 miles per hour, but can travel as fast as 70 miles per hour. Most tornadoes are only about 300 yards wide; however, one of the most destructive tornadoes ever to strike the United States was about one mile wide. Even though a tornado passes quickly, it can cause extreme destruction. The wind is so strong that blades of straw have been embedded in fence posts by tornadoes. In one case, a school with eighty-five students was destroyed and the students were carried about 450 feet by the twister. Surprisingly, not one of the students was injured.

1. Which of the following can you predict would suffer the most destruction from a tornado?

   A. a concrete apartment building
   B. an underground shelter
   C. an outdoor carnival
   D. a school's basement

2. If you knew exactly where a tornado was first sighted, which of the following details could help you predict how quickly to take cover?

   A. Tornadoes are usually about 300 yards wide.
   B. Winds can reach 300 miles per hour.
   C. Tornadoes can move at 30 miles per hour.
   D. Tornadoes cause terrible destruction.

3. Based on the passage, you can reasonably predict that—

   A. small items such as pencils or pens can become deadly in a tornado.
   B. most tornadoes will pass by without doing harm.
   C. tornadoes do not usually injure people.
   D. faster tornadoes pick up more debris.

4. What information is most helpful for predicting how much damage a tornado will cause?

   A. the amount of debris that it picks up
   B. the tornado's rotational speed
   C. the shape of the funnel cloud
   D. which storm generated the tornado

Writing for Assessment

Connecting Across Texts
What dangers might Jack have faced if he had not taken safety precautions? In a paragraph, use details from the two passages to support your answer.

www.PHLitOnline.com
- Online practice
- Instant feedback

Reading for Information

Analyzing Expository Texts

Feature Article

Newsletter

Common Core State Standards

Reading Informational Text

3. Analyze how the author unfolds an analysis or series of ideas or events, including the order in which the points are made, how they are introduced and developed, and the connections that are drawn between them.

4. Determine the meaning of words and phrases as they are used in a text, including figurative, connotative, and technical meanings; analyze the cumulative impact of specific word choices on meaning and tone.

Language

6. Acquire and use accurately general academic and domain-specific words and phrases, sufficient for reading, writing, speaking, and listening at the college and career readiness level; demonstrate independence in gathering vocabulary knowledge when considering a word or phrase important to comprehension or expression.

Reading Skill: Analyze Structure and Format

When you **analyze structure** and **format** in a text, you examine how the information is organized and presented. Authors make decisions about how words appear on a page in order to achieve specific **purposes.** Understanding how authors use structural features, or text features, can help you locate and analyze the information provided.

This chart shows some common structural features and their purposes.

Structural Feature	Purpose
Main heading	• Provides an overview of content
Subheading	• Introduces a specific topic within the main topic • Helps readers to quickly locate information
Bold or italic text	• Separates text on a page, making it easier to read • Calls attention to certain information
Illustration or other graphic	• Conveys visual information • Adds visual interest to a page

Content-Area Vocabulary

These words appear in the selections that follow. You may also encounter them in other content-area texts.

- **phrasings** (frāz´ ingz) *n.* groups of notes that form short, distinct passages of music

- **ensemble** (än säm´ bəl) *n.* group of musicians, actors, or dancers who perform together

- **repertoire** (rep´ ər twär) *n.* group of items, such as musical pieces, that are performed regularly

Feel the City's Pulse?

It's Be-bop man!

By Ann Douglas

> The main heading tells you that the article will be about be-bop music in the city.

In 1964, Thelonious Monk, one of the pioneers of be-bop and perhaps jazz's greatest composer, was asked by an interviewer to define jazz. Though Monk disliked questions and usually ignored them, this time he didn't miss a beat: "New York, man. You can feel it. It's around in the air. . . ."

Be-Bop was sometimes labeled "New York Jazz," and it is, in fact, the only major school of jazz to which the city can lay proprietary claim. Jazz of the '20s, dominated by Louis Armstrong, originated in New Orleans, migrating to New York only after a formative detour in Chicago. Armstrong inspired '30s swing, the music of the big bands led by Benny Goodman, Artie Shaw, Glenn Miller, Count Basie and Duke Ellington, the "mother bands," as Gillespie called them, whose music the be-boppers both emulated and revolutionized.

. . . Bop's wide-ranging allusiveness, its quicksilver expressivity, angular dissonance and shockingly extended palette of pitches and rhythms echoed the international mix, the fluidity and speed of New York life.

Jamming After Hours

Bop began at roughly the same time as World War II, in 1940 when Monk, then 23, was hired to play with Kenny (Klook) Clarke, the man who transformed jazz drumming, at Minton's Playhouse in Harlem. Gillespie jammed with them after his regular engagement, and Parker[1] joined them a year later. When Minton's closed for the night, they adjourned to Clark Monroe's Uptown House, an after-hours club where an extraordinary teen-age drummer named Max Roach played in the band.

The nation's entrance into the war in late 1941 imposed gas rationing, entertainment taxes and curfews, sharply restricting travel. The swing bands were touring bands, and some of them continued to tour, but now everyone was looking for a long-term base in a big city, easily accessible by public transit. What hurt swing helped be-bop. The expense and risks of touring (especially down South) had been far greater for black musicians than for white.

> The subheading breaks up the text for easier reading and explains what material will follow.

1. **Gillespie . . . Parker** Trumpeter Dizzy Gillespie and saxophonist Charlie Parker.

The cramped quarters of many city clubs suited the young bop musicians, eager to work with the small ensembles that maximized opportunities for experimentation. . . .

The word "be-bop," which both Monk and Gillespie claimed to have coined, described the music's unconventional stop-and-start form, especially Gillespie and Parker's witty eighth-note pair conclusions. The purpose of bop's irregular **phrasings,** side-sliding harmonies and whirlwind pace, was, in Kenny Clarke's words, to "raise the standards of musicianship," to tell people, "Whatever you go into, go into it intelligently." The be-boppers were the real New York intellectuals, the hippest, smartest men in town.

The map shows the locations of sites mentioned in the text.

SITES OF BOP'S TRIUMPHS AND TRAGEDIES

1. **Savoy Ballroom**, Lenox Avenue and 140th Street, Harlem. Charlie Parker played in this legendary jazz and dance hall with the Jay McShann Orchestra in his early days in New York.

2. **Minton's Playhouse**, 210 West 118th Street, Morningside Heights. Charlie Christian, Kenny Clarke, Thelonious Monk, Parker and Gillespie made musical history here in the early 1940s.

3. **St. Peter's Church**, 54th Street and Lexington Avenue, Manhattan (also its current site). Monk's funeral took place here on Feb. 22, 1982, with musicians playing for three hours.

4. **52nd Street**, between Fifth and Sixth Avenues, known as "The Street." A magical block of jazz clubs . . . including the Onyx, Spotlite, Three Deuces and Kelly's Stable.

Bold text helps to separate this list into clear sections.

5. **Birdland**, 1678 Broadway, at 53rd Street, Manhattan. It opened on Dec. 15, 1949, with dozens of (caged) birds on view and Charlie (Bird) Parker presiding.

6. **216 West 19th Street**
Eager to become "a New York musician," Gillespie lived here with his brother, . . . when he first came to town from Philadelphia in 1937, eating for 25 cents a day.

WINTER 2007
VOLUME 7
ISSUE 1

Newsletter

Features:
- regular publication intervals
- information about upcoming activities and events
- text written for a specific audience

Dig Deeper into Jazz

JAZZ APPRECIATION COURSE STARTS IN HEALDSBURG

The title indicates a specific area of interest—learning more about jazz.

What is this "jazz" thing all about, anyway? Though we all know what we like—and we like jazz!—most of us don't know as much about it as we wish. Whether you're a novice or a fan, if you dig jazz, this is your chance to dig it deeper. Three fun, informative, and inexpensive mid-week Jazz Appreciation classes will begin February 28 at the Raven Film Center. The classes will mix live and recorded music with the expertise of the guest instructor to bring jazz history alive.

"Adult education has always been a missing component in the Healdsburg Jazz Festival," said artistic director Jessica Felix as she announced a new grant from the Healdsburg Area Affiliate of the Community Foundation, Sonoma County. The grant makes it possible to offer this three-part series on the history of jazz for area adults, extending the reach of the Festival's Jazz Education Program out of the schools and into the community at large."

"The goal of this series is to bring us all closer to understanding the depth and history of an art form that has grown out of the American experience," Jessica Felix explained.

Take three giant steps toward jazz enjoyment with our first-ever Jazz Appreciation Series, starting the last day of February. To learn more, see page 2 of this newsletter.

LEARN MORE ABOUT Jazz Music With The

HEALDSBURG JAZZ FESTIVAL'S JAZZ APPRECIATION COURSE

THREE-PART SERIES AT THE RAVEN FILM CENTER, THEATER 2, 415 CENTER STREET

February 28th, March 28th, and May 9th. 6:30 to 9:30 pm

Open to all Ages, $10 per class, 3 for $25, half price for Senior Citizens (65 and over) and Students. Financial assistance available.

This class is made possible in part by a generous grant from the Healdsburg Area Affiliate of the Community Foundation, Sonoma County.

A subheading introduces the topic covered in the second section of the newsletter.

Class 1, February 28: Jazz History and Jazz Styles

Jazz educator, Ali Jackson explores the origins of jazz music with his celebrated *What is Jazz?*, a class, designed to make "America's Classical Music" accessible to a wide audience. What is jazz? Where did jazz come from? Who are the true pioneers and innovators of jazz? If you or a friend have asked these questions, *What is Jazz?* will provide the answers. *Class will use audio (CDs) and visual materials (DVDs).*

Boldface dates are followed by details for each event in the schedule.

Class 2, March 28: The Music Making Process

Dr. James Newton, internationally acclaimed musician, composer, educator and jazz historian, will introduce the class to the essential concepts of interaction within a jazz ensemble. The class will also demonstrate how a jazz combo approaches the interpretation of a composition, and Newton will be joined by a rhythm section to illustrate these concepts. *CDs, DVDs, and live music will be used as part of this class.*

Class 3, May 9: Artists and Music of the Healdsburg Jazz Festival

Also taught by Dr. James Newton, this class will give participants a more informed perspective on the bands appearing at the 2007 Healdsburg Jazz Festival. The class will cover the stylistic practices of the artists and highlights of their careers, and explore the use of different size ensembles particularly as they relate to the jazz repertoire. *CDs and DVDs will be used as part of this class.*

Comparing Expository Texts

1. Key Ideas and Details (a) What is the author's **purpose** in each of the two documents? **(b)** How do the **structure and format** of each document support that purpose? **(c)** Which document do you think uses structural features more effectively to achieve the author's purpose? Explain your response.

Content-Area Vocabulary

2. (a) List a synonym, or word with a similar meaning, for *ensemble* and for *repertoire*. **(b)** Use *phrasings, ensemble,* and *repertoire* in a brief paragraph about music.

⏱ Timed Writing

Argument: Essay

Format
The prompt directs you to write a persuasive essay. Therefore, you should express an opinion and convince readers to agree with you.

> Write a persuasive essay in which you take a position on the following quotation: "Music reflects culture. It is a central means by which a group asserts its relationship to past generations, distinguishes insiders from outsiders, and addresses the future." Support your response with details from the two texts. (25 minutes)

Academic Vocabulary
When you *take a position,* you state your opinion, or claim, on an issue. You *support* your position by defending it with evidence and examples.

5-Minute Planner

Complete these steps before you begin to write:

1. Read the prompt carefully to make sure you understand the assignment. Pay special attention to highlighted key words and phrases.
2. Review the article and newsletter, keeping in mind the quotation in the assignment. **TIP** Use structural features to find information.
3. Decide what position you will take on the quotation.
4. Note details from the two texts that support your position.
5. Prepare a quick outline for your essay. Then, refer to your notes and outline as you write.

Comparing Literary Works

Comparing Style

A writer's **style** is made up of the features that make his or her expression of ideas distinctive. Writers may use various styles, depending on their **purpose,** or reason for writing. Here are two important elements of style:

- **Diction,** or word choice, involves the types of words the writer uses. Writers may use words that are difficult or simple, abstract or concrete, old-fashioned or modern.

  Writers choose words that will help them achieve their purposes. In making their choices, writers consider the connotations, or emotional associations, of a word as well as its denotation, or definition.

- **Syntax,** or sentence structure, is related to the way words are organized to express ideas. When you analyze syntax, you consider the arrangement of words in phrases and sentences. You also consider what effect that arrangement has on the reader. One writer may write a series of short, punchy sentences, driving home each new idea. Another may play with readers, putting a key idea at the end of a long, twisty sentence.

Use a chart like the one shown to compare the writers' styles and purposes in "Marian Anderson, Famous Concert Singer" and "Tepeyac."

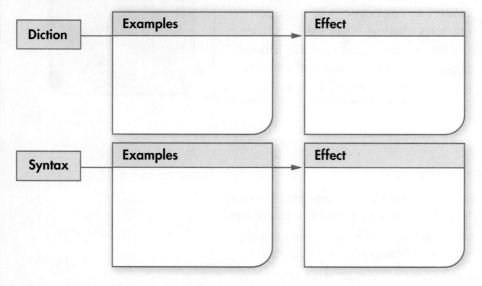

| Diction | Examples | → | Effect |
| Syntax | Examples | → | Effect |

Common Core State Standards

Reading Literature/ Informational Text

4. Determine the meaning of words and phrases as they are used in the text, including figurative, connotative, and technical meanings; analyze the cumulative impact of specific word choices on meaning and tone.

Writing

2. Write informative/explanatory texts to examine and convey complex ideas, concepts, and information clearly and accurately through the effective selection, organization, and analysis of content. *(Timed Writing)*

PHLit Online!
www.PHLitOnline.com

- Vocabulary flashcards
- Interactive journals
- More about the authors
- Selection audio
- Interactive graphic organizers

Is there a difference between *reality* and *truth?*

Writing About the Big Question

These selections show characters who grow as a result of the reality around them. Use this sentence starter to develop your ideas.

One person's **perception** of truth can be challenged when _____.

Meet the Authors

Langston Hughes (1902–1967)

Author of "Marian Anderson, Famous Concert Singer"

In the 1920s and 1930s, African American writers, artists, and musicians based in Harlem, a neighborhood in New York City, gave vivid, intense expression to the African American experience. The period is known as the Harlem Renaissance, and Langston Hughes is acknowledged as one of its dominant forces.

Jazz Rhythms on the Page Harlem Renaissance artists dedicated themselves to finding authentically African American styles. Hughes crafted a style, especially in his poetry, that reflected the rhythms and moods of jazz and blues music. (You can read one of Hughes's poems on page 736.)

Sandra Cisneros (b. 1954)

Author of "Tepeyac"

Born to a Mexican father and a Mexican American mother, Sandra Cisneros spent her childhood shuttling between Chicago and Mexico City. The only girl among seven children, Cisneros felt as if she had "seven fathers." Struggling to find her identity, she took refuge in reading and writing.

Winning Honors Although her family was not well-off, Cisneros managed to attend the prestigious Writers' Workshop at the University of Iowa. Her first novel, the autobiographical *The House on Mango Street* (1984), was a commercial and critical success, earning her the American Book Award from the Before Columbus Foundation in 1985.

Marian Anderson

FAMOUS CONCERT SINGER

Langston Hughes

Background Marian Anderson (1897?–1993) was one of the first African American singers to gain widespread recognition as a performer of classical music, including opera.

When Marian Anderson was born in a little red brick house in Philadelphia, a famous group of Negro singers, the Fisk Jubilee Singers, had already carried the spirituals all over Europe. And a colored woman billed as "Black Patti" had become famous on variety programs as a singer of both folk songs and the classics. Both

Negro and white minstrels had popularized American songs. The all-Negro musical comedies of Bert Williams and George Walker had been successful on Broadway. But no well-trained colored singers performing the great songs of Schubert, Handel, and the other masters, or the arias from famous operas, had become successful on the concert stage. And most people thought of Negro vocalists only in connection with spirituals. Roland Hayes[1] and Marian Anderson were the first to become famous enough to break this stereotype.

Marian Anderson's mother was a **staunch** church worker who loved to croon the hymns of her faith about the house, as did the aunt who came to live with them when Marian's father died. Both parents were from Virginia. Marian's mother had been a school-teacher there, and her father a farm boy. Shortly after they moved to Philadelphia where three daughters were born, the father died, and the mother went to work at Wanamaker's department store. But she saw to it that her children attended school and church regularly. The father had been an usher in the Union Baptist Church, so the congregation took an interest in his three little girls. Marian was the oldest and, before she was eight, singing in the Sunday school choir, she had already learned a great many hymns and spirituals by heart.

One day Marian saw an old violin in a pawnshop window marked $3.45. She set her mind on that violin, and began to save the nickels and dimes neighbors would give her for scrubbing their white front steps—the kind of stone steps so characteristic of Philadelphia and Baltimore houses—until she had $3.00. The pawnshop man let her take the violin at a reduced price. Marian never became very good on the violin. A few years later her mother bought a piano, so the child forgot all about it in favor of their newer instrument. By that time, too, her unusual singing voice had attracted the attention of her choir master, and at the age of fourteen she was promoted to a place in the main church choir. There she learned all four parts of all the hymns and anthems and could easily fill in anywhere from bass to soprano.

Sensing that she had exceptional musical talent, some of the church members began to raise money so that she might have singing lessons. But her first teacher, a colored woman, refused to accept any pay for instructing so talented a child. So the church folks put their money into a trust fund called "Marian Anderson's Future," banking it until the time came for her to have advanced training. Meanwhile, Marian attended South Philadelphia High School for Girls and took part in various group concerts, usually doing the solo parts. When she was fifteen she sang a group of

---

1. **Roland Hayes** (1887–1977) famous African American tenor.

Vocabulary
staunch (stônch) *adj.* steadfast; loyal

Literary Analysis
Style Identify an example of a direct, down-to-earth word or phrase in this passage.

Reading Check
What organization supported the development of Anderson's talent?

songs alone at a Sunday School Convention in Harrisburg and word of her talent began to spread about the state. When she was graduated from high school, the Philadelphia Choral Society, a Negro group, sponsored her further study and secured for her one of the best local teachers. Then in 1925 she journeyed to New York to take part, with three hundred other young singers, in the New York Philharmonic Competitions, where she won first place, and appeared with the orchestra at Lewisohn Stadium.

This appearance was given wide publicity, but very few lucrative engagements came in, so Marian continued to study. A Town Hall concert was arranged for her in New York, but it was unsuccessful. Meanwhile, she kept on singing with various choral groups, and herself gave concerts in churches and at some of the Negro colleges until, in 1930, a Rosenwald Fellowship made European study possible. During her first year abroad she made her debut in Berlin. A prominent Scandinavian concert manager read of this concert, but was attracted more by the name, *Anderson*, than by what the critics said about her voice. "Ah," he said, "a Negro singer with a Swedish name! She is bound to be a success in Scandinavia." He sent two of his friends to Germany to hear her, one of them being Kosti Vehanen who shortly became her accompanist and remained with her for many years.

Sure enough, Marian Anderson did become a great success in the Scandinavian countries, where she learned to sing in both Finnish and Swedish, and her first concert tour of Europe became a critical triumph. When she came back home to America, she gave several programs and appeared as soloist with the famous Hall Johnson Choir, but without financial success. However, the Scandinavian people, who had fallen in love with her, kept asking her to come back there. So, in 1933, she went again to Europe for 142 concerts in Norway, Sweden, Denmark, and Finland. She was decorated by the King of Denmark and the King of Sweden. Sibelius[2] dedicated a song to her. And the following spring she made her debut in Paris where she was so well received that she had to give three concerts that season at the Salle Gaveau.[3] Great successes followed in all the European capitals. In 1935 the famous conductor, Arturo Toscanini, listened to her sing at Salzburg.[4] He said, "What I heard today one is privileged to hear only once in a hundred years." It was in Europe that Marian Anderson began to be acclaimed by critics as "the greatest singer in the world."

When Marian Anderson again returned to America, she was a seasoned artist. News of her tremendous European successes

2. **Sibelius** (si bā′ lē oos) Jean Sibelius (1865–1957), a Finnish composer.
3. **Salle Gaveau** (sàl ga vō′) concert hall in Paris, France.
4. **Salzburg** city in Austria noted for its music festivals.

Vocabulary
lucrative (loo′ krə tiv) *adj.* producing wealth; profitable
debut (dā byoo′) *n.* first public appearance

Literary Analysis
Style How do the words *sure enough* contribute to the informal, conversational diction?

had preceded her, so a big New York concert was planned. But a few days before she arrived at New York, in a storm on the liner crossing the Atlantic, Marian fell and broke her ankle. She refused to allow this to interfere with her concert, however, nor did she even want people to know about it. She wore a very long evening gown that night so that no one could see the plaster cast on her leg. She propped herself in a curve of the piano before the curtains parted, and gave her New York concert standing on one foot! The next day Howard Taubman wrote enthusiastically in *The New York Times*:

> Marian Anderson has returned to her native land one of the great singers of our time. . . . There is no doubt of it, she was mistress of all she surveyed. . . . It was music making that probed too deep for words.

A coast-to-coast American tour followed. And, from that season on, Marian Anderson has been one of our country's favorite singers, rated, according to *Variety*,[5] among the top ten of the concert stage who earn over $100,000 a year. Miss Anderson has sung with the great symphony orchestras, and appeared on all the major radio and television networks many times, being a particular favorite with the millions of listeners to the Ford Hour. During the years she has returned often to Europe for concerts, and

---

5. *Variety* a show-business newspaper.

 ▲ Critical Viewing
Does this photograph of Anderson's concert in Washington, D.C., support Hughes's description of her success? Explain. **[Support]**

 Spiral Review
Central Idea What central idea about Anderson does the reviewer's opinion help develop?

Reading Check
In which region of the world did Anderson first find success?

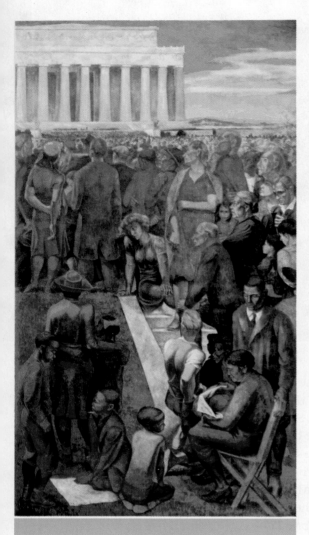

among the numerous honors accorded her abroad was a request for a command performance before the King and Queen of England, and a decoration from the government of Finland. Her concerts in South America and Asia have been as successful as those elsewhere. Since 1935 she has averaged over one hundred programs a year in cities as far apart as Vienna, Buenos Aires, Moscow, and Tokyo. Her recordings have sold millions of copies around the world. She has been invited more than once to sing at the White House. She has appeared in concert at the Paris Opera and at the Metropolitan Opera House in New York. Several colleges have granted her honorary degrees, and in 1944 Smith College made her a Doctor of Music.

In spite of all this, as a Negro, Marian Anderson has not been immune from those aspects of racial segregation which affect most traveling artists of color in the United States. In his book, *Marian Anderson*, her longtime accompanist, Vehanen, tells of hotel accommodations being denied her, and service in dining rooms often refused. Once after a concert in a Southern city, Vehanen writes that some white friends drove Marian to the railroad station and took her into the main waiting room. But a policeman ran them out, since Negroes were not allowed in that part of the station. Then they went into the smaller waiting room marked, COLORED. But again they were ejected, because *white* people were not permitted in the cubby hole allotted to Negroes. So they all had to stand on the platform until the train arrived.

The most dramatic incident of prejudice in all Marian Anderson's career occurred in 1939 when the Daughters of the American Revolution, who own Constitution Hall in Washington, refused to allow her to sing there. The newspapers headlined this and many Americans were outraged. In protest a committee of prominent people, including a number of great artists and distinguished figures in the government, was formed. Through the efforts of this committee, Marian Anderson sang in Washington, anyway—before the statue of Abraham Lincoln—to one of the largest crowds ever to hear a singer at one time in the history of the world. Seventy-five thousand people stood in the open air on a cold clear Easter Sunday afternoon to hear her. And millions more listened to Marian Anderson that day over the radio or heard her in the newsreels that recorded the event. Harold Ickes, then Secretary of the Interior, presented Miss Anderson to that enormous audience standing in the plaza to pay honor, as he said, not only to a great singer, but to the basic ideals of democracy and equality.

In 1943 Marian Anderson married Orpheus H. Fisher, an architect, and settled down—between tours—in a beautiful country house in Connecticut where she rehearses new songs to add to her already vast repertoire. Sometimes her neighbors across the fields can hear the rich warm voice that covers three octaves singing in English, French, Finnish, or German. And sometimes they hear in the New England air that old Negro spiritual, "Honor, honor unto the dying Lamb. . . ."

Friends say that Marian Anderson has invested her money in real estate and in government bonds. Certainly, throughout her career, she has lived very simply, traveled without a maid or secretary, and carried her own sewing machine along by train, ship, or plane to mend her gowns. When in 1941 in Philadelphia she was awarded the coveted Bok Award for outstanding public service, the $10,000 that came with the medallion she used to establish a trust fund for "talented American artists without regard to race or creed." Now, each year from this fund promising young musicians receive scholarships.

Vocabulary
repertoire (rep´ ər twär´) *n.* a stock of works, such as songs, that a performer is prepared to present

Literary Analysis
Style Which words and phrases here give a direct illustration of Anderson's lifestyle?

Critical Thinking

1. **Key Ideas and Details (a)** According to Hughes, in what area had African American singers not received recognition before Anderson? **(b) Infer:** How can you explain this lack of recognition?

2. **Key Ideas and Details (a)** Identify one action Anderson's congregation took to help her career. **(b) Infer:** What does their decision to help suggest about Anderson's talent as a young girl? Explain.

3. **Key Ideas and Details (a) Summarize:** What type of difficulties did Anderson face when traveling in the United States? **(b) Infer:** What attitude led to these difficulties? **(c) Analyze:** In what sense was Anderson's outdoor concert in Washington, D. C., a response to this attitude?

4. **Integration of Knowledge and Ideas** In this biography, the narrator describes the reality of racial segregation practices during the 1930s and 1940s. How did Marian Anderson's career help expose the truth about racism during this time? Using details from the text, explain your answer. *[Connect to the Big Question: Is there a difference between reality and truth?]*

Cite textual evidence to support your responses.

TEPEYAC

Sandra Cisneros

Vocabulary
canopied (kan´ ə pēd)
adj. covered by a cloth
suspended from poles
or a framework

Literary Analysis
Style How many sentences are included in this first paragraph?

When the sky of Tepeyac[1] opens its first thin stars and the dark comes down in an ink of Japanese blue above the bell towers of La Basílica de Nuestra Señora,[2] above the plaza photographers and their souvenir backdrops of La Virgen de Guadalupe, above the balloon vendors and their balloons wearing paper hats, above the red-canopied thrones of the shoeshine stands, above the wooden booths of the women frying lunch in vats of oil, above the *tlapalería*[3] on the corner of Misterios and Cinco de Mayo, when the photographers have toted up their tripods and big box cameras, have rolled away the wooden ponies I don't know where, when the balloon men have sold all but the ugliest balloons and herded these last few home, when the shoeshine men have grown tired of squatting on their little wooden boxes, and the women frying lunch have finished packing dishes, tablecloth, pots, in the big straw basket in which they came, then Abuelito[4] tells the boy with dusty hair, *Arturo, we are closed,* and in crooked shoes and purple elbows Arturo pulls down with a pole the corrugated metal curtains—first the one on Misterios, then the other on Cinco de Mayo—like an eyelid over each door, before Abuelito tells him he can go.

This is when I arrive, one shoe and then the next, over the sagging door stone, worn smooth in the middle from the huaraches of those who have come for tins of glue and to have their scissors sharpened, who have asked for candles and cans of boot polish,

---

1. **Tepeyac** (tep ā yäk´) Tepeyac Hill lies in the northern part of Mexico City.
2. **La Basílica de Nuestra Señora** (lä bä sil´ ē kä dä nwäs´ trä sen yō´ rä) the Basilica [Church] of Our Lady, lying at the foot of Tepeyac Hill on the site where, according to legend, Juan Diego had a vision in 1531.
3. **tlapalería** (tlä pä lä rē´ ä) *n.* the Mexican equivalent of a hardware store.
4. **Abuelito** (ä bwä lē´ tō) *n.* affectionate Spanish term for "grandfather."

a half-kilo sack of nails, turpentine, blue-specked spoons, paintbrushes, photographic paper, a spool of picture wire, lamp oil, and string.

Abuelito under a bald light bulb, under a ceiling dusty with flies, puffs his cigar and counts money soft and wrinkled as old Kleenex, money earned by the plaza women serving lunch on flat tin plates, by the souvenir photographers and their canvas Recuerdo[5] de Tepeyac backdrops, by the shoeshine men sheltered beneath their fringed and canopied kingdoms, by the blessed vendors of the holy cards, rosaries, scapulars, little plastic altars, by the good sisters who live in the convent across the street, counts and recounts in a whisper and puts the money in a paper sack we carry home.

I take Abuelito's hand, fat and dimpled in the center like a valentine, and we walk past the basilica, where each Sunday the Abuela[6] lights the candles for the soul of Abuelito. Past the very same spot where long ago Juan Diego brought down from the *cerro*[7] the miracle that has drawn everyone, except my Abuelito, on their knees, down the avenue one block past the bright lights of the *sastrería*[8] of Señor Guzmán who is still at work at his sewing machine, past the candy store where I buy my milk-and-raisin gelatins, past La Providencia *tortillería* where every afternoon Luz María and I are sent for the basket of lunchtime tortillas, past the house of the widow Márquez whose husband died last winter of a tumor the size of her little white fist, past La Muñeca's mother watering her famous dahlias with a pink rubber hose and a skinny string of water, to the house on La Fortuna, number 12, that has always been our house. Green iron gates that arabesque[9] and scroll like the initials of my name, familiar whine and clang, familiar lacework of ivy growing over and between except for one small clean square for the hand of the postman whose face I have never seen, up the twenty-two steps we count out loud together—*uno, dos, tres*—to the supper of *sopa de fideo* and *carne guisada*—*cuatro, cinco, seis*—the glass of *café con leche*—*siete, ocho, nueve*—shut the door against the mad parrot voice of the Abuela—*diez, once, doce*—fall asleep as we always do, with the television mumbling—*trece, catorce, quince*—the Abuelito snoring—*dieciséis, diecisiete, dieciocho*—the grandchild, the one who will leave soon for that borrowed country—

---

5. **Recuerdo** (rā kwer´ tho) Spanish for "souvenir."
6. **Abuela** (ä bwä´ lä) *n.* Spanish for "grandmother."
7. **cerro** (se´ rō) *n.* Spanish for "hill."
8. **sastrería** (säs tre rē´ ä) *n.* tailor's shop.
9. **arabesque** (ar´ ə besk´) *v.* branch out in complex, intertwining lines (usually a noun referring to such lines).

Reading Check

With whom does the narrator live in Tepeyac?

Central Idea The author is counting more than one thing as she recites these numbers. How does counting relate to the central idea of this piece?

Vocabulary
irretrievable
(ir´ i trēv´ ə bəl) *adj.*
impossible to regain or recover

Literary Analysis
Style What contrast does Cisneros create by ending the story with a shorter sentence?

diecinueve, veinte, veintiuno—the one he will not remember, the one he is least familiar with—*veintidós, veintitrés, veinticuatro*—years later when the house on La Fortuna, number 12, is sold, when the *tlapalería*, corner of Misterios and Cinco de Mayo, changes owners, when the courtyard gate of arabesques and scrolls is taken off its hinges and replaced with a corrugated sheet metal door instead, when the widow Márquez and La Muñeca's mother move away, when Abuelito falls asleep one last time—*veinticinco, veintiséis, veintisiete*—years afterward when I return to the shop on the corner of Misterios and Cinco de Mayo, repainted and redone as a pharmacy, to the basilica that is crumbling and closed, to the plaza photographers, the balloon vendors and shoeshine thrones, the women whose faces I do not recognize serving lunch in the wooden booths, to the house on La Fortuna, number 12, smaller and darker than when we lived there, with the rooms boarded shut and rented to strangers, the street suddenly dizzy with automobiles and diesel fumes, the house fronts scuffed and the gardens frayed, the children who played kickball all grown and moved away.

Who would've guessed, after all this time, it is me who will remember when everything else is forgotten, you who took with you to your stone bed something irretrievable without a name.

Critical Thinking

Cite textual evidence to support your responses.

1. **Key Ideas and Details** **(a)** List three details the narrator remembers about the market at Tepeyac. **(b) Synthesize:** What overall impression about the market do these details create? Explain your answer.

2. **Key Ideas and Details** **Interpret:** To what event is the narrator referring when she says, "the grandchild, the one who will leave soon for that borrowed country"?

3. **Key Ideas and Details** **(a) Analyze:** List two things that have changed in Tepeyac when the narrator returns. **(b) Draw Conclusions:** Why is the narrator surprised to discover at the end that "it is me who will remember"?

4. **Integration of Knowledge and Ideas** The narrator describes Tepeyac very realistically. What overall truth is she trying to convey with her detailed description? Explain. *[Connect to the Big Question: Is there a difference between reality and truth?]*

Comparing Styles

1. Craft and Structure (a) Explain how Hughes's **style** helps make Anderson seem accessible to readers, despite her fame. **(b)** How does Cisneros's style re-create the rushing flow of memories?

2. Craft and Structure (a) Using a chart like the one shown, compare each writer's style at the dramatic moment indicated.

	Hughes	**Cisneros**
Moment	**Washington, D.C., Concert**	**Concluding Realization**
type of words		
type of sentences		
similar to/different from rest of work?		

(b) Based on your chart, explain the ways in which each writer's style—or a shift in the writer's style—adds dramatic effect.

Timed Writing

Explanatory Text: Essay

Write an interpretive response to both texts that analyzes each author's specific purpose and the aesthetic effects of each author's use of stylistic devices. Then, decide which style is more effective in meeting the writer's purpose. **(30 minutes)**

5-Minute Planner

1. Read the prompt carefully and completely.
2. Consider these questions:
   - What is each writer's purpose for writing?
   - What stylistic devices, such as diction and syntax, does each author use?
   - What role do stylistic devices play in helping each writer achieve his or her purpose?
3. Provide evidence and examples from the texts, including quotations.
4. Reread the prompt, and then draft your essay.

Writing Workshop

Write a Narrative

Narration: Autobiographical Narrative

Defining the Form **Autobiographical narratives** tell a story from the writer's own life. They can be as simple as a remembrance of a weekend vacation or as complex as the entire story of the writer's life. You might use elements of autobiographical narratives in journals, eyewitness accounts, and reflective essays.

Assignment Write an autobiographical narrative about an event in your life that changed you or helped you grow. Include these elements:

✓ a *clear sequence of events* involving you, the writer

✓ a *problem or conflict*

✓ *effective descriptions* of people, places, and events

✓ use of *dialogue* to show character

✓ an *insight* you gained as a result of this experience

✓ error-free grammar, including *correct use of possessive nouns*

To preview the criteria on which your autobiographical narrative may be judged, see the rubric on page 113.

 Writing Workshop: *Work in Progress*

Review the work you did on pages 57 and 87.

Prewriting/Planning Strategy

Create character and setting cards. To select a story from your life, consider events that were funny, exciting, unusual, or puzzling. Choose one and prepare to focus your narrative by identifying the main conflict or insight you want to explain. Write an index card for each important character or setting.

- For characters, include facts like name, age, and appearance. Also note personality, habits, and the person's role in your story.

- For settings, jot down precise physical details and sensory details, such as sights and sounds, to use in your descriptions.

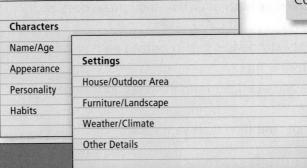

Characters	
Name/Age	
Appearance	
Personality	
Habits	

Settings	
House/Outdoor Area	
Furniture/Landscape	
Weather/Climate	
Other Details	

 Common Core State Standards

Writing

3. Write narratives to develop real or imagined experiences or events using effective technique, well-chosen details, and well-structured event sequences.

3.a. Engage and orient the reader by setting out a problem, situation, or observation, establishing one or multiple point(s) of view, and introducing a narrator and/or characters; create a smooth progression of experiences or events.

3.c. Use a variety of techniques to sequence events so that they build on one another to create a coherent whole.

3.d. Use precise words and phrases, telling details, and sensory language to convey a vivid picture of the experiences, events, setting, and/or characters.

5. Develop and strengthen writing as needed by planning, revising, editing, rewriting, or trying a new approach, focusing on addressing what is most significant for a specific purpose and audience.

Reading-Writing Connection

To get a feel for narrative nonfiction, read the excerpt from *Swimming to Antarctica* by Lynne Cox on page 62.

Telling the Story

Organization is the order in which you present your ideas or the events and actions in your narrative. One common and effective technique is to sequence events in *chronological* order. To create a smooth sequence, a writer might begin by setting the scene and introducing the characters. Then, he or she might describe the action or event that occurs first in time and continue presenting the details of the narrative in the order that they took place.

Writers may use other techniques, such as *flashbacks,* or going back in time to describe an event that has an impact on their narrative. Writers also pace the presentation of the actions to show the changes in time and in the mood of the characters. For example, the first part of a narrative contains the rising action, or the actions and events that lead to the *climax*—the point of highest interest. After reaching the climax, writers reduce the suspense of their narrative until they reach a resolution, which is the point where the author ties up the loose ends.

Decide the point you want to make. Consider the impression you want to make on your readers. You may want to show how another person influenced your life. You might want to describe a suspenseful and frightening incident in which you narrowly escaped from injury. Perhaps you want to show how you reached an important decision.

Choose your details. Telling every single detail of an event usually bores the reader. Choose only those details that help you make your point, and try to convey vivid images.

Pace the action. Be sure to identify the climax before you begin writing. Then, pace the presentation of the events or actions to create tension or suspense as you build to the key moment of the climax.

Devise a plan for telling your story. Sequence events so that they build on one another in a logical way. Use this plot diagram to help structure your narrative.

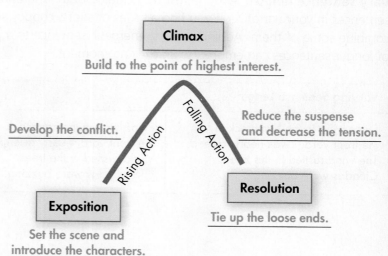

Climax

Build to the point of highest interest.

Develop the conflict.

Rising Action

Falling Action

Reduce the suspense and decrease the tension.

Resolution

Tie up the loose ends.

Exposition

Set the scene and introduce the characters.

Drafting Strategy

Use dialogue. *Dialogue*—the conversations between or among people in a narrative—can add interest to your writing. Use dialogue to advance the plot and show what characters are like. You might also create *interior monologues*, statements that reveal your exact thoughts at the time.

Narration	Dialogue
She told me not to go into the cave without a flashlight.	"Don't go into that cave without a flashlight," she warned me.

Dialogue also reflects the *point of view*, or perspective from which the narrative is told. In a *third-person* point of view, a voice outside the story relates the narrative. In a *first-person* point of view, the narrator or speaker is a character in the narrative. With a first-person point of view, the readers learn only what this character sees or hears.

Revising Strategies

Revise to clarify insight. Review your draft to make sure that you have clearly communicated the importance of the event you narrate. Underline sentences that show your reader what you learned. If necessary, add more of these sentences to explain your insight.

Check your conclusion. Provide a satisfying end to your narrative—one that follows from and reflects on the importance of the event you narrate.

Vary sentence length. Add interest by including both long and short sentences in your narrative. If you find a series of short, choppy sentences, combine some of them. Adding a short, energetic sentence to a passage of longer sentences can emphasize an exciting moment.

Varying Sentence Length	
I was lying in the hammock in the front yard. I was nearly asleep. The wind rustled in the trees. Cicadas were buzzing.	I was lying in the hammock in the front yard, nearly asleep. Wind rustled in the trees, and cicadas were buzzing.

Combining short sentences into a single longer one improves flow. Keeping a short sentence adds emphasis to the moment.

Common Core State Standards

Writing

3.a. Engage and orient the reader by setting out a problem, situation, or observation, establishing one or multiple point(s) of view, and introducing a narrator and/or characters; create a smooth progression of experiences or events.

3.b. Use narrative techniques, such as dialogue, pacing, description, reflection, and multiple plot lines, to develop experiences, events, and/or characters.

3.e. Provide a conclusion that follows from and reflects on what is experienced, observed, or resolved over the course of the narrative.

Language

2. Demonstrate command of the conventions of standard English capitalization, punctuation, and spelling when writing.

Using Possessive Nouns Correctly

A **possessive noun** indicates possession or ownership. An apostrophe must be used to form a possessive noun.

Identifying Incorrect Possessive Nouns You might find these three kinds of mistakes involving possessive nouns:

- nouns that are possessive but do not have an apostrophe
- possessive nouns that have an apostrophe in the wrong place
- nouns that are not possessive but include an apostrophe

Clarifying Your Meaning Thinking about what you mean will help you choose the correct possessive noun.

The student's essays were due on Friday. *(one student, many essays)*

The students' essays were due on Friday. *(more than one student)*

In the following example, the plural noun is not possessive. It should not have an apostrophe.

Wrong: The student's laughed.

Right: The students laughed.

> **PH** **WRITING COACH**
>
> Further instruction and practice are available in *Prentice Hall Writing Coach*.

Fixing Incorrect Possessive Nouns To fix the possessive nouns in your writing, look for any nouns that show ownership.

1. Ask yourself whether the noun is singular or plural.

2. Follow these rules to place the apostrophe correctly:

> A. Add an apostrophe and *s* to show the possessive case of most singular nouns.
>   the ocean's roar   Julia's bicycle   James's poem
>
> B. Add an apostrophe to show the possessive case of plural nouns ending in *s* or *es*.
>   the branches' leaves   the Canadians' houses
>
> C. Add an apostrophe and *s* to show the possessive case of plural nouns that do not end in *s* or *es*.
>   the people's stories   the children's department

Grammar in Your Writing

Scan your writing for apostrophes. You might find some in abbreviations, but others will be used in possessive nouns. Check that each possessive noun is punctuated correctly. Then, review your writing for possessives that are missing their apostrophes.

Student Model: Alexandria Symonds, Royersford, PA

 Common Core
State Standards

Language
2. Demonstrate command of the conventions of standard English capitalization, punctuation, and spelling when writing.

The Collision, or Hardly Extreme

Some people are simply not meant for extreme athletics, I thought to myself as I slowly regained consciousness. I am one of those people. I will never compete in the X Games; I should just stick to my orderly world where "sports" include Scrabble. I would have continued in this thought pattern, but a feeling like someone stabbing me in the eye with a dozen dull forks grabbed my attention instead.

I was bored that Saturday afternoon in May of 1998—so bored, in fact, that it seemed like a bright and creative idea to see if my old girly purple bike could be used for off-roading. The "off-road" in question was to be our front and back yards (the latter of which happened, incidentally, to back up to the North Carolina woods). I planned a fairly straightforward circuit around the house, complicated only slightly by the fact that our house sat on a hill.

It is prophesied that if the earth ever loses its gravitational pull, the moon will abandon its orbit and spin, instead, in a straight line into infinity. Something similar happened to me after a couple of laps around the house. I had reached a speed so high that I concentrated solely on pedaling to maintain it—forgetting, as it were, to turn at a pivotal point in the round. The difference, however, between the moon and me is that while the moon could spin into infinity unobstructed, there was a forest in my way.

I realized a split second too late that I hadn't made the turn and knew there was no use trying to do it now. In retrospect, I could have jumped off the bike, but logical thoughts rarely occur when one is hurtling toward a giant oak tree at 25 miles per hour. Instead, I stopped pedaling, closed my eyes, and braced myself for the impact.

I never actually felt it. When I opened my eyes, I was crumpled on the grass in a position I'm sure humans were never intended to take. My bike was tangled in my limbs, and a searing pain in my left eye was the only thing I could feel. After a bit of reflection about my "extreme" lack of foresight, I decided the best response was to scream as loudly as I could.

The events immediately following my ill-fated rendezvous with the tree are a blur; but I know that somehow I made it to the hospital, where I endured what seemed like endless tests and injections. I would be okay, but my recovery was a painful process. While the rest of me suffered only surface cuts and deep bruises, my left eye was swollen shut for a week. It was distended for months afterwards, and I still have some puffy scar tissue that causes my left eye to close more than the right when I smile.

Still, every time I get photos developed and notice this phenomenon, it serves as a reminder that I was simply not meant for any kind of physical activity more "extreme" than skipping.

Alexandria's thoughts provide an intriguing beginning for the narrative.

Specific details about Alexandria's state of mind and her bicycle add color and interest to the tale.

Alexandria's sense of humor gives a spark to the narrative.

Key details create a vivid picture and also keep the story moving.

Details here echo the beginning of the narrative and bring the story full circle.

Editing and Proofreading

Check your draft for errors in spelling, grammar, capitalization, and punctuation.

Focus on punctuating dialogue. Check that you have punctuated dialogue correctly. Quotation marks should surround a character's exact words or thoughts. As you edit, make sure that there is a closing quotation mark for every opening quotation mark. (For more on punctuating dialogue, see Quotation Marks on p. R53.)

Publishing and Presenting

Consider one of the following ways to share your writing:

Illustrate your narrative. Use photographs or drawings to illustrate people, places, or events in your narrative. Assemble a clean copy of your narrative, choosing an appropriate title and cover.

Deliver a narrative presentation. Rehearse reading your narrative aloud. Using a copy as a reading script, underline words that you will emphasize. Note places where you will vary your reading rate.

Reflecting on Your Writing

Jot down your answer to this question:

How did writing about the event help you to understand it?

Rubric for Self-Assessment

Find evidence in your writing to address each category. Then, use the rating scale to grade your work.

Spiral Review

Earlier in this unit, you learned about **common and proper nouns** (p. 56) and **abstract and concrete nouns** (p. 86). Check the capitalization of proper nouns in your narrative. Review your writing to make sure you used abstract and concrete nouns correctly.

Criteria	Rating Scale
	not very very
Focus: How clearly do you explain the insight gained from this experience?	1 2 3 4 5
Organization: How smooth is the progression of the sequence of events?	1 2 3 4 5
Support/Elaboration: How vivid and well structured are your descriptions of people, places, and events?	1 2 3 4 5
Style: How effective is your use of dialogue?	1 2 3 4 5
Conventions: How correct is your grammar, especially your use of possessive nouns?	1 2 3 4 5

Leveled Texts

Build your skills and improve your comprehension of fiction with texts of increasing complexity.

Read **"Contents of the Dead Man's Pocket"** to find out why a man risks his life on the ledge of a tall building.

Read **"Games at Twilight"** to experience the drama of a game of hide-and-seek from the point of view of a child.

Common Core State Standards

Meet these standards with either **"Contents of the Dead Man's Pocket"** (p. 118) or **"Games at Twilight"** (p. 139).

Reading Literature
5. Analyze how an author's choices concerning how to structure a text, order events within it, and manipulate time create such effects as mystery, tension, or surprise. *(Literary Analysis: Conflict and Resolution)*
Spiral Review: RL.9-10.2

Writing
3. Write narratives to develop real or imagined experiences or events using effective technique, well-chosen details, and well-structured event sequences. *(Writing: Anecdote)*

Speaking and Listening
1.a. Come to discussions prepared, having read and researched material under study; explicitly draw on that preparation by referring to evidence from texts and other research on the topic to stimulate a thoughtful,

well-reasoned exchange of ideas. **1.c.** Propel conversations by posing and responding to questions that relate the current discussion to broader themes or larger ideas; actively incorporate others into the discussion; and clarify, verify, or challenge ideas and conclusions. **1.d.** Respond thoughtfully to diverse perspectives, summarize points of agreement and disagreement, and qualify or justify their own views and understanding. *(Speaking and Listening: Problem-Solving Group)*

Language
1. Demonstrate command of the conventions of standard English grammar and usage when writing or speaking. *(Conventions: Personal Pronouns)*

Literary Analysis: Conflict and Resolution

The **conflict** in a short story is a struggle between two forces. Conflict drives a story's plot and influences the story's structure.

- In an **external conflict,** a character struggles against an outside force, such as an element of nature or another character.
- In an **internal conflict,** a character struggles with his or her own opposing desires, beliefs, or needs.

In many stories, the conflict intensifies until one force wins and a **resolution** of the conflict occurs. To build interest in a story's conflict, writers may hint at events to come or "stretch out" episodes that lead up to a crucial moment. In these ways, they create **suspense,** a rising curiosity or anxiety in readers.

Using the Strategy: Conflict Chart

As you read, use a chart like this one to record conflicts.

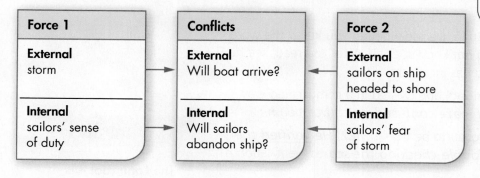

Force 1	Conflicts	Force 2
External storm	**External** Will boat arrive?	**External** sailors on ship headed to shore
Internal sailors' sense of duty	**Internal** Will sailors abandon ship?	**Internal** sailors' fear of storm

Reading Skill: Cause and Effect

A **cause** is an event, an action, or a situation that produces a result. An **effect** is the result produced. To better follow a story, **analyze causes and effects** as you read, determining which earlier events lead to which later events. Many stories are chains of cause and effect, in which one event leads to the next.

To analyze causes and effects, **reflect on key details** that the writer spends time explaining or describing. For example, a writer's description of a dangerous coastline prepares you to understand the cause-and-effect relationships leading to the sinking of a ship.

Is there a difference between *reality* and *truth?*

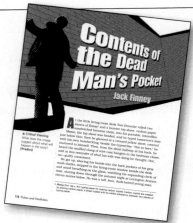

Writing About the Big Question

In "Contents of the Dead Man's Pocket," a man's perception of reality shifts because of a terrifying experience. He discovers the truth about his life and his priorities. Use this sentence starter to develop your ideas about the Big Question.

Life-threatening situations may cause people to **evaluate** _____ because _____.

While You Read Look for moments when the main character experiences changes in his understanding of reality or truth.

Vocabulary

Read each word and its definition. Decide whether you know the word well, know it a little bit, or do not know it at all. After you read, see how your knowledge of each word has increased.

- **convoluted** (kän′ və lōōt′ əd) *adj.* twisted in a complicated way (p. 121) *The convoluted maze confused us. convolution n.*

- **verified** (ver′ ə fīd) *v.* proved to be true (p. 122) *He verified the results of the test by double-checking the scores. verification n. verifiable adj.*

- **deftness** (deft′ nis) *n.* skillfulness (p. 126) *She climbed with the deftness of a mountain goat. deftly adv. deft adj.*

- **imperceptibly** (im′ pər sep′ tə blē) *adv.* so slowly or slightly as to be barely noticeable (p. 127) *I did not notice when the fish nibbled imperceptibly at my bait. imperceptible adj. perception n.*

- **reveling** (rev′ əl iŋ) *v.* taking great pleasure or delight (p. 127) *When she got her first job, she could not stop reveling in her newfound independence. revel v. reveler n. revelry v.*

- **interminable** (in tur′ mi nə bəl) *adj.* endless or seeming endless (p. 130) *The wait seemed interminable to the impatient shopper. interminably adv. terminate v.*

Word Study

The **Latin root -ver-** means "true."

In this story, Tom **verified** a situation when he made sure that it was true.

Meet
Jack Finney
(1911–1995)

Author of
Contents of the Dead Man's Pocket

While working at an advertising agency, Jack Finney dreamed of becoming a writer. He realized his dream when he entered his first short story in a contest sponsored by a magazine—and won!

Tales of Time Finney became especially well known for blending realistic and imaginary details into tales of time travel. In his popular works, the hero often escapes from the present into a simpler and calmer time in the past. However, Finney was happy to live in the present. "There's no past time I'd like to stay in," he said. "I want to stay here permanently."

DID YOU KNOW?

Finney's novel *Invasion of the Body Snatchers* has been made into a movie three times.

BACKGROUND FOR THE STORY
Before Computers

In the 1950s, when this story takes place, there were no computers or photocopiers. To make copies, people used carbon paper—black-coated sheets that transferred written or typed marks onto blank paper below. Without a carbon copy, a lost document might be gone forever—a possibility the main character in this story dreads.

Contents of the Dead Man's Pocket

Jack Finney

▲ **Critical Viewing**
What does this image suggest about what will happen in the story? **[Predict]**

At the little living-room desk Tom Benecke rolled two sheets of flimsy[1] and a heavier top sheet, carbon paper sandwiched between them, into his portable. Interoffice Memo, the top sheet was headed, and he typed tomorrow's date just below this; then he glanced at a creased yellow sheet, covered with his own handwriting, beside the typewriter. "Hot in here," he muttered to himself. Then, from the short hallway at his back, he heard the muffled clang of wire coat hangers in the bedroom closet, and at this reminder of what his wife was doing he thought: Hot, no—guilty conscience.

He got up, shoving his hands into the back pockets of his gray wash slacks, stepped to the living-room window beside the desk and stood breathing on the glass, watching the expanding circle of mist, staring down through the autumn night at Lexington Avenue, eleven stories below. He was a tall, lean, dark-haired young man

---

1. flimsy (flim′ zē) *n.* thin typing paper for making carbon copies. Carbon copies are created by placing carbon paper, a sheet coated with an inklike substance, between two pieces of typing paper.

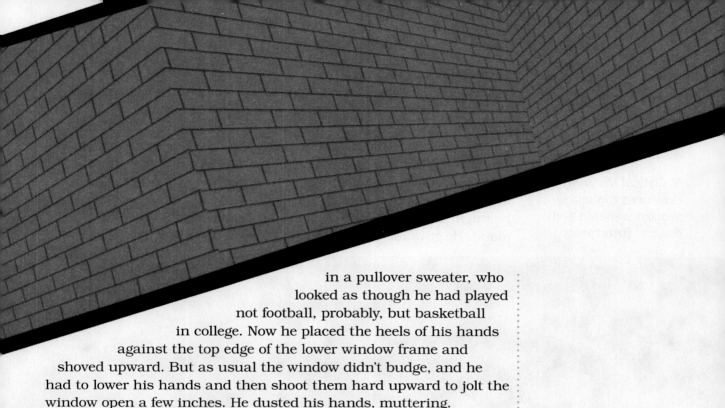

in a pullover sweater, who looked as though he had played not football, probably, but basketball in college. Now he placed the heels of his hands against the top edge of the lower window frame and shoved upward. But as usual the window didn't budge, and he had to lower his hands and then shoot them hard upward to jolt the window open a few inches. He dusted his hands, muttering.

But still he didn't begin his work. He crossed the room to the hallway entrance and, leaning against the doorjamb, hands shoved into his back pockets again, he called, "Clare?" When his wife answered, he said, "Sure you don't mind going alone?"

"No." Her voice was muffled, and he knew her head and shoulders were in the bedroom closet. Then the tap of her high heels sounded on the wood floor and she appeared at the end of the little hallway, wearing a slip, both hands raised to one ear, clipping on an earring. She smiled at him—a slender, very pretty girl with light brown, almost blonde, hair—her prettiness emphasized by the pleasant nature that showed in her face. "It's just that I hate you to miss this movie; you wanted to see it too."

"Yeah, I know." He ran his fingers through his hair. "Got to get this done though."

She nodded, accepting this. Then, glancing at the desk across the living room, she said, "You work too much, though, Tom—and too hard."

He smiled. "You won't mind though, will you, when the money comes rolling in and I'm known as the Boy Wizard of Wholesale Groceries?"

"I guess not." She smiled and turned back toward the bedroom. •

At his desk again, Tom lighted a cigarette, then a few moments later as Clare appeared, dressed and ready to leave, he set it on the

Literary Analysis
Conflict What internal conflict of Tom's does this paragraph show?

Reading
Check
Why has Tom decided to stay home?

rim of the ash tray. "Just after seven," she said. "I can make the beginning of the first feature."

He walked to the front-door closet to help her on with her coat. He kissed her then and, for an instant, holding her close, smelling the perfume she had used, he was tempted to go with her; it was not actually true that he had to work tonight, though he very much wanted to. This was his own project, unannounced as yet in his office, and it could be postponed. But then they won't see it till Monday, he thought once again, and if I give it to the boss tomorrow he might read it over the weekend . . . "Have a good time," he said aloud. He gave his wife a little swat and opened the door for her,

▼ **Critical Viewing**
How does this image suggest suspense and danger? **[Interpret]**

feeling the air from the building hallway, smelling faintly of floor wax, stream gently past his face.

He watched her walk down the hall, flicked a hand in response as she waved, and then he started to close the door, but it resisted for a moment. As the door opening narrowed, the current of warm air from the hallway, channeled through this smaller opening now, suddenly rushed past him with accelerated force. Behind him he heard the slap of the window curtains against the wall and the sound of paper fluttering from his desk, and he had to push to close the door.

Turning, he saw a sheet of white paper drifting to the floor in a series of arcs, and another sheet, yellow, moving toward the window, caught in the dying current flowing through the narrow

Reading Skill
Cause and Effect
Which key details explain why the paper floats off the desk?

opening. As he watched, the paper struck the bottom edge of the window and hung there for an instant, plastered against the glass and wood. Then as the moving air stilled completely, the curtains swinging back from the wall to hang free again, he saw the yellow sheet drop to the window ledge and slide over out of sight.

He ran across the room, grasped the bottom edge of the window and tugged, staring through the glass. He saw the yellow sheet, dimly now in the darkness outside, lying on the ornamental ledge a yard below the window. Even as he watched, it was moving, scraping slowly along the ledge, pushed by the breeze that pressed steadily against the building wall. He heaved on the window with all his strength and it shot open with a bang, the window weight rattling in the casing. But the paper was past his reach and, leaning out into the night, he watched it scud steadily along the ledge to the south, half plastered against the building wall. Above the muffled sound of the street traffic far below, he could hear the dry scrape of its movement, like a leaf on the pavement.

The living room of the next apartment to the south projected a yard or more farther out toward the street than this one; because of this the Beneckes paid seven and a half dollars less rent than their neighbors. And now the yellow sheet, sliding along the stone ledge, nearly invisible in the night, was stopped by the projecting blank wall of the next apartment. It lay motionless, then, in the corner formed by the two walls—a good five yards away, pressed firmly against the ornate corner ornament of the ledge, by the breeze that moved past Tom Benecke's face.

He knelt at the window and stared at the yellow paper for a full minute or more, waiting for it to move, to slide off the ledge and fall, hoping he could follow its course to the street, and then hurry down in the elevator and retrieve it. But it didn't move, and then he saw that the paper was caught firmly between a projection of the convoluted corner ornament and the ledge. He thought about the poker from the fireplace, then the broom, then the mop—discarding each thought as it occurred to him. There was nothing in the apartment long enough to reach that paper.

It was hard for him to understand that he actually had to abandon it—it was ridiculous—and he began to curse. Of all the papers on his desk, why did it have to be this one in particular! On four long Saturday afternoons he had stood in supermarkets counting the people who passed certain displays, and the results were scribbled on that yellow sheet. From stacks of trade publications, gone over page by page in snatched half hours at work and during evenings at home, he had copied facts, quotations, and figures onto that sheet. And he had carried it with him to the Public

Literary Analysis
Conflict Explain how an external conflict here helps create suspense.

Vocabulary
convoluted (kän´ və loot´ id) *adj.* twisted in a complicated way

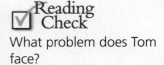
Reading Check
What problem does Tom face?

Library on Fifth Avenue, where he'd spent a dozen lunch hours and early evenings adding more. All were needed to support and lend authority to his idea for a new grocery-store display method; without them his idea was a mere opinion. And there they all lay, in his own improvised shorthand—countless hours of work—out there on the ledge.

For many seconds he believed he was going to abandon the yellow sheet, that there was nothing else to do. The work could be duplicated. But it would take two months, and the time to present this idea . . . was *now,* for use in the spring displays. He struck his fist on the window ledge. Then he shrugged. Even if his plan were adopted, he told himself, it wouldn't bring him a raise in pay—not immediately, anyway, or as a direct result. It won't bring me a promotion either, he argued—not of itself. •

But just the same, and he couldn't escape the thought, this and other independent projects, some already done and others planned for the future, would gradually mark him out from the score of other young men in his company. They were the way to change from a name on the payroll to a name in the minds of the company officials. They were the beginning of the long, long climb to where he was determined to be, at the very top. And he knew he was going out there in the darkness, after the yellow sheet fifteen feet beyond his reach.

By a kind of instinct, he instantly began making his intention acceptable to himself by laughing at it. The mental picture of himself sidling along the ledge outside was absurd—it was actually comical—and he smiled. He imagined himself describing it; it would make a good story at the office and, it occurred to him, would add a special interest and importance to his memorandum, which would do it no harm at all.

To simply go out and get his paper was an easy task—he could be back here with it in less than two minutes—and he knew he wasn't deceiving himself. The ledge, he saw, measuring it with his eye, was about as wide as the length of his shoe, and perfectly flat. And every fifth row of brick in the face of the building, he remembered—leaning out, he verified this—was indented half an inch, enough for the tips of his fingers, enough to maintain balance easily. It occurred to him that if this ledge and wall were only a yard aboveground—as he knelt at the window staring out, this thought was the final confirmation of his intention—he could move along the ledge indefinitely.

On a sudden impulse, he got to his feet, walked to the front closet and took out an old tweed jacket; it would be cold outside. He put

Reading Skill
Cause and Effect
What might cause Tom to go after the paper?

Reading Skill
Cause and Effect
What effect does Tom hope the story of his adventure will have on listeners?

Vocabulary
verified (ver´ ə fīd) *v.* proved to be true

it on and buttoned it as he crossed the room rapidly toward the open window. In the back of his mind he knew he'd better hurry and get this over with before he thought too much, and at the window he didn't allow himself to hesitate.

He swung a leg over the sill, then felt for and found the ledge a yard below the window with his foot. Gripping the bottom of the window frame very tightly and carefully, he slowly ducked his head under it, feeling on his face the sudden change from the warm air of the room to the chill outside. With infinite care he brought out his other leg, his mind concentrating on what he was doing. Then he slowly stood erect. Most of the putty, dried out and brittle, had dropped off the bottom edging of the window frame, he found, and the flat wooden edging provided a good gripping surface, a half inch or more deep, for the tips of his fingers.

Now, balanced easily and firmly, he stood on the ledge outside in the slight, chill breeze, eleven stories above the street, staring into his own lighted apartment, odd and different-seeming now.

First his right hand, then his left, he carefully shifted his fingertip grip from the puttyless window edging to an indented row of bricks directly to his right. It was hard to take the first shuffling sideways step then—to make himself move—and the fear stirred in his stomach, but he did it, again by not allowing himself time to think. And now—with his chest, stomach, and the left side of his face pressed against the rough cold brick—his lighted apartment was suddenly gone, and it was much darker out here than he had thought.

Without pause he continued—right foot, left foot, right foot, left—his shoe soles shuffling and scraping along the rough stone, never lifting from it, fingers sliding along the exposed edging of brick. He moved on the balls of his feet, heels lifted slightly; the ledge was not quite as wide as he'd expected. But leaning slightly inward toward the face of the building and pressed against it, he could feel his balance firm and secure, and moving along the ledge was quite as easy as he had thought it would be. He could hear the buttons of his jacket scraping steadily along the rough bricks and feel them

Reading Check

Describe Tom's progress on the first part of his journey.

catch momentarily, tugging a little, at each mortared crack. He
simply did not permit himself to look down, though the compulsion
to do so never left him; nor did he allow himself actually to think.
Mechanically—right foot, left foot, over and again—he shuffled
along crabwise, watching the projecting wall ahead loom steadily
closer . . .

Then he reached it, and, at the corner—he'd decided how he was
going to pick up the paper—he lifted his right foot and placed it
carefully on the ledge that ran along the projecting wall at a right
angle to the ledge on which his other foot rested. And now, facing
the building, he stood in the corner formed by the two walls, one
foot on the ledging of each, a hand on the shoulder-high indentation
of each wall. His forehead was pressed directly into the corner
against the cold bricks, and now he carefully lowered first one
hand, then the other, perhaps a foot farther down, to the next
indentation in the rows of bricks. •

Very slowly, sliding his forehead down the trough of the brick
corner and bending his knees, he lowered his body toward the
paper lying between his outstretched feet. Again he lowered his
fingerholds another foot and bent his knees still more, thigh
muscles taut, his forehead sliding and bumping down the

brick V. Half squatting now, he dropped his left hand to the next indentation and then slowly reached with his right hand toward the paper between his feet.

He couldn't quite touch it, and his knees now were pressed against the wall; he could bend them no farther. But by ducking his head another inch lower, the top of his head now pressed against the bricks, he lowered his right shoulder and his fingers had the paper by a corner, pulling it loose. At the same instant he saw, between his legs and far below, Lexington Avenue stretched out for miles ahead.

He saw, in that instant, the Loew's theater sign, blocks ahead past Fiftieth Street; the miles of traffic signals, all green now; the lights of cars and street lamps; countless neon signs; and the moving black dots of people. And a violent instantaneous explosion of absolute terror roared through him. For a motionless instant he saw himself externally—bent practically double, balanced on this narrow ledge, nearly half his body projecting out above the street far below—and he began to tremble violently, panic flaring through his mind and muscles, and he felt the blood rush from the surface of his skin.

In the fractional moment before horror paralyzed him, as he stared between his legs at that terrible length of street far beneath him, a fragment of his mind raised his body in a spasmodic jerk to an upright position again, but so violently that his head scraped hard against the wall, bouncing off it, and his body swayed outward to the knife edge of balance, and he very nearly plunged backward and fell. Then he was leaning far into the corner again, squeezing and pushing into it, not only his face but his chest and stomach, his back arching; and his fingertips clung with all the pressure of his pulling arms to the shoulder-high half-inch indentation in the bricks.

He was more than trembling now; his whole body was racked with a violent shuddering beyond control, his eyes squeezed so tightly shut it was painful, though he was past awareness of that. His teeth were exposed in a frozen grimace, the strength draining like water from his knees and calves. It was extremely likely, he knew, that he would faint, to slump down along the wall, his face scraping, and then drop backward, a limp weight, out into nothing. And to save his life he concentrated on holding onto consciousness, drawing deliberate deep breaths of cold air into his lungs, fighting to keep his senses aware.

Then he knew that he would not faint, but he could neither stop shaking nor open his eyes. He stood where he was, breathing deeply, trying to hold back the terror of the glimpse he had had of

Reading Skill
Cause and Effect
What is the effect of Tom's glimpse of the avenue below?

Literary Analysis
Conflict What internal conflict does Tom's external conflict cause?

Reading Check

What event introduces a new obstacle in Tom's journey?

what lay below him; and he knew he had made a mistake in not making himself stare down at the street, getting used to it and accepting it, when he had first stepped out onto the ledge.

It was impossible to walk back. He simply could not do it. He couldn't bring himself to make the slightest movement. The strength was gone from his legs; his shivering hands—numb, cold and desperately rigid—had lost all deftness; his easy ability to move and balance was gone. Within a step or two, if he tried to move, he knew that he would stumble clumsily and fall.

Seconds passed, with the chill faint wind pressing the side of his face, and he could hear the toned-down volume of the street traffic far beneath him. Again and again it slowed and then stopped, almost to silence; then presently, even this high, he would hear the click of the traffic signals and the subdued roar of the cars starting up again. During a lull in the street sounds, he called out. Then he was shouting "*Help!*" so loudly it rasped his throat. But he felt the steady pressure of the wind, moving between his face and the blank wall, snatch up his cries as he uttered them, and he knew they must sound directionless and distant. And he remembered how habitually, here in New York, he himself heard and ignored shouts in the night. If anyone heard him, there was no sign of it, and presently Tom Benecke knew he had to try moving; there was nothing else he could do.

Eyes squeezed shut, he watched scenes in his mind like scraps of motion-picture film—he could not stop them. He saw himself stumbling suddenly sideways as he crept along the ledge and saw his upper body arc outward, arms flailing. He saw a dangling shoestring caught between the ledge and the sole of his other shoe, saw a foot start to move, to be stopped with a jerk, and felt his balance leaving him. He saw himself falling with a terrible speed as his body revolved in the air, knees clutched tight to his chest, eyes squeezed shut, moaning softly.

Out of utter necessity, knowing that any of these thoughts might be reality in the very next seconds, he was slowly able to shut his mind against every thought but what he now began to do. With fear-soaked slowness, he slid his left foot an inch or two toward his own impossibly distant window. Then he slid the fingers of his shivering left hand a corresponding distance. For a moment he could not bring himself to lift his right foot from one ledge to the other; then he did it, and became aware of the harsh exhalation of air from his throat and realized that he was panting. As his right hand, then, began to slide along the brick edging, he was astonished to feel the yellow paper pressed to the bricks underneath his stiff fingers, and he uttered a terrible, abrupt bark

Vocabulary
deftness (deft′ nis)
n. skillfulness

Reading Skill
Cause and Effect
What causes Tom to begin moving?

that might have been a laugh or a moan. He opened his mouth and took the paper in his teeth, pulling it out from under his fingers. •

By a kind of trick—by concentrating his entire mind on first his left foot, then his left hand, then the other foot, then the other hand—he was able to move, almost **imperceptibly**, trembling steadily, very nearly without thought. But he could feel the terrible strength of the pent-up horror on just the other side of the flimsy barrier he had erected in his mind; and he knew that if it broke through he would lose this thin artificial control of his body.

During one slow step he tried keeping his eyes closed; it made him feel safer, shutting him off a little from the fearful reality of where he was. Then a sudden rush of giddiness swept over him and he had to open his eyes wide, staring sideways at the cold rough brick and angled lines of mortar, his cheek tight against the building. He kept his eyes open then, knowing that if he once let them flick outward, to stare for an instant at the lighted windows across the street, he would be past help.

He didn't know how many dozens of tiny sidling steps he had taken, his chest, belly, and face pressed to the wall; but he knew the slender hold he was keeping on his mind and body was going to break. He had a sudden mental picture of his apartment on just the other side of this wall—warm, cheerful, incredibly spacious. And he saw himself striding through it, lying down on the floor on his back, arms spread wide, **reveling** in its unbelievable security. The impossible remoteness of this utter safety, the contrast between it and where he now stood, was more than he could bear. And the barrier broke then, and the fear of the awful height he stood on coursed through his nerves and muscles.

A fraction of his mind knew he was going to fall, and he began taking rapid blind steps with no feeling of what he was doing, sidling with a clumsy desperate swiftness, fingers scrabbling along the brick, almost hopelessly resigned to the sudden backward pull and swift motion outward and down. Then his moving left hand slid

Reading Check

Why does Tom stop calling for help?

onto not brick but sheer emptiness, an impossible gap in the face of the wall, and he stumbled.

His right foot smashed into his left anklebone; he staggered sideways, began falling, and the claw of his hand cracked against glass and wood, slid down it, and his fingertips were pressed hard on the puttyless edging of his window. His right hand smacked gropingly beside it as he fell to his knees; and, under the full weight and direct downward pull of his sagging body, the open window dropped shudderingly in its frame till it closed and his wrists struck the sill and were jarred off.

For a single moment he knelt, knee bones against stone on the very edge of the ledge, body swaying and touching nowhere else, fighting for balance. Then he lost it, his shoulders plunging backward, and he flung his arms forward, his hands smashing against the window casing on either side; and—his body moving backward—his fingers clutched the narrow wood stripping of the upper pane.

For an instant he hung suspended between balance and falling, his fingertips pressed onto the quarter-inch wood strips. Then, with utmost delicacy, with a focused concentration of all his senses, he increased even further the strain on his fingertips hooked to these slim edgings of wood. Elbows slowly bending, he began to draw the full weight of his upper body forward, knowing that the instant his fingers slipped off these quarter-inch strips he'd plunge backward and be falling. Elbows imperceptibly bending, body shaking with the strain, the sweat starting from his forehead in great sudden drops, he pulled, his entire being and thought concentrated in his fingertips. Then suddenly, the strain slackened and ended, his chest touching the window sill, and he was kneeling on the ledge, his forehead pressed to the glass of the closed window.

Dropping his palms to the sill, he stared into his living room—at the red-brown davenport[2] across the room, and a magazine he had left there; at the pictures on the walls and the gray rug; the entrance to the hallway; and at his papers, typewriter and desk, not two feet from his nose. A movement from his desk caught his eye and he saw that it was a thin curl of blue smoke; his cigarette, the ash long, was still burning in the ash tray where he'd left it—this was past all belief—only a few minutes before.

His head moved, and in faint reflection from the glass before him he saw the yellow paper clenched in his front teeth. Lifting a hand from the sill he took it from his mouth; the moistened corner parted from the paper, and he spat it out.

---

2. davenport (dav´ ən pôrt´) *n.* large couch.

For a moment, in the light from the living room, he stared wonderingly at the yellow sheet in his hand and then crushed it into the side pocket of his jacket.

He couldn't open the window. It had been pulled not completely closed, but its lower edge was below the level of the outside sill; there was no room to get his fingers underneath it. Between the upper sash and the lower was a gap not wide enough—reaching up, he tried—to get his fingers into; he couldn't push it open. The upper window panel, he knew from long experience, was impossible to move, frozen tight with dried paint.

Very carefully observing his balance, the fingertips of his left hand again hooked to the narrow stripping of the window casing, he drew back his right hand, palm facing the glass, and then struck the glass with the heel of his hand.

His arm rebounded from the pane, his body tottering, and he knew he didn't dare strike a harder blow.

But in the security and relief of his new position, he simply smiled; with only a sheet of glass between him and the room just before him, it was not possible that there wasn't a way past it. Eyes narrowing, he thought for a few moments about what to do. Then his eyes widened, for nothing occurred to him. But still he felt calm: the trembling, he realized, had stopped. At the back of his mind there still lay the thought that once he was again in his home, he could give release to his feelings. He actually would lie on the floor, rolling, clenching tufts of the rug in his hands. He would literally run across the room, free to move as he liked, jumping on the floor, testing and reveling in its absolute security, letting the relief flood through him, draining the fear from his mind and body. His yearning for this was astonishingly intense, and somehow he understood that he had better keep this feeling at bay.

He took a half dollar from his pocket and struck it against the pane, but without any hope that the glass would break and with very little disappointment when it did not. After a few moments of thought he drew his leg up onto the ledge and picked loose the knot of his shoelace. He slipped off the shoe and, holding it across the instep, drew back his arm as far as he dared and struck the leather heel against the glass. The pane rattled, but he knew he'd been a long way from breaking it. His foot was cold and he slipped the shoe back on. He shouted again experimentally, and then once more, but there was no answer.

LITERATURE IN CONTEXT

Science Connection

Physics

Tom is on the ledge with only a pane of glass between him and safety. Yet he is reluctant to hit the window to break the glass—with good reason. Tom understands Newton's third law of motion: for every action, there is an equal and opposite reaction. For example, the *action* of throwing a ball against a wall has the opposite *reaction* of the ball bouncing away from the wall.

Connect to the Literature

What opposite reaction does Tom fear will result if he hits the glass hard but does not break it?

Reading Check ☑

In what way has Tom's situation improved? In what way does it remain the same?

The realization suddenly struck him that he might have to wait
here till Clare came home, and for a moment the thought was
funny. He could see Clare opening the front door, withdrawing her
key from the lock, closing the door behind her, and then glancing
up to see him crouched on the other side of the window. He could
see her rush across the room, face astounded and frightened, and
hear himself shouting instructions: "Never mind how I got here!
Just open the wind—" She couldn't open it, he remembered, she'd
never been able to; she'd always had to call him. She'd have to get
the building superintendent or a neighbor, and he pictured himself
smiling and answering their questions as he climbed in. "I just
wanted to get a breath of fresh air, so—" •

He couldn't possibly wait here till Clare came home. It was the
second feature she'd wanted to see, and she'd left in time to see the
first. She'd be another three hours or—He glanced at his watch;
Clare had been gone eight minutes. It wasn't possible, but only eight
minutes ago he had kissed his wife goodbye. She wasn't even at the
theater yet!

It would be four hours before she could possibly be home, and he
tried to picture himself kneeling out here, fingertips hooked to these
narrow strippings, while first one movie, preceded by a slow listing
of credits, began, developed, reached its climax and then finally
ended. There'd be a newsreel next, maybe, and then an animated
cartoon, and then interminable scenes from coming pictures. And
then, once more, the beginning of a full-length picture—while all
the time he hung out here in the night.

**Vocabulary
interminable** (in tur´
mi nə bəl) *adj.* endless
or seemingly endless

He might possibly get to his feet, but he was afraid to try. Already
his legs were cramped, his thigh muscles tired; his knees hurt, his
feet felt numb and his hands were stiff. He couldn't possibly stay
out here for four hours, or anywhere near it. Long before that his
legs and arms would give out; he would be forced to try changing
his position often—stiffly, clumsily, his coordination and strength
gone—and he would fall. Quite realistically, he knew that he would
fall; no one could stay out here on this ledge for four hours.

A dozen windows in the apartment building across the street
were lighted. Looking over his shoulder, he could see the top of
a man's head behind the newspaper he was reading; in another
window he saw the blue-gray flicker of a television screen. No
more than twenty-odd yards from his back were scores of people,
and if just one of them would walk idly to his window and glance
out. . . . For some moments he stared over his shoulder at the
lighted rectangles, waiting. But no one appeared. The man reading

his paper turned a page and then continued his reading. A figure passed another of the windows and was immediately gone.

In the inside pocket of his jacket he found a little sheaf of papers, and he pulled one out and looked at it in the light from the living room. It was an old letter, an advertisement of some sort; his name and address, in purple ink, were on a label pasted to the envelope. Gripping one end of the envelope in his teeth, he twisted it into a tight curl. From his shirt pocket he brought out a book of matches. He didn't dare let go the casing with both hands, but, with the twist of paper in his teeth, he opened the matchbook with his free hand; then he bent one of the matches in two without tearing it from the folder, its red-tipped end now touching the striking surface. With his thumb, he rubbed the red tip across the striking area.

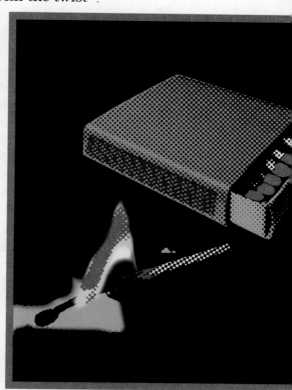

He did it again, then again, and still again, pressing harder each time, and the match suddenly flared, burning his thumb. But he kept it alight, cupping the matchbook in his hand and shielding it with his body. He held the flame to the paper in his mouth till it caught. Then he snuffed out the match flame with his thumb and forefinger, careless of the burn, and replaced the book in his pocket. Taking the paper twist in his hand, he held it flame down, watching the flame crawl up the paper, till it flared bright. Then he held it behind him over the street, moving it from side to side, watching it over his shoulder, the flame flickering and guttering in the wind.

There were three letters in his pocket and he lighted each of them, holding each till the flame touched his hand and then dropping it to the street below. At one point, watching over his shoulder while the last of the letters burned, he saw the man across the street put down his paper and stand—even seeming, to Tom, to glance toward his window. But when he moved, it was only to walk across the room and disappear from sight.

There were a dozen coins in Tom Benecke's pocket and he dropped them, three or four at a time. But if they struck anyone, or if anyone noticed their falling, no one connected them with their source, and no one glanced upward.

His arms had begun to tremble from the steady strain of clinging to this narrow perch, and he did not know what to do now and was terribly frightened. Clinging to the window stripping with one hand, he again searched his pockets. But now—he had left his wallet

Reading Skill
Cause and Effect
What effect does Tom hope the burning papers and the falling coins will have?

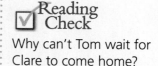
Reading Check

Why can't Tom wait for Clare to come home?

Reading Skill
Cause and Effect
What key details explain
why Tom grows angry?

Spiral Review
Theme What insight
about himself does
Tom experience? Is
this insight also the
story's theme? Explain.

on his dresser when he'd changed clothes—there was nothing left but the yellow sheet. It occurred to him irrelevantly that his death on the sidewalk below would be an eternal mystery; the window closed—why, how, and from where could he have fallen? No one would be able to identify his body for a time, either—the thought was somehow unbearable and increased his fear. All they'd find in his pockets would be the yellow sheet. *Contents of the dead man's pockets,* he thought, *one sheet of paper bearing penciled notations— incomprehensible.*

He understood fully that he might actually be going to die; his arms, maintaining his balance on the ledge, were trembling steadily now. And it occurred to him then with all the force of a revelation that, if he fell, all he was ever going to have out of life he would then, abruptly, have had. Nothing, then, could ever be changed; and nothing more—no least experience or pleasure— could ever be added to his life. He wished, then, that he had not allowed his wife to go off by herself tonight—and on similar nights. He thought of all the evenings he had spent away from her, working; and he regretted them. He thought wonderingly of his fierce ambition and of the direction his life had taken; he thought of the hours he'd spent by himself, filling the yellow sheet that had brought him out here. *Contents of the dead man's pockets,* he thought with sudden fierce anger, *a wasted life.*

He was simply not going to cling here till he slipped and fell; he told himself that now. There was one last thing he could try; he had been aware of it for some moments, refusing to think about it, but now he faced it. Kneeling here on the ledge, the fingertips of one hand pressed to the narrow strip of wood, he could, he knew, draw his other hand back a yard perhaps, fist clenched tight, doing it very slowly till he sensed the outer limit of balance, then, as hard as he was able from the distance, he could drive his fist forward against the glass. If it broke, his fist smashing through, he was safe; he might cut himself badly, and probably would, but with his arm inside the room, he would be secure. But if the glass did not break, the rebound, flinging his arm back, would topple him off the ledge. He was certain of that.

He tested his plan. The fingers of his left hand clawlike on the little stripping, he drew back his other fist until his body began teetering backward. But he had no leverage now—he could feel that there would be no force to his swing—and he moved his fist slowly forward till he rocked forward on his knees again and could sense that his swing would carry its greatest force. Glancing down, however, measuring the distance from his fist to the glass, he saw that it was less than two feet.

It occurred to him that he could raise his arm over his head, to bring it down against the glass. But, experimenting in slow motion, he knew it would be an awkward . . . blow without the force of a driving punch, and not nearly enough to break the glass. •

Facing the window, he had to drive a blow from the shoulder, he knew now, at a distance of less than two feet; and he did not know whether it would break through the heavy glass. It might; he could picture it happening, he could feel it in the nerves of his arm. And it might not; he could feel that too—feel his fist striking this glass and being instantaneously flung back by the unbreaking pane, feel the fingers of his other hand breaking loose, nails scraping along the casing as he fell.

He waited, arm drawn back, fist balled, but in no hurry to strike; this pause, he knew, might be an extension of his life. And to live even a few seconds longer, he felt, even out here on this ledge in the night, was infinitely better than to die a moment earlier than he had to. His arm grew tired, and he brought it down and rested it.

Then he knew that it was time to make the attempt. He could not kneel here hesitating indefinitely till he lost all courage to act, waiting till he slipped off the ledge. Again he drew back his arm, knowing this time that he would not bring it down till he struck. His elbow protruding over Lexington Avenue far below, the fingers of his other hand pressed down bloodlessly tight against the narrow stripping, he waited, feeling the sick tenseness and terrible excitement building. It grew and swelled toward the moment of action, his nerves tautening. He thought of Clare—just a wordless, yearning thought—and then drew his arm back just a bit more, fist so tight his fingers pained him, and knowing he was going to do it. Then with full power, with every last scrap of strength he could bring to bear, he shot his arm forward toward the glass, and he said, *"Clare!"*

He heard the sound, felt the blow, felt himself falling forward, and his hand closed on the living-room curtains, the shards and fragments of glass showering onto the floor. And then, kneeling there on the ledge, an arm thrust into the room up to the shoulder, he began picking away the protruding slivers and great wedges of glass from the window frame, tossing them in onto the rug. And, as he grasped the edges of the empty window frame and climbed into his home, he was grinning in triumph.

Literary Analysis
Conflict
How do Tom's imaginings of what might happen build suspense?

Contents of the Dead Man's Pocket **133**

He did not lie down on the floor or run through the apartment, as he had promised himself; even in the first few moments it seemed to him natural and normal that he should be where he was. He simply turned to his desk, pulled the crumpled yellow sheet from his pocket and laid it down where it had been, smoothing it out; then he absently laid a pencil across it to weight it down. He shook his head wonderingly, and turned to walk toward the closet.

There he got out his topcoat and hat and, without waiting to put them on, opened the front door and stepped out, to go find his wife. He turned to pull the door closed and the warm air from the hall rushed through the narrow opening again. As he saw the yellow paper, the pencil flying, scooped off the desk and, unimpeded by the glassless window, sail out into the night and out of his life, Tom Benecke burst into laughter and then closed the door behind him.

Critical Thinking

1. **Key Ideas and Details** **(a) Analyze Cause and Effect:** At the start of the story, what long-term goals does Tom hope to achieve? **(b) Draw Conclusions:** What does his plan tell you about his character?

2. **Key Ideas and Details** **(a)** Why does Tom go out on the ledge? **(b) Connect:** Is his decision surprising? Explain using details from the story.

3. **Key Ideas and Details** **(a) Compare and Contrast:** Contrast Tom's attitude toward life at the beginning of the story with his attitude at the end. **(b) Infer:** What causes his attitude to change? **(c) Speculate:** What changes, if any, will Tom make as a result of this insight?

4. **Integration of Knowledge and Ideas** **(a) Evaluate:** Do you think a movie based on Finney's story would be as effective as the story itself? Why or why not? **(b) Discuss:** Share your response with a partner. Then, discuss the changes a filmmaker might make to the story and the reasons for such changes. Explain your ideas to the class.

5. **Integration of Knowledge and Ideas** How do Tom's perceptions of reality change during the course of the story? How can you tell? *[Connect to the Big Question: Is there a difference between reality and truth?]*

Literary Analysis: Conflict and Resolution

1. Key Ideas and Details (a) What is the main **external conflict** in this story? Explain. **(b)** What is the main **internal conflict** in the story? Explain.

2. Craft and Structure (a) Identify a moment in the story that has great **suspense. (b)** Which conflict helps to create this suspense? Explain.

3. Craft and Structure (a) How are Tom's conflicts resolved? **(b)** Describe an alternative **resolution** the story might have had.

Reading Skill: Cause and Effect

4. (a) In your opinion, which single **cause** sets the story's cause-and-effect chain in motion? **(b)** Identify two **effects**—one short-term and one long-term—of this event. Use a diagram like this one.

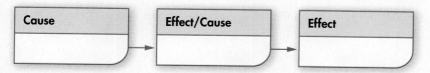

Cause	Effect/Cause	Effect

5. (a) Identify a **key detail** early in the story that becomes important later on. **(b)** Analyze the causes and effects linked to this detail.

Vocabulary

Acquisition and Use Answer each question. Explain your responses.

1. Should directions for dealing with an emergency be <u>convoluted</u>?

2. Can you trust information that has been <u>verified</u>?

3. Would you want a surgeon to display <u>deftness</u>?

4. If the temperature fell <u>imperceptibly</u>, would most people notice?

5. Is someone who is <u>reveling</u> expressing joy?

6. Would you be happy if your school day was <u>interminable</u>?

Word Study Use the context of the sentences and what you know about the **Latin root -ver-** to explain your answer to each question.

1. Does a judge expect *veracity* from those testifying in court?

2. Would you feel proud if your personal narrative was a *veritable* masterpiece?

Word Study

The **Latin root -ver-** means "true."

Apply It Explain how the root -ver- contributes to the meanings of these words. Consult a dictionary if necessary.

verification
aver
verdict

Is there a difference between *reality* and *truth?*

Writing About the Big Question

In "Games at Twilight," a boy tries to gain the respect of the older children by winning a game of hide-and-seek. Though it is just a game, it gives him a glimpse of a harsh reality. Use this sentence starter to develop your ideas about the Big Question.

Playing a game can change a person's **perception** of **reality** because _____.

While You Read Look for moments when the main character experiences changes in his understanding of reality or truth.

Vocabulary

Read each word and its definition. Decide whether you know the word well, know it a little bit, or do not know it at all. After you read, see how your knowledge of each word has increased.

- **livid** (liv´ id) *adj.* discolored, as by a bruise; red with anger (p. 140) *She became livid when she saw the bully bothering the first grade students.* lividly *adv.* lividness *n.*

- **intervened** (in´ tər vēnd´) *v.* came between (p. 140) *The moderator intervened because the two lawyers could not come to an agreement.* intervention *n.* interval *n.*

- **dejectedly** (dē jek´ tid lē) *adv.* in a depressed way (p. 142) *After losing the game, the players walked away dejectedly.* dejection *n.* dejected *adj.*

- **defunct** (dē fuŋkt´) *adj.* no longer in use or existence (p. 142) *The defunct computer now gathers cobwebs.* function *v.*

- **dogged** (dôg´ id) *adj.* stubborn (p. 146) *It took a day of dogged efforts to solve the puzzle.* doggedness *n.* doggedly *adv.*

- **elude** (ē lo͞od´) *v.* escape or avoid (p. 146) *The toddler tried to elude us by hiding under a blanket.* elusion *n.* elusive *adj.*

Word Study

The **Latin root -ven-** means "come" or "go."

In this story, an older child **intervened**, or came between, arguing children.

Games at Twilight

Anita Desai

It was still too hot to play outdoors. They had had their tea, they had been washed and had their hair brushed, and after the long day of confinement in the house that was not cool but at least a protection from the sun, the children strained to get out. Their faces were red and bloated with the effort, but their mother would not open the door, everything was still curtained and shuttered in a way that stifled the children, made them feel that their lungs were stuffed with cotton wool and their noses with dust and if they didn't burst out into the light and see the sun and feel the air, they would choke.

"Please, Ma, please," they begged. "We'll play in the veranda and porch—we won't go a step out of the porch."

"You will, I know you will, and then—"

"No—we won't, we won't," they wailed so horrendously that she actually let down the bolt of the front door so that they burst out like seeds from a crackling, over-ripe pod into the veranda, with such wild, maniacal yells that she retreated to her bath and the shower of talcum powder and the fresh sari[1] that were to help her face the summer evening.

They faced the afternoon. It was too hot. Too bright. The white walls of the veranda glared stridently in the sun. The bougainvillea hung about it, purple and magenta, in livid balloons. The garden outside was like a tray made of beaten brass, flattened out on the red gravel and the stony soil in all shades of metal—aluminum, tin, copper and brass. No life stirred at this arid time of day—the birds still drooped, like dead fruit, in the papery tents of the trees; some squirrels lay limp on the wet earth under the garden tap. The outdoor dog lay stretched as if dead on the veranda mat, his paws and ears and tail all reaching out like dying travelers in search of water. He rolled his eyes at the children—two white marbles rolling in the purple sockets, begging for sympathy—and attempted to lift his tail in a wag but could not. It only twitched and lay still.

Then, perhaps roused by the shrieks of the children, a band of parrots suddenly fell out of the eucalyptus tree, tumbled frantically in the still, sizzling air, then sorted themselves out into battle formation and streaked away across the white sky.

The children, too, felt released. They too began tumbling, shoving, pushing against each other, frantic to start. Start what? Start their business. The business of the children's day which is—play.

"Let's play hide-and-seek."

"Who'll be It?"

"You be It."

"Why should I? You be—"

"You're the eldest—"

"That doesn't mean—"

The shoves became harder. Some kicked out. The motherly Mira intervened. She pulled the boys roughly apart. There was a tearing sound of cloth but it was lost in the heavy panting and angry grumbling and no one paid attention to the small sleeve hanging loosely off a shoulder.

"Make a circle, make a circle!" she shouted, firmly pulling and pushing till a kind of vague circle was formed. "Now clap!" she

---

1. **sari** (sä´ rē) *n.* a long piece of cloth wrapped around the body, forming a skirt and draped over one shoulder; the main garment of Indian women.

roared and, clapping, they all chanted in melancholy unison: "Dip, dip, dip—my blue ship—" and every now and then one or the other saw he was safe by the way his hands fell at the crucial moment— palm on palm, or back of hand on palm—and dropped out of the circle with a yell and a jump of relief and jubilation.

Raghu was It. He started to protest, to cry "You cheated—Mira cheated—Anu cheated—" but it was too late, the others had all already streaked away. There was no one to hear when he called out, "Only in the veranda—the porch—Ma said—Ma said to stay in the porch!" No one had stopped to listen, all he saw were their brown legs flashing through the dusty shrubs, scrambling up brick walls, leaping over compost heaps and hedges, and then the porch stood empty in the purple shade of the bougainvillea and the garden was as empty as before; even the limp squirrels had whisked away, leaving everything gleaming, brassy and bare.

Only small Manu suddenly reappeared, as if he had dropped out of an invisible cloud or from a bird's claws, and stood for a moment in the center of the yellow lawn, chewing his finger and near to tears as he heard Raghu shouting, with his head pressed against the veranda wall, "Eighty-three, eighty-five, eighty-nine, ninety . . ." and then made off in a panic, half of him wanting to fly north, the other half counseling south. Raghu turned just in time to see the flash of his white shorts and the uncertain skittering of his red sandals, and charged after him with such a bloodcurdling yell that Manu

Reading Skill
Cause and Effect What key details suggest that the children use this rhyming game to choose who will be "it"?

Reading Check

What game do the children decide to play?

Games at Twilight **141**

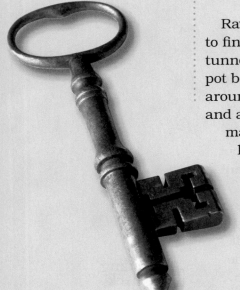

stumbled over the hosepipe, fell into its rubber coils and lay there weeping, "I won't be It—you have to find them all—all—All!"

"I know I have to, idiot," Raghu said, superciliously[2] kicking him with his toe. "You're dead," he said with satisfaction, licking the beads of perspiration off his upper lip, and then stalked off in search of worthier prey, whistling spiritedly so that the hiders should hear and tremble.

Ravi heard the whistling and picked his nose in a panic, trying to find comfort by burrowing the finger deep—deep into that soft tunnel. He felt himself too exposed, sitting on an upturned flower pot behind the garage. Where could he burrow? He could run around the garage if he heard Raghu come—around and around and around—but he hadn't much faith in his short legs when matched against Raghu's long, hefty, hairy footballer legs. Ravi had a frightening glimpse of them as Raghu combed the hedge of crotons and hibiscus, trampling delicate ferns underfoot as he did so. Ravi looked about him desperately, swallowing a small ball of snot in his fear.

The garage was locked with a great heavy lock to which the driver had the key in his room, hanging from a nail on the wall under his work-shirt. Ravi had peeped in and seen him still sprawling on his string-cot in his vest and striped underpants, the hair on his chest and the hair in his nose shaking with the vibrations of his phlegm-obstructed snores. Ravi had wished he were tall enough, big enough to reach the key on the nail, but it was impossible, beyond his reach for years to come. He had sidled away and sat dejectedly on the flower pot. That at least was cut to his own size.

But next to the garage was another shed with a big green door. Also locked. No one even knew who had the key to the lock. That shed wasn't opened more than once a year when Ma turned out all the old broken bits of furniture and rolls of matting and leaking buckets, and the white ant hills were broken and swept away and Flit sprayed into the spider webs and rat holes so that the whole operation was like the looting of a poor, ruined and conquered city. The green leaves of the door sagged. They were nearly off their rusty hinges. The hinges were large and made a small gap between the door and the walls—only just large enough for rats, dogs, and, possibly, Ravi to slip through.

Ravi had never cared to enter such a dark and depressing mortuary of defunct household goods seething with such

---

2. **superciliously** (soo´ pər sil´ ē əs lē) *adv.* haughtily; in a manner expressing pride in oneself and scorn for the other person.

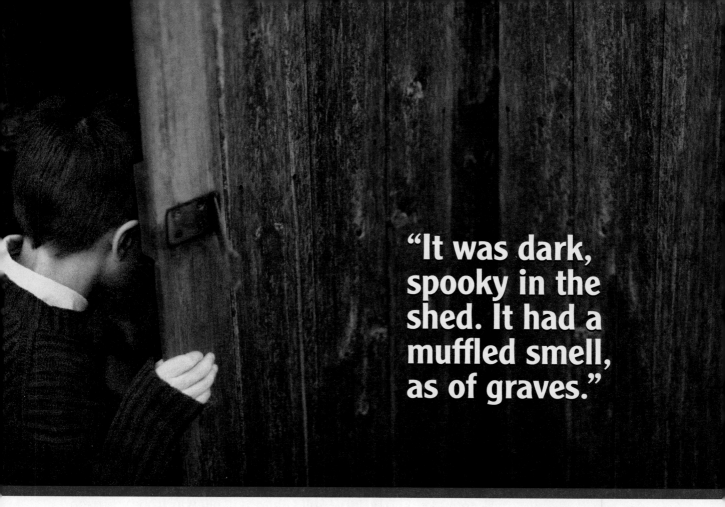

"It was dark, spooky in the shed. It had a muffled smell, as of graves."

unspeakable and alarming animal life but, as Raghu's whistling grew angrier and sharper and his crashing and storming in the hedge wilder, Ravi suddenly slipped off the flower pot and through the crack and was gone. He chuckled aloud with astonishment at his own temerity[3] so that Raghu came out of the hedge, stood silent with his hands on his hips, listening, and finally shouted "I heard you! I'm coming! Got you—" and came charging round the garage only to find the upturned flower pot, the yellow dust, the crawling of white ants in a mud-hill against the closed shed door—nothing. Snarling, he bent to pick up a stick and went off, whacking it against the garage and shed walls as if to beat out his prey.

Ravi shook, then shivered with delight, with self-congratulation. Also with fear. It was dark, spooky in the shed. It had a muffled smell, as of graves. Ravi had once got locked into the linen cupboard and sat there weeping for half an hour before he was rescued. But at least that had been a familiar place, and even

_____

3. **temerity** (tə mer´ ə tē) *n.* recklessness; foolish boldness.

▲ **Critical Viewing**
What might Ravi find in a shed like the one shown in the photograph? **[Speculate]**

Spiral Review
Theme Which details in the description of the shed suggest a possible theme?

Reading Check
Where does Ravi decide to hide?

smelled pleasantly of starch, laundry and, reassuringly, of his mother. But the shed smelled of rats, ant hills, dust and spider webs. Also of less definable, less recognizable horrors. And it was dark. Except for the white-hot cracks along the door, there was no light. The roof was very low. Although Ravi was small, he felt as if he could reach up and touch it with his finger tips. But he didn't stretch. He hunched himself into a ball so as not to bump into anything, touch or feel anything. What might there not be to touch him and feel him as he stood there, trying to see in the dark? Something cold, or slimy—like a snake. Snakes! He leapt up as Raghu whacked the wall with his stick—then quickly realizing what it was, felt almost relieved to hear Raghu, hear his stick. It made him feel protected.

But Raghu soon moved away. There wasn't a sound once his footsteps had gone around the garage and disappeared. Ravi stood frozen inside the shed. Then he shivered all over. Something had tickled the back of his neck. It took him a while to pick up the courage to lift his hand and explore. It was an insect—perhaps a spider—exploring him. He squashed it and wondered how many more creatures were watching him, waiting to reach out and touch him, the stranger.

There was nothing now. After standing in that position—his hand still on his neck, feeling the wet splodge of the squashed spider gradually dry—for minutes, hours, his legs began to tremble with the effort, the inaction. By now he could see enough in the dark to make out the large solid shapes of old wardrobes, broken buckets and bedsteads piled on top of each other around him. He recognized an old bathtub—patches of enamel glimmered at him and at last he lowered himself onto its edge.

Literary Analysis
Conflict What internal conflict does Ravi now experience?

He contemplated slipping out of the shed and into the fray. He wondered if it would not be better to be captured by Raghu and be returned to the milling crowd as long as he could be in the sun, the light, the free spaces of the garden and the familiarity of his brothers, sisters and cousins. It would be evening soon. Their games would become legitimate. The parents would sit out on the lawn on cane basket chairs and watch them as they tore around the garden or gathered in knots to share a loot of mulberries or black, teeth-splitting jamun from the garden trees. The gardener would fix the hosepipe to the water tap and water would fall lavishly through the air to the ground, soaking the dry yellow grass and the red gravel and arousing the sweet, the intoxicating scent of water on dry earth—that loveliest scent in the world. Ravi sniffed for a whiff of it. He half-rose from the bathtub, then heard the despairing scream of one of the girls as Raghu bore down upon her. There

was the sound of a crash, and of rolling about in the bushes, the shrubs, then screams and accusing sobs of, "I touched the den—" "You did not—" "I did—" "You liar, you did not" and then a fading away and silence again.

Ravi sat back on the harsh edge of the tub, deciding to hold out a bit longer. What fun if they were all found and caught—he alone left unconquered! He had never known that sensation. Nothing more wonderful had ever happened to him than being taken out by an uncle and bought a whole slab of chocolate all to himself, or being flung into the soda-man's pony cart and driven up to the gate by the friendly driver with the red beard and pointed ears. To defeat Raghu—that hirsute,[4] hoarse-voiced football champion—and to be the winner in a circle of older, bigger, luckier children—that would be thrilling beyond imagination. He hugged his knees together and smiled to himself almost shyly at the thought of so much victory, such laurels.[5] •

---

4. **hirsute** (hʉr´ sōōt´) *adj.* hairy.
5. **laurels** (lôr´ əlz) *n.* leaves of the laurel tree; worn in a crown as an ancient symbol of victory in a contest.

▲ **Critical Viewing**
Contrast the time of day in this image with the time of day at the beginning of the story. **[Contrast]**

Reading Check
What does Ravi hope happens?

There he sat smiling, knocking his heels against the bathtub, now and then getting up and going to the door to put his ear to the broad crack and listening for sounds of the game, the pursuer and the pursued, and then returning to his seat with the dogged determination of the true winner, a breaker of records, a champion.

It grew darker in the shed as the light at the door grew softer, fuzzier, turned to a kind of crumbling yellow pollen that turned to yellow fur, blue fur, gray fur. Evening. Twilight. The sound of water gushing, falling. The scent of earth receiving water, slaking its thirst in great gulps and releasing that green scent of freshness, coolness. Through the crack Ravi saw the long purple shadows of the shed and the garage lying still across the yard. Beyond that, the white walls of the house. The bougainvillea had lost its lividity, hung in dark bundles that quaked and twittered and seethed with masses of homing sparrows. The lawn was shut off from his view. Could he hear the children's voices? It seemed to him that he could. It seemed to him that he could hear them chanting, singing, laughing. But what about the game? What had happened? Could it be over? How could it when he was still not found?

It then occurred to him that he could have slipped out long ago, dashed across the yard to the veranda and touched the "den." It was necessary to do that to win. He had forgotten. He had only remembered the part of hiding and trying to elude the seeker. He had done that so successfully, his success had occupied him so wholly that he had quite forgotten that success had to be clinched by that final dash to victory and the ringing cry of "Den!"

With a whimper he burst through the crack, fell on his knees, got up and stumbled on stiff, benumbed legs across the shadowy yard, crying heartily by the time he reached the veranda so that when he flung himself at the white pillar and bawled, "Den! Den! Den!" his voice broke with rage and pity at the disgrace of it all and he felt himself flooded with tears and misery.

Out on the lawn, the children stopped chanting. They all turned to stare at him in amazement. Their faces were pale and triangular in the dusk. The trees and bushes around them stood inky and sepulchral,[6] spilling long shadows across them. They stared, wondering at his reappearance, his passion, his wild animal howling. Their mother rose from her basket chair and came toward him, worried, annoyed, saying, "Stop it, stop it, Ravi. Don't be a baby. Have you hurt yourself?" Seeing him attended to, the children went back to clasping their hands and chanting "The grass is green, the rose is red. . . . "

But Ravi would not let them. He tore himself out of his mother's grasp and pounded across the lawn into their midst, charging at them with his head lowered so that they scattered in surprise. "I won, I won, I won," he bawled, shaking his head so that the big tears flew. "Raghu didn't find me. I won, I won—"

It took them a minute to grasp what he was saying, even who he was. They had quite forgotten him. Raghu had found all the others long ago. There had been a fight about who was to be It next. It had been so fierce that their mother had emerged from her bath and made them change to another game. Then they had played another and another. Broken mulberries from the tree and eaten them. Helped the driver wash the car when their father returned from work. Helped the gardener water the beds till he roared at them and swore he would complain to their parents. The parents had come out, taken up their positions on the cane chairs. They had begun to play again, sing and chant. All this time no one had remembered Ravi. Having disappeared from the scene, he had disappeared from their minds. Clean.

"Don't be a fool," Raghu said roughly, pushing him aside, and even Mira said, "Stop howling, Ravi. If you want to play, you can

6. **sepulchral** (sə pul´ krəl) *adj.* of the tomb; gloomy.

Reading Skill
Cause and Effect
What effect had Ravi hoped for in hiding so well? What effect has it actually caused?

Reading Check
What rule of the game does Ravi forget?

stand at the end of the line," and she put him there very firmly.

The game proceeded. Two pairs of arms reached up and met in an arc. The children trooped under it again and again in a lugubrious[7] circle, ducking their heads and intoning

> "The grass is green,
> The rose is red;
> Remember me
> When I am dead, dead, dead, dead . . ."

And the arc of thin arms trembled in the twilight, and the heads were bowed so sadly, and their feet tramped to that melancholy refrain so mournfully, so helplessly, that Ravi could not bear it. He would not follow them, he would not be included in this funereal game. He had wanted victory and triumph—not a funeral. But he had been forgotten, left out and he would not join them now. The ignominy[8] of being forgotten—how could he face it? He felt his heart go heavy and ache inside him unbearably. He lay down full length on the damp grass, crushing his face into it, no longer crying, silenced by a terrible sense of his insignificance.

He would not follow them, he would not be included in this funereal game.

---

7. **lugubrious** (lə gōō´ brē əs) *adj.* very sad, especially in an exaggerated or ridiculous way.
8. **ignominy** (ig´ nə min´ ē) *n.* shame and dishonor.

Critical Thinking

Cite textual evidence to support your responses.

1. **Key Ideas and Details (a)** How does Ravi think it would feel to be "the winner in a circle of older, bigger, luckier children"? **(b) Draw Conclusions:** What do his feelings show about his view of the other children?

2. **Key Ideas and Details (a) Infer:** Why do the other children stop searching for Ravi? **(b) Draw Conclusions:** What do the other children think of Ravi? Give details from the story to support your answer.

3. **Key Ideas and Details (a) Interpret:** What bitter lesson does Ravi learn at the end of the story? **(b) Apply:** Do you think that Ravi's sense of his "insignificance" will remain strong? Explain.

4. **Integration of Knowledge and Ideas** When does Ravi discover that his ideas about reality are not true? How does this discovery affect him? *[Connect to the Big Question: Is there a difference between reality and truth?]*

Literary Analysis: Conflict and Resolution

© **1. Key Ideas and Details (a)** What is the main **external conflict** in this story? Explain. **(b)** What is the main **internal conflict** in the story? Explain.

© **2. Craft and Structure (a)** Identify a moment in the story that has great **suspense. (b)** Which conflict helps to create this suspense? Explain your thinking.

© **3. Craft and Structure (a)** Are Ravi's conflicts settled by the end of the story? Explain. **(b)** Describe an alternative **resolution** the story might have.

Reading Skill: Cause and Effect

4. (a) In your opinion, which **cause** sets the story's cause-and-effect chain in motion? **(b)** Identify two **effects** that depend on this event. Use a diagram like this one to record your answer.

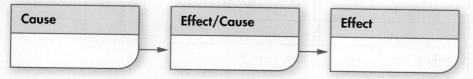

Cause	Effect/Cause	Effect

5. (a) Find a key detail about the shed that links to later events.
(b) Explain the causes and effects to which this detail is linked.

Vocabulary

© **Acquisition and Use** Answer each question. Explain your responses.

1. To inspire calm, would you paint a room in <u>livid</u> colors?

2. If a neutral person <u>intervened</u> in an argument, could it help the two sides resolve their differences?

3. Would an athlete sigh <u>dejectedly</u> after a game if she had won?

4. How many calls can you make on a <u>defunct</u> cell phone?

5. Is a lazy person likely to make a <u>dogged</u> effort?

6. Would you want to <u>elude</u> someone who has a gift for you?

Word Study Follow the directions for using a word that has the Latin root **-ven-**.

1. Use the verb *venture* to tell about a person who takes a risk.

2. Use the verb *convene* to tell about a group coming together.

Word Study

The **Latin root -ven-** means "come" or "go."

Apply It Explain how the root -ven- contributes to the meaning of these words. Consult a dictionary if necessary.

event
adventure
avenue

Integrated Language Skills

Contents of the Dead Man's Pocket • Games at Twilight

Conventions: Personal Pronouns

Pronouns are words that are used in place of nouns or of words that work together as a noun. The words that pronouns replace are called antecedents.

The most common pronouns are **personal pronouns.** First-person pronouns refer to the person speaking. Second-person pronouns refer to the person being spoken to. Third-person pronouns refer to the person, place, or thing being spoken about. Look at the chart below to see first-, second-, and third-person pronouns in both singular and plural forms.

Personal Pronouns	Singular	Plural
First Person	I, me, my, mine	we, us, our, ours
Second Person	you, your, yours	you, your, yours
Third Person	he, him, his, she, her, hers, it, its	they, them, their, theirs

Practice A Identify the personal pronoun or pronouns in each sentence. Then, indicate whether they are first-, second-, or third-person pronouns.

1. Tom loses his paper when the wind blows it out the window.
2. He goes out on the ledge to retrieve it.
3. "You will not die today," he tells himself.
4. Tom wishes Clare were there to save him.

Reading Application In "Contents of the Dead Man's Pocket," find one example of each type of personal pronoun. Write the sentences in which they appear, circling and labeling the pronouns.

Practice B Rewrite each sentence, using a pronoun for each underlined word or words. Then, explain how the effect of the sentence changes.

1. The children hope to elude Raghu.
2. Ravi has never won the game before.
3. Though Ravi is frightened in the shed, Ravi hides in the shed for a long time.
4. "Victory will be Ravi's," thought Ravi.

Writing Application Find three sentences in "Games at Twilight" in which you could replace a noun or nouns with a personal pronoun. Rewrite these sentences with the substituting pronoun. What effect do these changes have?

PH WRITING COACH Further instruction and practice are available in *Prentice Hall Writing Coach*.

Writing

 **Narrative Text** Both "Contents of the Dead Man's Pocket" and "Games at Twilight" end with **irony**—a strong contrast between what a character or reader expects and what actually happens. Write an **anecdote,** or brief story, that has an ironic ending.

- Pick a character, a conflict, an expected end, and a twist.
- As you draft, carefully choose details that set up the expected outcome, but include hints that could explain an unexpected one.
- Pace the presentation of actions to accommodate time or mood changes.
- Finally, resolve the conflict with a well-structured ironic ending.

Grammar Application As you write your anecdote, be aware of your use of personal pronouns. Be sure the antecedents are clear.

Writing Workshop: *Work in Progress*

Prewriting for Cause-and-Effect Essay For an essay you may write, list three *why* questions on topics that interest you. Note sources that might have information on each topic. Keep this Why List in your writing portfolio.

 **Common Core State Standards**

L.9-10.1; W.9-10.3; SL.9-10.1.a, SL.9-10.1.c, SL.9-10.1.d
[For the full wording of the standards, see page 114.]

Use this prewriting activity to prepare for the **Writing Workshop** on page 200.

Speaking and Listening

 **Comprehension and Collaboration** Form a **problem-solving group** with classmates to find solutions to either Tom's or Ravi's problem.

- Identify the problem the character faces.
- Generate questions about the problem to determine an appropriate approach.
- Discuss strategies, supporting your ideas with reasons and examples. Make sure every group member participates.
- Summarize and evaluate comments as the discussion unfolds. Respond to one another respectfully and ask for clarification of any points you do not understand.
- At the end of the discussion, formulate one or two possible conclusions.
- Produce concise notes summarizing main discussion points. Use the notes to explain the potential solutions to classmates.

Share your ideas with the rest of the class.

www.PHLitOnline.com
- Interactive graphic organizers
- Grammar tutorial
- Interactive journals

Ⓒ Leveled Texts

Build your skills and improve your comprehension of nonfiction with texts of increasing complexity.

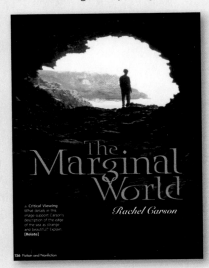

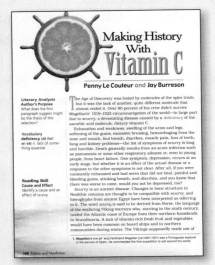

Read **"The Marginal World"** to learn about the enormous vitality of life at the edge of the sea.

Read **"Making History With Vitamin C"** to learn about the role vitamin C played in sea travel.

Ⓒ Common Core State Standards

Meet these standards with either **"The Marginal World"** (p. 156) or **"Making History with Vitamin C"** (p. 168).

Reading Informational Text

6. Determine an author's point of view or purpose in a text and analyze how an author uses rhetoric to advance that point of view or purpose. *(Literary Analysis: Author's Purpose)*

Writing

2.f. Provide a concluding statement or section that follows from the information or explanation presented. *(Research and Technology: Spreadsheet)*

9. Draw evidence from literary or informational texts to support analysis, reflection, and research. *(Writing: Proposal for a Documentary)*

Speaking and Listening

5. Make strategic use of digital media in presentations to enhance understanding of findings, reasoning, and evidence and to add interest. *(Research and Technology: Spreadsheet)*

Language

1.b. Use various types of phrases and clauses to convey specific meanings and add variety and interest to writing or presentations. *(Grammar: Relative Pronouns)*

5. Demonstrate understanding of figurative language, word relationships, and nuances in word meanings. *(Vocabulary: Antonyms)*

Literary Analysis: Author's Purpose

An **author's purpose** is his or her main reason for writing.

- An author may seek to inform, explain, persuade, describe, or entertain. He or she may also have more than one purpose.

- If an author's primary purpose is to inform or persuade, the author presents a **thesis**—the main point or claim about the subject. To explain and prove the thesis, the author supplies support: evidence, facts, and other details confirming the thesis.

- The author's purpose is also reflected in his or her rhetoric and style—the ways in which he or she uses language. Word choice, sentence length, and sentence complexity contribute to an author's style.

As you read, look for ways in which the authors achieve their purposes.

Reading Skill: Cause and Effect

A **cause** is an event, an action, or a situation that makes something happen. An **effect** is the event that results. To **analyze cause and effect,** determine which events cause which effects.

- **Reread** passages to determine whether some events in a sequence are the reason that other events happen.

- Look for cause-and-effect terms such as *because, as a result, for that reason,* and so on.

Using the Strategy: Sequence Chart

As you read, use a **sequence chart** like the one below to record connections between causes and effects.

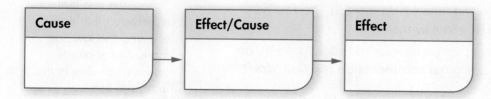

Cause	Effect/Cause	Effect

Is there a difference between *reality* and *truth*?

Writing About the Big Question

Successful scientists, such as Rachel Carson, seek to discover truths through scientific inquiry. Use these sentence starters to develop your ideas about the Big Question.

Reality is sometimes best discovered by _____.

Scientists can find **evidence** of the wonders that exist in nature by _____.

While You Read Decide what "truth" the author is expressing by describing real things in the tidal pool in an imaginative way.

Vocabulary

Read each word and its definition. Decide whether you know the word well, know it a little bit, or do not know it at all. After you read, see how your knowledge of each word has increased.

- **elusive** (ē loō′ siv) *adj.* hard to grasp mentally (p. 158) *The twisted plot made the movie too elusive for many viewers.* *elude v.*

- **mutable** (myoōt′ ə bəl) *adj.* changeable (p. 158) *His personality is mutable, and I never know how he will react.* *mutability n. mutation n.*

- **intertidal** (in′ tər tīd′′l) *adj.* pertaining to a shore zone bounded by the levels of low and high tide (p. 158) *When the tide is high, the intertidal zone is covered with water.* *tide n. tidal adj.*

- **ephemeral** (e fem′ ər əl) *adj.* short-lived (p. 160) *The fog was ephemeral; it lifted just after sunrise.*

- **marginal** (mär′ jə nəl) *adj.* at, on, or near the edge (p. 163) *The teacher wrote a few marginal comments on my final draft.* *margin n. marginally adv.*

- **manifestations** (man′ ə fes tā′ shənz) *n.* appearances; forms (p. 164) *Steam and ice are different manifestations of water.* *manifest v.*

Word Study

The **Latin prefix *inter-*** means "between" or "among."

In this selection, the author focuses on the part of the sea that is between the high tide and the low tide mark. Many plants and animals live in this **intertidal** zone.

Author of

The Marginal World

A lifelong lover of nature, Rachel Carson trained as a marine biologist at a time when few women pursued the study of the sea. She worked for the United States Fish and Wildlife Service and wrote poetically about nature in books like *The Sea Around Us,* which won the National Book Award.

A Crusade One day a friend wrote to complain that many birds had died on her property after it was sprayed for insects. Carson decided she had to show the world that people were damaging the environment with insecticides. In 1962, she published *Silent Spring,* a pioneering environmental work.

BACKGROUND FOR THE ESSAY
Tides

The pull of the moon's gravity is strongest on the part of Earth that is closest to the moon. As the Earth rotates, the area that is closest to the moon changes. The result is tides, the daily changes in the water level at the ocean shore. Each day, the edge of the shore is flooded and then exposed by the tides. Rachel Carson explores the creatures that live in this special zone.

DID YOU KNOW?
As a result of Carson's book *Silent Spring,* the insecticide DDT was eventually banned.

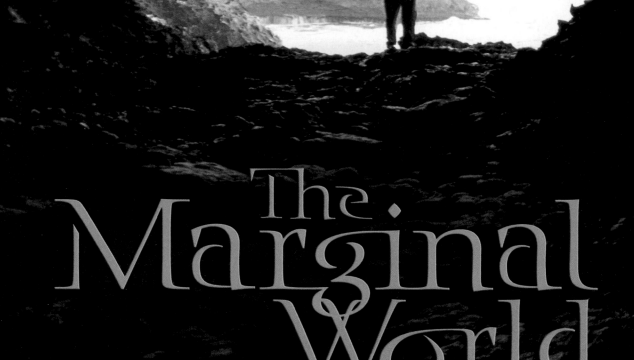

The Marginal World

Rachel Carson

▲ **Critical Viewing**
What details in this image support Carson's description of the edge of the sea as strange and beautiful? Explain. **[Relate]**

T he edge of the sea is a strange and beautiful place. All through the long history of Earth it has been an area of unrest where waves have broken heavily against the land, where the tides have pressed forward over the continents, receded, and then returned. For no two successive days is the shoreline precisely the same.

Vocabulary
elusive (ē lōō´ siv) *adj.* hard to grasp mentally
mutable (myōōt´ ə bəl) *adj.* changeable
intertidal (in tər tīd´ 'l) *adj.* pertaining to a shore zone bounded by the levels of low and high tide

Not only do the tides advance and retreat in their eternal rhythms, but the level of the sea itself is never at rest. It rises or falls as the glaciers melt or grow, as the floor of the deep ocean basins shifts under its increasing load of sediments, or as the earth's crust along the continental margins warps up or down in adjustment to strain and tension. Today a little more land may belong to the sea, tomorrow a little less. Always the edge of the sea remains an elusive and indefinable boundary.

The shore has a dual nature, changing with the swing of the tides, belonging now to the land, now to the sea. On the ebb tide it knows the harsh extremes of the land world, being exposed to heat and cold, to wind, to rain and drying sun. On the flood tide it is a water world, returning briefly to the relative stability of the open sea.

Only the most hardy and adaptable can survive in a region so mutable, yet the area between the tide lines is crowded with plants and animals. In this difficult world of the shore, life displays its enormous toughness and vitality by occupying almost every conceivable niche. Visibly, it carpets the intertidal rocks; or half hidden, it descends into fissures and crevices, or hides under boulders, or lurks in the wet gloom of sea caves. Invisibly, where the casual observer would say there is no life, it lies deep in the sand, in burrows and tubes and passageways. It tunnels into solid rock and bores into peat and clay. It encrusts weeds or drifting spars[1] or the hard, chitinous[2] shell of a lobster. It exists minutely, as the film of bacteria that spreads over a rock surface or a wharf piling; as spheres of protozoa, small as pinpricks, sparkling at the surface of the sea; and as Lilliputian[3] beings swimming through dark pools that lie between the grains of sand.

---

1. **spars** (spärz) *n.* pieces of wood or metal, such as masts or booms, for supporting sails on a ship.
2. **chitinous** (kī´ tin əs) *adj.* of the material that forms the tough outer covering of insects, crustaceans, and so on.
3. **Lilliputian** (lil´ ə pyōō´ shən) *adj.* tiny (from the name of the tiny people who inhabit Lilliput in *Gulliver's Travels* by Jonathan Swift).

The shore is an ancient world, for as long as there has been an earth and sea there has been this place of the meeting of land and water. Yet it is a world that keeps alive the sense of continuing creation and of the relentless drive of life. Each time that I enter it, I gain some new awareness of its beauty and its deeper meanings, sensing that intricate fabric of life by which one creature is linked with another, and each with its surroundings.

In my thoughts of the shore, one place stands apart for its revelation of exquisite beauty. It is a pool hidden within a cave that one can visit only rarely and briefly when the lowest of the year's low tides fall below it, and perhaps from that very fact it acquires some of its special beauty. Choosing such a tide, I hoped for a glimpse of the pool. The ebb was to fall early in the morning. I knew that if the wind held from the northwest and no interfering swell ran in from a distant storm the level of the sea should drop below the entrance to the pool. There had been sudden ominous showers in the night, with rain like handfuls of gravel flung on the roof. When I looked out into the early morning the sky was full of a gray dawn light but the sun had not yet risen. Water and air were pallid. Across the bay the moon was a luminous disc in the western sky, suspended above the dim line of distant shore—the full August moon, drawing the tide to the low, low levels of the threshold of the alien sea world. As I watched, a gull flew by, above the spruces. Its breast was rosy with the light of the unrisen sun. The day was, after all, to be fair.

Later, as I stood above the tide near the entrance to the pool, the promise of that rosy light was sustained. From the base of the steep wall of rock on which I stood, a moss-covered ledge jutted seaward

Reading Skill
Cause and Effect What effect does the changing region have on the creatures that live there?

The shore is an ancient world, for as long as there has been an earth and sea there has been this place of the meeting of land and water.

☑ Reading Check

Name three places creatures may live along the shore.

The Marginal World **159**

into deep water. In the surge at the rim of the ledge the dark fronds of oarweeds swayed, smooth and gleaming as leather. The projecting ledge was the path to the small hidden cave and its pool. Occasionally a swell, stronger than the rest, rolled smoothly over the rim and broke in foam against the cliff. But the intervals between such swells were long enough to admit me to the ledge and long enough for a glimpse of that fairy pool, so seldom and so briefly exposed.

And so I knelt on the wet carpet of sea moss and looked back into the dark cavern that held the pool in a shallow basin. The floor of the cave was only a few inches below the roof, and a mirror had been created in which all that grew on the ceiling was reflected in the still water below.

Literary Analysis
Author's Purpose
Which details indicate that the author's purpose here is to show the beauty of sea life?

Under water that was clear as glass the pool was carpeted with green sponge. Gray patches of sea squirts glistened on the ceiling and colonies of soft coral were a pale apricot color. In the moment when I looked into the cave a little elfin starfish hung down, suspended by the merest thread, perhaps by only a single tube foot. It reached down to touch its own reflection, so perfectly delineated that there might have been, not one starfish, but two. The beauty of the reflected images and of the limpid pool itself was the poignant beauty of things that are ephemeral, existing only until the sea should return to fill the little cave.

Vocabulary
ephemeral
(e fem´ ər əl) *adj.* short-lived

Whenever I go down into this magical zone of the low water of the spring tides, I look for the most delicately beautiful of all the shore's inhabitants—flowers that are not plant but animal, blooming on the threshold of the deeper sea. In that fairy cave I was not disappointed. Hanging from its roof were the pendent[4] flowers of the hydroid Tubularia, pale pink, fringed and delicate as the wind flower. Here were creatures so exquisitely fashioned that they seemed unreal, their beauty too fragile to exist in a world of crushing force. Yet every detail was functionally useful, every stalk and hydranth[5] and petallike tentacle fashioned for dealing with the realities of existence. I knew that they were merely waiting, in that moment of the tide's ebbing, for the return of the sea. Then in the rush of water, in the surge of surf and the pressure of the incoming tide, the delicate flower heads would stir with life. They would sway on their slender stalks, and their long tentacles would sweep the returning water, finding in it all that they needed for life.

And so in that enchanted place on the threshold

4. **pendent** (pen´ dənt) *adj.* dangling; hanging like a pendant on a necklace or charm.
5. **hydranth** (hī´ dranth´) *n.* one of the feeding individuals in a hydroid colony; the individuals are all attached at the base to a common tube.

of the sea the realities that possessed my mind were far from those of the land world I had left an hour before. In a different way the same sense of remoteness and of a world apart came to me in a twilight hour on a great beach on the coast of Georgia. I had come down after sunset and walked far out over sands that lay wet and gleaming, to the very edge of the retreating sea. Looking back across that immense flat, crossed by winding, waterfilled gullies and here and there holding shallow pools left by the tide, I was filled with awareness that this intertidal area, although abandoned briefly and rhythmically by the sea, is always reclaimed by the rising tide. There at the edge of low water the beach with its reminders of the land seemed far away. The only sounds were those of the wind and the sea and the birds. There was one sound of wind moving over water, and another of water sliding over the sand and tumbling down the faces of its own wave forms. The flats were astir with birds, and the voice of the willet[6] rang insistently. One of them stood at the edge of the water and gave its loud, urgent cry; an answer came from far up the beach and the two birds flew to join each other.

The flats took on a mysterious quality as dusk approached and the last evening light was reflected from the scattered pools and creeks. Then birds became only dark shadows, with no color discernible. Sanderlings[7] scurried across the beach like little ghosts, and here and there the darker forms of the willets stood out. Often I could come very close to them before they would start up in alarm—the sanderlings running, the willets flying up, crying. Black skimmers[8] flew along the ocean's edge silhouetted against the dull, metallic gleam, or they went flitting above the sand like large, dimly seen moths. Sometimes they "skimmed" the winding creeks of tidal water, where little spreading surface ripples marked the presence of small fish. •

The shore at night is a different world, in which the very darkness that hides the distractions of daylight brings into sharper focus the elemental realities. Once, exploring the night beach, I surprised a small ghost crab in the searching beam of my torch. He was lying in a pit he had dug just above the surf, as though watching the sea and waiting. The blackness of the night possessed water, air, and beach. It was the darkness of an older world, before

---

6. **willet** (wil´ it) *n.* shorebird, about 16 inches long, with a long bill, found by shallow shores and other waters of North and South America.
7. **sanderlings** (san´ dər liŋz) *n.* small, gray-and-white shorebirds.
8. **skimmers** (skim´ ərz) *n.* shorebirds with bladelike bills, which they use to skim the surface of the water for small fish and crustaceans.

▲ **Critical Viewing**
What features might make the skimmer particularly adept at catching fish? **[Interpret]**

☑ Reading Check

What main qualities does Carson associate with life along the seashore?

Spiral Review
Central Idea What meaning does Carson find in the ghost crab's existence at the edge of the sea?

Reading Skill
Cause and Effect Which details in this passage indicate cause-and-effect relationships?

Man. There was no sound but the all-enveloping, primeval sounds of wind blowing over water and sand, and of waves crashing on the beach. There was no other visible life—just one small crab near the sea. I have seen hundreds of ghost crabs in other settings, but suddenly I was filled with the odd sensation that for the first time I knew the creature in its own world—that I understood, as never before, the essence of its being. In that moment time was suspended; the world to which I belonged did not exist and I might have been an onlooker from outer space. The little crab alone with the sea became a symbol that stood for life itself—for the delicate, destructible, yet incredibly vital force that somehow holds its place amid the harsh realities of the inorganic world.

The sense of creation comes with memories of a southern coast, where the sea and the mangroves,[9] working together, are building a wilderness of thousands of small islands off the southwestern coast of Florida, separated from each other by a tortuous[10] pattern of bays, lagoons, and narrow waterways. I remember a winter day when the sky was blue and drenched with sunlight; though there was no wind one was conscious of flowing air like cold clear crystal. I had landed on the surf-washed tip of one of those islands, and then worked my way around to the sheltered bay side. There I found the tide far out, exposing the broad mud flat of a cove bordered by the mangroves with their twisted branches, their glossy leaves, and their long prop roots reaching down, grasping and holding the mud, building the land out a little more, then again a little more.

The mud flats were strewn with the shells of that small, exquisitely colored mollusk,[11] the rose tellin, looking like scattered

---

9. **mangroves** (maŋ´ grōvz) *n.* tropical trees that grow in swampy ground with spreading branches. The branches send down additional roots, forming a cluster of trunks for each tree.
10. **tortuous** (tôr´ chōō əs) *adj.* full of twists and turns.
11. **mollusk** (mäl´ əsk) *n.* one of a large group of soft-bodied animals with shells, including clams and snails.

petals of pink roses. There must have been a colony nearby, living buried just under the surface of the mud. At first the only creature visible was a small heron in gray and rusty plumage—a reddish egret that waded across the flat with the stealthy, hesitant movements of its kind. But other land creatures had been there, for a line of fresh tracks wound in and out among the mangrove roots, marking the path of a raccoon feeding on the oysters that gripped the supporting roots with projections from their shells. Soon I found the tracks of a shore bird, probably a sanderling, and followed them a little; then they turned toward the water and were lost, for the tide had erased them and made them as though they had never been.

Looking out over the cove I felt a strong sense of the interchangeability of land and sea in this marginal world of the shore, and of the links between the life of the two. There was also an awareness of the past and of the continuing flow of time, obliterating much that had gone before, as the sea had that morning washed away the tracks of the bird.

The sequence and meaning of the drift of time were quietly summarized in the existence of hundreds of small snails—the mangrove periwinkles—browsing on the branches and roots of the trees. Once their ancestors had been sea dwellers, bound to the salt waters by every tie of their life processes. Little by little over the thousands and millions of years the ties had been broken, the snails had adjusted themselves to life out of water, and now today they were living many feet above the tide to which they only occasionally returned. And perhaps, who could say how many ages hence, there would be in their descendants not even this gesture of remembrance for the sea.

The spiral shells of other snails—these quite minute—left winding tracks on the mud as they moved about in search of food. They were horn shells, and when I saw them I had a nostalgic

Vocabulary
marginal (mär´ jə nəl) *adj.* at, on, or near the edge

Reading Check

What realization does Carson come to during her encounter with the crab?

moment when I wished I might see what Audubon[12] saw, a century and more ago. For such little horn shells were the food of the flamingo, once so numerous on this coast, and when I half closed my eyes I could almost imagine a flock of these magnificent flame birds feeding in that cove, filling it with their color. It was a mere yesterday in the life of the earth that they were there; in nature, time and space are relative matters, perhaps most truly perceived subjectively in occasional flashes of insight, sparked by such a magical hour and place.

There is a common thread that links these scenes and memories—the spectacle of life in all its varied manifestations as it has appeared, evolved, and sometimes died out. Underlying the beauty of the spectacle there is meaning and significance. It is the elusiveness of that meaning that haunts us, that sends us again and again into the natural world where the key to the riddle is hidden. It sends us back to the edge of the sea, where the drama of life played its first scene on earth and perhaps even its prelude; where the forces of evolution are at work today, as they have been since the appearance of what we know as life; and where the spectacle of living creatures faced by the cosmic realities of their world is crystal clear.

12. **Audubon** (ôd´ ə bän´) John James Audubon (1785–1851), an ornithologist, a naturalist, and a painter famous for his paintings of North American birds.

Vocabulary
manifestations (man´ ə fes tā´ shənz) *n.* appearances; forms

Literary Analysis
Author's Purpose
In what way does this final paragraph relate to the thesis identified in the first paragraph?

Critical Thinking

Cite textual evidence to support your responses.

1. **Key Ideas and Details** **(a)** What does Carson mean when she says, "Only the most hardy and adaptable can survive in a place so mutable"? **(b)** How does she support this claim?

2. **Key Ideas and Details** **(a)** Name three creatures that Carson describes at length. **(b)** Explain how each demonstrates or symbolizes the power of life to endure in a harsh world.

3. **Key Ideas and Details** **Interpret:** What central idea, or lesson about life, does Carson draw from her observation of the "marginal world"? Support your answer with details from the work.

4. **Integration of Knowledge and Ideas** Carson wrote this essay about fifty years ago. Do you think she expresses a truth that is valid today? Explain your answer. *[Connect to the Big Question: Is there a difference between reality and truth?]*

Literary Analysis: Author's Purpose

1. Key Ideas and Details (a) Explain Carson's main **purpose. (b)** Write a brief, objective summary stating Carson's **thesis** and main points.

2. Key Ideas and Details (a) Use a diagram like this one to record details that **support** the author's thesis. Include at least five details. **(b)** Explain how each detail supports the thesis.

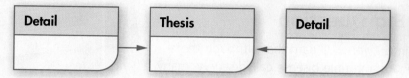

| Detail | → | Thesis | ← | Detail |

3. Key Ideas and Details Identify two examples that persuasively support Carson's thesis about the "spectacle of life." Explain your choices.

Reading Skill: Cause and Effect

4. Identify the **cause** of water level changes in the "marginal world."

5. (a) Name two **effects** on creatures in the tidal zone caused by the changing water level. **(b)** For each effect, explain how the changing water level brings it about.

Vocabulary

Acquisition and Use Antonyms are words that have opposite meanings, such as *day* and *night*. For each numbered word, choose the best antonym. Then, use each pair of antonyms in a sentence.

1. elusive: (a) unreal, (b) indefinable, (c) understandable

2. marginal: (a) buttery, (b) outside, (c) central

3. ephemeral: (a) enduring, (b) weak, (c) healthy

4. manifestations: (a) upheavals, (b) absences, (c) questions

5. mutable: (a) worried, (b) noisy, (c) permanent

6. intertidal: (a) watery, (b) deep-sea, (c) moving

Word Study Use the context of the sentences and what you know about the **Latin prefix *inter-*** to explain your answer to each question.

1. Would an *intermediate* course be very easy?

2. Does an *interstate* truck stay within the state?

Word Study

The **Latin prefix *inter-*** means "between" or "among."

Apply It Explain how the prefix *inter-* contributes to the meanings of these words. Consult a dictionary if necessary.

interfere
international
intermission

Is there a difference between *reality* and *truth?*

Writing About the Big Question

In "Making History With Vitamin C," you will learn that although there was proof that vitamin C prevented a terrible disease called scurvy, many people did not use this knowledge! Use this sentence starter to develop your ideas about the Big Question.

Even in the face of **evidence,** some people refuse to face the truth because _____.

While You Read Look for reasons that explain why many sailors ignored advice on avoiding scurvy.

Vocabulary

Read each word and its definition. Decide whether you know the word well, know it a little bit, or do not know it at all. After you read, see how your knowledge of each word has increased.

- **deficiency** (dē fish′ ən sē) *n.* lack of something essential (p. 168) *A calcium deficiency can cause weak bones. deficient adj.*

- **replenished** (ri plen′ isht) *v.* made complete or full again (p. 169) *She replenished the bowl with pretzels before it was empty. replenishment n. replenish v.*

- **incessant** (in ses′ ənt) *adj.* not stopping; constant (p. 169) *His incessant chatter gave me a headache. incessantly adv. cease v.*

- **alleviate** (ə lē′ vē āt′) *v.* lighten or relieve (p. 170) *The medicine should alleviate your headache and you will feel better. alleviation n.*

- **obscured** (əb skyo͞ord′) *v.* made dark; blocked from view; hid (p. 171) *The tall person sitting in front of me obscured my view of the screen. obscurely adv. obscurity n. obscure v., adj.*

- **compulsory** (kəm pul′ sə rē) *adj.* required, mandatory (p. 172) *It is compulsory that the hikers stay on the safe trail, or they must leave the park. compulsion n. compulsive adj. compel v.*

Word Study

The **Latin prefix ob-** means "against," "over," or "in front of."

In this selection, the authors explain that the use of ineffective remedies for scurvy may have **obscured,** or covered over, our understanding of the power of vitamin C.

Making History With Vitamin C

Penny Le Couteur (b. 1943)
Jay Burreson (b. 1942)

Authors of "Making History With Vitamin C"

Born in New Zealand, Penny Le Couteur (lə kōō′ tər) has taught chemistry for more than thirty years. Jay Burreson is also a chemist and runs a high-tech company. The two met in graduate school and have remained friends ever since.

Teaming Up The two friends decided to work together on a book "to tell the stories of the fascinating connections between chemical structures and historical episodes." Each chapter in this book, *Napoleon's Buttons*, examines a different molecule and its role in history.

Napoleon's Buttons takes its title from the chapter on tin. In extreme cold, tin will crumble. When the French leader Napoleon invaded Russia in 1812, his soldiers' tin buttons disintegrated in the freezing air. Many perished of cold in this defeat—some, perhaps, because of their tin buttons.

BACKGROUND FOR THE ESSAY

The Age of Discovery

In the 1300s, Europeans began sailing the known world in search of spices and other goods to trade. As navigation improved, they traveled farther. These adventurers risked shipwreck and losing their way. They also risked scurvy, the illness resulting from a lack of vitamin C, as "Making History With Vitamin C" explains.

DID YOU KNOW?

These two chemists propose that molecules helped shape history. For example, they claim that the pursuit of sugar led to the slave trade and the Industrial Revolution.

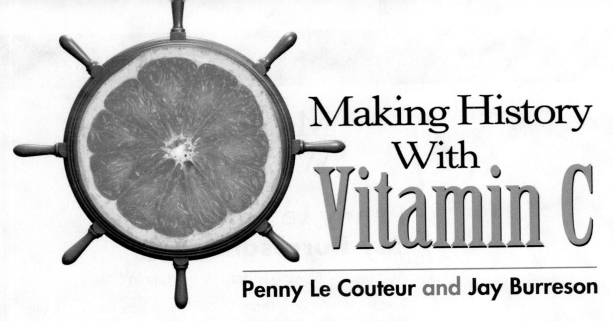

Making History With Vitamin C

Penny Le Couteur and Jay Burreson

Literary Analysis
Author's Purpose
What does the first paragraph suggest might be the thesis of this selection?

Vocabulary
deficiency (dē fish´ ən sē) *n.* lack of something essential

Reading Skill
Cause and Effect
Identify a cause and an effect of scurvy.

The Age of Discovery was fueled by molecules of the spice trade, but it was the lack of another, quite different molecule that almost ended it. Over 90 percent of his crew didn't survive Magellan's[1] 1519–1522 circumnavigation of the world—in large part due to scurvy, a devastating disease caused by a deficiency of the ascorbic acid molecule, dietary vitamin C.

Exhaustion and weakness, swelling of the arms and legs, softening of the gums, excessive bruising, hemorrhaging from the nose and mouth, foul breath, diarrhea, muscle pain, loss of teeth, lung and kidney problems—the list of symptoms of scurvy is long and horrible. Death generally results from an acute infection such as pneumonia or some other respiratory ailment or, even in young people, from heart failure. One symptom, depression, occurs at an early stage, but whether it is an effect of the actual disease or a response to the other symptoms is not clear. After all, if you were constantly exhausted and had sores that did not heal, painful and bleeding gums, stinking breath, and diarrhea, and you knew that there was worse to come, would you not be depressed, too?

Scurvy is an ancient disease. Changes in bone structure in Neolithic remains are thought to be compatible with scurvy, and hieroglyphs from ancient Egypt have been interpreted as referring to it. The word *scurvy* is said to be derived from Norse, the language of the seafaring Viking warriors who, starting in the ninth century, raided the Atlantic coast of Europe from their northern homelands in Scandinavia. A lack of vitamin-rich fresh fruit and vegetables would have been common on board ships and in northern communities during winter. The Vikings supposedly made use of

---

1. **Magellan's** (mə jel´ ənz) Ferdinand Magellan (ca. 1480–1521) was a Portuguese explorer in the service of Spain. He commanded the first expedition to sail around the world.

scurvy grass, a form of Arctic cress, on their way to America via Greenland. The first real descriptions of what was probably scurvy date from the Crusades in the thirteenth century. •

Scurvy at Sea

In the fourteenth and fifteenth centuries, as longer voyages were made possible by the development of more efficient sets of sails and fully rigged ships, scurvy became commonplace at sea. Oar-propelled galleys, such as those used by the Greeks and Romans, and the small sailing boats of Arab traders had stayed fairly close to the coast. These vessels were not seaworthy enough to withstand the rough waters and huge swells of the open ocean. Consequently, they would seldom venture far from the coast, and supplies could be replenished every few days or weeks. Access to fresh food on a regular basis meant that scurvy was seldom a major problem. But in the fifteenth century, long ocean voyages in large sailing ships heralded not only the Age of Discovery but also reliance on preserved food.

Bigger ships had to carry cargo and arms, a larger crew to handle the more complicated rigging and sails, and food and water for months at sea. An increase in the number of decks and men and the amount of supplies inevitably translated into cramped sleeping and living conditions for the crew, poor ventilation, and a subsequent increase in infectious diseases and respiratory conditions. Consumption (tuberculosis) and the "bloody flux" (a pernicious form of diarrhea) were common as, no doubt, were body and head lice, scabies, and other contagious skin conditions.

The standard sailor's food did nothing to improve his health. Two major factors dictated the seafaring diet. Firstly, aboard wooden ships it was extremely difficult to keep anything, including food, dry and mold free. Water was absorbed through wooden hulls, as the only water-proofing material available was pitch, a dark-colored, sticky resin obtained as a by-product of charcoal manufacture, applied to the outside of the hull. The inside of the hull, particularly where ventilation was poor, would have been extremely humid. Many accounts of sailing journeys describe incessant dampness, as mold and mildew grew on clothing, on leather boots and belts, on bedding, and on books. The standard sailor's fare was salted beef or pork and ship's biscuits known as hardtack, a mixture of flour and water without salt that was baked rock hard and used as a substitute for bread. Hardtack had the desirable characteristic of being relatively immune to mildew. It was baked to such a degree of hardness that it remained edible for

Vocabulary

replenished (ri plen´ isht) *v.* made complete or full again

incessant (in ses´ ənt) *adj.* not stopping; constant

Reading Check

What problems did the lack of vitamin C in sailors' diets cause?

As for Resolution, Robin Brooks, Private Collection

decades, but it was extremely difficult to bite into, especially for those whose gums were inflamed by the onset of scurvy. Typically, ship's biscuits were weevil-infested, a circumstance that was actually welcomed by sailors as the weevil holes increased porosity and made the biscuits easier to break and chew.

The second factor governing diet on wooden ships was the fear of fire. Wooden construction and liberal use of highly combustible pitch meant that constant diligence was necessary to prevent fire at sea. For this reason the only fire permitted on board was in the galley and then only in relatively calm weather. At the first sign of foul weather, galley fires would be extinguished until the storm was over. Cooking was often not possible for days at a time. Salted meat could not be simmered in water for the hours necessary to reduce its saltiness; nor could ship's biscuits be made at least somewhat palatable by dunking them in hot stew or broth.

At the outset of a voyage provisions would be taken on board: butter, cheese, vinegar, bread, dried peas, beer, and rum. The butter was soon rancid, the bread moldy, the dried peas weevil infested, the cheeses hard, and the beer sour. None of these items provided vitamin C, so signs of scurvy were often evident after as little as six weeks out of port. Was it any wonder that the navies of European countries had to resort to the press-gang[2] as a means of manning their ships?

Scurvy's toll on the lives and health of sailors is recorded in the logs of early voyages. By the time the Portuguese explorer Vasco da Gama sailed around the southern tip of Africa in 1497, one hundred of his 160-member crew had died from scurvy. Reports exist of the discovery of ships adrift at sea with entire crews dead from the disease. It is estimated that for centuries scurvy was responsible for more death at sea than all other causes; more than the combined total of naval battles, piracy, shipwrecks, and other illnesses. •

Astonishingly, preventives and remedies for scurvy during these years were known—but largely ignored. As early as the fifth century, the Chinese were growing fresh ginger in pots on board their ships. The idea that fresh fruit and vegetables could alleviate symptoms of scurvy was, no doubt, available to other countries in Southeast Asia in contact with Chinese trading vessels. It would have been passed on to the Dutch

Africa

Vocabulary
alleviate (ə lē′ vē āt′)
v. to lighten or relieve

---

2. press-gang men who round up other men to force them into naval or military service.

and been reported by them to other Europeans as, by 1601, the first fleet of the English East India Company is known to have collected oranges and lemons at Madagascar[3] on their way to the East. This small squadron of four ships was under the command of Captain James Lancaster, who carried bottled lemon juice with him on his flagship, the *Dragon*. Anyone who showed signs of scurvy was dosed with three teaspoons of lemon juice every morning. On arrival at the Cape of Good Hope, none of the men on board the *Dragon* was suffering from scurvy, but the toll on the other three ships was significant. Despite Lancaster's instructions and example, nearly a quarter of the total crew of this expedition died from scurvy—and not one of these deaths was on his flagship.

Some sixty-five years earlier the crew members on French explorer Jacques Cartier's second expedition to Newfoundland and Quebec were badly affected by a severe outbreak of scurvy, resulting in many deaths. An infusion of needles of the spruce tree, a remedy suggested by the local Indians, was tried with seemingly miraculous results. Almost overnight the symptoms were said to lessen and the disease rapidly disappeared. In 1593 Sir Richard Hawkins, an admiral of the British navy, claimed that within his own experience at least ten thousand men had died at sea from scurvy, but that lemon juice would have been an immediately effective cure.

There were even published accounts of successful treatments of scurvy. In 1617, John Woodall's *The Surgeon's Mate* described lemon juice as being prescribed for both cure and prevention. Eighty years later Dr. William Cockburn's *Sea Diseases, or the Treatise of their Nature, Cause and Cure* recommended fresh fruits and vegetables. Other suggestions such as vinegar, salt water, cinnamon, and whey were quite useless and may have obscured the correct action.

It was not until the middle of the following century that the effectiveness of citrus juice was proven in the first controlled clinical studies of scurvy. Although the numbers involved were very small, the conclusion was obvious. In 1747, James Lind, a Scottish naval surgeon at sea in the *Salisbury*, chose twelve of the crew suffering from scurvy for his experiment. He selected men whose symptoms seemed as similar as possible. He had them all eat the same diet: not the standard salted meat and hardtack, which these patients would have found very difficult to chew, but sweetened gruel, mutton broth, boiled biscuits, barley, sago, rice, raisins, currants, and wine. Lind added various supplements to this

---

3. **Madagascar** (mad´ ə gas´ kər) an island in the Indian Ocean off the southeast coast of Africa.

Literary Analysis
Author's Purpose
Which details in this paragraph support the idea that vitamin C is important?

Spiral Review
Central Idea The authors give a variety of examples of successful remedies for scurvy. What main idea do these examples support?

Vocabulary
obscured (əb skyoord´) *v.* made dark; blocked from view; hid

Reading Check
What factors limited sailors' diets on board a ship?

carbohydrate-based regime. Two of the sailors each received a quart of cider daily. Two others were dosed with vinegar, and another unfortunate pair received diluted elixir of vitriol (or sulfuric acid). Two more were required to drink half a pint of seawater daily, and another two were fed a concoction of nutmeg, garlic, mustard seed, gum myrrh, cream of tartar, and barley water. The lucky remaining pair was issued daily two oranges and one lemon each.

The results were sudden and visible and what we would expect with today's knowledge. Within six days the men who received the citrus fruit were fit for duty. Hopefully, the other ten sailors were then taken off their seawater, nutmeg, or sulfuric acid regimes and also supplied with lemons and oranges. Lind's results were published in *A Treatise of Scurvy,* but it was another forty years before the British navy began the compulsory issue of lemon juice.

If an effective treatment for scurvy was known, why wasn't it acted upon and used routinely? Sadly, the remedy for scurvy, though proven, seems to have not been recognized or believed. A widely held theory blamed scurvy on a diet of either too much salted meat or not enough fresh meat rather than a lack of fresh fruit and vegetables. Also, there was a logistical problem: it was difficult to keep fresh citrus fruit or juice for weeks at a time. Attempts were made to concentrate and preserve lemon juice, but such procedures were time consuming, costly, and perhaps not very effective, as we now know that vitamin C is easily destroyed by heat and light and that long-term storage reduces the amount in fruits and vegetables.

Because of expense and inconvenience, naval officers, physicians, the British admiralty, and shipowners could see no way of growing sufficient greens or citrus fruit on heavily manned vessels. Precious cargo space would have to be used for this purpose. Fresh or preserved citrus fruit was expensive, especially if it was to be allocated daily as a preventive measure. Economy and the profit margin ruled—although, in hindsight, it does seem that this was a false economy. Ships had to be manned above capacity to allow for a 30, 40 or even 50 percent death rate from scurvy. Even without a high death rate, the effectiveness of a crew suffering from scurvy would have been remarkably low. And then there was the humane factor—rarely considered during these centuries.

Vocabulary
compulsory (kəm pulʹ sə rē) *adj.* required, mandatory

Another element was the intransigence of the average crew. They were used to eating the standard ship's fare, and although they complained about the monotonous diet of salt meat and ship's biscuit when they were at sea, what they wanted in port was lots of fresh meat, fresh bread, cheese, butter, and good beer. Even if fresh fruit and vegetables were available, the majority of the crew would not have been interested in a quick stir-fry of tender crunchy greens. They wanted meat and more meat—boiled, stewed, or roasted. The officers, who generally came from a higher social class, where a wider and more varied diet was common, would have found eating fruit and vegetables in port to be normal and probably highly acceptable. It would not have been unusual for them to be interested in trying exotic new foodstuffs to be found in the locales where they made landfall. Tamarinds, limes, and other fruits high in vitamin C would have been used in the local cuisine that they, unlike the crew, might try. Scurvy was thus usually less of a problem among a ship's officers.

Reading Skill
Cause and Effect
In your own words, explain why the crew's food preferences were a cause of scurvy.

If an effective treatment for scurvy was known, why wasn't it acted upon and used routinely?

Cook: Hundreds—Scurvy: Nil

James Cook of the British Royal Navy was the first ship's captain to ensure that his crews remained scurvy free. Cook is sometimes associated with the discovery of antiscorbutics, as scurvy-curing foods are called, but his true achievement lay in the fact that he insisted on maintaining high levels of diet and hygiene aboard all his vessels. The result of his meticulous standards was an extraordinarily good level of health and a low mortality rate among his crew. Cook entered the navy at the relatively late age of twenty-seven, but his previous nine years of experience sailing as a merchant seaman mate in the North Sea and the Baltic, his intelligence, and his innate seamanship combined to ensure his rapid promotion within the naval ranks. His first experience with scurvy came aboard the *Pembroke,* in 1758, on his initial voyage across the Atlantic Ocean to Canada to challenge the French hold on the St. Lawrence River. Cook was alarmed by the devastation this common affliction caused and appalled that the deaths of so many crew, the dangerous reduction of working efficiency, and even actual loss of ships were generally accepted as inevitable.

His experience exploring and mapping around Nova Scotia, the Gulf of St. Lawrence, and Newfoundland and his accurate observations of the eclipse of the sun greatly impressed the Royal Society, a body founded in 1645 with the aim of "improving natural knowledge." He was granted command of the ship *Endeavour* and instructed to explore and chart the southern oceans, to investigate

Reading
Check
What was James Cook's contribution to maintaining sailors' health?

new plants and animals, and to make astronomical observations of the transit of planets across the sun.

Less known but nonetheless compelling reasons for this voyage and for Cook's subsequent later voyages were political. Taking possession in the name of Britain of already discovered lands; claiming of new lands still to be discovered, including Terra Australis Incognita, the great southern continent; and the hopes of finding a Northwest Passage were all on the minds of the admiralty. That Cook was able to complete so many of these objectives depended to a large degree on ascorbic acid.

Consider the scenario on June 10, 1770, when the *Endeavour* ran aground on coral of the Great Barrier Reef just south of present-day Cooktown, in northern Queensland, Australia. It was a near catastrophe. The ship had struck at high water; a resulting hole in the hull necessitated drastic measures. In order to lighten the ship, the entire crew heaved overboard everything that could be spared. For twenty-three hours straight they manned the pumps as seawater leaked inexorably into the hold, hauling desperately on cables and anchor in an attempt to plug the hole by fothering, a temporary method of mending a hole by drawing a heavy sail under the hull. Incredible effort, superb seamanship, and good fortune prevailed. The ship eventually slid off the reef and was beached for repairs. It had been a very close call—one that an exhausted, scurvy-inflicted crew could not have summoned the energy to answer.

A healthy, well-functioning crew was essential for Cook to accomplish what he did on his voyages. This fact was recognized by the Royal Society when it awarded him its highest honor, the Copley gold medal, not for his navigational feats but for his demonstration that scurvy was not an inevitable companion on long ocean voyages. Cook's methods were simple. He insisted on maintaining cleanliness throughout the ship, especially in the tight confines of the seamen's quarters. All hands were required to wash their clothes regularly, to air and dry their bedding when the weather permitted, to fumigate between decks, and in general to live up to the meaning of the term *shipshape*. When it was not possible to obtain the fresh fruit and vegetables he thought necessary for a balanced diet, he required that his men eat the sauerkraut he had included in the ship's provisions. Cook touched land at every

▲ Critical Viewing
Do the actions of James Cook described in the essay seem to fit with his personality as suggested by this painting? Explain.
[Connect]

possible opportunity to replenish stores and gather local grasses (celery grass, scurvy grass) or plants from which he brewed teas.

This diet was not at all popular with the crew, accustomed as they were to the standard seamen's fare and reluctant to try anything new. But Cook was adamant. He and his officers also adhered to this diet, and it was by his example, authority, and determination that his regimen was followed. There is no record that Cook had anyone flogged for refusing to eat sauerkraut or celery grass, but the crew knew the captain would not hesitate to prescribe the lash for opposing his rules. Cook also made use of a more subtle approach. He records that a "Sour Kroutt" prepared from local plants was initially made available only to the officers; within a week the lower ranks were clamoring for their share.

Success no doubt helped convince Cook's crew that their captain's strange obsession with what they ate was worthwhile. Cook never lost a single man to scurvy. On his first voyage of almost three years, one-third of his crew died after contracting malaria or dysentery in Batavia (now Jakarta) in the Dutch East Indies (now Indonesia). On his second voyage from 1772 to 1775,

Reading Skill
Cause and Effect
What factors caused Cook to be successful in the Navy?

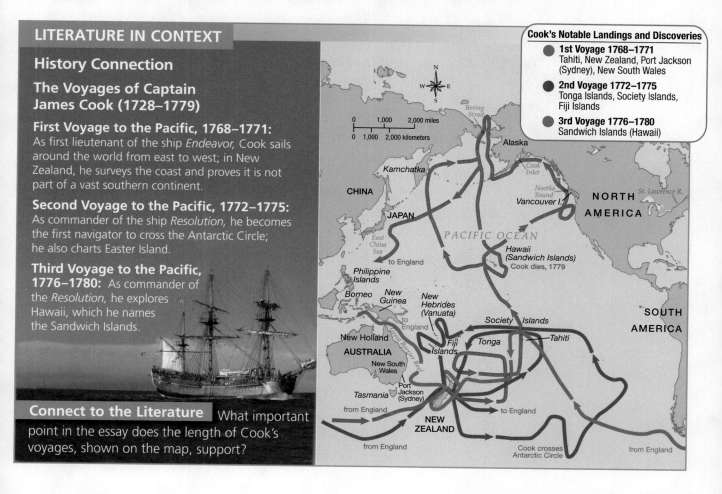

LITERATURE IN CONTEXT

History Connection

The Voyages of Captain James Cook (1728–1779)

First Voyage to the Pacific, 1768–1771: As first lieutenant of the ship *Endeavor,* Cook sails around the world from east to west; in New Zealand, he surveys the coast and proves it is not part of a vast southern continent.

Second Voyage to the Pacific, 1772–1775: As commander of the ship *Resolution,* he becomes the first navigator to cross the Antarctic Circle; he also charts Easter Island.

Third Voyage to the Pacific, 1776–1780: As commander of the *Resolution,* he explores Hawaii, which he names the Sandwich Islands.

Connect to the Literature What important point in the essay does the length of Cook's voyages, shown on the map, support?

Cook's Notable Landings and Discoveries

● **1st Voyage 1768–1771**
Tahiti, New Zealand, Port Jackson (Sydney), New South Wales

● **2nd Voyage 1772–1775**
Tonga Islands, Society Islands, Fiji Islands

● **3rd Voyage 1776–1780**
Sandwich Islands (Hawaii)

he lost one member of his crew to illness—but not to scurvy. Yet on that trip the crew of his companion vessel was badly affected by the problem. The commander, Tobias Furneaux, was severely reprimanded and instructed yet again by Cook on the need for preparation and administration of antiscorbutics. Thanks to vitamin C, the ascorbic acid molecule, Cook was able to compile an impressive list of accomplishments: the discovery of the Hawaiian Islands and the Great Barrier Reef, the first circumnavigation of New Zealand, the first charting of the coast of the Pacific Northwest, and first crossing of the Antarctic Circle.

Literary Analysis
Author's Purpose
What details about Captain Cook support the authors' thesis about the importance of vitamin C for the Age of Discovery?

Critical Thinking

Cite textual evidence to support your responses.

©1. Key Ideas and Details (a) Before the eighteenth century, what was included in a typical sailor's diet? **(b) Analyze Cause and Effect:** Using details from the selection, explain why this diet led to widespread illness.

©2. Key Ideas and Details (a) Connect: In what way did shipowners' concern about saving money add to the problem of scurvy? **(b) Interpret:** What does the delay in preventing and treating scurvy reveal about human nature?

©3. Key Ideas and Details Summarize: What was Captain James Cook's contribution to eliminating scurvy?

©4. Key Ideas and Details (a) Speculate: What modern food storage devices do you think would have been most helpful to navigators in the Age of Discovery? Why? **(b) Discuss:** Share your ideas with classmates in a group. Then, present your ideas to the class.

©5. Integration of Knowledge and Ideas What are some reasons sailors and ships' captains failed to see the truth about the effectiveness of vitamin C? *[Connect to the Big Question: Is there a difference between reality and truth?]*

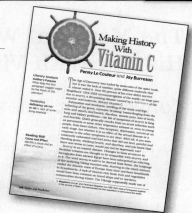

Literary Analysis: Author's Purpose

© **1. Key Ideas and Details (a)** What is the authors' main **purpose** for writing? Explain. **(b)** Write a brief, objective summary stating the authors' **thesis** and main points.

© **2. Key Ideas and Details (a)** Use a diagram like this one to record details that **support** the authors' thesis. Include at least five details. **(b)** Explain how each detail supports the thesis.

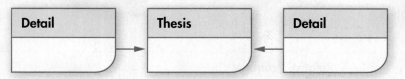

| Detail | | Thesis | | Detail |

© **3. Key Ideas and Details** Identify two examples that show how the writers' choice of words helps them accomplish their purpose.

Reading Skill: Cause and Effect

4. Why was scurvy such a problem during the Age of Discovery? Name two **causes** from the text.

5. Explain the **effect** Captain Cook's shipboard dietary policies had on his voyages in the 1770s.

Vocabulary

© **Acquisition and Use Antonyms** are words that have opposite meanings. For each numbered word below, choose the best antonym. Then, use each pair of antonyms in a sentence.

1. deficiency: (a) shortage, (b) obstacle, (c) surplus

2. replenished: (a) emptied, (b) forgave, (c) allowed

3. incessant: (a) failing, (b) brief, (c) filthy

4. alleviate: (a) oppose, (b) destroy, (c) increase

5. obscured: (a) revealed, (b) darkened, (c) pierced

6. compulsory: (a) necessary, (b) optional, (c) thoughtless

Word Study Use the context of the sentences and what you know about the **Latin prefix ob-** to explain your answer to each question.

1. Would a person who is *obstinate* be easily persuaded?

2. Would a lawyer *object* to a ruling in his favor?

Word Study

The **Latin prefix ob-** means "against," "over," or "in front of."

Apply It Explain how the prefix *ob-* contributes to the meanings of these words. Consult a dictionary if necessary.

obliterate
obstruction
obstacle

Integrated Language Skills

The Marginal World • Making History With Vitamin C

Conventions: Relative Pronouns

A **relative pronoun** is a pronoun that begins a subordinate clause. The relative pronoun relates the information in the clause to a noun or pronoun in the sentence.

Relative Pronouns				
that	**which**	**who**	**whom**	**whose**
This is the shell *that* my brother gave me.	Cook insisted his crew drink lemon juice, *which* saved many lives.	Carson is the author *who* ignited environmental awareness in the public.	Cook was the captain with *whom* men preferred to serve.	Captains *whose* crews suffered from scurvy could have saved their men with lemon juice.

Practice A Copy the sentences. Circle the relative pronoun. Underline the noun and the clause that are connected by this relative pronoun.

1. Low tides expose the myriad of life that exists at the shore's edge.

2. A delicate starfish, whose reflection appears in the water, clings to the roof of the cave.

3. The little crab, which was scurrying near the water, was the only visible sign of life.

4. Creatures whose ancestors inhabited the sea for millions of years still exist in tidal waters.

Ⓒ **Reading Application** In "The Marginal World," find two sentences that contain a relative pronoun. Write the relative pronouns and the nouns to which the relative pronouns relate.

Practice B Complete the following sentences using a relative pronoun and a clause that relates to the noun.

1. Vitamin C is an important nutrient _____.

2. Early sailors, _____, often died from scurvy.

3. Victims of scurvy, _____, could have been saved by drinking lemon juice.

4. Captain Cook was a man _____.

Ⓒ **Writing Application** Using this sentence as a model, write two sentences with relative pronouns and a clause that relates to the noun: *Eating oranges, which contain vitamin C, prevents scurvy.*

PH **WRITING COACH** | Further instruction and practice are available in *Prentice Hall Writing Coach*.

Writing

Explanatory Text Both of these essays address topics that could be presented well in a film version. Write a **proposal for a documentary** on life at the edge of the sea or on Cook's efforts to prevent scurvy. First, reread the essay you chose for ideas. Then, write your own essay describing the documentary you propose to create. Include these elements:

- The main impression you want to convey
- Details about objects to be filmed and the places to be filmed
- Summaries of the actions and quotations to use from the essay
- Topics for comment by the narrator and actors

Grammar Application Check your proposal to make sure you have used relative pronouns correctly in any clauses that include them.

Writing Workshop: *Work in Progress*

Prewriting for Cause and Effect Look at the Why List in your writing portfolio and identify a question to research. While researching, note the progression of causes and effects that produced the final result. Keep these Cause-Effect Notes in your writing portfolio.

Research and Technology

Build and Present Knowledge Use computer software to create a **spreadsheet** based on one of the selections you read.

- If you read "The Marginal World," create a wildlife spreadsheet about living things you observe in your area. Include dates, times, and your observations. At the end of a week, write a conclusion about your environment. Compare your observations to Carson's.
- If you read "Making History With Vitamin C," create a personal diet spreadsheet. For one week, keep track of what you eat at each meal. Then, write a conclusion in which you compare your diet to that of typical sailors in Cook's day.

Use these suggestions when working on the assignment.

- Record many details for each observation. For example, for a wildlife spreadsheet, include detailed descriptions of all the plants, animals, and insects you observe. For a diet spreadsheet, record the ingredients of packaged foods.
- Review all your data carefully. Then, present your spreadsheet and conclusions to your class. Make sure that all of your conclusions flow directly from the data you gathered and that the connections are clear.

Common Core State Standards

L.9-10.1.b; W.9-10.2.f, W.9-10.9; SL.9-10.5
[For the full wording of the standards, see page 152.]

Use this prewriting activity to prepare for the **Writing Workshop** on page 200.

PHLit Online!
www.PHLitOnline.com

- Interactive graphic organizers
- Grammar tutorial
- Interactive journals

Test Practice: Reading

Cause and Effect

Fiction Selection

Directions: *Read the selection. Then, answer the questions.*

"Ah-choo!" Lisa heard her brother George sneezing. He had been ill for two days, and Lisa could feel her throat getting itchy. "I knew I'd catch his cold," Lisa told her friend Keisha. "If he has a virus, I get it." Still, Lisa knew she could not miss school. "I need to review for the geometry exam tomorrow," she told her mother. "Keisha and I are studying after class."

"Okay, but be home early. If you don't get more rest, you will catch George's cold," her mother replied.

The next morning Lisa woke up with a throbbing headache. Her throat ached and she began sneezing and coughing.

"It looks like you're staying home today," her mother said. "You'll just have to miss the exam and make it up later."

That evening, Lisa phoned Keisha. "How was the exam?" asked Lisa.

"I didn't go to school," Keisha replied, wheezing. "I have a cold, too."

"Great!" said Lisa. "We'll both spend the weekend in bed and then have to make up the exam on Monday. And all because of George!"

1. Which event occurs first?

   A. Lisa studies with Keisha for the exam.
   B. George has a cold.
   C. Lisa has a geometry exam.
   D. Lisa misses school.

2. What does Lisa suspect is causing her itchy throat?

   A. anxiety about her geometry exam
   B. lack of rest.
   C. an oncoming cold
   D. a sore throat

3. Which event is both a cause and an effect?

   A. Lisa catches a cold.
   B. George has a cold.
   C. Lisa makes up a math exam.
   D. Keisha spends the weekend in bed.

4. Which effect of the cold do both Lisa and Keisha experience?

   A. a sick brother
   B. a trip to the doctor
   C. a day home from school
   D. a failed geometry exam

Writing for Assessment

In a paragraph, describe the chain of events that occurs in this passage. What additional effects might George's cold have on his school, community, or family?

Nonfiction Selection

Directions: *Read the selection. Then, answer the questions.*

Most people occasionally suffer from the common cold. Although a cold is rarely serious, it can be uncomfortable and downright annoying. The first signs of a cold are a runny nose and sneezing, which are often followed by coughing, headache, fatigue, sore throat, and sometimes chills. Usually, no fever is involved.

Colds are caused by viruses. As many as 200 different viruses can cause colds. Colds are passed from one person to another. In fact, people can be carriers of cold viruses without having cold symptoms themselves. It takes only a short time to catch a cold from another person—as little as one to four days. Many colds are contracted in the fall, and cold epidemics can continue throughout the winter months. Scientists believe most colds occur during the cooler months because people spend more time indoors and have closer contact with people carrying cold viruses. No medicine is available that can cure the cold. Cold medicines simply help relieve cold symptoms. The most common treatment is resting and drinking fluids.

1. Which of the following is the direct cause of a cold?

   A. contact with a sick person
   B. staying indoors
   C. a virus
   D. cold weather

2. Which of the following is an effect of a cold?

   A. a high fever
   B. being confined to bed
   C. headache and tiredness
   D. drinking more fluids

3. According to the selection, which of the following causes people to catch colds?

   A. change of seasons
   B. contact with someone carrying the cold virus
   C. being outside in cold weather
   D. sneezing and coughing

4. Which of the following helps cure a cold?

   A. getting plenty of rest
   B. taking cold medicine
   C. staying indoors
   D. none of the above

Writing for Assessment

Connecting Across Texts

Lisa gets angry with her brother when she misses a geometry exam. In a paragraph, explain whether she is right to feel this way. Use details from each passage to support your response.

www.PHLitOnline.com
- Online practice
- Instant feedback

Reading for Information

Analyzing Functional and Expository Texts

Web Site

Primary Source

Common Core State Standards

Reading Informational Text
6. Determine an author's point of view or purpose in a text.

Language
4.b. Identify and correctly use patterns of word changes that indicate different meanings or parts of speech.
6. Acquire and use accurately general academic and domain-specific words and phrases, sufficient for reading, writing, speaking, and listening at the college and career readiness level; demonstrate independence in gathering vocabulary knowledge when considering a word or phrase important to comprehension or expression.

Writing
2. Write informative/explanatory texts to examine and convey complex ideas, concepts, and information clearly and accurately through the effective selection, organization, and analysis of content. *(Timed Writing)*

Reading Skill: Evaluate Sources

When researching a topic, remember that not all the material you find will be completely accurate. Before you use material from a Web site or a primary source, **analyze the credibility** of the source. Do this by evaluating the text's validity and reliability. Use the following checklist.

Checklist for Evaluating Credibility of Sources

- ☐ Consider the author or sponsor. Might the source be biased?
- ☐ Check the information against a source you know is reliable.
- ☐ Check the date of the document or the "last updated" field on the Web page.
- ☐ For Web sites, check the ending of the URL.
  - Educational and governmental (".edu" and ".gov"): generally reliable
  - Nonprofit (".org"): may be unbiased, or may present only a specific point of view
  - Businesses and individuals (".com"): information of varying quality

Content-Area Vocabulary

These words appear in the selections that follow. You may also encounter them in other content-area texts.

- **excavate** (ek´ skə vāt´) *v.* create a hole by digging
- **millennia** (mə len´ ē ə) *n.* periods that each consist of one thousand years
- **vessels** (ves´ əlz) *n.* containers, often used to hold liquid, such as bowls or pots

The URL, or address, of the Web site, appears in the browser here. Check the ending of the URL to evaluate the site's credibility.

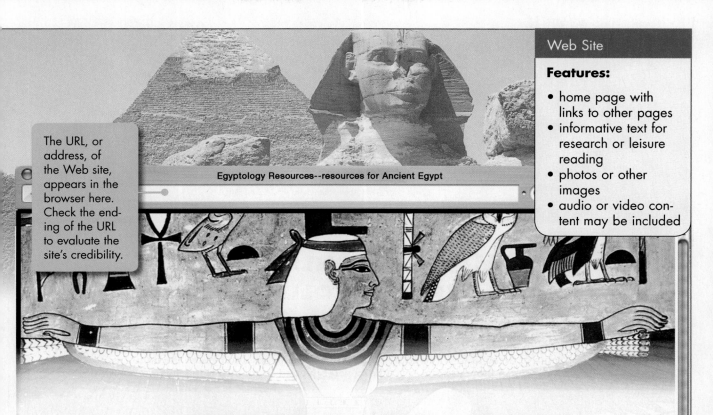

Egyptology Resources--resources for Ancient Egypt

EGYPTOLOGY RESOURCES

Popular local items

News & Gossip

Announcements

Bulletin Board

E-mail Addresses

Tomb of Sennefen

Beinlich Wordlist

Wilbour Library Acquisitions

Online Publications

Commercial Items

Server statistics

The first Egyptology site on the web

This page is set up with the kind assistance of the Newton Institute in the University of Cambridge to provide a World Wide Web resource for Egyptological information. The pages are not a publication of the Newton Institute, and all matters concerning them (e.g., comments, criticisms, and suggestions for items to include) should be sent to Nigel Strudwick.

Click here for guidelines on the format of material.

Click here for site history.

Main pages

Essential Resources

Institutions

Museums

Digs

Publishers, Booksellers

Journals, Magazines

Organizations, Societies

Interesting Egypt Pages

Personal Egypt Pages

Other Resources of Interest

Information on the individual who maintains this Web site is available by clicking his name. This information will help you evaluate the credibility of the site.

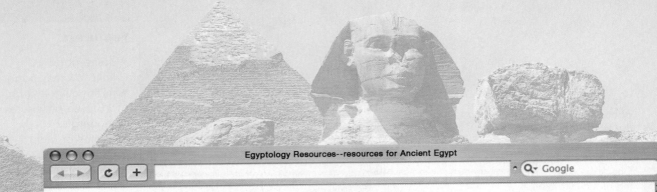

Q▾ Google

MUSEUMS ONLINE WITH EGYPTIAN COLLECTIONS

Many museums, of course, have WWW pages now. I have tried to select some of those which have more specific information on their Egyptian Collections, but I do also include the general Web presences of major museums with relevant material. Some of these links often go directly to the Egypt pages and bypass the home page. A more general set of links will be found in the ABZU indexes.

Each of these links brings users to the Web site of a museum that has Egyptian artifacts in its collection. Evaluate the credibility of any site you visit.

Egypt
- The Egyptian Museum, Cairo
- The Coptic Museum, Cairo

North America
- Museum of Fine Arts, Boston
- Metropolitan Museum, New York
- Michael C. Carlos Museum, Emory University, Atlanta
- Brooklyn Museum
- Oriental Institute, University of Chicago

Europe
- The British Museum, London COMPASS Project
- The Louvre, Paris
- Musées royaux d'art et d'art historie, Brussels
- Museo Egizio, Torino
- Agyptisches Museum und Papyrussammlung Berlin-Charlottenburg
- Allard Pierson Museum
- Carsten Niebuhr Institute, University of Copenhagen, Papyrus Collection

Back to Egyptology Resources home page

Interactive Dig

Primary Source

Features:

- informative text used for reference or research
- first-person perspective
- accounts of events given by an active participant or an eyewitness

Narmer's Temple: Week 1

by Renée Friedman

After a hiatus of 13 years, we've returned to the Predynastic Temple at Hierakonpolis. Dating to around 3500 B.C., it is Egypt's oldest. Excavations here in 1985, 1986–1987, and 1989 had revealed about half of a large (presumably) oval courtyard walled by a wooden fence, onto which fronted a main shrine with a façade composed of four large wooden pillars—now marked by four enormous postholes.

Our first order of business was to remove the sand that had accumulated over the **millennia** over the unexcavated portion of the courtyard floor in order to determine the full architectural layout of the vast complex. Of special interest was the area between the entrance to the compound and the entrance to the main shrine, as this might be where important things happened. With over 80cm of sand and debris covering this possible processional corridor, it is no wonder that the area was not cleared earlier. The volume of debris meant a lot of work, but it also, we hope, meant that the temple deposits below had a good chance of being undisturbed.

We got to work immediately. With Ramadan coming up, it was a race against time. We **excavate** with local workmen, who have worked with us for over 30 years. They come from the nearby village and ride their donkeys to work each day, since we can provide miles of free parking. Michael Hoffman, who directed the excavations, began training the villagers in 1969 and working for the expedition has become a family tradition. Now we are working with the sons and grandsons of the original crew, who have worked their way up from basket boy to valued excavator. They are not only skilled, but also interested and proud of their own local heritage. Trained to note the slightest change in the soil, they can point out areas of compaction, or texture differences, disturbance, etc. In a sandy site, where excavation balks are hard to maintain, and a prehistoric site, where detailed observation is critical, they make our work possible.

> The dig is described from a first-person perspective, which suggests the information is reliable.

Interactive Dig

The author demonstrates reliability by describing in detail how objects were found.

Our workers are very good-natured. During the first week, the plan was to remove as much of the windblown sand and mixed debris as possible. This made for somewhat boring work as once we reached a level that looked good, I made them stop, and move over to the next square (we dig in 10×10m squares divided into 5×5m subunits) and begin again, saving the detailed work, brush work, sieving, and other less arduous tasks for the fasting days of Ramadan.

In the first six digging days, working from six in the morning until noon, we managed to clear seven 5×5m squares of about 50cm of sand to layers that look promising. The sand over the courtyard floor, however, was not entirely devoid of interesting things. We found a number of fragments of once beautifully polished stone **vessels** made of exotic stones imported from the Red Sea hills—diorite, basalt, alabaster, marble. We also recovered a crescent drill of flint used in the manufacture of these stone vessels. It probably originated from the workshops that surround the temple complex. Microdrills for boring out beads, and fragments of carefully knapped bifacial knives also turned up. The fine micro-retouch on the edge of what may have been a lance is amazing.

These objects, however, are no longer in their original place because of fertilizer digging. In the early part of the last century and before, farmers mined the rich soil of archaeological deposits as fertilizer for their fields, which is called *sebakh* in Arabic. The decayed organic debris of ancient sites provided a supply of nitrogen, necessary for the crops and before chemical fertilizer was easily available, mining the ancient levels was the only alternative. As a result, the low desert at Hierakonpolis looks like the valleys of the moon, with sand-filled pits surrounded by mountains of discarded predynastic artifacts that were of no interest to the farmers, who only wanted the midden in which they were found. Piles of potsherds, animal bone, grinding stones, lithics, and assorted other wonderful things cover the site—over two square miles. It was years before I ever looked up while walking to work here—the wealth of goodies on the ground was riveting and after a good rain (like the one we had on our very first day this season!) or a major sand storm, new wonders can always be found.

The photo and caption indicate that the author was present for the work being described.

The men at work removing the sand.

Comparing Functional and Expository Texts

1. Key Ideas and Details (a) Compare and contrast the possible disadvantages of using Web sites and primary sources for research. **(b)** Under what circumstances would you use either of these two sources?

Content-Area Vocabulary

2. (a) Explain how each of the following words is formed by adding a suffix to *excavate* and how the suffix changes the base word's meaning and part of speech: *excavation, excavator.* **(b)** Use each word in a sentence that shows its meaning.

Timed Writing

Explanatory Text: Essay

> **Format**
> The prompt calls for a brief essay. Therefore, you will need to present and support your ideas in three to five paragraphs.

Write a brief essay in which you evaluate the credibility of the Web site and the primary source document as sources of information on ancient Egypt. Note the features or techniques that make each source seem credible, as well as improvements that would make each source seem more credible. (20 minutes)

> **Academic Vocabulary**
> When you *evaluate* the credibility of a source, you analyze and make judgments about the source's quality and reliability.

5-Minute Planner

Complete these steps before you begin to write:

1. Read the prompt carefully.

2. Review the Web site and primary source document. Make notes about clues to each author's credibility and the features and techniques that make each source seem more credible. **TIP** Credibility of primary sources written in the first person often depends upon the author's purpose for writing or biases the author may have.

3. Note what elements of these two sources might be improved or what could be added to improve their credibility. Refer to your notes as you draft your essay.

Comparing Literary Works

Comparing Irony and Paradox

Irony is the effect created when a writer sets up contrasts between readers' or characters' expectations and reality. Irony may involve a discrepancy between appearance and reality, between expectation and outcome, or between stated meaning and intended meaning. A writer's use of irony often adds emotional intensity to a story or creates a sense of surprise when readers learn that a situation or a character has a different truth.

There are three main types of irony:

- In **situational irony,** an event directly contradicts strong expectations.

  Example: In a story in which two companions hide from an enemy, one of the two turns out to be an enemy operative.

- In **verbal irony,** a character says the opposite of what he or she really means.

  Example: After the enemy operative gives up his companion, the one betrayed says, "I'm glad I trusted you."

- In **dramatic irony,** the reader knows something a character does not.

  Example: During the whole story, readers know that the operative is actually a long-lost brother of the one he betrays—but neither of the characters are aware of this.

In addition to irony, writers may use **paradox**—a statement that seems contradictory but actually reveals a deeper truth. For example, consider the following statement: "One must sometimes be cruel to be kind." At first, the statement seems impossible—how can cruelty be kind? However, the statement makes sense when you consider that seemingly unkind words or actions can actually help someone face a painful truth or develop stronger skills.

In "Like the Sun" and "The Open Window," the writers use irony and paradox to explore contradictory ideas of honesty and deceit. As you read, use a diagram like the one shown to note examples of irony and paradox in these stories.

Common Core State Standards

Reading Literature

5. Analyze how an author's choices concerning how to structure a text, order events within it, and manipulate time create such effects as mystery, tension, or surprise.

Writing

2. Write informative/explanatory texts to examine and convey complex ideas, concepts, and information clearly and accurately through the effective selection, organization, and analysis of content. *(Timed Writing)*

2.b. Develop the topic with well-chosen, relevant, and sufficient facts; extended definitions, concrete details, quotations, or other information; and examples appropriate to the audience's knowledge of the topic. *(Timed Writing)*

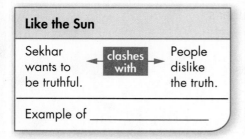

Like the Sun

| Sekhar wants to be truthful. | → clashes with → | People dislike the truth. |

Example of _____

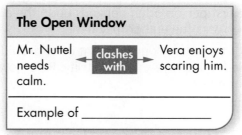

The Open Window

| Mr. Nuttel needs calm. | → clashes with → | Vera enjoys scaring him. |

Example of _____

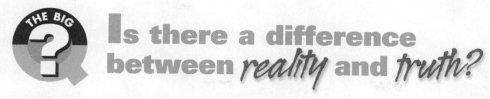

Is there a difference between *reality* and *truth?*

Writing About the Big Question

In these stories, characters plan reasonable goals, but the outcomes are far from what they expect. Think about a time when things did not turn out as you had planned. Use these sentence starters to develop your ideas.

My **perception** of the situation was that _____.

In **reality,** though, _____.

Meet the Authors

R. K. Narayan (1906–2001)

Author of "Like the Sun"

R. K. Narayan spun his tales from the stuff of real life. His hometown of Mysore in southern India probably served as the basis for Malgudi, the setting for much of his fiction. Like the main character in "Like the Sun," Narayan's father was a schoolteacher, and Narayan studied music, a key element of the story, as a youth.

Crossing Languages A native Tamil speaker, Narayan wrote his novels and stories in English, a second language to many Indians. In addition to fiction, he wrote a memoir, *My Days,* and a noted English translation of the ancient Indian epic the *Mahabharata.*

Saki (1870–1916)

Author of "The Open Window"

Saki is the pen name of Hector Hugh Munro. Born to British parents in Burma (now Myanmar), Saki lived in England for most of his life. He began his career writing political satires for newspapers and later turned to fiction.

Humor and Wit Today, Saki is best known for his witty, sometimes cruel short stories, many of which feature humorous surprise endings. Many readers consider "The Open Window" to be one of the best examples of Saki's style.

Like the Sun

R.K. Narayan

Truth,

Sekhar reflected, is like the sun. I suppose no human being can ever look it straight in the face without blinking or being dazed. He realized that, morning till night, the essence of human relationships consisted in tempering truth so that it might not shock. This day he set apart as a unique day—at least one day in the year we must give and take absolute Truth whatever may happen. Otherwise life is not worth living. The day ahead seemed to him full of possibilities. He told no one of his experiment. It was a quiet resolve, a secret pact between him and eternity.

The very first test came while his wife served him his morning meal. He showed hesitation over a tidbit, which she had thought was her culinary masterpiece. She asked, "Why, isn't it good?" At other times he would have said, considering her feelings in the matter, "I feel full up, that's all." But today he said, "It isn't good. I'm unable to swallow it." He saw her wince and said to himself, Can't be helped. Truth is like the sun.

Vocabulary
tempering (tem´ pər iŋ) *n.* changing to make more suitable, usually by mixing with something

Spiral Review
Theme Based on the first two paragraphs, what thematic ideas do you think the author is developing? Explain.

He always struck me as a mean and selfish brute.

His next trial was in the common room when one of his colleagues came up and said, "Did you hear of the death of so-and-so? Don't you think it a pity?" "No," Sekhar answered. "He was such a fine man—" the other began. But Sekhar cut him short with: "Far from it. He always struck me as a mean and selfish brute."

During the last period when he was teaching geography for Third Form A,[1] Sekhar received a note from the headmaster: "Please see me before you go home." Sekhar said to himself: It must be about these horrible test papers. A hundred papers in the boys' scrawls; he had shirked this work for weeks, feeling all the time as if a sword were hanging over his head. The bell rang, and the boys burst out of the class.

Sekhar paused for a moment outside the headmaster's room to button up his coat; that was another subject the headmaster always sermonized about.

He stepped in with a very polite "Good evening, sir."

The headmaster looked up at him in a very friendly manner and asked, "Are you free this evening?"

Sekhar replied, "Just some outing which I have promised the children at home."

"Well, you can take them out another day. Come home with me now."

"Oh . . . yes, sir, certainly. . ." And then he added timidly, "anything special, sir?"

"Yes," replied the headmaster, smiling to himself. . . ."You didn't know my weakness for music?"

"Oh, yes, sir. . ."

"I've been learning and practicing secretly, and now I want you to hear me this evening. I've engaged a drummer and a violinist to accompany me—this is the first time I'm doing it full-dress, and I want your opinion. I know it will be valuable."

Sekhar's taste in music was well known. He was one of the most dreaded music critics in the town. But he never anticipated his musical inclinations would lead him to this trial. . . . "Rather a surprise for you, isn't it?" asked the headmaster. "I've spent a fortune on it behind closed doors. . . ."

They started for the headmaster's house.

"God hasn't given me a child, but at least let him not deny me the consolation of music," the headmaster said, pathetically, as they walked. He incessantly chattered about music: how he began one day out of sheer boredom; how his teacher at first laughed at him and then gave him hope; how his ambition in life was to forget himself in music.

At home the headmaster proved very ingratiating. He sat Sekhar on a red silk carpet, set before him several dishes of delicacies, and

---

Literary Analysis
Irony and Paradox
Why is it ironic that this is the day the headmaster will ask for Sekhar's opinion about his musical abilities?

Vocabulary
ingratiating (in grā´ shē āt´ iŋ) *adj.* acting in a way intended to win someone's favor

---

1. **Third Form A** in British-style schools, an advanced class roughly equivalent to eighth grade in the United States school system.

fussed over him as if he were a son-in-law of the house. He even said, "Well, you must listen with a free mind. Don't worry about these test papers." He added half humorously, "I will give you a week's time."

"Make it ten days, sir," Sekhar pleaded.

"All right, granted," the headmaster said generously. Sekhar felt really relieved now—he would attack them at the rate of ten a day and get rid of the nuisance.

The headmaster lighted incense sticks. "Just to create the right atmosphere," he explained. A drummer and a violinist, already seated on a Rangoon mat, were waiting for him. The headmaster sat down between them like a professional at a concert, cleared his throat and began an alapana[2], and paused to ask, "Isn't it good Kalyani[3]?" Sekhar pretended not to have heard the question. The headmaster went on to sing a full song composed by Thyagaraja[4] and followed it with two more. All the time the headmaster was singing, Sekhar went on commenting within himself, He croaks like a dozen frogs. He is bellowing like a buffalo. Now he sounds like loose window shutters in a storm.

The incense sticks burnt low. Sekhar's head throbbed with the medley of sounds that had assailed his eardrums for a couple of hours now. He felt half stupefied. The headmaster had gone nearly hoarse, when he paused to ask, "Shall I go on?" Sekhar replied, "Please don't, sir; I think this will do. . . ." The headmaster looked stunned. His face was beaded with perspiration. Sekhar felt the greatest pity for him. But he felt he could not help it. No judge delivering a sentence felt more pained and helpless. Sekhar noticed that the headmaster's wife peeped in from the kitchen, with eager curiosity. The drummer and the violinist put away their burdens with an air of relief. The headmaster removed his spectacles, mopped his brow, and asked, "Now, come out with your opinion."

"Can't I give it tomorrow, sir?" Sekhar asked tentatively.

"No. I want it immediately—your frank opinion. Was it good?"

"No, sir. . . ." Sekhar replied.

"Oh! . . . Is there any use continuing my lessons?"

"Absolutely none, sir. . . ." Sekhar said with his voice trembling. He felt very unhappy that he could not speak more soothingly. Truth, he reflected, required as much strength to give as to receive. All the way home he felt worried. He felt that his official life was not going to be smooth sailing hereafter. There were questions of increment and

---

2. **alapana** (äl ä´ pä nä) in classical Indian music, an improvisational exploration of a melody, without a defined beat, and intended to showcase the talent of a singer.
3. **Kalyani** (käl yä´ nē) traditional Indian folk songs.
4. **Thyagaraja** (tē ä´ gä rä´ jä) (1767–1847) revered composer of Indian devotional songs.

▲ **Critical Viewing**
What can you conclude about the sitar (si tär´), a traditional Indian instrument, based on this image? Explain. **[Draw Conclusions]**

Reading Check

What does the headmaster request that Sekhar do that evening?

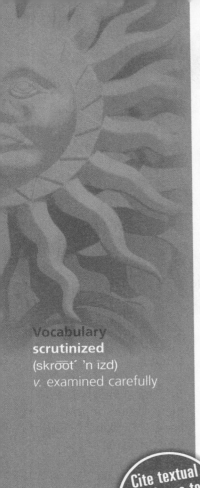

confirmation[5] and so on, all depending upon the headmaster's goodwill. All kinds of worries seemed to be in store for him. . . . Did not Harishchandra[6] lose his throne, wife, child, because he would speak nothing less than the absolute Truth whatever happened?

At home his wife served him with a sullen face. He knew she was still angry with him for his remark of the morning. Two casualties for today, Sekhar said to himself. If I practice it for a week, I don't think I shall have a single friend left.

He received a call from the headmaster in his classroom next day. He went up apprehensively.

"Your suggestion was useful. I have paid off the music master. No one would tell me the truth about my music all these days. Why such antics at my age! Thank you. By the way, what about those test papers?"

"You gave me ten days, sir, for correcting them."

"Oh, I've reconsidered it. I must positively have them here tomorrow. . . ." A hundred papers in a day! That meant all night's sitting up! "Give me a couple of days, sir. . . ."

"No. I must have them tomorrow morning. And remember, every paper must be thoroughly scrutinized."

"Yes, sir," Sekhar said, feeling that sitting up all night with a hundred test papers was a small price to pay for the luxury of practicing Truth.

Vocabulary
scrutinized
(skrōōt´ 'n izd)
v. examined carefully

---

5. **increment and confirmation** salary increase and job security.
6. **Harischchandra** (he rish chen´ dra) legendary Hindu king who was subject of many Indian stories. His name has come to symbolize truth and integrity.

Cite textual evidence to support your responses.

Critical Thinking

1. **Key Ideas and Details** **(a)** What experiment does Sekhar plan at the beginning of the story? **(b) Connect:** What conflict does this create for him?

2. **Key Ideas and Details** **Infer:** Is the headmaster pleased or angry that Sekhar has told him the truth about his music? Explain your inference.

3. **Key Ideas and Details** **(a) Draw Conclusions:** Are there any benefits to Sekhar's truth telling? **(b) Support:** Cite story details and logical reasons to support your conclusion.

4. **Integration of Knowledge and Ideas** Based on the results of Sekhar's experiment, do you think people prefer to hear reality through absolute truths, or do they prefer tempered truth? Explain. *[Connect to the Big Question: Is there a difference between reality and truth?]*

Literary Analysis
Irony and Paradox
How does Sekhar's experience contradict the idea that "honesty is the best policy"?

THE OPEN WINDOW

Saki (H.H. Munro)

"My aunt will be down presently, Mr. Nuttel," said a very self-possessed young lady of fifteen; "in the meantime you must try and put up with me."

Framton Nuttel endeavored to say the correct something that should duly flatter the niece of the moment without unduly discounting the aunt that was to come. Privately he doubted more than ever whether these formal visits on a succession of total strangers would do much towards helping the nerve cure which he was supposed to be undergoing.

"I know how it will be," his sister had said when he was preparing to migrate to this rural retreat; "you will bury yourself down there and not speak to a living soul, and your nerves will be worse than ever from moping. I shall just give you letters of introduction[1] to all the people I know there. Some of them, as far as I can remember, were quite nice."

Vocabulary
endeavored (en dev´ ərd) *v.* tried to achieve a set goal

---

1. **letters of introduction** letters introducing two strangers, written by someone who knows them both. The person to whom such a letter is written is obliged to provide hospitality to the person carrying the letter.

Framton wondered whether Mrs. Sappleton, the lady to whom he was presenting one of the letters of introduction, came into the nice division.

"Do you know many of the people round here?" asked the niece, when she judged that they had had sufficient silent communion.

"Hardly a soul," said Framton. "My sister was staying here, at the rectory, you know, some four years ago, and she gave me letters of introduction to some of the people here."

He made the last statement in a tone of distinct regret.

"Then you know practically nothing about my aunt?" pursued the self-possessed young lady.

"Only her name and address," admitted the caller. He was wondering whether Mrs. Sappleton was in the married or widowed state. An undefinable something about the room seemed to suggest masculine habitation.

"Her great tragedy happened just three years ago," said the child; "that would be since your sister's time."

"Her tragedy?" asked Framton; somehow in this restful country spot tragedies seemed out of place.

"You may wonder why we keep that window wide open on an October afternoon," said the niece, indicating a large French window that opened on to a lawn.

"It is quite warm for the time of the year," said Framton; "but has that window got anything to do with the tragedy?"

"Out through that window, three years ago to a day, her husband and her two young brothers went off for their day's shooting. They never came back. In crossing the moor to their favorite snipe-shooting ground[2] they were all three engulfed in a treacherous piece of bog.[3] It had been that dreadful wet summer, you know, and places that were safe in other years gave way suddenly without warning. Their bodies were never recovered. That was the dreadful part of it." Here the child's voice lost its self-possessed note and became falteringly human. "Poor aunt always thinks that they will come back some day,

2. **snipe-shooting ground** area for hunting snipe—wading birds that live chiefly in marshy places and have long, flexible bills.
3. **bog** small swamp; wet, spongy ground.

Spiral Review
Theme Why is Vera's question, in which she seeks confirmation of Mr. Nuttel's ignorance, important?

Vocabulary
falteringly (fôl′ tər in lē) *adv.* spoken hesitatingly or with a wavering voice

they and the little brown spaniel that was lost with them, and walk in at that window just as they used to do. That is why the window is kept open every evening till it is quite dusk. Poor dear aunt, she has often told me how they went out, her husband with his white waterproof coat over his arm, and Ronnie, her youngest brother, singing, 'Bertie, why do you bound?' as he always did to tease her, because she said it got on her nerves. Do you know, sometimes on still, quiet evenings like this, I almost get a creepy feeling that they will walk in through that window—"

She broke off with a little shudder. It was a relief to Framton when the aunt bustled into the room with a whirl of apologies for being late in making her appearance.

"I hope Vera has been amusing you?" she said.

"She has been very interesting," said Framton.

"I hope you don't mind the open window," said Mrs. Sappleton briskly; "my husband and brothers will be home directly from shooting, and they always come in this way. They've been out for snipe in the marshes today, so they'll make a fine mess over my poor carpets. So like you menfolk, isn't it?"

She rattled on cheerfully about the shooting and the scarcity of birds, and the prospects for duck in the winter. To Framton, it was all purely horrible. He made a desperate but only partially successful effort to turn the talk on to a less ghastly topic; he was conscious that his hostess was giving him only a fragment of her attention, and her eyes were constantly straying past him to the open window and the lawn beyond. It was certainly an unfortunate coincidence that he should have paid his visit on this tragic anniversary.

"The doctors agree in ordering me complete rest, an absence of mental excitement, and avoidance of anything in the nature of violent physical exercise," announced Framton, who labored under the tolerably widespread delusion that total strangers and chance acquaintances are hungry for the least detail of one's ailments and infirmities, their cause and cure. "On the matter of diet they are not so much in agreement," he continued.

"No?" said Mrs. Sappleton, in a voice which only replaced a yawn at the last moment. Then she suddenly brightened into alert attention— but not to what Framton was saying.

"Here they are at last!" she cried. "Just in time for tea, and don't they look as if they were muddy up to the eyes!"

Framton shivered slightly and turned towards the niece with a look intended to convey sympathetic comprehension. The child was staring out through the open window with dazed horror in her eyes. In a chill shock of nameless fear Framton swung round in his seat and looked in the same direction.

Literary Analysis
Irony and Paradox
What kind of irony is involved when Mrs. Sappleton does not know about the tall tale Vera told Mr. Nuttel?

Vocabulary
delusion (di lo͞o′ zhan) n. an erroneous belief that is held despite evidence to the contrary

Reading Check
What does Vera say is her aunt's great tragedy?

In the deepening twilight three figures were walking across the window...

In the deepening twilight three figures were walking across the lawn towards the window; they all carried guns under their arms, and one of them was additionally burdened with a white coat hung over his shoulders. A tired brown spaniel kept close at their heels. Noiselessly they neared the house, and then a hoarse young voice chanted out of the dusk: "I said, Bertie, why do you bound?"

Framton grabbed wildly at his stick and hat; the hall door, the gravel drive, and the front gate were dimly noted stages in his headlong retreat. A cyclist coming along the road had to run into the hedge to avoid imminent collision.

"Here we are, my dear," said the bearer of the white mackintosh,[4] coming in through the window; "fairly muddy, but most of it's dry. Who was that who bolted out as we came up?"

"A most extraordinary man, a Mr. Nuttel," said Mrs. Sappleton; "could only talk about his illnesses, and dashed off without a word of goodbye or apology when you arrived. One would think he had seen a ghost."

"I expect it was the spaniel," said the niece calmly; "he told me he had a horror of dogs. He was once hunted into a cemetery somewhere on the banks of the Ganges[5] by a pack of pariah dogs, and had to spend the night in a newly dug grave with the creatures snarling and grinning and foaming just above him. Enough to make anyone lose their nerve."

Romance at short notice was her specialty.

---

4. **mackintosh** (mak´ in täsh´) *n.* waterproof raincoat.
5. **Ganges** (gan´ jēz) river in northern India and Bangladesh.

Critical Thinking

Cite textual evidence to support your responses.

© 1. **Key Ideas and Details** **(a)** Why is Mr. Nuttel visiting the country? **(b) Interpret**: Why is this detail critical to the story?

© 2. **Key Ideas and Details** **(a) Speculate:** Why does Vera tell Mr. Nuttel the story about the hunters' deaths? **(b) Connect:** Is it unusual for her to tell such stories? Explain.

© 3. **Key Ideas and Details** **Compare and Contrast:** How are Mr. Nuttel and Vera similar and different? Use details from the story to support your answer.

© 4. **Integration of Knowledge and Ideas** **(a)** How does Vera use aspects of reality to shape her story? **(b)** How is Mr. Nuttel's perception of the situation at the end of the story different from reality? *[Connect to the Big Question: Is there a difference between reality and truth?]*

Comparing Irony and Paradox

1. Craft and Structure (a) Analyze one example of **irony** in each story. For each example, identify and explain the elements that contrast with one another. **(b)** Did you identify situational, verbal, or dramatic irony? Explain.

2. Key Ideas and Details Explain how each story explores a **paradox:**

(a) "Like the Sun": Telling the truth is a virtue that leads to punishment.

(b) "The Open Window": The cure for Mr. Nuttel's illness makes him worse.

3. Craft and Structure Complete a diagram like this one to show how irony and paradox affect each story. Consider whether these devices simply add humor or whether they emphasize the impossible dilemmas facing a character.

Like the Sun	The Open Window
Effect of Irony and Paradox:	Effect of Irony and Paradox:

Timed Writing

Explanatory Text: Essay

Both Narayan and Saki use irony or paradox to explore ideas. In an essay, compare and contrast how the authors present the concepts of truth and deception in these stories. Provide evidence from the texts to support your understanding. **(30 minutes)**

5-Minute Planner

1. Read the prompt carefully and completely.

2. Identify a few examples of irony or paradox in each story.

3. Draw a conclusion about the message each writer is expressing about truth, deception, and honesty.

4. Take notes on how the use of irony and paradox helps each writer express his message. Find quotations from the text that you can include to support your ideas.

5. Reread the prompt, and then draft your essay.

Writing Workshop

Write an Explanatory Text

Exposition: Cause-and-Effect Essay

Defining the Form Whenever something unusual happens, the first question most people ask is, "Why?" A **cause-and-effect essay** can satisfy a reader's curiosity. It might explain why a weird new fashion fad began or what happened as a result of a groundbreaking court decision. You might use elements of this form in research papers, informative articles, and reflective essays.

Assignment Write an essay in which you explain a cause-and-effect relationship. Include these elements:

✓ a thesis statement in which you clearly identify the cause-and-effect relationships you will explore

✓ an effective and *logical method of organization*

✓ well-chosen, relevant *supporting evidence* and examples that suit your audience and purpose

✓ *transitions* that smoothly and clearly connect your ideas

✓ error-free grammar, including *correct pronoun-antecedent agreement*

To preview the criteria on which your cause-and-effect essay may be judged, see the rubric on page 207.

 Writing Workshop: *Work in Progress*

Review the work you did on pages 151 and 179.

WRITE GUY
Jeff Anderson, M.Ed.

What Do You Notice?

Structure and Style

Read these sentences from Penny Le Couteur and Jay Burreson's "Making History with Vitamin C."

If an effective treatment for scurvy was known, why wasn't it acted upon and used routinely? Sadly, the remedy for scurvy, though proven, seems to have not been recognized or believed.

With a partner, discuss why these sentences are interesting. Consider the sentence structures and rhetorical strategies used.

 Common Core State Standards

Writing

2. Write informative/explanatory texts to examine and convey complex ideas, concepts, and information clearly and accurately through the effective selection, organization, and analysis of content.

5. Develop and strengthen writing as needed by planning, revising, editing, rewriting, or trying a new approach, focusing on addressing what is most significant for a specific purpose and audience.

7. Conduct short as well as more sustained research projects to answer a question or solve a problem; narrow or broaden the inquiry when appropriate.

Reading-Writing Connection

To get a feel for cause-and-effect essays, read "Making History With Vitamin C" by Penny Le Couteur and Jay Burreson on page 168.

Prewriting/Planning Strategies

Use one of the following ways to choose a topic and focus for your essay.

Make a list. Brainstorm for a list of scientific phenomena, historic events, or popular trends that you find interesting, important, or even confusing. Look over your list to choose a topic you would like to explore in an essay.

Scan a newspaper or magazine. Review print or online articles, looking for ideas that make you ask, "Why?" Identify possible topics and then conduct short research projects to learn more about the subjects that spark your interest. Review your research notes and choose a topic to address.

Narrow your topic. Once you have a topic, make sure that you can discuss it fully in your essay. If your topic is too broad, you may need to focus it. For example, you might not be able to answer "Why did the Great Depression happen?" in a short essay. Instead, you could focus your inquiry on why the stock market crashed in October of 1929.

Make a cause-and-effect chart. Organizing your ideas and details in a cause-and-effect chart can help you form a clear picture of the relationship you will discuss. One chart shown here presents three possible causes of one effect. The other chart classifies the possible effects of one cause.

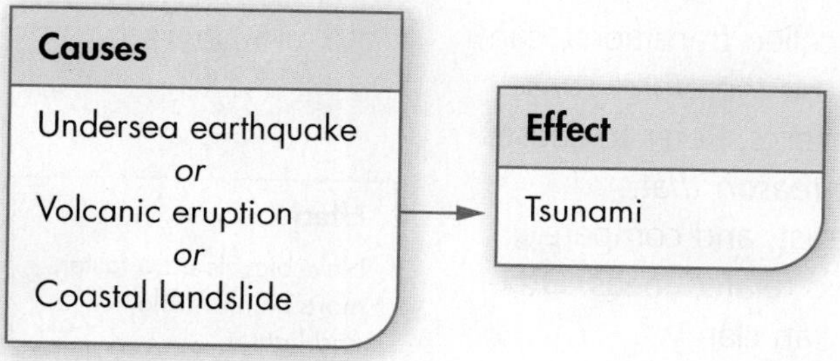

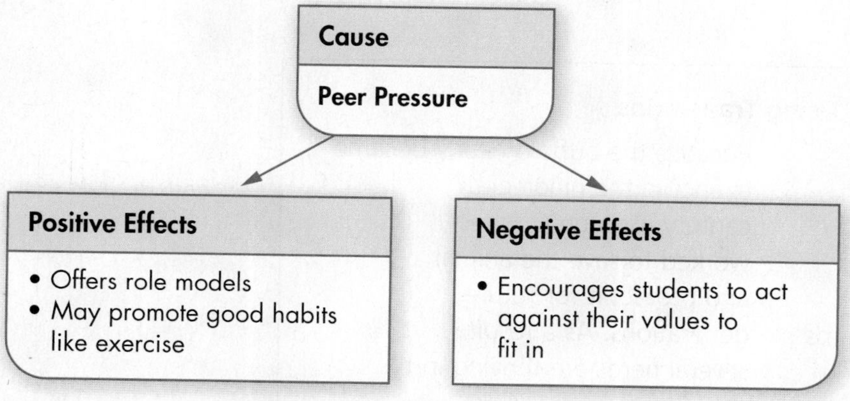

PHLit
Online!
www.PHLitOnline.com
- Author video: Writing Process
- Author video: Rewards of Writing

Causes
Undersea earthquake
or
Volcanic eruption
or
Coastal landslide

Effect
Tsunami

Cause
Peer Pressure

Positive Effects
• Offers role models
• May promote good habits like exercise

Negative Effects
• Encourages students to act against their values to fit in

Drafting Strategies

Clarify your analysis. Even if you are describing a complicated chain of effects, you will need a clear and direct introduction. Prepare a simplified cause-and-effect chart like the one shown on this page to organize your pre-writing ideas. It can show you which ideas are most essential to your topic.

Choose a logical organization. The structure you choose for your essay depends on the information you have.

- **Chronological order** makes sense for many cause-and-effect essays. You can start with the cause and then continue by describing its effects. Alternatively, you can start with the effect and then work through its causes one at a time.

- If you are describing multiple causes, consider using an **order-of-importance organization.** You might begin with your most important cause or save the most important cause for last.

When developing your organization, make sure your essay includes an introduction, a body, and a conclusion that supports your analysis.

Consider your audience. Think about how much your readers already know about your topic. Use precise words, and provide full explanations for any technical or unfamiliar words or events.

Use clear transitions. Specific words and phrases, called transitions, can help you introduce causes and effects. For example, use *therefore, consequently, as a result,* or *for that reason* to introduce effects. Refer to causes with transitions such as *because, since, as,* or *for the reason that.*

Also consider phrases that help you connect, contrast, and compare ideas. You might use *not only . . . but also* to join two related ideas. Other transitions, such as *however* and *on the other hand,* can clarify contrasting ideas.

Common Core State Standards

Writing

2.a. Introduce a topic, organize complex ideas, concepts, and information to make important connections and distinctions.

2.c. Use appropriate and varied transitions to link the major sections of the text, create cohesion, and clarify the relationships among complex ideas and concepts.

2.d. Use precise language and domain-specific vocabulary to manage the complexity of the topic.

2.f. Provide a concluding statement or section that follows from and supports the information or explanation presented.

Cause

Bicycles are built using new, stronger materials.

Effect

New bicycles are faster, more comfortable, and lighter.

Using Transitions

The buffalo nearly became extinct in the nineteenth century. George Grinnell worked to save the animal and protect it for future generations. Today, several herds are thriving in the wild.

Because the buffalo nearly became extinct in the nineteenth century, George Grinnell worked to save the animal and protect it for future generations. *As a result,* several herds are thriving in the wild today.

Writers on Writing

Susan Vreeland On Showing Causes and Effects

> Susan Vreeland is the author of "Magdalena Looking" (p. 10).

My story "Crayon, 1955" is drawn from a time in my childhood when my great-grandfather, an artist, came to our house to die. What occurred there in that intense time was magical: He introduced me to his world of art. The experience narrated here was the cause of my lifelong interest in art, and resulted, ultimately, in writing *Girl in Hyacinth Blue*.

"Re-visioning . . . is a coaxing process."
—Susan Vreeland

Professional Model:

from "Crayon, 1955"

"Jenny," he said the next day. His voice scraped [like a Popsicle stick across the sidewalk]. "Let me teach you to paint."

I wasn't sure I wanted him to. The room smelled bad, but not just because of his . . . paints. Once Mom said Gramp's blood ran with turpentine, which I thought was what made his skin waxy and yellow.

Practicing a secret style of shallow breathing, I sat on the edge of the bed and he held my hand inside his [spidery one] while I held the long brush. He squeezed so tightly, directing where my hand should go, that his long yellow nails jabbed into my palm. I curled up my toes and kept quiet. [Like a miracle,] in front of me appeared an unrolled white flower with an orange finger inside. "There's nothing so cheerful as a calla lily," he said as we worked. "They grow tall and graceful just like you, and one day, they open themselves to the world."

In my revision, I inserted images that a young girl might think — the simile of a Popsicle stick, and the visual adjective "spidery."

To convey sharply the resulting change in Jenny, in my revision I added, "like a miracle," an exaggerated simile revealing her astonishment.

In fiction, cause and effect are subtle, sometimes only a suggestion. Jenny's negative reactions to her grandfather change when the painting resulting from his teaching pleases her.

Revising Strategies

Look for careless repetition. Effective use of repetition helps to emphasize key ideas and create a memorable impact. Sloppy repetition, however, weakens your writing. Look for words that appear too often or too close together. Use a thesaurus to find words with related meanings or use a pronoun to replace a noun that you have used many times.

> **Too Much Repetition:** Bees *buzz* as a result of beating their wings *rapidly*. When an intruder approaches, bees beat their wings even more *rapidly*. As a result, *the bees' buzzing* grows louder.

> **More Effective:** Bees *buzz* as a result of beating their wings *rapidly*. When an intruder approaches, bees beat their wings *faster* and their *buzzing* grows louder.

Consider your style and tone. Use language that will further your purpose for writing. A formal style that is free of slang words and that creates a serious, objective tone is appropriate for cause-and-effect essays.

Color-code to identify related details. Each paragraph in your essay should have a strong, single focus. First, circle the topic sentence of each paragraph. If you cannot find a topic sentence, consider adding one. Then, underline sentences that contain details that support the topic of the paragraph.

Peer Review

After identifying topic sentences and supporting details, look at the sentences that are neither circled nor underlined. With a partner, discuss whether to rewrite or delete these sentences. You might also consider moving those sentences to a paragraph where they support the topic more effectively. After revising, explain your decisions to your partner.

Common Core State Standards

Writing
2.e. Establish and maintain a formal style and objective tone while attending to the norms and conventions of the discipline in which they are writing.
5. Develop and strengthen writing as needed by planning, revising, editing, rewriting, or trying a new approach, focusing on addressing what is most significant for a specific purpose and audience.

Language
1. Demonstrate command of the conventions of standard English grammar and usage when writing or speaking.

Model: Revising to Strengthen Focus
Ice storms caused devastation throughout the Northeast. Power lines were downed by the heavy coating of ice, causing widespread electric outages. ~~People became bored without access to television.~~ Roads coated with ice became impassable.

> The writer deleted a sentence that offered useful information but did not relate to the topic of the paragraph.

Revising Pronoun-Antecedent Agreement

Antecedents are the nouns for which pronouns stand. A pronoun must agree with its antecedent in number, person, and gender.

Identifying Incorrect Pronoun-Antecedent Agreement In your writing, check each pronoun to make sure it agrees with its antecedent. Ask three things about the antecedent:

- *Number:* Is it singular or plural?
- *Person:* Is it first person (the one speaking), second person (the one being spoken to), or third person (the one spoken about)?
- *Gender:* Is it masculine, feminine, or neuter?

> Antecedent   Pronoun
> <u>Marie Curie</u> is known for <u>her</u> work with radium.
>
> Antecedent   Pronoun
> <u>My father and I</u> saw the experiment. <u>We</u> were amazed.

PH | WRITING COACH

Further instruction and practice are available in *Prentice Hall Writing Coach.*

Special Problems With Agreement Use a plural personal pronoun with two or more antecedents joined by *and*.

<u>Lewis and Clark</u> described the expedition in <u>their</u> journal.

Use a singular personal pronoun with two or more antecedents joined by *or* or *nor*.

Neither <u>Lewis</u> nor <u>Clark</u> regretted <u>his</u> journey.

Fixing Agreement Errors To fix a pronoun and antecedent that do not agree, choose the pronoun that has the correct number, person, and gender.

1. Describe the number, person, and gender of the antecedent.
2. Choose a pronoun with the same number, person, and gender. Be sure you use the right pronoun case: nominative, objective, or possessive.

Grammar in Your Writing

Circle the pronouns in two paragraphs of your draft. Draw an arrow to the antecedent for each pronoun. Evaluate whether or not the pronoun and antecedent agree. Replace any incorrect pronouns.

Hurricane: Causes and Effects

Everyone dreads the hurricane season. When that time of year comes around, we all lock down and get ready for the harsh winds and power outages. The 2004 season started out with a bang. Large parts of the coast were torn apart as storms rolled in, one after another.

Causes of Hurricanes

Hurricanes form when weather patterns of different temperatures run into each other and start spinning. When a cold front out in the ocean, moving in one direction, comes in contact with a warm front moving in the opposite direction, winds start. These winds start moving in circular motions. As they spin, they pick up speed. These large areas of fast-moving winds generate tornadoes that pull water up into the storm. Hurricanes have high winds with tornadoes and carry large amounts of water.

When it starts, the storm is classified as a tropical depression. As it becomes stronger, it is called a tropical storm. If the wind speeds get high enough, the tropical storm is categorized as a hurricane.

Effects of Hurricanes: Damage to Property

When the storm hits land, it dumps all its water, and that is when it becomes the most destructive. Some of the water soaks into the ground, but often there is more water than the land can absorb. As a result, the water quickly runs off to lower areas. These run-offs are called flash floods. Flash floods can wash away land and possessions or destroy them by filling them with water. At the same time, hurricane winds can blow over trees and power lines. With the power out, repairs are hard to make quickly. This means power can be out for a week or longer. Hurricanes also bring lightning, which can cause fires in trees or houses.

Effects of Hurricanes: Damage to Business

During the late summer and fall of 2004, the state of Florida was hit by four major hurricanes: Charley, Frances, Ivan, and Jeanne. Each hurricane caused so much damage that it could not be repaired before the next storm hit. The damage was so bad that President Bush asked Congress for 7.1 billion dollars for repairs in Florida. Many people had to board up stores and wait in line for electric generators. In addition, relief workers were sent down to Florida to help deliver meals, water, and ice.

These storms not only caused trouble for the insurance companies, but also affected the citrus and tourism industries. The citrus growers in Florida lost about half of their grapefruit crop during Hurricane Frances. Tourism was also hurt because people do not want to travel into a disaster zone.

Conclusion

The hurricane season of 2004 was more intense than previous years. This is said to be from warm temperatures in the Atlantic Ocean and a decrease in wind shear. We hope that in the future we will better be able to predict and prepare for these hurricanes.

Andrew uses subheads to clearly organize the information. This paragraph explains what causes hurricanes.

Andrew breaks his discussion of the effects of hurricanes into two sections.

Andrew uses a specific detail to support his broader claims.

Editing and Proofreading

Review your draft to correct errors in grammar, spelling, capitalization, and punctuation.

Focus on usage errors. Check your writing for commonly confused words. Remember that *then* refers to time and *than* is used for comparisons. Use *since* to refer to a previous time, not to mean "because." If you are unsure about a word, consult a dictionary or usage guide.

Publishing and Presenting

Consider one of the following ways to share your writing:

Give a class presentation. Use your essay as the basis of a presentation. Use photographs, charts, maps, or diagrams to make your cause-and-effect relationships clear. Practice combining visuals with your writing, deciding when you will show each visual as you share the ideas from your essay.

Use e-mail. Share your writing electronically. Type your essay using word-processing software. Attach the file to an e-mail to a friend or relative. Save printouts of the essay and any responses in your writing portfolio.

Reflecting on Your Writing

Writer's Journal Jot down your answers to this question:
How did writing about your topic help you to understand it?

Rubric for Self-Assessment

Find evidence in your writing to address each category. Then, use the rating scale to grade your work.

Spiral Review
Earlier in the unit, you learned about **personal pronouns** (p. 150) and **relative pronouns** (p. 178). Review your draft carefully to be sure you have used these types of pronouns correctly.

Criteria	Rating Scale
	not very · · · very
Focus: How clearly do you identify the cause-and-effect relationship you explore?	1 2 3 4 5
Organization: How effectively do you organize your information?	1 2 3 4 5
Support/Elaboration: How strong are the details and examples you use as support?	1 2 3 4 5
Style: How effectively do you use transitions to connect your ideas?	1 2 3 4 5
Conventions: How correct is your grammar, especially your use of pronouns?	1 2 3 4 5

Vocabulary Workshop

Using a Dictionary and Thesaurus

A **dictionary** is an alphabetical listing of words. It gives definitions, parts of speech, etymologies, and more. Notice the information given in this dictionary entry.

Dictionary

Part of speech   Etymology

narrate (nar´āt; na āt´, nə-) *vt., vi.* -rat´ed, -rat´ing [< L *narratus*, pp. of *narrare*, to tell, akin to *gnarus*, acquainted with < IE *gnoro- < base *gen-, to KNOW] **1.** to tell (a story) in writing or speech **2.** to give an account of (happenings, etc.)

Definition

In addition to information about the work, a dictionary includes a guide to pronunciation. Most dictionaries provide a key to the symbols at the bottom of the page or in the front of the dictionary.

There are many kinds of dictionaries. One to know about is the *Oxford English Dictionary,* or OED. It tracks the usage of most English words over the past thousand years. The latest edition is available online and in a twenty-volume set. It is a very useful tool if you are studying the etymology, or origin, of a word in English.

A **thesaurus** is a reference book that lists synonyms, or words with similar meanings. You can use a thesaurus to increase your vocabulary or to find alternative words to express your meaning. Here's an example of a thesaurus entry:

Thesaurus

entertainer *n.* **1.** entertainer, performer, artist, dancer, hoofer **2.** actor, actress, player, thespian, mime, villain, character *v.* entertain, act, perform, dramatize, dance, play

Both dictionaries and thesauruses are available in print, in computer programs, and on the Internet.

Practice A Look up each word in a thesaurus. For each, write two words that have almost the same meaning.

1. disapproval
2. patience
3. talk
4. repeatedly
5. remember
6. joke

Common Core State Standards

Language
4. Determine or clarify the meaning of unknown and multiple-meaning words and phrases based on grades 9–10 reading and content, choosing flexibly from a range of strategies.
4.c. Consult general and specialized reference materials, both print and digital, to find the pronunciation of a word or determine or clarify its precise meaning, its part of speech, or its etymology.
4.d. Verify the preliminary determination of the meaning of a word or phrase.

Practice B Use a dictionary to answer questions 1–7 and a thesaurus to respond to questions 8 and 9.

1. Some words have more than one dictionary definition. **(a)** What is the definition of *idle* in the following sentence? *Eliot sat* <u>idle</u> *all afternoon.* **(b)** What is another definition for this word?

2. **(a)** What is the adverb form of the word *sleepy*? **(b)** How would you use it in a sentence?

3. What is the meaning of the word *cuff* when used as a verb?

4. If the situation is *fraught* with danger, is it safe? Explain.

5. Which dictionary definition is correct for *sorry* as it is used the following sentence? *In Aunt Sarah's opinion, I was one* <u>sorry</u> *entertainer.*

6. Is it possible to use the word *revise* as a noun? Explain.

7. How many definitions does your dictionary give for the word *frost*?

8. Find three synonyms for *deadly*.

9. Rewrite this sentence twice using synonyms for *genuine*: *The painting turned out to be a* <u>genuine</u> *Van Gogh.*

www.PHLitOnline.com

- Illustrated vocabulary words
- Interactive vocabulary games
- Vocabulary flashcards

Activity Create a note card like the one shown for each of these words:

allay   unkempt   linear   quandary   naive

Word:	
Definition:	
Pronunciation:	
Sentence:	

Read your sentences aloud. Then, in a group, trade cards and read each other's sentences. Check one another's pronunciation and usage. Refer to a dictionary if you disagree on the pronunciation or word meaning.

Comprehension and Collaboration

Look up the following words in a dictionary or reliable online source. Find the earliest usage of each word and its definition. Then, locate a more modern definition of each word. Talk with a group about how the meaning of each word has changed over the years. Is the original meaning still used?

flaunt
cab
fragile
vandal

Analyzing Media Messages

Some television, radio, and Internet sources are truthful, thorough, and objective. Others offer information that is inaccurate, incomplete, or reported in a biased way. To evaluate media messages, stay alert and analyze claims critically.

Common Core State Standards

Speaking and Listening
3. Evaluate a speaker's point of view, reasoning, and use of evidence and rhetoric, identifying any fallacious reasoning or exaggerated or distorted evidence.

Learn the Skills

Use the strategies to complete the activity on page 211.

Evaluate the content of the message. Carefully consider and evaluate what the message says.

- **Look for support for claims.** Note facts, statistics, quotations, and other evidence. If no support is provided, decide whether you have any reason to accept the claims in the message.

- **Consider bias.** People quoted in media may present biased, or one-sided, evidence. Consider the reasons a source might have to favor one version of events over another or to exaggerate or distort evidence. Note whether opposing viewpoints have been left out and why a speaker might omit them.

- **Look for faulty reasoning.** Ask yourself whether the claims made are contradictory or vague. Look for logical fallacies, such as insisting something is correct because most people think so.

- **Look for illegal statements.** There are laws to protect people from libel (false written statements) and slander (false spoken statements). Be alert to accusations that are not supported by facts.

Evaluate the style of the message. Once you understand a message's content, consider its delivery. Some media techniques sway viewers or misrepresent ideas.

- **Be aware of stereotypes.** Watch for stereotypes, or oversimplified ideas about a group of people. Many stereotypes are negative images based on race, gender, age, or role.

- **Detect cultural assumptions.** Media presentations can reflect basic assumptions about what is important or good. Think about whether you agree with such value judgments.

- **Be alert to charged or emotional language.** Listen for words and phrases that are meant to manipulate or affect your emotions.

- **Consider the impact of the medium.** Background music, images, and graphics may capture your attention. If they have been added only to stir emotions, they are not evidence.

Practice the Skills

Ⓒ Presentation of Knowledge and Ideas Use what you have learned in this workshop to perform the following task.

ACTIVITY: Analyze a Media Message

Using the Analysis Checklist as a guide, analyze a television newscast or advertisement. Then, share your analysis in a group discussion. Follow these steps.

• Watch the newscast or advertisement multiple times and observe carefully.
• As you watch, refer often to the Analysis Checklist.
• Take notes on your observations.
• Use your checklist and notes to present your ideas to a small group of classmates.

Analysis Checklist

Rating System

Poor   Excellent
1   2   3   4   5

Message Purpose

What is the main purpose of the message?

_____

_____

Use of Facts and Evidence

_____ Relevant Support   _____ Complete Support
_____ Unbiased Support   _____ Sound Reasoning

Message Style

_____ Relevance of Graphics or Images   _____ Avoidance of Charged Language
_____ Relevance of Music   _____ Avoidance of Stereotypes

Conclusions

Was the message trustworthy?

_____

_____

Did the message fulfill its purpose?

_____

_____

Ⓒ Comprehension and Collaboration After you present your analysis of the media message to a small group, lead a brief discussion. Ask group members whether your observations are similar to or different from theirs. Make sure that everyone participates in the discussion.

Cumulative Review

 **Common Core State Standards**

RL.9-10.1, RL.9-10.3, RL.9-10.4, RL.9-10.5; W.9-10.2
[For the full wording of the standards, see the standards chart in the front of your textbook.]

I. Reading Literature/Informational Text

Directions: *Read the passage. Then, answer each question that follows.*

The Mummy's Curse

Death Shall Come on Swift Wings to Him Who Disturbs the Peace of the King.

These words, supposedly inscribed on the tomb of Egyptian King Tutankhamen, did not <u>deter</u> the intrepid English archaeologist Howard Carter. After years of searching, in 1922 Carter located King Tut's tomb. Archaeologists had long known that pharaohs were mummified at death and buried with riches to accompany them to the afterworld. To protect them from grave robbers, tombs were sealed with stone blocks or contained false passages. In some cases, the tombs were guarded by a curse.

After visiting England, Carter brought a canary back to Egypt. When Carter returned to his house after locating the tomb, his servant met him holding the dead bird. The servant claimed the bird had been killed by a cobra, a symbol of ancient Egyptian royalty, because Carter had violated the tomb. Carter ignored the warning. Upon the arrival in Egypt of his wealthy backer, Lord Carnarvon, Carter prepared to open the tomb.

Lord Carnarvon watched as Carter drilled a hole in the tomb door. Carter leaned through the hole, a candle in his hand.

"Can you see anything?" asked Lord Carnarvon.

"Yes, wonderful things," answered Carter.

The tomb contained a treasure trove, including a stone sarcophagus in which rested three gold coffins, nested inside each other. The innermost coffin held the mummy of King Tut. Everyone was excited about the find, and no one considered the curse. According to rumor, Carter had found a tablet inscribed with the curse, but hid it from his superstitious workers.

Shortly after the tomb was opened, the curse struck. Lord Carnarvon died from an infected bug bite. When King Tut's mummy was unwrapped, it had a wound in the same position as Lord Carnarvon's bug bite.

Within ten years, eleven people related to the discovery of King Tut's tomb had died of unnatural causes. Newspapers sensationalized the "mummy's curse" and claimed there were as many as twenty-one victims of the curse. Was this the hype of a sensationalist press, or did the curse exist?

Later investigation showed that of twenty-two people present when the tomb was opened, only six had died by 1934. Carter himself lived to the age of sixty-six, dying of natural causes.

1. Which event in the selection occurs first?

   A. The canary dies.
   B. King Tut's tomb is discovered.
   C. Lord Carnarvon dies.
   D. King Tut's mummy is unwrapped.

2. Which event is an example of **foreshadowing?**

   A. the death of Lord Carnarvon
   B. the arrival of Lord Carnarvon in Egypt
   C. the discovery of King Tut's tomb
   D. the death of the canary

3. Which of the following represents an **internal conflict** of a character?

   A. The servant fears the Mummy's curse.
   B. Carter dismisses the superstition.
   C. Lord Carnarvon pays for Carter's work.
   D. The reporters tell stories about the "curse."

4. **Vocabulary** Which word is closest in meaning to the underlined word *deter*?

   A. encourage
   B. destroy
   C. stop
   D. include

5. Which of the following best states the **author's purpose?**

   A. to persuade readers that the "mummy's curse" may have been exaggerated
   B. to persuade readers to study archaeology
   C. to entertain readers with a comic tale
   D. to inform readers about King Tut

6. Which of the following best describes the **author's perspective?**

   A. The author believes in the "mummy's curse."
   B. The author supports archaeological studies.
   C. The author views the story objectively.
   D. The author wants tombs to be undisturbed.

7. Which of the following is an example of **irony?**

   A. Carter eventually locates King Tut's tomb after years of searching.
   B. Lord Carnarvon attends the tomb's opening.
   C. The canary dies when the tomb is found.
   D. The mummy has a wound in the same location as Lord Carnarvon's bug bite.

8. Which of these sentences *best* increases the tension in the selection?

   A. Carter leaned through the hole, a candle in his hand.
   B. After years of searching, in 1922 Carter located King Tut's tomb.
   C. On one of his trips to England, Carter had brought a yellow canary back to Egypt.
   D. Carter himself lived to the age of sixty-six, dying of natural causes.

9. Which element common to fiction is *not* present in this nonfiction piece?

   A. ordered events
   B. dialogue
   C. suspense
   D. exposition

⊙ Timed Writing

10. In a well-developed and logically organized essay, **explain** how the syntax and diction in the opening quotation reinforce the mysteriousness of the curse as described in the passage. **Support** your answer with details from the passage. [20 minutes]

GO ON

II. Reading Informational Text

Directions: *Read the passage. Then, answer each question that follows.*

 Common Core
State Standards

RI.9-10.3; L.9-10.1, L.9-10.3
[For the full wording of the standards, see the standards chart in the front of your textbook.]

The Ghost Crab

Have you ever taken an evening stroll on the beach and seen a small ghostly figure scurry across the sand and suddenly disappear? This was most probably a ghost crab, or *Ocypode quadrata,* also known as a sand crab. The name *ghost crab* comes from the creature's ability to blend in with the sand and to suddenly appear out of and disappear into the sand.

Habitat

Ghost crabs live on the sandy beaches along the eastern coastline of North America and South America. They live in burrows that can be as deep as three feet. Older crabs live farther from the water than younger crabs.

Appearance

Their body shell, or carapace, is usually square and can be up to two inches wide. They are gray or yellow-white on their top surface, but their underside is white. Ghost crabs have white or lavender pincers, are uneven in size, and have hairy legs. Their eyes, which sit atop long stalks, sense changes in light.

Diet

Ghost crabs are <u>omnivorous</u>. They will eat clams, insects, other crabs, and vegetation, as well as plant and animal detritus that washes up on the shore. They feed at night and burrow into the sand during daylight hours.

The following list shows some interesting facts about ghost crabs.
- At night, they face the moon when it is full.
- They can run up to ten miles per hour.
- At night, they wash water over their gills for oxygen.
- Their "periscope" eyes can see 360°.

1. If you wanted to draw a ghost crab, which feature in the text would help you locate the most useful information?

   A. the title
   B. the subhead *Habitat*
   C. the bulleted list
   D. the subhead *Appearance*

2. Which two ideas does the author connect?

   A. ghost crabs are pale / they seem to disappear
   B. crabs eat many things / they burrow
   C. crabs have pincers / they survive
   D. ghost crabs are fast / they feed at night

III. Writing and Language Conventions

Directions: *Read the passage. Then, answer each question that follows.*

(1) My dad and I had looked forward to our camping trip in the mountains for weeks. (2) Charlie, the family's black Labrador pup, was going along. (3) It was our first visit to the mountains.

(4) Our campsite was thickly lined with trees. (5) I inhaled the fresh mountain air, and, grabbing my fishing tackle, I strolled down the path to the lake with my dog. (6) The dog ran after me, ready for fun.

(7) "Watch out for bears, Joe," Dad called.

(8) "Okay!" I said, laughing. (9) As I rounded a bend, though, right in front of me was a small black bear ambling along the path. (10) Charlie's fur bristled. (11) The bear stopped cold, staring at me. (12) I froze, holding my breath until the bear finally turned and hurried off down the path.

(13) I've been camping a lot since then, but I'll never forget the dramatic events of that first trip.

1. Which of the following revisions to sentence 10 enhances the story's **conflict** and increases suspense?

A. Charlie's black fur bristled.

B. Charlie's fur bristled, his senses on full predator alert.

C. Charlie stopped and his fur bristled.

D. Charlie, his fur bristling, stopped suddenly.

2. How would you revise the **dialogue** in sentence 8 to better convey Joe's carefree attitude?

A. "Yeah, sure!" I said, laughing.

B. "Do you really think so?" I asked.

C. "Thanks for the reminder!" I said.

D. "Stop fooling around!" I cried.

3. What is the *best* way to add **sensory description** to sentence 4?

A. Replace "trees" with "fragrant green pines."

B. Replace "lined" with "wooded."

C. Replace "campsite" with "camping area."

D. Replace "Our campsite" with "Our chosen campsite."

4. Which **proper noun** should replace the **common noun** in sentence 6 for clarity?

A. Joe

B. Charlie

C. Dad

D. trail

5. Which **abstract noun** should be substituted for the phrase "the dramatic events" in sentence 13 in order to use precise language?

A. joy

B. boredom

C. excitement

D. melancholy

6. What is the correct way to write the **possessive noun** in sentence 2?

A. the families black Labrador pup

B. the familys' black Labrador pup

C. the families' black Labrador pup

D. Leave as is.

Performance Tasks

Directions: *Follow the instructions to complete the tasks below as required by your teacher.*

As you work on each task, incorporate both general academic vocabulary and literary terms you learned in this unit.

Common Core State Standards

RL.9-10.2, RL.9-10.4, RL.9-10.5;
RI.9-10.2, RI.9-10.4, RI.9-10.6;
W.9-10.2, W.9-10.9.a, W.9-10.9.b;
SL.9-10.1.a–b, SL.9-10.4, SL.9-10.5;
L.9-10.1, L.9-10.2

[For the full wording of the standards, see the standards chart in the front of your textbook.]

Writing

Task 1: Literature [RL.9-10.2; W.9-10.2, W.9-10.9.a]

Analyze Theme

Write an essay in which you analyze the development of the theme of a literary work from this unit.

- Choose a story from this unit that has a theme that you find interesting or compelling. Explain your choice.
- Provide a summary of the work, briefly describing the main characters and the story's key events.
- State the theme of the story in a sentence or two. Identify the theme as either stated or implied and provide justification for your decision.
- Explain how the theme is introduced in the story. For example, theme might first be suggested in dialogue or in descriptions of a character's inner struggles.
- Analyze the development of the theme by citing and explaining key details that shape the theme over the course of the story.
- Distinguish between significant details that contribute to the theme and minor or incidental details that do not shape the theme.
- Use all language conventions correctly, including capitalization of proper nouns.

Task 2: Informational Text [RI.9-10.2; W.9-10.2, W.9-10.9.b; L.9-10.1]

Analyze Central Idea

Write an essay in which you analyze the development of the central idea in a nonfiction work from this unit.

- Provide a brief summary of the work, explaining the central idea and the key points that support it.

- Explain how the author first presents the central idea. For example, it may be stated directly or implied though details.
- Analyze how the author supports and develops the central idea throughout the work. Cite key details from the work in your analysis and show how they help to deepen readers' understanding of the central idea.
- In your essay, be sure to follow the conventions of standard English grammar and usage.

Task 3: Informational Text [RI.9-10.6; W.9-10.9.b; L.9-10.1]

Analyze Author's Purpose

Write an essay in which you analyze an author's primary purpose in a nonfiction work from this unit.

- Select a nonfiction work from this unit, either functional text or literary nonfiction, in which the author's purpose is advanced by his or her style.
- State what you believe is the primary purpose of the text: to inform, to persuade, or to entertain. Then, discuss how the author's style—his or her special use of language—helps to achieve that purpose.
- Identify a specific purpose that the author is trying to achieve. Connect the author's style to the specific purpose by evaluating the effectiveness of the style he or she chose.
- Draw a conclusion about the relationship between the author's style and purpose.
- Establish and maintain a formal style in your essay.
- Be sure to follow the conventions of standard English grammar and usage. Check for correct pronoun-antecedent agreement.

Speaking and Listening

ⓔ Task 4: Informational Text [RI.9-10.6; SL.9-10.4]

Analyze Author's Point of View

Prepare an oral presentation in which you analyze an author's point of view, or perspective, in a nonfiction work from this unit.

- Select a work of nonfiction from this unit, and determine the author's point of view in the work.
- Explain how the author's point of view is conveyed. Support your ideas with evidence from the text.
- Present your analysis logically, so that listeners are able to follow your reasoning.
- Organize and develop your presentation in ways that are appropriate to your purpose, audience, and task.

ⓔ Task 5: Literature/Informational Text [RL.9-10.4; RI.9-10.4; SL.9-10.1.a–b]

Analyze an Author's Style

Lead a small group discussion analyzing the style of a work from this unit.

- Prepare for the discussion by analyzing the author's diction and syntax—his or her word choices and sentence structures. Consider the author's use of rhetorical devices or figurative language. Determine how these choices help to create the author's style.
- Create a list of discussion points, including specific questions you plan to ask. For example, to arrive at a description of the style of this work, you might ask whether the author's word choice is formal or informal, simple or sophisticated, or old-fashioned or contemporary. You might also discuss the function of style in the work (i.e., what style accomplishes), and how important style is to the overall meaning of the work.
- Make sure you guide the group to provide examples from the text to illustrate each point.
- As you lead the discussion, actively incorporate group members into the discussion. Clarify and challenge ideas while maintaining a collegial tone.

- At the conclusion of your discussion, review the key ideas that were expressed.

ⓔ Task 6: Literature [RL.9-10.5; SL.9-10.5]

Analyze Cause and Effect

Prepare and deliver an oral presentation in which you analyze cause and effect in a literary work from this unit.

- Select a work from this unit in which cause and effect is important to the plot. Identify the specific cause (or causes) and effect (or effects).
- Describe how cause and effect fits within the structure of the text, how it affects the development of the plot, and how it contributes to the overall theme of the work.
- Present your analysis in a clear and logical way. Include supporting evidence from the text to validate your points.
- Incorporate digital media, such as a slide show, to help communicate your ideas. You may also create a poster or a handout to add interest to your presentation.
- When you are speaking, use adequate volume and clear pronunciation so that your audience can hear you easily.

THE BIG ?

Is there a difference between reality and truth?

At the beginning of Unit 1, you participated in a discussion of the Big Question. Now that you have completed the unit, write a response to the question. Discuss how your initial ideas have deepened or changed. Support your response with at least one example from literature and one example from an additional subject area or your own life. Use Big Question vocabulary words (see p. 3) in your response.

Featured Titles

In this unit, you have read a variety of fiction and literary nonfiction. Continue to read on your own. Select books that you enjoy, but challenge yourself to explore new topics, new authors, and works of increasing depth and complexity. The titles suggested below will help you get started.

Literature

Lord of the Flies
by William Golding
Berkley Publishing Group, 1954

In this **novel,** a plane crash leaves a group of boys stranded without adults on a deserted island, and life feels like an exotic vacation. A dark influence soon casts a shadow over the young survivors, and life turns dangerous and deadly. The reality that the boys face may challenge your ideas about human nature.

Revolutionary Petunias and Other Poems
by Alice Walker   EXEMPLAR TEXT

Walker's collection of **poetry** explores the similarities between love and revolution— both in terms of the devastation each can cause and the possibilities for dramatic breakthrough.

41 Stories
by O. Henry   EXEMPLAR TEXT

This collection of O. Henry's finest **short stories** whisks readers from a bustling city to a seedy saloon to a prison shoe shop. Wherever O. Henry takes you, you will find yourself discovering that reality and truth may not always be as they appear.

Animal Farm
by George Orwell

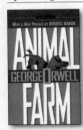

With idealism and stirring slogans, mistreated animals take over a farm and try to create a paradise of progress, justice, and equality. As the **novel** progresses, however, the reality of the situation points to far different truths. A hard-to-categorize mix of fable and political satire, this book is a bullet aimed squarely at totalitarianism in all its forms.

Rhinoceros
by Eugene Ionesco   EXEMPLAR TEXT

In this absurdist **drama,** Ionesco imagines a situation in which all the residents of a small French town slowly turn into rhinoceroses. This play is admired for its revealing look at the perils of conformity and the destructive nature of extremist ideologies.

Informational Texts

The Illustrated Book of Great Composers
by Wendy Thompson   EXEMPLAR TEXT

Herself a musician, Wendy Thompson has written a **reference book** that describes the lives and accomplishments of the most influential composers of classical music.

Euclid's Elements
by Euclid
Translated by Thomas L. Heath   EXEMPLAR TEXT

When the mathematician Euclid wrote this **treatise** in the third century B.C., he might as well have been planning a modern high school geometry course. Geometry students still learn the same axioms and proofs that Euclid proposed so many centuries ago. This translation includes all thirteen books written by this Greek "Father of Geometry."

Before Columbus: The Americas of 1491
by Charles C. Mann
Atheneum, 2009   EXEMPLAR TEXT

In this **nonfiction** book, the author vividly describes life in the Americas before Columbus. He tells how natives accomplished such feats as producing genetically engineered corn and building enormous pyramids.

Preparing to Read Complex Texts

Attentive Reading As you read literature on your own, bring your imagination and questions to the text. The questions shown below and others that you ask as you read will help you learn and enjoy literature even more.

 **Common Core State Standards**

Reading Literature/Informational Text 10. By the end of Grade 10, read and comprehend literature, including stories, dramas, poems, and literary nonfiction at the high end of the grades 9–10 text complexity band independently and proficiently.

When reading fiction, ask yourself...

- Who is telling the story? Do I like this character or voice?
- Does the story offer a message about life—a theme—that I appreciate? Why or why not?

Key Ideas and Details

- Is the world of the story convincing? Do any details jolt me out of that world or seem wrong?
- Does the plot pull me along? Do I care what happens?
- Do the characters seem real? Do the reasons they feel and act as they do ring true? Why or why not?
- Do their words and thoughts sound authentic? If not, why?
- Does the author use language well? Why or why not?

Craft and Structure

- Do I like the characters, or at least find them interesting? If not, why?
- Do I believe the events of this story? Why or why not?
- Is the work fresh and original? Why or why not?

Integration of Ideas

When reading nonfiction, ask yourself...

- Who is the author? Why did he or she write the work?
- Does the work meet my expectations? Why or why not?
- Are the ideas exciting? Do they give me a new way of looking at a topic?
- Do I learn something new? If so, what?
- Has the author made me care about the subject? Why or why not?

Key Ideas and Details

- Does the author organize ideas so that I can follow them? Why or why not?
- Does the author use strong, varied, and convincing evidence? Why or why not?
- Does the author use language well? Why or why not?
- Does the work ring true? Is any aspect of the work exaggerated?

Craft and Structure

- Do I agree or disagree with the author's ideas?
- Does the author omit viewpoints I think are important?

Integration of Ideas

THE BIG ? Can progress be made without *conflict?*

Short Stories

PHLit Online!
www.PHLitOnline.com

Hear It!
- Selection summary audio
- Selection audio
- BQ Tunes

See It!
- Author videos
- Big Question video
- Get Connected videos
- Background videos
- More about the authors
- Illustrated vocabulary words
- Vocabulary flashcards

Do It!
- Interactive journals
- Interactive graphic organizers
- Grammar tutorials
- Interactive vocabulary games
- Test practice

Can progress be made without *conflict?*

A **conflict** is a struggle between two or more opposing forces. Frequently, these opposing sides have different motives, or reasons for doing something, that spark the confrontation. Sometimes, progress, in the form of reconciliation, can be achieved. Progress involves change in a situation or a relationship. At times, adversaries must compromise and negotiate in order to resolve differences and move forward. Progress can take many forms, and at times, it can happen without conflict.

Exploring the Big Question

Collaboration: Group Discussion Start thinking about the Big Question by considering different ways people can make progress in their lives. List situations in which you or someone else has made progress. Give an example of each of the following circumstances that may lead to progress.

- Someone overcomes adversity in an athletic or academic competition.

- A change is made after an argument.

- A concession is offered for the sake of achieving a common goal.

- Internal conflict, a struggle within oneself, leads to personal progress.

- A change to a situation ends up causing a conflict.

Share your examples with a small group of classmates. Talk about whether progress was achieved and if there was any conflict involved. Listen carefully to group members' examples, and try to build on their ideas.

Connecting to the Literature The readings in this unit will help you think about different types of conflict and the different ways progess is, and is not, achieved. Each reading in this unit will give you additional insight into the Big Question.

PHLit
Online!
www.PHLitOnline.com
- Big Question video
- Illustrated vocabulary words
- Interactive vocabulary games
- BQ Tunes

Learning Big Question Vocabulary

Acquire and Use Academic Vocabulary Academic vocabulary is the language you encounter and use in classroom discussion, in textbooks, and on standardized tests. It is the language that helps to express and convey academic ideas. Review the definitions of these academic vocabulary words that relate to this unit's Big Question.

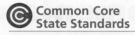
Common Core State Standards

Speaking and Listening
1. Initiate and participate effectively in a range of collaborative discussions with diverse partners on grades 9–10 topics, texts, and issues, building on others' ideas and expressing their own clearly and persuasively.

Language
6. Acquire and use accurately general academic and domain-specific words and phrases, sufficient for reading, writing, speaking, and listening at the college and career readiness level; demonstrate independence in gathering vocabulary knowledge when considering a word or phrase important to comprehension or expression.

debate (dē bāt´) *v.* argue or discuss

motive (mōt´ iv) *n.* something that causes a person to act a certain way

oppose (ə pōz´) *v.* set against

radical (rad´ i kəl) *adj.* tending to make extreme changes in existing views, conditions, or institutions

resolve (ri zälv´, -zôlv) *v.* reach a conclusion or decision

unify (yo͞o´ nə fi´) *v.* combine into one

Use these words as you complete Big Question activities in this unit that involve reading, writing, speaking, and listening. Because they are related to the themes of progress and conflict, they will help you to express your thoughts effectively.

Gather Vocabulary Knowledge Additional Big Question words are listed below. Categorize the words by deciding whether you know each one well, know it a little bit, or do not know it at all.

adversity	concession	progress
change	confrontation	reconciliation
compromise	negotiate	struggle

Then, do the following:

1. Write the definitions of the words you know.

2. Using a print or an online dictionary, look up the meanings of the words you do not know. Then, write the meanings.

3. If you think you know a word's meaning, write it down. Consult a dictionary to confirm the word's meaning. Revise your definition if necessary.

4. If you are not sure of a word's meaning, consult a dictionary. Then, record the meaning.

5. Use all the words in a brief paragraph about progress.

Elements of a Short Story

A short story is a brief work of fiction. Like all fiction, short stories focus on characters in conflict.

A **short story** is a brief work of fiction that can usually be read in one sitting. Because short stories are compact, writers usually limit the number of characters, the range of settings, and the scope of the action.

Characters are the personalities that take part in the action of a story. An author portrays characters by using a set of techniques that are collectively called **characterization**, or **character development**. Descriptive details, dialogue, and other literary elements help readers understand characters' qualities, including their feelings, thoughts, motivations, and behavior.

The characters in a story interact within a **setting,** or a particular time and place. In some stories, the setting is simply a backdrop for the action. In other stories, the setting exerts a strong influence on characters, shaping their personalities and motivations.

In every story, characters face a **conflict** that sets the plot in motion. The **plot** is the sequence of interrelated events that make up the action. As events unfold, the plot develops to a **climax,** or high point of tension. The tension subsides as the plot reaches the **resolution,** when events come to a close.

All of the elements of a short story work together to suggest a theme, or central insight about life. A **theme** is not a summary of a story's events. Instead, it is a generalization about what the events mean. A theme may be stated explicitly, but more often it is implied. The reader must then examine the relationships among the story's elements to arrive at an interpretation of its theme.

All of the elements of a short story contribute to its deeper meaning, or theme.

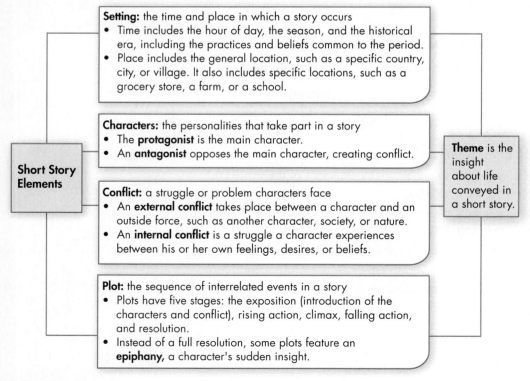

Setting: the time and place in which a story occurs
- Time includes the hour of day, the season, and the historical era, including the practices and beliefs common to the period.
- Place includes the general location, such as a specific country, city, or village. It also includes specific locations, such as a grocery store, a farm, or a school.

Short Story Elements

Characters: the personalities that take part in a story
- The **protagonist** is the main character.
- An **antagonist** opposes the main character, creating conflict.

Theme is the insight about life conveyed in a short story.

Conflict: a struggle or problem characters face
- An **external conflict** takes place between a character and an outside force, such as another character, society, or nature.
- An **internal conflict** is a struggle a character experiences between his or her own feelings, desires, or beliefs.

Plot: the sequence of interrelated events in a story
- Plots have five stages: the exposition (introduction of the characters and conflict), rising action, climax, falling action, and resolution.
- Instead of a full resolution, some plots feature an **epiphany,** a character's sudden insight.

Genre and Structure A **genre** is a classification of works of fiction that share certain elements, such as character types, moods, and common plot patterns. Genres include mysteries, fantasy, and realistic fiction. Short stories appear in all fictional genres, from traditional tales with formulaic plots, to online experiments in which the reader decides who the characters are and what they do.

A story's **structure** is the way in which the events of the plot unfold and the reader learns about characters and situations. A story's structure is shaped, in part, by the story's genre. For example, a mystery story is usually structured around an intriguing problem and a protagonist who seeks to solve it. The plot usually involves many twists and turns that finally arrive at a logical, but surprising, resolution. A mystery writer is not obliged to follow that pattern and may break from the genre conventions. Some mystery writers, for instance, are as interested in relating complex characters as they are in relating complex plots. In general, however, a story's genre helps shape its structure.

In This Section

Elements of a Short Story

Analyzing Characters in a Short Story

Analyzing Structure in a Short Story

Close Read: Character Development and Story Structure
- Model Text
- Practice Text

After You Read

 Common Core State Standards

RL.9-10.3, RL.9-10.5
[For the full wording of the standards, see the standards chart in the front of your textbook.]

Common Genres of Fiction	
Realistic	A story that portrays believable characters facing a true-to-life conflict in a realistic setting **Example:** A high-school athlete changes her priorities in life after an injury keeps her from playing sports.
Speculative (Science Fiction)	A story, often set in the future, in which actual or imagined science and technology play a central role **Example:** In the year 2090, humans declare war on androids after the machines attempt to overthrow the government.
Historical	A story set in the past that combines fictional characters with historical figures or events **Example:** A young man assists the Wright brothers at Kitty Hawk as they test various versions of their airplane.
Humorous	A story with comical characters and situations intended to amuse readers **Example:** Home alone, a bloodhound and a terrier join forces to track down and open a hidden bag of pet food.
Parody	An imitation of another story or writing style, intended to comment on or poke fun at the original **Example:** A retelling of a fairy tale in which characters are terrified, rather than delighted, by magical events.

Analyzing Characters in a Short Story

Common Core
State Standards

Reading Literature 3. Analyze how complex characters develop over the course of a text, interact with other characters, and advance the plot or develop the theme.

Complex characters are at the heart of most short stories.

Types of Characters Characters provide the moving force in most short stories. Their conflicts set off the plot and their actions and reactions keep it going. Characters can be classified according to the manner in which they are portrayed.

Types of Characters	
Flat, or Stock, Characters	Have just one or two traits
Round, or Complex, Characters	Have many traits, including both faults and virtues
Static Characters	Do not change during the story
Dynamic Characters	Change as a result of the experiences they undergo in the story

The main characters in most literary fiction are complex because they exhibit many different traits. Like real human beings, their personalities cannot be summed up in a word or simple phrase. However, complex characters may or may not be dynamic. For example, a complex character who undergoes a crisis may not change as a result.

All characters have **motivations,** or reasons for feeling and behaving as they do. Complex characters may have multiple or even **conflicting motivations.** For example, a character who desires to be true to his or her values may also want to fit in with a clique. Those two motivations conflict. They may cause the character to be confused, or to take actions that complicate his or her situation in unexpected ways.

Characterization is the method by which an author develops a character. In **direct characterization,** the **narrator**—the character or voice telling the story—directly states a character's traits.

> **Example: Direct Characterization**
> Lauren was always the first to volunteer to help, but then she never stopped reminding everyone about her good deeds. That was one of her greatest faults.

In **indirect characterization,** the narrator reveals a character's personality by describing a character's appearance, feelings, behavior, and thoughts, as well as his or her interactions with other characters. **Dialogue,** the words that characters speak, is one of the key tools an author uses to reveal character traits. The ways in which characters speak—their use of sarcasm, irony, body language, or hidden meanings—can be just as revealing as the statements they make. In the example shown below, dialogue reveals what the characters are like as well as what they think.

> **Example: Indirect Characterization**
> Matt stared at the huge pile of envelopes that he had to stuff for the fundraiser. "How will we finish in time?" he asked wearily.
>
> "Lauren said she'd be here to help," LaTise mumbled, rolling her eyes.
>
> Sarah added, "Then she'll spend the entire fundraiser announcing how she did it all by herself."
>
> Just then, Lauren walked in. "Never fear! I'm here to save the day!"

Analyzing Structure in a Short Story

 **Common Core State Standards**

Reading Literature 5.
Analyze how an author's choices concerning how to structure a text, order events within it, and manipulate time create such effects as mystery, tension, or surprise.

Story structure is the way in which events, characters, and situations are introduced and developed.

The foundation of a story's **structure** is its plot—the series of interrelated events that unfold as characters face a conflict. The order in which the author arranges events is an important part of that structure. **Chronological order,** in which events unfold in a sequence from beginning to end, is the most common structure. However, authors may vary that basic structure to create effects such as mystery, tension, or surprise. Consider the following narrative techniques.

Flashbacks interrupt the flow of a chronological sequence to describe earlier events. Flashbacks may take the form of a memory, a dream, or an actual relocation of the story into the past. Flashbacks may provide information about a character's past or insights into his or her motivations.

Flashback in a Chronological Sequence

Sequence	Event
First	Felicia waits for Nathan.
Second	Nathan arrives.
Third	They go to dinner.
Fourth	At dinner, Nathan asks Felicia to marry him.
Flashback	Felicia recalls the first time they met.
Fifth	Felicia says yes.

Parallel plots occur when an author develops two distinct storylines, with two sets of characters, in a single work. Parallel plots often explore similar conflicts among different groups of people. Often, these separate storylines ultimately join into a single, unified tale.

Pacing, the speed or rhythm of the writing, influences how readers experience a story. Slow pacing can create tension or suspense by delaying an anticipated event. Authors may slow the pace of events by adding detailed descriptions of the action or of a character's thoughts and feelings.

> **Example: Slow Pacing**
> Luis nervously stared at the clock. The hand trudged from one second to the next as though it were moving through mud. He counted along with each tick, dragging out the name of each number to match the sluggish twitches of the hand. "One . . . two . . . three . . ."
>
> His heart slowed, but his mind raced. If Jim arrived before the 3 o'clock train and found him, the whole scheme would fall apart.

By contrast, fast pacing creates a sense of energy and excitement. Short and even fragmented sentences and rapid cutting from detail to detail increase the story's pace.

> **Example: Fast Pacing**
> Luis stared at the clock. 2:55.
>
> He peered down the platform. A man in a suit was walking toward him. 2:56. He looked down the track. No train.
>
> The man drew closer. Was it Jim?
>
> Luis's heart pounded in his ears. 2:57. If Jim found him first the scheme would fail.
>
> The man was getting closer. Luis pulled down his hat. 2:58. Was that a train whistle? Time was running out.

Close Read: Character Development and Story Structure

Characters develop as a story progresses. Narrative structure organizes events and affects the reader's experience.

Complex, believable characters are the lifeblood of good stories. A character's history, perceptions, desires, and fears affect how he or she reacts to conflict. These reactions, in turn, move the plot forward and develop the theme. The story's structure helps the reader follow the unfolding of events and grasp the connections among details. As you read, look for clues to character and notice structural elements that organize the story.

Character Development	Structural Elements
Characterization Writers use many different techniques to reveal what characters are like. As you read, notice • direct statements that explain characters; • details that show characters' reactions to one another; • descriptions of how characters look, think, feel, and behave; • dialogue that indicates characters' attitudes, beliefs, or other qualities.	**Setting** The setting may be a backdrop or an active influence on the action. As you read, notice • details that describe the physical setting; • details that show values, beliefs, traditions, and cultural practices typical of the setting; • problems caused by the setting.
Characters' Motivations Characters' motivations, an aspect of characterization, play an essential role in a story. As you read, look for details that show • the reasons that characters feel, think, and behave as they do; • any opposing motivations that create internal conflict.	**Conflict and Plot** Conflict drives all plots. As you read, notice • the conflict that starts the story; • ways in which that conflict intensifies and is finally resolved; • the order of events; • causal relationships, or the way in which one event leads to another; • techniques that manipulate time, such as flashbacks or pacing.
Dynamic Characters Some characters are dynamic and change as a result of the events of a story, whereas others are static and do not. As you read, consider • how characters think, feel, and behave at the beginning of a story; • whether characters change by the end of the story; • what kinds of changes characters experience.	**Narrative Effects** Structural elements may create specific emotions in the reader. As you read, consider • emotional high points, such as suspense or excitement, and the story events that evoke these emotions; • changes in pacing and their effects.

Model

About the Text Langston Hughes (1902–1967) was a distinguished and prolific author who first came to prominence during the Harlem Renaissance of the 1920s. Although Hughes is probably best known as a poet, he was also a playwright, a song lyricist, a novelist, and an author of short stories.

In the following short story, Hughes depicts an unexpected meeting between former sweethearts in a New York City park. In little more than 400 words, Hughes vividly portrays a few moments in time—and a lifetime of regret.

"Early Autumn" by Langston Hughes

When Bill was very young, they had been in love. Many nights they had spent walking, talking together. Then something not very important had come between them, and they didn't speak. Impulsively, she had married a man she thought she loved. Bill went away, bitter about women.

Yesterday, walking across Washington Square, she saw him for the first time in years.

"Bill Walker," she said.

He stopped. At first he did not recognize her, to him she looked so old.

"Mary! Where did you come from?"

Unconsciously, she lifted her face as though wanting a kiss, but he held out his hand. She took it.

"I live in New York now," she said.

"Oh"—smiling politely. Then a little frown came quickly between his eyes.

"Always wondered what happened to you, Bill."

"I'm a lawyer. Nice firm, way downtown."

"Married yet?"

"Sure. Two kids."

"Oh," she said.

Setting The title suggests that the season of the year is important to the story's meaning. Autumn is a time of endings. The fact that the title says autumn comes early suggests that an ending comes too soon.

Conflict and Plot The first paragraph provides compact exposition that rapidly fills readers in on the characters' shared past and likely conflict.

Indirect Characterization Details emphasize the two characters' differences. Mary recognizes Bill, but she looks "so old" to him; she seems to seek a kiss, but he offers only his hand. Bill seems to have moved on, while Mary lingers over memories of this lost love.

Model continued

Dynamic Characters Mary has undergone many changes since she knew Bill. She is married, has children, and looks considerably older.

Conflict and Plot The chronological order is interrupted by a brief memory that provides important information about differences in the characters' ages.

Narrative Effects Autumn and dusk both represent endings. The fragmented description of the setting creates a broken and melancholy effect.

Motivation The detail about her son's name reinforces all the preceding details that suggest Mary still loves Bill. For Mary, their relationship did, indeed, end too early.

A great many people went past them through the park. People they didn't know. It was late afternoon. Nearly sunset. Cold.

"And your husband?" he asked her.

"We have three children. I work in the bursar's office at Columbia."

"You're looking very . . ." (he wanted to say *old*) ". . .well," he said.

She understood. Under the trees in Washington Square, she found herself desperately reaching back into the past. She had been older than he then in Ohio. Now she was not young at all. Bill was still young.

"We live on Central Park West," she said. "Come and see us sometime."

"Sure," he replied. "You and your husband must have dinner with my family some night. Any night. Lucille and I'd love to have you."

The leaves fell slowly from the trees in the Square. Fell without wind. Autumn dusk. She felt a little sick.

"We'd love it," she answered.

"You ought to see my kids." He grinned.

Suddenly the lights came on up the whole length of Fifth Avenue, chains of misty brilliance in the blue air.

"There's my bus," she said.

He held out his hand, "Good-bye."

"When . . ." she wanted to say, but the bus was ready to pull off. The lights on the avenue blurred, twinkled, blurred. And she was afraid to open her mouth as she entered the bus. Afraid it would be impossible to utter a word.

Suddenly she shrieked very loudly, "Good-bye!" But the bus door had closed.

The bus started. People came between them outside, people crossing the street, people they didn't know. Space and people. She lost sight of Bill. Then she remembered she had forgotten to give him her address—or to ask him for his—or tell him that her youngest boy was named Bill, too.

Independent Practice

About the Text C. J. Cherryh is known for her space opera series—books filled with romantic adventure, vivid details of alien cultures, and interstellar conflict. She enjoys excitement in her real life on Earth as well. Her adventures include outrunning a dog pack in Thebes, Greece, and falling down a chute in a cave on Crete. Referring to her home in the Pacific Northwest, Cherryh says, "I choose to live downwind of five active volcanoes."

In the following science-fiction story, Cherryh depicts the perils faced by the qhal, a human-like race, when they discover a way to travel through time. Cherryh says that "it's human to wish to relive yesterday or to leap ahead to a longed-for event. Science fiction allows you to fulfill that wish."

"The Threads of Time" by C. J. Cherryh

It was possible that the Gates were killing the qhal. They were everywhere, on every world, had been a fact of life for five thousand years, and linked the whole net of qhalur civilization into one present-tense coherency.

They had not, to be sure, invented the Gates. Chance gave them that gift . . . on a dead world of their own sun. One Gate stood—made by unknown hands.

And the qhal made others, imitating what they found. The Gates were instantaneous transfer, not alone from place to place, but, because of the motion of worlds and suns and the traveling galaxies—involving time.

There was an end of time. Ah, qhal *could* venture anything. If one supposed, if one believed, if one were very *sure,* one could step through a Gate to a Gate that would/might exist on some other distant world.

And if one were wrong?

If it did not exist?

If it never had?

Time warped in the Gate-passage. One could step across light-years, unaged; so it was possible to outrace light and time. Did one not want to die, bound to a single lifespan? Go forward. See the future. Visit the world/end worlds to come.

But never go back. Never tamper. Never alter the past.

There was an End of Time.

It was the place where qhal gathered, who had been farthest and lost their courage for traveling on. It was the point beyond which no one had courage, where descendants shared the world with living ancestors in greater and greater numbers, the jaded, the restless, who reached this age and felt their will erode away.

Setting Which clues in the opening paragraph suggest when and where this science fiction story takes place?

Narrative Effects How do the short, one-line paragraphs affect the p●ng of the story?

Conflict and Plot What do these details tell you about the unusual way time and events will be ordered in this story?

Practice continued

Conflict and Plot What internal conflict for the qhal is described in these lines?

Narrative Effects How do the varied lengths of paragraphs and sentences reinforce the sense of displacement in time the story describes?

It was the place where hope ended. Oh, a few went farther, and the age saw them—no more. They were gone. They did not return.

They went beyond, whispered those who had lost their courage. They went out a Gate and found nothing there.

They died.

Or was it death—to travel without end? And what was death? And was the universe finite at all?

Some went, and vanished, and the age knew nothing more of them.

Those who were left were in agony—of desire to go; of fear to go farther.

Of changes.

This age—did change. It rippled with possibilities. Memories deceived. One remembered, or remembered that one had remembered, and the fact grew strange and dim, contradicting what obviously *was.* People remembered things that never had been true.

And one must never go back to see. Backtiming—had direst possibilities. It made paradox.

But some tried, seeking a time as close to their original exit point as possible. Some came too close, and involved themselves in time-loops, a particularly distressing kind of accident and unfortunate equally for those involved as bystanders.

Among qhal, between the finding of the first Gate and the End of Time, a new kind of specialist evolved: time-menders, who in most extreme cases of disturbance policed the Gates and carefully researched afflicted areas. They alone were licensed to violate the back-time barrier, passing back and forth under strict noninvolvement regulations, exchanging intelligence only with each other, to minutely adjust reality.

Evolved.

Agents recruited other agents at need—but at whose instance? There might be some who knew. It might have come from the far end of time—in that last (or was it last?) age beyond which nothing seemed certain, when the years since the First Gate were more than five thousand, and the Now in which all Gates existed was—very distant. Or it might have come from those who had found the Gate, overseeing their invention. Someone knew, somewhen, somewhere along the course of the stars toward the end of time.

But no one said.

It was hazardous business, this time-mending, in all senses. Precisely *what* was done was something virtually unknowable after it was done, for alterations in the past produced (one believed) changes in future reality. Whole time-fields, whose events could be wiped and redone, with effects which widened the farther down the timeline they proceeded. Detection of time-tampering was almost impossible.

> *A stranger wanted something to eat, a long time ago. He shot himself his dinner.*
>
> *A small creature was not where it had been, when it had been.*
>
> *A predator missed a meal and took another . . . likewise small.*
>
> *A child lost a pet.*
>
> *And found another.*
>
> *And a friend she would not have had. She was happier for it.*
>
> *She met many people she had never/would never meet.*
>
> *A man in a different age had breakfast in a house on a hill.*

Agent Harrh had acquired a sense about disruptions, a kind of extrasensory queasiness about a just-completed timewarp. He was not alone in this. But the time-menders (Harrh knew three others of his own age) never reported such experiences outside their own special group. Such reports would have been meaningless to his own time, involving a past which (as a result of the warp) was neither real nor valid nor perceptible to those in Time Present. Some time-menders would reach the verge of insanity because of this. This was future fact. Harrh knew this.

He had been there.

And he refused to go again to Now, that Now to which time had advanced since the discovery of the Gate—let alone to the End of Time, which was the farthest that anyone imagined. He was one of a few, a very few, licensed to do so, but he refused.

He lived scattered lives in ages to come, and remembered the future with increasing melancholy.

He had visited the End of Time, and left it in the most profound despair. He had seen what was there, and when he had contemplated going beyond, that most natural step out the Gate which stood and beckoned—

He fled. He had never run from anything but that. It remained, a recollection of shame at his fear.

Conflict and Plot What information about the past—or, in this story of time travel, the future—do these flashbacks provide?

Characterization The protagonist, Agent Harrh, appears for the first time in this paragraph. What do you learn about his personality in this introduction?

Dynamic Characters How has the experience of time travel changed Harrh?

Practice continued

Characterization
Describe what Harrh and his wife are like. Cite specific details from the text, both explicit and implied.

Dynamic Characters What dramatic change in his life is Harrh contemplating?

A sense of a limit which he had never had before.

And this in itself was terrible, to a man who had thought time infinite and himself immortal.

In his own present of 1003 since the First Gate, Harrh had breakfast, a quiet meal. The children were off to the beach. His wife shared tea with him and thought it would be a fine morning.

"Yes," he said. "Shall we take the boat out? We can fish a little, take the sun."

"Marvelous," she said. Her gray eyes shone. He loved her—for herself, for her patience. He caught her hand on the crystal table, held slender fingers, not speaking his thoughts, which were far too somber for the morning.

They spent their mornings and their days together. He came back to her, time after shifting time. He might be gone a month; and home a week; and gone two months next time. He never dared cut it too close. They lost a great deal of each other's lives, and so much— so much he could not share with her.

"The island," he said. "Mhreihrrinn, I'd like to see it again."

"I'll pack," she said.

And went away.

He came back to her never aged; and she bore their two sons; and reared them; and managed the accounts: and explained his absences to relatives and the world. *He travels,* she would say, with that right amount of secrecy that protected secrets.

And even to her he could never confide what he knew.

"I trust you," she would say—knowing what he was, but never what he did.

He let her go. She went off to the hall and out the door— He imagined happy faces, holiday, the boys making haste to run the boat out and put on the bright colored sail. She would keep them busy carrying this and that, fetching food and clothes—things happened in shortest order when Mhreihrrinn set her hand to them.

He wanted that, wanted the familiar, the orderly, the homely. He was, if he let his mind dwell on things—afraid. He had the notion never to leave again.

He had been to the Now most recently—5045, and his flesh crawled at the memory. There was recklessness there. There was disquiet. The Now had traveled two decades and more since he had first begun, and he felt it more and more. The whole decade of the 5040s had a queasiness about it, ripples of instability as if the whole fabric of the Now were shifting like a kaleidoscope.

And it headed for the End of Time. It had become more and more like that age, confirming it by its very collapse.

People had illusions in the Now. They perceived what had not been true.

And yet it *was* when he came home.

It had grown to be so—while he was gone.

A university stood in Morurir, which he did not remember.

A hedge of trees grew where a building had been in Morurir.

A man was in the Council who had died.

He would not go back to Now. He had resolved that this morning.

He had children, begotten before his first time-traveling. He had so very much to keep him—this place, this home, this stability—He was very well to do. He had invested well—his own small tampering. He had no lack, no need. He was mad to go on and on. He was done.

But a light distracted him, an opal shimmering beyond his breakfast nook, arrival in that receptor which his fine home afforded, linked to the master gate at Pyvrrhn.

A young man materialized there, opal and light and then solidity, a distraught young man.

"Harrh," the youth said, disregarding the decencies of meeting, and strode forward unasked. "Harrh, is everything all right here?"

Harrh arose from the crystal table even before the shimmer died, beset by that old queasiness of things out of joint. This was Alhir from 390 Since the Gate, an experienced man in the force: he had used a Master Key to come here—had such access, being what he was.

"Alhir," Harrh said, perplexed. "What's wrong?"

"You don't know." Alhir came as far as the door.

"A cup of tea?" Harrh said. Alhir had been here before. They were friends. There were oases along the course of suns, friendly years, places where houses served as rest-stops. In this too Mhreihrrinn was patient. "I've got to tell you— No, don't tell me. I don't want to know. I'm through. I've made up my mind. You can carry that where you're going. —But if you want the breakfast—"

"There's been an accident."
"I don't want to hear."
"He got past us."

Motivation What are Harrh's reasons for wanting to stay?

Characterization What does the first rapid dialogue exchange between Harrh and Alhir tell you about these characters?

Conflict and Plot What does this paragraph reveal about the conflict between Harrh and the time-menders?

Narrative Effects What effect is created by hinting at events without providing full information?

Practice continued

"I don't want to know." He walked over to the cupboard, took another cup. "Mhreihrrinn's with the boys down at the beach. You just caught us." He set the cup down and poured the tea, where Mhreihrrinn had sat. "Won't you? You're always welcome here. Mhreihrrinn has no idea what you are. My young friend, she calls you. She doesn't know. Or she suspects. She'd never say.—Sit *down.*"

Alhir had strayed aside, where a display case sat along the wall, a lighted case of mementoes of treasures, of crystal. "Harrh, there was a potsherd here."

"No," Harrh said, less and less comfortable. "Just the glasses. I'm quite sure."

"Harrh, it was very old."

"No," he said. "—I promised Mhreihrrinn and the boys—I mean it.

I'm through. I don't want to know."

"It came from Silen. From the digs at the First Gate, Harrh. It was a very valuable piece. You valued it very highly.—You don't remember."

"No," Harrh said, feeling fear thick about him, like a change in atmosphere. "I don't know of such a piece. I never had such a thing. Check your memory, Alhir."

"It was from the ruins by the *First Gate,* don't you understand?"

And then Alhir did not exist.

Harrh blinked, remembered pouring a cup of tea. But he was sitting in the chair, his breakfast before him.

He poured the tea and drank.

He was sitting on rock, amid the grasses blowing gently in the wind, on a clifftop by the sea.

He was standing there. "Mhreihrrinn," he said, in the first chill touch of fear.

But that memory faded. He had never had a wife, nor children. He forgot the house as well.

Trees grew and faded.

Rocks moved at random.

The time-menders were in most instances the only ones who survived even a little while.

Wrenched loose from time and with lives rooted in many parts of it, they felt it first and lived it longest, and not a few were trapped in backtime and did not die, but survived the horror of it and begot children who further confounded the time-line.

Narrative Effects
How does Alhir's sudden disappearance affect you as a reader?

Dynamic Characters
How has the loss of his memories affected Harrh? What insight about the relationship between memory and identity does this passage develop?

Time, stretched thin in possibilities, adjusted itself.

He was Harrh.

But he was many possibilities and many names.

In time none of them mattered.

He was many names; he lived. He had many bodies; and the souls stained his own.

In the end he remembered nothing at all, except the drive to live.

And the dreams.

And none of the dreams were true.

After You Read — The Threads of Time

1. Key Ideas and Details (a) How did the qhal acquire the ability to travel in time? **(b) Infer:** To what extent did they at first understand the consequences of what they were doing?

2. Key Ideas and Details (a) In his present of 1003, what changes does Harrh notice? **(b) Draw Conclusions:** Why are these changes significant?

3. Key Ideas and Details (a) Describe: How would you describe Mhreihrrinn? **(b) Classify:** Is she a dynamic or static character? Explain.

4. Craft and Structure Analyze: Is the character of Harrh developed mainly through direct or indirect characterization? Explain.

5. Craft and Structure (a) Identify: Note two techniques the author uses to manipulate the pace of the story. **(b) Analyze:** What effect is produced?

6. Integration of Knowledge and Ideas (a) Use a chart like the one shown to define key terms from the story.

Term	What It Means	Why It Is Important
the qhal		
Gate		
time-mender		
the Now		
End of Time		

(b) Collaboration: In a group, discuss your definitions.

Leveled Texts

Build your skills and improve your comprehension of short stories with texts of increasing complexity.

Read **"A Visit to Grandmother"** to see what happens when a son confronts his mother about his childhood.

Read **"A Problem"** to see how a group of uncles debates the fate of their irresponsible nephew.

Common Core State Standards

Meet these standards with either **"A Visit to Grandmother"** (p. 242) or **"A Problem"** (p. 256).

Reading Literature
3. Analyze how complex characters develop over the course of a text, interact with other characters, and advance the plot or develop the theme. (*Literary Analysis: Character and Characterization*)

Writing
3.a. Engage and orient the reader by setting out a problem, situation, or observation, establishing one or multiple point(s) of view, and introducing a narrator and/or characters; create a smooth progression of experiences or events.

3.b. Use narrative techniques, such as dialogue, pacing, description, reflection, and multiple plot lines, to develop experiences, events, and/or characters.

3.d. Use precise words and phrases, telling details, and sensory language to convey a vivid picture of the experiences, events, setting, and/or characters. (*Writing: Retellings*)

8. Gather relevant information from multiple authoritative print and digital sources; assess the usefulness of each source in answering the research question; integrate information into the text selectively to maintain the flow of ideas, avoiding plagiarism and following a standard format for citation. (*Research and Technology: Report on Sources*)

Language
4. Determine or clarify the meaning of unknown and multiple-meaning words and phrases based on grades 9–10 reading and content, choosing flexibly from a range of strategies. (*Vocabulary: Word Study*)

Literary Analysis: Character and Characterization

Story **characters** are the people, animals, or even objects who perform the actions and experience the events of a narrative. Writers use two main types of **characterization** to bring characters to life.

- **Direct characterization:** The writer tells readers exactly what a character is like—for example, "Hugo is generous to a fault."
- **Indirect characterization:** The writer reveals a character's traits through **dialogue** (the character's words), the character's actions and thoughts, and the interactions between the character and others.

To better understand characters and gain insight into the theme of a story, take note of the **character development**—changes a complex character undergoes or new aspects of the character the writer reveals.

Reading Skill: Make Inferences

An **inference** is a logical assumption based on details in a story. Making inferences helps you more fully understand story characters and the reasons that they act as they do. To make inferences about a character, **relate characters and events to your own experience,** and make assumptions based on that information. For example, if a story character mumbles and avoids eye contact, you may think of people you know who act this way, and you may infer that the character is shy.

Using the Strategy: Inference Chart

Use an **inference chart** like this one to help you relate your reading to your experiences.

Story Detail		Your Experience		Inference
The new captain's palms are sweating as she addresses the crew.	+	New camp counselors are nervous about whether campers will obey them.	→	The new captain is unsure of herself.

Can progress be made without *conflict?*

Writing About the Big Question

In "A Visit to Grandmother," a man must decide if he can believe his mother's version of a longstanding family conflict. Use these sentence starters to develop your ideas about the Big Question:

When people experience a misunderstanding, a **confrontation** may be helpful because _____.

Following a conflict, relationships might **change** because _____ _____.

While You Read Look for details that build up to a confrontation and decide whether progress can be made.

Vocabulary

Read each word and its definition. Decide whether you know the word well, know it a little bit, or do not know it at all. After you read, see how your knowledge of each word has increased.

- **indulgence** (in dul´ jəns) *n.* leniency; readiness to tolerate or forgive bad behavior (p. 244) *If you show the child too much __indulgence__, you may spoil her.* indulge *v.* indulgent *adj.*

- **grimacing** (grim´ is iŋ) *v.* making a twisted face showing disgust or pain (p. 244) *She is __grimacing__ because she has a splinter in her toe.* grimace *n.*

- **meager** (mē´ gər) *adj.* of poor quality or small amount (p. 250) *Due to poor rainfall, there was only a __meager__ crop.* meagerly *adv.* meagerness *n.*

- **trace** (trās) *n.* tiny amount; hint (p. 250) *There was not even a __trace__ of cake left.*

- **fraud** (frôd) *n.* deceit; trickery (p. 251) *There are strict penalties for insurance __fraud__.* fraudulent *adj.* fraudulently *adv.*

- **engaging** (en gāj´ iŋ) *adj.* attractive; pleasant (p. 252) *The doctor's __engaging__ personality puts his patients at ease.* engage *v.* engagingly *adv.* engagement *n.*

Word Study

The **Latin suffix -ence** means "quality of" or "state of."

In this story, a mother treats one of her sons with **indulgence,** or the state of yielding to his wishes, by not punishing him for improper behavior.

Author of
A Visit to Grandmother

William Melvin Kelley is a man of questions. He says, "I am not a sociologist or a politician or a spokesman. Such people try to give answers. A writer, I think, should ask questions."

Kelley's questions often explore the problems of belonging to a group. His first novel, *A Different Drummer,* reflects his belief in individualism.

A Community Artist At the same time, Kelley's work shows a strong connection to community. He belongs to the Black Arts Movement, the generation of writers, artists, dancers, and musicians that emerged in the 1960s and 1970s. Like others in the movement, he often addresses the moral, cultural, and political questions African Americans face.

DID YOU KNOW?

Introducing his class on writing fiction, Kelley notes that "Art may come from the heart, but craft comes from the brain."

BACKGROUND FOR THE STORY
Dialect

Dialect is the variety of a language spoken in a region or community. Some characters in "A Visit to Grandmother" speak in a southern dialect. In this dialect, *I reckon* means "I believe." *Fixin' to* replaces "about to."

A Visit to Grandmother

William Melvin Kelley

Chig knew something was wrong the instant his father kissed her. He had always known his father to be the warmest of men, a man so kind that when people ventured timidly into his office, it took only a few words from him to make them relax, and even laugh. Doctor Charles Dunford cared about people.

But when he had bent to kiss the old lady's black face, something new and almost ugly had come into his eyes: fear, uncertainty, sadness, and perhaps even hatred.

Ten days before in New York, Chig's father had decided suddenly he wanted to go to Nashville to attend his college class reunion, twenty years out. Both Chig's brother and sister, Peter and Connie, were packing for camp and besides were too young for such an affair. But Chig was seventeen, had nothing to do that summer, and his father asked if he would like to go along. His father had given him additional reasons: "All my running buddies got their diplomas and were snapped up by them crafty young gals, and had kids within a year—now all those kids, some of them gals, are your age."

The reunion had lasted a week. As they packed for home, his father, in a far too offhand way, had suggested they visit Chig's grandmother. "We this close. We might as well drop in on her and my brothers."

Literary Analysis
Character and Characterization
What do you learn about GL through direct characterization?

Vocabulary
indulgence (in dul′ jəns)
n. leniency; readiness to tolerate or forgive bad behavior

So, instead of going north, they had gone farther south, had just entered her house. And Chig had a suspicion now that the reunion had been only an excuse to drive south, that his father had been heading to this house all the time.

His father had never talked much about his family, with the exception of his brother, GL, who seemed part con man, part practical joker and part Don Juan;[1] he had spoken of GL with the kind of indulgence he would have shown a cute, but ill-behaved and potentially dangerous, five-year-old.

Chig's father had left home when he was fifteen. When asked why, he would answer: "I wanted to go to school. They didn't have a Negro high school at home, so I went up to Knoxville and lived with a cousin and went to school."

They had been met at the door by Aunt Rose, GL's wife, and ushered into the living room. The old lady had looked up from her seat by the window. Aunt Rose stood between the visitors.

The old lady eyed his father. "Rose, who that? Rose?" She squinted. She looked like a doll, made of black straw, the wrinkles in her face running in one direction like the head of a broom. Her hair was white and coarse and grew out straight from her head. Her eyes were brown—the whites, too, seemed light brown—and were hidden behind thick glasses, which remained somehow on a tiny nose. "That Hiram?" That was another of his father's brothers. "No, it ain't Hiram; too big for Hiram." She turned then to Chig. "Now that man, he look like Eleanor, Charles's wife, but Charles wouldn't never send my grandson to see me. I never even hear from Charles." She stopped again.

"It Charles, Mama. That who it is." Aunt Rose, between them, led them closer. "It Charles come all the way from New York to see you, and brung little Charles with him."

The old lady stared up at them. "Charles? Rose, that really Charles?" She turned away, and reached for a handkerchief in the pocket of her clean, ironed, flowered housecoat, and wiped her eyes. "God have mercy, Charles." She spread her arms up to him, and he bent down and kissed her cheek. That was when Chig saw his face, grimacing. She hugged him; Chig watched the muscles in her arms as they tightened around his father's neck. She half rose out of her chair. "How are you, son?"

Chig could not hear his father's answer.

She let him go, and fell back into her chair, grabbing the arms. Her hands were as dark as the wood, and seemed to become part of it. "Now, who that standing there? Who that man?"

Reading Skill
Make Inferences What feelings does the grandmother have upon seeing her son? Which details support your inference?

Vocabulary
grimacing (grim′ is iŋ)
v. making a twisted face showing disgust or pain

---

1. **Don Juan** (dän′ wän′) a legendary nobleman, idle and immoral, who fascinates women.

"That's one of your grandsons, Mama." His father's voice cracked. "Charles Dunford, junior. You saw him once, when he was a baby, in Chicago. He's grown now."

"I can see that, boy!" She looked at Chig squarely. "Come here, son, and kiss me once." He did. "What they call you? Charles too?"

"No, ma'am, they call me Chig."

She smiled. She had all her teeth, but they were too perfect to be her own. "That's good. Can't have two boys answering to Charles in the same house. Won't nobody at all come. So you that little boy. You don't remember me, do you. I used to take you to church in Chicago, and you'd get up and hop in time to the music. You studying to be a preacher?"

"No, ma'am. I don't think so. I might be a lawyer."

"You'll be an honest one, won't you?"

"I'll try."

"Trying ain't enough! You be honest, you hear? Promise me. You be honest like your daddy."

"All right. I promise."

"Good. Rose, where's GL at? Where's that thief? He gone again?"

"I don't know, Mama." Aunt Rose looked embarrassed. "He say he was going by the store. He'll be back."

"Well, then where's Hiram? You call up those boys, and get them over here—now! You got enough to eat? Let me go see." She started to get up. Chig reached out his hand. She shook him off. "What they tell you about me, Chig? They tell you I'm all laid up? Don't believe it. They don't know nothing about old ladies. When I want help, I'll let you know. Only time I'll need help getting anywhere is when I dies and they lift me into the ground."

She was standing now, her back and shoulders straight. She came only to Chig's chest. She squinted up at him. "You eat much? Your daddy ate like two men."

"Yes, ma'am."

"That's good. That means you ain't nervous. Your mama, she ain't nervous. I remember that. In Chicago,

Literary Analysis
Character and Characterization
Name one trait of the grandmother that is suggested in the dialogue.

Reading Check
How does the grandmother react to the surprise visit?

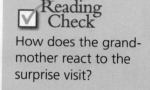

A Visit to Grandmother **245**

she'd sit down by a window all afternoon and never say nothing, just knit." She smiled. "Let me see what we got to eat."

"I'll do that, Mama." Aunt Rose spoke softly. "You haven't seen Charles in a long time. You sit and talk."

The old lady squinted at her. "You can do the cooking if you promise it ain't because you think I can't."

Aunt Rose chuckled. "I know you can do it, Mama."

"All right. I'll just sit and talk a spell." She sat again and arranged her skirt around her short legs.

Chig did most of the talking, told all about himself before she asked. His father spoke only when he was spoken to, and then, only one word at a time, as if by coming back home, he had become a small boy again, sitting in the parlor while his mother spoke with her guests. •

When Uncle Hiram and Mae, his wife, came they sat down to eat. Chig did not have to ask about Uncle GL's absence; Aunt Rose volunteered an explanation: "Can't never tell where the man is at. One Thursday morning he left here and next thing we knew, he was calling from Chicago, saying he went up to see Joe Louis[2] fight. He'll be here though; he ain't as young and footloose as he used to be." Chig's father had mentioned driving down that GL was about five years older than he was, nearly fifty.

Uncle Hiram was somewhat smaller than Chig's father; his short-cropped kinky hair was half gray, half black. One spot, just off his forehead, was totally white. Later, Chig found out it had been that way since he was twenty. Mae (Chig could not bring himself to call her Aunt) was a good deal younger than Hiram, pretty enough so that Chig would have looked at her twice on the street. She was a honey-colored woman, with long eyelashes. She was wearing a white sheath.

At dinner, Chig and his father sat on one side, opposite Uncle Hiram and Mae; his grandmother and Aunt Rose sat at the ends. The food was good; there was a lot and Chig ate a lot. All through the meal, they talked about the family as it had been thirty years before, and particularly about the young GL. Mae and Chig asked questions; the old lady answered; Aunt Rose directed the discussion, steering the old lady onto the best stories; Chig's father laughed from time to time; Uncle Hiram ate.

"Why don't you tell them about the horse, Mama?" Aunt Rose, over Chig's weak protest, was spooning mashed potatoes onto his plate. "There now, Chig."

---

2. **Joe Louis** (1914–1981) U.S. boxer and the world heavyweight champion from 1937 to 1949.

◄ **Critical Viewing**
What does this image suggest about the life the grandmother and her family lead? **[Connect]**

Reading Check
How does Chig's father act during their visit?

"I'm trying to think." The old lady was holding her fork halfway to her mouth, looking at them over her glasses. "Oh, you talking about that crazy horse GL brung home that time."

"That's right, Mama." Aunt Rose nodded and slid another slice of white meat on Chig's plate.

Mae started to giggle. "Oh, I've heard this. This is funny, Chig."

The old lady put down her fork and began: Well, GL went out of the house one day with an old, no-good chair I wanted him to take over to the church for a bazaar, and he met up with this man who'd just brung in some horses from out West. Now, I reckon you can expect one swindler[3] to be in every town, but you don't rightly think there'll be two, and God forbid they should ever meet—but they did, GL and his chair, this man and his horses. Well, I wished I'd-a been there; there must-a been some mighty high-powered talking going on. That man with his horses, he told GL them horses was half-Arab, half-Indian, and GL told that man the chair was an antique he'd stole from some rich white folks. So they swapped. Well, I was a-looking out the window and seen GL dragging this animal to the house. It looked pretty gentle and its eyes was most closed and its feet was shuffling.

"GL, where'd you get that thing?" I says.

"I swapped him for that old chair, Mama," he says. "And made myself a bargain. This is even better than Papa's horse."

Well, I'm a-looking at this horse and noticing how he be looking more and more wide awake every minute, sort of warming up like a teakettle until, I swears to you, that horse is blowing steam out its nose.

"Come on, Mama," GL says, "come on and I'll take you for a ride." Now George, my husband, God rest his tired soul, he'd brung home this white folks' buggy which had a busted wheel and fixed it and was to take it back that day and GL says: "Come on, Mama, we'll use this fine buggy and take us a ride."

"GL," I says, "no, we ain't. Them white folks'll burn us alive if we use their buggy. You just take that horse right on back." You see, I was sure that boy'd come by that animal ungainly.

"Mama, I can't take him back," GL says.

"Why not?" I says.

"Because I don't rightly know where that man is at," GL says.

"Oh," I says. "Well, then I reckon we stuck with it." And I turned around to go back into the house because it was getting late, near dinner time, and I was cooking for ten.

"Mama," GL says to my back. "Mama, ain't you coming for a ride with me?"

---

3. swindler (swind′ lər) *n.* a cheater; a person who takes the money or property of others using deception.

Literary Analysis
Character and Characterization
How does the writer use indirect characterization to reveal GL's character?

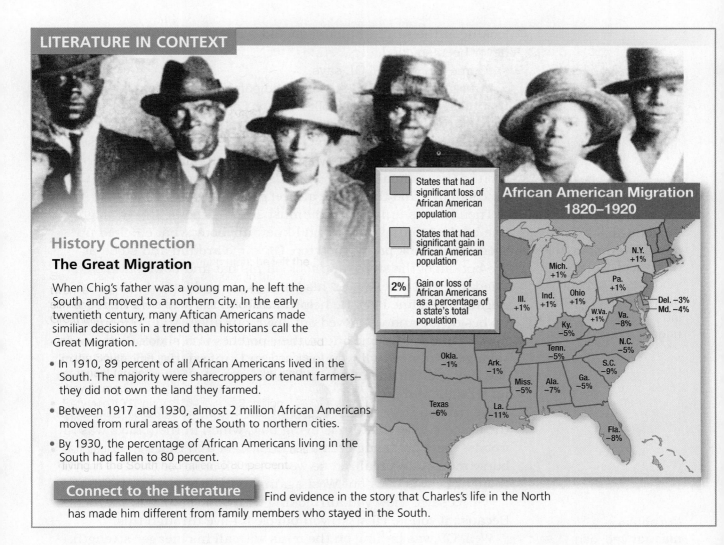

History Connection

The Great Migration

When Chig's father was a young man, he left the South and moved to a northern city. In the early twentieth century, many Aftican Americans made similiar decisions in a trend than historians call the Great Migration.

- In 1910, 89 percent of all African Americans lived in the South. The majority were sharecroppers or tenant farmers—they did not own the land they farmed.

- Between 1917 and 1930, almost 2 million African Americans moved from rural areas of the South to northern cities.

- By 1930, the percentage of African Americans living in the South had fallen to 80 percent.

Connect to the Literature   Find evidence in the story that Charles's life in the North has made him different from family members who stayed in the South.

"Go on, boy. You ain't getting me inside kicking range of that animal." I was eying that beast and it was boiling hotter all the time. I reckon maybe that man had drugged it. "That horse is wild, GL," I says.

"No, he ain't. He ain't. That man say he is buggy and saddle broke[4] and as sweet as the inside of a apple."

My oldest girl, Essie, had-a come out on the porch and she says: "Go on, Mama. I'll cook. You ain't been out the house in weeks."

"Sure, come on, Mama," GL says. "There ain't nothing to be fidgety about. This horse is gentle as a rose petal." And just then that animal snorts so hard it sets up a little dust storm around its feet.

"Yes, Mama," Essie says, "you can see he gentle." Well, I looked at Essie and then at that horse because I didn't think we could be

---

4. **buggy and saddle broke** trained to carry a mounted rider or to pull a carriage.

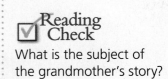

Reading Check

What is the subject of the grandmother's story?

looking at the same animal. I should-a figured how Essie's eyes ain't never been so good.

"Come on, Mama," GL says.

"All right," I says. So I stood on the porch and watched GL hitching that horse up to the white folks' buggy. For a while there, the animal was pretty quiet, pawing a little, but not much. And I was feeling a little better about riding with GL behind that crazy-looking horse. I could see how GL was happy I was going with him. He was scurrying around that animal buckling buckles and strapping straps, all the time smiling, and that made me feel good. •

Then he was finished, and I must say, that horse looked mighty fine hitched to that buggy and I knew anybody what climbed up there would look pretty good too. GL came around and stood at the bottom of the steps, and took off his hat and bowed and said: "Madam," and reached out his hand to me and I was feeling real elegant like a fine lady. He helped me up to the seat and then got up beside me and we moved out down our alley. And I remember how colored folks come out on their porches and shook their heads, saying: "Lord now, will you look at Eva Dunford, the fine lady! Don't she look good sitting up there!" And I pretended not to hear and sat up straight and proud.

We rode on through the center of town, up Market Street, and all the way out where Hiram is living now, which in them days was all woods, there not being even a farm in sight and that's when that horse must-a first realized he weren't at all broke or tame or maybe thought he was back out West again, and started to gallop.

"GL," I says, "now you ain't joking with your mama, is you? Because if you is, I'll strap you purple if I live through this."

Well, GL was pulling on the reins with all his meager strength, and yelling, "Whoa, you. Say now, whoa!" He turned to me just long enough to say, "I ain't fooling with you, Mama. Honest!"

I reckon that animal weren't too satisfied with the road, because it made a sharp right turn just then, down into a gulley and struck out across a hilly meadow. "Mama," GL yells. "Mama, do something!"

I didn't know what to do, but I figured I had to do something so I stood up, hopped down onto the horse's back and pulled it to a stop. Don't ask me how I did that; I reckon it was that I was a mother and my baby asked me to do something, is all.

"Well, we walked that animal all the way home; sometimes I had to club it over the nose with my fist to make it come, but we made it, GL and me. You remember how tired we was, Charles?"

"I wasn't here at the time." Chig turned to his father and found his face completely blank, without even a trace of a smile or a laugh.

Reading Skill
Make Inferences Think of a person you know who likes to get attention. How does knowing this person help you understand GL's actions?

Vocabulary
meager (mē′ gər) *adj.* of poor quality or small amount

trace (trās) *n.* tiny amount; hint

"Well, of course you was, son. That happened in . . . in . . . it was a hot summer that year and—"

"I left here in June of that year. You wrote me about it."

The old lady stared past Chig at him. They all turned to him; Uncle Hiram looked up from his plate.

"Then you don't remember how we all laughed?"

"No, I don't, Mama. And I probably wouldn't have laughed. I don't think it was funny." They were staring into each other's eyes.

"Why not, Charles?"

"Because in the first place, the horse was gained by fraud. And in the second place, both of you might have been seriously injured or even killed." He broke off their stare and spoke to himself more than to any of them: "And if I'd done it, you would've beaten me good for it."

"Pardon?" The old lady had not heard him; only Chig had heard.

Chig's father sat up straight as if preparing to debate. "I said that if I had done it, if I had done just exactly what GL did, you would have beaten me good for it, Mama." He was looking at her again.

"Why you say that, son?" She was leaning toward him.

"Don't you know? Tell the truth. It can't hurt me now." His voice cracked, but only once. "If GL and I did something wrong, you'd beat me first and then be too tired to beat him. At dinner, he'd always get seconds and I wouldn't. You'd do things with him, like ride in that buggy, but if I wanted you to do something with me, you were always too busy." He paused and considered whether to say what he finally did say: "I cried when I left here. Nobody loved me, Mama. I cried all the way up to Knoxville. That was the last time I ever cried in my life."

"Oh, Charles." She started to get up, to come around the table to him. He stopped her. "It's too late."

"But you don't understand."

"What don't I understand? I understood then; I understand now."

Tears now traveled down the lines in her face, but when she spoke, her voice was clear. "I thought you knew. I had ten children. I had to give all of them what they needed most." She nodded. "I paid more mind to GL. I had to. GL could-a ended up swinging if I hadn't. But you was smarter. You was more growed up than GL when you was five and he was ten, and I tried to show you that by letting you do what you wanted to do."

"That's not true, Mama. You know it. GL was light-skinned and had good hair and looked almost white and you loved him for that."

"Charles, no. No, son. I didn't love any one of you more than any other."

"That can't be true." His father was standing now, his fists

Spiral Review
Plot In what way does this family anecdote act as a flashback?

Vocabulary
fraud (frôd) *n.* deceit; trickery

Literary Analysis
Character and Characterization
What new information helps to develop Charles's character?

Reading Check

What happens when GL takes his mother for a buggy ride?

clenched tight. "Admit it, Mama . . . please!" Chig looked at him, shocked; the man was actually crying.

"It may not-a been right what I done, but I ain't no liar." Chig knew she did not really understand what had happened, what he wanted of her. "I'm not lying to you, Charles."

Chig's father had gone pale. He spoke very softly. "You're about thirty years too late, Mama." He bolted from the table. Silverware and dishes rang and jumped. Chig heard him hurrying up to their room.

They sat in silence for a while and then heard a key in the front door. A man with a new, lacquered[5] straw hat came in. He was wearing brown and white two-tone shoes with very pointed toes and a white summer suit. "Say now! Man! I heard my brother was in town. Where he at? Where that rascal?"

He stood in the doorway, smiling broadly, an engaging, open, friendly smile, the innocent smile of a five-year-old.

Vocabulary
engaging (en gāj´ iŋ)
adj. attractive; pleasant

---

5. **lacquered** (lak´ ərd) *adj.* coated with a hardened protective layer of resinous material, which gives a shine.

Critical Thinking

Cite textual evidence to support your responses.

1. Key Ideas and Details **(a)** What reason does Charles give for leaving home when he was fifteen? **(b) Hypothesize:** What other reasons might he have had? Support your answer with story details.

2. Key Ideas and Details **(a)** How does Charles react to Mama's story about GL and the horse? **(b) Compare and Contrast:** In what way does his reaction contrast with the way Mama feels about the story? **(c) Connect:** Explain why the story has this effect on Charles.

3. Key Ideas and Details **Speculate:** What might Charles's relationship with his mother be like in the future?

4. Key Ideas and Details **(a) Summarize:** Describe Mama's approach to raising her children. **(b) Evaluate:** Is her approach sound? Explain.

5. Integration of Knowledge and Ideas By finally confronting his mother about his feelings, has Chig's father made progress in repairing his relationship with his family? Explain. *[Connect to the Big Question: Can progress be made without conflict?]*

Literary Analysis: Character and Characterization

© 1. Key Ideas and Details Use details from the story to compare and contrast the **characters** of Charles and GL.

© 2. Key Ideas and Details Give examples of **indirect characterization** used to portray Charles. Use a chart like this one.

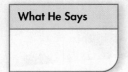

| What He Says | What He Does | What Others Say About Him |

© 3. Key Ideas and Details How does the character of Charles **develop** over the course of the story?

© 4. Key Ideas and Details **(a)** Give two examples of **dialogue** from Mama and two from Charles. **(b)** What do your examples show about how they differ?

Reading Skill: Make Inferences

5. Make an inference about Charles's feelings toward GL. On which story details is your inference based?

6. Make an inference about Chig's feelings toward his family. Support your inference with story details and your own experiences.

Vocabulary

© Acquisition and Use Answer each question. Explain how the meaning of the underlined word influences your answer.

1. Would unlimited playtime be an <u>indulgence</u> for a child?
2. On what occasions might you see someone <u>grimacing</u>?
3. If there is a <u>trace</u> of mud on the rug, is a big cleanup necessary?
4. Would a child with a <u>meager</u> allowance have a large savings?
5. Would a bank allow a man known as a <u>fraud</u> to open an account?
6. Why would a politician want to have an <u>engaging</u> personality?

Word Study Use the context of the sentences and what you know about the **Latin suffix -ence** to explain your answer to each question.

1. Would a person's *negligence* help or hurt others?
2. Would you trust someone who demonstrates *competence*?

Word Study

The **Latin suffix -ence** means "quality of" or "state of."

Apply It Explain how the suffix -ence contributes to the meanings of these words. Consult a dictionary if necessary.

fraudulence
dependence
diligence

Can progress be made without *conflict*?

Writing About the Big Question

In "A Problem," an uncle argues with other family members to give his wayward nephew a second chance. Use this sentence starter to develop your ideas about the Big Question.

In order to help a loved one make an important **change** in his or her life, one should _____.

While You Read Look for clues that suggest Ivan Markovitch is successful in his efforts to help his nephew.

Vocabulary

Read each word and its definition. Decide whether you know the word well, know it a little bit, or do not know it at all. After you read, see how your knowledge of each word has increased.

- **pretense** (prē tens´) *n.* a pretending; a false show of something (p. 257) *She maintained a <u>pretense</u> of being friendly, but was really quite mean.* pretend *v.* pretentious *adj.*

- **candid** (kan´ did) *adj.* honest; direct (p. 257) *Stop telling tales, and give me a <u>candid</u> answer.* candidly *adv.* candor *n.*

- **lofty** (lôf´ tē) *adj.* elevated in character; noble (p. 258) *The dignitary's <u>lofty</u> ideals, such as equality and peace, are admirable.* loftily *adv.* loftiness *n.* aloft *adj.*

- **detestable** (dē tes´ tə bəl) *adj.* deserving hate or scorn; offensive (p. 259) *The factory's thick, foul-smelling smoke was <u>detestable</u> to her.* detest *v.* detestation *n.*

- **subdued** (səb dōōd´) *adj.* quiet; lacking energy (p. 262) *The boy was <u>subdued</u> after he was scolded.* subdue *v.*

- **edifying** (ed´ i fī´ iŋ) *adj.* instructive in such a way as to improve morally or intellectually (p. 263) *The counselor's advice was generally quite helpful and <u>edifying</u>.* edify *v.* edification *n.*

Word Study

The **Latin suffix -able** means "worthy of; capable of being."

In this story, a character thinks his uncles are **detestable**, or worthy of being disliked, because they will not give in to his wishes.

Meet
Anton Chekhov
(1860–1904)

Author of
A Problem

Anton Chekhov grew up in the small coastal town of Taganrog in southern Russia. When the family moved to Moscow, he helped support them by writing comic sketches and light short stories. Although he attended medical school and became a doctor, Chekhov devoted himself to writing short stories and dramas.

A Diagnosis Chekhov said that "a writer is not a confectioner, a cosmetic dealer, or an entertainer. He is a man who has signed a contract with his conscience and his sense of duty." Some of Chekhov's works offer a diagnosis of nineteenth-century Russian society, showing how it trapped individuals into hopeless, unproductive lives. Other works humorously reveal universal human weaknesses. Today, he is regarded as one of the greatest modern writers and one of the most important dramatists of all time.

BACKGROUND FOR THE STORY

Money Lending

An IOU, or promissory note, is a promise to pay money or goods. In Russia at the time of this story, a person could "discount" an IOU, selling it to a moneylender for less than full value. Later, the person could "redeem" the note, buying it back by a certain date. In this story, a character commits a crime by forging an IOU and selling it to a moneylender.

DID YOU KNOW?

Chekhov's study of prisoner's lives, *The Island of Sakhalin*, helped reform the Russian prison system.

A Problem

ANTON CHEKHOV

translated by
Constance Garnett

The strictest measures were taken that the Uskovs' family secret might not leak out and become generally known. Half of the servants were sent off to the theater or the circus; the other half were sitting in the kitchen and not allowed to leave it. Orders were given that no one was to be admitted. The wife of the Colonel, her sister, and the governess, though they had been initiated into the secret, kept up a pretense of knowing nothing; they sat in the dining room and did not show themselves in the drawing room or the hall.

Sasha Uskov, the young man of twenty-five who was the cause of all the commotion, had arrived some time before, and by the advice of kind-hearted Ivan Markovitch, his uncle, who was taking his part, he sat meekly in the hall by the door leading to the study, and prepared himself to make an open, candid explanation.

The other side of the door, in the study, a family council was being held. The subject under discussion was an exceedingly disagreeable and delicate one. Sasha Uskov had cashed at one of the banks a false promissory note,[1] and it had become due for payment three days before, and now his two paternal uncles and Ivan Markovitch, the brother of his dead mother, were deciding the question whether they should pay the money and save the family honor, or wash their hands of it and leave the case to go to trial.

To outsiders who have no personal interest in the matter such questions seem simple; for those who are so unfortunate as to have to decide them in earnest they are extremely difficult. The uncles had been talking for a long time, but the problem seemed no nearer decision.

"My friends!" said the uncle who was a colonel, and there was a note of exhaustion and bitterness in his voice. "Who says that family honor is a mere convention? I don't say that at all. I am only warning you against a false view; I am pointing out the possibility of an unpardonable mistake. How can you fail to see it? I am not speaking Chinese; I am speaking Russian!"

"My dear fellow, we do understand," Ivan Markovitch protested mildly.

"How can you understand if you say that I don't believe in family honor? I repeat once more; fa-mil-y ho-nor false-ly un-der-stood is a prejudice! Falsely understood! That's what I say: whatever may be the motives for screening a scoundrel, whoever he may be, and helping him to escape punishment, it is contrary to law and unworthy of a gentleman. It's not saving the family honor; it's civic cowardice! Take the army, for instance. . . . The honor of the army is more precious to us than any other honor, yet we don't screen

---

1. **promissory note** written promise to pay a specified sum on demand; an IOU.

◀ **Critical Viewing**
Based on this painting, what do you expect the mood of the story will be? **[Predict]**

Vocabulary
pretense (prē tens´) *n.* a pretending; a false show of something
candid (kan´ did) *adj.* honest; direct

✓ Reading Check
Why is Sasha in trouble?

A Problem **257**

our guilty members, but condemn them. And does the honor of the army suffer in consequence? Quite the opposite!"

The other paternal uncle, an official in the Treasury, a taciturn, dull-witted, and rheumatic man, sat silent, or spoke only of the fact that the Uskovs' name would get into the newspapers if the case went for trial. His opinion was that the case ought to be hushed up from the first and not become public property; but, apart from publicity in the newspapers, he advanced no other argument in support of this opinion.

The maternal uncle, kind-hearted Ivan Markovitch, spoke smoothly, softly, and with a tremor in his voice. He began with saying that youth has its rights and its peculiar temptations. Which of us has not been young, and who has not been led astray? To say nothing of ordinary mortals, even great men have not escaped errors and mistakes in their youth. Take, for instance, the biography of great writers. Did not every one of them gamble, drink, and draw down upon himself the anger of right-thinking people in his young days? If Sasha's error bordered upon crime, they must remember that Sasha had received practically no education; he had been expelled from the high school in the fifth class; he had lost his parents in early childhood, and so had been left at the tenderest age without guidance and good, benevolent influences. He was nervous, excitable, had no firm ground under his feet, and, above all, he had been unlucky. Even if he were guilty, anyway he deserved indulgence[2] and the sympathy of all compassionate souls. He ought, of course, to be punished, but he was punished as it was by his conscience and the agonies he was enduring now while awaiting the sentence of his relations. The comparison with the army made by the Colonel was delightful, and did credit to his lofty intelligence; his appeal to their feeling of public duty spoke for the chivalry of his soul, but they must not forget that in each individual the citizen is closely linked with the Christian. . . .

"Shall we be false to civic duty," Ivan Markovitch exclaimed passionately, "if instead of punishing an erring boy we hold out to him a helping hand?"

Ivan Markovitch talked further of family honor. He had not the honor to belong to the Uskov family himself, but he knew their distinguished family went back to the thirteenth century; he did not

---

2. indulgence (in dul′ jəns) *n.* forgiveness; tolerance.

forget for a minute, either, that his precious, beloved sister had been the wife of one of the representatives of that name. In short, the family was dear to him for many reasons, and he refused to admit the idea that, for the sake of a paltry fifteen hundred rubles,³ a blot should be cast on the escutcheon⁴ that was beyond all price. If all the motives he had brought forward were not sufficiently convincing, he, Ivan Markovitch, in conclusion, begged his listeners to ask themselves what was meant by crime? Crime is an immoral act founded upon ill-will. But is the will of man free? Philosophy has not yet given a positive answer to that question. Different views were held by the learned. The latest school of Lombroso,⁵ for instance, denies the freedom of the will, and considers every crime as the product of the purely anatomical peculiarities of the individual.

"Ivan Markovitch," said the Colonel, in a voice of entreaty, "we are talking seriously about an important matter, and you bring in Lombroso, you clever fellow. Think a little, what are you saying all this for? Can you imagine that all your thunderings and rhetoric will furnish an answer to the question?" ●

Sasha Uskov sat at the door and listened. He felt neither terror, shame, nor depression, but only weariness and inward emptiness. It seemed to him that it made absolutely no difference to him whether they forgave him or not; he had come here to hear his sentence and to explain himself simply because kind-hearted Ivan Markovitch had begged him to do so. He was not afraid of the future. It made no difference to him where he was: here in the hall, in prison, or in Siberia.

"If Siberia, then let it be Siberia, damn it all!"

He was sick of life and found it insufferably hard. He was inextricably involved in debt; he had not a farthing⁶ in his pocket; his family had become detestable to him; he would have to part from his friends and his women sooner or later, as they had begun to be too contemptuous of his sponging on them. The future looked black.

Sasha was indifferent, and was only disturbed by one circumstance; the other side of the door they were calling him a scoundrel and a criminal. Every minute he was on the point of jumping up, bursting into the study and shouting in answer to the detestable metallic voice of the Colonel:

"You are lying!"

Reading Skill
Make Inferences Based on Sasha's thoughts, what can you infer about how mature he is?

Vocabulary
detestable (dē tes´ tə bəl) *adj.* deserving hate or scorn; offensive

Reading Check

What is one reason Ivan Markovitch wants to help Sasha?

---

3. **rubles** (roo͞´ belz) *n.* A ruble is the basic unit of Russian currency.
4. **escutcheon** (e skuch´ ən) *n.* shield displaying a family's coat of arms, symbol of its nobility.
5. **Lombroso** Cesare Lombroso (1835–1909), an Italian criminologist who believed that criminals were of a distinct human type and were led to crime by hereditary, inborn characteristics.
6. **farthing** (fär´ thiŋ) *n.* coin of little value.

"Criminal" is a dreadful word—that is what murderers, thieves, robbers are; in fact, wicked and morally hopeless people. And Sasha was very far from being all that. . . . It was true he owed a great deal and did not pay his debts. But debt is not a crime, and it is unusual for a man not to be in debt. The Colonel and Ivan Markovitch were both in debt. . . .

"What have I done wrong besides?" Sasha wondered.

He had discounted a forged note. But all the young men he knew did the same. Handrikov and Von Burst always forged IOU's from their parents or friends when their allowances were not paid at the regular time, and then when they got their money from home they redeemed them before they became due. Sasha had done the same, but had not redeemed the IOU because he had not got the money which Handrikov had promised to lend him. He was not to blame; it was the fault of circumstances. It was true that the use of another person's signature was considered reprehensible; but, still, it was not a crime but a generally accepted dodge, an ugly formality which injured no one and was quite harmless, for in forging the Colonel's signature Sasha had had no intention of causing anybody damage or loss.

"No, it doesn't mean that I am a criminal . . ." thought Sasha. "And it's not in my character to bring myself to commit a crime. I am soft, emotional. . . . When I have the money I help the poor. . . ."

Sasha was musing after this fashion while they went on talking the other side of the door.

"But, my friends, this is endless," the Colonel declared, getting excited. "Suppose we were to forgive him and pay the money. You know he would not give up leading a dissipated life, squandering money, making debts, going to our tailors and ordering suits in our names! Can you guarantee that this will be his last prank? As far as I am concerned, I have no faith whatever in his reforming!"

The official of the Treasury muttered something in reply; after him Ivan Markovitch began talking blandly and suavely again. The Colonel moved his chair impatiently and drowned the other's words with his detestable metallic voice. At last the door opened and Ivan Markovitch came out of the study; there were patches of red on his cleanshaven face.

"Come along," he said, taking Sasha by the hand. "Come and speak frankly from your heart. Without pride, my dear boy, humbly and from your heart."

Sasha went into the study. The official of the Treasury was sitting down; the Colonel was standing before the table with one hand in his pocket and one knee on a chair. It was smoky and stifling in the study. Sasha did not look at the official or the Colonel; he felt

W M Ireland

suddenly ashamed and uncomfortable. He looked uneasily at Ivan Markovitch and muttered:

"I'll pay it . . . I'll give it back. . . ."

"What did you expect when you discounted the IOU?" he heard a metallic voice.

"I . . . Handrikov promised to lend me the money before now."

Sasha could say no more. He went out of the study and sat down again on the chair near the door. He would have been glad to go away altogether at once, but he was choking with hatred and he awfully wanted to remain, to tear the Colonel to pieces, to say something rude to him. He sat trying to think of something violent and effective to say to his hated uncle, and at that moment a woman's figure, shrouded in the twilight, appeared at the drawing room door. It was the Colonel's wife. She beckoned Sasha to her, and, wringing her hands, said, weeping:

"*Alexandre*, I know you don't like me, but . . . listen to me; listen, I beg you. . . . But, my dear, how can this have happened? Why, it's awful, awful! For goodness' sake, beg them, defend yourself, entreat them."

Sasha looked at her quivering shoulders, at the big tears that were rolling down her cheeks, heard behind his back the hollow, nervous voices of worried and exhausted people, and shrugged his shoulders. He had not in the least expected that his aristocratic relations would raise such a tempest over a paltry fifteen hundred rubles! He could not understand her tears nor the quiver of their voices. •

An hour later he heard that the Colonel was getting the best of it; the uncles were finally inclining to let the case go for trial.

"The matter's settled," said the Colonel, sighing. "Enough."

After this decision all the uncles, even the emphatic Colonel, became noticeably depressed. A silence followed.

"Merciful Heavens!" sighed Ivan Markovitch. "My poor sister!"

And he began saying in a subdued voice that most likely his sister, Sasha's mother, was present unseen in the study at that moment. He felt in his soul how the unhappy, saintly woman was weeping, grieving, and begging for her boy. For the sake of her peace beyond the grave, they ought to spare Sasha.

The sound of a muffled sob was heard. Ivan Markovitch was weeping and muttering something which it was impossible to catch through the door. The Colonel got up and paced from corner to corner. The long conversation began over again.

But then the clock in the drawing room struck two. The family council was over. To avoid seeing the person who had moved him to

such wrath, the Colonel went from the study, not into the hall, but into the vestibule. . . . Ivan Markovitch came out into the hall. . . . He was agitated and rubbing his hands joyfully. His tear-stained eyes looked good-humored and his mouth was twisted into a smile.

"Capital," he said to Sasha. "Thank God! You can go home, my dear, and sleep tranquilly. We have decided to pay the sum, but on condition that you repent and come with me tomorrow into the country and set to work."

A minute later Ivan Markovitch and Sasha in their greatcoats and caps were going down the stairs. The uncle was muttering something edifying. Sasha did not listen, but felt as though some uneasy weight were gradually slipping off his shoulders. They had forgiven him; he was free! A gust of joy sprang up within him and sent a sweet chill to his heart. He longed to breathe, to move swiftly, to live! Glancing at the street lamps and the black sky, he remembered that Von Burst was celebrating his name day[7] that evening at the "Bear," and again a rush of joy flooded his soul. . . .

"I am going!" he decided.

But then he remembered he had not a farthing, that the companions he was going to would despise him at once for his empty pockets. He must get hold of some money, come what may!

"Uncle, lend me a hundred rubles," he said to Ivan Markovitch.

His uncle, surprised, looked into his face and backed against a lamppost.

"Give it to me," said Sasha, shifting impatiently from one foot to the other and beginning to pant. "Uncle, I entreat you, give me a hundred rubles."

---

7. **name day** feast day of the saint after whom a person is named.

Vocabulary
edifying (ed´ i fī´ iŋ)
adj. instructive in such a way as to improve morally or intellectually

> They had forgiven him; he was free! A gust of joy sprang up within him and sent a sweet chill to his heart. He longed to breathe, to move swiftly, to live!

Reading Check
What decision do the uncles come to regarding Sasha?

His face worked; he trembled, and seemed on the point of attacking his uncle. . . .

"Won't you?" he kept asking, seeing that his uncle was still amazed and did not understand. "Listen. If you don't, I'll give myself up tomorrow! I won't let you pay the IOU! I'll present another false note tomorrow!"

Petrified, muttering something incoherent in his horror, Ivan Markovitch took a hundred-ruble note out of his pocketbook and gave it to Sasha. The young man took it and walked rapidly away from him. . . .

Taking a sledge, Sasha grew calmer, and felt a rush of joy within him again. The "rights of youth" of which kind-hearted Ivan Markovitch had spoken at the family council woke up and asserted themselves. Sasha pictured the drinking party before him, and, among the bottles, the women, and his friends, the thought flashed through his mind:

"Now I see that I am a criminal; yes, I am a criminal."

Literary Analysis
Character and Characterization In what way does Sasha's character develop at the end of the story?

Critical Thinking

Cite textual evidence to support your responses.

@ 1. **Key Ideas and Details** **(a)** Why is Sasha in trouble? **(b) Compare and Contrast:** Use details from the story to compare the position each uncle takes toward Sasha's problem.

@ 2. **Key Ideas and Details** **Infer:** How does Ivan Markovitch change the Colonel's mind?

@ 3. **Key Ideas and Details** **(a)** Does Ivan Markovitch's attitude help or harm Sasha? Explain. **(b) Take a Position:** What should he have done when Sasha asked him for money after the family meeting?

@ 4. **Key Ideas and Details** **(a) Evaluate:** Do you think what Sasha did should be punished as a crime? Why or why not? **(b) Relate:** What would you have done if you were one of Sasha's uncles? Explain.

@ 5. **Integration of Knowledge and Ideas** **(a)** Did Ivan Markovitch make progress with the other uncles in his fight for Sasha? Why or why not? **(b)** Explain why you think Sasha did or did not learn his lesson after being given a second chance. *[Connect to the Big Question: Can progress be made without conflict?]*

Literary Analysis: Character and Characterization

© **1. Key Ideas and Details** Use details from the story to compare and contrast the **characters** of Ivan Markovitch and the Colonel.

© **2. Key Ideas and Details** Give three examples of **indirect characterization** used to portray Sasha. Use a chart like this one.

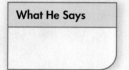

What He Says	What He Does	What Others Say About Him

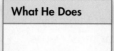

© **3. Key Ideas and Details** How does the character of Sasha **develop** over the course of the story?

© **4. Key Ideas and Details** **(a)** Give two examples of **dialogue** from Sasha and two from Ivan. **(b)** What do your examples reveal about their differences?

Reading Skill: Make Inferences

5. Make an inference about how Sasha feels having been caught doing wrong. On which story details is your inference based?

6. Make an inference about Ivan's feelings at the end of the story. Support your inference with story details and your own experience.

Vocabulary

© **Acquisition and Use** Answer each question. Explain how the meaning of the underlined word influences your answer.

1. Why might you expect a <u>candid</u> answer from a good friend?

2. When might it be a good idea to keep your conversation <u>subdued</u>?

3. Is someone who displays a <u>pretense</u> of wealth actually rich?

4. What <u>lofty</u> goals might an aspiring actor have?

5. Would you want to spend a lot of time with a <u>detestable</u> person?

6. When might a child expect an <u>edifying</u> speech from an adult?

Word Study Use the context of the sentences and what you know about the **Latin suffix -able** to explain your answer to each question.

1. If you have a *curable* disease, will you feel better soon?

2. When an athlete makes a *remarkable* play, do spectators cheer?

Word Study

The **Latin suffix -able** means "worthy of; capable of being."

Apply It Explain how the suffix -*able* contributes to the meanings of these words. Consult a dictionary if necessary.

admirable
calculable
negotiable

Integrated Language Skills

A Visit to Grandmother • A Problem

Conventions: Principal Parts of Regular Verbs

A **verb** is a word that expresses existence, action, or occurrence in a sentence. A verb has four **principal parts:** the present, the present participle, the past, and the past participle.

Most of the verbs in the English language form the present participle by adding *-ing* to the present. The past and the past participle of most verbs add *-ed* or *-d* to the present.

The Four Principal Parts of Verbs			
Present	**Present Participle**	**Past**	**Past Participle**
talk	(is) talking	talked	(have) talked
type	(is) typing	typed	(have) typed

Practice A Identify the verb in each sentence, and indicate whether it is the present, present participle, past, or past participle.

1. Chig has traveled with his father to the South.
2. Chig's grandmother tells stories about the past.
3. The aunts are passing the food to Chig.
4. Chig's father confronted his mother about his childhood.

ⓒ **Reading Application** In "A Visit to Grandmother," find one example of each principal verb part.

Practice B Identify the principal part of the italicized verb in each sentence. Then, rewrite each sentence using a different principal part.

1. Sasha *is waiting* for his uncles to finish their discussion.
2. "I always *borrow* money," Sasha explained.
3. Sasha *jumped* into a sledge and drove off.
4. Ivan Markovitch *has pleaded* Sasha's case to the uncles.

ⓒ **Writing Application** Rewrite this model sentence three times using the other principal parts of the verb: *Sasha prepared a candid explanation.*

PH **WRITING COACH**   Further instruction and practice are available in *Prentice Hall Writing Coach.*

Writing

Ⓖ Narrative Text Write two brief **retellings** of the events that took place in the selection you read. For "A Visit to Grandmother," retell the story first as Mama would tell it and then retell the story from GL's viewpoint. For "A Problem," retell the story from the point of view, or perspective, of one of the uncles and then from Sasha's perspective.

- Use a story map or plot diagram to list the main events. Aim for a smooth progression of events.
- Identify details that will show the difference between the characters' perspectives and convey a vivid picture of each character.
- Use the pronoun *I* to write from the character's point of view.
- When you have completed a first draft, evaluate the draft for appropriate point of view.

Grammar Application For clarity, make sure to use the principal parts of verbs correctly in your retelling.

Writing Workshop: *Work in Progress*

Prewriting for a Short Story Select a character trait that would be suitable for a protagonist in a short story. Then, choose a trait for an antagonist. Provide brief descriptions of these two characters based on these traits. Save your Character Descriptions in your writing portfolio.

Research and Technology

Build and Present Knowledge Write a **report on sources** for a research project about either the Great Migration from the rural South or nineteenth-century Russian society.

Follow these steps to complete the assignment:

- Find three to four sources of varied types, including books, online material, CD-ROM references, or audiovisual materials.
- Evaluate the reliability of each source. Consider its date, the author's credentials, and its accuracy.
- Identify and evaluate each source's text features, such as the table of contents, glossary, index, charts, and graphs.
- As you read, identify complexities, look for discrepancies between sources, and note your thoughts and opinions.
- Use a style manual to cite publication information for each source correctly.
- In your report, assess the value of each source. Then, present your report to your class.

Ⓒ **Common Core State Standards**

L.9-10.4; W.9-10.3.a, W.9-10.3.b, W.9-10.3.d, W.9-10.8
[For the full wording of the standards, see page 238.]

Use this prewriting activity to prepare for the **Writing Workshop** on page 328.

PHLit Online!
www.PHLitOnline.com
- Interactive graphic organizers
- Grammar tutorial
- Interactive journals

© Leveled Texts

Build your skills and improve your comprehension of short stories with texts of increasing complexity.

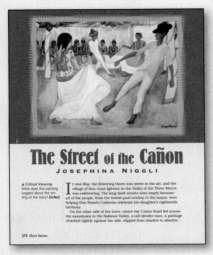

Read **"The Street of the Cañon"** to find out what happens when a mysterious stranger appears at a young woman's birthday party.

Read **"There Will Come Soft Rains"** to learn what happens when technology outlives its creators.

© Common Core State Standards

Meet these standards with either **"The Street of the Cañon"** (p. 272) or **"There Will Come Soft Rains"** (p. 284).

Reading Literature

1. Cite strong and thorough textual evidence to support analysis of what the text says explicitly as well as inferences drawn from the text. (*Reading Skill: Make Inferences*)

4. Determine the meaning of words and phrases as they are used in the text, including figurative and connotative meanings; analyze the cumulative impact of specific word choices on meaning and tone. (*Literary Analysis: Setting*)

Spiral Review: RL.9-10.3

Writing

1. Write arguments to support claims in an analysis of substantive topics or texts, using valid reasoning and relevant and sufficient evidence. (*Writing: Letter and Book Review*)

Speaking and Listening

6. Adapt speech to a variety of contexts and tasks, demonstrating command of formal English when indicated or appropriate. (*Speaking and Listening: Oral Reading*)

Language

4. Determine or clarify the meaning of unknown and multiple-meaning words and phrases based on *grades 9–10 reading and content,* choosing flexibly from a range of strategies. (*Vocabulary: Word Study*)

Literary Analysis: Setting

The time and the place of a story's events are called its **setting.** To establish a setting, writers use **description,** creating word-pictures that appeal to the senses. Settings shape stories in a few ways:

- Setting may affect a story's plot. In a story set in the Arctic wilderness, for example, characters will face challenges not found in a Caribbean resort hotel.

- A well-described setting helps readers understand the time and place of the action in a story. For example, a character from medieval times might be concerned with preserving his honor. A character from the Stone Age, however, might be concerned only with survival.

Before reading either selection, consult the author biographies and background notes. Then, consider the way the setting of the story reflects the time period in which it was written.

Using the Strategy: Setting Chart

To study setting, record details on a **setting chart** like this one.

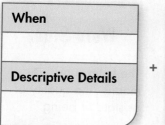
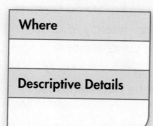

When
Descriptive Details

+

Where
Descriptive Details

Reading Skill: Make Inferences

An **inference** is a conclusion that you reach, based on evidence about information that is not stated in a text. Drawing inferences helps you make connections between facts or events. For instance, if a writer does not name a setting but describes extreme cold, hunters huddled in igloos, and a night that will last all winter, you can make the inference that the story is set in the Arctic.

After you make an inference, **read on** to find additional support for your inference. If new details contradict your inference, modify it.

Can progress be made without *conflict?*

Writing About the Big Question

In this selection, the towns of San Juan Iglesias and Hidalgo are in a quarrel. In the midst of the conflict, a mysterious man makes a bold move. Use these sentence starters to develop your ideas about the Big Question:

One possible **motive** for using humor during a quarrel is _____.

Forming personal connections with members of the opposing side is an important step towards **reconciliation** because _____.

While You Read Look for descriptions of the mysterious man's behavior and decide what may motivate his actions.

Vocabulary

Read each word and its definition. Decide whether you know the word well, know it a little bit, or do not know it at all. After you read, see how your knowledge of each word has increased.

- **nonchalantly** (nän´ shə länt´ lē) *adv.* casually; indifferently (p. 274) *Despite the insult, he shrugged <u>nonchalantly</u>. nonchalance n.*

- **audaciously** (ô dā´ shəs lē) *adv.* in a bold manner (p. 275) *He is usually so shy, so I was surprised to hear that he had behaved <u>audaciously</u>. audacious adj. audacity n.*

- **imperiously** (im pir´ ē əs lē) *adv.* arrogantly (p. 275) *She tends to be bossy and give orders <u>imperiously</u>. imperious adj.*

- **disdain** (dis dān´) *n.* a feeling or a show of a lack of respect (p. 276) *The men treated their captain with <u>disdain</u> by refusing to salute him when he walked by. disdainful adj. disdainfully adv.*

- **plausibility** (plô´ zə bil´ i tē) *n.* believability; seeming truth (p. 276) *Although his excuse has some <u>plausibility</u>, I just do not believe it. plausible adj. plausibly adv.*

- **apprehension** (ap´ rē hen´ shən) *n.* anxious feeling; fear (p. 280) *Filled with <u>apprehension</u>, the children slowly approached the abandoned house. apprehensive adj. apprehensively adv.*

Word Study

The **Latin suffix -ity** means "the quality of or state of being."

In this story, a man hopes the tone he uses has **plausibility,** or the quality of being believable, so his identity is not revealed.

Author of
The Street of the Cañon

Josephina Niggli was born in Monterrey, Mexico, but she grew up on both sides of the border between Mexico and the United States. When Niggli was fifteen, her parents sent her to San Antonio, Texas, to attend school.

Writing for Stage and Screen Niggli published her first book shortly after her high school graduation. Later, she wrote plays. She found theater thrilling, writing, "Once you have experienced the emotion of having a play produced, you are forever lost to the ordinary world."

Later, Niggli worked on movie scripts in Hollywood. In 1945, she published *Mexican Village*, a collection of ten stories that capture the rich local color of Mexico.

BACKGROUND FOR THE STORY

Courtship and Marriage in Old Mexico

Historically, in some parts of Mexico, a man had to ask a woman's family for permission to marry her. In others, the parents arranged the match. In the town in this story, a man and woman are considered engaged if they walk together in the plaza.

Did You Know?

While still in college, Niggli won several prizes for her writing.

Dance in Tehuantepec, 1935. Diego Rivera. Los Angeles County Museum of Art.

The Street of the Cañon

JOSEPHINA NIGGLI

▲ **Critical Viewing**
What does this painting suggest about the setting of the story? **[Infer]**

It was May, the flowering thorn was sweet in the air, and the village of San Juan Iglesias in the Valley of the Three Marys was celebrating. The long dark streets were empty because all of the people, from the lowest-paid cowboy to the mayor, were helping Don Roméo Calderón celebrate his daughter's eighteenth birthday.

On the other side of the town, where the Cañon Road led across the mountains to the Sabinas Valley, a tall slender man, a package clutched tightly against his side, slipped from shadow to shadow.

Once a dog barked, and the man's black suit merged into the blackness of a wall. But no voice called out, and after a moment he slid into the narrow, dirt-packed street again.

The moonlight touched his shoulder and spilled across his narrow hips. He was young, no more than twenty-five, and his black curly head was bare. He walked swiftly along, heading always for the distant sound of guitar and flute. If he met anyone now, who could say from which direction he had come? He might be a trader from Monterrey, or a buyer of cow's milk from farther north in the Valley of the Three Marys. Who would guess that an Hidalgo man dared to walk alone in the moonlit streets of San Juan Iglesias?

Carefully adjusting his flat package so that it was not too prominent, he squared his shoulders and walked jauntily across the street to the laughter-filled house. Little boys packed in the doorway made way for him, smiling and nodding to him. The long, narrow room with the orchestra at one end was filled with whirling dancers. Rigid-backed chaperones[1] were gossiping together, seated in their straight chairs against the plaster walls. Over the scene was the yellow glow of kerosene lanterns, and the air was hot with the too-sweet perfume of gardenias, tuberoses,[2] and the pungent scent of close-packed humanity.

The man in the doorway, while trying to appear at ease, was carefully examining every smiling face. If just one person recognized him, the room would turn on him like a den of snarling mountain cats, but so far all the laughter-dancing eyes were friendly.

Suddenly a plump, officious little man, his round cheeks glistening with perspiration, pushed his way through the crowd. His voice, many times too large for his small body, boomed at the man in the doorway. "Welcome, stranger, welcome to our house." Thrusting his arm through the stranger's, and almost dislodging the package, he started to lead the way through the maze of dancers. "Come and drink a toast to my daughter—to my beautiful Sarita. She is eighteen this night."

In the square patio the gentle breeze ruffled the pink and white oleander bushes. A long table set up on sawhorses held loaves of flaky crusted French bread, stacks of thin, delicate tortillas, plates of barbecued beef, and long red rolls of spicy sausages. But most of all there were cheeses, for the Three Marys was a cheese-eating valley. There were yellow cheese and white cheese and curded

Reading Skill
Make Inferences
Make an inference about the towns of Hidalgo and San Juan Iglesias. What kinds of details might confirm your inference?

Literary Analysis
Setting To which senses does this description of the setting appeal?

Reading Check

What occasion is the village of San Juan Iglesias celebrating?

---

1. **chaperones** (shap´ ər ōnz´) older or married women who accompany and supervise the behavior of a young person in public.
2. **gardenias** (gär dēn´ yəz), **tuberoses** (to͞ob´ rōz´ əs) two types of plant with especially sweet-smelling flowers.

Spanish Vocabulary

Set in Mexico, the story contains several Spanish words and terms, including

- **cañon** canyon; a narrow valley between high cliffs
- **tío** uncle
- **hola** Spanish exclamation meaning "hi"
- **don** title of respect meaning "sir"; often placed before a man's name
- **parada** literally, "parade"; a dance in which partners stride around together

Connect to the Literature

Why do you think Niggli included these terms in the story? **[Hypothesize]**

Vocabulary
nonchalantly (nän´ shə länt´ lē) *adv.* casually; indifferently

---

cheese from cow's milk. There was even a flat white cake of goat cheese from distant Linares, a delicacy too expensive for any but feast days.

To set off this feast were bottles of beer floating in ice-filled tin tubs, and another table was covered with bottles of mescal, of tequila, of maguey wine.

Don Roméo Calderón thrust a glass of tequila into the stranger's hand. "Drink, friend, to the prettiest girl in San Juan. As pretty as my fine fighting cocks, she is. On her wedding day she takes to her man, and may she find him soon, the best fighter in my flock. Drink deep, friend. Even the rivers flow with wine."

The Hidalgo man laughed and raised his glass high. "May the earth be always fertile beneath her feet."

Someone called to Don Roméo that more guests were arriving, and with a final delighted pat on the stranger's shoulder, the little man scurried away. As the young fellow smiled after his retreating host, his eyes caught and held another pair of eyes—laughing black eyes set in a young girl's face. The last time he had seen that face it had been white and tense with rage, and the lips clenched tight to prevent an outgushing stream of angry words. That had been in February, and she had worn a white lace shawl over her hair. Now it was May, and a gardenia was a splash of white in the glossy dark braids. The moonlight had mottled his face that February night, and he knew that she did not recognize him. He grinned impudently[3] back at her, and her eyes widened, then slid sideways to one of the chaperones. The fan in her small hand snapped shut. She tapped its parchment tip against her mouth and slipped away to join the dancing couples in the front room. The gestures of a fan translate into a coded language on the frontier. The stranger raised one eyebrow as he interpreted the signal.

But he did not move toward her at once. Instead, he inched slowly back against the table. No one was behind him, and his hands quickly unfastened the package he had been guarding so long. Then he nonchalantly walked into the front room.

The girl was sitting close to a chaperone. As he came up to her he swerved slightly toward the bushy-browed old lady.

"Your servant, señora. I kiss your hands and feet."

The chaperone stared at him in astonishment. Such fine manners were not common to the town of San Juan Iglesias.

"Eh, you're a stranger," she said. "I thought so."

---

3. **impudently** (im´ pyo͞o dənt lē) *adv.* in a shamelessly bold or provocative way.

"But a stranger no longer, señora, now that I have met you." He bent over her, so close she could smell the faint fragrance of talcum on his freshly shaven cheek.

"Will you dance the *parada* with me?"

This request startled her eyes into popping open beneath the heavy brows. "So, my young rooster, would you flirt with me, and I old enough to be your grandmother?"

"Can you show me a prettier woman to flirt with in the Valley of the Three Marys?" he asked audaciously.

She grinned at him and turned toward the girl at her side. "This young fool wants to meet you, my child."

The girl blushed to the roots of her hair and shyly lowered her white lids. The old woman laughed aloud.

"Go out and dance, the two of you. A man clever enough to pat the sheep has a right to play with the lamb."

The next moment they had joined the circle of dancers and Sarita was trying to control her laughter.

"She is the worst dragon in San Juan. And how easily you won her!"

"What is a dragon," he asked imperiously, "when I longed to dance with you?"

"Ay," she retorted, "you have a quick tongue. I think you are a dangerous man."

In answer he drew her closer to him, and turned her toward the orchestra. As he reached the chief violinist he called out, "Play the Virgencita, 'The Shy Young Maiden.'"

The violinist's mouth opened in soundless surprise. The girl in his arms said sharply, "You heard him, the *Borachita*, 'The Little Drunken Girl.'" ●

Vocabulary

audaciously (ô dā′ shəs lē) *adv.* in a bold manner

imperiously (im pir′ ē əs lē) *adv.* arrogantly

Reading Check

Why does the stranger ask the girl's chaperone to dance?

With a relieved grin, the violinist tapped his music stand with his bow, and the music swung into the sad farewell of a man to his sweetheart:

> *Farewell, my little drunken one,*
> *I must go to the capital*
> *To serve the master*
> *Who makes me weep for my return.*

The stranger frowned down at her. "Is this a joke, señorita?" he asked coldly.

"No," she whispered, looking about her quickly to see if the incident had been observed. "But the Virgencita is the favorite song of Hidalgo, a village on the other side of the mountains in the next valley. The people of Hidalgo and San Juan Iglesias do not speak."

"That is a stupid thing," said the man from Hidalgo as he swung her around in a large turn. "Is not music free as air? Why should one town own the rights to a song?"

The girl shuddered slightly. "Those people from Hidalgo—they are wicked monsters. Can you guess what they did not six months since?"

The man started to point out that the space of time from February to May was three months, but he thought it better not to appear too wise. "Did these Hidalgo monsters frighten you, señorita? If they did, I personally will kill them all."

She moved closer against him and tilted her face until her mouth was close to his ear. "They attempted to steal the bones of Don Rómolo Balderas."

"Is it possible?" He made his eyes grow round and his lips purse up in disdain. "Surely not that! Why, all the world knows that Don Rómolo Balderas was the greatest historian in the entire Republic. Every school child reads his books. Wise men from Quintana Roo to the Río Bravo bow their heads in admiration to his name. What a wicked thing to do!" He hoped his virtuous tone was not too virtuous for plausibility, but she did not seem to notice.

"It is true! In the night they came. Three devils!"

"Young devils, I hope."

"Young or old, who cares? They were devils. The blacksmith surprised them even as they were opening the grave. He raised such a shout that all of San Juan rushed to his aid, for they were fighting, I can tell you. Especially one of them—their leader."

"And who was he?"

"You have heard of him doubtless. A proper wild one named Pepe Gonzalez."

Vocabulary
disdain (dis dān´) *n.* a feeling or a show of a lack of respect

plausibility (plô´ zə bil´ i tē) *n.* believability; seeming truth

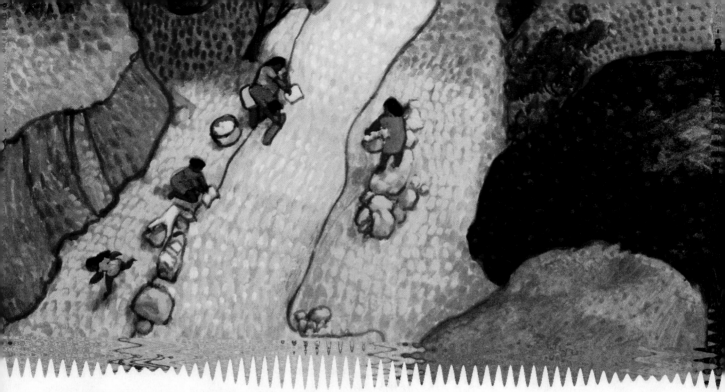

"And what happened to them?"

"They had horses and got away, but one, I think, was hurt."

The Hidalgo man twisted his mouth remembering how Rubén the candymaker had ridden across the whitewashed line high on the cañon trail that marked the division between the Three Marys' and the Sabinas' sides of the mountains, and then had fallen in a faint from his saddle because his left arm was broken. There was no candy in Hidalgo for six weeks, and the entire Sabinas Valley resented that broken arm as fiercely as did Rubén.

The stranger tightened his arm in reflexed anger about Sarita's waist as she said, "All the world knows that the men of Hidalgo are sons of the mountain witches."

"But even devils are shy of disturbing the honored dead," he said gravely.

"'Don Rómolo was born in our village,' Hidalgo says. 'His bones belong to us.' Well, anyone in the valley can tell you he died in San Juan Iglesias, and here his bones will stay! Is that not proper? Is that not right?"

To keep from answering, he guided her through an intricate dance pattern that led them past the patio door. Over her head he could see two men and a woman staring with amazement at the open package on the table.

▲ **Critical Viewing**
Compare the mood of this painting with the mood of the story. **[Compare and Contrast]**

Reading Skill
Make Inferences
Make an inference about the stranger's connection to the men who tried to raid the grave.

Reading Check

What did three men from Hidalgo try to do six months earlier?

His eyes on the patio, he asked blandly, "You say the leader was one Pepe Gonzalez? The name seems to have a familiar sound."

"But naturally. He has a talent." She tossed her head and stepped away from him as the music stopped. It was a dance of two *paradas*. He slipped his hand through her arm and guided her into place in the large oval of parading couples. Twice around the room and the orchestra would play again.

"A talent?" he prompted.

"For doing the impossible. When all the world says a thing cannot be done, he does it to prove the world wrong. Why, he climbed to the top of the Prow, and not even the long vanished Joaquín Castillo had ever climbed that mountain before. And this same Pepe caught a mountain lion with nothing to aid him but a rope and his two bare hands."

"He doesn't sound such a bad friend," protested the stranger, slipping his arm around her waist as the music began to play the merry song of the soap bubbles:

> *Pretty bubbles of a thousand colors*
> *That ride on the wind*
> *And break as swiftly*
> *As a lover's heart.*

The events in the patio were claiming his attention. Little by little he edged her closer to the door. The group at the table had considerably enlarged. There was a low murmur of excitement from the crowd.

"What has happened?" asked Sarita, attracted by the noise.

"There seems to be something wrong at the table," he answered, while trying to peer over the heads of the people in front of him. Realizing that this might be the last moment of peace he would have that evening, he bent toward her.

"If I come back on Sunday, will you walk around the plaza with me?"

She was startled into exclaiming, "Ay, no!"

"Please. Just once around."

"And you think I'd walk more than once with you, señor, even if you were no stranger? In San Juan Iglesias, to walk around the plaza with a girl means a wedding."

"Ha, and you think that is common to San Juan alone? Even the devils of Hidalgo respect that law," he added hastily at her puzzled upward glance. "And so they do in all the villages." To cover his lapse[4] he said softly, "I don't even know your name."

Literary Analysis

Setting How does the time and place of the story affect the way Sarita responds to the stranger?

---

4. **lapse** (laps) *n.* slip; error.

A mischievous grin crinkled the corners of her eyes. "Nor do I know yours, señor. Strangers do not often walk the streets of San Juan."

Before he could answer, the chattering in the patio swelled to louder proportions. Don Roméo's voice lay on top, like thick cream on milk. "I tell you it is a jewel of a cheese. Such flavor, such texture, such whiteness. It is a jewel of a cheese."

"What has happened?" Sarita asked of a woman at her elbow.

"A fine goat's cheese appeared as if by magic on the table. No one knows where it came from."

"Probably an extra one from Linares," snorted a fat bald man on the right.

"Linares never made such a cheese as this," said the woman decisively.

"Silence!" roared Don Roméo. "Old Tío Daniel would speak a word to us."

A great hand of silence closed down over the mouths of the people. The girl was standing on tiptoe trying vainly to see what was happening. She was hardly aware of the stranger's whispering voice although she remembered the words that he said. "Sunday night—once around the plaza."

She did not realize that he had moved away, leaving a gap that was quickly filled by the blacksmith.

Old Tío Daniel's voice was a shrill squeak, and his thin, stringy neck jutted forth from his body like a turtle's from its shell. "This is no cheese from Linares," he said with authority, his mouth sucking in over his toothless gums between his sentences. "Years ago, when the great Don Rómolo Balderas was still alive, we had such cheese as this—ay, in those days we had it. But after he died and was buried in our own sainted ground, as was right and proper . . ."

"Yes, yes," muttered voices in the crowd. He glared at the interruption. As soon as there was silence again, he continued:

"After he died, we had it no more. Shall I tell you why?"

"Tell us, Tío Daniel," said the voices humbly.

"Because it is made in Hidalgo!"

The sound of a waterfall, the sound of a wind in a narrow cañon, and the sound of an angry crowd are much the same. There were no distinct words, but the sound was enough.

"Are you certain, Tío?" boomed Don Roméo.

"As certain as I am that a donkey has long ears. The people of Hidalgo have been famous for generations for making cheese like

Reading Check

What has appeared on the table on the patio?

this—especially that wicked one, that owner of a cheese factory, Timotéo Gonzalez, father to Pepe, the wild one, whom we have good cause to remember."

"We do, we do," came the sigh of assurance.

"But on the whole northern frontier there are no vats like his to produce so fine a product. Ask the people of Chihuahua, of Sonora. Ask the man on the bridge at Laredo, or the man in his boat at Tampico, 'Hola, friend, who makes the finest goat cheese?' And the answer will always be the same, 'Don Timotéo of Hidalgo.'"

It was the blacksmith who asked the great question. "Then where did that cheese come from, and we haters of Hidalgo these ten long years?"

No voice said, "The stranger," but with one fluid movement every head in the patio turned toward the girl in the doorway. She also turned, her eyes wide with something that she realized to her own amazement was more apprehension than anger.

But the stranger was not in the room. When the angry, muttering men pushed through to the street, the stranger was not on the plaza. He was not anywhere in sight. A few of the more religious crossed themselves for fear that the Devil had walked in their midst. "Who was he?" one voice asked another. But Sarita, who was meekly listening to a lecture from Don Roméo on the propriety of dancing with strangers, did not have to ask. She had a strong suspicion that she had danced that night within the circling arm of Pepe Gonzalez.

Critical Thinking

Cite textual evidence to support your responses.

1. **Key Ideas and Details (a)** What adjectives does the author use to describe the way the Hidalgo man walks into the village? **(b) Infer:** What does the man wish to prevent others from learning?

2. **Key Ideas and Details (a)** Whom does the Hidalgo man first ask to dance? **(b) Infer:** Why does he ask her?

3. **Key Ideas and Details (a) Summarize:** Why are the towns quarreling? **(b) Hypothesize:** What might the villagers have done to the stranger if they had known his identity? Explain your answer.

4. **Integration of Knowledge and Ideas** Why does the stranger risk danger to dance with Sarita and leave the gift? Explain your answer using details from the story. *[Connect to the Big Question: Can progress be made without conflict?]*

Literary Analysis: Setting

© **1. Craft and Structure (a)** Identify these aspects of the story's **setting:** the country, the town, and the historical period. **(b)** For each aspect, give an example of a **description** that helps make the setting vivid for readers.

© **2. Craft and Structure** Explain why the dangers the man from Hidalgo faces might not apply in a story set in a different town or time.

Reading Skill: Make Inferences

3. (a) Based on the information in the first three paragraphs of the story, what two **inferences** could you make about the stranger's plans? **(b)** For each inference, note at least one detail later in the story that either confirms it or disproves it. Record your answers in a chart like the one shown.

Inference	Confirming Details	Disproving Details

4. Make an inference concerning Sarita's feelings about the stranger at the end of the story. Give three details to support your inference.

Vocabulary

© **Acquisition and Use** Match each statement with a word from the vocabulary list on page 270. Explain each choice.

1. Some say that a good story should have this quality.

2. A conceited individual might act this way.

3. A nervous person may have difficulty behaving this way.

4. People with many fears often feel a sense of this.

5. A captain who treated his or her officers with this attitude would be disliked.

6. Extreme situations call for people to act this way.

Word Study Use the context of the sentences and what you know about the **Latin suffix -ity** to explain your answer to each question.

1. Could you read a letter that lacked *legibility*?

2. Is a movie that is known for its *complexity* easy to understand?

Word Study

The **Latin suffix -ity** means "the quality of or state of being."

Apply It Explain how the suffix -ity contributes to the meanings of these words. Consult a dictionary if necessary.
accessibility
activity
responsibility

Can progress be made without *conflict*?

Writing About the Big Question

In this story, the human race has achieved a high level of technology, but at a terrible cost. Use these sentence starters to develop your ideas about the Big Question:

A benefit of technological **progress** is _____.

A possible downside of new technology is _____.

While You Read Notice what technology allows the house to do during the course of one day. Then, determine if these advances are positive or negative.

Vocabulary

Read each word and its definition. Decide whether you know the word well, know it a little bit, or do not know it at all. After you read, see how your knowledge of each word has increased.

- **titanic** (tī tan´ ik) *adj.* powerful; of great size (p. 287) *A single titanic wave sank the ship.* titan *n.*

- **paranoia** (par´ ə nɔi´ ə) *n.* mental disorder characterized by delusions (p. 287) *His irrational fear of crowded places could be a sign of paranoia.* paranoid *adj.*

- **fluttered** (flut´ ərd) *v.* flapped or vibrated rapidly (p. 288) *The papers fluttered in the wind and then blew away.* flutter *n.*

- **manipulated** (mə nip´ yōō lāt´ id) *v.* managed or controlled through clever moves (p. 288) *The sculptor molded and manipulated the clay into different shapes.* manipulative *adj.* manipulation *n.*

- **tremulous** (trem´ yōō ləs) *adj.* trembling; quivering; timid; fearful (p. 289) *The cup shook in his tremulous hands.* tremulously *adv.*

- **oblivious** (ə bliv´ ē əs) *adj.* unaware (p. 291) *Oblivious to the shark that was quickly approaching, the turtle swam peacefully.* oblivion *n.* obliviously *adv.*

Word Study

The **Greek suffix -ic** means "having the characteristic of" or "pertaining to."

In this story, an event of **titanic** proportions, pertaining to giant consequences, has occurred.

Meet
Ray Bradbury
(b. 1920)

Author of
There Will Come
Soft Rains

©Thomas Victor

Ray Bradbury, one of the world's most celebrated science-fiction and fantasy writers, was born in Waukegan, Illinois, and grew up near Lake Michigan. As a child, he was influenced by the stories of Edgar Allan Poe and developed a fascination with horror movies and futuristic fantasy.

Dreaming the Impossible Bradbury considers most of his work fantasy rather than science fiction, explaining, "Science fiction is the art of the possible. Fantasy is the art of the impossible." One of his dreams remains an impossible fantasy, at least for now—he wants to go to Mars. "But since it's not going to happen," he explains, "I don't worry about it."

Did You Know?
In 2002, Bradbury was commemorated with a star on the Hollywood Walk of Fame.

BACKGROUND FOR THE STORY
The Atomic Age
Ray Bradbury published this story in 1950. Five years earlier, the United States had dropped the first atomic bombs on Japan. One year before the story was published, the Soviet Union had tested its own atomic device. This story reflects the fear at that time that these rival nations might unleash their deadly technology and destroy humanity.

The Body of a House, #5 of 8. © Robert Beckmann 1993.
Collection: Nevada Museum of Art, Reno.

There Will Come Soft Rains

Ray Bradbury

In the living room the voice-clock sang, *Tick-tock, seven o'clock, time to get up, time to get up, seven o'clock!* as if it were afraid that nobody would. The morning house lay empty. The clock ticked on, repeating and repeating its sounds into the emptiness. *Seven-nine, breakfast time, seven-nine!*

In the kitchen the breakfast stove gave a hissing sigh and ejected from its warm interior eight pieces of perfectly browned toast, eight eggs sunnyside up, sixteen slices of bacon, two coffees, and two cool glasses of milk.

"Today is August 4, 2026," said a second voice from the kitchen ceiling, "in the city of Allendale, California." It repeated the date three times for memory's sake. "Today is Mr. Featherstone's birthday. Today is the anniversary of Tilita's marriage. Insurance is payable, as are the water, gas, and light bills."

Somewhere in the walls, relays clicked, memory tapes glided under electric eyes.

Eight-one, tick-tock, eight-one o'clock, off to school, off to work, run, run, eight one! But no doors slammed, no carpets took the soft tread of rubber heels. It was

The Body of a House, #1 of 8. © Robert Beckmann 1993. Collection: Nevada Museum of Art, Reno.

◀ **Critical Viewing**
What does this painting
suggest about the mood
of the story? **[Predict]**

The Body of a House, #2 of 8. © Robert Beckmann 1993. Collection, Nevada Museum of Art, Reno.

▶ **Critical Viewing**
Compare and contrast the house in this painting with the house at this point in the story. **[Compare and Contrast]**

Reading Skill
Make Inferences
Make an inference about the inhabitants of the house. What kinds of confirming details will you look for as you read on?

raining outside. The weather box on the front door sang quietly: "Rain, rain, go away; rubbers, raincoats for today . . ." And the rain tapped on the empty house, echoing.

Outside, the garage chimed and lifted its door to reveal the waiting car. After a long wait the door swung down again.

At eight-thirty the eggs were shriveled and the toast was like stone. An aluminum wedge scraped them into the sink, where hot water whirled them down a metal throat which digested and flushed them away to the distant sea. The dirty dishes were dropped into a hot washer and emerged twinkling dry.

Nine-fifteen, sang the clock, *time to clean.*

Out of warrens in the wall, tiny robot mice darted. The rooms were acrawl with the small cleaning animals, all rubber and metal. They thudded against chairs, whirling their mustached runners, kneading the rug nap, sucking gently at hidden dust. Then, like mysterious invaders, they popped into their burrows. Their pink electric eyes faded. The house was clean.

Ten o'clock. The sun came out from behind the rain. The house stood alone in a city of rubble and ashes. This was the one house left standing. At night the ruined city gave off a radioactive glow which could be seen for miles.

Ten-fifteen. The garden sprinklers whirled up in golden founts, filling the soft morning air with scatterings of brightness. The water pelted windowpanes, running down the charred west side where the house had been burned evenly free of its white paint. The entire west face of the house was black, save for five places. Here the silhouette[1] in paint of a man mowing a lawn. Here, as in a photograph, a woman bent to pick flowers. Still farther over, their images burned on wood in one titanic instant, a small boy, hands flung into the air; higher up, the image of a thrown ball, and opposite him a girl, hands raised to catch a ball which never came down.

The five spots of paint—the man, the woman, the children, the ball—remained. The rest was a thin charcoaled layer.

The gentle-sprinkler rain filled the garden with falling light.

Until this day, how well the house had kept its peace. How carefully it had inquired, "Who goes there? What's the password?" and, getting no answer from lonely foxes and whining cats, it had shut up its windows and drawn shades in an old-maidenly preoccupation with self-protection which bordered on a mechanical paranoia.

It quivered at each sound, the house did. If a sparrow brushed a window, the shade snapped up. The bird, startled, flew off! No, not even a bird must touch the house!

The house was an altar with ten thousand attendants, big, small, servicing, attending, in choirs. But the gods had gone away, and the ritual of the religion continued senselessly, uselessly. •

Twelve noon.

A dog whined, shivering, on the front porch.

The front door recognized the dog voice and opened. The dog, once huge and fleshy, but now gone to bone and covered with sores, moved in and through the house, tracking mud. Behind it whirred angry mice, angry at having to pick up mud, angry at inconvenience.

For not a leaf fragment blew under the door but what the wall panels flipped open and the copper scrap rats flashed swiftly out. The offending dust, hair, or paper, seized in miniature steel jaws, was raced back to the burrows. There, down tubes which fed into the cellar, it was dropped into the sighing vent of an incinerator which sat like evil Baal[2] in a dark corner.

The dog ran upstairs, hysterically yelping to each door, at last realizing, as the house realized, that only silence was here.

It sniffed the air and scratched the kitchen door. Behind the door, the stove was making pancakes which filled the house with a rich baked odor and the scent of maple syrup.

---

1. **silhouette** (sil´ ə wet´) *n.* outline of a figure, filled in with a solid color.
2. **Baal** (bā´ əl) *n.* ancient Near Eastern deity, later associated with evil.

Vocabulary
titanic (tī tan´ ik) *adj.* powerful; of great size

Literary Analysis
Setting What new information have you learned about the setting of the story?

Vocabulary
paranoia (par´ ə nɔi´ ə) *n.* mental disorder characterized by delusions

Reading Check
What has happened to the rest of the city?

Vocabulary
fluttered (flut´ ərd)
v. flapped or vibrated
rapidly

The dog frothed at the mouth, lying at the door, sniffing, its eyes turned to fire. It ran wildly in circles, biting at its tail, spun in a frenzy, and died. It lay in the parlor for an hour.

Two o'clock, sang a voice.

Delicately sensing decay at last, the regiments of mice hummed out as softly as blown gray leaves in an electrical wind.

Two-fifteen.

The dog was gone.

In the cellar, the incinerator glowed suddenly and a whirl of sparks leaped up the chimney.

Two thirty-five.

Bridge tables sprouted from patio walls. Playing cards fluttered onto pads in a shower of pips. Glasses manifested on an oaken bench with egg-salad sandwiches. Music played.

But the tables were silent and the cards untouched.

At four o'clock the tables folded like great butterflies back through the paneled walls.

Four-thirty.

The nursery walls glowed.

Literary Analysis
Setting How does this
description show that the
story is set in a time different from the present?

Animals took shape: yellow giraffes, blue lions, pink antelopes, lilac panthers cavorting in crystal substance. The walls were glass. They looked out upon color and fantasy. Hidden films clocked through well-oiled sprockets, and the walls lived. The nursery floor was woven to resemble a crisp, cereal meadow. Over this ran aluminum roaches and iron crickets, and in the hot still air butterflies of delicate red tissue wavered among the sharp aroma of animal spoors![3] There was the sound like a great matted yellow hive of bees within a dark bellows, the lazy bumble of a purring lion. And there was the patter of okapi[4] feet and the murmur of a fresh jungle rain, like other hoofs, falling upon the summer-starched grass. Now the walls dissolved into distances of parched weed, mile on mile, and warm endless sky. The animals drew away into thorn brakes and water holes.

It was the children's hour.

Five o'clock. The bath filled with clear hot water.

Six, seven, eight o'clock. The dinner dishes manipulated like magic tricks, and in the study a *click*. In the hearth a fire now blazed up warmly.

Vocabulary
manipulated (mə nip´
yoo lāt´ id) *v.* man-
aged or controlled
through clever moves

Nine o'clock. The beds warmed their hidden circuits, for nights were cool here.

Nine-five. A voice spoke from the study ceiling:

---

3. spoors (spoorz) *n.* droppings of wild animals.
4. okapi (ō kä´ pē) *n.* African animal related to the giraffe but with a much shorter neck.

The Body of a House, #4 of 8. © Robert Beckmann 1993.
Collection: Nevada Museum of Art, Reno.

"Mrs. McClellan, which poem would you like this evening?"
The house was silent.

The voice said at last, "Since you express no preference, I shall select a poem at random." Quiet music rose to back the voice. "Sara Teasdale. As I recall, your favorite. . . .

> There will come soft rains and the smell of the ground,
> And swallows circling with their shimmering sound;
>
> And frogs in the pools singing at night,
> And wild plum trees in tremulous white;
>
> Robins will wear their feathery fire,
> Whistling their whims on a low fence-wire;
>
> And not one will know of the war, not one
> Will care at last when it is done.
>
> Not one would mind, neither bird nor tree,
> If mankind perished utterly;

▲ **Critical Viewing**
What does this painting suggest about the future of the house in the story? **[Predict]**

Vocabulary
tremulous (trem′ yo͞o ləs) *adj.* trembling; quivering; timid; fearful

Reading Check
What happens to the dog?

There Will Come Soft Rains **289**

And Spring herself, when she woke at dawn
Would scarcely know that we were gone."

The fire burned on the stone hearth. The empty
chairs faced each other between the silent walls, and
the music played. ●

At ten o'clock the house began to die.

The wind blew. A falling tree bough crashed through the kitchen
window. Cleaning solvent, bottled, shattered over the stove. The
room was ablaze in an instant!

"Fire!" screamed a voice. The house lights flashed, water
pumps shot water from the ceilings. But the solvent spread on the
linoleum, licking, eating, under the kitchen door, while the voices
took it up in chorus: "Fire, fire, fire!"

The house tried to save itself. Doors sprang tightly shut, but the
windows were broken by the heat and the wind blew and sucked
upon the fire.

The house gave ground as the fire in ten billion angry sparks
moved with flaming ease from room to room and then up the stairs.
While scurrying water rats squeaked from the walls, pistoled their
water, and ran for more. And the wall sprays let down showers of
mechanical rain.

But too late. Somewhere, sighing, a pump shrugged to a stop.
The quenching rain ceased. The reserve water supply which had
filled baths and washed dishes for many quiet days was gone.

The fire crackled up the stairs. It fed upon Picassos and
Matisses[5] in the upper halls, like delicacies, baking off the oily
flesh, tenderly crisping the canvases into black shavings.

Now the fire lay in beds, stood in windows, changed the colors
of drapes!

And then, reinforcements.

From attic trapdoors, blind robot faces peered down with faucet
mouths gushing green chemical.

The fire backed off, as even an elephant must at the sight of a
dead snake. Now there were twenty snakes whipping over the floor,
killing the fire with a clear cold venom of green froth.

But the fire was clever. It had sent flame outside the house, up
through the attic to the pumps there. An explosion! The attic brain
which directed the pumps was shattered into bronze shrapnel on
the beams.

---

5. Picassos (pi kä´ sōz) **and Matisses** (mä tēs´ əz) paintings by the celebrated modern
painters Pablo Picasso (1881–1973) and Henri Matisse (1869–1954).

Spiral Review

Plot Which details make the house seem human? How does this characterization of the house intensify the rising action?

The fire rushed back into every closet and felt of the clothes hung there.

The house shuddered, oak bone on bone, its bared skeleton cringing from the heat, its wire, its nerves revealed as if a surgeon had torn the skin off to let the red veins and capillaries quiver in the scalded air. Help, help! Fire! Run, run! Heat snapped mirrors like the first brittle winter ice. And the voices wailed Fire, fire, run, run, like a tragic nursery rhyme, a dozen voices, high, low, like children dying in a forest, alone, alone. And the voices fading as the wires popped their sheathings like hot chestnuts. One, two, three, four, five voices died.

In the nursery the jungle burned. Blue lions roared, purple giraffes bounded off. The panthers ran in circles, changing color, and ten million animals, running before the fire, vanished off toward a distant steaming river. . . .

Ten more voices died. In the last instant under the fire avalanche, other choruses, oblivious, could be heard announcing the time, playing music, cutting the lawn by remote-control mower, or setting an umbrella frantically out and in the slamming and opening front door, a thousand things happening, like a clock shop when each clock strikes the hour insanely before or after the other, a scene of maniac confusion, yet unity; singing, screaming, a few last cleaning mice darting bravely out to carry the horrid ashes away! And one voice, with sublime disregard for the situation, read poetry aloud in

Reading Skill
Make Inferences
Based on the details in this paragraph, what do you infer is happening?

Vocabulary
oblivious (ə bliv´ ē əs) *adj.* unaware

Reading Check
What starts the fire in the house?

the fiery study, until all the film spools burned, until all the wires withered and the circuits cracked.

The fire burst the house and let it slam flat down, puffing out skirts of spark and smoke.

In the kitchen, an instant before the rain of fire and timber, the stove could be seen making breakfasts at a psychopathic rate, ten dozen eggs, six loaves of toast, twenty dozen bacon strips, which, eaten by fire, started the stove working again, hysterically hissing!

The crash. The attic smashing into kitchen and parlor. The parlor into cellar, cellar into subcellar. Deep freeze, armchair, film tapes, circuits, beds, and all like skeletons thrown in a cluttered mound deep under.

Smoke and silence. A great quantity of smoke.

Dawn showed faintly in the east. Among the ruins, one wall stood alone. Within the wall, a last voice said, over and over again and again, even as the sun rose to shine upon the heaped rubble and steam:

"Today is August 5, 2026, today is August 5, 2026, today is . . ."

Critical Thinking

1. **Key Ideas and Details** **(a)** List five automated tasks the house performs. **(b) Infer:** What is missing in the routine of activity that the house performs? **(c) Interpret:** What is a likely reason for this absence? Give details in support of your answer.

2. **Key Ideas and Details** **(a) Infer:** Why does the house continue its activity even when it no longer makes sense? **(b) Analyze:** What does this fact indicate about the human qualities the house lacks?

3. **Key Ideas and Details** **(a) Make a Judgment:** Do you think Bradbury gives a realistic view of the future of technology? Explain. **(b) Discuss:** Trade answers with a partner. After you have read your partner's response, discuss your answers. **(c) Reflect:** Afterward, write a sentence or two explaining whether your partner's views have influenced your own.

4. **Integration of Knowledge and Ideas** Are the technological advances described in the story more positive or negative? Explain. *[Connect to the Big Question: Can progress be made without conflict?]*

Cite textual evidence to support your responses.

Literary Analysis: Setting

© **1. Craft and Structure** **(a)** Identify these aspects of the story's **setting:** the place in which events occur; the historical period. **(b)** For each aspect, give an example of a **description** that helps make this setting vivid for readers.

© **2. Craft and Structure** Explain why the setting of the story is also its main character.

Reading Skill: Make Inferences

3. (a) Based on information in the first two pages of the story, what two **inferences** could you make about events that occurred before the story opens? **(b)** For each inference, note at least one detail later in the story that either confirms it or disproves it. Record your answers in a chart like the one shown.

Inference	Confirming Details	Disproving Details

4. (a) What can you infer about the future of the house when the fire starts in the kitchen? **(b)** What information can you learn by reading on to confirm this inference?

Vocabulary

© **Acquisition and Use** Match each statement with a word from the vocabulary list on page 282. Then, explain each choice.

1. This word might be used to describe a nervous person.

2. The flag did this in the breeze.

3. If you make an effort like this, you are working hard.

4. People who do not notice things can be described with this word.

5. People who see danger everywhere can be said to suffer from this.

6. If you adjusted a picture to make it brighter, you did this to it.

Word Study Use the context of the sentences and what you know about the **Greek suffix -ic** to explain your answer to each question.

1. Would a person be *emphatic* if he or she had a strong belief?

2. How might a person react to a *comedic* movie?

Word Study

The **Greek suffix -ic** means "having the characteristic of" or "pertaining to."

Apply It Explain how the suffix -ic contributes to the meanings of these words. Consult a dictionary if necessary.

dramatic
metallic
organic

Integrated Language Skills

The Street of the Cañon • There Will Come Soft Rains

Conventions: Irregular Verbs

> An **irregular verb** is a verb whose tenses are not formed according to the standard rules.

Unlike regular verbs, the past and the past participle of an irregular verb are not formed by adding *-ed* or *-d* to the present form. Some common irregular verbs are shown in the following chart.

The Four Principal Parts of Irregular Verbs			
Present	**Present Participle**	**Past**	**Past Participle**
lend	(is) lending	lent	(have) lent
fly	(is) flying	flew	(have) flown
spin	(is) spinning	spun	(have) spun
begin	(is) beginning	began	(have) begun

Practice A Identify which principal part each italicized verb represents.

1. The town church bells *rang* to announce the beginning of the party.
2. She *is eating* her birthday cake.
3. The guests *had begun* to dance.
4. People *ran* to see what the package contained.

Reading Application Find three sentences in "The Street of the Cañon" that contain irregular verbs. Write the irregular verbs and identify which of the principal parts the verbs represent.

Practice B Rewrite each sentence twice: once with the past form and once with the past participle form of the verb in parentheses.

1. The voice-clock _____ for the last time. (sing)
2. The garage door _____ up and down. (swing)
3. When the house _____ to die, it screamed, "Fire!" (begin)
4. The house _____ in its yard like a smoldering pile of trash. (sit)

Writing Application Write a paragraph about an automated machine such as a car alarm or an ATM. In your writing, use at least four different irregular verbs.

PH WRITING COACH Further instruction and practice are available in *Prentice Hall Writing Coach*.

Writing

Common Core State Standards

L.9-10.4; SL.9-10.6; W.9-10.1
[For the full wording of the standards, see page 268.]

Argumentative Text Write a brief **letter to a friend** summarizing either "The Street of the Cañon" or "There Will Come Soft Rains." Then, rewrite the summary as part of a **book review** for newspaper readers.

- As you transfer your ideas into a new format, exclude information and arguments that are irrelevant to your book review.
- Change your language as needed for your new audience, replacing informal words with formal ones.
- Add information that a newspaper audience would expect to find in a review, such as information about the author.
- State your claim, or opinion of the story, and support it with examples.

Grammar Application Check your writing to make sure you have used the correct forms of irregular verbs.

Writing Workshop: *Work in Progress*

Prewriting for Narration: Short Story Using the Character Descriptions in your writing portfolio, make a chart of potential conflicts that the protagonist and antagonist could have. Choose one of these conflicts and add notes about how the two characters could resolve this conflict during the course of the story. Save your Potential Conflict chart in your writing portfolio.

Use this prewriting activity to prepare for the **Writing Workshop** on page 328.

Speaking and Listening

Comprehension and Collaboration Each of these stories can be compared to a well-known poem: Niggli's story bears similarity to Alfred Noyes's "The Highwayman"; Bradbury's story shares many similarities to the poem for which it was named, "There Will Come Soft Rains" by Sara Teasdale. Give an **oral reading** of the poem "The Highwayman" or the poem "There Will Come Soft Rains."

- Use a dictionary to look up the definitions and pronunciations of any words you do not know.
- Vary your tone of voice to reflect the poem's meaning. In addition, try different pacing to best capture its emotion and rhythm.
- Use gestures as appropriate.
- Spend time practicing the reading in front of a mirror, or ask friends or family members to listen to your reading and offer you suggestions.

After reading the poem to the class, lead a class discussion in a comparison of the poem and the story.

www.PHLitOnline.com
- Interactive graphic organizers
- Grammar tutorial
- Interactive journals

Test Practice: Reading

Make Inferences

Fiction Selection

Directions: *Read the selection. Then, answer the questions.*

David pulled Teacher from his backpack. "Review math lesson," he said into the device. David curled up on his bed as he listened to Teacher's smooth, mechanical voice. "Give the test," David said. As test questions appeared on the small screen, David used a stylus to record his answers. A light on his device blinked, and he touched the *pause* button.

"What's up, Jake?" he said, as the image of his best friend appeared.

"Meet me in the sky gym for some hoops."

"I've got a Spanish class," David answered.

"Bring Teacher. We can do the class together later," said Jake.

"Good idea," answered David. "See you at the gym." David pushed a button, and Jake's face was replaced on the screen with David's test.

David touched the *send* button without hesitation. Pushing Teacher into his pocket, he slipped on his anti-grav sneakers and left for the gym.

1. What inference can you make about the setting of this selection?

   A. It takes place in the future.
   B. It takes place in the twentieth century.
   C. It takes place long, long ago.
   D. It takes place in the present.

2. What detail helps you infer that sports activities are influenced by technology?

   A. having live video of a friend on the phone
   B. wearing "anti-grav sneakers"
   C. studying with an electronic "Teacher"
   D. postponing a class to play sports

3. Based on details in this passage, what inference can you make about David's education?

   A. He only reviews Spanish with Jake.
   B. Technology plays a role in his education.
   C. He wants to attend class in a school room.
   D. Teacher has taught him to speak Spanish fluently.

4. What can you infer about how technology enhances David's education?

   A. Technology helps him excel in athletics.
   B. He can contact his friends from school using technology.
   C. He can review material and take tests at his own pace.
   D. Teacher can answer all of David's questions about any subject.

Writing for Assessment

Using your own knowledge and details from this passage, what inferences can you make about how other areas of David's life besides his education might be affected by technology? Write a paragraph in which you explain your ideas.

Nonfiction Selection

Directions: *Read the selection. Then, answer the questions.*

Let's explore the implications of technological advancement on our students' lives now and on the lives of students in the future. The use of computers, the Internet, wireless systems, and hand-held mobile devices already impact our students' daily routines and some aspects of how we teach them. Information that once took hours or even days of library research to find can be retrieved in milliseconds. Research tools such as primary source documents and specialized reference books—previously found only in select libraries—can now be accessed easily. Along with the ease of accessibility, however, comes dangers. For example, some material found on the Internet contains misinformation. The act of using technology itself may cause unforeseen changes. I predict that both the dangers of technology and the advances in education due to technology will only increase.

1. Using the details in this text, you can infer that the writer is—

   A. a student.
   B. a teacher.
   C. a salesperson.
   D. an inventor.

2. You can infer that the remainder of this essay will elaborate on—

   A. positive and negative aspects of technology.
   B. positive aspects of technology.
   C. negative aspects of technology.
   D. the removal of technology from education.

3. Using your own knowledge, you can infer from the second sentence that the author—

   A. is aware of the ways in which students currently use technology.
   B. has limited knowledge about students.
   C. is confused about students' use of technology.
   D. is angry about students' use of technology.

4. After reading the last sentence, you can reasonably infer that the author—

   A. is in favor of increasing use of technology.
   B. is opposed to increasing use of technology.
   C. is ignorant about technology.
   D. has an open mind about technology.

Writing for Assessment

Connecting Across Texts

The author of this passage maintains that technology can have both positive and negative effects on students. Based on details from these two passages, what inferences can you make about the positive and negative effects of technology on David's education? Describe your conclusions in a paragraph.

PHLit Online!
www.PHLitOnline.com

- Online practice
- Instant feedback

Reading for Information

Analyzing Expository Texts

Technical Article

News Release

Common Core State Standards

Reading Informational Text
4. Determine the meaning of words and phrases as they are used in a text, including figurative, connotative, and technical meanings; analyze the cumulative impact of specific word choices on meaning and tone.
6. Determine an author's point of view or purpose in a text and analyze how an author uses rhetoric to advance that point of view or purpose.

Language
5.b. Analyze nuances in the meaning of words with similar denotations

Reading Skill: Analyze Texts to Extend Ideas

When you **extend ideas** presented in informational texts, you consider, judge, and build on those ideas. You do this through **analysis, evaluation,** and **elaboration.** To extend ideas, consider these questions:

Extending Ideas	Questions to Ask
Analysis	• What is the text about? • What kinds of details are presented? • What characteristics—text features and structures—are used to present information?
Evaluation	• How well are the main ideas presented and supported? • Is the text suited for its audience? Does it achieve its purpose?
Elaboration	• What connections can I make with the text? • What additional ideas and questions do I have about this topic?

Content-Area Vocabulary

These words appear in the selections that follow. You may also encounter them in other content-area texts.

* **phenomenon** (fə nom′ ə non) *n.* fact or event that can be observed

* **monitor** (mon′ ə tər) *v.* watch closely in order to control

* **mission** (mish′ ən) *n.* special work or service done on behalf of a government or military group

Tides

Joseph D. Exline, Ed.D., Jay M. Pasachoff, Ph.D., et al.

Technical Article

Features:
- main headings and subheadings that organize the article into sections
- boldface words, phrases, or sentences that contain key ideas
- diagrams or charts that illustrate or summarize information
- text written for a specific audience

You're standing on a riverbank in the town of Saint John, Canada. In the distance there's a loud roaring sound, like a train approaching. Suddenly a wall of water twice your height thunders past. The surge of water rushes up the river channel so fast that it almost looks as if the river is flowing backward.

This thundering wall of water is an everyday event at Saint John. The town is located where the Saint John River enters the Bay of Fundy, an arm of the Atlantic Ocean. The Bay of Fundy is famous for its dramatic daily tides. When the tide comes in fishing boats float on the water near the piers, as shown in Figure 1A. But once the tide goes out, so much water flows back to sea that the boats are stranded on the muddy harbor bottom (Figure 1B).

Photographs, as well as diagrams and other graphics, are used to extend ideas presented in the text.

Figure 1 The Bay of Fundy in Canada is noted for its great differences in water level at high and low tide. **A.** Near the mouth of the bay, boats float in the Saint John River at high tide. **B.** At low tide, the boats are grounded.

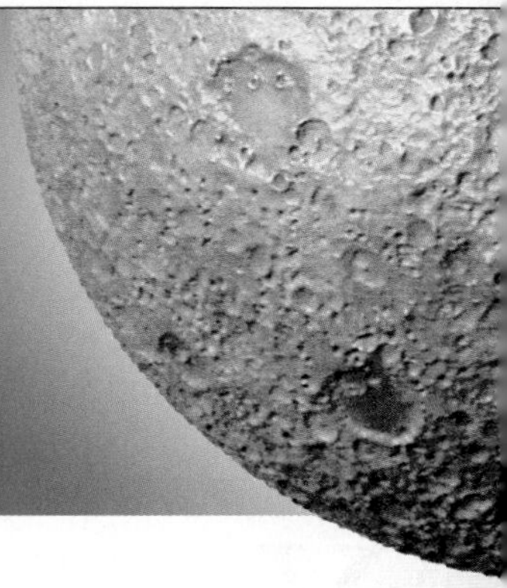

What Causes Tides?

The daily rise and fall of Earth's waters on its coastlines are called tides. As the tide comes in, the level of the water on the beach rises gradually. When the water reaches its highest point, it is high tide. Then the tide goes out, flowing back toward the sea. When the water reaches its lowest point, it is low tide. **Tides are caused by the interaction of Earth, the moon, and the sun.**

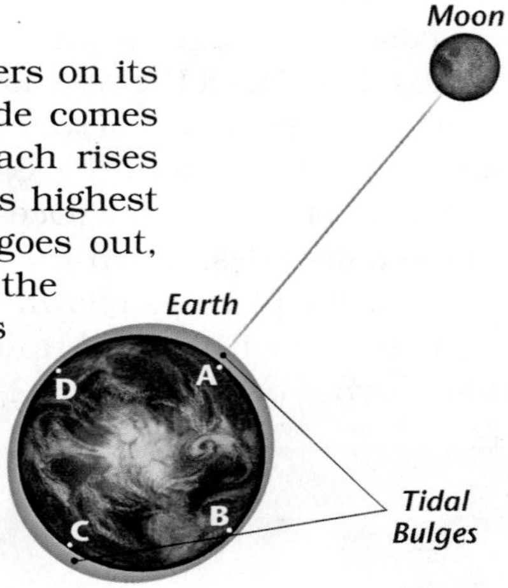

Figure 2 shows the effect of the moon's gravity on the water on Earth's surface. The moon pulls on the water on the side closest to it (point A) more strongly than it pulls on the center of the Earth. This pull creates a bulge of water, called a tidal bulge, on the side of Earth facing the moon. The water at point C is pulled toward the moon less strongly than is Earth as a whole. This water is "left behind," forming a second bulge.

In the places in Figure 2 where there are tidal bulges (points A and C), high tide is occurring along the coastlines. In the places between the bulges (points B and D), low tide is occurring. As Earth rotates, different places on the planet's surface pass through the areas of the tidal bulges and experience the change in water levels.

Moon

Earth

Tidal Bulges

Figure 2
The moon's pull on Earth's water causes tidal bulges to form on the side closest to the moon and the side farthest from the moon.

The Daily Tide Cycle

As Earth turns completely around once each day, people on or near the shore observe the rise and fall of the tides as they reach the area of each tidal bulge. The high tides occur about 12 hours and 25 minutes apart in each location. As Earth rotates, eastern-most points pass through the area of the tidal bulge before points farther to the west. Therefore, high tide occurs later the farther west you go along a coastline.

The Monthly Tide Cycle

Even though the sun is 150 million kilometers from Earth, it is so massive that its gravity also affects the tides. The sun pulls the water on Earth's surface toward it. In Figure 4 (next page), you can follow the positions of the Earth, moon, and sun at different times during a month.

Spring Tides Twice a month, at the new moon and the full moon, the sun and moon are lined up. Their combined gravitational pull produces the greatest range between high and low tide, called a spring tide. These tides get their name not because they occur during the spring season, but from an Old English word, *springen*, which means "to jump."

Day	Highest High Tide (m)	Lowest Low Tide (m)
1	1.9	0.2
2	2.1	0.1
3	2.3	0.0
4	2.4	-0.2
5	2.5	-0.2
6	2.6	-0.3
7	1.9	0.3

Figure 3
This table lists the highest high tides and lowest low tides at the mouth of the Savannah River at the Atlantic Ocean in Georgia for one week.

Tables present numerical data for you to analyze and evaluate.

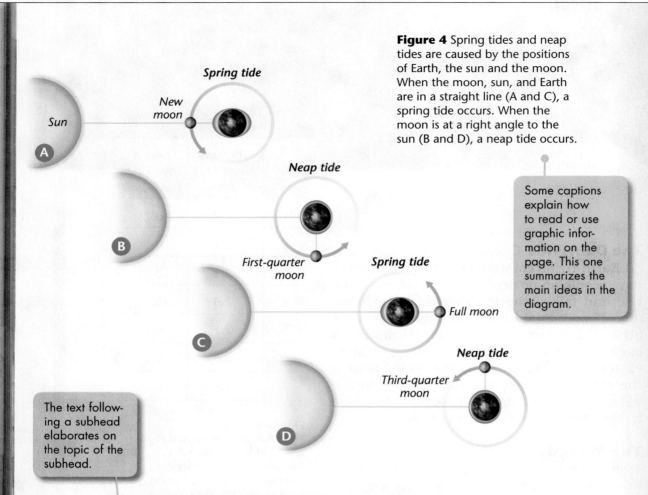

Figure 4 Spring tides and neap tides are caused by the positions of Earth, the sun and the moon. When the moon, sun, and Earth are in a straight line (A and C), a spring tide occurs. When the moon is at a right angle to the sun (B and D), a neap tide occurs.

Some captions explain how to read or use graphic information on the page. This one summarizes the main ideas in the diagram.

The text following a subhead elaborates on the topic of the subhead.

Neap Tides In between spring tides, at the first and third quarters of the moon, the sun and moon pull at right angles to each other. This line-up produces a neap tide, a tide with the least difference between low and high tide. During a neap tide, the sun's gravity pulls some of the water away from the tidal bulge facing the moon. This acts to "even out" the water level over Earth's surface, reducing the difference between high and low tides.

Features:
- current, sometimes time-sensitive or breaking news
- text written for a specific audience

Information in the text elaborates on the information provided in the headline.

NASA News
Date: April 17, 2003 - RELEASE NO: 03-39
Contact: Rob Gutro

Black Water Turns the Tide on Florida Coral

In early 2002, a patch of "black water" spanning over 60 miles in diameter formed off southwestern Florida and contributed to severe coral reef stress and death in the Florida Keys, according to results published from research funded by the National Aeronautics and Space Administration (NASA), the U.S. Environmental Protection Agency and the National Oceanic and Atmospheric Administration (NOAA). The "black water" contained a high abundance of toxic and non-toxic microscopic plants.

Chuanmin Hu and other colleagues at the Institute for Marine Remote Sensing of the University of South Florida (USF), St. Petersburg, Fla., and colleagues from the Florida Fish and Wildlife Conservation Commission (FFWCC) and the University of Georgia, co-authored an article on this **phenomenon** that appeared as the cover story of a recent issue of the American Geophysical Union's Geophysical Research Letters.

You might evaluate the credibility of this information by noting the author's credentials.

"The water appeared black in satellite imagery because the concentration of the microscopic plants and other dissolved matters were high," Hu said. Because plants and dissolved matter absorb sunlight, they reduce the amount of light normally reflected from the ocean. When a red-tide bloom occurs the water takes on various hues of red or brown. While not all microscopic plants contribute to red tides, the darker hue created by both the plankton and the harmful algal blooms made the water appear black when seen from the satellite.

When Hu and his colleagues examined the data collected by divers from the dark water area in the Florida Keys, they discovered a 70 percent decrease in stony coral cover, a 40 percent reduction of coral species, and a near-elimination of sponge colonies at two reef sites after the dark water passed. By examining satellite images and field survey data, the authors concluded that the coral reef ecosystem was stressed by microscopic organisms and toxins contained in the dark water.

The "black water" event caused alarm among local fishermen, divers, and the public, as the color of the water was unusual and fish seemed to avoid this large area of dark water. Satellite instruments such as the Sea-viewing Wide Field-of-view Sensor (SeaWiFS) aboard Orbimage's SeaStar satellite and the Moderate Resolution Imaging Spectroradiometer (MODIS) aboard NASA's Terra and Aqua satellites provide information on ocean color that allows scientists to **monitor** the health of the water and the shallow benthic (ocean bottom) environment. The SeaWiFS and MODIS measurements of the dark water led to a number of investigations to help clarify the issues and to provide answers to the public's concerns.

During January 2002, SeaWiFS detected the dark-colored water in the Florida Bight, just southwest of the Everglades. In fall 2001, the SeaWiFS images showed an extensive red tide off Florida's central west coast, near Charlotte Harbor.

Red tides occur every year off Florida and are known to cause fish kills, coral stress and mortality, and skin and respiratory problems in humans. They are caused by high concentration of microscopic plants called dinoflagellates. Other microorganisms called cyanobacteria can also cause harmful algal blooms. The waters containing this red tide migrated to the south along the coast. Winter storms caused large amounts of fresh water to drain from the Everglades into Florida Bight (the curve in the shoreline from the Keys north to Everglades National Park on the mainland), carrying high levels of nutrients such as silicate, phosphorus, and nitrogen to the sea. These caused a bloom of the microscopic marine plants known as diatoms in the same patch. The bloom turned the water dark and the "black water" patch re-circulated for several months in a slow clockwise motion off southwest Florida in the Florida Bight. Slowly, the dark water drifted farther south and toward the Florida Keys. By May 2002, the "black water" had moved through passages in the Florida Keys, dispersing into the Atlantic and the Gulf Stream. . . .

NASA funded part of this research as part of its Earth Science **mission** to understand and protect our home planet. NASA's Earth Science Enterprise is dedicated to understanding the Earth as an integrated system and applying Earth System Science to improve prediction of climate, weather, and natural hazards using the unique vantage point of space.

You can evaluate how well the data and statistics support the main idea of the article.

To elaborate on these ideas, you might consult a resource on recent incidents of red tides.

Comparing Expository Texts

1. Key Ideas and Details **(a) Extend ideas** presented in the two texts by **analyzing** and comparing them. What different kinds of details do the two texts present? **(b) Evaluate** how well those details support the main ideas of each text. Which text offers better support? Explain. **(c) Elaborate** by describing how to improve the text that has less support.

Content-Area Vocabulary

2. (a) Explain the difference in meaning between the words in each pair: *mission/work; phenomenon/event; monitor/watch.* **(b)** Choose a pair, and use each word in a sentence that shows its meaning.

⏱ Timed Writing

Analytical Text: Essay

Format
The prompt instructs you to write a *brief essay.* Therefore, your essay should be approximately three to five paragraphs long.

Both the technical article and the news release discuss tides, but from different perspectives. In a brief essay, identify each author's point of view and how it affects the tone and content of the text. Also, consider the combined information of the two sources and explain whether the authors' different perspectives cause discrepancies in the information presented. Support your response with details from the texts. (25 minutes)

Academic Vocabulary
When you *identify* something, you recognize and bring attention to it.

5-Minute Planner

Complete these steps before you begin to write:

1. Quickly review the two texts to compare the **perspectives,** tone, and content. **TIP** Consider the purpose of each text to better understand the author's perspective.

2. Note specific word and phrase choices to support your impressions.

3. **Synthesize,** or combine, the information in both texts by thinking about all the facts and details presented. Note any **discrepancies,** or conflicts, in the combined information.

4. Refer to your notes as you write your essay.

Comparing Literary Works

Comparing Points of View

Point of view is the perspective from which a story is told. Most stories are told from one of the following perspectives:

- **First-person point of view:** The narrator is one of the characters and refers to himself or herself with the pronouns *I* and *me*. One kind of first-person narrator is the **naïve first-person narrator.** This narrator understands less about events in the story than the readers do. For example, if the narrator of a story is a five-year-old, readers may have a clearer understanding of events in the story than does the child who describes them.

- **Third-person point of view:** The narrator does not participate in the action. Characters are referred to by the third-person pronouns *he, she, him, her, they,* and *them.* The narrator's point of view may be **omniscient** (all-knowing), or it may be **limited** (restricted to the perceptions of a single character).

By giving readers more information than the narrator or character has, writers can create **dramatic irony**—a contrast between what the readers know and what the narrator or character believes. Dramatic irony is a powerful device in fiction because it involves readers on an analytical, interpretative level as well as an emotional one. Effects such as tension and surprise can be created when readers' minds and hearts are engaged in a story.

Compare the use of point of view and its impact in "One Thousand Dollars" and "By the Waters of Babylon" by using a chart like the one shown.

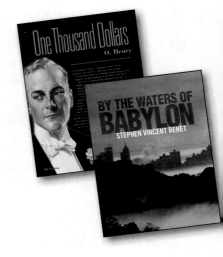

**Common Core
State Standards**

Reading Literature
5. Analyze how an author's choices concerning how to structure a text, order events within it, and manipulate time create such effects as mystery, tension, or surprise.

Writing
2. Write informative/explanatory texts to examine and convey complex ideas, concepts, and information clearly and accurately through the effective selection, organization, and analysis of content. *(Timed Writing)*

Story	Point of View	What Reader Knows	What Character Knows	Effect of Contrast in Knowledge	Impact on Story

www.PHLitOnline.com

- Vocabulary flashcards
- Interactive journals
- More about the authors
- Selection audio
- Interactive graphic organizers

Can progress be made without *conflict?*

Writing About the Big Question

In each of these stories, the main character finds himself challenged by unusual circumstances. Both of these characters use conflict as a springboard toward **progress.** Use these sentence starters to develop your ideas about the Big Question.

Facing **adversity** could teach someone _____.

After a disagreement is **resolved**, a person may be able to _____.

Meet the Authors

O. Henry (1862–1910)
Author of "One Thousand Dollars"

A native of North Carolina, William Sydney Porter dropped out of school at age fifteen and by his twenties had made his way to Texas. After working for more than a decade as a bank teller, he was convicted— perhaps unjustly—of embezzling bank funds. In prison, he began to write short stories and took on the pen name O. Henry.

Hundreds of Stories Later Upon his release from jail, O. Henry settled in New York City, where he became a full-time and hugely successful short-story writer. He turned out nearly 300 tales, most of them featuring ironic twists of fate.

Stephen Vincent Benét (1898–1943)
Author of "By the Waters of Babylon"

Born in Bethlehem, Pennsylvania, Stephen Vincent Benét grew up listening to his father read poetry in the evenings. During World War I, Benét was barred from active army duty because of poor eyesight. Still, he took time off from his studies at Yale University to serve in the State Department during the war.

Touch of the Poet Benét considered himself a poet first and foremost. Much of his work centers on American history and the quest for American ideals. His interest in American history and folklore influenced his epic poem *John Brown's Body*, which won a Pulitzer Prize in 1929.

One Thousand Dollars

O. Henry

"One thousand dollars," repeated Lawyer Tolman, solemnly and severely, "and here is the money."

Young Gillian gave a decidedly amused laugh as he fingered the thin package of new fifty-dollar notes.

"It's such a confoundedly awkward amount," he explained, genially, to the lawyer. "If it had been ten thousand a fellow might wind up with a lot of fireworks and do himself credit. Even fifty dollars would have been less trouble."

"You heard the reading of your uncle's will," continued Lawyer Tolman, professionally dry in his tones. "I do not know if you paid much attention to its details. I must remind you of one. You are required to render to us an account of the manner of expenditure of this $1,000 as soon as you have disposed of it. The will stipulates that. I trust that you will so far comply with the late Mr. Gillian's wishes."

"You may depend upon it," said the young man, politely, "in spite of the extra expense it will entail. I may have to engage a secretary. I was never good at accounts."

Gillian went to his club. There he hunted out one whom he called Old Bryson.

Old Bryson was calm and forty and sequestered. He was in a corner reading a book, and when he saw Gillian approaching he sighed, laid down his book and took off his glasses.

"Old Bryson, wake up," said Gillian. "I've a funny story to tell you."

"I wish you would tell it to someone in the billiard room," said Old Bryson. "You know how I hate your stories."

"This is a better one than usual," said Gillian . . . ; "and I'm glad to tell it to you. It's too sad and funny to go with the rattling of billiard balls. I've just come from my late uncle's firm of legal corsairs. He leaves me an even thousand dollars. Now, what can a man possibly do with a thousand dollars?"

"I thought," said Old Bryson, showing as much interest as a bee shows in a vinegar cruet, "that the late Septimus Gillian was worth something like half a million."

"He was," assented Gillian, joyously, "and that's where the joke comes in. He's left his whole cargo of doubloons[1] to a microbe. That is, part of it goes to the man who invents a new bacillus and the rest to establish a hospital for doing away with it again. There are one or two trifling bequests on the side. The butler and the housekeeper get a seal ring and $10 each. His nephew gets $1,000."

"You've always had plenty of money to spend," observed Old Bryson.

"Tons," said Gillian. "Uncle was the fairy godmother as far as an allowance was concerned."

"Any other heirs?" asked Old Bryson.

"None." Gillian frowned . . . and kicked the upholstered leather of a divan uneasily. "There is a Miss Hayden, a ward of my uncle, who lived in his house. She's a quiet thing—musical—the daughter of somebody who was unlucky enough to be his friend. I forgot to say that she was in on the seal ring and $10 joke, too. I wish I had been. Then I could have had two bottles of brut, tipped the waiter with the ring, and had the whole business off my hands. Don't be superior and insulting, Old Bryson—tell me what a fellow can do with a thousand dollars."

Old Bryson rubbed his glasses and smiled. And when Old Bryson smiled, Gillian knew that he intended to be more offensive than ever.

"A thousand dollars," he said, "means much or little. One man may buy a happy home with it and laugh at Rockefeller.[2] Another could send his wife South with it and save her life. A thousand dollars would buy pure milk for one hundred babies during June, July, and August and save fifty of their lives. You could count upon a half hour's diversion with it at faro in one of the fortified art galleries. It would furnish an education to an ambitious boy.

---

1. **doubloons** (də blōōnz´) *n.* old gold coins of Spanish or Spanish American origin, often associated with pirates.
2. **Rockefeller** John D. Rockefeller (1839–1937), a businessman who became the first American billionaire.

Vocabulary
stipulates (stip´ yə lāts´) *v.* includes specifically as part of an agreement

Literary Analysis
Point of View Whose thoughts are revealed in this short paragraph? Who reveals them?

Reading Check

What problem does young Gillian face?

I am told that a genuine Corot[3] was secured for that amount in an auction room yesterday. You could move to a New Hampshire town and live respectably two years on it. You could rent Madison Square Garden for one evening with it, and lecture your audience, if you should have one, on the precariousness of the profession of heir presumptive."

"People might like you, Old Bryson," said Gillian, almost unruffled, "if you wouldn't moralize. I asked you to tell me what I could do with a thousand dollars."

"You?" said Bryson, with a gentle laugh. "Why, Bobby Gillian, there's only one logical thing you could do. You can go buy Miss Lotta Lauriere a diamond pendant with the money, and then take yourself off to Idaho and inflict your presence upon a ranch. I advise a sheep ranch, as I have a particular dislike for sheep."

"Thanks," said Gillian, rising. "I thought I could depend upon you, Old Bryson. You've hit on the very scheme. I wanted to chuck the money in a lump, for I've got to turn in an account for it, and I hate itemizing."

Gillian phoned for a cab and said to the driver:

"The stage entrance of the Columbine Theatre."

Miss Lotta Lauriere was assisting nature with a powder puff, almost ready for her call at a crowded matinée, when her dresser mentioned the name of Mr. Gillian.

"Let it in," said Miss Lauriere. "Now, what is it, Bobby? I'm going on in two minutes."

"Rabbit-foot your right ear a little," suggested Gillian, critically. "That's better. It won't take two minutes for me. What do you say to a little thing in the pendant line? I can stand three ciphers[4] with a figure one in front of 'em."

"Oh, just as you say," carolled Miss Lauriere. "My right glove, Adams. Say, Bobby, did you see that necklace Della Stacey had on the other night? Twenty-two hundred dollars it cost at Tiffany's. But, of course—pull my sash a little to the left, Adams."

"Miss Lauriere for the opening chorus!" cried the call boy without.

Gillian strolled out to where his cab was waiting.

"What would you do with a thousand dollars if you had it?" he asked the driver.

"Open a s'loon," said the cabby promptly and huskily. "I know a place I could take money in with both hands. It's a four-story brick on a corner. I've got it figured out. Second story— . . . chop

---

3. **Corot** (kə rō′) a painting by Jean (zhän) Baptiste (bȧ tēst′) Camille (kȧ mē′y′) Corot (1796–1875), a famous French painter.
4. **ciphers** (sī′ fərz) n. zeroes.

suey; third floor—manicures and foreign missions; fourth floor—poolroom. If you was thinking of putting up the cap—"

"Oh, no," said Gillian, "I merely asked from curiosity. I take you by the hour. Drive till I tell you to stop."

Eight blocks down Broadway Gillian poked up the trap[5] with his cane and got out. A blind man sat upon a stool on the sidewalk selling pencils. Gillian went out and stood before him.

"Excuse me," he said, "but would you mind telling me what you would do if you had a thousand dollars?"

"You got out of that cab that just drove up, didn't you?" asked the blind man.

"I did," said Gillian.

"I guess you are all right," said the pencil dealer, "to ride in a cab by daylight. Take a look at that, if you like."

He drew a small book from his coat pocket and held it out. Gillian opened it and saw that it was a bank deposit book. It showed a balance of $1,785 to the blind man's credit.

Gillian returned the book and got into the cab.

"I forgot something," he said. "You may drive to the law offices of Tolman & Sharp, at —— Broadway."

Lawyer Tolman looked at him hostilely and inquiringly through his gold-rimmed glasses.

"I beg your pardon," said Gillian, cheerfully, "but may I ask you a question? It is not an impertinent one, I hope. Was Miss Hayden left anything by my uncle's will besides the ring and the $10?"

"Nothing," said Mr. Tolman.

"I thank you very much, sir," said Gillian, and out he went to his cab. He gave the driver the address of his late uncle's home.

Miss Hayden was writing letters in the library. She was small and slender and clothed in black. But you would have noticed her eyes. Gillian drifted in with his air of regarding the world as inconsequent.

"I've just come from old Tolman's," he explained. "They've been going over the papers down there. They found a"—Gillian searched his memory for a legal term—"they found an amendment or a postscript or something to the will. It seemed that the old boy loosened up a little on second thoughts and willed you a thousand dollars. I was driving up this way and Tolman asked me to bring you the money. Here it is. You'd better count it to see if it's right." Gillian laid the money beside her hand on the desk.

Miss Hayden turned white. "Oh!" she said, and again "Oh!"

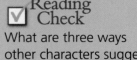

Reading Check

What are three ways other characters suggest Gillian spend the thousand dollars?

---

5. **poked up the trap** pushed open the roof door of the cab so that the driver would know that he wanted to get out.

Gillian half turned and looked out of the window.

"I suppose, of course," he said, in a low voice, "that you know I love you."

"I am sorry," said Miss Hayden, taking up her money.

"There is no use?" asked Gillian, almost light-heartedly.

"I am sorry," she said again.

"May I write a note?" asked Gillian, with a smile. He seated himself at the big library table. She supplied him with paper and pen, and then went back to her secrétaire.

Gillian made out his account of his expenditure of the thousand dollars in these words:

"Paid by the black sheep, Robert Gillian, $1,000 on account of the eternal happiness, owed by Heaven to the best and dearest woman on earth."

Gillian slipped his writing into an envelope, bowed and went his way.

His cab stopped again at the offices of Tolman & Sharp.

"I have expended the thousand dollars," he said, cheerily, to Tolman of the gold glasses, "and I have come to render account of it, as I agreed. There is quite a feeling of summer in the air—do you not think so, Mr. Tolman?" He tossed a white envelope on the lawyer's table. "You will find there a memorandum, sir, of the *modus operandi* of the vanishing of the dollars."

Without touching the envelope, Mr. Tolman went to a door and called his partner, Sharp. Together they explored the caverns of an immense safe. Forth they dragged as trophy of their search a big envelope sealed with wax. This they forcibly invaded, and wagged their venerable heads together over its contents. Then Tolman became spokesman.

"Mr. Gillian," he said, formally, "there was a codicil[6] to your uncle's will. It was intrusted to us privately, with instructions that it be not opened until you had furnished us with a full account of your handling of the $1,000 bequest in the will. As you have fulfilled the conditions, my partner and I have read the codicil. I do not wish to encumber your understanding with its legal phraseology, but I will acquaint you with the spirit of its contents.

"In the event that your disposition of the $1,000 demonstrates that you possess any of the qualifications that deserve reward, much benefit will accrue to you. Mr. Sharp and I are named as the judges, and I assure you that we will do our duty strictly according to justice—with liberality. We are not at all unfavorably disposed toward you, Mr. Gillian. But let us return to the letter of the codicil.

---

6. **codicil** (käd´ i səl) *n.* an addition to a will changing or explaining the instructions it gives.

Literary Analysis
Point of View How does the use of a limited third-person narrator help readers see what Gillian is doing in secret?

> "I have expended the thousand dollars," he said, cheerily, to Tolman of the gold glasses. . .

If your disposal of the money in question has been prudent, wise, or unselfish, it is in our power to hand you over bonds to the value of $50,000, which have been placed in our hands for that purpose. But if—as our client, the late Mr. Gillian, explicitly provides—you have used this money as you have used money in the past—I quote the late Mr. Gillian—in reprehensible dissipation among disreputable associates—the $50,000 is to be paid to Miriam Hayden, ward of the late Mr. Gillian, without delay. Now, Mr. Gillian, Mr. Sharp and I will examine your account in regard to the $1,000. You submit it in writing, I believe. I hope you will repose confidence in our decision."

Mr. Tolman reached for the envelope. Gillian was a little the quicker in taking it up. He tore the account and its cover leisurely into strips and dropped them into his pocket.

"It's all right," he said, smilingly. "There isn't a bit of need to bother you with this. I don't suppose you'd understand these itemized bets anyway. I lost the thousand dollars on the races. Good day to you, gentlemen."

Tolman & Sharp shook their heads mournfully at each other when Gillian left, for they heard him whistling gayly in the hallway as he started for the elevator.

Vocabulary
prudent (prōō′ dənt)
adj. exercising sound judgment; cautious

Literary Analysis
Point of View How does the use of a limited third-person narrator help readers know more about what is in the envelope than Mr. Tolman knows?

Critical Thinking

Cite textual evidence to support your responses.

1. **Key Ideas and Details (a)** According to his uncle's will, what must Bobby Gillian do after spending the thousand dollars?
(b) Infer: What are Gillian's feelings about inheriting this amount?

2. **Key Ideas and Details (a) Infer:** Why does Gillian decide to give Miss Hayden the money but not tell the lawyers? **(b) Draw Conclusions:** What do these decisions tell you about his character? **(c) Compare and Contrast:** Compare what these decisions indicate about his character with your first impressions of him.

3. **Key Ideas and Details (a)** Why do you think Gillian lets Miss Hayden think that the money was willed to her by his uncle?
(b) Interpret: What do you think Gillian hopes to gain by doing this?

4. **Integration of Knowledge and Ideas** Gillian deals with the conflict of being in love with Miss Hayden, who does not return his affection. **(a)** How does Gillian address this conflict? **(b)** Does dealing with this conflict help him to grow as a person? Explain. *[Connect to the Big Question: Can progress be made without conflict?]*

BY THE WATERS OF BABYLON

STEPHEN VINCENT BENÉT

The north and the west and the south are good hunting ground, but it is forbidden to go east. It is forbidden to go to any of the Dead Places except to search for metal, and then he who touches the metal must be a priest or the son of a priest. Afterwards, both the man and the metal must be purified! These are the rules and the laws: they are well made. It is forbidden to cross the great river and look upon the place that was the Place of the Gods—this is most strictly forbidden. We do not even say its name though we know its name. It is there that spirits live, and demons—it is there that there are the ashes of the Great Burning. These things are forbidden—they have been forbidden since the beginning of time.

My father is a priest; I am the son of a priest. I have been in the Dead Places near us, with my father—at first, I was afraid. When my father went into the house to search for the metal, I stood by the door and my heart felt small and weak. It was a dead man's house, a spirit house. It did not have the smell of man, though there were old bones in a corner. But it is not fitting that a priest's son should show fear. I looked at the bones in the shadow and kept my voice still.

Then my father came out with the metal—a good, strong piece. He looked at me with both eyes but I had not run away. He gave me the metal to hold—I took it and did not die. So he knew that I was truly his son and would be a priest in my time. That was when I was very young—nevertheless, my brothers would not have done it, though they are good hunters. After that, they gave me the good piece of meat and the warm corner by the fire. My father watched over me—he was glad that I should be a priest. But when I boasted or wept without a reason, he punished me more strictly than my brothers. That was right.

After a time, I myself was allowed to go into the dead houses and search for metal. So I learned the ways of those houses—and if I saw bones, I was no longer afraid. The bones are light and old—sometimes they will fall into dust if you touch them. But that is a great sin.

I was taught the chants and the spells—I was taught how to stop the running of blood from a wound and many secrets. A priest must know many secrets—that was what my father said. If the hunters think we do all things by chants and spells, they may believe so—it does not hurt them. I was taught how to read in the old books and how to make the old writings—that was hard and took a long time. My knowledge made me happy—it was like a fire in my heart. Most of all, I liked to hear of the Old Days and the stories of the gods. I asked myself many questions that I could not answer, but it was good to ask them. At night, I would lie awake and listen to the

Vocabulary
purified (pyo͞or´ ə fīd´)
v. rid of impurities or pollution; made pure

Literary Analysis
Point of View Which words in the second paragraph on this page tell you that the story is written from the first-person point of view?

Vocabulary
nevertheless (nev´ ər *thə* les´) *adv.* in spite of that; however

Reading Check
Why are the narrator and his father allowed to bring back metal from the "Dead Places"?

wind—it seemed to me that it was the voice of the gods as they flew through the air.

We are not ignorant like the Forest People—our women spin wool on the wheel, our priests wear a white robe. We do not eat grubs from the tree, we have not forgotten the old writings, although they are hard to understand. Nevertheless, my knowledge and my lack of knowledge burned in me—I wished to know more. When I was a man at last, I came to my father and said, "It is time for me to go on my journey. Give me your leave."

He looked at me for a long time, stroking his beard, then he said at last, "Yes. It is time." That night, in the house of the priesthood, I asked for and received purification. My body hurt but my spirit was a cool stone. It was my father himself who questioned me about my dreams.

He bade me look into the smoke of the fire and see—I saw and told what I saw. It was what I have always seen—a river, and, beyond it, a great Dead Place and in it the gods walking. I have always thought about that. His eyes were stern when I told him —he was no longer my father but a priest. He said, "This is a strong dream."

"It is mine," I said, while the smoke waved and my head felt light. They were singing the Star song in the outer chamber and it was like the buzzing of bees in my head.

He asked me how the gods were dressed and I told him how they were dressed. We know how they were dressed from the book, but I saw them as if they were before me. When I had finished, he threw the sticks three times and studied them as they fell.

"This is a very strong dream," he said. "It may eat you up."

"I am not afraid," I said and looked at him with both eyes. My voice sounded thin in my ears but that was because of the smoke.

He touched me on the breast and the forehead. He gave me the bow and the three arrows.

"Take them," he said. "It is forbidden to travel east. It is forbidden to cross the river. It is forbidden to go to the Place of the Gods. All these things are forbidden."

"All these things are forbidden," I said, but it was my voice that spoke and not my spirit. He looked at me again.

"My son," he said. "Once I had young dreams. If your dreams do not eat you up, you may be a great priest. If they eat you, you are still my son. Now go on your journey."

I went fasting, as is the law. My body hurt but not my heart. When the dawn came, I was out of sight of the village. I prayed and purified myself, waiting for a sign. The sign was an eagle. It flew east.

Literary Analysis
Point of View What details give the narrator credibility? Do you trust him? Why or why not?

▶ **Critical Viewing** Why do you think the tribes in the story refer to a city like the one in this image as "the Place of the Gods"? **[Infer]**

Sometimes signs are sent by bad spirits. I waited again on the flat rock, fasting, taking no food. I was very still—I could feel the sky above me and the earth beneath. I waited till the sun was beginning to sink. Then three deer passed in the valley, going east—they did not wind me or see me. There was a white fawn with them—a very great sign.

I followed them, at a distance, waiting for what would happen. My heart was troubled about going east, yet I knew that I must go. My head hummed with my fasting—I did not even see the panther spring upon the white fawn. But, before I knew it, the bow was in my hand. I shouted and the panther lifted his head from the fawn. It is not easy to kill a panther with one arrow but the arrow went through his eye and into his brain. He died as he tried to spring— he rolled over, tearing at the ground. Then I knew I was meant to go east—I knew that was my journey. When the night came, I made my fire and roasted meat.

It is eight suns' journey to the east and a man passes by many Dead Places. The Forest People are afraid of them but I am not. Once I made my fire on the edge of a Dead Place at night and, next morning, in the dead house, I found a good knife, little rusted. That was small to what came afterward, but it made my heart feel big. Always when I looked for game, it was in front of my arrow, and twice I passed hunting parties of the Forest People without their knowing. So I knew my magic was strong and my journey clean, in spite of the law.

Toward the setting of the eighth sun, I came to the banks of the great river. It was half-a-day's journey after I had left the god-road— we do not use the god-roads now for they are falling apart into great blocks of stone, and the forest is safer going. A long way off, I had seen the water through trees but the trees were thick. At last, I came out upon an open place at the top of a cliff. There was the great river below, like a giant in the sun. It is very long, very wide. It could eat all the streams we know and still be thirsty. Its name is Ou-dis-sun, the Sacred, the Long. No man of my tribe had seen it, not even my father, the priest. It was magic and I prayed.

Literary Analysis
Point of View What might the reader understand about the Dead Places that John does not?

Reading
Check

Where is the narrator journeying?

Then I raised my eyes and looked south. It was there, the Place of the Gods.

How can I tell what it was like—you do not know. It was there, in the red light, and they were too big to be houses. It was there with the red light upon it, mighty and ruined. I knew that in another moment the gods would see me. I covered my eyes with my hands and crept back into the forest.

Surely, that was enough to do, and live. Surely it was enough to spend the night upon the cliff. The Forest People themselves do not come near. Yet, all through the night, I knew that I should have to cross the river and walk in the places of the gods, although the gods ate me up. My magic did not help me at all and yet there was a fire in my bowels, a fire in my mind. When the sun rose, I thought, "My journey has been clean. Now I will go home from my journey." But, even as I thought so, I knew I could not. If I went to the place of the gods, I would surely die, but, if I did not go, I could never be at peace with my spirit again. It is better to lose one's life than one's spirit, if one is a priest and the son of a priest.

Nevertheless, as I made the raft, the tears ran out of my eyes. The Forest People could have killed me without fight, if they had come upon me then, but they did not come. When the raft was made, I said the sayings for the dead and painted myself for death. My heart was cold as a frog and my knees like water, but the burning in my mind would not let me have peace. As I pushed the raft from the shore, I began my death song—I had the right. It was a fine song.

"I am John, son of John," I sang. "My people are the Hill People.
    They are the men.
I go into the Dead Places but I am not slain.
I take the metal from the Dead Places but I am not blasted.
I travel upon the god-roads and am not afraid. E-yah! I have killed
    the panther, I have killed the fawn!
E-yah! I have come to the great river. No man has come there before.
It is forbidden to go east, but I have gone, forbidden to go on the
    great river, but I am there.
Open your hearts, you spirits, and hear my song.
Now I go to the Place of the Gods, I shall not return.
My body is painted for death and my limbs weak, but my heart is
    big as I go to the Place of the Gods!"

Literary Analysis
Point of View How does the use of a first-person narrator help readers appreciate John's thoughts and actions in this passage?

All the same, when I came to the Place of the Gods, I was afraid, afraid. The current of the great river is very strong—it gripped my raft with its hands. That was magic, for the river itself is wide and calm. I could feel evil spirits about me, in the bright morning; I could feel their breath on my neck as I was swept down the stream. Never have I been so much alone—I tried to think of my knowledge, but it was a squirrel's heap of winter nuts. There was no strength in my knowledge any more, and I felt small and naked as a new-hatched bird—alone upon the great river, the servant of the gods.

Yet, after a while, my eyes were opened and I saw. I saw both banks of the river—I saw that once there had been god-roads across it, though now they were broken and fallen like broken vines. Very great they were, and wonderful and broken—broken in the time of the Great Burning when the fire fell out of the sky. And always the current took me nearer to the Place of the Gods, and the huge ruins rose before my eyes.

I do not know the customs of rivers—we are the People of the Hills. I tried to guide my raft with the pole but it spun around. I thought the river meant to take me past the Place of the Gods and out into the Bitter Water of the legends. I grew angry then—my heart felt strong. I said aloud, "I am a priest and the son of a priest!" The gods heard me—they showed me how to paddle with the pole on one side of the raft. The current changed itself—I drew near to the Place of the Gods.

When I was very near, my raft struck and turned over. I can swim in our lakes—I swam to the shore. There was a great spike of rusted metal sticking out into the river—I hauled myself up upon it and sat there, panting. I had saved my bow and two arrows and the knife I found in the Dead Place but that was all. My raft went whirling downstream toward the Bitter Water. I looked after it, and thought if it had trod me under, at least I would be safely dead. Nevertheless, when I had dried my bow-string and restrung it, I walked forward to the Place of the Gods.

It felt like ground underfoot; it did not burn me. It is not true what some of the tales say, that the ground there burns forever, for I have been there. Here and there were the marks and stains of the Great Burning, on the ruins, that is true. But they were old marks and old stains. It is not true either, what some of our priests say, that it is an island covered with fogs and enchantments. It is not. It is a great Dead Place—greater than any Dead Place we know. Everywhere in it there are god-roads, though most are cracked and broken. Everywhere there are the ruins of the high towers of the gods.

◀ **Critical Viewing**
How does this image represent the natural dangers John has to overcome to get to the Place of the Gods? **[Infer]**

Spiral Review
Character What does John's anger about being taken past the Place of the Gods suggest about him?

How does John feel as he approaches the Place of the Gods?

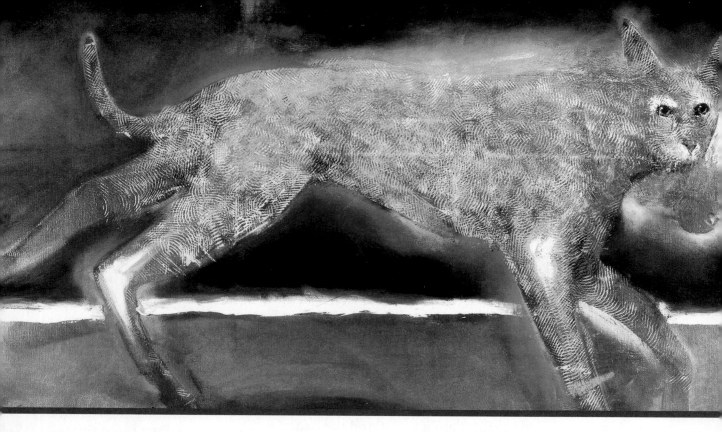

How shall I tell what I saw? I went carefully, my strung bow in
my hand, my skin ready for danger. There should have been the
wailings of spirits and the shrieks of demons, but there were not.
It was very silent and sunny where I had landed—the wind and
the rain and the birds that drop seeds had done their work—the
grass grew in the cracks of the broken stone. It is a fair island—no
wonder the gods built there. If I had come there, a god, I also would
have built.

How shall I tell what I saw? The towers are not all broken—here
and there one still stands, like a great tree in a forest, and the
birds nest high. But the towers themselves look blind, for the gods
are gone. I saw a fish-hawk, catching fish in the river. I saw a little
dance of white butterflies over a great heap of broken stones and
columns. I went there and looked about me—there was a carved
stone with cut-letters, broken in half. I can read letters but I could
not understand these. They said UBTREAS. There was also the
shattered image of a man or a god. It had been made of white stone
and he wore his hair tied back like a woman's. His name was
ASHING, as I read on the cracked half of a stone. I thought it wise
to pray to ASHING, though I do not know that god.

How shall I tell what I saw? There was no smell of man left,
on stone or metal. Nor were there many trees in that wilderness
of stone. There are many pigeons, nesting and dropping in the

towers—the gods must have loved them, or, perhaps, they used them for sacrifices. There are wild cats that roam the god-roads, green-eyed, unafraid of man. At night they wail like demons, but they are not demons. The wild dogs are more dangerous, for they hunt in a pack, but them I did not meet till later. Everywhere there are the carved stones carved with magical numbers or words.

I went North—I did not try to hide myself. When a god or a demon saw me, then I would die, but meanwhile I was no longer afraid. My hunger for knowledge burned in me—there was so much that I could not understand. After a while, I knew that my belly was hungry. I could have hunted for my meat, but I did not hunt. It is known that the gods did not hunt as we do—they got their food from enchanted boxes and jars. Sometimes these are still found in the Dead Places—once, when I was a child and foolish, I opened such a jar and tasted it and found the food sweet. But my father found out and punished me for it strictly, for, often, that food is death. Now, though, I had long gone past what was forbidden, and I entered the likeliest towers, looking for the food of the gods.

I found it at last in the ruins of a great temple in the mid-city. A mighty temple it must have been, for the roof was painted like the sky at night with its stars—that much I could see, though the colors were faint and dim. It went down into great caves and tunnels—perhaps they kept their slaves there. But when I started to climb down, I heard the squeaking of rats, so I did not go—rats are unclean, and there must have been many tribes of them, from the squeaking. But near there, I found food, in the heart of a ruin, behind a door that still opened. I ate only the fruits from the jars—they had a very sweet taste. There was drink, too, in bottles of glass—the drink of the gods was strong and made my head swim. After I had eaten and drunk, I slept on the top of a stone, my bow at my side.

When I woke, the sun was low. Looking down from where I lay, I saw a dog sitting on his haunches. His tongue was hanging out of his mouth; he looked as if he were laughing. He was a big dog, with a gray-brown coat, as big as a wolf. I sprang up and shouted at him but he did not move—he just sat there as if he were laughing. I did not like that. When I reached for a stone to throw, he moved swiftly out of the way of the stone. He was not afraid of me; he looked at me as if I were meat. No doubt I could have killed him with an arrow, but I did not know if there were others. Moreover, night was falling.

Reading Check

What are two things John sees in the Place of the Gods?

I looked about me—not far away there was a great, broken god-road, leading North. The towers were high enough, but not so high, and while many of the dead-houses were wrecked, there were some that stood. I went toward this god-road, keeping to the heights of the ruins, while the dog followed. When I had reached the god-road, I saw that there were others behind him. If I had slept later, they would have come upon me asleep and torn out my throat. As it was, they were sure enough of me; they did not hurry. When I went into the dead-house, they kept watch at the entrance—doubtless they thought they would have a fine hunt. But a dog cannot open a door and I knew, from the books, that the gods did not like to live on the ground but on high.

I had just found a door I could open when the dogs decided to rush. Ha! They were surprised when I shut the door in their faces—it was a good door, of strong metal. I could hear their foolish baying beyond it, but I did not stop to answer them. I was in darkness—I found stairs and climbed. There were many stairs, turning around till my head was dizzy. At the top was another door—I found the knob and opened it. I was in a long small chamber—on one side of it was a bronze door that could not be opened, for it had no handle. Perhaps there was a magic word to open it, but I did not have the word. I turned to the door in the opposite side of the wall. The lock of it was broken and I opened it and went in

Within, there was a place of great riches. The god who lived there must have been a powerful god. The first room was a small anteroom—I waited there for some time, telling the spirits of the place that I came in peace and not as a robber. When it seemed to me that they had had time to hear me, I went on. Ah, what riches! Few, even, of the windows had been broken—it was all as it had been. The great windows that looked over the city had not been broken at all though they were dusty and streaked with many years. There were coverings on the floors, the colors not greatly faded, and the chairs were soft and deep. There were pictures upon the walls, very strange, very wonderful—I remember one of a bunch of flowers in a jar—if you came close to it, you could see nothing but

Literary Analysis
Point of View In what ways does John's perception of the "gods" influence his beliefs about his surroundings?

bits of color, but if you stood away from it, the flowers might have been picked yesterday. It made my heart feel strange to look at this picture—and to look at the figure of a bird, in some hard clay, on a table and see it so like our birds. Everywhere there were books and writings, many in tongues that I could not read. The god who lived there must have been a wise god and full of knowledge. I felt I had right there, as I sought knowledge also.

Nevertheless, it was strange. There was a washing-place but no water—perhaps the gods washed in air. There was a cooking-place but no wood, and though there was a machine to cook food, there was no place to put fire in it. Nor were there candles or lamps— there were things that looked like lamps but they had neither oil nor wick. All these things were magic, but I touched them and lived—the magic had gone out of them. Let me tell one thing to show. In the washing-place, a thing said "Hot" but it was not hot to the touch—another thing said "Cold" but it was not cold. This must have been a strong magic but the magic was gone. I do not understand—they had ways—I wish that I knew.

It was close and dry and dusty in their house of the gods. I have said the magic was gone but that is not true—it had gone from the magic things but it had not gone from the place. I felt the spirits about me, weighing upon me. Nor had I ever slept in a Dead Place before—and yet, tonight, I must sleep there. When I thought of it, my tongue felt dry in my throat, in spite of my wish for knowledge. Almost I would have gone down again and faced the dogs, but I did not.

I had not gone through all the rooms when the darkness fell. When it fell, I went back to the big room looking over the city and made fire. There was a place to make fire and a box with wood in it, though I do not think they cooked there. I wrapped myself in a floor-covering and slept in front of the fire—I was very tired.

Now I tell what is very strong magic. I woke in the midst of the night. When I woke, the fire had gone out and I was cold. It seemed to me that all around me there were whisperings and voices. I closed my eyes to shut them out. Some will say that I slept again, but I do not think that I slept. I could feel the spirits drawing my spirit out of my body as a fish is drawn on a line.

Why should I lie about it? I am a priest and the son of a priest. If there are spirits, as they say, in the small Dead Places near us, what spirits must there not be in that great Place of the Gods? And would not they wish to speak? After such long years? I know that I felt myself drawn as a fish is drawn on a line. I had stepped out of my body—I could see my body asleep in front of the cold fire, but it was not I. I was drawn to look out upon the city of the gods.

Literary Analysis
Point of View What might the reader know about the "thing that said 'Cold'" that John does not know?

Reading Check

In what way was the life of the gods different from the life John's tribe leads?

It should have been dark, for it was night, but it was not dark. Everywhere there were lights—lines of light—circles and blurs of light—ten thousand torches would not have been the same. The sky itself was alight—you could barely see the stars for the glow in the sky. I thought to myself "This is strong magic" and trembled. There was a roaring in my ears like the rushing of rivers. Then my eyes grew used to the light and my ears to the sound. I knew that I was seeing the city as it had been when the gods were alive.

That was a sight indeed—yes, that was a sight: I could not have seen it in the body—my body would have died. Everywhere went the gods, on foot and in chariots—there were gods beyond number and counting and their chariots blocked the streets. They had turned night to day for their pleasure—they did not sleep with the sun. The noise of their coming and going was the noise of many waters. It was magic what they could do—it was magic what they did.

I looked out of another window—the great vines of their bridges were mended and the god-roads went East and West. Restless, restless, were the gods and always in motion! They burrowed tunnels under rivers—they flew in the air. With unbelievable tools they did giant works—no part of the earth was safe from them, for, if they wished for a thing, they summoned it from the other side of the world. And always, as they labored and rested, as they feasted and made love, there was a drum in their ears—the pulse of the giant city, beating and beating like a man's heart.

Were they happy? What is happiness to the gods? They were great, they were mighty, they were wonderful and terrible. As I looked upon them and their magic, I felt like a child—but a little more, it seemed to me, and they would pull down the moon from the sky. I saw them with wisdom beyond wisdom and knowledge beyond knowledge. And yet not all they did was well done—even I

Literary Analysis
Point of View
In what way is John's perception of these scenes different from what yours would be?

▼ **Critical Viewing**
Compare this picture with John's descriptions of the Place of the Gods. **[Compare and Contrast]**

could see that—and yet their wisdom could not but grow until all was peace.

Then I saw their fate come upon them and that was terrible past speech. It came upon them as they walked the streets of their city. I have been in the fights with the Forest People—I have seen men die. But this was not like that. When gods war with gods, they use weapons we do not know. It was fire falling out of the sky and a mist that poisoned. It was the time of the Great Burning and the Destruction. They ran about like ants in the streets of their city— poor gods, poor gods! Then the towers began to fall. A few escaped— yes, a few. The legends tell it. But, even after the city had become a Dead Place, for many years the poison was still in the ground. I saw it happen, I saw the last of them die. It was darkness over the broken city, and I wept.

All this, I saw. I saw it as I have told it, though not in the body. When I woke in the morning, I was hungry, but I did not think first of my hunger, for my heart was perplexed and confused. I knew the reason for the Dead Places but I did not see why it had happened. It seemed to me it should not have happened, with all the magic they had. I went through the house looking for an answer. There was so much in the house I could not understand—and yet I am a priest and the son of a priest. It was like being on one side of the great river, at night, with no light to show the way.

Then I saw the dead god. He was sitting in his chair, by the window, in a room I had not entered before and, for the first moment, I thought that he was alive. Then I saw the skin on the back of his hand—it was like dry leather. The room was shut, hot and dry—no doubt that had kept him as he was. At first I was afraid to approach him—then the fear left me. He was sitting looking out over the city—he was dressed in the clothes of the gods. His age was neither young nor old—I could not tell his age. But there was wisdom in his face and great sadness. You could see that he would have not run away. He had sat at his window, watching his city die—then he himself had died. But it is better to lose one's life than one's spirit—and you could see from the face that his spirit had not been lost. I knew that, if I touched him, he would fall into dust—and yet, there was something unconquered in the face.

That is all of my story, for then I knew he was a man—I knew then that they had been men, neither gods nor demons. It is a great knowledge, hard to tell and believe. They were men—they went a dark road, but they were men. I had no fear after that—I had no fear going home, though twice I fought off the dogs and once I was hunted for two days by the Forest People. When I saw my father again, I prayed and was purified. He touched my lips and my

Literary Analysis
Point of View In what way has John's view of the gods changed?

Reading Check

What event does John see in his vision?

breast, he said, "You went away a boy. You come back a man and a priest." I said, "Father, they were men! I have been in the Place of the Gods and seen it! Now slay me, if it is the law—but still I know they were men."

He looked at me out of both eyes. He said, "The law is not always the same shape—you have done what you have done. I could not have done it in my time but you come after me. Tell!"

I told and he listened. After that, I wished to tell all the people but he showed me otherwise. He said, "Truth is a hard deer to hunt. If you eat too much truth at once, you may die of the truth. It was not idly that our fathers forbade the Dead Places." He was right—it is better the truth should come little by little. I have learned that, being a priest. Perhaps, in the old days, they ate knowledge too fast.

Nevertheless, we make a beginning. It is not for the metal alone we go to the Dead Places now—there are the books and the writings. They are hard to learn. And the magic tools are broken—but we can look at them and wonder. At least, we make a beginning. And, when I am chief priest we shall go beyond the great river. We shall go to the Place of the Gods—the place newyork—not one man but a company. We shall look for the images of the gods and find the god ASHING and the others—the gods Lincoln and Biltmore[1] and Moses.[2] But they were men who built the city, not gods or demons. They were men. I remember the dead man's face. They were men who were here before us. We must build again.

---

1. **Biltmore** hotel in New York City.
2. **Moses** Robert Moses, former New York City municipal official who oversaw many large construction projects.

Literary Analysis
Point of View Does John's new understanding of the gods now match the reader's? Explain.

Critical Thinking

Cite textual evidence to support your responses.

1. **Key Ideas and Details** **(a) Infer:** What are the Dead Places and the Place of the Gods? **(b) Synthesize:** How does John's tribe view the Dead Places?

2. **Key Ideas and Details** **(a)** When is this story set? How can you tell? **(b) Infer:** What destroyed the city? Explain.

3. **Key Ideas and Details** **(a)** Why does John's father want to keep John's experience secret? **(b) Evaluate:** Do you agree with John's father? Explain.

4. **Integration of Knowledge and Ideas** **(a)** What progress does John make as a result of dealing with conflict? Explain. **(b)** Do you think he could have made this progress without facing conflict? Why or why not? *[Connect to the Big Question: Can progress be made without conflict?]*

Comparing Points of View

1. Craft and Structure Using a chart like the one shown, compare the way in which each author uses **point of view** to control the information his reader receives.

Story	Point of View	What Reader Knows	What Character Knows	Effect of Contrast in Knowledge	Impact of Story

2. Craft and Structure (a) Compare the ways in which the ending of each story surprises the reader. **(b)** For each story, explain how the author's choice of narrator helps prepare for this surprise.

3. Craft and Structure (a) Readers may find Gillian's final gesture moving because they see that none of the characters knows what he has done. How does point of view create this effect? **(b)** Compare this feeling with that created by the ending of "By the Waters of Babylon." Why might a modern reader feel humbled by the story's ending?

◐ Timed Writing

Explanatory Text: Essay

Both stories use dramatic irony. In an essay, compare and contrast how the irony is achieved in these stories. Support your response with details from the texts. **(40 minutes)**

5-Minute Planner

1. Read the prompt carefully and completely.
2. Consider these questions for both stories:
   - How does the point of view develop dramatic irony?
   - What is the character or persona of the narrator?
   - How much do you trust the narrator to tell you the truth?
   - What is the nature of the truth that is revealed in the ending?
   - How does irony affect your response to the selection?
3. Reread the prompt, and then draft your essay.

Writing Workshop

 Common Core State Standards

Writing

3. Write narratives to develop real or imagined experiences or events using effective technique, well-chosen details, and well-structured event sequences.

3.a. Engage and orient the reader by setting out a problem, situation, or observation, establishing one or multiple point(s) of view, and introducing a narrator and/or characters; create a smooth progression of experiences or events.

5. Develop and strengthen writing as needed by planning, revising, editing, rewriting, or trying a new approach, focusing on addressing what is most significant for a specific purpose and audience.

Write a Narrative

Narration: Short Story

Defining the Form **Short stories** are a brief form of fiction that usually focuses on a limited number of characters. You might use elements of the short story in anecdotes, scripts, and reflective essays.

Assignment Write a short story about a main character who undergoes a change or learns something. Include these elements:

- ✓ a clear *setting*—the time and place of the story
- ✓ a *plot,* or series of events, that builds to a dramatic climax
- ✓ a *narrator* to tell the story
- ✓ effective descriptions using *sensory details*
- ✓ a *theme* that is revealed by the story's conclusion
- ✓ error-free grammar, including use of *consistent verb tense*

To preview the criteria on which your short story may be judged, see the rubric on page 333.

 Writing Workshop: *Work in Progress*

Review the work you did on pages 267 and 295.

Prewriting/Planning Strategy

Gather details about characters. Before you begin your draft, get to know the characters you will develop. Use a character chart like this one.

Character Chart	
Name	Kei
Appearance	Small frame, dark hair, intense brown eyes
Three Key Adjectives	smart, clumsy, ambitious
Goals	to be a great trumpet player
Habits or Quirks	taps his fingers
Likes	jazz, football, reading
Dislikes	TV, his boss at his after school job

Reading-Writing Connection

To get a feel for short stories, read "A Problem" by Anton Chekhov, on p. 256.

Using Your Imagination

Ideas are the building blocks of your story. They shape the plot, setting, and characters. As you generate ideas, begin with any one element—plot, setting, or characters—and develop the other two elements from there. Use these tips to engage your imagination and develop story ideas.

Imagining the Setting Create a setting you would choose if you could live anywhere or at any historical time. You can adapt most universal themes to any setting. For example, Shakespeare's play *Romeo and Juliet* is set in medieval Italy. The musical *West Side Story*, based loosely on the same plot, is set in 1950s New York City. Consider the setting before starting plot and character development. Often, the setting suggests the plot and characters. For example, a setting of a colony on a distant, inhospitable planet might suggest a struggle for survival.

Imagining the Plot Think about a dramatic moment in your life or the life of someone you know, or use newspapers or TV news to find an intriguing story. Turn the outlines of the personal event or news story into a short story. Remember that a short story is fiction, so you can add details or change the facts in order to make the story more interesting.

You might also use one of the universal themes of stories that can be adapted to any time or place. Examples include the following:

- A couple whose love is doomed, such as in *Romeo and Juliet*
- A hero who leads a desperate fight of good against evil
- A young person on a quest to save his or her family, tribe, or world

Imagining the Characters Think about the kind of character who would live in the setting or fit the plot you have chosen. As you develop your ideas, use a chart like the one shown to jot down notes.

	Plot	Setting	Character
Idea 1	a young boy struggles for survival in the wilderness	a remote area of the Rocky Mountains	a young Boy Scout who has wandered away during a camping trip
Idea 2			
Idea 3			

Drafting Strategies

Make a plot diagram. The plot of your story should include exposition to set up the characters, setting, and conflict. Rising action will build to a climax, or point of highest tension. Then, the falling action leads to the resolution. Create a plot diagram like the one shown here. Note major story events to create a logical, smooth progression.

Keep pacing in mind. To keep your story moving, consider introducing the problem early in the story. Then, add details that intensify the problem. Using *flashbacks*—or material that occurred earlier than the present time of the narrative—is one way to add intensity. Flashbacks can be in the form of a character's memories, dreams, or accounts of past events, or they can simply be a shift in the narrative back to an earlier time. You might also delay the climax to create more suspense. After the climax, provide a conclusion in which a character or the narrator reflects on the events of the story.

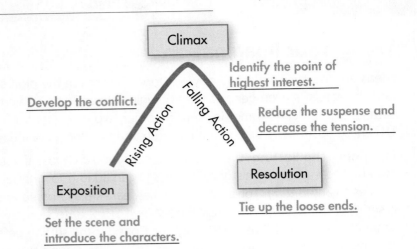

Climax — Identify the point of highest interest.

Develop the conflict.

Rising Action / Falling Action

Reduce the suspense and decrease the tension.

Exposition — Set the scene and introduce the characters.

Resolution — Tie up the loose ends.

Revising Strategies

Add dialogue to develop characters. Look for points where you can develop characters through dialogue and action. If your characters are from a specific region or background, including their dialect will help readers hear how they sound. Review your draft to identify direct statements that could be replaced with the characters' own words.

Revise to use active voice. Active voice is livelier and more engaging than the passive voice. In the passive voice, the action is done to the subject. In the active voice, the subject of the sentence performs the action.

Passive Voice: The deadline was met by Krista and Rachel.

Active Voice: Krista and Rachel met their deadline.

Add sensory details. Add sensory details to your writing to enable the reader to experience what you are describing. Sensory details are words that appeal to the senses: sight, smell, taste, touch, and hearing. Instead of writing *The pie smelled good,* you might say, *The freshly baked pie filled the house with the warm aroma of apples and cinnamon.* Using sensory language in this way allows readers to partake in your description.

Common Core State Standards

Writing

3.b. Use narrative techniques, such as dialogue, pacing, description, reflection, and multiple plot lines, to develop experiences, events, and/or characters.

3.c. Use a variety of techniques to sequence events so that they build on one another to create a coherent whole.

3.d. Use precise words and phrases, telling details, and sensory language to convey a vivid picture of the experiences, events, setting, and/or characters.

3.e. Provide a conclusion that follows from and reflects on what is experienced, observed, or resolved over the course of the narrative.

Revising to Apply Consistent Verb Tense

Correct use of verb tenses indicates when an event occurred. It is best to stay with a single tense. Mixing tenses unnecessarily can confuse the reader.

Six Basic Verb Tenses	
Present	He *arrives* today.
Past	He *arrived* yesterday.
Future	He *will arrive* tomorrow.
Present Perfect	He *has arrived* already.
Past Perfect	He *had arrived* earlier than expected.
Future Perfect	He *will have arrived* by next week.

Identifying Mixed Tenses To identify mixed tenses, first recognize the verb tenses you use. Compare these examples:

Mixed Tenses: Kei *has knocked* and *was waiting* patiently at the door. Nothing *happens*. Kei *had decided* to leave.

Consistent Tense: Kei *knocked* and *waited* patiently at the door. Nothing *happened*. Kei *decided* to leave.

Mixing tenses is necessary when your work refers to two different times.

> **Past Perfect**   **Past**
> Kei <u>*had waited*</u> for ten minutes before the door <u>*opened*</u>.

PH **WRITING COACH**

Further instruction and practice are available in *Prentice Hall Writing Coach*.

Fixing Errors To make sure that your verb tenses are consistent, find each verb in your writing.

1. Identify your overall verb tense as past, present, or future.

2. Review the verbs in your writing, circling each one.

3. If you find a verb that is not in your basic verb tense, make sure the tense shift is necessary.

4. Revise the verb if the shift is unnecessary.

Grammar in Your Writing

Review two paragraphs of your draft. Underline every verb and identify its tense. Use the steps you have just learned to fix confusing mixed tenses.

Student Model: Aubrey Weatherford,
Broken Arrow, OK

Common Core
State Standards

Language
2.b. Spell correctly.

And Then the Rain Came

"Is it wrong for us to have a voice in our lives? We have to fight!" said the woman speaking to the crowd. Scarlett flashed instantly to the night of the fire. She could feel the young man holding her back; she could hear the child screaming in the burning building. She struggled to free herself, tears running down her face. Shaking herself back into reality, Scarlett walked slowly away from the park, the speaker's words fading as she went. There was a dull rumble in the distance, and a flicker of light illuminated the city around her. The cool breeze rustled her long skirt, and she began to quicken her pace for fear of being caught in the storm. Scarlett's mind was spinning, the speaker's words stirring her thoughts. The thought of speaking her opinion and of being able to choose whomever she wanted for public office, though she had never learned exactly what their jobs were—just the thought of having the choice was enough to excite her.

"Little Lady, you had better hurry on home now. There's a gonna be quite a storm a comin'." An old, wrinkled man had approached Scarlett from the shadows, seemingly trying to help. She was looking at him patiently.

"Hey you, crazy man, leave the lady alone. You go on home now, you worthless old fool!" A middle-aged businessman had approached the two.

"Don't talk to him that way! He wasn't bothering me!" Scarlett said. "You don't need to associate with street people like him. Go on home!"

"You have no right to speak to me in that fashion, good sir. I may associate with whomever I choose."

The businessman turned on his heel and left. "Thank yer for standing up for me, little lady. Mighty appreciative."

"It was nothing. You remind me so much of, oh, never mind," Scarlett replied.

"I am sure I will walk by here again sometime. I will look for you. Good day, sir." Though Scarlett did not see it, the old man began to come out of the shadows as she made her way down the crowded street, though his appearance had greatly changed. He was no longer a wrinkled, old man but a tall, young man with sandy hair and piercing eyes. Carefully, he watched as Scarlett hurried along the sidewalk. Tiny drops of rain began to fall from the ashen sky as Scarlett disappeared into the crowd. . . .

Aubrey introduces the main character in the first paragraph.

Sensory details describe the setting.

Aubrey develops the conflict through dialogue.

These details reveal an interesting twist in the plot.

Editing and Proofreading

Reread your story to correct errors in grammar, usage, and mechanics.

Focus on complete sentences and spelling. Check that all sentences in your draft contain a subject and a verb and express a complete thought. Also check your spelling. Words with double letters, such as *dilemma*, and words with two sets of double letters, such as *embarrass*, are often spelled incorrectly. Make up clues to help yourself remember any word that you often misspell.

Publishing and Presenting

Consider one of the following ways to share your writing:

Give a dramatic reading. Practice reading your story aloud, experimenting with pace, emphasis, and tone. Then, read your story to a group of classmates. After the presentation, discuss which of your story's elements were especially effective when presented dramatically.

Compile an anthology. Join with your classmates to create a class story anthology. Organize the stories by theme and illustrate them with suitable photographs or drawings. Place the collection in your class, school, or community library.

Reflecting on Your Writing

Writer's Journal Jot down your answers to this question:

How did writing a short story help you better understand the form?

Rubric for Self-Assessment

Find evidence in your writing to address each category. Then, use the rating scale to grade your work.

Spiral Review

Earlier in the unit, you learned about the **principal parts of regular verbs** (p. 266) and **irregular verbs** (p. 294). Review your draft to ensure you have formed verb tenses correctly and consistently.

Criteria	Rating Scale				
	not very				very
	1	2	3	4	5
Focus: How clear is the story's theme or message?	1	2	3	4	5
Organization: How effectively does the plot build to a climax?	1	2	3	4	5
Support/Elaboration: How effective is your choice of details?	1	2	3	4	5
Style: How well do you describe the characters and setting?	1	2	3	4	5
Conventions: How correct is your grammar, especially your use of verb tense?	1	2	3	4	5
Ideas: How effective and interesting are your ideas for plot, setting, and characters?	1	2	3	4	5

Ⓒ Leveled Texts

Build your skills and improve your comprehension of short stories with texts of increasing complexity.

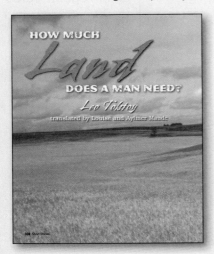

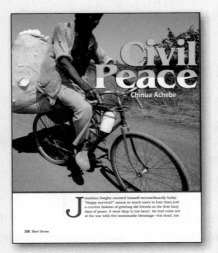

Read **"How Much Land Does a Man Need?"** to find out what happens when a man is never satisfied with what he has.

Read **"Civil Peace"** to find out what happens when a man chooses to make the most of what he has.

Ⓒ Common Core State Standards

Meet these standards with either **"How Much Land Does a Man Need?"** (p. 338) or **"Civil Peace"** (p. 358).

Reading Literature
2. Determine a theme or central idea of a text and analyze in detail its development over the course of the text, including how it emerges and is shaped and refined by specific details; provide an objective summary of the text. *(Literary Analysis: Theme)*

Spiral Review: RL.9-10.5
Writing
2.a. Introduce a topic; organize complex ideas, concepts, and information to make important connections and distinctions. **2.b.** Develop the topic with well-chosen, relevant, and sufficient facts, extended definitions, concrete details, quotations, or other information and examples appropriate to the audience's knowledge of the topic. **2.c.** Use appropriate and varied transitions to link the major sections of the text, create cohesion, and clarify the relationships among complex ideas and concepts.

(Writing: Character Analysis)
Speaking and Listening
1.c. Propel conversations by posing and responding to questions that relate the current discussion to broader themes or larger ideas; actively incorporate others into the discussion; and clarify, verify, or challenge ideas and conclusions. **1.d.** Respond thoughtfully to diverse perspectives, summarize points of agreement and disagreement, and, when warranted, qualify or justify their own views and understanding and make new connections in light of the evidence and reasoning presented. *(Speaking and Listening: Group Discussion)*

Language
5. Demonstrate understanding of figurative language, word relationships, and nuances in word meanings. *(Vocabulary: Antonyms)*

Literary Analysis: Theme

The **theme** of a literary work is the central idea it communicates about life. For example, a simple story might convey the theme "Honesty is the best policy." Another work might suggest, "Human suffering cannot be justified or explained." Frequently, writers' themes spring from the *historical context* of a selection, the social and cultural background of a story. The author's diction and use of figurative language contribute to the interpretation of the theme. To express a theme, a writer may take one of these approaches:

- Directly state the theme of the work, or have a character directly state it.
- Create patterns of story elements to suggest a larger meaning—for instance, by using language patterns or repeated phrases. In addition, a writer might contrast a generous man and his selfish brother to convey an idea about generosity.

In many cases, a theme reflects a **philosophical assumption**—the writer's basic beliefs about life. For instance, a writer may make the assumption that being generous leads to happiness and may explore that idea in his or her writing.

Reading Skill: Draw Conclusions

When you **draw a conclusion,** you reach a decision or form an opinion based on information in a text. To draw a conclusion identifying the theme of a work, **recognize key details.** Also, think about the characters' experiences and what they learn about life in the course of the story. Use that information to draw conclusions about theme.

Using the Strategy: Key Details Diagram

Use a **key details diagram** to help draw a conclusion about a selection.

Story Detail		Story Detail		Pattern
Greedy Joe invests in a crooked scheme. He loses his money.	+	Generous John tricks the crooks and saves Joe.	→	Being greedy causes harm. Being generous leads to solutions.

Can progress be made without *conflict?*

Writing About the Big Question

In "How Much Land Does a Man Need?", a man struggles to satisfy his desire for more land and prosperity. Use these sentence starters to help develop your ideas about the Big Question:

Making a **change** can improve the quality of your life as long as

_____ .

A person may **struggle** with finding happiness if _____ .

While You Read Note signs of the main character's discontent with his life. Then, decide whether he faces the biggest conflict with others or within himself.

Vocabulary

Read each word and its definition. Decide whether you know the word well, know it a little bit, or do not know it at all. After you read, see how your knowledge of each word has increased.

- **piqued** (pēkt) *adj.* annoyed or upset (p. 339) *I am piqued by the fact that you did not tell me that you would be late.* pique *n.* piqued *v.* piquant *adj.*

- **discord** (dis′ kôrd′) *n.* conflict; disagreement (p. 340) *The new referee's questionable call caused discord between the teams.* discordant *adj.* concord *n.* cordial *adj.*

- **forbore** (fôr bôr′) *v.* prevented oneself from doing something; refrained from (p. 342) *The quarterback forbore responding to the linebackers' taunts.* forbearance *n.* forbearingly *adv.*

- **aggrieved** (ə grēvd′) *adj.* wronged; suffering grief or injury (p. 343) *The tenants were aggrieved by the landlord's delay in fixing the hot-water tank.* aggrieve *v.* grievance *n.*

- **arable** (ar′ ə bəl) *adj.* suitable for growing crops (p. 344) *After two years of poor crops, the farmer was forced to seek out more arable land.* arability *adj.*

- **prostrate** (präs′ trāt′) *adj.* lying flat (p. 350) *After a tiring day, Randall lay prostrate on the couch.* prostration *n.*

Word Study

The **Latin prefix dis-** means "wrong," "bad," or "not."

In this story, **discord** arises when the peasants are not in accord, or agreement, with one another. They pursue individual interests instead of a common goal.

Meet
Leo Tolstoy
(1828–1910)

Author of
HOW MUCH *Land*
DOES A MAN NEED?

Leo Tolstoy is remembered almost as much for his unusual life as for his work. Born into a rich family, he inherited his family estate at age nineteen. He soon set about trying to improve the lives of the peasants who lived on his land.

Crisis and Renewal After the publication of two major masterpieces, the novels *War and Peace* (1865–1869) and *Anna Karenina* (1875–1877), Tolstoy fell into deep despair, questioning the value of his life and all his previous works. He found salvation and renewal in a mystical spirituality. He gave up small luxuries and worked in the fields. Tolstoy's beliefs about overcoming evil helped to inspire later activists such as Dr. Martin Luther King, Jr.

DID YOU KNOW?

Although the young Tolstoy volunteered for the army, he later came to believe that all forms of violence were wrong.

BACKGROUND FOR THE STORY
Landless in Russia

In Russia, from the sixteenth century to the mid-nineteenth century, peasants were serfs, bound by law to work land they could rent but not own. At the time of the story, peasants were allowed to own property. The memory of earlier times, however, kept peasants, like Pahom in this story, hungry for land.

HOW MUCH *Land* DOES A MAN NEED?

Leo Tolstoy

translated by Louise and Aylmer Maude

An elder sister came to visit her younger sister in the country. The elder was married to a shopkeeper in town, the younger to a peasant in the village. As the sisters sat over their tea talking, the elder began to boast of the advantages of town life, saying how comfortably they lived there, how well they dressed, what fine clothes her children wore, what good things they ate and drank, and how she went to the theater, promenades, and entertainments.

The younger sister was piqued, and in turn disparaged the life of a shopkeeper, and stood up for that of a peasant.

"I wouldn't change my way of life for yours," said she. "We may live roughly, but at least we're free from worry. You live in better style than we do, but though you often earn more than you need, you're very likely to lose all you have. You know the proverb, 'Loss and gain are brothers twain.' It often happens that people who're wealthy one day are begging their bread the next. Our way is safer. Though a peasant's life is not a rich one, it's long. We'll never grow rich, but we'll always have enough to eat."

The elder sister said sneeringly:

"Enough? Yes, if you like to share with the pigs and the calves! What do you know of elegance or manners! However much your good man may slave, you'll die as you live—in a dung heap—and your children the same."

"Well, what of that?" replied the younger sister. "Of course our work is rough and hard. But on the other hand, it's sure, and we need not bow to anyone. But you, in your towns, are surrounded by temptations; today all may be right, but tomorrow the Evil One may tempt your husband with cards, wine, or women, and all will go to ruin. Don't such things happen often enough?"

Pahom, the master of the house, was lying on the top of the stove and he listened to the women's chatter.

"It is perfectly true," thought he. "Busy as we are from childhood tilling mother earth, we peasants have no time to let any nonsense settle in our heads. Our only trouble is that we haven't land enough. If I had plenty of land, I shouldn't fear the Devil himself !"

The women finished their tea, chatted a while about dress, and then cleared away the tea things and lay down to sleep.

But the Devil had been sitting behind the stove and had heard all that had been said. He was pleased that the peasant's wife had led her husband into boasting and that he had said that if he had plenty of land he would not fear the Devil himself.

"All right," thought the Devil. "We'll have a tussle. I'll give you land enough; and by means of the land I'll get you into my power."

Vocabulary
piqued (pēkt) *adj.* annoyed or upset

Literary Analysis
Theme What theme about work do the younger sister's remarks suggest?

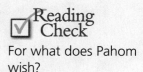
Reading Check
For what does Pahom wish?

Close to the village there lived a lady, a small landowner who had an estate of about three hundred acres. She had always lived on good terms with the peasants until she engaged as her manager an old soldier, who took to burdening the people with fines. However careful Pahom tried to be, it happened again and again that now a horse of his got among the lady's oats, now a cow strayed into her garden, now his calves found their way into her meadows—and he always had to pay a fine.

Pahom paid up, but grumbled, and, going home in a temper, was rough with his family. All through that summer Pahom had much trouble because of this manager, and he was actually glad when winter came and the cattle had to be stabled. Though he grudged the fodder when they could no longer graze on the pasture land, at least he was free from anxiety about them.

In the winter the news got about that the lady was going to sell her land and that the keeper of the inn on the high road was bargaining for it. When the peasants heard this they were very much alarmed.

"Well," thought they, "if the innkeeper gets the land, he'll worry us with fines worse than the lady's manager. We all depend on that estate."

So the peasants went on behalf of their village council and asked the lady not to sell the land to the innkeeper, offering her a better price for it themselves. The lady agreed to let them have it. Then the peasants tried to arrange for the village council to buy the whole estate, so that it might be held by them all in common. They met twice to discuss it, but could not settle the matter; the Evil One sowed discord among them and they could not agree. So they decided

Vocabulary
discord (dis´ kôrd´) *n.* conflict; disagreement

▼ **Critical Viewing**
Based on details of his appearance, does the peasant in this portrait lead a life similar to Pahom's? Explain. **[Infer]**

to buy the land individually, each according to his means; and the lady agreed to this plan as she had to the other.

Presently Pahom heard that a neighbor of his was buying fifty acres, and that the lady had consented to accept one half in cash and to wait a year for the other half. Pahom felt envious.

"Look at that," thought he, "the land is all being sold, and I'll get none of it." So he spoke to his wife.

"Other people are buying," said he, "and we must also buy twenty acres or so. Life is becoming impossible. That manager is simply crushing us with his fines."

So they put their heads together and considered how they could manage to buy it. They had one hundred rubles[1] laid by. They sold a colt and one half of their bees, hired out one of their sons as a farmhand and took his wages in advance, borrowed the rest from a brother-in-law, and so scraped together half the purchase money.

Having done this, Pahom chose a farm of forty acres, some of it wooded, and went to the lady to bargain for it. They came to an agreement, and he shook hands with her upon it and paid her a deposit in advance. Then they went to town and signed the deeds, he paying half the price down, and undertaking to pay the remainder within two years.

So now Pahom had land of his own. He borrowed seed and sowed it on the land he had bought. The harvest was a good one, and within a year he had managed to pay off his debts both to the lady and to his brother-in-law. So he became a landowner, plowing and sowing his own land, making hay on his own land, cutting his own trees, and feeding his cattle on his own pasture. When he went out to plow his fields, or to look at his growing corn, or at his grass meadows, his heart would fill with joy. The grass that grew and the flowers that bloomed there seemed to him unlike any that grew elsewhere. Formerly, when he had passed by that land, it had appeared the same as any other land, but now it seemed quite different. ●

3

So Pahom was well contented, and everything would have been right if the neighboring peasants would only not have trespassed on his wheatfields and meadows. He appealed to them most civilly, but they still went on: now the herdsmen would let the village cows stray into his meadows, then horses from the night pasture would get among his corn. Pahom turned them out again and again, and

Literary Analysis
Theme What do these details about Pahom's motives suggest about his "need" for land?

Reading Check
After acquiring his own land, how does Pahom feel at first?

---

1. **rubles** (rōō′ bəlz) *n.* A ruble is the basic unit of Russian currency.

Vocabulary
forbore (fôr bôr´) v.
prevented oneself
from doing some-
thing; refrained from

Reading Skill
Draw Conclusions
Which key details in
this passage show
that the desire for
land leads to discord
among the peasants?

Literary Analysis
Theme In what way
does this episode rein-
force the idea that the
desire for land leads
to division and
unhappiness?

forgave their owners, and for a long time he forbore to prosecute
anyone. But at last he lost patience and complained to the District
Court. He knew it was the peasants' want of land, and no evil intent
on their part, that caused the trouble, but he thought:

"I can't go on overlooking it, or they'll destroy all I have. They must
be taught a lesson."

So he had them up, gave them one lesson, and then another,
and two or three of the peasants were fined. After a time Pahom's
neighbors began to bear him a grudge for this, and would now and
then let their cattle onto his land on purpose. One peasant even
got into Pahom's wood at night and cut down five young lime trees
for their bark. Pahom, passing through the wood one day, noticed
something white. He came nearer and saw the stripped trunks lying
on the ground, and close by stood the stumps where the trees had
been. Pahom was furious.

"If he'd only cut one here and there it would have been bad
enough," thought Pahom, "but the rascal has actually cut down
a whole clump. If I could only find out who did this, I'd get even
with him."

He racked his brains as to who it could be. Finally he decided:
"It must be Simon—no one else could have done it." So he went to
Simon's homestead to have a look around, but he found nothing and
only had an angry scene. However, he now felt more certain than
ever that Simon had done it, and he lodged a complaint. Simon was
summoned. The case was tried, and retried, and at the end of it all
Simon was acquitted, there being no evidence against him. Pahom

felt still more aggrieved, and let his anger loose upon the Elders and the Judges.

"You let thieves grease your palms," said he. "If you were honest folk yourselves you wouldn't let a thief go free."

So Pahom quarreled with the judges and with his neighbors. Threats to burn his hut began to be uttered. So though Pahom had more land, his place in the community was much worse than before.

About this time a rumor got about that many people were moving to new parts.

"There's no need for me to leave my land," thought Pahom. "But some of the others may leave our village and then there'd be more room for us. I'd take over their land myself and make my estates somewhat bigger. I could then live more at ease. As it is, I'm still too cramped to be comfortable."

One day Pahom was sitting at home when a peasant, passing through the village, happened to drop in. He was allowed to stay the night, and supper was given him. Pahom had a talk with this peasant and asked him where he came from. The stranger answered that he came from beyond the Volga,[2] where he had been working. One word led to another, and the man went on to say that many people were settling in those parts. He told how some people from his village had settled there. They had joined the community there and had had twenty-five acres per man granted them. The land was so good, he said, that the rye sown on it grew as high as a horse, and so thick that five cuts of a sickle made a sheaf.[3] One peasant, he said, had brought nothing with him but his bare hands, and now he had six horses and two cows of his own.

Pahom's heart kindled with desire.

"Why should I suffer in this narrow hole, if one can live so well elsewhere?" he thought. "I'll sell my land and my homestead here, and with the money I'll start afresh over there and get everything new. In this crowded place one is always having trouble. But I must first go and find out all about it myself."

Toward summer he got ready and started out. He went down the Volga on a steamer to Samara, then walked another three hundred miles on foot, and at last reached the place. It was just as the stranger had said. The peasants had plenty of land: every man had twenty-five acres of communal land given him for his use, and anyone who had money could buy, besides, at a ruble and a half an acre, as much good freehold land[4] as he wanted.

Having found out all he wished to know, Pahom returned home as

---

2. **Volga** (väl´ gə) the major river in western Russia.
3. **sheaf** (shēf) *n.* bundle of grain.
4. **freehold land** privately owned land that the owner can lease to others for a fee.

Vocabulary
aggrieved (ə grēvd´) *adj.* wronged; suffering grief or injury

Reading Skill
Draw Conclusions
Based on the story so far, draw a conclusion about the amount of land Pahom will need before he is satisfied.

Reading Check
After quarreling with his neighbors, what does Pahom decide to do?

autumn came on, and began selling off his belongings. He sold his land at a profit, sold his homestead and all his cattle, and withdrew from membership in the village. He only waited till the spring, and then started with his family for the new settlement. •

4

As soon as Pahom and his family reached their new abode, he applied for admission into the council of a large village. He stood treat to the Elders and obtained the necessary documents. Five shares of communal land were given him for his own and his sons' use: that is to say—125 acres (not all together, but in different fields) besides the use of the communal pasture. Pahom put up the buildings he needed and bought cattle. Of the communal land alone he had three times as much as at his former home, and the land was good wheat land. He was ten times better off than he had been. He had plenty of arable land and pasturage, and could keep as many head of cattle as he liked.

At first, in the bustle of building and settling down, Pahom was pleased with it all, but when he got used to it he began to think that even here he hadn't enough land. The first year he sowed wheat on his share of the communal land and had a good crop. He wanted to go on sowing wheat, but had not enough communal land for the purpose, and what he had already used was not available, for in those parts wheat is sown only on virgin soil or on fallow land. It is sown for one or two years, and then the land lies fallow till it is again overgrown with steppe grass. There were many who wanted such land, and there was not enough for all, so that people quarreled about it. Those who were better off wanted it for growing wheat, and those who were poor wanted it to let to dealers, so that they might raise money to pay their taxes. Pahom wanted to sow more wheat, so he rented land from a dealer for a year. He sowed much wheat and had a fine crop, but the land was too far from the village—the wheat had to be carted more than ten miles. After a time Pahom noticed that some peasant dealers were living on separate farms and were growing wealthy, and he thought:

"If I were to buy some freehold land and have a homestead on it, it would be a different thing altogether. Then it would all be fine and close together."

The question of buying freehold land recurred to him again and again.

He went on in the same way for three years, renting land and sowing wheat. The seasons turned out well and the crops were good, so that he began to lay by money. He might have gone on living contentedly, but he grew tired of having to rent other people's land every year and having to scramble for it. Wherever there was good

Vocabulary
arable (ar´ ə bəl)
adj. suitable for growing crops

Literary Analysis
Theme What common idea comes across in each of the episodes in which Pahom acquires land?

land to be had, the peasants would rush for it and it was taken up at once, so that unless you were sharp about it, you got none. It happened in the third year that he and a dealer together rented a piece of pasture land from some peasants, and they had already plowed it up, when there was some dispute and the peasants went to law about it, and things fell out so that the labor was all lost.

"If it were my own land," thought Pahom, "I should be independent, and there wouldn't be all this unpleasantness."

So Pahom began looking out for land which he could buy, and he came across a peasant who had bought thirteen hundred acres, but having got into difficulties was willing to sell again cheap. Pahom bargained and haggled with him, and at last they settled the price at fifteen hundred rubles, part in cash and part to be paid later. They had all but clinched the matter when a passing dealer happened to stop at Pahom's one day to get feed for his horses. He drank tea with Pahom, and they had a talk. The dealer said that he was just returning from the land of the Bashkirs,[5] far away, where he had bought thirteen thousand acres of land, all for a thousand rubles. Pahom questioned him further, and the dealer said:

---

5. **Bashkirs** (bash kirz´) *n.* originally nomadic people who live in the plains of southwestern Russia.

▲ **Critical Viewing**
What assumptions could you make about the lifestyle of a peasant based on the details in this painting? **[Interpret]**

Reading Check

What information does the stranger who comes to visit give Pahom?

"All one has to do is to make friends with the chiefs. I gave away about one hundred rubles' worth of silk robes and carpets, besides a case of tea, and I gave wine to those who would drink it; and I got the land for less than three kopecks[6] an acre." And he showed Pahom the title deed, saying:

"The land lies near a river, and the whole steppe[7] is virgin soil."

Pahom plied him with questions, and the dealer said:

"There's more land there than you could cover if you walked a year, and it all belongs to the Bashkirs. They're as simple as sheep, and land can be got almost for nothing."

"There, now," thought Pahom, "with my one thousand rubles, why should I get only thirteen hundred acres, and saddle myself with a debt besides? If I take it out there, I can get more than ten times as much for my money."

5

Pahom inquired how to get to the place, and as soon as the grain dealer had left him, he prepared to go there himself. He left his wife to look after the homestead, and started on his journey, taking his hired man with him. They stopped at a town on their way and bought a case of tea, some wine, and other presents, as the grain dealer had advised.

---

6. **kopecks** (kō´ peks´) *n.* units of Russian money, each equal to one hundredth of a ruble.
7. **steppe** (step) *n.* high grassland plains stretching from Hungary through Russia into central Asia.

On and on they went until they had gone more than three hundred miles, and on the seventh day they came to a place where the Bashkirs had pitched their round tents. It was all just as the dealer had said. The people lived on the steppe, by a river, in felt-covered tents. They neither tilled the ground nor ate bread. Their cattle and horses grazed in herds on the steppe. The colts were tethered behind the tents, and the mares were driven to them twice a day. The mares were milked, and from the milk kumiss[8] was made. It was the women who prepared the kumiss, and they also made cheese. As far as the men were concerned, drinking kumiss and tea, eating mutton, and playing on their pipes was all they cared about. They were all stout and merry, and all the summer long they never thought of doing any work. They were quite ignorant, and knew no Russian, but were good-natured enough.

As soon as they saw Pahom, they came out of their tents and gathered around the visitor. An interpreter was found, and Pahom told them he had come about some land. The Bashkirs seemed very glad; they took Pahom and led him into one of the best tents, where they made him sit on some down cushions placed on a carpet, while they sat around him. They gave him some tea and kumiss, and had a sheep killed, and gave him mutton to eat. Pahom took presents out of his cart and distributed them among the Bashkirs, and divided the tea amongst them. The Bashkirs were delighted. They talked a great deal among themselves and then told the interpreter what to say.

"They wish to tell you," said the interpreter, "that they like you and that it's our custom to do all we can to please a guest and to repay him for his gifts. You have given us presents, now tell us which of the things we possess please you best, that we may present them to you."

"What pleases me best here," answered Pahom, "is your land. Our land is crowded and the soil is worn out, but you have plenty of land, and it is good land. I never saw the likes of it."

The interpreter told the Bashkirs what Pahom had said. They talked among themselves for a while. Pahom could not understand what they were saying, but saw that they were much amused and heard them shout and laugh. Then they were silent and looked at Pahom while the interpreter said:

"They wish me to tell you that in return for your presents they will gladly give you as much land as you want. You have only to point it out with your hand and it is yours."

---

8. **kumiss** (ko͞o′ mis) *n.* fermented mare's or camel's milk that is used as a drink.

Reading Skill
Draw Conclusions
What details in this passage suggest that the Bashkirs have different priorities than Pahom?

Reading
Check

Where does Pahom decide to go next?

The Bashkirs talked again for a while and began to dispute. Pahom asked what they were disputing about, and the interpreter told him that some of them thought they ought to ask their chief about the land and not act in his absence, while others thought there was no need to wait for his return.

6

While the Bashkirs were disputing, a man in a large fox-fur cap appeared on the scene. They all became silent and rose to their feet. The interpreter said: "This is our chief himself."

Pahom immediately fetched the best dressing gown and five pounds of tea, and offered these to the chief. The chief accepted them and seated himself in the place of honor. The Bashkirs at once began telling him something. The chief listened for a while, then made a sign with his head for them to be silent, and addressing himself to Pahom, said in Russian:

"Well, so be it. Choose whatever piece of land you like; we have plenty of it."

"How can I take as much as I like?" thought Pahom. "I must get a deed to make it secure, or else they may say: 'It is yours,' and afterward may take it away again."

"Thank you for your kind words," he said aloud. "You have much land, and I only want a little. But I should like to be sure which portion is mine. Could it not be measured and made over to me? Life and death are in God's hands. You good people give it to me, but your children might wish to take it back again."

"You are quite right," said the chief. "We will make it over to you."

"I heard that a dealer had been here," continued Pahom, "and that you gave him a little land, too, and signed title deeds to that effect. I should like to have it done in the same way."

The chief understood.

"Yes," replied he, "that can be done quite easily. We have a scribe, and we will go to town with you and have the deed properly sealed."

"And what will be the price?" asked Pahom.

"Our price is always the same: one thousand rubles a day."

Pahom did not understand.

"A day? What measure is that? How many acres would that be?"

"We do not know how to reckon it out," said the chief. "We sell it by the day. As much as you can go around on your feet in a day is yours, and the price is one thousand rubles a day."

Pahom was surprised.

"But in a day you can get around a large tract of land," he said.

The chief laughed.

Reading Skill
Draw Conclusions
What details suggest that the Bashkirs view the land differently from Pahom?

"It will all be yours!" said he. "But there is one condition: If you don't return on the same day to the spot whence you started, your money is lost."

"But how am I to mark the way that I have gone?"

"Why, we shall go to any spot you like and stay there. You must start from that spot and make your round, taking a spade with you. Wherever you think necessary, make a mark. At every turning, dig a hole and pile up the turf; then afterward we will go around with a plow from hole to hole. You may make as large a circuit as you please, but before the sun sets you must return to the place you started from. All the land you cover will be yours."

Pahom was delighted. It was decided to start early next morning. They talked a while, and after drinking some more kumiss and eating some more mutton, they had tea again, and then the night came on. They gave Pahom a featherbed to sleep on, and the Bashkirs dispersed for the night, promising to assemble the next morning at daybreak and ride out before sunrise to the appointed spot.

7

Pahom lay on the featherbed, but could not sleep. He kept thinking about the land.

"What a large tract I'll mark off!" thought he. "I can easily do thirty-five miles in a day. The days are long now, and within a circuit of thirty-five miles what a lot of land there will be! I'll sell the poorer land or let it to peasants, but I'll pick out the best and farm it myself. I'll buy two ox teams and hire two more laborers. About a hundred and fifty acres shall be plowland, and I'll pasture cattle on the rest."

Pahom lay awake all night and dozed off only just before dawn. Hardly were his eyes closed when he had a dream. He thought he was lying in that same tent and heard somebody chuckling outside. He wondered who it could be, and rose and went out, and he saw the Bashkir chief sitting in front of the tent holding his sides and rolling about with laughter. Going nearer to the chief, Pahom asked: "What are you laughing at?" But he saw that it was no longer the chief but the grain dealer who had recently stopped at his house and had told him about the land. Just as Pahom was going to ask: "Have you been here long?" he saw that it was not the dealer, but the peasant who had come up from the Volga long ago, to Pahom's old home. Then he saw that it was not the peasant either, but the Devil himself with hoofs and horns, sitting there and chuckling, and before him

"But there is one condition: If you don't return on the same day to the spot whence you started, your money is lost."

Reading Check

How large a tract of land does Pahom decide he will mark off?

History Connection

The Emancipation of the Serfs

Tolstoy published "How Much Land Does a Man Need?" in 1886, a year in which the question in the title was on many Russians' minds.

- In 1861, the ruler of Russia, Tsar Alexander II, freed the serfs
- The government bought land from the serfs' former masters and sold it to the serfs.
- In some parts of Russia, the price was unrealistically high. In other parts, the parcels were too small.
- To survive, some freed serfs rented land from landowners. Others worked for landowners or went to work in factories. Discontent grew, and many sought further reform.

Connect to the Literature

Tolstoy thought of land reform in Russia? Explain.

Russia

1460 The freedom of peasants to leave the land they farmed is limited.

1649 Russian peasants are enserfed.

1773–1774 Peasants rebel.

1861 Alexander II ends serfdom in Russia.

Other Countries England ends serfdom. **1600s**

France ends serfdom. **1789**

United States abolishes slavery. **1865**

Nineteenth Century Population of Russia

Privately Owned Serfs roughly two fifths

Nobles, Merchants, and Others roughly one fifth

State and Other Peasants roughly two fifths

Based on Pahom's story, what do you think

Vocabulary
prostrate (präs´ trāt´) *adj.* lying flat

lay a man, prostrate on the ground, barefooted, with only trousers and a shirt on. And Pahom dreamed that he looked more attentively to see what sort of man it was lying there, and he saw that the man was dead, and that it was himself. Horror-struck, he awoke.

"What things one dreams about!" thought he.

Looking around he saw through the open door that the dawn was breaking.

"It's time to wake them up," thought he. "We ought to be starting."

He got up, roused his man (who was sleeping in his cart), bade him harness, and went to call the Bashkirs.

"It's time to go to the steppe to measure the land," he said.

The Bashkirs rose and assembled, and the chief came, too. Then they began drinking kumiss again, and offered Pahom some tea, but he would not wait.

"If we are to go, let's go. It's high time," said he. ●

8

The Bashkirs got ready and they all started; some mounted on horses and some in carts. Pahom drove in his own small cart with his servant and took a spade with him. When they reached the steppe, the red dawn was beginning to kindle. They ascended a hillock (called by the Bashkirs a *shikhan*) and, dismounting from their carts and their horses, gathered in one spot. The chief came up to Pahom and, stretching out his arm toward the plain:

"See," said he, "all this, as far as your eye can reach, is ours. You may have any part of it you like."

Pahom's eyes glistened: it was all virgin soil, as flat as the palm of your hand, as black as the seed of a poppy, and in the hollows different kinds of grasses grew breast-high.

The chief took off his fox-fur cap, placed it on the ground, and said:

"This will be the mark. Start from here, and return here again. All the land you go around shall be yours."

Pahom took out his money and put it on the cap. Then he took off his outer coat, remaining in his sleeveless undercoat. He unfastened his girdle[9] and tied it tight below his stomach, put a little bag of bread into the breast of his coat, and, tying a flask of water to his girdle, he drew up the tops of his boots, took the spade from his man, and stood ready to start. He considered for some moments which way he had better go—it was tempting everywhere.

"No matter," he concluded, "I'll go toward the rising sun."

He turned his face to the east, stretched himself, and waited for the sun to appear above the rim.

"I must lose no time," he thought, "and it's easier walking while it's still cool."

The sun's rays had hardly flashed above the horizon when Pahom, carrying the spade over his shoulder, went down into the steppe.

Pahom started walking neither slowly nor quickly. After having gone a thousand yards he stopped, dug a hole, and placed pieces of turf one on another to make it more visible. Then he went on; and now that he had walked off his stiffness he quickened his pace. After a while he dug another hole.

Pahom looked back. The hillock could be distinctly seen in the sunlight, with the people on it, and the glittering iron rims of the cartwheels. At a rough guess Pahom concluded that he had walked three miles. It was growing warmer; he took off his undercoat, slung it across his shoulder, and went on again. It had grown quite warm now; he looked at the sun—it was time to think of breakfast.

"The first shift is done, but there are four in a day, and it's too soon yet to turn. But I'll just take off my boots," said he to himself.

He sat down, took off his boots, stuck them into his girdle, and went on. It was easy walking now.

"I'll go on for another three miles," thought he, "and then turn

---

9. **girdle** (gurd´'l) *n.* old term for a belt or sash for the waist.

Literary Analysis
Theme How do Pahom's thoughts and actions now reflect his earlier attitude toward acquiring land?

Reading
Check
At what sort of pace does Pahom set out?

to the left. This spot is so fine that it would be a pity to lose it. The further one goes, the better the land seems."

He went straight on for a while, and when he looked around, the hillock was scarcely visible and the people on it looked like black ants, and he could just see something glistening there in the sun.

"Ah," thought Pahom, "I have gone far enough in this direction; it's time to turn. Besides, I'm in a regular sweat, and very thirsty."

He stopped, dug a large hole, and heaped up pieces of turf. Next he untied his flask, had a drink, and then turned sharply to the left. He went on and on; the grass was high, and it was very hot.

Pahom began to grow tired: he looked at the sun and saw that it was noon.

"Well," he thought, "I must have a rest."

He sat down, and ate some bread and drank some water; but he did not lie down, thinking that if he did he might fall asleep. After sitting a little while, he went on again. At first he walked easily; the food had strengthened him; but it had become terribly hot and he felt sleepy. Still he went on, thinking: "An hour to suffer, a lifetime to live."

He went a long way in this direction also, and was about to turn to the left again, when he perceived a damp hollow: "It would be a pity to leave that out," he thought. "Flax would do well there." So he went on past the hollow and dug a hole on the other side of it before he made a sharp turn. Pahom looked toward the hillock. The heat made the air hazy: it seemed to be quivering, and through the haze the people on the hillock could scarcely be seen.

"Ah," thought Pahom, "I have made the sides too long; I must make this one shorter." And he went along the third side, stepping faster. He looked at the sun: it was nearly halfway to the horizon, and he had not yet done two miles of the third side of the square. He was still ten miles from the goal.

"No," he thought, "though it will make my land lopsided, I must hurry back in a straight line now. I might go too far, and as it is I have a great deal of land."

So Pahom hurriedly dug a hole and turned straight toward the hillock. •

Spiral Review
Plot In what way do Pahom's pacing and the pacing of this part of the story work in parallel?

9

Pahom went straight toward the hillock, but he now walked with difficulty. He was exhausted from the heat, his bare feet were cut and bruised, and his legs began to fail. He longed to rest, but it was impossible if he meant to get back before sunset. The sun waits for no man, and it was sinking lower and lower.

"Oh, Lord," he thought, "if only I have not blundered trying for

Reading Skill
Draw Conclusions
Based on details here and earlier, what conclusion can you draw about the chances for Pahom's success?

too much! What if I am too late?"

He looked toward the hillock and at the sun. He was still far from his goal, and the sun was already near the rim of the sky.

Pahom walked on and on; it was very hard walking, but he went quicker and quicker. He pressed on, but was still far from the place. He began running, threw away his coat, his boots, his flask, and his cap, and kept only the spade which he used as a support.

"What am I to do?" he thought again. "I've grasped too much and ruined the whole affair. I can't get there before the sun sets."

And this fear made him still more breathless. Pahom kept on running; his soaking shirt and trousers stuck to him, and his mouth was parched. His breast was working like a blacksmith's bellows, his heart was beating like a hammer, and his legs were giving way as if they did not belong to him. Pahom was seized with terror lest he should die of the strain.

Though afraid of death, he could not stop.

"After having run all that way they will call me a fool if I stop now," thought he.

And he ran on and on, and drew near and heard the Bashkirs yelling and shouting to him, and their cries inflamed his heart still more. He gathered his last strength and ran on.

The sun was close to the rim of the sky and, cloaked in mist, looked large, and red as blood. Now, yes, now, it was about to set! The sun was quite low, but he was also quite near his goal. Pahom could already see the people on the hillock waving their arms to make him hurry. He could see the fox-fur cap on the ground and the money in it, and the chief sitting on the ground holding his sides. And Pahom remembered his dream.

"There's plenty of land," thought he, "but will God let me live on it? I have lost my life, I have lost my life! Never will I reach that spot!"

Pahom looked at the sun, which had reached the earth: one side of it had already disappeared. With all his remaining strength he rushed on, bending his body forward so that his legs could hardly follow fast enough to keep him from falling. Just as he reached the hillock it suddenly grew dark. He looked up—the sun had already set!

"I can't get there before the sun sets."

Literary Analysis
Theme Rephrase Pahom's words as a statement of a theme in the story.

Reading Check
What are Pahom's fears as the sun begins to set?

He gave a cry: "All my labor has been in vain," thought he, and was about to stop, but he heard the Bashkirs still shouting and remembered that though to him, from below, the sun seemed to have set, they on the hillock could still see it. He took a long breath and ran up the hillock. It was still light there. He reached the top and saw the cap. Before it sat the chief, laughing and holding his sides. Again Pahom remembered his dream, and he uttered a cry: his legs gave way beneath him, he fell forward and reached the cap with his hands.

"Ah, that's a fine fellow!" exclaimed the chief. "He has gained much land!"

Pahom's servant came running up and tried to raise him, but he saw that blood was flowing from his mouth. Pahom was dead.

The Bashkirs clicked their tongues to show their pity.

His servant picked up the spade and dug a grave long enough for Pahom to lie in, and buried him in it.

Six feet from his head to his toes was all he needed.

Critical Thinking

Cite textual evidence to support your responses.

1. Key Ideas and Details (a) What event allows Pahom to buy his first parcel of land? **(b) Interpret:** What is his main reason for wanting this land? Support your answer with story details.

2. Key Ideas and Details (a) Explain the events that change Pahom's relations with his neighbors. **(b) Analyze Cause and Effect:** What effect does owning land have on his life?

3. Craft and Structure (a) If Pahom had no chances to acquire more land, do you think he could find happiness with what he already has? Explain. **(b) Discuss:** Share and discuss answers with a partner. **(c) Apply:** Based on your discussion, write a sentence explaining the author's attitude toward ambition.

4. Key Ideas and Details (a) Summarize: In a few sentences, sum up what happens on the last day of Pahom's life. Do not state your opinion of events; simply report them. **(b) Interpret:** Explain the meaning of the story's last sentence both as a description of Pahom's fate and as an answer to the title of the story.

5. Integration of Knowledge and Ideas (a) Is Pahom's main conflict with others or with himself? Explain. **(b)** Should Pahom's acquisition of increasingly large parcels of land be considered progress? Why or why not? *[Connect to the Big Question: Can progress be made without conflict?]*

Literary Analysis: Theme

1. Craft and Structure (a) Using a chart like the one shown, analyze the episodes in which Pahom is given the chance to acquire property. **(b)** How are these episodes related?

Episode	Character's Response	Reasons for the Response	Result: Peace of Mind/Problems

(c) State the **theme** of the story, explaining how each event helps convey it.

2. Key Ideas and Details Tolstoy makes the **philosophical assumption** that people should not waste their lives on material things. How could Pahom have applied this belief to his life?

Reading Skill: Draw Conclusions

3. (a) Draw a conclusion about the Bashkirs' values based on their attitude toward land. **(b)** Which details in Tolstoy's depiction of the tribe contribute to the story's theme? Explain.

Vocabulary

Acquisition and Use Antonyms are words with opposite meanings. Rewrite the following sentences by replacing each word or phrase in italics with its antonym from the vocabulary list on page 336. Then, explain which version of each sentence makes more sense.

1. He *indulged* and ate half the cake.

2. After he took my bicycle, I was *forgiving* and lent him my radio.

3. I was *not hurt* by his insults, and I found his company enjoyable.

4. The *harmony* between the siblings made family dinners peaceful.

5. His land was *desert*, so he had no success with his crops.

6. Her body was *upright* and at attention as she received her medal.

Word Study Use the context of the sentences and what you know about the **Latin prefix dis-** to explain your answer to each question.

1. Are people living in *disharmony* good at working together?

2. What happens when a person is *disabled* in some way?

Word Study

The **Latin prefix dis-** means "wrong," "bad," or "not."

Apply It Explain how the prefix dis- contributes to the meanings of these words. Consult a dictionary if necessary.

disconnect
disembody
disregard

Can progress be made without *conflict?*

Writing About the Big Question

In "Civil Peace," a man and most of his family survive a civil war only to face new conflicts during peacetime. Use this sentence starter to develop your ideas about the Big Question.

Understanding what things are truly important in life can help a person overcome **adversity** because _____.

While You Read Look for things Jonathan, the story's main character, counts as blessings after the conflict of war ends.

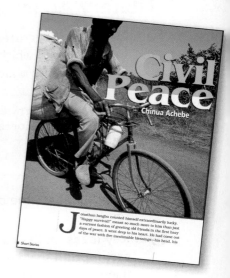

Vocabulary

Read each word and its definition. Decide whether you know the word well, know it a little bit, or do not know it at all. After you read, see how your knowledge of each word has increased.

- **disreputable** (dis rep′ yōō tə bəl) *adj.* not respectable; having or deserving a bad reputation (p. 359) *The travel guide warned against <u>disreputable</u> street vendors.* *disreputably adv. disrepute n.*

- **amenable** (ə mē′ nə bəl) *adj.* responsive; open (p. 359) *The plans are not set, so I will be <u>amenable</u> to your suggestions.* *amenability n. amenably adv.*

- **destitute** (des′ tə tōōt′) *adj.* lacking the basic necessities of life; poverty-stricken (p. 360) *The city provided housing for families left <u>destitute</u> by the flood.* *destitution n.*

- **inaudibly** (in ô′ də blē) *adv.* in a way that cannot be heard (p. 362) *No one can understand what Lydia says when she mumbles <u>inaudibly</u>.* *audible adj. inaudible adj. audio n.*

- **dissent** (di sent′) *n.* disagreement; refusal to accept a common opinion (p. 363) *The dictator would not tolerate <u>dissent</u> from his subjects.* *dissent v. dissenter n. assent v.*

- **commiserate** (kə miz′ ər āt′) *v.* sympathize with or show sorrow for (p. 364) *The coach will usually <u>commiserate</u> with his team after a tough loss.* *commiseration n. commiserative adj.*

Word Study

The **Latin prefix** *com-* means "together" or "with."

In this story, a character and his neighbors **commiserate**, or feel sorrow together, after he and his family are robbed.

Meet
Chinua Achebe
(b. 1930)

Author of
Civil Peace

Chinua (chin′ wä′) Achebe (ä chā′ bā) is renowned for novels and stories that explore the conflicts of modern Africans. Achebe was born into the Ibo tribe of Nigeria. He grew up to pursue a varied career as a university teacher and as a director for the Nigerian Broadcasting Corporation. According to one critic, "In the English language, he is the founding father of modern African literature."

Africans Face the West Achebe wrote his first and most celebrated novel, *Things Fall Apart* (1958), in an effort to accurately portray the disruption of Ibo tribal society by Western colonial rule.

BACKGROUND FOR THE STORY

The Nigerian Civil War

In 1960, the West African nation of Nigeria finally won independence from Britain. The Ibo (also spelled *Igbo*), one people of Nigeria, seceded from the new country, setting up the independent Republic of Biafra. A brutal civil war followed. In 1970, a defeated Biafra rejoined Nigeria. "Civil Peace" unfolds in the aftermath of this war.

DID YOU KNOW?

During the civil war in Nigeria, Achebe's house was bombed. He fled, leaving behind a book of his that he had nearly finished printing. When he returned, a single copy of the book remained.

Civil Peace

Chinua Achebe

Jonathan Iwegbu counted himself extraordinarily lucky. "Happy survival!" meant so much more to him than just a current fashion of greeting old friends in the first hazy days of peace. It went deep to his heart. He had come out of the war with five inestimable blessings—his head, his wife Maria's head and the heads of three out of their four children. As a bonus he also had his old bicycle—a miracle too but naturally not to be compared to the safety of five human heads.

The bicycle had a little history of its own. One day at the height of the war it was commandeered "for urgent military action." Hard as its loss would have been to him he would still have let it go without a thought had he not had some doubts about the genuineness of the officer. It wasn't his disreputable rags, nor the toes peeping out of one blue and one brown canvas shoe, nor yet the two stars of his rank done obviously in a hurry in biro,[1] that troubled Jonathan; many good and heroic soldiers looked the same or worse. It was rather a certain lack of grip and firmness in his manner. So Jonathan, suspecting he might be amenable to influence, rummaged in his raffia bag and produced the two pounds with which he had been going to buy firewood which his wife, Maria, retailed to camp officials for extra stock-fish and corn meal, and got his bicycle back. That night he buried it in the little clearing in the bush where the dead of the camp, including his own youngest son, were buried. When he dug it up again a year later after the surrender all it needed was a little palm-oil greasing. "Nothing puzzles God," he said in wonder.

He put it to immediate use as a taxi and accumulated a small pile of Biafran[2] money ferrying camp officials and their families across the four-mile stretch to the nearest tarred road. His standard charge per trip was six pounds and those who had the money were only glad to be rid of some of it in this way. At the end of a fortnight[3] he had made a small fortune of one hundred and fifteen pounds.

Then he made the journey to Enugu and found another miracle waiting for him. It was unbelievable. He rubbed his eyes and looked again and it was still standing there before him. But, needless to say, even that monumental blessing must be accounted also totally inferior to the five heads in the family. This newest miracle was his little house in Ogui Overside. Indeed nothing puzzles God! Only two houses away a huge concrete edifice some wealthy contractor had put up just before the war was a mountain of rubble. And here was Jonathan's little zinc house of no regrets built with mud blocks quite intact! Of course the doors and windows were missing and five sheets off the roof. But what was that? And anyhow he had returned to Enugu early enough to pick up bits of old zinc and wood and soggy sheets of cardboard lying around the neighborhood before thousands more came out of their forest holes looking for

---

1. **biro** (bī′ rō) *n.* British expression for "ballpoint pen."
2. **Biafran** (bē äf′ rən) *adj.* of the rebellious southeastern region of Nigeria, which declared itself the independent Republic of Biafra in the civil war of 1967.
3. **fortnight** (fôrt′ nīt′) *n.* British English for "two weeks."

Vocabulary
disreputable (dis rep′ yo͞o tə bəl) *adj.* not respectable; having or deserving a bad reputation

amenable (ə mē′ nə bəl) *adj.* responsive; open

Literary Analysis
Theme What do these stories of Jonathan's "blessings" have in common?

Reading Check

What are the five blessings for which Jonathan is grateful?

▲ **Critical Viewing**
Does the expression on this man's face suggest he has a personality similar to Jonathan's? Explain. **[Connect]**

Vocabulary
destitute (des´ tə tōot´) *adj.* lacking the basic necessities of life; poverty-stricken

the same things. He got a destitute carpenter with one old hammer, a blunt plane and a few bent and rusty nails in his tool bag to turn this assortment of wood, paper and metal into door and window shutters for five Nigerian shillings or fifty Biafran pounds. He paid the pounds, and moved in with his overjoyed family carrying five heads on their shoulders.

His children picked mangoes near the military cemetery and sold them to soldiers' wives for a few pennies—real pennies this time—and his wife started making breakfast akara balls[4] for neighbors in a hurry to start life again. With his family earnings he took his bicycle to the villages around and bought fresh palm-wine which he mixed generously in his rooms with the water which had recently started running again in the public tap down the road, and opened up a bar for soldiers and other lucky people with good money. ●

At first he went daily, then every other day and finally once a week, to the offices of the Coal Corporation where he used to be a miner, to find out what was what. The only thing he did find out in the end was that that little house of his was even a greater blessing than he had thought. Some of his fellow ex-miners who had nowhere to return at the end of the day's waiting just slept outside the doors of the offices and cooked what meal they could scrounge together in Bournvita tins. As the weeks lengthened and still nobody could say what was what Jonathan discontinued his weekly visits altogether and faced his palm-wine bar.

But nothing puzzles God. Came the day of the windfall when

---

4. **akara** (ə kär´ ə) **balls** *n.* deep-fried balls of ground beans.

after five days of endless scuffles in queues[5] and counterqueues in the sun outside the Treasury he had twenty pounds counted into his palms as ex-gratia[6] award for the rebel money he had turned in. It was like Christmas for him and for many others like him when the payments began. They called it (since few could manage its proper official name) *egg-rasher.*

As soon as the pound notes were placed in his palm Jonathan simply closed it tight over them and buried fist and money inside his trouser pocket. He had to be extra careful because he had seen a man a couple of days earlier collapse into near-madness in an instant before that oceanic crowd because no sooner had he got his twenty pounds than some heartless ruffian picked it off him. Though it was not right that a man in such an extremity of agony should be blamed yet many in the queues that day were able to remark quietly at the victim's carelessness, especially after he pulled out the innards of his pocket and revealed a hole in it big enough to pass a thief's head. But of course he had insisted that the money had been in the other pocket, pulling it out too to show

---

5. **queues** (kyo͞oz) *n.* British English for "lines."
6. **ex-gratia** (eks grā′ shē ə) as a favor (Latin).

Reading Skill
Draw Conclusions
What conclusion can you draw about Jonathan's attitude toward good and bad events? Explain.

Reading Check

What does Jonathan get in exchange for the rebel money he has saved?

Geography Connection

Nigerian Civil War

Jonathan is delighted that his home in Enugu still stands—and for good reason. Enugu was at the center of the civil war that broke out in Nigeria in 1967. The war began when the eastern region of Nigeria declared itself the independent Republic of Biafra, with Enugu as its capital. The city was invaded by Nigerian federal troops just five months after independence. The war resulted in horrific famine as well as violence. It ended in 1970 with the defeat of Biafra and the reunification of Nigeria.

Connect to the Literature

Which of Jonathan's experiences can you connect to events of the Nigerian Civil War? Explain.

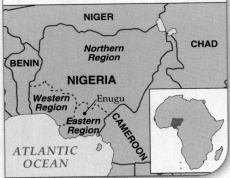

Vocabulary
inaudibly (in ôˊ də blē) *adv.* in a way that cannot be heard

its comparative wholeness. So one had to be careful.

Jonathan soon transferred the money to his left hand and pocket so as to leave his right free for shaking hands should the need arise, though by fixing his gaze at such an elevation as to miss all approaching human faces he made sure that the need did not arise, until he got home. ●

He was normally a heavy sleeper but that night he heard all the neighborhood noises die down one after another. Even the night watchman who knocked the hour on some metal somewhere in the distance had fallen silent after knocking one o'clock. That must have been the last thought in Jonathan's mind before he was finally carried away himself. He couldn't have been gone for long, though, when he was violently awakened again.

"Who is knocking?" whispered his wife lying beside him on the floor.

"I don't know," he whispered back breathlessly.

The second time the knocking came it was so loud and imperious that the rickety old door could have fallen down.

"Who is knocking?" he asked them, his voice parched and trembling.

"Na tief-man and him people," came the cool reply. "Make you hopen de door."[7] This was followed by the heaviest knocking of all.

Maria was the first to raise the alarm, then he followed and all their children.

"Police-o! Thieves-o! Neighbors-o! Police-o! We are lost! We are dead! Neighbors, are you asleep? Wake up! Police-o!"

This went on for a long time and then stopped suddenly. Perhaps they had scared the thief away. There was total silence. But only for a short while.

"You done finish?" asked the voice outside. "Make we help you small. Oya, everybody!"

"Police-o! Tief-man-so! Neighbors-o! we done loss-o! Police-o! . . ."

There were at least five other voices besides the leader's.

Jonathan and his family were now completely paralyzed by terror. Maria and the children sobbed inaudibly like lost souls. Jonathan groaned continuously.

The silence that followed the thieves' alarm vibrated horribly. Jonathan all but begged their leader to speak again and be done with it.

---

7. **"Na tief-man . . . hopen de door"** (dialect) "I am a thief with my accomplices. Open the door."

"My frien," said he at long last, "we don try our best for call dem but I tink say dem all done sleep-o . . . So wetin we go do now? Sometaim you wan call soja? Or you wan make we call dem for you? Soja better pass police. No be so?"

"Na so!" replied his men. Jonathan thought he heard even more voices now than before and groaned heavily. His legs were sagging under him and his throat felt like sandpaper.

"My frien, why you no de talk again. I de ask you say you wan make we call soja?"

"No."

"Awrighto. Now make we talk business. We no be bad tief. We no like for make trouble. Trouble done finish. War done finish and all the katakata wey de for inside. No Civil War again. This time na Civil Peace. No be so?"

"Na so!" answered the horrible chorus.

"What do you want from me? I am a poor man. Everything I had went with this war. Why do you come to me? You know people who have money. We . . ."

"Awright! We know say you no get plenty money. But we sef no get even anini. So derefore make you open dis window and give us one hundred pound and we go commot. Orderwise we de come for inside now to show you guitar-boy like dis . . ."

A volley of automatic fire rang through the sky. Maria and the children began to weep aloud again.

"Ah, missisi de cry again. No need for dat. We done talk say we na good tief. We just take our small money and go nwayorly. No molest. Abi we de molest?"

"At all!" sang the chorus.

"My friends," began Jonathan hoarsely. "I hear what you say and I thank you. If I had one hundred pounds . . ."

"Lookia my frien, no be play we come play for your house. If we make mistake and step for inside you no go like am-o. So derefore . . ."

"To God who made me; if you come inside and find one hundred pounds, take it and shoot me and shoot my wife and children. I swear to God. The only money I have in this life is this twenty-pounds *egg-rasher* they gave me today . . ."

"Ok. Time de go. Make you open dis window and bring the twenty pound. We go manage am like dat."

There were now loud murmurs of **dissent** among the chorus: "Na lie de man de lie; e get plenty money . . . Make we go inside and search properly well . . . Wetin be twenty pound? . . ."

"Shurrup!" rang the leader's voice like a lone shot in the sky and silenced the murmuring at once. "Are you dere? Bring the money quick!"

Vocabulary
dissent (di sent´)
n. disagreement;
refusal to accept a
common opinion

Reading Check

Who are the people at Jonathan's door, and what do they want?

"I am coming," said Jonathan fumbling in the darkness with the key of the small wooden box he kept by his side on the mat.

At the first sign of light as neighbors and others assembled to commiserate with him he was already strapping his five-gallon demijohn[8] to his bicycle carrier and his wife, sweating in the open fire, was turning over akara balls in a wide clay bowl of boiling oil. In the corner his eldest son was rinsing out dregs of yesterday's palm-wine from old beer bottles.

"I count it as nothing," he told his sympathizers, his eyes on the rope he was tying. "What is *egg-rasher*? Did I depend on it last week? Or is it greater than other things that went with the war? I say, let *egg-rasher* perish in the flames! Let it go where everything else has gone. Nothing puzzles God."

---

8. demijohn (dem´ i jän´) *n.* large glass or earthenware bottle with a wicker cover.

Critical Thinking

Ⓒ **1. Key Ideas and Details** **(a)** What are the "five inestimable bless-ings" for which Jonathan is grateful? **(b) Infer:** In what sense has the war enhanced Jonathan's appreciation for his life?

Ⓒ **2. Key Ideas and Details** **(a)** Explain how Jonathan reacts to the damage to his house. **(b) Connect:** Considering the other dam-age the war has caused, why might his reaction make sense?

Ⓒ **3. Key Ideas and Details** By giving the "egg-rasher" to the thieves, what does Jonathan hope to prevent? Explain.

Ⓒ **4. Key Ideas and Details** **(a)** In your own words, summarize Jonathan's reaction to the theft. **(b) Connect:** In what way is Jonathan's response consistent with his other responses to loss?

Ⓒ **5. Integration of Knowledge and Ideas** **(a)** How does Jonathan change as he experiences the conflicts in his life? **(b)** How might his life have changed without the conflict? *[Connect to the Big Question: Can progress be made without conflict?]*

Literary Analysis: Theme

1. **Craft and Structure** **(a)** Using a chart like the one shown, analyze the episodes that spark a response in Jonathan. **(b)** How are these episodes related?

Episode	Character's Response	Reasons for the Response	Result: Peace of Mind/Problems

(c) State the **theme** of the story, explaining how each event helps convey it.

2. **Key Ideas and Details** Achebe makes the **philosophical assumption** that in order to survive, we must be able to let go of what we have lost. How would Jonathan have behaved after the theft if he had refused to let go?

Reading Skill: Draw Conclusions

3. **(a) Draw a conclusion** about the thieves' response to the losses of war based on what they say and do. **(b)** Which details in Achebe's story contribute to its theme?

Vocabulary

Acquisition and Use **Antonyms** are words with opposite meanings. For each sentence, replace the word in italics with its antonym from the list on page 356. Explain which version makes more sense.

1. We should not give charity to the most *wealthy*.
2. People go to this bank because it is *respectable*.
3. In times of joy, people may get together to *celebrate*.
4. Ellen is *resistant* to trading bicycles with me because she likes hers.
5. His dog howled *audibly*, and the loud noise scared the cats away.
6. If there is *agreement* about going to the concert, I will buy a ticket.

Word Study Use the context of the sentences and what you know about the **Latin prefix com-** to explain your answer to each question.

1. What would happen to an egg under *compression*?
2. What effect would a *compromise* have on warring factions?

Word Study

The **Latin prefix com-** means "together" or "with."

Apply It Explain how the prefix com- contributes to the meanings of these words. Consult a dictionary if necessary.

compassion
compare
comfort

Integrated Language Skills

How Much Land Does a Man Need? • Civil Peace

Conventions: Action and Linking Verbs

An **action verb** is a verb that shows physical or mental action. A **linking verb** expresses state of being or tells what the subject is by linking it to one or more words in the predicate.

Examples:

Action Verb: Li *worries* about her grades. (shows mental action)

Linking Verb: She *is* a good student. (links *She* to *good student*)

The most common linking verb is *be* in one of its forms—*is, are, was, were,* and so on. Other linking verbs include *feel* when used in a sentence such as "I feel ill" and *grew* when used in a sentence such as "He grew tall." To tell whether a verb is functioning as a linking verb, replace it with the appropriate form of *be*. If the sentence still makes sense, then the verb is a linking verb.

Testing Verbs to See if They Are Linking Verbs:

Action Verb: I *smelled* a rose. (cannot replace with a form of *be*)

Linking Verb: The rose *smelled* fragrant. (can replace with *was*)

Practice A Identify the verb in each sentence, and tell whether it is an action verb or a linking verb.

1. Pahom grows wheat on his land.
2. The land on the steppe is rich and fertile.
3. Pahom's tea tastes delicious.
4. Each year Pahom's parcel of land grows larger.

Ⓒ **Reading Application** In "How Much Land Does a Man Need?," find two sentences with action verbs and two sentences with linking verbs.

Practice B For each word, write a sentence using the word as a linking verb and another sentence using the verb as an action verb.

1. look
2. grow
3. smell
4. feel

Ⓒ **Writing Application** Use this sentence as a model to write two sentences that contain both action and linking verbs: *Jonathan <u>realizes</u> that his family <u>is</u> more valuable than any possession.*

PH **WRITING COACH** Further instruction and practice are available in *Prentice Hall Writing Coach.*

Writing

Common Core State Standards

W.9-10.2.a, W.9-10.2.b, W.9-10.2.c; SL.9-10.1.c, SL.9-10.1.d
[For the full wording of the standards, see page 334.]

© **Explanatory Text** The fate of the characters in these selections is determined in large part by their personalities. Write a brief **character analysis** of Pahom or Jonathan. In your analysis, identify the character's main character traits including strengths and weaknesses.

- Review the text to analyze the character. Using a two-column chart, list strengths and weaknesses.

- As you draft, introduce the ideas you will convey. Elaborate on these strengths and weaknesses by providing examples of incidents and descriptions in the story that show these traits.

- Use phrases such as *for example* to link supporting details to your main idea. Include transitions such as *instead* to connect ideas.

Writing Workshop: *Work in Progress*

Prewriting for Problem-and-Solution Essay For an essay you may write, define a problem that you see in your school. Use this problem as the central circle of a web. Fill in spokes of the web with all the possible solutions. Put this Problem/Solution Web in your writing portfolio.

Use this prewriting activity to prepare for the **Writing Workshop** on page 420.

Speaking and Listening

© **Comprehension and Collaboration** Hold a **group discussion** about the theme in Tolstoy's or Achebe's story. Begin by proposing and agreeing on a statement of the author's message. With your group, discuss ways in which the theme applies to your life or the lives of people today. Use persuasive techniques to support your ideas. To aid the discussion, follow these tips:

- Express your ideas in clear and inoffensive ways.

- Add to others' ideas and support your own viewpoints with details from the text. Include quotations that help to prove your ideas. When appropriate, adjust your ideas in light of the evidence presented by others.

- Allow your position to be challenged by the contributions of others.

- Clarify, illustrate, or verify a response when asked to do so. Ask other students follow-up questions to help members of the group clarify their own positions and to make new connections with previous statements.

- Make sure all members of the group have a chance to participate.

- As a group, decide on a single idea to share with the class.

PHLit Online!
www.PHLitOnline.com

- Interactive graphic organizers
- Grammar tutorial
- Interactive journals

© Leveled Texts

Build your skills and improve your comprehension of short stories with texts of increasing complexity.

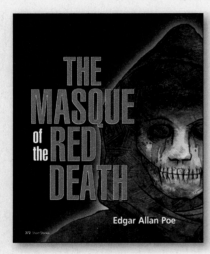

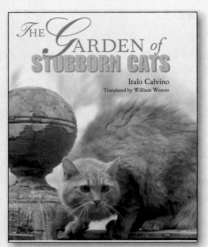

Read **"The Masque of the Red Death"** to see how a prince tries to use his power to evade death.

Read **"The Garden of Stubborn Cats"** to discover how the unexpected can spring up in the most ordinary places.

© Common Core State Standards

Meet these standards with either **"The Masque of the Red Death"** (p. 372) or **"The Garden of the Stubborn Cats"** (p. 384).

Reading Literature
4. Determine the meaning of words and phrases as they are used in the text, including figurative and connotative meanings; analyze the cumulative impact of specific word choices on meaning and tone. (*Literary Analysis: Symbolism and Allegory*)

Spiral Review: RL.9-10.5
Writing
3. Write narratives to develop real or imagined experiences or events using effective technique, well-chosen details, and well-structured event sequences. **3.a.** Engage and orient the reader by setting out a problem, situation, or observation, establishing one or multiple point(s) of view, and introducing a narrator and/or characters; create a

smooth progression of experiences or events. **3.b.** Use narrative techniques to develop experiences, events, and/or characters. (*Writing: Narrative*)

Speaking and Listening
2. Integrate multiple sources of information presented in diverse media or formats, evaluating the credibility and accuracy of each source. (*Research and Technology: Research Summary*)

Language
3. Apply knowledge of language to understand how language functions in different contexts, to make effective choices for meaning or style, and to comprehend more fully when reading or listening. (*Conventions: Active and Passive Voice*)

Literary Analysis: Symbolism and Allegory

Symbolism is a writer's use of symbols. A **symbol** is a type of figurative language in which a character, a place, a thing, or an event in a literary work stands for a larger idea. For example, a dog in a story may stand for loyalty. To create symbols, a writer may use these strategies:

- Call on traditional associations and connotations—a dog is a symbol of loyalty because dogs are often praised for that virtue.

- Create new associations—if a story character cherishes an object because it was his grandfather's, the object may come to symbolize family ties.

In most stories, the use of symbolism is subtle and open to interpretation. A story in which all characters, settings, events, and actions are clearly symbolic is called an **allegory.**

Using the Strategy: Symbol Diagram

Use a **symbol diagram** like this one to identify details that show that an object or a character symbolizes a larger meaning.

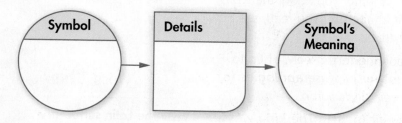

Reading Skill: Draw Conclusions

When you **draw a conclusion,** you make a decision or develop an opinion based on facts and details in a text. To draw a conclusion about the meaning of a symbol, **identify patterns** that suggest its larger meaning.

- Consider the repeated actions, qualities, and other details that the work associates with the symbol.

- Use any background knowledge you have to help you identify symbols.

- Develop an idea about the meaning of the symbol—the meaning that best explains its role in the work.

Can progress be made without *conflict?*

Writing About the Big Question

In "The Masque of the Red Death," a prince attempts to hide from a terrible death that is sweeping the kingdom. Use these sentence starters to develop your ideas about the Big Question.

People may **struggle** against the inevitable when _____.

Sometimes a **confrontation** is necessary in order to **resolve** a conflict because _____.

While You Read Look for descriptions of how the people behave at the masque, the grand ball that the prince hosts. Then, decide whether you think the writer believes people can avoid conflict.

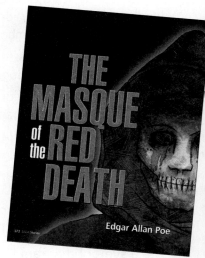

Vocabulary

Read each word and its definition. Decide whether you know the word well, know it a little bit, or do not know it at all. After you read, see how your knowledge of each word has increased.

- **profuse** (prō fyo͞os´) *adj.* giving or pouring forth freely, often to excess (p. 373) *Sheri offered her mother <u>profuse</u> apologies for forgetting her birthday.* profusely *adv.* profusion *n.*

- **august** (ô gust´) *adj.* impressive; majestic (p. 373) *The king was an <u>august</u> figure when he sat on his throne.* augustly *adv.* augustness *n.*

- **impeded** (im pēd´ əd) *v.* blocked; obstructed (p. 373) *The pillar I sat behind <u>impeded</u> my ability to see the stage.* impediment *n.*

- **cessation** (se sā´ shən) *n.* halt; stopping (p. 377) *After the sudden <u>cessation</u> of the car alarm, the silence seemed deep.* cease *v.*

- **decorum** (di kôr´ əm) *n.* behavior that is polite and correct for an occasion (p. 378) *The best man, lacking any <u>decorum</u>, showed up an hour late to the wedding.*

- **tangible** (tan´ jə bəl) *adj.* real and able to be touched (p. 380) *The dream was so vivid, that it almost seemed <u>tangible</u>.* tangibly *adv.* tangibility *n.*

Word Study

The **Latin suffix *-tion*** means "the act or quality of."

In this selection, there is a **cessation** of activity when the clock chimes the hour of midnight. All activity stops.

Meet
Edgar Allan Poe
(1809–1849)

Author of
The Masque of the Red Death

The son of traveling actors, Edgar Poe lost his mother at an early age. He was then raised by a wealthy Virginia family named Allan, from whom he took his middle name. After winning a writing contest with his story "MS. in a Bottle," Poe became a literary success, winning fame but not fortune. He died in poverty at the age of forty. Today, Poe is recognized as a master of the short story.

A Single Effect Poe believed that a work of fiction has the most impact if it can be read in one sitting and if all the elements work together to create a "single effect." He is best known for tales in which the single effect is horror. Poe also pioneered detective stories and science fiction.

DID YOU KNOW?
The Mystery Writers of America call their annual awards "Edgars" in Poe's honor.

BACKGROUND FOR THE STORY
The Black Death

In the 1300s, a plague called the Black Death swept across Europe, killing as many as 25 million people. Most of those who caught the disease died within three to five days after their symptoms appeared. Subsequent oubreaks of plague continued in Europe until recent times. Poe invented the "Red Death" for this story, but his tale plays on an age-old fear.

THE MASQUE of the RED DEATH

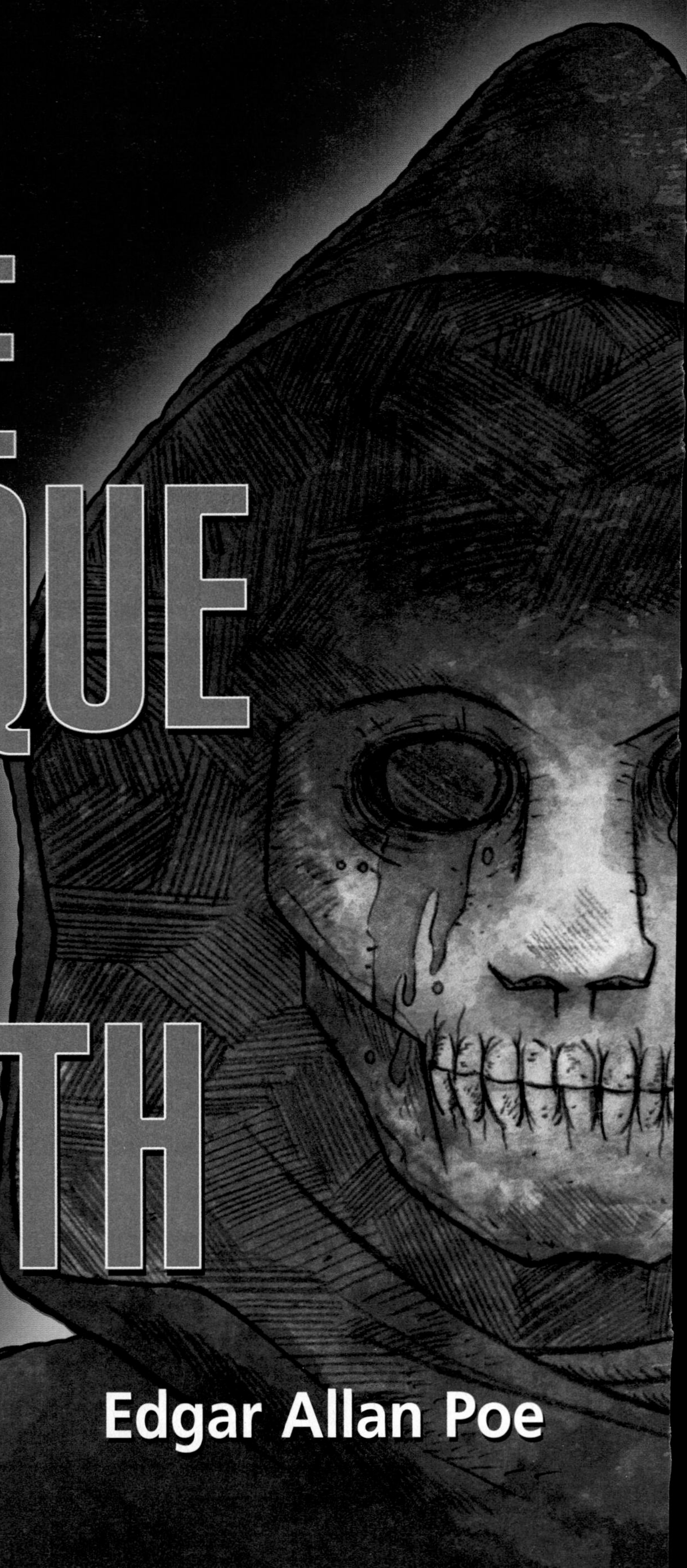

Edgar Allan Poe

Short Stories

The "Red Death" had long devastated the country. No pestilence had ever been so fatal, or so hideous. Blood was its Avatar[1] and its seal—the redness and the horror of blood. There were sharp pains, and sudden dizziness, and then profuse bleeding at the pores, with dissolution. The scarlet stains upon the body and especially upon the face of the victim, were the pest ban which shut him out from the aid and from the sympathy of his fellow men. And the whole seizure, progress and termination of the disease, were the incidents of half an hour.

But the Prince Prospero was happy and dauntless and sagacious. When his dominions were half depopulated, he summoned to his presence a thousand hale and lighthearted friends from among the knights and dames of his court, and with these retired to the deep seclusion of one of his castellated abbeys.[2] This was an extensive and magnificent structure, the creation of the prince's own eccentric yet august taste. A strong and lofty wall girdled it in. This wall had gates of iron. The courtiers, having entered, brought furnaces and massy hammers and welded the bolts. They resolved to leave means neither of ingress or egress[3] to the sudden impulses of despair or frenzy from within. The abbey was amply provisioned. With such precautions the courtiers might bid defiance to contagion. The external world could take care of itself. In the meantime it was folly to grieve, or to think. The prince had provided all the appliances of pleasure. There were buffoons, there were improvisatori, there were ballet dancers, there were musicians, there was Beauty, there was wine. All these and security were within. Without was the "Red Death."

It was toward the close of the fifth or sixth month of his seclusion, and while the pestilence raged most furiously abroad, that the Prince Prospero entertained his thousand friends at a masked ball of the most unusual magnificence.

It was a voluptuous scene, that masquerade. But first let me tell of the rooms in which it was held. There were seven—an imperial suite. In many palaces, however, such suites form a long and straight vista, while the folding doors slide back nearly to the walls on either hand, so that the view of the whole extent is scarcely impeded. Here the case was very different; as might have been expected from the duke's love of the bizarre. The apartments were so irregularly disposed that the vision embraced but little more than one at a time. There was a sharp turn at every twenty or thirty yards, and at each turn a novel effect. To the right and left, in the middle of each wall,

Vocabulary
profuse (prō fyo͞os´) *adj.*
giving or pouring forth freely, often to excess

august (ô gust´) *adj.*
impressive; majestic

Reading Skill
Draw Conclusions
What details here support the conclusion that the prince thinks he can escape the plague?

Vocabulary
impeded (im pēd´ əd)
v. blocked; obstructed

Reading
Check
Why has Prince Prospero locked himself and his guests in his castle?

---

1. **Avatar** (av´ ə tär´) *n.* sign; outward manifestation of an unseen force.
2. **castellated abbeys** (kas´ tə lāt´ əd ab´ ēz) monasteries or convents (religious retreats) with towers like those of a castle.
3. **ingress** (in´ gres´) or egress (è» gres«) entry or exit.

Reading Skill
Draw Conclusions
Judging from the title of the story and the colors of the seventh room, what might the room represent?

a tall and narrow Gothic window looked out upon a closed corridor which pursued the windings of the suite. These windows were of stained glass whose color varied in accordance with the prevailing hue of the decorations of the chamber into which it opened. That at the eastern extremity was hung, for example, in blue—and vividly blue were its windows. The second chamber was purple in its ornaments and tapestries, and here the panes were purple. The third was green throughout, and so were the casements. The fourth was furnished and lighted with orange—the fifth with white—the sixth with violet. The seventh apartment was closely shrouded in black velvet tapestries that hung all over the ceiling and down the walls, falling in heavy folds upon a carpet of the same material and hue. But in this chamber only, the color of the windows failed to correspond with the decorations. The panes here were scarlet—a deep blood color. Now in no one of the seven apartments was there any lamp or candelabrum amid the profusion of golden ornaments that lay scattered to and fro or depended from the roof. There was no light of any kind emanating from lamp or candle within the suite of chambers. But in the corridors that followed the suite, there stood, opposite to each window, a heavy tripod, bearing a brazier[4] of fire that projected its rays through the tinted glass and so glaringly illumined the room. And thus were produced a multitude of gaudy and fantastic appearances. But in the western or black chamber the effect of the firelight that streamed upon the dark hangings through the blood-tinted panes, was ghastly in the extreme, and produced so wild a look upon the countenances of those who entered, that there were few of the company bold enough to set foot within its precincts at all.

It was in this apartment, also, that there stood against the western wall a gigantic clock of ebony.[5] Its pendulum swung to and fro with a dull, heavy, monotonous clang; and when the minute-hand made the circuit of the face, and the hour was to be stricken, there came from the brazen lungs of the clock a sound which was clear and loud and deep and exceedingly musical, but of so peculiar a note and emphasis that, at each lapse of an hour, the musicians of the orchestra were constrained to pause, momentarily, in their performance, to hearken to the sound; and thus the waltzers perforce ceased their evolutions; and there was a brief disconcert[6] of the whole gay company; and, while the chimes of the clock yet rang, it was observed that the giddiest grew pale, and the more aged and sedate passed their hands over their brows as if in confused reverie or meditation. But when the echoes had fully ceased, a light laughter at once pervaded the assembly; the musicians looked at

---

4. **brazier** (brā´ zhər) *n.* metal pan or bowl used to hold burning coals.
5. **ebony** (eb´ ə nē) *n.* the black or dark wood of certain trees.
6. **disconcert** (dis kän´ sʉrt) *n.* embarrassment; confusion.

each other and smiled as if at their own nervousness and folly, and made whispering vows, each to the other, that the next chiming of the clock should produce in them no similar emotion; and then, after the lapse of sixty minutes, (which embrace three thousand and six hundred seconds of the Time that flies), there came yet another chiming of the clock, and then were the same disconcert and tremulousness and meditation as before. ●

But, in spite of these things, it was a gay and magnificent revel. The tastes of the duke were peculiar. He had a fine eye for colors and effects. He disregarded the decora of mere fashion. His plans were bold and fiery, and his conceptions glowed with barbaric luster. There are some who would have thought him mad. His followers felt that he was not. It was necessary to hear and see and touch him to be sure that he was not.

He had directed, in great part, the movable embellishments of the seven chambers, upon occasion of this great fête; and it was his own guiding taste which had given character to the masqueraders. Be sure they were grotesque.[7] There were much glare and glitter and piquancy and phantasm—much of what has been since seen in Hernani.[8] There were arabesque figures with unsuited limbs and

---

7. **grotesque** (grō tesk´) *adj.* fantastic; distorted; bizarre; marked by strange mismatches of characteristics.
8. *Hernani* (hʉr nä´ nē) extravagant drama by the French author Victor Hugo.

▲ **Critical Viewing**
What details does this scene share with the masque in the story? What differences can you find? **[Compare and Contrast]**

Reading Check

How do the partygoers and musicians react when the clock strikes?

appointments. There were delirious fancies such as the madman fashions. There was much of the beautiful, much of the wanton, much of the bizarre, something of the terrible, and not a little of that which might have excited disgust. To and fro in the seven chambers there stalked, in fact, a multitude of dreams. And these—the dreams—writhed in and about, taking hue from the rooms, and causing the wild music of the orchestra to seem as the echo of their steps. And, anon, there strikes the ebony clock which stands in the hall of the velvet. And then, for a moment, all is still, and all is silent save the voice of the clock. The dreams are stiff-frozen as they stand. But the echoes of the chime die away—they have endured but an instant—and a light, half-subdued laughter floats after them as they depart. And now again the music swells, and the dreams live, and writhe to and fro more merrily than ever, taking hue from the many-tinted windows through which stream the rays from the tripods. But to the chamber which lies most westwardly of the seven, there are now none of the maskers who venture; for the night is waning away; and there flows a ruddier light through the blood-colored panes; and the blackness of the sable[9] drapery appalls; and to him whose foot falls upon the sable carpet, there comes from the near clock of ebony a muffled peal more solemnly emphatic than any which reaches *their* ears who indulge in the more remote gaieties of the other apartments.

But these other apartments were densely crowded, and in them beat feverishly the heart of life. And the revel went whirlingly on, until at length there commenced the sounding of midnight upon the clock. And then the music ceased, as I have told; and the evolutions of the waltzers were quieted; and there was an uneasy cessation of all things as before. But now there were twelve strokes to be sounded by the bell of the clock; and thus it happened, perhaps, that more of thought crept, with more of time, into the meditations of the thoughtful among those who reveled. And thus, too, it happened, perhaps, that before the last echoes of the last chime had utterly sunk into silence, there were many individuals in the crowd who had found leisure to become aware of the presence of a masked figure which had arrested the attention of no single individual before. And the rumor of this new presence having spread itself whisperingly around, there arose at length from the whole company a buzz, or murmur, expressive of disapprobation and surprise—then, finally, of terror, of horror, and of disgust.

In an assembly of phantasms such as I have painted, it may well be supposed that no ordinary appearance could have excited such

---

9. **sable** (sā′ bəl) *adj.* black; made of the black fur of the marten, an animal in the weasel family.

◀ **Critical Viewing**
Does this illustration capture the mood of the seventh room as Poe describes it? Support your answer. **[Interpret]**

**Reading Skill
Draw Conclusions**
What does the contrast between activities in the first six rooms and the last one suggest about the symbolic meaning of this room?

**Vocabulary
cessation** (se sā′ shən) *n.* halt; stopping

Reading Check
Who draws the attention of the revelers?

Vocabulary
decorum (di kôr´
əm) *n.* behavior that
is polite and is cor-
rect for an occasion

Spiral Review
Order of Events
Why do you think
Poe chose to have
the stranger arrive at
midnight? What effect
does the midnight
stranger have on the
party?

sensation. In truth the masquerade license of the night was nearly unlimited; but the figure in question had out-Heroded Herod,[10] and gone beyond the bounds of even the prince's indefinite decorum. There are chords in the hearts of the most reckless which cannot be touched without emotion. Even with the utterly lost, to whom life and death are equally jests, there are matters of which no jest can be made. The whole company, indeed, seemed now deeply to feel that in the costume and bearing of the stranger neither wit nor propriety existed. The figure was tall and gaunt, and shrouded from head to foot in the habiliments[11] of the grave. The mask which concealed the visage was made so nearly to resemble the countenance of a stiffened corpse that the closest scrutiny must have had difficulty in detecting the cheat. And yet all this might have been endured, if not approved, by the mad revelers around. But the mummer[12] had gone so far as to assume the type of the Red Death. His vesture was dabbled in *blood*—and his broad brow, with all the features of the face, was besprinkled with the scarlet horror. •

When the eyes of Prince Prospero fell upon this spectral image (which with a slow and solemn movement, as if more fully to sustain its role, stalked to and fro among the waltzers) he was seen to be convulsed, in the first moment with a strong shudder either of terror or distaste; but, in the next, his brow reddened with rage.

"Who dares?" he demanded hoarsely of the courtiers who stood near him—"who dares insult us with this blasphemous mockery? Seize him and unmask him—that we may know whom we have to hang at sunrise, from the battlements!"

It was in the eastern or blue chamber in which stood the Prince Prospero as he uttered these words. They rang throughout the seven rooms loudly and clearly—for the prince was a bold and robust man, and the music had become hushed at the waving of his hand.

It was in the blue room where stood the prince, with a group of pale courtiers by his side. At first, as he spoke, there was a slight rushing movement of this group in the direction of the intruder, who at the moment was also near at hand, and now, with deliberate and stately step, made closer approach to the speaker. But from a certain nameless awe with which the mad assumptions of the mummer had inspired the whole party, there were found none who put forth hand to seize him; so that, unimpeded, he passed within a yard of the prince's person; and, while the vast assembly, as if with one impulse, shrank from the centers of the rooms to

---

10. out-Heroded Herod (her´ əd) behaved even more excessively than Herod, a Biblical figure noted for his shocking acts.
11. habiliments (hə bil´ ə mənts) *n.* clothing.
12. mummer (mum´ ər) *n.* masked and costumed person.

the walls, he made his way uninterruptedly, but with the same solemn and measured step which had distinguished him from the first, through the blue chamber to the purple—through the purple to the green—through the green to the orange—through this again to the white—and even thence to the violet, ere a decided movement had been made to arrest him. It was then, however, that the Prince Prospero, maddening with rage and the shame of his own momentary cowardice, rushed hurriedly through the six chambers, while none followed him on account of a deadly terror that had seized upon all. He bore aloft a drawn dagger, and had approached, in rapid impetuosity, to within three or four feet of the retreating figure, when the latter, having attained the extremity of the velvet apartment, turned suddenly and confronted his pursuer. There was a sharp cry—and the dagger dropped gleaming upon the sable carpet, upon which, instantly afterwards, fell prostrate in death the Prince Prospero. Then, summoning the wild courage

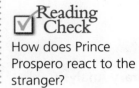

Reading Check

How does Prince Prospero react to the stranger?

◀ **Critical Viewing**
In what way does this image express the fears of the revelers?
[Connect]

Vocabulary
tangible (tan´ jə bəl)
adj. real and able
to be touched

Literary Analysis
Symbolism How does
the use of a number
of symbols—the black
room, the clock, the un-
invited guest—show that
the story is an allegory?

of despair, a throng of the revelers at once threw themselves into the black apartment, and, seizing the mummer, whose tall figure stood erect and motionless within the shadow of the ebony clock, gasped in unutterable horror at finding the grave cerements[13] and corpselike mask which they handled with so violent a rudeness, untenanted by any tangible form.

And now was acknowledged the presence of the Red Death. He had come like a thief in the night. And one by one dropped the revelers in the blood-bedewed halls of their revel, and died each in the despairing posture of his fall. And the life of the ebony clock went out with that of the last of the gay. And the flames of the tripods expired. And Darkness and Decay and the Red Death held illimitable dominion over all.

---

13. **cerements** (ser´ ə mənts) *n.* burial wrapping for a corpse; shroud.

Critical Thinking

Cite textual
evidence to
support your
responses.

1. **Key Ideas and Details (a)** Why does Prince Prospero hide in his palace? **(b) Contrast:** Contrast life outside the palace with life inside it.

2. **Key Ideas and Details (a)** Use details from the story to describe the rooms where the masquerade is held. **(b) Infer:** What do these details suggest about the prince's tastes and values?

3. **Key Ideas and Details (a)** Why does the prince decide to hold the masquerade? **(b) Evaluate:** What does the prince's response to the Red Death suggest about the kind of person he is? Explain.

4. **Integration of Knowledge and Ideas** What message does Poe convey about attempting to avoid conflict? Explain your answer. *[Connect to the Big Question: Can progress be made without conflict?]*

Literary Analysis: Symbolism and Allegory

1. Craft and Structure In the story, the stranger might be viewed as a **symbol** of death. **(a)** Describe two responses of the partygoers to the stranger. **(b)** How are these responses similar to ones associated with death? **(c)** Identify two other details supporting this interpretation of the stranger.

2. Craft and Structure This story can be read as an **allegory.** Explain what the ability of the uninvited guest to enter a fortified palace might symbolize.

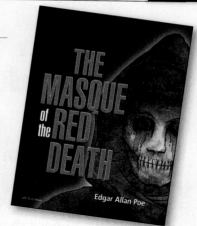

Edgar Allan Poe

Reading Skill: Draw Conclusions

3. (a) In a chart like the one shown, identify the pattern of details that shows the importance of the clock. **(b)** Based on your chart, **draw a conclusion** about what the clock symbolizes.

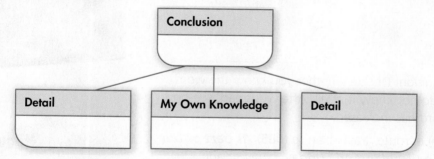

Vocabulary

Acquisition and Use Words with similar meanings are called **synonyms.** For each set, choose the word that is *not* a synonym for the other two words. Explain.

1. plentiful; efficient; profuse

2. august; dignified; anguished

3. aided; hindered; impeded

4. end; cessation; hesitation

5. propriety; decisiveness; decorum

6. tangible; touchable; flavorful

Word Study Use the context of the sentences and what you know about the **Latin suffix *-tion*** to explain your answer to each question.

1. How would a positive job *evaluation* make you feel?

2. If you received a letter of *rejection,* would you be pleased?

Word Study

The **Latin suffix *-tion*** means "the act or quality of."

Apply It Explain how the suffix *-tion* contributes to the meanings of these words. Consult a dictionary, if necessary.

justification
protection
participation

Can progress be made without *conflict?*

Writing About the Big Question

In this story, stubborn cats fight to preserve their space. Use these sentence starters to develop your ideas about the Big Question.

A person may **oppose change** because _____.

Progress can sometimes create conflict when _____.

While You Read Note the differences between the world of cats and the world of humans. Then, decide whether nature and people must be in conflict.

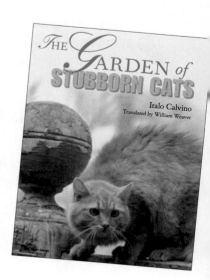

Vocabulary

Read each word and its definition. Decide whether you know the word well, know it a little bit, or do not know it at all. After you read, see how your knowledge of each word has increased.

- **itinerary** (ī tin′ ər er′ ē) *n.* route; travel plan (p. 385) *As part of our itinerary, we will be in Cleveland on Sunday. itinerant adj.*

- **intrigues** (in′ trēgz) *n.* plots; schemes (p. 386) *The twins whispered together and laughed, cooking up one of their intrigues. intrigue v. intriguing adj.*

- **squalid** (skwäl′ id) *adj.* foul or unclean (p. 387) *The restaurant was so squalid that the health board shut it down. squalor n. squalidly adv.*

- **futile** (fyo͞ot′ l) *adj.* not successful; useless (p. 390) *After a futile attempt to climb the steep and icy incline, the hikers had to seek another path. futilely adv. futility n.*

- **indigence** (in′ di jəns) *n.* poverty (p. 393) *Many lost their jobs, and the number of people living in indigence grew. indigent adj.*

- **consigned** (kən sīnd′) *v.* handed over; gave up or delivered (p. 395) *Thankfully, the stolen car was found and consigned to the owners. consignable adj. consignment n.*

Word Study

The **Latin suffix -id** means "the body of" or "connected with."

In this story, the cats lead Marcovaldo through **squalid** passageways, those that are filled with squalor, or dirt and grime.

Author of

THE GARDEN of STUBBORN CATS

The son of two Italian botanists, Italo Calvino was born in Cuba. He grew up in San Remo on the Italian Riviera and began his literary career in the Italian city of Turin.

A Writer of Fables According to Calvino, "A classic is a book that has never finished saying what it has to say." In this sense, Calvino's own works are classics. They say much more than appears on the page.

Though his ideas are complex, Calvino conveys them using events and characters as simple as those in a fable or fairy tale. Like a good fable, his stories blend reality and fantasy.

DID YOU KNOW?

During World War II, Calvino joined the Italian Resistance to fight Italy's fascist dictatorship.

BACKGROUND FOR THE STORY

Marcovaldo

This story is one of the interrelated short stories in Italo Calvino's *Marcovaldo: or The Seasons in the City.* Set in a grim Italian industrial city in the 1950s and 1960s, the collection presents the adventures of Marcovaldo, an ordinary working man, as he uses his imagination to escape his surroundings.

THE GARDEN of STUBBORN CATS

Italo Calvino

translated by William Weaver

The city of cats and the city of men exist one inside the other, but they are not the same city.

Few cats recall the time when there was no distinction: the streets and squares of men were also streets and squares of cats, and the lawns, courtyards, balconies, and fountains: you lived in a broad and various space. But for several generations now domestic felines have been prisoners of an uninhabitable city: the streets are uninterruptedly overrun by the mortal traffic of cat-crushing automobiles; in every square foot of terrain where once a garden extended or a vacant lot or the ruins of an old demolition, now condominiums loom up, welfare housing, brand-new skyscrapers; every entrance is crammed with parked cars; the courtyards, one by one, have been roofed by reinforced concrete and transformed into garages or movie houses or storerooms or workshops. And where a rolling plateau of low roofs once extended, copings, terraces, water tanks, balconies, skylights, corrugated-iron sheds, now one general superstructure rises wherever structures can rise; the intermediate differences in height, between the low ground of the street and the supernal[1] heaven of the penthouses, disappear; the cat of a recent litter seeks in vain the itinerary of its fathers, the point from which to make the soft leap from balustrade to cornice to drainpipe, or for the quick climb on the roof-tiles. But in this vertical city, in this compressed city where all voids tend to fill up and every block of cement tends to mingle with other blocks of cement, a kind of counter-city opens, a negative city, that consists of empty slices between wall and wall, of the minimal distances ordained by the

---

1. **supernal** (sŏŏ pʉr´ nəl) *adj.* of the heavens; divine.

Literary Analysis
Symbolism What associations with cats is the author creating?

Vocabulary
itinerary (ī tin´ ər er´ ē) *n.* route; travel plan

☑ Reading Check

Why is the city uninhabitable for cats?

**Reading Skill
Draw Conclusions**
Which details here
support the conclusion
that cats are not fully at
home in the city?

building regulations between two constructions, between the rear of one construction and the rear of the next; it is a city of cavities, wells, air conduits, driveways, inner yards, accesses to basements, like a network of dry canals on a planet of stucco and tar, and it is through this network, grazing the walls, that the ancient cat population still scurries.

On occasion, to pass the time, Marcovaldo would follow a cat. It was during the work-break, between noon and three, when all the personnel except Marcovaldo went home to eat, and he—who brought his lunch in his bag—laid his place among the packing-cases in the warehouse, chewed his snack, smoked a half-cigar, and wandered around, alone and idle, waiting for work to resume. In those hours, a cat that peeped in at a window was always welcome company, and a guide for new explorations. He had made friends with a tabby, well fed, a blue ribbon around its neck, surely living with some well-to-do family. This tabby shared with Marcovaldo the habit of an afternoon stroll right after lunch; and naturally a friendship sprang up.

Following his tabby friend, Marcovaldo had started looking at places as if through the round eyes of a cat and even if these places were the usual environs of his firm he saw them in a different light, as settings for cattish stories, with connections practicable only by light, velvety paws. Though from the outside the neighborhood seemed poor in cats, every day on his rounds Marcovaldo made the acquaintance of some new face, and a miau, a hiss, a stiffening of fur on an arched back was enough for him to sense ties and intrigues and rivalries among them. At those moments he thought he had already penetrated the secrecy of the felines' society: and then he felt himself scrutinized by pupils that became slits, under the surveillance of the antennae of taut whiskers, and all the cats around him sat impassive as sphinxes, the pink triangles of their noses convergent on the black triangles of their

**Vocabulary
intrigues** (in´ trēgz)
n. plots; schemes

lips, and the only things that moved were the tips of the ears, with a vibrant jerk like radar. They reached the end of a narrow passage, between squalid blank walls; and, looking around, Marcovaldo saw that the cats that had led him this far had vanished, all of them together, no telling in which direction, even his tabby friend, and they had left him alone. Their realm had territories, ceremonies, customs that it was not yet granted to him to discover.

On the other hand, from the cat city there opened unsuspected peepholes onto the city of men: and one day the same tabby led him to discover the great Biarritz Restaurant. ●

Anyone wishing to see the Biarritz Restaurant had only to assume the posture of a cat, that is, proceed on all fours. Cat and man, in this fashion, walked around a kind of dome, at whose foot some low, rectangular little windows opened. Following the tabby's example, Marcovaldo looked down. They were transoms through which the luxurious hall received air and light. To the sound of gypsy violins, partridges and quails swirled by on silver dishes balanced by the white-gloved fingers of waiters in tailcoats. Or, more precisely, above the partridges and quails the dishes whirled, and above the dishes the white gloves, and poised on the waiters' patent-leather shoes, the gleaming parquet floor, from which hung dwarf potted palms and tablecloths and crystal and buckets like bells with the champagne bottle for their clapper: everything was turned upside-down because Marcovaldo, for fear of being seen, wouldn't stick his head inside the window and confined himself to looking at the reversed reflection of the room in the tilted pane.

But it was not so much the windows of the dining-room as those of the kitchens that interested the cat: looking through the former you saw, distant and somehow transfigured, what in the

▲ **Critical Viewing**
In what way does this picture, like the story, express the idea of multiple perspectives on the world? **[Interpret]**

Reading Check
To what place does Marcovaldo follow the tabby?

LITERATURE IN CONTEXT

Architecture Connection

Architectural Features

The following building features are mentioned in the narrative:

- **balustrade** railing suported by posts
- **belvedere** long balcony with a roof
- **capitals** tops of columns
- **copings** top layer of a stone or brick wall, sloped to carry off water
- **cornice** overhanging part of a roof
- **transom** small window or shutter over a door or window

Connect to the Literature

Compare and contrast the purposes for which a cat and a person would use each of these features.

kitchens presented itself—quite concrete and within paw's reach—as a plucked bird or a fresh fish. And it was toward the kitchens, in fact, that the tabby wanted to lead Marcovaldo, either through a gesture of altruistic friendship or else because it counted on the man's help for one of its raids. Marcovaldo, however, was reluctant to leave his belvedere over the main room: first as he was fascinated by the luxury of the place, and then because something down there had riveted his attention. To such an extent that, overcoming his fear of being seen, he kept peeking in, with his head in the transom.

In the midst of the room, directly under that pane, there was a little glass fish tank, a kind of aquarium, where some fat trout were swimming. A special customer approached, a man with a shiny bald pate, black suit, black beard. An old waiter in tailcoat followed him, carrying a little net as if he were going to catch butterflies. The gentleman in black looked at the trout with a grave, intent air; then he raised one hand and with a slow, solemn gesture singled out a fish. The waiter dipped the net into the tank, pursued the appointed trout, captured it, headed for the kitchens, holding out in front of him, like a lance, the net in which the fish wriggled. The gentleman in black, solemn as a magistrate[2] who has handed down a capital sentence, went to take his seat and wait for the return of the trout, sautéed "à la meunière."[3]

If I found a way to drop a line from up here and make one of those trout bite, Marcovaldo thought, I couldn't be accused of theft; at worst, of fishing in an unauthorized place. And ignoring the miaus that called him toward the kitchens, he went to collect his fishing tackle.

Nobody in the crowded dining room of the Biarritz saw the long, fine line, armed with hook and bait, as it slowly dropped into the tank. The fish saw the bait, and flung themselves on it. In the fray one trout managed to bite the worm: and immediately it began to rise, rise, emerge from the water, a silvery flash, it darted up high, over the laid tables and the trolleys of hors d'oeuvres, over the blue flames of the crêpes Suzette, until it vanished into the heavens of the transom.

Marcovaldo had yanked the rod with the brisk snap of the expert fisherman, so the fish landed behind his back. The trout had barely touched the ground when the cat sprang. What little life the trout

---

2. magistrate (maj´ is trāt´) *n.* judge.

3. sautéed "à la meunière" (sô tād´ ä lä mə nyer´) rolled in flour, fried in butter, and sprinkled with lemon juice and chopped parsley.

still had was lost between the tabby's teeth. Marcovaldo, who had abandoned his line at that moment to run and grab the fish, saw it snatched from under his nose, hook and all. He was quick to put one foot on the rod, but the snatch had been so strong that the rod was all the man had left, while the tabby ran off with the fish, pulling the line after it. Treacherous kitty! It had vanished.

But this time it wouldn't escape him: there was that long line trailing after him and showing the way he had taken. Though he had lost sight of the cat, Marcovaldo followed the end of the line: there it was, running along a wall; it climbed a parapet, wound through a doorway, was swallowed up by a basement . . . Marcovaldo, venturing into more and more cattish places, climbed roofs, straddled railings, always managed to catch a glimpse—perhaps only a second before it disappeared—of that moving trace that indicated the thief's path.

Literary Analysis
Symbolism Which details reinforce the contrast between a cat's view of the city and a human's view?

Now the line played out down a sidewalk, in the midst of the traffic, and Marcovaldo, running after it, almost managed to grab it. He flung himself down on his belly: there, he grabbed it! He managed to seize one end of the line before it slipped between the bars of a gate.

Beyond a half-rusted gate and two bits of wall buried under climbing plants, there was a little rank⁴ garden, with a small, abandoned-looking building at the far end of it. A carpet of dry leaves covered the path, and dry leaves lay everywhere under the boughs of the two plane-trees, forming actually some little mounds in the yard. A

☑ Reading Check
Where does the tabby finally lead Marcovaldo?

4. **rank** (raŋk) *adj.* growing vigorously and coarsely.

The Garden of Stubborn Cats **389**

layer of leaves was yellowing in the green water of a pool. Enormous buildings rose all around, skyscrapers with thousands of windows, like so many eyes trained disapprovingly on that little square patch with two trees, a few tiles, and all those yellow leaves, surviving right in the middle of an area of great traffic.

And in this garden, perched on the capitals and balustrades, lying on the dry leaves of the flowerbeds, climbing on the trunks of the trees or on the drainpipes, motionless on their four paws, their tails making a question-mark, seated to wash their faces, there were tiger cats, black cats, white cats, calico cats, tabbies, angoras, Persians, house cats and stray cats, perfumed cats and mangy cats. Marcovaldo realized he had finally reached the heart of the cats' realm, their secret island. And, in his emotion, he almost forgot his fish.

It had remained, that fish, hanging by the line from the branch of a tree, out of reach of the cats' leaps; it must have dropped from its kidnapper's mouth at some clumsy movement, perhaps as it was defended from the others, or perhaps displayed as an extraordinary prize. The line had got tangled, and Marcovaldo, tug as he would, couldn't manage to yank it loose. A furious battle had meanwhile been joined among the cats, to reach that unreachable fish, or rather, to win the right to try and reach it. Each wanted to prevent the others from leaping: they hurled themselves on one another, they tangled in midair, they rolled around clutching each other, and finally a general war broke out in a whirl of dry, crackling leaves.

After many futile yanks, Marcovaldo now felt the line was free, but he took care not to pull it: the trout would have fallen right in the midst of that infuriated scrimmage of felines.

It was at this moment that, from the top of the walls of the gardens, a strange rain began to fall: fish-bones, heads, tails, even bits of lung and lights.[5] Immediately the cats' attention was distracted from the suspended trout and they flung themselves on the new delicacies. To Marcovaldo, this seemed the right moment to pull the line and regain his fish. But, before he had time to act, from a blind of the little villa, two yellow, skinny hands darted out: one was brandishing scissors; the other, a frying pan. The hand with the scissors was raised above the trout, the hand with the frying pan was thrust under it. The scissors cut the line, the trout fell into the pan; hands, scissors and pan withdrew, the blind closed: all in the space of a second. Marcovaldo was totally bewildered.

---

5. lights term for animal organs used for catfood.

"Are you also a cat lover?" A voice at his back made him turn round. He was surrounded by little old women, some of them ancient, wearing old-fashioned hats on their heads; others, younger, but with the look of spinsters; and all were carrying in their hands or their bags packages of leftover meat or fish, and some even had little pans of milk. "Will you help me throw this package over the fence, for those poor creatures?"

All the ladies, cat lovers, gathered at this hour around the garden of dry leaves to take the food to their protégés.[6]

"Can you tell me why they are all here, these cats?" Marcovaldo inquired.

"Where else could they go? This garden is all they have left! Cats come here from other neighborhoods, too, from miles and miles around . . ."

"And birds, as well," another lady added. "They're forced to live by the hundreds and hundreds on these few trees . . ."

"And the frogs, they're all in that pool, and at night they never stop croaking . . . You can hear them even on the eighth floor of the buildings around here."

"Who does this villa belong to anyway?" Marcovaldo asked. Now, outside the gate, there weren't just the cat-loving ladies but also other people: the man from the gas pump opposite, the apprentices from a mechanic's shop, the postman, the grocer, some passers-by. And none of them, men and women, had to be asked twice: all wanted to have their say, as always when a mysterious and controversial subject comes up.

"It belongs to a Marchesa.[7] She lives there, but you never see her . . ."

"She's been offered millions and millions, by developers, for this little patch of land, but she won't sell . . ."

"What would she do with millions, an old woman all alone in the world? She wants to hold on to her house, even if it's falling to pieces, rather than be forced to move . . ."

"It's the only undeveloped bit of land in the downtown area . . . Its value goes up every year . . . They've made her offers—"

"Offers! That's not all. Threats, intimidation, persecution . . . You don't know the half of it! Those contractors!"

"But she holds out. She's held out for years . . ."

"She's a saint. Without her, where would those poor animals go?"

> *M*arcovaldo realized he had finally reached the heart of the cats' realm, their secret island.

Reading Check

What happens to Marcovaldo's trout?

---

6. protégés (prōt´ ə zhāz´) *n.* those guided and helped by another.
7. Marchesa (mär kā´ zä) *n.* title of an Italian noblewoman.

"A lot she cares about the animals, the old miser! Have you ever seen her give them anything to eat?"

"How can she feed the cats when she doesn't have food for herself? She's the last descendant of a ruined family!"

"She hates cats. I've seen her chasing them and hitting them with an umbrella!"

"Because they were tearing up her flowerbeds!"

"What flowerbeds? I've never seen anything in this garden but a great crop of weeds!"

Marcovaldo realized that with regard to the old Marchesa opinions were sharply divided: some saw her as an angelic being, others as an egoist and a miser.

Literary Analysis
Symbolism What relationship with the city do the Marchesa and her property represent?

"It's the same with the birds; she never gives them a crumb!"

"She gives them hospitality. Isn't that plenty?"

"Like she gives the mosquitoes, you mean. They all come from here, from that pool. In the summertime the mosquitoes eat us alive, and it's all the fault of that Marchesa!"

"And the mice? This villa is a mine of mice. Under the dead leaves they have their burrows, and at night they come out . . ."

"As far as the mice go, the cats take care of them . . ."

"Oh, you and your cats! If we had to rely on them . . ."

"Why? Have you got something to say against cats?"

Here the discussion degenerated into a general quarrel.

"The authorities should do something: confiscate the villa!" one man cried.

"What gives them the right?" another protested.

"In a modern neighborhood like ours, a mouse-nest like this . . . it should be forbidden . . ."

"Why, I picked my apartment precisely because it overlooked this little bit of green . . ."

"Green, hell! Think of the fine skyscraper they could build here!"

Marcovaldo would have liked to add something of his own, but he couldn't get a word in. Finally, all in one breath, he exclaimed: "The Marchesa stole a trout from me!"

The unexpected news supplied fresh ammunition to the old woman's enemies, but her defenders exploited it as proof of the indigence to which the unfortunate noblewoman was reduced. Both sides agreed that Marcovaldo should go and knock at her door to demand an explanation. •

It wasn't clear whether the gate was locked or unlocked; in any case, it opened, after a push, with a mournful creak. Marcovaldo picked his way among the leaves and cats, climbed the steps to the porch, knocked hard at the entrance.

At a window (the very one where the frying pan had appeared), the blind was raised slightly and in one corner a round, pale blue eye was seen, and a clump of hair dyed an undefinable color, and a dry skinny hand. A voice was heard, asking: "Who is it? Who's at the door?", the words accompanied by a cloud smelling of fried oil.

"It's me, Marchesa. The trout man," Marcovaldo explained. "I don't mean to trouble you. I only wanted to tell you, in case you didn't know, that the trout was stolen from me, by that cat, and I'm the one who caught it. In fact the line . . ."

Vocabulary
indigence (in′ di jəns) *n.* poverty

"*S*he hates cats. I've seen her chasing them and hitting them with an umbrella!"

Reading Check

Who owns the garden where the cats gather?

"Those cats! It's always those cats . . ." the Marchesa said, from behind the shutter, with a shrill, somewhat nasal voice. "All my troubles come from the cats! Nobody knows what I go through! Prisoner night and day of those horrid beasts! And with all the refuse people throw over the walls, to spite me!"

"But my trout . . ."

"Your trout! What am I supposed to know about your trout!" The Marchesa's voice became almost a scream, as if she wanted to drown out the sizzle of oil in the pan, which came through the window along with the aroma of fried fish. "How can I make sense of anything, with all the stuff that rains into my house?"

"I understand, but did you take the trout or didn't you?"

"When I think of all the damage I suffer because of the cats! Ah, fine state of affairs! I'm not responsible for anything! I can't tell you what I've lost! Thanks to those cats, who've occupied house and garden for years! My life at the mercy of those animals! Go and find the owners! Make them pay damages! Damages? A whole life destroyed! A prisoner here, unable to move a step!"

"Excuse me for asking: but who's forcing you to stay?"

From the crack in the blind there appeared sometimes a round, pale blue eye, sometimes a mouth with two protruding teeth; for a moment the whole face was visible, and to Marcovaldo it seemed, bewilderingly, the face of a cat.

"They keep me prisoner, they do, those cats! Oh, I'd be glad to leave! What wouldn't I give for a little apartment all my own, in a nice clean modern building! But I can't go out . . . They follow me, they block my path, they trip me up!" The voice became a whisper, as if to confide a secret. "They're afraid I'll sell the lot . . . They won't leave me . . . won't allow me . . . When the builders come to offer me a contract, you should see them, those cats! They get in the way, pull out their claws; they even chased a lawyer off! Once I had the contract right here, I was about to sign it, and they dived in through the window, knocked over the inkwell, tore up all the pages . . ."

All of a sudden Marcovaldo remembered the time, the shipping department, the boss. He tiptoed off over the dried leaves, as the voice continued to come through the slats of the blind, enfolded in that cloud apparently from the oil of a frying pan. "They even scratched me . . . I still have the scar . . . All alone here at the mercy of these demons . . ."

Winter came. A blossoming of white flakes

"All my troubles come from the cats! Nobody knows what I go through!"

decked the branches and capitals and the cats' tails. Under the snow, the dry leaves dissolved into mush. The cats were rarely seen, the cat lovers even less; the packages of fish-bones were consigned only to cats who came to the door. Nobody, for quite a while, had seen anything of the Marchesa. No smoke came now from the chimneypot of the villa.

One snowy day, the garden was again full of cats, who had returned as if it were spring, and they were miauing as if on a moonlight night. The neighbors realized that something had happened: they went and knocked at the Marchesa's door. She didn't answer: she was dead.

In the spring, instead of the garden, there was a huge building site that a contractor had set up. The steam shovels dug down to great depths to make room for the foundations, cement poured into the iron armatures, a very high crane passed beams to the workmen who were making the scaffoldings. But how could they get on with their work? Cats walked along all the planks, they made bricks fall and upset buckets of mortar, they fought in the midst of the piles of sand. When you started to raise an armature, you found a cat perched on top of it, hissing fiercely. More treacherous

▲ **Critical Viewing**
Compare this image with the garden in the story. **[Compare and Contrast]**

Vocabulary
consigned (kən sīnd´)
v. handed over; gave up or delivered

Reading
Check

How does the Marchesa feel about the cats?

pusses climbed onto the masons' backs as if to purr, and there was
no getting rid of them. And the birds continued making their nests
in all the trestles, the cab of the crane looked like an aviary[8] . . .
And you couldn't dip up a bucket of water that wasn't full of frogs,
croaking and hopping . . .

---

8. aviary (ā´ vē er´ ē) *n.* building or large cage for housing many birds.

Critical Thinking

1. **Key Ideas and Details** **(a)** What is the "negative city"?
   (b) Infer: How have changes in the city altered the way cats live?

2. **Key Ideas and Details** **(a)** How does Marcovaldo find the secret
   garden of the cats? **(b) Analyze:** List two details from the story
   that suggest such a garden is rare in the city.

3. **Integration of Knowledge and Ideas** **(a) Take a Position:**
   Should the garden of cats remain as it is, or should developers be
   free to build over it? Support your position. **(b) Discuss:** Share and
   discuss your opinions with a small group. **(c) Evaluate:** Choose the
   two best-supported opinions and share them with the class.

4. **Integration of Knowledge and Ideas** **(a)** How are nature and
   development at war with one another in this story? **(b)** Do you
   think the two can ever peacefully coexist? Explain. *[Connect to
   the Big Question: Can progress be made without conflict?]*

Literary Analysis: Symbolism and Allegory

© **1. Craft and Structure** The stubborn cats might be viewed as a force challenging order—they resist human attempts to control the city. **(a)** List two other forces—natural or human—that resist people's control of city space and life. **(b)** Using your answer, explain the meaning of the cats as a **symbol.**

© **2. Craft and Structure** This story can be read as an **allegory.** What does the final conflict between cats and humans symbolize?

Reading Skill: Draw Conclusions

3. (a) In a chart like the one shown, list two details showing the pattern in the Marchesa's relationship to other people in the city.

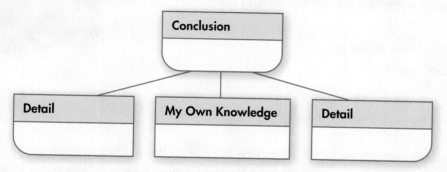

(b) Use your chart to **draw a conclusion** about what she may symbolize.

Vocabulary

© **Acquisition and Use** Words with similar meanings are called **synonyms**. For each set, choose the word that is *not* a synonym for the other two words. Explain.

1. schedule; itinerary; decision

2. intrigues; impulses; plots

3. dirty; nauseated; squalid

4. useless; futile; angry

5. indigence; poverty; laziness

6. delivered; agreed; consigned

Word Study Use the context of the sentences and what you know about the **Latin suffix -id** to explain your answer to each question.

1. If a deadline is *rigid*, can it be extended?

2. Should a mediator be *candid* in his or her judgments?

Word Study

The **Latin suffix -id** means "the body of" or "connected with."

Apply It Explain how the suffix *-id* contributes to the meanings of these words. Consult a dictionary if necessary.

valid
pallid
lucid

Integrated Language Skills

The Masque of the Red Death • The Garden of Stubborn Cats

Conventions: Active and Passive Voice

A verb is in the **active voice** when the subject performs the action. A verb is in the **passive voice** when the action is performed on the subject.

Verbs in the passive voice consist of a form of *be* followed by the past participle of the main verb. Usually, active voice is stronger. However, passive voice is used when the writer wants to emphasize the recipient of the action. Passive voice is also used when the subject performing the action is unknown.

Active Voice: The student *answered* the question.

Passive Voice: The question *was answered.*

Active Voice: Jeremy ate the last cookie.

Passive Voice: The last cookie was eaten by Jeremy.

Practice A Identify each verb or verb phrase as active or passive.

1. The costumes *produced* gaudy and fantastic appearances.
2. Thousands of friends *were invited* to the ball.
3. The clock's heavy clang *was heard* throughout the rooms.
4. The prince *stood* in the blue room.
5. The intruder *was* not *stopped* as he walked through the rooms.

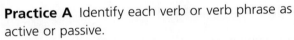 **Reading Application** Choose four sentences from "The Masque of the Red Death," two in the active voice and two in the passive voice. Rewrite each sentence in the opposite voice.

Practice B Change the following sentences from passive voice to active voice. You may need to add words to indicate who performed the action.

1. Marcovaldo is led through alleys by the cat.
2. Marcovaldo's trout is taken by the Marchesa.
3. The fish bones are eaten by the cats.
4. The garden is destroyed and covered with a building.
5. The Marchesa was kept prisoner in her own apartment.

Writing Application Write a brief paragraph in the passive voice describing a cat you have seen. Then, rewrite the paragraph in the active voice. Discuss the effect of each paragraph on a reader.

PH WRITING COACH   Further instruction and practice are available in *Prentice Hall Writing Coach*.

Writing

 Narrative Text In both stories, symbols help convey important messages. Poe turns a clock into a symbol of doom. Calvino turns cats into a symbol of mischief and mystery. Write a brief **narrative** using another object or animal as a symbol. Follow these steps:

- In your narrative, develop an interesting, engaging plot.
- Describe your symbol using precise and vivid adjectives that suggest the qualities it represents. Provide information about its location or situation and its actions.
- Link your symbol to important events or give it a name that hints at what it symbolizes.

Grammar Application Make sure you have used the active voice to make your writing lively. Use the passive voice only when necessary.

Writing Workshop: *Work in Progress*

Prewriting for Problem-and-Solution Essay Take the Problem/Solution Web from your portfolio and highlight one solution. Clarify the solution with additional evidence, such as facts, reasons, or expressions of commonly accepted beliefs. Save this Solution Support List in your portfolio.

 **Common Core State Standards**

L.9-10.3; W.9-10.3, W.9-10.3.a, W.9-10.3.b; SL.9-10.2
[For the full wording of the standards, see page 368.]

Use this prewriting activity to prepare for the **Writing Workshop** on page 420.

Research and Technology

Build and Present Knowledge Conduct library and Internet research to find out more about a topic related to one of the selections—either Poe's literary legacy or city planning. Consult three to four sources of varied types, including books, online sources, CD-ROM references, or audiovisual materials. Evaluate the accuracy and credibility of each source of information before you use it. Then, sum up your findings in a **research summary** and present it to your class. Use these suggestions:

- Use words suited to your audience's knowledge level. Explain technical terms such as *ratiocination* or *balustrade*.
- Anticipate and address listeners' potential misunderstandings and expectations. Make your ideas clear and easy to understand.
- At the end of your presentation, ask for questions and comments from the class.

Revise your summary based on feedback from the class.

PHLit Online!
www.PHLitOnline.com
- Interactive graphic organizers
- Grammar tutorial
- Interactive journals

Test Practice: Reading

Draw Conclusions

Fiction Selection

Directions: *Read the selection. Then, answer the questions.*

> Tiger had been Cassandra's cat since Cassandra was eight years old. Cassandra's father was in the army, and over the years her family moved from state to state, leaving behind friends, classmates, and favorite places. Then, Cassandra's father was sent overseas. Now, it was just Cassandra, her mom, and—until last weekend—Tiger. She and her mom had gone camping and had brought Tiger with them. He had enjoyed the trip, exploring the woods around the campground and snuggling up by Cassandra at night. As they packed to leave, they realized Tiger was gone. Cassandra and her mother spent hours searching for Tiger. Finally, they had to give up. Now at home, Cassandra lay on her bed, her mother sitting beside her. "You know, Sweetie," she said, "cats have amazing powers. We may yet see Tiger again." And somehow, Cassandra knew Tiger—and her dad—would come home someday.

1. Based on the passage, what can you conclude about Cassandra's life so far?

    A. It has been a life of upheaval and change.
    B. It has been exciting.
    C. It has been a life of stability and security.
    D. It has been happy.

2. What might Tiger symbolize to Cassandra?

    A. honesty and loyalty
    B. responsibility
    C. love and stability
    D. mystery

3. Based on details in this passage, what conclusion can you draw about how Cassandra probably feels about losing Tiger?

    A. She blames her mother for losing Tiger.
    B. She feels she has lost something important.
    C. She is glad to be relieved of the responsibility.
    D. She is excited about getting a new cat.

4. Which of the following is the *best* statement of this passage's theme?

    A. Pets are a great responsibility that most teenagers are not ready to handle.
    B. Pets can never replace a true friend.
    C. Cats are unpredictable and easily lost.
    D. Pets can be a source of comfort and stability in life.

Writing for Assessment

Consider the details in this passage. What conclusion can you draw about how Cassandra's mother feels about Tiger? Write a paragraph to explain your conclusion.

Nonfiction Selection

Directions: *Read the selection. Then, answer the questions.*

The ancestors of the domestic cat appeared in Egypt nearly 3,500 years ago. Ancient Egyptians considered the cat sacred and worshipped a cat-headed goddess called Bast. Egyptians often mummified cats, and even mummified mice, presumably as a source of food for the cats.

Cats first appeared in the art and literature of other cultures several thousand years ago: in Greece 2,600 years ago, in China 2,500 years ago, and in India 2,100 years ago. The cat appears in Arabia, Japan, and Britain by A.D. 900.

The cat is noted for its independence, frequent aloofness, and cleanliness, as well as its uncanny ability to find its way home over long distances. Over the centuries, it has been associated with superstitions. Black cats in particular have been associated with supernatural powers. Whatever the reason is, cats continue to fascinate many people. There are 37.7 million cat-owning households in the United States today.

1. Based on this passage, what can you conclude about humans' attitudes toward cats?

A. All humans generally revere cats.
B. Humans throughout the world have long been fascinated with cats.
C. Humans generally dislike cats.
D. Humans around the world find cats useful for removing pests from homes.

2. What can you conclude about the Egyptians' attitude toward cats?

A. Egyptians believed cats live on in the afterworld just as they believed humans do.
B. Egyptians believed that cats should be treated just like humans.
C. Egyptians grieved over the death of a cat.
D. Egyptians were afraid of cats.

3. Based on the details in this passage about cats, what could you reasonably conclude?

A. Most cats are very clingy pets and cannot be left alone.
B. The average cat has a good sense of direction.
C. Few people keep cats as pets.
D. Cats are not loyal to humans.

4. Based on details in the passage, the cat would make a good symbol for—

A. affection.
B. loyalty.
C. the mysterious.
D. justice.

Writing for Assessment

Connecting Across Texts

Based on details from these two passages, what can you conclude about the chances of Cassandra recovering Tiger? Explain your answer in a paragraph.

www.PHLitOnline.com
- Online practice
- Instant feedback

Reading for Information

Analyzing Argumentative and Expository Texts

Newspaper Editorial

Primary Source

Common Core State Standards

Reading Informational Text
3. Analyze how the author unfolds an analysis or series of ideas or events, including the order in which the points are made, how they are introduced and developed, and the connections that are drawn between them.

Language
4.b. Identify and correctly use patterns of word changes that indicate different meanings or parts of speech.
6. Acquire and use accurately general academic and domain-specific words and phrases, sufficient for reading, writing, speaking, and listening at the college and career readiness level; demonstrate independence in gathering vocabulary knowledge when considering a word or phrase important to comprehension or expression.

Reading Skills: Paraphrase to Connect Ideas

When you **paraphrase,** you use your own words to restate ideas presented in a text. Paraphrasing helps you to clarify meaning in a text so that you can determine the main idea and better understand how an author introduces, develops, and connects related ideas. Begin the process of paraphrasing by identifying key ideas and details in a text. Once you have identified the relevant ideas and details, restate them in your own words.

By paraphrasing ideas, you can better analyze how they are connected to each other. You can then more easily **connect** them to ideas in another text and **synthesize** content from the two sources. Use the following chart to guide your reading.

Guidelines for Paraphrasing and Connecting Ideas

- Paraphrase to identify the main ideas in source one.
- Look for similar or related ideas in source two.
- Synthesize the content from the sources by drawing a conclusion about the topic, based on your analysis of the main ideas.

Content-Area Vocabulary

These words appear in the selections that follow. You may also encounter them in other content-area texts.

- **regimes** (rə zhēmz´) *n.* systems or types of government; forms of rule
- **accelerate** (ak sel´ ər āt´) *v.* cause to happen sooner; speed up
- **proclaimed** (prō klāmd´) *v.* made known publicly and officially

Features:
• author's opinion about a current or a historical event
• background information and supporting arguments
• text written for a general or a specific audience

The New York Times

Editorial, November 10, 1999

The editorial begins with a statement of a main idea it will support: Gorbachev should be celebrated for his role in the fall of communism.

The Berlin Wall was bound to fall eventually. But that it came down as bloodlessly as it did 10 years ago this week is largely a tribute to one leader. Today Mikhail Gorbachev is a political pariah in Russia and increasingly forgotten in the West. But history will remember him generously for his crucial role in ending the cold war and pulling back the Iron Curtain that Stalin drew across Europe in 1945.[1]

Liquidating the Soviet empire was not what Mr. Gorbachev had in mind when he came to power in 1985. He was shrewd enough to recognize that radical changes were urgently needed to stave off economic and political bankruptcy in Russia and its European satellites.[2] . . .

Once Mr. Gorbachev lifted the lid with the openness of glasnost and the attempted economic restructuring of perestroika,[3] change took on a dynamic of its own. Similar energies were unleashed in the once-captive nations of Eastern Europe as it became clear that he would not send Soviet tanks to bail out the unpopular client **regimes** that had held sway there since World War II.

As political pressures began to build in the late 1980s, Mr. Gorbachev was left with two options. He could hurtle ahead toward full political and economic freedom. Or he could reverse course and crack down, as so many previous Soviet leaders had done. He chose to do neither. He was too much a creature of his Soviet Communist upbringing to subject his own power to the test of electoral democracy. But he was too enlightened to unleash the kind of thorough repression that might have preserved the Soviet empire for a few more years.

1. **Iron Curtain . . . 1945** At the end of the Second World War, in 1945, Europe was split between western countries, allied with the United States, and eastern countries, dominated by its rival, the Soviet Union, then led by Josef Stalin. West and East were said to be divided by an "iron curtain."
2. **European satellites** Eastern European countries dominated by the Soviet Union.
3. **glasnost** (glaz´ nōst) . . . **perestroika** (per´ ə stroi´ kə) policies of Gorbachev's designed to reform the Soviet Union. Glasnost involved lifting restrictions on free speech; perestroika referred to attempts to reform the government and economy.

Although *glasnost* and *perestroika* are footnoted in the text, paraphrasing these definitions will help you understand them better.

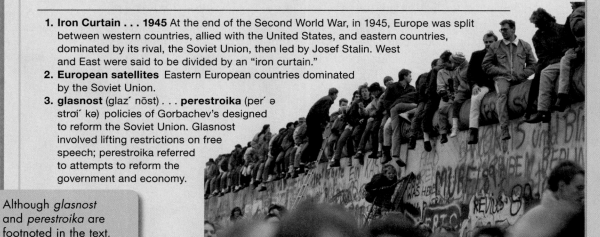

Others stepped in to **accelerate** the transformations Mr. Gorbachev had begun, and in 1989 fixtures of the Soviet empire began to crumble. . . .

Through it all, Mr. Gorbachev and his like-minded foreign minister, Eduard Shevardnadze, stayed their hand, reflecting not only their idealism about reshaping East-West relations but also a pragmatic calculation that the Soviet Union could no longer afford an empire. For permitting its dissolution, Mr. Gorbachev paid a high price. Within two years he had been pushed from power in Moscow. . . .

History has passed Mr. Gorbachev by. But this week, especially, he deserves to be remembered for what he did and, perhaps more important, what he refused to do. With a wisdom and decency that is sadly rare in international power politics, he chose not to defend a dying system with a final, futile spasm of murderous force.

The writer concludes the editorial with a statement that reinforces the main idea introduced in the first paragraph.

Voices from the Wall

Personal stories about the fall of the Berlin Wall

Where were you when the wall came down?

Not even two months after the Berlin Wall had been erected, I was born into the western part of this mysterious and fascinating city—I guess by accident. Who determined whether you were born to a family in the West or in the East? The small two-bedroom apartment where I grew up in the southern part of West Berlin (Neukoelln) was only 15 minutes walking distance from this world famous but horrific monument.

While graffiti was decorating the western exposure of this concrete monster, and interested tourists (and locals) could take a peek eastward from wooden watchtowers strategically positioned along the western demarcation line, a wide "death zone" or "no-man's land" extended from the Wall deep into East Berlin and was characterized by barbed wire, multiple rows of fences, wire-triggered explosive devices, watch dogs on mobile leashes and soldiers with rifles ready to shoot and kill those who dared to follow the soon-to-be-famous advertisement: "Let's Go West."

Seeing the Wall almost every day, being confined to "our" side and traveling on the rather bumpy East German autobahn "in transit" to West Germany, however, was part of our West Berlin normalcy.

In 1989, I was living in Schöneberg in the heart of West Berlin, right around the corner from Rathaus Schöneberg, the district's city hall. Rathaus Schöneberg had achieved some claim to fame when John F. Kennedy used it as the back-drop for his speech addressing a gigantic crowd of Berliners in 1963. The speech ended with the frequently quoted phrase: *"Ich bin ein Berliner"* (which does not mean: "I am a jelly-donut"). Kennedy's speech was directed to the population of West Berlin and was an assurance of America's commitment to—if necessary—defending the freedom of this encircled city. A few months after Kennedy's visit to West Berlin, he was assassinated in the streets of Dallas, Texas.

Paraphrasing the question the author poses will help clarify his main idea.

Paraphrasing this paragraph will ensure that you understand the situation described.

To break down these long sentences into simpler parts, consider one detail at a time and restate the information in your own words.

On November 9, 1989 late in the evening, I was watching the news on television in my cozy Schöneberg apartment. Gunter Schabowski, representative of the still-in-power East German government, was reading a declaration that surprisingly **proclaimed** East German citizens could—from now on—easily obtain travel permits to the West. It was apparently no longer required to provide unequivocal proof of a family emergency or similar hardship that would sometimes be accepted by East German authorities as justification for a "blitz-trip" to the golden West. Even in cases when a travel permit was granted, which was a rare event, the East German traveler's family had to stay behind to ensure his timely return to his beloved socialist fatherland. . . .

West Berliners lived in West Berlin and East Berliners were condemned to staying in East Berlin—that's the way it is. During the 28 years of my life that I had lived in this city, East Berliners traveling freely to West Berlin would be like running into polar bears in the Sahara desert. Thus, I did not pay too much attention to Schabowski's announcement and went to bed because I had to get up early the next day to go to work.

When I left my house the next morning I was stunned. Thousands of East German visitors had "arrived" and were hustling through the western part of the city. Visitors were waiting in long lines on sidewalks to receive their "Begrüssungsgeld" (welcome money), issued by the West German federal government through private banks. This was an unbelievable sight and the beginning of the probably most impressive political experience of my lifetime. The continuation of the story is well known.

I spent many days and nights in wintry Berlin witnessing pieces of the Wall being dismantled by East German soldiers and meeting people from the East. It was also the beginning of a period during which the West Berliners began to explore the other side of the iron curtain. Despite the physical proximity of East Berlin, this part of our city was largely unknown to us.

Four years after the fall of the Berlin Wall, in 1993, I moved to Seattle in the United States for job-related reasons. My wife is American. I am still captured by the events in November 1989 and will always remember them as a once-in-a-lifetime experience. . . .

Ich bin ein Berliner! And I will always be.

From Marco Mielcarek Seattle, Washington

Comparing Argumentative and Expository Texts

© 1. Key Ideas and Details (a) Paraphrase the first paragraph of the editorial.
(b) Paraphrase each succeeding paragraph. **(c)** Based on your paraphrases, explain how the author introduces and develops his analysis.

© 2. Key Ideas and Details (a) Paraphrase the first paragraph of the primary source.
(b) In what ways does the main idea in the editorial **connect** with the main idea of the primary source? Explain.

Content-Area Vocabulary

3. (a) Add the suffix *-ant* to the base word *accelerate*. Using a print or online dictionary, explain how changing the suffix alters the meaning and part of speech of the base word. **(b)** Do the same with the suffix *-ion*. **(c)** Use the words *accelerate, accelerant,* and *acceleration* in sentences that show their meanings.

⏱ Timed Writing

Argument: Response to Literature

Format
The prompt directs you to write a response to literature. Therefore, you must discuss your thoughts about a text you have read.

> Each of these texts presents a different perspective on the same historical event, the fall of the Berlin Wall in 1989. Choose one of the texts and write a response to literature in which you describe what you found compelling about the text. Explain what effect the author's writing had on you, citing and paraphrasing sections of text to support your response. (40 minutes)

Academic Vocabulary
When you *cite* a section or passage from a text, you quote it as support for the argument or ideas you are presenting.

5-Minute Planner

Complete these steps before you begin to write:

1. Read the prompt carefully and completely. Look for key words.

2. Consider both your first and later responses to each text. Then, decide which one you find more compelling. If a text is unclear to you, paraphrase to understand it better.

3. Skim the text you have chosen and take notes about details and information you will include as support in your response.

4. Use your notes to draft an outline. Then, use your outline and notes to draft your response.

Comparing Tone in Fiction and Nonfiction

The **tone** of a work is the writer's attitude toward his or her subject and audience. A writer may treat a subject seriously or playfully, with anger or sadness, or in an objective tone that shows no emotion.

Tone is closely related to **voice** and **persona**—the personality that a writer shows to readers. The tone of a selection may also be affected by the author's **cultural experiences,** since these may help shape his or her attitude toward a subject. The two works you are about to read express very different cultural experiences. One is a work of fiction by a Latin American writer who lived under an oppressive regime. That experience is reflected in both the events and tone of her story. The other work is a personal essay by a Mexican American writer who explores the legacy of family heritage. The cultural experiences she discusses and the tone she uses reflect her admiration for diversity.

Tone may be conveyed by the details the writer chooses to include. It can also be developed in the **diction,** or word choice, that the writer uses. Finally, tone may be revealed in direct statements of the writer's feelings.

In these two selections, "The Censors" and "The Leader in the Mirror," Luisa Valenzuela and Pat Mora look at perceptions and values created by society. However, each writer's work expresses different cultural experiences and takes a different tone. Use a chart like the one shown to note elements in each essay that create its distinctive tone.

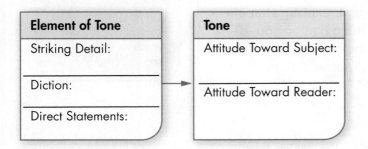

Element of Tone
Striking Detail:

Diction:

Direct Statements:

Tone
Attitude Toward Subject:

Attitude Toward Reader:

Common Core State Standards

Reading Literature
4. Determine the meaning of words and phrases as they are used in the text, including figurative and connotative meanings; analyze the cumulative impact of specific word choices on meaning and tone.

6. Analyze a particular point of view or cultural experience reflected in a work of literature from outside the United States, drawing on a wide reading of world literature.

Writing
1. Write arguments to support claims in an analysis of substantive topics or texts, using valid reasoning and relevant and sufficient evidence.

www.PHLitOnline.com

- Vocabulary flashcards
- Interactive journals
- More about the authors
- Selection audio
- Interactive graphic organizers

Can progress be made without *conflict?*

Writing About the Big Question

In these selections, authors present the idea that facing **adversity** in everyday life can change a person. Consider how dealing with challenges could help someone grow. Use these sentence starters to develop your ideas about the Big Question.

Because I have **struggled** with_____, I know _____.

If someone asked me for advice on handling **conflict**, I would say _____.

Meet the Authors

Luisa Valenzuela (b. 1938)
Author of "The Censors"

Born in Buenos Aires, the capital of Argentina, Luisa Valenzuela has lived in places ranging from bustling New York City to Tepoztlán, Mexico, a little village where people still speak the ancient Aztec language. Valenzuela brings the same sense of adventure to her writing by changing spellings, creating new words, and using puns.

Politics and Writing Having lived under a repressive regime, Valenzuela is a strong defender of human rights. In "The Censors," she explores the dilemmas that life in a repressive society poses.

Pat Mora (b. 1942)
Author of "The Leader in the Mirror"

Pat Mora was born in El Paso, Texas, just across the United States border from Juarez, Mexico. A graduate of the University of Texas, she taught school and served as a museum director before becoming a full-time writer.

Celebrating Heritage As a young girl, Mora spoke Spanish at home but did not want her friends at school to know. Now, she celebrates her Mexican American background. "I write in part because Hispanic perspectives need to be part of our literary heritage," she explains.

The Censors

Luisa Valenzuela   *translated by* David Unger

Background Like many other Latin American writers, Luisa
Valenzuela often addresses political issues in her writing. Her native
country, Argentina, now a democracy, has had an unfortunate history
of censorship and other human rights violations. In the 1970s, a military
regime took power, brutally hunting down suspected political foes and
censoring news and mail. In "The Censors," Valenzuela explores the
absurd aspects of such oppression.

Poor Juan! One day they caught him with his guard down
before he could even realize that what he had taken as a stroke of
luck was really one of fate's dirty tricks. These things happen the
minute you're careless, as one often is. Juancito let happiness—a
feeling you can't trust—get the better of him when he received from
a confidential source Mariana's new address in Paris and knew

that she hadn't forgotten him. Without thinking twice, he sat down at his table and wrote her a letter. The letter that now keeps his mind off his job during the day and won't let him sleep at night (what had he scrawled, what had he put on that sheet of paper he sent to Mariana?).

Juan knows there won't be a problem with the letter's contents, that it's irreproachable, harmless. But what about the rest? He knows that they examine, sniff, feel, and read between the lines of each and every letter, and check its tiniest comma and most accidental stain. He knows that all letters pass from hand to hand and go through all sorts of tests in the huge censorship offices and that, in the end, very few continue on their way. Usually it takes months, even years, if there aren't any snags; all this time the freedom, maybe even the life, of both sender and receiver is in jeopardy. And that's why Juan's so troubled: thinking that something might happen to Mariana because of his letters. Of all people, Mariana, who must finally feel safe there where she always dreamt she'd live. But he knows that the *Censor's Secret Command* operates all over the world and cashes in on the discount in air fares; there's nothing to stop them from going as far as that hidden Paris neighborhood, kidnapping Mariana, and returning to their cozy homes, certain of having fulfilled their noble mission.

Well, you've got to beat them to the punch, do what everyone tries to do: sabotage the machinery, throw sand in its gears, get to the bottom of the problem so as to stop it.

This was Juan's sound plan when he, like many others, applied for a censor's job—not because he had a calling or needed a job: no, he applied simply to intercept his own letter, a consoling albeit unoriginal idea. He was hired immediately, for each day more and more censors are needed and no one would bother to check on his references.

Ulterior motives couldn't be overlooked by the *Censorship Division,* but they needn't be too strict with those who applied. They knew how hard it would be for the poor guys to find the letter they wanted and even if they did, what's a letter or two when the new censor would snap up so many others? That's how Juan managed

Vocabulary
irreproachable (ir´ i prō´ chə bəl) *adj.* above criticism

ulterior (ul tir´ ē ər) *adj.* further; beyond what is openly stated or implied

Literary Analysis
Tone What does the author's use of phrases such as "beat them to the punch" and "throw sand in its gears" show you about her tone?

Reading Check
What does Juan fear may happen as a result of his letter?

The Censors **411**

to join the *Post Office's Censorship Division*, with a certain goal in mind.

The building had a festive air on the outside that contrasted with its inner staidness. Little by little, Juan was absorbed by his job, and he felt at peace since he was doing everything he could to get his letter for Mariana. He didn't even worry when, in his first month, he was sent to *Section K* where envelopes are very carefully screened for explosives.

It's true that on the third day, a fellow worker had his right hand blown off by a letter, but the division chief claimed it was sheer negligence on the victim's part. Juan and the other employees were allowed to go back to their work, though feeling less secure. After work, one of them tried to organize a strike to demand higher wages for unhealthy work, but Juan didn't join in; after thinking it over, he reported the man to his superiors and thus got promoted.

You don't form a habit by doing something once, he told himself as he left his boss's office. And when he was transferred to *Section F*, where letters are carefully checked for poison dust, he felt he had climbed a rung in the ladder.

By working hard, he quickly reached *Section E* where the job became more interesting, for he could now read and analyze the letters' contents. Here he could even hope to get hold of his letter, which, judging by the time that had elapsed, had gone through the other sections and was probably floating around in this one.

Soon his work became so absorbing that his noble mission blurred in his mind. Day after day he crossed out whole paragraphs in red ink, pitilessly chucking many letters into the censored basket. These were horrible days when he was shocked by the subtle and conniving ways employed by people to pass on subversive messages; his instincts were so sharp that he found behind a simple "the weather's unsettled" or "prices continue to soar" the wavering hand of someone secretly scheming to overthrow the Government.

▲ **Critical Viewing**
What similarities and differences exist between the building represented in this painting and the building in which Juan works? **[Connect]**

Vocabulary
staidness (stād´ nəs) *n.* state of being settled; calm

Literary Analysis
Tone Based on the details in this paragraph, what do you think is the author's attitude about Juan and his hard work as a censor?

His zeal brought him swift promotion. We don't know if this made him happy. Very few letters reached him in *Section B*—only a handful passed the other hurdles—so he read them over and over again, passed them under a magnifying glass, searched for microprint with an electronic microscope, and tuned his sense of smell so that he was beat by the time he made it home. He'd barely manage to warm up his soup, eat some fruit, and fall into bed, satisfied with having done his duty. Only his darling mother worried, but she couldn't get him back on the right track. She'd say, though it wasn't always true: Lola called, she's at the bar with the girls, they miss you, they're waiting for you. Or else she'd leave a bottle of red wine on the table. But Juan wouldn't overdo it: any distraction could make him lose his edge, and the perfect censor had to be alert, keen, attentive, and sharp to nab cheats. He had a truly patriotic task, both self-denying and uplifting.

His basket for censored letters became the best fed as well as the most cunning basket in the whole Censorship Division. He was about to congratulate himself for having finally discovered his true mission, when his letter to Mariana reached his hands. Naturally, he censored it without regret. And just as naturally, he couldn't stop them from executing him the following morning, another victim of his devotion to his work.

Spiral Review
Character Development How has Juan's job changed his attitude toward censorship?

Literary Analysis
Tone What does the last line of this selection contribute to the author's tone?

Critical Thinking

Cite textual evidence to support your responses.

1. **Key Ideas and Details (a)** What worries Juan at the start of the story? **(b) Infer:** From this concern, what can you tell about the situation in Juan's country?

2. **Key Ideas and Details (a)** Why does Juan apply for a job as a censor? **(b) Analyze:** What character traits make Juan a good censor?

3. **Key Ideas and Details (a)** How does Juan's career as a censor progress? **(b) Draw Conclusions:** Why does his attitude about censorship change?

4. **Integration of Knowledge and Ideas (a)** What advice would you give Juan on handling the conflicts he faces? **(b)** What details from the story would help you convince Juan to follow your advice? **(c)** Do you think this story suggests a positive outcome of the conflict? Why or why not? *[Connect to the Big Question: Can progress be made without conflict?]*

THE
LEADER
in the
MIRROR

Pat Mora

Each year, the newspaper in my hometown of El Paso, Texas, honors the top five academic achievers from the local high schools at an annual banquet. Last year when I addressed the group, the room at the fancy hotel was full of proud students and their relatives.

The aspirations of the students were like a dose of powerful vitamins, filling parents, educators and guests with energy.

I began by congratulating the family members and teachers for being steady beacons[1] for those young people. In a society that undervalues families and educators, they had truly lived their commitments.

As I was planning the talk I would give to this group, I wondered how best to create an occasion for reflection. What could I say to the audience about the daily struggle to create a meaningful life?

I remembered planning parties for my children when they were young: the careful selection of party favors, the mementos for the guests to carry away. Since this banquet was to be a party of sorts, an academic celebration, I asked myself what favors I would choose for each place at the table.

I knew I would be very popular with the students if I could give them keys to a new red car or tickets to an island vacation. But I am a writer, not a millionaire. So I decided to give them imaginary gifts: Each student would receive confetti, a tape recorder, a photograph and a mirror—symbols and metaphors to take with them through life.

I hoped that most of the students were going to enroll in college. The confetti would be for their private celebrations, those solitary moments when they had passed a test that worried them, finished a difficult paper at 2 a.m., found a summer internship.[2] Sometimes, even when no one else is around, it's important to celebrate when we have struggled and succeeded—to sprinkle a little confetti on our own heads.

Why a tape recorder? I read them my poem "Immigrants."

---

1. **beacons** (bē´ kənz) *n.* guiding lights; shining examples.
2. **internship** (in´ tʉrn´ ship´) *n.* temporary job providing training for an inexperienced young person.

Vocabulary
aspirations (as´ pə rā´ shənz) *n.* strong ambitions

Literary Analysis
Tone Which details here show you that the writer might be amused by students' values?

Reading Check

What does Mora say she used to do when planning parties for her children?

Immigrants
wrap their babies in the American flag,
feed them mashed hot dogs and apple pie,
name them Bill and Daisy,
buy them blonde dolls that blink blue
eyes or a football and tiny cleats
before the baby can even walk,
speak to them in thick English,
  hallo, babee, hallo,
whisper in Spanish or Polish
when the baby sleeps, whisper
in a dark parent bed, that dark
parent fear, "Will they like
our boy, our girl, our fine american
boy, our fine american girl?"

As a writer, I understand the value and necessity of knowing my past, of keeping that door open. My family stories are my **catalyst** for creativity. All of us have people in our lives whose voices merit saving if we'll only take the time.

Vocabulary
catalyst (kat´ ə list´) *n.* person or thing that triggers an event or action

▶ **Critical Viewing**
Drawing on the details in this photograph of El Paso, explain what sort of life Mora's audience might lead. **[Speculate]**

My own father was once a paper boy for the newspaper hosting the banquet. I might not have known that fact, nor his long history of hard work, had I not been listening to him with my tape recorder a few years ago. I did not want the students to wait as long as I had to begin preserving the rich inheritance of their family voices. The strength of their heritage would give them the courage to face the future.

My third gift was a photograph of the El Paso/Juarez border: the Chihuahua Desert. the Rio Grande,[3] a stern mountain, two sprawling border cities. Like our families, our geography is part of who we are.

When I was growing up on the U.S. side of that border, the society around me tried in subtle and not-so-subtle ways to convince me that my Mexican heritage was inferior to that of Anglo-Americans. I hope that today's educators on the border and throughout this nation are now committed to multiculturalism, to motivating the next generation to draw on their heritage as a resource for learning. The U.S. has been described as the first international country: Our varied cultures are our common wealth.

Borders—and if we're attentive, we realize we all live on borders, whether they are national or not—are sites of tension and sites for learning. Borders invite us to confront differences, inequities and stereotypes. They invite us to work for multicultural cooperation and to celebrate multilingual richness.

---

3. **El Paso** (el pas´ ō) / **Juárez** (hwä´ res) . . . **Chihuahua** (chi wä´ wä) . . . **Rio Grande** (rē´ ō grand´) El Paso is a city in Texas on the Rio Grande, the river forming the border between Texas and Mexico. Juárez, in the Mexican state of Chihuahua, is directly across the river.

Vocabulary
inheritance (in her´ i təns) *n.* gift handed down to a later generation

Literary Analysis
Tone What tone do the details and diction in this paragraph help to create?

Reading Check

What aspects of life does the writer intend the second and third gifts to reflect?

The final gift of the evening, a mirror, was for serious gazing. I asked the students if they saw a leader when they looked into their mirrors. My guess is that too many of our young people do not see themselves as leaders because they don't look, dress or sound like the images of leaders presented to us. But leaders come in all colors, shapes and sizes. Some are talkative while others are quiet, but they all share a determination to contribute to the society of the future.

I urged the students to look often in their mirrors and to ask themselves these questions: "Am I satisfied with this world? If not, what will I do to improve it?" For if we are shaped by our surroundings, we in turn shape them. We deceive ourselves if we believe that we can live neutral[4] lives.

One-third of this nation now traces its heritage to regions other than Western Europe. We will continue to squander[5] our talent if our leaders—in politics, science, business, education and the arts—do not reflect our grand variety. I urged the students (and all of us) to ponder the strength of the mountains around us, to rise to the challenges.

---

4. **neutral** (noō′ trəl) *adj.* not taking a position; lacking vivid color.
5. **squander** (skwän′ dər) *v.* spend or use wastefully or extravagantly.

Critical Thinking

Cite textual evidence to support your responses.

1. **Key Ideas and Details (a)** On what occasion does Mora give her speech? **(b) Infer:** What does the invitation to give this speech show about Mora's achievements?

2. **Key Ideas and Details (a)** What "gifts" does Mora give the students? **(b) Interpret:** Explain the meaning or purpose of each. **(c) Connect:** In what way is each gift connected to the idea of respect for one's own cultural experiences and heritage?

3. **Key Ideas and Details** Which of Mora's gifts would you value the most? Explain your choice.

4. **Integration of Knowledge and Ideas** In this speech, Mora mentions that borders are "sites of tension and sites of learning." **(a)** Using examples from the speech, explain how tension and adversity have affected Mora's life. **(b)** How might tension lead to learning? *[Connect to the Big Question: Can progress be made without conflict?]*

Comparing Tones

1. Key Ideas and Details What is each author's attitude toward the following concepts? Cite textual evidence.

Valenzuela: (a) censorship **(b)** governments that censor

Mora: (c) heritage **(d)** consumer goods

2. Craft and Structure (a) Use a chart like the one shown to record words and phrases that express each writer's **tone**. Analyze each writer's attitude toward the perceptions created by a society. **(b)** Based on your chart, write a sentence comparing the mixture of tones in each piece.

	Inspirational	Sarcastic	Analytical	Other
Diction				
Direct Statements				
Other Details				

3. Craft and Structure Based on the mix of tones in each piece, describe the **voice,** or "personality on the page," of each writer.

⏱ Timed Writing

Argumentative Text: Essay

In an argumentative essay, compare and evaluate the success of each author's writing style in conveying an idea to readers. Consider tone and diction and the way in which they shape readers' understanding. Support your response with details from each text. **(25 minutes)**

5-Minute Planner

1. Read the prompt carefully and completely.
2. Use these questions to gather details for your essay.
   - How would you categorize each writer's tone and diction?
   - How did each author's writing style affect your ability to understand her ideas?
   - Which author did you find more successful? Why?
3. Review each text to locate textual evidence to support your ideas.
4. Reread the prompt, and then draft your essay.

Writing Workshop

 **Common Core State Standards**

Writing

1. Write arguments to support claims in an analysis of substantive topics or texts, using valid reasoning and relevant and sufficient evidence.

1.a. Introduce precise claim(s), distinguish the claim(s) from alternate or opposing claims, and create an organization that establishes clear relationships among claim(s), counterclaims, reasons, and evidence.

Write an Argumentative Text

Exposition: Problem-and-Solution Essay

Defining the Form Individuals, schools, communities, and even entire nations face problems. **Problem-and-solution writing** helps identify the problems and offers reasonable remedies. In this workshop, you will write a problem-and-solution essay on a subject of your choice.

Assignment Write a problem-and-solution essay to identify a problem in your school or community and present one or more solutions. Your essay should feature these elements:

✓ *a clear description* of a specific, real-life problem

✓ an *analysis* of the most important parts of the problem

✓ *proof, such as facts, anecdotes, or examples,* that shows the significance of the problem in a way your readers can understand

✓ *transitions* that link the parts of the essay to form a coherent whole

✓ *a complete explanation* of one or more possible solutions

✓ *your personal evaluation* of any solutions you discuss

✓ error-free grammar, *including correct subject-verb agreement*

To preview the criteria on which your problem-and-solution essay may be assessed, see the rubric on page 427.

 **Writing Workshop:** *Work in Progress*

Review the work you did on pages 367 and 399.

WRITE GUY
Jeff Anderson, M.Ed.

What Do You Notice?

Word Choice

The following passage is from Edgar Allan Poe's "The Masque of the Red Death." Read the passage several times.

The abbey was amply provisioned. With such precautions the courtiers might bid defiance to contagion.

With a partner, discuss the qualities that make this passage interesting.

Now, think about ways you might use word choice in your problem-and-solution essay.

Reading-Writing Connection

To get a feel for problem-and-solution essays, read "Nobel Lecture" by Alexander Solzhenitsyn on page 548.

Prewriting/Planning Strategies

Browse media sources. Look through newspapers, magazines, and Internet sites for recent stories that discuss a problem. Jot down problems for which you think you can offer solutions. Choose a topic from among these ideas.

Analyze your audience. Decide which people you want to reach—community members, students, or others. Consider that group's interests and needs. Conduct brief interviews to identify a problem that troubles your audience, and then choose a topic to pursue.

Categorize to narrow your topic. Some problems may be too large for your essay. Focus on manageable, local aspects of an issue.

- Write these categories: World, Nation, State, Town, and School. Identify one aspect of the problem for each category.

- Focus your essay on the aspect that you wrote under the local categories, such as "Town" or "School." For example, you cannot solve the problem of war in a few pages. However, you can write about the problem of bullies at school.

Evaluate possible solutions. After you have focused your essay on a specific and manageable problem, think about potential solutions. Brainstorm for practical and logical ways to solve the issue. Before you draft, use a chart to evaluate potential solutions. Be sure each solution can be supported with specific and concrete details. Then, consider the advantages and disadvantages of each solution. As you get ready to write, plan to offer the best solutions in your essay.

PHLit
Online!
www.PHLitOnline.com
- Author video: Writing Process
- Author video: Rewards of Writing

Problem		Solutions	Pros	Cons
Overcrowded computer lab	→	1. Teachers split classes into three parts, each with separate deadlines.	Students won't need the lab at the same time.	Teachers will have to manage a lot of deadlines.
Details: students have the same deadlines; all need the lab at the same times		2. Students sign up for lab time one week in advance.	Students will have to plan their work.	Some students may not sign up.

Drafting Strategies

Create an essay map. For additional support during drafting, write each important idea on an index card. Then, write each supporting detail, such as a fact or an example, on an index card. Using the index cards, arrange the ideas and details in different orders. Consider placing your most powerful idea near the end of the essay, before your personal evaluation. Once you have determined the best order, number the cards and use them as a map for your writing.

Write an outline. An outline gives you a quick overview of all your points. It also lets you figure out how best to structure, or order, the information and reasoning you want to present. The outlines here show two possible organizations for a problem-and-solution essay.

Common Core State Standards

Writing

1.c. Use words, phrases, and clauses to link the major sections of the text, create cohesion, and clarify the relationships between claim(s) and reasons, between reasons and evidence, and between claim(s) and counterclaims.

1.d. Establish and maintain a formal style and objective tone while attending to the norms and conventions of the discipline in which they are writing.

Outline A

I. Description of Problem
    A. One aspect
    B. Another aspect
II. Explanation of Solution
    A. How it solves the first aspect
    B. How it solves the second aspect
III. Personal Evaluation

Outline B

I. Description of Problem
    A. One aspect
    B. Another aspect
II. Explanation of First Solution
    A. Advantages
    B. Disadvantages
III. Explanation of Second Solution
    A. Advantages
    B. Disadvantages
IV. Personal Evaluation

Address your audience. Some audiences, such as your friends or young readers, might respond best to informal language. In general, though, audiences will respect your thinking more if you use formal language.

    Informal: Face it—lots of us like to eat junk food for lunch.

    Formal: When choosing their own meals, many students select foods with little nutritional value.

Stick to the facts. To convince your audience that the problem you describe is genuine, present factual information in an objective way rather than personal opinions. Reserve your opinions for your personal evaluation in the conclusion of your essay. Your personal evaluation should judge the quality of the solutions you included in your essay.

Use appropriate transitions. Show the relationships between your ideas by linking them with transitions. To show contrast, use transitions like *on the other hand.* To show cause-and-effect relationships, use transitions like *as a result.*

Writers on Writing

C. J. Cherryh On Revising to Tighten Sentences

C. J. Cherryh is the author of "The Threads of Time" (p. 231).

Knowing what to delete is as important as knowing what to write in the first place. The value of that advice is illustrated both by "The Threads of Time" and by the passage below, which I have written especially for this workshop. The last few sentences of "Threads" relate to the novel that the story originally introduced. Now that the story exists on its own, I'd like to strike that final passage. It's too late for that, but in the passage below, I show how the timely deletion of unnecessary words can tighten a narrative.

"Perfect sentences are created by good editing."
—C. J. Cherryh

Professional Model:

Original writing by C. J. Cherryh

"Well," I said, ~~taking a moment to look out at the sunset~~ gazing over the *porch* railing *at the gathering dark,* ~~of the porch which my grandfather had built,~~ ~~"I really think, well,~~ "it was about this time of evening, yes—back ~~sometime~~ in June. ~~when~~ I saw ~~a truly~~ *something* terrible ~~thing over there~~ in the garden, right *over* there by the rose bushes."

~~The little girl who was standing next to me on the porch looked~~ *Eight-year-old Susan glanced* up at me, wide-eyed. ~~She had blue eyes. She was my sister's daughter. She was about eight. She looked very scared at first.~~

~~It wasn't fair to scare the girl. She was just like her mother. I used to tell her mother stories, too, when we were both kids in this house.~~ Then *those eyes narrowed:* "Mama said you~~'re~~ *were* a liar." ~~," she said.~~

Was I surprised? No. I knew my sister. ~~Her mother Louise never believed me, either.~~ Louise hated imagination: ~~and she missed a lot of~~ *ever so many* true things ~~sat~~ *that* ~~were~~ right under her nose, ~~but she never believed~~ *simply because she wouldn't believe* she saw them.

I really want the reader to hear the word "June." I set it off with a long dash. Then, I cut out the choppy, chattery little words, and set the rhythms of the sentence to land on "something terrible in the garden."

"Look" is a neutral word. "Glance" is sharp and fast. Choosing that word for "look" changes the impression in the reader's mind.

Do I need to spell out specifically who Louise is? Once the little girl talks about "mama" and I talk about "my sister," I trust my readers to figure it out.

Revising Strategies

Common Core State Standards

Writing
5. Develop and strengthen writing as needed by planning, revising, editing, rewriting, or trying a new approach, focusing on addressing what is most significant for a specific purpose and audience.

Language
3. Apply knowledge of language to make effective choices for meaning or style.

Ask questions to consider effectiveness. Review your draft to uncover illogical connections, weakly supported examples, or missing information. Ask yourself the following questions. If you have difficulty providing clear answers, adjust your writing.

- Is there a logical flow to my ideas?
- Did I provide enough details to support my ideas? Are there more facts, anecdotes, or examples that would be useful to include?
- Did I provide more details than I really need?
- Does every statement make sense? If not, what did I mean to say?
- Is this statement a fact or an opinion? If it is an opinion, am I sure I want to include it?
- Have I evaluated the solution I proposed?

Evaluate tone and style. The words you choose establish your **tone**—your attitude toward your subject and audience. When appropriate, you might want to present an optimistic or a pessimistic tone regarding a particular problem or solution.

Optimistic: Our challenge is to discover an effective solution.

Pessimistic: The difficulty will be in finding a workable solution.

Replace dull words. Word choice is also key to writing style. Replace any dull words and phrases with vivid, expressive writing, and define technical terms your readers may not know.

Flat: The board will make the final decision about the program.

Vivid: The fate of the program lies in the hands of the board.

Model: Revising to Replace Dull Words

        convincing   implemented immediately
The proposal is ~~good~~ and should be ~~used soon.~~

> The writer replaced dull, lifeless words with more precise and vivid choices.

Peer Review

Ask a partner to read your draft and then conduct a conference about your work. Your reader can ask about the overall structure as well as specific details. Use your discussion to guide your revisions.

Subject-Verb Agreement

For a subject and verb to agree, both must be singular or plural.

Identifying Errors Errors in agreement can occur when the subject and verb are separated by other words, phrases, or clauses. In the examples below, subjects are underlined, and verbs are set in italic type.

Singular Subject and Verb

Incorrect: The <u>decision</u> of the board members *are* final.

Correct: The <u>decision</u> of the board members *is* final.

Plural Subject and Verb

Incorrect: <u>Students</u> who park here seldom *follows* the rules.

Correct: <u>Students</u> who park here seldom *follow* the rules.

Agreement errors also occur with compound subjects and with indefinite pronouns serving as subjects.

Identifying Indefinite Pronouns These are the most common indefinite pronouns categorized by number:

Singular: anybody, anyone, each, either, every, everybody, neither, nobody, nothing, somebody, something

Plural: both, few, many, others, several

Singular or Plural: all, any, more, most, none, some

PH WRITING COACH

Further instruction and practice are available in *Prentice Hall Writing Coach.*

Fixing Errors To correct mismatched subjects and verbs, follow these steps:

1. Identify the subject and determine whether it is singular or plural.

2. Select the verb that matches the subject.

   - For compound subjects joined by *and*, use the plural form.

   - For singular subjects joined by *or* or *nor*, use the singular form.

   - When the subject is an indefinite pronoun, use the appropriate form of the verb.

Grammar in Your Writing

Circle all the subjects in two paragraphs of your draft. For each subject, draw an arrow to the verb that tells what it does. Make sure that you have used the form of the verb that agrees with the subject.

Student Model: Jacquelyn Simone, Endicott, NY

Brand Names

A great majority of youth today have become walking advertisements. A person's worth is not based on the content of their character, but on the contents of their wallets. Labels have become the measure of merit, and the right clothing can lead to success and popularity. Society has forgotten the value of self-expression. Individuality has been dissolved in a world full of expensive brand names and styles. The problem has several main parts:

Expense: Students experience great pressure to purchase brand name clothes. However, these articles cost more than regular clothes, making it a challenge for many people to afford them. Despite these realities, those teens who do not own a popular brand are often shunned or ridiculed.

Sameness: Clothes should be a reflection of who you are, not an imitation of what you wish you were. For many teens, clothes no longer express their individuality. Instead, brand names express someone else's idea of who teens are supposed to be.

Poor Self-Esteem: We have a certain image of the ideal body, which has been fed to us by magazines, television, and movies. Girls are expected to be thin and tall, while boys should be muscular. However, everyone has a different body, and few fit these unrealistic images. The clothes that we are told to buy often suit only that one uncommon body type. The rest of the population is left to try to squeeze into stylish clothes or feel inferior. For many teens, self-esteem drops with every outfit they cannot wear.

The problem is complex, but there are some solutions:

Change the media: Magazines should feature models with more common body types wearing flattering clothing. Fewer television programs should be dedicated to fashion, and more should focus on human character. Department stores should offer a greater selection of sizes, styles, and prices. Clothing manufacturers might be able to make attractive but inexpensive clothes, so that costly brands do not have a fashion monopoly.

Change values: Adults should try to build children's identities so that teens are able to express themselves instead of copying whatever they are told is stylish. Schools could offer seminars on celebrating our personal distinctiveness.

Diversity is beautiful, yet it is far too often hidden beneath layers of conformity. Making more affordable and unique styles could lessen the problem of people being judged based on the brand of their clothes. Clothing can be a wonderful medium of self-expression, but only if we eliminate the pressure of dressing the same as everyone else.

In her introduction, Jacquelyn clearly explains the problem she will discuss.

The writer breaks the problem down into its elements.

Jacquelyn organizes her solutions into two main categories.

In her conclusion, the writer restates her key points.

Editing and Proofreading

Check your draft for errors in grammar, spelling, capitalization, and punctuation.

Focus on clear references. Make sure you have used *that* and *which* correctly. Use *that* to introduce adjective clauses that are essential to the meaning of the noun and *which* to introduce clauses that are not essential to the meaning of the noun.

Publishing and Presenting

Consider one of the following ways to share your essay with others:

Launch a discussion. Read your essay to your classmates. Then, allow your audience members to ask questions and propose their own solutions.

Submit your essay. If your essay focused on a matter of local interest, send it to your school or community newspaper. If your school or town has its own Web site, consider posting your essay. Create links to appropriate background information, and update your essay as new information becomes available.

Reflecting on Your Writing

Writer's Journal Jot down your answers to these questions:
How did writing about the work help you understand it?
Which strategy would you use again? Why?

Spiral Review
Earlier in this unit, you learned about **action and linking verbs** (p. 366) and **active and passive voice** (tenses) (p. 398). Review your essay to be sure that you have often used action verbs and active voice.

PH WRITING COACH

Further instruction and practice are available in *Prentice Hall Writing Coach*.

Rubric for Self-Assessment

Find evidence in your writing to address each category. Then, use the rating scale to grade your work.

Criteria	Rating Scale not very → very
Focus: How well do you explain a problem?	1 2 3 4 5
Organization: How logically do you present one or more solutions?	1 2 3 4 5
Support/Elaboration: How effectively do you use facts, anecdotes, or examples to support your ideas?	1 2 3 4 5
Style: How confidently do you state your evaluations of the solutions?	1 2 3 4 5
Conventions: How correct is your grammar, especially your use of subject-verb agreement?	1 2 3 4 5

Vocabulary Workshop

Word Origins

Words come into the English language from many sources. A word's **origin,** or source, is shown in its **etymology.** A word's etymology identifies the language in which the word first appeared and tells how its spelling and meaning have changed over time.

English as a language dates back to about the year 500, when Germanic tribes including Angles, Saxons, and Jutes settled in England. This first English language is known as Old English. In the years following 1066, English changed dramatically as a result of the Norman invasion, which brought Old French to England and produced what we now call Middle English. During a period known as the Renaissance, roughly between 1300 and 1500, there was a renewed interest in the classical languages of Greek and Latin that greatly influenced the English language. As a result, grammar, spelling, and pronunciation changed and Modern English emerged.

This chart shows how a few words first entered the English language.

Word	Definition	Origin
Thursday	the fifth day of the week	Old Norse word *Thorsdagr,* which means "Thor's day," a reference to the god of thunder in Norse mythology
martial	of or suitable for war	Latin word *martialis,* which means "of Mars," a reference to the god of war in Roman mythology
narcissistic	showing excessive self-love	reference to Narcissus, a young man in Greek mythology who falls in love with his own reflection

Common Core State Standards

Language
4.c. Consult general and specialized reference materials, both print and digital, to find the pronunciation of a word or determine or clarify its precise meaning, its part of speech, or its etymology.

Practice A Look up each of the following words in a print or an online dictionary. Define each word and explain its origin.

1. psyche
2. algebra
3. Saturday
4. anger
5. sleuth
6. theater

Practice B Each numbered question contains a word that has come into the English language from the Greek, Latin, or Old Norse language or mythology. Use a dictionary to find each italicized word's origin and meaning. Then, use that information to answer the question.

1. How did the word *tantalizing* come to mean "tempting" or "enticing"?
2. What qualities does something *titanic* share with the Titans in Greek mythology?
3. What kind of days was the word *dismal* originally used to describe?
4. For which Norse god is *Wednesday* named?
5. What kind of journey is an *odyssey*, and which hero of Greek mythology took this kind of journey?
6. Why is the word *mercurial* used to describe someone who is lively and quick-witted?

Activity Use a print or an online dictionary to identify the source of each of the following English words. Then, use a graphic organizer like the one shown to explain how the English word and its source word are related. The first item has been completed as an example.

1. consequence
2. agony
3. detour
4. thespian
5. pendant

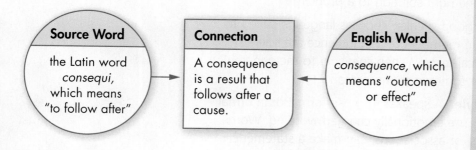

Source Word	Connection	English Word
the Latin word *consequi*, which means "to follow after"	A consequence is a result that follows after a cause.	*consequence*, which means "outcome or effect"

Comprehension and Collaboration

With a partner, research these words, which are all derived from ancient Greek theater. In writing, explain how each word's theatrical meaning relates to its everyday meaning.

catastrophe
antagonist
chorus

Communications Workshop

Viewing and Evaluating a Speech

Do not believe everything you hear in a speech, regardless of who presents it. Analyze the presenter's message and speaking skills as you listen.

Learn the Skills

Use the following strategies to help you complete the activity on page 431.

Identify the purpose. The purpose of a speech may be to pay tribute to someone, to inform, to entertain, or to persuade. Identifying the speaker's purpose will help you decide whether or not the presenter achieves his or her goal and therefore whether or not the speech is effective.

Assess the arguments. A speaker should present and support clear arguments, or ideas. Analyze the types of argument used by the speaker, such as *causation,* or making a connection between a cause and an effect; *analogy,* or comparing two situations to prove a point; and *authority,* or using an expert's credibility to support an argument.

Consider point of view. When listening to a speech, consider the speaker's point of view, which can be understood as the life experiences that have shaped the speaker and the perspective from which he or she presents information. A point of view can sometimes cause the speaker to be biased toward a certain way of thinking. An effective speaker presents both sides of an argument and anticipates opposing viewpoints.

Consider logic and accuracy. Use your knowledge to check the accuracy of statements. Look for fallacious, or faulty, reasoning, such as insisting that there is only one right solution to a problem.

Check language level. A good speaker chooses language suited to the audience. For example, if members of the audience are scientists, the speaker may use technical terms. When speaking to the general public, the speaker may use common terms instead.

Note word choice and style. A speaker may use formal or informal language, or he or she may use emotionally charged wording. Words with powerful connotations, or associations, can make a statement memorable or make opinions appear to be facts.

Look at nonverbal communication. A speaker communicates with more than words. The speaker's body language, eye contact, gestures, vocal tone, and pacing affect the audience's reaction.

Common Core State Standards

Speaking and Listening
3. Evaluate a speaker's point of view, reasoning, and use of evidence and rhetoric, identifying any fallacious reasoning or exaggerated or distorted evidence.

Practice the Skills

© Presentation of Knowledge and Ideas Use what you've learned in this workshop to perform the following task.

ACTIVITY: Evaluate an Argument

Listen to a speech presented in your school or find one online or on television. Take notes to evaluate how the style and structure support or undermine the speaker's purpose and the speech's meaning. Answer the following questions in your notes.

- What is the speaker's main argument?
- How well do the details support this argument?
- Does the speaker appear biased in his or her point of view? Explain.
- Does the speaker make logical and accurate statements and avoid faulty reasoning? Explain.
- Is the speaker's word choice and use of connotations and emotionally charged language effective and suited to his or her audience? Explain.

As you listen to the speech, use the following Speech Checklist to analyze the purpose, point of view, and communication skills.

Speech Checklist

Rate how well the speaker did each of the following on a scale of 1 (very poor) to 5 (very good). Explain your ratings.

Purpose and Support
- ❏ conveyed a clear purpose   Rating: _____
- ❏ presented sufficient supporting arguments   Rating: _____
- ❏ avoided faulty reasoning   Rating: _____

Point of View
- ❏ conveyed a clear position without bias   Rating: _____
- ❏ presented opposing viewpoints fairly   Rating: _____

Communication Skills
- ❏ chose words with audience in mind   Rating: _____
- ❏ used effective body language, eye contact, and vocal tone   Rating: _____

© Comprehension and Collaboration After you have evaluated the speech, work with a small group of classmates and compare your notes. Work together to build a consensus about whether the speaker's arguments, supporting details, and style effectively fulfilled his or her purpose.

Cumulative Review

I. Reading Literature

Directions: *Read the passage. Then, answer each question that follows.*

Common Core
State Standards

RL.9-10.1, RL.9-10.2, RL.9-10.3, RL.9-10.4; W.9-10.2
[For the full wording of the standards, see the standards chart in the front of your textbook.]

Futbol

Alex clutched the football under his arm and rubbed its rough surface. The plane was taking off. As he watched from his window seat, the cars on the freeway grew smaller and smaller, until they looked like toys. He gazed out over the city, trying to spot the football field at his old high school. He knew he would not see it again for a long time. Alex and his family were moving to Mexico City, Mexico. His dad had taken a job there.

"It will be an adventure, Alex," his dad had said when he announced the move. "You'll learn a new language and make new friends."

"But I'll have to leave my old friends—and football!" Alex had argued.

"They have football in Mexico—just not your kind."

"Very funny, dad! They call it *futbol*—we call it *soccer*. And I've never really played soccer." All during the conversation, Alex had tossed his football in the air, trying to imagine life without the game.

As soon as the family was settled in Mexico City, Alex enrolled in school. Although there were many English-speaking students, Alex still felt he didn't belong, like a <u>misfit.</u> He kept his football in his locker during the day and set it on the table by his bed at night.

One evening, a few months after the move, Alex's dad entered his room. "Alex, this is enough. You can't sit at home each night. I've enrolled you in a Saturday soccer league with kids from the neighborhood."

"You can't do that! I'm not going," Alex protested. "Those kids have played soccer all their lives!"

"Not all of them, Alex. Some are new to *futbol.*"

"Futbol. Soccer. I've never played it. I'll look stupid."

"You were a wide receiver on the football team, and you know how to move. You'll do fine."

Saturday after Saturday, Alex went to the field, but he always watched on the sidelines as the boys played. Alex was an outsider. Afterwards, he would go home and toss his football in the air for hours. One Saturday, the ball came flying towards his spot on the sidelines, high over the heads of the players. Without thinking, Alex stepped forward and butted it back into play with his head. "Bueno! Bueno!" a dark-haired boy shouted at Alex with a grin. That afternoon, Alex picked up his football, gave it a pat, and put it on the top shelf in his closet.

1. Which of the following sentences is an example of direct characterization?

   A. Alex was an outsider.
   B. "It will be an adventure, Alex."
   C. Alex's dad entered his room.
   D. "Some are new to *futbol.*"

2. Which statement best describes the **theme?**

   A. Change can be painful, but it opens doors to new experiences.
   B. People around the world are very similar.
   C. Moving to a different country is an exciting adventure.
   D. Not everyone is good at sports.

3. From which **point of view** is the story told?

   A. first person
   B. second person
   C. third person
   D. limited

4. **Vocabulary** What is the best definition of the underlined word *misfit?*

   A. someone who is not intelligent
   B. someone who feels out of place
   C. someone who feels superior
   D. someone who is disgusted

5. Which sentence best represents the **character development** that happens during the story?

   A. "Bueno! Bueno!" a dark haired boy shouted at Alex with a grin.
   B. That afternoon, Alex picked up his football, gave it a pat, and put it on the top shelf in his closet.
   C. He gazed out over the city, trying to spot the football field at his old high school.
   D. One Saturday, the ball came flying towards his spot on the sidelines, high over the heads of the players.

6. Which of the following statements includes the most **description?**

   A. He kept his football in his locker during the day and set it on the table by his bed at night.
   B. "And I've never really played soccer."
   C. He knew he would not see it again for a long time.
   D. As he watched from his window seat, the cars on the freeway grew smaller and smaller, until they looked like toys.

7. Which of the following best describes the **symbolic meaning** of Alex's football?

   A. his anger at his father for the move
   B. the family's move
   C. his source of comfort in new surroundings
   D. the football team's dedication

8. Which of the following does *not* describe the story's **setting?**

   A. an airplane
   B. a *futbol* field in Mexico City
   C. Alex's bedroom in Mexico
   D. a football field in the United States

9. The **dialogue** reveals that Alex's father—

   A. wants to leave Mexico City.
   B. believes Alex will adjust to *futbol.*
   C. has a high-paying job.
   D. knows how to play football.

⏱ Timed Writing

10. Write an informational essay in which you **describe** the character of Alex and **explain** how his character develops. Cite evidence from the text to support your analysis.

GO ON

II. Reading Informational Text

Directions: *Read the passage. Then, answer each question that follows.*

Common Core
State Standards

RI.9-10.7; W.9-10.5; L.9-10.1,
L.9-10.4.a
[For the full wording of the standards,
see the standards chart in the front of
your textbook.]

Association Football

In the United States, tens of thousands of kids play a game called *soccer.* Elsewhere the same ball game is called *association football,* or, in some countries, *futbol.* Around the world, about 40 million players are registered, plus there are thousands of others who play pickup games in streets, parks, school yards, and vacant lots, and even on beaches.

The game is played with two teams of eleven players each. The <u>ultimate</u> goal is to move the ball into the opposing team's goal net, without using the hands or arms. Players may bump the ball with their heads, hips, or knees, or they may kick the ball, but only the goalie, who stands in front of the goal, can touch the ball with his or her hands. The rules are simple, and the game can be played almost anywhere, which makes it the most popular game in the world, not only for players but for spectators as well.

Champions!

It was a brisk, overcast Sunday morning—the best kind for soccer. I walked on to the field and was greeted by high fives from my ten excited teammates. It was championship game day. Proud spectators with painted faces colored the stands, wildly waving striped flags and banners. "Today is the day," I thought to myself. "Nothing gets by these hands today." I put my gloves on and clapped my hands three times for good luck, a ritual I started years before on the streets in my neighborhood. The whistle sounded. I protected the goal, throwing my body in front of every shot. With 30 seconds of play left, the score was 1–0, our favor. Suddenly, I saw two fast and furious feet dribbling the ball toward my goal. I glanced at the clock—22 seconds left and counting down. I took a deep breath and put my hands up to block the shot I knew was coming. The fans roared. Teammates cheered. I did it! I shut the other team down. We had won the championship!

1. Both of these articles are about soccer. The article "Champions" would be more useful for—

A. learning how the game is played.
B. understanding the rules for playing soccer.
C. appreciating the excitement of watching a soccer game.
D. learning about the popularity of the game.

2. "Association Football" would be more useful for—

A. appreciating the fans.
B. understanding the stress on soccer players.
C. learning how soccer players feel.
D. learning the rules of soccer.

3. If these two articles were to continue, in which of them would you likely find statistics about soccer fans?

A. "Association Football"
B. "Champions"
C. Both articles
D. Neither article

4. Vocabulary What is the *best* definition of the underlined word *ultimate?*

A. most important
B. first
C. rule
D. lowest

III. Writing and Language Conventions

Directions: *Read the passage. Then, answer each question that follows.*

(1) The air lock doors were opened with a hiss. (2) As Mark stepped outside, he could feel the air, even through his protective suit. (3) Mark saw the sky as the sun set on Mars.

(4) "This is it, Joey," he is saying, looking down at the limp, furry, black body in his arms.

(5) He walked swiftly—bounced, really, in the thin gravity—away from the glowing glass dome of the city. (6) Carefully, Mark placed Joey's body in a shallow hole, kicking dirt back over it and mounding the grave with rocks. (7) Mark felt tears in his eyes, tears he couldn't wipe through his helmet. (8) Joey had been his first pet, brought to Mars when Mark's family moves there years earlier. (9) Losing him meant that his last tie to his old life on Earth was gone. (10) Mark was now completely Martian.

1. Which revision of sentence 3 most vividly describes the **setting** of the story?

  A. Mark could see the sun setting on Mars.
  B. Mark felt sadness as he watched the sun setting on Mars.
  C. The blackness of the sky was broken by the glow at the horizon—the sun setting on Mars.
  D. Mark watched the sun dip low in Mars's sky as he mourned the loss of his first pet, Joey.

2. What is the best way to incorporate **sensory details** in sentence 2?

  A. Replace "air" with "icy winds."
  B. Replace "he" with "Mark."
  C. Replace "suit" with "gear."
  D. Replace "protective" with "protecting."

3. How should the phrase "is saying" in sentence 4 be revised so that the **verb tense** is consistent in the story?

  A. says
  B. has said
  C. said
  D. keep as is

4. Which of the following is the *best* way to rewrite sentence 1 in the **active voice?**

  A. Hissing, the air lock doors were opened.
  B. Joey opened the air lock doors with a hiss.
  C. With a hiss, the air lock doors were opened.
  D. The air lock doors opened with a hiss.

5. How should sentence 8 be revised so that the **verb tense** in the sentence is consistent?

  A. Joey was his first pet, brought to Mars when Mark's family moved there.
  B. Joey was his first pet, brought to Mars when Mark's family moves there.
  C. Joey had been his first pet, brings to Mars when Mark's family had moved there.
  D. Joey is his first pet, brought to Mars when Mark's family will move there.

Performance Tasks

Directions: *Follow the instructions to complete the tasks below as required by your teacher.*

As you work on each task, incorporate both general academic vocabulary and literary terms you learned in this unit.

Common Core State Standards

RL.9-10.2, RL.9-10.3, RL.9-10.4, RL.9-10.5; RI.9-10.4; W.9-10.9.a, W.9-10.9.b; SL.9-10.1, SL.9-10.1.d, SL.9-10.4; L.9-10.1
[For the full wording of the standards, see the standards chart in the front of your textbook.]

Writing

Task 1: Literature [RL.9-10.3; W.9-10.9.a]
Analyze the Development of a Complex Character

From this unit, choose a story that has characters with many or conflicting motivations. Write an essay analyzing the development of one of these complex characters.

- Identify the character you will analyze, and explain why you chose to analyze him or her.
- Explain what motivates the character to behave as he or she does. Include times during which the character's motivations conflict with each other.
- Analyze changes the character undergoes as a result of his or her experiences.
- Cite evidence from the text, including well-chosen, relevant details and direct quotations, to support your analysis.
- Use conventions of standard English in your writing. Ensure that all irregular verbs in your essay are in the correct form.

Task 2: Literature [RL.9-10.4; W.9-10.9.a]
Analyze Setting

Write an essay analyzing how descriptions in a story from this unit evoke a sense of time and place.

- Identify the time and place in which the story is set.
- Quote vivid descriptions of setting from the story, including descriptions that appeal to one or more of the five senses.

- Evaluate the significance of setting in the story. For example, you might explain whether the setting helps shape the conflicts that characters experience or the events that take place in the story.
- Use conventions of standard English in your writing. Use the active voice throughout your essay unless you have a particular reason for using the passive voice.

Task 3: Literature [RL.9-10.2; W.9-10.9.a]
Analyze the Theme of a Story

Write an essay in which you analyze the development of the theme of a story from this unit.

- Provide a short summary of the story in which you briefly identify the main characters and describe key events in the story's plot.
- State the theme of the story, and explain whether the theme is directly stated in the story or is implied.
- Describe how the theme is first presented in the story, citing specific details to support your ideas.
- Explain how the theme is shaped and refined over the course of the story.
- Use conventions of standard English as you write. Avoid mixing verb tenses unnecessarily.

Speaking and Listening

©Task 4: Literature [RL.9-10.4, SL.9-10.1.d]
Analyze Symbolism

Deliver a speech to your class in which you analyze the meaning of one or more symbols in a story from this unit.

- From the story, select a character, place, object, or event that stands for a larger idea.
- Identify the symbol you have chosen, and explain your interpretation of what it represents. Support your ideas with key details from the story.
- Explain whether the symbol is traditional—that is, it calls on ideas that people traditionally associate with the object or event—or whether the symbol is unique to the story.
- After you have finished your speech, encourage your classmates to ask questions and to offer their interpretations of the symbol.
- Respond thoughtfully to your classmates' interpretations, summarize points of agreement and disagreement, and make new connections in light of the reasoning they present.

©Task 5: Informational Text
[RI.9-10.4; SL.9-10.4]
Analyze Word Choice

Prepare and deliver an oral presentation in which you analyze word choice in an informational text in this unit.

- Select an informational text in which word choice has a clear impact on meaning and tone. The text may be technical, historical, or reflective.
- Determine the tone, or author's attitude toward the subject, in the work. Provide examples of words and phrases that contribute to the tone.
- Analyze the specific word choices—for example, technical words, or words with specific connotations—that contribute to the meaning of the work.
- Draw a conclusion about the cumulative effect of word choice on the meaning and tone of the piece.

- Present your information clearly and in an organized way. Read portions of the text aloud to demonstrate your points.

©Task 6: Literature [RL.9-10.5; SL.9-10.1, SL.9-10.4]
Analyze the Point of View From Which a Story Is Told

Lead a small group discussion of the narrative point of view from which a story in this unit is told.

- Prepare for the discussion by identifying the story's point of view—first person, third person omniscient, or third person limited.
- Consider the effects of the narrative point of view on the story, including how it shapes readers' perceptions of the characters and whether a reader has more information or less information than the narrator or other characters have.
- Use details from the story to support your ideas about the narrative point of view.
- Prepare and pose relevant questions to the group. Involve all group members in the discussion. During the discussion, make new connections based on the points made by group members.
- To conclude your group discussion, review the main points made, as well as points of agreement and disagreement.

THE BIG ?

Can progress be made without conflict?

At the beginning of Unit 2, you participated in a discussion of the Big Question. Now that you have completed the unit, write a response to the question. Discuss how your understanding has deepened. Support your response with at least one example from literature and one example from an additional subject area or your own life. Use Big Question vocabulary words (see p. 223) in your response.

Featured Titles

In this unit, you have read a variety of short stories. Continue to read on your own. Select works that you enjoy, but challenge yourself to explore new authors and works of increasing depth and complexity. The titles suggested below will help you get started.

Literature

The Fall of the House of Usher and Other Tales
by Edgar Allan Poe

Poe's nightmarish **short stories** lead readers to the darkest experiences of the human condition—from a family confronting an ancient curse to a murderer losing his grasp on sanity.

Anton Chekhov: Selected Stories
by Anton Chekhov

Against the backdrop of Russia's bustling cities and rugged countryside, Chekhov brings vivid characters to life. This collection of renowned **short stories** shows everyday struggles portrayed with honesty and humor.

The Complete Poems of Percy Bysshe Shelley
by Percy Bysshe Shelley   **EXEMPLAR TEXT** Ⓒ

Shelley's collection of **poetry** explores many themes popularized by the nineteenth-century wave of writers known as The Romantics. His poems explore such topics as love, death, and nature with the type of passionate intensity for which the Romantic poets were famous.

The Prince and the Pauper
by Mark Twain
Signet, 1980

The sixteenth-century royal court and the boisterous London streets spring to life in this **novel** about a poor boy who exchanges identities with Edward Tudor, the prince of England.

The Collected Short Fiction of C. J. Cherryh
by C. J. Cherryh
Daw Books, 2008

From stories of an alien world threatened by a cooling sun to a tale of a woman cursed with unbelievable visions, this collection of **short stories** introduces readers to Cherryh's boundless imagination.

Informational Texts

Biography of an Atom
by Jacob Bronowski and
Millicent Selsam   **EXEMPLAR TEXT** Ⓒ

This **nonfiction** book by Millicent Selsam, a biologist and former science teacher, and Jacob Bronowski, an expert in both literature and science, explains atoms in a friendly, engaging way.

Up from Slavery
by Booker T. Washington
Signet, 2000

During his life, Booker T. Washington was a slave, an educator, an orator, and the founder of the Tuskegee University. In this **autobiography,** Washington tells the remarkable story of his struggles as he rose from houseboy to activist for social change.

Ancient Rome: Voyages Through Time
by Peter Ackroyd

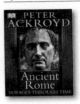

Spanning centuries of war and conquest, this work of **historical nonfiction** brings the reader face to face with famous and infamous Roman rulers, along with the architectural marvels of their age—aqueducts, amphitheaters, spectacular temples, and the Circus Maximus.

Preparing to Read Complex Texts

Attentive Reading As you read literature on your own, bring your imagination and questions to the text. The questions shown below and others that you ask as you read will help you learn and enjoy literature even more.

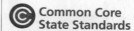 **Common Core State Standards**

Reading Literature/Informational Text 10. By the end of Grade 10, read and comprehend literature, including stories, dramas, poems, and literary nonfiction at the high end of the grades 9–10 text complexity band independently and proficiently.

When reading short stories, ask yourself...

- Who is narrating the story? Is this voice part of the story or an outside observer?

- Do I find the narrator's voice interesting and engaging? Why or why not?

- Who is the story's main character? Is he or she interesting to me? Why or why not?

- Which characters do I like or admire? Which do I dislike? How do my reactions to the characters make me feel about the story as a whole?

- Is the setting of the story—the place, time, and society—believable and interesting? Why or why not?

- What does the story mean to me? Does it convey a theme or insight that I find important and true? Why or why not?

Ⓒ Key Ideas and Details

- What aspects of the story grab my attention right away? Which fail to grab my attention?

- Do I find anything about the story confusing? Do my questions get answered? Why or why not?

- Is there anything different or unusual in the way the story is structured? Do I find that structure interesting or distracting?

- Are there any passages or details that I find especially strong or beautiful?

- Do I understand why characters act and feel as they do? Do their thoughts and actions seem real? Why or why not?

- What questions do I have about characters and events?

Ⓒ Craft and Structure

- Does the story remind me of others I have read? If so, how?

- Have I gained new knowledge from reading this story? If so, what have I learned?

- Would I recommend this story to others? If so, to whom?

- Would I like to read other stories by this author? Why or why not?

Ⓒ Integration of Ideas

What kind of *knowledge* changes our lives?

Types of Nonfiction

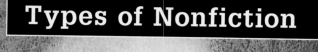

www.PHLitOnline.com

Hear It!
- Selection summary audio
- Selection audio
- BQ Tunes

See It!
- Author videos
- Big Question video
- Get Connected videos
- Background videos
- More about the authors
- Illustrated vocabulary words
- Vocabulary flashcards

Do It!
- Interactive journals
- Interactive graphic organizers
- Grammar tutorials
- Interactive vocabulary games
- Test practice

What kind of *knowledge* changes our lives?

Knowledge is a mastering of a body of facts or a range of information about a topic. As you learn, you may also develop **insight** into a problem or arrive at a deeper awareness and understanding of the world around you. You gain knowledge when you leave ignorance behind, question old attitudes, and revise ideas that are outdated or wrong. While not all information may cause a noticeable difference in your life, some knowledge—such as information that makes you think about people and important issues—can change your life and influence your actions

Exploring the Big Question

Collaboration: Group Discussion Start thinking about the Big Question by considering the different types of knowledge people gain throughout their lives. List the people, ideas, and subjects about which you have gained important knowledge. Describe one specific example of each of the following categories:

- discovering something new about a person that caused you to view that person differently

- a time you put a new skill to use

- an incident in history you studied that changed the way people live

- an essay or a book that altered how you view the world

- a problem or conflict that made you take action

Share your examples with others in a small group. Participate effectively in the group discussion by building on teammates' ideas and by presenting your own relevant ideas clearly and persuasively.

Connecting to the Literature Each reading in this unit will give you insight into the Big Question.

www.PHLitOnline.com

- Big Question video
- Illustrated vocabulary words
- Interactive vocabulary games
- BQ Tunes

Learning Big Question Vocabulary

Acquire and Use Academic Vocabulary Academic vocabulary is the language you encounter in textbooks and on standardized tests. Review the definitions of these academic vocabulary words.

adapt (ə dapt´) **v.** change or adjust

awareness (ə wer´ nis) **n.** having knowledge

evolve (ē välv´, -vôlv´) **v.** develop through gradual changes

insight (in´ sīt´) **n.** a clear idea about the true nature of something

modified (mäd´ ə fīd´) **v.** changed or altered slightly

revise (ri vīz´) **v.** reconsider and modify

Use these words as you complete Big Question activities in this unit that involve reading, writing, speaking, and listening.

Gather Vocabulary Knowledge Additional Big Question words are listed below. Categorize the words by deciding whether you know each one well, know it a little bit, or do not know it at all.

empathy	history	question
enlighten	ignorance	reflect
growth	influence	understanding

Then, do the following:

1. Write the definitions of the words you know.

2. Using a print or an online dictionary, look up the meanings of the words you do not know. Then, write the meanings.

3. If you think you know a word's meaning but are not certain, write your idea of the word's definition. Consult a dictionary to confirm the word's meaning. Revise your definition if necessary.

4. If a word sounds familiar but you do not know its meaning, consult a dictionary. Then, record the meaning.

5. Use all of the words in a brief paragraph about knowledge.

Common Core State Standards

Speaking and Listening
1. Initiate and participate effectively in a range of collaborative discussions with diverse partners on grades 9–10 topics, texts, and issues, building on others' ideas and expressing their own clearly and persuasively.

Language
6. Acquire and use accurately general academic and domain-specific words and phrases, sufficient for reading, writing, speaking, and listening at the college and career readiness level; demonstrate independence in gathering vocabulary knowledge when considering a word or phrase important to comprehension or expression.

Elements of Essays and Speeches

Essays and speeches express an author's point of view about a single topic.

An **essay** is a short nonfiction work that conveys a central idea or key concept about a specific topic. It also expresses its author's **point of view,** or perspective, on the topic.

A **speech** is a nonfiction work that a speaker delivers to an audience. Like an essay, a speech usually presents a central idea and expresses the speaker's point of view on a topic.

Whether an author is writing an essay or a speech, he or she always has a **purpose,** or reason, for writing. A writer chooses details to include in an essay or speech based on his or her purpose. For example, a writer who wishes to warn of the dangers of pollution might include facts about its impact on health. Certain types of writing lend themselves to specific purposes:

- Expository writing **informs or explains.**
- Argumentative writing **persuades,** or convinces readers to believe or to do something.
- Narrative writing **entertains** by telling a story.

An author may have more than one purpose in a single work. For example, he or she might inform by telling an entertaining story about a topic. Usually, however, an author has one overriding purpose.

Effective essays and speeches employ the following elements in ways that suit the material, the circumstances of the writing, and the audience.

Elements of Essays and Speeches

Element	Definition
Author's Purpose	The author's main reason for writing
Central Idea	The author's main, or central, point
Point of View	The author's overall stance on the subject; an author's point of view reflects his or her beliefs, experiences, and values.
Structure	The organizational pattern the author uses to develop and present his or her ideas
Style	The author's distinct approach to writing. Stylistic elements include the author's **syntax** (sentence structure, length and variety) and **diction** (word choice).
Rhetorical Devices	Patterns of word choice, syntax, and meaning used to emphasize ideas, including *parallelism*, the use of similar grammatical structures to express related ideas
Tone	The author's emotional attitude toward his or her subject and audience.

Types of Essays

Essays are often categorized by their general purposes.

- An **expository essay** explains a topic by providing information about it or by exploring an idea related to it.

- A **persuasive essay, or argument,** attempts to convince readers to accept the writer's point of view on an issue or to take a particular course of action.

- A **reflective essay** presents experiences that inspired the writer's thoughts or feelings about a topic.

- A **narrative essay** tells the story of real events or experiences.

- A **descriptive essay** provides specific details to create an impression of a person, an object, or an experience.

An author may combine elements of different types of essays in order to fulfill a purpose. For example, in an argumentative essay persuading readers to exercise, an author might narrate a story about personal experiences with an exercise program.

Types of Speeches

When developing a speech, a writer must consider several factors: his or her purpose for writing, the occasion or event at which the speech will be delivered, and the audience. Imagine, for example, the differences between a speech for a school graduation ceremony and a speech for a surprise birthday party. The chart below shows possible occasions and audiences for several common types of speeches.

In This Section

Elements of Essays and Speeches

Analyzing the Development of Ideas

Close Read: Development of Ideas
- Model Text
- Practice Text

After You Read

 Common Core State Standards

RI.9-10.3, RI.9-10.4, RI.9-10.5, RI.9-10.6, RI.9-10.9
[For the full wording of the standards, see the standards chart in the front of your textbook.]

Type of Speech	Possible Occasion and Audience
Address: a formal, prepared speech that is usually delivered by someone of importance	A graduation speech, delivered by a principal to an audience of parents, faculty, staff, and students
Lecture: a prepared, often formal speech that informs or instructs an audience	A speech explaining a medical discovery, delivered by a scientist to doctors at a medical convention
Talk: an informal speech delivered in a conversational style	A report on a fundraiser, delivered by a student to other members of a volunteer club
Sermon: a prepared, often formal speech intended to teach or inspire	A speech about a religious figure, delivered by a pastor to the congregation of a church
Presentation: a prepared speech about a topic; may include visual aids	A multimedia presentation about a historical event, delivered by a student to a history class
Extemporaneous Speech: a speech delivered without preparation, usually in a conversational style	A toast at a wedding, delivered by a wedding guest to the bride and groom

Analyzing the Development of Ideas

Common Core State Standards

Reading Informational Text

3. Analyze how the author unfolds an analysis or series of ideas or events, including the order in which the points are made, how they are introduced and developed, and the connections that are drawn between them.

5. Analyze in detail how an author's ideas or claims are developed and refined by particular sentences, paragraphs, or larger portions of a text.

Writers use a variety of techniques to **develop and support** the central ideas in their essays and speeches.

A writer will employ several different elements to fulfill his or her purpose and to develop the key ideas in an essay or speech. These elements include *support* for his or her claims; a specific *organizational structure; rhetorical devices; imagery and figurative language;* and effective *word choice.*

Types of Support Supporting a claim means giving readers valid reasons to believe it is true. Here are some types of support:

- **Facts,** or statements that can be proved true
- **Statistics,** or numerical data that presents important information on a subject
- **Descriptions,** or details that tell what something looks like, sounds like, and so on
- **Examples,** or specific cases that illustrate an idea
- **Reasons,** or statements that justify or explain a belief
- **Expert opinions,** or statements made by people who have special knowledge of a topic

The methods an author uses to support a claim depend upon his or her purpose and audience. Notice, for example, how the author relies on description in this persuasive speech to potential vacationers.

> **Example: Leave Winter Behind!**
> Take off those heavy boots and warm your feet on a soft, sandy beach. Listen to the call of the gulls as you gaze at aqua waves lapping a golden shore.

Organization of Ideas Authors organize ideas to emphasize the connections among them. In an effective essay or speech, key ideas are introduced, developed, and refined at all levels of the work. For example, a work may be divided into **sections** that introduce central ideas. **Paragraphs** develop and support those ideas, and **sentences** within the paragraphs present supporting details and connect one idea to another.

An author chooses the overall organizational structure that best fits his or her topic. In a long work, an author may employ several different methods of organization. The following are some common organizational patterns.

> **Example
> Organizational Structures**
> - **Chronological order** presents events in the order in which they happen.
> - **Spatial order** presents details from left to right, bottom to top, near to far, and so on.
> - **List organization** presents connected details consecutively or sorts them into categories.
> - **Comparison-and-contrast organization** groups ideas according to their similarities and differences.
> - **Cause-and-effect organization** shows how one event causes another.
> - **Problem-and-solution organization** identifies a problem, then presents ways to solve it.

Rhetorical Devices Rhetorical devices are language techniques that an author uses to support and emphasize central ideas, create rhythm, and make a work memorable. Although rhetorical devices by themselves are not sufficient to support a claim, they add force and appeal to a writer's work and aid readers in grasping, retaining, and accepting a writer's ideas. Some common rhetorical devices are listed below.

- **Repetition** is the reuse of a key word, phrase, or idea.

Example: We will play with pride. We will play with sportsmanship. We will play to win.

- **Parallel structure** is the use of similar grammatical structures to express related ideas.

Example: They will walk out of the darkness, into the light, beyond limitations.

- **Restatement** is the expression of the same idea in different words to strengthen a point.

Example: We won't give up. Quitting is not an option.

- **Rhetorical questions** are inquiries that have obvious answers and that are asked for effect.

Example: Do you really need to talk on your cell phone while you drive? Can't that call wait?

- **Analogies** are comparisons that show similarities between things that are otherwise not alike.

Example: Our belief in this mission is a fire that keeps us warm.

Common Core State Standards

Reading Informational Text
4. Determine the meaning of words and phrases as they are used in a text, including figurative, connotative, and technical meanings; analyze the cumulative impact of specific word choices on meaning and tone.

Imagery and Figurative Language In addition to rhetorical devices, authors use other creative methods to invigorate their writing. **Imagery** includes vivid details that appeal to the five senses of sight, sound, touch, taste, and smell. **Figurative language** is writing or speech that is not meant to be interpreted literally. It includes **figures of speech** that make unexpected comparisons or describe and explain in fresh, imaginative ways. Three common figures of speech are simile, metaphor, and personification.

- A **simile** is an indirect comparison that contains the word *like* or *as: My little brother is as annoying and tenacious as a swarm of mosquitoes.*

- A **metaphor** describes one thing as if it were another: *Each day is a gift.*

- **Personification** assigns human characteristics to a nonhuman subject: *The old car coughed, wheezed, and refused to move.*

Tone and Word Choice The tone of an essay or speech is the author's attitude toward his or her subject and audience. An author's tone may be formal or informal, ironic, amused, angry, sarcastic, or anything in between. Tone is revealed through an author's choice of words as well as the devices he or she uses. The **connotations,** or emotional associations, of words play a key part in creating tone.

Example: Humorous Essay
Finally, I finished writing my first draft. I admit it was a little rough. Well, maybe more than a little rough. To be honest, it was so rough you could sand wood with it.

Close Read: Development of Ideas

Analyzing literary nonfiction involves determining the author's point of view and evaluating the development of ideas within a work.

Writers of essays and speeches develop their ideas in ways that will fulfill their purpose and present their point of view. When you analyze a work, consider how the author introduces and supports a central idea. Identify the order in which ideas are presented, and note the logical connections among them. Finally, think about the elements the author uses to express ideas effectively, such as rhetorical devices and figures of speech, and consider how they work together to express meaning and create a tone. To guide you in your analysis, use the following questions:

Questions to Ask About Development of Ideas

Central Idea and Point of View
- What key point does the writer want me to understand?
- Where does the writer first introduce the point?
- What point of view, or position, does the author express in the central idea?
- What beliefs, values, or experiences are reflected in that point of view?

Methods of Development
- How does the author introduce and support the central idea or ideas?
- Does the author develop ideas in a way that strengthens his or her claims?
- Does the author provide enough support? If not, what ideas are unsupported?
- Is the support logical and convincing?

Organizational Structure
- What is the overall structure of the work?
- In what order are supporting details presented?
- What connections does the author make among the key ideas in the work?

Rhetorical Devices
- What rhetorical devices does the author use?
- Do these devices strengthen the author's arguments? Why or why not?
- Do these devices create emphasis or stir emotion? If so, how?

Imagery and Figurative Language
- Does the work contain vivid descriptions appealing to one or more of the five senses?
- Does the author make comparisons by using similes or metaphors?
- Does the author use personification to make a point?
- What are the effects of the figurative language in the work?

Tone and Word Choice
- Does the author use formal or informal language?
- What adjective or adjectives would you use to describe the author's tone?
- Does the tone fit the occasion? Does the tone support the author's purpose? How?

Model

About the Text When U.S. President Ronald Reagan addressed the students and faculty of Moscow State University in 1988, he stood before a "new" Soviet Union. The October Revolution of 1917 had helped establish the Soviet Union as a communist society, with a centrally planned economy and tight limits on freedom of speech and assembly. Now, led by Mikhail Gorbachev, the Soviets moved toward economic reform, including private ownership of some businesses, as well as expanded social freedoms.

Although reforms were taking root, President Reagan and other Western leaders pressed for faster, more comprehensive change.

Common Core State Standards

Reading Informational Text

9. Analyze seminal U.S. documents of historical and literary significance, including how they address related themes and concepts.

---

from Address to Students at Moscow State University by Ronald Reagan

But progress is not foreordained. The key is freedom—freedom of thought, freedom of information, freedom of communication. The renowned scientist, scholar, and founding father of this university, Mikhail Lomonosov, knew that. "It is common knowledge," he said, "that the achievements of science are considerable and rapid, particularly once the yoke of slavery is cast off and replaced by the freedom of philosophy." [...]

The explorers of the modern era are the entrepreneurs, men with vision, with the courage to take risks and faith enough to brave the unknown. These entrepreneurs and their small enterprises are responsible for almost all the economic growth in the United States. They are the prime movers of the technological revolution. In fact, one of the largest personal computer firms in the United States was started by two college students, no older than you, in the garage behind their home. Some people, even in my own country, look at the riot of experiment that is the free market and see only waste. What of all the entrepreneurs that fail? Well, many do, particularly the successful ones; often several times. And if you ask them the secret of their success, they'll tell you it's all that they learned in their struggles along the way; yes, it's what they learned from failing. Like an athlete in competition or a scholar in pursuit of the truth, experience is the greatest teacher. [...]

We are seeing the power of economic freedom spreading around the world. Places such as the Republic of Korea, Singapore, Taiwan have vaulted into the technological era, barely pausing in the industrial age along the way. Low-tax agricultural policies in the subcontinent mean that in some years India is now a net exporter of food. Perhaps most exciting are the winds of change that are

Point of View Here, Reagan expresses his central idea: that freedom is the key to progress. In doing so, he also reveals his point of view.

Methods of Development Reagan supports his central idea by connecting it to the related idea that freedom allows people to start businesses, which spurs economic growth.

Figurative Language Reagan uses similes to add emphasis and interest to his speech.

Ⓒ EXEMPLAR TEXT

Model continued

Methods of Development Reagan uses facts, statistics, and examples to support the key idea that Americans have the freedom to choose their presidents.

Tone and Word Choice Reagan uses simple, everyday language and sounds sincere, patriotic, and most importantly, believable.

Rhetorical Devices By using repetition and parallelism, Reagan emphasizes his key point that it is easy to find examples of the benefits of freedom.

blowing over the People's Republic of China, where one-quarter of the world's population is now getting its first taste of economic freedom. At the same time, the growth of democracy has become one of the most powerful political movements of our age. In Latin America in the 1970s, only a third of the population lived under democratic government; today over 90 percent does. In the Philippines, in the Republic of Korea, free, contested, democratic elections are the order of the day. Throughout the world, free markets are the model for growth. Democracy is the standard by which governments are measured.

We Americans make no secret of our belief in freedom. In fact, it's something of a national pastime. Every 4 years the American people choose a new president, and 1988 is one of those years. At one point there were 13 major candidates running in the two major parties, not to mention all the others, including the Socialist and Libertarian candidates—all trying to get my job. About 1,000 local television stations, 8,500 radio stations, and 1,700 daily newspapers—each one an independent, private enterprise, fiercely independent of the Government— report on the candidates, grill them in interviews, and bring them together for debates. In the end, the people vote; they decide who will be the next president. But freedom doesn't begin or end with elections.

Go to any American town, to take just an example, and you'll see dozens of churches, representing many different beliefs—in many places, synagogues and mosques—and you'll see families of every conceivable nationality worshiping together. Go into any schoolroom, and there you will see children being taught the Declaration of Independence, that they are endowed by their Creator with certain unalienable rights—among them life, liberty, and the pursuit of happiness—that no government can justly deny; the guarantees in their Constitution for freedom of speech, freedom of assembly, and freedom of religion. Go into any courtroom, and there will preside an independent judge, beholden to no government power. There every defendant has the right to a trial by a jury of his peers, usually 12 men and women—common citizens; they are the ones, the only ones, who weigh the evidence and decide on guilt or innocence. In that court, the accused is innocent until proven guilty, and the word of a policeman or any official has no greater legal standing than the word of the accused. Go to any university campus, and there you'll find an open, sometimes heated discussion of the problems in American society and what can be done to correct them. Turn on the television, and you'll see the legislature conducting the business of government right there before the camera, debating and voting on the legislation that will become the law of the land. March in any demonstration, and there are many of them; the people's right of assembly is guaranteed in the Constitution and protected by the police. Go into any union hall, where the members know their right to strike is protected by law. [...]

But freedom is more even than this. Freedom is the right to question and change the established way of doing things. It is the continuing revolution of the marketplace. It is the understanding that allows us to recognize shortcomings and seek solutions. It is the right to put forth an idea, scoffed at by the experts, and watch it catch fire among the people. It is the right to dream—to follow your dream or stick to your conscience, even if you're the only one in a sea of doubters. Freedom is the recognition that no single person, no single authority or government has a monopoly on the truth, but that every individual life is infinitely precious, that every one of us put on this world has been put there for a reason and has something to offer. [. . .]

Your generation is living in one of the most exciting, hopeful times in Soviet history. It is a time when the first breath of freedom stirs the air and the heart beats to the accelerated rhythm of hope, when the accumulated spiritual energies of a long silence yearn to break free. I am reminded of the famous passage near the end of Gogol's[1] *Dead Souls.* Comparing his nation to a speeding troika,[2] Gogol asks what will be its destination. But he writes, "There was no answer save the bell pouring forth marvelous sound."

We do not know what the conclusion will be of this journey, but we're hopeful that the promise of reform will be fulfilled. In this Moscow spring, this May 1988, we may be allowed that hope: that freedom, like the fresh green sapling planted over Tolstoy's[3] grave, will blossom forth at last in the rich fertile soil of your people and culture. We may be allowed to hope that the marvelous sound of a new openness will keep rising through, ringing through, leading to a new world of reconciliation, friendship, and peace. [. . .]

---

1. **Gogol's** (gô′ gôlz) reference to Nikolai (nē′ kô lī′) Gogol (1809–1852), famous Russian novelist.
2. **troika** (troi′ kə) a Russian sled or carriage drawn by three horses.
3. **Tolstoy's** (täl′ stoiz′) reference to Leo Tolstoy (1828–1910), famous Russian novelist and thinker.

Organizational Structure This section brings listeners full circle. Through rhetorical devices and memorable examples, Reagan sums up and explains the significance of his central idea.

Figurative Language Reagan ends his speech with a powerful appeal to his listeners, framed in figurative language: a comparison between freedom in Russia and a young tree.

Independent Practice

About the Selection The dangers of high-altitude mountain climbing are severe. Many climbers fall sick or even die from illnesses caused by reduced oxygen. Others freeze or plummet to their deaths. Despite these risks, Erik Weihenmayer, a blind climber, had successfully reached the summits of five of the world's highest peaks by 1999. In that year, when Pasquale "PV" Scaturro, a geophysicist and expert climber, suggested an expedition to the top of Mount Everest, Weihenmayer readily agreed. He arranged sponsorship from the National Federation of the Blind and, with Scaturro, organized the expedition. The other members of the team included Sherm Bull and his son Brad; Ang Pasang, a Sherpa who had climbed Everest twice; and Weihenmayer's longtime mountaineering buddies Eric "Erie" Alexander, Jeff Evans, Chris Morris, and Mike O'Donnell. On May 25, 2001, Weihenmayer and many of his teammates reached the top of Mount Everest. This excerpt describes the final leg of that adventure.

"Everest" from *Touch the Top of the World* by Erik Weihenmayer

We left our tents a little before 9:00 p.m. on May 24. Because of our twenty-four-hour delay and the apprehension of other expeditions to share a summit day with me, we moved across the South Col with only one other team behind us. We had no worries of the typical horde clogging the fixed lines but could direct our full focus toward the mountain. The wind was blowing so loudly through the col that I couldn't hear the bells jingling from Chris's ice axe. Chris and I expected this, so for the first two hours he clanked his metal axe against rocks he passed. Finally, we worked our way around to the mountain's leeward[1] side, where Everest itself protected us from the wind. Chris had lost his voice, so his verbal directions were sparse. At each anchor, he'd hold the new line with his hand, so I could locate it and clip in. Chris was moving in front of me at his usual rock-solid pace, and I was right on his heels. We were making unbelievable time.

As we got higher up the mountain, four distinct changes had begun to work in my favor. Earlier, in the icefall, each step was very specific, but the terrain above the South Col consisted of steep forty-five-degree snow faces a hundred yards wide, intermingled with ten-to-fifty-foot crumbly rock steps. I could stay in the kicked boot holes of Chris or kick my own steps. Where I stepped had become less important than maintaining internal balance. I could breathe, scan my ice axe, and count on the next step. The slope was often so steep that I could lean forward and feel the rock or snow steps with my gloved hands, and I had trained myself long ago to save energy by landing my feet in the same holds my hands had just left. Finally, when I needed it most, the mountain had given me a pattern.

Imagery To which of the five senses does this descriptive language appeal?

Organizational Structure In what way does this sentence indicate a possible organizational pattern?

---

1. leeward (lē′ wərd′) *adj.* away from the wind.

The thin oxygen of extreme altitude reduced us to a crawl. It was like moving through a bizarre atmosphere of syrup mixed with a narcotic. My team, struggling just to put one foot in front of the other, moved so slowly, it gave me more time to scan my axe across the snow and feel my way forward. The third equalizer was the darkness. With just a trickle of light produced by headlamps, my sighted team could only see a few feet in front of them. Bulky goggles blocked their side vision, and oxygen masks covered much of their visual field. Also, the pure oxygen trickling through their masks would flow up and freeze the lenses of their goggles so that they constantly had to remove them to wipe the lenses clean. Those brief moments when eyes are exposed to the elements, corneas will freeze, and the intense rays of the sun reflecting off the snow cause instant snow blindness. Not once did I ever have to worry about these complications.

In addition, my teammates had chosen smaller masks that rode low and tight across their cheeks and hung mostly below their chins. This allowed climbers to see better and prevented pure oxygen from seeping into their lenses, but also allowed plenty of pure oxygen to escape into the wind. I, on the other hand, had the luxury of choosing the largest mask I could find and wore it high on my face, getting the most benefit from the oxygen flow and the ambient air around the mask. I'm sure I made a freakish sight with my gigantic mask covering my goggles, like a day long ago in wrestling practice when I had put my sweatshirt on backward, with the hood covering my face, and chased the terrified freshmen around the mat. The consistent terrain, the altitude, the mask, and the darkness were great equalizers. I wouldn't go so far as to claim these gave me an advantage, but it was a matter of perspective. The mountain had gotten desperately harder for everyone else, while it had gotten slightly easier for me.

For two and a half months, all the decisions, the logistics, the backup safety plans had been implemented and executed by PV, and now, somewhere below the Balcony, the exhausting burden of leadership finally took its toll. Suddenly feeling listless and unable to catch his breath even with his oxygen bottle at full flow, PV had arduously turned back. He managed to convince Brad and Sherm, next to him, that he was strong enough to descend alone, in retrospect, a ploy that might have turned deadly, but PV's weary brain had never stopped calculating the big picture. He had refused to divert any energy from the team's summit effort. Through periodic radio checks as PV dropped altitude, I could hear his characteristically hyper voice growing flat, and just below a steep ice bulge, only an hour from Camp Four, PV sat down in the snow.

Tone and Word Choice Describe the tone of these passages, in which the author notes that his blindness helps him avoid some of the problems faced by the other climbers.

Practice continued

"I'm very tired," he said. "I don't know if I can make it. I might need some assistance." PV's one warning before we left the tent was "If you sit down, you'll stay there." So, beginning to panic, I ripped my radio out of my pocket. "Is anyone near PV who can help him down?" I asked. "Is anyone reading me?" I repeated myself several times to empty static.

A few weeks earlier, Dr. Gipe had received the sad news that a close family friend had been killed in a skiing accident; a three-thousand-foot day in the Death Zone just didn't seem fair to his family, so that night, he had never left his tent. His decision was a tough one to make, but extremely fortunate for PV's sake. "This is Gipe at the South Col," finally came over the radio. "I'm strapping on my crampons right now. I'm going out to get PV." Dr. Gipe met PV about a half an hour from camp, up again and staggering slowly toward the tents.

Methods of Development Why does Weihenmayer provide background details about Dr. Gipe?

With the first crisis of the night averted, Chris and I plodded up a steep gully, which led us to the Balcony, a flat snow platform, ten feet wide. Michael Brown arrived first at about 2:00 a.m., with Chris and me right behind. All night, the weather had remained clear, with high clouds to the southeast and distant lightning flashes illuminating the sky, but at the Balcony, our luck suddenly ran out. We walked into a blasting storm. Wind and horizontal snow raked our down suits and covered us with a layer of ice. The lightning strikes were now on top of us, exploding like a pyrotechnic[2] show. Chris later said he couldn't see his feet through the blowing snow, which stopped us short, since the southeast ridge above narrowed to fifteen feet wide. Mike O.'s and Didrik's headlamps had simultaneously flickered out, and one of Didrik's crampons had popped off. "Someone come and help us," Mike yelled over the radio. Charley headed back and found them sitting in the snow only twenty feet away.

Tone and Word Choice How would you describe the tone at this point? Identify two words that help to create this tone, and explain the connotations, or emotional associations, of each.

Chris and I huddled together in the wind, waiting for the others to arrive. "What do you think, Big E?" he asked. "It's lookin' pretty grim." When the others trickled in, Sherm wanted to go on; Charley wanted to turn back, and Erie thought we should wait. For forty-five minutes, we waited, periodic arguments breaking out whether to go on or descend. I was beginning to shiver and forced myself to bounce up and down, and to windmill my arms. We were so close, and I was feeling strong. Turning back was a crushing proposition, but I also wasn't willing to go bullheadedly forward and throw my life away. My mind was starting to settle on the possibility of turning back, when Kevin's voice from Base Camp crackled over my radio. Throughout the expedition, Kevin had been learning to read the satellite weather reports we received every few days over the Internet. From the weather map, it appeared the storm was moving rapidly to the northeast toward Bhutan, and where we

---

2. **pyrotechnic** (pī′ rə tek′ nik) *adj.* of or pertaining to fireworks; here, brilliant; dazzling.

stood on the Balcony, we were directly northeast of Base Camp. "Hey you guys, don't quit yet," his voice sounded urgent. "The storm's cleared down here. It just might pass over you."

"Weather is also clearing here," Kami said from Camp Two below. Chris glanced over at me. Beyond my right hip, shining through the storm clouds, he could see a star. "Let's see if this thing breaks up," he said. Sherm must have felt good tidings, too, because he pushed on. Chris and I followed.

Following the narrow exposed southeast shoulder, I felt the first warmth of the sun about 4:00 a.m.; so high up, no other mountain blocked the sunrise. The weather had thankfully turned spectacular.

Still hours below the South Summit, we were stalled out again. The fixed lines, running up the steepest slope yet, had been frozen over by a hard windswept crust of snow. Jeff and Brad moved ahead, pulling the lines free, an exhausting job at twenty-eight thousand feet. The job was quickly wearing Jeff down, but he said later that with each gasping breath as he heaved the rope free, he envisioned the two of us standing on top together. Soon he was beginning to feel faint and dizzy. As he knelt in the snow, Brad, behind him, examined his oxygen equipment and assessed that his regulator, connecting the long tube of his mask to his bottle, had malfunctioned. The internal valves responsible for regulating flow were notoriously prone to freezing shut. "Who's got an extra regulator?" Brad called out over the radio, but tired bodies and brains could not recall who had thrown in the extras in the presummit shuffle. "My day's finished if I can't find the extra," Jeff yelled testily.

It may not have been PV's time to summit, but he wasn't through benefiting the team. "Calm down," he advised, lying weakly on his back in his tent. "Everyone take a deep breath. Ang Pasang and Sherm are carrying the extra regulators." Luckily, Ang Pasang was only a hundred feet behind. Together, Brad and Ang Pasang screwed on Jeff's new regulator.

By 8:00 a.m., we had struggled on to the South Summit, 28,700 feet. After a short rest, Chris took off for the summit, cranking it into "Morris gear," and Luis took over in front of me. From the South Summit, the true summit is still at least two hours away across the three-hundred-foot-long knife-edge ridge, up the fifty-foot vertical Hillary Step, and finally traversing up a long slightly broader ridge to the summit.

Jeff, exhausted from his two-hour struggle pulling lines, stopped short in front of me. "I'm wasted. I've gotta go down," he said reluctantly. "This'll have to be my summit."

Central Idea Why are these details significant?

Organizational Structure What organizational structure is Weihenmayer using in this passage?

Practice continued

Tone and Word Choice What are two adjectives that describe the author's tone in this passage? Citing specific examples, explain how he uses the connotative meaning of words to create this tone.

Methods of Development What key idea is developed and supported by this anecdote?

For a moment I wanted to goad him on the way we had done each other on winter training climbs of Colorado fourteeners. "If you wanna turn back, just say the word," we'd jab. "Of course, I'll have to tell everyone you were a whiney little crybaby." But 28,700 feet above sea level wasn't the place to motivate with bravado or ego, so assessing that he was strong enough to get down, I rested a hand on Jeff's shoulder and wished him a safe descent. Jeff had been with me from the beginning, practically introducing me to the mountains. He had shown extraordinary patience as I stumbled along experimenting with brand-new trekking poles. We had even stood together on the summit of Denali[3] and El Capitan,[4] so I knew that reaching the summit of Mt. Everest without him wouldn't feel complete. Suddenly, a wave of heavy exhaustion passed over me, and I felt weary and crumpled. "Maybe I'll go down too," I readied my lips to say, but then Luis was crunching through the snow in front of me, and I forced myself to revive.

Down-climbing the twenty-foot vertical snow face on the backside of the South Summit leading onto the knife-edge ridge went against my survival instinct. The ridge is the width of a picnic table and always heavily corniced[5] with snow. To the left is an eight-thousand-foot drop into Nepal, and on the right, a twelve-thousand-foot drop into Tibet. PV had told me that while crossing the ridge on his 1998 attempt, he had driven his ice axe into the snow and, after withdrawing it, had stared through the small hole into the early morning light of Tibet. In 1995, on Brad's second attempt, a climber in front of him had taken his first step onto the ridge just before the entire right half of it dropped away. The climber jumped back to safety, but a second later he would have ridden the cornice into Tibet. This year, the ridge was drier and more stable. Frozen boot steps traversed along the lefthand side. I'd scan my pole until it dropped into a boot mark, then cautiously lower my foot. I knew I couldn't make a mistake here: six hard steady breaths, another solid step, and a relaxed, focused mind like clear water.

Climbing the Hillary Step, I felt I was in my element, feeling the rock under my gloves. I stuck the crampon points of my right foot tenuously into a tiny crack and the left points into a cornice of snow, slid my ascender as high as it would go on the rope, and stood up and quickly reached for the next knob of rock. At the top, I awkwardly belly-flopped onto a flat ledge, slowly pulled myself to my feet, and began traversing the last slope to the summit. For forty minutes I trudged upward. My heavy sluggish muscles felt as if they were pushing through wet cement. With each step closer, the real possibility of standing on

---

3. **Denali** (di nä´ lē) name of the National Park in which Mt. McKinley is located.
4. **El Capitan** (el´ ka´ pē tan´) a peak in the Sierra Nevada mountain range in the Yosemite Valley of central California.
5. **corniced** (kôr´ nist) *adj.* in architecture, having a projecting decorative strip atop a wall or building; here, characterized by overhanging masses of snow or ice.

top began to trickle through my focused brain. I had speculated success in a conceptual way and as a way to motivate myself when I was down, but it was dangerous to believe it as a fact. A team could be turned back for so many reasons at any time. Just keep moving, I thought. You're not there yet.

Then a body moved down the slope toward me and I felt thin wiry arms beneath a puffy down suit wrapping around me. "Big E!" The voice rasped, so hollow and wispy, I had trouble recognizing it as Chris. His voice tried to say more, but his quaking words dissipated in the wind. Then he leaned in against my ear. "Big E"—his voice gave way to tears, then struggled out in an immense effort— "you're about to stand on top of the world." Then he quickly let go and hurriedly moved down the slope.

Luis and I linked our arms, and in a few steps, the earth flattened and the massive sky closed around me on all sides. "This is Erik, Luis, and Ang Pasang," I said over the radio. "We're on the top. I can't believe it; we're on the top."

"You're the best, Big E!" Kevin yelled from Base Camp. "I love you guys." I could hear the entire Base Camp crew cheering behind him.

"You're the strongest man in the world," PV said.

I turned around, surprised to hear more crampons moving up behind me. "I wasn't gonna let you stand on top and hear about it the rest of my life," Jeff said, with a little pep left in his voice. One of the greatest joys of my summit was that Jeff hadn't turned back at all. From the South Summit, he had watched us down-climb onto the knife-edge ridge and move toward the Hillary Step. Later he told me, "I simply had to follow." Behind Jeff came Erie, Michael B., Didrik, Charley, and Mike O. Sherm had been the first on the team to summit, becoming the oldest man in history to stand on the top of the world, but better than his record was the fact that his son, Brad, had stepped onto the summit right behind him. Nineteen team members made it to the summit: eleven Westerners and eight Sherpas, the most from one team to reach the top in a single day. So it was a crowded summit as we all stood together, hugging and crying on a snow platform the size of a single-car garage.

Another storm was rolling in from the north. "Weather's changing fast," PV called up on the radio. "You guys need to go down immediately." I turned to head down with Erie, when Jeff said, "Wait a second, Big E. You'll only be here once in your life. Look around. Think about where you are and what you've done." So I suspended my nerves for a moment, reached down and touched the

Rhetorical Devices
What emotion is conveyed through the repetition in these sentences?

Practice continued

snow through my gloved hand, listened to the Sherpa prayer flags flapping in the wind, and heard the infinite sound of space around me, as on my first rock climb. After I had gone blind almost twenty years ago, I would have been proud to find the bathroom, so I said a quick prayer and thanked God for giving me so much. Then it was time to go down.

We descended through heavy snowfall but, thankfully, little wind. Erie took over guiding me, down the Hillary Step, across the knife edge, and contrary to his fears that he wouldn't be strong enough to make the top, he was stronger and more lucid on the way down from Everest's summit than most were on the top of a peak in Colorado. Reaching our tents at about 3:00 p.m., I hugged Erie. "Today," I said, "you were my guardian angel. I'm glad you're here."

That night, Kevin radioed up to report that he had called Ellie on the sat phone with the news. "She screamed loud enough to break the neighbors' windows." He laughed. The next days were exhausting as we fought our way through the screaming wind of the South Col, down the Lhotse Face—where my rubbery legs refused to obey my brain—and finally one last trip through the icefall. At the bottom, in Superman's Palace, of course, the whole team was waiting, and the party lasted long after the sun had sunk below Pumori.

Despite our success, plenty of detractors voiced their opinions on Internet chat rooms and in letters to the editor. I've heard all the ridiculous assumptions.

"Now that a blind guy's climbed it, everyone's going to want to climb it. They're going to think it's easy. People will probably get hurt."

"Why are people thinking this is such a big deal? Anyone can be short-roped to the top by nineteen seeing-eye guides."

My teammates constantly come to my rescue with carefully crafted comebacks like "Before you start spouting a bunch of lies over a public forum, get your facts straight, dude!"

"Don't let 'em get to you," Chris Morris said after I shared with him their comments. "You climbed every inch of that mountain, and then some."

I knew he was right. There were some who would never be convinced, others who still had no idea what to think, but many others for whom the climb forced a higher expectation of their own possibilities. I don't climb mountains to prove to anyone that blind people can do this or that. I climb for the same reason an artist paints a picture: because it brings me great joy. But I'd be lying if I didn't admit my secret satisfaction in facing those cynics and blowing through their doubts, destroying their negative stereotypes, taking their very narrow parameters of what's possible and what's not, and shattering them into a million pieces.

Point of View What is the author's point of view regarding his critics?

When those parameters are rebuilt, thousands and thousands of people will live with fewer barriers placed before them, and if my climbs can play a small role in opening doors of opportunity and hope for those who will come after us, then I am very proud of what we were able to achieve . . .

Central Idea What is the central idea of this selection?

After You Read

"Everest" *from* **Touch the Top of the World**

1. Integration of Knowledge and Ideas Speculate: Why might it matter to people around the world that a blind man climbed Mount Everest?

2. Integration of Knowledge and Ideas (a) Identify: Identify two challenges that the altitude presents to the climbers. **(b) Connect:** In what ways is Weihenmayer's blindness a benefit as he meets these challenges? **(c) Generalize:** Based on his experience, what statements can you make about turning negatives into positives?

3. Key Ideas and Details Analyze: Use a chart like the one shown to analyze decisions made by individuals or the team on Mount Everest.

4. Key Ideas and Details (a) How do some critics respond to Weihenmayer's success in reaching the summit of Mount Everest? **(b) Analyze:** Based on the details of Weihenmayer's climb, how would you answer those critics?

5. Craft and Structure Analyze: In what ways does Weihenmayer balance his own perspective with the views of others? Explain.

6. Integration of Knowledge and Ideas (a) What new insights and skills did Weihenmayer develop because he lost his sight? **(b) Connect:** In what ways could learning about Weihenmayer's climbing experiences change someone else's life?

Decision	Results of Decision	Importance to the Team's Success

Leveled Texts

Build your skills and improve your comprehension of nonfiction with texts of increasing complexity.

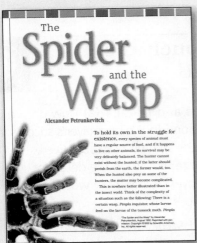

Read **"The Spider and the Wasp"** to find out how a wasp ensures the survival of its young by conquering a large and potentially deadly spider.

Read the excerpt from **Longitude** to learn how the demands of computing longitude have challenged people for hundreds of years.

Common Core State Standards

Meet these standards with either **"The Spider and the Wasp"** (p. 464) or the excerpt from **Longitude** (p. 474).

Reading Informational Text
2. Determine a central idea of a text and analyze its development over the course of the text, including how it emerges and is shaped and refined by specific details; provide an objective summary of the text. *(Reading Skill: Main Idea)*

4. Determine the meaning of words and phrases as they are used in a text, including figurative, connotative, and technical meanings; analyze the cumulative impact of specific word choices on meaning and tone. *(Literary Analysis: Expository Essay)*

Spiral Review: RI.9-10.3
Writing
2.e. Establish and maintain a formal style and objective tone while attending to the norms and conventions of the

discipline in which they are writing. *(Writing: Business Letter)*

Speaking and Listening
4. Present information, findings, and supporting evidence clearly, concisely, and logically such that listeners can follow the line of reasoning and the organization, development, substance, and style are appropriate to purpose, audience, and task. *(Speaking and Listening: Humorous Persuasive Speech)*

Language
3. Apply knowledge of language to understand how language functions in different contexts, to make effective choices for meaning or style, and to comprehend more fully when reading or listening. *(Literary Analysis: Expository Essay; Speaking and Listening: Humorous Persuasive Speech)*

Literary Analysis: Expository Essay

An **expository essay** is a brief nonfiction work in which an author informs by explaining, defining, or interpreting an idea. Often, the writer reaches a conclusion through reasoning, or logic.

   Diction, or the author's word choice, sets one expository essay off from another. Diction may be formal, informal, sophisticated, or slangy. It may include *technical language,* such as scientific terms. The writer's word choice and sentence structure have an impact on a text's meaning and **tone**. The tone reflects the author's attitude toward his or her subject and affects the reader's perception.

Using the Strategy: Diction and Tone Chart

As you read, use a diction and tone chart like this one to find examples of the author's diction and to describe the tone it creates.

	Example of Diction	Description of Diction	Tone
"The Spider and the Wasp"	The hunter cannot exist without the hunted; if the latter should perish from the earth, the former would, too.	**Formal:** latter, former **Old-fashioned:** perish	scholarly philosophical
Longitude	Any sailor worth his salt can gauge his latitude well enough by the length of the day...	**Technical language:** gauge his latitude **Idiomatic expression:** worth his salt	not too formal friendly informative

Reading Skill: Main Idea

To fully understand an essay, **analyze main,** or **central, ideas** and **supporting details**—recognize each main point the writer makes and identify its relation to the ideas or facts that explain or illustrate it. To help you organize your thoughts, pause occasionally to summarize what you have read. When you **summarize,** you briefly restate the central ideas and key details from the text.

What kind of *knowledge* changes our lives?

Writing About the Big Question

In "The Spider and the Wasp," a spider's instinctive responses leave it vulnerable to attack by a wasp. Use this sentence starter to develop your ideas about the Big Question.

An example of a situation in which it would be important to **adapt** or **revise** a behavior based on instinct and gut reaction is _____.

While You Read Look for examples of how the spider uses information provided by its body to protect itself under normal circumstances.

Vocabulary

Read each word and its definition. Decide whether you know the word well, know it a little bit, or do not know it at all. After you read, see how your knowledge of each word has increased.

- **instinct** (in´ stiŋkt´) *n.* an inborn pattern of behavior, as opposed to a learned skill (p. 465) *As soon as they hatch, sea turtles use instinct to find their way to the sea.* instinctive *adj.* instinctual *adj.*

- **customarily** (kus´ tə mer´ ə lē) *adv.* usually; by habit or tradition (p. 465) *Senior citizens customarily receive discounts.* custom *n.* customary *adj.*

- **distinct** (di stiŋkt´) *adj.* clearly different; separate (p. 466) *There are two distinct sides to the issue.* distinction *n.* distinctive *adj.*

- **tactile** (tak´ təl) *adj.* related to the sense of touch (p. 467) *I enjoy the tactile sensations of stroking a rabbit's fluffy fur.* tactility *n.* intact *adj.*

- **formidable** (fôr´ mə də bəl) *adj.* causing fear or dread (p. 467) *He is such a formidable enemy, that few dare to cross him.* formidably *adv.*

- **evoking** (ē vōk´ iŋ) *v.* drawing forth emotions or responses (p. 468) *His experimental plays are known for evoking mixed responses from the audience.* evocation *n.* evocative *adj.*

Word Study

The **Latin roots -tact-** and **-tang-** mean "touch" or "feel."

This essay describes a particular kind of tarantula that has three **tactile** responses that cause it to react when touched.

Author of
The Spider and the Wasp

The Russian thinker Alexander Petrunkevitch (pə trōōn´ kə vich) was one of the first scientists to explore the secret world of spiders. He classified at least 274 species.

From Politics to Poetry Although Petrunkevitch spent countless hours observing spiders, he did not bury himself away from the world in science. Inspired by his father, who had been jailed for supporting democratic reforms in the Russian government, the younger Petrunkevitch was politically active. He also translated many English poems into Russian.

BACKGROUND FOR THE ESSAY

Instinct vs. Intelligence
Petrunkevitch's essay helps readers understand the distinction between instinct and intelligence. An animal's instincts cannot change, even when they lead to harm. Some animals, however, show intelligence: They learn and adjust their behavior to fit their experience.

Did You Know?
The scientific names for several spider species are based on Petrunkevitch's name.

The Spider and the Wasp

Alexander Petrunkevitch

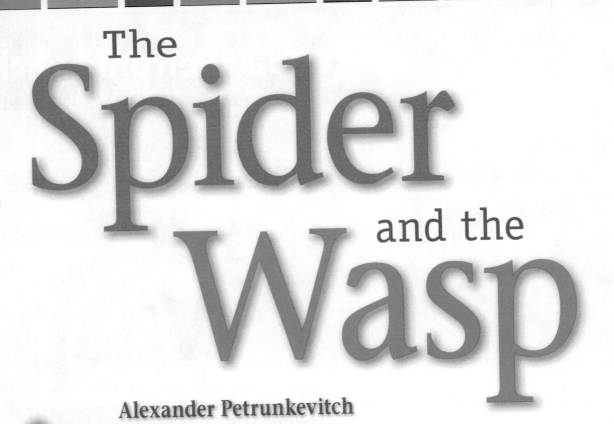

To hold its own in the struggle for existence, every species of animal must have a regular source of food, and if it happens to live on other animals, its survival may be very delicately balanced. The hunter cannot exist without the hunted; if the latter should perish from the earth, the former would, too. When the hunted also prey on some of the hunters, the matter may become complicated.

This is nowhere better illustrated than in the insect world. Think of the complexity of a situation such as the following: There is a certain wasp, *Pimpla inquisitor,* whose larvae feed on the larvae of the tussock moth. *Pimpla* larvae in turn serve as food for the larvae of a second wasp, and the latter in their turn nourish still a third wasp. What subtle balance between fertility and mortality must exist in the case of each of these four species to prevent the extinction of all of them! An excess of mortality over fertility in a single member of the group would ultimately wipe out all four.

This is not a unique case. The two great orders of insects, Hymenoptera and Diptera, are full of such examples of interrelationship. And the spiders (which are not insects but members of a separate order of arthropods) also are killers and victims of insects.

The picture is complicated by the fact that those species which are carnivorous in the larval stage have to be provided with animal food by a vegetarian mother. The survival of the young depends on the mother's correct choice of a food which she does not eat herself.

In the feeding and safeguarding of their progeny[1] the insects and spiders exhibit some interesting analogies to reasoning and some crass examples of blind instinct. The case I propose to describe here is that of the tarantula spiders and their arch-enemy, the digger wasps of the genus Pepsis. It is a classic example of what looks like intelligence pitted against instinct—a strange situation in which the victim, though fully able to defend itself, submits unwittingly to its destruction.

Most tarantulas live in the tropics, but several species occur in the temperate zone and a few are common in the southern U.S. Some varieties are large and have powerful fangs with which they can inflict a deep wound. These formidable-looking spiders do not, however, attack man; you can hold one in your hand, if you are gentle, without being bitten. Their bite is dangerous only to insects and small mammals such as mice; for a man it is no worse than a hornet's sting.

Tarantulas customarily live in deep cylindrical burrows, from which they emerge at dusk and into which they retire at dawn. Mature males wander about after dark in search of females and occasionally stray into houses. After mating, the male dies in a few weeks, but a female lives much longer and can mate several years in succession. In a Paris museum is a tropical specimen which is said to have been living in captivity for 25 years.

---

1. **progeny** (präj´ ə nē) *n.* offspring; young.

Literary Analysis
Expository Essay
What does the writer's choice of words tell you about his attitude toward the subject?

Vocabulary
instinct (in´ stiŋkt´) *n.* an inborn pattern of behavior, as opposed to a learned skill

customarily (kus´ tə mer´ ə lē) *adv.* usually; by habit or tradition

Reading Check
What two concepts will the writer explore in this essay?

A fertilized female tarantula lays from 200 to 400 eggs at a time; thus it is possible for a single tarantula to produce several thousand young. She takes no care of them beyond weaving a cocoon of silk to enclose the eggs. After they hatch, the young walk away, find convenient places in which to dig their burrows and spend the rest of their lives in solitude. Tarantulas feed mostly on insects and millipedes. Once their appetite is appeased, they digest the food for several days before eating again. Their sight is poor, being limited to sensing a change in the intensity of light and to the perception of moving objects. They apparently have little or no sense of hearing, for a hungry tarantula will pay no attention to a loudly chirping cricket placed in its cage unless the insect happens to touch one of its legs.

But all spiders, and especially hairy ones, have an extremely delicate sense of touch. Laboratory experiments prove that tarantulas can distinguish three types of touch: pressure against the body wall, stroking of the body hair, and riffling of certain very fine hairs on the legs called trichobothria.[2] Pressure against the body, by a finger or the end of a pencil, causes the tarantula to move off slowly for a short distance. The touch excites no defensive response unless the approach is from above where the spider can see the motion, in which case it rises on its hind legs, lifts its front legs, opens its fangs and holds this threatening posture as long as the object continues to move. When the motion stops, the spider drops back to the ground, remains quiet for a few seconds and then moves slowly away.

The entire body of a tarantula, especially its legs, is thickly clothed with hair. Some of it is short and woolly, some long and stiff. Touching this body hair produces one of two distinct reactions. When the spider is hungry, it responds with an immediate and swift attack. At the touch of a cricket's antennae the tarantula seizes the insect so swiftly that a motion picture taken at the rate of 64 frames per second shows only the result and not the process of capture. But when the spider is not hungry, the stimulation of its hairs merely causes it to shake the touched limb. An insect can walk under its hairy belly unharmed.

The trichobothria, very fine hairs growing from disklike membranes on the legs, were once thought to be the spider's hearing organs, but we now know that they have nothing to do with sound.

---

2. trichobothria (trik´ ə bäth´ rē ə)

Spiral Review
Series of Ideas
Explain how the ideas stated in this paragraph connect to those expressed in the paragraphs that immediately precede and follow it.

But **all** **spiders,** and especially **hairy ones,** have an extremely delicate **sense of touch.**

Vocabulary
distinct (di stiŋkt´) *adj.* clearly different; separate

Reading Skill
Main Idea Which sentence in this paragraph states the main idea?

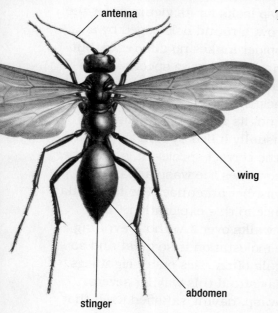

antenna

wing

stinger

abdomen

They are sensitive only to air movement. A light breeze makes them vibrate slowly, without disturbing the common hair. When one blows gently on the trichobothria, the tarantula reacts with a quick jerk of its four front legs. If the front and hind legs are stimulated at the same time, the spider makes a sudden jump. This reaction is quite independent of the state of its appetite.

These three tactile responses—to pressure on the body wall, to moving of the common hair, and to flexing of the trichobothria—are so different from one another that there is no possibility of confusing them. They serve the tarantula adequately for most of its needs and enable it to avoid most annoyances and dangers. But they fail the spider completely when it meets its deadly enemy, the digger wasp Pepsis.

These solitary wasps are beautiful and formidable creatures. Most species are either a deep shiny blue all over, or deep blue with rusty wings. The largest have a wing span of about four inches. They live on nectar. When excited, they give off a pungent odor—a warning that they are ready to attack. The sting is much worse than that of a bee or common wasp, and the pain and swelling last longer. In the adult stage the wasp lives only a few months. The female produces but a few eggs, one at a time at intervals of two or three days. For each egg the mother must provide one adult tarantula, alive but paralyzed. The tarantula must be of the correct species to nourish the larva. The mother wasp attaches the egg to the paralyzed spider's abdomen. Upon hatching from the egg, the larva is many hundreds of times smaller than its living but helpless victim. It eats no other food and drinks no water. By the time it has finished its single gargantuan meal and become ready for wasphood, nothing remains of the tarantula but its indigestible chitinous skeleton.[3]

The mother wasp goes tarantula-hunting when the egg in her ovary is almost ready to be laid. Flying low over the ground late on

Vocabulary

tactile (tak´ təl) *adj.* related to the sense of touch

formidable (fôr´ mə də bəl) *adj.* causing fear or dread

Reading Check

What three tactile responses do spiders have?

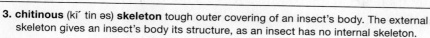

3. **chitinous** (kī´ tin əs) **skeleton** tough outer covering of an insect's body. The external skeleton gives an insect's body its structure, as an insect has no internal skeleton.

Science Connection

Studying Animal Behavior
Ethology—the scientific study of animal behavior in the wild—has helped scientists better understand the role of instinct in animal interactions. For instance, Konrad Lorenz (lōr´ ens´), shown below, discovered that instinct causes a baby bird to imprint on, or become attached to, the first moving creature it sees after hatching—even if that creature is a human scientist, not the bird's mother!

Connect to the Literature

Judging from Petrunkevitch's essay, what two concepts are a key concern for ethologists?

Vocabulary
evoking (ē vōk´ iŋ)
v. drawing forth emotions or responses

a sunny afternoon, the wasp looks for its victim or for the mouth of a tarantula burrow, a round hole edged by a bit of silk. The sex of the spider makes no difference, but the mother is highly discriminating as to species. Each species of Pepsis requires a certain species of tarantula, and the wasp will not attack the wrong species. In a cage with a tarantula which is not its normal prey, the wasp avoids the spider, and is usually killed by it in the night.

Yet when a wasp finds the correct species, it is the other way about. To identify the species the wasp apparently must explore the spider with her antennae. The tarantula shows an amazing tolerance to this exploration. The wasp crawls under it and walks over it without **evoking** any hostile response. The molestation is so great and so persistent that the tarantula often rises on all eight legs, as if it were on stilts. It may stand this way for several minutes. Meanwhile the wasp, having satisfied itself that the victim is of the right species, moves off a few inches to dig the spider's grave. Working vigorously with legs and jaws, it excavates a hole 8 to 10 inches deep with a diameter slightly larger than the spider's girth. Now and again the wasp pops out of the hole to make sure that the spider is still there.

When the grave is finished, the wasp returns to the tarantula to complete her ghastly enterprise. First she feels it all over once more with her antennae. Then her behavior becomes more aggressive. She bends her abdomen, protruding her sting, and searches for the soft membrane at the point where the spider's leg joins its body—the only spot where she can penetrate the horny skeleton. From time to time, as the exasperated spider slowly shifts ground, the wasp turns on her back and slides along with the aid of her wings, trying to get under the tarantula for a shot at the vital spot. During all this maneuvering, which can last for several minutes, the tarantula makes no move to save itself. Finally the wasp corners it against some obstruction and grasps one of its legs in her powerful jaws. Now at last the harassed spider tries a desperate but vain defense. The two contestants roll over and over on the ground. It is a terrifying sight and the outcome is always the same. The wasp finally manages to thrust her sting into the soft spot and holds it there for a few seconds while she pumps in the poison. Almost immediately the tarantula falls paralyzed on its back. Its legs stop twitching; its heart stops beating. Yet it is not dead, as is shown by the fact that if taken from the wasp it can be restored to some sensitivity by being kept in a moist chamber for several months.

After paralyzing the tarantula, the wasp cleans herself by dragging her body along the ground and rubbing her feet, sucks the drop of blood oozing from the wound in the spider's abdomen, then grabs a leg of the flabby, helpless animal in her jaws and drags it down to the bottom of the grave. She stays there for many minutes, sometimes for several hours, and what she does all that time in the dark we do not know. Eventually she lays her egg and attaches it to the side of the spider's abdomen with a sticky secretion. Then she emerges, fills the grave with soil carried bit by bit in her jaws, and finally tramples the ground all around to hide any trace of the grave from prowlers. Then she flies away, leaving her descendant safely started in life.

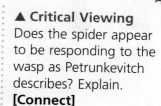

In all this the behavior of the wasp evidently is qualitatively different from that of the spider. The wasp acts like an intelligent animal. This is not to say that instinct plays no part or that she reasons as man does. But her actions are to the point; they are not automatic and can be modified to fit the situation. We do not know for certain how she identifies the tarantula—probably it is by some olfactory or chemotactile sense[4]—but she does it purposefully and does not blindly tackle a wrong species.

On the other hand, the tarantula's behavior shows only confusion. Evidently the wasp's pawing gives it no pleasure, for it tries to move away. That the wasp is not simulating sexual stimulation is certain, because male and female tarantulas react in the same way to its advances. That the spider is not anesthetized by some odorless secretion is easily shown by blowing lightly at the tarantula and making it jump suddenly. What, then, makes the tarantula behave as stupidly as it does?

No clear, simple answer is available. Possibly the stimulation by the wasp's antennae is masked by a heavier pressure on the spider's body, so that it reacts as when prodded by a pencil. But the explanation may be much more complex. Initiative in attack is not in the nature of tarantulas; most species fight only when

---

4. **olfactory** (äl fak´ tə rē) . . . **chemotactile** (kē´ mō tak´ təl) **sense** An olfactory sense is a sense of smell. A chemotactile sense involves sensitivity by touch to the presence of specific chemicals.

▲ **Critical Viewing**
Does the spider appear to be responding to the wasp as Petrunkevitch describes? Explain. **[Connect]**

Literary Analysis
Expository Essay How does the writer link his descriptions of behavior to the concepts identified at the beginning of the essay?

☑ Reading Check
What does the wasp do to the tarantula?

cornered so that escape is impossible. Their inherited patterns of behavior apparently prompt them to avoid problems rather than attack them. For example, spiders always weave their webs in three dimensions, and when a spider finds that there is insufficient space to attach certain threads in the third dimension, it leaves the place and seeks another, instead of finishing the web in a single plane. This urge to escape seems to arise under all circumstances, in all phases of life, and to take the place of reasoning. For a spider to change the pattern of its web is as impossible as for an inexperienced man to build a bridge across a chasm obstructing his way.

In a way the instinctive urge to escape is not only easier but often more efficient than reasoning. The tarantula does exactly what is most efficient in all cases except in an encounter with a ruthless and determined attacker dependent for the existence of her own species on killing as many tarantulas as she can lay eggs. Perhaps in this case the spider follows its usual pattern of trying to escape, instead of seizing and killing the wasp, because it is not aware of its danger. In any case, the survival of the tarantula species as a whole is protected by the fact that the spider is much more fertile than the wasp.

Critical Thinking

1. **Key Ideas and Details (a)** What do newly hatched digger wasps feed on? **(b) Compare and Contrast:** Using examples from the essay, compare the ways in which the wasp and the tarantula each provide for their young.

2. **Craft and Structure** The author says the tarantula rises "as if it were on stilts" to let the wasp explore it. How does this description help you picture the tarantula's actions?

3. **Key Ideas and Details (a) Classify:** In a two-column chart, collect examples of instinctive behavior and intelligent behavior from the essay. **(b) Analyze:** Identify the positive and the negative consequences of each behavior you list.

4. **Integration of Knowledge and Ideas** For an animal in conflict, do you think instinct or intelligence provides a greater advantage? Explain. *[Connect to the Big Question: What kind of knowledge changes our lives?]*

Cite textual evidence to support your responses.

Literary Analysis: Expository Essay

1. Key Ideas and Details (a) What phenomenon does Petrunkevitch explain in this **expository essay? (b)** How does the essay help readers see the difference between instinct and intelligence?

2. Craft and Structure Describe the **diction** in and the **tone** of the essay. Support your answer with analysis of specific word choices.

Reading Skill: Main Idea

3. Make a chart like the one shown to identify the **main**, or **central, ideas** and the **supporting details** in the essay. In each box, write the author's main idea about the topic in your own words. Then, find and record supporting details for each main idea.

Spider's Sense of Touch	Spider's Response to Wasp	Wasp's Handling of Spider
Detail Detail	Detail Detail	Detail Detail

4. In your own words, **summarize** the essay.

Vocabulary

Acquisition and Use Write a one-sentence answer to each question. Then, explain how the meaning of the underlined word helped you.

1. What is one <u>instinct</u> that all dogs have?

2. At what time do you <u>customarily</u> wake up?

3. How do scientists decide if two spiders belong to <u>distinct</u> species?

4. What fabric do you think has a lot of <u>tactile</u> appeal?

5. What traits make a grizzly bear a <u>formidable</u> creature?

6. Would a surprise party be effective in <u>evoking</u> a positive response?

Word Study Use the context of the sentences and what you know about the **Latin roots -tact-** and **-tang-** to explain your answers.

1. Why is it important for scientists to have *tangible* evidence?

2. Is someone who has *tact* in touch with the feelings of others?

Word Study

The **Latin roots -tact-** and **-tang-** mean "touch" or "feel."

Apply It Explain how the roots contribute to the meanings of these words. Consult a dictionary if necessary.

contact

intact

tangent

What kind of *knowledge* changes our lives?

from **Longitude**
Dava Sobel

Writing About the Big Question

In the excerpt from *Longitude*, the author presents a history of the search for information about longitude. Use this sentence starter to develop your ideas about the Big Question.

New discoveries and inventions allow for **growth** in a person's **understanding** of the world because _____.

While You Read Look for steps taken throughout history to reach an understanding of longitude.

Vocabulary

Read each word and its definition. Decide whether you know the word well, know it a little bit, or do not know it at all. After you read, see how your knowledge of each word has increased.

- **haphazardly** (hap´ haz´ ərd lē) *adv.* in an unplanned or a disorganized way (p. 476) *Dirty clothes lay <u>haphazardly</u> thrown about the messy room.* haphazard *adj.* haphazardness *n.*

- **configuration** (kən fig´ yə rā´ shən) *n.* arrangement of parts; pattern (p. 476) *We stood in a circular <u>configuration</u>.* configurative *adj.* configure *v.* figure *n.*

- **converge** (kən vʉrj´) *v.* to come together (p. 476) *Relatives from across the country will <u>converge</u> at the reunion.* convergence *n.*

- **derived** (di rīvd´) *v.* reached by reasoning (p. 477) *We <u>derived</u> the answer by solving the equation.* derivation *n.* derivative *n.*

- **contested** (kən test´ əd) *v.* tried to disprove or invalidate something; disputed (p. 481) *She <u>contested</u> the false charges with the credit card company.* contest *n.* contestant *n.*

- **impervious** (im pʉr´ vē əs) *adj.* not affected by (used with *to*) (p. 481) *In my new parka, I am <u>impervious</u> to cold weather.* imperviously *adv.* imperviousness *n.*

> **Word Study**
>
> The **Latin root -fig-** means "form" or "shape."
>
> In this essay, the author explains that although the world changes its **configuration**, its contours and how boundaries are formed, the lines of latitude and longitude stay fixed.

Meet
Dava Sobel
(b. 1947)

Author of
Longitude

As a child in the Bronx, New York, Dava Sobel enjoyed trips on her family's sailboat, navigated by one of her parents. Years later, she would transform a chapter of navigation history into her first bestseller, *Longitude*.

Curiosity and Inspiration Sobel attended the Bronx High School of Science and went on to become an award-winning science reporter for *The New York Times* and various magazines. In November 1993, she attended a conference about navigation. She became fascinated by the historic contributions of clockmaker John Harrison.

While researching the history of longitude, Sobel stumbled onto the topic of her next book: Italian Renaissance astronomer Galileo and his daughter. She wrote about their relationship in *Galileo's Daughter*.

BACKGROUND FOR THE ESSAY
Navigation

Navigation is the science of finding the position and direction of a craft such as a ship or plane. Since ancient times, mapmakers and sailors have used a system of imaginary lines—longitude and latitude—to identify positions on the Earth's surface.

Did You Know?

While researching *Longitude*, Sobel traveled to London for research and to stand directly on the prime meridian.

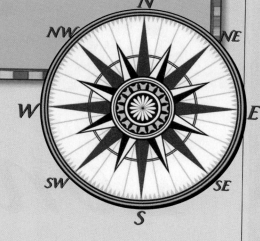

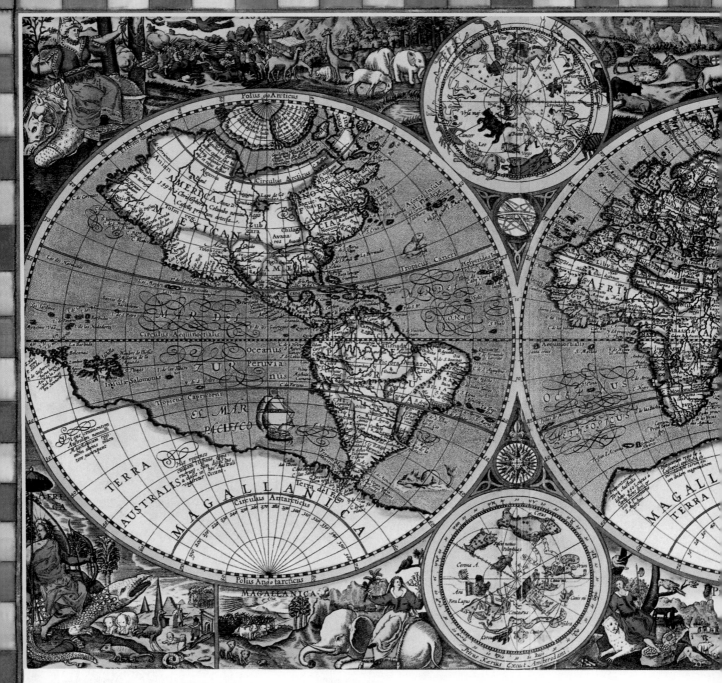

from Longitude

Dava Sobel

*W*hen I'm playful
I use the meridians
of longitude and parallels
of latitude for a seine, and
drag the Atlantic Ocean
for whales.

—Mark Twain
Life on the Mississippi

*O*nce on a Wednesday excursion when I was a little girl, my father bought me a beaded wire ball that I loved. At a touch, I could collapse the toy into a flat coil between my palms, or pop it open to make a hollow sphere. Rounded out, it resembled a tiny Earth, because its hinged wires traced the same pattern of intersecting circles that I had seen on the globe in my schoolroom—the thin black lines of latitude and longitude. The few colored beads slid along the wire paths haphazardly, like ships on the high seas.

My father strode up Fifth Avenue to Rockefeller Center with me on his shoulders, and we stopped to stare at the statue of Atlas,[1] carrying Heaven and Earth on his.

The bronze orb that Atlas held aloft, like the wire toy in my hands, was a see-through world, defined by imaginary lines. The Equator. The Ecliptic. The Tropic of Cancer. The Tropic of Capricorn. The Arctic Circle. The prime meridian. Even then I could recognize, in the graph-paper grid imposed on the globe, a powerful symbol of all the real lands and waters on the planet.

Today, the latitude and longitude lines govern with more authority than I could have imagined forty-odd years ago, for they stay fixed as the world changes its configuration underneath them—with continents adrift across a widening sea, and national boundaries repeatedly redrawn by war or peace.

As a child, I learned the trick for remembering the difference between latitude and longitude. The latitude lines, the *parallels*, really do stay parallel to each other as they girdle the globe from the Equator to the poles in a series of shrinking concentric[2] rings. The meridians of longitude go the other way: They loop from the North Pole to the South and back again in great circles of the same size, so they all converge at the ends of the Earth. •

Lines of latitude and longitude began crisscrossing our worldview in ancient times, at least three centuries before the birth of Christ. By A.D. 150, the cartographer and astronomer Ptolemy had plotted them on the twenty-seven maps of his first world atlas. Also for this landmark volume, Ptolemy listed all the place names in an index, in alphabetical order, with the latitude and longitude of each—as well as he could gauge them from travelers' reports. Ptolemy himself had only an armchair appreciation of the wider world. A common misconception of

Vocabulary

haphazardly (hap´ haz´ ərd lē) *adv.* in an unplanned or a disorganized way

configuration (kən fig´ yə rā´ shən) *n.* arrangement of parts; pattern

converge (kən vʉrj´) *v.* to come together

▼ **Critical Viewing**
How does this image convey the endurance of the system of longitude and latitude? **[Interpret]**

1. **Fifth Avenue . . . Rockefeller Center . . . Atlas** landmarks in the borough of Manhattan of New York City. Rockefeller Center features a statue of Atlas, the Greek giant condemned to carry the heavens on his shoulders.
2. **concentric** (kən sen´ trik) *adj.* having a center in common.

476 Types of Nonfiction: Essays and Speeches

his day held that anyone living below the Equator would melt into deformity from the horrible heat.

The Equator marked the zero-degree parallel of latitude for Ptolemy. He did not choose it arbitrarily but took it on higher authority from his predecessors, who had derived it from nature while observing the motions of the heavenly bodies. The sun, moon, and planets pass almost directly overhead at the Equator. Likewise the Tropic of Cancer and the Tropic of Capricorn, two other famous parallels, assume their positions at the sun's command. They mark the northern and southern boundaries of the sun's apparent motion over the course of the year.

Ptolemy was free, however, to lay his prime meridian, the zero-degree longitude line, wherever he liked. He chose to run it through the Fortunate Islands (now called the Canary and Madeira Islands) off the northwest coast of Africa. Later mapmakers moved the prime meridian to the Azores and to the Cape Verde Islands,[3] as well as to Rome, Copenhagen, Jerusalem, St. Petersburg, Pisa, Paris, and Philadelphia, among other places, before it settled down at last in London. As the world turns, any line drawn from pole to pole may serve as well as any other for a starting line of reference. The placement of the prime meridian is a purely political decision.

Here lies the real, hard-core difference between latitude and longitude—beyond the superficial difference in line direction that any child can see: The zero-degree parallel of latitude is fixed by the laws of nature, while the zero-degree meridian of longitude shifts like the sands of time. This difference makes finding latitude child's play, and turns the determination of longitude, especially at sea, into an adult dilemma—one that stumped the wisest minds of the world for the better part of human history.

Any sailor worth his salt can gauge his latitude well enough by the length of the day, or by the height of the sun or known guide stars above the horizon. Christopher Columbus followed a straight path across the Atlantic when he "sailed the parallel" on his 1492 journey, and the technique would doubtless have carried him to the Indies had not the Americas intervened.

The measurement of longitude meridians, in comparison, is tempered by time. To learn one's longitude at sea, one needs to know what time it is aboard ship and also the time at the home

Reading Skill
Main Idea What main idea does the writer support using examples like Rome and Copenhagen?

A common misconception of his day held that anyone living below the Equator would melt into deformity from the horrible heat.

Reading Check
Name an important contribution made to science or navigation by Ptolemy.

---

3. **Azores** (ā´ zôrz´) . . . **Cape Verde** (vʉrd) **Islands** two island groups in the Atlantic Ocean; the Azores are off Portugal and the Cape Verde Islands are off the westernmost point of Africa.

Science Connection

Longitude and Latitude

The lines of longitude and latitude form an imaginary grid that can be used to name the exact location of any place on Earth.

- The **equator** is the line of latitude on which all points are the same distance from the North and South poles. The sun appears directly overhead at the equator on March 21 and September 21 of each year.

- The **Tropic of Cancer** is 23° 27′ north of the equator. It marks the northernmost latitude at which the sun can appear directly overhead—an event that occurs at noon on June 20 or 21.

- The **Tropic of Capricorn,** at 23° 27′ south, is the southernmost latitude at which the sun can appear directly overhead. The sun reaches its highest position at this tropic at noon on December 20 or 21.

- The **prime meridian** is the line of longitude chosen as the 0° line.

Connect to the Literature

What does this information indicate about how sailors determine latitude by the sun?

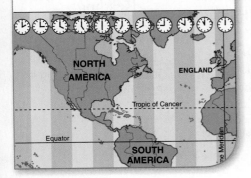

port or another place of known longitude—at that very same moment. The two clock times enable the navigator[4] to convert the hour difference into a geographical separation. Since the Earth takes twenty-four hours to complete one full revolution of three hundred sixty degrees, one hour marks one twenty-fourth of a spin, or fifteen degrees. And so each hour's time difference between the ship and the starting point marks a progress of fifteen degrees of longitude to the east or west. Every day at sea, when the navigator resets his ship's clock to local noon when the sun reaches its highest point in the sky, and then consults the home-port clock, every hour's discrepancy between them translates into another fifteen degrees of longitude.

Those same fifteen degrees of longitude also correspond to a distance traveled. At the Equator, where the girth of the Earth is greatest, fifteen degrees stretch fully one thousand miles. North or south of that line, however, the mileage value of each degree decreases. One degree of longitude equals four minutes of time the world over, but in terms of distance, one degree shrinks from sixty-eight miles at the Equator to virtually nothing at the poles.

Precise knowledge of the hour in two different places at once—a longitude prerequisite so easily accessible today from any pair of cheap wristwatches—was utterly unattainable up to and including the era of pendulum clocks.[5] On the deck of a rolling ship, such clocks would slow down, or speed up, or stop running altogether. Normal changes in temperature encountered en route from a cold country of origin to a tropical trade zone thinned or thickened a clock's lubricating oil and made its metal parts expand or contract with equally disastrous results. A rise or fall in barometric pressure, or the subtle variations in the Earth's gravity from one latitude to another, could also cause a clock to gain or lose time.

For lack of a practical method of determining longitude, every great captain in the Age of Exploration[6]

---

4. **navigator** (nav′ ə gāt′ ər) *n.* a person skilled in locating the position and plotting the course of a ship or an aircraft.
5. **pendulum** (pen′ dyo͞o ləm) **clocks** clocks whose timekeeping movement is regulated by a pendulum, a weight swinging freely from a fixed point.
6. **Age of Exploration** the period from about 1450 to about 1700, when European navigators sailed to new territories and founded colonies in Africa, the Americas, and Asia.

became lost at sea despite the best available charts and compasses. From Vasco da Gama to Vasco Núñez de Balboa, from Ferdinand Magellan to Sir Francis Drake[7]—they all got where they were going willy-nilly, by forces attributed to good luck or the grace of God.

As more and more sailing vessels set out to conquer or explore new territories, to wage war, or to ferry gold and commodities between foreign lands, the wealth of nations floated upon the oceans. And still no ship owned a reliable means for establishing her whereabouts. In consequence, untold numbers of sailors died when their destinations suddenly loomed out of the sea and took them by surprise. In a single such accident, on October 22, 1707, at the Scilly Isles near the southwestern tip of England, four home-bound British warships ran aground and nearly two thousand men lost their lives.

---

7. **Vasco da Gama** (väs´ kô də gä´ mə) . . . **Vasco Núñez de Balboa** (väs´ kô noo´ nyeth *the* bal bō´ ə) . . . **Ferdinand Magellan** (mə jel´ ən) . . . **Sir Francis Drake** famous explorers of the fifteenth and sixteenth centuries.

Reading Skill
Main Idea Which detail in this paragraph supports Sobel's idea that not knowing one's longitude was dangerous?

Reading Check
What key technical problem prevented sailors from measuring longitude accurately?

The active quest for a solution to the problem of longitude persisted over four centuries and across the whole continent of Europe. Most crowned heads of state eventually played a part in the longitude story, notably King George III of England and King Louis XIV of France. Seafaring men such as Captain William Bligh of the Bounty and the great circumnavigator Captain James Cook, who made three long voyages of exploration and experimentation before his violent death in Hawaii, took the more promising methods to sea to test their accuracy and practicability.

Renowned astronomers approached the longitude challenge by appealing to the clockwork universe: Galileo Galilei, Jean Dominique Cassini, Christiaan Huygens, Sir Isaac Newton, and Edmond Halley,[8] of comet fame, all entreated the moon and stars for help. Palatial observatories were founded at Paris, London, and Berlin for the express purpose of determining longitude by the heavens. Meanwhile, lesser minds devised schemes that depended on the yelps of wounded dogs, or the cannon blasts of signal ships strategically anchored—somehow—on the open ocean.

In the course of their struggle to find longitude, scientists struck upon other discoveries that changed their view of the universe. These include the first accurate determinations of the weight of the Earth, the distance to the stars, and the speed of light.

As time passed and no method proved successful, the search for a solution to the longitude problem assumed legendary proportions, on a par with discovering the Fountain of Youth, the secret of perpetual motion, or the formula for transforming lead into gold.[9] The governments of the great maritime nations—including Spain, the Netherlands, and certain city-states of Italy—periodically roiled the fervor by offering jackpot purses for a workable method. The British Parliament, in its famed Longitude Act of 1714, set the highest bounty of all, naming a prize equal to a king's ransom (several million dollars in today's currency) for a "Practicable and Useful" means of determining longitude.

▲ **King George III**

---

8. **Galileo Galilei** (gal´ ə lā´ ō gal´ ə lā ē) . . . **Jean-Dominique Cassini** (zhän dō mi nēk´ kä sē´ nē) . . . **Christiaan Huygens** (hī´ gənz) . . . **Sir Isaac Newton** . . . **Edmond Halley** (hal´ ē) pioneering astronomers and scientists of the sixteenth through the eighteenth centuries. Their work redefined people's picture of the universe, replacing traditional views with modern ones.

English clockmaker John Harrison, a mechanical genius who pioneered the science of portable precision timekeeping, devoted his life to this quest. He accomplished what Newton had feared was impossible: He invented a clock that would carry the true time from the home port, like an eternal flame, to any remote corner of the world.

Harrison, a man of simple birth and high intelligence, crossed swords with the leading lights of his day. He made a special enemy of the Reverend Nevil Maskelyne, the fifth astronomer royal, who contested his claim to the coveted prize money, and whose tactics at certain junctures can only be described as foul play.

With no formal education or apprenticeship to any watchmaker, Harrison nevertheless constructed a series of virtually friction-free clocks that required no lubrication and no cleaning, that were made from materials impervious to rust, and that kept their moving parts perfectly balanced in relation to one another, regardless of how the world pitched or tossed about them. He did away with the pendulum, and he combined different metals inside his works in such a way that when one component expanded or contracted with changes in temperature, the other counteracted the change and kept the clock's rate constant.

Vocabulary

contested (kən test′ əd) *v.* tried to disprove or invalidate something; disputed

impervious (im pʉr′ vē əs) *adj.* not affected by

Reading Check

What important device did Harrison invent?

---

9. Fountain of Youth . . . lead into gold three imaginary goals seriously pursued by inquirers. The Fountain of Youth was supposed to restore youth. Perpetual motion would allow people to generate power endlessly without consuming fuel. A formula to turn the cheap metal lead into the precious metal gold was sought for centuries by alchemists.

His every success, however, was parried by members of the scientific elite, who distrusted Harrison's magic box. The commissioners charged with awarding the longitude prize—Nevil Maskelyne among them—changed the contest rules whenever they saw fit, so as to favor the chances of astronomers over the likes of Harrison and his fellow "mechanics."[10] But the utility and accuracy of Harrison's approach triumphed in the end. His followers shepherded Harrison's intricate, exquisite invention through the design modifications that enabled it to be mass produced and enjoy wide use.

An aged, exhausted Harrison, taken under the wing of King George III, ultimately claimed his rightful monetary reward in 1773—after forty struggling years of political intrigue, international warfare, academic backbiting, scientific revolution, and economic upheaval.

All these threads, and more, entwine in the lines of longitude. To unravel them now—to retrace their story in an age when a network of orbiting satellites can nail down a ship's position within a few feet in just a moment or two—is to see the globe anew.

---

10. **"mechanics"** skilled workers and tradesmen, of a lower class than merchants or aristocrats.

Critical Thinking

Cite textual evidence to support your responses.

1. **Key Ideas and Details** **(a)** According to Sobel, what two methods can sailors use to estimate their latitude? **(b) Apply:** Using one of these methods, how could you tell whether you were at the equator—the zero-degree latitude?

2. **Key Ideas and Details** **Analyze:** Briefly explain why the invention of an accurate clock was crucial to solving the problem of determining longitude.

3. **Key Ideas and Details** **Analyze Cause and Effect:** Why did Harrison have difficulties getting his solution to the problem of longitude recognized?

4. **Integration of Knowledge and Ideas** **(a)** Identify two ways in which the world would be different without Harrison's clocks. **(b)** Would you say longitude is a life-changing development? Explain. *[Connect to the Big Question: What kind of knowledge changes our lives?]*

Literary Analysis: Expository Essay

1. Key Ideas and Details (a) What event does Sobel explain in this **expository essay? (b)** Briefly explain how she uses facts about astronomy and navigation to help readers understand the significance of this event.

2. Craft and Structure Describe the **diction** in and the **tone** of the essay. Support your answer with analysis of specific word choices.

Reading Skill: Main Idea

3. Using a chart like the one shown, identify the **main,** or **central, ideas** and the **supporting details** in the essay.

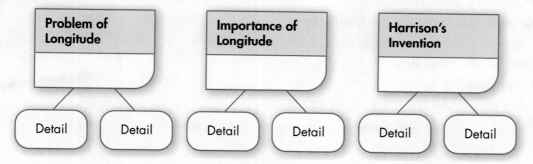

4. In your own words, **summarize** the essay.

Vocabulary

Acquisition and Use Write a one-sentence answer to each question. Then, explain how the meaning of the underlined word helped you.

1. What might a room look like if it is <u>haphazardly</u> decorated?

2. Has he <u>derived</u> a correct conclusion if he was missing information?

3. What is the <u>configuration</u> of the desks in your classroom?

4. Do you think anyone is truly <u>impervious</u> to criticism?

5. How could you determine if two streets <u>converge</u>?

6. What tone would you find at a debate over a <u>contested</u> election?

Word Study Use the context of the sentences and what you know about the **Latin root -fig-** to explain your answer to each question.

1. If a room becomes *transfigured,* will it look different?

2. What are you doing if you *reconfigure* a chart?

Word Study

The **Latin root -fig-** means "form" or "shape."

Apply It Explain how the root -fig- contributes to the meanings of these words. Consult a dictionary if necessary.

effigy
figment
figurine

Integrated Language Skills

The Spider and the Wasp •
from Longitude

Conventions: Direct and Indirect Objects

A **direct object** is a noun or pronoun that receives the action of an action verb. An **indirect object** is used with a direct object and names the person or thing that something is given to or done for.

To find the direct object of a verb, answer the question "[verb] *whom?"* or "[verb] *what?"*

> **Example:** Sam threw Fred the ball.
>
> *Threw what?* ANSWER: the ball (direct object)

To find the indirect object of a verb, answer the question "[verb] *to or for whom?"* or "[verb] *to or for what?"*

> **Example:** Sam threw Fred the ball.
>
> *Threw to whom?* ANSWER: Fred (indirect object)

Indirect objects may appear only between verbs and direct objects in sentences.

Practice A Identify the verb and direct and indirect objects in each sentence. Then, tell whether each object is a direct object or an indirect object.

1. Tarantulas attack insects.
2. Digger wasps give tarantulas a sting.
3. A spider's hair throws the brain impulses.
4. The wasp attaches her egg to the spider.
5. The writer told us the story of the spider and the wasp.

Practice B Identify the action verb and direct object in each sentence below. Then, rewrite each sentence, adding an indirect object, if possible.

1. The author's father bought a ball.
2. The sailors showed the compass.
3. Harrison presented a clock.
4. The king granted the prize money.
5. Astronomers gave the results of their long research study.

© **Reading Application** In "The Spider and the Wasp," find two sentences that have both direct and indirect objects. Identify and label the verb and the objects in each sentence.

© **Writing Application** Write two sentences about using maps using the following grammatical order: subject, action verb, indirect object, direct object.

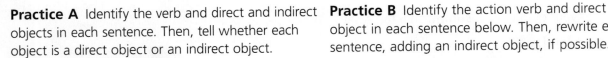
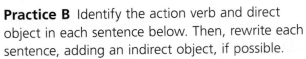

PH **WRITING COACH**   Further instruction and practice are available in *Prentice Hall Writing Coach.*

Writing

Common Core State Standards

W.9-10.2.e; SL.9-10.4; L.9-10.3
[For the full wording of the standards, see page 460.]

Explanatory Text Write a **business letter** in which you imagine that you are either a scientist requesting funds to do more research on tarantulas and wasps, or John Harrison explaining your invention to King George III. (For the format of a business letter, see page 532.) Maintain an objective style and formal tone appropriate for a business letter and for your audience and purpose.

If you read "The Spider and the Wasp," follow these suggestions.

- Explain why tarantulas and wasps are of scientific interest, and summarize what we currently know, as reported by Petrunkevitch.
- Tell what mysteries could be solved with additional research.

If you read the excerpt from *Longitude,* follow these suggestions.

- Briefly describe your clock and explain how it determines longitude.
- Mention the resistance you have met from the Royal Society.

Grammar Application In your letter, include at least one sentence with a direct object and indirect object.

Writing Workshop: *Work in Progress*

Prewriting for a Letter to the Editor For a letter to the editor you may write, list several issues in the news that spark your interest. Write two important facts or examples for each issue. Then, choose one issue about which to write. Put this Issues List in your writing portfolio.

Use this prewriting activity to prepare for the **Writing Workshop** on page 532.

Speaking and Listening

Comprehension and Collaboration Deliver a **humorous persuasive speech** in which you encourage your audience to view wasps and tarantulas as pets, or propose moving the prime meridian to your hometown.

- Plan humorous approaches to meet your audience's interests.
- Formulate a clear thesis—the main idea you want to get across.
- Support your ideas with facts, examples, and reasons.
- Address specific concerns your audience may have, anticipating and answering any objections.
- Choose effective language. Slang might seem contemporary, but formal language might command respect. Use figurative language such as similes, metaphors, or imagery to make your message vivid.

PHLit Online!
www.PHLitOnline.com
- Interactive graphic organizers
- Grammar tutorial
- Interactive journals

ⓒ Leveled Texts

Build your skills and improve your comprehension of nonfiction with texts of increasing complexity.

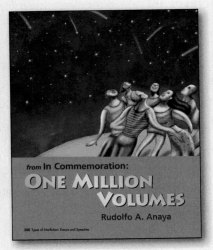

Read **"The Sun Parlor"** to learn what happens when a woman puts her pride in a room ahead of her respect for a child.

Read the excerpt from **"In Commemoration: One Million Volumes"** to see how a boy cultivates his love of books throughout his life.

ⓒ Common Core State Standards

Meet these standards with either **"The Sun Parlor"** (p. 490) or the excerpt from **"In Commemoration: One Million Volumes"** (p. 500).

Reading Informational Text
3. Analyze how the author unfolds an analysis or series of ideas or events, including the order in which the points are made, how they are introduced and developed, and the connections that are drawn between them. *(Literary Analysis: Reflective Essay)*

Spiral Review: RI.9-10.5

Writing
3.d. Use precise words and phrases, telling details, and sensory language to convey a vivid picture of the experiences, events, setting, and/or characters.

3.e. Provide a conclusion that follows from and reflects on what is experienced, observed, or resolved over the course of the narrative. *(Writing: Memoir)*

Speaking and Listening
4. Present information, findings, and supporting evidence clearly, concisely, and logically such that listeners can follow the line of reasoning and the organization, development, substance, and style are appropriate to purpose, audience, and task. *(Speaking and Listening: Oral Recollection)*

Language
6. Acquire and use accurately general academic and domain-specific words and phrases, sufficient for reading and writing at the college and career readiness level; demonstrate independence in gathering vocabulary knowledge when considering a word or phrase important to comprehension or expression. *(Vocabulary: Word Study)*

Literary Analysis: Reflective Essay

A **reflective essay** is a brief nonfiction work in which a writer presents the experiences that shaped or inspired his or her thoughts on a topic. In a reflective essay, a writer

- tells of an event, a time period, or an idea from his or her own life and experience.
- introduces and develops reflections on his or her topic, weaving connections between personal experience and a point of general interest, such as a lesson about life.
- may focus his or her reflections on a specific object, scene, occasion, place, or idea.

Look for these characteristics of a reflective essay as you read.

Reading Skill: Main Idea

To fully understand an essay, **analyze central,** or **main, ideas** and **supporting details**—recognize each main point that the writer makes and identify the ideas or facts that explain or illustrate it. To help you analyze, **ask questions** like these as you read:

- What is the topic of this passage?
- What is the main point being made?
- Which details support this point?

Using the Strategy: Main Ideas and Supporting Details Chart

As you read, record details on a **main ideas and supporting details chart** like this one. After you have read, consider what you know about the issue the writer develops and identify other questions you may have.

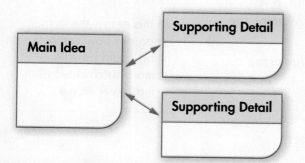

What kind of *knowledge* changes our lives?

The *Sun Parlor*
Dorothy West

Writing About the Big Question

In "The Sun Parlor," a woman learns an important lesson about values. Use these sentence starters to develop your ideas about the Big Question.

Understanding what is truly important in life is valuable because _____.

Learning from past mistakes can lead to personal **growth** when _____.

While You Read Notice the author's attitude toward the sun room, and compare it with the way she seems to feel about her niece.

Vocabulary

Read each word and its definition. Decide whether you know the word well, know it a little bit, or do not know it at all. After you read, see how your knowledge of each word has increased.

- **lavished** (lav´ isht) *v.* gave with extreme generosity (p. 491) *She lavished candy on us, and we had to borrow a bag to carry it home. lavish adj. lavishly adv. lavishness n.*

- **subordinate** (sə bôrd´ 'n it) *adj.* below another in importance or rank (p. 491) *A private is subordinate to a general. subordinate n. subordinately adv. subordination n.*

- **rejuvenation** (ri jo͞o´ və nā´ shən) *n.* the act of making new, youthful, or energetic again (p. 492) *A warm bath is a good method for rejuvenation. rejuvenate v. rejuvenator n. juvenile n.*

- **convalesce** (kän´ və les´) *v.* regain strength and health (p. 494) *A few days at home will give you time to convalesce after the accident. convalescence n. convalescent adj.*

- **cajoling** (kə jōl´ iŋ) *n.* coaxing with flattery (p. 494) *I resisted her cajoling and did not sign up for the play. cajole v. cajoler n. cajolingly adv.*

- **succinct** (sək siŋkt´) *adj.* clearly and briefly stated (p. 494) *If your essay is too wordy, revise to make it more succinct. succinctly adv. succinctness n.*

Word Study

The **Latin prefix suc-** is another spelling of the prefix **sub-,** meaning "under," "less or lower than," or "following after."

In this essay, the author imagines how something could be said in a more **succinct** way, using fewer words.

Meet
Dorothy West
(1907–1998)

Author of
The Sun Parlor

Dorothy West enjoyed a comfortable childhood—one made possible by her family's fiery ambition and hard work. Her father, a former slave, came north and built a successful business in Boston.

A Lifetime of Writing By the age of fourteen, West was winning local writing competitions in Boston. A few years later, in 1926, she moved to New York City and contributed to the Harlem Renaissance, an outpouring of African American creativity in the 1920s.

West wrote short stories, novels, and essays. She spent the last half of her life in Oak Bluffs, the village in Martha's Vineyard that is the setting for "The Sun Parlor."

BACKGROUND FOR THE ESSAY

Parlors and Sun Parlors

In past eras, many houses, like the one described in "The Sun Parlor," included a room called the parlor. An early version of the modern living room, the parlor was a place for family members to visit with guests or with each other. A sun parlor, or solarium, enclosed mostly by glass, was intended for enjoying the sun and for reading and talking.

Did You Know?

Oprah Winfrey made West's second novel, *The Wedding,* into a television movie.

The Sun Parlor

Dorothy West

This is a tale with a moral. I will try not to tax your attention too long. But I have to go way back to begin because it begins with my childhood. It is about houses and children, and which came first.

There were four of us children, well-schooled in good manners, well-behaved almost all of the time, and obedient to the commands of grown-ups, the power people who could make or break us.

We lived in a beautiful house. The reason I knew that is because all my mother's friends said so, and brought their other friends to see it. On the day appointed for the tour, which included inspection of every room on every floor, my mother would gather us around her and say in her gentlest voice, "I'm sorry, children, but Mrs. So-and-so is coming today and bringing a friend to see our house. You children keep clean and play quietly while they're here. It's not a real visit. They won't stay long. It'll be over before you can say Jack Robinson."

Most often a first-time caller, having **lavished** praise on everything she saw, including us, proceeded out without any further remarks. But there were others who, when they saw four children good as gold, did not see beyond their size, and asked my mother in outspoken horror, "How can you bear to let children loose in a lovely house like this?"

Every time it happened we were terrified. What would happen to us if my mother decided her house was too good for us and she hated the sight of us? What would we do, where would we go, would we starve?

My mother looked at our stricken faces, and her own face softened and her eyes filled with love. Then she would say to her inquisitor, though she did not say it rudely, "The children don't belong to the house. The house belongs to the children. No room says, *Do not enter*."

I did not know I could ever forget those sentiments. But once, to my lasting regret, I did. With the passage of years I took my place with grown-ups, and there was another generation, among them the little girl, Sis, who was my mother's treasure. The summer she was eight was the one time I forgot that a child is not **subordinate** to a house.

We had a cottage in the Highlands of Oak Bluffs of unimpressive size and appearance. My mother loved it for its easy care. It couldn't even stand in the shade of our city house, and there certainly were no special rules for children. No one had ever looked aghast at a child on its premises.

Except me, the summer I painted the sun parlor. I am not a painter, but I am a perfectionist. I threw my whole soul into the project, and worked with such diligence and

◀ **Critical Viewing**
Based on this painting, what feelings do you think will be described in the essay? **[Connect]**

Vocabulary
lavished (lav´ isht) *v.* gave with extreme generosity

subordinate (sə bôrd´ 'n it) *adj.* below another in importance or rank

Spiral Review
Development of Ideas What central idea does the author introduce in her opening paragraphs? What is its connection to the rest of the essay?

Reading Check
What does the author say she regrets forgetting?

painstaking care that when the uncounted hours ended I felt that I had painted the Sistine Chapel.[1]

School vacation began, and Sis arrived for the long holiday, the car pulling up at the edge of the brick walk, and Sis streaking into the house for a round of hugs, then turning to tear upstairs to take off her travel clothes and put on her play clothes, and suddenly her flying feet braking to a stop in front of the sun parlor, its open door inviting inspection.

She who was always in motion, she who never took time for a second look at anything, or cared whether her bed was smooth or crumpled, or noticed what was on her plate as long as it was something to eat—she, in the awakening that came when she was eight, in her first awareness of something outside herself, stood in the doorway of the sun parlor, her face filled with the joy of her discovery, and said in a voice on the edge of tears, "It's the most beautiful room I ever saw in my whole life."

I did not hear her. I did not really hear her. I did not recognize the magnitude of that moment. I let it sink to some low level of my subconscious. All I saw was that her foot was poised to cross the threshold of my chapel.

I let out a little cry of pain. "Sis," I said, "please don't go in the sun parlor. There's nothing in there to interest a child. It's not a place for children to play in. It's a place for grown-ups to sit in. Go and change. Summer is outside waiting for you to come and play wherever you please."

In a little while the sounds of Sis's soaring laughter were mingling with the happy sounds of other vacationing children. They kept any doubt I might have had from surfacing. Sis was surely more herself running free than squirming on a chair in the sun parlor.

All the same I monitored that room, looking for smudges and streaks, scanning the floor for signs of scuffing. The room bore no scars, and Sis showed no trace of frustration.

The summer flowed. My friends admired the room, though they did it without superlatives. To them it was a room I had talked about redoing for a long time. Now I had done it. So much for that.

The summer waned, and Sis went home for school's reopening, as did the other summer children, taking so much life and laughter with them that the ensuing days recovered slowly. •

Then my mother's sister, my favorite aunt, arrived from New York for her usual stay at summer's end. She looked ten years younger than her actual years. She seemed to bounce with energy, as if she had gone through some process of rejuvenation. We asked her for the secret.

Reading Skill
Main Idea Which details support the idea that Sis's reaction is exceptional?

Literary Analysis
Reflective Essay How is this experience connected to the lesson that the author learned from her mother?

Vocabulary
rejuvenation
(ri jōō′ və nā′ shən) *n.* the act of making new, youthful, or energetic again

---

1. **the Sistine Chapel** (sis′ tēn′ chap′ əl) place of worship in the Vatican, Rome, the Pope's residence. The chapel is famed for scenes painted on its walls and ceiling by Michelangelo.

I did not hear her. I did not really hear her.

There was no way for us to know in the brimful days that followed that there really was a secret she was keeping from us. She had had a heart attack some months before, and she had been ordered to follow a strict set of rules: plenty of rest during the day, early to bed at night, take her medicine faithfully, carefully watch her diet.

She was my mother's younger sister. My mother had been her babysitter. She didn't want my mother to know that she was back to being a baby again, needing to be watched over, having to be put down for a nap, having to be spoon-fed pap. She kept herself busy around the clock, walking, lifting, sitting up late, eating her favorite foods and forgetting her medicine.

▲ **Critical Viewing**
Do you think this painting reflects the author's description of the summer children? Why or why not? **[Connect]**

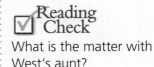

What is the matter with West's aunt?

The Sun Parlor **493**

▶ **Critical Viewing**
In what way does this painting suggest a room apart from the rest of the house, like the sun parlor? **[Connect]**

Reading Skill
Main Idea What main idea do these details about the aunt's stay in the sun parlor suggest?

Vocabulary
convalesce (kän′ və les′) *v.* regain strength and health
cajoling (kə jōl′ iŋ) *n.* coaxing with flattery
succinct (sək siŋkt′) *adj.* clearly and briefly stated

And then one day standing over the stove involved in the making of a meal that a master chef might envy, she collapsed, and the doctor was called, and the doctor called the ambulance.

She was in the hospital ten days. When she was ready to come home to convalesce, we turned the sun parlor into a sickroom, for the stairs to the upper story were forbidden to her. At night we who, when she slept upstairs, would talk family talk back and forth from our beds far into the night, without her we were now quiet, not wanting our voices to wake her if she was asleep, knowing her recovery depended on rest and quiet.

But at night she slept fitfully. The sleeping house and separation from the flock were unbearable. She was afraid of the sun parlor, seeing it as an abnormal offshoot from the main part of the house, its seven long windows giving access to so many imagined terrors. She did not know if we would hear her if she called. She did not know if she would ever get well.

She did not get well. She went back to the hospital, and for our sakes was brave in her last days, comforting us more than we comforted her.

When it was over, we took the sickbed away and restored the sun parlor to its natural look. But it did not look natural. The sadness resisted the sun's cajoling. It had settled in every corner. The seven long windows streaming light did not help. I closed the door and locked it.

My mother saw the closed door and the key in my hand. She said as a simple statement of fact, "A little girl wanted to love that room, and you wouldn't let her. We learn so many lessons as we go through life."

> "We learn so many lessons as we go through life."

"I know that now," I said. "I wish I had known it then." Another summer came, and with it Sis. The sun parlor door was open again, the room full of light with the sadness trying to hide itself whenever she passed. I did not know how to say to her, "You can go in the sun parlor if you want to." I did not know whether she knew it had been a sickroom, and might say, "Take your sun parlor and you-know-what," though in less succinct phrasing. I did not know if she yet knew that nothing can be the same once it has been different.

Other summers passed, older family members died, and mine became the oldest generation. I was living on the Island year-round in the winterized cottage. The sun parlor was just another everyday room, its seven long windows reduced to three of standard size, most of the furniture replaced for sturdier sitting.

Sis was married, a mother, coming to visit when she could—coming, I think, to look for bits and pieces of my mother in me, wanting to see her ways, hear her words through me.

It was a year ago that I asked her the question that had been on my mind, it seems, forever. A dozen times I had bitten it off my tongue because I did not know what she might answer.

"Sis," I said, "do you remember the summer I painted the sun parlor and acted as if I thought more of it than I thought of you? I'm not asking you to forgive me. All I want to know is if sometimes my mother said to you when I went out, 'She's gone.'" My mother always referred to me as "she" when she was annoyed with me. "'She said she'd be gone awhile. You go play in that sun parlor if you want to. There's nothing in there you can hurt. Nothing in that room is worth as much as a child.'"

I saw her lips beginning to part. And I felt my heart trembling.

"I don't want to know the answer. Please don't tell me the answer. I had to ask the question. It's enough for me that you listened."

She smiled.

Literary Analysis
Reflective Essay What lesson about life has the author learned?

Critical Thinking

Cite textual evidence to support your responses.

1. **Key Ideas and Details** **(a)** What project does West take on to improve the sun parlor? **(b) Infer:** Why does she tell Sis not to go into the room? **(c) Connect:** Does West's response to Sis reflect what her mother taught her about respect for children? Explain.

2. **Key Ideas and Details** **(a) Compare and Contrast:** Using details from the selection, contrast Sis's first reaction to the parlor with her reactions to other things. **(b) Interpret:** What does West mean by calling Sis's reaction part of an "awakening"?

3. **Craft and Structure** **(a)** At what point near the end of the essay does the author switch from the past to the present? **(b)** How does this order of ideas help her explain the lesson she learned?

4. **Integration of Knowledge and Ideas** **(a)** What does West mean when she says to Sis, "It's enough for me that you listened"? **(b)** Explain how the statement could also indicate the reason West wrote the essay. **(c)** In a group, discuss why it is important to West that people "listen." Work together to develop an explanation, and then present it to the class. *[Connect to the Big Question: What kind of knowledge changes our lives?]*

Literary Analysis: Reflective Essay

1. Key Ideas and Details Using a chart like the one shown, analyze West's use of the sun parlor as a focus for her **reflective essay.** For each detail you list, explain its connection to the sun parlor.

2. Craft and Structure **(a)** Explain what point the author makes through the feelings and events she connects with the sun parlor. **(b)** Explain how she organizes details in her essay to build toward this point.

The Sun Parlor
490 Types of Nonfiction: Essays and Speeches
Dorothy West

Reading Skill: Main Idea

3. (a) Reread the first six paragraphs. What is the topic of this section? **(b)** What is the **main idea? (c)** What details support it?

4. (a) What is the next main idea you find in the essay? **(b)** Identify three **supporting details** that develop this idea.

5. (a) After reading the essay, identify one further question you have. **(b)** Where could you look to find the answer?

Vocabulary

Acquisition and Use For each sentence, write a new sentence with the same meaning using a word from the list on page 488.

1. I gave in to my brother's wheedling and lent him my new game.

2. The lesser-known actors must share a dressing room.

3. They showered praise on us for our successful fund drive.

4. The complete recovery of her knee after surgery was a wonder.

5. After she broke her leg, my sister had to stay home for a month to regain her strength and health.

6. He is a good debater because his responses are clear and brief.

Word Study Use the context of the sentences and what you know about the **Latin prefix suc-** to explain your answer to each question.

1. If books you requested from the library arrive in *succession*, will you receive them all at the same time?

2. Will a person with strong willpower easily *succumb* to others?

Word Study

The **Latin prefix suc-** is another spelling of the prefix **sub-,** meaning "under," "less or lower than," or "following after."

Apply It Explain how the prefix -suc- contributes to the meanings of these words. Consult a dictionary if necessary.

succeed
successor
succor

What kind of *knowledge* **changes our lives?**

from **In Commemoration: ONE MILLION VOLUMES**

Rudolfo A. Anaya

Writing About the Big Question

In the excerpt from "In Commemoration: One Million Volumes," Anaya reflects on how a devotion to words and knowledge has shaped his life. Use these sentence starters to develop your ideas about the Big Question.

In addition to books and libraries, _____ may **influence** a person's desire to learn new things because _____.

One way to **enlighten** a person about new experiences and information is to _____.

While You Read Look for the different ways Anaya has gained knowledge throughout his life.

Vocabulary

Read each word and its definition. Decide whether you know the word well, know it a little bit, or do not know it at all. After you read, see how your knowledge of each word has increased.

- **infinite** (in´ fə nit) *adj.* beyond measure or comprehension; endless (p. 501) *The number of stars in the sky seems <u>infinite</u>. infinitely adv. infinity n. finite adj.*

- **inherent** (in hir´ ənt) *adj.* inborn; natural; characteristic (p. 502) *Her <u>inherent</u> sweetness makes it hard for her to get angry. inherently adv.*

- **paradox** (par´ ə däks´) *n.* a statement or situation that seems contradictory (p. 503) *What a <u>paradox</u> it is for him to confess that he never tells the truth! paradoxical adj. paradoxically adv.*

- **dilapidated** (də lap´ ə dāt´ id) *adj.* shabby; broken down (p. 503) *The <u>dilapidated</u> chair broke when I sat on it. dilapidate v. dilapidation n.*

- **enthralls** (en thrôlz´) *v.* captivates; fascinates (p. 505) *This book <u>enthralls</u> me, and I cannot wait to read more. enthrallment n.*

- **poignant** (poin´ yənt) *adj.* emotionally moving; piercing (p. 506) *The <u>poignant</u> scene with the abandoned puppies always makes me cry. poignancy n. poignantly adv.*

Word Study

The **Greek prefix** *para-* means "beside" or "beyond."

In this essay, the author explains that books are a **paradox** because they provide answers to questions but also make the reader want to go beyond that information in order to learn more.

Meet
Rudolfo A. Anaya
(b. 1937)

Author of
In Commemoration:
ONE MILLION VOLUMES

Rudolfo A. Anaya was born and raised in the rural village of Pastura in New Mexico. As a child, Anaya's imagination was nourished by *cuentos*—stories that Mexican Americans passed down from one generation to the next.

Teaching and Learning While teaching high school English, Anaya wrote *Bless Me, Ultima,* a highly praised novel about a young boy growing up in New Mexico. The novel was published in 1972. A strong voice of the Mexican American experience, Anaya is considered a founder of Chicano literature. He went on to teach at the University of New Mexico until his retirement in 1993. In his writing, though, he plays the student as much as the teacher. He explains, "Writing novels seems to be the medium which allows me to bring together all the questions I ask about life."

BACKGROUND FOR THE ESSAY
Libraries

In this essay, Anaya is astounded by the size of the University of New Mexico's library. Libraries perform a variety of functions. For example, a neighborhood library may preserve local history. A university library supports the research of scholars in a variety of subject areas. The Library of Congress guards the historical and cultural records of the United States.

DID YOU KNOW?
In 2002, Anaya was awarded a National Medal of the Arts; he has also received the Mexican Medal of Friendship.

from **In Commemoration:**

ONE MILLION VOLUMES

Rudolfo A. Anaya

A MILLION VOLUMES. A MAGIC NUMBER. A MILLION BOOKS TO READ, TO LOOK AT, TO HOLD IN ONE'S HAND, TO LEARN, TO DREAM. . . .

I have always known there were at least a million stars. In the summer evenings when I was a child, we, all the children of the neighborhood, sat outside under the stars and listened to the stories of the old ones, los viejitos.[1] The stories of the old people taught us to wonder and imagine. Their adivinanzas[2] induced the stirring of our first questioning, our early learning.

I remember my grandfather raising his hand and pointing to the swirl of the Milky Way which swept over us. Then he would whisper his favorite riddle:

> Hay un hombre con tanto dinero
> Que no lo puede contar
> Una mujer con una sábana tan grande
> Que no la puede doblar.

> There is a man with so much money
> He cannot count it
> A woman with a bedspread so large
> She cannot fold it

We knew the million stars were the coins of the Lord, and the heavens were the bedspread of his mother, and in our minds the sky was a million miles wide. A hundred million. Infinite. Stuff for the imagination. And what was more important, the teachings of the old ones made us see that we were bound to the infinity of that cosmic dance of life which swept around us. Their teachings created in us a thirst for knowledge. Can this library with its million volumes bestow that same inspiration?

I was fortunate to have had those old and wise viejitos as guides into the world of nature and knowledge. They taught me with their stories; they taught me the magic of words. Now

---

1. **los viejitos** (lôs byā hē´ tôs) *n.* Spanish for "the old ones."
2. **adivinanzas** (a *th*ē vē nan´ sas) *n.* Spanish for "riddles."

◀ **Critical Viewing**
How does this painting convey a sense of wonder and imagination? **[Connect]**

Vocabulary
infinite (in´ fə nit) *adj.* beyond measure or comprehension; endless

Reading Check
What does Anaya learn to appreciate from the *viejitos*?

Vocabulary
inherent (in hir´ ənt)
adj. inborn; natural;
characteristic

Literary Analysis
Reflective Essay Which
period in his life is the
writer describing?

Reading Skill
Main Idea What main
idea is supported by
details about the writer's
grandfather's stories?

Spiral Review
**Development of
Ideas** Explain how this
passage helps the writer
develop connections
between the theme of
wonder and the theme
of learning.

the words lie captured in ink, but the magic is still there, the power inherent in each volume. Now with book in hand we can participate in the wisdom of mankind.

Each person moves from innocence through rites of passage into the knowledge of the world, and so I entered the world of school in search of the magic in the words. The sounds were no longer the soft sounds of Spanish which my grandfather spoke; the words were in English, and with each new awareness came my first steps toward a million volumes. I, who was used to reading my oraciones en español[3] while I sat in the kitchen and answered the litany to the slap of my mother's tortillas,[4] I now stumbled from sound to word to groups of words, head throbbing, painfully aware that each new sound took me deeper into the maze of the new language. Oh, how I clutched the hands of my new guides then!

Learn, my mother encouraged me, learn. Be as wise as your grandfather. He could speak many languages. He could speak to the birds and the animals of the field.

Yes, I remember the cuentos[5] of my grandfather, the stories of the people. Words are a way, he said, they hold joy, and they are a deadly power if misused. I clung to each syllable which lisped from his tobacco-stained lips. That was the winter the snow came, he would say, it piled high and we lost many sheep and cattle, and the trees groaned and broke with its weight. I looked across the llano[6] and saw the raging blizzard, the awful destruction of that winter which was imbedded in our people's mind.

And the following summer, he would say, the grass of the llano grew so high we couldn't see the top of the sheep. And I would look and see what was once clean and pure and green. I could see a million sheep and the pastores[7] caring for them, as I now care for the million words that pasture in my mind.

But a million books? How can we see a million books? I don't mean just the books lining the shelves here at the University of New Mexico Library, not just the fine worn covers, the intriguing titles; how can we see the worlds that lie waiting in each book? A million worlds. A million million worlds. And the beauty of it is that each world is related to the next, as was taught to us by the old ones. Perhaps it is easier for a child to see. Perhaps it is easier for a child to ask: How many stars are there in the sky? How many leaves in the trees of the river? How many blades of grass in the llano? How many dreams in a night of dreams? ●

---

3. oraciones en español (ô ra syôn´ ās en es pa nyōl´) prayers in Spanish.
4. tortillas (tôr tē´ yəs) *n.* thin, flat, round cakes of unleavened cornmeal.
5. cuentos (kwen´ tôs) *n.* Spanish for "stories."
6. llano (ya´ nō) *n.* Spanish for "plain."
7. pastores (pas tô´ rās) *n.* Spanish for "shepherds."

Cultural Connection

Mexican American Pride
Anaya's celebration of his grandfather's *cuentos* shares in the spirit of the Chicano movement of the 1960s.

- Participants in the movement cultivated pride in their Mexican American heritage.

- Leaders included Cesar Chavez (shown in the mural), who unionized grape pickers in California.

- Chicano artists use the symbol of the eagle and serpent to reflect their connection with the Aztecs, founders of a great civilization in Mexico.

Connect to the Literature

What is one way in which Anaya's essay celebrates his Mexican American heritage? Explain your answer.

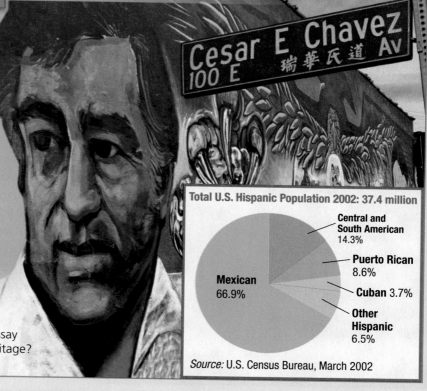

Total U.S. Hispanic Population 2002: 37.4 million

Central and South American 14.3%

Puerto Rican 8.6%

Cuban 3.7%

Other Hispanic 6.5%

Mexican 66.9%

Source: U.S. Census Bureau, March 2002

So I worked my way into the world of books, but here is the paradox, a book at once quenches the thirst of the imagination and ignites new fires. I learned that as I visited the library of my childhood, the Santa Rosa Library. It was only a dusty room in those days, a room sitting atop the town's fire department, which was comprised of one dilapidated fire truck used by the town's volunteers only in the direst emergencies. But in that small room I found my shelter and retreat. If there were a hundred books there we were fortunate, but to me there were a million volumes. I trembled in awe when I first entered that library, because I realized that if the books held as much magic as the words of the old ones, then indeed this was a room full of power.

Miss Pansy, the librarian, became my new guide. She fed me books as any mother would nurture her child. She brought me book after book, and I consumed them all. Saturday afternoons disappeared as the time of day dissolved into the time of distant worlds. In a world that occupied most of my other schoolmates with games, I took the time to read. I was a librarian's dream. My tattered library card was my ticket into the same worlds my grandfather had known, worlds of magic that fed the imagination.

Late in the afternoon, when I was satiated with reading, when I could no longer hold in my soul the characters that crowded there,

Vocabulary
paradox (par´ ə däks´) *n.* a statement or situation that seems contradictory

dilapidated (də lap´ ə dāt´ id) *adj.* shabby; broken down

Literary Analysis
Reflective Essay What general idea connects this new experience to those Anaya has already narrated?

Reading Check

How does Anaya pursue his love of words?

I heard the call of the llano, the real world of my father's ranchito, the solid, warm world of my mother's kitchen. Then to the surprise and bewilderment of Miss Pansy, I would rush out and race down the streets of our town, books tucked under my shirt, in my pockets, clutched tightly to my breast. Mad with the insanity of books, I would cross the river to get home, shouting my crazy challenge even at la Llorona,[8] and that poor spirit of so many frightening cuentos would wither and withdraw. She was no match for me.

Those of you who have felt the same exhilaration from reading—or from love—will know about what I'm speaking. Alas, the people of the town could only shake their heads and pity my mother. At least one of her sons was a bit touched. Perhaps they were right, for few will trade a snug reality to float on words to other worlds.

And now there are a million volumes for us to read here at the University of New Mexico Library. Books on every imaginable subject, in every field, a history of the thought of the world which we must keep free of censorship, because we treasure our freedoms. It is the word *freedom* which eventually must reflect what this collection, or the collection of any library, is all about. We know that as we preserve and use the literature of all cultures, we preserve and regenerate our own. The old ones knew and taught me this. They eagerly read the few newspapers that were available. They kept their diaries, they wrote décimas[9] and cuentos, and they survived on their oral stories and traditions.

Another time, another library. I entered Albuquerque[10] High School Library prepared to study, because that's where we spent our study time. For better or for worse, I received my first contracts as a writer there. It was a place where budding lovers spent most of their time writing notes to each other, and when my friends who didn't have the gift of words found out I could turn a phrase I quickly had all the business I could do. I wrote poetic love notes for a dime apiece and thus worked my way through high school.

▲ **Critical Viewing**
How might Anaya feel about a painting such as this one? How do you know? **[Connect]**

Reading Skill
Main Idea
Which details illustrate the main idea stated in the last sentence of this paragraph?

---

8. **la Llorona** (la yô rô′ na) *n.* spirit of many Spanish stories, famous for shouting and crying for her lost love.
9. **décimas** (dā′ sē mas) *n.* Spanish for "ten-line stanzas."
10. **Albuquerque** (al′ bə kʉr′ kē) *n.* city in central New Mexico.

And there were fringe benefits, because the young women knew very well who was writing the sweet words, and many a heart I was supposed to capture fell in love with me. And so, a library is also a place where love begins.

A library should be the heart of a city. With its storehouse of knowledge, it liberates, informs, teaches, and enthralls. A library indeed should be the cultural center of any city. Amidst the bustle of work and commerce, the great libraries of the world have provided a sanctuary where scholars and common man alike come to enlarge and clarify knowledge, to read and reflect in quiet solitude.

I knew a place like this. I spent many hours in the old library on Central Avenue and Edith Street. But my world was growing, and quite by accident I wandered up the hill to enroll in the University of New Mexico. And what a surprise lay in store for me. The libraries of my childhood paled in comparison to this new wealth of books housed in Zimmerman Library. Here there were stack after stack of books, and ample space and time to wander aimlessly in this labyrinth of new frontiers.

I had known the communal memory of my people through the newspapers and few books my grandfather read to me and through the rich oral tradition handed down by the old ones; now I discovered the collective memory of all mankind at my fingertips. I had only to reach for the books that laid all history bare. Here I could converse with the writers from every culture on earth, old and new, and at the same time I began my personal odyssey, which would add a few books to the collection which in 1981 would come to house a million volumes.

Those were exciting times. Around me swirled the busy world of the university, in many respects an alien world. Like many fellow undergraduates, I sought refuge in the library. My haven during those student university years was the reading room of the west wing of the old library. There I found peace. The carved vigas[11] decorating the ceiling, the solid wooden tables and chairs and the warm adobe color of the stucco were things with which I was familiar. There I felt comfortable. With books scattered around me, I could read and doze and dream. I took my breaks in the warm sun of the portal, where I ate my tortilla sandwiches, which I carried in my brown paper bag. There, with friends, I sipped coffee as we talked of changing the world and exchanged idealistic dreams.

---

11. **vigas** (bē´ gas) *n.* Spanish for "roof beams."

Vocabulary
enthralls (en thrôlz´) *v.* captivates; fascinates

> A LIBRARY INDEED SHOULD BE THE CULTURAL CENTER OF ANY CITY.

Literary Analysis
Reflective Essay What general idea does Anaya use to relate this new period in his life to previous ones?

Reading Check
What vital services do libraries provide to cities?

That is a rich and pleasant time in my memory. No matter how far across the world I find myself in the future, how deep in the creation of worlds with words, I shall keep the simple and poignant memories of those days. The sun set golden on the ocher walls, and the green pine trees and the blue spruce, sacred trees to our people, whispered in the breeze. I remembered my grandfather meeting with the old men of the village in the resolana[12] of one of the men's homes, or against the wall of the church on Sundays, and I remembered the things they said. Later, alone, dreaming against the sun-warmed wall of the library, I continued that discourse in my mind.

Yes, the library is a place where people should gather. It is a place for research, reading, and for the quiet fomentation of ideas, but because it houses the collective memory of our race, it should also be a place where present issues are discussed and debated and researched in order for us to gain the knowledge and insight to create a better future. The library should be a warm place that reflects the needs and aspirations of the people.

---

12. **resolana** (rā sô la´ na) *n.* Spanish for "place for enjoying the sun."

Critical Thinking

1. Key Ideas and Details **(a)** According to Anaya, what did the stories of *los viejitos* teach him and other children? **(b) Compare and Contrast:** Identify a difference and a similarity between the riddles and *cuento*s Anaya learned in childhood and the books he later read.

2. Craft and Structure **(a)** At what point near the end of the essay does the author switch from the past to the present? **(b)** How does this order of ideas help him develop his main idea about libraries?

3. Key Ideas and Details **Interpret:** Why does Anaya associate libraries with freedom?

4. Integration of Knowledge and Ideas **(a)** In what ways do libraries make an impact on individuals? **(b)** In today's world, what do you think is the best way to awaken wonder and imagination in people and inspire them to learn? *[Connect to the Big Question: What kind of knowledge changes our lives?]*

Cite textual evidence to support your responses.

Literary Analysis: Reflective Essay

1. Key Ideas and Details Using a chart like the one shown, analyze Anaya's use of libraries as a focus for his **reflective essay.** For each detail you list, explain its connection to libraries.

from In Commemoration:
ONE MILLION VOLUMES
Rudolfo A. Anaya

2. Craft and Structure (a) Choose an item from your chart, and explain its association with something endless—an uncountable number, for example. What truth about imagination does the item illustrate? **(b)** Explain how Anaya organizes details to develop this idea.

Reading Skill: Main Idea

3. (a) Reread up to the paragraph on page 502 that begins, "But a million books?" What is the topic of this section? **(b)** What is the **main idea? (c)** What details support it?

4. (a) What is the next main idea you find in the essay? **(b)** Identify three **supporting details** for the idea.

5. (a) After reading the essay, identify one further question you have. **(b)** Where could you look to find the answer?

Vocabulary

Acquisition and Use For each sentence, write a new sentence with the same meaning using a word from the list on page 498.

1. Getting wet is a risk that is a built-in part of boating.
2. Their reunion was very emotional and touching.
3. My broken-down old bike is dangerous to ride.
4. That comic book is wildly interesting to him.
5. When she takes care of her little brother, her patience is endless.
6. It seemed like a contradiction that she loved to grow vegetables but did not like to eat them.

Word Study Use the context of the sentences and what you know about the **Greek prefix *para-*** to explain your answer to each question.

1. Would two *parallel* boards be crossing or touching each other?
2. Should you postpone a task of *paramount* importance?

Word Study

The **Greek prefix *para-*** means "beside" or "beyond."

Apply It Explain how the prefix *para-* contributes to the meanings of these words. Consult a dictionary if necessary.

paramedic
parameter
paraphrase

Integrated Language Skills

The Sun Parlor • *from* In Commemoration: One Million Volumes

Conventions: Subject Complements

Predicate nominatives and **predicate adjectives** are subject complements. They appear after a linking verb such as *be, is,* or *seem,* and they rename, identify, or describe the subject of the sentence.

A subject and a predicate nominative both name the same person, place, or thing. The linking verb joins them and makes them equal.

Examples: Their first <u>choice</u> was <u>you</u>.
Our vacation <u>destination</u> is the <u>beach</u>.

A predicate adjective appears with the linking verb and describes the subject of the sentence.

Examples: <u>Roses</u> are <u>red</u>.
Soccer <u>equipment</u> is <u>expensive</u>.

Practice A Identify the subject complement in each sentence and label it *predicate nominative* or *predicate adjective.*

1. The author is the narrator.
2. The sun parlor was beautiful.
3. West's aunt seemed healthy.
4. Children are our greatest treasures.
5. West felt remorseful.

Practice B Add a predicate nominative or predicate adjective, as indicated, to complete each sentence.

1. Anaya is (predicate nominative).
2. Anaya is (predicate adjective).
3. The stories of Anaya's youth seemed (predicate adjective).
4. One feature of libraries is (predicate nominative).
5. Books are (predicate adjective).

© **Reading Application** In "The Sun Parlor," find and copy one sentence that has a predicate nominative and one sentence that has a predicate adjective. For each sentence, label the complements, and underline the subject once and the linking verb twice.

© **Writing Application** Write a brief paragraph about a library. At least two sentences should have predicate adjectives, and at least two sentences should have predicate nominatives. After you draft, identify the subject complements you have included.

PH **WRITING COACH**   Further instruction and practice are available in *Prentice Hall Writing Coach.*

Writing

Common Core State Standards

L.9-10.6; SL.9-10.4;
W.9-10.3.d-e
[For the full wording of the standards, see page 486.]

Narrative Text Both authors reflect on an earlier time in their lives. Write a brief **memoir,** or recollection based on your personal experience, of a room or a building that holds meaning for you.

- Memoirs are autobiographical; write in the first person, using the pronoun *I* to refer to yourself.
- Develop your memoir with *precise words* to paint a vivid picture of the space or place you are recalling.
- Use concrete *sensory details* to describe the sights, sounds, and smells of the scene, and organize your ideas in a logical order.
- Conclude by sharing your insights with readers and revealing why the place has special meaning for you. Write in a style appropriate for your purpose and audience.

Grammar Application As you write your memoir, use at least one predicate nominative and one predicate adjective.

Writing Workshop: *Work in Progress*

Prewriting for a Letter to the Editor Using the Issues List in your writing portfolio, write an opening sentence for each item that identifies the main point of your letter. Save this Main Idea List in your writing portfolio.

Use this prewriting activity to prepare for the **Writing Workshop** on page 532.

Speaking and Listening

Comprehension and Collaboration Prepare an **oral recollection.** Focus on someone you know who is interesting and important to you or on a group you've been involved in, such as a sports team or a community organization.

- Provide key details to develop your subject. Organize them logically, and build toward a central insight.
- Make sure to clearly establish your point of view and relationship with the subject of your recollection.
- Include sensory details and concrete images.
- First, present your recollection to a classmate. Then, revise your draft based on feedback from your partner. Make sure the reasoning you use to connect details to your central insight is clear and that the style of your speech is appropriate for your audience and purpose.
- Present a revised version of your recollection to the class.

PHLit Online!
www.PHLitOnline.com

- Interactive graphic organizers
- Grammar tutorial
- Interactive journals

Test Practice: Reading

Main Idea

Fiction Selection

Directions: *Read the selection. Then, answer the questions.*

Nahuaca's family were cultivators of the *chinampas,* the raised lake gardens of the Aztecs. Nahuaca worked beside his father, placing rows of long poles to form the sides of the chinampas in the shallow lake surrounding the great city of Tenochtitlán. He paddled the canoe, scooping mud and plants from the lake bottom to build the chinampas several feet above the lake. He transplanted the tiny tomato plants in the garden. As he worked, he marveled at the garden's beauty.

One day his father spoke to him. "Nahuaca, someday you will choose your own path, but know that if you choose to farm with your family, you will be contributing to your people. Growing these tomatoes, maize, and chilies allows us all to thrive. Without us, the people in our city would have no food. Food is not all we get from the lake gardens, though; they are an important part of our culture as well."

1. Which of the following *best* states the main idea of this passage?

  A. Aztec people were great warriors.
  B. Aztec people grew a variety of food in lake gardens.
  C. Tenochtitlán was a beautiful city.
  D. Aztec people lived on gardens in lakes and worked very hard.

2. Which detail supports the idea that Nahuaca appreciated the gardens?

  A. His family were cultivators of the chinampas.
  B. He worked alongside his father.
  C. His father told Nahuaca he would choose his own path someday.
  D. He marveled at the gardens' beauty.

3. Which of the following details *does not* tell how the Aztec people lived?

  A. Chinampas were raised lake gardens.
  B. "We grow tomatoes, maize, beans, and chilies."
  C. Nahuaca paddled a flat-bottom canoe.
  D. One day his father spoke to him.

4. To understand the Aztec way of life better, what question might you ask?

  A. Did Nahuaca continue to grow food?
  B. Is it difficult to grow tomatoes?
  C. What did Aztecs do for recreation?
  D. Why should people build lake gardens?

Writing for Assessment

Consider the main idea and details in this passage. Then write an appropriate title for it. In a paragraph, explain why your title makes sense.

Nonfiction Selection

Directions: *Read the selection. Then, answer the questions.*

You may not be able to imagine pizza without tomato sauce, but tomatoes have not always been such a popular food. Tomatoes began as a wild species in what is now Peru and Ecuador. The plant was probably domesticated in Mexico centuries before Europeans arrived. Its name is from the Náhuatl (Aztec) word *tomati*. In the early 1500s, the Spanish brought the tomato to Europe, where it was used as food by the Spanish and Italians. In England, France, and Northern Europe, however, the tomato was believed to be poisonous. The English used the plant simply for its beauty.

From Europe, the tomato was introduced to North America, where it was used as food in the early 1800s. By the early twentieth century, the tomato was widely popular as food, and by the late twentieth century, the United States led the world in tomato production.

1. Which of the following *best* states the main idea of the passage?

   A. Tomatoes originated in South America, probably in Ecuador and Peru, and were probably domesticated in Mexico.

   B. At one time, tomatoes were considered poisonous and planted for their beauty.

   C. The tomato has a long history that spans the world, but it did not become widely popular as a food until the 1900s.

   D. The Aztecs were the first to cultivate tomatoes.

2. Which of the following details *does not* support the main idea of the passage?

   A. Some believed tomatoes were poisonous.

   B. *Tomato* originated from a Náhautl word.

   C. Tomatoes originated in Ecuador and Peru.

   D. The Spanish brought the tomato to Europe.

3. The author's purpose is most likely to—

   A. entertain readers with a humorous story about pizza.

   B. describe what it is like to eat a tomato.

   C. inform readers about how the tomato became a popular food.

   D. explain the process of growing tomatoes.

4. To learn more about the popularity of tomatoes in the United States today, what question might you research?

   A. What caused people to believe that tomatoes might be poisonous?

   B. How many tomatoes were sold in the United States last year?

   C. Do Europeans still plant tomatoes for their beauty?

   D. Do wild tomatoes grow in the U.S.?

Writing for Assessment

Connecting Across Texts
What details from the nonfiction passage might be used to support the fiction passage? In a paragraph, explain your answer.

PHLit Online!
www.PHLitOnline.com
- Online practice
- Instant feedback

Reading for Information

Analyzing Functional Texts

Technical Directions

User's Guide

 **Common Core State Standards**

Reading Informational Text
3. Analyze how the author unfolds an analysis or series of ideas or events, including the order in which the points are made, how they are introduced and developed, and the connections that are drawn between them.

Writing
1. Write arguments to support claims in an analysis of substantive topics or texts, using valid reasoning and relevant and sufficient evidence. *(Timed Writing)*

Language
4.b. Identify and correctly use patterns of word changes that indicate different meanings or parts of speech.

Reading Skill:
Follow and Critique Technical Directions

You can better understand technical directions if you first scan the text to get a sense of the information provided. Then, **critique the logic of the document by examining the sequence,** or structure, of information and directions. Analyze the order in which points are made, how they are introduced, and the connections that are drawn between them. Consider the clarity of the structure and determine whether any elements might cause confusion for the reader.

Once you have analyzed the text, be sure you can answer the following questions before **following the technical directions.**

Questions for Technical Directions

- What does the device do?
- What tools or materials are needed?
- What steps or directions are provided?
- What information is given in charts, diagrams, and illustrations?
- What are the safety warnings?
- What should the user do if something goes wrong?

Content-Area Vocabulary
These words appear in the selections that follow. You may also encounter them in other content-area texts.

- **degrees** (di grēz´) *n.* units of measurement for points on a circle
- **aligns** (ə līnz´) *v.* arranges in a straight line
- **defects** (dē´ fekts) *n.* faults or blemishes

How to Use a
Compass

Our compasses have been the accurate and easy-to-use choice of foresters, geologists, surveyors, scientific explorers, sports enthusiasts, military personnel, and many others for 50 years. Most of our compasses include these features:

- Magnetized tungsten steel needle
- Friction-free sapphire bearing
- Permanently clear, antistatic liquid
- Accurate from − 40° to +140°F

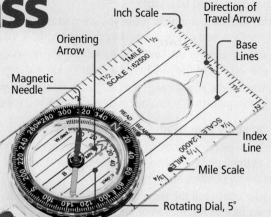

Inch Scale

Orienting Arrow

Magnetic Needle

Direction of Travel Arrow

Base Lines

Index Line

Mile Scale

Rotating Dial, 5°

Orienting Lines

Clear Base Plate

A diagram identifies the parts of the product with labels to help users follow the instructions.

Easy as 1-2-3

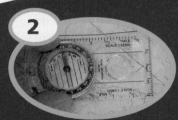

1

Point the Base Plate to Your Destination:
Place your compass on the map with the edge along the desired line of travel.

2

Set the Compass Heading:
Turn the compass Dial until "N" points to the north on your map. Your direction in degrees is read at the Index Line on the Dial.

NOTE: Align the Dial with magnetic north if it is marked on your map. If it is not marked on your map, align the Dial with true north and adjust for declination.

3

Follow Your Heading:
- Remove the compass from your map and hold it level, so the Magnetic Needle is free to turn.
- Turn your body until the red end of the Needle aligns with the Orienting Arrow and "N" on the Dial.

This section explains the easiest use of the compass. Other sections give instructions for other uses.

Find Your Way Without a Map:

Find a heading (field bearing):

1. Select a landmark along the route you want to travel. Hold the compass level and point the Direction of Travel Arrow at the landmark.
2. Find your heading to the landmark by turning the compass dial until the "N" aligns with the red end of the Needle. Read your heading in degrees to the Index Line.
3. Keep the Needle aligned with the "N"; look up; sight on your landmark and walk to it. Repeat this procedure until you reach your destination and walk to it.

When you know your heading:

1. If you've been given a heading in degrees to travel, turn the Dial so that the heading is set at the Index Line. Hold the compass level in front of you with the Direction of Travel Arrow pointing straight ahead.
2. Turn your body until the red end of the Needle is aligned with the "N" on the dial. You now face your direction of travel.
3. Pick out a landmark in line with your heading and move toward it. Repeat this procedure until you reach your destination.

NOTE: Be aware of nearby iron or steel objects. They may attract the Magnetic Needle if too close to the compass. Even a hidden nail can deflect the needle.

> Two ways of using the compass are explained, each in its own set of numbered steps.

Compass Warranty

What Is Covered?
We warrant your compass to be free from **defects** in materials or workmanship, and we guarantee its accuracy, for the life of the compass.

> Headings help users quickly locate answers to frequently asked warranty questions.

What Is Not Covered?
Normal wear, abrasion, melting, misuse, alteration, abuse, or taking apart the compass is not covered by this warranty.

How to Obtain Warranty Service or Repair of Your Compass
Should your compass become defective under the terms of this warranty, call the Customer Satisfaction Department toll free at 1 (800) 123-4567 for return authorization. If, after our inspection, we find that the product was defective in material or workmanship, we shall, at our option, either repair or replace it without charge. If repairs not covered under this warranty are required, we will contact you for approval to proceed. You will be charged for the components repaired or replaced, plus a nominal charge for labor.

There are no other express warranties beyond the terms of this limited warranty. In no event shall our company be liable for incidental or consequential damages arising from using our compasses.

GPS[1]
Quick-Start Guide

Features:
- instructions for how to operate a device
- explanations of the different functions and features of the device and how to access them
- diagrams, illustrations, or photographs of the device
- text written for a specific audience

Using the Find Feature:

1 Tap the **Find** icon on the Map Page tool bar to display the Find Menu.

The features of the Map Page are defined and explained. Instructions are provided for how to utilize them.

2 Then select a category icon and tap it to open the search list. To narrow the list of items, tap the second field to display the list of search options. Choose "Near Current Location".

3 To shorten the list even more, tap the category field to display a list of sub-categories to refine the type of map item you are searching for.

4 Select the desired destination and tap to highlight it. Then tap the **Routes** icon at bottom of the page to begin route calculation. From the pop-up options window, select the calculation preference and then tap **OK** to complete route calculation.

5 When complete the route will be displayed on the Map Page along with navigation instructions and voice prompts.

Two sets of instructions are provided. The steps are numbered, and icons highlight key actions.

Managing a Route

Once you have selected a destination and calculated a route, you can modify the route, preview turns, and save it for later reuse.

1 Tap the **Routes** icon on the Map Page tool bar to display the Routes Page. Then tap the desired **Routes Options** icon.

2 Tap the **Turns Page** to view a list of turns for the route. Tap a turn entry to preview the turn on the map.

3 Tap **Recalculate** if you have left the route and want to calculate from your current location.

4 Tap the **Detour** icon if you want to detour the route around a traffic jam or road construction.

5 Tap the **Stop Navigation** icon if you want to quit the route.

6 Tap the **Route Preferences** icon if you want to change the way a route is managed in order to meet your personal requirements.

7 Tap **Edit Vias** if you want to add some new points to alter your route.

8 Tap **Saved Routes** if you want to save the current route or view a previously saved route.

9 Tap **Speak** if you want to listen to current route status voice prompts.

---

1. GPS An abbreviation that stands for Global Positioning System, a navigational system based on receiving signals from satellites orbiting earth.

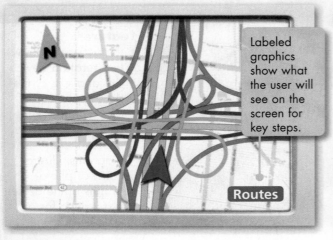

Labeled graphics show what the user will see on the screen for key steps.

Routes

Navigation Using the Map Page

Navigation is the process of going from your current location to another, and the Map Page has features to help you do that.

Data Fields—Provide GPS Status when not moving, Direction of Travel or Next Street Ahead, Compass Direction, Speed and Current Location

Map Detail—With downloaded detailed maps: Residential Streets, Rivers, Lakes, Points of Interest and Individual Addresses. Oriented with North Up unless in Track Up mode.

The Position Arrow—Indicates your current location. Tap to center it on the map page. Points in the direction of travel.

The Map Pointer—Marks map locations using the stylus. Displays information for a location if available.

The Map Scale—Tapping the Map Scale Box in the lower left corner of the map displays the moving Map Scale. Tap the arrows to move up or down the scale. Tap the desired scale to close.

Navigating to a Destination

A destination can be determined in two ways: you use the Map Pointer to mark a point on the map and then tap the Routes icon . . . or use the Find Feature to search for a destination form the map database and then, when found and highlighted, choose the "Route To It" option from the Find Options Menu.

Using the Map Pointer:

1. Tap the point on the Map Page that you want to navigate to. If there is information about that point in the map database, it will display next to the point.

2. Then tap the **Routes** icon to display the Routes Page.

3. Tap the "Route To" field and the route will begin to calculate.

4. A pop-up window will offer three preferences for calculating the route. Select an option and tap **OK** to return to the Map Page to complete calculation.

5. When the calculation is complete, the route will display as a purple overlay on top of the map.

6. The first maneuver on your route is displayed at the top of the map page and is complemented by a voice prompt.

7. To view all of the turns on the route, open the Routes Page and tap the **Turns Page** icon. A list of turns will display and a preview page for each turn will display when the turn on the list is tapped.

Comparing Functional Texts

1. Key Ideas and Details **(a) Critique the logic** of the sequence of information in the technical directions. Explain which aspects of the structure help clarify information and which, if any, might cause readers to be confused. **(b)** Do the same for the user's guide. **(c)** Compare the structures of the two documents. Explain which is more logically structured and why.

Content-Area Vocabulary

2. (a) Using your knowledge of the word *aligns* and of word patterns, explain the meanings of these words: *aligned* and *alignment*. **(b)** Use each word in a sentence that reveals its meaning.

Timed Writing

Argumentative Text: Letter

> **Format and Audience**
> The prompt gives instructions to write a letter. Because the letter will be addressed to a business, the tone should be formal.

> Write a letter in which you request a repair under warranty for your compass. In your letter, describe a specific problem with the compass. Then, cite details from the warranty to explain the reasons you believe that the repair is covered. (20 minutes)

> **Academic Vocabulary**
> When you *describe* something, you use precise words to create a vivid picture in your reader's mind.

5-Minute Planner

Complete these steps before you begin to write:

1. Read the prompt carefully and completely.

2. Reread the technical directions to identify a problem that might occur with the compass. Then, decide on the repair that you will request and make notes about how you will describe the problem.

3. Reread the compass warranty to be sure that the repair you are requesting is covered. Then, note passages you will use as evidence to show why the company is obligated to make the repair.

4. Decide how to structure your letter. For example, you might include a brief introductory paragraph before presenting the reasons why the company should repair your compass. **TIP:** Your letter will be more convincing if you anticipate and answer your readers' objections.

5. Use your notes to prepare a quick outline. Refer to your outline as you draft.

Comparing Humorous Writing

In a **humorous essay** or **speech,** a writer presents a subject in an unexpected, amusing way. The writer may treat a serious situation lightly or a ridiculous situation seriously. Techniques for creating humor include the following.

- Using **hyperbole,** or exaggeration, a writer describes people, things, or events as if they were much more important than they are—for instance, calling the discovery of a missing sock a "joyous reunion."

- Using **understatement,** a writer speaks of people, things, or events as if they were less important than they are—for instance, saying that "the weather was not ideal" after a tornado carries off picnic tables.

When a writer uses humor to point out the foolishness of a particular type of human behavior or of a particular institution, the result is called **satire.**

Mark Twain's speech "A Toast to the Oldest Inhabitant . . ." and James Thurber's essay "The Dog That Bit People" use humor, but their comic techniques are different. Use a chart like the one shown to compare the elements that make these selections humorous.

	Hyperbole	Understatement	Satire
Twain			
Thurber			

Diction, or word choice, is another literary element that contributes to humor. Authors try to select words that precisely convey the meaning they intend. To do so, they consider a word's **connotation**—the set of ideas associated with it—as well as the word's denotation, or definition. For example, the words *house* and *home* both mean "place to live," but the word *home* is associated with ideas like family and comfort. The word *house* does not have these connotations. As you read the selections, consider the connotations of the authors' diction and analyze how precise word choices contribute to both humorous meaning and **tone**, or the expression of the writer's attitude toward his or her subject and reader.

Common Core State Standards

Reading Literature
7. Analyze the representation of a subject or a key scene in two different artistic mediums, including what is emphasized or absent in each treatment.

Reading Informational Text
4. Determine the meaning of words and phrases as they are used in a text, including figurative, connotative, and technical meanings; analyze the cumulative impact of specific word choices on meaning and tone.

Writing
2. Write informative/explanatory texts to examine and convey complex ideas, concepts, and information clearly and accurately through the effective selection, organization, and analysis of content.
2.a. Introduce a topic; organize complex ideas, concepts, and information to make important connections and distinctions. *(Timed Writing)*

www.PHLitOnline.com

- Vocabulary flashcards
- Interactive journals
- More about the authors
- Selection audio
- Interactive graphic organizers

What kind of *knowledge* changes our lives?

Writing About the Big Question

In each story, the narrator tolerates something that would otherwise be intolerable—terrible weather or an exceptionally bad dog—by treating it with good humor. Think about a bad situation that you or someone else might typically experience. What knowledge might change your attitude? Use this sentence starter to develop your ideas about the Big Question.

When I need to **adapt** to a bad situation, I try to remember _____.

Meet the Authors

Mark Twain (1835–1910)

Author of "A Toast to the Oldest Inhabitant"

Mark Twain is the pen name of Samuel Langhorne Clemens, one of America's greatest writers. He is most famous for two classic novels: *The Adventures of Tom Sawyer* (1876) and *The Adventures of Huckleberry Finn* (1884).

A Standup Comic Mark Twain became a sought-after, highly paid public speaker. He delivered "A Toast to the Oldest Inhabitant . . ." at the annual dinner of the New England Society on December 22, 1876.

James Thurber (1894–1961)

Author of "The Dog That Bit People"

A native of Columbus, Ohio, James Thurber went to work for the U.S. State Department after college. Soon afterward, however, he found his true calling—he became a humorist, writing essays and drawing cartoons for *The New Yorker*, a famous magazine.

Growing Fame, Failing Vision Thurber won fame for his whimsical depictions of human (and animal) silliness. By the 1940s, though, his failing eyesight forced him to reduce the number of cartoon drawings he created. By 1952, Thurber was almost totally blind, but he still wrote stories and articles for the magazine. His collections, including *The Thurber Carnival* (1945), are considered classics of humor writing.

A Toast to the Oldest Inhabitant:

The WEATHER

of New England

Mark Twain

▲ **Critical Viewing**
Based on this scene, what comments do you think Twain makes about New England weather?
[Preview]

Who can lose it and forget it?
Who can have it and regret it?
Be interposer 'twixt us Twain.[1]
—The Merchant of Venice, William Shakespeare

Gentlemen: I reverently believe that the Maker who made us all, makes everything in New England[2]—but the weather. I don't know who makes that, but I think it must be raw apprentices in the Weather Clerk's factory, who experiment and learn how in New England, for board and clothes, and then are promoted to make

---

1. **Twain** archaic word for "two" (and a pun on Twain's name).
2. **New England** the states of the northeastern United States: Maine, Vermont, New Hampshire, Massachusetts, Rhode Island, and Connecticut.

weather for countries that require a good article, and will take their custom elsewhere if they don't get it. There is a **sumptuous** variety about the New England weather that compels the stranger's admiration—and regret. The weather is always doing something there; always attending strictly to business; always getting up new designs and trying them on the people to see how they will go. But it gets through more business in spring than in any other season. In the spring I have counted one hundred and thirty-six different kinds of weather inside of four and twenty hours. It was I that made the fame and fortune of that man that had that marvelous collection of weather on exhibition at the Centennial[3] that so astounded the foreigners. He was going to travel all over the world and get specimens from all the climes. I said, "Don't you do it; you come to New England on a favorable spring day." I told him what we could do, in the way of style, variety, and quantity. Well, he came, and he made his collection in four days. As to variety—why, he confessed that he got hundreds of kinds of weather that he had never heard of before. And as to quantity—well, after he had picked out and discarded all that was blemished in any way, he not only had weather enough, but weather to spare; weather to hire out; weather to sell; to deposit; weather to invest; weather to give to the poor.

---

3. **Centennial** international trade fair held in 1876 in Philadelphia to mark the hundredth anniversary of the Declaration of Independence. The fair featured scientific and technological marvels of the day.

Vocabulary
sumptuous (sump´ chōō əs) *adj.* lavish

Literary Analysis
Humorous Writing
What hyperbole does Twain use here to make his point about New England weather?

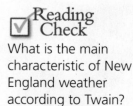
Reading Check

What is the main characteristic of New England weather according to Twain?

▼ **Critical Viewing**
Are you surprised there
is such a wide variety
of weather in such a
small area of the United
States? Why or why not?
[Make a Judgment]

The people of New England are by nature patient and forbearing; but there are some things which they will not stand. Every year they kill a lot of poets for writing about "Beautiful Spring." These are generally casual visitors, who bring their notions of spring from somewhere else, and cannot, of course, know how the natives feel about spring. And so, the first thing they know, the opportunity to inquire how they feel has permanently gone by.

Old Probabilities has a mighty reputation for accurate prophecy, and thoroughly well deserves it. You take up the papers and observe how crisply and confidently he checks off what today's weather is going to be on the Pacific, down South, in the Middle States, in the Wisconsin region; see him sail along in the joy and pride of his power till he gets to New England, and then—see his tail drop. *He* doesn't know what the weather is going to be like in New England. He can't any more tell than he can tell how many Presidents of the United States there's going to be next year.[4] Well, he mulls over it, and by and by he gets out something about like this: Probable nor'-east to sou'-west winds, varying to the southard and westard and eastard and points between; high and low barometer, swapping around from place to place; probable

---

4. **how many Presidents of the United States there's going to be next year** The United States presidential election of 1876 was one of the most disputed, with two declared "winners" when Twain gave this speech. Rutherford B. Hayes was declared the final victor on March 2, 1877.

areas of rain, snow, hail, and drought, succeeded or preceded by earthquakes, with thunder and lightning. Then he jots down this postscript from his wandering mind, to cover accidents: "But it is possible that the program may be wholly changed in the meantime."

Yes, one of the brightest gems in the New England weather is the dazzling uncertainty of it. There is only one thing certain about it, you are certain there is going to be plenty of weather—a perfect grand review; but you never can tell which end of the procession is going to move first. You fix up for the drought; you leave your umbrella in the house and sally out with your sprinkling pot, and ten to one you get drowned. You make up your mind that the earthquake is due; you stand from under, and take hold of something to steady yourself, and the first thing you know, you get struck by lightning. These are great disappointments. But they can't be helped. The lightning there is peculiar; it is so convincing! When it strikes a thing, it doesn't leave enough of that thing behind for you to tell whether—well, you'd think it was something valuable, and a Congressman had been there.

And the thunder. When the thunder commences to merely tune up, and scrape, and saw, and key up the instruments for the performance, strangers say, "Why, what awful thunder you have here!" But when the baton is raised and the real concert begins, you'll find that stranger down in the cellar, with his head in the ash barrel.

Now, as to the size of the weather in New England—lengthways, I mean. It is utterly disproportioned to the size of that little country. Half the time, when it is packed as full as it can stick, you will see that New England weather sticking out beyond the edges and projecting around hundreds and hundreds of miles over the neighboring states. She can't hold a tenth part of her weather. You can see cracks all about, where she has strained herself trying to do it.

I could speak volumes about the inhuman perversity of the New England weather, but I will give but a single specimen. I like to hear rain on a tin roof, so I covered part of my roof with tin, with an eye to that luxury. Well, sir, do you think it ever rains on the tin? No, sir; skips it every time.

Mind, in this speech I have been trying merely to do honor to the New England weather—no language could do it justice. But, after all, there are at least one or two things about that weather (or, if you please, effects produced by it) which we residents would not like to part with. If we hadn't our bewitching autumn foliage, we should still have to credit the weather with one

Literary Analysis
Humorous Writing
How does Twain use understatement here to add humor?

Literary Analysis
Humorous Writing
What does Twain satirically imply about congressmen in this paragraph?

Yes, one of the brightest gems in the New England weather is the dazzling uncertainty of it.

Reading Check
According to Twain, how easy is it to predict New England weather?

Vocabulary
vagaries (vā′ gər ēz) *n.*
erratic or unpredictable
actions

**Literary Analysis
Humorous Writing**
What makes this para-
graph different from the
rest of the essay?

feature which compensates for all its bullying vagaries—the ice
storm—when a leafless tree is clothed with ice from the bottom to
the top—ice that is as bright and clear as crystal; when every bough
and twig is strung with ice beads, frozen dewdrops, and the whole
tree sparkles, cold and white, like the Shah[5] of Persia's diamond
plume. Then the wind waves the branches, and the sun comes out
and turns all those myriads of beads and drops to prisms, that glow
and burn and flash with all manner of colored fires, which change
and change again, with inconceivable rapidity, from blue to red,
from red to green, and green to gold—the tree becomes a spraying
fountain, a very explosion of dazzling jewels; and it stands there
the acme, the climax, the supremest possibility in art or nature,
of bewildering, intoxicating, intolerable magnificence! One cannot
make the words too strong.

   Month after month I lay up my hate and grudge against the
New England weather; but when the ice storm comes at last, I say:
"There—I forgive you, now—the books are square between us, you
don't owe me a cent; go, and sin no more; your little faults and
foibles count for nothing—you are the most enchanting weather in
the world!"

---

5. **Shah** (shä) *n.* formerly, the title of the ruler of Persia (now Iran).

Critical Thinking

Cite textual
evidence to
support your
responses.

1. **Key Ideas and Details** **(a)** According to Twain, what quality or
feature of New England weather "compels the stranger's
admiration"? **(b) Connect:** What point does Twain support with
the story of the man who collected and exhibited weather?

2. **Key Ideas and Details** **(a) Infer:** What is the profession of "Old
Probabilities"? **(b) Interpret:** What point is Twain making in the
anecdote about this character?

3. **Craft and Structure** Twain describes New England weather as
having "inhuman perversity." **(a) Interpret:** Is the connotation of
these words positive or negative? **(b) Analyze:** How does the
connotation affect the tone of the writing?

4. **Integration of Knowledge and Ideas** What knowledge allows
Twain to appreciate New England's tumultuous weather?
*[Connect to the Big Question: What kind of knowledge
changes our lives?]*

The Dog That Bit People

James Thurber

Probably no one man should have as many dogs in his life as I have had, but there was more pleasure than distress in them for me except in the case of an Airedale named Muggs. He gave me more trouble than all the other fifty-four or -five put together, although my moment of keenest embarrassment was the time a Scotch terrier named Jeannie, who had just had six puppies in the clothes closet of a fourth floor apartment in New York, had the unexpected seventh and last at the corner of Eleventh Street and Fifth Avenue during a walk she had insisted on taking. Then, too, there was the prize winning French poodle, a great big black poodle—none of your little, untroublesome white miniatures—who got sick riding in the rumble seat[1] of a car with me on her way to the Greenwich Dog Show. She had a red rubber bib tucked around her throat and, since a rain storm came up when we were halfway through the Bronx, I had to hold over her a small green umbrella, really more of a parasol. The rain beat down fearfully and suddenly the driver of the car drove into a big garage, filled with mechanics. It happened so quickly that I forgot to put the umbrella down and I will always remember, with sickening distress, the look of incredulity mixed with hatred that came over the face of the particular hardened garage man that came over to see what we

---

1. **rumble seat** *n.* in some early automobiles, an open seat in the rear, behind the roofed seat, which could be folded shut when not in use.

▲ Analyze Representations

Which elements of this drawing by Thurber suggest that Muggs has a difficult personality? **[Analyze]**

Vocabulary

incredulity
(in´ krə d $\overline{oo}$´ lə tē) *n.* unwillingness to believe

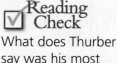

Reading Check

What does Thurber say was his most embarrassing moment?

wanted, when he took a look at me and the poodle. All garage men, and people of that intolerant stripe, hate poodles with their curious hair cut, especially the pom-poms that you got to leave on their hips if you expect the dogs to win a prize.

But the Airedale, as I have said, was the worst of all my dogs. He really wasn't my dog, as a matter of fact: I came home from a vacation one summer to find that my brother Roy had bought him while I was away. A big, burly, choleric dog, he always acted as if he thought I wasn't one of the family. There was a slight advantage in being one of the family, for he didn't bite the family as often as he bit strangers. Still, in the years that we had him he bit everybody but mother, and he made a pass at her once but missed. That was during the month when we suddenly had mice, and Muggs refused to do anything about them. Nobody ever had mice exactly like the mice we had that month. They acted like pet mice, almost like mice somebody had trained. They were so friendly that one night when mother entertained at dinner the Friraliras, a club she and my father had belonged to for twenty years, she put down a lot of little dishes with food in them on the pantry floor so that the mice would be satisfied with that and wouldn't come into the dining room. Muggs stayed out in the pantry with the mice, lying on the floor, growling to himself—not at the mice, but about all the people in the next room that he would have liked to get at. Mother slipped out into the pantry once to see how everything was going. Everything was going fine. It made her so mad to see Muggs lying there, oblivious of the mice—they came running up to her—that she slapped him and he slashed at her, but didn't make it. He was sorry immediately, mother said. He was always sorry, she said, after he bit someone, but we could not understand how she figured this out. He didn't act sorry.

Mother used to send a box of candy every Christmas to the people the Airedale bit. The list finally contained forty or more names. Nobody could understand why we didn't get rid of the dog. I didn't understand it very well myself, but we didn't get rid of him. I think that one or two people tried to poison Muggs—he acted poisoned once in a while—and old Major Moberly fired at him once with his service revolver near the Seneca Hotel in East Broad Street—but Muggs lived to be almost eleven years old and even when he could hardly get around he bit a Congressman who had called to see my father on business. My mother had never liked the Congressman—she said the signs of his horoscope showed he couldn't be trusted (he was Saturn with the moon in Virgo)—but she sent him a box of candy that Christmas. He sent it right back, probably because he suspected it was trick candy. Mother

Literary Analysis
Humorous Writing
Explain how Thurber uses understatement when comparing Muggs's treatment of family and strangers.

Literary Analysis
Humorous Writing
Which details in this paragraph seem to be hyperboles?

persuaded herself it was all for the best that the dog had bitten him, even though father lost an important business association because of it. "I wouldn't be associated with such a man," mother said, "Muggs could read him like a book."

We used to take turns feeding Muggs to be on his good side, but that didn't always work. He was never in a very good humor, even after a meal. Nobody knew exactly what was the matter with him, but whatever it was it made him irascible, especially in the mornings. Roy never felt very well in the morning, either, especially before breakfast, and once when he came downstairs and found that Muggs had moodily chewed up the morning paper he hit him in the face with a grapefruit and then jumped up on the dining room table, scattering dishes and silverware and spilling the coffee. Muggs' first free leap carried him all the way across the table and into a brass fire screen in front of the gas grate but he was back on his feet in a moment and in the end he got Roy and gave him a pretty vicious bite in the leg. Then he was all over it; he never bit anyone more than once at a time. Mother always mentioned that as an argument in his favor; she said he had a quick temper but that he didn't hold a grudge. She was forever defending him. I think she liked him because he wasn't well. "He's not strong," she would say, pityingly, but that was inaccurate; he may not have been well but he was terribly strong.

One time my mother went to the Chittenden Hotel to call on a woman mental healer who was lecturing in Columbus on the subject of "Harmonious Vibrations." She wanted to find out if it was possible to get harmonious vibrations into a dog. "He's a large tan-colored Airedale," mother explained. The woman said that she had never treated a dog but she advised my mother to hold the thought that he did not bite and would not bite. Mother was holding the thought the very next morning when Muggs got the iceman but she blamed that slip-up on the iceman. "If you didn't think he would bite you, he wouldn't," mother told him. He stomped out of the house in a terrible jangle of vibrations.

One morning when Muggs bit me slightly, more or less in passing, I reached down and grabbed his short stumpy tail and hoisted him into the air. It was a foolhardy thing to do and the last time I saw my mother, about six months ago, she said she didn't know what possessed me. I don't either, except that I was pretty mad. As long as I held the dog off the floor by his tail he couldn't get at me, but he twisted and jerked so, snarling all the time, that I realized I couldn't hold him that way very long. I carried him to the kitchen and flung him onto the floor and shut the door on him just as he crashed against it. But I forgot about the backstairs.

Vocabulary
irascible (i ras´ ə bəl)
adj. quick tempered

Spiral Review
Series of Ideas
Explain what the story of "harmonious vibrations" adds to your understanding of the mother.

Reading Check
How does Muggs generally respond to people?

Muggs at His Meals Was an Unusual Sight, James Thurber

▲ Analyze Representations

How does this drawing of Muggs compare and contrast with the behavior described in the essay? **[Compare and Contrast]**

Muggs went up the backstairs and down the frontstairs and had me cornered in the living room. I managed to get up onto the mantelpiece above the fireplace, but it gave way and came down with a tremendous crash throwing a large marble clock, several vases, and myself heavily to the floor. Muggs was so alarmed by the racket that when I picked myself up he had disappeared. We couldn't find him anywhere, although we whistled and shouted, until old Mrs. Detweiler called after dinner that night. Muggs had bitten her once, in the leg, and she came into the living room only after we assured her that Muggs had run away. She had just seated herself when, with a great growling and scratching of claws, Muggs emerged from under a davenport where he had been quietly hiding all the time, and bit her again. Mother examined the bite and put arnica[2] on it and told Mrs. Detweiler that it was only a bruise. "He just bumped you," she said. But Mrs. Detweiler left the house in a nasty state of mind.

Lots of people reported our Airedale to the police but my father held a municipal office at the time and was on friendly terms with the police. Even so, the cops had been out a couple of times—once when Muggs bit Mrs. Rufus Sturtevant and again when he bit Lieutenant-Governor Malloy—but mother told them that it hadn't been Muggs' fault but the fault of the people who were bitten. "When he starts for them, they scream," she explained, "and that excites him." The cops suggested that it might be a good idea to tie the dog up, but mother said that it mortified him to be tied up and that he wouldn't eat when he was tied up.

Muggs at his meals was an unusual sight. Because of the fact that if you reached toward the floor he would bite you, we usually put his food plate on top of an old kitchen table with a bench alongside the table. Muggs would stand on the bench and eat. I remember that my mother's Uncle Horatio, who boasted that he was the third man up Missionary Ridge,[3] was splutteringly indignant when he found out that we fed the dog on a table because we were afraid to put his plate on the floor. He said he wasn't afraid of any dog that ever lived and that he would put the dog's plate on the floor if we would give it to him. Roy said that if Uncle Horatio had fed Muggs on the ground just before the battle he would have been the first man up Missionary Ridge. Uncle Horatio was furious. "Bring him in! Bring him in now!" he shouted. "I'll feed the — on the floor!" Roy was all for giving him a chance, but my father wouldn't hear of it. He said that Muggs had already been fed. "I'll feed him again!" bawled Uncle Horatio. We had quite a time quieting him.

In his last year Muggs used to spend practically all of his time outdoors. He didn't like to stay in the house for some reason or other—perhaps it held too many unpleasant memories for him. Anyway, it was hard to get him to come in and as a result the garbage man, the iceman, and the laundryman wouldn't come near the house. We had to haul the garbage down to the corner, take the laundry out and bring it back, and meet the iceman a block from home. After this had gone on for some time we hit on an ingenious arrangement for getting the dog in the house so that we could lock him up while the gas meter was read, and so on. Muggs was afraid of only one thing, an electrical storm. Thunder and lightning frightened him out of his senses (I think he thought a storm had broken the day the mantelpiece fell). He would rush into the house and hide under

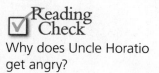

---

2. **arnica** (är′ ni kə) n. preparation once used for treating bruises.
3. **Missionary Ridge** hill near Chattanooga, Tennessee, that was the site of a Civil War battle.

Literary Analysis
Humorous Writing
Why is this anecdote
about the thunder
machine an example
both of hyperbole and
of understatement?

a bed or in a clothes closet. So we fixed up a thunder machine out of a long narrow piece of sheet iron with a wooden handle on one end. Mother would shake this vigorously when she wanted to get Muggs into the house. It made an excellent imitation of thunder, but I suppose it was the most roundabout system for running a household that was ever devised. It took a lot out of mother.

A few months before Muggs died, he got to "seeing things." He would rise slowly from the floor, growling low, and stalk stiff-legged and menacing toward nothing at all. Sometimes the Thing would be just a little to the right or left of a visitor. Once a Fuller Brush salesman[4] got hysterics. Muggs came wandering into the room like Hamlet[5] following his father's ghost. His eyes were fixed on a spot just to the left of the Fuller Brush man, who stood it until Muggs was about three slow, creeping paces from him. Then he shouted. Muggs wavered on past him into the hallway grumbling to himself but the Fuller man went on shouting. I think mother had to throw a pan of cold water on him before he stopped. That was the way she used to stop us boys when we got into fights.

Muggs died quite suddenly one night. Mother wanted to bury him in the family lot under a marble stone with some such inscription as "Flights of angels sing thee to thy rest" but we persuaded her it was against the law. In the end we just put up a smooth board above his grave along a lonely road. On the board I wrote with an indelible pencil "Cave Canem."[6] Mother was quite pleased with the simple classic dignity of the old Latin epitaph.

---

4. **Fuller Brush salesman** salesman for the Fuller Brush Company who went door-to-door demonstrating cleaning equipment; a figure celebrated in comic strips and movies of the 1920s through the 1940s.
5. **Hamlet** the main character of William Shakespeare's play *Hamlet*; in the play, he is visited by the ghost of his murdered father.
6 **"Cave Canem"** (kä´ vä kä´ nem´) Latin for "Beware of the dog."

Critical Thinking

Cite textual evidence to support your responses.

1. **Key Ideas and Details (a)** Which event was Thurber's "foolhardy" experience with Muggs? **(b) Analyze:** List reactions you expect the family to have to this experience, and explain which are missing in the essay.

2. **Key Ideas and Details Infer:** What do other people think of the family's tolerance for Muggs's behavior? Explain.

3. **Craft and Structure (a)** Is the connotation of Muggs's epitaph positive or negative? **(b)** Is the connotation appropriate? Explain.

4. **Integration of Knowledge and Ideas** Why did the family keep Muggs despite their knowledge of his bad nature? *[Connect to the Big Question: What kind of knowledge changes our lives?]*

Comparing Humorous Writing

© **1. Craft and Structure (a)** Find an example of **hyperbole** in each work. **(b)** Find an example of **understatement** in each work. **(c)** Compare Twain's and Thurber's use of these devices, explaining which device each writer uses most.

© **2. Craft and Structure (a)** Which author treats a potentially serious subject lightly? **(b)** Which treats an ordinary subject with exaggerated seriousness? **(c)** How do the forms—essay and speech—shape the way ideas are presented? Give examples.

© **3. Integration of Knowledge and Ideas (a)** Find an example of **satire** in each essay. **(b)** Identify the type of person satirized in each. Do you think satirizing such people is fair or justified? Explain.

⏱ Timed Writing

Explanatory Text: Essay

In an essay, compare how Twain and Thurber use conflict to develop their humorous writing. Analyze how they use hyperbole, understatement, and precise diction to portray those conflicts and make them funny. **(30 minutes)**

5-Minute Planner

1. Read the prompt carefully and completely.

2. Before you write, complete a chart like the one shown to identify each conflict and the comic details that depict it.

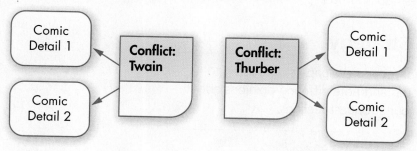

3. Analyze the authors' diction, tone, and use of hyperbole and understatement. Take notes on specific details that support your analysis.

4. Develop an outline logically organizing your points.

5. Reread the prompt, and then draft your essay.

Writing Workshop

Common Core State Standards

Writing

1. Write arguments to support claims in an analysis of substantive topics or texts, using valid reasoning and relevant and sufficient evidence.

1.d. Establish and maintain a formal style and objective tone while attending to the norms and conventions of the discipline in which they are writing.

Write an Argument

Persuasion: Letter to the Editor

Defining the Form A **letter to the editor** is a formal business letter that presents the writer's viewpoints about important issues and is addressed to the opinion page of a newspaper or magazine. You might use elements of this form in position papers, speeches, and proposals.

Assignment Write a letter to the editor of a magazine, newspaper, or Web site. Give your opinion about a current event. Include these elements:

✔ *standard business letter format*, including a heading, an inside address, a greeting, a body, a closing, and a signature

✔ *formal, polite language* that creates an objective tone

✔ *a clear statement of opinion, or claim,* supported by sufficient evidence and by an argument refuting an opposing opinion

✔ *persuasive techniques* to convince readers to agree with you

✔ a conclusion that explains the importance of the claim

✔ error-free grammar, including *well-combined sentences*

To preview the criteria on which your letter to the editor may be judged, see the rubric on page 537.

📖 Writing Workshop: *Work in Progress*

Review the work you did on pages 485 and 509.

Prewriting/Planning Strategy

Find a hot topic. Watch television, scan newspapers, and listen to neighborhood discussions. List issues and note differing opinions about each one. Decide which prompt your strongest feelings.

Pro	Hot Topic	Con
Professional athletes have a responsibility to the public.	**Sports heroes as role models**	Excellent athletes are not models for behavior outside the court or off the field.
Restrictions can protect our youngest citizens.	**Laws restricting the Internet**	Freedom of speech is denied by restrictions.

Finding Your Voice

Voice is the writer's distinctive "sound" or way of "speaking" on the page. It is created through elements such as word choice, sentence structure, and tone. Voice, in its written form, can be described in the same way the spoken word is described—fast, slow, blunt, and so on. Use the following tips to help you find the appropriate voice for your letter.

Choose effective words. Before you begin your letter, think about how you want to sound: for example, impassioned, concerned, reasoned, or detached. Your choice of words and the structure of your sentences communicate your voice. Try saying a few sentences aloud. You might tape-record your voice, or have a friend listen to you speak. Then, decide whether the sound of your voice is what you wish to convey on paper. Use a chart like the following to record words or phrases that reflect your voice.

> **PH WRITING COACH**
>
> Further instruction and practice are available in *Prentice Hall Writing Coach.*

Voice and/or Tone	Words and Phrases
impassioned	We urgently need…; So much is at stake…
concerned	I am concerned…; The problem is serious…
reasoned	We all will benefit from…; We have the resources to…; Some people may disagree with me…

Consider your audience and tone. Your voice in writing should reflect your audience. Your letter will address the general public, so include information that is essential to your case. Be respectful to your audience. Remember that the overall tone of a letter to the editor is usually objective. Even if you are voicing a complaint, maintain a calm and reasonable tone. Your goal is to persuade, not to insult.

Revise to create appropriate formality. Check that your tone is polite and your style is formal. Replace casual language with formal language.

Casual: The park's a big old mess.
Formal: The park is littered with trash.

Drafting Strategies

Use the proper format. Your letter to the editor must follow a standard business letter format. Here are two commonly accepted conventions:

- **Block Format:** Each part of the letter begins at the left margin.
- **Modified Block Format:** The heading, closing, and signature align and are indented to the center of the page by using the tab function.

Ensure that you include all six elements of a formal business letter: heading, inside address, salutation, body, closing, and signature. (For more on business letters, see page R34.)

Organize ideas. Logically organize your ideas and use clear transitional words, phrases, and clauses so that your readers can follow your argument. Distinguish your opinions or ideas from those of others.

Use persuasive techniques. As you write, include persuasive techniques and rhetorical devices to convince your readers to adopt your opinion or take a course of action. The chart shown here provides some examples.

Common Core State Standards

Writing

1. Write arguments to support claims in an analysis of substantive topics or texts, using valid reasoning and relevant and sufficient evidence.

1.a. Introduce precise claim(s), distinguish the claim(s) from alternate or opposing claims, and create an organization that establishes clear relationships among claim(s), counterclaims, reasons, and evidence.

1.c. Use words, phrases, and clauses to link the major sections of the text, create cohesion, and clarify the relationships between claim(s) and reasons, between reasons and evidence, and between claim(s) and counterclaims.

Persuasive Techniques	Rhetorical Devices
Appeal to Emotion Abandoned animals are suffering needlessly.	**Parallelism** Homeless animals deserve our compassion. Homeless animals deserve a home.
Appeal to Logic Taking care of these animals will help eliminate sources of diseases to our pets.	**Rhetorical Question** Can we allow this situation to continue?

Revising Strategy

Evaluate support. Review your draft, highlighting main ideas to ensure they are supported with sufficient evidence. Also ensure main ideas are valid and logical. If a point is not important or logical, omit it. If it is important, support it. Select different types of evidence to make your letter both convincing and interesting. Consider including evidence in these categories:

- facts and statistics
- real-life examples
- personal experiences
- expert opinions

> **Model: Highlighting to Add Supporting Details**
> Many pets in this city have been abandoned, left homeless by uncaring owners. These animals roam the city streets. Most are hungry, and many are sick and diseased. I personally rescued a puppy who was scavenging in our trash can for food. My vet said he had heartworms and fleas.

The writer adds support in the form of personal experience.

Sentence Fluency	Voice	Organization	Word Choice	Ideas	Conventions

Revising to Combine Short Sentences

If you use too many short sentences, your work can seem as if it was written for very young readers rather than a mature audience. To avoid this problem, combine short sentences that express related ideas.

Methods of Sentence Combining Use compound verbs to combine two short sentences:

Choppy: I *cancelled* my service. I *turned* my phone in for a refund.

Combined: I *cancelled* my service and *turned* my phone in for a refund.

You may use **compound objects:**

Choppy: I ate *a sandwich.* I ate *an ice cream cone.*

Combined: I ate *a sandwich* and *an ice cream cone.*

Use **compound predicate nominatives** or **predicate adjectives.**

predicate nominative	predicate adjective
a noun or pronoun that appears with a linking verb and identifies or explains the subject	an adjective that appears with a linking verb and describes the subject
Example: Parakeets are <u>birds.</u>	Example: Parakeets are <u>colorful.</u>

> **PH WRITING COACH**
> Further instruction and practice are available in *Prentice Hall Writing Coach.*

Choppy: My favorite celebrity *is a singer.* She is also *an actress.*

Combined: My favorite celebrity is *a singer and an actress.*

Choppy: The bicycle is *very lightweight.* It is *extremely fast.*

Combined: The bicycle is *very lightweight and extremely fast.*

Fixing Choppy Sentences Follow these steps to fix short sentences:

1. **Read your draft aloud,** listening for choppy sentences.

2. **Identify sentences to combine.** Determine which sentences share a common subject or a common predicate.

3. **Try a variety of sentence-combining techniques.** Use the methods above to create a variety of fluid sentences.

Grammar in Your Writing

Reread two paragraphs in your letter. Look for places where a single sentence would express related ideas better than a series of shorter sentences. Combine these sentences using one of the methods above.

Student Model: Clay Creamans, Independence, KY

Common Core State Standards

Language
2.c. Spell correctly.

Clay Creamans
2351 Any Drive
Independence, Kentucky 41051

September 25, 2005

Editor-in-Chief
The Daily Independent
552 Downtown Street
Ashland, Kentucky 41000

Dear Editor-in-Chief:

I am writing in response to the letter you published from Mr. Jones, who complained about our band's playing at the last football game.

The point of high school band programs is to train students to play together, to produce one stirring, harmonious sound. Because of a lack of instruction, education, and familiarity with music and instruments, this is difficult for some students. Band programs all over the country have inspired many students to go into the field of music, but many do not meet the requirements students need to compete after high school. I personally know students who have been denied scholarships and have had scholarships revoked because they have not been properly trained. The Kenton County School District needs to devise a class that will alleviate these problems.

This new music class should have a staff composed of teachers who can play and teach all of the band instruments. Students need one-on-one, as well as group, instruction. Of course, hiring a full staff of musicians for every school would cost a lot. Instead, full band directors could be hired for all the schools to share. This would allow students to gain a greater knowledge of music from a larger group of musicians. These teachers would offer more insight into the history and theory of music.

With so many young people interested in fine arts, band directors cannot offer everyone the instruction that is needed. For the band to improve as a whole, everyone has to grow. Many of today's band directors try hard to develop better musicians, yet, because of a lack of time and staffing, they feel disappointed and discouraged.

With adequate time and staffing, students will be able to make music together and demonstrate their talents. With an experienced music staff and better classes, I believe that Mr. Jones will be happier with our band's performance.

Sincerely,

Clay Creamans

Clay Creamans

Clay uses a correct modified block format.

Formal language shows that Clay takes both his opinion and his readers seriously.

Clay supports his argument with personal experiences.

Clay points out an opposing argument and suggests an alternative plan.

The conclusion reinforces Clay's ideas.

Editing and Proofreading

Check your draft for errors in format, grammar, and punctuation.

Focus on accuracy. Ensure that the names of people, periodicals, and quoted experts are spelled and capitalized correctly. Make sure that numerical data and street addresses are accurate.

Publishing and Presenting

Consider one of the following ways to share your writing:

Submit your letter. Send your letter to the editor of the media source you have addressed. When the letter is published, share the newspaper, periodical, or Web site with classmates.

Hold a speaker's corner. Organize a group of classmates in which you read your letters aloud and evaluate each speaker's point of view and reasoning. Point out any exaggerated claims or fallacious reasoning, such as overgeneralizations. As a group, set time limits for each speaker and negotiate rules, such as holding questions until a speaker is finished.

Reflecting on Your Writing

Writer's Journal Jot down your answers to this question:

How did writing about the issue you chose help you to understand it?

Rubric for Self-Assessment

Find evidence in your writing to address each category. Then, use the rating scale to grade your work.

© **Spiral Review**
Earlier in the unit, you learned about **subject complements** (p. 508). In your essay, write at least one sentence that has a predicate nominative and one sentence that has a predicate adjective. To write effectively, choose sentences in which it is appropriate to use linking verbs rather than action verbs.

Criteria	Rating Scale
	not very / very
Focus: How clearly do you state your opinion?	1 2 3 4 5
Organization: How accurately do you use standard business letter format?	1 2 3 4 5
Support/Elaboration: How relevant and logical are the facts, examples, or experiences you use to support your opinion?	1 2 3 4 5
Style: How formal and objective is your use of language?	1 2 3 4 5
Conventions: How correct is your grammar, especially your use of well-combined sentences?	1 2 3 4 5
Voice: How well do your word choice and sentence structure reflect your voice?	1 2 3 4 5

Ⓒ Leveled Texts

Build your skills and improve your comprehension of nonfiction with texts of increasing complexity.

Read **"Keep Memory Alive"** to learn why a man has devoted his life to ensuring that the horrors of the Holocaust are not forgotten.

Read the excerpt from a writer's **Nobel Lecture** to find out how one author uses literature to fight against global forces of injustice.

Ⓒ Common Core State Standards

Meet these standards with either **"Keep Memory Alive"** (p. 542) or the excerpt from Alexander Solzhenitsyn's **Nobel Lecture** (p. 548).

Reading Informational Text
6. Determine an author's point of view or purpose in a text and analyze how an author uses rhetoric to advance that point of view or purpose. *(Literary Analysis: Persuasive Writing and Rhetorical Devices)*
8. Delineate and evaluate the argument and specific claims in a text, assessing whether the reasoning is valid and the evidence is relevant and sufficient; identify false statements and fallacious reasoning. *(Reading Skill: Evaluate Persuasion)*

Spiral Review: RI.9-10.5
Writing
1.d. Establish and maintain a formal style and objective tone while attending to the norms and conventions of the discipline in which they are writing. *(Writing: Letter)*

Speaking and Listening
3. Evaluate a speaker's point of view, reasoning, and use of evidence and rhetoric, identifying any fallacious reasoning or exaggerated or distorted evidence. *(Speaking and Listening: Debate)*

Language
5. Demonstrate understanding of figurative language, word relationships, and nuances in word meanings. *(Vocabulary: Synonyms and Antonyms)*

Literary Analysis: Persuasive Writing and Rhetorical Devices

Persuasive writing, including **speeches,** is intended to convince people to take a particular action or position. Persuasive writers present **arguments,** or series of logically linked ideas that support a conclusion, to defend their ideas. They also use **rhetorical devices,** or verbal techniques that create emphasis and appeal to emotions. Writers use both arguments and rhetorical devices to achieve a persuasive purpose. While rhetorical devices cannot replace arguments, they can move readers, helping them to understand, remember, and accept a writer's ideas. Here are some common rhetorical devices:

- **repetition:** the reuse of a key word or idea for emphasis
- **parallelism:** similar grammatical structures expressing related ideas
- **slogans and saws:** short, catchy phrases
- **rhetorical questions:** questions that are intended to have obvious answers; asked for effect

Reading Skill: Evaluate Persuasion

When reading persuasive writing, **evaluate the writer's argument.** Consider whether the writer supports claims with sound evidence and logical reasoning.

Determine when **persuasive techniques** are effectively used to enhance the impact of the supporting evidence and reasoning, and recognize when they are used to cover up a lack of logical support.

Using the Strategy: Argument Chart

Use an **argument chart** like the one shown to take notes as you read.

Position	Claim	Support	Persuasive Technique
People should oppose a new mall.	Local businesses will suffer.	Prices at malls are lower.	Rhetorical question: Do you want your neighbor to lose his business?

What kind of *knowledge* changes our lives?

Keep Memory Alive Elie Wiesel

Writing About the Big Question

In "Keep Memory Alive," Wiesel shows that testifying to the evils of the past can be a difficult but important duty. He argues that studying history is important not just for the facts and information it teaches us, but for the important lessons it reveals. Use these sentence starters to develop your ideas about the Big Question.

The kinds of facts we may learn through studying **history** include _____, and _____.

From these facts, we can learn important lessons such as _____.

Living in **ignorance** of problems of the past and present can be dangerous because _____.

While You Read Look for lessons the author learns in childhood that he carries with him as an adult.

Vocabulary

Read each word and its definition. Decide whether you know the word well, know it a little bit, or do not know it at all. After you read, see how your knowledge of each word has increased.

- **transcends** (tran sendz´) *v.* goes beyond the limits of; exceeds (p. 543) *The indescribable beauty of the Grand Canyon transcends the words used to describe it.* transcendent *adj.* transcendence *n.*

- **presumptuous** (prē zump´ choo əs) *adj.* overstepping appropriate bounds; too bold (p. 543) *It would be presumptuous of me to give medical advice, because I am not a doctor.* presume *v.* presumption *n.* presumptuously *adv.*

- **accomplices** (ə käm´ plis iz) *n.* people who help another person commit a crime (p. 544) *His accomplices kept a lookout while he robbed the bank.*

Word Study

The **Latin root -scend-** means "climb."

In this speech, the author talks about receiving an honor that **transcends,** or climbs and goes beyond, him as just one person.

Author of
Keep Memory Alive

The Romanian-born teacher, philosopher, and writer Elie Wiesel was deported to the Nazi death camp at Auschwitz at age fifteen. His parents and sister all perished at the hands of the Nazis.

Survivor and Witness After surviving the war, Wiesel did not write a single word about his wartime experiences for ten years. Finally, in 1955, he wrote an account of his experiences, *And the World Kept Silent.* His English adaptation of the work, *Night,* was published in 1960. He says, "I wrote it for the other survivors who found it difficult to speak. And I wanted really to tell them, 'Look, you must speak . . . we must try.'"

BACKGROUND FOR THE SPEECH

The Holocaust

The Holocaust was the systematic persecution and murder of Jews and others deemed "unfit" by Germany's Nazi Party. The Nazis came to power in Germany in 1933. During World War II (1939–1945), Nazi forces killed Jews throughout German-occupied lands or sent them to concentration camps. There, prisoners like Elie Wiesel were worked to death, starved to death, or killed outright.

Did You Know?
Wiesel was perhaps the first to use the term *Holocaust* to describe the Nazis' brutal program of persecution.

Keep Memory Alive

Alive

Elie Wiesel

It is with a profound sense of humility that I accept the honor you have chosen to bestow upon me. I know: your choice transcends me. This both frightens and pleases me.

It frightens me because I wonder: do I have the right to represent the multitudes who have perished? Do I have the right to accept this great honor on their behalf? I do not. That would be presumptuous. No one may speak for the dead, no one may interpret their mutilated dreams and visions.

It pleases me because I may say that this honor belongs to all the survivors and their children, and through us, to the Jewish people with whose destiny I have always identified.

I remember: it happened yesterday or eternities ago. A young Jewish boy discovered the kingdom of night. I remember his bewilderment, I remember his anguish. It all happened so fast. The ghetto.[1] The deportation. The sealed cattle car. The fiery altar upon which the history of our people and the future of mankind were meant to be sacrificed.

---

1. **The ghetto** (get´ ō) During the Second World War, the Nazis forced Jews in European cities to live in crowded, restricted neighborhoods, or ghettos.

◀ **Critical Viewing** How does this image of children being sent to a Nazi concentration camp add force to Wiesel's point about the necessity of remembering? Explain. **[Support]**

Literary Analysis
Persuasive Writing
Identify two examples of parallelism in the second paragraph.

Vocabulary
transcends (tran sendz´)
v. goes beyond the limits of; exceeds

presumptuous
(prē zump´ choo əs) adj. overstepping appropriate bounds; too bold

I remember: he asked his father: "Can this be true? This is the 20th century, not the Middle Ages. Who would allow such crimes to be committed? How could the world remain silent?"

And now the boy is turning to me: "Tell me," he asks. "What have you done with my future? What have you done with your life?"

And I tell him that I have tried. That I have tried to keep memory alive, that I have tried to fight those who would forget. Because if we forget, we are guilty, we are accomplices.

And then I explained to him how naive we were, that the world did know and remain silent. And that is why I swore never to be silent whenever and wherever human beings endure suffering and humiliation. We must always take sides. Neutrality[2] helps the oppressor, never the victim. Silence encourages the tormentor, never the tormented.

Vocabulary
accomplices (ə käm′ plis iz) *n.* people who help another person commit a crime

---

2. **Neutrality** (noō tral′ ə tē) *n.* state of not taking sides in a conflict; quality of being unbiased.

Critical Thinking

© 1. **Key Ideas and Details (a)** On whose behalf does Wiesel accept the Nobel Prize? **(b) Draw Conclusions:** Why does he believe the award belongs to those people? **(c) Interpret:** Why does he say that receiving the award both "frightens and pleases" him?

© 2. **Key Ideas and Details (a)** What does the boy Wiesel ask the adult Wiesel? **(b) Interpret:** What do his questions imply about Wiesel's adult responsibilities? **(c) Draw Conclusions:** Why does Wiesel believe we have a moral duty to remember?

© 3. **Integration of Knowledge and Skills** Describe a situation in which silence might do harm.

© 4. **Integration of Knowledge and Skills** What lessons learned in a concentration camp have guided Weisel's actions as an adult? *[Connect to the Big Question: What kind of knowledge changes our lives?]*

Cite textual evidence to support your responses.

Literary Analysis: Persuasive Writing and Rhetorical Devices

© **1. Key Ideas and Details** Identify the central **argument** in Wiesel's **persuasive speech**, and summarize his point of view.

© **2. Craft and Structure** What **rhetorical devices** does Wiesel use in his speech? Use a chart like the one shown to analyze examples.

	Repetition	Parallelism	Slogans or Saws	Rhetorical Questions
Example				
Effect				

© **3. Integration of Knowledge and Skills (a)** What assumptions does Wiesel make about a person's obligation to the community? **(b)** With a small group, discuss whether you agree with the assumptions.

Reading Skill: Evaluate Persuasion

4. (a) Wiesel says, "Because if we forget, we are guilty, we are accomplices." What are his reasons for making the claim? **(b)** Explain whether there are any important facts he has not taken into account. **(c)** Is the claim logical? Why or why not?

5. Use your answers to **evaluate** this claim. Consider the rhetorical power of Wiesel's statement as well as the support he gives.

Vocabulary

© **Acquisition and Use** Words that have similar meanings are called **synonyms**. Words that have opposite meanings are called **antonyms.** Explain whether each word pair contains synonyms or antonyms. Then, write a sentence using both words.

1. presumptuous, modest
2. transcends, exceeds
3. accomplices, collaborators

Word Study Use the context of the sentences and what you know about the **Latin root -scend-** to explain your answer to each question.

1. Are you going uphill or downhill as you *ascend* a mountain?
2. If a person is a *descendant* of a mayor, are the two related?

Word Study

The **Latin root -scend-** means "climb."

Apply It Explain how the root -scend- contributes to the meanings of these words. Consult a dictionary if necessary.

condescend
descend
ascend

What kind of *knowledge* changes our lives?

Writing About the Big Question

In the excerpt from Nobel Lecture, the author insists that writers should be the voices of truth against the lies and oppression of corrupt governments. Use this sentence starter to develop your ideas about the Big Question.

In order to develop a better **awareness** of and **insight** into issues such as free speech, one can _____.

While You Read Look for ways Solzhenitsyn suggests that writers can help one another to be the voice of truth.

Vocabulary

Read each word and its definition. Decide whether you know the word well, know it a little bit, or do not know it at all. After you read, see how your knowledge of each word has increased.

- **aggregate** (ag´ rə git) *n.* a group of distinct things gathered into a whole; a sum (p. 549) *The aggregate of ants worked together to rebuild their colony.* aggregate *adj.* aggregate *v.* aggregation *n.*

- **reciprocity** (res´ ə präs´ ə tē) *n.* relations of exchange; interdependence (p. 549) *Reciprocity between nations means helping each other out during difficult times.* reciprocal *adj.* reciprocate *v.*

- **jurisdiction** (joor´ is dik´ shən) *n.* sphere of authority or power (p. 549) *The mayor's jurisdiction does not extend beyond this town.* jurisdictional *adj.* jury *n.*

- **condemn** (kən dem´) *v.* disapprove of; pass unfavorable judgment on (p. 551) *The court is certain to condemn the traitor for his crimes.* condemnable *adj.* condemnation *n.* condemned *adj.*

- **inexorably** (in eks´ ə rə blē) *adv.* without the possibility of being delayed or stopped (p. 551) *The hurricane moved inexorably up the coast.* inexorable *adj.* inexorability *n.*

- **oratory** (ôr´ ə tôr´ ē) *n.* act of public speaking; strategies used in such speaking (p. 551) *The speaker's oratory fired up the crowd.* orate *v.* orator *n.* oration *n.*

Word Study

The **Latin root -jur-** means "law" or "right."

In this speech, the author asserts that a nation's government should not have **jurisdiction,** or the right to make laws, over the literature produced there.

Meet
Alexander Solzhenitsyn
(1918–2008)

Author of
Nobel Lecture

Russian writer Alexander Solzhenitsyn spent years in prison camps because of his political views. Yet he was never intimidated into silence. He experienced the hardship of being a dissident—someone who publicly disagrees with an established system.

A Powerful Voice During the Second World War, Solzhenitsyn was imprisoned for writing letters to a friend that were critical of the Soviet leader, Joseph Stalin. In his first novel, *A Day in the Life of Ivan Denisovich,* he described the harsh climate, backbreaking work, and poor diet at the camp in which he was imprisoned. In 1974, after the publication in Paris of parts of *The Gulag Archipelago,* Solzhenitsyn was tried for treason and exiled. In 1994, three years after the fall of the Soviet Union, he returned to his homeland.

BACKGROUND FOR THE SPEECH

A Writer in Exile

By writing critically about the U.S.S.R. (now Russia and other nations), Alexander Solzhenitsyn faced punishment and censorship. As he explains in his Nobel Lecture, writers and publishers around the world offered their support. When Solzhenitsyn was exiled in 1974, he was first welcomed by fellow author and Nobel Prize winner Heinrich Böll.

Did You Know?
Solzhenitsyn won the Nobel Prize in Literature in 1970.

from Nobel Lecture

Alexander Solzhenitsyn

translated by F.D. Reeve

▲ **Critical Viewing**
Why is it surprising that
Solzhenitsyn was sent to
a prison camp, like this
one, for writing letters?
[Connect]

I am, however, encouraged by a keen sense of WORLD
LITERATURE as the one great heart that beats for the cares
and misfortunes of our world, even though each corner sees
and experiences them in a different way.

In past times, also, besides age-old national literatures there
existed a concept of world literature as the link between the

summits of national literatures and as the aggregate of reciprocal literary influences. But there was a time lag: readers and writers came to know foreign writers only belatedly, sometimes centuries later, so that mutual influences were delayed and the network of national literary high points was visible not to contemporaries but to later generations.

Today, between writers of one country and the readers and writers of another, there is an almost instantaneous reciprocity, as I myself know. My books, unpublished, alas, in my own country, despite hasty and often bad translations have quickly found a responsive world readership. Critical analysis of them has been undertaken by such leading Western writers as Heinrich Böll.[1] During all these recent years, when both my work and my freedom did not collapse, when against the laws of gravity they held on seemingly in thin air, seemingly on nothing, on the invisible, mute surface tension of sympathetic people, with warm gratitude I learned, to my complete surprise, of the support of the world's writing fraternity. On my fiftieth birthday I was astounded to receive greetings from well-known European writers. No pressure put on me now passed unnoticed. During the dangerous weeks when I was being expelled from the Writers' Union,[2] THE PROTECTIVE WALL put forward by prominent writers of the world saved me from worse persecution, and Norwegian writers and artists hospitably prepared shelter for me in the event that I was exiled from my country. Finally, my being nominated for a Nobel Prize was originated not in the land where I live and write but by François Mauriac[3] and his colleagues. Afterward, national writers' organizations expressed unanimous support for me.

As I have understood it and experienced it myself, world literature is no longer an abstraction or a generalized concept invented by literary critics, but a common body and common spirit, a living, heartfelt unity reflecting the growing spiritual unity of mankind. State borders still turn crimson, heated red-hot by electric fences and machine-gun fire; some ministries of internal affairs still suppose that literature is "an internal affair" of the countries under their jurisdiction; and newspaper headlines still herald, "They have no right to interfere in our internal affairs!" Meanwhile, no such thing as INTERNAL AFFAIRS remains on our crowded Earth. Mankind's salvation lies exclusively in everyone's making everything his business, in the people of the East being anything but indifferent to what is thought in the West, and in the

Vocabulary

aggregate (ag´ rə git) *n.* a group of distinct things gathered into a whole; a sum

reciprocity (res´ ə präs´ ə tē) *n.* relations of exchange; interdependence

jurisdiction (jŏŏr´ is dik´ shən) *n.* sphere of authority or power

Spiral Review Development of Ideas What do the details in this paragraph add to Solzhenitsyn's idea of "world literature"?

Literary Analysis Persuasive Writing How does repetition of the words *common, unity, West,* and *East* add to the power of this paragraph?

Name one way in which writers in other countries helped Solzhenitsyn.

---

1. **Heinrich** (hīn´ riH) **Böll** (böl) (1917–1985) German novelist and winner of the Nobel Prize in Literature.
2. **Writers' Union** official Soviet writers' organization, which enforced government policies on literature and gave privileges to writers. In addition to being expelled from this union, Solzhenitsyn was forbidden to live in Moscow.
3. **François** (frän swä´) **Mauriac** (mô´ rè ak´) (1885–1970) French novelist and essayist.

World Events Connection

Repression in the Soviet Union

◄ Many of Solzhenitsyn's difficulties with the Soviet authorities stemmed from his works exposing the evils of the Soviet Gulag.

The Gulag consisted of prison camps such as the one shown. Many were located in Siberia, where harsh weather, poor diet, and intensive labor led to much suffering among inmates. ►

1929–1953	1956–1964	mid-1960s–mid-1980s	1985–1991
Dictatorship of Josef Stalin Millions are imprisoned for allegedly opposing the government.	**The "Thaw"** New freedoms are permitted.	Renewed Repression	**Glasnost ("openness")** Mikhail Gorbachev introduces policies tolerating freedom of expression.

Connect to the Literature

Judging from Solzhenitsyn's Nobel Lecture, how might he have responded to news of Gorbachev's policies from 1985 to 1991?

people of the West being anything but indifferent to what happens in the East. Literature, one of the most sensitive and responsive tools of human existence, has been the first to pick up, adopt, and assimilate this sense of the growing unity of mankind. I therefore confidently turn to the world literature of the present, to hundreds of friends whom I have not met face to face and perhaps never will see.

My friends! Let us try to be helpful, if we are worth anything. In our own countries, torn by differences among parties, movements, castes, and groups, who for ages past has been not the dividing but the uniting force? This, essentially, is the position of writers, spokesmen of a national language, of the chief tie binding the nation, the very soil which the people inhabit, and, in fortunate circumstances, the nation's spirit too.

I think that world literature has the power in these frightening times to help mankind see itself accurately despite what is advocated by partisans and by parties. It has the power to transmit the condensed experience of one region to another, so that different scales of values are combined, and so that one people accurately and concisely knows the true history of another with a power of recognition and acute awareness as if it had lived through that history itself—and could thus be spared repeating old mistakes. At the same time, perhaps we ourselves may succeed in developing our own WORLDWIDE VIEW, like any man, with the center of the eye seeing what is nearby but the periphery of vision taking in what is happening in the rest of the world. We will make correlations and maintain worldwide standards.

Who, if not writers, are to condemn their own unsuccessful governments (in some states this is the easiest way to make a living; everyone who is not too lazy does it) as well as society itself, whether for its cowardly humiliation or for its self-satisfied weakness, or the lightheaded escapades of the young, or the youthful pirates brandishing knives?

We will be told: What can literature do against the pitiless onslaught of naked violence? Let us not forget that violence does not and cannot flourish by itself; it is inevitably intertwined with LYING. Between them there is the closest, the most profound and natural bond: nothing screens violence except lies, and the only way lies can hold out is by violence. Whoever has once announced violence as his METHOD must inexorably choose lying as his PRINCIPLE. At birth, violence behaves openly and even proudly. But as soon as it becomes stronger and firmly established, it senses the thinning of the air around it and cannot go on without befogging itself in lies, coating itself with lying's sugary oratory. It does not always or necessarily go straight for the gullet; usually it demands of its victims only allegiance to the lie, only complicity in the lie.

Vocabulary

condemn (kən dem´) v. disapprove of; pass unfavorable judgment on

inexorably (in eks´ ə rə blē) adv. without the possibility of being delayed or stopped

oratory (ôr´ ə tôr´ ē) n. act of public speaking; strategies used in such speaking

Reading Check

According to Solzhenitsyn, what does world literature have the power to do?

◀ **Critical Viewing** The Berlin Wall once separated East and West Berlin. How does this scene of newspaper readers by the wall support what the author says about truth? **[Connect]**

Reading Skill
Evaluate Persuasion
Does Solzhenitsyn
support his claim that
"art has always won and
always will"? Explain.

The simple act of an ordinary courageous man is not to take part, not to support lies! Let *that* come into the world and even reign over it, but not through me. Writers and artists can do more: they can VANQUISH LIES! In the struggle against lies, art has always won and always will. Conspicuously, incontestably for everyone. Lies can stand up against much in the world, but not against art.

Once lies have been dispelled, the repulsive nakedness of violence will be exposed—and hollow violence will collapse.

That, my friends, is why I think we can help the world in its red-hot hour: not by the nay-saying of having no armaments,[4] not by abandoning oneself to the carefree life, but by going into battle!

In Russian, proverbs about TRUTH are favorites. They persistently express the considerable, bitter, grim experience of the people, often astonishingly:

ONE WORD OF TRUTH OUTWEIGHS THE WORLD.

On such a seemingly fantastic violation of the law of the conservation of mass and energy are based both my own activities and my appeal to the writers of the whole world.

---

4. **the nay-saying of having no armaments** Solzhenitsyn is referring to the idea that nations should limit the number or kind of weapons that they hold ready for war.

ONE WORD OF TRUTH OUTWEIGHS THE WORLD.

Critical Thinking

Cite textual evidence to support your responses.

1. **Key Ideas and Details** **(a)** According to Solzhenitsyn, what is a key difference between world literature today and in the past? **(b)** **Interpret:** Why does he call world literature "one great heart"?

2. **Key Ideas and Details:** **(a)** According to Solzhenitsyn, what were two ways in which European writers showed support for him? **(b)** **Connect:** How does this support confirm his view of world literature?

3. **Key Ideas and Details** **Analyze:** What role does Solzhenitsyn believe artists have in the struggle against injustice?

4. **Integration of Knowledge and Ideas** Solzhenitsyn wants writers to write about "the truth." **(a)** What issues would he think are most in need of this truthful examination? **(b)** Does he want the truth about these issues to change people? Explain. *[Connect to the Big Question: What kind of knowledge changes our lives?]*

Literary Analysis: Persuasive Writing and Rhetorical Devices

1. **Key Ideas and Details** Identify the central argument in and main purpose of Solzhenitsyn's **persuasive speech.**

2. **Craft and Structure** What **rhetorical devices** does Solzhenitsyn use to emphasize his message and achieve his purpose? Use a chart like the one shown to analyze examples.

	Repetition	Parallelism	Slogans or Saws	Rhetorical Questions
Example				
Effect				

3. **Integration of Knowledge and Ideas** **(a)** What assumptions does Solzhenitsyn make about the rights of individuals as opposed to the dictates of the state? **(b)** In a group, discuss whether you agree with his assumptions.

Reading Skill: Evaluate Persuasion

4. **(a)** Solzhenitsyn writes, "Once lies have been dispelled . . . hollow violence will collapse." Explain his reasons for making the claim. **(b)** Explain whether there are any important facts he has not taken into account. **(c)** Explain whether the claim is logical.

5. Evaluate Solzhenitsyn's claim. In your answer, consider the rhetorical power of the statement as well as the support he gives.

Vocabulary

Acquisition and Use Words with the same or similar meanings are **synonyms.** Words with opposite meanings are **antonyms.** Explain whether each item contains synonyms or antonyms. Then, write a sentence using both words.

1. reciprocity, independence
2. inexorably, avoidably
3. oratory, rhetoric
4. aggregate, total
5. jurisdiction, authority
6. condemn, approve

Word Study Use the context of the sentences and what you know about the **Latin root -jur-** to explain your answer to each question.

1. Would you expect to see a *jury* in a courtroom or in a gymnasium?
2. Why would it be a bad idea to commit *perjury* during a trial?

Word Study

The **Latin root -jur-** means "law" or "right."

Apply It Explain how the root *-jur-* contributes to the meanings of these words. Consult a dictionary if necessary.

abjure

injury

jurisprudence

Integrated Language Skills

Keep Memory Alive • *from* Nobel Lecture

Conventions: Degrees of Adverbs

An **adverb** is a word that modifies a verb, an adjective, or another adverb.

Most adverbs have three different forms, called degrees of comparison—the *positive,* the *comparative,* and the *superlative.* Use the positive form to describe a single action or quality. Use the comparative to compare two items. Use the superlative to compare more than two items.

There are several ways to indicate these degrees. For single-syllable words, add -*er* or -*est.* For longer words, use *more* or *most.* Some adverbs take on a completely different form. Look at these examples:

Positive	Comparative	Superlative
soon	sooner	soonest
impressively	more impressively	most impressively
well	better	best

Practice A Underline the adverb in each sentence. Tell whether its form is positive, comparative, or superlative.

1. Of all the writers, Wiesel spoke most convincingly.

2. He wrote powerfully about the concentration camps.

3. Wiesel painfully recalled his experiences during World War II.

4. We must be stronger than the person who wants to hurt us.

ⓒ **Reading Application** In "Keep Memory Alive," find at least one example of a positive and a superlative adverb.

Practice B Rewrite each sentence, replacing each positive adverb with either a comparative or a superlative adverb. You may need to add words to the sentences.

1. Solzhenitsyn wrote <u>passionately</u>.

2. The Russian government searched <u>often</u> for dissenting voices.

3. A courageous author writes <u>truthfully</u>.

4. Dedicated writers work <u>diligently</u> at uniting people.

ⓒ **Writing Application** Write a brief paragraph about the importance of free speech. Make sure to include at least one example of a positive, a comparative, and a superlative adverb in your writing.

PH | **WRITING COACH** | Further instruction and practice are available in *Prentice Hall Writing Coach.*

Writing

Argumentative Text Write a **letter** taking a position on Weisel's claim that silence makes us accomplices *or* on Solzhenitsyn's claim that telling the truth can change the world.

If you are writing to Wiesel, follow these tips:

- Identify and state the general definition of "accomplice."
- Describe the specific results of silence that Wiesel points out.
- Use *rhetorical devices* to help reveal your point of view and purpose.

If you are writing to Solzhenitsyn, follow these tips:

- State a general definition of "changing the world."
- Describe the effects of truth that Solzhenitsyn identifies.
- Use *rhetorical devices* to help reveal your point of view and purpose.

In your letter, use evidence to support your reasoning. Also, be sure to use formal language and an objective tone. For example, use the objective word *illogical* instead of the emotional word *stupid*. Use the formal term *impressive* rather than the informal *awesome*.

Grammar Application Use the correct degree of adverbs in your letter.

Writing Workshop: *Work in Progress*

Prewriting for Persuasive Essay For a persuasive essay you may write, jot down five local or national practices that you would like to see changed or modified. Prioritize your list, numbering the items 1 through 5. Save this Topic List in your writing portfolio.

Speaking and Listening

Comprehension and Collaboration Hold a group **debate** about one of the following paraphrased claims.

Wiesel: *People who do not speak up against injustice are accomplices.*

Solzhenitsyn: *Telling the truth will bring down an unjust government.*

Choose a notetaker and moderator, and divide the group into teams to argue for and against the statement.

- Present your point of view, supporting it with evidence.
- During the debate, listen to the arguments presented and prepare to respond. Point out any instances of the opposing team's use of exaggerated evidence or fallacious reasoning.
- Conclude your argument by summarizing your position.

After the debate, review the notes to identify the best ideas.

Common Core State Standards

W.9-10.1.d; SL.9-10.3
[For the full wording of the standards, see page 538.]

Use this prewriting activity to prepare for the **Writing Workshop** on page 604.

PHLit Online!
www.PHLitOnline.com

- Interactive graphic organizers
- Grammar tutorial
- Interactive journals

© Leveled Texts

Build your skills and improve your comprehension of nonfiction with texts of increasing complexity.

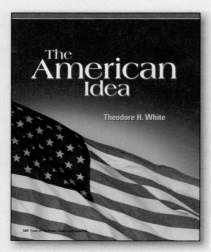

Read **"The American Idea"** to learn about the ideas that influenced the founding of the United States.

Read **"What Makes a Degas a Degas?"** to learn about a famous artist's life and work.

© Common Core State Standards

Meet these standards with either **"The American Idea"** (p. 560) or **"What Makes a Degas a Degas?"** (p. 568).

Reading Informational Text
5. Analyze in detail how an author's ideas or claims are developed and refined by particular sentences, paragraphs, or larger portions of a text. *(Literary Analysis: Analytic and Interpretive Essays)*

Spiral Review: RI.9-10.3
Writing
7. Conduct short as well as more sustained research projects to answer a question or solve a problem; narrow or broaden the inquiry when appropriate; synthesize multiple sources on the subject, demonstrating understanding of the subject under investigation. *(Research and Technology: Cover Letter and Résumé)*

Language
1. Demonstrate command of the conventions of standard English grammar and usage when writing or speaking. *(Conventions: Degrees of Adjectives)*
5. Demonstrate understanding of figurative language, word relationships, and nuances in word meanings. *(Vocabulary: Analogies)*

Literary Analysis: Analytic and Interpretive Essays

An **analytic essay** is a brief work of nonfiction in which a writer explores an idea or claim by breaking it into parts. In an **interpretive essay,** a writer offers a view of the meaning or significance of an issue of general interest. A single essay may combine features of both types of essay.

To bring readers to accept an analysis or interpretation, a writer may develop it using **appeals** of the following types:

- *appeals to authority,* or calls upon the opinions of experts or other respected people

- *appeals to reason,* or calls upon logic

- *emotional appeals,* or calls upon feelings like fear, sympathy, or pride

- *appeals to shared values,* or calls upon beliefs shared by many about what is good, right, or fair

Reading Skill: Evaluate Persuasion

To **evaluate a writer's appeals,** decide whether the writer balances logic with emotional appeals. **Distinguish between fact and opinion.**

- A statement of **fact** can be proved true.

- A statement of **opinion** expresses a belief or a viewpoint and should be supported by facts or reason.

A weak essay may rely too much on persuasive appeal and not enough on fact. As you evaluate persuasive writing, look for ways in which the writer supports and develops his or her claims and ideas.

Using the Strategy: Fact and Opinion Chart

Record details on a **fact and opinion chart** like this one to help you decide if the writer has made a strong argument for a position.

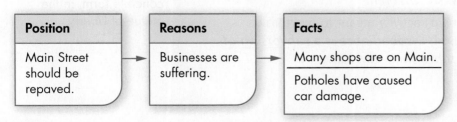

Position	Reasons	Facts
Main Street should be repaved.	Businesses are suffering.	Many shops are on Main.
		Potholes have caused car damage.

What kind of knowledge changes our lives?

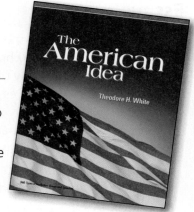

Writing About the Big Question

In "The American Idea," the author explores the concept of America as a nation tied together by an idea of freedom. Use these sentence starters to develop your ideas about the Big Question.

The kind of knowledge that may **influence** a person's decision to move to another country is _____.

_____ can make it easier to **adapt** to life in a new land.

While You Read Look for the statement that White believes was most important to those who drafted the idea of American freedom. Then, consider White's proposal that this idea meant different things to different people.

Vocabulary

Read each word and its definition. Decide whether you know the word well, know it a little bit, or do not know it at all. After you read, see how your knowledge of each word has increased.

- **embodied** (em bäd´ ēd) *v.* gave form to; made concrete (p. 561) *The poem <u>embodied</u> her most hidden hopes and dreams.* *body n. embodiment n.*

- **emigrants** (em´ i grənts) *n.* people who leave their country or region to settle elsewhere (p. 561) *Many <u>emigrants</u> left Ireland in the 1840s and moved to other countries.* *emigrate v. emigration n. migrant adj.*

- **successive** (sək ses´ iv) *adj.* following one after another in sequence (p. 563) *Phil received an award after winning all five <u>successive</u> tennis matches.* *succeed v. succession n.*

- **subversion** (səb vur´ zhən) *n.* activity meant to overthrow something established (p. 564) *Disobedience is a <u>subversion</u> of authority.* *subversive adj. subversively adv. subvert v.*

Word Study

The **Greek prefix em-** means "in" or "into."

In this essay, the author explains that Jefferson's ideas about liberty are **embodied**, or put into concrete form, in the Statue of Liberty.

Meet
Theodore H. White
(1915–1986)

Author of
The American Idea

A Boston native, Theodore H. White worked as a newsboy for the *Boston Globe* to help pay for his education at Harvard University. At Harvard, he studied Chinese history and Asian languages. After he graduated, Henry Luce, founder of *Time* magazine, made him *Time*'s correspondent in eastern Asia.

The Making of a Reporter White earned fame writing about the election of John F. Kennedy in *The Making of the President, 1960.* "There is no excitement anywhere in the world, short of war, to match the excitement of the American presidential campaign," White observed. Today, he is viewed as one of the finest political reporters of the twentieth century.

Did You Know?
President Kennedy's widow, Jacqueline Kennedy, chose White to write a magazine essay honoring her husband.

BACKGROUND FOR THE ESSAY

Coming to America

In his essay, Theodore H. White asserts that immigration is key to the idea of America. Since its founding, the United States has welcomed more immigrants than any other nation. From 1820 to 1930, about 60 percent of all immigration worldwide was to the United States. From 1905 to 1914, more than a million people immigrated to the United States each year, seeking opportunity or fleeing oppression.

The American Idea

Theodore H. White

*T*he idea was there at the very beginning, well before Thomas Jefferson put it into words—and the idea rang the call.

Jefferson himself could not have imagined the reach of his call across the world in time to come when he wrote:

"We hold these truths to be self-evident, that all men are created equal, that they are endowed by their Creator with certain unalienable rights, that among these are life, liberty, and the pursuit of happiness."

But over the next two centuries the call would reach the potato patches of Ireland, the ghettoes of Europe, the paddyfields of China, stirring farmers to leave their lands and townsmen their trades and thus unsettling all traditional civilizations.

It is the call from Thomas Jefferson, embodied in the great statue that looks down the Narrows of New York Harbor,[1] and in the immigrants who answered the call, that we now celebrate.

Some of the first European Americans had come to the new continent to worship God in their own way, others to seek their fortunes. But, over a century-and-a-half, the new world changed those Europeans, above all the Englishmen who had come to North America. Neither King nor Court nor Church could stretch over the ocean to the wild continent. To survive, the first emigrants had to learn to govern themselves.

---

1. **the great statue that looks down the Narrows of New York Harbor** Statue of Liberty.

Literary Analysis
Analytic and Interpretive Essays
What emotional appeals does White use in the opening paragraphs of this essay?

Vocabulary
embodied (em bäd´ ēd) *v.* gave form to; made concrete

emigrants (em´ i grənts) *n.* people who leave their country or region to settle elsewhere

Reading Check
According to Thomas Jefferson, what three rights do all men have?

But the freedom of the wilderness whetted their appetites for more freedoms. By the time Jefferson drafted his call, men were in the field fighting for those new-learned freedoms, killing and being killed by English soldiers, the best-trained troops in the world, supplied by the world's greatest navy. Only something worth dying for could unite American volunteers and keep them in the field—a stated cause, a flag, a nation they could call their own.

When, on the Fourth of July, 1776, the colonial leaders who had been meeting as a Continental Congress in Philadelphia voted to approve Jefferson's Declaration of Independence, it was not puffed-up rhetoric for them to pledge to each other "our lives, our fortunes and our sacred honor." Unless their new "United States of America" won the war, the Congressmen would be judged traitors as relentlessly as would the irregulars-under-arms in the field. . . .

The new Americans were tough men fighting for a very tough idea. How they won their battles is a story for the schoolbooks, studied by scholars, wrapped in myths by historians and poets. But what is most important is the story of the idea that made them into a nation, the idea that had an explosive power undreamed of in 1776.

All other nations had come into being among people whose families had lived for time out of mind on the same land where they were born. Englishmen are English, Frenchmen are French, Chinese are Chinese, while their governments come and go; their national states can be torn apart and remade without losing their nationhood. But Americans are a nation born of an idea; not the place, but the idea, created the United States Government.

The story we celebrate . . . is the story of how this idea worked itself out, how it stretched and changed and how the call for "life, liberty and the pursuit of happiness" does still, as it did in the beginning, mean different things to different people. ●

Reading Skill
Evaluate Persuasion
Identify one fact and one opinion expressed in the essay so far.

The new Americans were tough men fighting for a very tough idea.

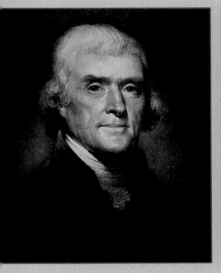

▲ Thomas Jefferson

▲ John Adams

LITERATURE IN CONTEXT

History Connection

The American Revolution
White makes a number of references to the era of the American Revolution.

- **The Declaration of Independence** Written by Thomas Jefferson, the Declaration announced the colonies' decision in 1776 to break away from Great Britain. In the opening paragraph, Jefferson refers to the phrase *unalienable* (un āl´ yən ə bəl) rights—those rights that cannot be taken or given away.

- **Irregulars-Under-Arms** The colonists who fought the British in the Revolution could be considered irregulars-under-arms. As rebels, they did not belong to a regularly established army.

Connect to the Literature

What contrasting views of the American idea are represented by Jefferson's "unalienable rights" and by Adams's views on immigration?

The debate began with the drafting of the Declaration of Independence. That task was left to Jefferson of Virginia, who spent two weeks in an upstairs room in a Philadelphia boarding house penning a draft, while John Adams and Benjamin Franklin questioned, edited, hardened his phrases. By the end of that hot and muggy June, the three had reached agreement: the Declaration contained the ringing universal theme Jefferson strove for and, at the same time, voiced American grievances toughly enough to please the feisty Adams and the pragmatic Franklin. After brief debate, Congress passed it.

As the years wore on, the great debate expanded between Jefferson and Adams. The young nation flourished and Jefferson chose to think of America's promise as a call to all the world, its promises universal. A few weeks before he died, he wrote, "May it be to the world, what I believe it will be (to some parts sooner, to others later, but finally to all), the signal of arousing men to burst their chains." To Adams, the call meant something else—it was the call for American independence, the cornerstone of an American state.

Their argument ran through their successive Administrations. Adams, the second President, suspected the French Revolutionaries; Alien and Sedition Acts[2] were passed during his term of office to protect the American state and its liberties

Vocabulary
successive (sək ses´ iv) *adj.* following one after another in sequence

Reading Check

What document did the Founders draft to present their ideals?

---

2. **Alien and Sedition Acts** laws passed by Congress in 1798 restricting immigration and regulating the expression of criticism of the government.

against French subversion. But Jefferson, the third President, welcomed the French. The two men, once close friends, became archrivals. Still, as they grew old, their rivalry faded; there was glory enough to share in what they had made; in 1812, they began a correspondence that has since become classic, remembering and taking comfort in the triumphs of their youth.

Adams and Jefferson lived long lives and died on the same day—the Fourth of July, 1826, 50 years to the day from the Continental Congress's approval of the Declaration. Legend has it that Adams breathed on his death bed, "Thomas Jefferson still survives." As couriers set out from Braintree[3] carrying the news of Adams's death, couriers were riding north from Virginia with the news of Jefferson's death. The couriers met in Philadelphia. Horace Greeley,[4] then a youth in Vermont, later remembered: ". . . When we learned . . . that Thomas Jefferson and John Adams, the author and the great champion, respectively, of the Declaration, had both died on that day, and that the messengers bearing South and North, respectively, the tidings of their decease, had met in Philadelphia, under the shadow of that Hall in which our independence was declared, it seemed that a Divine attestation had solemnly hallowed and sanctified the great anniversary by the impressive ministration of Death."

---

3. **Braintree** town in Massachusetts (now called Quincy) where John Adams lived and died.
4. **Horace Greeley** famous American newspaper publisher.

Critical Thinking

Cite textual evidence to support your responses.

1. **Key Ideas and Details** **(a)** Identify three groups that White says heard the call of the American idea. **(b) Infer:** How did the call of the American idea affect each of them?

2. **Key Ideas and Details** **Compare and Contrast:** What differences does White see between early American settlers and people living elsewhere?

3. **Key Ideas and Details** **Interpret:** What does White mean when he writes, "Americans are a nation born of an idea"?

4. **Integration of Knowledge and Ideas** **(a)** Do you agree with White that "life, liberty, and the pursuit of happiness" means different things to different people? Why or why not? **(b)** How might these ideals shape a person's life? *[Connect to the Big Question: What kind of knowledge changes our lives?]*

Literary Analysis: Analytic and Interpretive Essays

© **1. Key Ideas and Details** The author of this **interpretive essay** focuses on the "American idea." Briefly summarize White's view.

© **2. Craft and Structure (a)** Use a chart like this one to summarize the development of ideas in the **analytic** sections of White's essay. **(b)** Explain how White uses the story about Adams and Jefferson along with other details and **persuasive appeals** to strengthen his presentation of an "American idea."

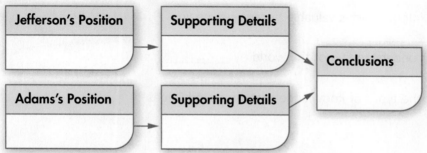

Reading Skill: Evaluate Persuasion

3. (a) List two **opinions** that White includes about people or events. **(b)** Which **facts** does he use to support each opinion?

4. Based on an analysis of his persuasive appeals and the facts and opinions presented, evaluate the validity of White's argument.

Vocabulary

© **Acquisition and Use** Word **analogies** match the relationship in one pair of words with that in another. For each item, choose the word that will make the relationships in the first and second pair of words most similar.

1. immigrants : enter :: emigrants : **(a)** leave, **(b)** stay, **(c)** build
2. entertainment : comedian :: subversion : **(a)** film, **(b)** spy, **(c)** ship
3. build : construct :: embodied : **(a)** formed, **(b)** chosen, **(c)** broke
4. many : few :: successive : **(a)** logical, **(b)** interrupted, **(c)** finished

Word Study Use the context of the sentences and what you know about the **Greek prefix em-** to explain your answer to each question.

1. Would a person feel *embittered* after winning the lottery?
2. Is someone who is *emboldened* courageous or fearful?

What kind of *knowledge* changes our lives?

What Makes a Degas a *Degas?*

566 Types of Nonfiction: Essays and Speeches   Richard Mühlberger

Writing About the Big Question

In "What Makes a Degas a Degas?," the author "reads" two Degas paintings by combining his own knowledge of art with his knowledge about Degas's life. Use these sentence starters to develop your ideas about the Big Question.

Understanding how to interpret art is valuable because you gain **insight** into _____.

Artists can **influence** our understanding of the world by _____ and _____.

While You Read Consider the types of knowledge that interested Degas and influenced his work.

Vocabulary

Read each word and its definition. Decide whether you know the word well, know it a little bit, or do not know it at all. After you read, see how your knowledge of each word has increased.

- **immaterial** (im′ ə tir′ ē əl) *adj.* not consisting of matter (p. 569) *The baby does not understand that his shadow is <u>immaterial</u> and cannot be touched. immaterialize v. immaterially adv. material adj.*

- **silhouette** (sil′ ə wet′) *n.* an outline drawing filled in with a solid color (p. 569) *He drew a solid black <u>silhouette</u> of Emily's profile. silhouette v.*

- **simulating** (sim′ yoo lāt′ iŋ) *v.* giving the appearance of (p. 569) *The machine trained new pilots by <u>simulating</u> a realistic crash. simulation n. simulator n.*

- **lacquered** (lak′ ərd) *adj.* covered in tough, sticky varnish (p. 570) *The artist combined charcoal and sap to coat this <u>lacquered</u> music box. lacquer n. lacquer v.*

Word Study

The **Latin prefix im-** means "not" or "opposite of."

In this essay, the author explains that a painted landscape has an **immaterial** quality, which makes the picture seem as though it is not made of physical materials.

Author of
What Makes a Degas a *Degas?*

Born in New Jersey, Richard Mühlberger has spent more than thirty-five years as an art critic and museum administrator. During the 1990s, he was vice-director in charge of education at the Metropolitan Museum of Art in New York City, one of the foremost art museums in the world.

Aiding in Art Appreciation While at the Metropolitan Museum of Art, Mühlberger began producing a series of books that make the works of famous artists accessible to the average viewer. The series includes *What Makes a Degas a Degas?*, from which this selection is taken, and similarly titled books on Van Gogh, Monet, and others.

BACKGROUND FOR THE ESSAY

Degas and Impressionism

In the 1860s, a group of French painters known as the Impressionists shocked the art world. Abandoning strict forms, they used short, dabbed brushstrokes to capture fleeting impressions of color and light. Their work had a great impact on Edgar Degas (ed gár´ də gä´; 1834–1917). At the same time, as Richard Mühlberger explains in his essay, Degas introduced his own innovative style.

Did You Know?

Mühlberger served as director of the Museum of Fine Art in Springfield, Massachusetts.

What Makes a Degas a *Degas?*

Richard Mühlberger

Dancers, Pink and Green

Degas's famous ballet paintings witness his enthusiasm for dance and his intimacy with the private backstage areas of the Paris Opéra, the huge complex where the ballet made its home. He was equally familiar with the theater's more public boxes and stalls, where he watched many performances. During his lifetime, he produced about fifteen hundred drawings, prints, pastels, and oil paintings with ballet themes.

In *Dancers, Pink and Green* [left], each ballerina is caught in a characteristic pose as she waits to go on the stage. One stretches and flexes her foot. Another secures her hair, while a third is almost hidden. The fourth dancer, who looks at her shoulder strap as she adjusts it, holds a pose that was a favorite of the artist and one he used in many paintings. An upright beam separates her from the fifth ballerina, who also turns her head but in the opposite direction, full of anticipation. Above her in the distance are the box seats, which Degas simplified into a stack of six red and orange rectangles along the edge of the canvas. The vertical beam the ballerina is touching extends to the top and the bottom of the painting. The multicolored vertical shapes behind the dancers represent a large, painted landscape used as a backdrop for one of the dances. It will provide an immaterial, dreamworld quality to the performance, as it does to the painting.

Subscribers to the Opéra were allowed backstage in the theater, and some took advantage of this access to pester dancers. On the far side of the tall wood column is the partial silhouette of a large man in a top hat. He seems to be trying to keep out of the way, but his protruding profile overlaps a ballerina. None of the dancers pay attention to him. They also ignore one another, for this scene represents the tense moments just before the curtain rises.

Degas discovered that with oil paints he could achieve the same fresh feeling conveyed with pastels. Although this painting took the same amount of time to finish as many of his others and was designed and executed in his studio, Degas wanted to make it look as though it had been executed quickly, backstage. To do this, he imitated the marks of a charcoal pencil with his brush, making narrow black lines that edge the dancers' bodies and costumes. Next, he used his own innovation of simulating the matte[1] finish of pastels by taking the sheen out of oil paint, then filling in the sketchy "charcoal" outlines of his figures with a limited range of colors. The colors he used for the dancers extend to the floor and

---

1. **matte** (mat) *adj.* dull; not shiny.

◄ **Critical Viewing**
Do you agree with Mühlberger that this painting looks as if Degas painted it hastily, on the spot? Why?
[Support]

Vocabulary
immaterial (im´ ə tir´ ē əl) *adj.* not consisting of matter
silhouette (sil´ ə wet´) *n.* an outline drawing filled in with a solid color
simulating (sim´ yo͞o lāt´ iŋ) *v.* giving the appearance of

Literary Analysis
Analytic and Interpretive Essays
What is analytic about this essay?

Reading Check
What materials did Degas use to execute *Dancers, Pink and Green?*

Spiral Review
Series of Ideas Reread the final two paragraphs of this section of the essay. Explain why Mühlberger presents ideas in the order in which he does.

the background. The technique gives the impression that he applied the colors hastily while standing in the wings watching the dancers get ready.

The results of Degas's experiments could have been executed much more quickly had he used pastels instead of oils. What Degas wanted, however, was to make paint look spontaneous. This was part of his lifelong quest: to make viewers feel that they were right there, beside him.

Carriage at the Races

Paul Valpinçon was Degas's best friend in school and remained close to the artist all his life. Degas was a frequent visitor to his country house in Normandy, the northwest region of France, a long journey from Paris. Degas thought that the Normandy countryside was "exactly like England," and the beautiful horse farms there inspired him to paint equestrian subjects. During a visit in 1869, however, Degas found horses secondary to Paul Valpinçon's infant son, Henri. This becomes apparent by looking at the painting *Carriage at the Races* [right].

At first, Degas's composition seems lopsided. In one corner are the largest and darkest objects, a pair of horses and a carriage. Against the lacquered body of the carriage, the creamy white tones of the passengers stand out. They are framed by the dark colors rather than overwhelmed by them.

Degas placed a cream-colored umbrella in the middle of the painting above some of the figures in the carriage. Near it, balanced on the back of the driver's seat, is a black bulldog. Paul Valpinçon himself is the driver. Both Paul and the dog are gazing at the baby, who lies in the shade of the umbrella. With pink, dimpled knees, Henri, not yet a year old, sprawls on the lap of his nurse while his mother looks on.

Vocabulary
lacquered (lak´ ərd) *adj.* covered in tough, sticky varnish

▶ **Critical Viewing**
Does the way in which the horses "are cut off" make the picture seem like a photograph, as the essay suggests? **[Assess]**

*T*his was part of his lifelong quest:
to make viewers feel that they were
right there, beside him.

Ideas From the Exotic, Old, and New

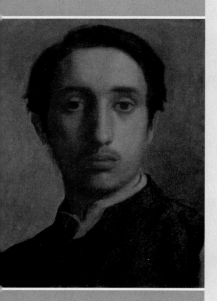

Degas always enjoyed looking at art. One of the thrills of his school years was being allowed to inspect the great paintings in the collection of Paul Valpinçon's father. Throughout his life, the artist drew inspiration from the masterpieces in the Louvre in Paris, one of the greatest museums in the world. He also found ideas in Japanese prints. They were considered cheap, disposable souvenirs in Japan, but were treasured by artists and others in the West as highly original, fascinating works of art. Photographs, then newly invented, also suggested to Degas ways of varying his paintings. He eventually became an enthusiastic photographer himself.

In *Carriage at the Races*, the way in which the horses and carriage are cut off recalls figures in photographs and Japanese prints. For Degas, showing only part of a subject made his paintings more intimate, immediate, and realistic. He wanted viewers to see the scene as if they were actually there.

▲ **Degas self-portrait**

Critical Thinking

Cite textual evidence to support your responses.

1. **Key Ideas and Details** **(a)** Use details from the essay to describe the effect Degas seeks by outlining the dancers in black lines in *Dancers, Pink and Green.* **(b) Analyze:** What other elements contribute to this effect?

2. **Key Ideas and Details** **(a)** What is the dominant image in *Carriage at the Races?* **(b) Analyze:** How does Degas focus attention on this image?

3. **Integration of Knowledge and Ideas** What qualities in Degas's paintings suggest that he might have been a good photographer when he took up that hobby? Explain.

4. **Integration of Knowledge and Ideas** Degas and his art developed and changed based on knowledge he acquired throughout his life. Based on this essay, what subjects and areas of interest do you think influenced Degas and his painting? *[Connect to the Big Question: What kind of knowledge changes our lives?]*

| After You Read | What Makes a Degas a Degas? |

Literary Analysis: Analytic and Interpretive Essays

1. Key Ideas and Details Briefly summarize Mühlberger's view of Degas's "lifelong quest" in this **interpretive essay.**

2. Craft and Structure (a) Use a chart like the one shown to analyze the development of ideas in the **analytic** sections of the essay. **(b)** Explain how **persuasive appeals** to reason strengthen Mühlberger's presentation of the idea that Degas intentionally incorporated qualities that might make his paintings seem incomplete.

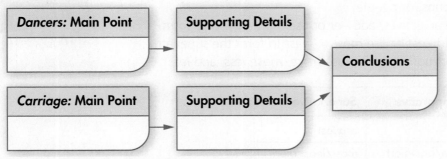

Reading Skill: Evaluate Persuasion

3. (a) List two **opinions** that Mühlberger includes about Degas. **(b)** What **facts** does he use to support each opinion?

4. Based on an analysis of his persuasive appeals and the facts and opinions presented, evaluate the validity of Mühlberger's argument.

Vocabulary

Acquisition and Use Word **analogies** match relationships between two pairs of words. For each item, choose the word that will make the relationships in the first and second pair of words most similar.

1. hatchback : car :: silhouette : **(a)** bracelet, **(b)** portrait, **(c)** carving
2. performing : do :: simulating : **(a)** pretend, **(b)** be, **(c)** own
3. chaotic : still :: immaterial : **(a)** dreamy, **(b)** personal, **(c)** solid
4. upholstered : chair :: lacquered : **(a)** table, **(b)** clean, **(c)** discolor

Word Study Use the context of the sentences and what you know about the **Latin prefix im-** to explain your answer to each question.

1. Would you be able to cross an *impassable* river?
2. Is it easy to solve a problem of *immeasurable* difficulty?

Word Study

The **Latin prefix im-** means "not" or "opposite of."

Apply It Explain how the prefix *im-* contributes to the meanings of these words. Consult a dictionary if necessary.

imbalance
immoderate
impudent

Integrated Language Skills

The American Idea •
What Makes a Degas a Degas?

Conventions: Degrees of Adjectives

An **adjective** is a word that describes a noun or a pronoun.

Most adjectives have three different forms, called degrees—the *positive degree*, the *comparative degree*, and the *superlative degree*. The positive is used to describe one item, group, or person. The comparative is used to compare two items, groups, or people. The superlative is used to compare three or more items, groups, or people.

For most two-syllable adjectives, add –*er* or use *more* or *less* to form the comparative, and add –*est* or use *most* or *least* to form the superlative. For adjectives of three or more syllables, use *more*, *most*, *less*, and *least*.

Positive	Comparative	Superlative
brave	braver	bravest
alert	more/less alert	most/least alert
good	better	best

Practice A Identify the degree of each italicized modifier.

1. Thomas Jefferson was a *brilliant* statesman.
2. Freedom is the *best* idea on which to build a nation.
3. The Declaration of Independence is an *important* document.
4. Some feel that Benjamin Franklin was *more pragmatic* than Thomas Jefferson.

Ⓒ **Reading Application** In "The American Idea," find an example of a positive and a superlative adjective.

Practice B Determine if the italicized modifier is used correctly. Explain your answer.

1. Degas's ballerina painting is *prettier*.
2. Oil paints are *shiniest* than pastels.
3. In *Carriage at the Races*, the baby is *more important* than the carriage.
4. The center ballerina is the *taller* dancer in the entire group.

Ⓒ **Writing Application** Write about a style of art or music you enjoy. Use this sentence as a model to write a new sentence that incorporates the three degrees of adjectives. *Degas's oil paintings were quick, his pastels were quicker, and his drawings were quickest.*

PH **WRITING COACH** | Further instruction and practice are available in *Prentice Hall Writing Coach*.

Writing

Argumentative Text Write a **critique,** or critical evaluation, of White's or Mühlberger's essay. Identify one of the central claims in the essay, and weigh the evidence the writer uses to support it.

Common Core State Standards

L.9-10.1; W.9-10.7
[For the full wording of the standards, see page 556.]

- Before you draft, gather examples of the writer's *evidence.* For each piece of evidence, note whether it is effective.
- Consider discussing each piece of evidence in a separate paragraph.
- Identify ambiguities, nuances, and complexities within the text by looking for sections that confused you. Decide whether the writer clarified ideas for you. If not, determine the effect of the ambiguity.
- Conclude with a statement that evaluates the overall strength of White's or Mühlberger's evidence.
- Present your evaluation to the class. Ask whether listeners agree with your ideas. Summarize points of agreement and disagreement.

Grammar Application In your critique, use the correct degree of adjectives.

Writing Workshop: *Work in Progress*

Prewriting for Persuasive Essay Make a flowchart for the first choice on your Topic List. In each supporting box, write a detail that shows why the change is needed or what positive result it would have. Save this Topic Defense List in your writing portfolio.

Use this prewriting activity to prepare for the **Writing Workshop** on page 604.

Research and Technology

Use multiple reliable sources to research one of the people associated with the essay you read. For example, you might learn more about one of the nation's founders, such as Thomas Jefferson, or study an artist associated with French Impressionism, such as Mary Cassatt. Then, write a **cover letter** and **résumé** that he or she might have submitted for either the job of "Founder of the Republic" or "French Impressionist."

- Conduct research to identify the education and experience that make your subject suitable for the job.
- Consult reference works to find a suitable format for cover letters and résumés. Use action verbs and vivid descriptions to make your writing engaging.
- Use appropriate principles of design, such as correct margins, tabs, columns, and use of white space, to create a visually interesting document.
- Proofread carefully to ensure that you follow the format and use language accurately.

PHLit Online!
www.PHLitOnline.com

- Interactive graphic organizers
- Grammar tutorial
- Interactive journals

Test Practice: Reading

Evaluate Persuasion

Fiction Selection

Directions: *Read the selection. Then, answer the questions.*

Aaron called his best friend, Danny. "I just came from the city pound, looking for Jake. He got lost again," he told Danny. "You should see that place—crowded and smelly, no room for the dogs to run, not enough people to care for the animals. We need to do something."

"Like what?" asked Danny.

"We need to convince our city council to give more funds to the pound. We should treat animals humanely. These dogs are locked in small cages, with no place to exercise. Some of them look sick. They need better medical care. Also, if the pound were cleaner and the animals better cared for, more people would adopt pets from there. That would save the city money."

"Okay," said Danny. "Count me in. By the way, did you find Jake?"

"Yeah. He came home by himself!"

1. Which of the following *best* states the claim made by Aaron?
- **A.** There are too many stray dogs.
- **B.** The city pound is not a humane place for animals.
- **C.** The city pound is dirty.
- **D.** The city council is negligent.

2. What is Aaron's position?
- **A.** People should be convinced to adopt more animals from the pound.
- **B.** The city council should give the pound more money.
- **C.** Dogs should be taken for walks.
- **D.** People should be more humane.

3. The statement "We should treat animals humanely" appeals to—
- **A.** logic.
- **B.** economics.
- **C.** a sense of humor.
- **D.** a sense of ethics.

4. Which of the following persuasive techniques is *not* found in Aaron's appeal?
- **A.** logic
- **B.** emotion
- **C.** statistics
- **D.** a sense of ethics

Writing for Assessment

Which of Aaron's appeals do you find most persuasive? Explain your answer in three or four sentences, using details from the passage.

Nonfiction Selection

Directions: *Read the selection. Then, answer the questions.*

Adopting a family dog is a long-term commitment, so it is important to choose a dog wisely. The Labrador retriever is the most popular dog in the United States. More Labs are registered to owners than any other breed—for good reason.

Labs are affectionate and playful. They love the company of humans, and they always welcome attention. Labs also love any kind of active play. They love to play fetch, especially in the water. Toss a stick into the lake or pool, and you can be sure the Lab will never tire of retrieving it. Labs love to be part of a family, and they are patient and gentle with children. Labs are also easy to train, an important characteristic in a puppy. So when looking for a family pet, choose a Lab. You will not be sorry.

1. Which of the following is the *best* summary of the author's opinion?
   A. You should choose a pet carefully.
   B. Labrador retrievers are superior to other dogs.
   C. A dog's temperament is important.
   D. A Labrador retriever is the best family dog.

2. Repeated use of the word *love* serves to—
   A. help the reader identify with the writer's statements.
   B. emphasize the Lab's enthusiasm and good nature.
   C. show the writer's knowledge.
   D. show the superiority of Labs.

3. Which of the following persuasive techniques is found in the sentence *"More Labs are registered to owners than any other breed"*?
   A. fact
   B. repetition
   C. example
   D. humor

4. Which of the following statements can be verified?
   A. Labs love to be part of a family.
   B. More Labs are registered to owners than any other breed.
   C. You will not be sorry.
   D. Toss a stick in a pool, and you can be sure the Lab will never tire of retrieving it.

Writing for Assessment

Connecting Across Texts
What general attitude toward dogs is expressed in these two passages? In a well-developed paragraph, use details from the two passages to support your answer.

www.PHLitOnline.com
• Online practice
• Instant feedback

Reading for Information

Analyzing Expository and Functional Texts

Research Source

Course Catalog

**Common Core
State Standards**

Reading Informational Text
3. Analyze how the author unfolds an analysis or series of ideas or events, including the order in which the points are made, how they are introduced and developed, and the connections that are drawn between them.

Language
6. Acquire and use accurately general academic and domain-specific words and phrases, sufficient for reading, writing, speaking, and listening at the college and career readiness level; demonstrate independence in gathering vocabulary knowledge when considering a word or phrase important to comprehension or expression.

Reading Skill: Analyze Text Structures

Authors **structure and format** their texts in order to help achieve their purposes. **Scan,** or glance over, titles, headings, and subheadings to analyze how these features support the **author's purpose.** Also, **critique the document** by **skimming,** or quickly reading, key parts of the text to determine the **sequence,** or order, of information. Then, decide whether that sequence is logical. This chart lists some common text structures.

Common Text Structures	
Cause and Effect	action followed by consequences
Chronological Order	in order of occurrence
Comparison and Contrast	according to the similarities and differences
List	connected items stated consecutively or sorted into categories
Order of Importance	in a logical progression from most to least important or from least to most important
Spatial Order	according to location

Content-Area Vocabulary

These words appear in the selections that follow. You may also encounter them in other content-area texts.

- **linguistic** (liŋ gwis´ tik) *adj.* having to do with language
- **endeavors** (en dev´ ərz) *n.* earnest tries or attempts
- **spectrum** (spek´ trəm) *n.* range or scope

The History of the Guitar
Thomas A. Hill

When we attempt to pinpoint the origins of deliberately produced, carefully designed instruments, we run into problems, because the very first instrument makers were not very concerned with posterity. They did not leave written records. One approach we might try, in an effort to find out where the guitar came from, would be an examination of languages.

This paragraph is organized using a cause-and-effect structure.

Ancient Beginnings

The ancient Assyrians,[1] four thousand years ago, had an instrument that they called a *chetarah*. We know little more about it other than that it was a stringed instrument with a sound-box, but the name is intriguing. The ancient Hebrews had their *kinnura,* the Chaldeans[2] their *qitra,* and the Greeks their *cithara* and *citharis*—which Greek writers of the day were careful to emphasize were *not* the same instrument. It is with the Greeks, in fact, that the first clear history of the evolution of an instrument begins; some of this history can again be traced with purely **linguistic** devices. The cithara and citharis were members of a family of musical instruments called *fides*—a word that is ancient Greek for "strings." From the fides family it is easy to draw lines to the medieval French *vielle,* the German *fiedel,* the English *fithele* or *fiddle,* and the *vihuela,* national instrument of medieval Spain. Significantly, much of the music for the vihuela (of which a great deal survives to the present day) can easily be transcribed[3] for the guitar. In England, the influences of the cithara and citharis led to the evolution of such instruments as the *cither, zither, cittern,* and *gittern,* with which instrument the linguistic parallel we seek is fairly easy to draw. Gitterns dating back to 1330 can be seen in the British Museum. In Spain, there is music for the vihuela that dates back at least that far. What did these instruments look like? Superficially, they bore a substantial resemblance to the guitar as we know it today, although the sides seldom curved in as far as do the sides of the modern

The author gives information in spatial order, according to the regions in which the events took place.

---

1. **Assyrians** (ə sir´ ē ənz) founders of an ancient empire in the Middle East, flourishing in the seventh century B.C.
2. **Chaldeans** (kal dē´ ənz) a people that rose to power in Babylon, an ancient empire of the Middle East, during the sixth century B.C.
3. **transcribed** (tran skrībd´) *v.* adapted piece of music for an instrument other than the one for which it was originally written.

A new pattern of organization—comparison and contrast—helps readers grasp details about instruments of the past.

guitar. They were usually strung with *pairs* of strings, or *courses,* much like a modern twelve-string guitar. The two strings of each course were tuned either in unison or an octave[4] apart. For a while, there seemed to be no standard for the number of courses an instrument should have; there are both vihuelas and gitterns with as few as four courses and as many as seven. By the fifteenth century, the vihuela seems to have settled on six as the standard number of courses. . . In England, the gittern settled down to four courses. . . . Historians of this period do note the existence in Spain of an instrument called the *guitarra.* . . . But no music was being written for this instrument, and nobody seems to have been paying much attention to it.

The African Link

Meanwhile, in Africa, the Arabs had been playing an instrument that they called *al-ud,* or "the wood," for centuries. When the Moors crossed the Straits of Gibraltar[5] in the twelfth century to conquer Spain, they brought this instrument with them. It quickly became popular, and by the time anybody who spoke English was talking about it, al-ud had become *lute.* The lute's main contribution to the evolution of the guitar as we know it today seems to

This paragraph uses a cause-and-effect structure to explain the evolution of the first fret.

have been the fret, a metal bar on the fingerboard. Until the arrival of the lute, the European forerunners of the guitar had no frets at all. Since the fret made it a little easier to play the same tune the same way more than once, and helped to standardize tunings, it was a resounding success. The first Arabic lutes in Europe had movable frets, tied to the neck, usually about eight in number. Consequently, the first vihuelas to which frets were added also had movable ones. The lute—or rather the people who brought it to Europe—made another important contribution. The Moorish artistic influence, blowing the cobwebs away from stodgy Spanish art and society, created an artistic climate that encouraged music to flourish. And so the instruments on which the music was played flourished as well, and continued to evolve and improve. This is a contribution that cannot be overestimated.

If any general lines can be drawn, perhaps it can be said that descendants of the original al-ud, crossing the Straits of Gibraltar, collided in Spain with the descendants of the Greek cithara and citharis. Sprinkled with a little bit of gittern influence from England, the result led ultimately to what we know today as the guitar.

---

4. unison (yoon´ e sen) . . . **octave** (äk´ tiv) A unison consists of two tones of the same pitch. An octave consists of two tones that are eight notes apart in the scale. The pitches in an octave sound "the same" and are named by the same note.

5. Moors (moorz) . . . **Gibraltar** (ji brôl´ tər) Groups of Moors, an Arab people of North Africa, invaded Spain at various times, beginning in the eighth century A.D. The Straits of Gibraltar are waters dividing Spain from Africa.

**CALIFORNIA STATE
UNIVERSITY AT FULLERTON
Course Catalog**

PROGRAMS OFFERED

Bachelor of Arts in Music

- Liberal Arts
- Music Education
- Music History and Theory

Bachelor of Music

- Composition
- Voice
- Instrumental
- Accompanying
- Keyboard
- Jazz and Commercial Music

Minor in Music

Master of Arts in Music

- Music History and Literature
- Music Education
- Piano Pedagogy

Master of Music

- Performance
- Theory-Composition

Single Subject (Secondary) Credential

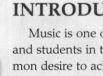

The text is organized by order of importance. The information becomes more specific through the document. This section lists all of the music programs offered.

INTRODUCTION

An introduction provides an overview of the university's music program.

Music is one of the most rewarding of all human endeavors, and the faculty and students in the Department of Music share a deep love for their art and a common desire to achieve excellence in it. The department offers a wide spectrum of degree programs and options with an overall emphasis in the area of performance. The curriculum provides basic preparation for careers in music, music education, or further graduate study, and is designed to provide a balanced education in the many facets of musical experience. Artist-teachers offer instruction in all areas of performance; practicing composers and theorists teach courses in theory and composition; active musicologists provide instruction in history and literature; and specialists in music education teach the courses in that area. It is the goal of the department to develop each student's musical and intellectual potential to the highest level of individual capability. California State University at Fullerton is fully accredited by the National Association of Schools of Music and the Western Association of Schools and Colleges.

MUSIC DEGREE PROGRAMS

The Department of Music offers a variety of courses that lead to baccalaureate and graduate degrees. The baccalaureate degree may be earned in either of two degree programs (Bachelor of Arts or Bachelor of Music). Within these programs, a student will pursue a concentration in Liberal Arts, Music History and Theory, Music Education, Performance, Composition, Accompanying, or Jazz and Commercial Music.

> This section provides more specific information about one music degree program.

BACHELOR OF MUSIC

This degree program is designed to provide training for highly gifted students who show promise and capability of becoming professional performers and composers.

The degree consists of 132 semester units. A minimum of 70 semester units in music are required, at least 32 of which must be upper-division.

Core Requirements for the Bachelor of Music (38 units)

Music theory (*Music 109, 111, 112, 121, 122, 211, 221, 319, 320*) (16 units)

Music history and literature (*Music 151; 351A, B, C*) (11 units)

Principal performance area (*applied music*) (6 units)

Major performance ensemble (*Music 406*) (4 units)

Recital (*Music 498*) (1 unit)

KEYBOARD CONCENTRATION (70 units)

Second Language Graduation Requirement

> You can skim the information provided here to determine if it is logically presented.

Since the Keyboard Concentration within the Bachelor of Music is a high-unit program, majors in this concentration are exempt from the Second Language Graduation Requirement.

Core Requirements for the Bachelor of Music (38 units)

Music theory (*Music 109, 111, 112, 121, 122, 211, 221, 319, 320*) (16 units)

Music history and literature (*Music 151; 351A, B, C*) (11 units)

Principal performance area (*applied music*) (6 units)

Major performance ensemble (*Music 406*) (4 units)

Recital (*Music 498*) (1 unit)

Additional Requirements (32 units)

Music theory (*two courses from Music 418, 420, 422*) (4–5 units)

Music history and literature (*Music 454A, B*) (4 units)

Conducting (*Music 382A or 383A*) (2 units)

Recital (*Music 398*) (1 unit)

Principal performance area (*applied music*) (6 units)

Chamber music (*Music 407D, E, M, Y and/or 408B, G, K, S, W, X*) (3 units)

Piano-Vocal Collaboration (*Music 386*) (1 unit)

Pedagogy (*Music 467A, B, C*) (6 units)

Harpsichord or organ class (*Music 372 or 373*) (1 unit)

Electives in music (3–4 units)

Comparing Expository and Functional Texts

1. **Key Ideas and Details** **(a)** Compare the **structures** and **formats** of each text. Make sure to explain the patterns of organization the writers use to order information, giving specific examples. **(b)** Explain ways in which structure and format affect how readers use each text.

Content-Area Vocabulary

2. The word *endeavor* can function as different parts of speech. Write one sentence using *endeavor* as a noun and another sentence using it as a verb. Use a dictionary if necessary.

Timed Writing

Explanatory Text: Letter

> **Format and Audience**
> The prompt directs you to write a letter to an author. Therefore, be sure you use letter formatting, formal language, and a respectful tone.

Write a letter to the author of the research source in which you comment on "The History of the Guitar" and the sequence of the information presented. Discuss whether the information was structured and developed effectively. Explain and support your comments with relevant details from the text. (25 minutes)

> **Academic Vocabulary**
> When you *explain* something, you describe it in terms that will help someone understand it more clearly.

5-Minute Planner

Complete these steps before you begin to write:

1. Read the prompt carefully. Look for key words, like those highlighted, to understand the assignment.
2. Scan the features and skim the text of the research source.
3. As you skim and scan, make notes about how the **sequence of information** helps you understand the text. Also note places where the sequence might confuse a reader.
4. Make a quick outline of your letter. Plan the order of the points you will make. Sequence your points in a way that will help the reader, the author, understand your ideas.
5. Use your outline and notes as you write to the author, Thomas A. Hill.

Comparing Literary Works

Comparing Authors' Purposes

An **author's purpose** is his or her main reason for writing. The following examples illustrate common purposes for nonfiction writers:

- A journalist might write to inform readers about a recent event.

- A humorist might write to entertain with a comical anecdote.

- An essayist might write to pay tribute to a person whom he or she thinks deserves honor.

A writer may have more than one purpose for writing. Generally, however, one purpose is the most important.

Both Yoshiko Uchida and N. Scott Momaday write about their personal connections to historic events. Both authors intend to inform readers about the past. However, writers who write about the past often have another, deeper purpose than informing: They may write to heal old wounds, to bear witness to past injustice, or to better understand themselves. As you read, use a chart like the one shown to compare Momaday's and Uchida's purposes and the details, or evidence, that they use for support.

	Uchida	Momaday
Details		
Purposes		

One important tool writers may use to accomplish a specific purpose in writing is **rhetoric,** or the use of language to persuade readers and shape their views of a subject. As you read, note the use of rhetorical strategies such as the following:

- Uchida's use of details appealing to readers' emotions, eliciting sympathy for her plight

- Momaday's blending of history with descriptions of landscapes and people to make vivid the Kiowa past and to help readers feel its loss

Common Core State Standards

Reading Informational Text
6. Determine an author's point of view or purpose in a text and analyze how an author uses rhetoric to advance that point of view or purpose.

Writing
2. Write informative/explanatory texts to examine and convey complex ideas, concepts, and information clearly and accurately through the effective selection, organization, and analysis of content.
2.a. Introduce a topic; organize complex ideas, concepts, and information to make important connections and distinctions. *(Timed Writing)*

www.PHLitOnline.com

- Vocabulary flashcards
- Interactive journals
- More about the authors
- Selection audio
- Interactive graphic organizers

What kind of *knowledge* changes our lives?

Writing About the Big Question

Both Yoshiko Uchida and N. Scott Momaday write to record a vanishing past with a belief that passing down history is critical. Use this sentence starter to develop your ideas about the Big Question.

Reflecting on the past is important because _____.

Meet the Authors

Yoshiko Uchida (1921–1992)

Author of *Desert Exile*

Yoshiko Uchida's childhood was fairly uneventful—until history struck. In 1942, the United States and Japan went to war, and the United States government forced Japanese American families like Uchida's into relocation camps. Uchida and her family were sent to Tanforan Racetrack near San Francisco, where they lived in a stable. Later, they were relocated to a camp in Utah.

Supporting Awareness After the war, Uchida attended Smith College in Massachusetts. She became a teacher and an award-winning author who wrote more than thirty fiction and nonfiction books. Her ultimate goal, she said, was "to write of meaningful relationships between human beings, to celebrate our common humanity."

N. Scott Momaday (b. 1934)

©Thomas Victor

Author of *The Way to Rainy Mountain*

Growing up on the Native American reservations where his parents taught, N. Scott Momaday learned the traditions of his father's Kiowa culture, as well as those of the Navajo, Apache, and Pueblo Indians. At the same time, he received a modern education. "I grew up in two worlds and straddle both those worlds even now," he says. "It has made for confusion and a richness in my life."

A Creative Heritage Momaday has made much of this "richness," celebrating Native American traditions in novels, poetry, and essays. His first novel, *House Made of Dawn*, received a Pulitzer Prize.

from
Desert Exile:
The Uprooting
of a
Japanese-American Family

Yoshiko Uchida

Background On December 7, 1941, Japan attacked the American naval base at Pearl Harbor, Hawaii. Two months later, under strong political pressure, President Franklin D. Roosevelt ordered more than 100,000 Japanese Americans from their homes and into government-run relocation camps. More than thirty years after the war, President Gerald Ford officially apologized to Japanese Americans and signed a proclamation officially ending the old order.

Yoshiko Uchida tells of her own family's experience of wartime internment. In 1942, her father was arrested and taken to Montana by the Federal Bureau of Investigation. A few months later, the rest of the family was ordered to report to the assembly camp at Tanforan.

As the bus pulled up to the grandstand, I could see hundreds of Japanese Americans jammed along the fence that lined the track. These people had arrived a few days earlier and were now watching for the arrival of friends or had come to while away the empty hours that had suddenly been thrust upon them.

As soon as we got off the bus, we were directed to an area beneath the grandstand where we registered and filled out a series of forms. Our baggage was inspected for contraband,[1] a cursory medical check made, and our living quarters assigned. We were to be housed in Barrack 16, Apartment 40. Fortunately, some friends who had arrived earlier found us and offered to help us locate our quarters.

It had rained the day before and the hundreds of people who had trampled on the track had turned it into a miserable mass of slippery mud. We made our way on it carefully, helping my mother who was dressed just as she would have been to go to church. She wore a hat, gloves, her good coat, and her Sunday shoes, because she would not have thought of venturing outside our house dressed in any other way.

Everywhere there were black tar-papered barracks[2] that had been hastily erected to house the 8,000 Japanese Americans of the area who had been uprooted from their homes. Barrack 16, however, was not among them, and we couldn't find it until we had traveled half the length of the track and gone beyond it to the northern rim of the racetrack compound.

Finally one of our friends called out, "There it is, beyond that row of eucalyptus trees." Barrack 16 was not a barrack at all, but a long stable raised a few feet off the ground with a broad ramp the horses had used to reach their stalls. Each stall was now numbered, and ours was number 40. That the stalls should have been called "apartments" was a euphemism so ludicrous it was comical.

---

1. **contraband** (kän´ trə band´) *n.* prohibited goods.
2. **barracks** (bar´ əks) *n.* large, plain, often temporary housing.

◀ **Critical Viewing**
Which details suggest that the family in this photograph is being forced to move to a relocation camp?

Literary Analysis
Author's Purpose
Which details here show that part of the author's purpose is to pay tribute, or honor the people she describes?

☑ **Reading Check**
What kind of building was Barrack 16 before it was turned into housing?

The Uprooting of a Japanese-American Family *from* Desert Exile **587**

Literary Analysis
Author's Purpose
In addition to informing, what purpose might details about dust and dirt serve?

Vocabulary
adept (ə dept´) adj.
expert; highly skilled

Literary Analysis
Author's Purpose
What might the author's purpose be in sharing such painful memories?

When we reached stall number 40, we pushed open the narrow door and looked uneasily into the vacant darkness. The stall was about ten by twenty feet and empty except for three folded Army cots lying on the floor. Dust, dirt, and wood shavings covered the linoleum that had been laid over manure-covered boards, the smell of horses hung in the air, and the whitened corpses of many insects still clung to the hastily white-washed walls.

High on either side of the entrance were two small windows which were our only source of daylight. The stall was divided into two sections by Dutch doors[3] worn down by teeth marks, and each stall in the stable was separated from the adjoining one only by rough partitions that stopped a foot short of the sloping roof. That space, while perhaps a good source of ventilation for the horses, deprived us of all but visual privacy, and we couldn't even be sure of that because of the crevices and knotholes in the dividing walls.

Because our friends had already spent a day as residents of Tanforan, they had become **adept** at scrounging for necessities. One found a broom and swept the floor for us. Two of the boys went to the barracks where mattresses were being issued, stuffed the ticking with straw themselves, and came back with three for our cots.

Nothing in the camp was ready. Everything was only half-finished. I wondered how much the nation's security would have been threatened had the Army permitted us to remain in our homes a few more days until the camps were adequately prepared for occupancy by families.

By the time we had cleaned out the stall and set up the cots, it was time for supper. Somehow, in all the confusion, we had not had lunch, so I was eager to get to the main mess hall, which was located beneath the grandstand.

The sun was going down as we started along the muddy track, and a cold, piercing wind swept in from the bay. When we arrived, there were six long weaving lines of people waiting to get into the mess hall. We took our place at the end of one of them, each of us clutching a plate and silverware borrowed from friends who had already received their baggage.

Shivering in the cold, we pressed close together trying to shield Mama from the wind. As we stood in what seemed a breadline for the destitute, I felt degraded, humiliated, and overwhelmed with a longing for home. And I saw the unutterable sadness on my mother's face.

This was only the first of many lines we were to endure, and we soon discovered that waiting in line was as inevitable a part of Tanforan as the north wind that swept in from the bay stirring up all the dust and litter of the camp.

---

3. Dutch doors two-part door in which the top half and the bottom half can be opened separately.

Once we got inside the gloomy cavernous mess hall, I saw hundreds of people eating at wooden picnic tables, while those who had already eaten were shuffling aimlessly over the wet cement floor. When I reached the serving table and held out my plate, a cook reached into a dishpan full of canned sausages and dropped two onto my plate with his fingers. Another man gave me a boiled potato and a piece of butterless bread.

With 5,000 people to be fed, there were few unoccupied tables, so we separated from our friends and shared a table with an elderly man and a young family with two crying babies. No one at the table spoke to us, and even Mama could seem to find no friendly word to offer as she normally would have done. We tried to eat, but the food wouldn't go down.

"Let's get out of here," my sister suggested.

We decided it would be better to go back to our barrack than to linger in the depressing confusion of the mess hall. It had grown dark by now and since Tanforan had no lights for nighttime occupancy, we had to pick our way carefully down the slippery track.

Once back in our stall, we found it no less depressing, for there was only a single electric light bulb dangling from the ceiling, and a one-inch crevice at the top of the north wall admitted a steady draft of the cold night air. We sat huddled on our cots, bundled in our coats, too cold and miserable even to talk. My sister and I worried about Mama, for she wasn't strong and had recently been troubled with neuralgia,[4] which could easily be aggravated by the cold. She in turn was worrying about us, and of course we all worried and wondered about Papa.

Suddenly we heard the sound of a truck stopping outside.

"Hey, Uchida! Apartment 40!" a boy shouted.

I rushed to the door and found the baggage boys trying to heave our enormous "camp bundle" over the railing that fronted our stall.

"What ya got in here anyway?" they shouted good-naturedly as they struggled with the unwieldy bundle. "It's the biggest thing we got on our truck!"

I grinned, embarrassed, but I could hardly wait to get out our belongings. My sister and I fumbled to undo all the

4. **neuralgia** (noo ral′ jə) *n.* severe pain along the path of a nerve.

Literary Analysis
Author's Purpose
How might these details affect the reader's opinion of the government relocation program?

Spiral Review
Development of Ideas How does Uchida develop the idea that the camp is an unpleasant place?

Vocabulary
unwieldy (un wēl′ dē) *adj.* hard to manage because of shape or weight

Reading Check

Identify three details showing that the family's first day in the camp is miserable.

The Uprooting of a Japanese-American Family *from* Desert Exile   **589**

Literary Analysis
Author's Purpose
What do these details show readers about the family?

knots we had tied into the rope around our bundle that morning and eagerly pulled out the familiar objects from home.

We unpacked our blankets, pillows, sheets, tea kettle, and, most welcome of all, our electric hot plate. I ran to the nearest washroom to fill the kettle with water, while Mama and Kay made up the Army cots with our bedding. Once we hooked up the hot plate and put the kettle on to boil, we felt better. We sat close to its warmth, holding our hands toward it as though it were our fireplace at home.

Before long some friends came by to see us, bringing with them the only gift they had—a box of dried prunes. Even the day before, we wouldn't have given the prunes a second glance, but now they were as welcome as the boxes of Maskey's chocolate my father used to bring home from San Francisco.

Mama managed to make some tea for our friends, and we sat around our steaming kettle, munching gratefully on our prunes. We spent much of the evening talking about food and the lack of it, a concern that grew obsessive over the next few weeks, when we were constantly hungry.

Our stable consisted of twenty-five stalls facing north which were back to back with an equal number facing south, so we were surrounded on three sides. Living in our stable were an assortment of people—mostly small family units—that included an artist, my father's barber and his wife, a dentist and his wife, an elderly retired couple, a group of Kibei[5] bachelors (Japanese born in the United States but educated in Japan), an insurance salesman and his wife, and a widow with two daughters. To say that we all became intimately acquainted would be an understatement. It was, in fact, communal living, with semi-private cubicles provided only for sleeping.

Our neighbors on one side spent much of their time playing cards, and at all hours of the day we could hear the sound of cards being shuffled and money changing hands. Our other neighbors had a teenage son who spent most of the day with his friends, coming home to his stall at night only after his parents were asleep. Family life began to show signs of strain almost immediately, not only in the next stall but throughout the entire camp.

One Sunday our neighbor's son fell asleep in the rear of his stall with the door bolted from inside. When his parents came home from church, no amount of shouting or banging on the door could awaken the boy.

"Our stupid son has locked us out," they explained, coming to us for help.

I climbed up on my cot and considered pouring water on him over the partition, for I knew he slept just on the other side of it. Instead

Literary Analysis
Author's Purpose
Which details suggest that the author relates this incident to amuse readers?

---

5. Kibei (kē´ bā´)

I dangled a broom over the partition and poked and prodded with it, shouting, "Wake up! Wake up!" until the boy finally bestirred himself and let his parents in. We became good friends with our neighbors after that.

About one hundred feet from our stable were two latrines and two washrooms for our section of camp, one each for men and women. The latrines were crude wooden structures containing eight toilets, separated by partitions, but having no doors. The washrooms were divided into two sections. In the front section was a long tin trough spaced with spigots of hot and cold water where we washed our faces and brushed our teeth. To the rear were eight showers, also separated by partitions but lacking doors or curtains. The showers were difficult to adjust and we either got scalded by torrents of hot water or shocked by an icy blast of cold. Most of the Issei[6] were unaccustomed to showers, having known the luxury of soaking in deep pine-scented tubs during their years in Japan, and found the showers virtually impossible to use.

Our card-playing neighbor scoured the camp for a container that might serve as a tub, and eventually found a large wooden barrel. She rolled it to the showers, filled it with warm water, and then climbed in for a pleasant and leisurely soak. The greatest compliment she could offer anyone was the use of her private tub.

The lack of privacy in the latrines and showers was an embarrassing hardship especially for the older women, and many would take newspapers to hold over their faces or squares of cloth to tack up for their own private curtain. The Army, obviously ill-equipped to build living quarters for women and children, had made no attempt to introduce even the most common of life's civilities into these camps for us.

During the first few weeks of camp life everything was erratic and in short supply. Hot water appeared only sporadically, and the minute it was available, everyone ran for the showers or the laundry. We had to be clever and quick just to keep clean, and my

Once we hooked up the hot plate and put the kettle on to boil, we felt better.

Reading Check
Name two major problems Uchida and other residents of the camp face.

---

6. **Issei** (ē′ sā′) *n.* Japanese immigrants to North America, especially those who came after 1907 and were ineligible until 1952 to become U.S. citizens.

sister and I often walked a mile to the other end of the camp where hot water was in better supply, in order to boost our morale with a hot shower.

Even toilet paper was at a premium, for new rolls would disappear as soon as they were placed in the latrines. The shock of the evacuation compounded by the short supply of every necessity brought out the baser instincts of the internees,[7] and there was little inclination for anyone to feel responsible for anyone else. In the early days, at least, it was everyone for himself or herself.

One morning I saw some women emptying bed pans into the troughs where we washed our faces. The sight was enough to turn my stomach, and my mother quickly made several large signs in Japanese cautioning people against such unsanitary practices. We posted them in conspicuous spots in the washroom and hoped for the best.

Across from the latrines was a double barrack, one containing laundry tubs and the other equipped with clotheslines and ironing boards. Because there were so many families with young children, the laundry tubs were in constant use. The hot water was often gone by 9:00 a.m., and many women got up at 3:00 and 4:00 in the morning to do their wash, all of which, including sheets, had to be done entirely by hand.

We found it difficult to get to the laundry by 9:00 a.m., and by then every tub was taken and there were long lines of people with bags of dirty laundry waiting behind each one. When we finally got to a tub, there was no more hot water. Then we would leave my mother to hold the tub while my sister and I rushed to

▼ **Critical Viewing**
This photograph shows the Manzanar Relocation Center. Compare this camp with Tanforan. **[Compare and Contrast]**

7. **internees** (in´ tʉrn´ ēz´) *n.* people detained or confined as prisoners of war or enemy aliens.

the washroom where there was a better supply and carried back bucketfuls of hot water as everyone else learned to do. By the time we had finally hung our laundry on lines outside our stall, we were too exhausted to do much else for the rest of the day.

For four days after our arrival we continued to go to the main mess hall for all our meals. My sister and I usually missed breakfast because we were assigned to the early shift and we simply couldn't get there by 7:00 a.m. Dinner was at 4:45 p.m., which was a terrible hour, but not a major problem, as we were always hungry. Meals were uniformly bad and skimpy, with an abundance of starches such as beans and bread. I wrote to my non-Japanese friends in Berkeley shamelessly asking them to send us food, and they obliged with large cartons of cookies, nuts, dried fruit, and jams.

Literary Analysis
Author's Purpose
Which details here reveal something about Uchida's personality?

We looked forward with much anticipation to the opening of a half dozen smaller mess halls located throughout the camp. But when ours finally opened, we discovered that the preparation of smaller quantities had absolutely no effect on the quality of the food. We went eagerly to our new mess hall only to be confronted at our first meal with chili con carne, corn, and butterless bread. To assuage our disappointment, a friend and I went to the main mess hall which was still in operation, to see if it had anything better. Much to our amazement and delight, we found small lettuce salads, the first fresh vegetables we had seen in many days. We ate ravenously and exercised enormous self-control not to go back for second and third helpings.

The food improved gradually, and by the time we left Tanforan five months later, we had fried chicken and ice cream for Sunday dinner. By July tubs of soapy water were installed at the mess hall exits so we could wash our plates and utensils on the way out. Being slow eaters, however, we usually found the dishwater tepid and dirty by the time we reached the tubs, and we often rewashed our dishes in the washroom.

Most internees got into the habit of rushing for everything. They ran to the mess halls to be first in line, they dashed inside for the best tables and then rushed through their meals to get to the washtubs before the suds ran out. The three of us, however, seemed to be at the end of every line that formed and somehow never managed to be first for anything.

Reading Check
Name two necessities that were in short supply at the camp.

The Uprooting of a Japanese-American Family *from* Desert Exile **593**

One of the first things we all did at Tanforan was to make our living quarters as comfortable as possible. A pile of scrap lumber in one corner of camp melted away like snow on a hot day as residents salvaged whatever they could to make shelves and crude pieces of furniture to supplement the Army cots. They also made ingenious containers for carrying their dishes to the mess halls, with handles and lids that grew more and more elaborate in a sort of unspoken competition.

Because of my father's absence, our friends helped us in camp, just as they had in Berkeley, and we relied on them to put up shelves and build a crude table and two benches for us. We put our new camp furniture in the front half of our stall, which was our "living room," and put our three cots in the dark windowless rear section, which we promptly dubbed "the dungeon." We ordered some print fabric by mail and sewed curtains by hand to hang at our windows and to cover our shelves. Each new addition to our stall made it seem a little more like home.

One afternoon about a week after we had arrived at Tanforan, a messenger from the administration building appeared with a telegram for us. It was from my father, telling us he had been released on parole from Montana and would be able to join us soon in camp. Papa was coming home. The wonderful news had come like an unexpected gift, but even as we hugged each other in joy, we didn't quite dare believe it until we actually saw him. . . .

Critical Thinking

Cite textual evidence to support your responses.

1. **Key Ideas and Details** (a) Describe stall number 40.
(b) **Analyze:** Why does Uchida feel that calling it an "apartment" was "ludicrous"?

2. **Key Ideas and Details** **Analyze Cause and Effect:** How do the shortages at the camp affect people's attitudes and behavior? Support your answer.

3. **Integration of Knowledge and Ideas** **Draw Conclusions:** What do the conditions at the camp suggest about the government's attitude toward Japanese Americans?

4. **Integration of Knowledge and Ideas** (a) In what ways did Uchida's experiences at the relocation camp change her? Support your answer with details from the selection. (b) What impact do you think Uchida hopes her narrative will have on readers? *[Connect to the Big Question: What kind of knowledge changes our lives?]*

from The Way to Rainy Mountain

N. Scott Momaday

Background Like other Great Plains tribes, the Kiowa were buffalo hunters. When white settlers came to the Plains, the Kiowa fought them. By the late 1800s, however, United States troops had broken Kiowa resistance and white hunters had all but exterminated the buffalo. Traditional Kiowa life came to an end. In 1868, the Kiowas went to live on a reservation in southwestern Oklahoma.

A single knoll rises out of the plain in Oklahoma, north and west of the Wichita Range.[1] For my people, the Kiowas, it is an old landmark, and they gave it the name Rainy Mountain. The hardest weather in the world is there. Winter brings blizzards, hot tornadic winds arise in the spring, and in summer the prairie

---

1. Wichita (wich´ ə tô´) **Range** mountain range in southwestern Oklahoma.

► Chief Sa-tan-ta of
the Kiowas

▲ **Critical Viewing**
Judging from Momaday's
account, what hardships
might this Kiowa person
have experienced?
[Speculate]

Spiral Review
**Development of
Ideas** How does
Momaday develop
the idea that the
land was lonely and
isolated?

is an anvil's edge. The grass turns brittle and brown, and it
cracks beneath your feet. There are green belts along the rivers
and creeks, linear groves of hickory and pecan, willow and witch
hazel. At a distance in July or August the steaming foliage seems
almost to writhe in fire. Great green and yellow grasshoppers are
everywhere in the tall grass, popping up like corn to sting the flesh,
and tortoises crawl about on the red earth, going nowhere in the
plenty of time. Loneliness is an aspect of the land. All things in
the plain are isolate; there is no confusion of objects in the eye, but
one hill or one tree or one man. To look upon that landscape in the
early morning, with the sun at your back, is to lose the sense of
proportion. Your imagination comes to life, and this, you think, is
where Creation was begun.

I returned to Rainy Mountain in July. My grandmother had died in
the spring, and I wanted to be at her grave. She had lived to be very
old and at last infirm. Her only living daughter was with her when
she died, and I was told that in death her face was that of a child.

I like to think of her as a child. When she was born, the Kiowas
were living the last great moment of their history. For more than
a hundred years they had controlled the open range from the

Smoky Hill River to the Red, from the headwaters of the Canadian to the fork of the Arkansas and Cimarron.[2] In alliance with the Comanches,[3] they had ruled the whole of the southern Plains. War was their sacred business, and they were among the finest horsemen the world has ever known. But warfare for the Kiowas was preeminently a matter of disposition rather than of survival, and they never understood the grim, unrelenting advance of the U.S. Cavalry. When at last, divided and ill-provisioned, they were driven onto the Staked Plains in the cold rains of autumn, they fell into panic. In Palo Duro Canyon they abandoned their crucial stores to pillage and had nothing then but their lives. In order to save themselves, they surrendered to the soldiers at Fort Sill[4] and were imprisoned in the old stone corral that now stands as a military museum. My grandmother was spared the humiliation of those high gray walls by eight or ten years, but she must have known from birth the affliction of defeat, the dark brooding of old warriors.

Her name was Aho, and she belonged to the last culture to evolve in North America. Her forebears came down from the high country in western Montana nearly three centuries ago. They were a mountain people, a mysterious tribe of hunters whose language has never been positively classified in any major group. In the late seventeenth century they began a long migration to the south and east.

It was a journey toward the dawn, and it led to a golden age. Along the way the Kiowas were befriended by the Crows,[5] who gave them the culture and religion of the Plains. They acquired horses, and their ancient nomadic spirit was suddenly free of the ground. They acquired Tai-me, the sacred Sun Dance doll, from that moment the object and symbol of their worship, and so shared in the divinity of the sun. Not least, they acquired the sense of destiny, therefore courage and pride. When they entered upon the southern Plains they had been transformed. No longer were they slaves to the simple necessity of survival; they were a lordly and dangerous society of fighters and thieves, hunters and priests of the sun. According to their origin myth, they entered the world through a hollow log. From one point of view, their migration was the fruit of an old prophecy, for indeed they emerged from a sunless world.

---

2. **Smoky Hill River . . . Cimarron** (sim´ ə rän´) these rivers all run through or near Oklahoma. The area Momaday is defining stretches from central Kansas south through Oklahoma and from the Texas panhandle east to Tulsa, Oklahoma.

3. **Comanches** (kə man´ chēz) *n.* formerly warlike Native American people of the southern Great Plains, famed for their horsemanship.

4. **Fort Sill** fort established by the United States government in 1869 to guard against Kiowa and Comanche attacks.

5. **Crows** members of a Native American tribe of the northern Plains; like other Plains tribes, they hunted buffalo.

Vocabulary
nomadic (nō mad´ ik) *adj.* moving from place to place; without a permanent home

Reading
Check

Who gave the Kiowa the culture and religion of the Plains?

Literary Analysis
Author's Purpose
What does this paragraph suggest about Momaday's purpose in writing about the Kiowa?

Although my grandmother lived out her long life in the shadow of Rainy Mountain, the immense landscape of the continental interior lay like memory in her blood. She could tell of the Crows, whom she had never seen, and of the Black Hills,[6] where she had never been. I wanted to see in reality what she had seen more perfectly in the mind's eye, and traveled fifteen hundred miles to begin my pilgrimage.

Yellowstone,[7] it seemed to me, was the top of the world, a region of deep lakes and dark timber, canyons and waterfalls. But, beautiful as it is, one might have the sense of confinement there. The skyline in all directions is close at hand, the high wall of the woods and deep cleavages of shade. There is a perfect freedom in the mountains, but it belongs to the eagle and the elk, the badger and the bear. The Kiowas reckoned their stature by the distance they could see, and they were bent and blind in the wilderness.

Descending eastward, the highland meadows are a stairway to the plain. In July the inland slope of the Rockies is luxuriant with flax and buckwheat, stonecrop and larkspur.[8] The earth unfolds and the limit of the land recedes. Clusters of trees, and animals grazing far in the distance, cause the vision to reach away and wonder to build upon the mind. The sun follows a longer course in the day, and the sky is immense beyond all comparison. The great billowing clouds that sail upon it are shadows that move upon the brain like water, dividing light. Farther down, in the land of the Crows and Blackfeet,[9] the plain is yellow. Sweet clover takes hold of the hills and bends upon itself to cover and seal the soil. There the Kiowas paused on their way; they had come to the place where they must change their lives. The sun is at home on the plains. Precisely there does it have the certain character of a god. When the Kiowas came to the land of the Crows, they could see the dark lees of the hills at dawn across the Bighorn River, the profusion of light on the grain shelves, the oldest deity ranging after the solstices. Not yet would they veer southward to the caldron[10] of the land that lay below; they must wean their blood from the northern winter and hold the mountains a while longer in their view. They bore Tai-me in procession to the east.

Devil's Tower

Wyoming

South Dakota

Colorado

Nebraska

Kansas

New Mexico

Texas

Oklahoma

Kiowa habitat

▲ **Critical Viewing**
Based on this map and the details in the text, why might the Kiowa journey from Wyoming to Oklahoma have been challenging and rewarding at the same time? **[Connect]**

---

6. **Black Hills** mountain range running from southwestern South Dakota to northeastern Wyoming.
7. **Yellowstone** Yellowstone National Park, lying mostly in Wyoming but including strips in southern Montana and eastern Idaho.
8. **flax and buckwheat, stonecrop and larkspur** various types of plants.
9. **Blackfeet** tribe of the region that includes present-day Montana and parts of Canada.
10. **caldron** (kôl′ drən) *n.* pot for boiling liquids; large kettle.

A dark mist lay over the Black Hills, and the land was like iron. At the top of a ridge I caught sight of Devil's Tower upthrust against the gray sky as if in the birth of time the core of the earth had broken through its crust and the motion of the world was begun. There are things in nature that engender an awful quiet in the heart of man; Devil's Tower is one of them. Two centuries ago, because they could not do otherwise, the Kiowas made a legend at the base of the rock. My grandmother said:

> *Eight children were there at play, seven sisters and their brother. Suddenly the boy was struck dumb; he trembled and began to run upon his hands and feet. His fingers became claws, and his body was covered with fur. Directly there was a bear where the boy had been. The sisters were terrified; they ran, and the bear after them. They came to the stump of a great tree, and the tree spoke to them. It bade them climb upon it, and as they did so it began to rise in the air. The bear came to kill them, but they were just beyond its reach. It reared against the tree and scored the bark all around with its claws. The seven sisters were borne into the sky, and they became the stars of the Big Dipper.*

From that moment, and so long as the legend lives, the Kiowas have kinsmen in the night sky. Whatever they were in the mountains, they could be no more. However tenuous their well-being, however much they had suffered and would suffer again, they had found a way out of the wilderness.

▲ **Critical Viewing**
Judging from this photograph of Devil's Tower, why might the landmark inspire Kiowa legends? **[Connect]**

Vocabulary
tenuous (ten´ yo͞o əs) *adj.* flimsy; not strong

Reading Check

What change did the Kiowa's beliefs undergo after they left the mountains?

Literary Analysis
Author's Purpose
In this section, how does Momaday link his grandmother's life to the history of the Kiowa?

▼ **Critical Viewing**
Based on the attire of this Kiowa dancer, what would you expect to see at a Kiowa Sun Dance?
[Infer]

My grandmother had a reverence for the sun, a holy regard that now is all but gone out of mankind. There was a wariness in her, and an ancient awe. She was a Christian in her later years, but she had come a long way about, and she never forgot her birthright. As a child she had been to the Sun Dances; she had taken part in those annual rites, and by them she had learned the restoration of her people in the presence of Tai-me. She was about seven when the last Kiowa Sun Dance was held in 1887 on the Washita River above Rainy Mountain Creek. The buffalo were gone. In order to consummate the ancient sacrifice—to impale the head of a buffalo bull upon the medicine tree—a delegation of old men journeyed into Texas, there to beg and barter for an animal from the Goodnight herd. She was ten when the Kiowas came together for the last time as a living Sun Dance culture. They could find no buffalo; they had to hang an old hide from the sacred tree. Before the dance could begin, a company of soldiers rode out from Fort Sill under orders to disperse the tribe. Forbidden without cause the essential act of their faith, having seen the wild herds slaughtered and left to rot upon the ground, the Kiowas backed away forever from the medicine tree. That was July 20, 1890, at the great bend of the Washita. My grandmother was there. Without bitterness, and for as long as she lived, she bore a vision of deicide.[11]

Now that I can have her only in memory, I see my grandmother in the several postures that were peculiar to her: standing at the wood stove on a winter morning and turning meat in a great iron skillet; sitting at the south window, bent above her beadwork, and afterwards, when her vision failed, looking down for a long time into the fold of her hands; going out upon a cane, very slowly as she did when the weight of age came upon her; praying. I remember her most often at prayer. She made long, rambling prayers out of suffering and hope, having seen many things. I was never sure that I had the right to hear, so exclusive were they of all mere custom and company. The last time I saw her she prayed standing by the side of her bed at night, naked to the waist, the light of a kerosene lamp moving upon her dark skin. Her long, black hair, always drawn and braided in the day, lay upon her shoulders and against her breasts like a shawl. I do not speak Kiowa, and I never understood her prayers, but there was something inherently sad in the sound, some merest hesitation upon the syllables of sorrow. She began in a high and

---

11. **deicide** (dē´ ə sīd´) *n.* killing of a god.

descending pitch, exhausting her breath to silence; then again and again—and always the same intensity of effort, of something that is, and is not, like urgency in the human voice. Transported so in the dancing light among the shadows of her room, she seemed beyond the reach of time. But that was illusion; I think I knew then that I should not see her again.

Houses are like sentinels in the plain, old keepers of the weather watch. There, in a very little while, wood takes on the appearance of great age. All colors wear soon away in the wind and rain, and then the wood is burned gray and the grain appears and the nails turn red with rust. The windowpanes are black and opaque; you imagine there is nothing within, and indeed there are many ghosts, bones given up to the land. They stand here and there against the sky, and you approach them for a longer time than you expect. They belong in the distance; it is their domain.

Once there was a lot of sound in my grandmother's house, a lot of coming and going, feasting and talk. The summers there were full of excitement and reunion. The Kiowas are a summer people; they abide the cold and keep to themselves, but when the season turns and the land becomes warm and vital they cannot hold still; an old love of going returns upon them. The aged visitors who came to my grandmother's house when I was a child were made of lean and leather, and they bore themselves upright. They wore great black hats and bright ample shirts that shook in the wind. They rubbed fat upon their hair and wound their braids with strips of colored cloth. Some of them painted their faces and carried the scars of old and cherished enmities. They were an old council of warlords, come to remind and be reminded of who they were. Their wives and daughters served them well. The women might indulge themselves; gossip was at once the mark and compensation of their servitude. They made loud and elaborate talk among themselves, full of jest and gesture, fright and false alarm. They went abroad in fringed and flowered shawls, bright beadwork and German silver. They were at home in the kitchen, and they prepared meals that were banquets.

There were frequent prayer meetings, and great nocturnal feasts. When I was a child I played with my cousins outside, where the lamplight fell upon the ground and the singing of the old people rose up around us and carried away into the darkness. There were a lot of good things to eat, a lot of laughter and surprise. And afterwards, when the quiet returned, I lay down with my grandmother and could hear the frogs away by the river and feel the motion of the air.

Now there is a funeral silence in the rooms, the endless wake of some final word. The walls have closed in upon my grandmother's

Literary Analysis
Author's Purpose
Which details here suggest Momaday writes to better understand his memories? Which details suggest he wants to pay tribute to his grandmother?

> I do not speak Kiowa, and I never understood her prayers, but there was something inherently sad in the sound . . .

Reading Check

Who comes to visit Momaday's grandmother's house in the summer?

Literary Analysis
Author's Purpose
Which details here
suggest that Momaday
writes to understand
himself?

house. When I returned to it in mourning, I saw for the first time in my life how small it was. It was late at night, and there was a white moon, nearly full. I sat for a long time on the stone steps by the kitchen door. From there I could see out across the land; I could see the long row of trees by the creek, the low light upon the rolling plains, and the stars of the Big Dipper. Once I looked at the moon and caught sight of a strange thing. A cricket had perched upon the handrail, only a few inches away from me. My line of vision was such that the creature filled the moon like a fossil. It had gone there, I thought, to live and die, for there, of all places, was its small definition made whole and eternal. A warm wind rose up and purled like the longing within me.

The next morning I awoke at dawn and went out on the dirt road to Rainy Mountain. It was already hot, and the grasshoppers began to fill the air. Still, it was early in the morning, and the birds sang out of the shadows. The long yellow grass on the mountain shone in the bright light, and a scissortail hied above the land. There, where it ought to be, at the end of a long and legendary way, was my grandmother's grave. Here and there on the dark stones were ancestral names. Looking back once, I saw the mountain and came away.

Critical Thinking

Cite textual evidence to support your responses.

© 1. **Key Ideas and Details** **(a)** Describe two activities at Momaday's grandmother's house in summer. **(b) Connect:** In what ways are these activities connected to a vanishing way of life?

© 2. **Key Ideas and Details** **(a) Support:** In what sense is Momaday's grandmother one of the last representatives of traditional Kiowa culture? **(b) Draw Conclusions:** How does Momaday seem to feel about the disappearance of this way of life? Support your answer with details from the selection.

© 3. **Integration of Knowledge and Ideas** **(a) Interpret:** When Momaday imagines the cricket on the moon, why does he say, "there . . . was its small definition made whole and eternal"? **(b) Draw Conclusions:** In what sense is Momaday's memory of his grandmother similar to his vision of the cricket?

© 4. **Integration of Knowledge and Ideas** **(a)** In what ways did Momaday's relationship with his grandmother shape his appreciation of Kiowa culture? **(b)** How did his knowledge of Kiowa history impact his view of his grandmother? **(c)** How has the experience Momaday narrates changed his life? *[Connect to the Big Question: What kind of knowledge changes our lives?]*

Comparing Authors' Purposes

1. Key Ideas and Details **(a)** Choose two powerful details from each selection. Using a chart like the one shown, analyze the writer's use of these details. **(b)** In a statement, identify the writer's purpose in sharing the details you have chosen. Explain your reasoning.

	Detail	Writer's Response to Detail	What Detail Adds to Meaning
Uchida			
Momaday			

2. Key Ideas and Details **(a)** What general purpose for writing do Momaday and Uchida share? **(b)** Identify one major difference in their views of the events and scenes they describe.

3. Craft and Structure Give an example of each writer's use of **rhetoric,** or powerful language, and explain how it helps the writer achieve his or her purpose.

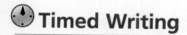 Timed Writing

Informative Text: Essay

Identify each author's purpose. Then, write a response to compare the effectiveness of the two selections. Address the success of both authors in meeting the purpose you have identified. Support your ideas with details from the selections. **(40 minutes)**

5-Minute Planner

1. Read the prompt carefully and completely.

2. Use these questions to get started:

- Which passages best convey the author's purpose?
- In these passages, are the details comprehensive enough to make the writing convincing or moving? Why or why not?

3. Plan your introduction to the topic. Make an outline in which you organize the ideas and concepts you plan to present. Think of ways to distinguish your ideas from alternative interpretations.

4. Reread the prompt, and then draft your essay.

Writing Workshop

 **Common Core State Standards**

Writing

1. Write arguments to support claims in an analysis of substantive topics or texts, using valid reasoning and relevant and sufficient evidence.

1.a. Introduce precise claim(s), distinguish the claim(s) from alternate or opposing claims, and create an organization that establishes clear relationships among claim(s), counterclaims, reasons, and evidence.

5. Develop and strengthen writing as needed by planning, focusing on addressing what is most significant for a specific purpose and audience.

7. Conduct short as well as more sustained research projects to answer a question or solve a problem; narrow or broaden the inquiry when appropriate; synthesize multiple sources on the subject.

Write an Argument

Argument: Persuasive Essay

Defining the Form Persuasion is a part of daily life. Friends may use persuasion to convince you to try a new food or volunteer for a cause. A **persuasive essay** is a nonfiction literary work in which the writer tries to convince readers to accept a particular point of view or take a specific action. You might use elements of the persuasive essay in editorials, position papers, letters to the editor, and proposals.

Assignment Write a persuasive essay supporting your opinion about an issue that matters to you. Include these elements:

✓ a clear *description of the issue* and a clear, precise *statement of your opinion*—your position, or claim, about the issue

✓ reliable and varied *evidence* that supports your opinion, or claim

✓ *arguments* that acknowledge and refute opposing claims

✓ vivid, *persuasive language* that appeals to your audience

✓ a logical *organization* that shows the relationship among claims, counterclaims, and evidence

✓ error-free grammar, including *correct use of parallel structures*

To preview the criteria on which your persuasive essay may be judged, see the rubric on page 611.

 Writing Workshop: *Work in Progress*

Review the work you did on pages 555 and 575.

WRITE GUY
Jeff Anderson, M.Ed.

What Do You Notice?

Voice and Tone

Read the following sentences from Alexander Solzhenitsyn's *Nobel Lecture* several times.

The simple act of an ordinary courageous man is not to take part, not to support lies! Let that come into the world and even reign over it, but not through me. Writers and artists can do more: they can VANQUISH LIES!

Jot down the qualities that make the sentences interesting. Then, consider how to use voice and tone similarly in your essay.

Reading-Writing Connection

To get a feel for persuasive writing, read the excerpt from Alexander Solzhenitsyn's *Nobel Lecture* on page 548.

Prewriting/Planning Strategies

Brainstorm and freewrite. Think about topics that cause you and others to argue. Using a chart like the one shown, make a list of the subjects and issues that have prompted emotional reactions and circle the one that most intrigues you. Then, freewrite for three minutes about that topic. Review what you have written and circle any statements of opinion that have emerged. Select the subject with the clearest statement and use it as the starting point for your essay.

www.PHLitOnline.com
- Author video: Writing Process
- Author video: Rewards of Writing

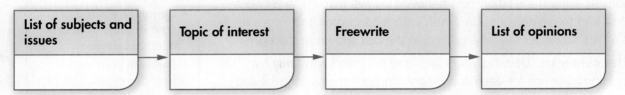

Conduct research. You may not have enough details about your topic to focus your ideas. More information can help you break the topic into meaningful parts. For example, freedom of speech is far too broad to discuss in a brief essay. However, after you learn more about it, you may choose to narrow your inquiry and research questions and write about balanced reporting in television news. Conduct research to identify an aspect of the topic that is manageable in the space of your essay.

Look at both sides of the issue. An effective persuasive essay anticipates and addresses differing opinions. It considers the knowledge level and concerns of readers and addresses their expectations. Use a pro-and-con chart like the one shown to identify counterarguments. In the left-hand column, list arguments that support your opinion, or claim. In the right-hand column, list opposing arguments. Use the chart to brainstorm for ideas, reasons, and evidence that counter the opposing claims.

Pro-and-Con Chart	
Topic: Honor Students Should Be Rewarded	
Supporting	**Opposing**
• Honor-roll students are responsible and dedicated. • They know the material.	• It is unfair to other students. • There would be inequality.

Drafting Strategies

Evaluate your arguments. Write each idea on a separate notecard. Then, consider whether your reasoning is valid and persuasive to your *intended audience*. Delete cards with faulty ideas that may not persuade readers. Then, organize the cards in order of persuasiveness.

Emphasize your strongest argument. Introduce your topic and state your claim in a precisely worded *thesis statement*. In the body of your essay, support your thesis with arguments and reasons. Use transitions to show the relationships between claims, reasons, and counterclaims and to create cohesion. Finish with a conclusion that urges readers to act. Consider the organization in the box shown at the right.

Offer evidence. Develop your claim and counterclaims fairly by providing evidence for each and by pointing out their strengths and limitations. For each point you make, provide convincing *support*, such as these types of evidence:

- **Facts:** information that can be proved true
- **Statistics:** numerical evidence
- **Expert opinion:** information or quotations from experts
- **Case studies:** analyses of examples that illustrate your opinions
- **Anecdotes:** relevant experiences, either your own or those of others

> **Model: Supporting Opinion With Evidence**
> Final exams are meant to test students' overall grasp of the course material. However, honor-roll students have already shown that they have mastered the course. School records show over 95% of honor-roll students have a straight "A" average.

Convincing statistical evidence supports the writer's opinion.

Identify your sources. The inclusion of *reliable sources* strengthens your arguments. When you present a fact or detail from your research, use a style guide to correctly provide the *source of the information*. If you quote someone, use quotation marks. When you use expert opinion, identify the expert and his or her qualifications. In addition, make sure to build a strong link between the quotation and your argument.

Organizing a Persuasive Essay

- Begin with a precise statement of your claim.
- Explain your second-best argument.
- Present and argue against a counterclaim.
- Organize the rest of your arguments in order of persuasiveness.
- End with your best argument.
- Wrap up with a concluding statement that follows from and supports the argument.

 **Common Core State Standards**

Writing

1.a. Introduce precise claim(s), distinguish the claim(s) from alternate or opposing claims, and create an organization that establishes clear relationships among claim(s), counterclaims, reasons, and evidence.

1.b. Develop claim(s) and counterclaims fairly, supplying evidence for each while pointing out the strengths and limitations of both in a manner that anticipates the audience's knowledge level and concerns.

1.c. Use words, phrases, and clauses to link the major sections of the text, create cohesion, and clarify the relationships between claim(s) and reasons, between reasons and evidence, and between claim(s) and counterclaims.

1.e. Provide a concluding statement or section that follows from and supports the argument presented.

Writers on Writing

Erik Weihenmayer On Persuasive Techniques

Erik Weihenmayer is the author of "Everest" from *Touch the Top of the World* (p. 452).

Atop Mt. Kilimanjaro, a sign reads, "You Are Now at the Uhuru Peak. . . ." Sitting on the summit, feeling exhausted, nauseated, and dizzy, I asked my guide, Baltazar, what "Uhuru" meant. He replied, "Freedom." In this passage, I try to persuade you to accept the conclusion about freedom I reached.

"Writing enables me to climb the mountain again."
—Erik Weihenmayer

Professional Model:

from *Touch the Top of the World*

Freedom. It was a word I didn't understand. Freedom from what? Freedom from the limits of my body? From pain? From disappointment? What did it mean? I wanted to believe that by standing atop mountains around the world, I was achieving this kind of freedom, . . . but when standing in these high places, the immense power of the mountains only served to magnify my own fragility, my human need for food, for oxygen, for the help that I received from my team. . . .

Then it came to me . . . Perhaps it was the freedom to make of my life what I wanted it to be, or at least the freedom to try, or to fail in the trying. Perhaps freedom itself was unobtainable and the goal was only to reach for it, strive for it, knowing all along that I would fall well short. Perhaps the importance was in the reaching out, and in the impossibility of it all, and in the reaching out through the impossibility, my body planted heavily on the earth but my spirit soaring up and coming impossibly close to its goal.

First, I ask you a series of difficult questions, which lead you to ponder whether freedom is obtainable.

Second, I try to shatter your traditional definition of freedom by emphasizing the obvious limits of our minds and bodies.

Lastly, I find the answer and suggest, without insisting on, a surprising new understanding of what freedom means.

Revising Strategies

Common Core State Standards

Writing

1. Write arguments to support claims in an analysis of substantive topics or texts, using valid reasoning and relevant and sufficient evidence.

1.d. Establish and maintain a formal style and objective tone while attending to the norms and conventions of the discipline.

5. Develop and strengthen writing as needed by planning, revising, editing, rewriting, or trying a new approach, focusing on addressing what is most significant for a specific purpose and audience.

Language

1.a. Use parallel structure.

Test your support. Every paragraph in your essay should play a clear role in *supporting your argument*. Use these steps to test each paragraph:

- Underline the sentence that states the main idea of the paragraph. If a topic sentence is missing, consider adding one.

- Put a star next to each sentence that supports the main idea. If a sentence is not starred, consider modifying or deleting it.

- If a topic sentence has fewer than two supporting details, add more evidence or reconsider whether the point is worth including.

Model: Revising to Strengthen a Paragraph

Even though honor-roll students have spent many hours studying for classes and completing assignments, they are forced to face even more stress in taking final exams. ★ Most honor-roll students are high performers who will spend extra time preparing for exams even though they do not need to.

★ A good friend of mine stayed up all night studying for his final chemistry exam, even though he already had an "A" in the class.

Additional anecdotal evidence helps to support the writer's claim.

Choose powerful words. Clear, strong language will help make your ideas memorable. Consider these options:

- **Comparatives and Superlatives** Comparative adjectives, such as *sharper* and *bolder*, clarify your ideas. Avoid overuse of predictable or subjective superlatives, such as *best, smartest, strongest,* or *bravest*.

- **Action Verbs** Strong verbs make your ideas more compelling.

   Linking verb: The policy *is* unfair. (weak)

   Action verb: The policy *cheats* us all. (strong)

- **Connotation** Be aware of **connotations,** the emotions a word sparks. Positive connotations can support ideas. Negative connotations can stress drawbacks of opposing arguments, but being overly negative can backfire. A neutral, objective tone shows fair-mindedness.

   Objective: We can look into this problem.

   Positive: We can rise to meet this challenge.

   Negative: We can attempt to approach this impossible task.

Peer Review

Review a classmate's work. Circle ten weak words in your partner's essay. In a peer conference, discuss possible replacements.

Revising to Create Parallelism

Parallelism is the use of similar grammatical forms or patterns to express similar ideas. Effective use of parallelism can connect your ideas and make them memorable.

Identifying Faulty Parallelism Parallel constructions place equal ideas in words, phrases, or clauses of similar types. Ideas are not parallel if the grammatical structure shifts.

	Nonparallel	Parallel
use of verbs	We want <u>to be learning, growing, and to succeed.</u>	We want <u>to learn, to grow, and to succeed.</u>
use of direct objects	Students benefit from <u>limits that are respectful, reasonable freedoms, and being inspired by classes.</u>	Students benefit from <u>respectful limits, reasonable freedoms, and inspiring classes.</u>

Fixing Errors Follow these steps to revise nonparallel constructions:

1. **Identify similar or equivalent ideas within a sentence.**

2. **Identify the form in which the ideas are expressed.** Then, read the sentence aloud to hear changes in rhythm or pattern.

3. **Rewrite the sentence so that all the elements match the stronger pattern.** Choose forms that produce the smoothest rhythm or require the fewest words. Look at these examples:

   Nouns: hand, heart, and mind

   Verbs: to seek, to question, and to learn

   Phrases: defining the borders, preserving our resources, securing the future

   Adverb clauses: wherever we go, whatever we do

   Adjective clauses: she who commits, who practices, who focuses

4. **Punctuate correctly.** Use commas to separate three or more words, phrases, or clauses in a parallel series.

PH WRITING COACH

Further instruction and practice are available in *Prentice Hall Writing Coach*.

Grammar in Your Writing

Review three paragraphs in your essay, circling sentences that present a series of equivalent ideas. If they have varying grammatical structures, revise them to build parallelism.

Student Model: Esther Herrera, Hialeah, FL

Common Core State Standards

Writing
6. Use technology, including the Internet, to produce, publish, and update individual or shared writing products, taking advantage of technology's capacity to link to other information and to display information flexibly and dynamically.

Language
2.c. Spell correctly.

True Reward for Our Achievements

Straight-A students have been rewarded in different ways for their hard work. They have been given the chance to eat breakfast with the principal, they have received gifts and certificates, and they have been publicly acknowledged. Schools hope that these policies will not only serve as a reward to students but also as an inspiration to others to do well in their classes. However, these honor-roll students show little interest in the awards; they want something else. These students should be exempt from taking the final exam because they have demonstrated responsibility and dedication, they know the material, and most importantly they feel that other students will likely be inspired to achieve the ultimate honor-roll goal.

Primarily, honor-roll students should be exempt from taking the final exam because they are responsible and dedicated. These students have stayed on task throughout the year, going out of their way to turn in a job well done. Sometimes, they sacrificed by staying up late to finish homework assignments. As one honor student recalled, "One time, I stayed up, literally, all night so that I could finish a project. The problem was not finishing it but making sure that it would come out perfect; it did."

In addition, teachers should not have to give these students the final examination. Because they got A's in the first, second, third, and fourth quarters, it is clear that the students know the material very well. Furthermore, the final exam is added stress, because students worry and get nervous taking tests.

On the other hand, eleven out of twenty-five students whom I interviewed believe that such an exemption policy would not be fair to the other students. However, all students were given the same opportunity to get A's. The striking thing about this survey is that many students who were in favor of an exemption policy were not honor students. Instead, they were students who might work harder to earn the privilege of not taking the final exam. What I say to the first eleven students is: Accept the challenge.

In conclusion, honor-roll students should be exempt from taking the final exam because they have already proved themselves. These students deserve a true reward: the knowledge that their efforts have been recognized.

Esther clearly states her opinion on the issue.

The writer states the argument and then supports it with valid evidence.

By referring to a survey she conducted, Esther shows her research and writes with authority.

Here, the writer addresses those who oppose her ideas.

Esther restates her opinion in her conclusion.

Editing and Proofreading

Review your draft to correct errors in grammar, spelling, capitalization, and punctuation.

Focus on spelling. Some vowel sounds in words are silent, which can make correct spelling difficult. Generally, two vowels are used to spell a sound that usually takes only one vowel, as in the final syllable of *porcelain*. If a word gives you problems, create a memory aid to remember the spelling. For example, you may say, *"u hides in camouflage."*

Publishing and Presenting

Consider one of the following ways to share your writing:

Publish for an audience. If your topic relates to a school or community issue, submit your essay to a school or local newspaper, or post it on a class Web site. If you post on a Web site, create links to relevant information. Update the links when new information becomes available.

Deliver a speech. Use your persuasive essay as the basis for an in-class speech followed by a question-and-answer session. Survey your audience before and after your speech to see if you have changed their minds about your topic. Encourage the entire class to join in the question-and-answer period and clarify, verify, or challenge ideas.

Reflecting on Your Writing

Writer's Journal Jot down your answers to this question:
How did writing about an issue help you better understand it?

Rubric for Self-Assessment

Find evidence in your writing to address each category. Then, use the rating scale to grade your work.

Spiral Review
Earlier in the unit, you learned about **degrees of adjectives** (p. 574). Check your essay to be sure you have used the correct forms of adjectives.

Criteria	Rating Scale not very very
Focus: How clearly do you explain both the issue and your opinion?	1 2 3 4 5
Organization: How well do you organize the elements of your arguments?	1 2 3 4 5
Support/Elaboration: How reliable and varied is your evidence?	1 2 3 4 5
Style: How vivid and persuasive is your language?	1 2 3 4 5
Conventions: How correct is your grammar, especially your use of parallel structures?	1 2 3 4 5

Vocabulary Workshop

Words With Multiple Meanings

Common Core State Standards

Language

4. Determine or clarify the meaning of unknown and multiple-meaning words and phrases based on grades 9–10 reading and content.

4.a. Use context as a clue to the meaning of a word or phrase.

4.c. Consult general and specialized reference materials, both print and digital, to find the pronunciation of a word or determine or clarify its precise meaning, its part of speech, or its etymology.

4.d. Verify the preliminary determination of the meaning of a word or phrase.

Many words in English have **multiple meanings.** Look at this dictionary entry for *coast*:

Dictionary

The first part of the entry gives meanings for the noun *coast*.

The second part of the entry gives meanings for the verb *coast*.

coast (kōst) *n.* [ME *coste*, coast < OFr, a rib, hill, shore, coast < L *costa*, a rib, side] **1.** land alongside the sea; seashore **2.** [Obs] frontier borderland **3.** a slide or ride, as on a sled going down an incline by the force of gravity— *vi.* **1.** to sail along or near a coast, esp. from port to port **2.** to go down an incline, as on a sled **3.** to continue in motion on momentum or by the force of gravity after propelling power has stopped **4.** to continue without serious effort, letting one's past efforts carry one along

This means "obsolete," or no longer useful.

To determine which meaning a writer is using in a sentence, look at the **context clues.** Context clues are in the information surrounding a word and can be used to determine the word's meaning. Look at the following sentence to identify context clues that help you determine the meaning used here:

My brother *coasted* through law school without opening a book.

One context clue is that *coast* is used as a verb. Another clue is *without opening a book,* which suggests "without much effort." Try each of the four definitions for verbs in the sentence. The definition that fits is 4— "to continue without serious effort, letting one's past efforts carry one along."

Practice A Read each sentence. Choose the multiple-meaning word that makes sense in each sentence pair: *vacuum, break, negative, police.*

1. (a) His _____ attitude kept him from succeeding in school.
(b) The _____ of a picture shows light and dark in reverse.

2. (a) I need to _____ the rug before company arrives.
(b) The absence of air creates a _____.

3. (a) We must _____ the campus for litter.
(b) My older sister went to the _____ academy when she was twenty.

4. (a) We definitely wanted to _____ free of our routine.
(b) The sun shone through a _____ in the clouds.

Practice B Using context clues, write your own definition for the underlined word in each sentence. With a partner, discuss which context clues helped you to determine the meaning of the word. Then, look up the word in a dictionary to confirm or correct your definition.

PHLit
Online!
www.PHLitOnline.com
- Illustrated vocabulary words
- Interactive vocabulary games
- Vocabulary flashcards

1. The map didn't show the <u>cardinal</u> directions!

2. A cold <u>draft</u> came in under the door and through cracks around the window.

3. She didn't seem to <u>harbor</u> any hard feelings over what I'd said.

4. The <u>launch</u> sped across the choppy bay.

5. How can you <u>gauge</u> someone's interest in the drama?

6. To prepare for the long Alaskan winter, Andrew stocked his cabin with flour, cereal, potatoes, and other <u>staples</u>.

7. The truck bounced its way across the sandy <u>wash</u>.

8. Their <u>plot</u> to avoid the extra work failed completely.

9. Don't <u>force</u> the lock or you may break the key off.

10. The sailor could hardly stay on his feet as he walked across the heaving <u>deck</u> of the ship.

Activity Look in a dictionary to find the multiple definitions of these words: *litter, fan, coat, pump,* and *contract*. Write each word on a separate notecard like the one shown. Fill in the left column of the notecard according to one of the word's meanings. Fill in the right column according to another of the word's meanings. Then, trade notecards with a partner and discuss the different meanings and uses of the words that each of you found.

Word	First Meaning	Second Meaning

Comprehension and Collaboration

Find each of these words in a dictionary: *craft, switch, exhaust.* Select one of the meanings for each and write a sentence in which the context clearly illustrates the meaning. Trade sentences with a partner. Identify the definition of the word in each of your partner's sentences.

Communications Workshop

Delivering a Persuasive Speech

A convincing persuasive speech depends on two key elements: strong writing and a powerful delivery. Your words and presentation style must connect with your audience, so use standard grammar and language.

Learn the Skills

Use the strategies to complete the activity on page 615.

Support your opinion. Your persuasive speech will define and support a claim—your position, or point of view. Gather supporting evidence, such as facts, expert opinions, expressions of commonly accepted beliefs, and relevant anecdotes. Evaluate your evidence from your audience's point of view. Ensure that your line of reasoning is logical and free of fallacies, such as overgeneralizations and exaggerations.

Consider your purpose. Think about your purpose—to persuade—as well as your specific goals. For example, you might want to persuade your audience to take a particular action as well as to share your position. Organize your speech in a way that will make it easy for your audience to follow your reasoning.

Use rhetorical devices. Strengthen the argument by using rhetorical devices, such as repetition and parallel structure. Choose words carefully, paying attention to both their sounds and connotations. Work to appeal to your audience's emotions and beliefs while using formal English to maintain their respect.

Focus on your opening and closing. Grab your audience's attention in your introduction, and summarize your points in a memorable way in your conclusion.

Prepare a reader's script. Once you have written your speech, plan how you will present it. Mark a copy of your speech to show words you will emphasize and places you will pause, as modeled in the sample reader's script. Use effective pacing. Slow down to stress key statements; speed up to emphasize emotion. Use a casual tone when telling a personal anecdote. Use a serious tone when quoting an expert.

Establish eye contact. Keep your audience interested by making frequent eye contact. Practice your speech so that it is familiar to you.

Common Core State Standards

Writing

1. Write arguments to support claims in an analysis of substantive topics or texts, using valid reasoning and relevant and sufficient evidence.

Speaking and Listening

3. Evaluate a speaker's point of view, reasoning, and use of evidence and rhetoric, identifying any fallacious reasoning or exaggerated or distorted evidence.

4. Present information, findings, and supporting evidence clearly, concisely, and logically such that listeners can follow the line of reasoning and the organization, development, substance, and style are appropriate to purpose, audience, and task.

6. Adapt speech to a variety of contexts and tasks, demonstrating command of formal English when indicated or appropriate.

SAMPLE READER'S SCRIPT

start gradually
The plans for the new park at Elm Street call for a baseball field,‖a

energetic
playground,‖and a big lawn. It sounds <u>great</u>, but it could be <u>better</u>.

There is one thing missing:‖dogs!‖ We need a dog run. We do not

slower
have a <u>single</u> public dog run in our city.   ‖ = pause

Practice the Skills

ⓒ **Presentation of Knowledge and Ideas** Use what you have learned in this workshop to perform the following task.

ACTIVITY: Deliver a Persuasive Speech

Choose a topic that has two sides. Organize a presentation in which you take a stand. Practice in front of a classmate. Based on the feedback you receive, revise your presentation. Then, deliver the speech for the full class. Consider the following criteria as you develop your speech:

- How clear is the position, point of view, or claim?
- Is it supported by convincing evidence?
- Is the evidence logically organized?
- Is the line of reasoning easy for readers to follow?

As your classmates make their presentations, listen carefully. Use the Presentation Checklist to analyze and evaluate their presentations, and invite your classmates to use the checklist to analyze and evaluate your presentation.

Presentation Checklist

Presentation Content
Did the presentation meet all the requirements of the activity?
Check all that apply.
- ☐ Its organization and style supported the purpose and task.
- ☐ It did not contain fallacies; the reasoning was logical.
- ☐ It met all of the criteria listed in the activity assignment.

Presentation Delivery
Did the speaker effectively deliver the speech?
Check all that apply.
- ☐ The speaker used standard grammar and effective language.
- ☐ The speaker used effective pacing.
- ☐ The speaker made frequent eye contact with the audience.

ⓒ **Comprehension and Collaboration** After all the class members have delivered their speeches, discuss which ones were the most effective and why. Offer positive suggestions for approaches or techniques that will help each student strengthen his or her presentation.

Cumulative Review

I. Reading Literary Nonfiction

Common Core State Standards

RI.9-10.1, RI.9-10.4, RI.9-10.6; W.9-10.1

[For the full wording of the standards, see the standards chart in the front of your textbook.]

Directions: *Read the passage. Then, answer each question that follows.*

Playing the Piano

You have heard it before: practice, practice, practice! Whether it is kicking a soccer ball, shooting hoops, or playing the piano, practice makes perfect. My parents sincerely believed that.

When I was nine years old, they bought a second-hand piano, hoping that my older sister would become the musical genius of our family. Unfortunately (or fortunately) she had about as much musical talent as I had athletic talent—in other words, zilch. On the other hand, I thought the piano wasn't the worst thing ever. I was <u>intrigued</u> that simply by pressing the right "buttons," you could make a song. I begged my parents for piano lessons. They agreed, on the condition that I vow to practice every day. I promised. I was excited. My music teacher told me I had "promise."

At first, I practiced every day. My parents marveled at my budding genius. My practice filled the house with heavenly music every day. Everyone but my sister thought I was wonderful. Gradually, the novelty of the piano and the praise grew stale. I still loved the piano, and I still loved to play—when I was in the mood. When spring came, I would rather be out riding my bike. When summer came, I would rather go to the beach. When fall came, I would rather be downloading music online.

So it went. Gradually, the praise stopped and the nagging started: "Have you practiced piano today?" Finally, the piano lessons were stopped. I didn't mind. I enjoyed the free time, and I still played the piano when I felt like it.

There is a moral to this story, of course: practice. Why? There are many reasons, but becoming a superstar is not necessarily one of them. With a physical skill, remember that muscles have "memories." Once you master a skill, such as biking, you never lose it. Even if the skill is more complex, such as playing a musical instrument, which requires both physical motor skills and mental skills, you never lose it. I have not played the piano for years, but I can still pick out a tune, and I can still read music. I still love the piano—and I love to bike-ride, too. So if there is something you enjoy doing, practice until you have mastered it. Then you will always have it. You may get rusty, but the skills will remain with you to enrich, expand, and enhance the rest of your life.

1. The second paragraph of this passage is an example of which type of **essay** writing?

   A. narrative
   B. argumentative
   C. humorous
   D. explanatory

2. The following passage is an example of which **persuasive** or **rhetorical device**?

   When spring came, I would rather be out riding my bike. When summer came, I would rather go to the beach. When fall came, I would rather be downloading music online.
   A. rhetorical question
   B. appeal to logic
   C. parallelism
   D. appeal to emotion

3. What best describes the **author's purpose**?

   A. to persuade readers to practice to become superstars
   B. to describe how it feels to practice
   C. to analyze the effect of practice
   D. to persuade readers to practice something they enjoy

4. Which sentence from the passage contains an example of **understatement**?

   A. My parents sincerely believed that.
   B. On the other hand, I thought the piano wasn't the worst thing ever.
   C. My parents marveled at my budding genius.
   D. There is a moral to this story of course: practice.

5. Which paragraph contains a **rhetorical question**?

   A. paragraph 2
   B. paragraph 3
   C. paragraph 4
   D. paragraph 5

6. Which of the following sentences from the passage contains **hyperbole**?

   A. I begged my parents for piano lessons.
   B. My practice filled the house with heavenly music every day.
   C. Gradually, the novelty of the piano and the praise grew stale.
   D. Finally, the piano lessons were stopped.

7. This passage reflects elements of which types of essays?

   A. analytic, argumentative
   B. reflective, humorous
   C. argumentative, humorous
   D. explanatory, reflective

8. **Vocabulary** Which is the closest definition of the underlined word *intrigued*?

   A. confused by   C. attracted by
   B. frightened by   D. angered by

9. With which of the following statements might the author agree?

   A. You should practice until you are perfect.
   B. An athlete should always strive to be the best in the world.
   C. Becoming skilled in a wide variety of activities is better than being perfect in one.
   D. Practicing daily makes you a better person.

Timed Writing

10. Write a brief essay to **explain** whether you agree or disagree with the author's "moral." Cite evidence from the text to support your **argument**.

II. Reading Functional Texts

Directions: *Read the passage. Then, answer each question that follows.*

Common Core
State Standards

RI.9-10.3, RI.9-10.5;
W.9-10.1, W.9-10.1.d,
W.9-10.4; L.9-10.1
[For the full wording
of the standards, see the
standards chart in the
front of your textbook.]

Using the Easy Smoothie Maker

Now create a nutritious, energy-packed smoothie in just a few seconds.

Read Safety Precautions Before Operation

- Do not immerse cord or base in water.
- Operate only on a clean, flat surface.
- Handle the cutting blade carefully to avoid injury.

Before beginning—

- Wash blade assembly and the cup in warm soapy water before using.
- Firmly place the four rubber suction cups on the feet of the base.

To create your own delicious smoothie—

1) Place the base on the counter, pressing firmly to secure the suction cups.
- Make sure the counter is free of water or grease.
- Do NOT plug in the Easy Smoothie until it is completely assembled.

2) Place ingredients in Smoothie Cup and screw on cutting blade.
- Place the solid ingredients in the cup, and then add milk or yogurt.
- Screw the cutting blade <u>assembly</u> on top of the filled Smoothie Cup.

3) Set the filled Smoothie Cup on base and engage the motor.
- Turn the cup over and place on the base, clicking it into place.
- Plug in the Smoothie base and press the "on" button for 10 seconds.
- Remove the cup from the base, unscrew the blade assembly, and enjoy!

1. Which of the following parts should you handle first when making a smoothie?

   A. the base assembly
   B. the suction cups
   C. milk or yogurt
   D. the plug

2. Why should you handle the blade carefully?

   A. It is worth a lot of money.
   B. It can be difficult to replace if you lose it.
   C. It is very sharp and can cause injuries.
   D. It can contaminate the cup's ingredients.

3. By **skimming** the article, one could learn—

   A. the dangers of improper appliance use.
   B. the steps for making a smoothie.
   C. how to care for the appliance.
   D. recipes for smoothies.

4. According to the directions, when should the Smoothie Maker be plugged in?

   A. before adding the ingredients
   B. after unscrewing the blade assembly
   C. before screwing on the cutting blade
   D. after placing the filled cup on the base

III. Writing and Language Conventions

Directions: *Read the passage. Then, answer each question that follows.*

(1) October 9, 2008

(2) Editor-in-Chief
The Sentinel Dispatch
700 Viewmont Street
Sentinel, South Dakota 96501

(3) Dear Editor-in-Chief:
(4) The school board of Sentinel High School has cut funds for after-school music programs. (5) I am writing to protest this action and to ask citizens of Sentinel to write to the school board to protest this as well.
(6) Students need options. (7) Music programs should receive as much funding as sports programs. (8) For students who are not athletic, music is an alternative to athletics. (9) All students should receive opportunities. (10) Please to the school board write. (11) Ask them not to cut funds.

(12) Sincerely,
Damon Fitzgerald

1. What section needs to be added to this letter?

   A. greeting

   B. closing

   C. return address

   D. date

2. The author's **tone** can best be described as—

   A. angry and disappointed.

   B. calm and reasonable.

   C. fearful and anxious.

   D. enraged and bitter.

3. Which sentences should be **combined?**

   A. sentences 4 and 5

   B. sentences 6 and 7

   C. sentences 8 and 9

   D. sentences 10 and 11

4. The author of this letter uses _____ language.

   A. formal

   B. informal

   C. sarcastic

   D. emotional

5. What is the correct way to revise sentence 10?

   A. To the school board write please.

   B. The school board please be written to.

   C. Writing to the school board please.

   D. Please write to the school board.

Performance Tasks

Common Core State Standards

RI.9-10.2, RI.9-10.3, RI.9-10.4, RI.9-10.5, RI.9-10.6, RI.9-10.8; W.9-10.2.d., W.9-10.9.b.; SL.9-10.1, SL.9-10.1.a., SL.9-10.4; L.9-10.1.a., L.9-10.2.c

[For the full wording of the standards, see the standards chart in the front of your textbook.]

Directions: *Follow the instructions to complete the tasks below as required by your teacher.*

As you work on each task, incorporate both general academic vocabulary and literary terms you learned in this unit.

Writing

Task 1: Informational Text [RI.9-10.2; W.9-10.2.d.]
Analyze the Development of a Central Idea

Write an essay in which you analyze the development of the central idea in a nonfiction work from this unit.

- Provide a brief summary of the work in which you explain its most important points, especially the central idea.

- Explain how the author initially presents the central idea.

- Describe how the author shapes and refines the central idea throughout the work. Include specific details to support your analysis.

- Present your ideas concisely. Look for places where you can eliminate wordiness or choose more precise language.

Task 2: Informational Text [RI.9-10.6; L.9-10.2.c.]
Determine an Author's Point of View and Analyze Use of Rhetoric

Write an essay in which you determine an author's point of view and analyze his or her use of rhetoric in a speech or an essay from this unit.

- Describe the author's point of view and explain how it affects his or her discussion of the topic.

- Discuss specific ways in which the author's rhetoric advances his or her point of view.

- Cite specific examples from the text to support your analysis.

- Edit your essay for correct capitalization and punctuation. Ensure that words are spelled correctly.

Task 3: Informational Text [RI.9-10.8]
Evaluate an Argument

Write an essay in which you evaluate the argument in a persuasive work from this unit.

- Present the author's argument, delineating both the author's specific claims and his or her supporting evidence.

- Determine whether the author's argument is sound, the reasoning valid, and the evidence both relevant and sufficient. Explain your position.

- Identify any faulty reasoning or fallacious arguments in the work.

- Follow your class style guide when quoting sentences or short paragraphs from the argument.

Task 4: Informational Text [RI.9-10.3, RI.9-10.5]
Analyze the Order and Development of Ideas

Write an essay in which you analyze the order and development of ideas in a nonfiction work from this unit.

- Identify the author's central idea.

- Describe the overall structure of the work, including the order in which supporting ideas are introduced.

- Discuss specific structural choices the writer makes, such as the ways in which he or she connects ideas. For example, explain how the writer uses transitional words and phrases, defines sections, or introduces contrasts and comparisons.

- Explain how the writer organizes sections, paragraphs, and individual sentences to develop key points and establish a logical flow of ideas.

- Maintain a consistent style and formal tone throughout your essay.

Speaking and Listening

ⒸTask 5: Informational Text [RI.9-10.6; SL.9-10.4]

Analyze an Author's Purpose

Deliver a speech in which you analyze an author's purpose in one work from this unit.

- Provide both a brief summary of the work and basic information about the author, including the era in which he or she wrote and his or her style and customary topics.

- Describe the author's purpose for writing this work. Explain specific concepts, attitudes, or feelings you think the author wanted to convey. Cite details from the work to support your thinking.

- Note specific ways in which the author uses rhetoric to support his or her purpose, and evaluate its effectiveness.

- Present your findings and supporting evidence clearly so that your audience can follow your reasoning.

ⒸTask 6: Informational Text [RI.9-10.4; SL.9-10.4; L.9-10.1.a.]

Analyze the Effect of Word Choice on Tone

Deliver an oral presentation in which you analyze the effect of word choice on tone in two works from this unit.

- Choose two works that offer clear and distinct tones. Explain your choices, describing how the tones of the two works differ.

- Identify specific word choices from each work and explain how these choices affect both meaning and tone.

- Use a graphic organizer to show how the tones of the two works differ.

- Present your ideas clearly and concisely so that your listeners can follow your reasoning.

- Use parallel structures to help engage your listeners.

ⒸTask 7: Informational Text [RI.9-10.5; SL.9-10.1, SL.9-10.1.a.]

Analyze an Author's Ideas

Lead a class discussion in which you analyze the ideas presented in a reflective essay from this unit.

- Prepare for the discussion by completing your own analysis of the work. Plan the key points you will address during the discussion.

- Introduce the discussion by offering a summary of the central ideas expressed in the work.

- Then, lead the class in a discussion of the work, including the significance of the title, as well as the development of ideas in specific paragraphs and sentences.

- Consider the author's uses of language, including rhetorical devices, word choices, and connotative meanings.

- As you lead the discussion, summarize points of agreement and disagreement and make connections among ideas.

What kind of knowledge changes our lives?

At the beginning of Unit 3, you participated in a discussion of the Big Question. Now that you have completed the unit, write a response to the question. Discuss how your initial ideas have changed or been reinforced. Support your response with at least one example from literature and one example from an additional subject area or your own life. Use Big Question vocabulary words (see page 443) in your response.

Featured Titles

In this unit, you have read a variety of informational text, including literary nonfiction. Continue to read on your own. Select works that you enjoy, but challenge yourself to explore new topics, new authors, and works of increasing depth and complexity. The titles suggested below will help you get started.

Informational Text

Night
by Elie Wiesel

During World War II, approximately 6 million European Jews were killed in concentration camps set up by the Nazi regime. *Night* is a **memoir** that describes the author's experiences as a 15-year-old boy who survived the camps but was tormented by what he had seen and experienced.

Immigrant Voices: Twenty-Four Narratives on Becoming an American
Edited by Gordon Hutner
Signet, 1999

This collection of **autobiographical narratives** and **essays** explores the experience of becoming American from many different points of view, including those of a female doctor from Germany forbidden to practice and a man from India struggling to become a writer.

Today's Nonfiction

This collection of **autobiographical narratives** brings together different styles and cultures. From Ernesto Galarza's story of learning English in school to Joan Didion's description of her visit to Pearl Harbor, each real-life story in this collection vividly captures a moment as unique as it is universal.

Touch the Top of the World
by Erik Weihenmayer
Signet, 1999

Erik Weihenmayer had already climbed five of the world's highest peaks when he decided to climb Mount Everest—the "top of the world." Despite having lost his eyesight when he was a child, Weihenmayer achieved his goal. In this **memoir,** he recounts the challenges he faced and the fulfillment he experienced on his high-altitude adventure.

Bury My Heart at Wounded Knee
by Dee Brown
H. Holt, 1991   EXEMPLAR TEXT

In this work of **historical nonfiction,** Dee Brown explores the conflicts between nineteenth-century American settlers and native peoples. The author includes first-hand accounts by Native Americans, who reveal the hardships they faced in trying to maintain their culture and way of life.

The Longitude Prize
by Joan Dash
Farrar, Straus and Giroux, 2000   EXEMPLAR TEXT

During the eighteenth century, the British government offered a large monetary prize to the first person to develop a method for measuring longitude at sea. The government hoped to reduce the losses of both sailors and ships. This work of **historical nonfiction** tells the story of clockmaker John Harrison, who invented a creative answer to a national problem.

Literature

To Kill a Mockingbird
by Harper Lee
Warner Books, 1960   EXEMPLAR TEXT

In this classic **novel,** Harper Lee tells a story of racial prejudice in a fictional Alabama town during the Great Depression. The narrator is eight-year-old Scout Finch, a young girl whose father defends an innocent man in a trial that raises questions about race and justice in America.

In the Time of the Butterflies
by Julia Alvarez
Algonquin Books, 2010   EXEMPLAR TEXT

This **novel** is set in the Dominican Republic during the mid-twentieth century. It is based on the real-life stories of the Mirabal sisters, who took part in a plot to topple their oppressive government. Beginning with their childhoods, the author gives life to these courageous sisters and traces their development as political revolutionaries.

Preparing to Read Complex Texts

Attentive Reading As you read on your own, bring your imagination and questions to the text. The questions shown below and others that you ask as you read will help you learn and enjoy reading even more.

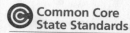
When reading literary nonfiction, ask yourself...

- Who is the author? Why did he or she write the work?
- Are the ideas the author conveys important? Do they merit my attention? If not, why?
- When did the author live and write? Do the attitudes of a particular time and place affect the ideas the author expresses? If so, how?
- Does any one idea strike me as being the most important? Why?
- How might the author's background and life experiences affect his or her views on the topic?
- How might the author's background and life experiences affect his or her use of language?
- How do my life experiences affect what I understand about the work? How do they affect what I feel about the work?
- What can I learn from this text?

© Key Ideas and Details

- Does the author organize ideas so that I can follow them? If not, what is wrong with the way the text is ordered?
- Does the author capture my interest right from the beginning, or do I have to work to get into the text? Why do I think that is?
- Does the author give me a new way of looking at a topic? If so, how? If not, why?
- Is the author an expert on the topic? How do I know?
- Has the author made me care about the subject? If so, how? If not, why?
- Does the author use strong evidence? Do I find any of the evidence unconvincing? If so, why?

© Craft and Structure

- Does the work seem authentic and true? Does any aspect of the work seem exaggerated, false, or unsupported?
- Do I agree or disagree with the author's basic premise? Why?
- Have I read other works about this or a related topic? What does this work add to my knowledge of the topic?
- How would I write about a similar topic? Would I follow an approach similar to the author's, or would I handle the topic differently?

© Integration of Ideas

Does all *communication* serve a positive purpose?

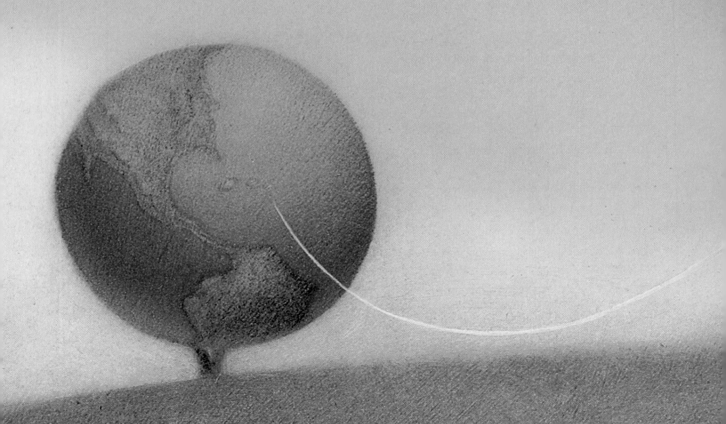

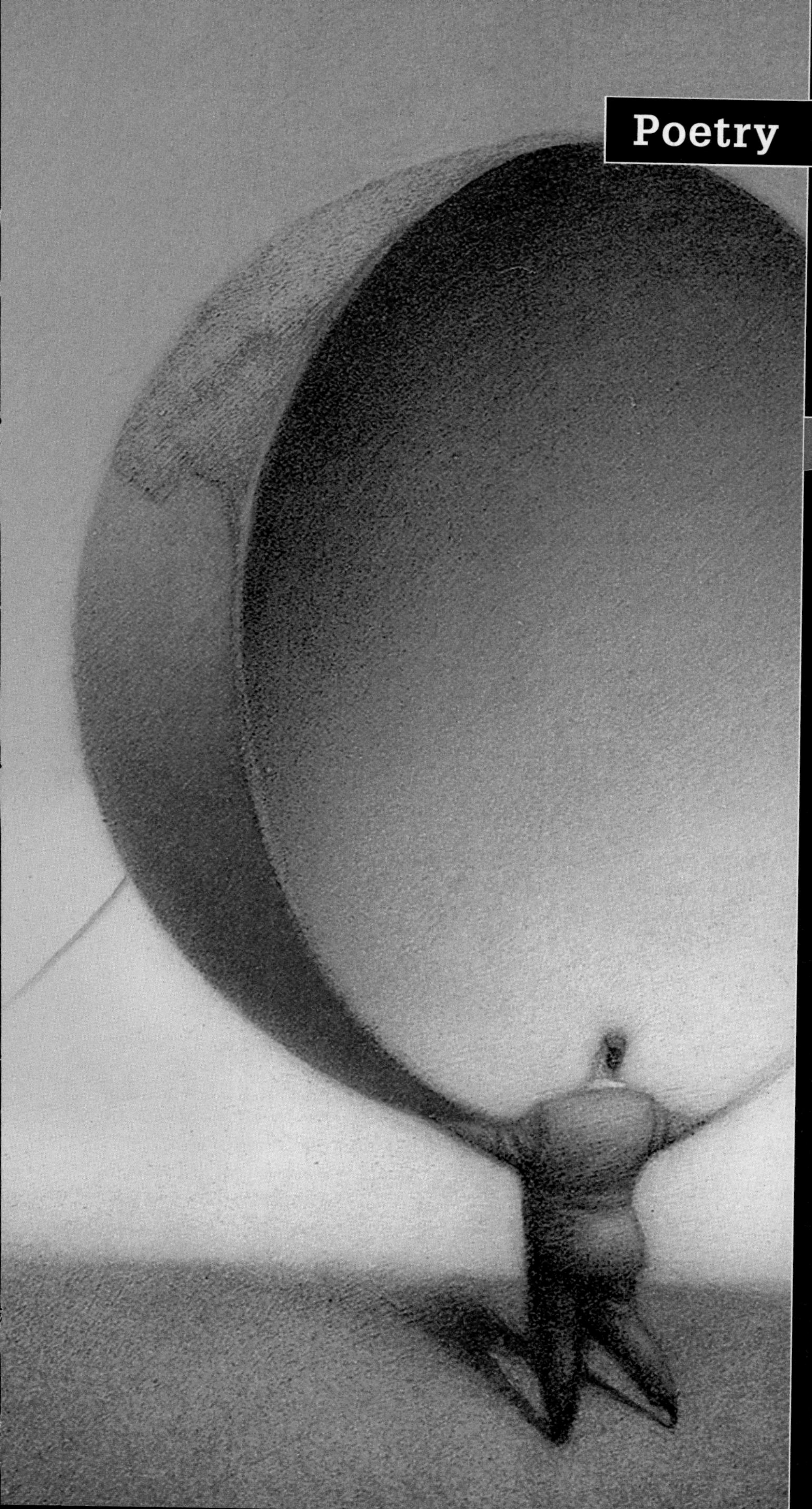

Poetry

Unit 4

PHLit Online!

www.PHLitOnline.com

Hear It!
- Selection summary audio
- Selection audio
- BQ Tunes

See It!
- Author videos
- Big Question video
- Get Connected videos
- Background videos
- More about the authors
- Illustrated vocabulary words
- Vocabulary flashcards

Do It!
- Interactive journals
- Interactive graphic organizers
- Grammar tutorials
- Interactive vocabulary games
- Test practice

Does all *communication* serve a positive purpose?

Communication, the act of exchanging information, can take on many forms: it can be verbal, visual, or auditory. For example, people may convey ideas and emotion through language, art, or music. People communicate for various reasons. If, for instance, a person feels as though he or she is isolated, communicating can help the person make a connection or interact with others. Communication allows people to provide an explanation or help clear up a source of confusion. Communication is not always positive, however, and can lead to problems when words are taken out of context or are misinterpreted.

Exploring the Big Question

Collaboration: Group Discussion Start thinking about the Big Question by identifying why people communicate with each other. In a small group, list reasons for communicating that you have experienced or know of. Give a specific example of each of the following categories:

- Informing people of a problem or an important issue
- Using art or music as a form of self-expression
- Clearing up a misunderstanding
- Understanding the feelings and experiences of others
- Passing along the latest gossip to a friend
- Telling a current news story or explaining historical events

Discuss why someone would communicate in each situation and whether the communication would have a positive or negative effect.

Connecting to the Literature Each reading in this unit will give you additional insight into the Big Question.

> **PHLit Online!**
> www.PHLitOnline.com
> - Big Question video
> - Illustrated vocabulary words
> - Interactive vocabulary games
> - BQ Tunes

Learning Big Question Vocabulary

 **Common Core State Standards**

Speaking and Listening
1. Initiate and participate effectively in a range of collaborative discussions with diverse partners on grades 9–10 topics, texts, and issues, building on others' ideas and expressing their own clearly and persuasively.

Language
6. Acquire and use accurately general academic and domain-specific words and phrases, sufficient for reading, writing, speaking, and listening at the college and career readiness level; demonstrate independence in gathering vocabulary knowledge when considering a word or phrase important to comprehension or expression.

Acquire and Use Academic Vocabulary Academic vocabulary is the language you encounter in textbooks and on standardized tests. Review the definitions of these academic vocabulary words.

context (kän´ tekst´) *n.* circumstances that form an event's setting

convey (kən vā´) *v.* communicate or make known

discourse (dis´ kors) *n.* ongoing communication of ideas and information

explanation (eks´ plə nā´ shən) *n.* something that makes meaning clear

interact (in´ tər akt´) *v.* act on one another

isolation (ī´sə lā´ shən) *n.* being alone or set apart

meaning (mē niŋ) *n.* significance of something

misinterpret (mis´ in tur´ prit) *v.* understand incorrectly

respond (ri spänd´) *v.* answer

Use these words as you complete Big Question activities in this unit that involve reading, writing, speaking, and listening.

Gather Vocabulary Knowledge Additional Big Question words are listed below. Categorize the words by deciding whether you know each one well, know it a little bit, or do not know it at all.

confusion	connection	emotion
language	self-expression	verbal

Then, do the following:

1. Write the definitions of the words you know.

2. Consult a dictionary to confirm the definitions of the words you know. Revise your definitions if necessary.

3. Using a print or an online dictionary, look up the meanings of the words you do not know. Then, write the meanings.

4. Use all the words in a brief paragraph about communication.

Elements of Poetry

Poetry combines structural elements with concise, musical, and emotionally charged language to express multiple layers of meaning.

Poetry is a musical form of literature in which words may suggest multiple layers of meaning. These layers emerge through the structure of the poem, the sounds and meanings of words, and the speaker's voice.

Structure and Meter Poems consist of lines that may be organized into groups called **stanzas. Meter** is the rhythmic pattern established by stresses, or beats, within each line of a poem. Meter is measured in units called **feet.**

Readers identify meter by **scanning** each line of a poem, or marking each stressed syllable with an accent (´) and each unstressed syllable with a horseshoe symbol (˘). Vertical lines (|) are used to divide each line into feet. Most metrical feet consist of one stressed and one or more unstressed syllables. The chart below explains common types of metrical feet.

Types of Metrical Feet

Name	Symbol	Example
iamb	˘ ´	*begin*
trochee	´ ˘	*catching*
anapest	˘ ˘ ´	*understand*
dactyl	´ ˘ ˘	*bicycle*
spondee	´ ´	*heartthrob*
Pyrrhus	˘ ˘	*in a*

By counting the number of feet in each line, readers can identify metrical patterns. One classic pattern is **iambic tetrameter,** which contains eight syllables—four iambic feet—as in the following line.

Example: Iambic Tetrameter
Wĕ wéar | thĕ másk | thăt gríns | ănd liés,
from "We Wear the Mask," Paul Laurence Dunbar

Another classic pattern is **iambic pentameter,** which contains ten syllables—five iambic feet— as in the following example.

Example: Iambic Pentameter
Aňd súm|mĕr's leáse|hăth áll|tŏo shórt|ă dáte:
from Sonnet 18, William Shakespeare (page 687)

Enjambment To maintain a metrical pattern, a poet may carry a thought over from one line to the next. When a line breaks before completing a grammatical unit that can stand on its own, the line is said to be **enjambed.** In the following example, lines 2–4 are enjambed.

Example: Enjambment
It is a beauteous evening, calm and free,
The holy time is quiet as a Nun
Breathless with adoration; the broad sun
Is sinking down in its tranquillity.
from "It Is a Beauteous Evening," William Wordsworth

Though line 2—"The holy time is quiet as a Nun"—appears to make sense by itself, line 3—"Breathless with adoration; the broad sun"— does not. Line 2 is enjambed with line 3, as indicated by the blue type. Similarly, line 3 is enjambed with line 4, as indicated by the green type. Enjambment allows Wordsworth to maintain five strong beats per line.

Example: Enjambment and Meter
Thĕ hó | lY tiḿe | ĭs qúi | ĕt ás | ă Nún
Bréathlĕss | wĭth ád | ŏ rá | tiŏn; thé | brŏad sún

Sound in Poetry

Meter is just one element of rhythm in poetry, and not all poems make use of it. For example, poems written in **free verse** do not follow regular metrical patterns. They do, however, include rhythmic elements that are often created through the combinations of word sounds. Sound devices are forms of repetition. Poets may repeat words and phrases to emphasize important ideas. They may also employ more sophisticated sound devices to add meaning and music to their work.

Rhyme and Rhyme Scheme

Rhyme is the repetition of vowel and consonant sounds at the ends of words, as in the words *proud* and *allowed*. Rhymes at the end of lines are called **end rhymes.** Rhymes that appear within lines are called **internal rhymes.**

Exact rhymes can sometimes be heavy or predictable. Poets may employ **slant rhyme,** which uses words with similar, but not exact, end sounds, as in *gill* and *shell* or *understand* and *find.*

Rhyme scheme is the pattern of end rhymes in a poem. Readers identify a rhyme scheme by assigning a letter of the alphabet to each line. When two end words rhyme, the lines are marked with the same letter, as in the following example.

Example: Rhyme Scheme

The bride hath paced into the hall,	**a**
Red as a rose is she;	**b**
Nodding their heads before her goes	**c**
The merry minstrelsy.	**b**

from "Rime of the Ancient Mariner," Samuel Taylor Coleridge

A **couplet** is a pair of rhyming lines, usually of the same meter and length. A couplet usually expresses a single idea and often functions as a complete stanza.

Example: Couplet

So long as men can breathe, or eyes can see,

So long lives this, and this gives life to thee.

from Sonnet 18, William Shakespeare (page 687)

Other Sound Devices

Poets may also use sound devices other than rhyme. Like rhyme, these devices emphasize key ideas, create connections between words, and elicit emotional responses. The chart that follows defines and provides examples of sound devices often used in poetry.

Example: Poetic Sound Devices

Alliteration is the repetition of initial consonant sounds.

Example: Loquacious locals like to talk to the town.

Assonance is the repetition of vowel sounds within stressed syllables that end in different consonant sounds.

Example: We dully trudged along the dusty tunnel.

Consonance is the repetition of final consonant sounds within stressed syllables that have different vowel sounds.

Example: The nervous move at every living sound.

Onomatopoeia is an actual or invented word that imitates the sound of what it names or describes.

Example: The galumphing runner huffed and puffed.

In This Section

Elements of Poetry

Determining Poetic Meaning

Close Read: Determining Meaning and Tone
- Model Text
- Practice Text

After You Read

 Common Core State Standards

RL.9-10.4
[For the full wording of the standards, see the standards chart in the front of your textbook.]

Determining Poetic Meaning

To fully understand a poem, consider the voice of the **speaker** as well as the literal and **figurative** meanings of words.

Common Core State Standards

Reading Literature 4. Determine the meaning of words and phrases as they are used in the text, including figurative and connotative meanings; analyze the cumulative impact of several word choices on meaning and tone.

Speaker and Tone

While structural elements support a poem's message, poetic meaning is largely determined by voice, tone, and language.

Voice emerges from a poem's **speaker,** who serves the same function as the narrator in a story. Even in a personal poem in which the speaker uses the first-person pronoun *I,* the speaker is not the poet but rather an imaginary voice created by the poet to tell the poem.

Tone is the attitude projected toward the subject and the audience. Tone is supported by meter and sound devices, but it is primarily established through word choice. A *formal tone* features standard English and formal grammar, as in the following example.

> ### Example: Formal Tone
> Tears, idle tears, I know not what they mean,
> Tears from the depth of some divine despair
> Rise in the heart, and gather to the eyes,
> In looking on the happy Autumn-fields,
> And thinking of the days that are no more.
>
> from "Tears, Idle Tears," Alfred, Lord Tennyson

An *informal tone* may feature colloquial language—local idioms and slang expressions—as in the example below.

> ### Example: Informal Tone
> "I'm dreadin' what I've got to watch," the
>   Color-Sergeant said.
>
> from "Danny Deever," Rudyard Kipling (page 653)

Kinds of Poetic Language

Poets combine literal and figurative language to generate layers of meaning or to invite a deeper understanding of a subject.

Denotation is a word's definition. Poems benefit from the use of specific words and phrases. For example, the word *store* communicates a general concept, but the phrase *lumber warehouse* conjures up a particular image.

Connotations are the emotional associations a word evokes. For example, the word *car* is a neutral word. However, *junker* suggests an old, broken-down vehicle, while *classic* implies a car worthy of showing off.

Sensory details, which appeal to sight, sound, hearing, taste, and touch, create imagery in the mind of the reader and evoke emotional associations. For example, the phrase "crispy, tart green apple" evokes sense memories about how apples sound, taste, and look.

Figurative Language is not meant to be taken literally. These words and phrases draw comparisons between ideas or images.

- **Similes** make direct comparisons using *as* or *like: Her glance hit me* <u>*like a spear*</u>.

- **Metaphors** make direct comparisons by stating that one thing is another: *Her glance* <u>*was a spear*</u>.

- **Personification** gives human qualities to nonhuman things: *The* <u>*lights* in the window *winked*</u> *at me.*

- **Hyperbole** is an extreme exaggeration: *After* <u>*three eons*</u>, *I saw him again.*

Forms and Types of Poetry

A poem's form can help convey its message and tone.

Free verse may use rhyme, sound devices, meter, and varied stanzas, but does not follow a fixed pattern. In the following free verse poem, the repetition of words and phrases helps emphasize ideas and creates a rhythm.

> **Example: Free Verse**
>
> A noiseless patient spider,
>
> I mark'd, where, on a little promontory, it stood, isolated;
>
> Mark'd how, to explore the vacant, vast surrounding,
>
> It launch'd forth filament, filament, filament, out of itself;
>
> Ever unreeling them—ever tirelessly speeding them.
>
> from "A Noiseless, Patient Spider," Walt Whitman

Formal verse follows established patterns. Each standard poetic form has specific requirements regarding rhyme scheme, meter, and line or stanza structure.

Types of Poetry

Though poems employ many different formats, most poems fall into one of three categories: narrative poems, dramatic poems, and lyric poems.

Narrative poetry tells a story and has a plot, characters, and a setting. Two common types of narrative poems are epic poems and ballads. An **epic poem** is a long narrative poem about gods or heroes. A **ballad** is a shorter poem that describes a single event and may be set to music. Most ballads include short stanzas and a refrain that repeats several times, like the chorus in a song.

Dramatic poetry, which tells a story using a character's own thoughts or spoken statements, is a component of many classical plays. In these plays, noble characters may deliver rhythmic, poetic speeches, while lower-class characters speak in regular prose. The term *dramatic poetry* is also used to refer to poems in which one or more characters speak.

Lyric poetry expresses the feelings of a single speaker, using melodic language, imagery, rhythm, and sound devices to express emotions. Lyric is the most common category of poetry in modern literature. Common lyric forms include the ode, elegy, sonnet, haiku, and tanka.

- **Odes** are poems of praise that often exhibit complex metrical patterns, specific rhyme schemes, and stanzas of ten or more lines each.

- **Elegies** are poems of loss that express both praise for the dead and an element of consolation.

- **Sonnets** are fourteen-line poems in which each line consists of five iambic feet (iambic pentameter). In a **Petrarchan sonnet,** an eight-line stanza with an *abbaabba* rhyme scheme is followed by a six-line stanza with a *cdecde* rhyme scheme. In a **Shakespearean sonnet,** three stanzas of four lines apiece have an *abab/cdcd/efef* rhyme scheme, followed by a two-line stanza with a *gg* rhyme scheme.

- A **haiku** is a form of Japanese poetry that consists of three unrhymed lines of five, seven, and five syllables. A **tanka** is a form of Japanese poetry that has five unrhymed lines consisting of five, seven, five, seven, and seven syllables. Both forms often describe a scene from nature and use imagery to convey a single vivid emotion or impression.

> **Example: Haiku**
>
> A crusty snowdrift,
> sooty from a week's traffic:
> Oh, for a warm day!

> **Example: Tanka**
>
> The sun is blinding.
> Glaring on the frozen lake,
> It's fire without warmth.
> Beneath the ice, the fish swim,
> Oblivious to season.

Close Read: Determining Meaning and Tone

Meter, sound devices, and language combine to express the meaning and tone of a poem.

Careful readers conduct multiple readings in order to fully understand the compact language of poetry. Reading a poem aloud is a great way to start. Listen for the impact of meter, rhyme, and other sound elements. In a second reading, concentrate on the language, both literal and figurative. Finally, put it all together as you read once more and reflect on how all these elements work together to produce a poetic message and tone. Ask the questions below to evaluate elements as you read.

Language and Tone	Sound Elements
Language Words and their meanings are the building blocks of poetry. Ask yourself • What is the literal definition of this word? Does this word have strong positive or negative connotations? • What images does it call to mind? • What emotions does it evoke?	**Rhythm and Meter** A poem's meter contributes to its rhythm, message, and mood. Ask yourself • Does this poem display a regular metrical pattern? • If so, what kinds of metrical feet does the poem employ? • If not, how is a sense of rhythm created?
Figurative Language Figurative language creates vivid impressions by comparing dissimilar things. Ask yourself • What comparisons are made in this poem? • What forms do the comparisons take (simile, metaphor, personification, hyperbole)? • What is the effect of the comparisons?	**Rhyme** Rhyme can reinforce rhythm and highlight relationships among ideas. Ask yourself • Does the poem include end rhymes? If so, do they follow a rhyme scheme? • Are there any internal rhymes? • Are the poem's rhymes exact rhymes or slant rhymes? • What words or ideas are emphasized through the use of rhyme?
Tone To determine the tone, or attitude, of the speaker in a poem, ask yourself • Is the tone formal or informal? • What tone of voice feels appropriate when I read the poem aloud? • Does the poem contain colloquial language or slang?	**Other Sound Devices** Repetition, alliteration, assonance, consonance, and onomatopoeia emphasize key words and support the poem's message. Ask yourself • When I read aloud, what words and sounds are most prominent? • What ideas or emotions do these sounds echo or reinforce?

Model

About the Text Jimmy Santiago Baca (b. 1952) is an American poet of Apache and Chicano descent. Orphaned at an early age, he grew up on the streets. While serving a prison sentence, he taught himself to read and now holds poetry workshops in schools, community centers, housing projects, and prisons throughout the United States.

"I Am Offering This Poem" by Jimmy Santiago Baca

I am offering this poem to you,
since I have nothing else to give.
Keep it like a warm coat
when winter comes to cover you,
5   or like a pair of thick socks
the cold cannot bite through,
          I love you,

I have nothing else to give you,
so it is a pot full of yellow corn
10 to warm your belly in winter,
it is a scarf for your head, to wear
over your hair, to tie up around your face,
          I love you,

Keep it, treasure this as you would
15 if you were lost, needing direction,
in the wilderness life becomes when mature;
and in the corner of your drawer,
tucked away like a cabin or hogan
in dense trees, come knocking,
20 and I will answer, give you directions,
and let you warm yourself by this fire,
rest by this fire, and make you feel safe,
          I love you,

It's all I have to give,
25 and all anyone needs to live,
and to go on living inside,
when the world outside
no longer cares if you live or die;
remember,
          I love you.

Figurative Language The poet personifies winter and cold as things that have a purpose: to cover or to bite.

Sound Devices The repetition of "I love you" keeps the reader focused on the topic of love and the ways in which the poem is an expression of love.

Figurative Language Unlike the opening simile that says what the poem is *like*, the poet now uses metaphors to say that the poem *is* a full pot and a scarf.

Language Here, precise nouns paint a vivid picture; a *hogan* is a traditional Navajo dwelling, made of logs and mud.

Rhyme The exact and slant rhymes in the last stanza link ideas and create a musicality that reinforces the optimistic tone of the poem.

Independent Practice

About the Text Cornelius Eady (b. 1954) listened to a lot of jazz, blues, and gospel music during his childhood in Rochester, New York. These musical traditions frequently inform his poetry. He says that he was inspired to write this poem when he read that "The Twist" dance craze "marked the end of couples holding each other on the dance floor. This started me thinking about how we danced that step where I grew up."

"The Poetic Interpretation of the Twist" by Cornelius Eady

I know what you're expecting to hear.
You think to yourself: Here's a guy who must understand
    what the twist was all about.
Look at the knuckles of his hands,
Look at his plain, blue shirt hanging out of the back
    of his trousers.
5 The twist must have been the equivalent of
    the high sign
In a secret cult.

I know
I know
I know

10 But listen: I am still confused by the mini-skirt
As well as the deep meaning of vinyl on everything.
The twist was just a children's game to us.
I know you expect there ought to be more to this,
The reason the whole world decided to uncouple,

15 But why should I lie to you? Let me pull up a chair
And in as few words as possible,
Re-create my sister,
Who was renowned for running like a giraffe.
Let me re-create my neighborhood,
20 A dead-end street next to the railroad tracks.
Let me re-create
My father, who would escape the house by bicycle
And do all the grocery shopping by himself.

Let's not forget the pool hall and the barbershop,

Figurative Language How does the metaphor in lines 5–6 characterize the twist?

Rhythm and Meter Although this poem is written in free verse, the poet creates a variety of musical rhythms. What is the meter of the repeated line "I know"? How do these lines affect your understanding of the poem's speaker?

Tone What tone do the rhetorical question and the statement "Let me pull up a chair" create?

Language What are the denotation and connotations of the phrase "a dead-end street"?

25 Each with their strange flavors of men,
And while we're on the subject,
I must not slight the ragweed,
The true rose of the street.

All this will still not give you the twist.
30 Forgive me for running on like this.
Your question has set an expectation
That is impossible to meet

Your question has put on my shoulders
A troublesome responsibility

35 Because the twist is gone.
It is the foundation of a bridge
That has made way for a housing project

And I am sorry to admit
You have come to the wrong person.
40 I recall the twist
The way we recall meeting a distant aunt as a baby
Or the afternoons spent in homeroom
Waiting for the last bell.

My head hurts.
45 I am tired of remembering.
Perhaps you can refresh my memory
And tell me
How we got on this topic?
As a favor to me,
50 Let's not talk anymore about old dances.

I have an entire world on the tip of my tongue.

Figurative Language
What is the effect of the metaphor in lines 27–28?

Tone How does the speaker's request for forgiveness contribute to the poem's tone?

Figurative Language
What idea about the twist does this metaphor convey?

Figurative Language
How does the hyperbole in the last line contribute to the poem's message?

About the Text In this poem, Eady contrasts poetic and scientific language, focusing on the concept of *inertia*. In physics, inertia describes the tendency of matter at rest to remain at rest, or, if moving, to keep moving in the same direction unless affected by an outside force.

Tone What tone does the speaker establish in the opening stanza?

"The Empty Dance Shoes" by Cornelius Eady

My friends,
As it has been proven in the laboratory,
An empty pair of dance shoes
Will sit on the floor like a wart
5 Until it is given a reason to move.

Those of us who study inertia
(Those of us covered with wild hair and sleep)
Can state this without fear:
The energy in a pair of shoes at rest
10 Is about the same as that of a clown

Rhythm and Meter Describe the meter of lines 10 and 11 and tell how it reinforces the simile.

Knocked flat by a sandbag.
This you can tell your friends with certainty:
A clown, flat on his back,
Is a lot like an empty pair of
15   dancing shoes.

Sound Devices What effect does the poet achieve by repeating this phrase throughout the poem?

An empty pair of dancing shoes
Is also a lot like a leaf
Pressed in a book.
And now you know a simple truth:
20 A leaf pressed in, say, *The Colossus*
        by Sylvia Plath,[1]
Is no different from an empty pair of dance shoes

Even if those shoes are in the middle of the Stardust Ballroom
With all the lights on, and hot music shakes the windows
25   up and down the block.
This is the secret of inertia:
The shoes run on their own sense of the world.
They are in sympathy with the rock the kid skips
        over the lake

Figurative Language Explain the meaning of the metaphor comparing empty dance shoes with a rock.

30 After it settles to the mud.
Not with the ripples,
But with the rock.

---

1. *The Colossus* by Sylvia Plath volume of poetry by American poet Sylvia Plath (1932–1963).

A practical and personal application of inertia
Can be found in the question:
35 Whose Turn Is It
To Take Out The Garbage?
An empty pair of dance shoes
Is a lot like the answer to this question,
As well as book-length poems
40 Set in the Midwest.

To sum up:
An empty pair of dance shoes
Is a lot like the sand the 98-pound weakling
    brushes from his cheeks
45 As the bully tows away his girlfriend.
Later,

When he spies the coupon at the back of the comic book,
He is about to act upon a different set of scientific principles.
He is ready to dance.

Sound Devices How does alliteration in line 33 contribute to the impact of the line?

Language The poem concludes with an allusion to the well-known 1950s ad campaign for a bodybuilding program. How does this allusion help you interpret the final lines of the poem?

After You Read

The Poetic Interpretation of the Twist • The Empty Dance Shoes

© **1. Key Ideas and Details (a)** In "The Poetic Interpretation of the Twist," what memories does the speaker mention as he tries to remember the dance? **(b) Analyze Cause and Effect:** How is the speaker affected by those memories?

© **2. Key Ideas and Details (a) Connect:** Note three examples the speaker uses to illustrate the principle of inertia. **(b) Compare and Contrast:** How are these examples both similar and different?

© **3. Craft and Structure** Examine the line structure of each poem. How does this structure affect each poem's **rhythm?**

© **4. Craft and Structure** How is the tone of "The Poetic Interpretation of the Twist"

different from the tone of "The Empty Dance Shoes"?

© **5. Integration of Knowledge and Ideas (a)** In the first column of a chart like the one shown, list examples of **figurative language** from "The Empty Dance Shoes" that compare the shoes to other things. In the second column, describe the effect of each example. In the third column, explain the meaning of the shoes in that example.

What It Says	Feeling It Creates	What It Means

(b) Collaboration: Discuss your chart with a partner, and use the feedback to revise your statements.

Leveled Texts

Build your skills and improve your comprehension of poetry with texts of increasing complexity.

The artistic works in **Poetry Collection 1** explore conflicts, choices, and challenges.

In **Poetry Collection 2** each poem shows something—an ancient story, a road, people mowing, a fist—from a fresh perspective.

Common Core State Standards

Meet these standards with either **Poetry Collection 1** (p. 642) or **Poetry Collection 2** (p. 658).

Reading Literature
4. Determine the meaning of words and phrases as they are used in a text, including figurative and connotative meanings; analyze the cumulative impact of specific word choices on meaning and tone. *(Literary Analysis: Spiral Review)*

9. Analyze how an author draws on and transforms source material in a specific work. *(Speaking and Listening: Oral Interpretation)*

Writing
4. Produce clear and coherent writing in which the development, organization, and style are appropriate to task, purpose, and audience. *(Writing: Lyric Poem)*

Speaking and Listening
6. Adapt speech to a variety of contexts and tasks, demonstrating command of formal English when indicated or appropriate. *(Speaking and Listening: Oral Interpretation)*

Language
1.b. Use various types of phrases and clauses to convey specific meanings and add variety and interest to writing or presentations. *(Conventions: Prepositions and Prepositional Phrases)*

4. Determine or clarify the meaning of unknown and multiple-meaning words and phrases based on grades 9–10 reading and content, choosing flexibly from a range of strategies. *(Vocabulary: Word Study)*

Literary Analysis: The Speaker in Poetry

The **speaker** is the voice that says the words of a poem. The speaker may be a character that the poet invents. The speaker may also bear a close resemblance to the poet. However, it is wrong to assume that the poet and the speaker are identical. The speaker is a persona, or an assumed, imagined voice.

- In **narrative poetry,** the speaker tells a story from a particular point of view.
- In **lyric poetry,** the speaker shares thoughts, feelings, and insights to create a single, unified impression.

Most poems employ **imagery,** which is language that appeals to the senses. Likewise, many poems use **figurative language**—words and phrases that create unexpected comparisons or play with meanings.

Reading Skill: Read Fluently

Read aloud to appreciate and share the musical qualities of poetry. As you read aloud, **read fluently**—with expression and understanding. To achieve reading fluency, **adjust your reading rate.**

- First, read the poem slowly and carefully. Make sure that you understand it and that you can pronounce all the words.
- Pay attention to punctuation, and group words for meaning. Do not pause at line ends unless punctuation indicates that you should.
- Slow down to emphasize an idea or the sounds of words.
- Reread the poem. Listen for the **tone,** or emotional attitude, the words create.

Using the Strategy: Reading Rate Chart

To prepare to read aloud, mark a copy of the poem to indicate adjustments to your reading rate. Use a **reading rate chart** like this one:

Mark the Text	Adjust Reading Rate
Circle punctuation marks.	Pause.
Underline words or sounds to emphasize.	Slow down.
Bracket phrases or groups of words to read together.	Speed up.

Does all *communication* serve a positive purpose?

Writing About the Big Question

The poems in Poetry Collection 1 conjure up complicated feelings such as suspense, wonder, and melancholy. Use these sentence starters to develop your ideas about the Big Question.

> One way to **convey** an **emotion** or communicate how you feel about something is to _____. Another method might be _____.

While You Read Notice the different feelings that arise in you as you read these poems.

Vocabulary

Read each word and its definition. Decide whether you know the word well, know it a little bit, or do not know it at all. After you read, see how your knowledge of each word has increased.

- **foreboding** (fôr bōd´ iŋ) *n.* a feeling that something bad will happen (p. 643) *Alone in the spooky house, I was filled with foreboding.* forebode *v.*

- **tumult** (tōō´ mult) *n.* noisy commotion (p. 645) *The tumult from the crowd at the parade in the street below kept me awake for most of the night.* tumultuous *adj.* tumultuously *adv.*

- **monotonously** (mə nät´ 'n əs lē) *adv.* in a dull, unvarying way (p. 649) *The official's boring speech continued monotonously.* monotonous *adj.* monotony *n.*

- **venerable** (ven´ ər ə bəl) *adj.* worthy of respect because of age or character (p. 650) *He asked for the wise advice of his venerable elders.* venerability *n.* venerate *v.*

- **sullen** (sul´ ən) *adj.* gloomy and showing resentment (p. 651) *The children were sullen when they had to leave the playground.* sullenly *adv.* sullenness *n.*

- **comrade** (käm´ rad´) *n.* a close companion (p. 653) *A soldier and his comrade share many experiences during a battle.* comradeship *n.* comradery *n.*

Word Study

The **Old English prefix *fore-*** means "before," "in front," or "beforehand."

In "The Bridegroom," when a young girl arrives home distraught, her parents are filled with **foreboding,** sensing something bad before it actually happens.

Alexander Pushkin

(1799–1837)

Author of "The Bridegroom" (p. 642)

Alexander Pushkin is considered the father of modern Russian literature. Though a nobleman, he had great sympathy for poor Russian peasants. In literature, too, he was a rebel, drawing on folklore to express his democratic ideas.

Federico García Lorca

(1898–1936)

Author of "The Guitar" (p. 648)

Poet and playwright Federico García Lorca is considered one of the greatest Spanish writers. A native of rural Andalusia, García Lorca wrote many of his poems shortly after World War I.

Elizabeth Bishop

(1911–1979)

Author of "The Fish" (p. 650)

In 1945, Elizabeth Bishop won a poetry contest, leading to the publication of her first poetry collection, *North and South,* which included "The Fish." Her work is noted for its powerful images.

Rudyard Kipling

(1865–1936)

Author of "Danny Deever" (p. 652)

Rudyard Kipling was born in India to English parents. He worked as a journalist in India, eventually moving to England. In 1907, he was awarded the Nobel Prize in Literature.

The Bridegroom

Alexander Pushkin *translated by D. M. Thomas*

The Lights of Marriage (detail), Marc Chagall, Kunsthaus, Zurich. © 1998 Artists Rights Society (ARS), New York/ADAGP, Paris.

Critical Viewing
Which details in this painting suggest that a single marriage is significant to the whole world? **[Interpret]**

Background An **allusion** is a reference to a person, event, place, or artistic work (often, to one that is well known). Pushkin's poem is an extended allusion to a folk tale, "The Robber Bridegroom." From the opening lines, Pushkin's Russian readers would have recognized the story, in which a woman witnesses a horrible crime—and nearly marries the person who committed it.

For three days Natasha,
The merchant's daughter,
Was missing. The third night,
She ran in, distraught.
5   Her father and mother
Plied her with questions.
She did not hear them,
She could hardly breathe.

Stricken with foreboding
10 They pleaded, got angry,
But still she was silent;
At last they gave up.
Natasha's cheeks regained
Their rosy color.
15 And cheerfully again
She sat with her sisters.

Once at the shingle-gate
She sat with her friends
—And a swift troika[1]
20 Flashed by before them;
A handsome young man
Stood driving the horses;
Snow and mud went flying,
Splashing the girls.

25 He gazed as he flew past,
And Natasha gazed.
He flew on. Natasha froze.
Headlong she ran home.
"It was he! It was he!"
30 She cried. "I know it!
I recognized him! Papa,
Mama, save me from him!"

Full of grief and fear,
They shake their heads, sighing.
35 Her father says: "My child,
Tell me everything.
If someone has harmed you,
Tell us . . . even a hint."
She weeps again and
40 Her lips remain sealed.

---

1. **troika** (troi´ kə) *n.* Russian carriage or sleigh drawn by a team of three horses.

Vocabulary
foreboding (fôr bōd´ iŋ)
n. a feeling that something bad will happen

Literary Analysis
The Speaker in Poetry
Which details in this stanza does the speaker use to tell a story?

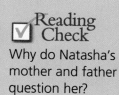
Reading Check
Why do Natasha's mother and father question her?

The next morning, the old
Matchmaking woman
Unexpectedly calls and
Sings the girl's praises;
45 Says to the father: "You
Have the goods and I
A buyer for them:
A handsome young man.

"He bows low to no one,
50 He lives like a lord
With no debts nor worries;
He's rich and he's generous,
Says he will give his bride,
On their wedding-day,
55 A fox-fur coat, a pearl,
Gold rings, brocaded[2] dresses,

"Yesterday, out driving,
He saw your Natasha;
Shall we shake hands
60 And get her to church?"
The woman starts to eat
A pie, and talks in riddles,
While the poor girl
Does not know where to look.

65 "Agreed," says her father;
"Go in happiness
To the altar, Natasha;
It's dull for you here;
A swallow should not spend
70 All its time singing,
It's time for you to build
A nest for your children."

Natasha leaned against
The wall and tried
75 To speak—but found herself
Sobbing; she was shuddering
And laughing. The matchmaker
Poured out a cup of water,
Gave her some to drink,
80 Splashed some in her face.

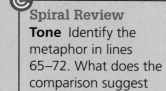
2. **brocaded** (brō kād′ əd) *adj.* with raised designs woven into the cloth.

Her parents are distressed.
Then Natasha recovered,
And calmly she said:
"Your will be done. Call
85 My bridegroom to the feast,
Bake loaves for the whole world,
Brew sweet mead[3] and call
The law to the feast."

"Of course, Natasha, angel!
90 You know we'd give our lives
To make you happy!"
They bake and they brew;
The worthy guests come,
The bride is led to the feast,
95 Her maids sing and weep;
Then horses and a sledge[4]

With the groom—and all sit.
The glasses ring and clatter,
The toasting-cup is passed
100 From hand to hand in tumult,
The guests are drunk.

BRIDEGROOM
"Friends, why is my fair bride
Sad, why is she not
Feasting and serving?"

105 The bride answers the groom:
"I will tell you why
As best I can. My soul
Knows no rest, day and night
I weep; an evil dream
110 Oppresses me." Her father
Says: "My dear child, tell us
What your dream is."

"I dreamed," she says, "that I
Went into a forest,
115 It was late and dark;

---

3. **mead** (mēd) *n.* drink made of fermented honey and water.
4. **sledge** (slej) *n.* sleigh.

Vocabulary
tumult (tōō´ mult) *n.*
noisy commotion

The Fiances, Marc Chagall, Giraudon / Art Resource, NY/ © Artists Rights Society (ARS), New York

Reading Check
What plans does Natasha's father make for her?

The moon was faintly
Shining behind a cloud;
I strayed from the path;
Nothing stirred except
120 The tops of the pine-trees.

"And suddenly, as if
I was awake, I saw
A hut. I approach the hut
And knock at the door
125 —Silence. A prayer on my lips
I open the door and enter.
A candle burns. All
Is silver and gold."

BRIDEGROOM
"What is bad about that?
130 It promises wealth."

BRIDE
"Wait, sir, I've not finished.
Silently I gazed
On the silver and gold,
The cloths, the rugs, the silks
135 From Novgorod,[5] and I
Was lost in wonder.

"Then I heard a shout
And a clatter of hoofs . . .
Someone has driven up
140 To the porch. Quickly
I slammed the door and hid
Behind the stove. Now
I hear many voices . . .
Twelve young men come in,

145 "And with them is a girl,
Pure and beautiful.
They've taken no notice
Of the ikons,[6] they sit
To the table without
150 Praying or taking off

The Fiancée with a Fan, 1911, Marc Chagall, Banque d'Images, ADAGP / Art Resource, NY/ © Artists Rights Society (ARS), New York

▲ Critical Viewing
What traits does this young woman seem to share with Natasha? Explain which details in the painting support your answer. [Interpret]

5. **Novgorod** (näv´ gə räd´) city in northwestern Russia.
6. **ikons** (ī´ känz´) *n.* sacred religious images.

Their hats. At the head,
The eldest brother,
At his right, the youngest;
At his left, the girl.
155 Shouts, laughs, drunken clamor . . . "

BRIDEGROOM
"That betokens merriment."

BRIDE
"Wait, sir, I've not finished.
The drunken din goes on
And grows louder still.
160 Only the girl is sad.

"She sits silent, neither
Eating nor drinking;
But sheds tears in plenty;
The eldest brother
165 Takes his knife and, whistling,
Sharpens it; seizing her by
The hair he kills her
And cuts off her right hand."

"Why," says the groom, "this
170 Is nonsense! Believe me,
My love, your dream is not evil."
She looks him in the eyes.
"And from whose hand
Does this ring come?"
175 The bride said. The whole throng
Rose in the silence.

With a clatter the ring
Falls, and rolls along
The floor. The groom blanches,
180 Trembles. Confusion . . .
"Seize him!" the law commands.
He's bound, judged, put to death.
Natasha is famous!
Our song at an end.

Literary Analysis
The Speaker in Poetry
What details help the bride's narrative grow in excitement?

The Old Guitarist, 1903, Pablo Picasso. The Art Institute of Chicago. ©2004 Estate of Pablo Picasso/Artists Rights Society (ARS), New York.

▲ **Critical Viewing** How does the man's pose add to the sad mood of this image? **[Analyze]**

The GUITAR

Federico García Lorca
translated by Elizabeth du Gué Trapier

Now begins the cry
Of the guitar,
Breaking the vaults
Of dawn.
5 Now begins the cry
Of the guitar.
Useless
To still it.
Impossible
10 To still it.
It weeps monotonously
As weeps the water,
As weeps the wind
Over snow.
15 Impossible
To still it.
It weeps
For distant things,
Warm southern sands
20 Desiring white camellias.
It mourns the arrow without a target,
The evening without morning.
And the first bird dead
Upon a branch.
25 O guitar!
A wounded heart,
Wounded by five swords.

Vocabulary
monotonously (mə nät´ 'n əs lē) *adv.* in a dull, unvarying way

Literary Analysis
The Speaker in Poetry
What feelings do the speaker's use of images in lines 19–24 convey?

The Fish

Elizabeth Bishop

Vocabulary
venerable (ven´ ər
ə bəl) *adj.* worthy
of respect because
of age or character

I caught a tremendous fish
and held him beside the boat
half out of water, with my hook
fast in a corner of his mouth.
5   He didn't fight.
He hadn't fought at all.
He hung a grunting weight,
battered and venerable
and homely. Here and there
10 his brown skin hung in strips
like ancient wallpaper,
and its pattern of darker brown
was like wallpaper:
shapes like full-blown roses
15 stained and lost through age.
He was speckled with barnacles,
fine rosettes of lime,
and infested
with tiny white sea-lice,
20 and underneath two or three
rags of green weed hung down.
While his gills were breathing in
the terrible oxygen
—the frightening gills,
25 fresh and crisp with blood,
that can cut so badly—
I thought of the coarse white flesh
packed in like feathers,
the big bones and the little bones,
30 the dramatic reds and blacks
of his shiny entrails,
and the pink swim-bladder
like a big peony.
I looked into his eyes
35 which were far larger than mine
but shallower, and yellowed,
the irises backed and packed
with tarnished tinfoil

Reading Skill
Read Fluently
Identify the pauses
signaled by punctua-
tion marks in lines
34–40.

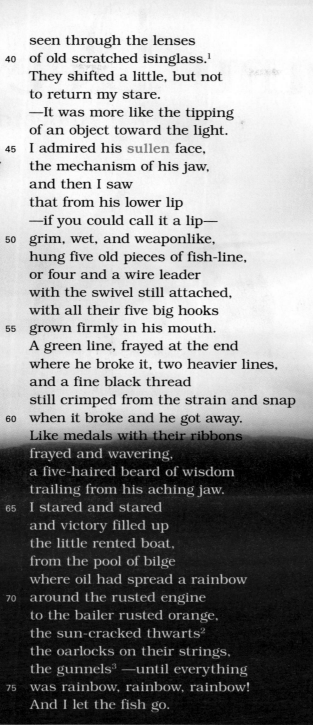

seen through the lenses
40 of old scratched isinglass.[1]
They shifted a little, but not
to return my stare.
—It was more like the tipping
of an object toward the light.
45 I admired his sullen face,
the mechanism of his jaw,
and then I saw
that from his lower lip
—if you could call it a lip—
50 grim, wet, and weaponlike,
hung five old pieces of fish-line,
or four and a wire leader
with the swivel still attached,
with all their five big hooks
55 grown firmly in his mouth.
A green line, frayed at the end
where he broke it, two heavier lines,
and a fine black thread
still crimped from the strain and snap
60 when it broke and he got away.
Like medals with their ribbons
frayed and wavering,
a five-haired beard of wisdom
trailing from his aching jaw.
65 I stared and stared
and victory filled up
the little rented boat,
from the pool of bilge
where oil had spread a rainbow
70 around the rusted engine
to the bailer rusted orange,
the sun-cracked thwarts[2]
the oarlocks on their strings,
the gunnels[3] —until everything
75 was rainbow, rainbow, rainbow!
And I let the fish go.

Vocabulary
sullen (sul´ ən) *adj.*
gloomy and show-
ing resentment

◀ **Critical Viewing**
Does this fish look
like the "vener-
able" old warrior
described in the poem?
Explain. **[Analyze]**

Literary Analysis
The Speaker in Poetry
What details in the
speaker's conclusion pro-
vide a dramatic insight
and a surprising action?

---

1. **isinglass** (i´ zin glas´) *n.* transparent material once used in windows.
2. **thwarts** (*th*wôrtz) *n.* seats in a boat for rowers.
3. **gunnels** (gun´ əlz) *n.* upper edges of the sides of a ship or boat.

Danny Deever

Rudyard Kipling

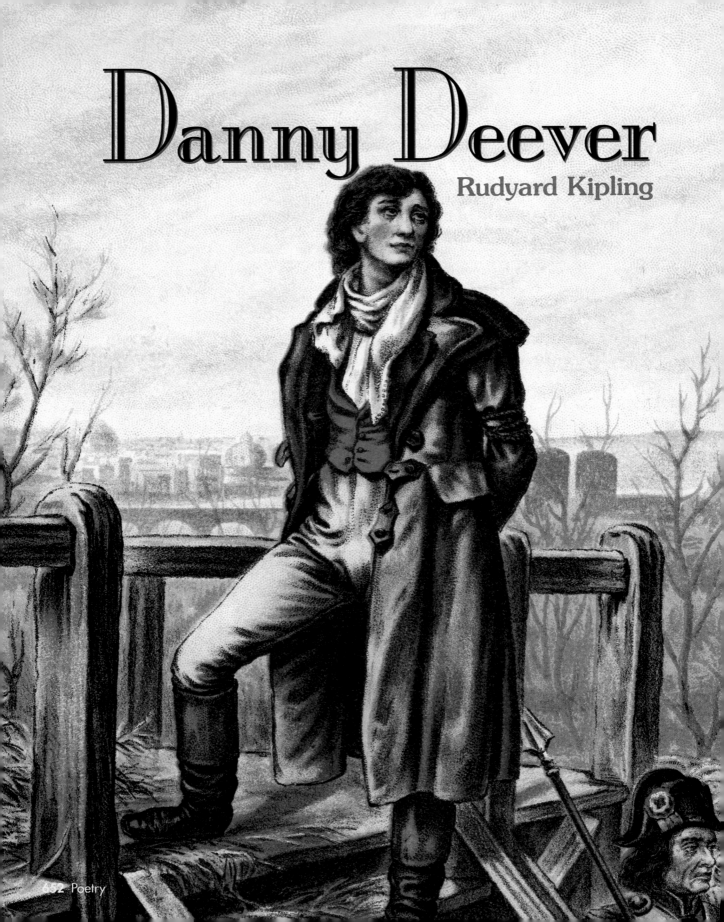

Background In this poem, Kipling writes in **dialect,** a distinct form of a language, spoken by people living in a particular region or belonging to a particular group. The characters' dialect reflects their working-class British origins.

"What are the bugles blowin' for?" said Files-on-Parade.[1]
"To turn you out, to turn you out," the Color-Sergeant[2] said.
"What makes you look so white, so white?" said Files-on-
  Parade.
"I'm dreadin' what I've got to watch," the Color-Sergeant said.
5   For they're hangin' Danny Deever, you can hear the Dead
       March play,
     The regiment's in 'ollow square[3] —they're hangin' him
       today;
     They've taken of his buttons off an' cut his stripes away,
     An' they're hangin' Danny Deever in the mornin'.

"What makes the rear-rank breathe so 'ard?" said Files-on-
   Parade.
10 "It's bitter cold, it's bitter cold," the Color-Sergeant said.
"What makes that front-rank man fall down?" says Files-on-
   Parade.
"A touch o' sun, a touch o' sun," the Color-Sergeant said.
     They are hangin' Danny Deever, they are marchin' of 'im
       round,
     They 'ave 'alted Danny Deever by 'is coffin on the ground;
15   An' 'e'll swing in 'arf a minute for a sneakin' shootin'
       hound—
     O they're hangin' Danny Deever in the mornin'!

"'Is cot was right-'and cot to mine," said Files-on-Parade.
"'E's sleepin' out an' far tonight," the Color-Sergeant said.
"I've drunk 'is beer a score o' times," said Files-on-Parade.
20 "'E's drinkin' bitter beer alone," the Color-Sergeant said.
     They are hangin' Danny Deever, you must mark 'im to
       'is place,
     For 'e shot a comrade sleepin'—you must look 'im in the face;
     Nine 'undred of 'is county an' the regiment's disgrace,
     While they're hangin' Danny Deever in the mornin'.

---

1. **Files-on-Parade** soldier who directs marching formations.
2. **Color-Sergeant** flag-bearer.
3. **'ollow square** At a hanging, soldiers standing in ranks form three sides of a square; the gallows occupies the fourth side.

Reading Skill
Read Fluently How should the punctuation in lines 13–16 affect your reading rate and pace?

Vocabulary
comrade (käm´ rad´)
n. a close companion

25 "What's that so black agin the sun?" said Files-on-Parade.
"It's Danny fightin' 'ard for life," the Color-Sergeant said.
"What's that that whimpers over'ead?" said Files-on-Parade.
It's Danny's soul that's passin' now," the Color-Sergeant said.
   For they're done with Danny Deever, you can 'ear the
      quick-step play,
30   The regiment's in column, an' they're marchin' us away;
   Ho! the young recruits are shakin', an' they'll want their
      beer to-day,
   After hangin' Danny Deever in the mornin'.

Critical Thinking

1. **Key Ideas and Details (a)** In "The Bridegroom," how does Natasha react during the matchmaker's visit? **(b)** Explain what her "dream" reveals about the reasons for her reaction.

2. **Craft and Structure (a)** At the end of "The Guitar," to what does the speaker compare the guitar? **(b)** What are the "five swords" that "wound" the guitar? **(c)** Explain the meaning of the figurative language in the last two lines of the poem.

3. **Key Ideas and Details (a)** What decision does the speaker of "The Fish" make at the end of the poem? **(b)** What realization about the fish motivates this decision? Support your answer with details.

4. **Key Ideas and Details (a)** Who are the two characters who speak in "Danny Deever"? **(b)** How are these two characters different?

5. **Integration of Knowledge and Ideas** Choose one of the poems and describe the emotions it conveys. Would you say the poem serves a positive purpose? Explain. *[Connect to the Big Question: Does all communication serve a positive purpose?]*

Literary Analysis: The Speaker in Poetry

© 1. Craft and Structure What do you think is the best example of **narrative poetry** in Poetry Collection 1? Explain why.

© 2. Craft and Structure On a chart like the one shown, give an example of visual imagery—one that appeals to the sense of sight. Quote details that develop the imagery. Then, note their effect.

Image	Sensory Language	Effect

© 3. Craft and Structure Compare the speakers in "The Guitar" and "The Fish." In your response, consider whether the speaker is a character in a story or another type of persona. In addition, compare the emotional attitudes the speakers express.

Reading Skill: Read Fluently

4. Choose one of the poems and identify two points at which you chose to **adjust your reading rate**. Explain your reasoning, citing details from the poem as support.

Vocabulary

© Acquisition and Use For each item, write a sentence about the situation described. In each sentence, use a word from the vocabulary list for Poetry Collection 1, on page 640.

1. a visit with an elderly, much-admired jazz drummer

2. a terrible feeling about whether you lost something important

3. a dripping faucet

4. a loud and crowded city council meeting

5. a camping trip with a close friend

6. a rainy day causes someone to feel gloomy and sad

Word Study Use the context of the sentences and what you know about the **Old English prefix fore-** to explain your answers.

1. Why should you check the weather *forecast* before going outside?

2. Would you *forewarn* a friend if you thought he was in danger?

Word Study

The **Old English prefix *fore-*** means "before," "in front," or "beforehand."

Apply It Explain how the prefix *fore-* contributes to the meanings of these words. Consult a dictionary if necessary.

forerunner
foreshadow
foretell

Does all *communication* serve a positive purpose?

Writing About the Big Question

In Poetry Collection 2, the speakers in the poems communicate unusual perspectives about a variety of things, many of them found in nature. Use this sentence starter to develop your ideas about the Big Question.

Looking at a familiar object or situation in a different way can give it a new **meaning** because _____.

While You Read As you read these poems, look for items, stories, or people that change in surprising ways.

Vocabulary

Read each word and its definition. Decide whether you know the word well, know it a little bit, or do not know it at all. After you read, see how your knowledge of each word has increased.

- **idle** (īd´ 'l) *adj.* useless; not busy (p. 658) *Idle hands are not help- ing hands.* idle *v.* idleness *n.* idly *adv.*

- **earnest** (ur´ nist) *adj.* serious and intense; not joking (p. 658) *The earnest effort of the farmer saved the crops from the drought.* earnestly *adv.* earnestness *n.*

- **rejoiced** (ri joist´) *v.* showed happiness (p. 661) *The team members rejoiced when they won the tournament.* rejoicingly *adv.* joy *n.*

- **anguish** (aŋ´ gwish) *n.* extreme suffering, as from grief or pain (p. 662) *Her anguish at the funeral was obvious.* anguish *v.* anguished *adj.*

- **clenching** (klench´ iŋ) *v.* closing or holding tightly (p. 664) *The child was clenching her fist in anger.* clench *n.* clenched *adj.*

- **stark** (stärk) *adj.* bare; harsh (p. 666) *The stark room contained only a table and chair.* starkly *adv.* starkness *n.*

Word Study

The **Latin prefix re-** means "again" or "anew."

In "A Tree Telling of Orpheus," a tree **rejoiced**, or experi- enced new happiness, when it heard Orpheus' music.

Robert Frost

(1874–1963)

Author of "Mowing" (p. 658)

Robert Frost worked as a farmer, an editor, and a schoolteacher, absorbing the ebb and flow of New England life. He went on to become one of America's most successful poets, winning many awards, including four Pulitzer Prizes.

Denise Levertov

(1923–1997)

Author of "A Tree Telling of Orpheus" (p. 659)

When Denise Levertov moved to the United States from England in 1948, she became associated with an experimental community of writers. She said that the freewheeling "open forms" she used allowed her to "explore chaos."

Naomi Shihab Nye

(b. 1952)

Author of "Making a Fist" (p. 664)

Naomi Shihab Nye began publishing poetry in magazines when she was in high school. Her poetry often draws inspiration from the places where she has lived—St. Louis, Missouri, and Jerusalem, in Israel, as well as her current home, San Antonio, Texas.

William Carlos Williams

(1883–1963)

Author of "Spring and All" (p. 665)

William Carlos Williams was both a doctor and a poet. When asked how he managed his double career, he replied that he treated his patients like poems and his poems like patients. Williams also said that a poet should listen "to the language of his locality."

Mowing

ROBERT FROST

▶ **Critical Viewing**
Which word in the poem names one of the tools shown in the painting? Explain how you know. **[Integrate Vocabulary]**

Background A **dialect** is the distinct form of a language spoken by people in a particular region or group. The speaker of this poem uses New England dialect words such as *swale,* referring to a marshland, and *make,* referring to the process of drying out hay. He also uses the outdated word *fay,* meaning "fairy" or "elf." Through these words, Frost creates a speaker who is a man of the land, a traditional New England farmer.

There was never a sound beside the wood but one,
And that was my long scythe whispering to the ground.
What was it it whispered? I knew not well myself;
Perhaps it was something about the heat of the sun,

5   Something, perhaps, about the lack of sound—
And that was why it whispered and did not speak.
It was no dream of the gift of idle hours,
Or easy gold at the hand of fay or elf:
Anything more than the truth would have seemed too weak

10   To the earnest love that laid the swale in rows,
Not without feeble-pointed spikes of flowers
(Pale orchises), and scared a bright green snake.
The fact is the sweetest dream that labor knows.
My long scythe whispered and left the hay to make.

Vocabulary
idle (īd´ 'l) *adj.* useless; not busy

earnest (ʉr´ nist) *adj.* serious and intense; not joking

A Tree Telling of Orpheus

Denise Levertov

Background An **allusion** is a reference to a person, event, place, or artistic work. Levertov's poem is an extended allusion to the classic Greek myth of Orpheus. Orpheus' skill on the lyre, an ancient stringed instrument, was so great and his voice so beautiful that trees were said to uproot themselves to follow him. In the end, he was torn limb from limb by his frenzied followers, the Maenads (mē′ nadz ´). Flung into a nearby river, his head was said to continue singing as it floated downstream.

White dawn. Stillness.   When the rippling began
    I took it for sea-wind, coming to our valley with rumors
    of salt, of treeless horizons. But the white fog
didn't stir; the leaves of my brothers remained outstretched,
5 unmoving.
          Yet the rippling drew nearer—and then
my own outermost branches began to tingle, almost as if
fire had been lit below them, too close, and their twig-tips
were drying and curling.
10   Yet I was not afraid, only
          deeply alert.

> **Literary Analysis**
> **The Speaker in Poetry**
> What clue to the speaker's identity appears in line 4?

A Tree Telling of Orpheus **659**

I was the first to see him, for I grew
                    out on the pasture slope, beyond the forest.
He was a man, it seemed: the two
15 moving stems, the short trunk, the two
arm-branches, flexible, each with five leafless
                              twigs at their ends,
and the head that's crowned by brown or gold grass,
bearing a face not like the beaked face of a bird,
20   more like a flower's.
                              He carried a burden made of
some cut branch bent while it was green,
strands of a vine tight-stretched across it. From this,
when he touched it, and from his voice
25 which unlike the wind's voice had no need of our
leaves and branches to complete its sound,
                              came the ripple,
But it was now no longer a ripple (he had come near and
stopped in my first shadow) it was a wave that bathed me
30   as if rain
                         rose from below and around me
                    instead of falling.
And what I felt was no longer a dry tingling:

        I seemed to be singing as he sang, I seemed to know
35   what the lark knows; all my sap
                was mounting towards the sun that by now
                    had risen, the mist was rising, the grass
was drying, yet my roots felt music moisten them
deep under earth.
40   He came still closer, leaned on my trunk:
                the bark thrilled like a leaf still-folded.
Music! There was no twig of me not
                              trembling with joy and fear.

Then as he sang
45 it was no longer sounds only that made the music:
he spoke, and as no tree listens I listened, and language
                    came into my roots
                              out of the earth,
                    into my bark
50   out of the air,
                    into the pores of my greenest shoots
                         gently as dew

Literary Analysis
The Speaker in Poetry
What do lines 14–20
tell you about the
speaker who provides
the description?

▼ **Critical Viewing**
This ancient Greek
vessel depicts Orpheus.
Which details match
the picture of Orpheus
you form as you read
the poem? Which
do not? **[Compare
and Contrast]**

and there was no word he sang but I knew its meaning.
He told of journeys,
55   of where sun and moon go while we stand in dark,
       of an earth-journey he dreamed he would take some day
deeper than roots . . .
He told of the dreams of man, wars, passions, griefs,
       and I, a tree, understood words—ah, it seemed
60 my thick bark would split like a sapling's that
                         grew too fast in the spring
when a late frost wounds it.

<!-- vocabulary sidebar -->

Vocabulary
rejoiced (ri joist´) *v.*
showed happiness

                              Fire he sang,
that trees fear, and I, a tree, rejoiced in its flames.
65 New buds broke forth from me though it was full summer.
     As though his lyre (now I knew its name)
      were both frost and fire, its chords flamed
up to the crown of me.
           I was seed again.
70   I was fern in the swamp.
                I was coal.

And at the heart of my wood
(so close I was to becoming man or a god)
     there was a kind of silence, a kind of sickness,
75   something akin to what men call boredom,
                    something

(the poem descended a scale, a stream over stones)
            that gives to a candle a coldness
               in the midst of its burning, he said.

80 It was then,
        when in the blaze of his power that
                  reached me and changed me
       I thought I should fall my length,
that the singer began
85   to leave me.   Slowly
        moved from my noon shadow
                   to open light,
words leaping and dancing over his shoulders
back to me
90   rivery sweep of lyre-tones becoming

Reading Check

What does Orpheus
do to cause the tree to
respond so powerfully to
him?

Literary Analysis
The Speaker in Poetry
Why might lines 85–92
be said to have a lyrical
quality?

Vocabulary
anguish (aṇˊ gwish) *n.*
extreme suffering, as
from grief or pain

slowly again
               ripple.
And I
      in terror
95   but not in doubt of
                   what I must do
in anguish, in haste,
             wrenched from the earth root after root,
the soil heaving and cracking, the moss tearing asunder—
100 and behind me the others: my brothers
forgotten since dawn. In the forest
they too had heard,
and were pulling their roots in pain
out of a thousand years' layers of dead leaves,
105   rolling the rocks away,
                breaking themselves
                      out of
                   their depths.
You would have thought we would lose the sound of the lyre,
110   of the singing
so dreadful the storm-sounds were, where there was no storm,
         no wind but the rush of our
       branches moving, our trunks breasting the air.
        But the music!
115   The music reached us.

Clumsily,
       stumbling over our own roots,
            rustling our leaves
              in answer,
120 we moved, we followed.
All day we followed, up hill and down.
          We learned to dance,
for he would stop, where the ground was flat,
         and words he said
125 taught us to leap and to wind in and out
around one another   in figures   the lyre's measure designed.
The singer
       laughed till he wept to see us, he was so glad.
           At sunset
130 we came to this place I stand in, this knoll[1]
with its ancient grove that was bare grass then.
      In the last light of the day his song became
farewell.
      He stilled our longing.

---

1. knoll (nōl) *n.* small hill.

135   He sang our sun-dried roots back into earth,
watered them: all-night rain of music so quiet
                                    we could almost
                    not hear it in the
                                    moonless dark.
140 By dawn he was gone.
                            We have stood here since,
in our new life.
                    We have waited.
                                    He does not return.
145 It is said he made his earth-journey, and lost
what he sought.
                    It is said they felled him
and cut up his limbs for firewood.
                                    And it is said
150 his head still sang and was swept out to sea singing.
Perhaps he will not return.
                            But what we have lived
comes back to us.
                    We see more.
155   We feel, as our rings increase,
something that lifts our branches, that stretches our furthest
                                                    leaf-tips
further.
            The wind, the birds,
160   do not sound poorer but clearer,
recalling our agony, and the way we danced.
The music!

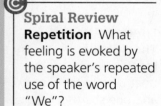

Literary Analysis
The Speaker in
Poetry What key
event does the narra-
tive relate?

Spiral Review
Repetition What
feeling is evoked by
the speaker's repeated
use of the word
"We"?

◄ **Critical Viewing**
How does the tree
pictured here sug-
gest the images in the
poem? **[Analyze]**

Making a Fist

Naomi Shihab Nye

Literary Analysis
The Speaker in Poetry
Identify one detail the poet uses to tell a story and one she uses to present an image or convey a feeling.

For the first time, on the road north of Tampico,[1]
I felt the life sliding out of me,
a drum in the desert, harder and harder to hear.
I was seven, I lay in the car
5   watching palm trees swirl a sickening pattern
       past the glass.
My stomach was a melon split wide inside my skin.

"How do you know if you are going to die?"
I begged my mother.
We had been traveling for days.
10   With strange confidence she answered,
"When you can no longer make a fist."

Years later I smile to think of that journey,
the borders we must cross separately,
stamped with our unanswerable woes.
15   I who did not die, who am still living,
still lying in the backseat behind all my questions,
clenching and opening one small hand.

Vocabulary
clenching (klench´ iŋ) v.
closing or holding tightly

---

1. Tampico (täm pē´ kō) seaport in eastern Mexico.

Spring & All

William Carlos Williams

By the road to the contagious hospital
under the surge of the blue
mottled clouds driven from the
northeast—a cold wind. Beyond, the
5 waste of broad, muddy fields
brown with dried weeds, standing
  and fallen

patches of standing water
the scattering of tall trees

All along the road the reddish
10 purplish, forked, upstanding, twiggy
stuff of bushes and small trees
with dead, brown leaves under them
leafless vines—

Literary Analysis
The Speaker in Poetry
To what senses do the
images in these stanzas
appeal?

Reading Skill
Read Fluently What
punctuation mark indi-
cates a pause at the end
of the third stanza?

Lifeless in appearance, sluggish
dazed spring approaches—

They enter the new world naked,
cold, uncertain of all
save that they enter. All about them
the cold, familiar wind—

Now the grass, tomorrow
the stiff curl of wildcarrot leaf
One by one objects are defined—
It quickens: clarity, outline of leaf

But now the stark dignity of
entrance—Still, the profound change
has come upon them: rooted, they
grip down and begin to awaken

15

20

25

Vocabulary
stark (stärk) *adj.*
bare; harsh

Critical Thinking

Cite textual evidence to support your responses.

© **1. Key Ideas and Details** **(a)** What is the speaker doing in "Mowing"? **(b)** What does he imply about accomplishing a task when he says, "The fact is the sweetest dream that labor knows"?

© **2. Key Ideas and Details** **(a)** In "A Tree Telling of Orpheus," how do the trees respond when Orpheus begins to leave them? **(b) Analyze:** Why do they react this way?

© **3. Key Ideas and Details** **(a)** At the end of "Making a Fist," in what sense is the speaker still a child? **(b)** What are the borders that she says we "must cross separately"? Explain the meaning of this figurative language.

© **4. Key Ideas and Details** **(a)** List three details of the landscape in "Spring and All." **(b) Synthesize:** What is the general quality of the landscape?

© **5. Integration of Knowledge and Ideas** **(a)** Choose one of the poems and describe how the poet presents the subject in a unique way. Explain what this fresh perspective adds to your understanding of the subject. **(b)** Would you say the poem serves a positive purpose? Why or why not? *[Connect to the Big Question: Does all communication serve a positive purpose?]*

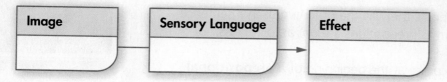

Literary Analysis: The Speaker in Poetry

1. Craft and Structure What do you think is the best example of **narrative poetry** in Poetry Collection 2? Explain why.

2. Craft and Structure On a chart like the one shown, give an example of visual imagery—one that appeals to the sense of sight. Quote details that develop the imagery. Then, note their effect.

Image	Sensory Language	Effect

3. Craft and Structure Compare the **speakers** in "Spring and All" and "Making a Fist." In your response, consider whether the speaker is a character in a story or another type of persona. In addition, compare the emotional attitudes the speakers express.

Reading Skill: Read Fluently

4. Choose one of the poems and identify two points at which you chose to **adjust your reading rate**. Explain your reasoning, citing details from the poem as support.

Vocabulary

Acquisition and Use For each item, write a sentence about the situation described. In each sentence, use a word from the vocabulary list for Poetry Collection 2, on page 656.

1. watching a race while holding something tightly

2. getting a cavity filled

3. a prison cell

4. waiting for the bus with nothing to do

5. receiving news that creates great happiness

6. delivering an important and serious speech

Word Study Use the context of the sentences and what you know about the **Latin prefix re-** to explain your answer to each question.

1. If you *recount* a story, are you telling it for the first time?

2. When someone is thirsty, should you *replenish* his or her glass?

Word Study

The **Latin prefix re-** means "again" or "anew."

Apply It Explain how the prefix re- contributes to the meanings of these words. Consult a dictionary if necessary.

reaccustom

reassurance

rejuvenate

Integrated Language Skills

Poetry Collections 1 and 2

Poetry Collection 1

Conventions:
Prepositions and Prepositional Phrases

A **preposition** is a word that relates the noun or pronoun that appears with it to another word in the sentence.

The choice of preposition affects the way the other words in a sentence relate to one another. Common prepositions are *on, at, of, across, to, under,* and *with.*

In English, a preposition comes at the beginning of a **prepositional phrase.** This is a group of words that includes a preposition and a noun or pronoun, which is called the **object of the preposition.**

In each of these examples, the preposition is underlined and the object of the preposition is in boldface.

Poetry Collection 2

Examples:

<u>on</u> the **couch**	<u>under</u> the **couch**	<u>beside</u> the **couch**
<u>in</u> the **backpack**	<u>near</u> the **backpack**	<u>behind</u> the **backpack**
<u>in</u> my **lifetime**	<u>after</u> the **rainstorm**	<u>before</u> the **party**

Practice A Write each of the following sentences, underlining the prepositions and circling all the objects of the prepositions.

1. The girl hid behind the stove in the house.

2. The guitar sings into the distance.

3. A hook stuck through the fish's lip.

4. The soldiers marched without Danny Deever away from the gallows in the middle of the square.

5. The poem was written by Rudyard Kipling.

Ⓒ **Reading Application** Find two examples of prepositional phrases in Poetry Collection 1. Identify the preposition and the object of the preposition.

Practice B Rewrite the sentence, substituting the numbered prepositions for the preposition *to.* Then, write a brief explanation of how the change in preposition changes the sentence.

Orpheus walks <u>to</u> the trees.

1. away from

2. with

3. behind

4. through

Ⓒ **Writing Application** Write three sentences based on the model below. Use different prepositions and prepositional phrases in each.

Sam showed up in the morning without his coat.

PH **WRITING COACH** | Further instruction and practice are available in *Prentice Hall Writing Coach.*

Writing

Poem Write your own **lyric poem** in response to any of the poems in Poetry Collection 1 or Poetry Collection 2.

- List *figurative language* you find in the poems. Refer to these examples as you create your own poetic style.
- Collect ideas for imagery in a chart with columns labeled *sight, hearing, taste, touch,* and *smell.*
- Remember your purpose. Review your draft to ensure that your writing communicates an emotion. Note ideas in your poem that might be clarified by the use of an allusion to another classic or contemporary work, and add an allusion to the original poem if appropriate.
- Read your draft aloud to a partner, and ask whether any ideas are unclear. Use your partner's answers to guide you in revising your poem.

Grammar Application If you have included prepositional phrases in your poem, make sure the prepositions accurately convey your ideas.

Writing Workshop: *Work in Progress*

Prewriting for Descriptive Essay For a descriptive essay you might write, fold a piece of paper into three columns: label one *spatial organization,* one *chronological organization,* and one *casual organization.* In each column, note two things, events, or actions that could be described using the given structure. Put this Organization Chart in your portfolio.

Speaking and Listening

 Comprehension and Collaboration Present an **oral interpretation** of the Pushkin poem or Levertov poem that you read. First, reread the background notes on pages 642 and 659. Then, go online or use library resources to find and study the source material upon which the poet based his or her poem. Write an introduction in which you analyze how the author uses the source material to create a new work. Answer these questions in your introduction:

- Which elements from the source material appear in the newer work?
- Which elements from the source material have been changed in the newer work?
- Do the source material and the newer work share a common theme?

After you have written your introduction, prepare your oral interpretation. Practice reading the poem aloud with fluency, making sure to pay attention to the punctuation marks within the poem. As you practice, ensure your reading conveys the poem's emotion and main idea. After your presentation, lead a group discussion about whether the dialect helps create a believable speaker.

 **Common Core State Standards**

L.9-10.1.b; W.9-10.4; RL.9-10.9; SL.9-10.6
[For the full wording of the standards, see page 638.]

Use this prewriting activity to prepare for the **Writing Workshop** on page 708.

www.PHLitOnline.com
- Interactive graphic organizers
- Grammar tutorial
- Interactive journals

ⓒ Leveled Texts

Build your skills and improve your comprehension of poetry with texts of increasing complexity.

The poems in **Poetry Collection 3** include vivid images of landscapes, both real and imagined.

In **Poetry Collection 4,** the speaker of each poem shares insight gained in moments of solitary reflection.

ⓒ Common Core State Standards

Meet these standards with either **Poetry Collection 3** (p. 676) or **Poetry Collection 4** (p. 684).

Reading Literature
5. Analyze how an author's choices concerning how to structure a text, order events within it, and manipulate time create such effects as mystery, tension, or surprise. *(Literary Analysis: Poetic Forms)*

Spiral Review: RL.9-10.4

Writing
4. Produce clear and coherent writing in which the development, organization, and style are appropriate to task, purpose, and audience. *(Writing: Tanka)*

Speaking and Listening
1. Initiate and participate effectively in a range of collaborative discussions with diverse partners. *(Speaking and Listening: Poetry Reading Discussion)*

Language
1. Demonstrate command of the conventions of standard English grammar and usage when writing or speaking. *(Conventions: Direct Objects)*

6. Acquire and use accurately general academic and domain-specific words and phrases. *(Vocabulary: Word Study)*

Literary Analysis: Poetic Forms

To unify sounds and ideas in a poem, a poet may follow a **poetic form,** or defined structure. Each poetic form uses a set number of lines and a distinctive **meter** and pattern of **rhymes.** (For more on these elements, see pp. 630–631.) The following are some traditional poetic forms.

Tanka is a five-line, unrhymed Japanese form.

- The first and third lines of tanka contain five syllables. The second, fourth, and fifth lines have seven syllables. (The number of syllables can vary when a tanka is translated into English.) Thus, the syllable pattern is 5-7-5-7-7.

  Example:
The flowing river	(5)
Twists and turns and runs away	(7)
Thinking of the sea	(5)
Through the forests light and dark	(7)
At last kissing salty waves.	(7)

- The author's choice of form is related to the effect that he or she wishes to create. The tanka's brief and concise structure, for example, helps the poet express a strong feeling, a powerful thought, or a focused image or idea. In the above example, the poet concentrates on a river's journey through varied landscapes as it flows toward and empties into the ocean.

A **sonnet** is a fourteen-line form with a specific line count, rhyme scheme, and rhythmic pattern. In a **Shakespearean sonnet,** the lines are grouped into three **quatrains** (groups of four lines) and a **couplet,** a pair of rhymed lines. The rhyme scheme is *abab, cdcd, efef, gg.* This form is so common in English poetry and was so identified with William Shakespeare and the time period during which he lived that these sonnets are also called *English sonnets* or *Elizabethan sonnets.*

- In a Shakespearean sonnet, the first quatrain introduces a situation or a topic to be considered, identifies a problem, or presents a question.

- The second and third quatrains develop the issue introduced in the first quatrain.

- Often, at the beginning of the third quatrain or in the couplet, the writer presents a turning point in which the situation is explained, the problem is solved, or the question is answered.

- The couplet often provides a final commentary on or summary of the ideas explored in the first twelve lines.

PHLit Online!
www.PHLitOnline.com

Hear It!
- Selection summary audio
- Selection audio

See It!
- Get Connected video
- Background video
- More about the author
- Vocabulary flashcards

Do It!
- Interactive journals
- Interactive graphic organizers
- Self-test
- Internet activity
- Grammar tutorial
- Interactive vocabulary games

Literary Analysis: Poetic Forms (continued)

- Beyond their specific rhyme scheme and formula for content, sonnets also follow a strict rhythmic pattern called *iambic pentameter*. An *iamb* is a poetic foot with one unstressed syllable followed by a stressed syllable, as in the word *again. Pentameter* is verse written in five-foot lines. In a sonnet, each line contains five unaccented and five accented syllables in a pattern like this: "da-DUM, da-DUM, da-DUM, da-DUM, da-DUM."

Another common sonnet form is known as the **Italian sonnet,** or the **Petrarchan sonnet,** named for the Italian poet Petrarch, who lived from 1304 to 1374. In this format, the sonnet's fourteen lines are split into an *octet*, or a group of eight lines, and a *sestet*, or a group of six lines. The octet follows a set rhyme scheme of *abba abba,* but the sestet may vary in its rhyme scheme. For example, it might have a pattern of *cdecde,* or *ccddee,* or *cddcdd.*

A **villanelle** is a nineteen-line form with a pattern of repeated lines and a specific rhyme scheme.

- The lines of a villanelle are grouped into five three-line stanzas and one four-line stanza. The lines rhyme *aba, aba, aba, aba, aba, abaa.*
- Line 1 is repeated in lines 6, 12, and 18. Line 3 is repeated in lines 9, 15, and 19.
- This deliberate repetition can create a chanting effect—such as "I wake to sleep, and take my waking slow" in "The Waking"—or suggest intense passion.

Using the Strategy: Analyze Poetic Form Chart

Use a **Poetic Form Chart** like the one shown to analyze poetic forms as you read.

Analyzing the Form of a Poem			
Number of lines?	Number of syllables in each line?	Pattern of accented and unaccented syllables in each line?	Which lines rhyme?

Reading Skill: Read Fluently

When you **read fluently,** you read smoothly and with understanding, placing emphasis appropriately and pausing where necessary. To increase your fluency when reading a poem, **preview** the work, looking over the text in advance.

- Use footnotes and other text aids to learn unfamiliar words. Practice saying each unfamiliar word by following the pronunciation given, and learn each word's definition. Pay special attention to which syllables are accented.

- Determine where each sentence in the poem begins and ends. If you notice that a sentence stretches over more than one line, prepare to read it "through" the end of each line, pausing only when the punctuation indicates you should. Try not to stop at the end of a line if there is no punctuation there. Refer to the chart below for the type of pause associated with common marks.

Punctuation	Type of Pause
. Period	Full stop
: Colon	Almost as strong as a period. End with your voice raised just enough so that a listener knows to expect more.
; Semicolon	Less strong than a colon. Pause briefly, with your voice raised.
, Comma	A slight pause

- Form a rough idea of the *topic* and *mood* of the work. A quick look at the type of words and images used in the poem may show you whether the mood of the poem is sad or happy, serious or humorous. For example, a poem about a robin that "chirps" on a "sunny" day is probably a happy poem.

- Read the poem with its *mood* in mind. You might change the *tone of your voice*, whispering or speaking loudly. You may read at a quicker pace if the action is exciting, or at a slower pace if the mood is suspenseful.

Does all *communication* serve a positive purpose?

Writing About the Big Question

In Poetry Collection 3, the authors present their messages using images from a variety of landscapes. Use these sentence starters to develop your ideas about the Big Question:

When people **interact** and **respond** to nature they might feel

_____.

Poets, in particular, might feel a **connection** to nature because

_____.

While You Read Look for different elements of nature as you read these poems. Consider what the poet communicates to you about nature.

Vocabulary

Read each word and its definition. Decide whether you know the word well, know it a little bit, or do not know it at all. After you read, see how your knowledge of each word has increased.

- **threshold** (thresh´ ōld´) *n.* the bottom of a doorway; entrance or a point of beginning (p. 677) *She opened the door and stepped across the threshold.*

- **keenest** (kēn´ ist) *adj.* sharpest; most cutting (p. 677) *The keenest disappointment was losing the last game.* *keen adj. keenly adv. keenness n.*

- **clustering** (klus´ tər iŋ) *adj.* gathering; forming in a group (p. 680) *I knew from the clustering wasps that their hive had been disturbed.* *cluster n. cluster v.*

- **lunar** (lōō´ nər) *adj.* of the moon (p. 680) *Neil Armstrong was the first person to set foot on the lunar surface.*

Word Study

The **Latin root -lun-** means "moon."

In the tanka by Minamoto no Toshiyori, the speaker refers to **lunar** shadows, or shadows made by the light of the moon.

James Weldon Johnson

(1871–1938)

Author of "My City" (p. 677)

Born in Jacksonville, Florida, James Weldon Johnson became the first African American allowed to practice law in Florida. Johnson also published a newspaper and was a leader in civil rights work.

Dylan Thomas

(1914–1953)

Author of "Do Not Go Gentle into That Good Night" (p. 679)

Born in Wales, in Great Britain, Dylan Thomas fell in love with words early in life. Poems poured out of him, and by the age of twenty, he had written most of the poems for which he is famous today.

Minamoto no Toshiyori

(1055?–1129?)

Author of "The clustering clouds . . ." (p. 680)

Japanese poet and critic Minamoto no Toshiyori (mi′ nä′ mō′ tō′ nō′ tō′ shē′ yō′ rē′) rebelled against tradition and helped forge a new style. In addition to writing poetry, Toshiyori judged poetry contests.

Ki no Tsurayuki

(ca. 872–945)

Author of "When I went to visit . . ." (p. 680)

Ki no Tsurayuki (kē′ nō tso͞or′ ĭ′ o͞o′ kē′) was one of the leading Japanese poets, critics, and diarists of his time. In his preface to a major literary anthology, he said that "The poetry of Japan . . . springs from the heart of man."

MY CITY

JAMES WELDON JOHNSON

Background Contemporary poets who write Shakespearean sonnets
may slightly modify the rhyme scheme. In this sonnet, Johnson uses
a modified scheme in the first two quatrains, or groups of four lines.
In the rest of the poem, however, he follows classic Shakespearean
form.

When I come down to sleep death's endless night,
   The threshold of the unknown dark to cross,
   What to me then will be the keenest loss,
When this bright world blurs on my fading sight?
5 Will it be that no more I shall see the trees
   Or smell the flowers or hear the singing birds
   Or watch the flashing streams or patient herds?
No, I am sure it will be none of these.
But, ah! Manhattan's sights and sounds, her smells,
10 Her crowds, her throbbing force, the thrill that comes
From being of her a part, her subtile spells,
   Her shining towers, her avenues, her slums—
   O God! the stark, unutterable pity,
To be dead, and never again behold my city!

Vocabulary
threshold (thresh´ ōld´)
n. the bottom of a
doorway; entrance or
a point of beginning

keenest (kēn´ ist) *adj.*
sharpest; most cutting

Literary Analysis
Poetic Forms Which
syllables are stressed in
the iambic pentameter
of line 9?

◄ **Critical Viewing** Which lines in the poem does this painting best
illustrate? Explain. **[Connect]**

Do Not Go
Gentle into That
Good Night

Dylan Thomas

Do not go gentle into that good night,
Old age should burn and rave at close of day;
Rage, rage against the dying of the light.

Though wise men at their end know dark is right,
5   Because their words had forked no lightning they
Do not go gentle into that good night.

Good men, the last wave by, crying how bright
Their frail deeds might have danced in a green bay,
Rage, rage against the dying of the light.

10   Wild men who caught and sang the sun in flight,
And learn, too late, they grieved it on its way,
Do not go gentle into that good night.

Grave men, near death, who see with blinding sight
Blind eyes could blaze like meteors and be gay,
15   Rage, rage against the dying of the light.

And you, my father, there on the sad height,
Curse, bless, me now with your fierce tears, I pray.
Do not go gentle into that good night.
Rage, rage against the dying of the light.

Literary Analysis
Poetic Forms Where are the first and third lines of the first stanza repeated in this villanelle?

Spiral Review
Figurative Language What type of figurative language does the author employ in line 14? Explain your answer.

Reading Skill
Read Fluently Where will you pause when reading lines 16–19? What punctuation indicates each pause?

◀ **Critical Viewing** Which of the four types of men do you think is represented in this painting? Explain. **[Interpret]**

TANKA

Vocabulary
clustering (klus´ tər iŋ)
adj. gathering; forming
in a group

lunar (loō´ nər) *adj.*
of the moon

The clustering clouds—
Can it be they wipe away
The lunar shadows?
Every time they clear a bit
The moonlight shines the brighter.
     — Minamoto no Toshiyori
     translated by Donald Keene

When I went to visit
The girl I love so much,
That winter night
The river blew so cold
That the plovers[1] were crying.
     — Ki no Tsurayuki
     translated by Geoffrey Bownas

1. **plovers** (pluv´ ərz) *n.* shorebirds with short tails and long, pointed wings.

Critical Thinking

Cite textual evidence to support your responses.

1. **Key Ideas and Details (a) Contrast:** Contrast the landscape the speaker prefers in "My City" with the one he first describes. **(b) Evaluate:** Did the contrast help you appreciate his perspective? Explain.

2. **Key Ideas and Details (a)** In "Do Not Go Gentle . . . ," what does the speaker mean when he says, "Old age should burn and rave at close of day"? **(b)** Do you agree? Why or why not?

3. **Key Ideas and Details (a) Contrast:** Contrast the events actually taking place in "The clustering clouds" with the speaker's interpretation of those events. **(b) Interpret:** What does the poem suggest about the effect of contrasts on our perceptions?

4. **Key Ideas and Details (a)** What is the weather like when the speaker goes visiting in "When I went to visit..."? **(b) Infer:** What does his reaction to such weather indicate about his love? Explain.

5. **Integration of Knowledge and Ideas** Select two poems from this collection and describe what message or feeling about nature each poem conveys. *[Connect to the Big Question: Does all communication serve a positive purpose?]*

Literary Analysis: Poetic Forms

1. Craft and Structure Which features of **tanka** appear in "The clustering clouds..." and "When I went to visit..."?

2. Craft and Structure On a chart like this one, analyze the three quatrains and the couplet in the **sonnet** "My City."

Message of Quatrain 1	Connection: Quatrains 1 and 2	Connection: Quatrains 2 and 3	Connection: Couplet to Quatrains

3. Craft and Structure **(a)** Identify the repeated lines in the **villanelle** "Do Not Go Gentle into That Good Night." **(b)** What feeling does the repetition of these lines help create? **(c)** Discuss your answers with a partner. Explain how discussion affected your thoughts and your understanding of the poem.

Reading Skill: Read Fluently

4. (a) Preview the first eight lines of "My City." What information about vocabulary and sentence structure can you learn? **(b)** Explain how this information might help you **read fluently.**

Vocabulary

Acquisition and Use Identify the word that does not belong in each group, and explain why it does not belong.

1. clustering, crowding, repairing

2. lunar, rectangular, earthly

3. threshold, doorway, harvest

4. keenest, sharpest, silliest

Word Study Use the context of the sentences and what you know about the **Latin root -lun-** to explain your answer to each question.

1. If someone displays *lunatic* behavior, is that person behaving rationally?

2. If the emblem over a door is a *lune,* is the emblem in the shape of a square?

Word Study

The **Latin root -lun-** means "moon."

Apply It Explain how the root -lun- contributes to the meanings of these words. Consult a dictionary if necessary.

lunate
lunette
lunacy

Making Connections
Poetry Collection 4

The Waking • Sonnet 18 •
One cannot ask loneliness . . . •
Was it that I went to sleep . . .

Does all *communication* serve a positive purpose?

Writing About the Big Question

In Poetry Collection 4, the speakers communicate insights they have gained through solitary reflection. Use these sentence starters to develop your ideas about the Big Question:

Isolation and thinking something through on your own can be useful when _____.

It is also important at times to **interact** and communicate with others because _____.

While You Read As you read these poems, look for the insights reached by each of the speakers about the relationship between isolation and communication.

Vocabulary

Read each word and its definition. Decide whether you know the word well, know it a little bit, or do not know it at all. After you read, see how your knowledge of each word has increased.

- **fate** (fāt) *n.* destiny; what happens to a person or thing; final outcome (p. 685) *The judge decided the defendant's <u>fate</u>.* *fated adj. fateful adj. fatefully adv.*

- **lowly** (lō′ lē) *adj.* humble; of low rank (p. 685) *Starting as a <u>lowly</u> stable boy, he worked hard to become a top trainer. lowliness n.*

- **temperate** (tem′ pər it) *adj.* mild; kept within limits (p. 687) *I prefer <u>temperate</u> weather much more than the snow. temper v. temperately adv. temperateness n.*

- **eternal** (ē tur′ nəl) *adj.* without beginning or end; everlasting (p. 687) *Our friendship is <u>eternal</u> and will last forever. eternally adv. eternalness n. eternity n.*

Word Study

The **Latin root -temp-** means "regulate," "moderate," or "time."

In Sonnet 18 by Shakespeare, the speaker explains that his beloved is more **temperate,** or moderate and less extreme, than the weather on a summer's day.

Theodore Roethke

(1908–1963)

Author of "The Waking" (p. 685)

Born in Michigan, Theodore Roethke developed his great love of nature from observing the plants in his family's commercial greenhouses. This love is often reflected in his poetry. In 1954, Roethke received a Pulitzer Prize for his poetry.

William Shakespeare

(1564–1616)

Author of Sonnet 18 (p. 687)

Even though he is most famous as a playwright, Shakespeare also wrote brilliant sonnets. Today, the English sonnet, which he perfected, is also known as the Shakespearean sonnet. (For more about Shakespeare and his career, see pages 890–891.)

Priest Jakuren

(1139–1202)

Author of "One cannot ask loneliness . . " (p. 688)

Priest Jakuren (jä´ ko͞o´ rən´) was a Buddhist priest whose poems are filled with beautiful yet melancholy imagery. After entering the priesthood at the age of twenty-three, he traveled the Japanese countryside.

Ono Komachi

(active ca. 833–857)

Author of "Was it that I went to sleep . . ." (p. 688)

A beautiful woman with a strong personality, Ono Komachi (ō´ nō´ kō´ mä´ chē´) was an early Japanese tanka poet. Her poems are marked by passion and energy. The few details known about her life have inspired many legends.

The Waking
Theodore Roethke

I wake to sleep, and take my waking slow.
I feel my fate in what I cannot fear.
I learn by going where I have to go.

We think by feeling. What is there to know?
5 I hear my being dance from ear to ear.
I wake to sleep, and take my waking slow.

Of those so close beside me, which are you?
God bless the Ground! I shall walk softly there,
And learn by going where I have to go.

10 Light takes the Tree; but who can tell us how?
The lowly worm climbs up a winding stair;
I wake to sleep, and take my waking slow.

Great Nature has another thing to do
To you and me; so take the lively air,
15 And, lovely, learn by going where to go.

This shaking keeps me steady. I should know.
What falls away is always. And is near.
I wake to sleep, and take my waking slow.
I learn by going where I have to go.

Vocabulary
fate (fāt) *n.* destiny; what happens to a person or thing; final outcome

lowly (lō´ lē) *adj.* humble; of low rank

Literary Analysis
Poetic Forms How has the repetition of lines 1 and 3 changed their significance or associated feelings by the end of the villanelle?

◄ **Critical Viewing** Which stanza of the poem might this painting illustrate best? **[Connect]**

Sonnet 18

William Shakespeare

Background The Italian poet Petrarch (pē´ trärk´) wrote during the 14th century. His sonnets, overflowing with enthusiastic, exaggerated comparisons in praise of his beloved Laura, inspired Shakespeare and other poets living in 17th century England. In Sonnet 18, Shakespeare offers a unique perspective on the comparisons that were popular in the sonnets of the time.

Shall I compare thee to a summer's day?
Thou art more lovely and more temperate:
Rough winds do shake the darling buds of May,
And summer's lease hath all too short a date:
5 Sometime too hot the eye of heaven shines,
And often is his gold complexion dimmed;
And every fair from fair sometime declines,
By chance or nature's changing course untrimmed;[1]
But thy eternal summer shall not fade,
10 Nor lose possession of that fair thou owest;[2]
Nor shall Death brag thou wander'st in his shade,
When in eternal lines to time thou grow'st:
     So long as men can breathe, or eyes can see,
     So long lives this, and this gives life to thee.

---

1. **untrimmed** *adj.* stripped of ornaments or beautiful features.
2. **owest** (ō´ ist) *v.* own.

Vocabulary
temperate (tem´ pər it) *adj.* mild; kept within limits

eternal (ē tʉr´ nəl) *adj.* without beginning or end; everlasting

Literary Analysis
Poetic Forms In what way does the couplet at the conclusion summarize the main idea of the poem?

◀ **Critical Viewing** Which characteristics of the woman in the sonnet does this woman seem to share? Explain. **[Connect]**

TANKA

Reading Skill
Read Fluently How might the mood, or general feeling, of each poem affect the way that you read it?

One cannot ask loneliness
How or where it starts.
On the cypress-mountain,[1]
Autumn evening.
    — Priest Jakuren
    translated by Geoffrey Bownas

Was it that I went to sleep
Thinking of him,
That he came in my dreams?
Had I known it a dream
I should not have wakened.
    — Ono Komachi
    translated by Geoffrey Bownas

---

1. **cypress-mountain** Cypress trees are cone-bearing evergreen trees native to North America, Europe, and Asia.

Critical Thinking

Cite textual evidence to support your responses.

1. **Key Ideas and Details Interpret:** What advice about life is implied in line 19 of "The Waking"?

2. **Key Ideas and Details (a) Analyze:** Identify three ways in which, according to the speaker in Sonnet 18, a summer day may become less than perfect. **(b) Infer:** What is the speaker's main reason for saying the woman is superior to a summer's day?

3. **Key Ideas and Details (a)** What question cannot be asked in "One cannot ask loneliness…"? **(b) Connect:** How does the image of the mountain relate to the speaker's thoughts about loneliness?

4. **Key Ideas and Details (a)** What reason does the speaker in "Was it that I went to sleep…" give for dreaming about the man? **(b) Infer:** What do the speaker's comments reveal about her feelings for the man?

5. **Integration of Knowledge and Ideas** "Isolation" and "communication" seem to be opposite ideas. How are these ideas connected in each poem? *[Connect to the Big Question: Does all communication serve a positive purpose?]*

After You Read
Poetry Collection 4

**The Waking • Sonnet 18 •
One cannot ask loneliness... •
Was it that I went to sleep...**

Literary Analysis: Poetic Forms

1. Craft and Structure Which features of **tanka** appear in "One cannot ask loneliness..." and "Was it that I went to sleep..."?

2. Craft and Structure On a chart like this one, analyze the three quatrains and the couplet in Sonnet 18.

Message of Quatrain 1	Connection: Quatrains 1 and 2	Connection: Quatrains 2 and 3	Connection: Couplet to Quatrains

3. Craft and Structure (a) Identify the repeated lines in the **villanelle** "The Waking." **(b)** What feeling does the repetition of these lines help create?

Reading Skill: Read Fluently

4. (a) Preview the first eight lines of Sonnet 18. What information about vocabulary and sentence structure can you learn?
(b) Explain how this information might help you **read fluently.**

Vocabulary

Acquisition and Use For each item, identify the word that does not belong in the group and explain why.

1. fate, destiny, loneliness

2. temperate, experienced, extreme

3. lowly, humble, clever

4. eternal, everlasting, terminal

Word Study Use the context of the sentences and what you know about the **Latin root -temp-** to explain your answer to each question.

1. If you describe the *temporal* aspect of a plan, are you talking about time, space, or rules?

2. Is a *temporary* building characterized by how long it will last or how tall it is?

Word Study

The **Latin root -temp-** means "regulate," "moderate," or "time."

Apply It Explain how the root -temp- contributes to the meanings of these words. Consult a dictionary if necessary.

contemporary
extemporaneous
tempo

Integrated Language Skills

Poetry Collections 3 and 4

Poetry Collection 3

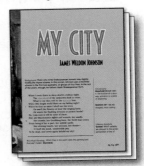

Conventions: Direct Objects

A **direct object** is a noun or pronoun that receives the action of a verb. (Action verbs that take a direct object are called *transitive verbs*.)

A direct object's function in a sentence is to add specific information. A direct object answers the question formed by putting *what* or *whom* after an action verb, as in the following examples. Verbs such as *am, is, are, was,* and *were* are linking verbs. They do not take direct objects.

Poetry Collection 4

Examples:

> DO
> <u>Tyrell</u> **steers** the (car.) (Tyrell **steers** *what*? Answer: the car)
> DO
> <u>Erin</u> **admires** her (friend.) (Erin **admires** *whom*? Answer: her friend)
>
> <u>The twins</u> **were** happy. (**Were** is a linking verb, so there is no direct object.)

Practice A Copy each sentence. Underline the action verb and circle the direct object in each sentence.

1. The poet describes the clouds.
2. Ki no Tsurayuki heard the plovers.
3. The sonnet contains fourteen lines.
4. Johnson celebrates his city.
5. The poet implores his father to fight death.

© Reading Application Find and label two examples of action verbs with direct objects in any of the poems in Poetry Collection 3.

Practice B The following phrases require a direct object to complete the thought. Copy each phrase and complete it by adding a direct object.

1. Priest Jakuren created beautiful

   _____.

2. Ono Komachi wrote _____.

3. Hikers navigate _____.

4. A beautiful woman inspired

   _____.

© Writing Application Rewrite each sentence by keeping the subject and choosing a new action verb and direct object.

PH WRITING COACH | Further instruction and practice are available in *Prentice Hall Writing Coach*.

Writing

Poetry Write your own **tanka,** following the traditional Japanese form. Follow these steps:

- Think of a subject for your poem. Focus on a single strong image or idea.
- Review the definition of a tanka on page 671.
- As you draft, choose words that will allow you to follow the prescribed syllable pattern for each line.
- After you draft, read your tanka aloud. Jot down ideas and then rephrase them to fit the form. If necessary, *invert* normal word order as long as your meaning is clear. For example, you might write, "To the store did he run."

Grammar Application Check that you have included direct objects where they will strengthen your tanka.

Writing Workshop: *Work in Progress*

Prewriting for Descriptive Essay Using the Organization Chart from your writing portfolio, choose one item to describe. Outline your description using the corresponding organizational structure. Then, use the outline to list sensory details that describe the item. Put this Outline in your writing portfolio.

Speaking and Listening

Comprehension and Collaboration In a small group, listen several times to a recording of either Dylan Thomas reading "Do Not Go Gentle into That Good Night" or someone reading Shakespeare's Sonnet 18. Afterward, hold a **poetry reading discussion** in which you explore what the reading added to your understanding and appreciation of the poem.

Answer the following questions as you hold your discussion, building on each other's ideas.

- Does the reader speed up at certain parts of the poem? Does he or she slow down at other parts?
- Does the reader put emphasis on certain words? Are there similarities in the words that the reader emphasizes?
- Does the reader stress the rhythm?
- Does the reader emphasize the rhyme?
- Does the reader convey a specific emotion or mood?
- Did hearing the poem aloud help your understanding of it?

After your discussion, have several people in your group read the poem aloud. Assess how the different readings impact the audience.

Common Core State Standards

L.9-10.1; W.9-10.4; SL.9-10.1
[For the full wording of the standards, see page 670.]

Use this prewriting activity to prepare for the **Writing Workshop** on page 708.

www.PHLitOnline.com
- Interactive graphic organizers
- Grammar tutorial
- Interactive journals

Test Practice: Reading

Read Fluently

Fiction Selection

Directions: *Read the selection. Then, answer the questions.*

> O Rose, thou art sick.
> The invisible worm
> That flies in the night,
> In the howling storm,
>
> Has found out thy bed
> Of crimson joy,
> And his dark secret love
> Does thy life destroy.
>
> —"The Sick Rose" by William Blake

1. How many sentences does this poem consist of?
- **A.** 8
- **B.** 4
- **C.** 2
- **D.** 1

2. The reader should expect to read this poem—
- **A.** faster than a grocery list.
- **B.** slower than a science text.
- **C.** faster than directions for building a radio.
- **D.** at the same pace as song lyrics.

3. Which lines should you read without pausing?
- **A.** Of crimson joy, - And his dark secret love
- **B.** thou art sick. - The invisible worm
- **C.** the howling storm, - has found out thy bed
- **D.** the invisible worm - that flies in the night

4. Which statement best conveys the basic meaning of the poem?
- **A.** A rose befriends a worm.
- **B.** A rain storm causes the destruction of a rose.
- **C.** A rose's petals are soft and inviting.
- **D.** A worm has a secret love for the rose.

Writing for Assessment

Explain how the mood and tone of this poem affect the way it should be read aloud. In a brief paragraph, use details from the passage to support your answer.

Nonfiction Selection

Directions: *Read the selection. Then, answer the questions.*

Introduction to Black Spot

(1) A common disease that affects roses is Black Spot. (2) The disease can be identified by round black spots on the upper surface of the leaves. (3) Each spot has a yellow halo around it. (4) Over time, the blemishes grow and join, until the entire leaf becomes yellow and drops from the plant.

Black Spot: Preventing the Spread of the Disease

(5) The cause of Black Spot is a fungus that thrives in humid and rainy conditions. (6) There is no simple chemical treatment. (7) The best remedy is to prune infected stems in early spring and apply an anti-fungal spray before the leaves open. (8) Wet leaves provide a hospitable environment for germinating fungus spores; thus, to avoid Black Spot, do not water rose plants from above. (9) Instead, soak the soil around the plants. (10) If a plant is infected, remove yellowed leaves from the plant and the ground around it. (11) Spray nearby plants with a fungicide to prevent the disease from spreading.

1. Based on the first few lines, at what speed should the reader read this passage?

A. The reader should read as fast as he or she would read a shopping list.

B. The reader should read as fast as he or she would read a magazine article.

C. The reader should read as fast as he or she would read a textbook.

D. The reader should read as fast as he or she would read poetry.

2. What should the reader do before reading this passage?

A. Preview the headings.

B. Scan to find any unfamiliar words.

C. Read the last sentence.

D. Research the background of this topic.

3. When reading this passage aloud, which of the following would be appropriate?

A. Read paragraph 1 more quickly than paragraph 2.

B. Stop at the end of sentence 7.

C. Reread sentence 5 aloud.

D. Pause at the end of sentence 4.

4. Which sentence requires the reader to pause in three places?

A. sentence 2

B. sentence 7

C. sentence 8

D. sentence 10

Writing for Assessment

Connecting Across Texts

How would your purpose for reading affect the rate at which you would read the two passages aloud? In a paragraph, use details from the passages to support your answer.

www.PHLitOnline.com
- Online practice
- Instant feedback

Reading for Information

Analyzing Functional Texts

Signs

Web Site

Common Core State Standards

Reading Informational Text
6. Determine an author's point of view or purpose in a text and analyze how an author uses rhetoric to advance that point of view or purpose.

Language
4.b. Identify and correctly use patterns of word changes that indicate different meanings or parts of speech.
6. Acquire and use accurately general academic and domain-specific words and phrases, sufficient for reading, writing, speaking, and listening at the college and career readiness level; demonstrate independence in gathering vocabulary knowledge when considering a word or phrase important to comprehension or expression.

Reading Skill: Make Predictions: Purpose

Along with precise wording, authors use many techniques and elements to achieve their purposes. Previewing a document—**analyzing the structure, format, and features** of a text—allows you to **make predictions,** or educated guesses, about the **purpose** of that text. Before reading, look at the document and use a chart like this one to record your predictions about the author's purpose. Then, after you have read the text, confirm whether your predictions were correct.

Previewing Observation	Prediction About Purpose	Confirmation
large, colorful graphics	grab readers' attention	
headings that categorize text	present several key ideas about a subject	
bulleted lists	provide examples	

Content-Area Vocabulary

These words appear in the selections that follow. You may also encounter them in other content-area texts.

- **exhibitions** (ek´ sə bish´ ənz) *n.* displays or shows of objects, art, materials, and so on that are open to public view

- **confidential** (kän´ fə den´ shəl) *adj.* kept private or secret

- **privileges** (priv´ li jez) *n.* special rights given to a person

FOLGER

S H A K E S P E A R E   L I B R A R Y

VISITOR ENTRANCE

ELIZABETHAN THEATRE

BOX OFFICE OPENS
ONE HOUR BEFORE EVENTS

EXHIBITIONS

◀ELIZABETHAN GARDEN

MONDAY–SATURDAY
10:00 A.M. – 4:00 P.M.

RESEARCH ENTRANCE▶

READING ROOM • MUSEUM SHOP
ADMINISTRATIVE OFFICES

CLOSED ALL FEDERAL HOLIDAYS

The purpose behind large, bold letters is usually to draw the reader's attention.

Because the text is presented simply and in short lines, you can predict that the writer is trying to convey short, simple ideas.

Elizabeth I

"TO BE A KING AND WEAR A CROWN IS a thing more glorious to them that see it than it is pleasant to them that bear it." These words, spoken by Elizabeth I to her Parliament in 1601, might just as well be echoed by any head of state today. All the perks of office—the fine clothes, jewels, servants, and now, private planes and media attention—are there to be enjoyed, but they come with the high price of responsibility to the people and the nation. Elizabeth was not elected, she inherited this responsibility from her father, Henry VIII, but she took it seriously and was educated to be a prince. In 1558 after the death of her Catholic sister Mary, Elizabeth came to the throne and reigned for forty-four years. Though she restored the Protestant church to England, she resisted extremes in religion as well as policy. She also resisted pressure by her male council and Parliament to marry, turning the many offers for her hand into a game of political chess. She was a true "career woman" long before the term was coined; her job was her life.

Now, four hundred years after Elizabeth's death in March of 1603, the Folger Library honors her memory and her reign. Because Emily and Henry Folger focused their collecting on the age of Shakespeare, when Elizabeth was queen, the Folger Library has the largest collection of artifacts relating to Elizabeth in America. She has never really gone out of style. Every generation has re-read her through their own ideas of womanhood, and today perhaps we can appreciate her political skills more than did any other era. In her "Golden Speech" quoted above, she also said: "though you have had and may have many princes more mighty and wise sitting in this seat, yet you never had or shall have any that will be more careful and loving."

Major support for this exhibition comes from the Winton and Carolyn Blount Exhibition Fund of the Folger Shakespeare Library.

Features:
- information about the source of the Web site
- links to other areas of the site
- graphic elements that highlight information

Atlanta-Fulton Public Library System

Library Cards

Your Library Card

Our Free Service Area

Children's Cards

Non-Residents' Cards

Your Privacy

Borrowing & Returning Items

Fines / Lost & Damaged Items

This list of links could lead you to predict that the purpose of the Web site is to present information on various subjects.

Your Library Card

Your Atlanta-Fulton Public Library card can open the door to a world of information. The Library System offers books, audiocassettes, compact discs, and videos for you to take home to use and enjoy. Here's how to get a valid Atlanta-Fulton Public Library System library card to check out library materials.

Our Free Service Area

Residents within all of Fulton County and residents within all of the City of Atlanta. This means that people who reside inside the incorporated city limits of the City of Atlanta, including that portion of the incorporated city of Atlanta that is in DeKalb County, are eligible for a free card. However, please note: Having an Atlanta mailing address is not the same thing as living within the incorporated City of Atlanta. Many people have an Atlanta postmark, but do not live within the incorporated Atlanta city limits. If you live in Dekalb County you must live within the incorporated city limits of Atlanta to be eligible for a free AFPL Library Card.

When you register for a library card you will need to verify your current name and address by presenting one piece of identification with your current residential address. Among the items you may present are your

- driver's license
- student identification card
- voter registration card
- printed checks with current address
- rental receipts or lease
- social services identification
- Fulton County property tax receipts or
- current utility bill.

Children's Cards

Children under the age of 13 who want to register for a library card must have the library card application signed by a parent or legal guardian. The parent or guardian must supply identification that shows the current residential address. By signing the child's application, the parent or guardian accepts the responsibility for all items borrowed on the child's library card.

Non-residents' cards

Non-residents may apply for a library card by paying a non-refundable fee of $25.00 per person per year.

Your Privacy

The Library System will keep **confidential** all records relating to your library card registration and the materials you borrow.

> The text in the section headings indicates that this Web site is intended to provide patrons with information about library policies and procedures.

Borrowing & Returning Items

Loan Periods: You may borrow items for the following time periods:

Popular or "Browse" Materials............14 days *(no renewals)*
CDs...28 days *(10 per card, two renewals)*
DVDs and VHS....................................7 days *(5 per card, two renewals)*
All other materials................................28 days

Renewals: You may renew MOST materials one time. Popular or "Browse" materials, books on hold can NOT be renewed. You may renew materials over the phone by using our TeleLibrarian Service or Go Online.

We strongly encourage you to return materials by the due date. Overdue materials will impact your borrowing **privileges**.

Fines/Lost & Damaged Items

Fines for overdue materials are as follows:

Adult Books and other materials.........10 cents a day, *maximum $5.00 per item.*
Adult Videos...$1.00 per day, *maximum $5.00 per item.*
Children's books....................................5 cents a day, *maximum $3.00 per item.*
Children's VHS and DVD's....................$1.00 per day, *maximum $3.00 per item.*
Lost library cards:.................................Replacement cards cost $1.00 each.

Lost & Damaged Materials: Replacement cost for lost or damaged materials is based on the library's average cost charts. Please save your receipt when you pay for lost or damaged material. If you find library material that you have paid for within 30 days of the payment date, bring the material and your receipt to your branch to receive a refund.

Theft: Anyone caught stealing or damaging material with intent to steal will be prosecuted in accordance with the law.

Comparing Functional Texts

1. Craft and Structure (a) Compare and contrast the **structures and formats** of the signs and Web site. **(b)** Explain how these elements help you **make predictions about the purpose** of each text.

Content-Area Vocabulary

2. (a) Remove the suffix *-ions* from the word *exhibitions*. Using a print or an online dictionary, explain how removing the suffix reveals a new word with a different part of speech. **(b)** Use the words *exhibitions* and *exhibit* in a brief paragraph about a school art show.

⏱ Timed Writing

Explanatory Text: Essay

> **Format**
> The prompt directs you to write an evaluation. Therefore, your response should include observations and judgments about the elements mentioned in the prompt.

Write an evaluation of either the signs or the Web site. Assess the usefulness of the text structures and formatting in helping the reader to understand the content and make predictions. Suggest improvements to features, such as graphics and headings, which will help better achieve the author's purpose. (30 minutes)

> **Academic Vocabulary**
> When you *assess*, you make a determination about something's value.

5-Minute Planner

Complete these steps before you begin to write:

1. Read the prompt carefully and completely. Look for key words, like the ones highlighted, that will help you understand the assignment.

2. Quickly review the signs and Web site. Decide which to evaluate.

3. Examine the text you chose in greater detail. Make notes about the text structures and formatting you find helpful.

4. Consider the author's purpose and improvements that could be made to better achieve that purpose. **TIP** Think about when you first read the text. Did you have to reread any sections in order to fully understand them? Consider improvements that would have made those sections clearer to you when you first read them.

5. Create an outline for your evaluation. Then, refer to your notes and outline as you write.

Comparing Tone and Mood

The overall feeling or impression conveyed by a literary work can be affected by two elements: **tone** and **mood.**

- **Tone** is the author's attitude toward the reader or the subject of the work. It can be described with adjectives such as *formal* or *informal*, *scolding* or *encouraging*, or *humorous* or *serious*.

- **Mood,** or atmosphere, is a general, unified feeling conveyed by the details of a literary work. The mood of a work may be described with adjectives such as *gloomy* or *joyous*, *menacing* or *cozy*.

Writers create tone and mood through their use of descriptive details and figurative language. Writers also create mood and tone by using words with specific connotations. A word's connotations are the ideas or emotions associated with the word in addition to its literal meaning. For example, *arrogant* has the same literal meaning as *proud*, but it suggests a negative feeling. A writer's choice of subject and setting can also help to define a mood.

In the selections presented here, the authors create unique worlds, defined by tone, mood, and the characters and events in the works. For example, the mood of "Fear" captures the emotional world of a mother. In contrast, the tone of "How to React to Familiar Faces" is mostly analytical, revealing a hint of humor and mild accusation. As you read, compare the moods and tones of the selections. List specific words and details that influence tone and mood. Then, consider the overall impact on tone and mood of the words and details that you listed. Use a diagram like this to help you.

**Common Core
State Standards**

Reading Literature
4. Determine the meaning of words and phrases as they are used in the text, including figurative and connotative meanings; analyze the cumulative impact of specific word choices on meaning and tone.

Writing
1. Write arguments to support claims in an analysis of substantive topics or texts, using valid reasoning and relevant and sufficient evidence. *(Timed Writing)*

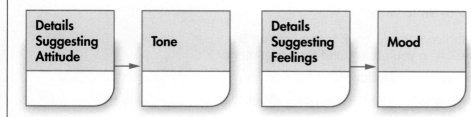

| Details Suggesting Attitude | → | Tone | | Details Suggesting Feelings | → | Mood |

www.PHLitOnline.com

- Vocabulary flashcards
- Interactive journals
- More about the authors

- Selection audio
- Interactive graphic organizers

Does all *communication* serve a positive purpose?

Writing About the Big Question

In these selections, the writer describes human interactions. Think about how people you know communicate with each other. Use this sentence starter to develop your ideas.

When one person **misinterprets** what another has said, it can lead to _____.

Meet the Authors

Gabriela Mistral (1889–1957)
Author of "Fear" (p. 702)

At fifteen, Gabriela Mistral (gä brē ä′ lä mē sträl′) was already a full-time grade-school teacher in her native Chile. Mistral, born Lucila Godoy y Alcayaga (lōō sī′ lə gō doʼī ē ȧl kī ä′ gə), published her poetry under a variety of pen names before she settled on Gabriela Mistral. In 1945, she became the first Latin American to receive the Nobel Prize in Literature.

Gwendolyn Brooks (1917–2000)
Author of "The Bean Eaters" (p. 703)

Gwendolyn Brooks began writing poetry at the age of seven. Encouraged by her family, she published her first poem at thirteen. In 1950, Brooks became the first African American writer to win a Pulitzer Prize. She is one of the most admired American poets of the twentieth century.

Umberto Eco (b. 1932)
Author of "How to React to Familiar Faces" (p. 704)

Italian author Umberto Eco has a personal library of more than 30,000 volumes—larger than many school libraries! He is interested in communication of every kind. At the University of Bologna, he teaches semiotics, the study of communication through signs and symbols. He also follows the information revolution with great interest.

Fear

Gabriela Mistral

translated by Doris Dana

I don't want them to turn
my little girl into a swallow.
She would fly far away into the sky
and never fly again to my straw bed,
5 or she would nest in the eaves[1]
where I could not comb her hair.
I don't want them to turn
my little girl into a swallow.

    I don't want them to make
10 my little girl a princess.
In tiny golden slippers
how could she play on the meadow?
And when night came, no longer
would she sleep at my side.
15 I don't want them to make
my little girl a princess.

    And even less do I want them
one day to make her queen.
They would put her on a throne
20 where I could not go to see her.
And when nighttime came
I could never rock her . . .
I don't want them to make
my little girl a queen!

---

1. **eaves** (ēvz) *n.* lower edges of a roof.

▲ **Critical Viewing**
Does the mother's expression in this painting express the fears described in the poem? Explain. **[Interpret]**

Literary Analysis
Tone and Mood In what tone of voice do you imagine the mother uttering lines 9–12? Why?

The Bean Eaters

Gwendolyn Brooks

They eat beans mostly, this old yellow pair.
Dinner is a casual affair.
Plain chipware on a plain and creaking wood,
Tin flatware.

5   Two who are Mostly Good.
Two who have lived their day,
But keep on putting on their clothes
And putting things away.

And remembering . . .
10   Remembering, with twinklings and twinges,
As they lean over the beans in their rented back room
    that is full of beads and receipts and dolls and cloths,
    tobacco crumbs, vases and fringes.

Literary Analysis
Tone and Mood What attitude toward her subject does the speaker show in her repetition of *plain*?

Vocabulary
twinges [twinj´ əz] *n.* sharp pains, either physical or mental

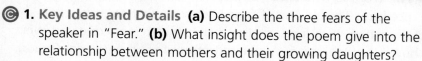

Critical Thinking

Cite textual evidence to support your responses.

© **1. Key Ideas and Details (a)** Describe the three fears of the speaker in "Fear." **(b)** What insight does the poem give into the relationship between mothers and their growing daughters?

© **2. Craft and Structure (a)** In "The Bean Eaters," what items are listed as being in the rented room? **(b)** Consider the author's choice of items. What overall tone does it create?

© **3. Craft and Structure** In "The Bean Eaters," why do you think the author capitalized the phrase "Mostly Good"?

© **4. Integration of Knowledge and Ideas (a)** If you were the daughter in "Fear," would you see the poem as a positive or negative expression of love? Explain. **(b)** Which poem do you think paints a truer picture of an attachment between people? Explain. *[Connect to the Big Question: Does all communication serve a positive purpose?]*

HOW TO REACT TO FAMILIAR FACES

UMBERTO ECO

Marilyn Monroe, Andy Warhol. © Andy Warhol Foundation.

▲ **Critical Viewing**
Artist Andy Warhol made these prints repeating movie star Marilyn Monroe's face. Which of Eco's points do the prints help illustrate? **[Connect]**

Background In this essay, Umberto Eco mentions several celebrities with whom you may not be familiar:

- Anthony Quinn was a film actor who won two Academy Awards.
- Charlton Heston, another film actor, won an Academy Award for his role in the film *Ben-Hur*.
- Johnny Carson was the host of the nighttime talk show *The Tonight Show* for thirty years.
- Oprah Winfrey is a successful talk-show host. She produces her show, publishes a magazine, and has a significant influence on public opinion.

Vocabulary
context (kän´ tekst´) *n.* situation in which something is found

A few months ago, as I was strolling in New York, I saw, at a distance, a man I knew very well heading in my direction. The trouble was that I couldn't remember his name or where I had met him. This is one of those sensations you encounter especially when, in a foreign city, you run into someone you met back home, or vice versa. A face out of context creates confusion. Still, that face was so familiar that, I felt, I should certainly stop, greet him, converse; perhaps he would immediately respond, "My dear Umberto, how are you?" or "Were you able to do that thing you were telling me about?" And I would be at a total loss. It was too late to flee. He was still looking at the opposite side of the street, but now he was beginning to turn his eyes towards me. I might as well make the first move; I would wave and then, from his voice, his first remarks, I would try to guess his identity.

We were now only a few feet from each other, I was just about to break into a broad, radiant smile, when suddenly I recognized him. It was Anthony Quinn. Naturally, I had never met him in my life, nor he me. In a thousandth of a second I was able to check myself, and I walked past him, my eyes staring into space.

Marilyn Monroe, Andy Warhol. © Andy Warhol Foundation.

Marilyn Monroe, Andy Warhol. © Andy Warhol Foundation.

Afterwards, reflecting on this incident, I realized how totally normal it was. Once before, in a restaurant, I had glimpsed Charlton Heston and had felt an impulse to say hello. These faces inhabit our memory; watching the screen, we spend so many hours with them that they are as familiar to us as our relatives', even more so. You can be a student of mass communication, debate the effects of reality, or the confusion between the real and the imagined, and expound the way some people fall permanently into this confusion; but still you are not immune to the syndrome.[1] And there is worse.

I have received confidences from people who, appearing fairly frequently on TV, have been subjected to the mass media over a certain period of time. I'm not talking about Johnny Carson or Oprah Winfrey, but public figures, experts who have participated in panel discussions often enough to become recognizable. All of them complain of the same disagreeable experience. Now, as a rule, when we see someone we don't know personally, we don't stare into his or her face at length, we don't point out the person to the friend at our side, we don't speak of this person in a loud voice when he or she can overhear. Such behavior would be rude, even—if carried too far—aggressive. But the same people who would never point to a customer at a counter and remark to a friend that the man is wearing a smart[2] tie behave quite differently with famous faces.

My guinea pigs[3] insist that, at a newsstand, in the tobacconist's, as they are boarding a train or entering a restaurant toilet, they

Literary Analysis
Tone and Mood What does the writer's choice of the verb *subjected* tell you about his attitude toward mass media?

Reading Check

How does the writer react at first when he sees Anthony Quinn?

---

1. **syndrome** (sin´ drōm´) *n.* set of symptoms or characteristics occurring together and defining a disease or condition.
2. **smart** *adj.* stylish; fashionable.
3. **guinea** (gin´ ē) **pigs** subjects of an experiment (so-called because of the use of guinea pigs in laboratory experiments).

encounter others who, among themselves, say aloud, "Look there's X." "Are you sure?" "Of course I'm sure. It's X, I tell you." And they continue their conversation amiably, while X hears them, and they don't care if he hears them: it's as if he didn't exist.

Such people are confused by the fact that a protagonist of the mass media's imaginary world should abruptly enter real life, but at the same time they behave in the presence of the real person as if he still belonged to the world of images, as if he were on a screen, or in a weekly picture magazine. As if they were speaking in his absence.

I might as well have grabbed Anthony Quinn by the lapel, dragged him to a phone booth, and called a friend to say, "Talk about coincidence! I've run into Anthony Quinn. And you know something? He seems real!" (After which I would throw Quinn aside and go on about my business.)

The mass media first convinced us that the imaginary was real, and now they are convincing us that the real is imaginary; and the more reality the TV screen shows us, the more cinematic[4] our everyday world becomes.

---

4. **cinematic** (sin´ ə mat´ ik) *adj.* of or like movies.

Critical Thinking

1. **Key Ideas and Details (a)** Whom does the author see while strolling in New York City? **(b)** Why does he plan to wave and then change his mind? **(c) Analyze Cause and Effect:** How does Eco explain his reaction to this familiar face?

2. **Key Ideas and Details (a)** According to Eco, how do many people behave when they run into a celebrity? **(b) Infer:** What does Eco suggest is the reason for their behavior?

3. **Key Ideas and Details (a) Analyze:** Explain Eco's understanding of the role that media plays in our attitude toward reality. **(b)** According to Eco, what changes in society may the media be causing?

4. **Integration of Knowledge and Ideas** In this essay, the speaker describes how some people talk about a celebrity—in his or her presence—as if the celebrity were not there. Does this kind of communication serve a positive purpose? Why or why not? *[Connect to the Big Question: Does all communication serve a positive purpose?]*

Comparing Tone and Mood

C 1. Key Ideas and Details (a) Identify two details in "Fear" and two in "The Bean Eaters" that give each poem a dreamlike feeling. **(b)** Explain the differences in mood between the two poems.

C 2. Key Ideas and Details (a) In "The Bean Eaters," what is the speaker's attitude toward the couple? **(b)** Give two examples of descriptive words and details in the poem that convey this attitude.

C 3. Craft and Structure Explain how the formal, sophisticated language in "How to React to Familiar Faces" creates an analytical tone. Support your answer with examples.

C 4. Craft and Structure Give an example of a time that Eco departs from his serious tone.

C 5. Craft and Structure (a) Using a chart like the one shown, compare the tone and mood in the selections. **(b)** Use your chart to compare each speaker's emotional connection with his or her subject. Explain which is most direct and which is most distant.

Tone	Similarities/ Differences	Mood	Similarities/ Differences

⏱ Timed Writing

Argumentative Text: Essay

In an essay, analyze the way the author generates a mood in each selection. Then, draw a conclusion about the world of each selection. Is it the inner world of a person, the outer world of everyday experience, or a special world in which outer things reflect an inward state?

5-Minute Planner

1. Read the prompt carefully and completely.

2. Use these questions to get started:
   - How is the mood of the selection linked to the speaker's emotions?
   - How is the mood conveyed by descriptive details or figurative language?
   - How is the mood connected to the scenes and objects described?

3. Analyze the aesthetic, or artistic, effects of the authors' use of these stylistic devices.

4. Reread the prompt, and then draft your essay.

Writing Workshop

Write an Explanatory Essay

Explanatory Text: Descriptive Essay

Defining the Form **Descriptive writing** portrays people, places, objects, experiences, or ideas in vivid detail so that the reader can create a mental picture of the subject. You might use elements of descriptive writing in short stories, reflective essays, and scientific observations.

Assignment Write a descriptive essay about someone or something that is important to you or that you find interesting. Include these elements:

- ✔ *precise word choices* that create a strong impression
- ✔ *sensory details* of sight, sound, smell, taste, texture, and movements
- ✔ *figurative language*, such as personification, simile, and metaphor
- ✔ a logical *organization* that clarifies the connections between details
- ✔ error-free grammar, including correct use of *prepositional phrases*

To preview the criteria on which your descriptive essay may be judged, see the rubric on page 713.

 Writing Workshop: *Work in Progress*

Review the work you did on pages 669 and 691.

Prewriting/Planning Strategy

Gather details to develop figurative language. After you have found a topic that interests you, list key details in a chart like the one shown. Create figurative language by comparing these details with something that is familiar to your readers.

Detail	Reminds Me of...	Figure of Speech
a star pitcher's fastball	a knife slicing through the air	Metaphor: His <u>fastball is a knife slicing through the air.</u>
	a runaway train	Simile: His fastball is <u>like a runaway train that stops for nothing.</u>
	an emotion, such as anger	Personification: His <u>angry fastball</u> makes batters want to run!

Writing

2. Write informative/explanatory texts to examine and convey complex ideas, concepts, and information clearly and accurately through the effective selection, organization, and analysis of content.

2.a. Introduce a topic; organize complex ideas, concepts, and information to make important connections and distinctions; include formatting, graphics, and multimedia when useful to aiding comprehension.

2.b. Develop the topic with well-chosen, relevant, and sufficient facts, extended definitions, concrete details, quotations, or other information and examples appropriate to the audience's knowledge of the topic.

2.d. Use precise language and domain-specific vocabulary to manage the complexity of the topic.

5. Develop and strengthen writing as needed by planning, revising, editing, rewriting, or trying a new approach, focusing on addressing what is most significant for a specific purpose and audience.

Creating a Memorable Image

Word choice refers to the specific words or figures of speech that a writer chooses to create a memorable impression in the reader's mind. To create vivid and memorable images, writers of descriptive essays choose words that appeal to the five senses of sight, sound, smell, taste, and touch. Use the tips below to create descriptions that will move your readers and make your essay memorable.

Choosing Appropriate Images Think about what impression you wish to create about the person or object you are describing. Be sure to consider your readers. For example, if you are describing a favorite uncle, readers will want to know what is most memorable about him—his sense of humor, his quiet wisdom, or his kindness. Use a chart like this one for help in choosing appropriate images and sensory details.

Characteristic	Words and Phrases
humor	*His soft blue eyes, edged with tiny laugh wrinkles, always had a smile behind them. When he laughed his whole body shook; just watching him made others laugh along with him.*

Reviewing Word Choice Think about not only the meaning, or *denotation* of the words you choose, but also their *connotation*—the set of ideas and emotions associated with the word. For example, consider the following:

> *His jaw was set in <u>firm</u> lines.*

> *His jaw was set in <u>hard</u> lines.*

Even though the words *firm* and *hard* have similar denotations, *firm* has a more positive connotation. It implies that the person has a strong character. In contrast, the word *hard* implies that the person is unbending or lacking in compassion for others.

Personalize Voice To create a genuine voice that "sounds" like you, choose words that both create vivid descriptions and reflect your personality. Review your essay, circling words or phrases that sound forced. Consider revising your essay with words that are truer to your voice.

Forced: *Father always sported a fedora of unobtrusive green.*

Genuine: *Dad always wore a hat that was a soft, faded green.*

PH **WRITING COACH**

Further instruction and practice are available in *Prentice Hall Writing Coach*.

Drafting Strategies

Present a controlling idea. Select details that build toward conveying a single main impression. Write one sentence that captures the main idea you want to express. Present this sentence in your introduction. Then, develop that idea in the rest of your essay.

Organize to describe. Choose an organization that showcases the details you will feature. These plans are useful when drafting descriptive writing:

- **General to specific:** Use this structure when describing a person, thing, or idea.
- **Chronological organization:** Use time order to bring events to life for reader.
- **Spatial organization:** Use this plan to show where things are located in relation to each other; for example, a place, a building, or an object.

Fully develop your ideas. Begin each paragraph with a statement that conveys the main idea. Next, extend that idea by restating or explaining the first sentence. Then, elaborate by providing supporting details.

Statement: At track meets, my coach shows few of her reactions.

Extension: She watches quietly from the sidelines.

Elaboration: She offers a smile and an encouraging word before we compete, but she rarely explodes with emotion.

Common Core State Standards

Writing

2.a. Introduce a topic; organize complex ideas, concepts, and information to make important connections and distinctions; include formatting, graphics, and multimedia when useful to aiding comprehension.

2.b Develop the topic with well-chosen, relevant, and sufficient facts, extended definitions, concrete details, quotations, or other information and examples appropriate to the audience's knowledge of the topic.

2.d. Use precise language to manage the complexity of the topic.

5. Develop and strengthen writing as needed by planning, revising, editing, rewriting, or trying a new approach, focusing on addressing what is most significant for a specific purpose and audience.

Language

1.b. Use various types of phrases and clauses to convey specific meanings and add variety and interest to writing.

Revising Strategies

Frame your description. Make sure your opening and closing paragraphs frame your work. Circle details in the opening that vividly introduce your topic. Circle details in your conclusion that add insight about your topic. If too few details are circled, consider adding some.

Model: Revising to Add Detail

Barney's fur was ragged-looking, filled with burrs and bits of leaves. A deep bloody gash on his left hind leg He moved, caused him to move slowly, with a severe limp.

> The addition of vivid details clearly establishes the topic.

Choose vivid words. Review your essay, circling vague or dull word choices. Consider replacements that appeal to the senses.

Dull: The blanket felt good.

Vivid: The soft flannel blanket felt smooth, warm, and cozy.

Revising to Vary Sentence Patterns

To make your writing more fluid and engaging, vary your style by beginning some sentences with prepositional phrases.

Identifying Prepositional Phrases A preposition and its object—the accompanying noun or pronoun—is called a prepositional phrase. Some prepositional phrases act as adjectives and some act as adverbs.

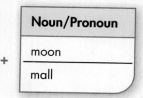

Preposition		Noun/Pronoun		Prepositional Phrase
of		moon		of the silvery moon
at	+	mall	=	at the local mall

Many prepositions express spatial or time-order relationships, which make them useful tools when writing a description.

> **Time:** after the game; before dinner; at two o'clock; for a day

> **Space:** under the table; near the river; in school; in my hand

Varying Sentences With Prepositional Phrases In these examples, subjects are italicized, verbs are underlined, and prepositional phrases appear in parentheses:

Repeated subject-verb pattern: *She* <u>wakes</u> up early. *She* <u>makes</u> breakfast. *She* <u>makes</u> lunch (after that).

Revision: *She* <u>wakes</u> up early. *She* <u>makes</u> breakfast. (After that), *she* <u>makes</u> lunch.

Follow these steps to vary your sentences in your own writing.

1. Read your draft aloud. Listen for overuse of the subject-verb sentence pattern.

2. Identify sentences that contain a prepositional phrase.

3. Rewrite the sentence, starting with the prepositional phrase. Be sure the phrase is close to the word it modifies.

4. If the prepositional phrase contains four or more words, set it off from the words that follow with a comma.

Grammar in Your Writing
Reread the first two paragraphs of your descriptive essay, looking for overuse of the subject-verb sentence pattern. Rewrite some sentences by beginning them with prepositional phrases.

Ⓒ Common Core
State Standards

Language
2.c. Spell correctly.

Hands

My hands are ragged. They look like the hands of a messy toddler in a way, with bitten cuticles and visibly clammy palms. But they are also covered in small scars, tiny and white, or larger and more raw-looking red marks. They were unmarked when I was a baby, but not anymore. I scar easily.

> Jordan establishes her topic with vivid details.

We had an assignment in drawing class to draw our hands holding an object. The teacher didn't tell us that the object had to be important in our lives until we'd already brought them in, so apparently handcuffs are important to me. The drawing wasn't terrible, but I never spent that much time staring at my hands before. My usual attention span for drawing is, at most, a half an hour, and I usually tend to give up once the shading gets complicated and careful attention must be paid to detail. I'm not a detail person. But in this assignment, I was forced to look at all the craggy grossness of my hands. I tried to stop biting my nails so that I wouldn't have to attempt the stubby, oddly textured things that pass for my fingernails, but it's a habit. I didn't start biting my nails until high school; whenever I have a lot of stress in my life, my nails look like they have been through a shredder.

I often find myself with my hands in my mouth when talking to someone, making for an extremely socially awkward moment. I never know if I should finish the nail-biting process or stop in mid-bite, leaving a partially severed nail.

> Jordan discusses what her topic means, not just what it looks like.

I can't leave my hands alone. An unpicked cuticle is an incomplete cuticle; a long, unbitten nail is not a true nail. I also have calluses on my fingertips from playing bass, guitar, and violin, and those provide endless fodder for fidgeting. Other people choose to stare off into space; I choose, or am compelled, to endlessly pick at my hands.

My hands are also extremely cold. They are the long-fingered, clammy hands of the Grim Reaper, un-holdable hands. Even my mother has told me that they are cold and clammy. Cold, clammy hands are things that cannot possibly be put in a good light. There is no bright side. I can imagine a palm reader, one who has seen countless hands, recoiling in horror from my hands, pointing at my life line from a distance instead of mapping it out on the skin.

> Jordan's genuine voice comes through here. Her sense of humor is evident.

Novels from a certain era always take care to point out the condition of a lady's hands. Long, white, glove-enclosed fingers are ladies' hands. Cracked red hands are scullery maid hands. My hands place me squarely in the pot-scrubbing set.

But I'm not sure that I'd want ladies' hands. I have a friend who has uncallused, soft and feminine hands. Her fingers are faintly chubby in an extremely cute, cherubic way. They don't look strong or capable, just soft and helpless as those of a baby. My hands, callused, bony, and cold, look strong and capable, not dainty, lily-white, and frail, but tough.

> Jordan draws a clear and interesting conclusion in her essay.

Editing and Proofreading

Check your draft for errors in grammar, punctuation, and capitalization.

Focus on spelling. Remember to check your spelling even if you use a word processor's spelling software. Spell-checkers cannot tell if you have spelled a word correctly but have used the wrong word. For example, you might have used a *homophone*—a word that sounds like another but is spelled differently, such as *site* and *sight* or *role* and *roll*.

Publishing and Presenting

Consider one of the following ways to share your writing:

Organize a display. Work with classmates to create a display of your essays. Select an appropriate title and organization. For example, you might use one area of the display for essays that describe people. Add artwork or photographs to complement the essays. Consider posting the collection online.

Prepare an oral reading. Select music or sound effects to accompany your essay in an oral reading. Practice until you are confident. Then, deliver your reading for the class. When you are done, gracefully accept applause and express your thanks. If possible, record the reading on audiotape.

Reflecting on Your Writing

Jot down your answers to this question:

How did writing to describe your subject help you understand it?

Rubric for Self-Assessment

Find evidence in your writing to address each category. Then, use the rating scale to grade your work.

© **Spiral Review**
Earlier in this unit, you learned about **prepositions and prepositional phrases** (p. 668) and **direct objects** (p.690). Check the sentences in your essay to make sure that you have used correct prepositions and that action verbs have direct objects when appropriate.

Criteria	Rating Scale				
	not very				very
Focus: How clear is the impression you create of your subject?	1	2	3	4	5
Organization: How logical is your organization?	1	2	3	4	5
Support/Elaboration: How well do you use sensory details?	1	2	3	4	5
Style: How effective is your use of figurative language?	1	2	3	4	5
Conventions: How correct is your grammar, especially your use of prepositional phrases?	1	2	3	4	5
Word Choice: How effective are the words and images you have chosen?	1	2	3	4	5

Leveled Texts

Build your skills and improve your comprehension of poetry with texts of increasing complexity.

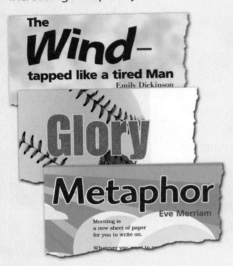

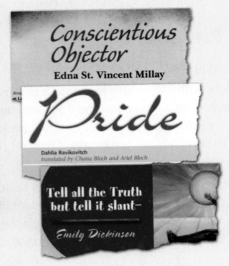

The poets in **Poetry Collection 5** remind us that even ordinary events contain a little bit of the extraordinary.

In each of the poems in **Poetry Collection 6,** the poet confronts life's limitations.

Common Core State Standards

Meet these standards with either **Poetry Collection 5** (p. 718) or **Poetry Collection 6** (p. 726).

Reading Literature

2. Determine a theme or central idea of a text. *(Reading Skill: Paraphrase)*

4. Determine the meaning of words and phrases as they are used in a text, including figurative and connotative meanings; analyze the cumulative impact of specific word choices on meaning and tone. *(Literary Analysis: Figurative Language)*

Writing

1. Write arguments to support claims in an analysis of substantive topics or texts, using valid reasoning and relevant and sufficient evidence. *(Writing: Critical Essay)*

6. Use technology, including the Internet, to produce, publish, and update individual or shared writing products, taking advantage of technology's capacity to link to other information and to display information flexibly and

dynamically. *(Research and Technology: Literary History Report)*

9. Draw evidence from literary or informational texts to support analysis, reflection, and research. *(Writing: Critical Essay)*

Language

1.b. Use various types of phrases and clauses to convey specific meanings and add variety and interest to writing or presentations. *(Conventions: Prepositional Phrases)*

5.a. Interpret figures of speech in context and analyze their role in the text.

6. Acquire and use accurately general academic and domain-specific words and phrases. *(Vocabulary: Word Study)*

Literary Analysis: Figurative Language

Figurative language is language that is not meant to be taken literally. Poets often use the following **figures of speech,** or specific types of figurative language, to convey their ideas in fresh and innovative ways.

Each of these figures of speech is a comparison of two things that are alike in certain respects but not in others.

- A **simile** is a comparison of unlike things using the word *like* or *as*. *Example:* He runs *like* a cheetah.
- In a **metaphor,** one thing is spoken about as if it were something else. *Example:* During the holidays, the stores *are* zoos.
- In **personification,** an object, animal, or idea is spoken of as if it were human. *Example:* The trees danced in the wind.

By making unexpected and surprising comparisons, figurative language helps the reader to think about familiar ideas in new ways. Because figurative language often expresses meaning in concrete pictures, it is an important source of **imagery,** or word-pictures, in poetry.

Reading Skill: Paraphrase

To understand a poem's central idea, **paraphrase** it, or restate the meaning of lines in your own words.

- Begin by **picturing the imagery,** forming clear pictures of the descriptive details in the poem.
- Then, consider how ideas in the lines you paraphrase are related to these pictures.

Using the Strategy: Paraphrase Chart

Use a chart like the one shown to paraphrase passages as you read.

Descriptive Details	What I Picture	My Paraphrase
"A snapshot in the radiant flood, / Raccoon glares, as any outlaw should. / His craft lies knotted in his paws; / His canny forest ways undo suburban laws."	a raccoon caught in the light when someone opens the back door	The raccoon freezes in the light of an open door. He is clever with his paws and can outsmart the person whose yard he is visiting.

Does all *communication* serve a positive purpose?

Writing About the Big Question

In Poetry Collection 5, the poets communicate their reflections about details associated with ordinary events. Use these sentence starters to develop your ideas about the Big Question.

People can make a deeper **connection** to everyday experiences by

_____.

Meaning can be found in ordinary things or events when

_____.

While You Read Look for interesting, unusual, or positive descriptions of ordinary people, actions, or things.

Vocabulary

Read each word and its definition. Decide whether you know the word well, know it a little bit, or do not know it at all. After you read, see how your knowledge of each word has increased.

- **countenance** (kount´ 'n əns) *n.* a person's face or expression (p. 718) *Danielle's <u>countenance</u> showed the calm she felt.*

- **tremulous** (trem´ yoō ləs) *adj.* trembling; quivering (p. 718) *I could tell the speaker was nervous by his <u>tremulous</u> voice.* *tremulously adv. tremulousness n.*

- **stance** (stans) *n.* the way one stands, especially the placement of the feet (p. 721) *The hockey player's <u>stance</u> was relaxed and upright as he swung. stand n. stand v.*

- **conjured** (kän´ jərd) *v.* performed tricks in which things seem to appear, disappear, or change as if by magic (p. 721) *As a child, I believed my mother <u>conjured</u> perfect weather for my party. conjurer n.*

Word Study

The **Latin suffix -ous** means "characterized by" or "having the quality of."

In "The Wind—tapped like a tired Man," the wind makes a **tremulous** sound, like the sound glass makes when it shakes or quivers.

Emily Dickinson

(1830–1886)

Author of "The Wind—tapped like a tired Man" (p. 718)

Now regarded as one of America's greatest poets, Emily Dickinson was scarcely known during her own time. She never married and spent almost her entire life in the home of her family. As she grew older, she rarely left her house. Although she wrote 1,775 poems, only seven were published during her life—and those were published anonymously.

Yusef Komunyakaa

(b. 1947)

Author of "Glory" (p. 720)

Poet Yusef Komunyakaa has come a long way in his life. Born in the small rural town of Bogalusa, Louisiana, he is now a creative writing professor at Princeton University in New Jersey. Komunyakaa's collection *Neon Vernacular* earned him a Pulitzer Prize in 1994. He has said that "the writer has to get down to the guts of the thing. . . . "

Eve Merriam

(1916–1992)

Author of "Metaphor" (p. 722)

Eve Merriam developed a fascination with poetry at an early age. She has written poetry for both children and adults. Merriam has called poetry the most immediate and richest form of communication.

The *Wind–*
tapped like a tired Man

Emily Dickinson

Reading Skill
Paraphrase Describe two images that the third stanza suggests, and then paraphrase the stanza to understand its content.

Vocabulary
countenance (kount´'n əns) *n.* a person's face or expression
tremulous (trem´ yoo ləs) *adj.* trembling; quivering

The Wind—tapped like a tired Man—
And like a Host—"Come in"
I boldly answered—entered then
My Residence within

5   A Rapid—footless Guest—
To offer whom a Chair
Were as impossible as hand
A Sofa to the Air—

No Bone had He to bind Him—
10 His Speech was like the Push
Of numerous Humming Birds at once
From a superior Bush—

His Countenance—a Billow—
His Fingers, as He passed
15 Let go a music—as of tunes
Blown tremulous in Glass—

He visited—still flitting—
Then like a timid Man
Again, He tapped—'twas flurriedly—
20 And I became alone—

The Wind—tapped like a tired Man **719**

Glory

Yusef Komunyakaa

Most were married teenagers
Working knockout shifts daybreak
To sunset six days a week—
Already old men playing ball
5   In a field between a row of shotgun houses
& the Magazine Lumber Company.
They were all Jackie Robinson
& Willie Mays, a touch of
Josh Gibson & Satchell Paige[1]
10 In each **stance** & swing, a promise
Like a hesitation pitch always
At the edge of their lives,
Arms sharp as rifles.
The Sunday afternoon heat
15 Flared like thin flowered skirts
As children & wives cheered.
The men were like cats
Running backwards to snag
Pop-ups & high-flies off
20 Fences, stealing each other's glory.
The old deacons & raconteurs[2]
Who umpired made an *Out* or *Safe*
Into a song & dance routine.
Runners hit the dirt
25 & slid into homeplate,
Cleats catching light,
As they **conjured** escapes, outfoxing
Double plays. In the few seconds
It took a man to eye a woman
30 Upon the makeshift bleachers,
A stolen base or homerun
Would help another man
Survive the new week.

Vocabulary
stance (stans) *n.*
the way one stands,
especially the place-
ment of the feet

conjured (kän´ jərd)
v. performed tricks in
which things seem to
appear, disappear, or
change as if by magic

---

1. **Jackie Robinson / & Willie Mays . . . / Josh Gibson &
Satchell Paige** African American baseball stars of the 1920s
through the 1970s.
2. **deacons & raconteurs** (rak´ än tʉrz´) assistant officers of a
church and skilled storytellers.

Metaphor

Eve Merriam

Morning is
a new sheet of paper
for you to write on.

Whatever you want to say,
5 all day,
until night
folds it up
and files it away.

The bright words and the dark words
10 are gone
until dawn
and a new day
to write on.

Literary Analysis
Figurative Language
What image does the poet use to convey the idea that each morning is a new start?

Critical Thinking

1. **Key Ideas and Details** **(a)** Who is the guest in "The Wind—tapped like a tired Man"? **(b)** Identify three ways in which the guest is unlike any other. **(c)** Does the speaker see the wind as menacing or kind? Use details from the poem to explain.

2. **Key Ideas and Details** **(a)** What hours do the men in "Glory" work? **(b)** What does the phrase "already old men" suggest about the effect of this work schedule? **(c)** In what way might a "stolen base or home run" help a man "survive the new week"?

3. **Craft and Structure** **(a)** In "Metaphor," to what does the speaker compare the morning? **(b)** To what does she compare a person's actions during the day? **(c)** What attitude toward a new day might this poem inspire in readers? Explain.

4. **Integration of Knowledge and Ideas** **(a)** Identify the ordinary events described in these poems. Then, explain how the poets present these events in a new light. **(b)** Do you see these as positive poems? Explain. *[Connect to the Big Question: Does all communication serve a positive purpose?]*

Literary Analysis: Figurative Language

© 1. Craft and Structure Among the three poems in Poetry Collection 5, find two examples of a **simile.**

© 2. Craft and Structure Find a **metaphor** in one of the poems.

© 3. Craft and Structure Identify an example of **personification** in one of the poems.

© 4. Craft and Structure (a) Using a chart like the one below, explain and evaluate each device you identified. **(b)** Discuss your evaluations with a partner. **(c)** In the chart's last column, explain whether your discussion changed your appreciation of the poems.

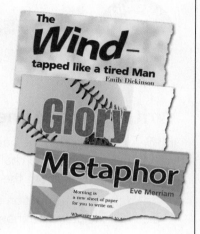

Poem	Device	Explanation	First Evaluation	Final Evaluation

Reading Skill: Paraphrase

5. (a) Describe the image you picture when reading the third stanza of "The Wind—tapped like a tired Man." **(b) Paraphrase** this stanza. **(c)** How does paraphrasing this stanza help you understand its central idea?

6. (a) Choose either "Glory" or "Metaphor" and paraphrase it to write a brief summary. **(b)** Compare your paraphrase to the original. What qualities does the poem have that your paraphrase does not?

Vocabulary

© Acquisition and Use Use each word pair correctly in a sentence.

1. countenance; mirror

2. tremulous; speech

3. stance; feet

4. conjured; thought

Word Study Use the context of the sentences and what you know about the **Latin suffix -ous** to explain your answer to each question.

1. Will a *joyous* person want to skip, jump, and laugh?

2. Could a *disastrous* situation be fixed quickly with little effort?

Word Study

The **Latin suffix -ous** means "characterized by" or "having the quality of."

Apply It Explain how the suffix -*ous* contributes to the meanings of these words. Consult a dictionary if necessary.

bilious
dexterous
garrulous

Does all *communication* serve a positive purpose?

Writing About the Big Question

In Poetry Collection 6, the poems' speakers present their plans for dealing with life's limitations and challenges. Use these sentence starters to develop your ideas about the Big Question.

An example of a situation or challenge that a person may not completely understand or know how to **respond** to appropriately is

_____.

Our limitations as humans can lead to **isolation** if _____.

While You Read Look for the the ways the poets characterize complex concepts such as death, pride, and truth. Then, determine whether literature like this can help us get through difficult times.

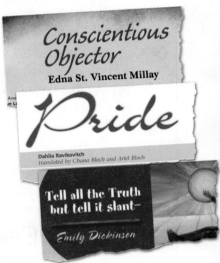

Vocabulary

Read each word and its definition. Decide whether you know the word well, know it a little bit, or do not know it at all. After you read, see how your knowledge of each word has increased.

- **overcome** (ō´ vər kum´) *v.* to master or prevail over (p. 726) *I knew I could <u>overcome</u> my poor start and win the race.*

- **flourishes** (flɐr´ ish əs) *v.* grows vigorously; thrives (p. 727) *This plant <u>flourishes</u> in sunlight but has a hard time growing in shade. flourish n. flourishing adj.*

- **circuit** (sɐr´ kit) *n.* act of going around something (p. 728) *The moon makes a monthly <u>circuit</u> of Earth. circuit v. circuitous adj. circuitously adj.*

- **infirm** (in fɐrm´) *adj.* weak; feeble (p. 728) *Our <u>infirm</u> uncle had trouble walking up the stairs. infirmly adv. infirmity n. infirmary n.*

Word Study

The **Latin suffix -ary** means "relating to" or "like."

"Tell all the Truth but tell it slant," describes an **infirm** delight, or one that is "weak" or "frail." An **infirmary** is a place for people who are frail or sick.

Edna St. Vincent Millay

(1892–1950)

Author of "Conscientious Objector" (p. 726)

Edna St. Vincent Millay was not yet in college when she first won fame as a poet. After graduating from Vassar, in Poughkeepsie, New York, she moved to New York City, where she acted in plays and pursued her writing career. Beautiful and outspoken, she received both praise and scorn for her controversial opinions on issues such as women's rights.

Dahlia Ravikovitch

(1936–2005)

Author of "Pride" (p. 727)

The Israeli poet Dahlia Ravikovitch was born in a town near Tel Aviv and was raised on a kibbutz, a cooperative settlement. Her father's death in an accident when she was six was a powerful influence. Her intensely personal poems are charged with images from nature, history, and religion.

Emily Dickinson

(1830–1886)

Author of "Tell all the Truth but tell it slant—" (p. 728)

Although Emily Dickinson led a reclusive life—she rarely left her home and saw only seven of her poems published in her lifetime—today she shines as one of the brightest stars of American poetry. It was only in 1955 that a scholar, Thomas H. Johnson, was able to assemble her complete works in one book. Dickinson is widely considered a truly individual voice in poetry.

Conscientious Objector[1]

Edna St. Vincent Millay

I shall die, but that is all that I shall do for Death.

I hear him leading his horse out of the stall; I hear the
    clatter on the barn-floor.
He is in haste; he has business in Cuba, business in the
    Balkans, many calls to make this morning.
But I will not hold the bridle while he cinches the girth.[2]
5 And he may mount by himself: I will not give him a leg up.

Though he flick my shoulders with his whip, I will not tell
    him which way the fox ran.
With his hoof on my breast, I will not tell him where the
    black boy hides in the swamp.
I shall die, but that is all that I shall do for Death; I am not
    on his pay-roll.

I will not tell him the whereabouts of my friends nor of my
    enemies either.
10 Though he promise me much, I will not map him the route to
    any man's door.

Am I a spy in the land of the living, that I should deliver men
    to Death?
Brother, the password and the plans of our city are safe with
    me; never through me
Shall you be overcome.

Literary Analysis
Figurative Language
Identify two details in this stanza that contribute to the personification of Death.

Vocabulary
overcome (ō´vər kum´) v. to master or prevail over

---

1. **conscientious** (kän´ shē en´ shəs) **objector** one who refuses to participate in warfare for religious or ethical reasons.
2. **cinches the girth** securely fastens the band that goes around a horse's belly to hold the saddle on.

Pride

Dahlia Ravikovitch
translated by Chana Bloch and Ariel Bloch

I tell you, even rocks crack,
and not because of age.
For years they lie on their backs
in the heat and the cold,
5 so many years,
it almost seems peaceful.
They don't move, so the cracks stay hidden.
A kind of pride.
Years pass over them, waiting.
10 Whoever is going to shatter them
hasn't come yet.
And so the moss flourishes, the seaweed
whips around,
the sea pushes through and rolls back—
15 the rocks seem motionless.
Till a little seal comes to rub against them,
comes and goes away.
And suddenly the rock has an open wound.
I told you, when rocks break, it happens by surprise.
20 And people, too.

Vocabulary
flourishes (flʊr´ ish əs) *v.*
grows vigorously; thrives

▼ **Critical Viewing**
In what ways does this image show both the strength and the fragility identified in the poem? **[Analyze]**

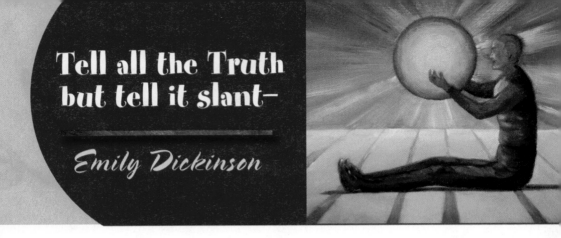

Tell all the Truth but tell it slant—

Emily Dickinson

Reading Skill

Paraphrase Restate the first line in your own words.

Vocabulary

circuit (sur´ kit) *n.* act of going around something

infirm (in furm´) *adj.* weak; feeble

Tell all the Truth but tell it slant—
Success in Circuit lies
Too bright for our infirm Delight
The Truth's superb surprise
5 As Lightning to the Children eased
With explanation kind
The Truth must dazzle gradually
Or every man be blind—

Critical Thinking

Cite textual evidence to support your responses.

1. **Key Ideas and Details** **(a)** What are two things the speaker in "Conscientious Objector" will not do? **(b)** Give your own example of a specific action the speaker would not take. Explain your choice.

2. **Key Ideas and Details** **(a)** According to the speaker in "Pride," what may rocks hide from view? **(b) Interpret:** Why might "a kind of pride" lead them to hide this thing? **(c) Extend:** What advice would the speaker in "Pride" give to someone dealing with stress or grief?

3. **Key Ideas and Details** **(a)** According to the speaker in "Tell all the Truth but tell it slant—," how much of the truth should be told? **(b) Interpret:** What does the speaker mean by the expression "tell it slant"? **(c)** Do you agree that truth often takes the form of a "surprise"? Explain.

4. **Integration of Knowledge and Ideas** **(a)** In what ways does each poem reflect limitations that all people share? **(b)** Why might people choose to read poetry that reflects these common elements? **(c)** Do you think these poems present workable solutions to difficult problems? Explain. *[Connect to the Big Question: Does all communication serve a positive purpose?]*

After You Read
Poetry Collection 6

Conscientious Objector •
Pride • Tell all the Truth
but tell it slant—

Literary Analysis: Figurative Language

Ⓒ 1. Craft and Structure Among the three poems in Poetry Collection 6, find one example of a **simile.**

Ⓒ 2. Craft and Structure Find a **metaphor** in one of the poems.

Ⓒ 3. Craft and Structure Identify an example of **personification** in one of the poems.

Ⓒ 4. Craft and Structure (a) Using a chart like the one below, explain and evaluate each device you identified. **(b)** Discuss your evaluations with a partner. **(c)** In the chart's last column, explain whether your discussion changed your appreciation of the poems.

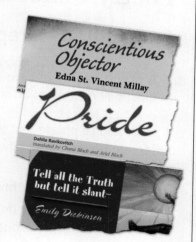

Poem	Device	Explanation	First Evaluation	Final Evaluation

Reading Skill: Paraphrase

5. (a) Paraphrase the last two stanzas of "Conscientious Objector."
(b) Compare your paraphrase to the original. What qualities does the poem have that your paraphrase does not? **(c)** Based on your paraphrase, what do you think is this poem's central idea?

6. (a) Describe an image you pictured when reading "Tell all the Truth but tell it slant—" or "Pride." **(b)** Write a brief summary of one of these two poems by paraphrasing it.

Vocabulary

Ⓒ Acquisition and Use Use each word pair correctly in a sentence.

1. flourishes; talent
2. circuit; speed
3. overcome; adversity
4. infirm; recuperate

Word Study Use the context of the sentences and what you know about the **Latin suffix -ary** to explain your answer to each question.

1. Would a *mortuary* be a place to help people after an illness?
2. If your activities after school are *customary,* are you doing them for the first time?

Word Study

The **Latin suffix -ary** means "relating to" or "like."

Apply It Explain how the suffix -*ary* contributes to the meanings of these words. Consult a dictionary if necessary.
emissary
tributary
proprietary

Integrated Language Skills

Poetry Collections 5 and 6

Conventions: Prepositional Phrases

Poetry Collection 5

A **prepositional phrase** is a phrase that can modify other words by functioning either as an adjective or as an adverb within sentences.

A prepositional phrase that serves as an adjective is called an **adjective phrase.** It modifies a noun or pronoun and tells *what kind* or *which one.*

Example: Adjective Phrase: The woman *in the blue dress* is a singer.

The phrase *in the blue dress* modifies *woman,* a noun, by telling *which one:* Which woman? the one *in the blue dress*

A prepositional phrase that serves as an adverb is called an **adverb phrase.** It modifies a verb and tells *where, when, in what way,* or *to what extent.*

Poetry Collection 6

Example: Adverb Phrase: Her music group sings *at the folk festival.*

The phrase *at the folk festival* modifies *sings,* a verb, by telling *where:* Where does her music group sing? *at the folk festival*

Practice A Identify the prepositional phrase in each sentence and tell whether it is an adjective phrase or an adverb phrase.

1. The runner slid into second base.
2. The sun rises in the sky.
3. Children in the bleachers cheered.
4. Dickinson's ideas leap from the page.

Reading Application Find two examples of prepositional phrases, either adjective phrases or adverb phrases, in the poems in Poetry Collection 5.

Practice B Add a prepositional phrase in the blank. The phrase should act as an adjective or adverb phrase and give additional information.

1. Death walks _____.
2. The rocks _____ lie motionless.
3. The crack _____ can open wide.
4. Emily Dickinson lived _____.

Writing Application Look at the model sentence and tell which prepositional phrase is an adjective and which is an adverb. Then, following the model, write three sentences of your own.

The seal at the seashore rubs its back on the rock.

PH | **WRITING COACH** | Further instruction and practice are available in *Prentice Hall Writing Coach.*

Writing

Argumentative Text Write a **critical essay** in which you reflect on and argue which of the **language techniques** in the poems you found most effective. Choose a poem from either Poetry Collection 5 or Poetry Collection 6.

- Decide on the criteria you will use in your evaluation. For example, you might judge the poem on the basis of how clever the use of language is.
- Review the poems carefully, using your criteria as a guide. For additional insight, research what critics have said about the language techniques of the poet.
- Note any words, lines, or sections of the poem that still confuse you. To clarify the text, try finding the word in a dictionary, paraphrasing the lines, describing the image, or discussing possible interpretations with a partner.
- As you draft, present your evaluation concisely. Then, support each claim with relevant quotations from the poems.

Grammar Application In your draft, vary your sentences by beginning at least one sentence with a prepositional phrase. Label any prepositional phrases in your essay as adjective or adverb phrases.

Writing Workshop: *Work in Progress*

Prewriting for an Analytical Response For an analytical response you might write, choose a story or poem that you like. Write five questions about the work's quality. Then, write five questions about how the work achieves its purpose. Put your Questions List in your writing portfolio.

Research and Technology

Build and Present Knowledge Write and present a brief **literary history report** explaining how Dickinson's poems were eventually published *or* describing Edna St. Vincent Millay's career. Follow these guidelines:

- Conduct research by using a variety of sources, including encyclopedias, biographical encyclopedias, and the Internet.
- Check the claims in one source against the claims in the others, considering the reliability of each source.
- Choose information to present that is significant, such as specific facts and dates. Omit details that do not support your purpose.
- Integrate the information from your sources into an informational report.

Present your report to the class and invite discussion about the information you have gathered.

Common Core State Standards

L.9-10.1.b; W.9-10.1, W.9-10.6, W.9-10.9
[For the full wording of the standards, see page 714.]

Use this prewriting activity to prepare for the **Writing Workshop** on page 768.

PHLit Online!
www.PHLitOnline.com
- Interactive graphic organizers
- Grammar tutorial
- Interactive journals

ⓒ Leveled Texts

Build your skills and improve your comprehension of poetry with texts of increasing complexity.

The poems in **Poetry Collection 7** describe the beauty of sight and sound.

Each poem in **Poetry Collection 8** uses descriptive language to capture a specific mood.

ⓒ Common Core State Standards

Meet these standards with either **Poetry Collection 7** (p. 736) or **Poetry Collection 8** (p. 744).

Reading Literature
2. Determine a theme or central idea of a text. *(Reading Skill: Paraphrase)*
4. Determine the meaning of words and phrases as they are used in a text, including figurative and connotative meanings; analyze the cumulative impact of specific word choices on meaning and tone. *(Literary Analysis: Spiral Review)*

Writing
4. Produce clear and coherent writing in which the development, organization, and style are appropriate to task, purpose, and audience. *(Writing: Poem)*

6. Use technology, including the Internet, to produce, publish, and update individual or shared writing products. *(Research and Technology: Visual Arts Presentation)*
7. Conduct short as well as more sustained research projects to answer a question or solve a problem; synthesize multiple sources on the subject. *(Research and Technology: Visual Arts Presentation)*

Language
1. Demonstrate command of the conventions of standard English grammar. *(Conventions: Infinitives)*
6. Acquire and use accurately general academic and domain-specific words and phrases. *(Vocabulary: Word Study)*

Literary Analysis: Sound Devices

To tap the music in words, poets use a variety of **sound devices,** or patterns of word sounds. These include the following:

- **Alliteration:** repetition of consonant sounds at the beginnings of nearby words, as in *"silent song"*
- **Assonance:** repetition of vowel sounds in nearby stressed syllables, as in *"<u>deep</u> and <u>dream</u>less."* Unlike rhyming syllables, assonant syllables end in different consonants.
- **Consonance:** repetition of consonant sounds at the ends of nearby stressed syllables with different vowel sounds, as in the words *"<u>heat</u> of <u>light</u>ning"*
- **Onomatopoeia:** use of words to imitate actual sounds, such as *buzz, tap,* or *splash*

Sound devices can add to the mood of a poem, imitate the sound of events, or reflect a poem's meaning. As you read, note how poets use sound devices to create a mood or emphasize their ideas.

Reading Skill: Paraphrase

To help you understand the central idea of a poem and relate it to other reading and experiences in your life, **paraphrase** the text, restating the ideas in your own words. First, **break down long sentences** into parts. Identify the main actions and who or what performs them. Next, identify details that show when, where, how, or why each action is performed. Then, write the paraphrase in your own words.

Using the Strategy: Paraphrase Chart

As you read, use a paraphrase chart like this to break down sentences.

Breaking Down Long Sentences to Paraphrase
"When fighting for his country, he lost an arm and was suddenly afraid: 'From now on, I shall only be able to do things by halves....'" from "A Man," by Nina Cassian
Who? he **Did what?** lost, was suddenly afraid
Paraphrase: He lost his arm fighting in a war and was afraid of what his life would be like.

Does all *communication* serve a positive purpose?

Writing About the Big Question

These poems show how music and a cemetery's striking visual scene can communicate and express human emotions. Use these sentence starters to develop your ideas.

Photographs or stunning scenes can tap **emotion** without words because _____.

One reason a person may feel a **connection** to a particular song or piece of music is _____.

While You Read Look for different ways the subjects of these poems convey emotion to readers.

Vocabulary

Read each word and its definition. Decide whether you know the word well, know it a little bit, or do not know it at all. After you read, see how your knowledge of each word has increased.

- **pallor** (pal´ ər) *n.* lack of color; unnatural paleness (p. 737) *When I saw the pallor of his face, I knew that he was frightened.* pale *adj.* pallid *adj.*

- **ebony** (eb´ ə nē) *adj.* black (p. 737) *The ebony floor contrasts with the white walls.* ebony *n.*

- **melancholy** (mel´ ən käl´ ē) *adj.* sad (p. 737) *The melancholy tone in her voice revealed how much she missed her best friend.* melancholy *n.*

- **foe** (fō) *n.* enemy (p. 738) *Judging by how kindly he treats everyone, I doubt he has a single foe.*

Word Study

The **Latin suffix -or** means "one who takes part in" or "condition, quality, or property of something."

In "The Weary Blues," an old gaslight has the quality of being pale. Its **pallor** provides a backdrop for the blues-playing pianist.

Langston Hughes

(1902–1967)

Author of "The Weary Blues" (p. 736)

As a young man, Langston Hughes moved from Missouri to Kansas to Illinois to Cleveland, Ohio, where he was voted class poet in high school. Later, he settled in the Harlem section of New York City. He contributed to the Harlem Renaissance, a flowering of African American artistic activity in the 1920s and 1930s. Hughes once defined poetry as "the human soul entire, squeezed like a lemon or lime, drop by drop, into atomic words."

John McCrae

(1872–1918)

Author of "In Flanders Fields" (p. 738)

Soldier, poet, doctor—John McCrae was a man of many talents. As a teenager in Ontario, Canada, McCrae joined the militia his father commanded. He also began writing poetry, and he published his first poems as a student at the University of Toronto. After earning a degree in medicine, McCrae fought in the Boer War in South Africa (1899–1902) and served as a medical officer in World War I (1914–1918). He died before the war ended.

Carl Sandburg

(1878–1967)

Author of "Jazz Fantasia" (p. 739)

Carl Sandburg once observed that some poetry was perfect only in form: "All dressed up with nowhere to go." In contrast, his own poetry dresses in blue jeans, going everywhere and speaking in the voices of everyday people. Born in Galesburg, Illinois, Sandburg settled for a time in Chicago. In addition to poetry, Sandburg is famous for his biography of Abraham Lincoln.

The Weary Blues

Langston Hughes

Autumn Lamp (Guitar Player, 1983), Romare Bearden. From the Mecklenburg Autumn Series. Private Collection. ©1997 Romare Bearden Foundation/Licensed by VAGA, New York, NY

Droning a drowsy syncopated[1] tune,
Rocking back and forth to a mellow croon,
    I heard a Negro play.
Down on Lenox Avenue[2] the other night
5 By the pale dull pallor of an old gas light
    He did a lazy sway. . . .
    He did a lazy sway. . . .
To the tune o' those Weary Blues.
With his ebony hands on each ivory key
10 He made that poor piano moan with melody.
    O Blues!
Swaying to and fro on his rickety stool
He played that sad raggy tune like a musical fool.
    Sweet Blues!
15 Coming from a black man's soul.
    O Blues!
In a deep song voice with a melancholy tone
I heard that Negro sing, that old piano moan—
    "Ain't got nobody in all this world,
20   Ain't got nobody but ma self.
    I's gwine to quit ma frownin'
    And put ma troubles on the shelf."
Thump, thump, thump, went his foot on the floor.
He played a few chords then he sang some more—
25   "I got the Weary Blues
    And I can't be satisfied.
    Got the Weary Blues
    And can't be satisfied—
    I ain't happy no mo'
30   And I wish that I had died."
And far into the night he crooned that tune.
The stars went out and so did the moon.
The singer stopped playing and went to bed
While the Weary Blues echoed through his head.
35 He slept like a rock or a man that's dead.

---

1. **syncopated** (siŋ´ kə pāt´ id) *adj.* with a catchy or an emphatic rhythm created by accenting beats that are usually unaccented.
2. **Lenox Avenue** street in Harlem, a historic African American neighborhood in New York City.

Vocabulary
pallor (pal´ ər) *n.* lack of color; unnatural paleness

ebony (eb´ ə nē) *adj.* black

melancholy (mel´ ən käl´ ē) *adj.* sad

Literary Analysis
Sound Devices Why is "thump, thump, thump" an example of onomatopoeia?

◀ **Critical Viewing** Does this painting express the same mood as Hughes's poem? Explain. **[Interpret]**

The Weary Blues **737**

In FLANDERS FIELDS

John McCrae

Background The devastation of the First World War (1914–1918) brought forth a sad beauty. In the torn-up battlegrounds of Flanders, a region of Belgium, thousands of poppies sprang up, flourishing in the fields cleared by war. McCrae turned these flowers into a symbol that generations have worn to honor the dead.

In Flanders fields the poppies blow
Between the crosses, row on row,
   That mark our place; and in the sky
   The larks, still bravely singing, fly
5 Scarce heard amid the guns below.

We are the Dead. Short days ago
We lived, felt dawn, saw sunset glow,
   Loved and were loved, and now we lie
    In Flanders fields.

10 Take up our quarrel with the foe:
To you from failing hands we throw
   The torch; be yours to hold it high.
   If ye break faith with us who die
We shall not sleep, though poppies grow
15   In Flanders fields.

Vocabulary
foe (fō) *n.* enemy

Jazz Fantasia

Carl Sandburg

◀ **Critical Viewing**
What details in the painting suggest that the music being played is filled with energy and life? **[Analyze]**

Drum on your drums, batter on your banjoes,
sob on the long cool winding saxophones.
Go to it, O jazzmen.

Sling your knuckles on the bottoms of the happy
5   tin pans, let your trombones ooze, and go husha-
husha-hush with the slippery sand-paper.

Moan like an autumn wind high in the lonesome treetops,
moan soft like you wanted somebody terrible, cry like a
racing car slipping away from a motorcycle cop,
10 bang-bang! you jazzmen, bang altogether drums, traps,
banjoes, horns, tin cans—make two people fight on the
top of a stairway and scratch each other's eyes in a
clinch[1] tumbling down the stairs.

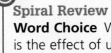

Spiral Review
Word Choice What is the effect of using the verb *batter* to refer to playing the banjo?

Reading Skill
Paraphrase Who or what performs the main action in this stanza?

---

1. **clinch** *n.* in boxing, the act of gripping the opponent's body with the arms.

Can[2] the rough stuff . . . now a Mississippi steamboat
15 pushes up the night river with a hoo-hoo-hoo-oo . . . and
the green lanterns calling to the high soft stars . . . a red
moon rides on the humps of the low river hills . . . go to it,
O jazzmen.

---

2. **Can** *v.* slang for "stop" or "cease."

Critical Thinking

Cite textual evidence to support your responses.

1. **Craft and Structure (a)** List four adjectives that Hughes uses to describe the music in "The Weary Blues." **(b)** Why do you think he chose to use the verb "moan" rather than "play" to describe the piano music? **(c) Infer:** What mood do the adjectives, verb, and song lyrics create?

2. **Key Ideas and Details (a)** Who is the speaker of "In Flanders Fields"? **(b)** Explain the contrasts in the first stanza and the contrasts in the second stanza. **(c)** Do these contrasts help make the speaker's concluding warning effective? Explain.

3. **Craft and Structure (a)** Contrast three of the musical moods described in the third and fourth stanzas of "Jazz Fantasia." **(b)** What do these changing moods suggest about the power of jazz to capture human experience?

4. **Integration of Knowledge and Ideas (a)** In each poem, what emotion do you think the poet wants to convey? **(b)** How does each poet's use of the style and sound of poetry support this goal? **(c)** Do you think the expression of emotion in poetry is a worthy goal? Explain. *[Connect to the Big Question: Does all communication serve a positive purpose?]*

Literary Analysis: Sound Devices

1. Craft and Structure (a) Using a chart like the one below, identify examples of **sound devices** in "The Weary Blues" and "Jazz Fantasia." **(b)** Explain what each example adds to the poem.

Alliteration	Consonance	Assonance	Onomatopoeia

2. Craft and Structure (a) Compare the effects of sound devices in "In Flanders Fields" with those in another poem in Poetry Collection 7. **(b)** Discuss your answer with a partner. **(c)** Together, draw a conclusion about the ways that sound devices can be used in poetry. Present your conclusion to the class.

Reading Skill: Paraphrase

3. (a) Break down the sentence in the first stanza of "In Flanders Fields" by identifying the action and the person or thing completing the action. **(b) Paraphrase** the poem in a brief summary.

4. (a) Paraphrase the third stanza of "Jazz Fantasia." **(b)** How does this paraphrase help you understand the poem's central idea?

Vocabulary

Acquisition and Use An **oxymoron** is a phrase combining contradictory or opposing ideas, often used for poetic effect. Explain whether each phrase below is an oxymoron.

1. healthy pallor

2. dark ebony

3. melancholy celebration

4. friendly foe

Word Study Use the context of the sentences and what you know about the **Latin suffix -or** to explain your answer to each question.

1. Would you press an *accelerator* to make a car go slower?

2. Would you ever put a *conductor* in charge of anything?

Word Study

The **Latin suffix -or** means "one who takes part in" or "condition, quality, or property of something or someone."

Apply It Explain how the suffix -or contributes to the meanings of these words. Consult a dictionary if necessary.

candor
compactor
competitor

Does all *communication* serve a positive purpose?

Writing About the Big Question

In Poetry Collection 8, these poets use sound devices to create a dreamlike mood in their poems. Use these sentence starters to develop your ideas about the Big Question:

Poets use **language** to communicate **meaning** and mood in various ways, such as _____.

Sometimes readers **respond** to the **meaning** of the words and other times they react to the _____.

While You Read Look for examples of sound devices that create "special effects" in the poems.

Vocabulary

Read each word and its definition. Decide whether you know the word well, know it a little bit, or do not know it at all. After you read, see how your knowledge of each word has increased.

- **quench** (kwench) *v.* satisfy; to fulfill a need (p. 744) *I quench my thirst with cold water in the summer.* quenchable *adj.*

- **abysmal** (ə biz′ məl) *adj.* immeasurably deep (p. 745) *The canyon was so abysmal that they could not see the bottom of it.* abyss *n.* abysmally *adv.*

- **millennial** (mi len′ ē əl) *adj.* of 1,000 years (p. 745) *Built in 1023, the abbey will hold its millennial celebration in 2023.* millennium *n.*

- **slumbering** (slum′ bər iŋ) *adj.* sleeping (p. 745) *Do not wake a slumbering bear.* slumber *v.* slumber *n.*

Word Study

The **Latin suffix -ial** means "relating to," "characterized," or "a function of."

In "The Kraken," the **millennial** growth of the huge sea sponges suggests that their size reflects their growth over a millennium, or a thousand years.

Robert Browning

(1812–1889)

Author of "Meeting at Night" (p. 744)

During his lifetime, Robert Browning was not as famous as his wife, poet Elizabeth Barrett Browning. Today, though, it is Robert who is considered the more innovative poet. He is admired especially for his dramatic monologues, poems in which characters speak directly to readers or other characters. Browning's eerie poem "Childe Roland to the Dark Tower Came" helped inspire Stephen King's *Dark Tower* series.

Alfred, Lord Tennyson

(1809–1892)

Author of "The Kraken" (p. 745)

In an age when poets were often celebrities, Alfred, Lord Tennyson was perhaps the most celebrated of all. Named Great Britain's poet laureate in 1850, Tennyson cut quite a figure, dressing in a dashing cape and large-brimmed felt hat. When not in London, he lived on the Isle of Wight in a large home that is now an inn. As laureate, he often wrote patriotic verse and poems drawn from history and legend.

Jean Toomer

(1894–1967)

Author of "Reapers" (p. 746)

"My position in America has been a curious one," Jean Toomer once observed. His maternal grandfather was the first African American ever to serve as a state governor (of Louisiana). Reflecting on his diverse ethnic background—French, Dutch, German, and Native American, as well as African American—Toomer called himself the "human race." He won early fame with the 1923 publication of his book *Cane*, an exploration of African American culture.

Meeting at Night

Robert Browning

▲ **Critical Viewing**
Compare the mood of
this scene with the mood
in the poem. **[Compare
and Contrast]**

Vocabulary
quench (kwench) *v.*
satisfy; to fulfill a need

Literary Analysis
Sound Devices Why is
"sea-scented beach" an
example of both allitera-
tion and of assonance?

1

The gray sea and the long black land;
And the yellow half-moon large and low;
And the startled little waves that leap
In fiery ringlets from their sleep,
5 As I gain the cove with pushing prow,
And quench its speed i' the slushy sand.

2

Then a mile of warm sea-scented beach;
Three fields to cross till a farm appears;
A tap at the pane, the quick sharp scratch
10 And blue spurt of a lighted match,
And a voice less loud, through its joys and fears,
Than the two hearts beating each to each!

The Kraken

Alfred, Lord Tennyson

Below the thunders of the upper deep;
Far, far beneath in the abysmal sea,
His ancient, dreamless, uninvaded sleep
The Kraken[1] sleepeth: faintest sunlights flee
5 About his shadowy sides: above him swell
Huge sponges of millennial growth and height;
And far away into the sickly light,
From many a wondrous grot[2] and secret cell
Unnumbered and enormous polypi[3]
10 Winnow[4] with giant arms the slumbering green.
There hath he lain for ages and will lie
Battening[5] upon huge seaworms in his sleep,
Until the latter fire[6] shall heat the deep;
Then once by man and angels to be seen,
15 In roaring he shall rise and on the surface die.

---

1. **Kraken** (krä´ kən) *n.* in Scandinavian folklore, a sea monster resembling a giant squid.
2. **grot** (grät) *n.* grotto; cave.
3. **polypi** (päl´ i pē) *n.* sea creatures with long, waving tentacles around the mouth, such as the sea anemone or hydra.
4. **Winnow** (win´ ō) *v.* fan; beat with wings or, here, tentacles.
5. **Battening** (bat´ 'n iŋ) *v.* feeding on; growing fat on.
6. **the latter fire** the apocalypse; the end of the world.

Vocabulary

abysmal (ə biz´ məl) *adj.* immeasurably deep

millennial (mi len´ ē əl) *adj.* of 1,000 years

slumbering (slum´ bər iŋ) *adj.* sleeping

Reading Skill

Paraphrase What is the main action in lines 7–10, and who or what performs that action?

REAPERS

Jean Toomer

▲ **Critical Viewing**
Identify one similarity and one difference between this scene and the scene in the poem. **[Compare and Contrast]**

Black reapers with the sound of steel on stones
Are sharpening scythes. I see them place the hones¹
In their hip-pockets as a thing that's done,
And start their silent swinging, one by one.

5   Black horses drive a mower through the weeds,
And there, a field rat, startled, squealing bleeds,
His belly close to ground. I see the blade,
Blood-stained, continue cutting weeds and shade.

---

1. **scythes** (sīthz) . . . **hones** A scythe is a tool for cutting grain or grass, consisting of a sharp blade attached to a long handle. A hone is a hard stone used to sharpen a metal blade.

Critical Thinking

Cite textual evidence to support your responses.

1. **Key Ideas and Details (a)** Identify the series of colors named or suggested in "Meeting at Night." **(b)** How might this series reflect the speaker's emotional and physical journey?

2. **Key Ideas and Details (a)** In "The Kraken," what are the "thunders of the upper deep"? **(b)** Why do you think Tennyson chose the word "thunders" to describe the sounds? **(c)** What has the Kraken been doing? **(d)** According to the poem, what is the only thing that could cause a change in the Kraken's activity?

3. **Key Ideas and Details (a)** According to "Reapers," will the reapers stop their work before it is done? Explain. **(b)** What contrasting ideas are expressed in the last description of the blade?

4. **Integration of Knowledge and Ideas (a)** How does the poets' use of sensory language help convey the main message of each poem? **(b)** What do you think was the purpose of each of the three poems? *[Connect to the Big Question: Does all communication serve a positive purpose?]*

Literary Analysis: Sound Devices

Ⓒ 1. Craft and Structure (a) Using a chart like the one below, identify examples of **sound devices** in "The Kraken" and "Reapers." **(b)** Explain what each example adds to the poem.

Alliteration	Consonance	Assonance	Onomatopoeia

Ⓒ 2. Craft and Structure (a) Compare the effects of sound devices in "Meeting at Night" with those in one of the other poems. **(b)** With a partner, draw a conclusion about the use of sound devices in poetry. Present your conclusion to the class.

Reading Skill: Paraphrase

3. (a) Break down the first clause (ending on the colon) of "The Kraken" by identifying the action and who or what is completing the action. **(b) Paraphrase** the clause.

4. (a) Paraphrase the second stanza of "Meeting at Night." **(b)** How does this paraphrase help you understand the poem?

Vocabulary

Ⓒ Acquisition and Use An **oxymoron** is a phrase combining contradictory or opposing ideas, often used as a figure of speech for poetic effect. Explain whether each phrase below is an oxymoron.

1. millennial instant
2. restful slumber
3. abysmally shallow
4. quenchable thirst

Word Study Use the context of the sentences and what you know about the **Latin suffix -ial** to explain your answer to each question.

1. If you have a *managerial* role, are you in charge of other people or is someone else in charge of you?

2. Will an *industrial* area of a city be filled with parks and wildlife?

Word Study

The **Latin suffix -ial** means "relating to," "characterized," or "a function of."

Apply It Explain how the suffix -ial contributes to the meanings of these words. Consult a dictionary if necessary.

celestial
financial
territorial

Integrated Language Skills

Poetry Collection 7 and 8

Conventions: Infinitives

An **infinitive** is a form of the verb that generally appears with the word *to* and acts as a noun, an adjective, or an adverb.

Example:
Infinitive (*noun*): Last year, my friend Ana learned *to drive.*
Infinitive (*adjective*): She was motivated by a desire *to succeed.*
Infinitive (*adverb*): Unfortunately. I am still unable *to drive.*

An **infinitive phrase** consists of an infinitive along with any modifiers or complements, all acting together as a single part of speech. In standard English, the word *to* should not be split or separated from its verb—its modifiers follow the verb.

Example:
Infinitive phrase: He tried *to answer decisively.* (*decisively* modifies the infinitive *to answer*)

Notice that an infinitive phrase always includes *to* and a verb, as in *to remember.* When *to* is used in a prepositional phrase, it is followed by a noun or pronoun and its modifier, as in *to the store.*

Practice A Identify the infinitive in each sentence and tell whether it acts as a noun, an adjective, or an adverb.

1. The speaker wants to hear the blues.
2. The dead have a longing to be remembered.
3. The band prepared to play their instruments.
4. The sound of music began to fill the air.
5. My goal in life is to play the saxophone.

© **Reading Application** Find and identify two lines from the poems in Poetry Collection 7 that include examples of infinitives.

Practice B Identify the infinitive or infinitive phrase in each sentence. Then, use the infinitive or infinitive phrase in an original sentence.

1. The Kraken's death is due to come later.
2. The sea is able to hide the squid.
3. The speaker is driven by his longing to see his beloved.
4. The reapers are able to continue their cutting.

© **Writing Application** Choose one illustration from Poetry Collection 8 and write three sentences about this image. In each sentence, include an infinitive or infinitive phrase that functions as a noun, an adjective, or an adverb.

PH WRITING COACH | Further instruction and practice are available in *Prentice Hall Writing Coach.*

Writing

Poem Write a **poem,** like "The Weary Blues" or "Jazz Fantasia," that tells about your favorite kind of music *or* write a poem, like "The Kraken" or "Reapers," that tells about a collision between nature and the world of people. Use sound devices to help create a mood, make your ideas memorable, or capture the sounds that you describe.

- Jot down the emotions your favorite type of music inspires in you *or* list details of a situation that pits nature against people or the developed world. From your list, determine the mood you want to convey.

- As you draft, work sound devices such as alliteration and onomatopoeia into your poem.

- Read your draft aloud. Then, revise to achieve the sounds, tone, and perspective you want to express. Review your word choice to delete weak words. Replace them with specific language that suits your purpose better.

Grammar Application Make sure that the infinitives in your poem are vivid and in the correct form.

Writing Workshop: *Work in Progress*

Prewriting for an Analytical Response Use the Questions List from your writing portfolio. Answer each question with both a statement of your opinion and a textual detail that supports that opinion. Put this Analysis Work in your writing portfolio.

Research and Technology

Build and Present Knowledge Choose a visual artist associated with the Harlem Renaissance, and prepare a **visual arts presentation** about three of his or her works. Follow these tips:

- Research the artist's style, subjects, and most famous work.

- As you draft your presentation, incorporate your research and compare the artwork to a poem by a Harlem Renaissance poet, such as Langston Hughes or Jean Toomer.

- Use props and visual aids to enhance the appeal of your presentation and make it easier for your audience to understand your main ideas.

- After you have delivered your presentation, publish your work on a class or school Web site and provide links to appropriate Web sites that display art of the Harlem Renaissance period.

Common Core State Standards

L.9-10.1; W.9-10.4, W.9-10.6, W.9-10.7
[For the full wording of the standards, see page 732.]

Use this prewriting activity to prepare for the **Writing Workshop** on page 768.

www.PHLitOnline.com
- Interactive graphic organizers
- Grammar tutorial
- Interactive journals

Test Practice: Reading

Paraphrase

Fiction Selection

Directions: *Read the selection. Then, answer the questions.*

Marta propped her elbows on the windowsill and rested her chin in her hands, watching the boxcars rumble by. She had to get up early the next morning and knew she should have been in bed slumbering deeply, but she'd never been able to resist.

She could feel the rumble in her chest, in her spine long before the huge black engine roared into sight. Each night at midnight, car after car thundered past. And every night for as long as she could remember, she played the same game in her head. *How many cars tonight?* She'd make a guess, sometimes realistic: *ninety.* Sometimes wildly improbable: *six hundred!* And then she'd count each one as it went by. *One, two, three, four, five, six . . .* It got harder with the large numbers; she couldn't say them as quickly as the cars raced by. *Sixtyonesixtytwosixtythree . . .* And then, after all the noise and shaking, suddenly it was over. It was as if all that sound and motion got chopped off as the last car whipped by her.

1. Which sentence would form the main idea of a paraphrase of this passage?
- **A.** Marta is watching cars drive by her.
- **B.** Marta is watching a train.
- **C.** Marta is waiting for a train.
- **D.** Marta is thinking about a train ride.

2. Which of the following *best* paraphrases this phrase: "feel the rumble in her chest, in her spine long before the huge black engine roared into sight"?
- **A.** "imagine the train even when it wasn't there"
- **B.** "feel the shaking of her house as the train went by"
- **C.** "predict when the train would pass by each night"
- **D.** "feel the vibrations of the train even before she could see it"

3. In a paraphrase, the words "slumbering deeply" would *best* be replaced with—
- **A.** the word "snoring."
- **B.** the phrase "dreaming of tomorrow."
- **C.** the word "sleeping."
- **D.** the phrase "asleep beneath the covers."

4. Which of the following statements *best* paraphrases the last two sentences?
- **A.** When the last train car went by, the noise and shaking stopped suddenly.
- **B.** The noise and shaking got louder as the last train car passed by.
- **C.** The train slowed down as it went by.
- **D.** The front of the train was louder than the back of the train.

Writing for Assessment

In a few sentences, describe the images that you would picture to help you paraphrase the first paragraph of this passage.

Nonfiction Selection

Directions: *Read the selection. Then, answer the questions.*

More than 500 individual railroad systems span from coast to coast of the United States, but the seven largest rail carriers generate over 90% of the country's total rail revenue. Passenger rail service is only a small part of rail operations; the most important use of the country's railways is for the transportation of freight.

The Federal Railroad Administration (FRA), one of the many agencies of the U.S. Department of Transportation, is in charge of the railroads. The key mission of the FRA is to enforce rail safety, but its functions also include research, financial assistance, and technical assistance. Other government entities that participate in regulating, assisting, and ensuring the safety of freight carriers in the U.S. are the Surface Transportation Board, the Department of Homeland Security, the Transportation Security Agency, the Railroad-Shipper Transportation Advisory Council, the National Grain Car Council, and various offices and bureaus of the U.S. Department of the Treasury.

1. The phrase "span from coast to coast of the United States" could *best* be reworded as—
   A. "spread the broad width of the U.S."
   B. "are all over"
   C. "exist in the United States"
   D. "span wide tracks of land"

2. How would you paraphrase this phrase so that an elementary student could understand it? *"Other government entities that participate in . . ."*
   A. The entire government participates
   B. Other government groups that help with
   C. More than one government group takes part in
   D. Participation by other governments

3. What is the *best* paraphrase of the sentence, "The key mission of the FRA is to enforce rail safety, but its functions also include research, financial assistance, and technical assistance"?
   A. The FRA mainly enforces rail safety but performs other functions as well.
   B. The FRA performs many functions.
   C. In addition to enforcing rail safety, the FRA is involved in research, financial, and technical assistance.
   D. The FRA is very important for railroads.

4. To paraphrase this passage, you might do all of the following *except*—
   A. restate the meaning in your own words.
   B. break down long sentences into parts.
   C. identify main actions and crucial details.
   D. brainstorm for questions to ask.

Writing for Assessment

Connecting Across Texts

If you were making recommendations for reading, to whom would you suggest each passage? Write a paragraph to support your recommendations by explaining why each is a good choice for the readers you select.

www.PHLitOnline.com
- Online practice
- Instant feedback

Reading for Information

Analyzing Functional and Expository Texts

Atlas Entry

Magazine Article

**Common Core
State Standards**

Reading Informational Text
1. Cite strong and thorough textual evidence to support analysis of what the text says explicitly as well as inferences drawn from the text.
Language
6. Acquire and use accurately general academic and domain-specific words and phrases, sufficient for reading, writing, speaking, and listening at the college and career readiness level; demonstrate independence in gathering vocabulary knowledge when considering a word or phrase important to comprehension or expression.

Reading Skill:
Synthesize: Make Generalizations

When researching a topic, you often need to consult several sources. Compare and contrast the texts to see what types of information are presented in each. Then, **synthesize,** or bring together, the facts and ideas from the various sources so that you can **find connections** between them and make generalizations. When you **make generalizations,** you examine details and then make inferences—conclusions based on what is not directly stated—to sum up the facts in a text. The following chart shows how to use two facts to form a generalization that is not directly stated in the text.

Fact		Fact		Generalization
Desertification in Mali is causing a scarcity of basic resources.	+	Poverty is a main political issue.	=	Many people in Mali struggle to make a living.

Content-Area Vocabulary

These words appear in the selections that follow. You may also encounter them in other content-area texts.

- **landlocked** (land´ läkt´) *adj.* shut in, or nearly shut in, by land
- **nomads** (nō´ madz´) *n.* people without a permanent home who move around in search of pasture land, food, and so on
- **resources** (rē´ sôrs´ ez) *n.* things in a region or country that can be used by people for food, energy, and so on

Features:

- visuals, such as maps, graphs, charts, icons, and symbols
- headings and subheadings
- statements of fact rather than opinion

Adapted from *Dorling Kindersley World Reference Atlas*

Central and Western Africa

MALI

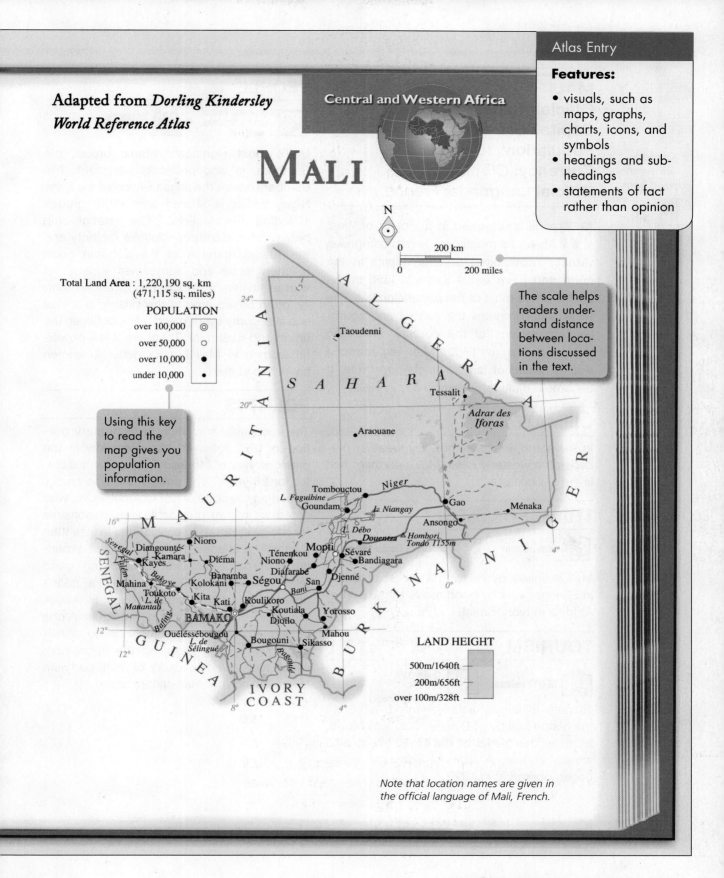

N

0 200 km

0 200 miles

The scale helps readers understand distance between locations discussed in the text.

Total Land Area : 1,220,190 sq. km (471,115 sq. miles)

POPULATION

over 100,000 ◎

over 50,000 ○

over 10,000 ●

under 10,000 •

Using this key to read the map gives you population information.

ALGERIA

SAHARA

Taoudenni

Tessalit

Adrar des Iforas

Araouane

MAURITANIA

Tombouctou

L. Faguibine

Goundam

Niger

L. Niangay

Gao

Ménaka

Ansongo

L. Débo

Douentza

Hombori Tondo 1155m

Nioro

Diangounté-Kamara

Diéma

Ténenkou

Mopti

Sévaré

Bandiagara

NIGER

Kayes

Niono

Diafarabé

Banamba

Ségou

San

Djenné

Senegal

Falémé

Mahina

Bakoye

Kolokani

Bani

Toukoto

L. de Manantali

Kita

Kati

Koulikoro

Koutiala

Yorosso

SENEGAL

Bafing

BAMAKO

Diolio

Ouéléssébougou

L. de Sélingué

Bougouni

Mahou

Sikasso

BURKINA

GUINEA

Bagoué

IVORY COAST

LAND HEIGHT

500m/1640ft

200m/656ft

over 100m/328ft

24°

20°

16°

12°

12°

8°

4°

4°

0°

Note that location names are given in the official language of Mali, French.

MALI

Official Name: *Republic of Mali*
Capital: *Bamako*
Population: *10.8 million*
Currency: *CFA franc*
Official Language: *French*

Mali is landlocked in the heart of West Africa. Its mostly flat terrain comprises virtually uninhabited Saharan plains in the north and more fertile savanna land in the south, where most of the population live. The River Niger irrigates the central and south-western regions of the country. Following independence in 1960, Mali experienced a long period of largely single-party rule. It became a multiparty democracy in 1992.

CLIMATE

In the south, intensely hot, dry weather precedes the westerly rains. Mali's northern half is almost rainless.

TRANSPORTATION

 Has no fleet   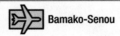 Bamako-Senou

Mali is linked by rail with the port of Dakar in Senegal, and by good roads to the port of Abidjan in Ivory Coast.

TOURISM

 16,000 visitors   Down 33% in 1994

Tourism is largely safari-oriented, although the historic cities of Djénné, Gao and Mopti, lying on the banks of the River Niger, also attract visitors. A national domestic airline began operating in 1990.

PEOPLE

 Bambara, Fulani, Senufo, Soninke, French   24 people per sq. mile

Mali's most significant ethnic group, the Bambara, is also politically dominant. The Bambara speak the lingua franca of the River Niger, which is shared with other groups including the Malinke. The relation-ship between the Bambara–Malinke majority and the Tuareg nomads of the Saharan north is often tense and sometimes violent. As with elsewhere in Africa, the extended family, often based around the village, is a vital social security system and a link between the urban and rural poor. There are a few powerful women in Mali but, in general, women have little status.

POLITICS

The successful transition to multi-party politics in 1992 followed the overthrow in the previous year of Moussa Traoré, Mali's dictator for 23 years. The army's role was crucial in leading the coup, while Colonel Touré, who acted as interim president, was responsible for the swift return to civilian rule in less than a year. The change marks Mali's first experience of multi-partyism. Maintaining good relations with the Tuaregs, after a peace agreement in 1991, is a key issue. However, the main challenge facing President Alpha Oumar Konaré's government is to alleviate poverty while placating the opposition, which feels that the luxury of multi-partyism is something that Mali cannot afford.

Will All the Blue Men End Up in Timbuktu?

'Desertification' forces nomads into the city

BY STEFAN LOVGREN

Posted 11/29/98

TIMBUKTU, Mali—To most people, this outpost on the southern fringe of the Sahara suggests the end of the world. To the blue-turbaned nomads known as the Tuareg, Timbuktu is the opposite, a busy city that does not agree with their unhurried ways. In the solitude of the surrounding desert, there are no telephones, newspapers, schools, or government services. Fathers teach their sons to care for goats and camels, then spend a lifetime following rain clouds in search of water.

But rains and the green pastures they yield have become increasingly scarce. Sweeping sand dunes now blanket what used to be fertile grazing lands. Tuaregs who once owned hundreds of animals are down to a dozen. Many have been forced to do the unthinkable and settle in the bustle of the town. Like some other wandering tribes in Africa, the proud and fiercely independent Tuareg now question their cultural survival. Is this the end of their nomadic ways?

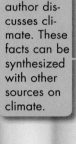

Here, the author discusses climate. These facts can be synthesized with other sources on climate.

The area around Timbuktu has suffered greatly from "desertification." Decades of overgrazing and drought have converted this land into a near desert. It is difficult to imagine that elephants and giraffes once roamed here; now, the only vegetation is an occasional thorn tree, and sandstorms flare up in seconds. Calling desertification "the biggest threat facing Africa," the presidents of Mali and neighboring Burkina Faso warned recently that the battle for shrinking resources will lead to civil wars and famines. The United Nations estimates the worldwide annual losses to desertification at $42 billion, much of it in Africa, where two thirds of the continent is desert or dry land. This week, representatives of some 150 countries will meet in Senegal to discuss how to involve local communities, like the Tuareg, in combating the problem.

Arab Berbers, ancestors of the Tuaregs, first arrived here 900 years ago. But with only 500,000 of Mali's 8.9 million people, the Tuareg have long felt neglected. In the early 1990s, they revolted against the government. The conflict ended in 1996 with the nomads earning greater representation in both the government and the army. Most of the 150,000 Tuaregs who fled to neighboring countries to escape the fighting are now back in Mali.

This information builds on information given about Tuaregs on p. 754.

Paris-Dakar. Abdou Ag Alhassane used to live in the desert, herding animals and making traditional swords for slaughtering camels. As camels dwindled in number, he moved to Timbuktu. He still makes swords but only to sell to tourists. Business is good when the Paris-Dakar auto rally passes through town, he says, but usually there are few travelers adventurous enough to make the eight-hour desert drive from the town of Douentza to Timbuktu. "If I had animals tonight, I would leave for the desert tomorrow," he says.

You can connect this text to the map on p. 753 by finding the locations mentioned (Douentza and Timbuktu [Tombouctou]) and tracing the route between them.

Other Tuaregs are determined to live out their days in the desert. In a dried-out creek at the foot of the Farach escarpment, 50 miles west of Timbuktu, a desert chieftain named Mohamed Aly Ag Moctar resides in a camp with his wife and two children. Seven other children have moved to towns. The heat in the camp reaches a staggering 120 degrees; flies are everywhere. But there are compensations. "Life here is simple," the 61-year-old chief says. "I don't need a watch."

As the traditional leader of 160,000 Tuaregs, Moctar mediates everything from family quarrels to political issues. These days, the most common dispute is over the use of pastoral wells—whose animals get to drink. "If we have animals, we can stay out here," the chief says. "If we have no animals, it is our obligation to go to town."

Instead of erecting ad-hoc camps every three months, some Tuaregs have begun rotating between a handful of semipermanent desert villages, all built around one well. The men may move their herds for up to a month before returning to one of the villages, where the women generally stay put. "This is a new tendency," says Sidebe Draman, an engineer with CARE, an American aid organization that helps rebuild pastoral wells in the region. Draman believes it could evolve into a new kind of nomadism.

Sipping tea in the sand of Farach, Chief Moctar says the Tuareg realize that they must change to survive. "I want to die here in the Sahara," he says. "But I don't want our way of life to die with me."

Comparing Functional and Expository Texts

1. Key Ideas and Details **(a)** Compare and contrast the types of information found in the atlas entry and magazine article. **(b) Synthesize** the texts. Choose a specific topic and use details and information from both selections to **make a generalization** about that topic.

Content-Area Vocabulary

2. (a) Review the definitions of the words *landlocked, nomads,* and *resources,* noting how the meanings are each related to land in some way. **(b)** Use the words in a brief paragraph about people who move from place to place in search of food and pasture land.

Timed Writing

Explanatory Text: Essay

> **Format**
> The prompt directs you to write an essay. Therefore, be sure your response includes an introduction, several supporting paragraphs, and a conclusion.

Write an essay in which you synthesize the information presented in the atlas entry and magazine article. In your essay, include only the most important information presented in each text. Support your response with details from the texts.
(35 minutes)

> **Academic Vocabulary**
> When you *support* your response, you use details and examples to show that your ideas are reasonable and correct.

5-Minute Planner

Complete these steps before you begin to write:

1. Read the prompt carefully, noting the key highlighted words.

2. Review the atlas entry and the magazine article and take notes on the most important points presented in each.

3. Compare and contrast the key points of each text to determine how they are similar and might be brought together.

4. Synthesize the texts by bringing together the ideas that are similar. **TIP** Exclude parts of the atlas entry that do not relate to the plight of the nomads described in the magazine article.

5. Refer to your notes as you draft your essay.

Comparing Literary Works

Comparing Theme

A **theme** is the essential idea that the author of a literary work conveys. Paying attention to an author's *diction,* or choice of words, can help a reader grasp the main message that an author wants to convey. Authors use diction, among other aspects of style, to guide readers to their theme. Some authors present a theme by dramatizing the contradictions, conflicts, or complications of life, including the following:

- By having hopes and making plans, people make their lives meaningful—yet if their plans fail, their lives may seem empty.
- People strive for what they desire—yet they may long most intensely for what they have lost or can never have.

By presenting such contradictions or conflicts, writers remind us that life is not just what happens to us. It is also the desires, fears, and joys that define us—even in the face of failure. Each of the authors in this group asks whether our actions add up to something, whether we should strive for success or find peace in ourselves.

Though their general topic is the same, each writer's theme, or insight into that topic, is different. In addition, a writer may develop his or her theme in different ways. For example, the writer may use slang, formal language, or another specific choice of words to emphasize his or her particular theme. As you read, use a chart like the one shown to note which specific word choices develop the theme.

Key Word / Phrase / Detail	Relationship to Message / Theme

Common Core State Standards

Reading Literature
2. Determine a theme or central idea of a text and analyze in detail its development over the course of the text, including how it emerges and is shaped and refined by specific details.

Writing
2. Write informative/explanatory texts to examine and convey complex ideas, concepts, and information clearly and accurately. **2.a.** Introduce a topic; organize complex ideas, concepts, and information to make important connections and distinctions; include formatting, graphics, and multimedia when useful to aiding comprehension. **2.b.** Develop the topic with well-chosen, relevant, and sufficient facts, extended definitions, concrete details, quotations, or other information and examples. *(Timed Writing)*

PHLit Online!
www.PHLitOnline.com

- Vocabulary flashcards
- Interactive journals
- More about the authors
- Selection audio
- Interactive graphic organizers

Does all *communication* serve a positive purpose?

Writing About the Big Question

In these selections, the speaker communicates a positive or negative vision for the future. Use this sentence starter to develop your ideas.

I think it is (important / not important) to make a positive **connection** to the future because _____.

Meet the Authors

Billy Joel (b. 1949)
Author of "Hold Fast Your Dreams— and Trust Your Mistakes" (p. 760)

Billy Joel grew up on Long Island, in the suburbs of New York City. He studied classical music as a child, but it was a performance by the Beatles that convinced him to become a professional musician. One of the most successful artists of his generation, Joel has sold more than 100 million records worldwide. He was inducted into the Rock and Roll Hall of Fame in 1999.

Bei Dao (b. 1949)
Author of "All" (p. 764)

In the 1970s, Bei Dao's poems became rallying cries for those Chinese who wanted their country to become more democratic. Since 1989, when government troops gunned down protesters in Tiananmen Square in Beijing, China's capital, Bei Dao has lived abroad.

Shu Ting (b. 1952)
Author of "Also All" (p. 765)

As a teenager, Shu Ting (the pen name of Gong Peiyu) was forced by political events in China to leave Beijing, the capital, and live in a small peasant village. She gained fame as a poet while still in her twenties, winning China's National Poetry Award in 1981 and 1983.

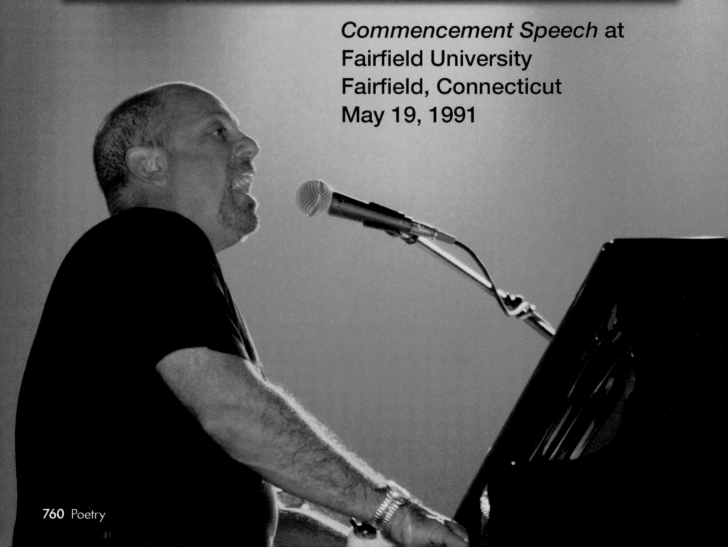

Hold Fast Your Dreams—and Trust Your Mistakes

Billy Joel

Commencement Speech at
Fairfield University
Fairfield, Connecticut
May 19, 1991

When I was first asked to speak to the graduating class of Fairfield University, my initial reaction was not too dissimilar to a certain philosophy professor who is a member of the faculty here. I had to ask myself, What makes me qualified to do this? What relevance do I have to the future lives of these young people? After all, I did not even go to college, and I did write a song called "Only the Good Die Young." So, why me?

After meeting with a group of Fairfield students, I realized what I might be able to share with you from my perspective. I have lived what many would consider to be an **unorthodox** life, but it has always been an interesting one.

It is true that I did not graduate from high school; but like you, I did spend years majoring in my own area of study. I am a graduate of the University of Rock and Roll, Class of 1970. My diploma was a check—a week's worth of wages earned from playing long nights in smoky, crowded clubs in the New York area. Through the years, I have been given platinum albums, Grammys, keys to cities, and many other awards which are considered prestigious in my profession. But the greatest award I have ever received was that check—my diploma—made out to Billy Joel in 1970. This particular check was enough to cover my rent and my expenses. It was also enough to convince me that I no longer needed to work in a factory or be a short-order cook or pump gas or paint houses or do any of the other day jobs I had done in order to make ends meet. That check meant that I was now able to make a living solely by doing

Vocabulary
unorthodox (un ôr´ thə daks´) *adj.* not traditional

Spiral Review
Imagery How does Joel describe the clubs where he played? What effect does the description create?

Reading Check

What does Joel say was his area of study?

Vocabulary

idealistic (i´dē ə lis´ tik)
adj. thinking or acting
based on how things
should be rather than
how they are

Literary Analysis
Theme What does Joel's
imagined relationship
with his 21-year-old self
reveal about his lifelong
hopes and dreams?

Literary Analysis
Theme What does the
use of words "flubs" and
"foul-ups" show about
Joel's attitude towards
mistakes?"

the thing that I loved most—making music. It meant that I had become self-reliant as a musician. I will never forget that day. I consider it to be one of the most important days in my life.

I also remember the twenty-one-year-old Billy Joel and I often wonder what it would be like if we could, somehow, meet each other. Here I am, forty-two, exactly twice his age. What would I think of him? Would I find him to be naive, arrogant, simplistic, crude, noble, hopelessly idealistic? Perhaps all of these things. But more important, what would he think of me? Have I fulfilled his dream? Have I created the kind of music he would have wanted to have written? Have I compromised any of his ideals? Have I broken any of the promises I made to him? Have I lost the desire to be the best he could be? Would he be disappointed in me? Would he even like me?

That twenty-one-year-old has been the biggest pain in the neck I have had to endure in my life. Yet he has had more influence on the work I have done than anyone else for the last twenty-one years. He has been my greatest teacher, my deepest conscience, my toughest editor, and my harshest critic. He has significantly shaped my life. I can say to you today that what you are at this moment in your lives you will always be in your hearts.

When I met with your fellow students, they asked me what is the most powerful lesson I have learned. After eleven years of classical training, I learned to play the piano, but I realized that I was not destined to be another Van Cliburn. I learned to write songs, although what I really wanted to write were symphonies like Beethoven. I have learned to perform, but somehow I knew I would never be able to move like Michael Jackson or sing like Ray Charles.

Out of respect for things that I was never destined to do, I have learned that my strengths are a result of my weaknesses, my success is due to my failures, and my style is directly related to my limitations. You see, the only original things I have ever done have been accidents, mistakes, flubs, foul-ups, and their attendant solutions. I have an inherent talent for stumbling onto something. I am an expert at making bad choices and illogical decisions. I have discovered that after all those years of musical instruction, after all that practice to be perfect, after all that hard work trying to compose the right notes, I am gifted with the knack of hitting exactly the wrong notes at precisely the right time.

This is the secret of originality. Think about it. You may have learned all there is to know about reproducing the art of someone else, but only you can commit a colossal blunder in your own exquisite style. This is what makes you unique. But then you are faced with solving the problem. This is what makes you inventive. Commit enough blunders and you become an artist. Solve all the problems you have created and they will call you a genius.

I have learned that no matter how successful or proficient or accomplished I might think I am, I am always going to make mistakes. I will always have to face some difficulties. I am always going to have to deal with the possibility of failure, and I will always be able to utilize these things in my work. So I am no longer afraid of becoming lost, because the journey back always reveals to me something new about my life and about my own humanity, and that is, ultimately, good for the artist.

Literary Analysis
Theme Why doesn't Joel fear "becoming lost"?

Critical Thinking

1. **Key Ideas and Details (a)** What was Joel's "college diploma"? **(b) Infer:** How did getting it change his life? Explain.

2. **Key Ideas and Details (a) Interpret:** Why do you think Joel says that his younger self has been "the biggest pain in [his] neck"? **(b)** What four roles has his younger self played in his life? **(c)** What effect does Joel create by listing the roles in a series?

Cite textual evidence to support your responses.

3. **Craft and Structure (a)** What does Joel say is the source of his strengths? His success? **(b)** What is the impact of Joel's use of antonyms to identify the sources?

4. **Integration of Knowledge and Ideas (a)** What positive effects might Joel's speech have on his audience? Explain. **(b)** In what ways could giving this speech serve a positive purpose in Joel's life? Explain. *[Connect to the Big Question: Does all communication serve a positive purpose?]*

All

Bei Dao

translated by
Donald Finkel and Xueliang Chen

Literary Analysis
Theme What doubt about people's ability to trust one another is implied in line 8?

All is fated,
all cloudy,

all an endless beginning,
all a search for what vanishes,

5 all joys grave,
all griefs tearless,

every speech a repetition,
every meeting a first encounter,

all love buried in the heart,
10 all history prisoned in a dream,

all hope hedged with doubt,
all faith drowned in lamentation.

Every explosion heralds an instant of stillness,
every death reverberates forever.

Vocabulary
lamentation
(lam´ ən tā´ shən) n. act of crying out in grief; wailing

Also All

Shu Ting

In answer to Bei Dao's "All"

Background Bei Dao and Shu Ting both belonged to a group of Chinese writers known as the Misty Poets. Influenced by Western poets and breaking with Chinese tradition, the Misty Poets used vivid imagery and expressed strong personal emotions. By speaking up for individual feelings, they expressed a quiet opposition to the government of China. In "Also All," Shu Ting answers Bei Dao's poem "All."

> Not all trees are felled by storms.
> Not every seed finds barren soil.
> Not all the wings of dream are broken,
> nor is all affection doomed
> 5   to wither in a desolate heart.

▲ **Critical Viewing**
This photograph shows a lone protester confronting a tank in China. Which poem do you think the image illustrates best? Explain.
[Apply]

Vocabulary
wither (*with′ər*) *v.* shrivel from loss of moisture

Also All **765**

No, not all is as you say.

Not all flames consume themselves,
shedding no light on other lives.
Not all stars announce the night
10 and never dawn. Not every song
will drift past every ear and heart.

No, not all is as you say.

Not every cry for help is silenced,
nor every loss beyond recall.
15 Not every chasm spells disaster.
Not only the weak will be brought to their knees,
nor every soul be trodden under.

It won't all end in tears and blood.
Today is heavy with tomorrow—
20 the future was planted yesterday.
Hope is a burden all of us shoulder
though we might stumble under the load.

Critical Thinking

Cite textual evidence to support your responses.

@ 1. **Key Ideas and Details (a)** What does the speaker in "All" say about "all joys" and about "all hope"? **(b) Infer:** What do these statements suggest about the speaker's view of life?

@ 2. **Craft and Structure (a)** What words does the speaker of "All" repeat at the beginning of lines? **(b)** What is the impact of the repetition in expressing main ideas in the poem?

@ 3. **Key Ideas and Details (a)** What does the speaker in "Also All" point out about the effect of a storm on trees? **(b) Infer:** Is her viewpoint basically optimistic or pessimistic? Support your answer.

@ 4. **Key Ideas and Details (a) Connect:** In what way does "Also All" answer the speaker's points in "All"? **(b) Speculate:** How might the speaker in "All" answer the point in the last two lines of "Also All"?

@ 5. **Integration of Knowledge and Ideas (a)** What is Bei Dao's attitude about life and the future? **(b)** What is Shu Ting's attitude about the present and the future? **(c)** Do both poems serve a positive purpose? Explain. *[Connect to the Big Question: Does all communication serve a positive purpose?]*

Comparing Theme

1. Craft and Structure (a) Sum up the central insights in "Hold Fast Your Dreams . . . ." **(b)** Would you view the central insights differently if Joel had used more formal diction? Explain.

2. Craft and Structure (a) Sum up the insights expressed in each poem. **(b)** List three phrases in each poem that help reveal these insights.

3. Key Ideas and Details What reaction might the speaker in "All" have to Joel's speech? Explain, using details from the selections.

4. Key Ideas and Details (a) The diagram lists four possible responses to disappointment and failure. Copy the diagram, and list details from the selections that reflect these responses. **(b)** Use your analysis to compare the insights into success and failure in these selections.

Timed Writing

Explanatory Text: Essay

In an essay, compare each writer's insights about success. Consider how each writer's style conveys this message. **(35 minutes)**

5-Minute Planner

1. Read the prompt carefully and completely.

2. Consider the theme or central message of each work. Gather your ideas by jotting down answers to these questions:

- What is the attitude of each author toward hope and success?
- How does each writer's word choice help reveal this attitude?
- Which details in each selection support its theme most strongly?

3. Choose an organizing structure appropriate to the purpose of the essay. Note that the prompt requires you to compare the selections.

4. Reread the prompt, and then draft your essay.

Writing Workshop

 **Common Core State Standards**

Writing

2. Write informative/explanatory texts to examine and convey complex ideas, concepts, and information clearly and accurately through the effective selection, organization, and analysis of content.

2.a. Introduce a topic; organize complex ideas, concepts, and information to make important connections and distinctions.

2.b. Develop the topic with well-chosen, relevant, and sufficient facts, extended definitions, concrete details, quotations, or other information and examples appropriate to the audience's knowledge of the topic.

9. Draw evidence from literary or informational texts to support analysis, reflection, and research.

Write an Explanatory Essay

Explanatory Text: Analytic Response to Literature

Defining the Form An analytic response to literature presents a reader's critical response to an entire literary work or focuses on a specific aspect. You might use elements of this type of writing in book reviews, annotated bibliographies, articles, and readers' journals.

Assignment Write an analytic response to a favorite piece of literature. Analyze a poem, a play, a story, or a screenplay. Include these elements:

✓ an opening that introduces the topic and contains a *thesis statement* that presents your personal response to the work being analyzed

✓ *references* to specific literary aspects of the work, such as theme or style, expressed in literary terms appropriate for the audience

✓ well-chosen, relevant *evidence* from the literary work or other texts, including accurate quotations, to support your opinions

✓ logical *organization* that clarifies the relationship between ideas

✓ error-free grammar, including *correct formation of comparisons*

To preview the criteria on which your analytic response to literature may be judged, see the rubric on page 775.

 Writing Workshop: *Work in Progress*

Review the work you did on pages 731 and 749.

WRITE GUY
Jeff Anderson, M.Ed.

What Do You Notice?

Expressing Ideas Clearly

The following sentence is from Umberto Eco's essay "How to React to Familiar Faces." Read the sentence several times.

Still, that face was so familiar that, I felt, I should certainly stop, greet him, converse; perhaps he would immediately respond, "My dear Umberto, how are you?" or "Were you able to do that thing you were telling me about?"

With a partner, discuss what you notice about the sentence. Then, think about ways you might embed quotations in your writing to express your ideas clearly.

Prewriting/Planning Strategies

Use these strategies to find a topic:

Hold a group discussion. With a small group, list the literary works that have provoked strong feelings in you. For each item, briefly describe any memorable details about the work or your experience reading it. Review your ideas and choose one work as your topic.

Ask your own questions. Decide which aspects of the literary work interested you, bothered you, or raised questions. For example, the actions or personality of one character may have seemed ambiguous or confusing. The complexity of the plot and characters may cause you to wonder how each character's action affects the others and how the actions of a particular character affect the unfolding of the plot. Jot down two or three questions that you hope to answer by writing your analytical response.

PHLit Online!
www.PHLitOnline.com
- Author video: Writing Process
- Author video: Rewards of Writing

Example Questions
In *Julius Caesar*, why do Antony and Cassius meet different fates?
Does Sasha learn a lesson in "A Problem"?
Why does "Contents of the Dead Man's Pocket" end as it does?

Consider your audience. Identify your audience and assess their knowledge of your topic. If you need to cover subjects that are unfamiliar to your readers, plan to include details that will help them understand. Use a chart like the one shown to plan your response.

My Topic and Audience
Topic: Tennyson's Kraken and the giant squid
Audience: classmates
What they know: They are familiar with the poem "The Kraken" because we read it in class.
What they do not know: They may not be familiar with giant squid, the real sea creatures that might have inspired the legend.

Go back to the source. Find the information you need by skimming the work for details and examples that relate to your topic. For additional insight, research what critics have said about the work. Write each detail or quotation on a separate index card. Then, organize the cards into general categories.

Drafting Strategies

Write a thesis statement. Review your notes and consider the main point you want to make about the literary work. Write a statement that expresses that point. Include this thesis in your introduction and use it to direct the rest of your essay.

Organize your response. A compelling response to literature can be organized into three parts: the introduction; the body, in which you analyze key elements and support with examples; and the conclusion, in which you summarize and explain why your ideas are important. Each part should relate directly to your thesis to create unity and coherence.

Use information from the text in various ways. For every major idea in your essay, provide evidence from the literary work or another relevant source. Consider these options:

- Use **exact quotations** to show a character's personality, a poet's use of imagery, or a writer's style. Identify all quotations clearly and use quotation marks. Check the form of your citations using a reliable style manual.

- Use **paraphrases**—your own restatement of ideas—in the text to clarify a conflict, to present a writer's theme, or to include key concepts. Be sure that your paraphrase accurately reflects the original text and that you cite sources for any ideas that are not your own.

- Use **summaries** to provide an overview of a writer's opinion or to explain a series of events. However, do not use summaries to fill up pages with material that is not relevant to your thesis.

<table>
<tr><td colspan="2">Using Information From the Text</td></tr>
<tr><td>Exact quotation</td><td>"BRUTUS. Into what dangers would you lead me, Cassius,
That you would have me seek into myself
For that which is not in me?"
(Julius Caesar, Act I, sc. ii, ll. 63–65)</td></tr>
<tr><td>Paraphrase</td><td>What dangerous situation are you leading me into, Cassius, by telling me I have greatness in me when I do not?</td></tr>
<tr><td>Summary</td><td>Brutus asks Cassius why Cassius is leading him into a dangerous situation by flattering him.</td></tr>
</table>

Whatever format you use for supporting your ideas, use transitional words and phrases to explain the link between the literature and your thesis.

Use strong, precise language. As you draft, choose vivid, precise language. Avoid the use of general or vague statements that will not illuminate your point of view.

Common Core State Standards

Writing

2. Write informative/explanatory texts to examine and convey complex ideas, concepts, and information clearly and accurately through the effective selection, organization, and analysis of content.

2.a. Introduce a topic; organize complex ideas, concepts, and information to make important connections and distinctions.

2.b. Develop the topic with well-chosen, relevant, and sufficient facts, quotations, or other information and examples appropriate to the audience's knowledge of the topic.

2.c. Use appropriate and varied transitions to link the major sections of the text, create cohesion, and clarify the relationships among complex ideas and concepts.

2.d. Use precise language and domain-specific vocabulary to manage the complexity of the topic.

2.f. Provide a concluding statement or section that follows from and supports the information or explanation presented.

9. Draw evidence from literary or informational texts to support analysis, reflection, and research.

Language

3.a. Write and edit work so that it conforms to the guidelines in a style manual.

Writers on Writing

Cornelius Eady On Writing Poetry About Music

> Cornelius Eady is the author of "The Poetic Interpretation of the Twist" (p. 634) and "The Empty Dance Shoes" (p. 636).

In my poem "Thelonious Monk"—named for the famous jazz composer and pianist—I was finding a way of duplicating the playfulness in Monk's music. I also wanted to capture another quality—his music is very rhythmic, but also very hard. It's as if you can hear body language—lots of elbows and knees. He forces you to pay attention to melody in a way you wouldn't ordinarily.

There's a link there in terms of the way poetry operates. Poetry makes you look at details or highlights within language that you wouldn't other-wise catch in other circumstances.

"Writing a poem about a certain song can yield some really wonderful results."
—Cornelius Eady

Professional Model:

from "Thelonious Monk"

I know what to do with this math.
Listen to this. It's
Arithmetic, a soundtrack. The motion

Frozen in these lampposts, it
Can be sung. I can lift away
Its logic, make it spin

Like an orbital satellite, find
Gambling's true pitch.
It can be *played*:

Adventure, the trying of
Patience, holding back, holding
Up, laying out, stop-time . . .

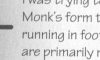

I was trying to get at the quality of Monk's form that's like broken-field running in football. Most of the lines are primarily monosyllabic, and I like to end them with hard percussive words like *It's*.

These lines came out of a story someone told me about Monk. He said he'd seen Monk go up to a lamppost and listen to it, and then Monk went home and tried to play the sound he heard in the lamppost.

I imagined the poem could be Monk saying, "Look, *this* is what I'm up to." I wanted the poem to be representing Monk representing himself.

Revising Strategies

Common Core
State Standards

Writing

2.d. Use precise language and domain-specific vocabulary to manage the complexity of the topic.

5. Develop and strengthen writing as needed by planning, revising, editing, rewriting, or trying a new approach, focusing on addressing what is most significant for a specific purpose and audience.

Use specific terms. The correct use of formal or specialized terms can help you express shades of meaning and add a sense of serious scholarship to your work. Use a dictionary and/or a thesaurus to locate the words with the precise meaning you want to express. Formal terminology may include literary terms, the names of literary movements, references to periods in history, or place names. Review your use of such terms to make sure they are correct.

Nonspecific:	the old system of government
Specific:	the ancient Roman republic

Cut excess writing. When revising, one of your most important goals is to delete words, phrases, sentences, and even paragraphs that do not add meaning or depth to your essay. As you review your draft, look for these types of unnecessary material:

- **Repeated Ideas:** Extend important ideas with fresh information, but cut repetitions that add nothing new.

- **Unrelated Details:** Be sure that every detail relates directly to your thesis. Eliminate material that seems off target, or revise to show its relationship to your thesis.

- **Inconsistencies:** Make sure that every sentence and every paragraph clearly relates to those that precede and follow.

Peer Review

Exchange drafts with a partner. Highlight passages that include ineffective repetition, unrelated details, or inconsistent statements. Discuss whether to delete the highlighted material. Then, revise your draft, cutting unnecessary language.

Model: Eliminating Unnecessary Writing

In Act I, Scene ii, Cassius shows his careful attention to others' moods and intentions. Cassius tells Brutus that he senses Brutus has something on his mind. ~~Cassius sees that something is bothering Brutus.~~ Brutus assures Cassius that what is troubling him has nothing to do with Cassius, who is one of his good friends. ~~He is not upset with Cassius.~~

> This writer deletes repeated ideas to make this paragraph more effective.

Revising Common Usage Problems

Many students misuse certain words when making comparisons.

Identifying Usage Problems With *like*, *as*, and *as if* When it is not used as a verb (I *like* baseball), the word *like* is a preposition meaning "similar to" or "such as." The word *like* should not be used in place of *as*, *as if*, or *as though*, which are conjunctions that introduce clauses.

Incorrect: The sand felt *like* it was a warm slipper. (before a clause)
Correct: The sand felt *like* a warm slipper. (before a noun)
Correct: The sand felt *as if* it were a warm slipper. (before a clause)

Prepositional Phrase vs. Clause

A **prepositional phrase** includes a preposition and a noun or pronoun. It has no subject or verb.

    like a feather   like a snoring elephant

A **clause** has a subject and a verb.

              S   V
    My friend looked [as if *she* <u>had overslept</u>.]
                        clause

Identifying Usage Problems With *among* and *between* Use *between* to compare two things. Use *among* to compare three or more things.

Incorrect: The cloud hovered *among* the horizon and infinity.
Correct: The cloud hovered *between* the horizon and infinity.

Incorrect: The sunlight danced *between* the many clouds.
Correct: The sunlight danced *among* the many clouds.

PH WRITING COACH
Further instruction and practice are available in *Prentice Hall Writing Coach*.

Fixing Usage Problems To revise usage problems with *like*, *as*, or *as if*:

If you have used *like* to introduce a clause, replace it with the conjunction *as*, *as if*, or *as though*.

To correct usage problems with *among* and *between*, follow these steps:

1. Identify the number of elements involved in the sentence.

2. Use between with phrases involving two elements.

3. Use among with phrases involving three or more elements.

Grammar in Your Writing

Review two paragraphs of your essay and circle uses of the words *like*, *as*, *as if*, *between*, and *among*. Revise any incorrect usage.

Student Model: Christopher Rich, Omaha, Nebraska

 Common Core
State Standards

Language
2.c. Spell correctly.

Response to *The Tragedy of Julius Caesar*

In all tales, modern or ancient, characters at odds often differ in obvious ways. One may be likable and honest—a natural leader. The other may be unpleasant and sneaky. However, sometimes enemies are actually very similar. No exception to this rule, Shakespeare's Antony and Cassius of *The Tragedy of Julius Caesar* share many characteristics but come to very different ends.

> Christopher includes a clear thesis statement in his introduction.

Marcus Antonius and Caius Cassius, both patricians and warriors, are presented as two of Rome's most noble citizens. Both are seen by plebians as noble and honest, if humanly flawed, men. In truth, they are among the most manipulative characters in the play. Cassius is the first to exploit his power to manipulate, using it to coerce Brutus onto the side of the conspirators. Flattering Brutus, ("I know that virtue to be in you, Brutus, / As well as I do know your outward favor") (I, ii, 90–91) and challenging his honor as a Roman, Cassius wins the support of his brother-in-law. Antony, however, shows his ability in a far less conspicuous way. After the assassination of Caesar in Act III, Antony cleverly manipulates the commoners. His subtle and smooth way of controlling the crowd with a pause in his voice reflects his manipulative ability.

> Christopher accurately quotes significant passages from the text.

Despite their powers of persuasion, these two show great allegiance to their loved ones. Over Caesar's body, in Act III, Scene i, Antony says he is willing to throw his country into civil war. Later, Cassius kills himself when he thinks that his best friend has been killed, taking loyalty to the extreme.

Though people may have many similarities, it is the differences that separate warriors and politicians. Always at the beck and call of the dictator who would be king, Antony is known by the common folk to be a possible successor to the "coronet." Cassius, however, is opposed to Caesar, not only politically but also personally, and is one of Caesar's least favorite people: *"Yon Cassius has a lean and hungry look"* (I, ii, 194). Cassius himself admits to his own dislike of Caesar by telling a story from their youth, in Act I, Scene ii, lines 97–131. It is their differences that determine the eventual fate of the characters.

> A point-by-point plan of organization focuses first on similarities and then moves onto differences.

In the end, the obvious similarities of these characters are not as important as their differences. The fate that each meets—Cassius commits suicide and Antony becomes part of the triumvirate that rules Rome—is determined by how each uses his personality traits.

> In his conclusion, Christopher restates his thesis and provides an insight that takes the analysis further.

Editing and Proofreading

Review your draft to correct errors in grammar, spelling, and punctuation.

Focus on spelling. Endings that sound the same or almost the same, such as *-ize*, *-ise*, and *-yze*, can be tricky to spell. Usually, *-ize* is added to another word to make a verb, such as *civilize* or *characterize*. For *-ise* and *-yze*, there are no dependable rules. Memorize the spellings or refer to a dictionary if you are unsure of the spelling.

Publishing and Presenting

Consider one of the following ways to share your writing:

Present your response to a book club. Share your response to literature with members of a book club. Invite a group of students, friends, or family members to read the work of literature you will address. Set a meeting time and give a brief introduction to the work. Then, read your essay aloud. Follow your reading with a general discussion to share ideas and responses. As you discuss the literature and your analysis, be open to the ideas of others rather than simply defending your own.

Publish an online review. Post a literary review on a student or bookstore Web site. Remember to check each site for specific submission requirements. Then, follow the correct procedures to retrieve and reproduce your document across platforms.

Reflecting on Your Writing

Writer's Journal Jot down your answers to this question:
How did writing about the work help you understand it?

Rubric for Self-Assessment

Find evidence in your writing to address each category. Then, use the rating scale to grade your work.

Spiral Review

Earlier in this unit, you learned about **prepositional phrases** (p. 730) and **infinitives** (p. 748). Review your response to literature to be sure you have used prepositional phrases and infinitives correctly.

Criteria	Rating Scale
	not very · · · very
Focus: How clear is your thesis statement?	1 2 3 4 5
Organization: How logical is your organization?	1 2 3 4 5
Support/Elaboration: How effectively do you include evidence from the literary work to support your opinions?	1 2 3 4 5
Style: How precise and vivid is your use of language?	1 2 3 4 5
Conventions: How correct is your grammar, especially your formation of comparisons?	1 2 3 4 5

Vocabulary Workshop

Connotation and Denotation

A word's **denotation** is its dictionary meaning, independent of other associations that the word may have. In contrast, a word's **connotations** are the ideas or emotions associated with the word in addition to its meaning. Often, words have positive, negative, or neutral connotations, which can affect how people respond to them when the words appear in writing.

For example, the denotations of *illustrious*, *famous*, and *notorious* all describe someone who is well known. However, the connotation of *illustrious* is of someone who is admired, while *notorious* suggests someone who is well known for something bad. *Famous* has a more neutral connotation. This chart shows other words that illustrate differences in the connotations of words.

Common Core State Standards

Language
4.c. Consult general and specialized reference materials, both print and digital, to find the pronunciation of a word or determine or clarify its precise meaning, its part of speech, or its etymology.
5.b. Analyze nuances in the meaning of words with similar denotations.

Positive ➝	Neutral ➝	Negative
prudent	timid	cowardly
self-confident	proud	arrogant
thrifty	economical	miserly

Dictionaries can give clues to connotations. The entry for *miserly*, for instance, might read, "greedy and stingy" to suggest the negative connotations of the word. Some dictionaries will also give example phrases or sentences that show how the word is used and that suggest its connotations.

Practice A Choose the word that has the more negative connotation in each item.

1. My parents lived in that (shack, house) for twenty years.
2. Christy's uncle has always lived a/an (reckless, adventurous) life.
3. As she looked his way, the (smile, smirk) on Jarod's face disappeared.
4. When I stumbled against the stranger, he (gazed, glared) at me.
5. The two families had been (feuding, quarreling) for years.
6. The football player turned and (stomped, walked) off the field.

Practice B Make a chart like the one shown and classify each of the words below as *positive, neutral,* or *negative*. There is one word that will fit in each blank space. Use a dictionary or thesaurus if necessary.

dreamer

strategy

persistent

high-strung

visionary

scheme

overwrought

new

laughable

slender

save

aggressive

skinny

pushy

drudgery

newfangled

employment

stubborn

Positive ⟶	Neutral ⟶	Negative
1. persevering	_____	_____
2. _____	nervous	_____
3. up-to-date	_____	_____
4. _____	inventor	_____
5. _____	store	hoard
6. _____	thin	
7. hilarious	_____	ludicrous
8. assertive	_____	_____
9. _____	work	_____
10. _____	plan	_____

Comprehension and Collaboration

Using neutral connotations, write an ad about a product. Then, trade ads with a classmate and rewrite each other's ads, using words with negative connotations. Trade ads with a third classmate. Rewrite the ad using positive connotations. Read your ad and talk about the changes in meaning.

PHLit Online!
www.PHLitOnline.com
- Illustrated vocabulary words
- Interactive vocabulary games
- Vocabulary flashcards

Activity Make a note card for each of the following words: *bossy, daring, glamorous, scrawny.* Look up each word in a dictionary and write its denotation. Then, write its connotation. Finally, use the word in an original sentence that shows its connotative meaning.

Word:

Denotation:

Connotation:

Sentence:

Communications Workshop

Delivering an Oral Interpretation of a Literary Work

You can share your ideas about a poem—or anything else you read—by **delivering an oral interpretation** for an audience in which you combine a careful analysis of the work with your own response.

Learn the Skills

Use the strategies to complete the activity on page 779.

Advance a judgment about significant ideas. Clearly state the main ideas in the literature. Discuss ways in which the ideas are developed and why they are important. Formulate a thesis statement that clearly reflects your view of the literature.

Support ideas and viewpoints. Your views will carry more weight if you support them with details from the text. Read excerpts from the work to share the writer's style and tone with your audience. Choose sections that illustrate key ideas and are pleasing or powerful when read aloud.

Pose questions. Authors do not state all of their ideas directly. Introduce some of the unstated themes or complexities of a work by asking a question and then answering it using examples from the works.

Prepare your delivery. Preparation is the key to feeling relaxed in front of an audience. These techniques can help you deliver a confident and effective presentation:

- **Organize your ideas.** Write each key idea on a separate note card. As you rehearse, experiment with the order of the cards. Then, number the cards in the best order.

- **Communicate with your voice.** Speak clearly and comfortably without rushing. Use the tone and pitch of your voice to add variety.

- **Use effective body language.** Your gestures and posture send a signal to your audience. Energetic body language shows that you think your subject is important. Maintain eye contact to keep your audience's attention.

 Common Core State Standards

Speaking and Listening

1. Initiate and participate effectively in a range of collaborative discussions with diverse partners on grades 9–10 topics, texts, and issues, building on others' ideas and expressing their own clearly and persuasively.

1.b. Work with peers to set rules for collegial discussions and decision-making, clear goals and deadlines, and individual roles as needed.

6. Adapt speech to a variety of contexts and tasks, demonstrating command of formal English when indicated or appropriate.

Practice the Skills

© **Presentation of Knowledge and Ideas** Use what you have learned in this workshop to perform the following task.

ACTIVITY: Deliver an Oral Interpretation

Select a poem, short story, or piece of nonfiction. Prepare a three-minute interpretation in which you respond to this work. Develop your interpretation by answering the following questions in your presentation:

- What is your claim, or thesis, about the work?
- Which details from the work most clearly explain and support your thesis?
- Why are these details powerful to you?
- What questions should your classmates ask themselves about the work?
- What examples from the work help answer the questions?

As your classmates make their presentations, listen attentively. Use the Presentation Evaluation Guide below to analyze their presentations.

Presentation Evaluation Guide

Rate each statement on a scale of 1 (not accurate) to 5 (completely accurate). Explain your ratings.

_____ The presentation was focused around a clear thesis statement.
_____ The thesis was sufficiently supported with details from the text.
_____ The presentation analyzed subtleties in the text.
_____ The presentation was logically organized.
_____ The speaker had a clear speaking voice.
_____ The speaker used a variety of speaking tones and pitches.
_____ The speaker used effective gestures and other body language.

What was most effective about this presentation?

_____

© **Comprehension and Collaboration** With a group of classmates, discuss which presentations were easiest to follow and why. To keep your discussion on track, set a time limit for your discussion, and choose roles, such as discussion leader, timekeeper, summarizer, and clarifier. Together, decide what rules you will follow. For example, determine whether listeners may interrupt a speaker to ask questions or whether they should hold questions until the speaker is finished.

Cumulative Review

**Common Core
State Standards**

RL.9-10.4, RL.9-10.5; W.9-10.9.a
[For the full wording of the standards, see the standards chart in the front of your textbook.]

I. Reading Literature

Directions: *Read the passage. Then, answer each question.*

TO AUTUMN

I
Season of mists and mellow fruitfulness,
  Close bosom-friend of the maturing sun;
<u>Conspiring</u> with him how to load and bless
  With fruit the vines that round the thatch-eves run;
To bend with apples the mossed cottage-trees,
  And fill all fruit with ripeness to the core;
    To swell the gourd, and plump the hazel shells
With a sweet kernel; to set budding more,
  And still more, later flowers for the bees,
  Until they think warm days will never cease,
    For Summer has o'er-brimmed their clammy cells.

II
Who hath not seen thee oft amid thy store?
  Sometimes whoever seeks abroad may find
Thee sitting careless on a granary floor,
  Thy hair soft-lifted by the winnowing wind;
Or on a half-reaped furrow sound asleep,
  Drowned with the fume of poppies, while thy hook
    Spares the next swath and all its twinèd flowers:
And sometimes like a gleaner thou dost keep
  Steady thy laden head across a brook;
  Or by a cider-press, with patient look,
    Thou watchest the last oozings hours by hours.

III
Where are the songs of Spring? Ay, where are they?
  Think not of them, thou hast thy music too,—
While barrèd clouds bloom the soft-dying day,
  And touch the stubble-plains with rosy hue;
Then in a wailful choir the small gnats mourn
  Among the river sallows, borne aloft
    Or sinking as the light wind lives or dies;
And full-grown lambs loud bleat from hilly bourn;
  Hedge-crickets sing; and now with treble soft
  The red-breast whistles from a garden-croft;
    And gathering swallows twitter in the skies.
                              —by John Keats

1. Which of the following best describes the **speaker** of the poem?

   A. someone who prefers Spring
   B. a farmer
   C. someone who admires Autumn
   D. a friend of the sun

2. When the speaker says, *Where are the songs of Spring? Ay, where are they? / Think not of them, thou has thy music too,*— he means—

   A. There are more songs written about Autumn than Spring.
   B. Spring is a beautiful season.
   C. The birds sing lovely songs in Autumn.
   D. Autumn is beautiful in its own way.

3. What is the dominant sensory **imagery** in stanza III?

   A. sight/sound
   B. smell/taste
   C. touch/taste
   D. sound/touch

4. **Vocabulary** Which of the following is the closest definition of the underlined word *conspiring*?

   A. secretly working together with
   B. finding fault with
   C. making an argument against
   D. separating from by a great distance

5. Which **sound device** is represented in the following line?

   While barrèd clouds bloom the soft-dying day,

   A. assonance
   B. alliteration
   C. rhyme
   D. rhyme scheme

6. Which of the following **rhyme schemes** is represented in the first seven lines of the poem?

   A. abbacdc
   B. ababcdc
   C. ababcde
   D. aabbcde

7. Who or what is the speaker addressing in this poem?

   A. a close friend
   B. the sun
   C. autumn
   D. spring

8. Which best describes the **tone** of this poem?

   A. reverent
   B. playful
   C. bitter
   D. sad

9. Which of the following lines is an example of **personification?**

   A. With a sweet kernel; to set budding more,
   B. And full-grown lambs loud bleat from hilly bourn
   C. Then in a wailful choir the small gnats mourn
   D. Among the river sallows, borne aloft

⏱ Writing for Assessment

10. Write a paragraph in which you **describe** the **mood** or feeling that you think the poet is trying to express in this poem. **Explain** how you think the speaker feels about the subject of the poem. **Support** your answer with details from the passage.

GO ON

II. Reading Informational Text

Directions: *Read the passage. Then, answer each question that follows.*

Common Core
State Standards

RI.9-10.2, RI.9-10.3, RI.9-10.4
[For the full wording of the standards, see the standards chart in the front of your textbook.]

The Bees

Bees, known for their fearful sting and their delicious honey, are a common sight in flower gardens. The flowers provide bees with their food—pollen and nectar. Bees have specialized adaptations for collecting food. They have hairy bodies, pollen baskets, and special tongues for collecting nectar.

Honeybees

Honeybees, the most commonly known type of bee, are organized social insects. Honeybees live in complex colonies in which large numbers of individuals act together nearly as a single organism. The bee colony consists of specialized individuals: the queen bee, worker bees, and drones.

Queen bee. The queen bee is a fully developed female. Her only job is to lay eggs. When summer flowers begin blooming, the queen begins to lay her eggs, as many as a thousand or more per day.

Worker bees. Worker bees are undeveloped females. A colony can have up to 60,000 female bees. They collect nectar and pollen, convert it into honey, raise the young, and build their honeycomb. As they collect pollen, some clings to the hairs on their bodies. As they fly from blossom to blossom, they pollinate flowers, fruit trees, and vegetable plants.

Drones. The drones are male bees. Their only job is to mate with the queen. When fall arrives, drones are driven out of the hive to die. The queen can lay drone, or unfertilized eggs, which develop into adult drones. This process of producing life from unfertilized eggs is known as <u>parthenogenesis</u>.

1. If you wanted to learn about dangerous insects, after **scanning** this passage you would—

   A. read the entire article
   B. move on to another source
   C. skim the article
   D. look for more information on honeybees

2. To learn how insects reproduce, the section most useful to you would be—

   A. the entire article
   B. the introduction
   C. "Drones"
   D. "Queen bee"

3. What **generalization** can you make about the queen bee?

   A. She has an easy life.
   B. Her worker bees are jealous of her.
   C. The colony would not survive without her.
   D. The other bees are more important than she is.

4. **Vocabulary** What is the best definition of the underlined word *parthenogenesis?*

   A. growth of undeveloped bees
   B. reproduction without fertilization
   C. the creation of honeybees
   D. mating with queen bees

III. Writing and Language Conventions

Descriptive Essay

Directions: *Read the passage. Then, answer each question that follows.*

© Common Core
State Standards

L.9-10.5.a, L.6.3.a; W.9-10.3.d
[For the full wording of the standards, see the standards chart in the front of your textbook.]

(1) I hear my dad's huge green hiking boots crunching on the leaves about ten feet ahead of me. (2) I struggle to keep up with him during our hike. (3) Although I was born and raised in the city, my dad is determined to make me appreciate what he calls "the great outdoors."

(4) Each November, he and I drive miles from the city to a state park. (5) When I was younger, I begged not to go, but he refused to listen. (6) Now, as I walk behind him up a steep hill, I take a deep breath of the air. (7) The trees around me are as tall as city skyscrapers, and just as impressive, in their own way. (8) Light is dancing across the floor of the forest, flickering here and there. (9) The forest is quiet; you can actually hear the breeze. (10) For the first time, I view the forest as my father does, and acknowledge its exquisiteness.

1. Which type of **figurative language** can be found in sentence 7?

   A. metaphor
   B. personification
   C. simile
   D. symbol

2. How could you incorporate more **sensory details** in sentence 6?

   A. Add "crisp, clear" before "air."
   B. Replace "deep" with "shallow."
   C. Add "very, very" before "steep."
   D. Replace "hill" with "mountain."

3. How should sentence 10 be revised to keep the **voice** consistent throughout the passage?

   A. Now, for the first time, do I enjoy this beautiful scenery as my papa has for years.
   B. For the first time, I see the forest as my dad does, and appreciate its beauty.
   C. Suddenly, I enjoy nature's rustic beauty.
   D. Like daddy said, the forest isn't bad.

4. How might you best revise sentence 2 to **vary the pattern** using a **prepositional phrase**?

   A. During our hike, I struggle to keep up with him.
   B. I struggle, to keep up, during our hike.
   C. Keep up with him, I struggle, during our hike.
   D. I struggle to keep up, during our hike, with him.

5. Which sentence uses **personification** to paint a picture in the reader's mind?

   A. sentence 1
   B. sentence 4
   C. sentence 8
   D. sentence 10

6. Which phrase would be *best* to add to the end of sentence 9 to appeal to the senses?

   A. "which distracted me from my thoughts"
   B. "coming out of the southeast"
   C. "blowing around"
   D. "rustling the leaves on the ground"

Performance Tasks

Directions: *Follow the instructions to complete the tasks below as required by your teacher.*

As you work on each task, incorporate both general academic vocabulary and literary terms you learned in this unit.

**Common Core
State Standards**

RL.9-10.1, RL.9-10.2, RL.9-10.4, RL.9-10.5; RI.9-10.6; W.9-10.2, W.9-10.4, W.9-10.7, W.9-10.9; SL.9-10.1, SL.9-10.1.c, SL.9-10.6; L.9-10.1, L.9-10.5

[For the full wording of the standards, see the standards chart at the front of your textbook.]

Writing

Task 1: Informational Text [RI.9-10.6; W.9-10.2]
Analyze Author's Purpose

Write an essay in which you analyze the author's purpose in a nonfiction text in this unit.

- Select a nonfiction text from this unit, such as an essay, speech, or article.
- Determine the author's purpose in the work as well as his or her perspective on the topic.
- Analyze the ways in which the author achieves his or her purpose. For example, purpose may be advanced through genre, text structure, or word choices. Discuss the significance of the author's perspective as it relates to author's purpose.
- Support your ideas with details and examples from the text.
- Use conventions of standard English grammar in your writing.

Task 2: Literature [RL.9-10.4; W.9-10.2]
Analyze Figurative Language

Write an essay in which you analyze the poet's use of figurative language in a poem.

- Select a poem from this unit that contains striking examples of figurative language, such as metaphors, similes, or personification.
- Cite the examples of figurative language and interpret them. Explain what the poet is expressing through the use of figurative language.

- Analyze the effect of figurative language on the poem's meaning.
- Cite specific examples from the text to support your analysis.
- Make sure you use correct capitalization and punctuation in your writing.

Task 3: Literature [RL.9-10.2; W.9-10.4]
Analyze Speaker and Theme

Write an essay in which you analyze how a poem's speaker helps to develop and convey the theme.

- Select a poem and describe its speaker.
- Use details from the poem to support your description.
- Explain how the speaker helps to develop the theme of the poem. The speaker may reveal information, attitudes, feelings, or impressions that contribute to the theme of the poem.
- Use precise language in your essay, and be sure to correctly punctuate any direct quotations from the poem.
- Provide a concluding statement that follows from and supports the information in your essay.

Speaking and Listening

ⓔTask 4: Literature [RL.9-10.4; SL.9-10.6]
Analyze Sound Devices

Prepare and deliver an oral presentation in which you analyze the use of sound devices in a poem from this unit.

- Select a poem that makes interesting and significant use of sound devices, such as alliteration, assonance, consonance, and onomatopoeia.

- Identify the sound devices and analyze the effect that they have on the meaning of the poem, as well as how they contribute to the mood of the poem.

- As you present your analysis, read key passages aloud to demonstrate the effects of the sound devices.

- Draw conclusions about the role of sound devices in poetry.

- Present your ideas in a clear and logical way.

ⓔTask 5: Literature [RL.9-10.5; SL.9-10.1.c, SL.9-10.6]
Compare Poetic Structures

Prepare and give an oral presentation in which you compare the effect of structure in two poems.

- Select two poems from this unit that are recognized poetic forms, such as a sonnet, villanelle, or tanka. Identify the poems and forms you will be discussing.

- Analyze the relationship between form and meaning. Determine what the form of each poem contributes to its meaning. For example, you may decide that repetition in a villanelle has an impact on meaning, or that a sonnet presents a logical argument.

- Compare the different effects of each structure. Use details from the poem to support your ideas.

- During your oral presentation, use formal English, good volume, and clear pronunciation.

- Invite questions after your presentation. Respond with further elaboration, referring back to the poems.

ⓔTask 6: Literature [RL.9-10.1; SL.9-10.1]
Compare Speakers

Conduct a small group discussion in which you compare and contrast the speakers in two poems.

- Identify two poems in this unit that have distinctive speakers.

- Analyze each speaker. Consider the effect the speakers have on theme, meaning, and mood.

- Determine what the significant differences are between the two speakers. For example, one speaker may tell a story while another may share insights.

- Based on your analysis, prepare questions designed to propel a discussion.

- During the discussion, keep track of key ideas expressed, whether on a chalkboard, on paper, or electronically, so that group members will find it easier to build on the ideas of others.

- Conclude the discussion by summarizing the main ideas expressed, including points of agreement and disagreement.

THE BIG ?

Does all communication serve a positive purpose?

At the beginning of Unit 4, you participated in a discussion of the Big Question. Now that you have completed the unit, write a response to the question. Discuss how your initial ideas have changed or been reinforced. Support your response with at least one example from literature and one example from an additional subject area or your own life. Use Big Question vocabulary words (see p. 627) in your response.

Featured Titles

In this unit, you have read a wide variety of poems by many different poets. Continue to read on your own. Select works that you enjoy, but challenge yourself to explore new poets and works of increasing depth and complexity. The titles suggested below will help you get started.

Literature

Immigrants in Our Own Land and Selected Early Poems
by Jimmy Santiago Baca   EXEMPLAR TEXT

Baca learned to read and write in prison and then wrote an extraordinary collection of **poetry** while still behind bars. The collection includes "I Am Offering This Poem," a plea from Baca asking someone he loves to accept his words since he has nothing else to give.

The Complete Poetry of Edgar Allan Poe
by Edgar Allan Poe   EXEMPLAR TEXT

Poems that have delighted and frightened generations of readers are collected in this anthology. Poe is a master of communicating feelings of fear and horror, as in his famous poem "The Raven."

The Song of the Lark
by Willa Cather

This **novel** tells the story of a small-town girl who sets herself apart due to her musical abilities. It is a lonely, isolated path she chooses as she pursues a career as an opera singer and dedicates herself to her art.

Victims of the Latest Dance Craze
by Cornelius Eady
Carnegie Mellon University Press, 1997

The **poems** in this collection invite readers to experience the world as a rhythmic place alive with sound and motion. Inventive language is woven throughout.

Lift Every Voice and Sing
by James Weldon Johnson   EXEMPLAR TEXT

Johnson wrote the title poem of this **poetry** collection in 1900 for a Lincoln birthday celebration. Its dual message, acknowledging past suffering while expressing hope for the future, has moved and inspired generations of African Americans.

Informational Texts

Roughing It
by Mark Twain

In this **semi-autobiographical account,** Twain recounts his years in the American West, when vigilantes ruled the land and gold prospecting was the rage. A unique mixture of true account and tall tale, this book is humorous and wildly entertaining.

Native American Literature

This collection of **myths, essays, poems,** and other types of writing communicates the diversity and spirit of Native American cultures. The writing invites readers to consider the importance of telling stories and sharing ideas for preserving a way of life.

The Story of Art: A Pocket Edition
by E. H. Gombrich   EXEMPLAR TEXT

This **nonfiction history** traces the development of art, from prehistoric cave painting to the twentieth century. The director of the famous Louvre Museum wrote about this book, "Almost as well known as the *Mona Lisa,* ... *The Story of Art* unites learning and pleasure."

Preparing to Read Complex Texts

Attentive Reading As you read literature on your own, bring your imagination and questions to the text. The questions shown below and others that you ask as you read will help you learn and enjoy literature even more.

 **Common Core State Standards**

Reading Literature/Informational Text 10. By the end of Grade 10, read and comprehend literature, including stories, dramas, poems, and literary nonfiction at the high end of the grades 9–10 text complexity band independently and proficiently.

When reading poetry, ask yourself...

- What, if anything, do I understand about the poem from its title?
- Who is the speaker of the poem? What is the speaker telling me?
- What subject matter does the poem address?
- Is the poem telling a story? If so, who are the characters, and what are they doing?
- What theme, meaning, or insight, does the poem express? Does any one line or section simply state that theme? If so, which one? If not, which details help me understand the poem's deeper meaning?

Ⓒ Key Ideas and Details

- How does the poem look on the page? How does the poem's appearance affect the way I read it?
- Is the poem an example of a particular form, such as a sonnet, ballad, or haiku? If so, what do I expect from the poem based on its form?
- Is the poem an example of free verse? If so, does it have any formal elements?
- How does the form affect what I understand and feel about the poem?
- What do I notice about the stanzas? Are they always a set number of lines, or do they vary in length? What new idea or piece of information does each stanza give me?
- What do I notice about the way the poem sounds? Does the poet use repetition? Does the poet use rhyme, and, if so, what kind? Does the poet use other sound devices?
- How do sound devices affect my enjoyment of the poem? How do they emphasize the meaning?
- What do I notice about any symbols or images? Does any one symbol or image repeat? What connections do I see between the symbol or image and the poem's deeper meaning?

Ⓒ Craft and Structure

- Even if I do not understand every word, do I like this poem? Why or why not?
- Has the poem helped me understand something in a new way? If so, how?
- In what ways is this poem similar to others I have read? In what ways is it different from others I have read?
- What insights have I gained from reading this poem?
- Would I like to read more poems by this poet? Why or why not?
- Could this poem serve as an inspiration to other writers, artists, or musicians? Why or why not?

Ⓒ Integration of Ideas

Q To what extent does *experience* determine what we *perceive?*

PHLit
Online!
www.PHLitOnline.com

Hear It!
- Selection summary audio
- Selection audio
- BQ Tunes

See It!
- Author videos
- Big Question video
- Get Connected videos
- Background videos
- More about the authors
- Illustrated vocabulary words
- Vocabulary flashcards

Do It!
- Interactive journals
- Interactive graphic organizers
- Grammar tutorials
- Interactive vocabulary games
- Test practice

To what extent does *experience* determine what we *perceive?*

A person's **experience** is everything he or she has lived through, seen, read, or heard about. It is the background that shapes his or her perspective, or point of view, about the world. Every individual uses knowledge and insight to try to make sense of his or her life.

Universal experiences are those that most people in a culture have known. Such experiences help people in a society share a sense of identity. Each person's experiences are unique, however, and shape the person's perceptions. For example, a person who has always struggled with schoolwork might perceive a college entrance test as a frightening prospect, whereas a person who has always had positive educational experiences might look forward to the same test as an exciting challenge.

Exploring the Big Question

© Collaboration: Small Group Discussion Start thinking about the Big Question by working with a small group of classmates to describe how different background experiences might affect two people's perception of each situation listed below.

- Moving to a new city or town and having to attend a new school
- Deciding whether or not someone is being truthful about a situation
- Persuading someone to do the right thing
- Trying to get a person of another generation to understand your point of view
- Attempting a new sport that requires a high level of athleticism
- Encountering an emergency situation that requires a quick response

Discuss how each person's experiences would affect his or her point of view. Present your ideas clearly and persuasively, and try to build on your classmates' ideas.

Connecting to the Literature Each reading in this unit will give you additional insight into the Big Question.

PHLit Online!
www.PHLitOnline.com
- Big Question video
- Illustrated vocabulary words
- Interactive vocabulary games
- BQ Tunes

Learning Big Question Vocabulary

Acquire and Use Academic Vocabulary Academic vocabulary is the language you encounter in textbooks and on standardized tests. Review the definitions of these academic vocabulary words.

anticipate (an tis´ ə pāt´) *v.* look forward to

background (bak´ ground´) *n.* all of a person's education, training, and experience

bias (bī´ əs) *n.* a preference for one thing, person, or group, often in a way considered unfair

distortion (di stôr´ shən) *n.* anything that shows something in an untrue way

individual (in´ də vij´ ōō əl) *adj.* relating to a single person or thing

insight (in´ sīt´) *n.* a clear idea of the nature of things

interpretation (in tur´ prə tā´ shən) *n.* a person's idea of the meaning of something

manipulate (mə nip´ yōō lāt´) *v.* control by use of influence, often in an unfair way

perspective (pər´ spek´ tiv) *n.* the way one sees things

Use these words as you complete Big Question activities in this unit that involve reading, writing, speaking, and listening.

Gather Vocabulary Knowledge Additional Big Question words are listed below. Categorize the words by deciding whether you know each one well, know it a little bit, or do not know it at all.

| expectations | impression | stereotype |
| identity | knowledge | universal |

Then, do the following:

1. Write the definitions of the words you know.

2. Consult a dictionary to confirm the definitions of the words you know. Revise your definitions if necessary.

3. Using a print or an online dictionary, look up the meanings of the words you do not know. Then, write the meanings.

4. Use all the words in a brief paragraph in which you describe how life experience has changed the way you perceive something or someone.

 Common Core State Standards

Speaking and Listening
1. Initiate and participate effectively in a range of collaborative discussions with diverse partners on grades 9–10 topics, texts, and issues, building on others' ideas and expressing their own clearly and persuasively.

Language
6. Acquire and use accurately general academic and domain-specific words and phrases, sufficient for reading, writing, speaking, and listening at the college and career readiness level; demonstrate independence in gathering vocabulary knowledge when considering a word or phrase important to comprehension or expression.

Elements of Drama

Drama is storytelling brought to life through performance.

Drama is a story that is written as a script and intended for performance by actors on a stage or in a film.

Like other narratives, a drama portrays characters caught up in conflict. The struggles that characters face in a drama spark a sequence of events, called the **plot,** which eventually reaches a **climax,** the point of highest intensity in the action. The **resolution,** or settling of the conflict, allows the story to wind down and leads to the drama's conclusion.

Character and conflict work together in a drama, or play, to engage readers or viewers. As events unfold, characters react and change, revealing their personalities and motives.

In performance, the various elements of drama combine to produce the illusion of reality known as **dramatic effect.** Through this effect, the author, or **playwright,** explores a **theme**—an insight or message about life. The example above explains how elements in a play create dramatic effect.

> **Example: Dramatic Effect**
> In *The Tragedy of Romeo and Juliet,* two lovers cannot marry because their families are sworn enemies. The play retains its dramatic effect, even centuries after it was first performed, because its key ideas are timeless. The **characters** of two people in love, the **conflict** of circumstances that keep the lovers apart, and **themes** about the power, difficulties, and danger of love, are concepts that still have relevance in the modern world.

A playwright divides a **script** into basic units called **acts.** Within acts, there may be further divisions known as **scenes.** Scenes often serve to shift the action's setting or time or to introduce new characters. Characters' speech is called **dialogue,** and notes in the script on how the play should be performed are called **stage directions.** The chart below further defines and explains these basic elements of drama.

The Elements of Drama

Acts and Scenes	Acts and scenes are the basic divisions of drama. Dramas may contain a varying number of acts, each of which may contain a number of scenes.
Stage Directions	Stage directions are notes that tell how a play should be performed or staged. They appear in italics and/or are set off by brackets or parentheses. Stage directions may include the following information: • Background about the setting or characters • Instructions that tell how actors should move and speak • Abbreviations such as *O.S.* (offstage), *D.S.* (downstage, or closer to the audience), and *U.S.* (upstage, or farther from the audience) • Details about scenery, lighting, and costumes
Sets	Sets define the area in which the play's action occurs. They include the physical elements placed on the stage. A set may be realistic and look like an actual place, or it may be more abstract and merely suggest a place.
Props	A prop is a movable object, such as a book, a pen, or a flashlight. Props add realism to the action in a play.

Dramatic Forms

The ancient Greeks, who developed drama as an organized literary form, created two basic types of plays. These broad categories still define drama today.

> **Tragedy**
>
> A **tragedy** traces the downfall of the main character, or **protagonist,** who is often called the **tragic hero.**
>
> - In classic drama, the tragic hero is an important person, such as a general or a king.
> - The hero is admirable but is defeated by a **tragic flaw,** a mistake or character defect.

> **Comedy**
>
> A **comedy** has a happy ending for the protagonist.
>
> - Comedies often feature events in which the world's order or balance is disrupted.
> - The ending restores order and may reward the hero.

Comedies are often funny, but they can make a serious point. The main distinction between tragedy and comedy is how the story ends: Tragedies end in death, defeat, or exile; comedies end in weddings or other joyful events.

Dramatic Structures Classic dramas, such as most ancient Greek and Shakespearean works, take place in five acts and thus are called **five-act plays.** The acts typically follow this plot structure:

Act 1: introduction/exposition;
Act 2: rising action;
Act 3: climax;
Act 4: falling action;
Act 5: resolution.

In most dramatic works, the five segments of plot are compressed into fewer acts. Many **screenplays, teleplays,** and **operas** are framed in three acts. Act 1 introduces main characters and sets the conflict in motion. Act 2 escalates the conflict and increases tension for the protagonist. Act 3 takes the conflict to a climax and reveals the outcome in a resolution.

Shorter dramatic works may consist of only a single act. **One-act plays** may be divided into several scenes.

Dramatic Dialogue In most dramatic works, dialogue is the playwright's main tool. Many ancient Greek plays also employ the convention of the **chorus,** a group of actors onstage who observe the action but do not participate in it. The members of the chorus would most often sing their lines, but sometimes their lines were spoken aloud in unison instead. The chorus provides background information and reacts to events. Some modern plays feature a chorus.

In other modern dramas, a **narrator** may replace the chorus. In certain films, for example, the voice of an unseen narrator may introduce the story, set up a scene, or tell viewers about a character.

Playwrights may use other types of dramatic speeches to advance plot and reveal character.

- A **monologue** is a long speech that one character delivers to other characters onstage.
- A **soliloquy** is a speech in which a character, alone on stage, "thinks aloud," revealing private thoughts.
- An **aside** is a remark that a character makes to the audience but that other characters do not hear.

In This Section

Elements of Drama

Analyzing Complex Characters

Close Read: Character Development, Conflict, and Theme
- Model Text
- Practice Text

After You Read

 Common Core
State Standards

RL.9-10.3
[For the full wording of the standards, see the standards chart in the front of your textbook.]

Analyzing Complex Characters

The ways that complex characters react to conflict help develop theme in a dramatic work.

Common Core State Standards

Reading Literature 3. Analyze how complex characters develop over the course of a text, interact with other characters, and advance the plot or develop the theme.

Characters in Conflict

In both tragedies and comedies, characters face **conflict,** a struggle between opposing forces. There are two main types of conflict:

- **External Conflict:** An external conflict is a struggle against an outside force, such as nature, another character, or the pressures of society. For example, a character who faces pressure from bullies at school experiences an external conflict.

- **Internal Conflict:** An internal conflict is a struggle within the mind of a character. For example, a character who struggles with his desire to support his family while following his dream to become an actor experiences an internal conflict.

The most interesting dramatic works feature conflicts that engage the audience. For tragic characters, the conflict may be life threatening. For comedic characters, the threat may be perceived. For example, a character in a romantic comedy may think that a coworker is trying to win over the woman he loves, when in reality, the coworker is not interested in the woman.

Protagonist and Antagonist Most plays and movies focus on a single main character—the **protagonist.** The character who opposes the main character and either creates or intensifies the conflict is called the **antagonist.**

Characterization and Motivation Through the use of **characterization**— the dialogue and actions that reveal a character's personality— a playwright provides clues about the human qualities of a character as well as clues about the character's **motivation,** or reasons for behaving a certain way. It is up to the reader or audience to infer what these clues mean.

Clues	Motivation
A young, thin boy eyes a loaf of bread; then he steals it.	The child is hungry.
A policeman detains the child; then he lets him go.	The policeman feels sorry for the child.

Complex Characters Great dramas present interesting protagonists and antagonists. Such characters are referred to as *complex*, which means they have strengths and weaknesses and experience mixed emotions. Complex characters have **multiple motivations,** or a variety of reasons for behaving as they do. In literary terms, complex characters are **round,** rather than flat, and **dynamic,** rather than static. **Flat** or **static** characters often represent stereotypes and do not change or develop over the course of a play. The arch-villain and the selfless best friend are two examples of flat or static characters.

Complex Characters	Limited Characters
• **Round:** multidimensional; possess more than one motivation; display many qualities, including strengths and weaknesses • **Dynamic:** undergo change during the course of play; grow in terms of improvement or self-realization	• **Flat:** one-dimensional; have only one motivation; display only one quality or trait • **Static:** remain the same throughout the play; resist or are unable to adjust to changing circumstances

Complex Characters and Theme

In the most compelling dramas, complex characters change or grow as the result of their responses to internal or external conflicts. In portraying such journeys of transformation, a playwright tries to bring insight to aspects of the human condition—and ultimately reveals a message about life that audiences can understand and appreciate. That message is the **theme.**

Character Development In any work of literature, a writer uses the tools of character development, or **characterization,** to create characters and reveal their personality traits.

In **direct characterization,** a writer directly states a character's traits. A playwright might use stage directions, a chorus, a narrator, or another character to convey information that tells what a character is like.

> **Example: Direct Characterization**
>
> **RAFAEL.** Yo! Mauricio! Where you going, man? Get back here! *[turns to face audience]* I hate to say it, but you just can't trust Mauricio. He is the most unreliable man you will ever meet. Whenever you need him, he just disappears.

In **indirect characterization,** a writer shows what a character is like in any of these ways:

- Descriptions of a character's physical appearance;
- The character's own words;
- The character's actions and behavior;
- Other characters' reactions to the character.

An actor brings a character to life on the stage or in a movie by using his or her voice, facial expressions, and gestures, as well as the pitch, pacing, and phrasing of his or her speech. Actors work under the guidance of the director, the interpreter and manager of the creative aspects of a dramatic or film production. Costumes, sets, and props also help emphasize elements of a character's personality.

Reading Drama

Actors speak the words in a script and breathe life into them. When you read a drama, make the play come alive by using textual clues to understand characters' motivations, feelings, actions, and thoughts. As you read, picture details of the performance.

To read a play effectively, look at dialogue, stage directions, punctuation, and word choice. In these elements, you will find clues about a character's emotions, relationships, social class, education, and environment.

> **Example:**
> **Characterization in Drama**
>
> **Stage Directions Suggesting Attitude:** *[Yuki lifts her cup and sips loudly, eyes glaring.]*
>
> **Punctuation Showing Emotion:** STANLEY. I don't buy your act. Not for one minute!
>
> **Dialogue Suggesting Social/Economic Class:** JASON. I have a social engagement this afternoon. I don't have time to deal with this. Where's my butler? *[Calls out]* Edward, get in here!
>
> **Word Choice Revealing Traits or Qualities:** MANUELITO. Lucy is a ridiculous creature. She's insufferable!

Dramatic Speeches Through monologues, soliloquies, and asides, playwrights provide critical clues to characters' motivations and actions. These dramatic speeches help propel the plot because they explain why characters do what they do. In addition, these speeches may express ideas that are key to the play's theme. For example, in a monologue or soliloquy, a character can explain what he or she thinks and feels. The audience learns about the character's conflicts and even his or her secrets.

Analyzing all the details a playwright provides through a complex character's words and actions will lead you to fully appreciate a drama and understand its deeper meaning.

Close Read: Character Development, Conflict, and Theme

In the best dramatic works, playwrights develop theme through complex characters and conflict.

A powerful drama provides a window to life as well as a form of entertainment. When you read or view a drama, notice how the playwright develops complex characters that point to the central message of the work. The chart below can help you make connections between characters and conflict and show you how to use clues the playwright provides to get at the deeper meaning of a drama.

Clues to Analyzing Character, Conflict, and Theme in a Dramatic Work

Characters
- What do characters want? What do they do to attain their goals?
- Who is the protagonist? What traits make him or her complex—round and dynamic? What motivates his or her decisions?
- Who is the antagonist? What is his or her motivation? Is the antagonist complex?
- Are there flat or static characters? What role do they play? What effect do they have?

Characterization
- How does the playwright use direct characterization? What do the descriptions reveal?
- How does indirect characterization, including a character's appearance, actions, words, or others characters' words and reactions, add to your understanding?
- How do characters' actions, motivations, behaviors, feelings, or thoughts reveal traits, motivations, and conflicts?

Actions and Events
- What actions do characters take, and what motivates them to act?
- What other events do the characters' actions cause?
- How do characters react to events or to the actions of other characters?
- How do actions advance the plot and theme?

Conflicts
- What is the main conflict?
- What other conflicts influence characters?
- Are the main character's conflicts internal, external, or both?
- How do different characters contribute or react to the conflicts?
- What themes do the conflicts suggest?

Dialogue and Dramatic Speeches
- What do the characters say to each other? What do they hide from each other?
- Do characters reveal to the audience things that they conceal from each other?
- What do characters' word choices suggest?
- Does the playwright use monologues, asides, or soliloquies? For what purpose?

Stage Directions
- Does the playwright make direct statements about the setting or characters?
- What notes does the playwright include about characters' speech, movement, or behavior?
- Do stage directions suggest characters' emotions?

Model

About the Text The Norwegian playwright Henrik Ibsen finished *A Doll House* in 1879. The play opened to shocked audiences. While many Victorian playwrights conveyed moral lessons, Ibsen lifted the veil from social institutions to show their hypocritical constructs. In *A Doll House,* for instance, the sexism of a Victorian marriage emerges in painful detail. Some critics view its heroine, Nora, as drama's first feminist. Nora, who has loved her husband, comes to be greatly disappointed in him. The drama broke precedent by ending not with a tragic downfall but an argument, after which Nora leaves her family in order to regain herself. In the play's last action, she slams the door.

With *A Doll House,* Ibsen sealed his reputation with progressive critics, establishing himself as a serious artist. Many dramatists and critics see Ibsen as the greatest Western playwright after Shakespeare.

The play is set in 1879 in the Helmer family's middle-class Norwegian home. Torvald Helmer has recently been hired as a banker, a great relief to the family, which has experienced financial difficulties. In this scene, the first of Act I, Nora has just returned from Christmas shopping.

---

from *A Doll House* by Henrik Ibsen

HELMER (in his room). Is that my lark twittering there?

NORA (busy opening some of her parcels). Yes, it is.

HELMER. Is it the squirrel frisking around?

NORA. Yes!

HELMER. When did the squirrel get home?

NORA. Just this minute. (Hides the bag of macaroons in her pocket and wipes her mouth.) Come here, Torvald, and see what I've been buying.

HELMER. Don't interrupt me. (A little later he opens the door and looks in, pen in hand.) Buying, did you say? What! All that? Has my little spendthrift been making the money fly again?

NORA. Why, Torvald, surely we can afford to launch out a little now. It's the first Christmas we haven't had to pinch.

Dialogue Torvald's nicknames for Nora seem endearing, but actually show his negative view of her.

Stage Directions In these stage directions, Ibsen conveys Nora's need to hide her actions from her husband.

Characterization Torvald's words reveal his controlling personality and condescending attitude toward Nora.

Conflict Torvald's wish to control the family budget clashes with Nora's need for cheer and freedom. Torvald sees Nora as undisciplined, and she sees him as inhibited.

Actions and Events Nora's proposal causes Torvald to tug at her ear. Ibsen notes that Torvald does this playfully, but in reality, Torvald treats his wife like a child.

Characters Torvald's words show his one motivation: control. Nora's words show that she is warm and loving. She appears, at this point, to be a round character, while Torvald seems static.

HELMER. Come, come; we can't afford to squander money.

NORA. Oh yes, Torvald, do let us squander a little, now—just the least little bit! You know you'll soon be earning heaps of money.

HELMER. Yes, from New Year's Day. But there's a whole quarter before my first salary is due.

NORA. Never mind; we can borrow in the meantime.

HELMER. Nora! (He goes up to her and takes her playfully by the ear.) Still my little featherbrain! Supposing I borrowed a thousand crowns to-day, and you made ducks and drakes of them during Christmas week, and then on New Year's Eve a tile blew off the roof and knocked my brains out.

NORA (laying her hand on his mouth). Hush! How can you talk so horridly?

HELMER. But supposing it were to happen—what then?

NORA. If anything so dreadful happened, it would be all the same to me whether I was in debt or not.

HELMER. But what about the creditors?

NORA. They! Who cares for them? They're only strangers.

HELMER. Nora, Nora! What a woman you are! But seriously, Nora, you know my principles on these points. No debts! No borrowing! Home life ceases to be free and beautiful as soon as it is founded on borrowing and debt. We two have held out bravely till now, and we are not going to give in at the last.

NORA (going to the fireplace). Very well—as you please, Torvald.

Independent Practice

About the Text The following excerpt comes from Act II of David Henry Hwang's dramatic adaptation of Peter Sís's illustrated book *Tibet Through the Red Box*. The story is set in Czechoslovakia and Tibet between the years 1950 and 1952. During that period, the Soviet Union occupied Czechoslovakia and China, a Soviet rival, invaded Tibet.

In Act I, the Russian government sent Peter's father, Vladimir, from their home in Czechoslovakia to Tibet to make a documentary film about the Chinese invasion. During his father's absence, Peter was injured while making trouble for the Russian troops. As a result, he has been confined to his bed. At the same time, an avalanche has stranded Vladimir in Tibet, keeping him away from his family for more than a year. With the aid of various unusual characters, father and son communicate through messages and dreams.

---

from *Tibet Through the Red Box* by David Henry Hwang

CHARACTERS

PETER a boy

ALENKA Peter's mother

THE BOY SPIRIT a guiding spirit who assumes many forms including a cat and Jingle-Bell Boy

VLADIMIR Peter's father, a filmmaker

YETI Abominable Snowman

ENSEMBLE 1 & 2 Groups of characters who act as a chorus and serve various functions

from Act II

ALENKA. *(O.S.)* Peter, we received another letter—from your Father!

Lights reveal ALENKA *and* PETER, *in bed. She holds the same letter that the* JINGLE-BELL BOY *pinched from* VLADIMIR.

ALENKA. All covered with a strange postmark, and these odd little stamps, and characters that can only be Chinese or maybe Japanese or—Peter, he's still alive!

(pause)

I had to run down to the post office to sign for it, and on the way home, of course, I couldn't wait to read it. He is having the most amazing adventures. In a land so strange—lamas, castles, even an abominable snowman! Here— read it.

PETER. I read the last one.

ALENKA. What is wrong with you?

> **Characters** What hint about the play do these character descriptions provide?

> **Dialogue** What do Alenka's comments suggest about her feelings for her husband?

Practice continued

Characters What feelings motivate Peter's reaction to the letter? What internal conflict is he experiencing?

Characterization What thoughts about his father's character do Peter's comments convey?

Conflict How does this question further illuminate Peter's internal conflict?

Dialogue What do Alenka's lines reveal about her character? Point out specific words and phrases to support your inference.

Characterization With this banter, what does the playwright suggest about the relationship between Peter and The Boy Spirit?

PETER. Every time we get a letter, it's like we have a big party. If he really cares about us, how come he's not home yet?

ALENKA. You are so brave, Peter. The hardest thing of all is not knowing. Where he is, or whether he's even still—whether he's all right. You don't know how strong you are.

PETER. Does Father know?

ALENKA. Oh, I bet he does. And when he returns you'll be all better, running around like your old self.

PETER. How can I get better unless he comes home?

(pause)

How much money does Father make?

ALENKA. Why are you—? Enough to survive, like everyone else.

PETER. How come, all of a sudden, we can afford paints?

ALENKA. I make it a priority, what kind of—?

PETER. Is Father a traitor?

ALENKA. Who says such a—?

PETER. It doesn't matter.

ALENKA. Do your friends talk like that? The delinquents?

PETER. Mother, they're not—

ALENKA. He was sent away by the Russians. But he had no choice!

PETER. You said he did.

ALENKA. I never said any such—

PETER. Before he left.

ALENKA. Who are you? The secret police? You tell your friends, your Father loves his country, he's a man of peace. Then send them to me—and I'll cuff them on their pointed heads!

ALENKA *exits, leaving the letter behind.* THE BOY SPIRIT *enters, as the cat.*

THE BOY SPIRIT. Meow. Spreading joy and happiness everywhere?

PETER. Want me to pull your tail?

THE BOY SPIRIT. (*re: the letter*) Oh, you got it.

PETER. But I'm not gonna read it. That'll show him.

THE BOY SPIRIT. Show him what?

PETER. He can't soften me up with, "I miss you, I love you." Not when I know the truth about him.

THE BOY SPIRIT. Does that mean you're not even curious about the Abominable Snowman?

The YETI, *an abominable snowman, enters. He is very tall.*

PETER. "Abominable snowman."

The YETI *approaches* THE BOY SPIRIT, *who flees, running around the stage.*

PETER. Who ever heard of such a stupid—?

The YETI is tall enough to stand eye to eye with PETER in his bed.

YETI. Hello, there!

THE BOY SPIRIT. Meow meow meow!

PETER. What the—?

YETI. Could you help me?

PETER. It's the abominable snowman!

YETI. Oh my god! Where?

PETER. "Where?" You *are* the abominable snowman!

YETI. Snowmen are made of snow. This is fur. I am a Yeti. I'm trying to find a city called Prague. In a country called Chicken-slovakia. A boy, about twelve years old, who's stuck in a bed, and can't get himself out. You know anyone like that?

PETER. You've got to be kidding.

(*off* YETI*'s confusion*)

Boy? Twelve? Bed?

YETI. Oh! Oh! Oh! So *you're* Peter. When he sent me on this mission, I wasn't sure—

PETER. "He?"

YETI. I mean, to travel all the way to Europe—and, you know, no one will issue me a passport.

PETER. Who sent you?

YETI. Your Father, of course. Haven't you read his letter yet?

PETER. Why's everyone keep asking me that?

Stage Directions What important information do these stage directions convey?

Dialogue What does this dialogue reveal about the tone of the play?

Characters What does this dialogue suggest about Peter?

Practice continued

YETI. Not to be boastful or anything, but . . . a lot of it is about me. (*pause*) If you read it, I'll grant you a magical wish.

PETER. Anything?

YETI. Anything.

PETER. (*pulls out the letter*) All right . . . sucker. (*reads:*) "I was crossing a mountain pass when suddenly—"

Paper cutouts of snowflakes are projected onto the U.S. wall, moving. MUSICIANS *enter with percussion, simulating the sounds of a snowstorm.* U.S., VLADIMIR *enters, fighting his way against a blizzard.*

VLADIMIR. "A snowstorm took me by surprise. I was looking for shelter, but the winds and snow pushed me to the ground."

U.S., VLADIMIR *is forced to the ground. He sits in a cross-legged meditation position for the rest of the scene.*

VLADIMIR. "I probably lost consciousness, but have some vague memory—like a dream—"

PETER. "Of being lifted up—" Hey!

The YETI *mimes lifting* PETER, *as he flies out of his bed.*

VLADIMIR. "Lifted up and carried!"

PETER *flies across the stage, with the* YETI *beneath, "carrying" him. Together, they move O.S.*

PETER. (*to* YETI) What are you doing?

YETI. Welcome to the Land of Magic.

YETI *releases* PETER. *He finds he can stand on his own two legs.*

VLADIMIR. I awoke in a dark cave, on a bed of leaves. Beside me was a potion of honey and herbs. I drank this potion, and soon my strength began to return.

The projections of snowflakes become silhouettes of YETIS, *moving across the stage.*

VLADIMIR. One day, I finally felt well-enough to venture out of my dark cave.

PETER *re-enters* (*having detached his wires*), *carried by the* YETI.

DANCERS *enter in Yeti-like costumes, begin to move through a series of warm-up rituals resembling Tai Chi.*

Stage Directions What changes to the scene do these stage directions indicate?

Characterization What do these lines tell the audience about Vladimir's effect on his son?

Actions and Events What do you expect happened to Vladimir when he drank the potion?

VLADIMIR. After my eyes had adjusted to the light, I could see giant fairy beings moving gently in a kind of slow motion throughout the valley.

YETI *starts to put* PETER *down amidst the* DANCERS.

VLADIMIR. They seemed to be working, gathering, tending to young ones, playing in the streams and waterfalls. Was this a lost civilization? I did not know. I crawled back into the cave, but this time I managed not to fall asleep. And I saw . . .

One of the YETIS *places food before* VLADIMIR.

VLADIMIR. Slowly, these gentle giants nursed me to recovery.

The DANCERS *begin to assume the almost martial exercises lamas perform when practicing their theological dialectics.*

PETER. (*to* YETI) What are they doing now?

YETI. Practicing for battle.

PETER. How tough are you guys, anyway?

YETI. Look at us—we're big, we're strong, and we love to work out.

PETER. And you've got big teeth.

YETI. With excellent gums.

PETER. OK, I order you to help me fight the Russians. This is gonna be a heck of a lot better than stealing their lunches.

YETI. Wait a second.

PETER. You promised, remember? Want the whole world to learn Yetis are big liars?

YETI. (*to other* YETIS) Guys, we're being called to battle!

ENSEMBLE 1. Battle?

PETER. We're gonna get the Russians.

ENSEMBLE 2. The who?

YETI. I . . . granted the boy a wish.

ENSEMBLE 2. Oh. Great.

YETI. It's a long story, but a wish is a wish!

ENSEMBLE 1 Where are we going?

PETER. Prague. Czechoslovakia.

Dialogue What is the main purpose of Vladimir's monologue?

Characterization What does this dialogue tell you about the Yeti's personality?

Conflict What kind of conflict do you expect will result from Peter's challenge?

Dialogue Sometimes, comedic dialogue addresses serious subjects. What serious subject is addressed here?

Practice continued

Stage Directions The word *reprise* means "repeat." Why might the playwright want to repeat music from an earlier scene?

Actions and Events What action does Peter want to take? Why?

Characters How does the character of The Boy Spirit help Peter tell his story?

ENSEMBLE 2. Is the food any good?

Musicians reprise the drumbeat which underscored the attack on the Russians in Act One.

PETER. All right. Let's go back to when everything went wrong. I threw the rock at the Russian soldier, then he followed me into the dead-end alley.

ENSEMBLE 1, ENSEMBLE 2, *and the* YETI *criss-cross the stage, recalling the sequence in Act I.*

PETER. This time he's in for a surprise!

THE BOY SPIRIT *enters, dressed as a Russian soldier.*

PETER. And here comes the Rooskie!

THE BOY SPIRIT. Nyet! Nyet!

PETER. I climb up the wall—the exit's blocked!

THE BOY SPIRIT. (*bad Russian accent*) Stop, you stupid kid-ski!

PETER. He sees me!

THE BOY SPIRIT. I say, stop!

PETER. Only this time, I don't even try to escape.

THE BOY SPIRIT. Nyet! We have you cornered!

PETER. I just stand there, spitting down at them.

THE BOY SPIRIT. I never again will lose another lunch to you!

PETER. Doing my little victory dance.

THE BOY SPIRIT. That's disgusting! Come down—else, I shoot!

PETER. Suddenly, out of nowhere—

THE BOY SPIRIT. One, two—

PETER. The Yeti cavalry appears!

THE BOY SPIRIT. What?

YETIS *rush* THE BOY SPIRIT.

YETIS. Roar!

THE BOY SPIRIT. Oh my god-ski!

PETER. He's so scared, he can't even move!

THE BOY SPIRIT. The Abominable Snowman?

YETI. We're Yeti, why does everyone get that wrong?

PETER. Tries to use his gun—

THE BOY SPIRIT. N-n-nice snowman . . .

PETER. —but his hands are shaking.

YETIS. Roar!

THE BOY SPIRIT. Bang, bang-ski!

YETI. Bullets can't go through our fur.

THE BOY SPIRIT. Mama!

ENSEMBLE 2. They only make us angrier!

YETIS. Roar, roar!

YETIS *duplicate their martial exercises, which buffet the "Soldier" without actually touching him.*

PETER. They close in, clutching their paws around the soldier's throat —

YETIS *mime the action, as the "Soldier" falls, clutching his throat.*

THE BOY SPIRIT. Aaaargh!

PETER. He falls to his knees—

THE BOY SPIRIT. (*choking*) Please, please spare me—

PETER. I see fear in his eyes—

THE BOY SPIRIT. You don't understand— I didn't want to come here—

PETER. (*to* YETIS) Well hurry up? Aren't you supposed to—you know—?

YETI. We're waiting for your command.

PETER. Me?

ENSEMBLE 2. After all, this is *your* wish.

ENSEMBLE 1. We're waiting.

THE BOY SPIRIT. I have wife and a son . . . just like you.

PETER. No you don't. You're nothing like me. You're a monster.

YETI. Actually, *we're* the monsters here.

PETER. (*to* YETI:) Shut up! (*to* THE BOY SPIRIT:) I mean you're not a human being.

THE BOY SPIRIT. In my back pocket . . .

Stage Directions What can you tell about the action and events from these stage directions? Consider the playwright's use of quotation marks around *Soldier*.

Conflicts What internal conflict is Peter struggling with now?

Characters What does this statement reveal about Peter's character? What does it reveal about the theme of the play?

Practice continued

Characterization
What do these lines and this stage direction reveal about Peter?

Characters How has Peter changed? What theme might Peter's feelings suggest?

Actions and Events Alenka's gift shows she has confidence in Peter's future. What does this tell the audience?

PETER. Not a real one anyway.

THE BOY SPIRIT. A letter . . .

PETER. You're . . . you're . . .

THE BOY SPIRIT. Send it to my son.

YETI. Hey, um, Peter, it's hard to hold this position.

ENSEMBLE 2. Yeah, so will you make up your mind?

PETER *screams in frustration.*

PETER. All right, let him go.

YETIS release THE BOY SPIRIT.

THE BOY SPIRIT. Thank you, thank you for showing mercy.

PETER. Get out of here. Before I change my mind.

THE BOY SPIRIT. I will remember you always

PETER. (*to* YETIS:) All of you!

YETI. But your wish . . .

PETER. I don't want any wishes, I'm sick of magic, of Tibet, of this whole stupid business!

(*he flies back into his bed*)

Everyone just leave me alone.

All exit.

ALENKA. (*O.S.*) Peter? I have something to show you.

ALENKA *enters, carrying a beautifully lacquered red box.*

ALENKA. Isn't it beautiful?

PETER. Where'd you get this?

ALENKA. I made it—with my own two hands. You think your old mother can only cook and clean and nag?

(*pause*)

I thought you might like a box—to store your paintings in.

PETER. What makes you think I'm painting?

ALENKA. Oh, I know you're not. But maybe you will someday. So I am giving you this beautiful red box . . . for all the paintings you have never made.

ALENKA *exits.*

1. **Key Ideas and Details** Why is Peter in bed at the beginning of the excerpt? What has happened?

2. **Key Ideas and Details** **(a)** Where is Vladimir, Peter's father? **(b) Infer:** What accusations have Peter's peers leveled at Vladimir? Use text evidence to explain your answers.

3. **Key Ideas and Details** **(a) Infer:** Based on specific dialogue, what is Peter's internal conflict? **(b)** What role do inner conflicts play in Peter's behavior?

4. **Craft and Structure** **Interpret:** Why might the playwright have chosen The Boy Spirit to take on so many different roles?

5. **Integration of Knowledge and Ideas** **Synthesize:** How does Peter's dilemma transcend the time and place of this drama to apply to children of any time and place?

6. **Integration of Knowledge and Ideas** **(a)** In a chart like the one shown, list the **conflicts** Peter experiences in this **drama.** Then, note **dialogue** and **stage directions** that Hwang uses to dramatize each conflict, and tell what these details reveal about each situation.

Peter's Conflicts	Stage Direction and Dialogue	What It Shows

(b) Collaborate: Compare charts with a partner. How do your partner's details add to your understanding of Peter's character?

Preparing to Read *Antigone*

The cultural and political influence of ancient Greece extended throughout the Mediterranean and into central Asia.

Historical Background: Ancient Greece

The Earliest Greeks More than one thousand years before the birth of Sophocles, the playwright who wrote *Antigone*, a people that we call the Mycenaeans (mī' sə nē' ənz) began to settle throughout the Greek mainland, which juts down from Europe into the Mediterranean Sea. They established strongholds in Thebes, Pylos, Athens, Mycenae, and elsewhere, building thick-walled palaces decorated with bronze metalwork. From the Minoans (mi nō' ənz), a sophisticated people who lived on the southern Greek island of Crete, they learned about writing, and they recorded palace business and other transactions on clay tablets. Many of these tablets have survived. The writings reveal a complex society that included administrative officials, priests, slaves, tradesmen, craftsmen and artisans, and an active warrior class. At the top of the social pyramid in each stronghold was a wanax, or king. If a historical Antigone existed, she would have been royalty, the daughter of the king of Thebes.

In about 1450 B.C., Minoan civilization collapsed, and the Mycenaeans became the dominant culture on Crete. Their influence spread throughout the Mediterranean islands and into western Asia Minor, or present-day Asian Turkey. On one of their most famous military ventures, the Mycenaeans successfully attacked the city of Troy in northern Asia Minor. We know that conflict as the Trojan War, which later became the subject of Homer's epic poems the *Iliad* and the *Odyssey*. It was among the last of the Mycenaean military successes. Soon afterward, Mycenaean civilization collapsed into a period called the Greek Dark Ages. The art of writing was lost, and the kingdoms broke down into small tribal units.

Re-emerging from Darkness In about 850 B.C., a vibrant Greek culture began to re-emerge, spurred by flourishing trade throughout the Mediterranean. Along with the economic boom came a resurgence of arts and learning capped by Homer's masterful epics. Although Homer composed in the oral tradition,

▲ This fresco depicting the Prince of Lilies is a beautiful example of Minoan art. It appears on a wall in the Minoan Palace of Knossos on the Greek island of Crete.

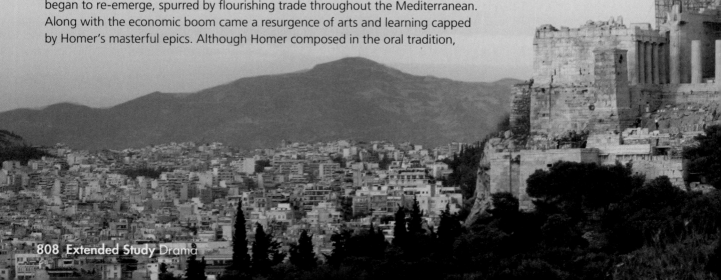

the Greeks soon began writing again, this time adapting the Phoenician writing system into the first true alphabet. They also began regrouping into city-states, or cities that functioned independently, just as countries do. By 500 B.C., the two most powerful city-states were Sparta, on Greece's Peloponnesian (**pel'ə pə nē' shən**) peninsula, and Athens, which stood east of Sparta in an area called Attica. Sparta was a monarchy with a powerful ruling council and a strong military tradition. Athens developed a government in which decision-making was shared by all adult males (other than slaves). It was, in short, the world's first democracy.

The Rise and Fall of Athens From 490 to 479 B.C., Athens and Sparta fought as allies in the Persian Wars, when the powerful Persian Empire (present-day Iran) twice tried to invade Greece. Despite Sparta's military prowess, it was Athens that led two important victories: the Battle of Marathon in the beginning and the Battle of Salamis later. These victories helped usher in a Golden Age of prosperity and achievement for Athens. Led by the statesman Pericles (**per' ə klēz'**), Athens became a great intellectual center, attracting artists, poets, scientists, and philosophers. Impressive new buildings were constructed, and civic festivals grew more splendid. Among those who contributed greatly to this cultural flowering was Sophocles: playwright, government official, and—briefly—general in the Athenian military.

Unfortunately, Pericles' foreign policy aroused the resentment of other Greek city-states. In 432 B.C., Sparta and its allies joined against Athens and its allies in what became known as the Peloponnesian War. Athens was defeated, and for a time, Sparta, and later Thebes, exerted control over the Greek world. In the end, however, it was Philip of Macedon, a monarch from a kingdom to the north of Greece, who rose to ascendancy. Philip's son Alexander would embark on an amazing series of military conquests that would spread Greek influence all the way into central Asia. His exploits would earn him the title by which he is still known today: Alexander the Great.

According to legend, after the Battle of Marathon, an Athenian soldier raced 26 miles back to Athens to share news of the victory. He then collapsed and died. The 26-mile race known as a marathon originated in his honor.

▼ The Parthenon, a temple dedicated to the goddess Athena, appears in the foreground of this photo of the Acropolis in Athens. The temple is among the most important surviving structures from Greece's Golden Age.

Ancient Greek Theater

*An art form rooted in religious ritual gave
rise to plays of enduring power.*

Religious Foundations Greek theater was rooted in Greek
religion, which was based on a belief in many gods. Each god
was associated with one or more aspects of nature or human
behavior. Poseidon (pə sī′ dən), for example, was god of the
seas, while Apollo was the god of light. Athena (ə thē′ nə) was the
goddess of wisdom, while Aphrodite (af′ rə dī′ tē) was the goddess
of love. Zeus (zoos′) ruled over all the gods, yet even he was not all-
powerful. Like human beings and lesser gods, Zeus could not alter fate.

The gods are key characters in Greek **mythology,** the set of stories the
Greeks told to explain the world around them. In these myths, the gods
often behave like human beings at our worst—they are angry, jealous,
and petty. They are even deceitful and often vengeful. They are especially
quick to punish human beings guilty of **hubris** (hyoo′ or hoo′ bris), or
excessive pride.

From Ritual to Art Theater in ancient Greece originated at annual
festivals called Dionysia (dī′ ə nī′ sē ə), which were dedicated to Dionysus,
the god of wine. At these festivals, a **chorus,** or group of singers, honored
Dionysus by chanting hymns called **dithyrambs** (dith′ ə ramz′). According
to legend, at one festival a poet named Thespis stepped away from the
chorus. He began a dialogue with the chorus leader while role-playing
figures from the Greek myths. Thus, drama was born. The playwright
Aeschylus developed the dramatic form further by adding a second actor,
and the playwright Sophocles later introduced a third player to the stage.

By the time Sophocles was writing, plays had become great spectacles each
performed in a large outdoor amphitheater with thousands in attendance.
The amphitheater was built on a slope with seating that rose in a semicircle
from the performing area, or **orchestra.** There was no curtain, but painted
scenery could be hung at the back. Performers wore large masks that
allowed the same actor to perform different roles.

At the Dionysia, prizes were awarded to the best playwright. By 501 B.C.,
the three-day festival featured work by three competitors. Each playwright
presented a **tetralogy,** or group of four plays, on a different day. The plays
usually included a bawdy drama called a **satyr** (sāt′ ər) **play,** as well as three
tragedies. About fifteen years later, a separate competition for comedies
was added.

▲ This mask depicts
Dionysus, the god of wine,
adorned with full beard
and a grapevine crown.

From the name of Thespis,
the first actor, comes the
English word *thespian,* an
elegant term for an actor.
The Greek word for an
actor, however, was
hypokrites, meaning "someone acting a part." That
term, of course, is the origin
of our word *hypocrite.*

Dramatic Structure Greek plays are **verse drama,** in which the dialogue takes the form of poetry. Typically, the plays follow a consistent format. They open with a **prologue,** or exposition, that presents the background of the conflict. The chorus then performs a **parados** (par´ əd əs), or opening song. This is followed by the first scene. Additional songs, called **odes,** divide scenes, as a curtain does in most modern theaters. At the end of a tragedy, the chorus performs a **paean** (pē´ ən) of thanksgiving to Dionysus. The tragedy then concludes with an **exodus** (eks´ ə dəs), or final scene.

The chorus is central to the production, providing key background information and commentary on the action. Chorus recitals often divide into a **strophe** (strō´ fē) and an answering **antistrophe.** During the strophe, the chorus sings while twisting or dancing from right to left. During the antistrophe, the chorus moves in the opposite direction. Some odes have a concluding stanza, or **epode,** when the chorus may have stood still. To help propel the plot, the chorus leader, or **choragos** (kō rā´ gəs; also spelled *choragus*), often exchanges thoughts with the rest of the chorus as well as with the actors.

Strophe is Greek for "twist." Originally, a *catastrophe* was simply the ending, or final plot twist, of a play. Because the endings of Greek tragedies involved disastrous events, the word has come to have its current meaning of a disastrous outcome.

THE THEATER OF DIONYUS IN ATHENS

The earliest dramas were likely performed in the Agora, or marketplace, in Athens. Later, the Theater of Dionysus (shown below as it appears today) was built on the slope of the Acropolis, the upper part of the city where other important buildings also stood. Stone seating was not used at first; instead, theater-goers probably sat on wooden benches.

Aristotle and Greek Tragedy

In Poetics, *Aristotle examined the mechanisms that make tragedy so compelling for audiences. His work remains the most influential discussion of drama the world has seen.*

Fundamentals of Tragedy In his landmark work *Poetics*, the Greek philosopher Aristotle (ar´ is tät´ l; 384–322 B.C.) provides a famous examination of tragedy. He describes a **tragedy** as a serious play recounting related events in the life of a person of high rank or importance who is brought low and often meets his or her doom. The main character, called the **tragic hero** or **protagonist,** experiences this reversal of fortune as a result of what the Greeks called **hamartia** (hä´ mär tē´ ə), a tragic flaw or profound error in judgment. When a **tragic flaw** is involved, it usually takes form as **hubris,** or excessive pride. Fate, too, plays a decisive role in ensuring the tragic hero's downfall. In addition, the protagonist may face an **antagonist,** a rival character whose opposition contributes to his or her downfall.

Although the plot and its outcome are central to a tragedy, the events come as no surprise to most audience members. Greek audiences knew the myths upon which the plays were based; they knew what would happen. Nevertheless—according to Aristotle—the audience becomes caught up in the action because the play arouses their feelings of pity and fear. At the end of the play, explains Aristotle, the audience experiences a **catharsis** (kə thär´ sis), a cleansing or release of these emotions. Aristotle believed that the best plays engender fear and pity through the story and characters, not through the spectacle of the production itself.

Three Masters Three playwrights are considered the grand masters of Greek tragedy: Aeschylus (es´ ki ləs; c. 525–456 B.C.), Sophocles (säf´ ə klēz´; 496–406 B.C.), and Euripides (yōō rip´ ə dēz; 480–406 B.C.). Between them, the three won first prize forty-two times in the annual drama competitions at Athens. Aeschylus, the pioneer of tragedy, is praised especially for his poetic language. Sophocles is most famous for his character development and insight into human nature. Euripides is noted for his efforts to address social concerns and humanitarian themes in his plays.

▲ This Roman bust of Aristotle is based on a fourth century B.C. Greek bronze.

Aristotle was the pupil of another famous Greek philosopher, Plato (plāt´ ō; c. 427–c. 347 B.C.), who himself studied under yet another famous Greek philosopher, Socrates (sok´ rə tēz; c. 470–399 B.C.). Aristotle had a famous pupil too—Alexander the Great, whose conquests spread Greek culture throughout Europe, North Africa, and much of Asia.

◄ This painting by nineteenth-century French artist Jean Auguste Ingres depicts Aeschylus, (with scroll), Sophocles, and Euripides. The work is a study for a much larger work entitled *The Apotheosis of Homer.*

Sophocles (496–406 B.C.) Although he lived and wrote more than two thousand years ago, Sophocles is still considered one of the finest and most influential playwrights who ever lived. He won first prize at the annual Dionysia in Athens twenty-four times; never once did he place below second.

A Golden Time to Live Sophocles grew up in a prosperous family in Colonus, near Athens. At sixteen, he was one of the young men chosen to perform in a choral ode celebrating the Athenian victory over the Persians at Salamis, the event that marks the beginning of Athens's golden age. Throughout his long life, he remained a leading figure of that era. Admired for his good looks and athleticism, he was also a talented musician and a frequent contributor to Athenian public life. He served for a time as a city treasurer and also as a general in the conflict with Samos, an island that revolted against Athens in 441 B.C. Late in life, he was elected to a special committee to investigate the disastrous failure of the Athenian military expedition to Sicily.

A Leading Light It was in theater, however, that Sophocles truly shone. His career as a dramatist began in 468 B.C., when he entered the annual Dionysia and beat the celebrated dramatist Aeschylus to take first prize. Over the next 62 years he wrote more than 120 plays, seven of which have survived. Among the most celebrated are *Oedipus Rex*, the tragedy Aristotle considered the best example of the form, and *Antigone*, the story of Oedipus' daughter. Sophocles is known for strong female characters and for his insight into human nature. He is credited with introducing a third actor to drama and also with the practice of using painted scenery. He died two years before Athens surrendered to Sparta in the Peloponnesian War, the event that marks the end of Athens's Golden Age.

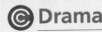 | Antigone, Prologue
through Scene 2

Drama

Build your skills and improve your comprehension of drama with this selection.

Read **Antigone** to find out how members of a family battle each other over their different values.

Common Core State Standards

Meet these standards with **Antigone, Prologue through Scene 2** (p. 814).

Reading Literature

2. Provide an objective summary of the text. *(Reading Skill: Summarize)*

3. Analyze how complex characters develop over the course of a text, interact with other characters, and advance the plot or develop the theme *(Literary Analysis: Protagonist and Antagonist)*

Writing

2. Write informative/explanatory texts to examine and convey complex ideas, concept, and information clearly and accurately through effective selection, organization, and analysis of content. **2.a.** Introduce a topic; organize complex ideas, concepts, and information to make important connections and distinctions. **2.b.** Develop the topic with well-chosen, relevant, and sufficient facts, extended definitions, concrete details, quotations, or other information and examples. *(Writing: Essay)*

Speaking and Listening

4. Present information, findings, and supporting evidence clearly, concisely, and logically such that listeners can follow the line of reasoning. *(Speaking and Listening: Oral Report)*

Language

1. Demonstrate command of the conventions of standard English grammar and usage when writing or speaking. *(Conventions: Participles and Gerunds)*

6. Acquire and use accurately general academic and domain-specific words and phrases *(Vocabulary: Word Study)*

Literary Analysis:
Protagonist and Antagonist

Greek tragedies, like many other plays and stories, typically focus on a **protagonist,** or main character, and an **antagonist,** the character who is in conflict with the protagonist. In fact, these two literary terms were first applied to Greek tragedies such as *Antigone*.

In a play, the struggle between a protagonist and an antagonist may take the form of a dramatic life-or-death conflict. At the same time, the two characters may stand for larger conflicting ideas or values. The characters' struggle may reflect deep questions of concern to people of all times and places. Here are some of the conflicting ideas in *Antigone*:

- Antigone, the protagonist, breaks the law because she believes that the laws of the gods are higher than human laws.

- Her antagonist, Creon, insists that everyone must obey the law. He believes that no one is above the law.

Reading Skill: Summarize

A **summary** is a short statement of the main ideas and events in a work. To summarize, pause occasionally to **retell** what you have read, using only the most important information. Summarizing improves your understanding of a work because it leads you to identify the key elements of the text.

As you read *Antigone*, pause to summarize scenes and conversations.

Using the Strategy: Summary Chart

Use a **summary chart** like this one to identify the key elements of this part of *Antigone*.

Who is the most important character?	What does the character want?	Who or what gets in the character's way?	What is the outcome?

PHLit Online!
www.PHLitOnline.com

Hear It!
- Selection summary audio
- Selection audio

See It!
- Get Connected video
- Background video
- More about the author
- Vocabulary flashcards

Do It!
- Interactive journals
- Interactive graphic organizers
- Self-test
- Internet activity
- Grammar tutorial
- Interactive vocabulary games

Extended Study: Antigone **811**

Making Connections

Antigone, Prologue through Scene 2

Prologue through Scene 2

To what extent does *experience* determine what we *perceive?*

Writing About the Big Question

In the first part of *Antigone*, a woman breaks the king's law in order to uphold her deeply felt beliefs. Use these sentence starters to develop your ideas about the Big Question.

An **individual** may go against what others say when _____.

The **interpretation** of an action or an event can differ between two people because _____.

While You Read Look for moments when Antigone and Creon express their own points of view about what is right and what is wrong.

Vocabulary

Read each word and its definition. Decide whether you know the word well, know it a little bit, or do not know it at all. After you read, see how your knowledge of each word has increased.

- **sated** (sāt´ əd) *adj.* satisfied; provided with more than enough (p. 818) *We were sated after the big lunch.* sate *v.*

- **sententiously** (sen ten´ shəs lē) *adv.* in a way that shows excessive fondness for wise sayings; in lecturing tones (p. 822) *I told him I felt ill, and he answered sententiously, "An apple a day keeps the doctor away."* sententious *adj.* sententiousness *n.*

- **deflects** (dē flekts´) *v.* turns or makes go to one side (p. 824) *He deflects his opponent's blows by blocking with his forearm.* deflection *n.* deflective *adj.* deflector *n.*

- **edict** (ē´ dikt´) *n.* a public order; decree (p. 827) *At the press conference, the mayor gave his edict about stray animals.*

- **brazen** (brā´ zən) *adj.* shameless; bold (p. 828) *There was chocolate all over her mouth, but she told a brazen lie about the cookies.* brazenly *adv.* brazenness *n.*

- **waver** (wā´ vər) *v.* show indecision; fluctuate (p. 831) *He dipped his toe into the icy water and began to waver about diving in.* waveringly *adv.*

Word Study

The **Latin root** *-dict-* means "speak" or "say."

In this play, a king issues an **edict**, publicly saying that no one is permitted to bury his enemy.

Background for the Play

"Be Witnesses for Me"

The Theban Plays *Antigone* is one of three surviving plays by Sophocles centering on the Greek myth of Oedipus (**ed´ i pəs**), king of Thebes; the other two are *Oedipus Rex* (*Oedipus the King*) and *Oedipus at Colonus*. Known as the Theban plays, they are now often published as a chronological trilogy, with *Antigone* last. However, Sophocles did not write the plays for the same Dionysia, and he apparently wrote *Antigone* first.

The Oedipus Myth The myth of Oedipus was well known to Greek audiences; in fact, Aeschylus wrote several earlier plays about it, although only his *Seven Against Thebes* has survived. In the myth, a prophecy informs Laius (or Laïos; **lā´ yəs**), king of Thebes, and his wife Jocasta (or Iocaste) that their son will grow up to kill his father and marry his mother. Horrified, they send the infant off to be destroyed, but he is instead saved and adopted by a couple from Corinth. When the child, called Oedipus, grows up, he learns of the prophecy. Believing the warning refers to his adoptive parents, he flees in order to protect them. At a crossroads, he quarrels with and kills a stranger. Then, on the road to Thebes, he discovers the city is being plagued by a monstrous sphinx. In Greek mythology, the sphinx is a creature with a lion's body, bird's wings, and a woman's head. Waiting near the entrance to the city, the sphinx poses a riddle to all those who approach and eats anyone who cannot answer. The sphinx refuses to abandon its hold on the city until someone can solve the riddle. Oedipus does so, thereby saving the city and becoming a hero. As compensation, the recently widowed queen marries him, and he becomes king.

▲▼ (above) Nineteenth-century artist Frederic Leighton painted actress Dorothy Dene as Antigone. (below) This relief depicts Oedipus as he solves the riddle of the Sphinx.

Years later, Oedipus discovers that the man he killed at the crossroads was his birth father, the Theban king, and that the queen is his mother. Filled with horror, Oedipus blinds himself, and Jocasta commits suicide. Oedipus goes to live in exile with his daughter Antigone (**an tig´ ə nē**). After Oedipus' death, Antigone returns to Thebes. Earlier, Oedipus' two sons, Polyneices (**päl´ i nī´ sēz**) and Eteocles (**ē tē´ ə klēz´**), decided to share the throne, ruling in alternate years. However, when the time comes for Eteocles to give up the throne, he refuses, and the two brothers kill each other. Creon (**krē´ än**), Jocasta's brother, then assumes the throne.

It is at this point in the larger story that the play *Antigone* begins.

The famous riddle that Oedipus answered was "What has four legs in the morning, two at noon, and three in the evening?" The answer is a human being—crawling as a child, walking upright as an adult, and using a cane in old age.

Antigone
Sophocles
translated by Dudley Fitts and Robert Fitzgerald

Persons Represented

ANTIGONE (an tig´ ə nē´), daughter of Oedipus, former King of Thebes

ISMENE (is mē´ nē), another daughter of Oedipus

EURYDICE (yo͞o rid´ i sē´), wife of Creon

CREON (krē´ än´), King of Thebes, uncle of Antigone and Ismene

HAIMON (hī´ mən), Creon's son, engaged to Antigone

TEIRESIAS (tī rē´ sē əs), a blind prophet

A SENTRY

A MESSENGER

CHORUS

CHORAGOS (kō rā´ gəs), leader of the chorus

A BOY who leads Teiresias

GUARDS

SERVANTS

Prologue—Scene 2

Scene. *Before the palace of* CREON, *King of Thebes. A central double door, and two lateral doors. A platform extends the length of the facade, and from this platform three steps lead down into the "orchestra," or chorus-ground.*

Time. *Dawn of the day after the repulse of the Argive[1] army from the assault on Thebes.*

Prologue

[ANTIGONE *and* ISMENE *enter from the central door of the Palace.*]

 ANTIGONE. Ismene, dear sister,
  You would think that we had already suffered enough
  For the curse on Oedipus:[2]
  I cannot imagine any grief
5 That you and I have not gone through. And now—
  Have they told you of the new decree of our King Creon?

 ISMENE. I have heard nothing: I know
  That two sisters lost two brothers, a double death
  In a single hour; and I know that the Argive army
10 Fled in the night; but beyond this, nothing.

 ANTIGONE. I thought so. And that is why I wanted you
  To come out here with me. There is something we must do.

 ISMENE. Why do you speak so strangely?

 ANTIGONE. Listen, Ismene:
15 Creon buried our brother Eteocles
  With military honors, gave him a soldier's funeral,
  And it was right that he should; but Polyneices,
  Who fought as bravely and died as miserably,—
  They say that Creon has sworn
20 No one shall bury him, no one mourn for him,
  But his body must lie in the fields, a sweet treasure
  For carrion birds[3] to find as they search for food.
  That is what they say, and our good Creon is coming here
  To announce it publicly; and the penalty—
25 Stoning to death in the public square!
        There it is,

◄ **Critical Viewing** What do you predict will be the mood of the play based on the actors' expressions? **[Predict]**

1. **Argive** (är´ gīv´) from Argos, the capital of a section of ancient Greece.

2. **curse on Oedipus** reference to the fate of Oedipus, who was doomed by a decree of the gods to kill his father and marry his mother while ignorant of their true identities.

Literary Analysis
Protagonist and Antagonist What conflict between Antigone and Creon does Antigone begin explaining here?

3. **carrion** (kar´ ē ən) **birds** scavenger birds, such as vultures.

Reading Check
What order will Creon give about Polyneices' body?

And now you can prove what you are:
A true sister, or a traitor to your family.

ISMENE. Antigone, you are mad! What could I possibly do?

30 **ANTIGONE.** You must decide whether you will help me or not.

ISMENE. I do not understand you. Help you in what?

ANTIGONE. Ismene, I am going to bury him. Will you come?

ISMENE. Bury him! You have just said the new law forbids it.

ANTIGONE. He is my brother. And he is your brother, too.

35 **ISMENE.** But think of the danger! Think what Creon will do!

ANTIGONE. Creon is not strong enough to stand in my way.

ISMENE. Ah sister!
Oedipus died, everyone hating him
For what his own search brought to light, his eyes
40 Ripped out by his own hand; and Iocaste died,
His mother and wife at once: she twisted the cords
That strangled her life; and our two brothers died,
Each killed by the other's sword. And we are left:
But oh, Antigone,
45 Think how much more terrible than these
Our own death would be if we should go against
     Creon
And do what he has forbidden! We are only women,
We cannot fight with men, Antigone!
The law is strong, we must give in to the law
50 In this thing, and in worse. I beg the Dead
To forgive me, but I am helpless: I must yield
To those in authority. And I think it is dangerous
     business
To be always meddling.

ANTIGONE.   If that is what you think,
55 I should not want you, even if you asked to come.
You have made your choice, you can be what you want to be.
But I will bury him; and if I must die,
I say that this crime is holy: I shall lie down
With him in death, and I shall be as dear
60 To him as he to me.
                    It is the dead,
Not the living, who make the longest demands;
We die for ever . . .
                    You may do as you like,

Reading Skill
Summarize Review
Ismene's speech and
then retell the tragic
history of Antigone's
family.

Literary Analysis
Protagonist and
Antagonist What
details in Antigone's
speech give the reader
reason to sympathize
with Antigone?

65 Since apparently the laws of the gods mean
nothing to you.

ISMENE. They mean a great deal to me; but I
have no strength
To break laws that were made for the
public good.

ANTIGONE. That must be your excuse, I
suppose. But as for me,
I will bury the brother I love.

70 ISMENE.   Antigone,
I am so afraid for you!

ANTIGONE.   You need not be:
You have yourself to consider, after
all.

ISMENE. But no one must hear of this,
you must tell no one!
75 I will keep it a secret, I promise!

ANTIGONE.   Oh tell it! Tell
everyone!
Think how they'll hate you when it
all comes out
If they learn that you knew about
it all the time!

ISMENE. So fiery! You should be
cold with fear.

80 ANTIGONE. Perhaps. But I am doing only what I must.

ISMENE. But can you do it? I say that you cannot.

ANTIGONE. Very well: when my strength gives out, I shall do no
more.

ISMENE. Impossible things should not be tried at all.

ANTIGONE. Go away, Ismene:
85 I shall be hating you soon, and the dead will too,
For your words are hateful. Leave me my foolish plan:
I am not afraid of the danger; if it means death,
It will not be the worst of deaths—death without honor.

ISMENE. Go then, if you feel that you must.
90 You are unwise,
But a loyal friend indeed to those who love you.
[*Exit into the Palace.* ANTIGONE *goes off, left. Enter the* CHORUS.]

▲ **Critical Viewing**
Which details of this image convey the intense emotions of Antigone and Ismene's conversation? **[Analyze]**

© **Spiral Review**
Conflict What conflict is introduced when Antigone says, "I will bury the brother I love" in line 69? Explain.

 Reading Check
What does Antigone ask Ismene to decide?

Antigone, Prologue **817**

Parodos

CHORUS. [STROPHE 1]

Now the long blade of the sun, lying
Level east to west, touches with glory
Thebes of the Seven Gates.[4] Open, unlidded
Eye of golden day! O marching light

5 Across the eddy and rush of Dirce's stream,[5]
Striking the white shields of the enemy
Thrown headlong backward from the blaze of morning!

CHORAGOS. Polyneices their commander
Roused them with windy phrases,

10 He the wild eagle screaming
Insults above our land,
His wings their shields of snow,
His crest their marshalled helms.

CHORUS. [ANTISTROPHE 1]

Against our seven gates in a yawning ring

15 The famished spears came onward in the night;
But before his jaws were sated with our blood,
Or pinefire took the garland of our towers,
He was thrown back; and as he turned, great Thebes—
No tender victim for his noisy power—

20 Rose like a dragon behind him, shouting war.

CHORAGOS. For God hates utterly
The bray of bragging tongues;
And when he beheld their smiling,
Their swagger of golden helms,

25 The frown of his thunder blasted
Their first man from our walls.

CHORUS. [STROPHE 2]

We heard his shout of triumph high in the air
Turn to a scream; far out in a flaming arc
He fell with his windy torch, and the earth struck him.

30 And others storming in fury no less than his
Found shock of death in the dusty joy of battle.

CHORAGOS. Seven captains at seven gates
Yielded their clanging arms to the god
That bends the battle-line and breaks it.

35 These two only, brothers in blood,
Face to face in matchless rage,
Mirroring each the other's death,
Clashed in long combat.

4. Seven Gates The city of Thebes was defended by walls containing seven entrances.

5. Dirce's (dur´ sēz) **stream** small river near Thebes into which the body of Dirce, one of the city's early queens, was thrown after her murder.

Vocabulary
sated (sāt´ əd) *adj.*
satisfied; provided with more than enough

Reading Skill
Summarize Reread the Parodos, and summarize Polyneices' attack on Thebes.

CHORUS.   [ANTISTROPHE 2]

But now in the beautiful morning of victory

40   Let Thebes of the many chariots sing for joy!

With hearts for dancing we'll take leave of war:

Our temples shall be sweet with hymns of praise,

And the long night shall echo with our chorus.

Scene 1

CHORAGOS. But now at last our new King is coming:

Creon of Thebes, Menoikeus'[6] son.

In this auspicious dawn of his reign

What are the new complexities

5   That shifting Fate has woven for him?

What is his counsel? Why has he summoned

The old men to hear him?

[*Enter* CREON *from the Palace, center. He addresses the* CHORUS *from the top step.*]

CREON. Gentlemen: I have the honor to inform you that our

Ship of State, which recent storms have threatened to

10   destroy, has come safely to harbor at last, guided by the

merciful wisdom of Heaven. I have summoned you here this

morning because I know that I can depend upon you: your

devotion to King Laïos was absolute; you never hesitated in

your duty to our late ruler Oedipus; and when Oedipus died,

15   your loyalty was transferred to his children. Unfortunately,

as you know, his two sons, the princes Eteocles and

Polyneices, have killed each other in battle; and I, as

the next in blood, have suceeded to the full power of

the throne.

20 I am aware, of course, that no Ruler can expect complete

loyalty from his subjects until he has been tested in

office. Nevertheless, I say to you at the very outset

6. Menoikeus' (me nɔi´ kē əs)

Reading Check

Why is Creon named king?

that I have nothing but contempt for the kind of
Governor who is afraid, for whatever reason, to follow
25 the course that he knows is best for the State; and as for
the man who sets private friendship above the public
welfare,—I have no use for him, either. I call God to
witness that if I saw my country headed for ruin, I
should not be afraid to speak out plainly; and I need
30 hardly remind you that I would never have any dealings
with an enemy of the people. No one values friendship more
highly than I; but we must remember that friends made at the
risk of wrecking our Ship are not real friends at all.
  These are my principles, at any rate, and that is why I
35 have made the following decision concerning the sons of
Oedipus: Eteocles, who died as a man should die,
fighting for his country, is to be buried with full military
honors, with all the ceremony that is usual when the greatest
heroes die; but his brother Polyneices, who broke his
40 exile to come back with fire and sword against his native
city and the shrines of his fathers' gods, whose one idea
was to spill the blood of his blood and sell his own people into
slavery—Polyneices, I say, is to have no burial: no man is to
touch him or say the least prayer for him; he shall lie
45 on the plain, unburied; and the birds and the scavenging
dogs can do with him whatever they like.
  This is my command, and you can see the wisdom behind
it. As long as I am King, no traitor is going to be honored
with the loyal man. But whoever shows by word and
50 deed that he is on the side of the State,—he shall have
my respect while he is living, and my reverence when he
is dead.

CHORAGOS. If that is your will, Creon son of Menoikeus,
  You have the right to enforce it: we are yours.

55 CREON. That is my will. Take care that you do your part.

CHORAGOS. We are old men: let the younger ones carry it out.

CREON. I do not mean that: the sentries have been appointed.

CHORAGOS. Then what is it that you would have us do?

CREON. You will give no support to whoever breaks this law.

60 CHORAGOS. Only a crazy man is in love with death!

CREON. And death it is; yet money talks, and the wisest
  Have sometimes been known to count a few coins too many.

Literary Analysis
Protagonist and
Antagonist How do
Creon's words in lines
42–49 show that he is
Antigone's antagonist?

Reading Skill
Summarize
Summarize the main
points in Creon's speech.

[*Enter* SENTRY *from left.*]

SENTRY. I'll not say that I'm out of breath from running, King,
   because every time I stopped to think about what I have to
65   tell you, I felt like going back. And all the time a voice kept
   saying, "You fool, don't you know you're walking straight into
   trouble?"; and then another voice: "Yes, but if you let somebody
   else get the news to Creon first, it will be even worse than
   that for you!" But good sense won out, at least I hope it was
70   good sense, and here I am with a story that makes no sense
   at all; but I'll tell it anyhow, because, as they say, what's going to happen's going to happen, and—

CREON. Come to the point. What have you to say?

SENTRY. I did not do it. I did not see who did it. You must not
75   punish me for what someone else has done.

CREON. A comprehensive defense! More effective, perhaps,
   If I knew its purpose. Come: what is it?

SENTRY. A dreadful thing . . . I don't know how to put it—

CREON. Out with it!

80 SENTRY.   Well, then;
   The dead man—
                 Polyneices—

[*Pause. The* SENTRY *is overcome, fumbles for words.* CREON *waits
impassively.*]

                              out there—
                                   someone,—
85   New dust on the slimy flesh!

[*Pause. No sign from* CREON.]

   Someone has given it burial that way, and
   Gone . . .

[*Long pause.* CREON *finally speaks with deadly control.*]

CREON. And the man who dared do this?

SENTRY.   I swear I
90   Do not know! You must believe me!
                              Listen:
   The ground was dry, not a sign of digging, no,
   Not a wheeltrack in the dust, no trace of anyone.
   It was when they relieved us this morning: and one of them,

▲ **Critical Viewing**
What elements of this
actor's appearance
reflect Creon's status
as king? **[Interpret]**

**Reading
Check**
What has happened to
Polyneices' body?

Antigone, Scene 1 **821**

95   The corporal, pointed to it.
                                    There it was,
      The strangest—
            Look:
      The body, just mounded over with light dust: you see?
100   Not buried really, but as if they'd covered it
      Just enough for the ghost's peace. And no sign
      Of dogs or any wild animal that had been there.

      And then what a scene there was! Every man of us
      Accusing the other: we all proved the other man did it,
105   We all had proof that we could not have done it.
      We were ready to take hot iron in our hands,
      Walk through fire, swear by all the gods,
      It was not I!
      I do not know who it was, but it was not I!

[CREON's *rage has been mounting steadily, but the* SENTRY *is too
intent upon his story to notice it.*]

110   And then, when this came to nothing, someone said
      A thing that silenced us and made us stare
      Down at the ground: you had to be told the news,
      And one of us had to do it! We threw the dice,
      And the bad luck fell to me. So here I am,
115   No happier to be here than you are to have me:
      Nobody likes the man who brings bad news.

      CHORAGOS. I have been wondering, King: can it be that the
          gods have done this?

      CREON. [*Furiously*] Stop!
          Must you doddering wrecks
120   Go out of your heads entirely? "The gods!"
      Intolerable!
      The gods favor this corpse? Why? How had he served them?
      Tried to loot their temples, burn their images,
      Yes, and the whole State, and its laws with it!
125   Is it your senile opinion that the gods love to honor bad men?
      A pious thought!—
                        No, from the very beginning
      There have been those who have whispered together,
      Stiff-necked anarchists, putting their heads together,
130   Scheming against me in alleys. These are the men,
      And they have bribed my own guard to do this thing.

      Money!   [*Sententiously*]

Reading Skill
Summarize
Summarize the sentry's
report through line 102.

Literary Analysis
Protagonist and
Antagonist What does
Creon's fear of people
scheming against him
show about his conflict
with Antigone?

Vocabulary

sententiously (sen ten´
shəs lē) *adv.* in a way
that shows excessive
fondness for wise say-
ings; in lecturing tones

There's nothing in the world so demoralizing as money.
Down go your cities,
135 Homes gone, men gone, honest hearts corrupted,
Crookedness of all kinds, and all for money!
[*To* SENTRY]   But you—!
I swear by God and by the throne of God,
The man who has done this thing shall pay for it!
140 Find that man, bring him here to me, or your death
Will be the least of your problems: I'll string you up
Alive, and there will be certain ways to make you
Discover your employer before you die;
And the process may teach you a lesson you seem
to have missed:
145 The dearest profit is sometimes all too dear:
That depends on the source. Do you understand
me?
A fortune won is often misfortune.

SENTRY. King, may I speak?

CREON.   Your very voice distresses me.

150 **SENTRY.** Are you sure that it is my voice, and not your
conscience?

CREON. By God, he wants to analyze me now!

SENTRY. It is not what I say, but what has been done,
that hurts you.

CREON. You talk too much.

SENTRY.   Maybe; but I've done nothing.

155 **CREON.** Sold your soul for some silver: that's all you've done.

SENTRY. How dreadful it is when the right judge judges wrong!

CREON. Your figures of speech
May entertain you now; but unless you bring me the man,
You will get little profit from them in the end.

[*Exit* CREON *into the Palace.*]

160 **SENTRY.** "Bring me the man"—!
I'd like nothing better than bringing him the man!
But bring him or not, you have seen the last of me here.
At any rate, I am safe!

[*Exit* SENTRY.]

▲ **Critical Viewing**
What does this ancient
Greek helmet indicate
about the type of weap-
ons against which the
sentry was prepared to
defend himself? **[Infer]**

**Reading
Check**
What does Creon order
the sentry to do?

Ode I

CHORUS. [STROPHE 1]

Numberless are the world's wonders, but none
More wonderful than man; the stormgray sea
Yields to his prows, the huge crests bear him high;
Earth, holy and inexhaustible, is graven
5 With shining furrows where his plows have gone
Year after year, the timeless labor of stallions.

[ANTISTROPHE 1]

The lightboned birds and beasts that cling to cover,
The lithe fish lighting their reaches of dim water,
All are taken, tamed in the net of his mind;
10 The lion on the hill, the wild horse windy-maned,
Resign to him; and his blunt yoke has broken
The sultry shoulders of the mountain bull.

[STROPHE 2]

Words also, and thought as rapid as air,
He fashions to his good use; statecraft is his,
15 And his the skill that deflects the arrows of snow,
The spears of winter rain: from every wind
He has made himself secure—from all but one:
In the late wind of death he cannot stand.

Vocabulary
deflects (dē flekts´)
v. turns or makes
go to one side

▼ **Critical Viewing**
Judging from this image,
what is Antigone's
reaction to her capture?
[Connect]

O clear intelligence, force beyond all measure!
20   O fate of man, working both good and evil!
When the laws are kept, how proudly his city stands!
When the laws are broken, what of his city then?
Never may the anarchic man find rest at my hearth,
Never be it said that my thoughts are his thoughts.

Scene 2

[*Re-enter* SENTRY *leading* ANTIGONE.]

CHORAGOS. What does this mean? Surely this captive woman
Is the Princess, Antigone. Why should she be taken?

SENTRY. Here is the one who did it! We caught her
In the very act of burying him.—Where is Creon?

5   **CHORAGOS.** Just coming from the house.

[*Enter* CREON, *center.*]

CREON.   What has happened?
Why have you come back so soon?

SENTRY. [*Expansively*]   O King,
A man should never be too sure of anything:
10   I would have sworn
That you'd not see me here again: your anger
Frightened me so, and the things you
   threatened me with;
But how could I tell then
That I'd be able to solve the case so soon?

15   No dice-throwing this time: I was only too
   glad to come!
Here is this woman. She is the guilty one:
We found her trying to bury him.
Take her, then; question her; judge her as you will.
I am through with the whole thing now, and glad of it.

20   **CREON.** But this is Antigone! Why have you brought her here?

SENTRY. She was burying him, I tell you!

CREON. [*Severely*]   Is this the truth?

SENTRY. I saw her with my own eyes. Can I say more?

CREON. The details: come, tell me quickly!

25 **SENTRY.**   It was like this:
After those terrible threats of yours, King,
We went back and brushed the dust away from the body.
The flesh was soft by now, and stinking,
So we sat on a hill to windward and kept guard.
30 No napping this time! We kept each other awake.
But nothing happened until the white round sun
Whirled in the center of the round sky over us:
Then, suddenly,
A storm of dust roared up from the earth, and the sky
35 Went out, the plain vanished with all its trees
In the stinging dark. We closed our eyes and endured it.
The whirlwind lasted a long time, but it passed;
And then we looked, and there was Antigone!
I have seen
40 A mother bird come back to a stripped nest, heard
Her crying bitterly a broken note or two
For the young ones stolen. Just so, when this girl
Found the bare corpse, and all her love's work wasted,
She wept, and cried on heaven to damn the hands
45 That had done this thing.
                                        And then she brought more dust
And sprinkled wine three times for her brother's ghost.

We ran and took her at once. She was not afraid,
Not even when we charged her with what she had done.
50 She denied nothing.
                              And this was a comfort to me,
And some uneasiness: for it is a good thing
To escape from death, but it is no great pleasure
To bring death to a friend.
                                    Yet I always say
55 There is nothing so comfortable as your own safe skin!

CREON. [*Slowly, dangerously*] And you, Antigone,
You with your head hanging,—do you confess this thing?

ANTIGONE. I do. I deny nothing.

60 **CREON.** [*To* SENTRY]   You may go.
                                                    [*Exit* SENTRY.]

[*To* ANTIGONE] Tell me, tell me briefly:
Had you heard my proclamation touching this matter?

**Literary Analysis
Protagonist and
Antagonist** Has
Creon realized that he
is Antigone's antago-
nist before this point?
Explain.

ANTIGONE. It was public. Could I help hearing it?

CREON. And yet you dared defy the law.

65 **ANTIGONE.**   I dared.
It was not God's proclamation. That final Justice
That rules the world below makes no such laws.

Your edict, King, was strong,
But all your strength is weakness itself against

70 The immortal unrecorded laws of God.
They are not merely now: they were, and shall be,
Operative forever, beyond man utterly.

I knew I must die, even without your decree:
I am only mortal. And if I must die

75 Now, before it is my time to die,
Surely this is no hardship: can anyone
Living, as I live, with evil all about me,
Think Death less than a friend? This death of mine
Is of no importance; but if I had left my brother

80 Lying in death unburied, I should have suffered.
Now I do not.
            You smile at me. Ah Creon,
Think me a fool, if you like; but it may well be
That a fool convicts me of folly.

85 **CHORAGOS.** Like father, like daughter: both headstrong, deaf to
            reason!
She has never learned to yield.

CREON.   She has much to learn.
The inflexible heart breaks first, the toughest iron
Cracks first, and the wildest horses bend their necks

90 At the pull of the smallest curb.
                                    Pride? In a slave?
This girl is guilty of a double insolence,
Breaking the given laws and boasting of it.
Who is the man here,

95 She or I, if this crime goes unpunished?
Sister's child, or more than sister's child,
Or closer yet in blood—she and her sister
Win bitter death for this!
[*To* SERVANTS]   Go, some of you,

100 Arrest Ismene. I accuse her equally.
Bring her: you will find her sniffling in the house there.

Vocabulary
edict (ē´ dikt´) *n.* public
order; decree

Literary Analysis
**Protagonist and
Antagonist** Which
details in this scene
solidify Antigone's role as
protagonist and Creon's
role as antagonist?

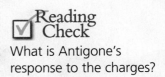
**Reading
Check**
What is Antigone's
response to the charges?

Her mind's a traitor: crimes kept in the dark
Cry for light, and the guardian brain shudders;
But how much worse than this
105   Is brazen boasting of barefaced anarchy!

Vocabulary
brazen (brā´ zən) *adj.*
shameless; bold

ANTIGONE. Creon, what more do you want than my death?

CREON.   Nothing.
That gives me everything.

ANTIGONE.   Then I beg you: kill me.
110   This talking is a great weariness: your words
Are distasteful to me, and I am sure that mine
Seem so to you. And yet they should not seem so:
I should have praise and honor for what I have done.
All these men here would praise me
115   Were their lips not frozen shut with fear of you.

                                                    [*Bitterly*]

Ah the good fortune of kings,
Licensed to say and do whatever they please!

CREON. You are alone here in that opinion.

ANTIGONE. No, they are with me. But they keep their tongues in
   leash.

▼ **Critical Viewing**
What feelings are
conveyed in this photo
of Antigone and
Creon? **[Interpret]**

CREON. Maybe. But you are guilty, and they are not.

ANTIGONE. There is no guilt in reverence for the dead.

CREON. But Eteocles—was he not your brother too?

ANTIGONE. My brother too.

CREON. And you insult his memory?

125 **ANTIGONE.** [*Softly*] The dead man would not say that I insult it.

CREON. He would: for you honor a traitor as much as him.

ANTIGONE. His own brother, traitor or not, and equal in blood.

CREON. He made war on his country. Eteocles defended it.

ANTIGONE. Nevertheless, there are honors due all the dead.

130 **CREON.** But not the same for the wicked as for the just.

ANTIGONE. Ah Creon, Creon,
Which of us can say what the gods hold wicked?

CREON. An enemy is an enemy, even dead.

ANTIGONE. It is my nature to join in love, not hate.

135 **CREON.** [*Finally losing patience*] Go join them, then; if you
must have your love,
Find it in hell!

CHORAGOS. But see, Ismene comes:

[*Enter* ISMENE, *guarded.*]

Those tears are sisterly, the cloud
That shadows her eyes rains down gentle sorrow.

140 **CREON.** You too, Ismene,
Snake in my ordered house, sucking my blood
Stealthily—and all the time I never knew
That these two sisters were aiming at my throne!

Ismene,

145 Do you confess your share in this crime, or deny it?
Answer me.

ISMENE. Yes, if she will let me say so. I am guilty.

ANTIGONE. [*Coldly*] No, Ismene. You have no right to say so.
You would not help me, and I will not have you help me.

150 **ISMENE.** But now I know what you meant; and I am here
To join you, to take my share of punishment.

Reading Skill
Summarize Summarize
the argument in lines
120–130.

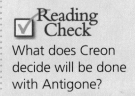
Reading
Check

What does Creon
decide will be done
with Antigone?

Literary Analysis
Protagonist and
Antagonist How does
the contrast between
the sisters emphasize
Antigone's role as the
protagonist?

ANTIGONE. The dead man and the gods who rule the dead
 Know whose act this was. Words are not friends.

ISMENE. Do you refuse me, Antigone? I want to die with you:
155 I too have a duty that I must discharge to the dead.

ANTIGONE. You shall not lessen my death by sharing it.

ISMENE. What do I care for life when you are dead?

ANTIGONE. Ask Creon. You're always hanging on his opinions.

ISMENE. You are laughing at me. Why, Antigone?

160 **ANTIGONE.** It's a joyless laughter, Ismene.

ISMENE.   But can I do nothing?

ANTIGONE. Yes. Save yourself. I shall not envy you.
 There are those who will praise you; I shall have honor, too.

ISMENE. But we are equally guilty!

165 **ANTIGONE.**   No more, Ismene.
 You are alive, but I belong to Death.

CREON. [*To the* CHORUS] Gentlemen, I beg you to observe these
 girls:

LITERATURE IN CONTEXT

Humanities Connection

Greek Chorus

In ancient Greek theater, the chorus was central to both the production and the meaning of the play. The chorus helped to tell the story, commented on the action, and divided scenes with odes, or songs. The chorus's commentary often expressed the audience's feelings. For Sophocles, a member of the chorus was an Everyman, an average Athenian citizen. A Greek chorus consisted of 12 or 15 men who sang and danced while wearing large masks.

▲ Objects like this vase reveal the importance of music and dance to Greek culture.

◀ In a modern-day production, this chorus reacts to events taking place onstage.

Connect to the Literature Identify a speech by the chorus in Scene 2 that probably mirrored the thoughts and feelings of the audience. Explain your choice.

One has just now lost her mind; the other,
It seems, has never had a mind at all.

170 **ISMENE.** Grief teaches the steadiest minds to waver, King.

CREON. Yours certainly did, when you assumed guilt with the guilty!

ISMENE. But how could I go on living without her?

CREON.   You are.
    She is already dead.

175 **ISMENE.**   But your own son's bride!

CREON. There are places enough for him to push his plow.
    I want no wicked women for my sons!

ISMENE. O dearest Haimon, how your father wrongs you!

CREON. I've had enough of your childish talk of marriage!

180 **CHORAGOS.** Do you really intend to steal this girl from your son?

CREON. No; Death will do that for me.

CHORAGOS.   Then she must die?

CREON. [*Ironically*] You dazzle me.
                        —But enough of this talk!
185 [*To* GUARDS] You, there, take them away and guard them well:
    For they are but women, and even brave men run
    When they see Death coming.

                [*Exit* ISMENE, ANTIGONE, *and* GUARDS.]

Ode II

CHORUS.   [STROPHE 1]
    Fortunate is the man who has never tasted God's vengeance!
    Where once the anger of heaven has struck, that house is
        shaken
    For ever: damnation rises behind each child
    Like a wave cresting out of the black northeast,
5   When the long darkness under sea roars up
    And bursts drumming death upon the windwhipped sand.
                                        [ANTISTROPHE 1]
    I have seen this gathering sorrow from time long past
    Loom upon Oedipus' children: generation from generation

Vocabulary
waver (wā´ vər) *v.* show
indecision; fluctuate

Literary Analysis
**Protagonist and
Antagonist** What fact
may force Haimon to
become involved in the
conflict between Creon
and Antigone?

Reading
Check
What does Ismene say
she wants to do?

Takes the compulsive rage of the enemy god.

10 So lately this last flower of Oedipus' line
Drank the sunlight! but now a passionate word
And a handful of dust have closed up all its beauty.

[STROPHE 2]

What mortal arrogance
Transcends the wrath of Zeus?[7]
15 Sleep cannot lull him, nor the effortless long months
Of the timeless gods: but he is young for ever,
And his house is the shining day of high Olympos.[8]
All that is and shall be,
And all the past, is his.
20 No pride on earth is free of the curse of heaven.

[ANTISTROPHE 2]

The straying dreams of men
May bring them ghosts of joy:
But as they drowse, the waking embers burn them;
Or they walk with fixed eyes, as blind men walk.
25 But the ancient wisdom speaks for our own time:
Fate works most for woe
With Folly's fairest show.
Man's little pleasure is the spring of sorrow.

7. **Zeus** (zōōs) King of all Greek gods, he was believed to throw lightning bolts when angry.

8. **Olympos** (ō lim′ pəs) mountain in Greece where the gods were believed to live in ease and splendor (also spelled "Olympus").

Reading Skill

Summarize Summarize the main ideas in the concluding ode.

Critical Thinking

Cite textual evidence to support your responses.

1. **Key Ideas and Details (a)** At the opening of the play, what does Antigone tell Ismene she plans to do? **(b) Analyze:** What reasons does Ismene give as she urges Antigone not to disobey Creon? **(c) Infer:** What does their argument reveal about the personality of each character? Support your answer with details.

2. **Key Ideas and Details (a)** Identify two of the accusations Creon makes against Polyneices in his speech about "the Ship of State." **(b) Analyze:** What is the key belief or principle that he states in this speech?

3. **Key Ideas and Details (a) Interpret:** What does Antigone mean when she says, "Your edict, King, was strong, / But all your strength is weakness itself against / The immortal unrecorded laws of God"? **(b) Compare and Contrast:** Compare Antigone's position with Creon's.

4. **Integration of Knowledge and Ideas** How does each individual's view of "right" and "wrong" determine how a reader views the conflict between Antigone and Creon? *[Connect to the Big Question: To what extent does experience determine what we perceive?]*

After You Read

Antigone, Prologue through Scene 2

Literary Analysis: Protagonist and Antagonist

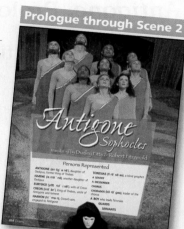

Prologue through Scene 2

© **1. Craft and Structure (a)** Using a chart like the one shown, identify words and actions that present Antigone, the **protagonist,** sympathetically. **(b)** Identify passages that show Creon, the **antagonist,** as hostile to her.

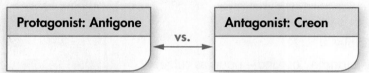

Protagonist: Antigone		Antagonist: Creon
	vs.	

© **2. Key Ideas and Details (a)** In Ode I, what powers does the Chorus say humanity possesses? **(b)** Against what force is humanity powerless? **(c)** Does the Chorus favor Creon or Antigone in this ode? Explain.

Reading Skill: Summarize

3. (a) Summarize the following conversations:
- between Antigone and Ismene at the end of Scene 2
- between Ismene and Creon at the end of Scene 2

(b) How does summarizing aid your understanding of the work?

Vocabulary

© **Acquisition and Use** In each item, find the two words that make the most logical pair, and identify the word that does not belong. Explain your choices.

1. sated, full, standing

2. sententiously, pompously, randomly

3. deflects, reverses, admires

4. edict, law, forecast

5. brazen, shy, cooked

6. waver, decide, smooth

Word Study Use the context of the sentences and what you know about the **Latin root -dict-** to explain your answer to each question.

1. If someone *dictates* a letter, is she typing silently on a computer?

2. Is it useful to have good *diction* if you are an actor?

Word Study

The **Latin root -dict-** means "speak" or "say."

Apply It Explain how the root -dict- contributes to the meanings of these words. Consult a dictionary if necessary.

indict
predict
valediction

PERFORMANCE TASKS
Integrated Language Skills

Antigone, Prologue through Scene 2

Conventions: Participles and Gerunds

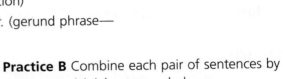
Prologue through Scene 2

A **participle** is a verb form used as an adjective to modify a noun or pronoun. A **gerund** is a verb form ending in *-ing* that acts as a noun.

Examples: a *creaking* floor (present participle)

a *fried* egg (past participle)

Dancing is my favorite pastime. (gerund—noun as subject)

I enjoy *singing*. (gerund—noun as direct object)

A **participial phrase** consists of a participle and its complements and modifiers. Participial phrases can add details to descriptions. A **gerund phrase** includes a gerund with its modifiers and complements.

Examples: a dress *designed by her aunt* (participial phrase)

Limping badly, the hiker continued down the slope. (participial phrase)

David was incapable of *reciting the poem.* (gerund phrase—noun as object of a preposition)

Quickly gathering details is important. (gerund phrase—noun as subject)

Practice A Underline and identify the participle, participial phrase, or gerund in each sentence.

1. Fighting was an important concern of the royal families of ancient Greece.

2. Ismene worries about the emotions expressed by Antigone.

3. Antigone used dried earth to cover the body of Polyneices.

4. A running messenger delivered the news to Creon.

© **Reading Application** Identify and label two participles and two gerunds in the Prologue, Scene 1, or Scene 2 of *Antigone*.

Practice B Combine each pair of sentences by using a participial or gerund phrase.

1. Antigone hatched a plan. The plan shocked her family.

2. The Chorus sings. The Chorus comments on the action of the play.

3. Antigone debates. She argues with her uncle.

4. Creon orchestrated a punishment. Creon's punishment was harsh.

© **Writing Application** Write a brief paragraph about events that happen in the first half of the play. Include at least one participial phrase and one gerund phrase in your paragraph.

PH WRITING COACH Further instruction and practice are available in *Prentice Hall Writing Coach.*

Writing

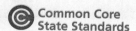

Explanatory Text In *Antigone*, Sophocles explores the universal theme of conflict between the individual and society. Write an **essay** exploring this theme. Use these tips to make sure your essay follows a logical organization:

- Identify the message Sophocles communicates about this conflict in Scenes 1 and 2 of the play. Find details to support your ideas.
- Explain what that message might mean to people today.
- Then, explain why that message is still important centuries after the play was written and performed. As you draft, provide relevant contemporary examples to help readers understand your thinking.

Grammar Application Use participles and gerunds correctly when writing your essay.

Common Core State Standards

L.9-10.1; W.9-10.2, W.9-10.2.a, W.9-10.2.b; SL.9-10.4
[For the wording of the standards, see page 810.]

Writing Workshop: *Work in Progress*

Prewriting for a Reflective Essay For a reflective essay you may write, work in a small group to brainstorm a list of ten small, everyday events. Then, for five of those events, note specific ways in which they affect people. Include these Event Notes in your writing portfolio.

Use this prewriting activity to prepare for the **Writing Workshop** on page 878.

Speaking and Listening

Presentation of Ideas The myths that drive the story of Antigone continue to influence culture today. Present an **oral report** on the influence of Greek mythology on contemporary literature and language. Include at least three examples of English words, such as *titanic* or *narcissist*, that are related to figures in Greek myths. Follow these steps:

- Use a dictionary, thesaurus, and digital tools to research the origins of words.
- Convey information and ideas from the sources accurately and coherently.
- Use notes, if necessary, and make eye contact with audience members as you speak.
- Watch for confusion in your audience and clarify points as needed.
- Ask classmates to share their examples of Greek influences.

PHLit Online!
www.PHLitOnline.com

- Interactive graphic organizers
- Grammar tutorial
- Interactive journals

Before You Read

Antigone, Scenes 3 through 5

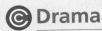 **Drama**

Build your skills and improve your comprehension of drama with this selection.

Review and Anticipate
In Scenes 1 and 2, Antigone defies the order of her uncle, King Creon of Thebes, and symbolically buries her brother Polyneices. When Creon discovers her guilt, he sentences Antigone to death, refusing to pardon her just because she is his niece. As Scene 2 ends, the chorus sings, *"Fate works most for woe / With Folly's fairest show."* The remaining scenes play out the truth of these words.

 Common Core State Standards

Meet these standards with *Antigone, Scenes 3 through 5* (p. 839).

Reading Literature
2. Determine a theme or central idea of a text and analyze in detail its development over the course of the text, including how it emerges and is shaped and refined by specific details. *(Literary Analysis: Greek Tragedies)*
Spiral Review: RL.9-10.3

Writing
1. Write arguments to support claims in an analysis of substantive topics or texts, using valid reasoning and relevant and sufficient evidence. *(Writing: Reflective Essay)*

Speaking and Listening
1.b. Work with peers to set rules for collegial discussions and decision-making, clear goals and deadlines, and individual roles as needed.

1.c. Propel conversations by posing and responding to questions that probe reasoning and evidence.

1.d. Respond thoughtfully to diverse perspectives; synthesize comments, claims, and evidence on all sides of an issue; resolve contradictions when possible; and determine what additional information is required.

3. Evaluate a speaker's point of view, reasoning, and use of evidence and rhetoric, identifying any fallacious reasoning or exaggerated or distorted evidence. *(Speaking and Listening: Mock Trial)*

Language
1.b. Use various types of phrases and clauses to convey specific meanings and add variety and interest to writing or presentations. *(Conventions: Independent and Subordinate Clauses)*

6. Acquire and use accurately general academic and domain-specific words and phrases. *(Vocabulary: Word Study)*

Literary Analysis: Greek Tragedies

Greek tragedies are serious dramas that share certain characteristics:

- They are based on myths that were familiar to the original audience.
- They tell of a reversal of fortune, from good to bad, experienced by a man or woman of noble birth.
- The main character may have a *tragic flaw,* a characteristic that leads to his or her downfall.
- Tragedy often presents audiences with a dilemma about understanding the hero's demise. The character's downfall results from his or her own actions. At the same time, this doom is clearly destined; it is brought about by *fate,* a force beyond the character's control.

The **theme,** or central message, of a Greek tragedy is often a warning against excess, such as pride or passion. Tragedies demonstrate the limitations of human knowledge, sympathy, and foresight. They remind us that every decision has consequences—often unforeseen.

Reading Skill: Summarize

To **summarize** a play, briefly state the most important actions and ideas in your own words. To gather details for a summary, **take notes.** Write down the most important elements of what you read; for example, note the characters, the places, the problems, and the key events.

Using the Strategy: Summary Chart

Use a **summary chart** like this one to take notes that will help you summarize *Antigone.*

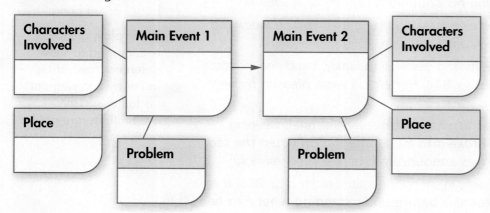

PHLit Online!
www.PHLitOnline.com

Hear It!
- Selection summary audio
- Selection audio

See It!
- Get Connected video
- Background video
- More about the author
- Vocabulary flashcards

Do It!
- Interactive journals
- Interactive graphic organizers
- Self-test
- Internet activity
- Grammar tutorial
- Interactive vocabulary games

Making Connections | Antigone, Scenes 3 through 5

To what extent does *experience* determine what we *perceive?*

Scenes 3 through 5

Writing About the Big Question

In the last three scenes of *Antigone*, Creon is unwilling and unable to accept anyone else's perception of events or anyone else's advice about what to do. Use these sentence starters to develop your ideas about the Big Question.

People try to **manipulate** the truth because _____.

Bias against others can distort a person's perception and lead to

_____.

While You Read Look for the reasons Creon gives to explain why he will not pardon Antigone. Decide whether you agree or disagree with him.

Vocabulary

Read each word and its definition. Decide whether you know the word well, know it a little bit, or do not know it at all. After you read, see how your knowledge of each word has increased.

- **deference** (def´ ər əns) *n.* a yielding to the ideas, wishes, and so on of another (p. 839) *Out of <u>deference</u> to him, she gave up her seat. defer v. deferential adj.*

- **contempt** (kən tempt´) *n.* scorn; the attitude of someone who looks down on something or someone else (p. 840) *He expressed his <u>contempt</u> by ignoring his opponent. contemptible adj.*

- **vile** (vīl) *adj.* evil; low; extremely disgusting (p. 843) *The week-old food tasted <u>vile</u>. vilely adv. vileness n.*

- **piety** (pī´ ə tē) *n.* loyalty and devotion to family, the divine, or some other object of respect (p. 844) *Her elders were pleased by her <u>piety</u>. pious adj. piously adv.*

- **lamentation** (lam´ ən tā´ shən) *n.* expression of grief; weeping (p. 847) *The crowd broke into loud <u>lamentation</u> when the sad news of the death was announced. lament v. lamentable adj.*

- **rash** (rash) *adj.* too hasty in speech or action; reckless (p. 858) *It was <u>rash</u> to yell at the toddler before understanding what had happened. rashly adv. rashness n.*

Word Study

The **Latin root -fer-** means "to carry," "to bear," or "to bring."

In this play, a son is encouraged to show **deference** toward his father by carrying out his father's wishes— even if these are not his own.

838 Drama

Scenes 3-5

Scene 3

CHORAGOS. But here is Haimon, King, the last of all your sons.
Is it grief for Antigone that brings him here,
And bitterness at being robbed of his bride?

[Enter HAIMON.*]*

CREON. We shall soon see, and no need of diviners.[1]
5 　　　　　　　　　　　　　　　　　—Son,
You have heard my final judgment on that girl:
Have you come here hating me, or have you come
With deference and with love, whatever I do?

HAIMON. I am your son, father. You are my guide.

1. **diviners** (də vīn´ ərz)
   n. those who claim to
   forecast the future.

Vocabulary
deference (def´ ər əns)
n. a yielding to the
ideas, wishes, and
so on of another

▼ **Critical Viewing**
What details of this
image suggest that
the chorus is pleading?
Explain. **[Analyze]**

Reading Skill
Summarize As you read Creon's speech in lines 12–51, take brief notes. Then, summarize the speech.

Vocabulary
contempt (kən tempt´) *n.* scorn; the attitude of someone who looks down on something or someone else

Literary Analysis
Greek Tragedies
What flaw in Creon's character do lines 28–29 reveal?

10 You make things clear for me, and I obey you.
No marriage means more to me than your continuing
   wisdom.

CREON. Good. That is the way to behave: subordinate
Everything else, my son, to your father's will.
This is what a man prays for, that he may get
15 Sons attentive and dutiful in his house,
Each one hating his father's enemies,
Honoring his father's friends. But if his sons
Fail him, if they turn out unprofitably,
What has he fathered but trouble for himself
20 And amusement for the malicious?
                              So you are right
Not to lose your head over this woman.
Your pleasure with her would soon grow cold, Haimon,
And then you'd have a hellcat in bed and elsewhere.
25 Let her find her husband in Hell!
Of all the people in this city, only she
Has had contempt for my law and broken it.

Do you want me to show myself weak before the people?
Or to break my sworn word? No, and I will not.
30 The woman dies.
I suppose she'll plead "family ties." Well, let her.
If I permit my own family to rebel,
How shall I earn the world's obedience?
Show me the man who keeps his house in hand,
35 He's fit for public authority.
                        I'll have no dealings
With law-breakers, critics of the government:
Whoever is chosen to govern should be obeyed—
Must be obeyed, in all things, great and small,
40 Just and unjust! O Haimon,
The man who knows how to obey, and that man only,
Knows how to give commands when the time comes.
You can depend on him, no matter how fast
The spears come: he's a good soldier, he'll stick it out.

45 Anarchy, anarchy! Show me a greater evil!
This is why cities tumble and the great houses rain down,
This is what scatters armies!

No, no: good lives are made so by discipline.
We keep the laws then, and the lawmakers,

50　And no woman shall seduce us. If we must lose,
　　Let's lose to a man, at least! Is a woman stronger than we?

CHORAGOS. Unless time has rusted my wits,
　　What you say, King, is said with point and dignity.

HAIMON. [*Boyishly earnest*] Father:
55　Reason is God's crowning gift to man, and you are right
　　To warn me against losing mine. I cannot say—
　　I hope that I shall never want to say!—that you
　　Have reasoned badly. Yet there are other men
　　Who can reason, too; and their opinions might be helpful.
60　You are not in a position to know everything
　　That people say or do, or what they feel:
　　Your temper terrifies them—everyone
　　Will tell you only what you like to hear.
　　But I, at any rate, can listen; and I have heard them
65　Muttering and whispering in the dark about this girl.
　　They say no woman has ever, so unreasonably,
　　Died so shameful a death for a generous act:
　　"She covered her brother's body. Is this indecent?
　　She kept him from dogs and vultures. Is this a crime?
70　Death?—She should have all the honor that we can give her!"

　　This is the way they talk out there in the city.

　　You must believe me:
　　Nothing is closer to me than your happiness.
　　What could be closer? Must not any son
75　Value his father's fortune as his father does his?
　　I beg you, do not be unchangeable:
　　Do not believe that you alone can be right.
　　The man who thinks that,
　　The man who maintains that only he has the power
80　To reason correctly, the gift to speak, the soul—
　　A man like that, when you know him, turns out empty.

　　It is not reason never to yield to reason!

　　In flood time you can see how some trees bend,
　　And because they bend, even their twigs are safe,
85　While stubborn trees are torn up, roots and all.
　　And the same thing happens in sailing:
　　Make your sheet fast, never slacken,—and over you go,
　　Head over heels and under: and there's your voyage.
　　Forget you are angry! Let yourself be moved!
90　I know I am young; but please let me say this:
　　The ideal condition

Literary Analysis
Greek Tragedies What basic limitation of human beings does Haimon describe?

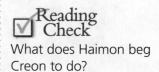
Reading Check
What does Haimon beg Creon to do?

Would be, I admit, that men should be right by instinct;
But since we are all too likely to go astray,
The reasonable thing is to learn from those who can teach.

95 **CHORAGOS.** You will do well to listen to him, King,
If what he says is sensible. And you, Haimon,
Must listen to your father.—Both speak well.

CREON. You consider it right for a man of my years and
     experience
To go to school to a boy?

100 **HAIMON.**   It is not right
If I am wrong. But if I am young, and right,
What does my age matter?

CREON. You think it right to stand up for an
     anarchist?

HAIMON. Not at all. I pay no respect to criminals.

105 **CREON.** Then she is not a criminal?

HAIMON. The City would deny it, to a man.

CREON. And the City proposes to teach me
     how to rule?

HAIMON. Ah. Who is it that's talking like a
     boy now?

▼ **Critical Viewing**
Which details of this image from a production of *Antigone* show that Creon and Haimon are father and son? **[Analyze]**

CREON. My voice is the one voice giving orders
in this City!

110 **HAIMON.** It is no City if it takes orders from one voice.

CREON. The State is the King!

HAIMON.   Yes, if the State is
a desert.

                                                           [*Pause*]

CREON. This boy, it seems, has sold out to
a woman.

HAIMON. If you are a woman: my concern is only
for you.

115 **CREON.** So? Your "concern"! In a public brawl
with your father!

HAIMON. How about you, in a public brawl with
justice?

CREON. With justice, when all that I do is
within my rights?

HAIMON. You have no right to trample on God's right.

CREON. [*Completely out of control*] Fool, adolescent fool! Taken in
by a woman!

120 **HAIMON.** You'll never see me taken in by anything vile.

CREON. Every word you say is for her!

HAIMON. [*Quietly, darkly*]   And for you.
And for me. And for the gods under the earth.

CREON. You'll never marry her while she lives.

125 **HAIMON.** Then she must die.—But her death will cause another.

CREON. Another?
Have you lost your senses? Is this an open threat?

HAIMON. There is no threat in speaking to emptiness.

CREON. I swear you'll regret this superior tone of yours!
130   You are the empty one!

HAIMON.   If you were not my father,
I'd say you were perverse.

CREON. You girlstruck fool, don't play at words with me!

Vocabulary
vile (vīl) *adj.* evil; low;
extremely disgusting

Literary Analysis
Greek Tragedies
How do Haimon's words
in line 125 warn of the
fateful consequences of
Creon's decision?

**Reading
Check**
How does Creon respond
to Haimon's arguments?

Ancient Greek Funeral Rites
In ancient Greek funeral ritual, the body was washed and laid out. Mourners sang ritual songs of grief. A funeral procession followed. The body was in many cases burned, and its ashes were buried in a grave or tomb. Without rites such as these, the Greeks believed, the soul would remain trapped between the underworld and the world of the living.

Connect to the Literature

How do Creon's decisions about Polyneices and Antigone blur the boundaries between the dead and the living?

Vocabulary
piety (pī´ ə tē) *n.*
loyalty and devotion to family, the divine, or some other object of respect

HAIMON. I am sorry. You prefer silence.

135 **CREON.** Now, by God—!
I swear, by all the gods in heaven above us,
You'll watch it, I swear you shall!
[*To the* SERVANTS] Bring her out!
Bring the woman out! Let her die before his eyes!
140 Here, this instant, with her bridegroom beside her!

HAIMON. Not here, no; she will not die here, King.
And you will never see my face again.
Go on raving as long as you've a friend to endure you.

[*Exit* HAIMON.]

CHORAGOS. Gone, gone.
145 Creon, a young man in a rage is dangerous!

CREON. Let him do, or dream to do, more than a man can.
He shall not save these girls from death.

CHORAGOS. These girls?
You have sentenced them both?

150 **CREON.** No, you are right.
I will not kill the one whose hands are clean.

CHORAGOS. But Antigone?

CREON. [*Somberly*] I will carry her far away
Out there in the wilderness, and lock her
155 Living in a vault of stone. She shall have food,
As the custom is, to absolve the State of her death.
And there let her pray to the gods of hell:
They are her only gods:
Perhaps they will show her an escape from death,
160 Or she may learn,
though late,
That **piety** shown the dead is pity in vain.

[*Exit* CREON.]

Ode III

CHORUS. Love, unconquerable [STROPHE 1]
Waster of rich men, keeper
Of warm lights and all-night vigil
In the soft face of a girl:
5 Sea-wanderer, forest-visitor!
Even the pure Immortals cannot escape you,
And mortal man, in his one day's dusk,
Trembles before your glory.

Surely you swerve upon ruin   [ANTISTROPHE]
10 The just man's consenting heart,
As here you have made bright anger
Strike between father and son—
And none has conquered but Love!
A girl's glance working the will of heaven:
15 Pleasure to her alone who mocks us,
Merciless Aphrodite.[2]

Scene 4

CHORAGOS. [*As* ANTIGONE *enters guarded*] But I can no longer
  stand in awe of this,
Nor, seeing what I see, keep back my tears.
Here is Antigone, passing to that chamber
Where all find sleep at last.

5 **ANTIGONE.** Look upon me, friends, and pity me   [STROPHE 1]
Turning back at the night's edge to say
Good-by to the sun that shines for me no longer;
Now sleepy Death
Summons me down to Acheron,[3] that cold shore:
10 There is no bridesong there, nor any music.

CHORUS. Yet not unpraised, not without a kind of honor,
You walk at last into the underworld;
Untouched by sickness, broken by no sword.
What woman has ever found your way to death?

ANTIGONE   [ANTISTROPHE 1]
15 How often I have heard the story of Niobe,[4]
Tantalos'[5] wretched daughter, how the stone
Clung fast about her, ivy-close: and they say
The rain falls endlessly
And sifting soft snow; her tears are never done.
20 I feel the loneliness of her death in mine.

CHORUS. But she was born of heaven, and you
Are woman, woman-born. If her death is yours,
A mortal woman's, is this not for you
Glory in our world and in the world beyond?

ANTIGONE.   [STROPHE 2]
25 You laugh at me. Ah, friends, friends,
Can you not wait until I am dead? O Thebes,
O men many-charioted, in love with Fortune,

2. **Aphrodite** (af´ rə dīt´ ē) goddess of beauty and love who is sometimes vengeful in her retaliation for offenses.

3. **Acheron** (ak´ ər än´) In Greek mythology, river in the underworld over which the dead are ferried.

4. **Niobe** (nī´ ō bē´) a queen of Thebes who was turned to stone while weeping for her slain children. Her seven sons and seven daughters were killed by Artemis and Apollo, the divine twins of Leto, after Leto complained that Niobe insulted her by bragging of maternal superiority. It was Zeus who turned the bereaved Niobe to stone, but her lament continued and her tears created a stream.

5. **Tantalos'** (tan´ tə ləs) Niobe's father, who was condemned to eternal frustration in the underworld because he revealed the secrets of the gods.

Reading Skill
Summarize
Summarize the conversation between Antigone and the chorus in lines 1–20.

✓ **Reading Check**
What punishment for Antigone does Creon announce?

Dear springs of Dirce, sacred Theban grove,
Be witnesses for me, denied all pity,
30 Unjustly judged! and think a word of love
For her whose path turns
Under dark earth, where there are no more tears.

CHORUS. You have passed beyond human daring and come
     at last
Into a place of stone where Justice sits.
35 I cannot tell
What shape of your father's guilt appears in this.

ANTIGONE.   [ANTISTROPHE 2]
You have touched it at last: that bridal bed
Unspeakable, horror of son and mother mingling:
Their crime, infection of all our family!
40 O Oedipus, father and brother!
Your marriage strikes from the grave to murder mine.
I have been a stranger here in my own land:
All my life
The blasphemy of my birth has followed me.

45 **CHORUS.** Reverence is a virtue, but strength
     Lives in established law: that must prevail.
     You have made your choice,
     Your death is the doing of your conscious hand.

ANTIGONE.   [EPODE]
Then let me go, since all your words are bitter,
50 And the very light of the sun is cold to me.

Literary Analysis
Greek Tragedies In lines 45–48, which does the chorus say is responsible for Antigone's doom—fate or her own choices?

▼ **Critical Viewing**
What does the actress's pose in this image suggest about Antigone's attitude toward her fate? Explain. **[Interpret]**

Lead me to my vigil, where I must have
Neither love nor lamentation: no song, but silence.

[CREON *interrupts impatiently.*]

CREON. If dirges and planned lamentations could put off death,
    Men would be singing forever.
55 [*To the* SERVANTS]   Take her, go!
    You know your orders: take her to the vault
    And leave her alone there. And if she lives or dies,
    That's her affair, not ours: our hands are clean.

ANTIGONE. O tomb, vaulted bride-bed in eternal rock,
60 Soon I shall be with my own again
    Where Persephone[6] welcomes the thin ghosts underground:
    And I shall see my father again, and you, mother,
    And dearest Polyneices—

                            dearest indeed
65 To me, since it was my hand
    That washed him clean and poured the ritual wine:
    And my reward is death before my time!

    And yet, as men's hearts know, I have done no wrong,
    I have not sinned before God. Or if I have,
70 I shall know the truth in death. But if the guilt
    Lies upon Creon who judged me, then, I pray,
    May his punishment equal my own.

CHORAGOS.   O passionate heart,
    Unyielding, tormented still by the same winds!

75 **CREON.** Her guards shall have good cause to regret their
        delaying.

ANTIGONE. Ah! That voice is like the voice of death!

CREON. I can give you no reason to think you are mistaken.

ANTIGONE. Thebes, and you my fathers' gods,
    And rulers of Thebes, you see me now, the last
80 Unhappy daughter of a line of kings,
    Your kings, led away to death. You will remember
    What things I suffer, and at what men's hands,
    Because I would not transgress the laws of heaven.

                        [*To the* GUARDS, *simply*]

    Come: let us wait no longer

                        [*Exit* ANTIGONE, *left, guarded.*]

Ode IV

CHORUS. [STROPHE 1]

All Danae's beauty[7] was locked away
In a brazen cell where the sunlight could not come:
A small room, still as any grave, enclosed her.
Yet she was a princess too,
5   And Zeus in a rain of gold poured love upon her.
O child, child,
No power in wealth or war
Or tough sea-blackened ships
Can prevail against untiring Destiny!

[ANTISTROPHE 1]

10   And Dryas' son[8] also, that furious king,
Bore the god's prisoning anger for his pride:
Sealed up by Dionysos[9] in deaf stone,
His madness died among echoes.
So at the last he learned what dreadful power
15   His tongue had mocked:
For he had profaned the revels,
And fired the wrath of the nine
Implacable Sisters[10] that love the sound of the flute.

[STROPHE 2]

And old men tell a half-remembered tale
20   Of horror done where a dark ledge splits the sea
And a double surf beats on the gray shores:
How a king's new woman, sick
With hatred for the queen he had imprisoned,
Ripped out his two sons' eyes with her bloody hands
25   While grinning Ares[11] watched the shuttle plunge
Four times: four blind wounds crying for revenge,

[ANTISTROPHE 2]

Crying, tears and blood mingled.—Piteously born,
Those sons whose mother was of heavenly birth!
Her father was the god of the North Wind
30   And she was cradled by gales,
She raced with young colts on the glittering hills
And walked untrammeled in the open light:
But in her marriage deathless Fate found means
To build a tomb like yours for all her joy.

---

7. Danae's (dan´ ā ēz´) **beauty** Danae was imprisoned when it was foretold that she would mother a son who would kill her father, King Acrisios. Her beauty attracted Zeus, who visited her in the form of a shower of gold. Perseus was born of the union, and Danae was exiled with the child. Years later, as prophesied, the boy did kill Acrisios, whom he failed to recognize as his grandfather.

8. Dryas' (drī´ əs) **son** Lycorgos (lī kɯr´ gəs), whose opposition to the worship of Dionysos was severely punished by the gods. He drove the followers of Dionysos from Thrace and was driven insane. Lycorgos recovered from his madness while imprisoned in a cave, but he was later blinded by Zeus as additional punishment.

9. Dionysos (dī´ ə nī´ səs) god of wine, in whose honor the Greek plays were performed.

10. nine / Implacable Sisters nine Muses, or goddesses, of science and literature. Implacable (im plak´ ə bəl) means "unforgiving."

11. Ares (er´ ēz´) god of war.

Scene 5

[*Enter blind* TEIRESIAS, *led by a boy. The opening speeches of* TEIRESIAS *should be in singsong contrast to the realistic lines of* CREON.]

TEIRESIAS. This is the way the blind man comes, Princes, Princes,
Lock-step, two heads lit by the eyes of one.

CREON. What new thing have you to tell us, old Teiresias?

TEIRESIAS. I have much to tell you: listen to the prophet, Creon.

5 **CREON.** I am not aware that I have ever failed to listen.

TEIRESIAS. Then you have done wisely, King, and ruled well.

CREON. I admit my debt to you.[12] But what have you to say?

TEIRESIAS. This, Creon: you stand once more on the edge of fate.

CREON. What do you mean? Your words are a kind of dread.

10 **TEIRESIAS.** Listen, Creon:
I was sitting in my chair of augury,[13] at the place
Where the birds gather about me. They were all a-chatter,
As is their habit, when suddenly I heard
A strange note in their jangling, a scream, a
15 Whirring fury; I knew that they were fighting,
Tearing each other, dying
In a whirlwind of wings clashing. And I was afraid.
I began the rites of burnt-offering at the altar,
But Hephaistos[14] failed me: instead of bright flame,

12. **my debt to you** Creon is admitting that he would not have acquired the throne if Teiresias had not moved the former king, Oedipus, to undertake an investigation that led eventually to his own downfall.

13. **chair of augury** the seat near the temple from which Teiresias would deliver his predictions about the future. Augury is the practice of reading the future from omens, such as the flight of birds.

14. **Hephaistos** (hē fes′ təs) god of fire and the forge, who would be invoked, as he was by Teiresias, for aid in the starting of ceremonial fires.

▼ **Critical Viewing**
Judging from this image of Teiresias, how does he feel about Creon? Explain. **[Infer]**

20 There was only the sputtering slime of the fat thigh-flesh
Melting: the entrails dissolved in gray smoke,
The bare bone burst from the welter. And no blaze!

This was a sign from heaven. My boy described it,
Seeing for me as I see for others.

25 I tell you, Creon, you yourself have brought
This new calamity upon us. Our hearths and altars
Are stained with the corruption of dogs and carrion birds
That glut themselves on the corpse of Oedipus' son.
The gods are deaf when we pray to them, their fire
30 Recoils from our offering, their birds of omen
Have no cry of comfort, for they are gorged
With the thick blood of the dead.
                                              O my son,
These are no trifles! Think: all men make mistakes,
35 But a good man yields when he knows his course is wrong,
And repairs the evil. The only crime is pride.

Give in to the dead man, then: do not fight with a corpse—
What glory is it to kill a man who is dead?
Think, I beg you:
40 It is for your own good that I speak as I do.
You should be able to yield for your own good.

CREON. It seems that prophets have made me their
            especial province.
All my life long
I have been a kind of butt for the dull arrows
45 Of doddering fortunetellers!
                                          No, Teiresias:
If your birds—if the great eagles of God
   himself
Should carry him stinking bit by bit to
   heaven,
I would not yield. I am not afraid of
   pollution:
50 No man can defile the gods.
                                          Do what you will,
Go into business, make money,
   speculate
In India gold or that synthetic gold from
   Sardis,[15]
Get rich otherwise than by my consent to
   bury him.

15. Sardis (sär´ dis) capital of ancient Lydia, which produced the first coins made from an alloy of gold and silver.

55   Teiresias, it is a sorry thing when a wise man
     Sells his wisdom, lets out his words for hire!

TEIRESIAS. Ah Creon! Is there no man left in the world—

CREON. To do what?—Come, let's have the aphorism!¹⁶

TEIRESIAS. No man who knows that wisdom outweighs any wealth?

60 **CREON.** As surely as bribes are baser than any baseness.

TEIRESIAS. You are sick, Creon! You are deathly sick!

CREON. As you say: it is not my place to challenge a prophet.

TEIRESIAS. Yet you have said my prophecy is for sale.

CREON. The generation of prophets has always loved gold.

65 **TEIRESIAS.** The generation of kings has always loved brass.

CREON. You forget yourself! You are speaking to your King.

TEIRESIAS. I know it. You are a king because of me.

CREON. You have a certain skill; but you have sold out.

TEIRESIAS. King, you will drive me to words that—

70 **CREON.**   Say them, say them!
     Only remember: I will not pay you for them.

TEIRESIAS. No, you will find them too costly.

CREON.   No doubt. Speak:
     Whatever you say, you will not change my will.

75 **TEIRESIAS.** Then take this, and take it to heart!
     The time is not far off when you shall pay back
     Corpse for corpse, flesh of your own flesh.
     You have thrust the child of this world into living night,
     You have kept from the gods below the child that is theirs:
80   The one in a grave before her death, the other,
     Dead, denied the grave. This is your crime:
     And the Furies¹⁷ and the dark gods of Hell
     Are swift with terrible punishment for you.

     Do you want to buy me now, Creon?

Literary Analysis
Greek Tragedies What ideas in Creon's speech to Teiresias reflect the king's tragic flaw?

16. **aphorism** (af´ ə riz´ əm) *n.* brief saying. Creon is taunting the prophet and suggesting that the old man relies on profound-sounding expressions to make an impression.

17. **Furies** (fyo͝or´ ēz) goddesses of vengeance who punished those who committed crimes against their own families.

Reading Check
What does Teiresias come to tell Creon?

▲ **Critical Viewing** In what way do both the play and this vessel show the importance of conflict in Greek art? **[Synthesize]**

85 Not many days,
And your house will be full of men and women weeping,
And curses will be hurled at you from far
Cities grieving for sons unburied, left to rot
Before the walls of Thebes.

90 These are my arrows, Creon: they are all for you.

[*To* BOY] But come, child: lead me home.
Let him waste his fine anger upon younger men.
Maybe he will learn at last
To control a wiser tongue in a better head.

[*Exit* TEIRESIAS.]

95 **CHORAGOS.** The old man has gone, King, but his words
Remain to plague us. I am old, too,
But I cannot remember that he was ever false.

CREON. That is true. . . . It troubles me.
Oh it is hard to give in! but it is worse
100 To risk everything for stubborn pride.

CHORAGOS. Creon: take my advice.

CREON. What shall I do?

CHORAGOS. Go quickly: free Antigone from her vault
And build a tomb for the body of Polyneices.

105 **CREON.** You would have me do this?

CHORAGOS. Creon, yes!
And it must be done at once: God moves
Swiftly to cancel the folly of stubborn men.

CREON. It is hard to deny the heart! But I
110 Will do it: I will not fight with destiny.

CHORAGOS. You must go yourself, you cannot leave it to others.

CREON. I will go.
—Bring axes, servants:
Come with me to the tomb. I buried her, I
115 Will set her free.
Oh quickly!
My mind misgives—
The laws of the gods are mighty, and a man must serve them
To the last day of his life!

[*Exit* CREON.]

Pæan

CHORAGOS.
God of many names [STROPHE 1]

CHORUS.   O Iacchos[18]
                        son
of Kadmeian Semele[19]
                        O born of the Thunder!
Guardian of the West
                Regent
of Eleusis' plain[20]
                O Prince of maenad Thebes[21]
10 and the Dragon Field by rippling Ismenos:[22]

CHORAGOS. [ANTISTROPHE 1]
God of many names

CHORUS.
                the flame of torches
flares on our hills
                the nymphs of Iacchos
15 dance at the spring of Castalia:[23]

from the vine-close mountain
                        come ah come in ivy:
Evohe evohe![24] sings through the streets of Thebes

CHORAGOS. [STROPHE 2]
God of many names

20 **CHORUS.**   Iacchos of Thebes
heavenly Child
                of Semele bride of the Thunderer!
The shadow of plague is upon us:
                        come
25 with clement[25] feet
                oh come from Parnasos[26]
down the long slopes
                across the lamenting water

CHORAGOS. [ANTISTROPHE 2]
Io[27] Fire! Chorister of the throbbing stars!
30 O purest among the voices of the night!
Thou son of God, blaze for us!

CHORUS. Come with choric rapture of circling Maenads
        Who cry *Io Iacche!*[28]
                God of many names!

---

18. **Iacchos** (ē′ ə kəs) one of several alternate names for Dionysos.

19. **Kadmeian Semele** (sem′ ə lē′) Semele was a mortal and the mother of Dionysos. She was the daughter of Thebes' founder, Kadmos.

20. **Eleusis'** (e lōō′ sis) **plain** Located north of Athens, this plain was a site of worship for Dionysos and Demeter.

21. **maenad** (mē′ nad′) **Thebes** The city is here compared to a maenad, one of Dionysos' female worshipers. Such a follower would be thought of as uncontrolled or disturbed.

22. **Dragon Field . . . Ismenos** (is mē′ nas) The Dragon Field was located by the banks of Ismenos, a river near Thebes. Kadmos created warriors by sowing in the Dragon Field the teeth of the dragon he killed there.

23. **Castalia** (kas tā′ lē ə) location of a site sacred to Apollo.

24. **Evohe** (ē vō′ ē) triumphant shout of affirmation.

25. **clement** kind; favorable

26. **Parnasos** (pär nas′ əs) mountain that was sacred to both Dionysos and Apollo, located in central Greece.

27. **Io** (ē′ ō′) Greek word for "behold" or "hail."

28. **Io Iacche** (ē′ ō′ ē′ ə ke) cry of celebration used by Dionysian worshipers.

Reading Check

In the Pæan, from whom does the chorus ask help?

Exodus

[*Enter* MESSENGER, *left.*]

29. **Kadmos** (kad´ məs) founder of the city of Thebes, whose daughter, Semele, gave birth to Dionysos.

30. **Amphion's** (am fī´ ənz) **citadel** Amphion was a king of Thebes credited with erecting the walls of the fortress, or citadel, by using a magic lyre.

31. **Pallas'** (pal´ əs) Pallas Athena, the goddess of wisdom.

MESSENGER. Men of the line of Kadmos,[29] you who live
Near Amphion's citadel:[30]
                     I cannot say
Of any condition of human life "This is fixed,
This is clearly good, or bad." Fate raises up,

5 And Fate casts down the happy and unhappy alike:
No man can foretell his Fate.
                         Take the case of Creon:
Creon was happy once, as I count happiness:

10 Victorious in battle, sole governor of the land,
Fortunate father of children nobly born.
And now it has all gone from him! Who can say
That a man is still alive when his life's joy fails?
He is a walking dead man. Grant him rich,

15 Let him live like a king in his great house:
If his pleasure is gone, I would not give
So much as the shadow of smoke for all he owns.

CHORAGOS. Your words hint at sorrow: what is your news for us?

MESSENGER. They are dead. The living are guilty of their death.

20 **CHORAGOS.** Who is guilty? Who is dead? Speak!

MESSENGER.   Haimon.
Haimon is dead; and the hand that killed him
Is his own hand.

CHORAGOS.   His father's? or his own?

25 **MESSENGER.** His own, driven mad by the murder his father had
done.

CHORAGOS. Teiresias, Teiresias, how clearly you saw it all!

MESSENGER. This is my news: you must draw what conclusions
you can from it.

CHORAGOS. But look: Eurydice, our Queen:
Has she overheard us?

[*Enter* EURYDICE *from the Palace, center.*]

30 **EURYDICE.** I have heard something, friends:
As I was unlocking the gate of Pallas'[31] shrine,
For I needed her help today, I heard a voice
Telling of some new sorrow. And I fainted

▼ **Critical Viewing**
Do you think the actress portraying Eurydice effectively conveys tragic grief? Explain. **[Evaluate]**

There at the temple with all my maidens about me.
35 But speak again: whatever it is, I can bear it:
    Grief and I are no strangers.

MESSENGER.   Dearest Lady,
    I will tell you plainly all that I have seen.
    I shall not try to comfort you: what is the use,
40 Since comfort could lie only in what is not true?
    The truth is always best.

                            I went with Creon
    To the outer plain where Polyneices was lying,
    No friend to pity him, his body shredded by dogs.
45 We made our prayers in that place to Hecate[32]
    And Pluto,[33] that they would be merciful. And we bathed
    The corpse with holy water, and we brought
    Fresh-broken branches to burn what was left of it,
    And upon the urn we heaped up a towering barrow
50 Of the earth of his own land.

                            When we were done, we ran
    To the vault where Antigone lay on her couch of stone.
    One of the servants had gone ahead,
    And while he was yet far off he heard a voice
55 Grieving within the chamber, and he came back
    And told Creon. And as the King went closer,
    The air was full of wailing, the words lost,
    And he begged us to make all haste. "Am I a prophet?"
    He said, weeping, "And must I walk this road,
60 The saddest of all that I have gone before?
    My son's voice calls me on. Oh quickly, quickly!
    Look through the crevice there, and tell me
    If it is Haimon, or some deception of the gods!"

    We obeyed; and in the cavern's farthest corner
65 We saw her lying:
    She had made a noose of her fine linen veil
    And hanged herself. Haimon lay beside her,
    His arms about her waist, lamenting her,
    His love lost underground, crying out
70 That his father had stolen her away from him.

    When Creon saw him the tears rushed to his eyes
    And he called to him: "What have you done, child? Speak
        to me.
    What are you thinking that makes your eyes so strange?
    O my son, my son, I come to you on my knees!"

Reading Skill

Summarize Identify three details in lines 37–50 that you would not include in summarizing the speech.

32. **Hecate** (hek´ ə tē) A goddess of the underworld, the resting place of dead souls in Greek mythology.
33. **Pluto** (plōō t´ ō) Chief god of the underworld, who ruled the souls of the dead in Greek mythology.

Reading Check

What has happened to Antigone and Haimon?

75 But Haimon spat in his face. He said not a word,
    Staring—
                    And suddenly drew his sword
    And lunged. Creon shrank back, the blade missed; and the
        boy,
    Desperate against himself, drove it half its length
80 Into his own side, and fell. And as he died
    He gathered Antigone close in his arms again,
    Choking, his blood bright red on her white cheek.
    And now he lies dead with the dead, and she is his
    At last, his bride in the houses of the dead.

                    [*Exit* EURYDICE *into the Palace.*]

85 **CHORAGOS.** She has left us without a word. What can this mean?

    MESSENGER. It troubles me, too; yet she knows what is best,
        Her grief is too great for public lamentation,
        And doubtless she has gone to her chamber to weep
        For her dead son, leading her maidens in his dirge.

90 **CHORAGOS.** It may be so: but I fear this deep silence.

                                        [*Pause*]

    MESSENGER. I will see what she is doing. I will go in.

                    [*Exit* MESSENGER *into the Palace.*]

    [*Enter* CREON *with attendants, bearing* HAIMON'S *body.*]

    CHORAGOS. But here is the King himself: oh look at him,
        Bearing his own damnation in his arms.

    CREON. Nothing you say can touch me any more.
95   My own blind heart has brought me
        From darkness to final darkness. Here you see
        The father murdering, the murdered son—
        And all my civic wisdom!

        Haimon my son, so young, so young to die,
100   I was the fool, not you; and you died for me.

    CHORAGOS. That is the truth; but you were late in learning it.

    CREON. This truth is hard to bear. Surely a god
        Has crushed me beneath the hugest weight of heaven,
        And driven me headlong a barbaric way
105   To trample out the thing I held most dear.

    The pains that men will take to come to pain!

Literary Analysis
Greek Tragedies
In what sense might Creon's loss of his son be fitting punishment for his misjudgment?

Ⓒ
Spiral Review
Character How do Creon's words in line 100 show that he has changed?

[*Enter* MESSENGER *from the Palace.*]

MESSENGER. The burden you carry in your hands is heavy,
But it is not all: you will find more in your house.

CREON. What burden worse than this shall I find there?

110 **MESSENGER.** The Queen is dead.

CREON. O port of death, deaf world,
Is there no pity for me? And you, Angel of evil,
I was dead, and your words are death again.
Is it true, boy? Can it be true?

115 Is my wife dead? Has death bred death?

MESSENGER. You can see for yourself.

[*The doors are opened, and the body of* EURYDICE *is disclosed within.*]

CREON. Oh pity!
All true, all true, and more than I can bear!
O my wife, my son!

120 **MESSENGER.** She stood before the altar, and her heart
Welcomed the knife her own hand guided,
And a great cry burst from her lips for Megareus[34] dead,
And for Haimon dead, her sons; and her last breath
Was a curse for their father, the murderer of her sons.

125 And she fell, and the dark flowed in through her closing eyes.

CREON. O God, I am sick with fear.
Are there no swords here? Has no one a blow for me?

MESSENGER. Her curse is upon you for the deaths of both.

CREON. It is right that it should be. I alone am guilty.

130 I know it, and I say it. Lead me in,
Quickly, friends.
I have neither life nor substance. Lead me in.

CHORAGOS. You are right, if there can be right in
so much wrong.
The briefest way is best in a world of sorrow.

34. Megareus (mə ga′ rē əs)
oldest son of Creon and
Eurydice, who was killed
in the civil war by Argive
forces invading Thebes.

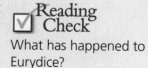

Reading
Check
What has happened to
Eurydice?

135 **CREON.** Let it come,
Let death come quickly, and be kind to me.
I would not ever see the sun again.

CHORAGOS. All that will come when it will; but we, meanwhile,
Have much to do. Leave the future to itself.

140 **CREON.** All my heart was in that prayer!

CHORAGOS. Then do not pray any more: the sky is deaf.

CREON. Lead me away. I have been rash and foolish.
I have killed my son and my wife.
I look for comfort; my comfort lies here dead.
145 Whatever my hands have touched has come to nothing.
Fate has brought all my pride to a thought of dust.

[*As* CREON *is being led into the house, the* CHORAGOS *advances and speaks directly to the audience.*]

CHORAGOS. There is no happiness where there is no wisdom;
No wisdom but in submission to the gods.
Big words are always punished,
150 And proud men in old age learn to be wise.

Vocabulary
rash (rash) *adj.* too hasty in speech or action; reckless

Critical Thinking

Cite textual evidence to support your responses.

© 1. **Key Ideas and Details** **(a)** In Scene 3, lines 55–94, what advice does Haimon give his father? **(b) Analyze:** Describe Creon's response to the advice. **(c) Contrast:** Contrast Haimon's main concerns with Creon's.

© 2. **Key Ideas and Details** **(a)** What does Creon rule must be done to Antigone? **(b) Make a Judgment:** Is upholding the law Creon's only motive, or is he also guided by a desire to appear strong? Support your answer with details from the play.

© 3. **Key Ideas and Details** **(a)** What prophecy does Teiresias make about Creon? **(b) Analyze Cause and Effect:** What action does Creon take because of the prophecy? **(c) Connect:** In what way is Teiresias' prophecy fulfilled?

© 4. **Integration of Knowledge and Ideas** How do Antigone's sense of herself as Oedipus' daughter and Creon's sense of himself as king determine the paths they each take in the play? *[Connect to the Big Question: To what extent does experience determine what we perceive?]*

After You Read | Antigone, Scenes 3 through 5

Literary Analysis: Greek Tragedies

Scenes 3 through 5

© **1. Key Ideas and Details** Identify three characteristics of a **Greek tragedy** that *Antigone* displays. Support your answer.

© **2. Key Ideas and Details (a)** What is Antigone's **tragic flaw?** Explain. **(b)** To what extent does this flaw lead to her downfall? To what extent is her downfall due to **fate?** Explain.

© **3. Key Ideas and Details (a)** What is Creon's tragic flaw? Explain. **(b)** To what extent does this flaw lead to his downfall? To what extent is his downfall due to fate? Explain.

© **4. Integration of Knowledge and Ideas** Who is the true tragic hero of this play? Defend your response.

© **5. Integration of Knowledge and Ideas (a)** Use a chart like this one to explore the play's **theme. (b)** Share and discuss answers with a partner. **(c)** Explain whether your discussion has changed your thoughts on the theme of the play.

Lines from Exodus	What Does It Say?	What Does It Mean?	Why Is It Important?
lines 94–106			
lines 142–150			

Reading Skill: Summarize

6. Summarize Scenes 3 through 5 scene by scene.

Vocabulary

© **Acquisition and Use** Replace each italicized word with its synonym from the vocabulary list on page 838. Then, use the phrase correctly in a sentence.

1. a great *wailing*

2. a *thoughtless* action

3. a *nasty* remark

4. show *meekness* before

5. given out of *reverence*

6. his *disdain* for

Word Study Use the context of the sentences and what you know about the **Latin root -fer-** to explain your answer to each question.

1. If an award has been *conferred* for a heroic act, has the award been taken away from someone?

2. Is *fertile* land good for farming?

Word Study

The **Latin root -fer-** means "to carry," "to bear," or "to bring."

Apply It Explain how the root *-fer-* contributes to the meanings of these words. Consult a dictionary if necessary.

circumference
ferry
transfer

PERFORMANCE TASKS
Integrated Language Skills

Antigone, Scenes 3 through 5

Conventions: Independent and Subordinate Clauses

A **clause** is a group of words that has both a subject and a verb. An **independent clause** can stand by itself as a sentence. A **subordinate clause,** however, cannot stand by itself. There are three types of subordinate clauses: **adjective clauses, adverb clauses,** and **noun clauses.**

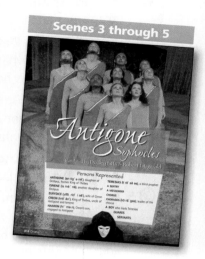

- **Independent clause:** *We visited the mountains.*
- **Adjective Clause:** Sam forgot to return the calculator *that he borrowed from Tito.* (modifies *calculator*)
- **Adverb Clause:** *Although it was cold out,* we jumped in the pool. (modifies *jumped*)
- **Noun Clause:** *Whatever you decide* is fine with me. (functions as the subject of the independent clause)

Practice A Identify the clause in each item. Then, state whether it is an independent or a subordinate clause. Classify subordinate clauses as adjective, adverb, or noun clauses.

1. Although Creon was angry, he listened to Teiresias.
2. Antigone dies in the tomb.
3. Wherever Creon lives will be filled with sorrow.
4. Haimon used the sword that he brought with him to the stone.

© **Reading Application** Identify two dependent clauses and two independent clauses in the second half of *Antigone.*

Practice B Complete each sentence by adding the type of clause named in parentheses.

1. (Independent clause) when Teiresias gave his prophecy.
2. Antigone was engaged to Haimon (adjective clause).
3. (Noun clause) was meaningless now.
4. The queen listened to the messenger (adverb clause).

© **Writing Application** Write a brief paragraph about the events that happen in the second half of *Antigone.* Your paragraph should include at least two independent and two subordinate clauses. Label your writing by identifying the types of subordinate clauses you used.

PH | **WRITING COACH** | Further instruction and practice are available in *Prentice Hall Writing Coach.*

Writing

Common Core State Standards

L.9-10.1, L.9-10.6; W.9-10.2, W.9-10.2.a, W.9-10.2.b; SL.9-10.4

[For the full wording of the standards, see page 836.]

© **Explanatory Text** In *Antigone*, Creon puts the state above family loyalty—and loses his family. Write a brief **reflective essay** on Creon's fate. As you write, consider these questions:

- Is Creon's fate just punishment for his decisions?
- Was there a single right course of action for him to take?
- What does his fate suggest about human action in general?

To develop your ideas in a logical organization, write a clear statement of your opinion about Creon at the beginning of your essay. Outline your main points before expanding them in the body of your essay. Use quotations and details from the play to support and elaborate on your ideas.

Grammar Application Include both independent and subordinate clauses in your essay.

Writing Workshop: *Work in Progress*

Prewriting for a Reflective Essay Use the Event Notes from your writing portfolio. For each of the five events you chose, write a brief answer to this question: What might be different if this event had not taken place? Put the Answer File in your writing portfolio.

Use this prewriting activity to prepare for the **Writing Workshop** on page 878.

Speaking and Listening

© **Presentation of Ideas** Hold a **mock trial** in which both sides in the dispute between Antigone and Creon are presented before the class. Select students to play various roles: judge, several defense attorneys, several prosecuting attorneys, and witnesses. Have attorneys for both sides provide witnesses. As you prepare for the trial, consider these suggestions:

- Attorneys should develop points they will make to support their client and choose a logical organization to inform and persuade the jury.
- Attorneys should identify points that could be argued against their client and develop counterarguments.
- Attorneys should use rhetorical devices such as appeals to logic or emotion to support their argument or testimony.
- One attorney on each side should be chosen to make closing remarks that summarize the strongest arguments before the jury.

The class should act as a jury to decide which argument is more convincing. During the deliberations, the jury should work to negotiate a unanimous decision.

PHLit Online!
www.PHLitOnline.com
- Interactive graphic organizers
- Grammar tutorial
- Interactive journals

Test Practice: Reading

Summarize

Drama Selection

Directions: *Read the selection. Then, answer the questions.*

In Sophocles' Oedipus at Colonus, *Creon is holding Oedipus' daughters Antigone and Ismene against their will in order to capture Oedipus himself. Theseus, the king of Athens, intervenes on behalf of Oedipus. Creon's response to Theseus is retold in the following passage.*

CREON. It is not that I believe this city lacks courage, King Theseus, or wisdom . . . that I have sought to capture Oedipus . . . I knew that your people would not allow a murderer—a polluted man who married his own mother—to enter this great city. Knowing that outlaws are not permitted to live in your land, I came here to hunt for the former king of Thebes, Oedipus. . .

    King Theseus, I know you will do what you think is right in this situation; although I believe my actions were right, the lack of support makes me weak: however, even though I feel old, I will not willingly give up my quest to destroy this man.

1. Who is speaking in the excerpt?

  A. Oedipus
  B. Creon
  C. Antigone
  D. Theseus

2. What is the main idea of the speech?

  A. Oedipus should be forgiven.
  B. The people of Athens are untrustworthy.
  C. Athens should not welcome Oedipus.
  D. I hope to reconcile with Oedipus.

3. What is Creon's most significant action in this excerpt?

  A. He kidnaps Antigone and Ismene.
  B. He answers Theseus.
  C. He forgives Oedipus.
  D. He kills Oedipus.

4. Which of the following details would be *least* important to include in a summary of this excerpt?

  A. Creon has captured Antigone and Ismene.
  B. Creon seeks to capture Oedipus.
  C. Creon is speaking to Theseus.
  D. Creon is feeling weak.

Writing for Assessment

Write a paragraph in which you summarize Creon's opinion of Oedipus. Include details from this excerpt in your summary.

Nonfiction Selection

Directions: *Read the selection. Then, answer the questions.*

All tragedies have a tragic hero, who is the protagonist. This character is usually of high or noble birth. The tragic hero is in a difficult situation for one of two reasons: Either he or she creates the situation because of a character flaw, or the situation itself is fated. Sometimes, the situation involves a combination of the two. For example, Oedipus is doomed by fate but makes his situation worse. The tragic hero ultimately experiences disaster.

Tragedies are timeless: The protagonist is a character with whom any audience will sympathize. The audience can identify with the hero's feelings of helplessness as he or she tries to fix past mistakes.

1. What is the *best* one-sentence summary of paragraph 1?

   A. For a tragic hero, fate interferes and the main character experiences disaster.

   B. The main character in a tragedy is a person of high status who faces a downfall due to fate or a character flaw.

   C. A tragedy is a play about a character who cannot avoid fate no matter what.

   D. Oedipus is a tragic hero because, no matter what he does, he cannot avoid the tragic fate that is waiting for him.

2. Which trait does *not* apply to a tragic hero?

   A. experiences disaster

   B. of high or noble birth

   C. doomed by fate

   D. sympathizes with the gods

3. What is the *best* paraphrase of the first sentence in paragraph 2?

   A. A tragic hero appeals to readers in any period of time.

   B. A tragic hero's feelings don't make sense to most readers.

   C. Readers always want to see the protagonist fail.

   D. Readers want to learn more about the protagonist.

4. Which of the following details could be left out of a summary of this selection?

   A. The protagonist is a character for whom the audience feels sympathy.

   B. The audience can identify with the main character's feelings of helplessness.

   C. Oedipus makes his situation worse.

   D. The tragic hero experiences disaster.

Writing for Assessment

Connecting Across Texts

Based on the passage on the left, in what ways does Oedipus fit the criteria of a tragic hero? Explain your answer in a paragraph. Support your response with details from both selections.

- Online practice
- Instant feedback

Reading for Information

Analyzing Argumentative Texts

Drama Review

Drama Review

**Common Core
State Standards**

Reading Informational Text
2. Determine a central idea of a text and analyze its development over the course of the text, including how it emerges and is shaped and refined by specific details; provide an objective summary of the text.

Language
6. Acquire and use accurately general academic and domain-specific words and phrases, sufficient for reading, writing, speaking, and listening at the college and career readiness level; demonstrate independence in gathering vocabulary knowledge when considering a word or phrase important to comprehension or expression.

Reading Skill Synthesize: Connect Ideas

When you read multiple texts dealing with a single issue, you will often find agreement and disagreement among the texts. To draw your own conclusions about the issue, **synthesize** the content from those sources by **connecting ideas** presented in the texts.

Begin by **paraphrasing,** or restating, the key ideas in one of the texts. Next, examine the ideas you have paraphrased to determine the work's central idea. Then, turn to the next text, and repeat the process, noting related ideas between the texts. For example, if you read two reviews of a single theatrical production, you might look for what each reviewer says about the play's staging, or overall appearance. You can synthesize the content of the two reviews by analyzing what each one says and drawing conclusions about the production, based on your analysis. This chart shows an example.

Idea in Text One	Idea in Text Two	Synthesis
The set design is plain, but it looks good and sometimes surprises.	Few props are used, but they are used in clever ways.	The staging of the production is simple but effective.

Content-Area Vocabulary

These words appear in the selections that follow. You may also encounter them in other content-area texts.

- **interpretation** (in tur´ prə tā´ shən) *n.* the way a person thinks of and expresses a work of art

- **collaboration** (kə lab´ ə rā shən) *n.* something, such as an artistic or a literary project, that is the product of people working together

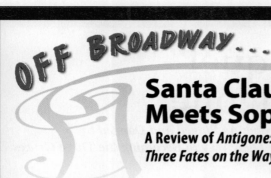

OFF BROADWAY...

Drama Review

Features:

- a summary of the play's plot
- a critique of the direction and acting
- support for opinions
- judgments about the staging

Santa Claus Meets Sophocles

A Review of *Antigone: As Played and Danced by the Three Fates on the Way to Becoming the Three Graces*

MATTHEW MURRAY

If you're familiar with Sophocles' classic Greek tragedy and have a solid working knowledge of Greek mythology, you might well appreciate the opportunity to see Big Dance Theater's production of Wellman's **interpretation** of the story, which is playing at Classic Stage Company through May 23. If you don't know Sophocles' original, or you have only a casual familiarity with it, chances are you'll be utterly baffled by what you see onstage.

The full title of Wellman's play is *Antigone: As Played and Danced by the Three Fates on Their Way to Becoming the Three Graces.* That should give you an idea of what you're in for: a highly deconstructed[1] take on Sophocles' story.

As the Fates (one who spins the thread of life, one who weaves it into actions, and one who determines when it must be snipped) existed eons before Sophocles, this story bears only a perfunctory similarity to his. The story the Fates enact features a handful of characters from the play, and is overseen by a narrator (and disc jockey) named E Shriek, whom Wellman describes as "an unknown god of unknown origin."

As the play progresses, the Fates become the Three Graces, and pass along the story of the young Antigone and the steadfast uncle she defied to Sophocles himself. (Well, as represented by a hand puppet.) The story is told and retold until it reaches the version we currently know, at which point the play stops: what is is of no interest to Wellman. He's more concerned with what was and what might have been.

That idea, and the stagecraft used to present it, are the most engaging parts of this *Antigone*. Director Paul Lazar and choreographer[2] Annie-B Parson have done an excellent job of making the play visually appealing, providing almost constant movement onstage, and no shortage of surprises in the way the Fates' journeys are conveyed. (They employ microphones, dust busters, yellow slippers and toy pianos.)

Cynthia Hopkins has provided a few attractive songs for the production; Joanne Howard's set design is spartan[3], but handsome and occasionally surprising; Claudia Stephens's costumes provide nice definition for the characters; Jay Ryan's lights are colorful and inventive; and Jane Shaw's sound design is never overdone. Leroy Logan, as E Shriek, is a fine combination of paternal and frightening, Santa Claus by way of Socrates (and Sophocles).

It's the lack of immediacy and freshness that hurts this *Antigone* more than anything else: the production never feels as crisp and well-defined as it needs to be. The theatrical concept on which Wellman and Lazar have collaborated is daring and intelligent, but it's currently missing the piquant[4] energy needed to really put it across.

> Paraphrasing these comments about the staging of the play can help you to connect the reviewer's ideas to related ideas in another review.

1. **deconstructed** (dē kən strukt´ id) *adj.* (said of a text) having been broken into its elements in order to question its meaning.
2. **choreographer** (kôr´ ē äg´ rə fər) *n.* a person who creates and directs dances.
3. **spartan** (spärt´ n) *adj.* very plain; lacking ornament.
4. **piquant** (pē´ kənt) *adj.* exciting agreeable interest or curiosity.

A "Prequel" to Antigone

A Review of *Antigone: As Played and Danced by the Three Fates on Their Way to Becoming the Three Graces*

Elyse Sommers

The 55-minute dance theater piece currently at the Classic Stage Theater is a **collaboration** made in avant-garde[1] heaven: a text by the wizard of word play Mac Wellman, direction and musical staging by the Big Dance Theater's director Paul Lazar and choreographer Annie-B Parson.

The prolific and always surprising Wellman's first journey into Greek myth is more musical tone poem than play. His deconstruction or prequel to Sophocles' *Antigone* is brilliantly acted out and danced by the production's four performers.

Wellman has kept all the traditional parts: Creon, Antigone's sister Ismene, Creon's son Haemon, Creon's wife Eurydice (who in Wellman's version is also Teiresias) and the chorus of Theban citizens. But in this highly stylized collaboration, all these parts are played by the chameleonic,[2] maskless Three Fates (Deirdre O'Connell, Molly Hickock and Rebecca Wisocky), who are also Three Fates, on their way to becoming the Three Graces. O'Connell is a moving Antigone. Wisocky, an actor-dancer whose enormous range I've long admired, is a mesmerizing and quite humorous Creon whose kingly edicts are delivered into a microphone. Hickock takes on the roles of Teiresias and Eurydice, as well as sharing the Chorus scenes with a fourth Fate, Nancy Ellis.

If all this sounds more than a little confusing and inaccessible, anyone not well schooled in the Greek tale is indeed likely to be swept with a sense of "this is all Greek to me." Still, if you just sit back and watch the four women dance and deliver the bursts of babbling dialogue, you'll gradually get the general sense if not all of it.

To add to the fun (yes, much of this IS fun with quite a few laugh-out-loud moments), there's a nondancing narrator with the intriguing name of Shriek Operator. This character is zestfully portrayed by Leroy Logan. The staging overall is appropriately spare with just a few simple but apt and often amusing props.

> Like the writer of the preceding review, this reviewer describes the adaptation of *Antigone* as a deconstruction of Sophocles' original.

Author: Mac Wellman
Director: Paul Lazar
Choreography & Musical Staging: Annie-B Parson
Cast: Nancy Ellis, Molly Hickock, Leroy Logan, Deirdre O'Connell & Rebecca Wisocky
Songs: Cynthia Hopkins
Running time: 60 minutes without intermission

Classic Stage
136 East 13th Street
(212/123-4567)
4/27/04 through 5/23/04;
opening 5/02/04
Tuesday through Friday
8:00pm / Saturday 2:00pm &
8:00pm / Sunday 3:00pm

---

1. **avant-garde** (ə vänt´ gärd´) *n.* any new or unconventional movement, especially in the arts.

2. **chameleonic** (kə mē´ lē än´ ik) *adj.* capable of assuming a variety of appearances.

Comparing Argumentative Texts

 1. Key Ideas and Details (a) In what ways are the two reviewers' critiques of the actors' performances similar? **(b)** In what ways are they different? **(c)** When you **synthesize** information from both reviews, what is one conclusion you can draw about the actors' performances? Explain your response.

Content-Area Vocabulary

2. (a) Review the definitions of the words *interpretation* and *collaboration,* noting how the definitions of the words are each related to art and how the words might be applied to the performing arts, such as theater. **(b)** Use the words in a brief paragraph about a favorite story, novel, or movie that your class might turn into a play.

Timed Writing

Persuasive Text: Essay

Format
The prompt directs you to write a persuasive essay. Therefore, you should use vivid, convincing language and support your ideas with strong evidence.

Your school will perform *Antigone: As Played.* . . . Write a persuasive essay offering suggestions for the performance. Combine criticism and praise from the reviews, synthesizing the ideas. Then, connect those ideas to your own ideas about drama to make suggestions. Cite details from the reviews as support. (35 minutes)

Academic Vocabulary
When you *connect* ideas, you find links between them, joining them together to draw conclusions and form new ideas.

5-Minute Planner

Complete these steps before you begin to write:

1. Read the prompt carefully and completely.

2. Skim the reviews to find criticisms and praise. Synthesize these ideas by combining them and making a list of points and details.

3. Think about what makes a good theatrical performance. Make a list of your ideas.

4. Review your lists, noting connections between the items.

5. Formulate suggestions based on the connections you found in your lists.

6. Consider the order in which you will present your suggestions. **TIP** List ideas for which you have the strongest support first.

7. Create an outline, and refer to it and your notes as you draft your essay.

Comparing Universal and Culturally Specific Themes

The **theme** of a literary work is its message. Often, the changes that a main character experiences in a literary work are related to the work's theme. For example, a character may be faced with a **moral dilemma**—a conflict that challenges the character's beliefs about right and wrong. How the character resolves the dilemma or what he or she learns from facing the dilemma may point toward the theme.

Themes may have aspects that are **culturally specific,** reflecting the circumstances and beliefs of the writer's culture and time period. In contrast, the theme may also have aspects that are **universal,** or that are meaningful to people of all times and places.

For instance, an ancient poem might tell of an arrogant warrior who does not obey his people's traditions and who is punished by the gods.

- The poem's theme is culturally specific because it reflects the beliefs of the culture: "The gods punish those who do not obey our traditions."

- The poem also expresses a universal theme, one that people of all times and places can appreciate: "No one is above the law."

In the ancient Greek play *Antigone*, Antigone bravely defies a king. In the nineteenth-century European drama *An Enemy of the People,* a doctor bravely defies his brother and boss, the mayor. The "local" or culturally specific elements of each play are different. Yet both plays express an important universal theme: "People may be torn between duty to authority and some higher value."

Use a diagram like the one shown to **compare and contrast themes** expressed in the two plays from different time periods.

Common Core State Standards

Reading Literature
2. Determine a theme or central idea of a text and analyze in detail its development over the course of the text, including how it emerges and is shaped and refined by specific details; provide an objective summary of the text.

Writing
2. Write informative/explanatory texts to examine and convey complex ideas, concepts, and information clearly and accurately through the effective selection, organization, and analysis of content.
2.b. Develop the topic with well-chosen, relevant, and sufficient facts, extended definitions, concrete details, quotations, or other information and examples appropriate to the audience's knowledge of the topic. *(Timed Writing)*

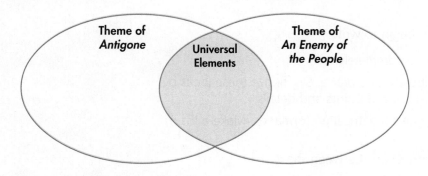

Theme of *Antigone* · Universal Elements · Theme of *An Enemy of the People*

www.PHLitOnline.com

- Vocabulary flashcards
- Interactive journals
- More about the authors
- Selection audio
- Interactive graphic organizers

To what extent does *experience* determine what we *perceive?*

Writing About the Big Question

In both *Antigone* and *An Enemy of the People,* characters must decide between following a person in power and following their own perception of what is morally right. Use these sentence starters to develop your ideas about the Big Question.

Individuals must balance respect for authority with _____.

When people in power try to **distort** your views of right and wrong, thinking about your own experiences can help you _____.

Meet the Author

Henrik Ibsen (1828–1906)
Author of *An Enemy of the People*

Born in Skien, Norway, Henrik Ibsen was a pioneer of modern realistic drama. The popular drama of his day specialized in idealized heroes, ridiculous buffoons, and happy endings. Breaking with convention, Ibsen showed ordinary people facing grimly realistic problems. Instead of developing perfect heroes and utter villains, he presented psychologically complex characters with a mix of good and bad motives.

Creating Controversy Ibsen also offered a brutally honest look at cutting-edge issues of his day. For instance, his play *A Doll House* concerns women's rights, a subject that was highly controversial in the nineteenth century. Outraged by such inflammatory subject matter, critics condemned him. In the end, though, Ibsen triumphed. Today, his plays are considered classics, and his realistic approach to character, plot, dialogue, and staging continues to influence drama.

from An Enemy of the People

Henrik Ibsen

Background At the opening of the play, the future looks good for Dr. Thomas Stockmann's hometown. The town has finally opened a health resort for visitors, who come to drink and bathe in the local water, which is said to have healthful effects. Just when the town is beginning to benefit from the new business, however, Dr. Stockmann makes an alarming discovery. Sewage from a nearby industrial town is polluting the water. As Dr. Stockmann explains to his wife, his oldest child, Petra, and a few friends, the town will have to relocate the pipes that feed the baths in order to prevent the spread of disease. He has sent a report on the problem to his brother Peter, mayor of the town. The next morning, Peter pays him a visit.

MAYOR STOCKMANN. (*entering from the hall*). Good morning.

DR. STOCKMANN. Good to see you, Peter!

MRS. STOCKMANN. Morning, Peter. How's everything with you?

MAYOR STOCKMANN. Just so-so, thank you. (*To the* DOCTOR.) Yesterday, after office hours, I received a report from you, discussing the condition of the water at the baths.

DR. STOCKMANN. Yes. Have you read it?

MAYOR STOCKMANN. I have.

DR. STOCKMANN. What have you got to say about it?

MAYOR STOCKMANN. (*glancing at the others*). Hm—

MRS. STOCKMANN. Come along, Petra.

(She and PETRA *go into the room on the left.)*

MAYOR STOCKMANN. *(after a moment).* Was it necessary to press all these investigations behind my back?

DR. STOCKMANN. Well, as long as I didn't have absolute proof, then—

MAYOR STOCKMANN. And now you think you do?

DR. STOCKMANN. You must be convinced of that yourself.

MAYOR STOCKMANN. Is it your object to put this document before the board of directors by way of an official recommendation?

DR. STOCKMANN. Of course. Something has to be done about this. And fast.

MAYOR STOCKMANN. As usual, in your report you let your language get out of hand. You say, among other things, that what we're offering our summer visitors is guaranteed poison.

DR. STOCKMANN. But, Peter, how else can you describe it? You've got to realize—this water is poison for internal or external use! And it's foisted on poor, suffering creatures who turn to us in good faith and pay us exorbitant fees to gain their health back again!

MAYOR STOCKMANN. And then you arrive at the conclusion, by your line of reasoning, that we have to build a sewer to drain off these so-called impurities from Mølledal,[1] and that all the water mains have to be relaid.

DR. STOCKMANN. Well, do you see any other way out? I don't.

MAYOR STOCKMANN. I invented a little business this morning down at the town engineer's office. And in a half-joking way, I brought up these proposals as something we perhaps ought to take under advisement[2] at some time in the future.

DR. STOCKMANN. Some time in the future!

MAYOR STOCKMANN. He smiled at my whimsical extravagance—naturally. Have you gone to the trouble of estimating just what these proposed changes would cost? From the information I received, the expenditure would probably run up into several hundred thousand crowns.[3]

DR. STOCKMANN. As high as that?

MAYOR STOCKMANN. Yes. But that's not the worst. The work would extend over at least two years.

---

1. **Mølledal** (möl′ ə däl′) fictional Norwegian town.
2. **to take under advisement** to think over carefully.
3. **crowns** *n.* A crown is the Norwegian unit of currency; krone (krō′ nə).

◄ **Critical Viewing**
Judging from Dr. Stockmann's expression in this film still, how might others respond to his discovery? **[Predict]**

Vocabulary
exorbitant (eg zôr′ bi tənt) *adj.* excessive

Literary Analysis
Themes What details of the issue raised by Dr. Stockmann are characteristic of life in modern, industrial times?

Reading Check
What problem does Dr. Stockmann's town face?

DR. STOCKMANN. Two years? Two full years?

MAYOR STOCKMANN. At the least. And meanwhile what do we do with the baths? Shut them down? Yes, we'll have to. Do you really think anyone would make the effort to come all the distance here if the rumor got out that the water was contaminated?

DR. STOCKMANN. Yes, but Peter, that's what it is.

Literary Analysis
Themes What ideas in the mayor's speech might provoke feelings of guilt in most people?

MAYOR STOCKMANN. And then all this happens now—just now, when the baths were being recognized. Other towns in this area have the same resources for development as health resorts. Don't you think they'll leap at the chance to attract the whole flow of tourists to them? No question of it. And there we are, left stranded. We'll most likely have to abandon the whole costly enterprise; and then you'll have ruined the town you were born in.

DR. STOCKMANN. I—ruined—!

MAYOR STOCKMANN. It's through the baths alone that this town has any future to speak of. You can see that just as plain as I can.

DR. STOCKMANN. But then what do you think ought to be done?

MAYOR STOCKMANN. From your report I'm unable to persuade myself that the condition of the baths is as critical as you claim.

DR. STOCKMANN. Look, if anything, it's worse! Or it'll be that by summer, when the warm weather comes.

MAYOR STOCKMANN. Once again. I think you're exaggerating considerably. A capable doctor must know the right steps to take—he should be able to control toxic[4] elements, and to treat them if they make their presence too obvious.

DR. STOCKMANN. And then—? What else—?

MAYOR STOCKMANN. The water system for the baths as it now stands is simply a fact and clearly has to be accepted as such. But in time the directors will more than likely agree to take under consideration to what extent—depending on the funds available—they can institute certain improvements.

DR. STOCKMANN. And you can think I'd play along with that kind of trickery!

MAYOR STOCKMANN. Trickery?

DR. STOCKMANN. Yes, it's a trick—a deception, a lie, an out-and-out crime against the public and society at large!

MAYOR STOCKMANN. As I've already observed, I've not yet persuaded

---

4. toxic (täk´ sik) *adj.* poisonous.

myself that there's any real impending danger here.

DR. STOCKMANN. Yes, you have! There's no alternative. My report is perfectly accurate, I know that! And you're very much aware of it, Peter, but you won't admit it. You're the one who got the baths and the water system laid out where they are today; and it's this—it's this hellish miscalculation that you won't concede. Pah! You don't think I can see right through you?

MAYOR STOCKMANN. And even if it were true? Even if I seem a bit overanxious about my reputation, it's all for the good of the town. Without moral authority I could hardly guide and direct affairs in the way I believe serves the general welfare. For this reason—among many others—it strikes me as imperative[5] that your report not be submitted to the board of directors. It has to be withheld for the common good. Then, later, I'll bring the matter up for discussion, and we'll do the very best we can, as quietly as possible. But nothing—not the slightest word of this catastrophe must leak out to the public.

DR. STOCKMANN. My dear Peter, there's no stopping it now.

MAYOR STOCKMANN. It must and it will be stopped.

DR. STOCKMANN. I'm telling you, it's no use. Too many people know already.

MAYOR STOCKMANN. Know already! Who? Not those fellows from the *Courier*—?

DR. STOCKMANN. Why, of course they know. The independent liberal press is going to see that you do your duty.

MAYOR STOCKMANN (*after a short pause*). You're an exceptionally thoughtless man, Thomas. Haven't you considered the consequences that can follow for you?

DR. STOCKMANN. Consequences? For me?

MAYOR STOCKMANN. For you and your family as well.

DR. STOCKMANN. What the devil does *that* mean?

MAYOR STOCKMANN. I think, over the years, I've proved a helpful and accommodating brother to you.

DR. STOCKMANN. Yes, you have, and I'm thankful to you for that.

MAYOR STOCKMANN. I'm not after thanks. Because, in part, I was forced into it—for my own sake. I always hoped I could keep you in check somewhat if I helped better your economic status.

---

5. **imperative** (im per´ ə tiv) *adj.* absolutely necessary; urgent.

Vocabulary
impending (im pend´ iŋ) *adj.* about to happen

Literary Analysis
Themes What situations in modern life does Peter's suggestion call to mind?

Literary Analysis
Themes Which details of this scene emphasize the universal theme of "brother against brother"?

Reading Check
What does the mayor wish to do about Dr. Stockmann's discovery?

DR. STOCKMANN. What? Just for your own sake—!

MAYOR STOCKMANN. In part, I said. It's embarrassing for a public servant when his closest relative goes and compromises himself again and again.

DR. STOCKMANN. And that's what you think I do?

MAYOR STOCKMANN. Yes, unfortunately you do, without your knowing it. You have a restless, unruly, combative nature. And then this unhappy knack[6] of bursting into print on all kinds of likely and unlikely subjects. You're no sooner struck by an idea than right away you have to scribble a newspaper article on it, or a whole pamphlet even.

DR. STOCKMANN. Well, but isn't it a citizen's duty to inform the public if he comes on a new idea?

MAYOR STOCKMANN. Oh, the public doesn't need new ideas. The public is served best by the good, old, time-tested ideas it's always had.

DR. STOCKMANN. That's putting it plainly!

MAYOR STOCKMANN. I have to talk to you plainly for once. Up till now I've always tried to avoid that because I know how irritable you are; but now I'm telling you the truth, Thomas. You have no conception how much you injure yourself with your impetuosity. You complain about the authorities and, yes, the government; you rail against them—and insist you're being passed over and persecuted. But what can you expect—someone as troublesome as you.

DR. STOCKMANN. Ah—so I'm troublesome, too?

MAYOR STOCKMANN. Yes, Thomas, you're a very troublesome man to work with. I know from experience. You show no consideration at all. You seem to forget completely that I'm the one you can thank for your post here as staff physician at the baths—

DR. STOCKMANN. I was the inevitable[7] choice—I and nobody else! I was the

Vocabulary
impetuosity
(im pech´ oo äs´ i
tē) *n.* sudden action
with little thought

▼ **Critical Viewing**
How might concern
for his children, one of
whom is shown here,
affect Dr. Stockmann's
handling of his conflict with the town?
Why? **[Speculate]**

---

6. **knack** (nak) *n.* trick; particular skill.
7. **inevitable** (in ev´ i tə bəl) *adj.* certain to happen; that which cannot be avoided.

first to see that this town could become a flourishing spa;[8] and I was the *only* one who could see it then. I stood alone fighting for that idea for years; and I wrote and wrote—

MAYOR STOCKMANN. Unquestionably. But the right moment hadn't arrived yet. Of course you couldn't judge that from up there in the wilds. But when the opportune time came, and I—and a few others—took the matter in hand—

DR. STOCKMANN. Yes, and bungled the whole magnificent plan. Oh yes, it's really coming out now what a brilliant crew you've been!

MAYOR STOCKMANN. All that's coming out, to my mind, is your usual hunger for a good fight. You want to attack your superiors—it's your old pattern. You can't stand any authority over you; you resent anyone in a higher position and regard him as a personal enemy—and then one weapon's as good as another to use. But now I've acquainted you with the vital interests at stake here for this whole town—and, naturally, for me as well. And so I'm warning you, Thomas, I'll be adamant about the demand I am going to make of you.

DR. STOCKMANN. What demand?

MAYOR STOCKMANN. Since you've been so indiscreet as to discuss this delicate issue with outsiders, even though it should have been kept secret among the directors, it of course can't be hushed up now. All kinds of rumors will go flying around, and the maliciously inclined will dress them up with trimmings of their own. It'll therefore be necessary that you publicly deny these rumors.

DR. STOCKMANN. I! How? I don't understand.

MAYOR STOCKMANN. We can expect that, after further investigation, you'll arrive at the conclusion that things are far from being as critical or dangerous as you'd first imagined.

DR. STOCKMANN. Ah—you expect that!

MAYOR STOCKMANN. Moreover, we expect that you'll support and publicly affirm your confidence in the present directors to take thorough and conscientious measures, as necessary, to remedy any possible defects.

DR. STOCKMANN. But that's utterly out of the question for me, as long as they try to get by with patchwork. I'm telling you that, Peter; and it's my unqualified opinion—!

---

8. **spa** (spä) *n.* health resort where people drink and bathe in mineral waters.

Spiral Review
Character Development What does the discussion about the baths reveal about Mayor Stockmann's character?

Vocabulary
adamant (ad´ ə mənt) *adj.* firm

Literary Analysis
Themes What ideas about rumors lead to Dr. Stockmann's new predicament?

Reading Check
What does the mayor tell Dr. Stockmann he must do?

MAYOR STOCKMANN. As a member of the staff, you're not entitled to any personal opinions.

DR. STOCKMANN. (*stunned*). Not entitled—?

MAYOR STOCKMANN. As a staff member, I said. As a private person— why, that's another matter. But as a subordinate official at the baths, you're not entitled to express any opinions that contradict your superiors.

DR. STOCKMANN. That's going too far! I, as a doctor, a man of science, aren't entitled to—!

MAYOR STOCKMANN. What's involved here isn't a purely scientific problem. It's a mixture of both technical and economic consider-ations.

DR. STOCKMANN. I don't care what the hell it is! I want the freedom to express myself on any problem under the sun!

MAYOR STOCKMANN. Anything you like—except for the baths. We forbid you that.

DR. STOCKMANN (*shouting*). You forbid—! You! A crowd of—!

MAYOR STOCKMANN. *I* forbid it—*I*, your supervisor. And when I forbid you, then you obey.

Literary Analysis
Themes Why might the idea of obedience to authority be universal?

Critical Thinking

Cite textual evidence to support your responses.

1. **Key Ideas and Details** **(a)** What problem does Dr. Stockmann report to his brother? **(b) Connect:** What solution does he propose?

2. **Key Ideas and Details** **(a)** What information does the mayor acquire from an engineer about the proposed solution? **(b) Infer:** What effect does this information have on his reaction?

3. **Key Ideas and Details** **(a) Draw Conclusions:** What is the mayor's main goal with regard to the problem? Explain. **(b) Connect:** What is the mayor willing to sacrifice to achieve this goal? **(c) Make a Judgment:** Is he being realistic or immoral? Explain.

4. **Integration of Knowledge and Ideas** Do you think this con-versation will change Dr. Stockmann's perception of the mayor as both a brother and a leader? Explain your answer. *[Connect to the Big Question: To what extent does experience determine what we perceive?]*

Comparing Universal and Culturally Specific Themes

© **1. Integration of Knowledge and Ideas (a)** Use a chart like the one shown to analyze both universal and culturally specific elements of Dr. Stockmann's dilemma in *An Enemy of the People*. **(b)** Complete another chart like the one shown, using details from Antigone's speech in *Antigone*, Scene 2, lines 65–84. **(c)** Referring to your charts, draw a conclusion about the universal **themes** in each play.

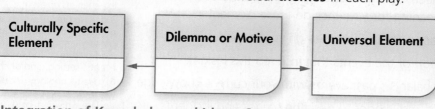

Culturally Specific Element	Dilemma or Motive	Universal Element

© **2. Integration of Knowledge and Ideas** Compare Antigone's situation and motives to Dr. Stockmann's. Quote from both plays to support your ideas.

© **3. Integration of Knowledge and Ideas (a)** Review Creon's speech in *Antigone*, Scene 1, lines 8–53, and describe his situation and attitude. **(b)** Compare Creon's reasoning with Mayor Stockmann's, quoting from both plays in support of your answer. Discuss how each character's reasoning reflects the time period in which he lives.

⏱ Timed Writing

Explanatory Text: Essay

In an essay, compare and contrast differences in the themes expressed in *Antigone* and *An Enemy of the People*. Introduce your discussion with a brief summary of each work. **(35 minutes)**

5-Minute Planner

1. Read the prompt carefully and completely.
2. Use these questions to get started:
   • What are the culturally specific elements in each work?
   • How do the different time periods affect the theme?
   • What universal ideas does each play suggest?
3. Note that the prompt asks you to compare and contrast the themes. Therefore, your essay should contain discussion of both the similarities and the differences in the two themes.
4. Reread the prompt, and then draft your essay.

Writing Workshop

Write a Narrative

Narration: Reflective Essay

Defining the Form A **reflective essay** describes a personal experience, memory, object, or idea and explains why and how it is significant. You might use elements of the reflective essay in journals, responses to literature, autobiographical narratives, and travel reports.

Assignment Write a reflective essay that describes a personal experience and explains its special meaning for you. Include these elements:

✓ an *insight* or *observation* about life based on your experiences

✓ a *thorough explanation* of the events that inspired this insight

✓ an *organization* that balances past events with your current knowledge

✓ use of *sensory details and images* to describe scenes and incidents

✓ error-free grammar, especially the use of *verbal phrases to vary sentence structures*

To preview the criteria on which your reflective essay may be judged, see the rubric on page 883.

Writing

3. Write narratives to develop real or imagined experiences or events using effective technique, well-chosen details, and well-structured event sequences.

3.a. Engage and orient the reader by setting out a problem, situation, or observation, establishing one or multiple point(s) of view, and introducing a narrator and/or characters; create a smooth progression of experiences or events.

3.d. Use precise words and phrases, telling details, and sensory language to convey a vivid picture of the experiences, events, setting, and/or characters.

6. Use technology, including the Internet, to produce, publish, and update individual or shared writing products, taking advantage of technology's capacity to link to other information and to display information flexibly and dynamically. *(p. 883)*

 Writing Workshop: *Work in Progress*

Review the work you did on pages 835 and 861.

Prewriting/Planning Strategy

Gather sensory details. Create a list of words and phrases that describe your experience and appeal to the senses of sight, hearing, touch, taste, and smell. Include words that form clear, vivid pictures of the setting, people, and events. Identify a strong image that captures a key part of your central insight. Use a chart like this one to record sensory details.

	Detail	Detail
Sight:	snowy trails through dark trees	
Hearing:	lonesome sound of birds in woods	
Smell:	scent of pines	
Touch:	the velvety feel of wet snow falling on my face	
Taste:	the warm, rich taste of double hot chocolate	

Finding an Effective Idea

Finding the right **idea** for your reflective essay is the most important task. When searching for the right idea, remember that a reflective essay must include a dramatic incident from your past that influenced your beliefs, way of thinking, and/or future behavior. Your essay must include a lively description of the event and a reflection on the meaning of that event and how it influenced you.

Thinking About the Past Think about events or experiences from your past and ask yourself why you find them memorable. You might look in journals, scrapbooks, or photo albums to refresh your memories about your past. Choose an event from your early childhood that you still find vivid, or choose a more recent event. Whatever the time period in which the event occurred, it should have made a lasting impression on you.

Considering the Significance The event you choose should be one that taught you an important lesson. It should also hold the reader's interest. For example, if the topic of your essay is the time you and a friend were lost in the woods and were later found by the authorities, you may have learned not to go into unfamiliar areas unprepared or without a guide. To make the story come alive for readers, however, you should include striking descriptions, such as how you and your friend worked together to escape, giving each other courage and hope. By including such descriptions, you can expand the lesson you learned to include the value of friendship and the importance of working together.

> **PH** **WRITING COACH**
>
> Further instruction and practice are available in *Prentice Hall Writing Coach.*

Refining Your Idea As you consider events from your past, jot them down in a chart like the one below. Also, include the lessons you learned from the event. Then, choose the event that has had the most significance and has taught you an important lesson.

How Old Was I?	What Happened/Where?	What Did I Learn?

Drafting Strategies

Choose a logical organization. Balance the description of events from the past with your present thoughts. Consider using *chronological order* to describe the events in sequence. Alternatively, consider using *order-of-importance organization* to emphasize the most important moment in your narrative.

Chronological Order	Order of Importance
Introduction Setting and first event: what happened Next events: what happened **Conclusion:** Explanation of overall insight gained through this experience	**Introduction** Setting: why it is meaningful Each event: why each one is meaningful Most important moment: why it is critical **Conclusion:** Explanation of overall insight gained

Use effective imagery. Use figurative language to create word pictures.

- A **simile** compares two unlike things using the words *like* or *as*. (My eyes were <u>as wide as saucers.</u>)

- A **metaphor** compares two unlike things by stating that one thing *is* the other. (After Joe walked home in the snow, <u>his feet were icebergs</u>.)

- **Personification** applies human qualities or behavior to something nonhuman. (<u>Disappointment grabbed me</u> and would not let go.)

Revising Strategies

Revise for unity. Reread your draft and highlight any sentences that do not support your intended meaning. Cut or rewrite those sentences.

Revise to replace vague words. Review your essay, circling vague words. Consider more descriptive replacements that will add liveliness to your writing. Use the following chart as a model for identifying and replacing vague words and phrases.

Vague	Precise
It was one of the *best things* I had ever seen.	It was one of the *most colorful packages* I had ever seen.
It was very cold.	My breath made frosty clouds in the bitter cold.

 **Common Core State Standards**

Writing

3.a. Engage and orient the reader by setting out a problem, situation, or observation, establishing one or more points of view, and introducing a narrator or characters; create a smooth progression of experiences or events.

3.c. Use a variety of techniques to sequence events so that they build on one another to create a coherent whole.

3.d. Use precise words and phrases, telling details, and sensory language to convey a vivid picture of the experiences, events, setting, and/or characters.

3.e. Provide a conclusion that follows from and reflects on what is experienced, observed, or resolved over the course of the narrative.

Language

1.b. Use various types of phrases (verb) to convey specific meanings and add variety and interest to writing or presentations.

Revising to Combine Sentences With Verbal Phrases

The repetition of too many sentences with the same structure can create choppy, uninteresting writing. Use verbal phrases to combine a series of short choppy sentences into longer, more flowing ones.

Identifying Verbal Phrases Verbal phrases use verbs and act as nouns, adjectives, or adverbs.

The Three Types of Verbal Phrases

Participial Phrase	Gerund Phrase	Infinitive Phrase
a participle — a form of a verb that can act as an **adjective** — and its modifiers	a gerund — a verb ending in -ing that functions as a **noun** — and its modifiers	an infinitive — a form of verb that appears with the word *to* and acts as a **noun, adjective,** or **adverb** — and its modifiers
Walking by *herself,* Sara felt peaceful. *(modifies Sara)*	*Speaking in public* is scary. *(acts as subject)*	Her advice was *to start small.* *(acts as predicate nominative)*

A verbal phrase should be close to the word it modifies.

Misplaced: *Eating fish,* the scientists saw a baby seal.

Correct: The scientists saw a baby seal *eating fish.*

Combining Sentences Using Verbal Phrases Use verbal phrases to combine choppy sentences. Follow these steps:

1. **Express the ideas from a short sentence as a verbal phrase.**

2. **Insert the phrase into a new sentence, locating it near the word or words being modified.**

3. **Punctuate the new sentence correctly.** Look at this example:

    Choppy sentences: The cheetah moves silently. It stalks its prey.

    Combined into one sentence: Stalking its prey, the cheetah moves silently.

Grammar in Your Writing

Review your essay, looking for short sentences that might be combined using verbal phrases. Avoid misplaced modifiers by placing phrases in your combined sentences as close as possible to the word or words they modify.

PH **WRITING COACH**

Further instruction and practice are available in *Prentice Hall Writing Coach.*

The Dollhouse

I was sitting on my couch eating chocolate chip ice cream when the front door was flung open. Suddenly, a huge colorfully wrapped box with a giant red bow appeared. The only other thing I could see was the strong hands of a man gripping the box tightly. He placed it carefully on the table in front of me.

My father, glowing with pleasure, emerged from behind the box and said, "My daughter deserves the best present that money can buy for her birthday, and here it is. Go on, open it. What are you waiting for?"

I stood up and ripped the shiny paper from the box, but I could not help but stare when I saw what the paper had been hiding.

"Thank you, Daddy, it's truly beautiful," I said, hoping my eyes did not reveal the confusion I felt as I looked at the item.

In front of me was a delicately handcrafted dollhouse, and inside was a family of tiny porcelain dolls. The furniture in the dollhouse looked real, except that it had no flaws. There were pretty paintings on the wall and little glass chandeliers. It was amazing how peaceful and perfect the family inside appeared.

It would have been a terrific birthday present except for one thing: The magical miniature world was enclosed in a glass case. My father brought it up to my bedroom and warned me never to touch the glass for fear I would destroy its perfection. The dollhouse was there for me to admire but never to touch or play with.

The dollhouse sat in the same place for many years. I obeyed my father and never touched it. At first, I was intrigued by this beautiful world and did as I was supposed to: I admired it. Time passed, though, and I started to find it boring and useless. I began to look at the dollhouse in a new light. Those pretty porcelain dolls had no expression. They would never experience life or feel the way real people do because in that perfect world there was no emotion.

On my eighth birthday, I received a gift that taught me a lot about what I want out of life: Many times I had imagined myself in that house, never being able to interact with the outside world. I do not think I could stand to be so closed off. I would much rather be a part of the world and feel and see everything possible. The dollhouse made me realize that as long as I opened myself up to the world, I would never be lonely. But if I shut the world out of my life, like one of those porcelain perfections, then I would be completely by myself.

The essay focuses on Samantha's personal experience.

Samantha orders events sequentially.

She clearly sets events in a specific place and time of her life.

Samantha shares the insight she gained through reflection.

Samantha includes a truth about life that she learned through personal experience.

Editing and Proofreading

Check your draft for errors in spelling, grammar, and punctuation.

Focus on punctuation. Check that you have used commas correctly. Read the essay aloud and notice where you pause naturally. Consider whether or not these pauses need to be punctuated with commas.

Publishing and Presenting

Consider one of the following ways to share your writing:

Publish electronically. As a class, design a blog about reflective essays. Organize your essays by topic or theme and locate them in logically labeled folders. Invite other classes in your school to visit the blog and post constructive feedback.

Give a reading. Practice reading your essay aloud to yourself. Emphasize specific emotions or ideas by varying the speed and volume of your reading. Mark your draft to indicate these changes. Then, read your essay aloud to your class, making use of your notes.

Reflecting on Your Writing

Writer's Journal Jot down your answers to this question:

How did writing about the topic help you discover its importance?

Rubric for Self-Assessment

Find evidence in your writing to address each category. Then, use the rating scale to grade your work.

Spiral Review

Earlier in this unit, you learned about **participles and gerunds** (p. 834) and **independent and subordinate clauses** (p. 860). Check your essay to make sure that you have used participles and gerunds correctly and that you have properly combined independent and subordinate clauses.

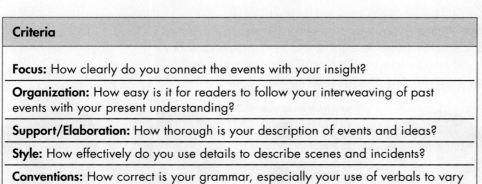

Criteria	Rating Scale				
	not very				*very*
Focus: How clearly do you connect the events with your insight?	1	2	3	4	5
Organization: How easy is it for readers to follow your interweaving of past events with your present understanding?	1	2	3	4	5
Support/Elaboration: How thorough is your description of events and ideas?	1	2	3	4	5
Style: How effectively do you use details to describe scenes and incidents?	1	2	3	4	5
Conventions: How correct is your grammar, especially your use of verbals to vary sentence length?	1	2	3	4	5
Ideas: How significant is the event and the lesson you learned from it?	1	2	3	4	5

Preparing to Read
The Tragedy of Julius Caesar

William Shakespeare wrote masterpieces of drama and poetry during an extraordinary era in English history.

Historical Background: Elizabethan England

A Golden Age Queen Elizabeth I came to the throne following a tumultuous period in English history. During the reign of her father, King Henry VIII, thousands of people had been executed. Warfare had been frequent, and the royal treasury was drained. The brief reigns of Elizabeth's half-brother Edward and half-sister Mary were equally stormy. Elizabeth, by contrast, proved to be a strong and successful ruler, frugal with money and popular with her people. Her long reign (1558–1603) is often seen as a golden age in English history. The relative stability that Elizabeth created allowed commerce and culture to thrive.

The Renaissance Elizabeth ruled toward the end of a flowering of European learning known as the Renaissance (ren´ ə sans´). The Renaissance began in Florence and other Italian city-states around 1350, and then spread throughout Europe. The word "renaissance" means "rebirth," and the era saw renewed interest in the arts and sciences that hearkened back to ancient Greece and Rome. The cultural pursuit of art and learning had diminished in Western Europe after the fall of the Roman Empire. Influenced by the achievements of the ancients, Renaissance writers and architects created new forms and designs that emphasized individual human expression. Painters and sculptors studied ancient Greek and Roman art to explore a new focus on the human form. Philosophers and religious reformers challenged old ideas, as did scientists who strove to unlock the hidden secrets of the natural world. With new knowledge of the skies, navigators sailed the globe, expanding trade and exploring distant lands.

The English Renaissance Elizabeth I encouraged commercial enterprise and the efforts of English navigators, such as Sir Walter Raleigh, who tried to establish a colony in Virginia, and Sir Francis Drake, who sailed around the globe. Profiting particularly from the wool trade, a strong merchant class developed in England, narrowing the

▲ Elizabeth I was crowned at the age of 25. This painting by Italian artist Federico Zuccaro is one of hundreds of portraits made of the queen during her reign.

Sixteenth-Century English Monarchs

King Henry VIII ruled from **1509 to 1547**

King Edward VI ruled from **1547 to 1553**

Queen Mary I ruled from **1553 to 1558**

Queen Elizabeth I ruled from **1558 to 1603**

THE GREAT CHAIN OF BEING

In *Shakespeare Alive*, Joseph Papp, founder of the New York Shakespeare Festival, and his co-author Elizabeth Kirkland explain how Shakespeare and his audience viewed nature and society:

In the heavenly kingdom . . . several levels of archangels and angels spread downwards from God's throne, and each level knew its place. . . . The universe was a hierarchy too, and each planet and star was assigned to a specific position...The animal world was another very stratified society in which each species had its king: the eagle was the king of birds; the whale was the king of fish; and the lion, of course, was king of beasts.

The Great Chain of Being, stretching from the lowliest creature in the natural world all the way up to God, connected these worlds to each other, and the hierarchy of one was mirrored in the others. . . .

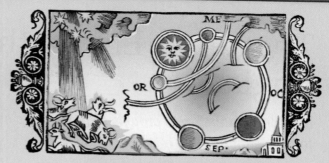

De circulis repentinis, & effectibus cometarum.

Since all living things were linked by the Great Chain of Being, violations of order in society were thought to set off violent disturbances in the heavens or the world of nature. . . .In *Julius Caesar* [Act I, Scene iii], strange and terrible goings-on are reported in Rome as the conspirators hatch an assassination plot against the emperor. . .

---

gap between rich and poor. London, with nearly 200,000 people, became Europe's largest city. It was a bustling if dirty cultural and political capital that attracted newcomers from overseas as well as from the English countryside. In 1588, the English army defeated the Spanish Armada, a fleet of warships sent by King Philip II of Spain to invade England. The victory contributed to Elizabeth's legend as well as to the country's sense of national pride. It also set England firmly on the path to becoming ruler of the seas.

Elizabeth's reign was not only remarkable for its commercial and military successes. Indeed, her court was a center for musicians and artists, both Continental and native born. The philosopher Sir Francis Bacon, who pioneered the informal essay as a literary form, became an unofficial member of the queen's group of advisers. Sir Philip Sidney, a popular courtier and diplomat, wrote a series of love sonnets that were much imitated. The poet Edmund Spenser wrote an adventure-packed epic called *The Faerie Queene* that he dedicated to Queen Elizabeth. The greatest Elizabethan literature, however, was written for the stage. The greatest of these voices were the playwrights Christopher Marlowe, Ben Jonson, and—greatest of them all—William Shakespeare.

The Concern for Stability Elizabeth's father, King Henry VIII, had married six times. He divorced three of his wives and executed two others, including Elizabeth's mother, Anne Boleyn. Queen Mary, Elizabeth's half-sister, infuriated the nation by wedding Phillip II of Spain, who abandoned her soon afterward. Perhaps because of these examples, or perhaps because she worried about sharing power, Elizabeth I never married. By the late 1590s, when Shakespeare wrote *The Tragedy of Julius Caesar*, she was quite advanced in years, and many were concerned about the nation's stability after her death. That concern is echoed in several of Shakespeare's plays, including *Julius Caesar*.

A *sonnet*, from the Italian for "little song," is a fourteen-line poem originally developed in Italy. Sidney's sonnets ushered in a sonnet-writing craze: Edmund Spenser, William Shakespeare, and just about every other Elizabethan poet produced a *sonnet sequence*, or series.

Theater in Elizabethan England

London theaters drew crowds that are large even by today's standards.

During the Elizabethan era, the religious plays of the Middle Ages gave way to English tragedies and comedies modeled on those of ancient Greece and Rome. Scholars at Oxford and Cambridge universities studied and translated the ancient plays into English. The first great Elizabethan playwrights attended those universities, which is why they are sometimes called the University Wits. The most prominent of the Wits, Christopher Marlowe, pioneered the use of blank verse in drama. (For more on blank verse, see p. 915.)

For a time, Elizabethan acting companies still traveled the countryside as their medieval counterparts had done. They performed at festivals, inns, and castles. Gradually, however, the better acting companies acquired noble patrons, or sponsors, and began staging private performances in their patrons' homes. They also gave performances at court, where elaborate masques—productions featuring singing and dancing—were especially popular.

From the Theatre to the Globe England's first public theater opened in 1576. Known simply as the Theatre, it was built by the actor James Burbage, whose company would later attract the young William Shakespeare. Since the performance of plays was banned in London proper, Burbage built the Theatre just outside the city walls. When its lease expired, Richard Burbage, who took charge of the company after his father's death, decided to move operations to Southwark (suth´ ərk), just south across the River Thames (temz) from London. He built a new theater, called the Globe, which opened in 1599. Shakespeare's first play to be performed there was probably *The Tragedy of Julius Caesar*.

Theater Structure England's first theaters were two- to three-story structures with a central space open to the sky. The open space was surrounded by enclosed seating in two or three tiers, or galleries, that faced inward. On the ground floor, a stage projected into an area called the pit. Audience members called groundlings paid a small fee to stand in the pit and watch the play. Wealthier audience members, including aristocrats, occupied the more expensive sheltered gallery seats. Since artificial light was not used, performances generally took place in the afternoon. Audiences were boisterous, cheering and booing loudly. Most theaters could hold up to 3,000 people and drew the largest crowds on holidays.

▲ This image from the late sixteenth century shows the Globe theater as the audience arrives for a performance.

Theater Stagecraft The portion of the building behind the stage was used to mount the production. This area included dressing rooms, storage rooms, and waiting areas from which actors could enter and exit the stage. The second-level gallery directly above the stage served as a performance space. There was no scenery; instead, settings were communicated through dialogue. Special effects were very simple—smoke might accompany a battle scene, for example. Actors playing members of the nobility or royalty wore elegant clothes. These were not really costumes as we think of them today, but simply the same types of clothing worn by high-ranking Elizabethans. Since acting was not considered proper for women, female roles were played by boys of about eleven or twelve, before their voices changed. Given the constraints of the era's stagecraft, the productions were unrealistic by modern standards. However, they were also fast-paced, colorful, and highly entertaining.

The Blackfriars In 1609, Shakespeare's company, the King's Men, began staging plays at an indoor theater called the Blackfriars. They still used the Globe during the summer months. The Blackfriars was one of the first English theaters to include artificial lighting, which enabled nighttime performances. Designed to appeal to wealthy patrons only, the Blackfriars did not have inexpensive seats or a space set aside for groundlings. Indoor theaters of this sort, attracting a fashionable crowd, would become the norm in centuries to come.

> The upper stage could be used for particular scenes, or to stage a scene with actors on two levels. It was also the seating area for musicians, an important part of many productions. Several of Shakespeare's plays, particularly the comedies, contain songs.

▼ Shakespeare's Globe, a reconstruction of the original theater, was completed in 1997 near the site of the original building. The modern convenience of artificial lighting allows for nighttime performances, such as the one shown in the photo.

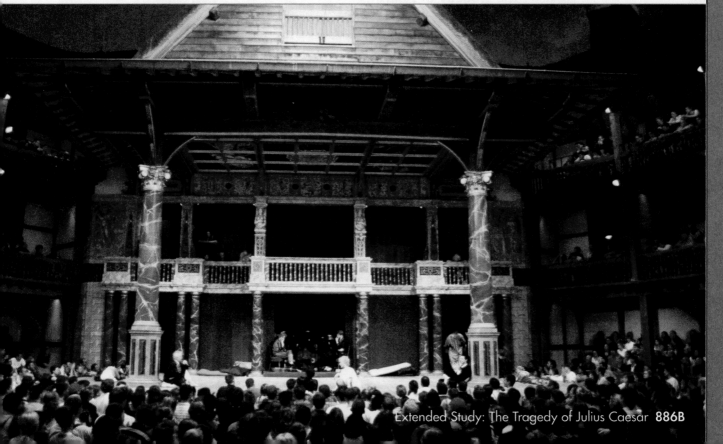

Before You Read

The Tragedy of Julius Caesar, Act I

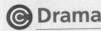 **Drama**

Build your skills and improve your comprehension of drama with this selection.

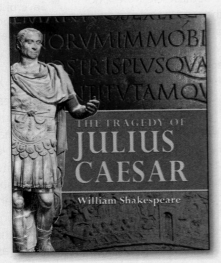

Read **The Tragedy of Julius Caesar** to learn how acts of betrayal and loyalty shaped the history of ancient Rome.

Common Core State Standards

Meet these standards with **The Tragedy of Julius Caesar Act 1** (p. 886)

Reading Literature

3. Analyze how complex characters develop over the course of a text, interact with other characters, and advance the plot or develop the theme (*Literary Analysis: Shakespeare's Tragedies*)

5. Analyze how an author's choices concerning how to structure a text, order events within it, and manipulate time create such effects as mystery, tension, or surprise. (*Literary Analysis: Shakespeare's Tragedies*)

10. Read and comprehend literature, including stories, dramas, and poems, independently and proficiently. (*Reading Skill: Use Text Aids*)

Language

6. Acquire and use accurately general academic and domain-specific words and phrases, sufficient for reading, writing, speaking, and listening at the college and career readiness level; demonstrate independence in gathering vocabulary knowledge when considering a word or phrase important to comprehension or expression. (*Vocabulary: Word Study*)

RL.9-10.7; L.9-10.1.b; W.9-10.1, W.9-10.1.b, W.9-10.1.e, W.9-10.4, W.9-10.6, W.9-10.7; SL.9-10.1, SL.9-10.1.c, SL.9-10.d, SL.9-10.6
These standards are covered on pages 1002–1005. For the full wording of the standards, see the standards chart in the front of your textbook.

Literary Analysis: Shakespeare's Tragedies

Like other tragedies, **Shakespeare's tragedies** are plays that tell of a reversal of fortune, from good to bad, experienced by a man or woman, usually of noble birth. Shakespeare's tragedies also have these distinctive features:

- They are sometimes based on **historical characters.**
- The **hero** often displays a **tragic flaw,** a characteristic that brings about his downfall.
- Shakespeare emphasizes the hero's **internal conflict.**
- Commoners often play key **supporting roles** and provide **comic relief** in humorous scenes that serve as a break from the intense emotions of the play.

Shakespeare's plays are structured in five acts. In his tragedies, the **crisis**—the turning point that determines how the play will end—occurs in Act III. The **climax,** or point of greatest emotional intensity, often occurs in Act V, when the **catastrophe,** or disaster, befalls the hero.

Using the Strategy: Plot Diagram

Record the events of a play on a **plot diagram** such as this one.

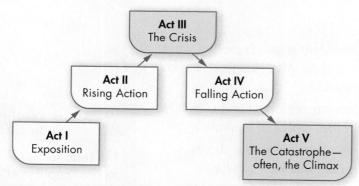

Act III — The Crisis

Act II — Rising Action

Act IV — Falling Action

Act I — Exposition

Act V — The Catastrophe—often, the Climax

Reading Skill: Use Text Aids

Because they were written in the sixteenth and seventeenth centuries, Shakespeare's plays contain unfamiliar language and references. When **reading Shakespearean drama, use text aids:**

- Review the list of *dramatis personae* (the cast of characters).
- Read the background information provided (p. 889).
- As you read the play, consult the notes, called **glosses,** beside the text. These notes define words and explain references.

Making Connections | The Tragedy of Julius Caesar, Act I

To what extent does *experience* determine what we *perceive?*

Writing About the Big Question

In *The Tragedy of Julius Caesar,* Shakespeare reveals the dangers of misinterpreting people and their intentions. Use these sentence starters to develop your ideas about the Big Question.

A person might form an **impression** of someone based on _____.

Our own values and beliefs may also affect the way we see others because _____.

While You Read Look for the opinions different characters have of Caesar, and look for signs that tell you why these characters' views of the leader differ.

Vocabulary

Read each word and its definition. Decide whether you know the word well, know it a little bit, or do not know it at all. After you read, see how your knowledge of each word has increased.

- **replication** (rep´ li kā´ shən) *n.* duplicate; reproduction (p. 894) *His house is an exact replication of mine.* *replica n. replicate v.*

- **servile** (sur´ vəl) *adj.* slavelike; humbly submissive to authority (p. 896) *The butler bowed in a servile manner.* *serve v. servility n. servitude n.*

- **spare** (sper) *adj.* lean; thin (p. 903) *She has a spare frame and is underweight.*

- **infirmity** (in fur´ mə tē) *n.* weakness; physical defect (p. 905) *A doctor cured his infirmity.* *infirm adj. infirmary n. infirmness n.*

- **portentous** (pôr ten´ təs) *adj.* ominous; giving signs of evil to come (p. 908) *The portentous clouds promised snow.* *portent n. portentously adv.*

- **prodigious** (prō dij´ əs) *adj.* of great size or power (p. 909) *The runner made a prodigious effort just before the finish line.* *prodigiously adv.*

Word Study

The **Latin suffix -ile** means "capable of" or "having the quality of."

In the play, a character is worried that he will become **servile** and take on the qualities of a slave if Caesar becomes king.

Background for the Play

A NOBLE ROMAN

William Shakespeare may be the most famous person ever to write in England, but Julius Caesar, Roman general and statesman, was one of the first ever to write about it. In his account of his military exploits in Gaul (modern-day France and Belgium), Caesar describes the island of Britain and its inhabitants. Caesar invaded the island twice, in 55 and 54 B.C., but he did not remain there long. About a century later, however, the Romans returned to make the area of Britain that we now call England an outpost of their empire. The land remained in Roman hands until about A.D. 400, when the empire was collapsing and Roman troops were called home to defend their capital. As part of English history, Julius Caesar and ancient Rome were of particular interest to English writers and audiences.

Rome in Caesar's Day Since about 509 B.C., Rome had been a republic, a society ruled by a democratically elected government. Two public officials called consuls shared governing authority with the Senate and the Assemblies. Members of the Senate were high-born Romans called patricians, while members of the Assemblies were low-born Romans called plebeians (plē bēʹ ənz). By the era of Julius Caesar (100–44 B.C.), Rome controlled a great empire through military expansion. However, the popularity of military leaders threatened the balance of power, and civil war became common. When a general named Pompey tried to make himself sole consul, another popular general, Julius Caesar, defeated him. As Shakespeare's play opens, all of Rome wonders whether Caesar will appoint himself emperor, thus ending the republic.

> From the name Caesar come the German word *kaiser* and the Russian word *czar*, both meaning "emperor." From Julius Caesar's first name comes *July*, our word for the month named in Julius Caesar's honor.

Plutarch, Shakespeare's Source

Shakespeare's source for *The Tragedy of Julius Caesar* was *The Lives of the Noble Grecians and Romans*, Sir Thomas North's 1579 English translation of a book by the Greek philosopher Plutarch (plo͞oʹ tärkʹ). Written late in the first century, Plutarch's *Lives* included literary sketches of Julius Caesar, Marcus Brutus, and Marcus Antonius (Mark Antony), who had lived just over a century earlier. Plutarch researched his information carefully, although he focused less on historical facts than on the personalities of his subjects. Shakespeare based his plot on the events Plutarch describes, but he condensed the timeline and added dramatic elements. For example, Plutarch writes that Antonius gave a funeral oration that stirred the common people to compassion and rage; Shakespeare did not know what Mark Antony actually said, but he gives us the speech as he imagined it.

THE PLAY THROUGH THE CENTURIES

Often cited as Shakespeare's first great tragedy, *The Tragedy of Julius Caesar* has been drawing crowds ever since its premiere at the Globe Theatre in 1599. In 1916, to commemorate the three-hundredth anniversary of Shakespeare's death, a famous outdoor production was staged in the Hollywood hills, starring Douglas Fairbanks, Sr., and Tyrone Power. Students from area high schools reenacted the battle scenes. Just before World War II, Orson Welles produced a controversial adaptation that likened Caesar to Italian dictator Benito Mussolini. In 2005, a production starring Denzel Washington was mounted on Broadway. Ironically, this play about assassination is also one of the few in which Abraham Lincoln's assassin, John Wilkes Booth, performed. In an 1864 production, Booth played the role of Mark Antony.

WILLIAM SHAKESPEARE (1564–1616)

Unlike other famed writers of his time, William Shakespeare was neither a lofty aristocrat nor a university scholar. Nevertheless, he is widely regarded as the greatest writer in the English language.

"What's Past Is Prologue" Shakespeare was born in Stratford-upon-Avon, a market town on the Avon River about seventy-five miles northwest of London. His father, John, was a successful glove maker who served for a time as town mayor. His mother, born Mary Arden, was the daughter of a wealthy farmer who owned the land on which John Shakespeare's father lived. Although the records have been lost, it is believed that Shakespeare attended the Stratford Grammar School, where he would have studied logic, history, Latin grammar, some Greek, and works by the Roman poets Ovid, Horace, and Virgil and Roman playwrights Plautus and Terence. When he left school, he would thus have had a solid foundation in classical literature.

"All the World's a Stage" In 1582, when he was eighteen, Shakespeare married a woman named Anne Hathaway, who was twenty-six. The couple had a daughter, Susanna, in 1583 and twins, Judith and Hamnet, two years later. No one knows what Shakespeare did for the next several years, but in the early 1590s his name began to appear in the world of the London theater. Working first as an actor, Shakespeare soon began writing plays. By 1594, he was part owner and principal playwright of the Lord Chamberlain's Men, the acting company run by the Burbages. As the leading actor in most of Shakespeare's plays, Richard Burbage was also becoming famous. Soon he decided to move the company to the new theater district in Southwark. There, Burbage oversaw the construction of the Globe theater, which was larger than the company's old home in London. With bigger audiences, profits increased for Burbage, Shakespeare, and all the other co-owners.

The Lord Chamberlain's Men was named for its sponsors, first Henry Carey, Lord Hunsdon, and then his son George. Both men served in the high government post of Lord Chamberlain. After Queen Elizabeth I died in 1603, her successor, James I, became the company's patron. In his honor, the company changed its name to the King's Men.

"Parting Is Such Sweet Sorrow" In 1609, the King's Men began to perform year-round, using the Globe theater in summer and the Blackfriars during the colder months. Profits increased even more, and about a year later Shakespeare was able to retire. He returned to his childhood home of Stratford, where he bought the second-largest house in town, invested in land, and continued to write. Shakespeare died in 1616, leaving the bulk of his estate to his elder daughter, Susanna, and a smaller sum to Judith. (Hamnet had died in 1596.)

THERE IS NO DARKNESS BUT IGNORANCE

SHAKESPEARE'S INFLUENCE

Nearly four hundred years after his death, William Shakespeare remains the most influential writer in the English language. His characters are known by name around the world. Filmmakers, painters, novelists, and composers reuse his plots, and phrases he coined still slip into daily conversation. You have probably quoted Shakespeare without even knowing it. Here are just a few examples of expressions made famous in his plays.

All the world's a stage. *(As You Like It)*
Brave new world *(The Tempest)*
Brevity is the soul of wit. *(Hamlet)*
Come full circle *(King Lear)*
Dish fit for the gods *(Julius Caesar)*
A foregone conclusion *(Othello)*
It was Greek to me. *(Julius Caesar)*
Lend me your ears. *(Julius Caesar)*
Loved not wisely, but too well *(Othello)*
More sinned against than sinning *(King Lear)*
Neither a borrower nor a lender be. *(Hamlet)*
Once more unto the breach *(Henry V)*
Parting is such sweet sorrow. *(Romeo and Juliet)*
Strange bedfellows *(The Tempest)*
Throw cold water on it. *(The Merry Wives of Windsor)*
Too much of a good thing *(As You Like It)*
What's past is prologue. *(The Tempest)*

THE AUTHORSHIP QUESTION

Because the documentary evidence of Shakespeare's life is slim and his roots fairly humble, some have questioned whether he really wrote the plays with which he is credited. Shakespeare scholars believe that the surviving texts of the plays were edited and that a few late plays even had co-authors, but nearly all dismiss the notion that Shakespeare did not write them. Nevertheless, the theories persist. Several suggest that Will Shakespeare, actor and Burbage business partner, served as a front for some high-born person (the Earl of Oxford, the Countess of Pembroke, and so on). Some theories center around philosopher and essayist Sir Francis Bacon as the true author—ignoring the fact that Bacon's writing style is completely different from Shakespeare's. The most interesting theories surround the playwright Christopher Marlowe, who was killed in a tavern brawl in 1593. According to these theories, Marlowe used Shakespeare as a front after faking his own death to escape retribution for blasphemous writings or his career as a government spy.

THE TRAGEDY OF

JULIUS CAESAR

William Shakespeare

CHARACTERS

JULIUS CAESAR

OCTAVIUS CAESAR ⎤
MARCUS ANTONIUS ⎥ Triumvirs* After
M. AEMILIUS LEPIDUS ⎦ the Death of
Julius Caesar

CICERO ⎤
PUBLIUS ⎥ Senators
POPILIUS LENA ⎦

MARCUS BRUTUS ⎤
CASSIUS ⎥
CASCA ⎥
TREBONIUS ⎥
LIGARIUS ⎥ Conspirators
DECIUS BRUTUS ⎥ Against Julius
METELLUS CIMBER ⎥ Caesar
CINNA ⎦

FLAVIUS ⎤ Tribunes
MARULLUS ⎦

ARTEMIDORUS OF CNIDOS ⎤ Teacher of Rhetoric

CINNA ⎤ Poets
ANOTHER POET ⎦

LUCILIUS ⎤
TITINIUS ⎥
MESSALA ⎥ Friends to Brutus
YOUNG CATO ⎥ and Cassius
VOLUMNIUS ⎦

VARRO ⎤
CLITUS ⎥
CLAUDIUS ⎥
STRATO ⎥ Servants to
LUCIUS ⎥ Brutus
DARDANIUS ⎦

PINDARUS ⎤ Servant to Cassius
CALPURNIA ⎤ Wife of Caesar
PORTIA ⎤ Wife of Brutus
SOOTHSAYER
SENATORS, CITIZENS, GUARDS,
ATTENDANTS, and so on

Scene: During most of the play, at Rome; afterwards near Sardis, and near Philippi.

*Triumvirs (trī um′ virz) *n.* in ancient Rome, a group of three leaders who shared power equally.

ACT I

Scene i. Rome. A street.

[*Enter* FLAVIUS, MARULLUS, *and certain* COMMONERS[1] *over the stage.*]

    FLAVIUS. Hence! Home, you idle creatures, get you home!
      Is this a holiday? What, know you not,
      Being mechanical,[2] you ought not walk
      Upon a laboring day without the sign
5   Of your profession?[3] Speak, what trade art thou?

    CARPENTER. Why, sir, a carpenter.

    MARULLUS. Where is thy leather apron and thy rule?
      What dost thou with thy best apparel on?
      You, sir, what trade are you?

10 **COBBLER.** Truly, sir, in respect of a fine workman,[4] I am but, as
      you would say, a cobbler.[5]

1. **COMMONERS** (kam′ ən ərz) *n.* people not of the nobility or upper classes.
2. **mechanical** of the working class.
3. **sign/Of your profession** work clothes and tools.
4. **in respect of a fine workman** in relation to a skilled worker.
5. **cobbler** (a pun) "mender of shoes" or "a clumsy, bungling worker."

Reading Check

What fact about the commoners attracts Flavius' attention?

6. **knave** (nāv) *n.* tricky rascal; rogue.

7. **be not out . . . if you be out** be not angry . . . if you have worn-out shoes.

8. **mend you** (a pun) "mend your shoes" or "improve your disposition."

Reading Skill

Use Text Aids

Explain how glosses, or sidenotes, 7 and 8 help you to understand Marullus' reaction in lines 19–20.

9. **awl** (ôl) *n.* small, pointed tool for making holes in leather.

10. **withal** (with ôl´) *adv.* nevertheless (also a pun on "with awl").

11. **neat's leather** leather made from the hides of cattle.

12. **triumph** (trī´ əmf) *n.* procession celebrating the return of a victorious general.

13. **tributaries** (trib´ yōō ter´ ēz) *n.* captives.

14. **Pompey** (päm´ pē) A Roman general and triumvir defeated by Caesar in 48 b.c. and later murdered.

15. **Tiber** (tī´ bər) river that flows through Rome.

16. **concave shores** hollowed-out banks; overhanging banks.

17. **cull out** pick out; select.

Vocabulary

replication (rep´ li kā´ sh ən) *n.* duplicate; reproduction

▶ **Critical Viewing**

Judging from this Roman painting, how might the characters be dressed? Explain. **[Connect]**

MARULLUS. But what trade art thou? Answer me directly.

COBBLER. A trade, sir, that, I hope, I may use with a safe conscience, which is indeed, sir, a mender of bad soles.

15 **FLAVIUS.** What trade, thou knave?[6] Thou naughty knave what trade?

COBBLER. Nay, I beseech you, sir, be not out with me: yet, if you be out,[7] sir, I can mend you.[8]

MARULLUS. What mean'st thou by that? Mend me, thou saucy
20 fellow?

COBBLER. Why, sir, cobble you.

FLAVIUS. Thou art a cobbler, art thou?

COBBLER. Truly, sir, all that I live by is with the awl:[9] I meddle
with no tradesman's matters, nor women's matters;
25 but withal,[10] I am indeed, sir, a surgeon to old shoes:
when they are in great danger, I recover them. As proper
men as ever trod upon neat's leather[11] have gone upon
my handiwork.

FLAVIUS. But wherefore art not in thy shop today?
30 Why dost thou lead these men about the streets?

COBBLER. Truly, sir, to wear out their shoes, to get myself into
more work. But indeed, sir, we make holiday to see Caesar
and to rejoice in his triumph.[12]

MARULLUS. Wherefore rejoice? What conquest brings he home?
35 What tributaries[13] follow him to Rome,
To grace in captive bonds his chariot wheels?
You blocks, you stones, you worse than senseless things!
O you hard hearts, you cruel men of Rome,
Knew you not Pompey?[14] Many a time and oft
40 Have you climbed up to walls and battlements,
To tow'rs and windows, yea, to chimney tops,
Your infants in your arms, and there have sat
The livelong day, with patient expectation,
To see great Pompey pass the streets of Rome.
45 And when you saw his chariot but appear,
Have you not made an universal shout,
That Tiber[15] trembled underneath her banks
To hear the **replication** of your sounds
Made in her concave shores?[16]
50 And do you now put on your best attire?
And do you now cull out[17] a holiday?

And do you now strew flowers in his way
That comes in triumph over Pompey's blood?[18]
Be gone!
55 Run to your houses, fall upon your knees,
Pray to the gods to intermit the plague[19]
That needs must light on this ingratitude.

FLAVIUS. Go, go, good countrymen, and, for this fault,
Assemble all the poor men of your sort;
60 Draw them to Tiber banks and weep your tears
Into the channel, till the lowest stream
Do kiss the most exalted shores of all.[20]

[All the commoners exit.]

18. **Pompey's blood**
Pompey's sons, whom Caesar has just defeated.
19. **intermit the plague** (plāg) stop the calamity or trouble.
20. **the most exalted shores of all** the highest banks.

Reading Check

What does Marullus think about the people celebrating in the streets?

21. whe'r their basest mettle whether the most inferior material of which they are made.

22. Disrobe the images . . . decked with ceremonies strip the statues . . . covered with decorations.

23. feast of Lupercal (lōō′ pər kal) ancient Roman festival celebrated on February 15.

24. vulgar (vul′ gər) *n.* common people.

25. pitch upward flight of a hawk.

Vocabulary
servile (sʉr′ vəl) *adj.* slavelike; humbly submissive to authority

See, whe'r their basest mettle[21] be not moved,
They vanish tongue-tied in their guiltiness.
65 Go you down that way toward the Capitol;
This way will I. Disrobe the images,
If you do find them decked with ceremonies.[22]

MARULLUS. May we do so?
You know it is the feast of Lupercal.[23]

70 **FLAVIUS.** It is no matter; let no images
Be hung with Caesar's trophies. I'll about
And drive away the vulgar[24] from the streets;
So do you too, where you perceive them thick.
These growing feathers plucked from Caesar's wing
75 Will make him fly an ordinary pitch,[25]
Who else would soar above the view of men
And keep us all in servile fearfulness.   [*Exit*]

▼ **Critical Viewing** What do the actors' poses in this movie still imply about the relation between Caesar (left) and Antony (middle)? **[Infer]**

Scene ii. A public place.

[*Enter* CAESAR, ANTONY (*for the course*),[1] CALPURNIA, PORTIA, DECIUS, CICERO, BRUTUS, CASSIUS, CASCA, *a* SOOTHSAYER; *after them,* MARULLUS *and* FLAVIUS.]

CAESAR. Calpurnia!

CASCA. Peace, ho! Caesar speaks.

CAESAR. Calpurnia!

CALPURNIA. Here, my lord.

CAESAR. Stand you directly in Antonius' way
When he doth run his course. Antonius!

5 **ANTONY.** Caesar, my lord?

CAESAR. Forget not in your speed, Antonius,
To touch Calpurnia; for our elders say
The barren, touchèd in this holy chase,
Shake off their sterile curse.[2]

ANTONY. I shall remember:
10 When Caesar says "Do this," it is performed.

CAESAR. Set on, and leave no ceremony out.

SOOTHSAYER. Caesar!

CAESAR. Ha! Who calls?

CASCA. Bid every noise be still; peace yet again!

15 **CAESAR.** Who is it in the press[3] that calls on me?
I hear a tongue, shriller than all the music,
Cry "Caesar." Speak; Caesar is turned to hear.

SOOTHSAYER. Beware the ides of March.[4]

CAESAR. What man is that?

BRUTUS. A soothsayer bids you beware the ides of March.

20 **CAESAR.** Set him before me; let me see his face.

CASSIUS. Fellow, come from the throng; look upon Caesar.

CAESAR. What say'st thou to me now? Speak once again.

SOOTHSAYER. Beware the ides of March.

CAESAR. He is a dreamer, let us leave him. Pass.

[*A trumpet sounds. Exit all but* BRUTUS *and* CASSIUS.]

1. **for the course** ready for the foot race that was part of the Lupercal festivities.

Reading Skill
Use Text Aids
What information about the relationship between Caesar and Calpurnia do you find in the "Characters" list, on page 893?

Literary Analysis
Shakespeare's Tragedies What is Caesar's rank?

2. **barren . . . sterile curse** It was believed that women who were unable to bear children (such as Calpurnia), if touched by a runner during this race, would then be able to bear children.

3. **press** *n.* crowd.

4. **ides of March** in the ancient Roman calendar, March 15.

Reading Check
How does Caesar respond to the soothsayer's warning?

5. **order of the course** the race.

6. **gamesome** (gām´ səm) *adj.* having a liking for sports.

7. **quick spirit** lively disposition.

8. **wont** (wōnt) *adj.* accustomed.

9. **bear . . . hand** treat too harshly and too like a stranger.

10. **if I . . . upon myself** if I have been less open, it is because I am troubled with myself.

11. **passions** *n.* feelings; emotions.

12. **of some difference** in conflict.

13. **Conceptions . . . myself** thoughts that concern only me.

14. **soil** *n.* blemish.

15. **By means . . . buried** because of which I have kept to myself.

16. **cogitations** (käj ə tā´ shənz) *n.* thoughts.

17. **'Tis just** it is true.

18. **lamented** (lə men´ təd) *v.* regretted.

19. **turn . . . shadow** reflect your hidden noble qualities so you could see their image.

20. **the best respect** the best reputation.

21. **this age's yoke** the tyranny of Caesar.

CASSIUS. Will you go see the order of the course?[5]   25

BRUTUS. Not I.

CASSIUS. I pray you do.

BRUTUS. I am not gamesome:[6] I do lack some part
    Of that quick spirit[7] that is in Antony.
    Let me not hinder, Cassius, your desires;   30
    I'll leave you.

CASSIUS. Brutus, I do observe you now of late;
    I have not from your eyes that gentleness
    And show of love as I was wont[8] to have;
    You bear too stubborn and too strange a hand[9]   35
    Over your friend that loves you.

BRUTUS.   Cassius,
    Be not deceived: if I have veiled my look,
    I turn the trouble of my countenance
    Merely upon myself.[10] Vexèd I am
    Of late with passions[11] of some difference,[12]   40
    Conceptions only proper to myself,[13]
    Which give some soil,[14] perhaps, to my behaviors;
    But let not therefore my good friends be grieved
    (Among which number, Cassius, be you one)
    Nor construe any further my neglect   45
    Than that poor Brutus, with himself at war,
    Forgets the shows of love to other men.

CASSIUS. Then, Brutus, I have much mistook your passion;
    By means whereof this breast of mine hath buried[15]
    Thoughts of great value, worthy cogitations.[16]   50
    Tell me, good Brutus, can you see your face?

BRUTUS. No, Cassius; for the eye sees not itself
    But by reflection, by some other things.

CASSIUS. 'Tis just.[17]
    And it is very much lamented,[18] Brutus,   55
    That you have no such mirrors as will turn
    Your hidden worthiness into your eye,
    That you might see your shadow.[19] I have heard
    Where many of the best respect[20] in Rome
    (Except immortal Caesar), speaking of Brutus,   60
    And groaning underneath this age's yoke,[21]
    Have wished that noble Brutus had his eyes.

BRUTUS. Into what dangers would you lead me, Cassius,
   That you would have me seek into myself
65   For that which is not in me?

CASSIUS. Therefore, good Brutus, be prepared to hear;
   And since you know you cannot see yourself
   So well as by reflection, I, your glass
   Will modestly discover to yourself
70   That of yourself which you yet know not of.²²
   And be not jealous on²³ me, gentle Brutus:
   Were I a common laughter,²⁴ or did use
   To stale with ordinary oaths my love
   To every new protester;²⁵ if you know
75   That I do fawn on men and hug them hard,
   And after scandal²⁶ them; or if you know
   That I profess myself in banqueting
   To all the rout,²⁷ then hold me dangerous.

   [Flourish of trumpets and shout]

22. **your glass . . . know not of** your mirror will make known to you without exaggeration the qualities you have of which you are unaware.
23. **be not jealous on** do not be suspicious of.
24. **common laughter** object of ridicule.
25. **To stale . . . new protester** to cheapen my friendship by avowing it to anyone who promises to be my friend.
26. **scandal** *v.* slander; gossip about.
27. **profess myself . . . rout** declare my friendship to the common crowd.

Reading Check

According to Cassius, what does Brutus not realize about himself?

◄ **Critical Viewing**
What does the expression of this actor in the role of Cassius convey about Cassius' intelligence? Explain. **[Infer]**

28. **aught . . . good** anything
to do with the public
welfare.
29. **indifferently** (in difʹ
ər ənt lē) *adv.* without
preference; impartially.
30. **speed** *v.* give good
fortune to.

31. **favor** *n.* face;
appearance.

32. **as lief not be** just as soon
not exist.
33. **such a thing as I myself**
another human being
(Caesar).
34. **chafing with** raging
against.

BRUTUS. What means this shouting? I do fear the people
Choose Caesar for their king.

80 **CASSIUS.**   Ay, do you fear it?
Then must I think you would not have it so.

BRUTUS. I would not, Cassius, yet I love him well.
But wherefore do you hold me here so long?
What is it that you would impart to me?

85 If it be aught toward the general good,[28]
Set honor in one eye and death i' th' other,
And I will look on both indifferently;[29]
For let the gods so speed[30] me, as I love
The name of honor more than I fear death.

90 **CASSIUS.** I know that virtue to be in you, Brutus,
As well as I do know your outward favor.[31]
Well, honor is the subject of my story.
I cannot tell what you and other men
Think of this life, but for my single self,

95 I had as lief not be,[32] as live to be
In awe of such a thing as I myself.[33]
I was born free as Caesar; so were you:
We both have fed as well, and we can both
Endure the winter's cold as well as he:

100 For once, upon a raw and gusty day,
The troubled Tiber chafing with[34] her shores,

LITERATURE IN CONTEXT

History Connection
Roman Society

Brutus and Cassius fear that the common people will
support Caesar in his bid to become emperor. Their fear
reflects tensions in Roman society of the time.

- Poor *plebeians* (commoners), including farmers who
  could no longer compete with wealthy landowners,
  flooded Rome.
- They created a restless mass of unemployed poor.
- Some leaders took their side and won power with
  their support.
- Other leaders took the side of the *patricians*
  (aristocrats) and the wealthy plebeians.
- The conflict between rich and poor led to civil unrest,
  including riots and assassinations.

Connect to the Literature

Which scenes in Act I best reflect the division in Roman society? Explain.

Caesar said to me "Darest thou, Cassius, now
Leap in with me into this angry flood,
And swim to yonder point?" Upon the word,
105 Accout'red[35] as I was, I plungèd in
And bade him follow: so indeed he did.
The torrent roared, and we did buffet[36] it
With lusty sinews,[37] throwing it aside
And stemming it with hearts of controversy.[38]
110 But ere we could arrive the point proposed,
Caesar cried "Help me, Cassius, or I sink!"
I, as Aeneas,[39] our great ancestor,
Did from the flames of Troy upon his shoulder
The old Anchises bear, so from the waves of Tiber
115 Did I the tired Caesar. And this man
Is now become a god, and Cassius is
A wretched creature, and must bend his body
If Caesar carelessly but nod on him.
He had a fever when he was in Spain,
120 And when the fit was on him, I did mark
How he did shake: 'tis true, this god did shake.
His coward lips did from their color fly,[40]
And that same eye whose bend[41] doth awe the world
did lose his[42] luster: I did hear him groan;
125 Ay, and that tongue of his, that bade the Romans
Mark him and write his speeches in their books,
Alas, it cried, "Give me some drink, Titinius,"
As a sick girl. Ye gods! It doth amaze me,
A man of such a feeble temper[43] should
130 So get the start of[44] the majestic world,
And bear the palm[45] alone.   [*Shout. Flourish of trumpets*]

BRUTUS. Another general shout?
I do believe that these applauses are
For some new honors that are heaped on Caesar.

135 **CASSIUS.** Why, man, he doth bestride the narrow world
Like a Colossus,[46] and we petty men
Walk under his huge legs and peep about
To find ourselves dishonorable[47] graves.
Men at some time are masters of their fates:
140 The fault, dear Brutus, is not in our stars,[48]
But in ourselves, that we are underlings.[49]
Brutus and Caesar: what should be in that "Caesar"?
Why should that name be sounded[50] more than yours?
Write them together, yours is as fair a name;

35. **Accout'red** (ə kōō′ trəd) *adj.* dressed in armor.
36. **buffet** (buf′ it) *v.* struggle against.
37. **lusty sinews** (sin′ yōōz) strong muscles.
38. **stemming it . . . controversy** making progress against it with our intense rivalry.
39. **Aeneas** (i nē′ əs) Trojan hero of the poet Virgil's epic poem *Aeneid*, who carried his old father, Anchises, from the burning city of Troy and later founded Rome.
40. **His coward lips . . . fly** color fled from his lips, which were like cowardly soldiers fleeing from a battle.
41. **bend** *n.* glance.
42. **his** *pron.* its.
43. **feeble temper** weak physical constitution.
44. **get the start of** outdistance.
45. **palm** *n.* leaf of a palm tree carried or worn as a symbol of victory; victor's prize.
46. **Colossus** (kə läs′ əs) *n.* gigantic ancient statue of Apollo, a Greek and Roman god, that was set at the entrance to the harbor of Rhodes; ships would sail under its legs.
47. **dishonorable** (dis än′ ər ə bəl) *adj.* shameful (because they will not be of free men).
48. **stars** *n.* destinies. The stars were thought to control people's lives.
49. **underlings** *n.* inferior people.
50. **sounded** *v.* spoken or announced by trumpets.

Reading Check

What has Cassius done to help Caesar in the past?

51. **conjure** (kän´ jər) *v.* summon a spirit by a magic spell.

52. **start** *v.* raise.

53. **great flood** in Greek mythology, a flood that drowned everyone except Deucalion and his wife Pyrrha, who were saved by the god Zeus because of their virtue.

54. **But it was famed with** without the age being made famous by.

55. **Brutus** Lucius Junius Brutus had helped expel the last king of Rome and had helped found the Republic in 509 B.C.

56. **brooked** *v.* put up with.

Reading Skill
Use Text Aids
How does the Background on page 889 along with note 55 help you understand Cassius' appeal to Brutus?

57. **nothing jealous** not at all doubting.

58. **work me to** persuade me of.

59. **aim** *n.* idea.

60. **meet** *adj.* fit; suitable.

61. **chew upon** think about.

Literary Analysis
Shakespeare's Tragedies What tragic flaw in Brutus' character might lines 172–175 reveal?

62. **train** *n.* attendants.

63. **chidden train** scolded attendants.

145　Sound them, it doth become the mouth as well;
　　Weigh them, it is as heavy; conjure[51] with 'em,
　　"Brutus" will start[52] a spirit as soon as "Caesar."
　　Now, in the names of all the gods at once,
　　Upon what meat doth this our Caesar feed,
150　That he is grown so great? Age, thou art shamed!
　　Rome, thou hast lost the breed of noble bloods!
　　When went there by an age, since the great flood,[53]
　　But it was famed with[54] more than with one man?
　　When could they say (till now) that talked of Rome,
155　That her wide walks encompassed but one man?
　　Now is it Rome indeed, and room enough,
　　When there is in it but one only man.
　　O, you and I have heard our fathers say,
　　There was a Brutus[55] once that would have brooked[56]
160　Th' eternal devil to keep his state in Rome
　　As easily as a king.

　　BRUTUS. That you do love me, I am nothing jealous;[57]
　　What you would work me to,[58] I have some aim;[59]
　　How I have thought of this, and of these times,
165　I shall recount hereafter. For this present,
　　I would not so (with love I might entreat you)
　　Be any further moved. What you have said
　　I will consider; what you have to say
　　I will with patience hear, and find a time
170　Both meet[60] to hear and answer such high things.
　　Till then, my noble friend, chew upon[61] this:
　　Brutus had rather be a villager
　　Than to repute himself a son of Rome
　　Under these hard conditions as this time
　　Is like to lay upon us.

175　**CASSIUS.**　　　　　　　　I am glad
　　That my weak words have struck but thus much show
　　Of fire from Brutus.

[*Enter* CAESAR *and his* TRAIN.][62]

　　BRUTUS. The games are done, and Caesar is returning.

　　CASSIUS. As they pass by, pluck Casca by the sleeve,
180　And he will (after his sour fashion) tell you
　　What hath proceeded worthy note today.

　　BRUTUS. I will do so. But look you, Cassius,
　　The angry spot doth glow on Caesar's brow,
　　And all the rest look like a chidden train:[63]

185   Calpurnia's cheek is pale, and Cicero
Looks with such ferret[64] and such fiery eyes
As we have seen him in the Capitol,
Being crossed in conference[65] by some senators.

CASSIUS. Casca will tell us what the matter is.

190 **CAESAR.** Antonius.

ANTONY. Caesar?

CAESAR. Let me have men about me that are fat,
Sleek-headed men, and such as sleep a-nights.
Yond Cassius has a lean and hungry look;
195   He thinks too much: such men are dangerous.

ANTONY. Fear him not, Caesar, he's not dangerous;
He is a noble Roman, and well given.[66]

CAESAR. Would he were fatter! But I fear him not.
Yet if my name were liable to fear,
200   I do not know the man I should avoid
So soon as that spare Cassius. He reads much,
He is a great observer, and he looks
quite through the deeds of men.[67] He loves no plays,
As thou dost, Antony; he hears no music;
205   Seldom he smiles, and smiles in such a sort[68]
As if he mocked himself, and scorned his spirit
That could be moved to smile at anything.
Such men as he be never at heart's ease
Whiles they behold a greater than themselves,
210   And therefore are they very dangerous.
I rather tell thee what is to be feared
Than what I fear; for always I am Caesar.
Come on my right hand, for this ear is deaf,
And tell me truly what thou think'st of him.

             [*A trumpet sounds.* CAESAR *and his* TRAIN *exit.*]

215 **CASCA.** You pulled me by the cloak; would you speak with me?

BRUTUS. Ay, Casca; tell us what hath chanced[69] today,
That Caesar looks so sad.

CASCA. Why, you were with him, were you not?

BRUTUS. I should not then ask Casca what had chanced.

220 **CASCA.** Why, there was a crown offered him; and being
offered him, he put it by[70] with the back of his hand, thus;
and then the people fell a-shouting.

---

64. ferret (fer´ it) *n.* small animal, like a weasel, with reddish eyes.
65. crossed in conference opposed in debate.
66. well given well disposed.
67. looks . . . deeds of men sees through people's actions to their motives.

Vocabulary
spare (sper) *adj.* lean; thin

68. sort way.

69. hath chanced has happened.
70. put it by pushed it away.

Reading Check

Why does Cassius compare Brutus and Caesar?

71. **marry** *interjection* truly.

BRUTUS. What was the second noise for?

CASCA. Why, for that too.

225 **CASSIUS.** They shouted thrice; what was the last cry for?

CASCA. Why, for that too.

BRUTUS. Was the crown offered him thrice?

CASCA. Ay, marry,[71] was't, and he put it by thrice, every time gentler than other; and at every putting-by mine honest
230 neighbors shouted.

CASSIUS. Who offered him the crown?

CASCA. Why, Antony.

BRUTUS. Tell us the manner of it, gentle Casca.

CASCA. I can as well be hanged as tell the manner of it:
235 it was mere foolery; I did not mark it. I saw Mark Antony offer him a crown—yet 'twas not a crown neither, 'twas one of these coronets[72]—and, as I told you, he put it by once; but for all that, to my thinking, he would fain[73] have had it. Then he offered it to him again; then he
240 put it by again; but to my thinking, he was very loath to lay his fingers off it. And then he offered it the third time. He put it the third time by; and still[74] as he refused it, the rabblement[75] hooted, and clapped their chopt[76] hands, and threw up their sweaty
245 nightcaps,[77] and uttered such a deal of stinking breath because Caesar refused the crown, that it had, almost, choked Caesar; for he swounded[78] and fell down at it. And for mine own part, I durst not laugh, for fear of opening my lips
250 and receiving the bad air.

72. **coronets** (kôr´ ə nets´) *n.* ornamental bands used as crowns.
73. **fain** (fān) *adv.* gladly.

74. **still** *adv.* every time.
75. **rabblement** (rab´ əl mənt) *n.* mob.
76. **chopt** (chäpt) *adj.* chapped.
77. **nightcaps** *n.* workers' caps.
78. **swounded** *v.* swooned; fainted.

CASSIUS. But, soft,[79] I pray you; what, did Caesar swound?

79. **soft** *adv.* slowly.

CASCA. He fell down in the market place, and foamed at mouth, and was speechless.

BRUTUS. 'Tis very like he hath the falling-sickness.[80]

80. **falling-sickness** *n.* epilepsy.
81. **we have the falling-sickness** We are losing power and falling in status under Caesar's rule.

255 **CASSIUS.** No, Caesar hath it not; but you, and I,
And honest Casca, we have the falling-sickness.[81]

82. **tag-rag people** the rabble; lower-class people.
83. **use** *v.* are accustomed.

CASCA. I know not what you mean by that, but I am sure Caesar fell down. If the tag-rag people[82] did not clap him and hiss him, according as he pleased and displeased
260 them, as they use[83] to do the players in the theater, I am no true man.

BRUTUS. What said he when he came unto himself?

CASCA. Marry, before he fell down, when he perceived the common herd was glad he refused the crown, he plucked me 265 ope his doublet[84] and offered them his throat to cut. An I had been a man of any occupation,[85] if I would not have taken him at a word, I would I might go to hell among the rogues. And so he fell. When he came to himself again, he said, if he had done or said anything amiss, he desired their worships 270 to think it was his infirmity.[86] Three or four wenches,[87] where I stood, cried "Alas, good soul!" and forgave him with all their hearts; but there's no heed to be taken of them; if Caesar had stabbed their mothers, they would have done no less.

275 **BRUTUS.** And after that, he came thus sad away?

CASCA. Ay.

CASSIUS. Did Cicero say anything?

CASCA. Ay, he spoke Greek.

CASSIUS. To what effect?

280 **CASCA.** Nay, an I tell you that, I'll ne'er look you i' th' face again. But those that understood him smiled at one another and shook their heads; but for mine own part, it was Greek to me. I could tell you more news too: Marullus and Flavius, for 285 pulling scarfs off Caesar's images, are put to silence.[88] Fare you well. There was more foolery yet, if I could remember it.

CASSIUS. Will you sup with me tonight, Casca?

CASCA. No, I am promised forth.[89]

290 **CASSIUS.** Will you dine with me tomorrow?

CASCA. Ay, if I be alive, and your mind hold,[90] and your dinner worth the eating.

CASSIUS. Good; I will expect you.

CASCA. Do so. Farewell, both. [*Exit*]

295 **BRUTUS.** What a blunt[91] fellow is this grown to be! He was quick mettle[92] when he went to school.

CASSIUS. So is he now in execution[93] Of any bold or noble enterprise, However he puts on this tardy form.[94]

84. **doublet** (dub´ lit) *n.* close-fitting jacket.
85. **An I . . . occupation** if I had been a workingman (or a man of action).
86. **infirmity** *n.* Caesar's illness is epilepsy.
87. **wenches** (wench´ ez) *n.* young women.

Vocabulary
infirmity (in fur´ mə tē) *n.* weakness; physical defect

88. **for pulling . . . silence** For taking decorations off statues of Caesar, they have been silenced (by being forbidden to take part in public affairs, exiled, or perhaps even executed).
89. **am promised forth** have a previous engagement.
90. **hold** *v.* does not change.
91. **blunt** *adj.* dull; not sharp.
92. **quick mettle** of a lively disposition.
93. **execution** *n.* carrying out; doing.
94. **tardy form** sluggish appearance.

Reading Check

How does Caesar respond when he is offered the crown?

95. **wit** *n.* intelligence.
96. **disgest** *v.* digest.
97. **the world** present state of affairs.
98. **wrought . . . is disposed** shaped (like iron) in a way different from its usual form.

300   This rudeness is a sauce to his good wit,[95]
Which gives men stomach to disgest[96] his words
With better appetite.

BRUTUS. And so it is. For this time I will leave you.
Tomorrow, if you please to speak with me,
305   I will come home to you; or if you will,
Come home to me, and I will wait for you.

CASSIUS. I will do so. Till then, think of the world.[97]

                                 [*Exit* BRUTUS.]

   Well, Brutus, thou art noble; yet I see
Thy honorable mettle may be wrought
310   From that it is disposed;[98] therefore it is meet
That noble minds keep ever with their likes;
For who so firm that cannot be seduced?

▼ **Critical Viewing**
How does this idyllic scene of Rome contrast with the events taking place in the play? **[Contrast]**

Caesar doth bear me hard,[99] but he loves Brutus.
If I were Brutus now, and he were Cassius,
315 He should not humor me.[100] I will this night,
In several hands,[101] in at his windows throw,
As if they came from several citizens,
Writings, all tending to the great opinion[102]
That Rome holds of his name; wherein obscurely
320 Caesar's ambition shall be glancèd at.[103]
And after this, let Caesar seat him sure;[104]
For we will shake him, or worse days endure. [*Exit*]

Scene iii. A street.

[*Thunder and lightning. Enter from opposite sides,* CASCA *and* CICERO.]

CICERO. Good even, Casca; brought you Caesar home?
Why are you breathless? And why stare you so?

CASCA. Are not you moved, when all the sway of earth[1]
Shakes like a thing unfirm? O Cicero,
5 I have seen tempests, when the scolding winds
Have rived[2] the knotty oaks, and I have seen
Th' ambitious ocean swell and rage and foam,
To be exalted with[3] the threat'ning clouds;
But never till tonight, never till now,
10 Did I go through a tempest dropping fire.
Either there is a civil strife in heaven,
Or else the world, too saucy[4] with the gods,
Incenses[5] them to send destruction.

CICERO. Why, saw you anything more wonderful?

15 CASCA. A common slave—you know him well by sight—
Held up his left hand, which did flame and burn
Like twenty torches joined, and yet his hand,
Not sensible of[6] fire, remained unscorched.
Besides—I ha' not since put up my sword—
20 Against[7] the Capitol I met a lion,
Who glazed[8] upon me and went surly by
Without annoying me. And there were drawn
Upon a heap[9] a hundred ghastly[10] women,
Transformèd with their fear, who swore they saw
25 Men, all in fire, walk up and down the streets.
And yesterday the bird of night[11] did sit
Even at noonday upon the market place,
Hooting and shrieking. When these prodigies[12]
Do so conjointly meet,[13] let not men say,
30 "These are their reasons, they are natural,"

99. bear me hard dislike me.
100. humor me win me over.
101. several hands different handwritings.
102. tending to the great opinion pointing out the great respect.
103. glancèd at hinted at.
104. seat him sure establish himself securely.

1. all the sway of earth the stable order of Earth.
2. Have rived have split.
3. exalted with lifted up to.
4. saucy *adj.* rude; impudent.
5. Incenses *v.* enrages.

Reading Skill
Use Text Aids
According to the information on page 889, why would Shakespeare's audience have connected these unnatural events with the political situation in the play?

6. sensible of sensitive to.
7. Against *prep.* opposite or near.
8. glazed *v.* stared.
9. were drawn . . . heap huddled together.
10. ghastly (gast´ lē) *adj.* ghostlike; pale.
11. bird of night owl.
12. prodigies (präd´ ə jēz) *n.* extraordinary happenings.
13. conjointly meet occur at the same time and place.

Reading Check

After his conversation with Brutus, what does Cassius say he will do?

14. **portentous** (pôr tenʹ təs) **. . . upon** bad omens for the country they point to.
15. **strange-disposèd** abnormal.
16. **construe . . . fashion** explain in their own way.
17. **Clean from the purpose** different from the real meaning.

18. **unbracèd** *adj.* with jacket open.
19. **thunder-stone** *n.* thunderbolt.
20. **cross** *adj.* zigzag.
21. **part** *n.* role.
22. **by tokens . . . to astonish** by portentous signs send such awful announcements to frighten and stun.
23. **want** *v.* lack.
24. **put on . . . in wonder** show fear and are amazed.
25. **from quality and kind** acting contrary to their nature.
26. **calculate** *v.* make predictions.

For I believe they are portentous things
Unto the climate that they point upon.[14]

CICERO. Indeed, it is a strange-disposèd[15] time:
But men may construe things after their fashion,[16]
Clean from the purpose[17] of the things themselves.
Comes Caesar to the Capitol tomorrow?

CASCA. He doth; for he did bid Antonius
Send word to you he would be there tomorrow.

CICERO. Good night then, Casca; this disturbèd sky
Is not to walk in.

CASCA.   Farewell, Cicero.   [*Exit* CICERO.]

[*Enter* CASSIUS.]

CASSIUS. Who's there?

CASCA.   A Roman.

CASSIUS.   Casca, by your voice.

CASCA. Your ear is good. Cassius, what night is this?

CASSIUS. A very pleasing night to honest men.

CASCA. Who ever knew the heavens menace so?

CASSIUS. Those that have known the earth so full of faults.
For my part, I have walked about the streets,
Submitting me unto the perilous night,
And thus unbracèd,[18] Casca, as you see,
Have bared my bosom to the thunder-stone;[19]
And when the cross[20] blue lightning seemed to open
The breast of heaven, I did present myself
Even in the aim and very flash of it.

CASCA. But wherefore did you so much tempt the heavens?
It is the part[21] of men to fear and tremble
When the most mighty gods by tokens send
Such dreadful heralds to astonish[22] us.

CASSIUS. You are dull, Casca, and those sparks of life
That should be in a Roman you do want,[23]
Or else you use not. You look pale, and gaze,
And put on fear, and cast yourself in wonder,[24]
To see the strange impatience of the heavens;
But if you would consider the true cause
Why all these fires, why all these gliding ghosts,
Why birds and beasts from quality and kind,[25]
Why old men, fools, and children calculate,[26]

35

40

45

50

55

60

65

Why all these things change from their ordinance,[27]
Their natures and preformèd faculties,
To monstrous quality,[28] why, you shall find
That heaven hath infused them with these spirits[29]

70 To make them instruments of fear and warning
Unto some monstrous state.[30]
Now could I, Casca, name to thee a man
Most like this dreadful night,
That thunders, lightens, opens graves, and roars

75 As doth the lion in the Capitol;
A man no mightier than thyself, or me,
In personal action, yet prodigious grown
And fearful,[31] as these strange eruptions are.

CASCA. 'Tis Caesar that you mean, is it not, Cassius?

80 **CASSIUS.** Let it be who it is; for Romans now
Have thews[32] and limbs like to their ancestors;
But, woe the while![33] Our fathers' minds are dead,
And we are governed with our mothers' spirits;
Our yoke and sufferance[34] show us womanish.

85 **CASCA.** Indeed, they say the senators tomorrow
Mean to establish Caesar as a king;
And he shall wear his crown by sea and land,
In every place save here in Italy.

CASSIUS. I know where I will wear this dagger then;
90 Cassius from bondage will deliver[35] Cassius.
Therein,[36] ye gods, you make the weak most strong;
Therein, ye gods, you tyrants do defeat.
Nor stony tower, nor walls of beaten brass,
Nor airless dungeon, nor strong links of iron,

95 Can be retentive to[37] the strength of spirit;
But life, being weary of these worldly bars,
Never lacks power to dismiss itself.
If I know this, know all the world besides,
That part of tyranny that I do bear
I can shake off at pleasure.   [*Thunder still*]

100 **CASCA.**   So can I;
So every bondman in his own hand bears
The power to cancel his captivity.

CASSIUS. And why should Caesar be a tyrant then?
Poor man, I know he would not be a wolf
105 But that he sees the Romans are but sheep;
He were no lion, were not Romans hinds.[38]

---

27. **ordinance** (ôrd´ 'n əns) *n.* regular behavior.
28. **preformèd . . . quality** established function to unnatural behavior.
29. **infused . . . spirits** filled them with supernatural powers.
30. **monstrous state** abnormal condition of government.

Vocabulary
prodigious (prō dij´ əs) *adj.* of great size or power

31. **fearful** *adj.* causing fear.
32. **thews** (thyo͞oz) *n.* muscles or sinews; strength.
33. **woe the while** alas for the times.
34. **yoke and sufferance** slavery and meek acceptance of it.
35. **will deliver** will set free.
36. **Therein** (ther in´) *adv.* in that way (that is, by giving the weak the power to end their own lives).

Literary Analysis
Shakespeare's Tragedies What main conflict has Shakespeare established in Act I?

37. **be retentive to** confine.
38. **hinds** (hīndz) *n.* female deer; peasants; servants.

Reading Check
What connection does Cassius make between the night's strange events and Caesar's rise to power?

39. **offal** (ôf′ əl) *n.* refuse; waste.

40. **base matter** inferior or low material; foundation materials.

41. **speak this . . . answer must be made** say this before a willing servant of Caesar's; then I know I will have to answer for my words.

42. **fleering tell-tale** sneering tattletale.

43. **factious** (fak′ shəs) *adj.* active in forming a faction or a political party.

44. **redress** (ri dres′) **of all these griefs** setting right all these grievances.

45. **undergo** (un′ dər gō′) *v.* undertake.

46. **consequence** (kän′ sə kwens′) *n.* importance.

47. **by this** by this time.

48. **Pompey's porch** portico of Pompey's Theater.

49. **complexion of the element** condition of the sky; weather.

50. **In favor's like** in appearance is like.

51. **close** *adj.* hidden.

52. **gait** (gāt) *n.* style of walking.

53. **incorporate** (in kôr′ pə rit) / **To our attempts** part of our efforts.

54. **stayed for** waited for.

55. **on't** (ônt) contraction of it.

56. **praetor's** (prē′ tərz) **chair** Roman magistrate's (or judge's) chair.

Those that with haste will make a mighty fire
Begin it with weak straws. What trash is Rome,
What rubbish and what offal,[39] when it serves
110 For the base matter[40] to illuminate
So vile a thing as Caesar! But, O grief,
Where hast thou led me? I, perhaps, speak this
Before a willing bondman; then I know
My answer must be made.[41] But I am armed,
115 And dangers are to me indifferent.

CASCA. You speak to Casca, and to such a man
That is no fleering tell-tale.[42] Hold, my hand.
Be factious[43] for redress of all these griefs,[44]
And I will set this foot of mine as far
As who goes farthest.   [*They clasp hands.*]

120 **CASSIUS.**   There's a bargain made.
Now know you, Casca, I have moved already
Some certain of the noblest-minded Romans
To undergo[45] with me an enterprise
Of honorable dangerous consequence;[46]
125 And I do know, by this[47] they stay for me
In Pompey's porch;[48] for now, this fearful night,
There is no stir or walking in the streets,
And the complexion of the element[49]
In favor's like[50] the work we have in hand,
130 Most bloody, fiery, and most terrible.

[*Enter* CINNA.]

CASCA. Stand close[51] awhile, for here comes one in haste.

CASSIUS. 'Tis Cinna; I do know him by his gait;[52]
He is a friend. Cinna, where haste you so?

CINNA. To find out you. Who's that? Metellus Cimber?

135 **CASSIUS.** No, it is Casca, one incorporate
To our attempts.[53] Am I not stayed for,[54] Cinna?

CINNA. I am glad on't.[55] What a fearful night is this!
There's two or three of us have seen strange sights.

CASSIUS. Am I not stayed for? Tell me.

CINNA.   Yes, you are.
140 O Cassius, if you could
But win the noble Brutus to our party—

CASSIUS. Be you content. Good Cinna, take this paper,
And look you lay it in the praetor's chair,[56]

Reading Skill
Use Text Aids Why might you need to consult glosses 56 and 57 to understand Cassius' plan?

▲ **Critical Viewing** Which details in this relief sculpture indicate the respect and awe with which Romans regarded their leaders? **[Interpret]**

57. **Where . . . find it** where only Brutus (as the chief magistrate) will find it.
58. **old Brutus'** Junius Brutus, the founder of the Roman Republic.
59. **Repair** *v.* go.
60. **hie** (hī) *v.* hurry.

Where Brutus may but find it;[57] and throw this
145   In at his window: set this up with wax
Upon old Brutus'[58] statue. All this done,
Repair[59] to Pompey's porch, where you shall find us.
Is Decius Brutus and Trebonius there?

CINNA. All but Metellus Cimber, and he's gone
150   To seek you at your house. Well, I will hie,[60]
And so bestow these papers as you bade me.

CASSIUS. That done, repair to Pompey's Theater.   [*Exit* CINNA.]
Come, Casca, you and I will yet ere day
See Brutus at his house; three parts of him
155   Is ours already, and the man entire
Upon the next encounter yields him ours.

61. **offense** (ə fens´) *n.* crime.
62. **countenance** (koun´ tə nəns) *n.* support.
63. **alchemy** (al´ kə mē) *n.* an early form of chemistry in which the goal was to change metals of little value into gold.
64. **conceited** (kən sēt´ id) *v.* understood.

CASCA. O, he sits high in all the people's hearts;
And that which would appear offense[61] in us,
His countenance,[62] like richest alchemy,[63]
160   Will change to virtue and to worthiness.

CASSIUS. Him, and his worth, and our great need of him,
You have right well conceited.[64] Let us go,
For it is after midnight, and ere day
We will awake him and be sure of him.   [*Exit*]

Critical Thinking

Cite textual evidence to support your responses.

© 1. Key Ideas and Details (a) At the opening of the play, how do common Romans such as the Cobbler react to Caesar's return? **(b) Interpret:** What do noble Romans such as Flavius and Cassius fear or resent about Caesar's success? Support your answer with quotations.

© 2. Key Ideas and Details (a) What warning does the soothsayer give Caesar? **(b) Infer:** What does Caesar's reaction show about him?

© 3. Integration of Knowledge and Ideas Hypothesize: Why is it important for Cassius and his co-conspirators to win Brutus' support for their plan against Caesar?

© 4. Integration of Knowledge and Ideas (a) Analyze Brutus' values as expressed in the speech in Scene ii, lines 82–89. **(b)** Then, analyze Cassius' speech appealing to those values in lines 135–161 of Scene ii. **(c)** How do these speeches help you understand how each character feels about Caesar? *[Connect to the Big Question: To what extent does experience determine what we perceive?]*

After You Read | The Tragedy of Julius Caesar, Act I

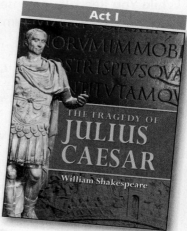

Literary Analysis: Shakespeare's Tragedies

© **1. Key Ideas and Details** Summarize what you learned in Act I of this **Shakespearean tragedy.**

© **2. Craft and Structure** Given what you have read so far, explain what **tragic flaw** in Brutus' character might lead him to disaster.

Reading Skill: Use Text Aids

3. The **text aids** before the play include a background section on ancient Rome (p. 889). Using a chart like the one shown, identify two passages in Act I that are clarified by this background information. Explain your choices.

	Location of passage	Text aids	What text aids add to understanding
Passage 1			
Passage 2			

4. In Scene ii, how do glosses 73 and 74 help readers understand what happened in the marketplace?

Vocabulary

© **Acquisition and Use** Replace the italicized word with an **antonym,** a word that is opposite in meaning. Then, decide which sentence makes better sense. Explain your answers.

1. The fine-art collector bought the *replication.*

2. His *servile* behavior makes me uncomfortable.

3. This suit was not tailored for someone with a *spare* build.

4. His *infirmity* is due to chance, not to the way he lives.

5. I found the unlocked door *portentous.*

6. She has a *prodigious* appetite.

Word Study Use the context of the sentences and what you know about the **Latin suffix -ile** to explain your answer to each question.

1. If all efforts to find your missing keys are *futile,* should you keep looking?

2. If a person's behavior is *infantile,* is he or she acting like an adult?

Word Study

The **Latin suffix -ile** means "capable of" or "having the quality of."

Apply It Explain how the suffix -ile contributes to the meanings of these words. Consult a dictionary if necessary.

facile
mobile
projectile

Before You Read

The Tragedy of Julius Caesar, Act II

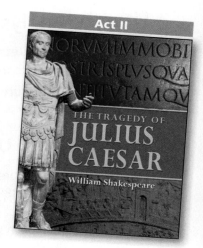

While You Read In response to the state of unrest in Rome, Calpurnia has a cryptic dream. Look for different characters' perceptions of her dream.

Common Core State Standards

Meet these standards with *The Tragedy of Julius Caesar*, **Act II** (p. 916).

Reading Literature
2. Determine a theme or central idea of a text. *(Reading Skill: Paraphrase)*
5. Analyze how an author's choices concerning how to structure a text, order events within it, and manipulate time create such effects as mystery, tension, or surprise. *(Literary Analysis: Blank Verse)*

Integrated Language Skills:
Pages 1002–1005

Writing
1. Write arguments to support claims. *(Writing: Editorial)*
4. Produce clear and coherent writing. *(Writing: Obituary; Research and Technology: Advertising Poster)*

6. Use technology, including the Internet. *(Research and Technology: Multimedia Presentation)*
7. Conduct short research projects. *(Research and Technology: Women's History Report)*

Speaking and Listening
1. Initiate and participate effectively in discussions. *(Speaking and Listening: Group Screening)*
6. Adapt speech to a variety of contexts and tasks. *(Speaking and Listening: Dramatic Reading)*

Vocabulary

Read each word and its definition. Decide whether you know the word well, know it a little bit, or do not know it at all. After you read, see how your knowledge of each word has increased.

- **augmented** (ôg ment´ id) *adj.* made greater; enhanced (p. 917)
  Her augmented library has hundreds more books than mine.
  augment *v.* augmentation *n.*

- **entreated** (en trēt´ id) *v.* begged; pleaded with (p. 919)
  He entreated her for mercy. entreatingly adv. entreaty n.

- **insurrection** (in´ sə rek´ shən) *n.* rebellion (p. 919) *The insurrection against the government started in the town square.*
  insurgence n. insurgent adj.

- **resolution** (rez´ ə lōō´ shən) *n.* strong determination; a plan or decision (p. 920) *Lou stuck to his plans with firm resolution.*
  resolute adj. resolutely adv. resolve n.

- **wrathfully** (rath´ fəl lē) *adv.* with intense anger (p. 922) *She shook her fist wrathfully at the tailgating driver. wrath n. wrathful adj.*

- **imminent** (im´ ə nənt) *adj.* about to happen (p. 931) *The lightning flash meant thunder was imminent. imminence n. imminently adv.*

Word Study

The **Latin prefix en-** means "in, into, or within."

In the play, a character wonders if he is being **entreated,** or asked in earnest, to act for the good of his country.

Literary Analysis: Blank Verse

The Tragedy of Julius Caesar is written in blank verse. **Blank verse** is a poetic form characterized by unrhymed lines written in iambic pentameter.

- An **iamb** is a *foot* (unit of rhythm) in which an unstressed syllable is followed by a stressed syllable: da-DUH.
- **Pentameter** refers to a rhythmic pattern in which each line has five *feet*.
- In **iambic pentameter,** the typical line has five iambs, or five stressed syllables each preceded by an unstressed syllable: And THERE | fore THINK | him AS | a SER | pent's EGG

Shakespeare's "upper-class" characters speak in iambic pentameter. Lower-born characters speak in prose. Sometimes, Shakespeare breaks the rhythmic pattern in a line to add contrast or emphasis. As you read, analyze the effect Shakespeare creates by having certain characters speak in blank verse.

Reading Skill: Paraphrase

Paraphrasing a line or passage from a work means restating its meaning in your own words. To paraphrase when **reading Shakespearean drama,** follow these steps:

- Look for punctuation showing where sentences end.
- For each sentence, identify the subject and verb and put them into the usual order. You may also need to add helping verbs.

Using the Strategy: Paraphrase Diagram

As you read, record details on a **paraphrase diagram** like the one shown.

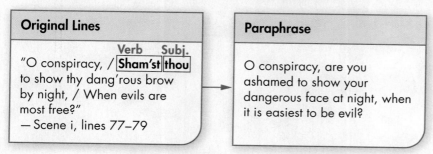

Original Lines	Paraphrase
Verb **Subj.** "O conspiracy, / Sham'st thou to show thy dang'rous brow by night, / When evils are most free?" — Scene i, lines 77–79	O conspiracy, are you ashamed to show your dangerous face at night, when it is easiest to be evil?

REVIEW AND ANTICIPATE

In Act I, as Caesar returns victorious from war, the common people are calling for him to be crowned emperor. Fearful of Caesar's ambitions and unwilling to surrender their own power, Cassius and others conspire against Caesar. Cassius attempts to win the support of Brutus, a highly respected Roman. Although Brutus is a friend of Caesar's, he worries about Caesar's ambition. In the meantime, Caesar receives a warning to "beware the ides of March." Act II opens on the evening before that fateful day. As you read, note how Caesar's own pride leads him to ignore danger. Note also the contrasts that emerge between Brutus and the conspirators.

◀ **Critical Viewing** What details in this painting of Caesar and his wife foreshadow tragedy? **[Interpret]**

ACT II

Scene i. Rome.

[*Enter* BRUTUS *in his orchard.*]

BRUTUS. What, Lucius, ho!
    I cannot, by the progress of the stars,
    Give guess how near to day. Lucius, I say!
    I would it were my fault to sleep so soundly.
5   When, Lucius, when? Awake, I say! What, Lucius!

[*Enter* LUCIUS.]

LUCIUS. Called you, my lord?

BRUTUS. Get me a taper in my study, Lucius.
    When it is lighted, come and call me here.

LUCIUS. I will, my lord.   [*Exit*]

10 **BRUTUS.** It must be by his death; and for my part,
    I know no personal cause to spurn at[1] him,
    But for the general.[2] He would be crowned.
    How that might change his nature, there's the question.
    It is the bright day that brings forth the adder,[3]
15   And that craves[4] wary walking. Crown him that,
    And then I grant we put a sting in him
    That at his will he may do danger with.
    Th' abuse of greatness is when it disjoins
    Remorse from power;[5] and, to speak truth of Caesar,
20   I have not known when his affections swayed[6]
    More than his reason. But 'tis a common proof[7]
    That lowliness[8] is young ambition's ladder,
    Whereto the climber upward turns his face;
    But when he once attains the upmost round,
25   He then unto the ladder turns his back,
    Looks in the clouds, scorning the base degrees[9]
    By which he did ascend. So Caesar may;
    Then lest he may, prevent.[10] And, since the quarrel
    Will bear no color for the thing he is,[11]
30   Fashion it[12] thus: that what he is, augmented
    Would run to these and these extremities;[13]
    And therefore think him as a serpent's egg
    Which hatched, would as his kind grow mischievous,
    And kill him in the shell.

[*Enter* LUCIUS.]

Literary Analysis

Blank Verse Explain which character, Brutus or Lucius, speaks in blank verse and why.

---

1. **spurn at** kick against; rebel against.
2. **the general** the public good.
3. **adder** (ad´ ər) *n.* poisonous snake.
4. **craves** *v.* requires.
5. **disjoins . . . power** separates mercy from power.
6. **affections swayed** emotions ruled.
7. **proof** *n.* experience.
8. **lowliness** (lō´ lē nəs) *n.* humility.
9. **base degrees** low steps or people in lower positions.
10. **lest . . . prevent** in case he may, we must stop him.
11. **the quarrel . . . the thing he is** our complaint cannot be justified in terms of what he now is.
12. **Fashion it** state the case.
13. **extremities** (ek strem´ ə tēz) *n.* extremes (of tyranny).

Vocabulary

augmented
(ôg ment´ id) *adj.* made greater; enhanced

Reading Check

What does Brutus fear may happen if Caesar is crowned?

14. **closet** *n.* study; small, private room for reading, meditation, and so on.
15. **flint** *n.* hard stone which, when struck with steel, makes sparks.

16. **exhalations** (eks´ hə lā´ shənz) *n.* meteors.
17. **&c.** et cetera (et set´ ər ə); Latin for "and so forth."
18. **instigations** (in´ stə gā´ shənz) *n.* urgings, incitements, or spurs to act.
19. **piece it out** figure out the meaning.
20. **under one man's awe** in fearful reverence of one man.
21. **Tarquin** (tär´ kwin) king of Rome driven out by Lucius Junius Brutus, Brutus' ancestor.

35 **LUCIUS.** The taper burneth in your closet,[14] sir.
Searching the window for a flint,[15] I found
This paper thus sealed up, and I am sure
It did not lie there when I went to bed.   [*Gives him the letter*]

BRUTUS. Get you to bed again; it is not day.
40   Is not tomorrow, boy, the ides of March?

LUCIUS. I know not, sir.

BRUTUS. Look in the calendar and bring me word.

LUCIUS. I will, sir.   [*Exit*]

BRUTUS. The exhalations[16] whizzing in the air
45   Give so much light that I may read by them.
                              [*Opens the letter and reads*]

    "Brutus, thou sleep'st; awake, and see thyself.
    Shall Rome, &c.[17] Speak, strike, redress.
    Brutus, thou sleep'st; awake."

Such instigations[18] have been often dropped
50 Where I have took them up.
"Shall Rome, &c." Thus must I piece it out:[19]
Shall Rome stand under one man's awe?[20] What, Rome?
My ancestors did from the streets of Rome
The Tarquin[21] drive, when he was called a king.

LITERATURE IN CONTEXT

Language Connection
Archaic Word Forms
Shakespeare uses some word forms that are now archaic, or out of date. For modern readers, these words give his work a tone that is both more formal and more poetic than contemporary English. These archaic forms include the following:

thou *pron.* subjective case of a pronoun meaning "you" (the form used with family, friends, or the young)

thee *pron.* you (objective case of *thou*)

thy *pron.* your (possessive case of *thou*)

burneth *v.* third-person singular present tense of *burn*

'tis *contraction* it is

doth *v.* third-person singular present tense of *do*

dost *v.* second-person singular present tense of *do* (used with *thou*)

sham'st *v.* second-person singular present tense of *shame* (used with *thou*)

Connect to the Literature

What does this archaic language add to your experience of the play? What challenges does it pose?

55 "Speak, strike, redress." Am I entreated
To speak and strike? O Rome, I make thee promise,
If the redress will follow, thou receivest
Thy full petition at the hand of[22] Brutus!

[*Enter* LUCIUS.]

LUCIUS. Sir, March is wasted fifteen days.   [*Knock within*]

60 BRUTUS. 'Tis good. Go to the gate; somebody knocks.

[*Exit* LUCIUS.]

Since Cassius first did whet[23] me against Caesar,
I have not slept.
Between the acting of a dreadful thing
And the first motion,[24] all the interim is
65 Like a phantasma,[25] or a hideous dream.
The genius and the mortal instruments[26]
Are then in council, and the state of a man,
Like to a little kingdom, suffers then
The nature of an insurrection.

[*Enter* LUCIUS.]

70 LUCIUS. Sir, 'tis your brother[27] Cassius at the door,
Who doth desire to see you.

BRUTUS.   Is he alone?

LUCIUS. No, sir, there are moe[28] with him.

BRUTUS.   Do you know them?

LUCIUS. No, sir; their hats are plucked about their ears,
And half their faces buried in their cloaks,
75 That by no means I may discover them
By any mark of favor.[29]

BRUTUS.   Let 'em enter.   [*Exit* LUCIUS.]
They are the faction. O conspiracy,
Sham'st thou to show thy dang'rous brow by night,
When evils are most free? O, then by day
80 Where wilt thou find a cavern dark enough
To mask thy monstrous visage? Seek none, conspiracy;
Hide it in smiles and affability:
For if thou path, thy native semblance on,[30]
Not Erebus[31] itself were dim enough
85 To hide thee from prevention.[32]

[*Enter the conspirators*, CASSIUS, CASCA, DECIUS, CINNA, METELLUS
CIMBER, *and* TREBONIUS.]

33. **upon** *adv.* in interfering with.

CASSIUS. I think we are too bold upon[33] your rest.
Good morrow, Brutus; do we trouble you?

BRUTUS. I have been up this hour, awake all night.
Know I these men that come along with you?

Reading Skill
Paraphrase
Paraphrase Cassius'
words in lines 90–93.

90 **CASSIUS.** Yes, every man of them; and no man here
But honors you; and every one doth wish
You had but that opinion of yourself
Which every noble Roman bears of you.
This is Trebonius.

BRUTUS. He is welcome hither.

CASSIUS. This, Decius Brutus.

95 **BRUTUS.** He is welcome too.

CASSIUS. This, Casca; this, Cinna; and this, Metellus Cimber.

BRUTUS. They are all welcome.
What watchful cares do interpose themselves
Betwixt your eyes and night?[34]

34. **watchful . . . night**
worries keep you from
sleep.
35. **entreat** (in trēt´) **a**
word ask for a chance to
speak with you.
36. **fret** (fret) *v.* decorate with
a pattern.
37. **growing on** tending
toward.
38. **Weighing** *v.* considering.
39. **high** *adj.* due.

100 **CASSIUS.** Shall I entreat a word?[35] [*They whisper.*]

DECIUS. Here lies the east; doth not the day break here?

CASCA. No.

CINNA. O, pardon, sir, it doth; and yon gray lines
That fret[36] the clouds are messengers of day.

105 **CASCA.** You shall confess that you are both deceived.
Here, as I point my sword, the sun arises,
Which is a great way growing on[37] the south,
Weighing[38] the youthful season of the year.
Some two months hence, up higher toward the north
110 He first presents his fire; and the high[39] east
Stands as the Capitol, directly here.

BRUTUS. Give me your hands all over, one by one.

CASSIUS. And let us swear our resolution.

Vocabulary
resolution (rez´ ə lōō´
shən) *n.* strong determination; a plan or decision

BRUTUS. No, not an oath. If not the face of men,
115 The sufferance of our souls, the time's abuse[40]—
If these be motives weak, break off betimes,[41]
And every man hence to his idle bed.
So let high-sighted[42] tyranny range on
Till each man drop by lottery.[43] But if these
120 (As I am sure they do) bear fire enough
To kindle cowards and to steel with valor

40. **the face . . . time's**
abuse the sadness on
men's faces, the patient
endurance of our souls,
the present abuses (that
is, Caesar's abuses of
power).
41. **betimes** (bē tīmz´)
adv. quickly.
42. **high-sighted** *adj.*
arrogant (a reference to
a hawk about to swoop
down on prey).
43. **by lottery** by chance or in
his turn.

The melting spirits of women, then, countrymen,
What need we any spur but our own cause
To prick us to redress?[44] What other bond
125   Than secret Romans, that have spoke the word,
And will not palter?[45] And what other oath
Than honesty to honesty[46] engaged
That this shall be, or we will fall for it?
Swear priests and cowards and men cautelous,[47]
130   Old feeble carrions[48] and such suffering souls
That welcome wrongs; unto bad causes swear
Such creatures as men doubt; but do not stain
The even[49] virtue of our enterprise,
Nor th' insuppressive mettle[50] of our spirits,
135   To think that or our cause or[51] our performance
Did need an oath; when every drop of blood
That every Roman bears, and nobly bears,
Is guilty of a several bastardy[52]
If he do break the smallest particle
140   Of any promise that hath passed from him.

CASSIUS. But what of Cicero? Shall we sound him?[53]
I think he will stand very strong with us.

CASCA. Let us not leave him out.

CINNA.   No, by no means.

METELLUS. O, let us have him, for his silver hairs
145   Will purchase us a good opinion,
And buy men's voices to commend our deeds.
It shall be said his judgment ruled our hands;
Our youths and wildness shall no whit[54] appear,
But all be buried in his gravity.

150 **BRUTUS.** O, name him not! Let us not break with him;[55]
For he will never follow anything
That other men begin.

CASSIUS.   Then leave him out.

CASCA. Indeed, he is not fit.

DECIUS. Shall no man else be touched but only Caesar?

155 **CASSIUS.** Decius, well urged. I think it is not meet
Mark Antony, so well beloved of Caesar,
Should outlive Caesar; we shall find of[56] him
A shrewd contriver;[57] and you know, his means,
If he improve[58] them, may well stretch so far

Spiral Review

Character What is Metellus's motivation for including Cicero in the plot against Caesar?

Reading Check

Why does Brutus think the conspirators should not swear an oath?

59. **annoy** *n.* harm.
60. **Like . . . envy afterwards**
    as if we were killing
    in anger with hatred
    afterward.
61. **come by Caesar's
    spirit** get hold of the
    principles of tyranny for
    which Caesar stands.
62. **gentle** *adj.* honorable;
    noble.

**Vocabulary
wrathfully** (ra*th*´ fəl lē)
adv. with intense anger

160   As to annoy[59] us all; which to prevent,
       Let Antony and Caesar fall together.

    BRUTUS. Our course will seem too bloody, Caius Cassius,
       To cut the head off and then hack the limbs,
       Like wrath in death and envy afterwards;[60]
165   For Antony is but a limb of Caesar.
       Let's be sacrificers, but not butchers, Caius.
       We all stand up against the spirit of Caesar,
       And in the spirit of men there is no blood.
       O, that we then could come by Caesar's spirit,[61]
170   And not dismember Caesar! But, alas,
       Caesar must bleed for it. And, gentle[62] friends,
       Let's kill him boldly, but not wrathfully;
       Let's carve him as a dish fit for the gods,
       Not hew him as a carcass fit for hounds.

▼ **Critical Viewing** What details of this image emphasize the differences between Brutus, on the left, and the other conspirators? **[Analyze]**

175 And let our hearts, as subtle masters do,
Stir up their servants[63] to an act of rage,
And after seem to chide 'em.[64] This shall make
Our purpose necessary, and not envious;
Which so appearing to the common eyes,
180 We shall be called purgers,[65] not murderers.
And for Mark Antony, think not of him;
For he can do no more than Caesar's arm
When Caesar's head is off.

CASSIUS.   Yet I fear him;
For in the ingrafted[66] love he bears to Caesar—

185 **BRUTUS.** Alas, good Cassius, do not think of him.
If he love Caesar, all that he can do
Is to himself—take thought[67] and die for Caesar.
And that were much he should,[68] for he is given
To sports, to wildness, and much company.

190 **TREBONIUS.** There is no fear in him; let him not die,
For he will live and laugh at this hereafter.

[*Clock strikes.*]

BRUTUS. Peace! Count the clock.

CASSIUS.   The clock hath stricken three.

TREBONIUS. 'Tis time to part.

CASSIUS.   But it is doubtful yet
Whether Caesar will come forth today or no;
195 For he is superstitious grown of late,
Quite from the main[69] opinion he held once
Of fantasy, of dreams, and ceremonies.[70]
It may be these apparent prodigies,[71]
The unaccustomed terror of this night,
200 And the persuasion of his augurers[72]
May hold him from the Capitol today.

DECIUS. Never fear that. If he be so resolved,
I can o'ersway him;[73] for he loves to hear
That unicorns may be betrayed with trees,[74]
205 And bears with glasses,[75] elephants with holes,[76]
Lions with toils,[77] and men with flatterers;
But when I tell him he hates flatterers
He says he does, being then most flatterèd.
Let me work;
210 For I can give his humor the true bent,[78]
And I will bring him to the Capitol.

63. their servants that is, the hands or the passions.
64. chide 'em scold them.
65. purgers (purj ərz) *n.* healers.

66. ingrafted (in graft´ id) *adj.* deeply rooted.
67. take thought become melancholy.
68. that were much he should It is unlikely he would do that.

69. Quite from the main quite changed from the strong.
70. ceremonies *n.* omens.
71. apparent prodigies obvious omens of disaster.
72. augurers (ô´ gər ərz) *n.* augurs; officials who interpreted omens to decide if they were favorable or unfavorable for an undertaking.
73. I can o'ersway him I can change his mind.
74. unicorns . . . trees reference to the belief that standing in front of a tree as a unicorn charges and then stepping aside at the last moment causes the unicorn to bury its horn in the tree and so allows it to be caught.
75. glasses *n.* mirrors.
76. holes *n.* pitfalls.
77. toils *n.* nets; snares.
78. give his humor the true bent bend his feelings in the right direction.

Reading Check

According to Brutus, why should Antony not be killed?

79. **uttermost** *adj.* latest.
80. **doth bear Caesar hard** has a grudge against Caesar.
81. **rated** *v.* berated; scolded forcefully.

82. **fashion** *v.* mold.
83. **put on** show.
84. **bear it** carry it off.
85. **formal constancy** consistent dignity.

Reading Skill
Paraphrase Paraphrase Brutus' speech in lines 229–233 and explain which punctuation mark helps you identify the conclusion he draws.

Literary Analysis
Blank Verse How does shifting the accent to the first and fourth syllables in line 240 add dramatic energy to this speech?

86. **wafter** (wäf´ tər) *n.* wave.

CASSIUS. Nay, we will all of us be there to fetch him.

BRUTUS. By the eighth hour; is that the uttermost?[79]

CINNA. Be that the uttermost, and fail not then.

215　**METELLUS.** Caius Ligarius doth bear Caesar hard,[80]
　　Who rated[81] him for speaking well of Pompey.
　　I wonder none of you have thought of him.

BRUTUS. Now, good Metellus, go along by him.
　　He loves me well, and I have given him reasons;
220　Send him but hither, and I'll fashion[82] him.

CASSIUS. The morning comes upon 's; we'll leave you, Brutus.
　　And, friends, disperse yourselves; but all remember
　　What you have said, and show yourselves true Romans.

BRUTUS. Good gentlemen, look fresh and merrily.
225　Let not our looks put on[83] our purposes,
　　But bear it[84] as our Roman actors do,
　　With untired spirits and formal constancy.[85]
　　And so good morrow to you every one.　　[*Exit all but* BRUTUS.]
　　Boy! Lucius! Fast asleep? It is no matter;
230　Enjoy the honey-heavy dew of slumber.
　　Thou hast no figures nor no fantasies
　　Which busy care draws in the brains of men;
　　Therefore thou sleep'st so sound.

[*Enter* PORTIA.]

PORTIA.　　　　　　　　　　　Brutus, my lord.

BRUTUS. Portia, what mean you? Wherefore rise you now?
235　It is not for your health thus to commit
　　Your weak condition to the raw cold morning.

PORTIA. Nor for yours neither. Y'have ungently, Brutus,
　　Stole from my bed; and yesternight at supper
　　You suddenly arose and walked about,
240　Musing and sighing, with your arms across;
　　And when I asked you what the matter was,
　　You stared upon me with ungentle looks.
　　I urged you further; then you scratched your head,
　　And too impatiently stamped with your foot.
245　Yet I insisted, yet you answered not,
　　But with an angry wafter[86] of your hand
　　Gave sign for me to leave you. So I did,
　　Fearing to strengthen that impatience
　　Which seemed too much enkindled, and withal

250   Hoping it was but an effect of humor,
Which sometime hath his[87] hour with every man.
It will not let you eat, nor talk, nor sleep,
And could it work so much upon your shape
As it hath much prevailed on your condition,[88]
255   I should not know you[89] Brutus. Dear my lord,
Make me acquainted with your cause of grief.

BRUTUS. I am not well in health, and that is all.

PORTIA. Brutus is wise and, were he not in health,
He would embrace the means to come by it.

260 **BRUTUS.** Why, so I do. Good Portia, go to bed.

PORTIA. Is Brutus sick, and is it physical[90]
To walk unbracèd and suck up the humors[91]
Of the dank morning? What, is Brutus sick,
And will he steal out of his wholesome bed,
265   To dare the vile contagion of the night,
And tempt the rheumy and unpurgèd air[92]
To add unto his sickness? No, my Brutus:
You have some sick offense[93] within your mind,
Which by the right and virtue of my place
270   I ought to know of; and upon my knees
I charm[94] you, by my once commended[95] beauty,
By all your vows of love, and that great vow[96]
Which did incorporate and make us one,
That you unfold to me, your self, your half,
275   Why you are heavy,[97] and what men tonight
Have had resort to you; for here have been
Some six or seven, who did hide their faces
Even from darkness.

BRUTUS.   Kneel not, gentle Portia.

PORTIA. I should not need, if you were gentle Brutus.
280   Within the bond of marriage, tell me, Brutus,
Is it excepted[98] I should know no secrets
That appertain[99] to you? Am I your self
But, as it were, in sort or limitation,[100]
To keep with you at meals, comfort your bed,
285   And talk to you sometimes? Dwell I but in the suburbs[101]
Of your good pleasure? If it be no more,
Portia is Brutus' harlot, not his wife.

87. **his** *pron.* its.
88. **condition** *n.* disposition; mood.
89. **I should not know you** I would not recognize you as.

90. **physical** *adj.* healthy.
91. **walk unbracèd . . . humors** walk with jacket unfastened and take in the dampness.
92. **tempt . . . air** risk exposing yourself to the night air, which is likely to cause rheumatism and has not been purified by the sun.
93. **sick offense** harmful sickness.
94. **charm** *v.* beg.
95. **commended** *adj.* praised.
96. **great vow** marriage vow.
97. **heavy** *adj.* sorrowful.

98. **excepted** *v.* made an exception that.
99. **appertain** (ap´ ər tān´) *v.* belong.
100. **in sort or limitation** in a limited way (legal terms).
101. **suburbs** *n.* outskirts.

Reading Check
What does Portia ask of Brutus?

▲ **Critical Viewing**

What do the pose and expressions of Brutus and Portia in this film still reveal about their feelings? **[Interpret]**

102. **ruddy drops** blood.
103. **withal** (wi*th* ôl´) *adv.* nevertheless.
104. **Cato's daughter** Marcus Porcius (pôr´ shəs) Cato (Cato the Younger; 95–46 B.C.) supported Pompey in his quarrel with Caesar and killed himself rather than allow himself to be captured by Caesar.
105. **counsels** *n.* secrets.

BRUTUS. You are my true and honorable wife,
    As dear to me as are the ruddy drops[102]
290   That visit my sad heart.

PORTIA. If this were true, then should I know this secret.
    I grant I am a woman; but withal[103]
    A woman that Lord Brutus took to wife.
    I grant I am a woman; but withal
295   A woman well reputed, Cato's daughter.[104]
    Think you I am no stronger than my sex,
    Being so fathered and so husbanded?
    Tell me your counsels,[105] I will not disclose 'em.
    I have made strong proof of my constancy,
300   Giving myself a voluntary wound
    Here in the thigh; can I bear that with patience,
    And not my husband's secrets?

BRUTUS.   O ye gods,
    Render[106] me worthy of this noble wife!   [*Knock*]
    Hark, hark! One knocks. Portia, go in a while,
305 And by and by thy bosom shall partake
    The secrets of my heart.
    All my engagements[107] I will construe to thee,
    All the charactery of my sad brows.[108]
    Leave me with haste.   [*Exit* PORTIA.]

[*Enter* LUCIUS *and* CAIUS LIGARIUS.]

                            Lucius, who's that knocks?

310 **LUCIUS.** Here is a sick man that would speak with you.

    BRUTUS. Caius Ligarius, that Metellus spake of.
        Boy, stand aside. Caius Ligarius! How?

    CAIUS. Vouchsafe good morrow from a feeble tongue.

    BRUTUS. O, what a time have you chose out,[109] brave Caius,
315   To wear a kerchief![110] Would you were not sick!

    CAIUS. I am not sick, if Brutus have in hand
        Any exploit worthy the name of honor.

    BRUTUS. Such an exploit have I in hand, Ligarius,
        Had you a healthful ear to hear of it.

320 **CAIUS.** By all the gods that Romans bow before,
        I here discard my sickness! Soul of Rome,
        Brave son, derived from honorable loins,[111]
        Thou, like an exorcist,[112] hast conjured up
        My mortifièd spirit.[113] Now bid me run,
325   And I will strive with things impossible.
        Yea, get the better of them. What's to do?

    BRUTUS. A piece of work that will make sick men whole.

    CAIUS. But are not some whole that we must make sick?

    BRUTUS. That must we also. What it is, my Caius,
330   I shall unfold[114] to thee, as we are going
        To whom it must be done.

    CAIUS.   Set on[115] your foot,
        And with a heart new-fired I follow you,
        To do I know not what; but it sufficeth[116]
        That Brutus leads me on.   [*Thunder*]

    BRUTUS.   Follow me, then.   [*Exit*]

---

106. Render (ren´ dər) *v.*
make.

Literary Analysis
Blank Verse By break-
ing the pattern of iambic
pentameter, which
words are emphasized in
lines 307 and 308?

107. engagements *n.*
commitments.
**108. All the charactery of
my sad brows** all that is
written on my sad face.

109. chose out picked out.
110. To wear a kerchief
Caius wears a scarf to
protect himself from
drafts because he is sick.

**111. derived from honorable
loins** descended from
Lucius (lōō´ shē əs) Junius
Brutus, founder of the
Roman Republic.
112. exorcist (ek´ sôr sist)
n. one who calls up
spirits.
113. mortifièd (môrt´ ə fī ed)
adj. deadened.
114. unfold *v.* disclose.
115. Set on advance.
116. sufficeth (sə fīs´ eth)
v. is enough.

Reading Check

Why does Portia feel that
Brutus should confide in
her?

Scene ii. Caesar's house.

Reading Skill
Paraphrase Paraphrase Caesar's remarks in lines 1–3, rearranging the subject and verb in line 2.

[*Thunder and lightning. Enter* JULIUS CAESAR *in his nightgown.*]

    CAESAR. Nor heaven nor earth have been at peace tonight:
      Thrice hath Calpurnia in her sleep cried out,
      "Help, ho! They murder Caesar!" Who's within?

[*Enter a* SERVANT.]

    SERVANT. My lord?

1. **present** *adj.* immediate.

5   **CAESAR.** Go bid the priests do present[1] sacrifice,
      And bring me their opinions of success.

    SERVANT. I will, my lord.   [*Exit*]

[*Enter* CALPURNIA.]

    CALPURNIA. What mean you, Caesar? Think you to walk forth?
      You shall not stir out of your house today.

10   **CAESAR.** Caesar shall forth. The things that threatened me
      Ne'er looked but on my back; when they shall see
      The face of Caesar, they are vanishèd.

LITERATURE IN CONTEXT

Culture Connection
Roman Augurs

In Scene ii, Caesar orders his "priests," or augurs (ô´ gə rz), to make a sacrifice to determine whether he should go to the Senate.

- In ancient Rome, augurs were officials who examined signs to determine whether the gods would grant success to a particular venture or plan.

- After receiving a negative judgment from the augurs, a Roman leader might postpone an attack or cancel a meeting.

- By the first century A.D., there were sixteen official augurs.

Augurs watched for signs ▶ such as thunder and lightning and the flights of birds. They also observed the pecking of sacred chickens. Omens related to birds were called auspices.

▲ Another class of priest, the *haruspices* (hə rus´ pə sēs´), examined the patterns in the innards of a sacrificed animal.

Connect to the Literature What does Caesar's own interpretation of his augurs' omen show about the straightforwardness of augury?

CALPURNIA. Caesar, I never stood on ceremonies,[2]
    Yet now they fright me. There is one within,
15   Besides the things that we have heard and seen,
    Recounts most horrid sights seen by the watch.[3]
    A lioness hath whelpèd[4] in the streets,
    And graves have yawned, and yielded up their dead;
    Fierce fiery warriors fought upon the clouds
20   In ranks and squadrons and right form of war,[5]
    Which drizzled blood upon the Capitol;
    The noise of battle hurtled[6] in the air,
    Horses did neigh and dying men did groan,
    And ghosts did shriek and squeal about the street.
25   O Caesar, these things are beyond all use,[7]
    And I do fear them.

CAESAR.   What can be avoided
    Whose end is purposed[8] by the mighty gods?
    Yet Caesar shall go forth; for these predictions
    Are to the world in general as to Caesar.[9]

30 **CALPURNIA.** When beggars die, there are no comets seen;
    The heavens themselves blaze forth[10] the death of princes.

CAESAR. Cowards die many times before their deaths;
    The valiant never taste of death but once.
    Of all the wonders that I yet have heard,
35   It seems to me most strange that men should fear,
    Seeing that death, a necessary end,
    Will come when it will come.

[*Enter a* SERVANT.]

                      What say the augurers?

SERVANT. They would not have you to stir forth today.
    Plucking the entrails of an offering forth,[11]
40   They could not find a heart within the beast.

CAESAR. The gods do this in shame of[12] cowardice:
    Caesar should be a beast without a heart
    If he should stay at home today for fear.
    No, Caesar shall not; Danger knows full well
45   That Caesar is more dangerous than he.
    We are two lions littered[13] in one day,
    And I the elder and more terrible,
    And Caesar shall go forth.

CALPURNIA.   Alas, my lord,
    Your wisdom is consumed in confidence.[14]

---

2. **stood on ceremonies** paid attention to omens.
3. **Recounts . . . watch** tells about the awful sights seen by the watchman.
4. **whelpèd** *v.* given birth.

5. **right form of war** proper military formation of war.
6. **hurtled** (hurt′ əld) *v.* clashed.
7. **beyond all use** contrary to all experience.

8. **is purposed** is intended.
9. **for these . . . as to Caesar** because these predictions apply to the rest of the world as much as they apply to Caesar.
10. **blaze forth** proclaim with meteors and comets.

Reading Skill
Paraphrase
Paraphrase the ideas in lines 32–33.

11. **Plucking . . . forth** pulling out the insides of a sacrificed animal (which were then "read" by augurs).
12. **in shame of** in order to shame.
13. **littered** *v.* born.
14. **confidence** *n.* overconfidence.

Reading Check
Why does Calpurnia urge Caesar to stay home?

50   Do not go forth today. Call it my fear
     That keeps you in the house and not your own.
     We'll send Mark Antony to the Senate House,
     And he shall say you are not well today.
     Let me, upon my knee, prevail in this.

55   **CAESAR.** Mark Antony shall say I am not well,
       And for thy humor,[15] I will stay at home.

[*Enter* DECIUS.]

     Here's Decius Brutus, he shall tell them so.

     DECIUS. Caesar, all hail! Good morrow, worthy Caesar;
       I come to fetch you to the Senate House.

60   **CAESAR.** And you are come in very happy time[16]
       To bear my greeting to the senators,
       And tell them that I will not come today.
       Cannot, is false; and that I dare not, falser:
       I will not come today. Tell them so, Decius.

     CALPURNIA. Say he is sick.

15. humor *n.* whim.

16. in very happy time at just the right moment.

LITERATURE IN CONTEXT

History Connection

The Roman Senate

Caesar is preparing to meet the Senate, the oldest Roman political institution. By this time, the Senate had evolved into the most powerful part of the Roman government:

- Before Caesar's rise to power, the Senate was made up of 500 to 600 members.
- The Senate met in the Curia in the Roman Forum (see page 942).
- Senators were appointed for life. Originally, all were from the *patrician*, or aristocratic, class.
- The Senate shaped policy through advice it issued to various officials, its powers to appoint officials, and its power to negotiate with foreign countries.
- After Caesar won his victory over Pompey, he eliminated his enemies in the Senate and packed it with supporters, including men of lower rank and people from outlying provinces.

Connect to the Literature   How does this information help explain the motives of the conspirators, many of whom are senators?

CAESAR. Shall Caesar send a lie?
Have I in conquest stretched mine arm so far
To be afeard to tell graybeards[17] the truth?
Decius, go tell them Caesar will not come.

DECIUS. Most mighty Caesar, let me know some cause,
70 Lest I be laughed at when I tell them so.

CAESAR. The cause is in my will: I will not come.
That is enough to satisfy the Senate.
But for your private satisfaction,
Because I love you, I will let you know.
75 Calpurnia here, my wife, stays me at home.
She dreamt tonight she saw my statue,
Which, like a fountain with an hundred spouts,
Did run pure blood, and many lusty Romans
Came smiling and did bathe their hands in it.
80 And these does she apply for[18] warnings and portents
And evils imminent, and on her knee
Hath begged that I will stay at home today.

DECIUS. This dream is all amiss interpreted;
It was a vision fair and fortunate:
85 Your statue spouting blood in many pipes,
In which so many smiling Romans bathed,
Signifies that from you great Rome shall suck
Reviving blood, and that great men shall press
For tinctures, stains, relics, and cognizance.[19]
90 This by Calpurnia's dream is signified.

CAESAR. And this way have you well expounded[20] it.

DECIUS. I have, when you have heard what I can say;
And know it now, the Senate have concluded
To give this day a crown to mighty Caesar.
95 If you shall send them word you will not come,
Their minds may change. Besides, it were a mock
Apt to be rendered,[21] for someone to say
"Break up the Senate till another time,
When Caesar's wife shall meet with better dreams."
100 If Caesar hide himself, shall they not whisper
"Lo, Caesar is afraid"?
Pardon me, Caesar, for my dear dear love
To your proceeding[22] bids me tell you this,
And reason to my love is liable.[23]

17. **afeard to tell graybeards** afraid to tell old men (the senators).
18. **apply for** consider to be.

Vocabulary
imminent (im´ ə nənt) *adj.* about to happen

19. **shall press . . . cognizance** Decius interprets Calpurnia's dream with a double meaning. To Caesar he suggests that people will beg for badges to show they are Caesar's servants; to the audience, that people will seek remembrances of his death.
20. **expounded** (eks pound´ id) *v.* interpreted; explained.
21. **mock . . . rendered** jeering comment likely to be made.
22. **proceeding** *n.* advancing in your career.
23. **reason . . . liable** my judgment about what I should or should not say is not as strong as my affection for you is.

Reading Check

What does Decius say about the dream?

24. robe *n.* toga.

105 **CAESAR.** How foolish do your fears seem now, Calpurnia!
I am ashamèd I did yield to them.
Give me my robe,²⁴ for I will go.

[*Enter* BRUTUS, LIGARIUS, METELLUS CIMBER, CASCA, TREBONIUS, CINNA, *and* PUBLIUS.]

And look where Publius is come to fetch me.

PUBLIUS. Good morrow, Caesar.

CAESAR.   Welcome, Publius.
110 What, Brutus, are you stirred so early too?
Good morrow, Casca. Caius Ligarius.

25. Caius Ligarius . . . your enemy Caesar had recently pardoned Ligarius for supporting Pompey during the civil war.
26. ague (āˊ gyoo͞) *n.* fever.
27. revels (revˊ əlz) *v.* makes merry.

Caesar was ne'er so much your enemy²⁵
As that same ague²⁶ which hath made you lean.
What is't o'clock?

BRUTUS.   Caesar, 'tis strucken eight.

115 **CAESAR.** I thank you for your pains and courtesy.

[*Enter* ANTONY.]

See! Antony, that revels²⁷ long a-nights,
Is notwithstanding up. Good morrow, Antony.

ANTONY. So to most noble Caesar.

28. prepare *v.* set out refreshments.

CAESAR.   Bid them prepare²⁸ within.
I am to blame to be thus waited for.
120 Now, Cinna; now, Metellus; what Trebonius,
I have an hour's talk in store for you;
Remember that you call on me today;
Be near me, that I may remember you.

Reading Skill
Paraphrase Paraphrase lines 124–125.

TREBONIUS. Caesar, I will [*aside*] and so near will I be,
125 That your best friends shall wish I had been further.

CAESAR. Good friends, go in and taste some wine with me,
And we (like friends) will straightway go together.

29. That every like . . . the same that is, that everyone who seems *like* a friend may actually be an enemy.
30. earns *v.* sorrows.

BRUTUS. [*Aside*] That every like is not the same,²⁹ O Caesar,
The heart of Brutus earns³⁰ to think upon.   [*Exit*]

Scene iii. A street near the Capitol, close to Brutus' house.

[*Enter* ARTEMIDORUS, *reading a paper.*]

ARTEMIDORUS. "Caesar, beware of Brutus; take heed off Cassius;
come not near Casca; have an eye to Cinna; trust not
Trebonius; mark well Metellus Cimber; Decius Brutus loves

thee not; thou hast wronged Caius Ligarius. There is but
one mind in all these men, and it is bent against Caesar. If
thou beest not immortal, look about you: security gives way
to conspiracy.[1] The mighty gods defend thee!

Thy lover,[2] ARTEMIDORUS."

Here will I stand till Caesar pass along,
And as a suitor[3] will I give him this.
My heart laments that virtue cannot live
Out of the teeth of emulation.[4]
If thou read this, O Caesar, thou mayest live;
If not, the Fates with traitors do contrive.[5]   [*Exit*]

Scene iv. *Another part of the street.*

[*Enter* PORTIA *and* LUCIUS.]

PORTIA. I prithee,[1] boy, run to the Senate House;
Stay not to answer me, but get thee gone.
Why dost thou stay?

LUCIUS.   To know my errand, madam.

PORTIA. I would have had thee there and here again
Ere I can tell thee what thou shouldst do there.

1. **security . . . conspiracy**
overconfident
carelessness allows the
conspiracy to proceed.
2. **lover** *n.* devoted friend.
3. **suitor** (sōōt´ ər) *n.* person
who requests, petitions, or
entreats.
4. **Out of the teeth of
emulation** beyond the
reach of envy.
5. **contrive** *v.* conspire.

1. **prithee** (pri*th*´ ē) "pray
thee"; ask you please.

Reading Check

What does Artemidorus
plan to do?

◄ **Critical Viewing**
When might Caesar
have participated in
an event like the one
depicted on this cup?
Explain. **[Speculate]**

O constancy,[2] be strong upon my side;
Set a huge mountain 'tween my heart and tongue!
I have a man's mind, but a woman's might.[3]
How hard it is for women to keep counsel![4]
Art thou here yet?

10 **LUCIUS.**　　　　　　　Madam, what should I do?
Run to the Capitol, and nothing else?
And so return to you, and nothing else?

PORTIA. Yes, bring me word, boy, if thy lord look well,
For he went sickly forth; and take good note

15 What Caesar doth, what suitors press to him.
Hark, boy, what noise is that?

LUCIUS. I hear none, madam.

PORTIA.　　　　　　　Prithee, listen well.
I heard a bustling rumor like a fray,[5]
And the wind brings it from the Capitol.

20 **LUCIUS.** Sooth,[6] madam, I hear nothing.

[*Enter the* SOOTHSAYER.]

PORTIA. Come hither, fellow. Which way hast thou been?

SOOTHSAYER. At mine own house, good lady.

PORTIA. What is't o'clock?

SOOTHSAYER.　　　　　About the ninth hour, lady.

PORTIA. Is Caesar yet gone to the Capitol?

25 **SOOTHSAYER.** Madam, not yet; I go to take my stand,
To see him pass on the Capitol.

PORTIA. Thou hast some suit[7] to Caesar, hast thou not?

SOOTHSAYER. That I have, lady; if it will please Caesar
To be so good to Caesar as to hear me,

30 I shall beseech him to befriend himself.

PORTIA. Why, know'st thou any harm's intended towards him?

SOOTHSAYER. None that I know will be, much that I fear may
　　chance.
Good morrow to you. Here the street is narrow;
The throng that follows Caesar at the heels,

35 Of senators, of praetors,[8] common suitors,

◄ **Critical Viewing** Judging from its ruins, how might the
Forum in Rome have compared to a modern city center?

2. **constancy** (kän´ stən sē)
   n. firmness of mind or
   purpose; resoluteness.
3. **might** *n.* strength.
4. **keep counsel** keep
   secrets.

Literary Analysis
Blank Verse Why might
Shakespeare present
Lucius' lines in blank
verse in this scene?

5. **fray** (frā) *n.* fight; brawl.
6. **Sooth** (sōōth) interjection
   truly.

7. **suit** (sōōt) *n.* petition.
8. **praetors** (prē´ tərz) *n.*
   Roman officials of the rank
   below consul.

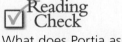

Reading
Check
What does Portia ask of
Lucius?

9. **void** (void) *adj.* empty.

Will crowd a feeble man almost to death.
I'll get me to a place more void,[9] and there
Speak to great Caesar as he comes along.

[*Exit*]

10. **speed** *v.* make successful.
11. **enterprise** (en′ tər prīz′) *n.* undertaking; project.
12. **command me** give my kind regard.

PORTIA. I must go in. Ay me, how weak a thing
40 The heart of woman is! O Brutus,
The heavens speed[10] thee in thine enterprise![11]
Sure, the boy heard me—Brutus hath a suit
That Caesar will not grant—O, I grow faint.
Run, Lucius, and commend me[12] to my lord;
45 Say I am merry; come to me again,
And bring me word what he doth say to thee.

[*Exit separately*]

Critical Thinking

Cite textual evidence to support your responses.

1. **Key Ideas and Details (a)** In Act II, Scene i, what coming event disturbs Brutus? **(b) Interpret:** In Scene i, lines 32–34, what point does Brutus make in comparing Caesar to a serpent's egg? **(c) Evaluate:** Are Brutus' reasons for joining the conspiracy convincing or flawed? Explain.

2. **Key Ideas and Details (a)** What does the writer of the letter that Lucius finds urge Brutus to do? **(b) Infer:** Why do you think the writer leaves gaps in the letter? **(c) Infer:** What inferences can you draw from the way Brutus fills in these gaps?

3. **Key Ideas and Details (a) Analyze:** Why does Brutus decide to join the conspirators? **(b) Assess:** Which of Brutus' reasons do you find most convincing? Explain.

4. **Integration of Knowledge and Ideas** Calpurnia and Decius Brutus have different interpretations of Calpurnia's dream. **(a)** What is Calpurnia's perception of her dream? What information contributes to her point of view? **(b)** What is Decius Brutus' interpretation of her dream? What information underlies his explanation? *[Connect to the Big Question: To what extent does experience determine what we perceive?]*

After You Read | The Tragedy of Julius Caesar, Act II

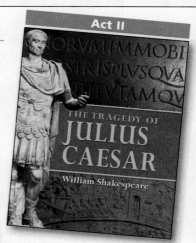

Literary Analysis: Blank Verse

© **1. Craft and Structure (a)** Copy lines 42–43 of Scene ii and mark them to indicate the stressed (´) and unstressed (~) syllables.
(b) Which line of **blank verse** illustrates perfect iambic pentameter?
(c) Explain how the rhythm of the other line reinforces the importance of certain words.

© **2. Craft and Structure** Using a chart like the one shown, examine the dialogue of the characters in Acts I and II. **(a)** Indicate whether each typically speaks in blank verse or prose. **(b)** Identify each as an aristocrat or a commoner based on your findings.

Character	Blank Verse or Prose?	Aristocrat or Commoner?
Flavius		
The Cobbler		
Brutus		
Portia		

Reading Skill: Paraphrase

3. **Paraphrase** Brutus' two questions in line 234 of Scene i.

4. **(a)** List four words in Portia's final speech in Scene iv that are no longer used or no longer used in the same sense. For each, give a modern word that means the same thing. **(b) Paraphrase** the speech.

Vocabulary

© **Acquisition and Use** A **synonym** of a word is a word that has a similar meaning: for example, *start* is a synonym of *begin*. For each of the following items, explain whether or not the words are synonyms.

1. augmented, angered
2. entreated, appealed
3. insurrection, revolt
4. resolution, glory
5. wrathfully, furiously
6. imminent, enduring

Word Study Use the context of the sentences and what you know about the **Latin prefix en-** to explain your answer to each question.

1. Are children safe if the new toy *endangers* them?
2. If critics are *enthralled* by a movie, would they give it bad reviews?

Word Study

The **Latin prefix en-** means "in," "into," or "within."

Apply It Explain how the prefix *en-* contributes to the meanings of these words. Consult a dictionary if necessary.

enamor
encircle
enlighten

Before You Read | The Tragedy of Julius Caesar, Act III

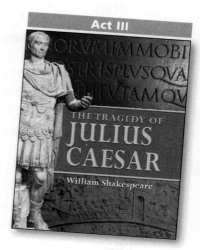

While You Read Act III features a key moment of the plot. Consider the way Brutus and Antony perceive the event and the way they try to sway others' perceptions.

Ⓒ Common Core State Standards

Meet these standards with **The Tragedy of Julius Caesar, Act III** (p. 940).

Reading Literature
3. Analyze how complex characters develop over the course of a text, interact with other characters, and advance the plot or develop the theme. *(Literary Analysis: Dramatic Speeches)*
4. Determine the meaning of words and phrases as they are used in the text, including figurative and connotative meanings; analyze the cumulative impact of word choices on meaning and tone. *(Reading Skill: Analyze Imagery)*

Integrated Language Skills:
Pages 1002–1005
Writing
1. Write arguments to support claims. *(Writing: Editorial)*

4. Produce clear and coherent writing. *(Writing: Obituary; Research and Technology: Advertising Poster)*
6. Use technology, including the Internet. *(Research and Technology: Multimedia Presentation)*
7. Conduct short research projects. *(Research and Technology: Women's History Report)*
Speaking and Listening
1. Initiate and participate effectively in discussions. *(Speaking and Listening: Group Screening)*
6. Adapt speech to a variety of contexts and tasks. *(Speaking and Listening: Dramatic Reading)*

Vocabulary

Read each word and its definition. Decide whether you know the word well, know it a little bit, or do not know it at all. After you read, see how your knowledge of each word has increased.

- **confounded** (kən foun´ did) *adj.* made to feel confused (p. 945) *Confounded by the difficult puzzle, he gave up.* confound *v.* confoundedly *adv.*

- **spectacle** (spek´ tə kəl) *n.* strange or remarkable sight (p. 949) *I was fascinated by the spectacle of ten acrobats performing.* spectacular *adj.*

- **prophesy** (präf´ ə sī´) *v.* predict what will happen (p. 950) *Who can truly prophesy the future?* prophecy *n.* prophet *n.* prophetic *adj.*

- **strife** (strīf) *n.* struggle; conflict (p. 950) *Afraid of causing strife, I did not take sides.*

- **discourse** (dis´ kôrs´) *v.* speak on a topic formally and at length (p. 951) *He wanted to discourse on seashells.* discourse *n.*

- **interred** (in tʉrd´) *v.* buried (said of a dead body) (p. 955) *They interred the body at the cemetery.* interment *n.*

Word Study

The **Latin root -spect-** means "to look at" or "behold."

In the play, a character refers to the **spectacle**, or remarkable sight, of Caesar's death and wonders how others will view it.

Literary Analysis: Dramatic Speeches

In plays, most of the information is expressed through characters' words and actions. Plays feature the following types of **dramatic speeches:**

- **Dialogue:** the conversations between characters
- **Soliloquy:** a long speech in which a character, usually alone on stage, speaks to himself or herself, unheard by any other character
- **Aside:** a remark a character makes, usually to the audience, that is not heard by other characters on stage
- **Monologue:** a long speech by one character usually heard by the other characters

Each type of dramatic speech serves multiple purposes. For example, a monologue may reveal the play's theme. It can also advance the plot by inspiring the other characters to take action. As you read, analyze how each type of dramatic speech advances the plot and develops the play's theme.

Reading Skill: Analyze Imagery

Writers sometimes use **imagery,** language that appeals to the senses, to make abstract ideas vivid and concrete. In Act III, Shakespeare uses many images that focus on words and the body, including these:

- Wounds that speak
- Burying Caesar's body rather than speaking praise of him
- "Plucking" a poet's name out of his heart

In each case, a reference to words—speech, praise, names—is coupled with an image of a person's physical body—a corpse, wounds, the heart. In this way, Shakespeare links physical violence in Rome with disrespect for laws—the words that bind society.

Using the Strategy: Imagery Chart

Record details on an **imagery chart** like this one.

Reference to Words	Imagery of the Body	Connection
And waving our red weapons o'er our heads, Let's all cry **"Peace, freedom, and liberty!"**	Swords covered in **blood** from Caesar's body	The words name the ideals the conspirators use to justify killing Caesar.

REVIEW AND ANTICIPATE

Having ignored the warnings of the soothsayer in Act I and those of his wife, Calpurnia, in Act II, Caesar proceeds to the Capitol on the ides of March. Decius has told him that the Senate is ready to confer a crown upon him. Caesar is accompanied by the conspirators, led by Cassius and Brutus, as well as by his friend Mark Antony. Meanwhile, Artemidorus plans to reveal the conspiracy to Caesar. As Act III unfolds, Caesar approaches the Capitol, and events take a fateful, irreversible turn.

ACT III

Scene i. Rome. Before the Capitol.

[*Flourish of trumpets. Enter* CAESAR, BRUTUS, CASSIUS, CASCA, DECIUS, METELLUS CIMBER, TREBONIUS, CINNA, ANTONY, LEPIDUS, ARTEMIDORUS, PUBLIUS, POPILIUS, *and the* SOOTHSAYER.]

CAESAR. The ides of March are come.

SOOTHSAYER. Ay, Caesar, but not gone.

ARTEMIDORUS. Hail, Caesar! Read this schedule.[1]

DECIUS. Trebonius doth desire you to o'er-read,
5   At your best leisure, this his humble suit.[2]

ARTEMIDORUS. O Caesar, read mine first; for mine's a suit
    That touches[3] Caesar nearer. Read it, great Caesar.

CAESAR. What touches us ourself shall be last served.

ARTEMIDORUS. Delay not, Caesar; read it instantly.

CAESAR. What, is the fellow mad?

10 **PUBLIUS.**   Sirrah, give place.[4]

CASSIUS. What, urge you your petitions in the street?
    Come to the Capitol.

[CAESAR *goes to the Capitol, the rest following*.]

POPILIUS. I wish your enterprise today may thrive.

CASSIUS. What enterprise, Popilius?

POPILIUS.   Fare you well.

[*Advances to* CAESAR]

15 **BRUTUS.** What said Popilius Lena?

CASSIUS. He wished today our enterprise might thrive.
    I fear our purpose is discoverèd.

BRUTUS. Look how he makes to[5] Caesar; mark him.

CASSIUS. Casca, be sudden,[6] for we fear prevention.
20   Brutus, what shall be done? If this be known,
    Cassius or Caesar never shall turn back,[7]
    For I will slay myself.

---

1. **schedule** (ske′ jool) *n.* paper.
2. **suit** *n.* petition; plea.
3. **touches** *v.* concerns.

Literary Analysis
Dramatic Speeches
How does the dialogue between Artemidorus and Caesar create suspense?

4. **give place** get out of the way.

5. **makes to** approaches.
6. **be sudden** be quick.
7. **Cassius . . . back** either Cassius or Caesar will not return alive.

Reading Check
What does Artemidorus want Caesar to do?

8. **constant** *adj.* firm; calm.
9. **change** *v.* that is, change the expression on his face.

10. **presently prefer his suit** immediately present his petition.
11. **addressed** *adj.* ready.
12. **second** *v.* support.
13. **amiss . . . redress** wrong that Caesar and his Senate must correct.
14. **puissant** (pyoo´ i sənt) *adj.* powerful.

BRUTUS.   Cassius, be constant.[8]
  Popilius Lena speaks not of our purposes;
  For look, he smiles, and Caesar doth not change.[9]

25 **CASSIUS.** Trebonius knows his time; for look you, Brutus,
  He draws Mark Antony out of the way.

[*Exit* ANTONY *and* TREBONIUS.]

DECIUS. Where is Metellus Cimber? Let him go
  And presently prefer his suit[10] to Caesar.

BRUTUS. He is addressed.[11] Press near and second[12] him.

30 **CINNA.** Casca, you are the first that rears your hand.

CAESAR. Are we all ready? What is now amiss
  That Caesar and his Senate must redress?[13]

METELLUS. Most high, most mighty, and most puissant[14] Caesar,
  Metellus Cimber throws before thy seat
  An humble heart.   [*Kneeling*]

LITERATURE IN CONTEXT

History Connection

The Roman Forum

Caesar receives petitioners at the Senate House in the Roman Forum. Consisting of a plaza, or open space lined with buildings, the Forum (shown here) was the center of government and commercial activity in ancient Rome.

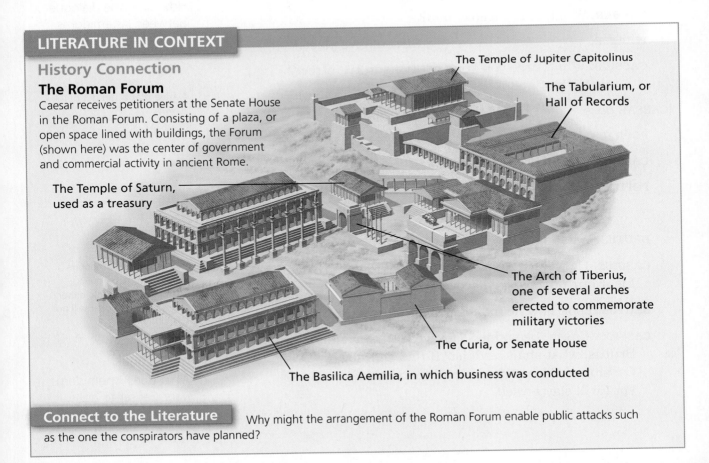

The Temple of Jupiter Capitolinus

The Tabularium, or Hall of Records

The Temple of Saturn, used as a treasury

The Arch of Tiberius, one of several arches erected to commemorate military victories

The Curia, or Senate House

The Basilica Aemilia, in which business was conducted

Connect to the Literature   Why might the arrangement of the Roman Forum enable public attacks such as the one the conspirators have planned?

35 **CAESAR.**   I must prevent thee, Cimber.
These couchings and these lowly courtesies[15]
Might fire the blood of ordinary men,
And turn preordinance and first decree
Into the law of children.[16] Be not fond[17]
40 To think that Caesar bears such rebel blood
That will be thawed from the true quality[18]
With that which melteth fools—I mean sweet words,
Low-crookèd curtsies, and base spaniel fawning.[19]
Thy brother by decree is banishèd.
45 If thou dost bend and pray and fawn for him,
I spurn[20] thee like a cur out of my way.
Know, Caesar doth not wrong, nor without cause
Will he be satisfied.

METELLUS. Is there no voice more worthy than my own,
50 To sound more sweetly in great Caesar's ear
For the repealing[21] of my banished brother?

BRUTUS. I kiss thy hand, but not in flattery, Caesar,
Desiring thee that Publius Cimber may
Have an immediate freedom of repeal.[22]

CAESAR. What, Brutus?

15. **couchings . . . courtesies** low bowings and humble gestures of reverence.
16. **And turn . . . law of children** and change what has already been decided as children might change their minds.
17. **fond** *adj.* foolish (enough).
18. **rebel . . . quality** unstable disposition that will lose its firmness.
19. **base spaniel fawning** low doglike cringing.
20. **spurn** *v.* kick disdainfully.
21. **repealing** *n.* recalling; ending the banishment.
22. **freedom of repeal** permission to be recalled.

Reading Check
What worries Cassius?

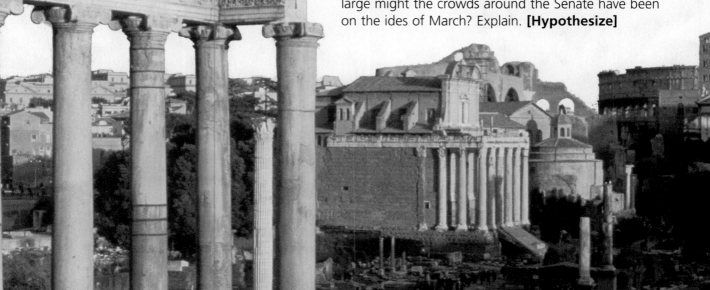

▼ Critical Viewing
Judging from these ruins of the Roman Forum, how large might the crowds around the Senate have been on the ides of March? Explain. **[Hypothesize]**

23. enfranchisement (en fran´ chīz mənt) *n.* freedom.

24. pray to move beg others to change their minds.

25. resting *adj.* immovable.

26. fellow *n.* equal.

27. firmament (fʉ r´ mə mənt) *n.* sky.

28. his *pron.* its.

29. apprehensive (ap´ rə hen´ siv) *adj.* able to understand.

30. one/That unassailable . . . rank one who, unattackable, maintains his position.

31. Unshaked of motion unmoved by his own or others' impulses.

▼ **Critical Viewing**
Which details in this picture suggest Caesar's ignorance? **[Analyze]**

55 **CASSIUS.**   Pardon, Caesar; Caesar, pardon!
       As low as to thy foot doth Cassius fall
       To beg enfranchisement[23] for Publius Cimber.

     CAESAR. I could be well moved, if I were as you;
       If I could pray to move,[24] prayers would move me;
60   But I am constant as the Northern Star,
       Of whose true-fixed and resting[25] quality
       There is no fellow[26] in the firmament.[27]
       The skies are painted with unnumb'red sparks,
       They are all fire and every one doth shine;
65   But there's but one in all doth hold his[28] place.
       So in the world; 'tis furnished well with men,
       And men are flesh and blood, and apprehensive;[29]
       Yet in the number I do know but one
       That unassailable holds on his rank,[30]
70   Unshaked of motion;[31] and that I am he,

Let me a little show it, even in this—
That I was constant³² Cimber should be banished,
And constant do remain to keep him so.

CINNA. O Caesar—

CAESAR.   Hence! Wilt thou lift up Olympus?³³

DECIUS. Great Caesar—

75 **CAESAR.**   Doth not Brutus bootless³⁴ kneel?

CASCA. Speak hands for me!   [*They stab* CAESAR.]

CAESAR. *Et tu, Brutè?*³⁵ Then fall, Caesar.   [*Dies*]

CINNA. Liberty! Freedom! Tyranny is dead!
Run hence, proclaim, cry it about the streets.

80 **CASSIUS.** Some to the common pulpits,³⁶ and cry out
"Liberty, freedom, and enfranchisement!"

BRUTUS. People, and senators, be not affrighted.
Fly not; stand still; ambition's debt is paid.³⁷

CASCA. Go to the pulpit, Brutus.

DECIUS.   And Cassius too.

85 **BRUTUS.** Where's Publius?³⁸

CINNA. Here, quite **confounded** with this mutiny.³⁹

METELLUS. Stand fast together, lest some friend of Caesar's
Should chance—

BRUTUS. Talk not of standing. Publius, good cheer;
90 There is no harm intended to your person,
Nor to no Roman else. So tell them, Publius.

CASSIUS. And leave us, Publius, lest that the people
Rushing on us should do your age some mischief.

BRUTUS. Do so; and let no man abide⁴⁰ this deed
95 But we the doers.

[*Enter* TREBONIUS.]

CASSIUS. Where is Antony?

TREBONIUS.   Fled to his house amazed.⁴¹
Men, wives, and children stare, cry out and run,
As⁴² it were doomsday.

BRUTUS.   Fates, we will know your pleasures.

32. **constant** *adj.* determined.
33. **Olympus** (ō lim´ pəs)
    n. mountain in Greece
    on which the Greek gods
    were said to live.
34. **bootless** (boot´ lis)
    adv. uselessly.

Reading Skill
Analyze Imagery
In what way does line 76
combine ideas of words
with images of violence?

35. *Et tu, Brutè?* Latin for
    "And you, too, Brutus?"
36. **pulpits** (pul´ pits) *n.*
    speakers' platforms.
37. **ambition's . . .**
    paid ambition received
    what it deserved.
38. **Publius** (pōōb´ lē əs) an
    elderly senator.

Vocabulary
confounded (kən
foun´ did) *adj.* made
to feel confused

39. **mutiny** (myoot´ 'n ē)
    n. revolt against authority,
    such as a rebellion of
    soldiers against their
    officers.
40. **let no man abide** let no
    man take responsibility for.
41. **amazed** *adj.* astounded.
42. **As** *conj.* as if.

Reading
Check
What do the conspirators
do to Caesar?

43. 'tis but the time . . . upon
It is only the time of death
and the length of life that
people care about.

Reading Skill
Analyze Imagery
Find an example of an
image linking blood and
words in lines 103–110.

44. market place the open
area of the Roman Forum,
the center of government,
business, and public life in
ancient Rome.

45. in sport for amusement;
the deed will be acted out
in plays.

**46. on Pompey's basis lies
along** by the pedestal
of Pompey's statue lies
stretched out.

47. knot *n.* group.

48. grace his heels do honor
to his heels; follow him.
49. Soft *interjection* wait

50. royal *adj.* showing noble
generosity.

51. be resolved have it
explained.

That we shall die, we know; 'tis but the time,
100 And drawing days out, that men stand upon.⁴³

CASCA. Why, he that cuts off twenty years of life
Cuts off so many years of fearing death.

BRUTUS. Grant that, and then is death a benefit.
So are we Caesar's friends, that have abridged
105 His time of fearing death. Stoop, Romans, stoop,
And let us bathe our hands in Caesar's blood
Up to the elbows, and besmear our swords.
Then walk we forth, even to the market place,⁴⁴
And waving our red weapons o'er our heads,
110 Let's all cry "Peace, freedom, and liberty!"

CASSIUS. Stoop then, and wash. How many ages hence
Shall this our lofty scene be acted over
In states unborn and accents yet unknown!

BRUTUS. How many times shall Caesar bleed in sport,⁴⁵
115 That now on Pompey's basis lies along⁴⁶
No worthier than the dust!

CASSIUS.   So oft as that shall be,
So often shall the knot⁴⁷ of us be called
The men that gave their country liberty.

DECIUS. What, shall we forth?

CASSIUS.   Ay, every man away.
120 Brutus shall lead, and we will grace his heels⁴⁸
With the most boldest and best hearts of Rome.

[*Enter a* SERVANT.]

BRUTUS. Soft,⁴⁹ who comes here? A friend of Antony's.

SERVANT. Thus, Brutus, did my master bid me kneel;
Thus did Mark Antony bid me fall down;
125 And, being prostrate, thus he bade me say:
Brutus is noble, wise, valiant, and honest;
Caesar was mighty, bold, royal,⁵⁰ and loving.
Say I love Brutus and I honor him;
Say I feared Caesar, honored him, and loved him.
130 If Brutus will vouchsafe that Antony
May safely come to him and be resolved⁵¹
How Caesar hath deserved to lie in death,
Mark Antony shall not love Caesar dead
So well as Brutus living; but will follow
135 The fortunes and affairs of noble Brutus

Thorough the hazards of this untrod state[52]
With all true faith. So says my master Antony.

BRUTUS. Thy master is a wise and valiant Roman;
I never thought him worse.
140 Tell him, so[53] please him come unto this place,
He shall be satisfied and, by my honor,
Depart untouched.

SERVANT. I'll fetch him presently.[54]

[*Exit* SERVANT]

BRUTUS. I know that we shall have him well to friend.[55]

CASSIUS. I wish we may. But yet have I a mind
145 That fears him much; and my misgiving still
Falls shrewdly to the purpose.[56]

[*Enter* ANTONY.]

BRUTUS. But here comes Antony. Welcome, Mark Antony.

ANTONY. O mighty Caesar! Dost thou lie so low?
Are all thy conquests, glories, triumphs, spoils,
150 Shrunk to this little measure? Fare thee well.
I know not, gentlemen, what you intend,
Who else must be let blood,[57] who else is rank.[58]
If I myself, there is no hour so fit
As Caesar's death's hour, nor no instrument
155 Of half that worth as those your swords, made rich
With the most noble blood of all this world.
I do beseech ye, if you bear me hard,[59]
Now, whilst your purpled hands[60] do reek and smoke,
Fulfill your pleasure. Live[61] a thousand years,
160 I shall not find myself so apt[62] to die;
No place will please me so, no mean of death,[63]
As here by Caesar, and by you cut off,
The choice and master spirits of this age.

BRUTUS. O Antony, beg not your death of us!
165 Though now we must appear bloody and cruel,
As by our hands and this our present act
You see we do, yet see you but our hands
And this the bleeding business they have done.
Our hearts you see not; they are pitiful;[64]
170 And pity to the general wrong of Rome—
As fire drives out fire, so pity pity[65]—
Hath done this deed on Caesar. For your part,
To you our swords have leaden[66] points, Mark Antony:

Literary Analysis
Dramatic Speeches
What is Antony's purpose in delivering this monologue?

Reading Check
What does Antony ask of the conspirators?

67. Our arms . . . / Of brothers' temper our arms strengthened with the desire to do harm and our hearts filled with brotherly feelings.

68. voice *n.* vote.

69. dignities *n.* offices.

70. deliver *v.* tell to.

Literary Analysis
Dramatic Speeches
In this monologue, what image of his state of mind does Antony create for the conspirators?

71. credit *n.* reputation.
72. conceit (kən sē t') *v.* think of.
73. dearer *adv.* more deeply.
74. corse *n.* corpse.
75. close (clōz) *v.* reach an agreement.
76. bayed *v.* cornered.
77. hart (härt) *n.* deer.

Reading Skill
Analyze Imagery
What images of the body does Antony use to contrast his real grief with his words of friendship?

78. Signed in thy spoil marked by signs of your slaughter.
79. Lethe (lē´ *thē*) river in Hades, the mythological Greek underworld inhabited by the dead; here, a river of blood.
80. stroken *v.* struck down.

Our arms in strength of malice, and our hearts
175 Of brothers' temper,[67] do receive you in
With all kind love, good thoughts, and reverence.

CASSIUS. Your voice[68] shall be as strong as any man's
In the disposing of new dignities.[69]

BRUTUS. Only be patient till we have appeased
180 The multitude, beside themselves with fear,
And then we will deliver[70] you the cause
Why I, that did love Caesar when I struck him,
Have thus proceeded.

ANTONY.   I doubt not of your wisdom.
Let each man render me his bloody hand.
185 First, Marcus Brutus, will I shake with you;
Next, Caius Cassius, do I take your hand;
Now, Decius Brutus, yours; now yours, Metellus;
Yours, Cinna; and, my valiant Casca, yours;
Though last, not least in love, yours, good Trebonius.
190 Gentlemen all—alas, what shall I say?
My credit[71] now stands on such slippery ground
That one of two bad ways you must conceit[72] me,
Either a coward or a flatterer.
That I did love thee, Caesar, O, 'tis true!
195 If then thy spirit look upon us now,
Shall it not grieve thee dearer[73] than thy death
To see thy Antony making his peace,
Shaking the bloody fingers of thy foes,
Most noble, in the presence of thy corse?[74]
200 Had I as many eyes as thou hast wounds,
Weeping as fast as they stream forth thy blood,
It would become me better than to close[75]
In terms of friendship with thine enemies.
Pardon me, Julius! Here wast thou bayed,[76] brave hart;[77]
205 Here didst thou fall, and here thy hunters stand,
Signed in thy spoil[78] and crimsoned in thy Lethe.[79]
O world, thou wast the forest to this hart;
And this indeed, O world, the heart of thee.
How like a deer, stroken[80] by many princes.
210 Dost thou here lie!

CASSIUS. Mark Antony—

ANTONY.   Pardon me, Caius Cassius.
   The enemies of Caesar shall say this;
   Then, in a friend, it is cold modesty.[81]

CASSIUS. I blame you not for praising Caesar so;
215   But what compact[82] mean you to have with us?
   Will you be pricked[83] in number of our friends,
   Or shall we on,[84] and not depend on you?

ANTONY. Therefore I took your hands, but was indeed
   Swayed from the point by looking down on Caesar.
220   Friends am I with you all, and love you all,
   Upon this hope, that you shall give me reasons
   Why, and wherein, Caesar was dangerous.

BRUTUS. Or else were this a savage spectacle.
   Our reasons are so full of good regard[85]
225   That were you, Antony, the son of Caesar,
   You should be satisfied.

ANTONY.   That's all I seek;
   And am moreover suitor that I may
   Produce[86] his body to the market place,
   And in the pulpit, as becomes a friend,
230   Speak in the order[87] of his funeral.

BRUTUS. You shall, Mark Antony.

CASSIUS.   Brutus, a word with you.
   [*Aside to* BRUTUS] You know not what you do; do not consent
   That Antony speak in his funeral.
   Know you how much the people may be moved
   By that which he will utter?

235 **BRUTUS.**   By your pardon:
   I will myself into the pulpit first,
   And show the reason of our Caesar's death.
   What Antony shall speak, I will protest[88]
   He speaks by leave and by permission,
240   And that we are contented Caesar shall
   Have all true rites and lawful ceremonies.
   It shall advantage more than do us wrong.[89]

CASSIUS. I know not what may fall;[90] I like it not.

BRUTUS. Mark Antony, here, take you Caesar's body.
245   You shall not in your funeral speech blame us,
   But speak all good you can devise of Caesar,

81. **cold modesty** calm, moderate speech.
82. **compact** (käm´ pakt) *n.* agreement.

83. **pricked** *v.* marked down; included.
84. **on** proceed.

Vocabulary
spectacle (spek´ tə kəl)
n. strange or remarkable
sight

85. **so full of good regard** so carefully considered.
86. **Produce** *v.* bring forth.
87. **order** *n.* course of the ceremonies.

Literary Analysis
Dramatic Speeches
Why does Cassius wish
to prevent others from
hearing what he says in
this aside to Brutus?

88. **protest** *v.* declare.
89. **advantage . . . wrong** benefit us more than hurt us.
90. **what may fall** what may happen.

Reading Check
What rules must Antony
follow in delivering his
funeral speech for Caesar?

And say you do't by our permission;
Else shall you not have any hand at all
About his funeral. And you shall speak
250 In the same pulpit whereto I am going,
After my speech is ended.

ANTONY.   Be it so;
I do desire no more.

BRUTUS. Prepare the body then, and follow us.

[*Exit all but* ANTONY.]

ANTONY. O pardon me, thou bleeding piece of earth,
255 That I am meek and gentle with these butchers!
Thou art the ruins of the noblest man
That ever livèd in the tide of times.[91]
Woe to the hand that shed this costly blood!
Over thy wounds now do I prophesy
260 (Which like dumb mouths do ope their ruby lips
To beg the voice and utterance of my tongue),
A curse shall light upon the limbs of men;
Domestic fury and fierce civil strife
Shall cumber[92] all the parts of Italy;
265 Blood and destruction shall be so in use,[93]
And dreadful objects so familiar,
That mothers shall but smile when they behold
Their infants quartered with the hands of war,
All pity choked with custom of fell deeds;[94]
270 And Caesar's spirit, ranging[95] for revenge,
With Atè[96] by his side come hot from hell,
Shall in these confines[97] with a monarch's voice
Cry "Havoc,"[98] and let slip[99] the dogs of war,
That this foul deed shall smell above the earth
275 With carrion[100] men, groaning for burial.

[*Enter* OCTAVIUS' SERVANT.]

You serve Octavius Caesar, do you not?

SERVANT. I do, Mark Antony.

ANTONY. Caesar did write for him to come to Rome.

SERVANT. He did receive his letters and is coming,
280 And bid me say to you by word of mouth—
O Caesar!   [*Seeing the body*]

▲ **Critical Viewing** Which scene in the play might this image depict? Explain. **[Connect]**

ANTONY. Thy heart is big;[101] get thee apart and weep.
Passion, I see, is catching, for mine eyes,
Seeing those beads of sorrow stand in thine,
285   Began to water. Is thy master coming?

SERVANT. He lies tonight within seven leagues[102] of Rome.

ANTONY. Post[103] back with speed, and tell him what hath
  chanced.[104]
Here is a mourning Rome, a dangerous Rome,
No Rome of safety for Octavius yet.
290   Hie hence and tell him so. Yet stay awhile;
Thou shalt not back till I have borne this corse
Into the market place; there shall I try[105]
In my oration[106] how the people take
The cruel issue[107] of these bloody men;
295   According to the which, thou shalt **discourse**
To young Octavius of the state of things.
Lend me your hand.   [*Exit*]

101. **big** *adj.* swollen with grief.
102. **leagues** (lēgz) *n.* units of measure, each equivalent in Roman times to about a mile and a half.
103. **Post** *v.* hasten.
104. **hath chanced** has happened.
105. **try** *v.* test.
106. **oration** (ō rā´ shən) *n.* formal public speech.
107. **cruel issue** outcome of the cruelty.

Vocabulary

discourse (dis´ kôrs´)
v. speak on a topic formally and at length

Reading Check

What is Antony's real response to Caesar's death?

Scene ii. The Forum

[*Enter* BRUTUS *and goes into the pulpit, and* CASSIUS, *with the* PLEBEIANS.[1]]

PLEBEIANS. We will be satisfied![2] Let us be satisfied!

BRUTUS. Then follow me, and give me audience, friends.
Cassius, go you into the other street
And part the numbers.[3]

5   Those that will hear me speak, let 'em stay here;
Those that will follow Cassius, go with him;
And public reasons shall be renderèd
Of Caesar's death.

FIRST PLEBEIAN.   I will hear Brutus speak.

SECOND PLEBEIAN. I will hear Cassius, and compare their reasons,
10   When severally[4] we hear them renderèd.

[*Exit* CASSIUS, *with some of the* PLEBEIANS.]

THIRD PLEBEIAN. The noble Brutus is ascended. Silence!

BRUTUS. Be patient till the last.
Romans, countrymen, and lovers,[5] hear me for my
cause, and be silent, that you may hear. Believe me
15   for mine honor, and have respect to mine honor, that
you may believe. Censure[6] me in your wisdom, and
awake your senses,[7] that you may the better judge. If
there be any in this assembly, any dear friend of
Caesar's, to him I say that Brutus' love to Caesar was
20   no less than his. If then that friend demand why
Brutus rose against Caesar, this is my answer: Not
that I loved Caesar less, but that I loved Rome more.
Had you rather Caesar were living, and die all slaves,
than that Caesar were dead, to live all free men? As
25   Caesar loved me, I weep for him; as he was fortunate,
I rejoice at it; as he was valiant, I honor him; but, as
he was ambitious, I slew him. There is tears, for his
love; joy, for his fortune; honor, for his valor; and
death, for his ambition. Who is here so base,[8] that
30   would be a bondman?[9] If any, speak; for him have I
offended. Who is here so rude,[10] that would not be a
Roman? If any, speak; for him have I offended. Who is
here so vile,[11] that will not love his country? If any,
speak; for him have I offended. I pause for a reply.

35   **ALL.** None, Brutus, none!

---

1. **Plebeians** (ple bē´ənz) *n.* commoners; members of the lower class.
2. **be satisfied** get an explanation.
3. **part the numbers** divide the crowd.

4. **severally** (sev´ ər əl ē) *adv.* separately.
5. **lovers** *n.* dear friends.
6. **Censure** (sen´ shər) *v.* judge.
7. **senses** *n.* powers of reason.

Literary Analysis
Dramatic Speeches
What is Brutus' purpose in delivering this monologue?

8. **base** *adj.* low.
9. **bondman** *n.* slave.
10. **rude** *adj.* uncivilized.
11. **vile** (vīl) *adj.* mean; low-born; of low character.

BRUTUS. Then none have I offended. I have done no
more to Caesar than you shall do to Brutus. The
question of his death is enrolled in the Capitol;[12] his
glory not extenuated,[13] wherein he was worthy, nor
40   his offenses enforced,[14] for which he suffered death.

[*Enter* MARK ANTONY, *with* CAESAR's *body.*]

Here comes his body, mourned by Mark Antony,
who, though he had no hand in his death, shall receive
the benefit of his dying, a place in the commonwealth,
as which of you shall not? With this I depart, that, as
45   I slew my best lover for the good of Rome, I have the
same dagger for myself, when it shall please my
country to need my death.

ALL. Live, Brutus! Live, live!

FIRST PLEBEIAN. Bring him with triumph home unto his house.

50   **SECOND PLEBEIAN.** Give him a statue with his ancestors.

THIRD PLEBEIAN. Let him be Caesar.

FOURTH PLEBEIAN.   Caesar's better parts[15]
Shall be crowned in Brutus.

FIRST PLEBEIAN. We'll bring him to his house with shouts and
clamors.

BRUTUS. My countrymen—

SECOND PLEBEIAN.   Peace! Silence! Brutus speaks.

55   **FIRST PLEBEIAN.** Peace, ho!

BRUTUS. Good countrymen, let me depart alone,
And, for my sake, stay here with Antony.
Do grace to Caesar's corpse, and grace his speech
Tending to Caesar's glories,[16] which Mark Antony
60   By our permission, is allowed to make.
I do entreat you, not a man depart,
Save I alone, till Antony have spoke.   [*Exit*]

FIRST PLEBEIAN. Stay, ho! And let us hear Mark Antony.

THIRD PLEBEIAN. Let him go up into the public chair;
65   We'll hear him. Noble Antony, go up.

ANTONY. For Brutus' sake, I am beholding[17] to you.

FOURTH PLEBEIAN. What does he say of Brutus?

12. **The question . . . in the
    Capitol** The issues that
    led to his death are on
    record in the Capitol.
13. **extenuated** (ek sten´ yōō
    āt´ id) *adj.* undervalued;
    made less of.
14. **enforced** (en fôrs'd´)
    adj. exaggerated.

**Literary Analysis
Dramatic Speeches**
In this monologue, how
does Brutus emphasize
his sincerity?

15. **parts** *n.* qualities.

16. **Do grace . . . glories**
    Show respect for Caesar's
    body and for the speech
    telling of Caesar's
    achievements.
17. **beholding** *adj.* indebted.

**Reading
Check**
What reason for killing
Caesar does Brutus offer
to the plebeians?

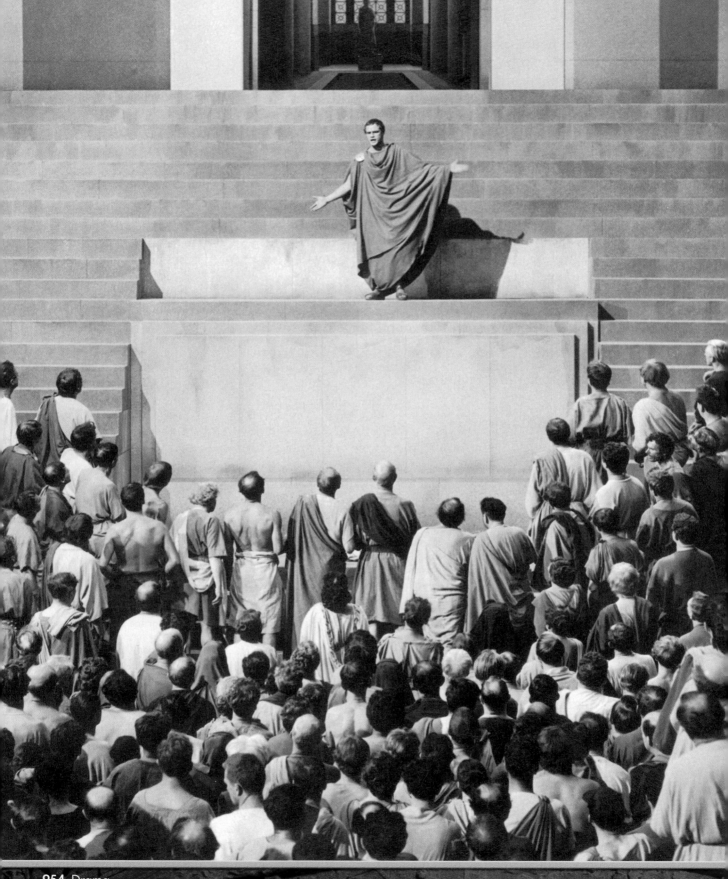

THIRD PLEBEIAN.   He says, for Brutus' sake,
He finds himself beholding to us all.

FOURTH PLEBEIAN. 'Twere best he speak no harm of Brutus
here!

FIRST PLEBEIAN. This Caesar was a tyrant.

70 **THIRD PLEBEIAN.**   Nay, that's certain.
We are blest that Rome is rid of him.

SECOND PLEBEIAN. Peace! Let us hear what Antony can say.

ANTONY. You gentle Romans—

ALL.   Peace, ho! Let us hear him.

ANTONY. Friends, Romans, countrymen, lend me your ears;
75   I come to bury Caesar, not to praise him.
The evil that men do lives after them,
The good is oft interrèd with their bones;
So let it be with Caesar. The noble Brutus
Hath told you Caesar was ambitious.
80   If it were so, it was a grievous fault,
And grievously hath Caesar answered[18] it.
Here, under leave of Brutus and the rest
(For Brutus is an honorable man,
So are they all, all honorable men),
85   Come I to speak in Caesar's funeral.
He was my friend, faithful and just to me;
But Brutus says he was ambitious,
And Brutus is an honorable man.
He hath brought many captives home to Rome,
90   Whose ransoms did the general coffers[19] fill;
Did this in Caesar seem ambitious?
When that the poor have cried, Caesar hath wept;
Ambition should be made of sterner stuff.
Yet Brutus says he was ambitious;
95   And Brutus is an honorable man.
You all did see that on the Lupercal
I thrice presented him a kingly crown,
Which he did thrice refuse. Was this ambition?
Yet Brutus says he was ambitious;
100   And sure he is an honorable man.
I speak not to disprove what Brutus spoke,
But here I am to speak what I do know.
You all did love him once, not without cause;
What cause withholds you then to mourn for him?

◀ **Critical Viewing**
What does this film still
of Antony addressing the
plebeians suggest about
the power of his words?
Explain. **[Interpret]**

Literary Analysis
Dramatic Speeches
How is Antony's mono-
logue both similar to and
different from Brutus' in
lines 12–34?

Vocabulary
interred (in tʉrd´) v.
buried (said of a
dead body)

18. **answered** v. paid the
penalty for.

19. **general coffers** public
treasury.

Literary Analysis
Dramatic Speeches
Contrast Antony's stated
purpose in this mono-
logue with the probable
effect of lines 92–100 on
his audience.

Reading
Check
How does Antony
describe Brutus'
character?

Reading Skill
Analyze Imagery In lines 106–108, which images link Antony's heart and inability to continue speaking?

105 O judgment, thou art fled to brutish beasts,
And men have lost their reason! Bear with me;
My heart is in the coffin there with Caesar,
And I must pause till it come back to me.

FIRST PLEBEIAN. Methinks there is much reason in his sayings.

110 **SECOND PLEBEIAN.** If thou consider rightly of the matter,
Caesar has had great wrong.

THIRD PLEBEIAN.   Has he, masters?
I fear there will a worse come in his place.

FOURTH PLEBEIAN. Marked ye his words? He would not take
the crown,
Therefore 'tis certain he was not ambitious.

20. **dear abide it** pay dearly for it.

115 **FIRST PLEBEIAN.** If it be found so, some will dear abide it.[20]

SECOND PLEBEIAN. Poor soul, his eyes are red as fire with
weeping.

THIRD PLEBEIAN. There's not a nobler man in Rome than
Antony.

FOURTH PLEBEIAN. Now mark him, he begins again to speak.

ANTONY. But yesterday the word of Caesar might

21. **so poor to** low enough in rank to.

120 Have stood against the world; now lies he there,
And none so poor to[21] do him reverence.
O masters! If I were disposed to stir
Your hearts and minds to mutiny and rage,
I should do Brutus wrong and Cassius wrong,

125 Who, you all know, are honorable men.
I will not do them wrong; I rather choose
To wrong the dead, to wrong myself and you,
Than I will wrong such honorable men.
But here's a parchment with the seal of Caesar;

22. **commons** n. plebeians; commoners.
23. **napkins** n. handkerchiefs.

130 I found it in his closet; 'tis his will.
Let but the commons[22] hear this testament,
Which, pardon me, I do not mean to read,
And they would go and kiss dead Caesar's wounds,
And dip their napkins[23] in his sacred blood;

135 Yea, beg a hair of him for memory,
And dying, mention it within their wills,
Bequeathing it as a rich legacy

24. **issue** n. children; offspring.

Unto their issue.[24]

FOURTH PLEBEIAN. We'll hear the will; read it, Mark Antony.

140 **ALL.** The will, the will! We will hear Caesar's will!

ANTONY. Have patience, gentle friends, I must not read it.
It is not meet[25] you know how Caesar loved you.
You are not wood, you are not stones, but men;
And being men, hearing the will of Caesar,
145 It will inflame you, it will make you mad.
'Tis good you know not that you are his heirs;
For if you should, O, what would come of it?

FOURTH PLEBEIAN. Read the will! We'll hear it, Antony!
You shall read us the will, Caesar's will!

150 **ANTONY.** Will you be patient? Will you stay awhile?
I have o'ershot myself[26] to tell you of it.
I fear I wrong the honorable men
Whose daggers have stabbed Caesar; I do fear it.

FOURTH PLEBEIAN. They were traitors. Honorable men!

155 **ALL.** The will! The testament!

SECOND PLEBEIAN. They were villains, murderers! The will!
Read the will!

ANTONY. You will compel me then to read the will?
Then make a ring about the corpse of Caesar,
160 And let me show you him that made the will.
Shall I descend? And will you give me leave?

ALL. Come down.

SECOND PLEBEIAN. Descend.   [ANTONY *comes down*.]

THIRD PLEBEIAN. You shall have leave.

165 **FOURTH PLEBEIAN.** A ring! Stand round.

FIRST PLEBEIAN. Stand from the hearse,[27] stand from the body!

SECOND PLEBEIAN. Room for Antony, most noble Antony!

ANTONY. Nay, press not so upon me; stand far[28] off.

ALL. Stand back! Room! Bear back.

170 **ANTONY.** If you have tears, prepare to shed them now.
You all do know this mantle;[29] I remember
The first time ever Caesar put it on:
'Twas on a summer's evening, in his tent,
That day he overcame the Nervii.[30]
175 Look, in this place ran Cassius' dagger through;
See what a rent[31] the envious[32] Casca made;
Through this the well-belovèd Brutus stabbed,
And as he plucked his cursèd steel away,

25. **meet** *adj.* fitting; suitable.

Spiral Review
Character What is Antony's real motivation for telling the crowd they should not read Caesar's testament?

26. **o'ershot myself** gone further than I meant to.

Reading Skill
Analyze Imagery
In what way does the action on stage connect Caesar's body and the words in his will?

27. **hearse** (hʉrs) *n.* coffin.
28. **far** *adv.* farther.
29. **mantle** (man´ təl) *n.* cloak; toga.
30. **Nervii** (nʉr´ vē ī) *n.* warlike European tribe conquered by Caesar in 57 B.C.
31. **rent** *n.* hole; tear; rip.
32. **envious** (en´ vē əs) *adj.* spiteful.

Reading Check
What effect does Antony's speech have on the crowd?

▲ **Critical Viewing**
Compare this image with the one on page 954. Which details here suggest Antony's growing bond with his audience? **[Contrast]**

33. **As** *conj.* as if.
34. **to be resolved** to learn for certain.
35. **unkindly** *adj.* cruelly; also, unnaturally.
36. **flourished** (flur´ ish ´d) *v.* swaggered; waved a sword in triumph.
37. **dint** *n.* stroke; blow.
38. **what** *adv.* why.
39. **vesture** (ves´ chər) *n.* clothing.
40. **with** *prep.* by.

Mark how the blood of Caesar followed it,
180 As[33] rushing out of doors, to be resolved[34]
If Brutus so unkindly[35] knocked, or no;
For Brutus, as you know, was Caesar's angel.
Judge, O you gods, how dearly Caesar loved him!
This was the most unkindest cut of all;
185 For when the noble Caesar saw him stab,
Ingratitude, more strong than traitors' arms,
Quite vanquished him. Then burst his mighty heart;
And, in his mantle muffling up his face,
Even at the base of Pompey's statue
190 (Which all the while ran blood) great Caesar fell.
O, what a fall was there, my countrymen!
Then I, and you, and all of us fell down,
Whilst bloody treason flourished[36] over us.
O, now you weep, and I perceive you feel
195 The dint[37] of pity; these are gracious drops.
Kind souls, what[38] weep you when you but behold
Our Caesar's vesture[39] wounded? Look you here,
Here is himself, marred as you see with[40] traitors.

FIRST PLEBEIAN. O piteous spectacle!

200 **SECOND PLEBEIAN.** O noble Caesar!

THIRD PLEBEIAN. O woeful day!

FOURTH PLEBEIAN. O traitors, villains!

FIRST PLEBEIAN. O most bloody sight!

SECOND PLEBEIAN. We will be revenged.

205 **ALL.** Revenge! About![41] Seek! Burn! Fire! Kill! Slay!
Let not a traitor live!

ANTONY. Stay, countrymen.

FIRST PLEBEIAN. Peace there! Hear the noble Antony.

SECOND PLEBEIAN. We'll hear him, we'll follow him, we'll die
210 with him!

ANTONY. Good friends, sweet friends, let me not stir you up
To such a sudden flood of mutiny.
They that have done this deed are honorable.
What private griefs[42] they have, alas, I know not,
215 That made them do it. They are wise and honorable,
And will, no doubt, with reasons answer you.
I come not, friends, to steal away your hearts;
I am no orator, as Brutus is;
But (as you know me all) a plain blunt man
220 That love my friend, and that they know full well
That gave me public leave to speak[43] of him.
For I have neither writ, nor words, nor worth,
Action, or utterance,[44] nor the power of speech
To stir men's blood; I only speak right on.[45]
225 I tell you that which you yourselves do know,
Show you sweet Caesar's wounds, poor poor dumb mouths,
And bid them speak for me. But were I Brutus,
And Brutus Antony, there were an Antony
Would ruffle up your spirits, and put a tongue
230 In every wound of Caesar's that should move
The stones of Rome to rise and mutiny.

ALL. We'll mutiny.

FIRST PLEBEIAN. We'll burn the house of Brutus.

THIRD PLEBEIAN. Away, then! Come, seek the conspirators.

ANTONY. Yet hear me, countrymen. Yet hear me speak.

235 **ALL.** Peace, ho! Hear Antony, most noble Antony!

ANTONY. Why, friends, you go to do you know not what: Wherein
hath Caesar thus deserved your loves?

41. About let's go.

42. private griefs personal
grievances.
43. public leave to speak
permission to speak in
public.
44. neither writ . . . utterance
(ut´ ər əns) neither a
written speech, nor
fluency, nor reputation,
nor gestures, nor style of
speaking.
45. right on directly.

Reading Skill
Analyze Imagery
Which images in Antony's speech combine ideas of words, the body, and violence?

Reading Check
How does the crowd feel toward the conspirators after Antony's speech?

Alas, you know not; I must tell you then: You have forgot the
will I told you of.

240 **ALL.** Most true, the will! Let's stay and hear the will.

ANTONY. Here is the will, and under Caesar's seal.
To every Roman citizen he gives,
To every several[46] man, seventy-five drachmas.

SECOND PLEBEIAN. Most noble Caesar! We'll revenge his death!

245 **THIRD PLEBEIAN.** O royal[47] Caesar!

ANTONY. Hear me with patience.

ALL. Peace, ho!

ANTONY. Moreover, he hath left you all his walks,
His private arbors, and new-planted orchards,[48]
250 On this side Tiber; he hath left them you,
And to your heirs forever: common pleasures,[49]
To walk abroad and recreate yourselves.
Here was a Caesar! When comes such another?

FIRST PLEBEIAN. Never, never! Come, away, away!
255 We'll burn his body in the holy place,
And with the brands[50] fire the traitors' houses.
Take up the body.

SECOND PLEBEIAN. Go fetch fire.

THIRD PLEBEIAN. Pluck down benches.

260 **FOURTH PLEBEIAN.** Pluck down forms, windows,[51] anything!

[*Exit* PLEBEIANS *with the body.*]

ANTONY. Now let it work:[52] Mischief, thou art afoot,
Take thou what course thou wilt.

[*Enter* SERVANT.]

How now, fellow?

SERVANT. Sir, Octavius is already come to Rome.

ANTONY. Where is he?

265 **SERVANT.** He and Lepidus are at Caesar's house.

ANTONY. And thither[53] will I straight to visit him;
He comes upon a wish.[54] Fortune is merry,
And in this mood will give us anything.

SERVANT. I heard him say, Brutus and Cassius
270 Are rid[55] like madmen through the gates of Rome.

---

46. **several** *adj.* individual.
47. **royal** *adj.* showing noble generosity.
48. **walks . . . orchards** parks, his private stands of trees, and newly planted gardens.
49. **common pleasures** public places of recreation.

Reading Skill
Analyze Imagery
Moved by news of Caesar's words, what action does the crowd take involving Caesar's body?

50. **brands** *n.* torches.
51. **forms, windows** benches and shutters.
52. **work** *v.* spread and expand, as yeast does; follow through to a conclusion.

53. **thither** *adv.* there.
54. **upon a wish** as I wished.
55. **Are rid** have ridden.

ANTONY. Belike[56] they had some notice of the people,[57]
How I had moved them. Bring me to Octavius. [*Exit*]

Scene iii. A street.

[*Enter* CINNA THE POET, *and after him the* PLEBEIANS.]

CINNA. I dreamt tonight[1] that I did feast with Caesar,
And things unluckily charge my fantasy.[2]
I have no will to wander forth of doors,[3]
Yet something leads me forth.

5 **FIRST PLEBEIAN.** What is your name?

SECOND PLEBEIAN. Whither are you going?

THIRD PLEBEIAN. Where do you dwell?

FOURTH PLEBEIAN. Are you a married man or a bachelor?

SECOND PLEBEIAN. Answer every man directly.[4]

10 **FIRST PLEBEIAN.** Ay, and briefly.

FOURTH PLEBEIAN. Ay, and wisely.

THIRD PLEBEIAN. Ay, and truly, you were best.

CINNA. What is my name? Whither am I going? Where do I
dwell? Am I a married man or a bachelor? Then, to answer
15 every man directly and briefly, wisely and truly: wisely I say,
I am a bachelor.

SECOND PLEBEIAN. That's as much as to say, they are fools that
marry; you'll bear me a bang[5] for that, I fear. Proceed
directly.

56. **Belike** *adv.* probably.
57. **notice of the people** word about the mood of the people.

Literary Analysis
Dramatic Speeches
To whom is Cinna's speech addressed?

1. **tonight** *adv.* last night.
2. **things . . . fantasy** the events that have happened give an unlucky meaning to my dream.
3. **forth of doors** outdoors.
4. **directly** *adv.* in a straightforward manner.
5. **bear me a bang** get a blow from me.

Reading Check

What has Caesar left the citizens of Rome in his will?

Extispicium relief (inspection of entrails) from the Forum of Trajan, Rome. Louvre, Paris, France.

CINNA. Directly, I am going to Caesar's funeral.

FIRST PLEBEIAN. As a friend or an enemy?

CINNA. As a friend.

SECOND PLEBEIAN. That matter is answered directly.

FOURTH PLEBEIAN. For your dwelling, briefly.

25 **CINNA.** Briefly, I dwell by the Capitol.

THIRD PLEBEIAN. Your name, sir, truly.

CINNA. Truly, my name is Cinna.

FIRST PLEBEIAN. Tear him to pieces! He's a conspirator.

CINNA. I am Cinna the poet! I am Cinna the poet!

30 **FOURTH PLEBEIAN.** Tear him for his bad verses! Tear him for his bad verses!

CINNA. I am not Cinna the conspirator.

FOURTH PLEBEIAN. It is no matter, his name's Cinna; pluck but his name out of his heart, and turn him going.[6]

35 **THIRD PLEBEIAN.** Tear him, tear him! [*They attack him.*]
Come, brands, ho! Firebrands![7] To Brutus', to Cassius'!
Burn all! Some to Decius' house, and some to
Casca's; some to Ligarius'! Away, go!

[*Exit all the* PLEBEIANS *with* CINNA.]

Reading Skill
Analyze Imagery
How does a confusion about Cinna's name place his body in danger?

6. **turn him going** send him on his way.
7. **Firebrands** *n.* burning pieces of wood; also, people who stir up others to revolt.

Critical Thinking

Cite textual evidence to support your responses.

1. **Key Ideas and Details (a)** What does Caesar say when he sees Brutus among the assassins? **(b) Infer:** What feelings do these words convey?

2. **Key Ideas and Details (a)** How does Antony respond to the conspirators after the assassination? **(b) Analyze:** What are the motives for his actions?

3. **Integration of Knowledge and Ideas** **Make a Judgment:** Is Caesar responsible for his death? Explain.

4. **Integration of Knowledge and Ideas** The crowd's perception of Caesar's death changes based on the different accounts given. **(a) Summarize:** Explain how Brutus justifies the assassination in his speech to the crowd. **(b) Analyze:** Explain how Antony turns the crowd against the conspirators. *[Connect to the Big Question: To what extent does experience determine what we perceive?]*

After You Read | The Tragedy of Julius Caesar, Act III

Literary Analysis: Dramatic Speeches

Ⓒ 1. Craft and Structure On a chart like the one shown, identify each speech as an **aside,** a **soliloquy,** or a **monologue.** Then, complete the other columns.

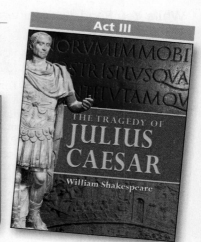

Lines	Type of Speech	Paraphrase	Who Hears It?
Scene i, lines 218–222			
Scene i, lines 254–275			
Scene ii, lines 261–262			

Ⓒ 2. Craft and Structure (a) Contrast the style and purpose of Antony's and Brutus' funeral speeches. **(b)** What does each speech reveal about the speaker? **(c)** What happens as a result of each speech?

Reading Skill: Analyze Imagery

3. (a) Give three examples of **imagery** in Act III related to the human body and to words. **(b) Analyze the imagery** by explaining how words and bodies are linked in each example.

Vocabulary

Ⓒ Acquisition and Use In word study, **analogies** show relationships between pairs of words. In each item, match the relationship between the first two words by choosing the correct word to complete the second pair.

1. vague : definite :: confounded : **(a)** certain, **(b)** lost, **(c)** unclear

2. insult : offended :: spectacle : **(a)** learned, **(b)** fascinated, **(c)** tired

3. remember : past :: prophesy : **(a)** sky, **(b)** present, **(c)** future

4. tuxedo : T-shirt :: discourse : **(a)** jeans, **(b)** lecture, **(c)** chat

5. stored : attic :: interred : **(a)** museum, **(b)** cemetery, **(c)** exit

6. merriment : laughter :: strife : **(a)** yelling, **(b)** singing, **(c)** blushing

Word Study Use the context of the sentences and what you know about the **Latin root -*spect*-** to explain your answer to each question.

1. Why is it important to *inspect* a car before buying it?

2. If you *speculate* about how to build a bookcase, are you actively building it?

Word Study

The **Latin root -*spect*-** means "to look at" or "behold."

Apply It Explain how the root -*spect*- contributes to the meanings of these words. Consult a dictionary if necessary.

perspective
spectator
spectrum

Before You Read

The Tragedy of Julius Caesar, Act IV

While You Read Look for ways that Brutus' experiences in Act III affect him in Act IV.

Common Core State Standards

Meet these standards with *The Tragedy of Julius Caesar,* **Act IV** (p. 966).

Reading Literature
1. Cite strong and thorough textual evidence to support inferences drawn from the text. *(Reading Skill: Read Between the Lines)*

5. Analyze how an author's choices concerning how to structure a text, order events within it, and manipulate time create such effects as mystery, tension, or surprise. *(Literary Analysis: External and Internal Conflict)*

Integrated Language Skills:
Pages 1002–1005
Writing
1. Write arguments to support claims. *(Writing: Editorial)*

4. Produce clear and coherent writing. *(Writing: Obituary; Research and Technology: Advertising Poster)*

6. Use technology, including the Internet. *(Research and Technology: Multimedia Presentation)*

7. Conduct short research projects. *(Research and Technology: Women's History Report)*

Speaking and Listening
1. Initiate and participate effectively in discussions. *(Speaking and Listening: Group Screening)*

6. Adapt speech to a variety of contexts and tasks. *(Speaking and Listening: Dramatic Reading)*

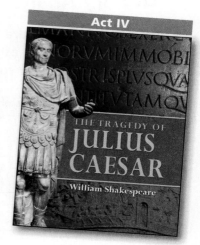

Act IV

THE TRAGEDY OF
JULIUS CAESAR
William Shakespeare

Vocabulary

Read each word and its definition. Decide whether you know the word well, know it a little bit, or do not know it at all. After you read, see how your knowledge of each word has increased.

- **legacies** (leg´ ə sēz) *n.* money, property, or position left in a will to someone (p. 967) *The legacies in his will included a gift to charity.* *legacy n.*

- **condemned** (kən demd´) *v.* declared to be guilty of wrongdoings (p. 970) *The reporter condemned the politician for failing to keep his promise.* *condemnable adj. condemnation n. condemnatory adj.*

- **chastisement** (chas´ tiz mənt) *n.* severe criticism; punishment (p. 971) *As chastisement, the child was sent to bed early.* *chastise v. chastiser n.*

- **rash** (rash) *adj.* given to acting without thinking; impulsive (p. 971) *Do not be so rash; think before you act.* *rashly adv. rashness n.*

- **mirth** (murth) *n.* joyfulness; merriment (p. 972) *The children were full of mirth and laughed joyfully.* *mirthful adj. mirthfully adv.*

- **presume** (prē zoom´) *v.* rely too much on; take advantage of (p. 972) *Do not presume on their good nature and expect them to pay for everything.* *presumable adj. presumption n. presumptive adj.*

Word Study

The **Latin root -sum-** means "to take" or "to use."

In the play, Cassius tells Brutus not to **presume** upon his friendship or take for granted his good will.

Literary Analysis: External and Internal Conflict

Conflict, a struggle between opposing forces, creates drama:

- In an **external conflict,** a character struggles with an outside force, such as another character, or a force such as the weather.

- In an **internal conflict,** the character struggles with his or her own opposing beliefs, desires, or values.

The Tragedy of Julius Caesar features both internal and external conflicts. The different conflicts help form the structure of the play. For example, earlier in the play, the external conflict between Brutus and Caesar creates an internal conflict for Brutus—he wishes to check Caesar's ambition, but he also considers Caesar a friend.

Reading Skill: Read Between the Lines

When **reading Shakespearean drama,** combine clues in the text with your own knowledge to **make inferences** about what Shakespeare suggests but does not directly say.

- Always begin with evidence from the text. For example, early in Act IV, Antony describes Lepidus as "Meet to be sent on errands." Antony has been deciding which of his rivals will share power. Between the lines, he is saying, "Fit to run errands—and nothing else."

- Follow indirect references. When Lucilius reports on Cassius, Brutus says, "Thou has described / A hot friend cooling." "A hot friend" refers to Cassius, whom Brutus worries is no longer his ally.

- Notice what details the author provides, and think about what larger ideas those clues suggest.

Using the Strategy: Inference Chart

Citing details on an **inference chart** will help you read between the lines.

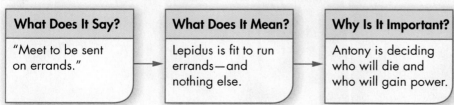

What Does It Say?	What Does It Mean?	Why Is It Important?
"Meet to be sent on errands."	Lepidus is fit to run errands—and nothing else.	Antony is deciding who will die and who will gain power.

Hear It!
- Selection summary audio
- Selection audio

See It!
- Get Connected video
- Background video
- More about the author
- Vocabulary flashcards

Do It!
- Interactive journals
- Interactive graphic organizers
- Self-test
- Internet activity
- Grammar tutorial
- Interactive vocabulary games

REVIEW AND ANTICIPATE

In Act III, after the conspirators assassinate Caesar, Brutus and Antony both speak at his funeral. Brutus explains that Caesar's death was necessary to keep Romans free. Antony, however, convinces the crowd that Caesar was a great man while Brutus is a traitor. The crowd rushes off to find and destroy the conspirators.

As Act IV opens, Antony and his allies Octavius and Lepidus are deciding which of their political rivals are to be killed. Meanwhile, conflict is brewing between their enemies, Cassius and Brutus.

▶ **Critical Viewing** Which of the qualities that Antony has shown in the play are portrayed in this sculpture of him? **[Connect]**

ACT IV

Scene i. A house in Rome.

[*Enter* ANTONY, OCTAVIUS, *and* LEPIDUS.]

ANTONY. These many then shall die; their names are pricked.[1]

OCTAVIUS. Your brother too must die; consent you, Lepidus?

LEPIDUS. I do consent—

OCTAVIUS.   Prick him down, Antony.

LEPIDUS. Upon condition Publius shall not live,

5   Who is your sister's son, Mark Antony.

ANTONY. He shall not live; look, with a spot I damn him.[2]
       But, Lepidus, go you to Caesar's house;
       Fetch the will hither, and we shall determine
       How to cut off some charge in legacies.[3]

10   **LEPIDUS.** What, shall I find you here?

OCTAVIUS. Or[4] here or at the Capitol.   [*Exit* LEPIDUS.]

ANTONY. This is a slight unmeritable[5] man,
       Meet[6] to be sent on errands; is it fit,
       The threefold world[7] divided, he should stand
       One of the three to share it?

15   **OCTAVIUS.**   So you thought him,
       And took his voice[8] who should be pricked to die
       In our black sentence and proscription.[9]

ANTONY. Octavius, I have seen more days[10] than you;
       And though we lay these honors on this man,

20   To ease ourselves of divers sland'rous loads,[11]
       He shall but bear them as the ass bears gold,
       To groan and sweat under the business,
       Either led or driven, as we point the way;
       And having brought our treasure where we will,

25   Then take we down his load, and turn him off,
       (Like to the empty ass) to shake his ears
       And graze in commons.[12]

OCTAVIUS.   You may do your will;
       But he's a tried and valiant soldier.

ANTONY. So is my horse, Octavius, and for that

30   I do appoint him store of provender.[13]

The Tragedy of Julius Caesar, Act IV, Scene i **967**

Side notes:

1. **pricked** *v.* checked off.

2. **with a spot . . . him** with a mark on the tablet, I condemn him.

3. **cut off some charge in legacies** save costs by changing the amount of gifts left in the will.

Vocabulary
legacies (leg´ ə sēz) *n.* money, property, or position left in a will to someone

4. **Or** *conj.* either.

5. **slight unmeritable** insignificant and without merit.

6. **Meet** *adj.* suitable.

7. **threefold world** three areas of the Roman Empire—Europe, Asia, and Africa.

8. **voice** *n.* vote; opinion.

9. **black . . . proscription** list of those sentenced to death or exile.

10. **have seen more days** am older.

11. **divers sland'rous loads** various burdens of blame.

12. **in commons** on public pasture.

13. **appoint . . . provender** give him a supply of food.

Reading Check
What is the conflict between Antony and Octavius?

14. **wind** (wīnd) *v.* turn.
15. **His . . . spirit** his bodily movements governed by my mind.
16. **taste** *n.* degree; measure.
17. **barren-spirited** without ideas of his own.
18. **feeds / On objects, arts, and imitations** enjoys curiosities, clever ways, and fashions.
19. **staled** *v.* cheapened.
20. **Begin his fashion** he begins to use. (He is hopelessly behind the times.)
21. **property** *n.* tool; object.
22. **levying powers** enlisting troops.
23. **straight make head** quickly gather soldiers.
24. **best friends made** closest allies chosen.
25. **stretched** *adj.* used to full advantage.
26. **presently** *adv.* immediately.
27. **How . . . answerèd** how hidden dangers may be discovered and known dangers met.
28. **at the stake . . . enemies** surrounded by enemies like a bear tied to a stake and set upon by many dogs. (Bear-baiting was a popular amusement in Elizabethan England.)
29. **mischiefs** *n.* plans to injure us.

1. **To do you salutation** to bring you greetings.
2. **In his own . . . done undone** Whether his actions are due to a change in his feelings toward me or to bad advice from subordinates, he has made me wish we did not do what we did.
3. **be satisfied** obtain an explanation.
4. **full of regard** worthy of respect.
5. **resolved** *adj.* fully informed.

It is a creature that I teach to fight,
To wind,[14] to stop, to run directly on,
His corporal motion governed by my spirit.[15]
And, in some taste,[16] is Lepidus but so.
35   He must be taught, and trained, and bid go forth.
A barren-spirited[17] fellow; one that feeds
On objects, arts, and imitations,[18]
Which, out of use and staled[19] by other men,
Begin his fashion.[20] Do not talk of him
40   But as a property.[21] And now, Octavius,
Listen great things. Brutus and Cassius
Are levying powers;[22] we must straight make head.[23]
Therefore let our alliance be combined,
Our best friends made,[24] our means stretched;[25]
45   And let us presently[26] go sit in council
How covert matters may be best disclosed,
And open perils surest answerèd.[27]

OCTAVIUS. Let us do so; for we are at the stake,
And bayed about with many enemies;[28]
50   And some that smile have in their hearts, I fear,
Millions of mischiefs.[29]   [*Exit*]

Scene ii. Camp near Sardis.

[*Drum. Enter* BRUTUS, LUCILIUS, LUCIUS, *and the* ARMY. TITINIUS *and* PINDARUS *meet them.*]

BRUTUS. Stand ho!

LUCILIUS. Give the word, ho! and stand.

BRUTUS. What now, Lucilius, is Cassius near?

LUCILIUS. He is at hand, and Pindarus is come
5   To do you salutation[1] from his master.

BRUTUS. He greets me well. Your master, Pindarus,
In his own change, or by ill officers,
Hath given me some worthy cause to wish
Things done undone;[2] but if he be at hand,
I shall be satisfied.[3]

10 **PINDARUS.** I do not doubt
But that my noble master will appear
Such as he is, full of regard[4] and honor.

BRUTUS. He is not doubted. A word, Lucilius,
How he received you; let me be resolved.[5]

15 **LUCILIUS.** With courtesy and with respect enough,
But not with such familiar instances,[6]
Nor with such free and friendly conference[7]
As he hath used of old.

BRUTUS.   Thou hast described
A hot friend cooling. Ever note, Lucilius,
20 When love begins to sicken and decay
It useth an enforcèd ceremony.[8]
There are no tricks in plain and simple faith;
But hollow[9] men, like horses hot at hand,[10]
Make gallant show and promise of their mettle;[11]

[*Low march within*]

25 But when they should endure the bloody spur,
They fall their crests, and like deceitful jades
Sink in the trial.[12] Comes his army on?

6. **familiar instances** marks of friendship.
7. **conference** *n.* conversation.
8. **enforcèd ceremony** forced formality.
9. **hollow** *adj.* insincere.
10. **hot at hand** full of spirit when reined in.
11. **mettle** *n.* spirit; high character; courage.
12. **They fall . . . the trial** They drop their necks, and like worn-out, worthless horses, fail the test.

Reading Check

What is Brutus' present attitude toward Cassius?

▼ **Critical Viewing** Which details in this film still reflect the fact that Antony dominates over both Lepidus and Octavius? **[Interpret]**

13. quartered *v.* provided with places to stay.
14. horse in general cavalry.
15. *Powers n.* forces; troops.

16. gently *adv.* slowly.

17. sober form serious manner.

18. be content be patient.

Reading Skill
Read Between the Lines Brutus and Cassius are standing near their troops. Why does Brutus suggest meeting in his tent?

19. enlarge *v.* freely express.
20. charges *n.* troops.

Vocabulary
condemned (kən demd´) *v.* declared to be guilty of wrongdoings

1. noted *v.* publicly denounced.
2. praying on his side pleading on his behalf.
3. slighted off disregarded.

LUCILIUS. They mean this night in Sardis to be quartered;[13]
The greater part, the horse in general,[14]
Are come with Cassius.

[*Enter* CASSIUS *and his Powers.*[15]]

30   **BRUTUS.**   Hark! He is arrived.
March gently[16] on to meet him.

CASSIUS. Stand, ho!

BRUTUS. Stand, ho! Speak the word along.

FIRST SOLDIER. Stand!

35   **SECOND SOLDIER.** Stand!

THIRD SOLDIER. Stand!

CASSIUS. Most noble brother, you have done me wrong.

BRUTUS. Judge me, you gods! Wrong I mine enemies?
And if not so, how should I wrong a brother?

40   **CASSIUS.** Brutus, this sober form[17] of yours hides wrongs;
And when you do them—

BRUTUS.   Cassius, be content.[18]
Speak your griefs softly; I do know you well.
Before the eyes of both our armies here
(Which should perceive nothing but love from us)
45   Let us not wrangle. Bid them move away;
Then in my tent, Cassius, enlarge[19] your griefs,
And I will give you audience.

CASSIUS.   Pindarus,
Bid our commanders lead their charges[20] off
A little from this ground.

50   **BRUTUS.** Lucilius, do you the like, and let no man
Come to our tent till we have done our conference.
Let Lucius and Titinius guard our door.

[*Exit all but* BRUTUS *and* CASSIUS]

Scene iii. Brutus' tent.

CASSIUS. That you have wronged me doth appear in this:
You have condemned and noted[1] Lucius Pella
For taking bribes here of the Sardians;
Wherein my letters, praying on his side,[2]
5   Because I knew the man, was slighted off.[3]

BRUTUS. You wronged yourself to write in such a case.

CASSIUS. In such a time as this it is not meet
    That every nice offense should bear his comment.[4]

BRUTUS. Let me tell you, Cassius, you yourself
10 Are much condemned to have an itching palm,[5]
    To sell and mart[6] your offices for gold
    To undeservers.

CASSIUS.   I an itching palm?
    You know that you are Brutus that speaks this,
    Or, by the gods, this speech were else your last.

15 **BRUTUS.** The name of Cassius honors[7] this corruption,
    And chastisement doth therefore hide his head.

CASSIUS. Chastisement!

BRUTUS. Remember March, the ides of March remember.
    Did not great Julius bleed for justice' sake?
20 What villain touched his body, that did stab,
    And not[8] for justice? What, shall one of us,
    That struck the foremost man of all this world
    But for supporting robbers,[9] shall we now
    Contaminate our fingers with base bribes,
25 And sell the mighty space of our large honors[10]
    For so much trash[11] as may be graspèd thus?
    I had rather be a dog, and bay[12] the moon,
    Than such a Roman.

CASSIUS.   Brutus, bait[13] not me;
    I'll not endure it. You forget yourself
30 To hedge me in.[14] I am a soldier, I,
    Older in practice, abler than yourself
    To make conditions.[15]

BRUTUS.   Go to! You are not, Cassius.

CASSIUS. I am.

BRUTUS. I say you are not.

35 **CASSIUS.** Urge[16] me no more, I shall forget myself;
    Have mind upon your health;[17] tempt me no farther.

BRUTUS. Away, slight[18] man!

CASSIUS. Is't possible?

BRUTUS.   Hear me, for I will speak.
    Must I give way and room to your rash choler?[19]
40 Shall I be frighted when a madman stares?

---

4. **every . . . comment** every petty fault should receive his criticism.
5. **condemned . . . palm** accused of having a hand eager to accept bribes.
6. **mart** *v.* trade.
7. **honors** *v.* gives respectability to.

Vocabulary
chastisement (chas´tiz mənt) *n.* severe criticism; punishment

rash (rash) *adj.* given to acting without thinking; impulsive

Reading Skill
Read Between the Lines When Brutus asks who stabbed Caesar "not for justice," what is he suggesting about Cassius?

8. **And not** except.
9. **But . . . robbers** Here Brutus says, for the first time, that Caesar's officials were also involved in taking bribes and that this was a motive in his assassination.
10. **honors** *n.* reputations.
11. **trash** *n.* that is, money.
12. **bay** *v.* howl at.
13. **bait** harass (as a bear tied to a stake is harassed by dogs).
14. **hedge me in** restrict my actions.
15. **make conditions** manage affairs.
16. **Urge** *v.* drive onward.
17. **health** *n.* safety.
18. **slight** *adj.* insignificant.
19. **choler** (käl´ ə r) *n.* anger.

Reading
Check
Of what does Brutus accuse Cassius?

20. choleric (käl´ ə rik) *adj.* quick-tempered.
21. bondmen *n.* slaves.
22. budge *v.* flinch away from you.
23. observe you show reverence toward you.
24. crouch *v.* bow.
25. testy humor irritability.
26. digest . . . spleen eat the poison of your spleen. (The spleen was thought to be the source of anger.)

Vocabulary

mirth (murth) *n.*
joyfulness; merriment

27. waspish *adj.* bad-tempered.
28. vaunting (vônt´ iŋ) *n.* boasting.
29. learn of hear about; learn from.
30. durst *v.* dared.
31. moved *v.* angered.

Vocabulary

presume (prē zo͞om´)
v. rely too much on; take advantage of

32. drachmas (drak´ məz) *n.* silver coins of ancient Greece.
33. indirection *n.* irregular methods.

CASSIUS. O ye gods, ye gods! Must I endure all this?

BRUTUS. All this? Ay, more: fret till your proud heart break.
  Go show your slaves how choleric[20] you are,
  And make your bondmen[21] tremble. Must I budge?[22]
45 Must I observe you?[23] Must I stand and crouch[24]
  Under your testy humor?[25] By the gods,
  You shall digest the venom of your spleen,[26]
  Though it do split you; for, from this day forth,
  I'll use you for my mirth, yea, for my laughter,
  When you are waspish.[27]

50 **CASSIUS.**   Is it come to this?

BRUTUS. You say you are a better soldier:
  Let it appear so; make your vaunting[28] true,
  And it shall please me well. For mine own part,
  I shall be glad to learn of[29] noble men.

55 **CASSIUS.** You wrong me every way; you wrong me, Brutus;
  I said, an elder soldier, not a better.
  Did I say, better?

BRUTUS.   If you did, I care not.

CASSIUS. When Caesar lived, he durst[30] not thus have
  moved[31] me.

BRUTUS. Peace, peace, you durst not so have tempted him.

60 **CASSIUS.** I durst not?

BRUTUS. No.

CASSIUS. What? Durst not tempt him?

BRUTUS.   For your life you durst not.

CASSIUS. Do not presume too much upon my love;
  I may do that I shall be sorry for.

65 **BRUTUS.** You have done that you should be sorry for.
  There is no terror, Cassius, in your threats;
  For I am armed so strong in honesty
  That they pass by me as the idle wind,
  Which I respect not. I did send to you
70 For certain sums of gold, which you denied me;
  For I can raise no money by vile means.
  By heaven, I had rather coin my heart
  And drop my blood for drachmas[32] than to wring
  From the hard hands of peasants their vile trash
75 By any indirection.[33] I did send

◀ **Critical Viewing**
What does this ancient Roman sculpture suggest about the Roman attitude toward war? **[Interpret]**

To you for gold to pay my legions,[34]
Which you denied me. Was that done like Cassius?
Should I have answered Caius Cassius so?
When Marcus Brutus grows so covetous[35]
80   To lock such rascal counters[36] from his friends,
Be ready, gods, with all your thunderbolts,
Dash him to pieces!

CASSIUS.   I denied you not.

BRUTUS. You did.

CASSIUS.   I did not. He was but a fool
That brought my answer back. Brutus hath rived[37] my heart.

34. **legions** *n.* Roman military divisions of several thousand soldiers.
35. **covetous** (kuv´ ət əs) *adj.* greedy.
36. **rascal counters** worthless coins.
37. **rived** (rīvd) *v.* broken.

Reading Check

What is the second accusation Brutus makes against Cassius?

85 A friend should bear his friend's infirmities;
But Brutus makes mine greater than they are.

BRUTUS. I do not, till you practice them on me.

CASSIUS. You love me not.

BRUTUS.   I do not like your faults.

CASSIUS. A friendly eye could never see such faults.

90 **BRUTUS.** A flatterer's would not, though they do appear
As huge as high Olympus.

CASSIUS. Come, Antony, and young Octavius, come,
Revenge yourselves alone[38] on Cassius,
For Cassius is aweary of the world:
95 Hated by one he loves; braved[39] by his brother;
Checked like a bondman;[40] all his faults observed,
Set in a notebook, learned and conned by rote[41]
To cast into my teeth. O, I could weep
My spirit from mine eyes! There is my dagger,

38. **alone** *adv.* only.
39. **braved** *adj.* defied;
    challenged.
40. **Checked like a
    bondman** scolded like a
    slave.
41. **conned by rote**
    memorized.

▼ **Critical Viewing** In
this film still, do Brutus
and Cassius look as
if they will be able to
settle their conflict?
Explain. **[Hypothesize]**

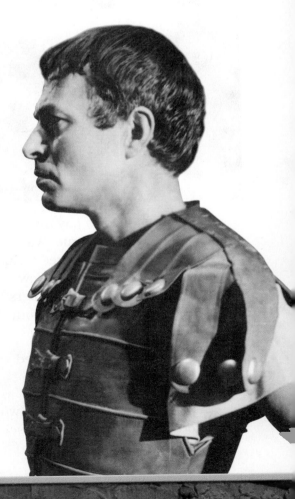

100 And here my naked breast; within, a heart
Dearer than Pluto's mine,[42] richer than gold;
If that thou be'st a Roman, take it forth.
I, that denied thee gold, will give my heart.
Strike as thou didst at Caesar; for I know,
105 When thou didst hate him worst, thou lovedst him better
Than ever thou lovedst Cassius.

BRUTUS.   Sheathe your dagger.
Be angry when you will, it shall have scope.[43]
Do what you will, dishonor shall be humor.[44]
O Cassius, you are yokèd[45] with a lamb
110 That carries anger as the flint[46] bears fire,
Who, much enforcèd,[47] shows a hasty spark,
And straight[48] is cold again.

CASSIUS.   Hath Cassius lived
To be but mirth and laughter to his Brutus
When grief and blood ill-tempered vexeth him?

115 **BRUTUS.** When I spoke that, I was ill-tempered too.

CASSIUS. Do you confess so much? Give me your hand.

BRUTUS. And my heart too.

CASSIUS.   O Brutus!

BRUTUS.   What's the matter?

CASSIUS. Have not you love enough to bear with me
When that rash humor[49] which my mother gave me
Makes me forgetful?

120 **BRUTUS.**   Yes, Cassius, and from henceforth,
When you are overearnest with your Brutus,
He'll think your mother chides, and leave you so.[50]

[*Enter a* POET, *followed by* LUCILIUS, TITINIUS, *and* LUCIUS.]

POET. Let me go in to see the generals;
There is some grudge between 'em; 'tis not meet
125 They be alone.

LUCILIUS. You shall not come to them.

POET. Nothing but death shall stay me.

CASSIUS. How now? What's the matter?

POET. For shame, you generals! What do you mean?
130 Love, and be friends, as two such men should be;
For I have seen more years, I'm sure, than ye.

42. **Pluto's mine** all the riches in the Earth.
43. **scope** *n.* free play.
44. **dishonor . . . humor** I will consider any insults to be just the effect of your irritable disposition.
45. **yokèd** *adj.* in partnership.
46. **flint** *n.* hard mineral that, when struck by steel, makes sparks.
47. **enforcèd** *adj.* provoked.
48. **straight** *adv.* immediately.

Reading Skill
Read Between the Lines In this situation, what does Cassius' use of the phrase "his Brutus" suggest?

49. **humor** *n.* temperament.
50. **your mother . . . so** it is just your inherited disposition and let it go at that.

Reading
Check

What happens in the quarrel between Cassius and Brutus?

53. **I'll know . . . time** I'll accept his eccentricity when he chooses a proper time to exhibit it.
54. **jigging** *adj.* rhyming.
55. **Companion** *n.* fellow (used to show contempt).

Literary Analysis

Conflict How does the arrival of the poet help end the conflict between Cassius and Brutus?

56. **Of your philosophy . . . evils** As a Stoic, Brutus believed that chance misfortunes should not disturb his peace of mind.

CASSIUS. Ha, ha! How vilely doth this cynic[51] rhyme!

BRUTUS. Get you hence, sirrah! Saucy[52] fellow, hence!

CASSIUS. Bear with him, Brutus, 'tis his fashion.

135 **BRUTUS.** I'll know his humor when he knows his time.[53]
　　　What should the wars do with these jigging[54] fools?
　　　Companion,[55] hence!

CASSIUS. 　　　　　　　　Away, away, be gone!　　　*[Exit POET.]*

BRUTUS. Lucilius and Titinius, bid the commanders
　　　Prepare to lodge their companies tonight.

140 **CASSIUS.** And come yourselves, and bring Messala with you
　　　Immediately to us.　　　*[Exit LUCILIUS and TITINIUS.]*

BRUTUS. 　　　　　　　　Lucius, a bowl of wine.　　　*[Exit LUCIUS.]*

CASSIUS. I did not think you could have been so angry.

BRUTUS. O Cassius, I am sick of many griefs.

CASSIUS. Of your philosophy you make no use,
145　　　If you give place to accidental evils.[56]

BRUTUS. No man bears sorrow better. Portia is dead.

CASSIUS. Ha? Portia?

BRUTUS. She is dead.

LITERATURE IN CONTEXT

Humanities Connection

Stoicism

Brutus follows a philosophy called Stoicism (stō´ i siz´ əm), a school of thought established by the ancient Greek thinker Zeno sometime after 312 B.C. Stoicism stresses the following ideas:

- The universe is ruled by unchanging natural laws.
- A wise person lives a virtuous life, using reason to understand natural laws and to act accordingly.
- A wise person is not ruled by his or her emotions.
- Using reason, a wise person distinguishes between what is truly in his or her power and what is not.
- A wise person does not allow events that he or she does not control—even the loss of a loved one—to affect him or her.

Connect to the Literature

How do Brutus' Stoic beliefs affect his actions in Act IV?

CASSIUS. How scaped I killing when I crossed you so?[57]

150   O insupportable and touching[58] loss!

Upon[59] what sickness?

BRUTUS.   Impatient of my absence,

And grief that young Octavius with Mark Antony

Have made themselves so strong—for with her death

That tidings[60] came—with this she fell distract,[61]

155   And (her attendants absent) swallowed fire.

CASSIUS. And died so?

BRUTUS.   Even so.

CASSIUS.   O ye immortal gods!

[*Enter* LUCIUS, *with wine and tapers.*]

BRUTUS. Speak no more of her. Give me a bowl of wine.

In this I bury all unkindness, Cassius.   [*Drinks*]

CASSIUS. My heart is thirsty for that noble pledge.

160   Fill, Lucius, till the wine o'erswell the cup;

I cannot drink too much of Brutus' love.

                          [*Drinks. Exit* LUCIUS.]

[*Enter* TITINIUS *and* MESSALA.]

BRUTUS. Come in, Titinius! Welcome, good Messala.

Now sit we close about this taper here,

And call in question[62] our necessities.

CASSIUS. Portia, art thou gone?

165 **BRUTUS.**   No more, I pray you.

Messala, I have here receivèd letters

That young Octavius and Mark Antony

Come down upon us with a mighty power,[63]

Bending their expedition toward Philippi.[64]

170 **MESSALA.** Myself have letters of the selfsame tenure.[65]

BRUTUS. With what addition?

MESSALA. That by proscription and bills of outlawry[66]

Octavius, Antony, and Lepidus

Have put to death an hundred senators.

175 **BRUTUS.** Therein our letters do not well agree.

Mine speak of seventy senators that died

By their proscriptions, Cicero being one.

CASSIUS. Cicero one?

---

57. **How scaped . . . you so?** How did I escape being killed when I opposed you so?
58. **touching** *adj.* deeply wounding.
59. **Upon** *prep.* as a result of.

Literary Analysis

Conflict With what internal conflict has Brutus been struggling?

60. **with . . . tidings came** That is, Brutus received two messages at the same time: news of Portia's death and news of Octavius and Antony's success.
61. **fell distract** became distraught.

62. **call in question** examine.

63. **power** *n.* army.
64. **Bending . . . Philippi** (fi lip´ ī) directing their rapid march toward Philippi, a city in Macedonia.
65. **selfsame tenure** same message.
66. **proscription . . . outlawry** proclamation of death sentences and lists of those condemned.

Reading Check

What has happened to Brutus' wife, Portia?

Reading Skill

Read Between the Lines In this situation, why might Messala ask Brutus about news of Portia?

67. **aught** (ôt) *n.* anything at all.

MESSALA.   Cicero is dead,
And by that order of proscription.
180   Had you your letters from your wife, my lord?

BRUTUS. No, Messala.

MESSALA. Nor nothing in your letters writ of her?

BRUTUS. Nothing, Messala.

MESSALA.   That methinks is strange.

BRUTUS. Why ask you? Hear you aught[67] of her in yours?

185 **MESSALA.** No, my lord.

BRUTUS. Now as you are a Roman, tell me true.

MESSALA. Then like a Roman bear the truth I tell,
For certain she is dead, and by strange manner.

BRUTUS. Why, farewell, Portia. We must die, Messala.
190   With meditating that she must die once,
I have the patience to endure it now.

MESSALA. Even so great men great losses should endure.

68. **have . . . art** have as much Stoicism in theory.
69. **to our work alive** Let us go about the work we have to do as living men.
70. **presently** *adv.* immediately.

CASSIUS. I have as much of this in art[68] as you,
But yet my nature could not bear it so.

195 **BRUTUS.** Well, to our work alive.[69] What do you think
Of marching to Philippi presently?[70]

CASSIUS. I do not think it good.

BRUTUS.   Your reason?

CASSIUS.   This it is:
'Tis better that the enemy seek us;
So shall he waste his means, weary his soldiers,

71. **offense** *n.* harm.
72. **of force** of necessity.
73. **Do stand . . . affection** support us only out of fear of force.
74. **grudged us contribution** given us aid and supplies grudgingly.
75. **shall make . . . up** will add more to their numbers.
76. **new-added** reinforced.

200   Doing himself offense,[71] whilst we, lying still,
Are full of rest, defense, and nimbleness.

BRUTUS. Good reasons must of force[72] give place to better.
The people 'twixt Philippi and this ground
Do stand but in a forced affection;[73]
205   For they have grudged us contribution.[74]
The enemy, marching along by them,
By them shall make a fuller number up,[75]
Come on refreshed, new-added[76] and encouraged;
From which advantage shall we cut him off
210   If at Philippi we do face him there,
These people at our back.

CASSIUS. Hear me, good brother.

BRUTUS. Under your pardon.[77] You must note beside
That we have tried the utmost of our friends,
Our legions are brimful, our cause is ripe.
215 The enemy increaseth every day;
We, at the height, are ready to decline.
There is a tide in the affairs of men
Which, taken at the flood, leads on to fortune;
Omitted,[78] all the voyage of their life
220 Is bound[79] in shallows and in miseries.
On such a full sea are we now afloat,
And we must take the current when it serves,
Or lose our ventures.[80]

CASSIUS. Then, with your will,[81] go on;
We'll along ourselves and meet them at Philippi.

225 **BRUTUS.** The deep of night is crept upon our talk,
And nature must obey necessity,
Which we will niggard with a little rest.[82]
There is no more to say?

CASSIUS. No more. Good night.
Early tomorrow will we rise and hence.[83]

[*Enter* LUCIUS.]

BRUTUS. Lucius, my gown.[84]   [*Exit* LUCIUS.]
230   Farewell, good Messala.
Good night, Titinius. Noble, noble Cassius,
Good night, and good repose.

CASSIUS. O my dear brother,
This was an ill beginning of the night.
Never come[85] such division 'tween our souls!
Let it not, Brutus.

[*Enter* LUCIUS, *with the gown.*]

235 **BRUTUS.** Everything is well.

CASSIUS. Good night, my lord.

BRUTUS. Good night, good brother.

TITINIUS, MESSALA. Good night, Lord Brutus.

BRUTUS. Farewell, every one.

[*Exit*]

Give me the gown. Where is thy instrument?[86]

Reading Skill
Read Between the Lines What does Brutus' speech indicate about the chances that he and Cassius will lose the war?

Reading Check

What do Brutus and Cassius plan to do?

LUCIUS. Here in the tent.

BRUTUS.   What, thou speak'st drowsily?
240   Poor knave,[87] I blame thee not; thou art o'erwatched.[88]
       Call Claudius and some other of my men;
       I'll have them sleep on cushions in my tent.

LUCIUS. Varro and Claudius!

[*Enter* VARRO *and* CLAUDIUS.]

VARRO. Calls my lord?

245   **BRUTUS.** I pray you, sirs, lie in my tent and sleep.
       It may be I shall raise[89] you by and by
       On business to my brother Cassius.

VARRO. So please you, we will stand and watch your pleasure.[90]

BRUTUS. I will not have it so; lie down, good sirs;
250   It may be I shall otherwise bethink me.[91]

                                   [VARRO *and* CLAUDIUS *lie down.*]

       Look. Lucius, here's the book I sought for so;
       I put it in the pocket of my gown.

LUCIUS. I was sure your lordship did not give it me.

BRUTUS. Bear with me, good boy, I am much forgetful.
255   Canst thou hold up thy heavy eyes awhile,
       And touch thy instrument a strain or two?[92]

LUCIUS. Ay, my lord, an't[93] please you.

BRUTUS.   It does, my boy.
       I trouble thee too much, but thou art willing.

LUCIUS. It is my duty, sir.

260   **BRUTUS.** I should not urge thy duty past thy might;
       I know young bloods[94] look for a time of rest.

LUCIUS. I have slept, my lord, already.

BRUTUS. It was well done, and thou shalt sleep again;
       I will not hold thee long. If I do live,
265   I will be good to thee.

[*Music, and a song*]

       This is a sleepy tune. O murd'rous[95] slumber!
       Layest thou thy leaden mace[96] upon my boy,
       That plays thee music? Gentle knave, good night;
       I will not do thee so much wrong to wake thee.
270   If thou dost nod, thou break'st thy instrument;

---

87. knave (nāv) *n.* servant.
88. o'erwatched *adj.* weary with too much watchfulness.

89. raise *v.* wake.
90. watch your pleasure stay alert for your command.
91. otherwise bethink me change my mind.

92. touch . . . a strain or two? play a melody or two on your instrument.
93. an't if it.

94. young bloods young bodies.

95. murd'rous *adj.* deathlike.
96. mace (mās) *n.* staff of office (an allusion to the practice of tapping a person on the shoulder with a mace when arresting him).

I'll take it from thee; and, good boy, good night.
Let me see, let me see; is not the leaf[97] turned down
Where I left reading? Here it is, I think.

[*Enter the ghost of* CAESAR.]

How ill this taper burns. Ha! Who comes here?
275 I think it is the weakness of mine eyes
That shapes this monstrous apparition.[98]
It comes upon[99] me. Art thou anything?
Art thou some god, some angel, or some devil,
That mak'st my blood cold, and my hair to stare?[100]
280 Speak to me what thou art.

GHOST. Thy evil spirit, Brutus.

BRUTUS.   Why com'st thou?

GHOST. To tell thee thou shalt see me at Philippi.

BRUTUS. Well; then I shall see thee again?

GHOST. Ay, at Philippi.

285 **BRUTUS.** Why, I will see thee at Philippi then.

[*Exit* GHOST.]

Now I have taken heart thou vanishest.
Ill spirit, I would hold more talk with thee.
Boy! Lucius! Varro! Claudius! Sirs, awake!
Claudius!

290 **LUCIUS.** The strings, my lord, are false.[101]

BRUTUS. He thinks he still is at his instrument.
Lucius, awake!

LUCIUS. My lord?

BRUTUS. Didst thou dream, Lucius, that thou so criedst out?

295 **LUCIUS.** My lord, I do not know that I did cry.

BRUTUS. Yes, that thou didst. Didst thou see anything?

LUCIUS. Nothing, my lord.

BRUTUS. Sleep again, Lucius. Sirrah Claudius!
[*To* VARRO] Fellow thou, awake!

300 **VARRO.** My lord?

CLAUDIUS. My lord?

BRUTUS. Why did you so cry out, sirs, in your sleep?

97. leaf *n.* page.
98. monstrous apparition ominous ghost.
99. upon *prep.* toward.
100. stare *n.* stand on end.

Reading Skill
Read Between the Lines Brutus is planning to march to battle at Philippi. In this situation, what might the ghost's warning mean?

101. false *adj.* out of tune.

Literary Analysis
Conflict What internal conflict might the ghost's warning create for Brutus?

☑ Reading Check

What frightens Brutus in his sleep?

BOTH. Did we, my lord?

BRUTUS.   Ay. Saw you anything?

VARRO. No, my lord, I saw nothing.

CLAUDIUS.   Nor I, my lord.

305 **BRUTUS.** Go and commend me[102] to my brother
        Cassius;
    Bid him set on his pow'rs betimes before,[103]
    And we will follow.

BOTH.   It shall be done, my lord.   [*Exit*]

102. **commend me** carry my greetings.
103. **set on . . . before** advance his troops early, before me.

◀ **Critical Viewing**
What does this ancient Roman coin suggest about how war was fought at the time? **[Interpret]**

Critical Thinking

Cite textual evidence to support your responses.

1. Key Ideas and Details (a) In Scene i, what opinion of Lepidus does Antony express? **(b) Infer:** Why is Octavius surprised to hear this opinion? **(c) Connect:** In what way is Antony's behavior toward Lepidus similar to his manipulation of the crowd at Caesar's funeral?

2. Key Ideas and Details (a) What are two accusations Brutus makes against Cassius in Scene iii? **(b) Compare and Contrast:** What difference in their characters does their argument emphasize?

3. Integration of Knowledge and Ideas (a) Make a Judgment: Which character in Act IV do you think would make the best leader for Rome? Explain. **(b) Discuss:** Share your ideas and the reasons for them in a small group discussion. **(c) Evaluate:** As a group, choose the two best candidates and present the reasons for your choices to the class.

4. Integration of Knowledge and Ideas (a) How do Brutus' past actions contribute to the appearance of Caesar's ghost? **(b)** What does Caesar's ghost represent? *[Connect to the Big Question: To what extent does experience determine what we perceive?]*

After You Read — The Tragedy of Julius Caesar, Act IV

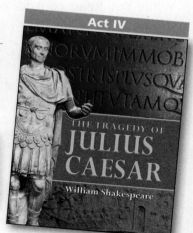
Act IV

THE TRAGEDY OF
JULIUS
CAESAR
William Shakespeare

Literary Analysis: External and Internal Conflict

Ⓒ **1. Craft and Structure (a)** Using a diagram like the one shown, identify two **external conflicts** shown or referred to in Act IV. **(b)** Describe two of the **internal conflicts** Brutus experiences in Act IV.

Force 1	Conflict: External/Internal	Force 2
→ →		← ←

Ⓒ **2. Craft and Structure (a)** Explain the connection Brutus makes in Scene iii, lines 18–28 between his reasons for joining the conspirators and his conflict with Cassius. **(b)** Do you think Brutus will feel an internal conflict over his decision to join the conspirators? Explain.

Reading Skill: Read Between the Lines

3. (a) To whom is Brutus referring as "a brother" in Scene ii, lines 38–39? **(b)** What is the meaning of what he says?

4. (a) What does Cassius say in Scene iii, lines 92–98? **(b)** What is the situation? **(c) Read between the lines** to explain the unspoken significance of his words.

Vocabulary

Ⓒ **Acquisition and Use** For each word from the vocabulary list on page 964, write a definition in your own words. Then, write a brief paragraph in which you use the words correctly to describe a profession or career.

1. legacies   **4.** rash

2. chastisement   **5.** condemned

3. mirth   **6.** presume

Word Study Use the context of the sentences and what you know about the **Latin root -sum-** to explain your answer to each question.

1. If Rafael *assumes* the role of class president, has he stepped down from the position?

2. Does her *presumptuous* remark reveal her modesty?

Word Study

The **Latin root -sum-** means "to take" or "to use."

Apply It Explain how the root -sum- contributes to the meanings of these words. Consult a dictionary if necessary.

consume
resume
sumptuous

Before You Read

The Tragedy of Julius Caesar, Act V

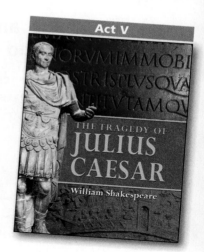

Act V

THE TRAGEDY OF
JULIUS CAESAR
William Shakespeare

While You Read Look for evidence that explains how Brutus perceives the world, and consider the way his ideas shape his actions.

© Common Core State Standards

Meet these standards with *The Tragedy of Julius Caesar,* **Act V** (p. 986).

Reading Literature

3. Analyze how complex characters develop over the course of a text, interact with other characters, and advance the plot or develop the theme. *(Literary Analysis: Tragic Heroes; Reading Skill: Compare and Contrast Characters)*

7. Analyze the representation of a subject or a key scene in two different artistic mediums, including what is emphasized or absent in each treatment. *(Speaking and Listening: Group Screening)*

Integrated Language Skills:
Pages 1002–1005
Writing
1. Write arguments to support claims. *(Writing: Editorial)*

4. Produce clear and coherent writing. *(Writing: Obituary; Research and Technology: Advertising Poster)*

6. Use technology, including the Internet. *(Research and Technology: Multimedia Presentation)*

7. Conduct short research projects. *(Research and Technology: Women's History Report)*

Speaking and Listening
6. Adapt speech to a variety of contexts and tasks. *(Speaking and Listening: Dramatic Reading)*

Language
1.b. Use various types of phrases and clauses to convey specific meanings. *(Conventions: Absolutes and Absolute Phrases)*

Vocabulary

Read each word and its definition. Decide whether you know the word well, know it a little bit, or do not know it at all. After you read, see how your knowledge of each word has increased.

- **fawned** (fônd) *v.* flattered; acted with excessive concern for the wishes and moods of another, as a servant might (p. 988) *She fawned on her new boss as if he were a king.* fawner *n.* fawningly *adv.*

- **presage** (prē sāj´) *v.* give a warning sign about a future event (p. 989) *His frown seemed to presage a stern lecture.* presage *n.*

- **demeanor** (di mēn´ ər) *n.* way of conducting oneself; behavior (p. 990) *The child's good demeanor earned him a gold star.*

- **disconsolate** (dis kän´ sə lit) *adj.* so unhappy that nothing brings comfort (p. 994) *Disconsolate, he would not stop weeping for his loss.* console *v.* disconsolately *adv.*

- **misconstrued** (mis´ kən strood´) *v.* misinterpreted (p. 994) *I misconstrued the directions and wound up lost.* construe *v.* misconstruction *n.*

- **meditates** (med´ ə tāts´) *v.* thinks deeply (p. 997) *The philosopher quietly meditates on a new idea.* meditation *n.* meditative *adj.*

Word Study

The **Latin root -stru-** means "pile up" or "build."

In the play, a scene on the battlefield is **misconstrued,** or interpreted incorrectly.

Literary Analysis: Tragic Heroes

Traditionally, a **tragic hero** is a person, usually of noble birth, who suffers a catastrophe. The hero's choices leading to the catastrophe may reflect a personal shortcoming, such as pride, called a **tragic flaw.** While **Shakespeare's tragic heroes** incorporate these traditional elements, he develops them in new ways:

- He adds complexity to his heroes, who may have opposing desires and who may suffer hesitation and doubt before acting.
- He presents a character's inner turmoil directly, through devices like the *soliloquy,* a speech in which a character thinks aloud.
- He focuses on the choices characters make rather than on fate.
- His characters' problems often concern the difference between the reasons for an action and its outcome. For example, Brutus acts for reasons of honor—the right reasons—but in a world of men who are less than honorable, the results are disastrous.

Reading Skill: Compare and Contrast Characters

Shakespeare often emphasizes the important qualities of one character by presenting another character with contrasting qualities. A **foil** is a character who sets off another character by providing a strong contrast. When **reading Shakespearean drama,** you can often gain understanding by **comparing and contrasting characters.** Look for similarities and differences in the characters' personalities, situations, behaviors, and attitudes.

Using the Strategy: Character Chart

Record details on a **character chart** to compare and contrast characters' qualities.

Brutus	Cassius
nobleman	nobleman
idealistic	practical

REVIEW AND ANTICIPATE

By the end of Act IV, Cassius and Brutus have patched up their quarrel. Brutus persuades Cassius to agree to his strategy—taking the battle to the enemy. He reasons that they should march to the city of Philippi and attack before Octavius and Antony swell their forces with new recruits. The act ends ominously as Brutus is visited by Caesar's ghost. Before disappearing, the ghost tells Brutus that they will meet again at Philippi. As Act V opens, the two armies are poised for battle on the plains of Philippi. Nothing less than the future of Rome is at stake.

▶ **Critical Viewing** Does Brutus' personality, as suggested by this statue, fit with his personality in the story? Explain. **[Connect]**

ACT V

Scene i. *The plains of Philippi.*

[*Enter* OCTAVIUS, ANTONY, *and their Army.*]

OCTAVIUS. Now, Antony, our hopes are answerèd;
You said the enemy would not come down,
But keep the hills and upper regions.
It proves not so; their battles[1] are at hand;
5   They mean to warn[2] us at Philippi here,
Answering before we do demand of them.[3]

ANTONY. Tut, I am in their bosoms,[4] and I know
Wherefore[5] they do it. They could be content
To visit other places, and come down
10 With fearful bravery,[6] thinking by this face[7]
To fasten in our thoughts[8] that they have courage;
But 'tis not so.

[*Enter a* MESSENGER.]

MESSENGER.   Prepare you, generals,
The enemy comes on in gallant show;
Their bloody sign[9] of battle is hung out,
15 And something to be done immediately.

ANTONY. Octavius, lead your battle softly[10] on
Upon the left hand of the even[11] field.

OCTAVIUS. Upon the right hand I; keep thou the left.

ANTONY. Why do you cross me in this exigent?[12]

20 **OCTAVIUS.** I do not cross you; but I will do so.   [*March*]

[*Drum. Enter* BRUTUS, CASSIUS, *and their Army;* LUCILIUS, TITINIUS,
MESSALA, *and others.*]

BRUTUS. They stand, and would have parley.[13]

CASSIUS. Stand fast, Titinius, we must out and talk.

OCTAVIUS. Mark Antony, shall we give sign of battle?

ANTONY. No, Caesar, we will answer on their charge.[14]
25 Make forth;[15] the generals would have some words.

OCTAVIUS. Stir not until the signal.

BRUTUS. Words before blows; is it so, countrymen?

OCTAVIUS. Not that we love words better, as you do.

1. **battles** *n.* armies.
2. **warn** *v.* challenge.
3. **Answering . . . of them** appearing in opposition to us before we challenge them.
4. **am in their bosoms** know what they are thinking.
5. **Wherefore** *conj.* why.
6. **fearful bravery** show of magnificence and pretend courage concealing fear.
7. **face** *n.* appearance.
8. **fasten in our thoughts** convince us.

Reading Skill
Compare and Contrast Characters
What contrast between Octavius and Antony is suggested by their opening speeches?

9. **bloody sign** red flag.
10. **softly** *adv.* slowly.
11. **even** *adj.* level.
12. **exigent** *n.* critical situation.
13. **parley** *n.* conference between enemies.
14. **answer on their charge** meet them when they attack.
15. **Make forth** go forward.

Reading Check
What news does the messenger bring Octavius and Antony?

The Tragedy of Julius Caesar, Act V, Scene i **987**

BRUTUS. Good words are better than bad strokes, Octavius.

30 **ANTONY.** In your bad strokes, Brutus, you give good words;
Witness the hole you made in Caesar's heart,
Crying "Long live! Hail, Caesar!"

CASSIUS.   Antony,
The posture[16] of your blows are yet unknown;
But for your words, they rob the Hybla bees,[17]
And leave them honeyless.

35 **ANTONY.**   Not stingless too.

BRUTUS. O, yes, and soundless too;
For you have stol'n their buzzing, Antony,
And very wisely threat before you sting.

ANTONY. Villains! You did not so, when your vile daggers
40 Hacked one another in the sides of Caesar.
You showed your teeth[18] like apes, and fawned like hounds,
And bowed like bondmen,[19] kissing Caesar's feet;
Whilst damnèd Casca, like a cur,[20] behind
Struck Caesar on the neck. O you flatterers!

45 **CASSIUS.** Flatterers! Now, Brutus, thank yourself;
This tongue had not offended so today,
If Cassius might have ruled.[21]

OCTAVIUS. Come, come, the cause.[22] If arguing make us sweat,
The proof[23] of it will turn to redder drops.
50 Look,
I draw a sword against conspirators.
When think you that the sword goes up[24] again?
Never, till Caesar's three and thirty wounds
Be well avenged; or till another Caesar
55 Have added slaughter to the sword of traitors.[25]

BRUTUS. Caesar, thou canst not die by traitors' hands,
Unless thou bring'st them with thee.

OCTAVIUS.   So I hope.
I was not born to die on Brutus' sword.

BRUTUS. O, if thou wert the noblest of thy strain,[26]
60 Young man, thou couldst not die more honorable.

CASSIUS. A peevish[27] schoolboy, worthless[28] of such honor,
Joined with a masker and a reveler.[29]

ANTONY. Old Cassius still!

OCTAVIUS.   Come, Antony; away!

---

16. **posture** *n.* quality.
17. **Hybla bees** bees from the town of Hybla in Sicily, noted for their sweet honey.

Vocabulary

fawned (fônd) *v.* flattered; acted with excessive concern for the wishes and moods of another, as a servant might

18. **showed your teeth** grinned.
19. **bondmen** *n.* slaves.
20. **cur** *n.* dog.
21. **If Cassius might have ruled** if Cassius had had his way when he urged that Antony be killed.

Literary Analysis

Tragic Heroes Which of Brutus' earlier decisions would Cassius call tragic?

22. **cause** *n.* business at hand.
23. **proof** *n.* test.
24. **goes up** goes into its scabbard.
25. **till another Caesar . . . traitors** until I, another Caesar, have also been killed by you.
26. **noblest of thy strain** best of your family.
27. **peevish** silly.
28. **worthless** *adj.* unworthy.
29. **a masker and a reveler** one who attends masquerades and parties; Antony.

Defiance, traitors, hurl we in your teeth.
65   If you dare fight today, come to the field;
If not, when you have stomachs.[30]

[*Exit* OCTAVIUS, ANTONY, *and Army.*]

CASSIUS. Why, now blow wind, swell billow, and swim bark![31]
The storm is up, and all is on the hazard.[32]

BRUTUS. Ho, Lucilius, hark, a word with you.

[LUCILIUS *and* MESSALA *stand forth.*]

LUCILIUS.   My lord?

[BRUTUS *and* LUCILIUS *converse apart.*]

CASSIUS. Messala.

MESSALA.   What says my general?

70   **CASSIUS.**   Messala,
This is my birthday; as this very day
Was Cassius born. Give me thy hand, Messala:
Be thou my witness that against my will
(As Pompey was)[33] am I compelled to set[34]
75   Upon one battle all our liberties.
You know that I held Epicurus strong,[35]
And his opinion; now I change my mind.
And partly credit things that do presage.
Coming from Sardis, on our former ensign[36]
80   Two mighty eagles fell,[37] and there they perched,
Gorging and feeding from our soldiers' hands,
Who to Philippi here consorted[38] us.
This morning are they fled away and gone,
And in their steads do ravens, crows, and kites[39]
85   Fly o'er our heads and downward look on us
As we were sickly prey; their shadows seem
A canopy most fatal,[40] under which
Our army lies, ready to give up the ghost.

MESSALA. Believe not so.

CASSIUS.   I but believe it partly,
90   For I am fresh of spirit and resolved
To meet all perils very constantly.[41]

BRUTUS. Even so, Lucilius.

CASSIUS.   Now, most noble Brutus,
The gods today stand friendly, that we may,
Lovers[42] in peace, lead on our days to age!

---

30. **stomachs** appetites for battle.
31. **bark** ship.
32. **on the hazard** at stake.

33. **As Pompey was** Against his own judgment, Pompey was urged to do battle against Caesar. The battle resulted in Pompey's defeat and murder.
34. **set** stake.
35. **held Epicurus strong** believed in Epicurus' philosophy that the gods do not interest themselves in human affairs and that omens are merely superstitions.

Vocabulary

presage (prē sāj´) *v.* give a warning sign about a future event

36. **former ensign** (en´ sīn´) standard-bearer (soldier carrying a flag) farthest in front.
37. **fell** swooped down.
38. **consorted** *v.* accompanied.
39. **ravens, crows, and kites** scavenger birds, said to gather before a battle.
40. **A canopy most fatal** a rooflike covering foretelling death.
41. **very constantly** most resolutely.
42. **Lovers** *n.* true friends.

Reading Check

What is Cassius' complaint about the battle they are about to fight?

43. **rests still incertain**
always remain uncertain.
44. **reason . . . befall** reason
about the worst that may
happen.
45. **that philosophy** here,
Stoicism.
46. **Cato** Marcus Porcius
Cato (Cato the Younger)
supported Pompey in his
quarrel with Caesar and
killed himself after
Pompey's defeat.
47. **so to prevent . . .
life** thus to anticipate the
natural end of life.
48. **stay the providence**
await the ordained fate.

Reading Skill
Compare and Contrast
Characters Contrast the
outlook Brutus expresses
here with Cassius' mis-
givings in lines 70–88.

49. **in triumph** as a captive in
the victor's procession.
50. **Thorough** *prep.* through.

Literary Analysis
Tragic Heroes What
details of Brutus' preoc-
cupation with honor,
expressed here, reflect
his decision to join the
conspirators?

1. **bills** written orders.
2. **other side** wing of the
army commanded by
Cassius.
3. **cold demeanor** (di mēn´ ər)
lack of spirit in their
conduct.

Vocabulary
demeanor (di mēn´ ər)
n. way of conduct-
ing oneself; behavior

95 But since the affairs of men rests still incertain,[43]
    Let's reason with the worst that may befall.[44]
    If we do lose this battle, then is this
    The very last time we shall speak together.
    What are you then determinèd to do?

100 **BRUTUS.** Even by the rule of that philosophy[45]
    By which I did blame Cato[46] for the death
    Which he did give himself; I know not how,
    But I do find it cowardly and vile,
    For fear of what might fall, so to prevent
105 The time of life,[47] arming myself with patience
    To stay the providence[48] of some high powers
    That govern us below.

    CASSIUS.   Then, if we lose this battle,
    You are contented to be led in triumph[49]
    Thorough[50] the streets of Rome?

110 **BRUTUS.** No, Cassius, no; think not, thou noble Roman,
    That ever Brutus will go bound to Rome;
    He bears too great a mind. But this same day
    Must end that work the ides of March begun;
    And whether we shall meet again I know not.
115 Therefore our everlasting farewell take.
    Forever, and forever, farewell, Cassius!
    If we do meet again, why, we shall smile;
    If not, why then this parting was well made.

    CASSIUS. Forever, and forever, farewell, Brutus!
120 If we do meet again, we'll smile indeed;
    If not, 'tis true this parting was well made.

    BRUTUS. Why then, lead on. O, that a man might know
    The end of this day's business ere it come!
    But it sufficeth that the day will end,
125 And then the end is known. Come, ho! Away!   [*Exit*]

Scene ii. *The field of battle.*

[*Call to arms sounds. Enter* BRUTUS *and* MESSALA.]

    BRUTUS. Ride, ride, Messala, ride, and give these bills[1]
    Unto the legions on the other side.[2]

                              [*Loud call to arms*]

    Let them set on at once; for I perceive
    But cold demeanor[3] in Octavius' wing,

History Connection

Roman Triumphs

Brutus and Cassius reflect on the humiliation they will experience if they are defeated and brought in triumph to Rome. A *triumph*, held to celebrate a general's victory, included these events:

- Temples were decorated and sacrifices were held.

- The victorious general and his troops marched through the city to the Capitol, preceded by the Roman Senators and trumpeters.

- The triumphant general, dressed in a royal purple toga and holding a laurel branch, rode in a golden chariot drawn by four white horses.

- On display were the spoils of war, including carts full of treasure, and exotic animals.

- Captive enemy leaders—and even their children—were marched in front of the general.

- The people of Rome gathered to view and cheer the spectacle.

Connect to the Literature Why would Cassius and Brutus wish to escape at any cost being led as prisoners in a triumph?

---

5   And sudden push gives them the overthrow,[4]
       Ride, ride, Messala! Let them all come down.[5]

[*Exit*]

4. **sudden push . . . overthrow** sudden attack will defeat them.
5. **Let . . . down** attack all at once.

Scene iii. *The field of battle.*

[*Calls to arms sound. Enter* CASSIUS *and* TITINIUS.]

   CASSIUS. O, look, Titinius, look, the villains[1] fly!
   Myself have to mine own turned enemy.[2]
   This ensign here of mine was turning back;
   I slew the coward, and did take it[3] from him.

1. **villains** here, cowards among his own men.
2. **Myself . . . enemy** I have become an enemy to my own soldiers.
3. **it** here, the ensign's banner.
4. **fell to spoil** began to loot.

5 **TITINIUS.** O Cassius, Brutus gave the word too early,
   Who, having some advantage on Octavius,
   Took it too eagerly; his soldiers fell to spoil,[4]
   Whilst we by Antony are all enclosed.

[*Enter* PINDARUS.]

   PINDARUS. Fly further off, my lord, fly further off!
10   Mark Antony is in your tents, my lord.
   Fly, therefore, noble Cassius, fly far off!

Reading Check

How well is the battle going for Cassius and his forces?

CASSIUS. This hill is far enough. Look, look, Titinius!
  Are those my tents where I perceive the fire?

TITINIUS. They are, my lord.

CASSIUS.   Titinius, if thou lovest me,
15 Mount thou my horse and hide[5] thy spurs in him
  Till he have brought thee up to yonder troops
  And here again, that I may rest assured
  Whether yond troops are friend or enemy.

TITINIUS. I will be here again even with a thought.[6]   [*Exit*]

20 **CASSIUS.** Go, Pindarus, get higher on that hill;
  My sight was ever thick.[7] Regard[8] Titinius,
  And tell me what thou not'st about the field.

                                    [*Exit* PINDARUS.]

  This day I breathèd first. Time is come round,
  And where I did begin, there shall I end.
25 My life is run his compass.[9] Sirrah, what news?

PINDARUS. [*Above*] O my lord!

CASSIUS. What news?

PINDARUS. [*Above*] Titinius is enclosèd round about
  With horsemen that make to him on the spur;[10]
30 Yet he spurs on. Now they are almost on him.
  Now, Titinius! Now some light.[11] O, he lights too!
  He's ta'en![12] [*Shout*] And, hark! They shout for joy.

CASSIUS. Come down; behold no more.
  O, coward that I am, to live so long,
35 To see my best friend ta'en before my face!

[*Enter* PINDARUS.]

  Come hither, sirrah.
  In Parthia did I take thee prisoner;
  And then I swore thee, saving of thy life,[13]
  That whatsoever I did bid thee do,
40 Thou shouldst attempt it. Come now, keep thine oath.
  Now be a freeman, and with this good sword,
  That ran through Caesar's bowels, search[14] this bosom.
  Stand not[15] to answer. Here, take thou the hilts,
  And when my face is covered, as 'tis now,
45 Guide thou the sword—Caesar, thou art revenged,
  Even with the sword that killed thee.   [*Dies*]

---

5. hide sink.

6. even with a thought as quick as a thought.

7. thick dim.

8. Regard observe.

9. his compass its full course.

10. make . . . spur ride toward him at top speed.

11. light dismount from their horses.

12. ta'en taken; captured.

13. swore thee . . . thy life made you promise when I spared your life.

14. search penetrate.

15. Stand not do not wait.

Literary Analysis
Tragic Heroes What heroic qualities does Cassius show?

▲ **Critical Viewing** Can you tell whether the horseman in this picture is the friend or enemy of the foot soldiers? Explain what your answer shows about the conclusions Cassius draws in battle. **[Connect]**

PINDARUS. So, I am free; yet would not so have been,
Durst[16] I have done my will. O Cassius!
Far from this country Pindarus shall run,
50 Where never Roman shall take note of him.   [*Exit*]

[*Enter* TITINIUS *and* MESSALA.]

MESSALA. It is but change,[17] Titinius; for Octavius
Is overthrown by noble Brutus' power,
As Cassius' legions are by Antony.

TITINIUS. These tidings[18] will well comfort Cassius.

MESSALA. Where did you leave him?

16. **Durst** if I had dared.

17. **change** an exchange.
18. **these tidings** *n.* this news.

Reading Check

What does Cassius think has happened to Titinius?

Vocabulary
disconsolate (dis kän´ sə lit) *adj.* so unhappy that nothing brings comfort

19. **dews** *n.* in Shakespeare's day, dew was considered harmful to the health
20. **Mistrust . . . success** fear that I would not succeed.

Literary Analysis
Tragic Heroes According to Messala, what flaw doomed Cassius?

21. **Melancholy's child** one of gloomy temperament.
22. **Why dost . . . are not?** Why do you fill the receptive imagination of men with false ideas?
23. **conceived** *v.* created.
24. **mother . . . thee** Cassius (in this case), who conceived the error.
25. **envenomèd** poisoned.
26. **Hie** *v.* hurry.
27. **brave** *adj.* noble.

Vocabulary
misconstrued
(mis´ kən strōōd´) *v.* misinterpreted

28. **hold thee** wait a moment.
29. **apace** *adv.* quickly.
30. **regarded** *v.* honored.
31. **By your leave** with your permission.
32. **part** *n.* role; duty.

55   **TITINIUS.**   All disconsolate,
      With Pindarus his bondman, on this hill.

MESSALA. Is not that he that lies upon the ground?

TITINIUS. He lies not like the living. O my heart!

MESSALA. Is not that he?

TITINIUS.   No, this was he, Messala,
60   But Cassius is no more. O setting sun,
      As in thy red rays thou dost sink to night,
      So in his red blood Cassius' day is set.
      The sun of Rome is set. Our day is gone;
      Clouds, dews,[19] and dangers come; our deeds are done!
65   Mistrust of my success[20] hath done this deed.

MESSALA. Mistrust of good success hath done this deed.
      O hateful Error, Melancholy's child,[21]
      Why dost thou show to the apt thoughts of men
      The things that are not?[22] O Error, soon conceived,[23]
70   Thou never com'st unto a happy birth,
      But kill'st the mother that engend'red thee![24]

TITINIUS. What, Pindarus! Where art thou, Pindarus?

MESSALA. Seek him, Titinius, whilst I go to meet
      The noble Brutus, thrusting this report
75   Into his ears. I may say "thrusting" it;
      For piercing steel and darts envenomèd[25]
      Shall be as welcome to the ears of Brutus
      As tidings of this sight.

TITINIUS.   Hie[26] you, Messala,
      And I will seek for Pindarus the while.   [*Exit* MESSALA.]
80   Why didst thou send me forth, brave[27] Cassius?
      Did I not meet thy friends, and did not they
      Put on my brows this wreath of victory,
      And bid me give it thee? Didst thou not hear their shouts?
      Alas, thou hast misconstrued everything!
85   But hold thee,[28] take this garland on thy brow;
      Thy Brutus bid me give it thee, and I
      Will do his bidding. Brutus, come apace,[29]
      And see how I regarded[30] Caius Cassius.
      By your leave,[31] gods. This is a Roman's part:[32]
90   Come, Cassius' sword, and find Titinius' heart.   [*Dies*]

[*Call to arms sounds. Enter* BRUTUS, MESSALA, YOUNG CATO, STRATO, VOLUMNIUS, *and* LUCILIUS.]

BRUTUS. Where, where, Messala, doth his body lie?

MESSALA. Lo, yonder, and Titinius mourning it.

BRUTUS. Titinius' face is upward.

CATO.   He is slain.

BRUTUS. O Julius Caesar, thou art mighty yet!
95   Thy spirit walks abroad, and turns our swords
        In our own proper entrails.[33]   [*Low calls to arms*]

CATO.   Brave Titinius!
        Look, whe'r[34] he have not crowned dead Cassius.

BRUTUS. Are yet two Romans living such as these?
        The last of all the Romans, fare thee well!
100   It is impossible that ever Rome
        Should breed thy fellow.[35] Friends, I owe moe[36] tears
        To this dead man than you shall see me pay.
        I shall find time, Cassius; I shall find time.
        Come, therefore, and to Thasos[37] send his body;
105   His funerals shall not be in our camp,
        Lest it discomfort us.[38] Lucilius, come,
        And come, young Cato; let us to the field.
        Labeo and Flavius set our battles[39] on.
        'Tis three o'clock; and, Romans, yet ere night
110   We shall try fortune in a second fight.   [*Exit*]

Scene iv. *The field of battle.*

[*Call to arms sounds. Enter* BRUTUS, MESSALA, YOUNG CATO, LUCILIUS, *and* FLAVIUS.]

BRUTUS. Yet, countrymen, O, yet hold up your heads!

                                        [*Exit, with followers*]

CATO. What bastard[1] doth not? Who will go with me?
        I will proclaim my name about the field.
        I am the son of Marcus Cato,[2] ho!
5   A foe to tyrants, and my country's friend.
        I am the son of Marcus Cato, ho!

[*Enter* SOLDIERS *and fight.*]

LUCILIUS. And I am Brutus, Marcus Brutus, I;
        Brutus, my country's friend; know me for Brutus![3]

                                        [YOUNG CATO *falls.*]

        O young and noble Cato, art thou down?

33. **own proper entrails** very own inner organs.

34. **whe'r** whether.

Literary Analysis
Shakespeare's Tragic Heroes What noble or heroic qualities does Brutus display in his reactions to Cassius' death?

35. **fellow** equal.
36. **moe** *n.* more.
37. **Thasos** an island not far from Philippi.

38. **discomfort us** discourage our soldiers.
39. **battles** armies.

1. **bastard** person who is not a true Roman.
2. **Marcus Cato** Brutus' wife's father.
3. **And I am Brutus** Lucilius impersonates Brutus in order to protect him and confuse the enemy.

Reading Check

What error has led to Cassius' and Titinius' deaths?

10 Why, now thou diest as bravely as Titinius,
       And mayst be honored, being Cato's son.

    FIRST SOLDIER. Yield, or thou diest.

    LUCILIUS.   Only I yield to die.[4]
       There is so much that thou wilt kill me straight;[5]
       Kill Brutus, and be honored in his death.

15 **FIRST SOLDIER.** We must not. A noble prisoner!

    [*Enter* ANTONY.]

    SECOND SOLDIER. Room, ho! Tell Antony, Brutus is ta'en.

    FIRST SOLDIER. I'll tell thee news. Here comes the general.
       Brutus is ta'en, Brutus is ta'en, my lord.

    ANTONY. Where is he?

20 **LUCILIUS.** Safe, Antony; Brutus is safe enough.
       I dare assure thee that no enemy
       Shall ever take alive the noble Brutus.
       The gods defend him from so great a shame!
       When you do find him, or alive or dead,
25   He will be found like Brutus, like himself.[6]

    ANTONY. This is not Brutus, friend, but, I assure you,
       A prize no less in worth. Keep this man safe;
       Give him all kindness. I had rather have
       Such men my friends than enemies. Go on,
30   And see whe'r Brutus be alive or dead,
       And bring us word unto[7] Octavius' tent
       How everything is chanced.[8]   [*Exit*]

    ### Scene v. The field of battle.

    [*Enter* BRUTUS, DARDANIUS, CLITUS, STRATO, *and* VOLUMNIUS.]

    BRUTUS. Come, poor remains[1] of friends, rest on this rock.

    CLITUS. Statilius showed the torchlight,[2] but, my lord,
       He came not back; he is or ta'en or slain.

    BRUTUS. Sit thee down, Clitus. Slaying is the word;
5   It is a deed in fashion. Hark thee, Clitus. [*Whispers*]

    CLITUS. What, I, my lord? No, not for all the world!

    BRUTUS. Peace then, no words.

    CLITUS.   I'll rather kill myself.

    BRUTUS. Hark thee, Dardanius. [*Whispers*]

---

4. **Only . . . die** I will surrender only to die.
5. **much . . . straight** much honor in it that you will kill me immediately.

6. **like himself** behaving in a noble way.
7. **unto** in.
8. **How everything is chanced** how everything has turned out; what has happened.

1. **poor remains** pitiful survivors.
2. **showed the torchlight** signaled with a torch.

DARDANIUS.   Shall I do such a deed?

CLITUS. O Dardanius!

10 **DARDANIUS.** O Clitus!

CLITUS. What ill request did Brutus make to thee?

DARDANIUS. To kill him, Clitus. Look, he meditates.

CLITUS. Now is that noble vessel[3] full of grief,
That it runs over even at his eyes.

15 **BRUTUS.** Come hither, good Volumnius; list[4] a word.

VOLUMNIUS. What says my lord?

BRUTUS.   Why, this, Volumnius:
The ghost of Caesar hath appeared to me
Two several[5] times by night; at Sardis once,
And this last night here in Philippi fields.
I know my hour is come.

20 **VOLUMNIUS.**   Not so, my lord.

BRUTUS. Nay, I am sure it is, Volumnius.
Thou seest the world, Volumnius, how it goes;
Our enemies have beat us to the pit.[6]

                    [*Low calls to arms*]

It is more worthy to leap in ourselves
25 Than tarry till they push us.[7] Good Volumnius,
Thou know'st that we two went to school together;
Even for that our love of old, I prithee[8]
Hold thou my sword-hilts whilst I run on it.

VOLUMNIUS. That's not an office[9] for a friend, my lord.

                    [*Call to arms still*[10]]

30 **CLITUS.** Fly, fly, my lord, there is no tarrying here.

BRUTUS. Farewell to you; and you; and you, Volumnius.
Strato, thou hast been all this while asleep;
Farewell to thee too, Strato. Countrymen,
My heart doth joy that yet in all my life
35 I found no man but he was true to me.
I shall have glory by this losing day
More than Octavius and Mark Antony
By this vile conquest shall attain unto.[11]
So fare you well at once, for Brutus' tongue
40 Hath almost ended his life's history.

Vocabulary
meditates (med´ ə tāts´)
v. thinks deeply

3. **vessel** container of liquid;
   here, a metaphor for
   Brutus.
4. **list** hear.

5. **several** separate.

Literary Analysis
Tragic Heroes Why
does this scene of Brutus
weeping add complexity
or depth to his character?

6. **pit** trap or grave.
7. **tarry . . . us** wait until they
   kill us.
8. **prithee** (pri*th*´ ē)
   interjection ask you,
   please; "pray thee."
9. **office** task.
10. **still** continuing.

Literary Analysis
Tragic Heroes What
tragic flaw in Brutus is
revealed in lines 33–35?

11. **By this . . . unto** by this
    evil victory shall gain.
    (Brutus sees the victory of
    Octavius and Antony as
    causing the downfall of
    Roman freedom.)

**Reading
Check**

What does Brutus ask of
his servants?

Night hangs upon mine eyes; my bones would rest,
That have but labored to attain this hour.[12]

[*Call to arms sounds. Cry within, "Fly, fly, fly!"*]

CLITUS. Fly, my lord, fly!

BRUTUS.   Hence! I will follow.

[*Exit* CLITUS, DARDANIUS, *and* VOLUMNIUS.]

12. **this hour** time of death.

13. **respect** reputation.
14. **smatch** smack or taste.

I prithee, Strato, stay thou by thy lord,
45   Thou art a fellow of a good respect.[13]
Thy life hath had some smatch[14] of honor in it;
Hold then my sword, and turn away thy face,
While I do run upon it. Wilt thou, Strato?

STRATO. Give me your hand first. Fare you well, my lord.

50   **BRUTUS.** Farewell, good Strato—Caesar, now be still;
I killed not thee with half so good a will.
[*Dies*]

Reading Skill
Compare and Contrast Characters What do the differences in the way in which Brutus and Cassius meet death show about their characters?

[*Call to arms sounds. Retreat sounds. Enter* ANTONY, OCTAVIUS, MESSALA, LUCILIUS, *and the Army.*]

OCTAVIUS. What man is that?

MESSALA. My master's man.[15] Strato, where is thy master?

15. **man** servant.
16. **Brutus only overcame himself** only Brutus, no one else, defeated Brutus.
17. **no man else hath honor** no other man gains honor.
18. **Lucilius' saying** See Act V, Scene iv, lines 21–22.
19. **entertain them** take them into my service.
20. **bestow** spend.
21. **prefer** recommend.

STRATO. Free from the bondage you are in, Messala;
55   The conquerors can but make a fire of him
For Brutus only overcame himself,[16]
And no man else hath honor[17] by his death.

LUCILIUS. So Brutus should be found. I thank thee, Brutus,
That thou hast proved Lucilius' saying[18] true.

60   **OCTAVIUS.** All that served Brutus, I will entertain them.[19]
Fellow, wilt thou bestow[20] thy time with me?

STRATO. Ay, if Messala will prefer[21] me to you.

OCTAVIUS. Do so, good Messala.

MESSALA. How died my master, Strato?

65   **STRATO.** I held the sword, and he did run on it.

MESSALA. Octavius, then take him to follow thee,
That did the latest service to my master.

ANTONY. This was the noblest Roman of them all.
All the conspirators save[22] only he
70   Did that[23] they did in envy of great Caesar;

22. **save** except.
23. **that** what.

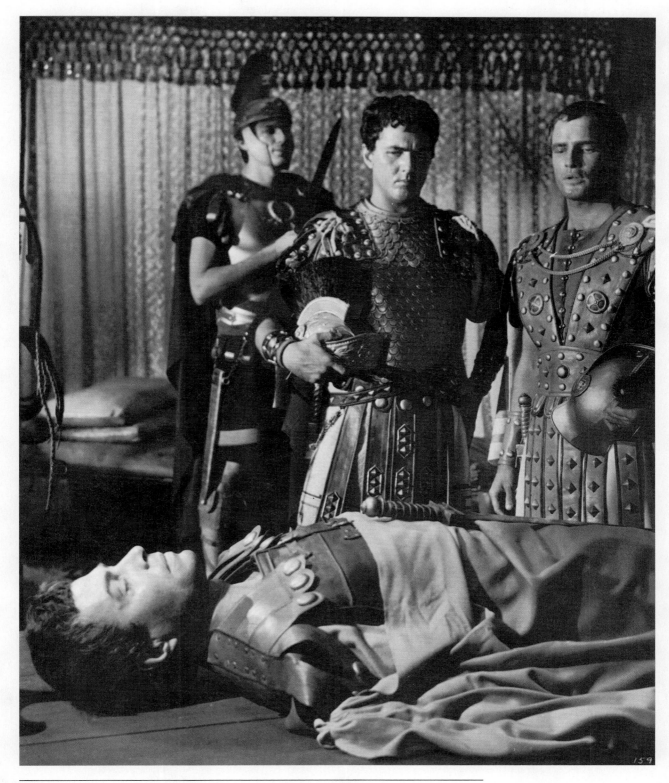

▲ **Critical Viewing** Which details in this film still suggest the respect that Octavius and Antony have for Brutus, even in defeat? **[Analyze]**

24. **only in a general honest thought** with only public-minded motives.
25. **made one of them** became one of the conspirators.
26. **gentle** noble.
27. **So mixed** well balanced.
28. **virtue** excellence.
29. **use** treat.
30. **ordered honorably** treated with honor.
31. **field** army.
32. **part** share.

He, only in a general honest thought[24]
And common good to all, made one of them.[25]
His life was gentle,[26] and the elements
So mixed[27] in him that Nature might stand up
75 And say to all the world, "This was a man!"

OCTAVIUS. According to his virtue,[28] let us use[29] him
With all respect and rites of burial.
Within my tent his bones tonight shall lie,
Most like a soldier ordered honorably.[30]
80 So call the field[31] to rest, and let's away
To part[32] the glories of this happy day.   [*Exit all.*]

Critical Thinking

Cite textual evidence to support your responses.

1. **Key Ideas and Details (a)** What do Cassius and Brutus each plan to do if they lose the battle? **(b) Analyze Cause and Effect:** In making these plans, what do they hope to avoid? Support your answer. **(c) Draw Conclusions:** What do their plans show about their values?

2. **Key Ideas and Details (a)** What does Cassius believe has happened to Titinius when Titinius rides to his tents? **(b) Analyze Cause and Effect:** What does his interpretation of events lead him to do? **(c) Connect:** In what way is this reaction like his reaction in Act I to signs that Caesar would become king?

3. **Key Ideas and Details (a)** How has Antony felt toward Brutus throughout most of the play? **(b) Infer:** How and why does Antony's attitude toward Brutus change at the end?

4. **Integration of Knowledge and Ideas (a)** Give two examples of situations in which Brutus expects others to act honorably and they fail to do so. **(b)** What is the outcome of each situation? **(c)** What do these situations suggest about Brutus' view of himself and the world? *[Connect to the Big Question: To what extent does experience determine what we perceive?]*

After You Read | The Tragedy of Julius Caesar, Act V

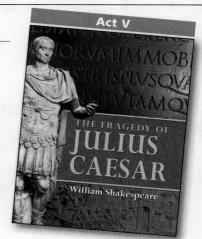

Literary Analysis: Tragic Heroes

Ⓒ **1. Craft and Structure (a)** Using a chart like the one shown, give examples showing that Brutus and Caesar have the qualities of traditional **tragic heroes.**

Noble Birth	Suffers Catastrophe	Tragic Flaw

(b) Which character has more characteristics of Shakespeare's tragic heroes? Support your answer with details from the text.

Ⓒ **2. Key Ideas and Details (a) Interpret:** What does Brutus mean when he says, "My heart doth joy that yet in all my life / I found no man but he was true to me"? **(b) Make a Judgment:** Do these lines express a positive attitude or a blindness toward others? Explain. **(c) Discuss:** Discuss your interpretation with a partner.

Reading Skill: Compare and Contrast Characters

3. (a) Compare and contrast Cassius and Brutus. Give specific examples in support of your points. **(b)** Find an example from the text to show that the two men are **foils. (c)** What do the differences between the two help to emphasize about Brutus' character?

Vocabulary

Ⓒ **Acquisition and Use** Use a vocabulary word from the list on page 984 to write a complete sentence about each numbered item. Explain your choices.

1. being too eager to please

2. watching the sun set

3. learning a new language

4. losing a friend

5. hearing distant thunder

6. making a good impression

Word Study Use the context of the sentences and what you know about the **Latin root -stru-** to explain your answer to each question.

1. If someone *obstructs* a doorway, is he or she allowing you to pass through it?

2. If a mathematician breaks a challenging code, has he or she *construed* its meaning?

Word Study

The **Latin root -stru-** means "pile up" or "build."

Apply It Explain how the root -stru- contributes to the meanings of these words. Consult a dictionary if necessary.

construction
instruct
structural

PERFORMANCE TASKS
Integrated Language Skills

The Tragedy of Julius Caesar, Acts I–V

Conventions: Absolutes and Absolute Phrases

An **absolute adjective** is an adjective that has no comparative or superlative form: *complete, infinite, perfect, unique, dead, empty, full, definite,* or *equal.* Logically, one cannot be *less equal* or *more full.*

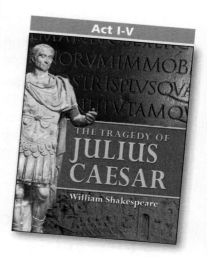

Examples

- Her dog is *bigger* than mine. (*non-absolute adjective:* The adjective *bigger* is the comparative form of *big.*)
- The bouquet of flowers is *perfect.* (*absolute adjective:* The flowers cannot be *more perfect.*)

An absolute phrase is a phrase that modifies an entire sentence, but does not modify any specific word in it. An absolute phrase usually acts as a comment on the main clause.

Example

All things considered, she decided that it was more important to help her brother than to attend the dance. (*absolute phrase*)

Practice A Identify the absolute adjective or absolute phrase in each sentence.

1. Given human nature, Caesar was bound to become too ambitious.
2. Brutus thinks that all Romans should be equal.
3. Cassius will be happy when Caesar is dead and no longer rules Rome.

Practice B Complete each sentence by adding the type of word or phrase in parentheses.

1. The list of conspirators was (absolute adjective) when Brutus joined the group.
2. Caesar expressed (absolute adjective) sorrow when he saw that Brutus had betrayed him.
3. (Absolute phrase), Antony mourned Brutus' death.

ⓒ **Reading Application** Find an example of an absolute adjective and an absolute phrase in the first two acts of *Julius Caesar.*

ⓒ **Writing Application** Write a brief paragraph about the battle between the conspirators and Antony's forces using two absolute adjectives and two absolute phrases.

PH WRITING COACH | Further instruction and practice are available in *Prentice Hall Writing Coach.*

Writing

 **Argumentative Text** Imagine that you are a journalist at the time of Caesar's murder. Write an **editorial** to express your opinion on Rome's future.

- Jot down notes on the major events and issues in the play.
- List consequences Rome faces because of the battle between the conspirators and Antony's allies.
- Mark each consequence as desirable or undesirable and add a note explaining why.
- As you draft your editorial, explain the consequences you foresee. Give reasons for each opinion you express.
- Anticipate your reader's concerns and biases. For each opinion you provide, add a sentence that deflects a counterargument someone might make against it.
- Include a concluding sentence that summarizes your overall opinion.

 **Explanatory Text** An **obituary** is a notice that someone has died. In addition to details about the death, an obituary often reports on the life and values of its subject. Write an obituary for a character who dies in *Julius Caesar*.

- Review the play for details about the character's life and personality.
- Choose an effective organization. For example, open with the circumstances of the character's death and provide brief background of the character's life.
- Use details from the text to construct a unified picture of the character's life.

Grammar Application Include absolutes and absolute phrases as you write your editorial and obituary.

Writing Workshop: *Work in Progress*

Prewriting for a Research Report For a research report you might write, brainstorm for topics by considering several different purposes. Fold a piece of paper in three and label the three sections as follows: "to persuade," "to make a recommendation," and "to inform." Under each label, write one or two topics on which you might write a report with the purpose described. Put these Purpose Notes in your portfolio.

 **Common Core State Standards**

L.9-10.1; W.9-10.1, W.9-10.1.b, W.9-10.1.e, W.9-10.4

[For the full wording of the standards, see the standards chart in the front of your textbook.]

Use this prewriting activity to prepare for the **Writing Workshop** on page 1020.

www.PHLitOnline.com
- Interactive graphic organizers
- Grammar tutorial
- Interactive journals

Integrated Language Skills **1003**

PERFORMANCE TASKS
Integrated Language Skills

Speaking and Listening

©**Comprehension and Collaboration** With a partner, give a **dramatic reading** of Cassius' discussion with Brutus in lines 132–177 of Act I, Scene ii. Review Act I for hints about the personality of each man. Let your knowledge of the character guide your tone of voice and attitude. Follow these suggestions:

- Make notes about how you want to pronounce certain lines: with contempt, with surprise, with suspicion, or with concern.
- Remember to project your voice strongly if you want to say a line loudly. Lower your voice if you want to convey a softer, quieter tone.
- Practice your parts and present your reading to the class.

Lead the class in a discussion to compare and contrast the experience of reading the scene silently to oneself with the experience of hearing it performed with different voices for the different roles.

©**Comprehension and Collaboration** With a small group of students, hold a **group screening** of a filmed production of *Julius Caesar.* Afterward, discuss the production, starting with these questions:

- How effective was each actor in a major role?
- How effective was the staging of the action?
- In what ways did the production surprise you, given your reading of the play and the way you "saw" the play in your mind as you read?
- Identify and discuss the influence of the director on the production, using questions like these to guide you: How appropriate was the actors' performance style? Were the costumes effective? Did you agree with the director's overall interpretation of the story?
- During the discussion, listen to understand and evaluate your classmate's ideas.

Have two members of the group serve as note takers. Afterward, review the discussion notes, and analyze the differences in members' responses. Make a chart showing the reactions to the film.

Research and Technology

 **Common Core State Standards**

RL.9-10.7; SL.9-10.1, SL.9-10.1.c, SL.9-10.1.d, SL.9-10.6; W.9-10.4, W.9-10.6, W.9-10.7
[For the full wording of the standards, see the standards chart in the front of your textbook.]

© **Build and Present Knowledge** Using books, reference articles, and reliable Internet sources, find out more about the life that married aristocratic women like Calpurnia and Portia led in ancient Rome. Then, write a **women's history report.** Follow these guidelines:

- Develop a comprehensive search plan to find and evaluate information from primary and secondary sources.

- Compare these two characters with the typical upper-class woman of the time.

- Consider the role of each in political affairs and each woman's role in relation to her husband.

© **Build and Present Knowledge** Create an **advertising poster** for a historically accurate performance of *Julius Caesar.* Include an illustration and appropriate text that capture the essence of the performance. Conduct research to find information about the following:

- The design of the Elizabethan theater

- The costumes

- The actors: were they men or women or both?

Include information to attract spectators' interest in the play, such as enticing details about the plot. As you develop your poster, be alert to the appeal of the layout you create. Choose a readable font or write legibly.

© **Build and Present Knowledge** Using computer software, produce a **multimedia presentation** on the philosophy of Stoicism. Conduct research to identify the main beliefs of the movement. Follow these research strategies:

- Paraphrase the information you find in your research sources. This step will let you know whether you fully understand the ideas you are using.

- Find visuals or music to accompany the information you will present.

- Organize the information you will use from most to least important. Put main ideas and evidence that supports your ideas at the top of the list. Add interesting but less relevant details at the bottom.

- Be sure to collect full information about each source you use: title, author, page number on which the information is found. Also note which ideas come from primary and which from secondary sources.

In your presentation, explain ways in which Brutus' behavior and attitudes reflect or do not reflect the ideas of Stoicism.

PHLit Online!
www.PHLitOnline.com

- Interactive graphic organizers
- Grammar tutorial
- Interactive journals

Test Practice: Reading

Reading Shakespearean Drama

Fiction Selection

Directions: *Read the selection. Then, answer the questions.*

Dunsinane. Within the castle.
[*Enter* MACBETH, SEYTON, *and* SOLDIERS, *with drum and colors.*]
    MACBETH. Hang out our banners on the outward walls.
    The cry is still "They come!" Our castle's strength
    Will laugh a siege to scorn. Here let them lie
    Till famine and the ague eat them up.
5   Were they not forced[1] with those that should be ours,
    We might have met them dareful,[2] beard to beard,
    And beat them backward home.
                [*A cry within of women.*]
                       What is that noise?
    SEYTON. It is the cry of women, my good lord.   [*Exit.*]
    MACBETH. I have almost forgot the taste of fears:
10   The time has been, my senses would have cooled
    To hear a night-shriek; and my fell[3] of hair
    Would at a dismal treatise[4] rouse and stir
    As life were in't. I have supped full with horrors.
    Direness,[5] familiar to my slaughterous thoughts,
    Cannot once start[6] me.
[*Enter SEYTON.*]
15   Wherefore was that cry?
    SEYTON. The queen, my lord, is dead.
    MACBETH. She should have died hereafter;[7]
    There would have been a time for such a word.[8]
    Tomorrow, and tomorrow, and tomorrow
20   Creeps in this petty pace from day to day,
    To the last syllable of recorded time;
    And all our yesterdays have lighted fools
    The way to dusty death. Out, out, brief candle!
    Life's but a walking shadow, a poor player
25   That struts and frets his hour upon the stage
    And then is heard no more. It is a tale
    Told by an idiot, full of sound and fury
    Signifying nothing.
—from *The Tragedy of Macbeth*, Act V, Scene v, by William Shakespeare

1. **forced** reinforced; **those that should be ours** deserters.
2. **dareful** boldly.

3. **fell** scalp.
4. **dismal treatise** horror.

5. **Direness** horror.
6. **start** startle.

7. **She should have died hereafter** She should have picked a more convenient time for her death.
8. **word** message.

1. By reading lines 1–4, what inference can you make about Macbeth's state of mind?

   A. He is enthusiastic.
   B. He is angry.
   C. He is full of despair.
   D. He feels optimistic.

2. Which is the *best* paraphrase of "here let them lie / Till famine and the ague eat them up" in lines 3–5?

   A. Our enemies will be very hungry.
   B. Let them lie here until they die of hunger and illness.
   C. They will lie here while we prepare to fight.
   D. Invading armies are often plagued by a variety of illnesses.

3. When Macbeth speaks in lines 10 through 15, his words reveal that he no longer—

   A. worries about the health of his wife.
   B. finds anything frightening or shocking.
   C. wants to be the king.
   D. hears people shrieking at night.

4. Which word could replace "signifying nothing" (line 28) in a paraphrase?

   A. meaningless
   B. significant
   C. amazing
   D. furious

5. Which state of mind is conveyed by the image "Out, out, brief candle" (line 23)?

   A. longing for death
   B. wish for personal safety
   C. curiosity about the future
   D. sorrow over the cruelty of nature

6. Which of the following images appeals to the sense of hearing?

   A. last syllable
   B. dusty death
   C. lighted fools
   D. poor player

7. Which of the following is the *best* paraphrase of the phrase "sound and fury" in line 27?

   A. delight and disappointment
   B. pain and natural disasters
   C. sensation and emotion
   D. music and excitement

8. For what purpose are glosses, or annotations, provided?

   A. to illustrate the imagery
   B. to define the vocabulary
   C. to depict the characters
   D. to explain the setting

Writing for Assessment

Would Shakespearean drama be readable by the average student without glosses and stage directions? Explain your answer in a paragraph. Use examples from this selection to help support your response.

www.PHLitOnline.com
- Online practice
- Instant feedback

Reading for Information

Analyzing Functional and Expository Texts

Job Application

Public Document

Common Core State Standards

Reading Informational Text
5. Analyze in detail how an author's ideas or claims are developed and refined by particular sentences, paragraphs, or larger portions of a text.

Language
4.b. Identify and correctly use patterns of word changes that indicate different meanings or parts of speech.

Reading Skill: Analyze Workplace Documents

Workplace documents often include bold or italic type, headers, and other structural features. Authors use these features to achieve their **purposes** and aid readers' understanding. These elements help organize the information presented, clarifying it and helping to convey an author's ideas. Use this chart to **analyze the structure and format** of a text.

Structural Feature	Purpose
title	states topic or main idea
heading or subheading	shows where to find categories of information
bulleted or numbered list	provides a quick way to reference essential information
diagram or graphic	provides additional or more specific information in a visual format
italic or boldface type	draws attention to key words
signature or write-on line	provides space for applicant to supply required information

Content-Area Vocabulary

These words appear in the selections that follow. You may also encounter them in other content-area texts.

- **vocational** (vō kā′ shə nəl) *adj.* of or about some occupation, business, profession, or trade
- **statistics** (stə tis′ tiks) *n.* numerical facts about people, the weather, business conditions, and so on
- **certified** (ser′ tə fīd) *adj.* having a document showing that certain requirements for a job or task have been met

Features:

- space to fill in requested information
- a signature line
- text written for a specific audience

The County of Sonoma
VOLUNTEER PROGRAM
Human Resources Department

VOLUNTEER APPLICATION

Date:

OFFICE USE ONLY		
Referred to:	**Job**	**Status**

Volunteer area of interest

1.

First Name   **Last Name**

2.

3.

Home Phone | **Work Phone** | **E-mail Address** | **Best Time to Reach You**

Address   **City**   **State**   **Zip Code**

MAJOR WORK EXPERIENCE
If unemployed, are you job hunting? ☐ Yes ☐ No   Career Goal:

Job Title	Company/Organization/Agency	Duties	How Long
Current position:			
Work History:			

VOLUNTEER EXPERIENCE

Job Title	Organization/Agency	Duties	How Long
Current position:			
Prior positions:			

EDUCATION

Are you currently a student?	☐ Yes ☐ No	If so, where?	
High School	Through what grade: 9 10 11 12	School	Major
College	Circle last year completed: 1 2 3 4	School	Major
Graduate School	Circle last year completed: 1 2 3 4	School	Major
Vocational School or Other Training	Subject:	School	

This chart allows the applicant to provide education information in an organized way.

GOALS: What do you hope to gain through volunteering? **(To help to contribute to our community, to gain work experience, to reenter the work world, to stay active, to test a new career field, etc.)**

> A column format is used here to organize and clarify options.

TIME AVAILABLE FOR VOLUNTEER WORK

Number of hours willing to give per week:	Availability:	Hours Preferred	Length of Assignment: (Some jobs may have minimum requirement.)
	☐ Mon ☐ Fri ☐ Tues ☐ Sat ☐ Wed ☐ Sun ☐ Thurs	☐ Mornings ☐ Afternoons ☐ Evenings	☐ Short Term ☐ 1 Year ☐ Months ☐ 2 Year ☐ Months ☐ On going

SPECIAL SKILLS, CERTIFICATES OR LICENSES

Interpreter: Language(s)

In times of county-wide disaster, can we call you to assist in any of the above areas?
☐ Yes   ☐ No

AREAS OF INTEREST OR HOBBIES (Tell us what you enjoy doing)

> Headings organize questions about different topics into categories.

TRANSPORTATION

Do you drive?   ☐ Yes   ☐ No   Do you have auto insurance?   ☐ Yes   ☐ No

If you don't drive, how will you reach your volunteer job?
Have you been put on probation or has your driver's license been suspended or revoked within the last five years? ☐ Yes   ☐ No
If yes, please explain:

Some jobs may require a background check. Please fill this section in if you are applying for such a position.

Birth Date: CA Driver's License #:   Social Security #:

I authorize the County to perform a background check as necessitated by the volunteer position I am applying for.

SIGNATURE _____

BLS Career Information

U.S. Department of Labor | Bureau of Labor Statistics

Urban Planner

- What is this job like?
- How do you get ready?
- How much does this job pay?
- How many jobs are there?
- What about the future?
- Are there other jobs like this?
- Where can you find more information?

> A bulleted list clearly and concisely states what questions will be answered in the text.

WHAT IS THIS JOB LIKE?

City planners figure out the best way to use the land in cities and neighborhoods. They report on the best location for houses, stores, and parks. They try to solve a lot of problems. These include things such as too much traffic and increases in air pollution. Planners want to make sure that people can get to a bus or subway. They need to plan where people should drive their cars and where they can park.

Planners make new plans when more people move into a community. They might tell community leaders that they need new schools or roads.

Planners also are concerned about saving the wetlands, and trees. They try to find safe places for getting rid of trash.

Before making plans for a community, planners need to know where everything is. They find out how many people use the streets, highways, water, sewers, schools, libraries, museums, and parks. Planners listen to the advice of people who live in the communities. With these and many other facts, they explain their new plans. They tell how much the changes will cost.

Planners use computers all the time. They make reports. They draw new maps showing changes for the future.

City planners spend much of their time in offices. They spend time outside to learn more about the areas that are changing.

Most planners work 40 hours per week. Sometimes they go to meetings in the evening or on weekends. Sometimes they have meetings with the people whose neighborhoods will be changed.

Planners have to work quickly to get their work finished because they have many other plans to make. Sometimes different groups do not agree with the plans for their community.

BLS Career Information

U.S. Department of Labor | Bureau of Labor Statistics

HOW DO YOU GET READY?

Employers want workers who have advanced training. Most employers seek persons who have a master's degree in city planning or urban design. Sometimes employers will hire persons who have worked as a planner for a long time, but do not have a master's degree. A bachelor's degree in planning and a master's degree in a related field are good to have when persons look for their first job. Persons who are interested in becoming a city planner should take courses in computer science and **statistics**.

Persons who are interested in becoming a city planner also should learn how to use a computer.

Local government planning offices often hire college students to work during the summer. Students can learn a lot before they get their first job after they graduate.

To become a **certified** planner, persons must take the right amount of classes. They must work in a planning office and pass a test. Planners must be able to speak and write well. They must be good at making things fit in place so that everyone can shop, work, and go to school.

HOW MUCH DOES THIS JOB PAY?

The middle half of all urban and regional planners earned between $41,950 and $67,530 a year in 2004. The lowest-paid 10 percent earned less than $33,840. The highest-paid 10 percent earned more than $82,610 a year.

HOW MANY JOBS ARE THERE?

Urban and regional planners held about 32,000 jobs in 2004. Most of them worked for local governments. Some planners work in private companies. Others work for State agencies. A small number of planners work for the Federal Government.

WHAT ABOUT THE FUTURE?

The number of jobs for planners is expected to grow about as fast as the average for all occupations through 2014. Most of their work will result from population growth. Most new jobs will be in rapidly expanding communities.

> Bold subheadings allow readers to quickly locate information that interests them.

ARE THERE OTHER JOBS LIKE THIS?

- Architects
- City managers
- Civil engineers
- Community development directors
- Environmental engineers
- Landscape architects
- Social scientists (*geographers*)

WHERE CAN YOU FIND MORE INFORMATION?

More BLS information about urban and regional planners can be found in the Occupational Outlook Handbook. The Handbook also shows where to find out even more about this job.

Comparing Functional and Expository Texts

1. Craft and Structure **(a) Analyze workplace documents** by comparing and contrasting the **structures and formats** of the job application and the public document. **(b)** How does the structure and format of each text aid the reader's understanding?

Content-Area Vocabulary

2. (a) Using a print or an online dictionary, explain how a change in suffix alters the meanings and parts of speech of these words: *certified, certifiable,* and *certification.* **(b)** Use each of the words in a sentence that shows its meaning.

Timed Writing

Informative Text: Essay

Format
The prompt directs you to write an essay. Therefore, be sure your response includes an introduction, several supporting paragraphs, and a conclusion.

Using details and information from the texts, write an essay in which you discuss the authors' purposes in the job application and the public document. Explain how the structure and format of each text help the author achieve his or her purpose. Also, explain why you think the authors are or are not successful in achieving their purposes. (40 minutes)

Academic Vocabulary
When you *discuss* a subject, you write or speak about various aspects of that subject in detail.

5-Minute Planner

Complete these steps before you begin to write:

1. Read the prompt carefully and completely. Highlighting indicates key words and phrases. **TIP** The assignment contains several points you must address. Be sure you understand all parts of the prompt.

2. Review the job application and public document. Consider the reason each text was written.

3. Analyze and make notes about the structures and formats and how those elements help achieve the purposes of the documents.

4. Consider whether each document achieves its purpose.

5. Create an outline, and refer to your outline and notes as you write.

Comparing Characters' Motivations

A **character's motivation** consists of the passions, convictions, ideas, and even illusions that guide his or her actions and shape his or her words. Characters' motivations are almost always at the heart of a story's action, motivating the plot and providing clues to its deeper meaning, or **theme.** To develop your own understanding of a character's motivation, answer the following questions as you read:

- What goals or desires does a character reveal in a dramatic speech, such as a soliloquy or a monologue?

- What personality traits and goals does the dialogue reveal?

- How does the character feel and behave toward other characters?

- What is the character's family and social background? How does social status contribute to the character's desires?

- Are there any striking similarities or differences between this character and others? If so, what are they?

A character can have more than one motivation. Often, these different motivations conflict with each other. For example, a character's closeness to her family may clash with her desire to travel the world.

Both William Shakespeare's *The Tragedy of Julius Caesar* and Lorraine Hansberry's *A Raisin in the Sun* feature characters with multiple motivations, such as personal ambition and a desire for dignity.

Compare the ideas of dignity that motivate Walter and Mama in *A Raisin in the Sun* with those motivating Cassius, Brutus, and Caesar in *Julius Caesar.* Use a diagram like the one shown to provide evidence from the text to support your understanding of the characters' motivations.

Common Core State Standards

Reading Literature
3. Analyze how complex characters (e.g., those with multiple or conflicting motivations) develop over the course of a text, interact with other characters, and advance the plot or develop the theme.

Writing
2. Write explanatory texts to examine and convey complex ideas, concepts, and information clearly and accurately through the effective selection, organization, and analysis of content. *(Timed Writing)*

Character	Challenge to Character's Dignity	Character's Response	What Character Finds Essential

www.PHLitOnline.com

- Vocabulary flashcards
- Interactive journals
- More about the authors
- Selection audio
- Interactive graphic organizers

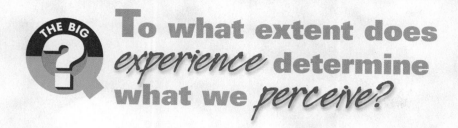

To what extent does *experience* determine what we *perceive?*

Writing About the Big Question

In both *Julius Caesar* and *A Raisin in the Sun,* characters experience conflicts between what they believe is right and what is actually happening around them. Consider how a person's background influences his or her expectations. Use these sentence starters to develop your ideas.

All people should **expect** to be treated _____, but that is not everyone's experience.

Individual opinions about whether the world can be a just, fair place vary greatly because _____.

Meet the Author

Lorraine Hansberry (1930–1965)
Author of *A Raisin in the Sun*

An important voice of the civil rights era, Lorraine Hansberry grew up in Chicago. "Both of my parents were strong-minded, civic-minded, exceptionally race-minded people who made enormous sacrifices on behalf of the struggle for civil rights throughout their lifetimes," she once recalled.

Biographical Inspiration When Hansberry was about eight years old, her parents tried to move to a white neighborhood. Property owners in the neighborhood blocked African American families from purchasing homes there. Hansberry's father fought the restrictions all the way to the U.S. Supreme Court, where he eventually won his case. Years later, Hansberry used that experience as the basis of her award-winning play *A Raisin in the Sun*, which opened on Broadway in 1959.

from

A Raisin in the Sun

Lorraine Hansberry

from Act 1, Scene II

Background The Youngers are an African American family living in Chicago some time after World War II. During this period, African Americans faced a shortage of economic opportunities and were deprived of many civil rights. Walter Younger, his wife Ruth, and their son Travis live with Walter's mother and his younger sister, Beneatha. Walter's father has passed away. When the family learns that Walter's mother is to receive a check from the father's insurance, Walter pleads with his mother to give him money to invest in a store he wants to open with friends. She wants instead to purchase a new home and to pay for Beneatha's education.

WALTER. (*Picks up the check*) Do you know what this money means to me? Do you know what this money can do for us? (*Puts it back*) Mama—Mama—I want so many things . . .

MAMA. Yes, son—

WALTER. I want so many things that they are driving me kind of crazy . . . Mama—look at me.

MAMA. I'm looking at you. You a good-looking boy. You got a job, a nice wife, a fine boy and—

WALTER. A job. (*Looks at her*) Mama, a job? I open and close car doors all day long. I drive a man around in his limousine and I say, "Yes, sir; no, sir; very good, sir; shall I take the Drive, sir?" Mama, that ain't no kind of job . . . that ain't nothing at all. (*Very quietly*) Mama, I don't know if I can make you understand.

MAMA. Understand what, baby?

WALTER. (*Quietly*) Sometimes it's like I can see the future stretched out in front of me—just plain as day. The future, Mama. Hanging over there at the edge of my days. Just waiting for me—a big, looming blank space—full of nothing. Just waiting for me. But it don't have to be. (*Pause. Kneeling beside her chair*) Mama—sometimes when I'm downtown and I pass them cool, quiet-looking restaurants where them white boys are sitting back and talking 'bout things . . . sitting there turning deals worth millions of dollars . . . sometimes I see guys don't look much older than me—

Literary Analysis
Character Motivation
Explain what type of life Walter seems to desire.

Vocabulary
looming (lōōm′ iŋ) *adj.* appearing unclearly but in a threatening form; threatening to occur

Reading Check
What good things does Mama see in Walter's life?

MAMA. Son—how come you talk so much 'bout money?

WALTER. (*With immense passion*) Because it is life, Mama!

MAMA. (*Quietly*) Oh—(*Very quietly*) So now it's life. Money is life. Once upon a time freedom used to be life—now it's money. I guess the world really do change . . .

WALTER. No—it was always money, Mama. We just didn't know about it.

MAMA. No . . . something has changed. (*She looks at him*) You something new, boy. In my time we was worried about not being lynched and getting to the North if we could and how to stay alive and still have a pinch of dignity too . . . Now here come you and Beneatha—talking 'bout things we ain't never even thought about hardly, me and your daddy. You ain't satisfied or proud of nothing we done. I mean that you had a home; that we kept you out of trouble till you was grown; that you don't have to ride to work on the back of nobody's streetcar—You my children—but how different we done become.

WALTER. (*A long beat. He pats her hand and gets up*) You just don't understand, Mama, you just don't understand.

Vocabulary
dignity (dig´ nə tē) *n.* quality of deserving respect and honor; self-respect

Critical Thinking

Cite textual evidence to support your responses.

1. **Key Ideas and Details** **(a)** What does Walter do for a living? **(b) Infer:** How does this job make him feel about the future? Support your answer with a quotation from the selection.

2. **Key Ideas and Details** **(a) Interpret:** Why does Walter think that money "is life"? **(b) Make a Judgment:** Do you agree with him? Explain why or why not.

3. **Key Ideas and Details** **(a) Summarize:** What is Mama's reaction to Walter's complaint? **(b) Compare and Contrast:** Compare Mama's goals in life with Walter's.

4. **Integration of Knowledge and Ideas** **(a)** In what ways do Mama's past experiences affect her perception of freedom and dignity? **(b)** How do Walter's past experiences influence his view of what it means to be free and have dignity? Explain your answer. *[Connect to the Big Question: To what extent does experience determine what we perceive?]*

Comparing Characters' Motivations

1. Integration of Knowledge and Ideas (a) Using a chart like the one shown, analyze Walter's **motivation** in the scene from *A Raisin in the Sun.* **(b)** Complete a similar chart about Cassius' motivation in *The Tragedy of Julius Caesar,* Act I, Scene ii, lines 90–161. **(c)** What comparisons can you identify?

Social Background	Personality	Feelings	Values	Goals

2. Integration of Knowledge and Ideas (a) What ideals motivate Brutus' speech in Act II, Scene i, lines 114–140? **(b)** Compare these ideals to those described by Walter's mother. **(c)** What is one difference between Brutus' goal in joining the conspiracy and Walter's dream of having a business?

3. Integration of Knowledge and Ideas (a) Summarize Caesar's ideas about dignity, as expressed in *Julius Caesar,* Act III, Scene i, lines 58–73. **(b)** Is his notion of dignity more like that of Walter or of Mama, or is it different from both? Explain.

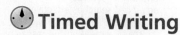 Timed Writing

Explanatory Text: Essay

These dramas were written more than 300 years apart, but they address similar themes. Write a brief essay in which you compare the ideas of dignity that motivate characters in *The Tragedy of Julius Caesar* with those that motivate Walter and his mother in *A Raisin in the Sun.* **(30 minutes)**

5-Minute Planner

1. Read the prompt carefully and completely.

2. Gather your ideas by jotting down answers to these questions:

- What are each character's beliefs, goals, and personality traits?

- Which statements reveal each character's view of dignity?

- What do each character's interactions with others show about his or her motivations?

- In what ways do specific character's motivations affect the plots and hint at the themes of each work?

3. Reread the prompt, and then draft your essay.

Writing Workshop

Write an Informative Text

Research Writing: Research Report

Defining the Form **Research writing** presents, interprets, and analyzes information gathered through comprehensive study of a subject. Writing a research report is a good way to learn about a topic that is outside your own experience. You might use elements of research writing in biographies, opinion papers, lab reports, and annotated bibliographies.

Assignment Write a research report on a topic that interests you and is substantial enough to merit an in-depth study. Include these elements:

✓ a *specific, narrow topic* that is summarized in a *thesis statement*

✓ relevant information from *primary and secondary sources*

✓ a *logical organization* of details and ideas

✓ *correct documentation of sources*, following an accepted format

✓ error-free grammar, including correct use of *adverb clauses*

To preview the criteria on which your research report may be judged, see the rubric on page 1031.

 Writing Workshop: *Work in Progress*

If you have completed the Work in Progress assignment on page 1003, you already have ideas to use in your research report. Work with these ideas, or explore a new idea as you complete the Writing Workshop.

WRITE GUY
Jeff Anderson, M.Ed.

What Do You Notice?

Controlling Idea

Read the following sentence from Theodore H. White's essay "The American Idea" several times.

The story we celebrate . . . is the story of how this idea worked itself out, how it stretched and changed and how the call for 'life, liberty and the pursuit of happiness' does still, as it did in the beginning, mean different things to different people.

With a partner, discuss what you notice about the sentence. Then, think about the ways you might present a controlling idea in your research report.

Prewriting/Planning Strategies

Scan your notebooks. Follow your instincts and interests when looking for a topic. Review the notes you have taken in any subject—from history to math to drama. Use a marker or self-sticking notes to highlight ideas that fascinate you. Then, choose one that you want to investigate further.

Review periodicals. Flip through print and online newspaper and magazine articles for topics that you find intriguing. For example, you might consider researching the history behind a story that is currently in the news. Determine what you already know about the topic and what you would like to learn. Use a chart like the one shown to organize your thoughts.

www.PHLitOnline.com
- Author video: Writing Process
- Author video: Rewards of Writing

What I Know	What I Want to Know

Develop a research plan. Generate questions to drive your study. After a brief overview of information, continue your research by developing a *working thesis statement*. This statement will summarize the idea you intend to address in your report. Based on this statement, determine the types of sources you will need to consult. For example, you may need to gain a broad overview of a subject before investigating specific categories. Conduct advanced searches to assess the availability of information on your topic.

Working Thesis Statement: Dreams are important in a variety of ways.

My Research Plan	Possible Sources
Step 1: Get a solid overview about dreams and dream theory.	• Books on dream theory • Web sites (credible ones)
Step 2: Gather specific details and current information.	• Psychology journals (online and print) • Biographies of historical figures • Interviews with working psychologists

Your working thesis statement will guide your research—it should be flexible to help focus your study and you may need to change it to reflect what you have learned. As you gather information and refine your ideas, revise your thesis statement so that it is more precise. Include the final version of your thesis statement in the introduction of your report.

Make a list of open-ended research questions. Create a list of questions you would like to answer through research. The information you find may also inspire other ideas. Include new questions, but be sure that you continue to focus or narrow your topic rather than expand it.

Use a variety of primary and secondary sources. Consult *primary sources*—firsthand or original accounts of events. Primary sources include interview transcripts, journals, letters, eyewitness accounts, and speeches.

Also consult *secondary sources*, such as books, encyclopedia entries, magazine articles, and newspapers that present a report, a retelling, or an analysis of primary sources. Consider using specialized types of secondary sources as well, such as those listed in this chart.

Resource	Information
Almanacs	Social, political, and economic statistics
Atlases	Tables, charts, maps, and illustrations
Government publications	Information on laws, government programs, and topics such as agriculture and economics
Microfiche	Back issues of periodicals
Databases	Indexes to online and print sources

Evaluate sources. Be critical of your sources, looking for *bias* that may lead the writer to obscure or misrepresent the facts. Decide which of your sources are most reliable and objective.

Document sources and organize your notes. As you gather information, carefully record each key detail and its source.

- **Source cards:** Write the identifying information—title, author, publisher, and date of publication—of every resource you consult. Use a separate note card for each source. Label each card with a letter (A, B, C, and so on) or with a code word, such as the author's last name.

- **Note cards:** Record each relevant fact or idea on its own notecard. *Paraphrase,* or restate in your own words, the ideas of other authors. If you quote passages directly, use quotation marks and make sure your quotations are accurate. Include the letter or code word you have chosen to identify the source of the information.

Evaluate the credibility of information and the bias of sources. As you gather information, evaluate its *credibility,* or trustworthiness. Make sure the authors have the education, training, or personal experience to speak with authority. Notice any evidence of bias, or a tendency to make unfair judgments about certain topics. Bias includes the use of stereotypes, unsupported statements, or overly dramatic claims. Opinions should be based on factual evidence. Note your evaluations on your source cards. Later, you can decide whether to use the information and how to present it.

Source Card

[A]

Kreisler, Kristin V. "Why We Dream What We Dream." Reader's Digest, Feb. 1995: 28, 30, 34–36,38.

Note Card

a dream helped Jack Nicklaus fix his golf swing

Source Card: A

Drafting Strategies

Refine your thesis statement. Your working thesis statement should have evolved into a focused declaration as you gathered information. Now, make sure it can be proved using the facts and ideas you have compiled through research.

> **Final Thesis Statement:** Dreams make a difference in people's lives—not only to the individuals who dream them, but to society.

Organize your information. Choose an organizational strategy that matches the content and purpose of your writing. Consider using one of the strategies described in this chart.

Common Core State Standards

W.9-10.2.a–b, W.9-10.7, W.9-10.8
[For the full wording of the standards, see page 1020.]

Organizational Strategy	Uses
Chronological Order offers information in the sequence in which it happened	historical topics; science experiments
Part-to-Whole Order examines how categories affect a larger subject	analysis of social issues; historical topics
Order of Importance presents information in order of increasing or decreasing importance	persuasive arguments; supporting a bold or challenging thesis
Comparison-and-Contrast Organization presents similarities and differences	addressing two or more subjects

Synthesize ideas. Effective research writing does not merely present facts and details but synthesizes—gathers, orders, and interprets—those elements. As you draft, synthesize information into a unified whole that is driven by your original thoughts.

Use and credit sources. You may choose any of the following methods to present the ideas, facts, and examples you discover in your research. In all cases, you must credit your source.

- **Direct quotation:** Use the author's exact words when they are interesting or persuasive. Indicate any omissions with ellipsis points. Enclose direct quotations in quotation marks.

- **Paraphrase:** Restate an author's ideas in your own words.

- **Summary:** Compress a complex idea into a briefer version.

- **Facts:** If a fact is available only in one source, include documentation.

Incorporate graphic aids and visuals. Consider using illustrations, photographs, maps, graphs, or charts to clarify facts, highlight trends, or add dramatic power. You may include visuals you discover in your research materials. If so, provide full citations for them.

Writers on Writing

David Henry Hwang On Using Research

David Henry Hwang is the author of *Tibet Through the Red Box* (p. 799).

As someone born and raised in California, I disliked New York very much. However, I have grown to love the city and now call it my home. The one aspect of New York I did enjoy was discovering Broadway. When I later wrote an article about Broadway, I relied on research as well as my own observations.

> *"My first Broadway producer . . . once told me that a success here is 'a shot fired round the world.'"*
> —David Henry Hwang

Professional Model:

from *Place of a Lifetime . . .*

Shows premiered here that helped a young nation define its identity: plays like *A Streetcar Named Desire* (at the Ethel Barrymore Theatre, on West 47th Street), musicals like *Guys and Dolls* (at the 46th Street Theatre, now renamed the Richard Rodgers).

I just *don't* know in my head which great plays were produced in which theatres; I had to look this information up.

Along with most theatre artists, I believe each of these theatres is home to at least one ghost; before leaving each evening, a stagehand will turn on the "ghost light," a single bulb that burns all night, to scare away bad spirits and attract good ones. Very little else about New York captured my imagination on that first visit; I only lasted four days before fleeing back to the West Coast, vowing never to return.

As with most legends, there are several different explanations for the origin of the "ghost light." Among the explanations I found in different books, this one seemed most common.

Now, more than 20 years later, I am a devoted New Yorker who has been privileged to see five of my shows performed on Broadway. I sometimes feel that my first hit, *M. Butterfly*, afflicted me with a Broadway virus: an unshakable affection for those aging theatres—roughly 40 in total—and the life that inhabits and surrounds them. . . .

Here, I jump forward in time to demonstrate how my views of New York have completely changed.

Revising Strategies

Step back from your work. If time allows, leave yourself time between drafting and revising. Reading your work with new energy will allow you to see your work with more clarity.

Revise for conciseness. Your research report will be more effective if you avoid unnecessary complexity or wordiness. Reread your draft, circling any words that add clutter without meaning. Consider omitting those words or replacing them with better choices.

> **Model: Revising for Conciseness**
>
> In
> ~~Thus, in~~ conclusion, ~~one can see from careful observation that~~ political conflict often leads to economic change.

Revise to avoid plagiarism. To avoid plagiarism—the unethical presentation of someone else's ideas as if they were your own—you must cite sources for direct quotations, paraphrased information, or facts that are specific to a single source. Reread your draft, circling any words or ideas that are not your own. Follow the instructions on page 1026 and pages R36–R37 to correctly cite those passages.

Revise to strengthen coherence. Make sure that all of the elements in your draft follow your organizational strategy and appear in logical, or coherent, order.

- On a separate piece of paper, write the main idea of each paragraph.

- Review this list—an abbreviated version of your report—to decide whether your ideas flow logically from paragraph to paragraph.

- Check that the ideas in your introduction and conclusion match.

- Rearrange paragraphs or sections that do not build in a logical way. Consider eliminating any that stray from your thesis statement.

- Add transitional words or sentences to help readers see the connections you want to emphasize.

Peer Review

Share your draft and list of main ideas with a partner. Ask your partner to consider how well each main idea builds on the last in a logical flow. Consider moving paragraphs or sections to improve your report's coherence. Explain to your partner your reasons for specific revision choices.

Common Core State Standards

Writing

2.c. Use appropriate and varied transitions to link the major sections of the text, create cohesion, and clarify the relationships among complex ideas and concepts.

2.d. Use precise language and domain-specific vocabulary to manage the complexity of the topic.

5. Develop and strengthen writing as needed by revising, focusing on addressing what is most significant for a specific purpose and audience.

8. Integrate information into the text selectively to maintain the flow of ideas, avoiding plagiarism and following a standard format for citation.

Documenting Sources

Citing Sources in the Body of a Report When citing sources in your report, follow a specific format. Modern Language Association (MLA) style calls for parenthetical citations or references. For print works, the citation usually gives the author's or editor's name followed by a page number. If the work does not have an author, use a keyword or phrase from the title. For Web sources, use the author's name if it is available, the title of the article, if any, or the title of the site itself. Include a screen number if screens on the site are numbered.

> **Citing a Print Work:** . . . men have more action-oriented dreams, while women imagine more emotional one-on-one struggles with loved ones (Van de Castle 45).

> **Citing a Web Source:** Unsolvedmysteries.com shows how dreams can bring luck with the report of a lottery winner from Maine ("Winning the Lottery," screen 1).

Creating a Works-Cited List or Bibliography Publication information for each source you cite must appear at the end of your report. MLA style calls for a Works-Cited list, in which you list alphabetically the works you cite.

- For books, the Works-Cited entry usually takes the form of the author's name, last name first, followed by the title of the work. The entry gives full publication information, including the city of publication, the name of the publisher, and the year of publication.

- For articles in periodicals, the entry usually takes the form of the author's name, last name first, followed by the title of the article, then the name of the magazine. Publication information includes the date of the issue, the volume and issue number if any, and the pages on which the article appears. If the article is continued on a later, non-consecutive page, give the number of the first page, followed by a plus sign.

- For general Web sites, give any of the following information that is available, in the order indicated: author's name, the title of the page, the title of the site, the date of last update, and the name of the sponsoring organization. Give screen numbers, if any. Give the date that you consulted the site, and conclude with the full URL, or address, for the material.

For more information on MLA style, see pages R40–R41.

Common Core State Standards

Writing

8. Gather relevant information from multiple authoritative print and digital sources, using advanced searches effectively; assess the usefulness of each source in answering the research question; integrate information into the text selectively to maintain the flow of ideas, avoiding plagiarism and following a standard format for citation.

Language

1. Demonstrate command of the conventions of standard English grammar and usage when writing or speaking.

1.b. Use various types of clauses to convey specific meanings and add variety and interest to writing or presentations.

3. Apply knowledge of language to understand how language functions in different contexts, to make effective choices for meaning or style, and to comprehend more fully when reading or listening.

Revising to Combine Sentences Using Adverb Clauses

Avoid choppy writing by combining some sentences using adverb clauses.

Two sentences: She had sent the letter. The mail was delayed.

Combined: Although the mail was delayed, she had sent the letter.

Identifying Adverb Clauses A clause is a group of words with a subject and a verb. An *independent clause* can stand alone as a complete sentence, but a *subordinate clause* cannot stand alone. An adverb clause is a subordinate clause that begins with a subordinating conjunction and tells *where, when, in what way, to what extent, under what condition,* or *why.*

When: *Before I got on the plane,* I was afraid of flying.

Condition: Dave will carry the box *if you will open the door.*

Why: I gave her my number *so she could call me later.*

In what way: The child swam *as if she had been born in the water.*

Combining Sentences When using adverb clauses to combine two shorter sentences, follow these steps:

1. Identify the relationship between the ideas in the sentences.

2. Select a subordinate conjunction that clarifies that relationship. Put the adverb clause at the beginning or end of the sentence.

3. When a subordinate clause begins a sentence, use a comma to separate it from the rest of the sentence.

| PH | WRITING COACH |

Further instruction and practice are available in *Prentice Hall Writing Coach.*

Subordinating Conjunctions			
after	although	as	as if
as long as	because	before	even though
if	since	so that	than
though	unless	until	when
whenever	where	wherever	while

Grammar in Your Writing

Review the introduction and conclusion of your report and highlight any short sentences. Look for a relationship between the ideas in the sentences that could be clarified with an adverb clause, and combine them using an appropriate subordinating conjunction.

In Your Dreams

Ever since humans have existed, dreams have made a difference in people's lives. Julius Caesar's wife, Calpurnia, once dreamed that Caesar's statue spurted blood like a fountain while the Romans smiled and bathed in it. This nightmarish picture foreshadowed reality when Caesar was later assassinated. In 1793, Marie Antoinette had a dream of a red sun and pillar. After the sun rose, it suddenly set; this immediately preceded her beheading. Then, there is Robert Louis Stevenson, who believed his best stories came from dreams, including the infamous "Dr. Jekyll and Mr. Hyde." Neils Bohr dreamed of sitting on the sun with planets whizzing around him on small cords; he then developed the model of an atom. Even Genghis Khan claimed to receive his battle plans from his sleepy nights.

Who were the early interpreters of such dreams? Aristotle and Freud, of course, were among the scholars who labored over dream interpretation. Aristotle suggested that dreams were formed by disturbances in the body. Freud, however, believed that dreams were powerful tools for uncovering unconscious wishes. He said, "The purpose of dreams is to allow us to satisfy in fantasies the instinctual urges that society judges unacceptable" (Dreams: History, 2000).

Even today, creative people use their dreams in solving problems. A 1995 *Reader's Digest* article entitled "Why We Dream What We Dream" provides many examples. One such dreamer was the scientist Dmitri Ivanovich Mendeleev. He "saw" the periodic table of the elements in a dream and wrote it down the following day. Later, only one correction was needed. Screenwriter James Cameron dreamed of a robot with a red eye staring back at him. He woke up and wrote the script for *The Terminator*. Steve Allen's hit song "This Could Be the Start of Something Big" also began from a dream, as did the new way of swinging the club that allowed Jack Nicklaus to overcome his golfing problem (Kreisler, 28–38).

Besides being helpful in the creative aspect, dreams have, in many cases, foretold the future. In the weeks prior to his murder, Abraham Lincoln dreamed the White House was in mourning for an assassinated president. The video *The Secret World of Dreams* tells of a man whose dreams indicated a chronic illness even before it was diagnosed, as well as a man whose recurring nightmares of an explosion prepared him for the real thing and enabled him to save the life of a coworker. Unsolvedmysteries.com shows how dreams can bring luck with the report of a lottery winner from Maine whose dreams revealed a winning ticket (Unsolved Mysteries Home Page, screen 1). Given such cases as these, it is no mystery that modern psychology still believes in the prophetic power of dreams.

Lisa begins by introducing the topic in a concise sentence.

She correctly quotes and cites one of her sources.

Lisa incorporates the source of her information into the flow of her discussion.

Lisa demonstrates the wide variety of sources she consulted in her research.

However, to understand one's dreams, one must uncover the meaning of dream symbols. Psychoanalyst Sigmund Freud said that the secret to the symbols in dreams lies within the dreamer (Bentley, p. 4). In other words, individuals can interpret dream symbols from their own lives and the imagery around them—not just by using a dream dictionary. Sleeps.com gives just a few examples of these symbols. For instance, to most dreamers, clothing symbolizes mood, attitude, or state of mind. One who wears a uniform in a dream may be influenced too much by society, while having clothes that are too short may suggest a longing for the pleasures of youth now gone. Death is also a recurring symbol. Whether the dreamer attends a funeral or is in a coffin, these pictures signify a change in one's attitude toward life or one's emotional balance. Finally, other people occur in dreams as reflections of the dreamer's own personality traits. For instance, if a dreamer is faced by the stares of others, that person may be worried about making a bad impression on other people (Dream Analysis and Interpretation, screens 6, 7).

While dreams can be interpreted according to symbols, the most common types of dreams vary throughout the human life cycle. People at different places in their lives tend to dream differently. Children's dreams reflect new impressions that they encounter each day. Bold geometric shapes are not just building blocks with which they play—they represent a fixation with family relationships. For example, a triangle would signify the relationship among the father, mother, and child. Dreams of giants indicate a child's impression of his or her own size and sense of self-worth. Naturally, everything is bigger to a child, but a child with giant proportions compared to the world around him may have an increasing self-awareness (Bentley, p. 25). Much like a scene from *The Nutcracker*, toys come to life as the child lives out fantasies, showing developments of the young person's persona. As children become teens, they dream more about romance. Among adults, men and women dream differently. "It's biology and social conditioning," says Milton Kramer, director of the Bethesda Oak Hospital's Sleep Center in Cincinnati. Research has shown that men dream twice as often of other men as they do of women, while women tend to have an equal number of dreams of both sexes (New Scientist, p. 2). A study by Robert Van de Castle, author of *Our Dreaming Mind*, analyzed 1,000 dreams and found that men have more action-oriented dreams, while women imagine more emotional one-on-one struggles with loved ones (Van de Castle, p. 45).

Studies are also beginning to show that a person's attitude can influence his or her dreams. University of Pennsylvania professor Aaron Beck found that angry

Each paragraph includes a topic sentence, which is then supported in the paragraph with details.

people are the ones throwing the punches in their dream, while depressed people often find themselves the victims of rejection. However, people who have a hard time standing up for themselves are the ones likely to suffer from restless nightmares (Kreisler, 36).

Through the fascinating history of dreams, the interpretation of some dream symbols, and the secret dreams of different sleepers, it is evident that dreams are important. They provide valuable insights, help solve problems, spark new thoughts and creations, and even foretell the future. Maybe people should pay more attention to their dreams. The hours one spends sleeping could be the key to a better life.

Works Cited

Bentley, Peter. *Book of Dream Symbols.* Chronicle Books, 1995.

"Dream Analysis and Interpretation, Doing It!" 9 March 2000: 6, 7.
    <http://www.sleeps.com/analysis.html>

"Dreams: History." 22 March 2000.
    <http://library.thinkquest.org/11130/data/history/history.html>

"Get Real, Siggi." *New Scientist*, 26 April 1997: 2,5. 21 March 2000.
    <http://www.newscientist.com/ns/970426/siggi.html>

Great Moments in Dream History Home Page. 7 March 2000: 1–3.
    <http://www.dr-dream.com/hist.htm>

Kreisler, Kristin V. "Why We Dream What We Dream." *Reader's Digest*, Feb. 1995: 28, 30, 34–36, 38.

Kramer, Milton. Personal Interview. 10 March 2000.

The Secret World of Dreams. Videotape. Questar Video, 1997. 80 Min.

Van de Castle, Robert L. *Our Dreaming Mind.* Ballantine, 1995.

"Winning the Lottery in Your Dreams." Unsolved Mysteries Home Page.
    11 March 2000: 1.
    <http://unsolvedmysteries.com/usm397.html>

Lisa lists, in a standard format, the sources from which her information was drawn.

Editing and Proofreading

Review your draft to correct errors in grammar, spelling, and punctuation.

Focus on accuracy in citations. Carefully check the spelling, punctuation, and format of title, including the use of quotation marks, underlining, and italics. Check the spelling of authors' names, and make sure that you have capitalized titles correctly. Be sure that your draft follows the proper manuscript format, including title page and correct page numbering.

Publishing and Presenting

Consider one of the following ways to share your writing:

Publish on the Internet. Post your research report on a Web site that publishes student writing, or send it to the Web site editors as an e-mail.

Share a multimedia presentation. Use your research report as the basis for a multimedia presentation, and include graphics, music, props, and other elements to engage your audience. If possible, rehearse your presentation with a live audience to coordinate the smooth combination of elements. Incorporate audience feedback to improve your report or presentation. Make sure you allow time for your audience to ask questions.

Reflecting on Your Writing

Writer's Journal Jot down your answers to this question:

How did writing a research report help you understand your topic?

Rubric for Self-Assessment

Find evidence in your writing to address each category. Then, use the rating scale to grade your work.

Spiral Review

Earlier in this unit, you learned about **absolutes and absolute phrases** (p. 1002). Check your research to be sure that you have used absolutes and absolute phrases correctly.

PH **WRITING COACH**

Further instruction and practice are available in *Prentice Hall Writing Coach*.

Criteria	Rating Scale
	not very very
Focus: How specific is your thesis statement?	1 2 3 4 5
Organization: How logical and effective is your organization?	1 2 3 4 5
Support/Elaboration: How varied and reliable is your evidence?	1 2 3 4 5
Style: How concise is your phrasing of ideas?	1 2 3 4 5
Conventions: How accurately and thoroughly have you cited sources for ideas that are not your own?	1 2 3 4 5

Vocabulary Workshop

Borrowed and Foreign Words

Common Core State Standards

Language

4.a. Use context as a clue to the meaning of a word or phrase.

4.c. Consult general and specialized reference materials, both print and digital, to find the pronunciation of a word or determine or clarify its precise meaning, its part of speech, or its etymology.

Many words in English have been taken directly from other languages. The meaning of these **borrowed words** may stay the same as in the original language, as in these examples: *pajamas* (Hindi), *sauna* (Finnish), and *plaza* (Spanish). In other cases, the meaning has changed. *Sleuth*, for example, comes from an Old Norse word meaning "trail." It has changed in English to mean "the person who follows a trail; a detective." Borrowed words include some of the most common words in English.

A **foreign word** is a borrowed word that is still treated as a foreign term in English. A foreign word or phrase is frequently set in italics. Some dictionaries indicate words that should be written in italics. Examples of foreign words that are frequently used in English include *mano a mano*, *mot juste*, *ex post facto*, and *quid pro quo*.

This chart shows some of the ways that new words enter a language.

Entry Point	Explanation	Examples
War	Conflict brings soldiers in contact with new people so new words enter the language.	*brigade, cavalry, infantry* (French); *arsenal* (Italian); *blitzkrieg* (German)
Immigration	When people settle in new countries, they bring their language with them.	*delicatessen* (German); *cappuccino, pasta, pizza* (Italian)
Travel and Trade	People who travel and do business in other countries bring words home with them.	*cruise, reef* (Dutch); *shampoo* (Hindi); *guitar, canyon* (Spanish)

Practice A Look up each word in a dictionary. Identify the language from which the word was borrowed and write the definition.

1. *persona non grata*
2. ad hoc
3. *je ne sais quoi*
4. hoi polloi
5. *verboten*
6. nom de guerre

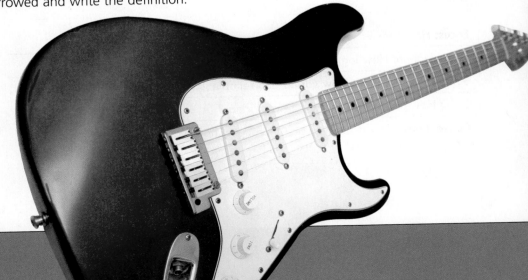

Practice B Rewrite each sentence substituting the correct borrowed or foreign word from the box for the word or phrase in italics. Use context clues to determine the word's meaning. Use a dictionary if necessary.

niche	clique	bazaar	tempo	carte blanche
faux pas	prima facie	passé	grotesque	vis-à-vis

1. My brother had *the freedom* to visit the millionaire whenever he wanted to.
2. The ugly gargoyle sitting on the roof was *distorted and strange*.
3. After many years, Trudy found her *special place* as a fashion designer.
4. I bought these boots at the *market*.
5. The strangers fell in love *at first sight*.
6. The people on a soccer team have their own *exclusive group*.
7. Rafael had a discussion about his future *face to face* with his guidance counselor.
8. That style of skirt from the 1990s is *old-fashioned*.
9. Please, slow down the *speed* of that song or I will not be able to sing along with you.
10. By taking a bite of the salad before the hostess was served, Tiffany made a serious *social blunder*.

Activity Prepare a note card like the following for each of these words: *arsenal, garage, précis, déjà vu, caveat, klutz.* Look up each word in a dictionary and write its pronunciation. Then, write the meaning of the word in its original language. Next, write the meaning of the word in English. Finally, write a sentence using the word correctly in English.

Comprehension and Collaboration

Develop a vocabulary quiz based on Practice B. Following the model, write sentences with clues for these words: *cul-de-sac, ad nauseum, southpaw, ensemble,* and *sayonara.* Have a partner figure out which of the words fits in the sentence. If it is not clear, you may have to rewrite the sentence with better context clues.

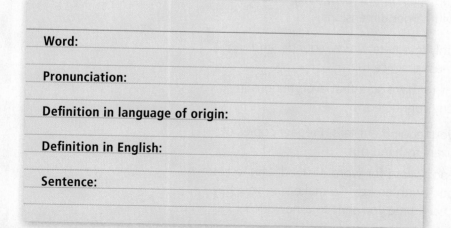

Word:

Pronunciation:

Definition in language of origin:

Definition in English:

Sentence:

www.PHLitOnline.com
- Illustrated vocabulary words
- Interactive vocabulary games
- Vocabulary flashcards

Communications Workshop

Delivering a Multimedia Presentation

Common Core State Standards

Speaking and Listening
5. Make strategic use of digital media in presentations to enhance understanding of findings, reasoning, and evidence and to add interest.

Transform your research report into a **multimedia presentation** by adding sounds and visuals that create drama and interest for an audience. A successful multimedia presentation offers clear ideas and information about a topic using a variety of supporting media such as images, music, charts, graphs, or video clips.

Learn the Skills

Use the strategies to complete the activity on page 1035.

Prepare the Content Consider your topic, audience, and available media and equipment when choosing which media to use.

- Decide which parts of your research report can be enhanced with the use of visuals or sounds.

- Choose media that suit your topic. For example, you might play music of a time period appropriate to your report as a soundtrack.

- Choose media that suit your audience. For example, you might choose certain music for an audience of classmates but other music if the audience is your parents.

- Use media that will help your audience understand the presentation. For example, if your research paper is about Gothic architecture, use images to show examples of Gothic-style buildings.

- Make sure any media and technology you choose is used ethically. Consult copyright notices and cite your sources to avoid plagiarism.

- Verify that all visual images can be seen by the entire audience. If you are presenting pictures on paper, photocopy and enlarge small images. If you are presenting images on a screen, make sure the resolution, or clarity, works with larger dimensions.

Prepare Your Delivery To smoothly integrate words, sounds, and images in your presentation, you must practice it.

- Double-check your equipment to make sure that everything is in working condition and properly connected.

- Have a backup plan in case your equipment fails. Prepare copies of illustrations or graphic organizers to hand out.

- Do not read your research report word for word. Instead, talk to your audience, articulating your ideas with energy. To make sure you stay on track, refer to your notes each time you shift to a new idea.

Practice the Skills

© **Presentation of Knowledge and Ideas** Use what you have learned in this workshop to perform the following task.

> ## ACTIVITY: Produce a Multimedia Presentation
>
> Use the steps shown to prepare a multimedia presentation of your research paper to deliver to your class.
> - Identify the most important ideas in your report.
> - Consider creative ways to define, illustrate, or summarize those ideas with media, such as images or sounds.
> - Research sources of graphics and other images that can help explain challenging concepts.
> - Incorporate sounds and images that convey your point of view on your subject and that appeal to your target audience.
> - Write an outline of your presentation that explains how you will integrate text, visuals, and sounds effectively.
> - Preview the Presentation Checklist to anticipate how your audience will evaluate your presentation.
> - Record your work or present it to the class in person.

Use the Presentation Checklist to analyze your classmates' use of visual and sound techniques in their multimedia presentations.

> ## Presentation Checklist
>
> Rate each statement on a scale of 1 (strongly disagree) to 5 (strongly agree). Explain your ratings.
>
> **Content**
> - The presentation conveys a clear message.   Rating:_____
> - The presenter supports main ideas with appropriate details. Rating:_____
>
> **Use of Visual Techniques**
> - The visuals help explain concepts.   Rating:_____
> - The visuals convey the presenter's thesis.   Rating:_____
> - The visual techniques appeal to me.   Rating:_____
>
> **Use of Sound Techniques**
> - The sounds support the presentation's purpose.   Rating:_____
> - The sounds convey the presenter's thesis.   Rating:_____
> - The sounds appeal to me.   Rating:_____

© **Comprehension and Collaboration** Take notes as you listen to your classmates' multimedia presentations. Analyze how speakers convey their ideas using visual and sound techniques. Based on this analysis, discuss which techniques were most successful.

Cumulative Review

Common Core
State Standards

RL.9-10.2, RL.9-10.3, RL.9-10.5;
W.9-10.2; L.4.a
[For the full wording of the standards, see the standards chart in the front of your textbook.]

I. Reading Literature

Directions: *Read the passage. Then, answer each question that follows.*

Scene: The king's bedchamber. The king lies asleep in his bed.
[*Enter:* a ghost dressed in kingly robes]

> [*Ghost stands looking down on the sleeping king.*]

1 **Ghost.** [*in a hoarse, rasping, heavy whisper*] Arise! Arise! The hour has struck
2 midnight. The new day is upon us.

> [*King awakens; looks at the Ghost with horror.*]

3 **King.** What is this! What are you?
4 **Ghost.** You know me well.
5 **King.** No, I do not know you! [*The King turns away.*]
6 You are a figment of my mind, a black and horrible nightmare.
7 **Ghost.** Then look on this!

> [*The Ghost tears open his shirt, revealing a deep gash in his chest*]

8 Know you now? This is your handiwork!
9 **King.** God save us! Is this Leopold?
10 **Ghost.** Ay. Your king, to whom you have sworn <u>fealty</u>,
11 And whose life and crown you robbed.
12 **King.** No, it was not I!
13 We have found the murderer and sent him to hell!
14 **Ghost.** You lie! Another bore the knife, but your gold was in his purse.
15 You bought my throne with murder and with gold!
16 Now you try to wash your hands of blood.

> [*The Ghost glides closer to the King and reaches out his bloody hand.*

17 **King.** [*King recoils in horror.*] No! No! It was not I, I say!
18 **Ghost.** The time has come to answer for your lies.
19 The dawn is near, but you'll not see another sun arise.
20 **King.** No, no! [*King clutches his chest, falls to the floor dead.*]

> [*Ghost dissolves into mist, just as sunrise appears through the window.*]

1. Which is the best statement of the **external conflict** between the King and the ghost of Leopold?

   A. The Ghost is angry that he is no longer king and wants to destroy the King.
   B. The new king had Leopold murdered, and the Ghost wants revenge.
   C. The Ghost is angry because the new king does not fear him.
   D. The King has been a poor leader, and the Ghost wants him replaced.

2. What is the Ghost's **motivation** for appearing to the King?

   A. to announce his anger
   B. to seek revenge
   C. to regain his power
   D. to frighten the King

3. The author has the Ghost speak in **blank verse** to show that—

   A. the Ghost is from the upper class.
   B. the King should not trust the Ghost.
   C. the Ghost was murdered during his life.
   D. the King might doubt what the Ghost says.

4. **Vocabulary** Which of the following is the closest definition of the underlined word *fealty*?

   A. jealousy
   B. laughter
   C. feudalism
   D. faithfulness

5. Based on lines 15–16, what is the King's **internal conflict**?

   A. He enjoys being the king too much.
   B. He fears his kingdom will go to war.
   C. He suffers guilt for having Leopold murdered.
   D. He wants to have more power.

6. Which of the following **universal themes** is represented in this passage?

   A. the loyalty of friends
   B. the desire for power
   C. the fear of death
   D. the need for love

7. In a **Shakespearean tragedy,** the murdering King might represent which of the following?

   A. the tragic hero
   B. the antagonist
   C. the foil
   D. the supporting character

8. Which line represents the **climax** of the passage?

   A. line 9
   B. line 14
   C. line 16
   D. line 20

9. What is the *most important information* that the **dialogue** in lines 4–11 reveals?

   A. The Ghost and the King are enemies.
   B. The King murdered Leopold to gain power.
   C. The King was the brother of Leopold.
   D. The Ghost was King Leopold in life.

Timed Writing

10. In a developed paragraph, **describe** the character of the King. **Explain** what you think motivated him, and how he related to King Leopold before Leopold's murder. **Support** your answer with details from the passage.

II. Reading Informational Text

Directions: *Read the copy below from an informational sign. Then, answer each question that follows.*

Common Core State Standards

RI.9-10.3, RI.9-10.4, RI.9-10.5; L.9-10.1.b, L.9-10.3, L.9-10.4.a
[For the full wording of the standards, see the standards chart in the front of your textbook.]

Welcome to the Exhibit on the Origins of World Theater!

This **exhibit** presents the costumes, sets, staging, and music of some of the world's greatest drama from Asian and Western cultures. The **art of drama** ranges from the kabuki theater in Japan to the English plays of Shakespeare, from the Javanese puppet plays to the modern social drama. This sign can help you decide where to begin.

Hall One

Asian Drama Asian theater's roots are the classical theater of Hindu India, which influenced theater in Burma, Thailand, Java, Bali, Japan, and China. Asian theater does not focus on individual authors or on advancing drama as an art form, as in the West. Classical Asian theater is nonrealistic and does not emphasize <u>chronology</u>, or tell stories in time order. The actors used stylized performances that developed over time into formalized traditions of high sophistication and visual beauty. To learn more, visit Hall One.

Hall Two

Western Drama From its beginnings in ancient Greece, Western drama originated as community ritual meant to celebrate myth and affirm the moral beliefs of the time. Much of the aspect of the ritual was lost with Roman theater, with the development of individual characters. The idea of religious ritual resurfaced in the Middle Ages with the mystery plays, meant to impart values to the audience. Western drama became more realistic over the centuries and reached a high level of sophistication in character and plot by the Renaissance. To learn more, visit Hall Two.

1. Based on this informational sign, which research topics might be covered in this exhibit?

   A. how the Renaissance was a flowering of art

   B. the themes of Oscar Wilde's plays

   C. how Western drama developed

   D. the artistry of Roman architecture

2. In Hall One, you would most likely see—

   A. a display of a play about medieval values.

   B. an actor giving a soliloquy.

   C. a costume of a kabuki actor.

   D. an image of a Roman amphitheater.

3. What visual aid might you find on this sign?

   A. a map to help you locate the halls

   B. a graph reflecting the number of visitors

   C. an illustration of a soap-opera star

   D. a timeline of early film history

4. Vocabulary What is the best definition of the underlined word *chronology*?

   A. the study of the Greek god Chronos

   B. the sequence of events in time

   C. the study of time

   D. the history of events

III. Writing and Language Conventions

Directions: *Read the passage. Then, answer each question that follows.*

(1) But I was ten years old, my mother took me to a live theater performance for the first time. (2) I knew I would be bored. (3) As we filed into the theater and took our seats, I noticed no one was eating popcorn or candy. (4) This was not the movies or even TV! (5) I love horror movies! (6) The houselights dimmed. (7) The stage lights brightened at the same time. (8) Everyone became perfectly silent. (9) I was astonished as the characters began to speak. (10) I could have reached out and touched them. (11) I could see and almost *feel* the texture of their clothing, smell the stage. (12) This was real! (13) I could feel the sadness ripple through the audience when the hero died! (14) Applauding in unison, the play ended, everyone stood. (15) I felt part of it all.

1. Which statement should be added to the end of this passage to best express the writer's **main insight?**

  A. To this day, I love live theater.
  B. Horror movies are the best.
  C. Some people enjoy live theater, but I do not.
  D. Theater is not for everyone.

2. In what way should the **subordinate clause** in sentence 1 be revised?

  A. Remove the comma.
  B. Replace "but" with "when."
  C. Replace "was" with "will be."
  D. Leave as is.

3. Which of the following is the *best* use of **independent and subordinate clauses** to combine sentence 6 with sentence 7?

  A. The houselights dimmed unless the stage lights brightened.
  B. Why the houselights dimmed, the stage lights brightened.
  C. The houselights dimmed that the stage lights brightened.
  D. While the houselights dimmed, the stage lights brightened.

4. Which sentence should be removed so this passage has unity?

  A. sentence 1
  B. sentence 3
  C. sentence 5
  D. sentence 15

5. To incorporate more descriptive **sensory details** in sentence 11, add—

  A. "touch and" before "texture."
  B. "the faintly dusty odor of" after "smell."
  C. "new costumes or" before "their clothing."
  D. "and touch" after "I could see."

6. How should sentence 14 be revised for clarity?

  A. As the play ended, everyone stood, applauding in unison.
  B. Standing, the play ended, and everyone applauded in unison.
  C. The play ended by applauding in unison, and everyone stood.
  D. When the play stood and applauded, we ended the play.

STOP

Performance Tasks

Common Core State Standards

RL.9-10.2, RL.9-10.3, RL.9-10.4, RL.9-10.5; W.9-10.2, W.9-10.9.a; SL.9-10.1, SL.9-10.4, SL.9-10.6; L.9-10.1, L.9-10.3, L.9-10.5
[For the full wording of the standards, see the standards chart in the front of your textbook.]

Directions: *Follow the instructions to complete the tasks below as required by your teacher.*

As you work on each task, incorporate both general academic vocabulary and literary terms you learned in this unit.

Writing

Task 1: Literature [RL.9-10.3; W.9-10.9.a]
Analyze Character Development

Write an essay in which you analyze the development of a complex character over the course of a play in the unit.

- Select a character with multiple or conflicting motivations from one of the plays in this unit. You might select an antagonist, a protagonist, or a tragic hero.
- Explain which work and character you chose to discuss.
- Analyze the development of this character over the course of the text. Cite details that describe the character at the play's beginning. Then, trace the critical points at which the character develops and changes. Explain how the character develops from the beginning to the end of the drama.
- Support your analysis with evidence from the text, using direct quotations when appropriate.
- Provide a concluding statement that supports the analysis in your essay.
- Use standard English grammar, punctuation, spelling, and capitalization in your writing.

Task 2: Literature [RL.9-10.2; W.9-10.2]
Analyze Theme

Write an essay in which you analyze the development of the theme in a play in the unit.

- State which play you chose and briefly summarize the story.
- State your interpretation of the theme and analyze how it develops over the course of the play.

- Cite relevant details from the play, including plot events and specific dialogue, that support your interpretation of the theme.
- Establish and maintain a formal tone throughout your essay.
- Use standard conventions of English grammar in your writing, including correct subject-verb and pronoun-antecedent agreement.

Task 3: Literature [RL.9-10.4; W.9-10.2]
Analyze Word Choice

Write an essay in which you analyze word choice in a dramatic speech.

- Choose a major dramatic speech, such as a soliloquy or a monologue, from a play in this unit. Explain which work and speech you chose.
- Determine what the character is saying and why. Then, analyze word choices in the speech. Consider the use of figurative language and imagery that adds to the meaning of the speech. Also consider significant connotative word choices that contribute to the development of the characters or theme.
- Use precise language, including literary and academic terms, to convey your ideas.
- Correctly use the conventions of standard English grammar and usage.

Speaking and Listening

Task 4: Literature [RL.9-10.5; SL.9-10.4, SL.9-10.6]

Compare Dramatic Elements

Prepare and deliver an oral presentation comparing and contrasting the function of the chorus in Greek tragedy and soliloquies in Shakespearean tragedy, noting that both are structural elements of the dramas in which they appear.

- Select chorus passages and soliloquies from this unit. Examples of soliloquies, in which characters speak alone onstage, are Brutus' speech in *Julius Caesar* Act II and Antony's in Act III.

- Analyze the function of the Greek chorus and the function of Shakespeare's soliloquies.

- Explain the type of information that is revealed to the audience through each dramatic element.

- Draw a conclusion about the relationships that an audience might have to a Greek chorus and to a Shakespearean character.

- Throughout your presentation, support your ideas with details from the text.

- Use formal English during your presentation.

Task 5: Literature [RL.9-10.3; SL.9-10.4]

Compare Characters

Write and deliver a speech in which you analyze and compare two characters from one of the plays in this unit.

- Choose two key characters from one of the plays in this unit and compare their roles and functions within the play. For example, you might choose a hero and a foil or a protagonist and an antagonist.

- Discuss the ways in which the characters interact with each other.

- Examine the motivations of each character, or the reasons for his or her actions. Provide evidence from the text to support your ideas.

- Provide examples of the ways in which both characters grow and change over the course of the play.

- Analyze the way in which each character advances the play's plot.

- Sequence your ideas clearly, concisely, and logically so that listeners can easily follow your reasoning.

Task 6: Literature [RL.9-10.1; SL.9-10.1]

Analyze Conflict

Conduct a small group discussion focusing on conflict, both internal and external, in one of the plays in this unit. Analyze the connections between the types of conflict and the way in which all conflict drives the plot.

- Choose one of the plays in this unit and identify the conflicts within it. Determine whether each conflict is internal or external.

- Analyze the effect that each conflict has on the development of the drama's plot. Make note of supporting details from the play.

- Prepare a list of questions for discussion. Design the questions to be interesting. Be sure you have also formulated possible answers to the questions in advance.

- As the leader of the discussion, initiate the conversation and keep it going. Actively incorporate all group members into the discussion.

- Respond thoughtfully to diverse perspectives, referring to the text to support your positions.

- At the conclusion of the discussion, summarize the main ideas the discussion yielded, including points of agreement and disagreement.

> **THE BIG ?**
>
> **To what extent does experience determine what we perceive?**
>
> At the beginning of Unit 5, you participated in a discussion of the Big Question. Now that you have completed the unit, write a response to the question. Discuss how your initial ideas have changed or been reinforced. Support your response with at least one example from literature and one example from an additional subject area or your own life. Use Big Question vocabulary words (see p. 791) in your response.

Featured Titles

In this unit, you have read a variety of dramatic works. Continue to read on your own. Select works that you enjoy, but challenge yourself to explore new playwrights and works of increasing depth and complexity. The titles suggested below will help you get started.

Literature

Sophocles: The Theban Plays
by Sophocles   EXEMPLAR TEXT

In this book of three ancient Greek **plays**—*Oedipus the King, Oedipus at Colonus,* and *Antigone*—Sophocles tells the stories of the ill-fated characters Oedipus and his daughter Antigone. Oedipus becomes the victim of a tragic prophecy while Antigone suffers the consequences of taking a principled stand.

The Grapes of Wrath
by John Steinbeck   EXEMPLAR TEXT

This Pulitzer Prize–winning **novel** is set during the Great Depression. The novel traces the path of an Oklahoma family as they lose their farm to drought and decide to make their way to California to find work. It is a story of desperate people chasing any glimmer of hope they can find.

The Collected Poetry of W. H. Auden
by W. H. Auden   EXEMPLAR TEXT

Auden's diverse collection of **poetry** includes poems that speak to readers in a deeply personal way. The collection includes Auden's famous poems "Musée des Beaux Arts" and "Funeral Blues."

Ibsen: Four Major Plays
by Henrik Ibsen
Signet, 1965   EXEMPLAR TEXT

Ibsen's innovative dramas show conflicted people whose inner struggles mirror their external dilemmas. In this collection of **plays,** which includes the classic *A Doll House,* Ibsen creates finely detailed worlds in which the secrets usually hidden by social conventions are revealed.

A Raisin in the Sun
by Lorraine Hansberry
Vintage Books, 1994

What would you do if you received a check for $10,000? This is the challenge the African American Younger family must confront. In Hansberry's **play,** family members clash over their perceptions of success and what this $10,000 should mean for them.

"Master Harold" . . . *and the boys*
by Athol Fugard
Vintage, 2009   EXEMPLAR TEXT

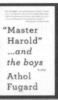

This one-act **play** is set in a tea room in South Africa during the racial segregation of the apartheid era. The play slowly builds to a climax that shows how one character, a teenager, has absorbed many of the society's racist values.

Girl in Hyacinth Blue
by Susan Vreeland
MacMurray & Beck, 2000

In this **novel,** a mysterious painting surfaces after being hidden for years, and secrets begin to unravel. As the work passes from owner to owner, it illuminates the changing realities it has witnessed.

Informational Text

Black, Blue & Gray: African Americans in the Civil War
by Jim Haskins
Simon & Schuster, 1998   EXEMPLAR TEXT

In this engaging **nonfiction** book, Haskins describes the contributions of black soldiers—178,000 fighting for the North—during the Civil War. The book brings the story of these men to life with photographs, as well as authentic letters and diary entries.

Preparing to Read Complex Texts

Attentive Reading As you read literature on your own, bring your imagination and questions to the text. The questions shown below and others that you ask as you read will help you learn and enjoy literature even more.

 **Common Core State Standards**

Reading Literature/Informational Text 10. By the end of Grade 10, read and comprehend literature, including stories, dramas, poems, and literary nonfiction at the high end of the grades 9–10 text complexity band independently and proficiently.

When reading drama, ask yourself...

- Who is the main character? What struggles does this character face?
- What other characters are important? How do these characters relate to the main character?
- Is there more than one conflict? If so, how do they connect?
- What is the setting of the play? Does the setting cause conflicts or affect the characters' actions? Why or why not?
- Is there more than one setting? If so, do the settings create different moods or conflicts?
- Are the characters, setting, and events believable? Why or why not?
- Does the play end happily, sadly, or somewhere in between? How does the ending make me feel?
- What theme or insight do I think the play conveys? Is that theme or insight important and true?

Ⓒ Key Ideas and Details

- How is the play structured? How many acts does it have? What events unfold in each act?
- Are there multiple plots—a main plot and a subplot? If so, how do the different plots relate to each other?
- Does the dialogue sound authentic and believable? Why or why not?
- What do the stage directions tell me about the characters and situations? In what other ways do I learn about the characters?
- At what point in the play do I feel the most concern for the characters? Why?
- What point of view does the main character express? Do other characters express similar points of view? If not, is this difference a point of conflict?
- If characters express different points of view, which one do I think the playwright shares? Why? Which point of view do I share? Why?

Ⓒ Craft and Structure

- What do I find most interesting, unusual, or powerful about this play?
- In what ways is the play similar to or different from others I have read or seen?
- What insights have I gained from reading this play?
- What actors would I choose to play the roles in this play?
- If I were to be cast in this play, which role would I want? Why?
- If I were directing this play, how might I stage it?
- After reading this play, do I want to read others by this playwright? Why or why not?

Ⓒ Integration of Ideas

Can anyone be a *hero?*

THE BIG ?

Themes in Literature:
Heroes and Dreamers

PHLit
Online!
www.PHLitOnline.com

Hear It!
• Selection summary audio
• Selection audio
• BQ Tunes

See It!
• Author videos
• Big Question video
• Get Connected videos
• Background videos
• More about the authors
• Illustrated vocabulary words
• Vocabulary flashcards

Do It!
• Interactive journals
• Interactive graphic organizers
• Grammar tutorials
• Interactive vocabulary games
• Test practice

Can anyone be a *hero?*

A hero is often thought of as someone who displays attributes such as selflessness and courage in order to help others. You may think of a hero as a noble figure, such as a legendary knight who goes on dangerous quests and is dedicated to his king. On the other hand, you might imagine a hero as an everyday person whose character is defined by his or her honesty, sincerity, and desire to do good. Such a person may perform small, often unnoticed acts of heroism simply because he or she wishes to do the right thing. Although there are different kinds of heroes, they all strive to act with honor.

Exploring the Big Question

© **Collaboration: One-on-One Discussion** Start thinking about the Big Question by making a list of the different people you have known, heard about, or read about who can be considered heroes. Describe one specific example of each of the following types of heroes:

- a legendary or mythical person who performs great deeds
- someone who helps others on a daily basis
- a person who makes a personal sacrifice in order to help others
- a courageous individual with a dangerous job
- a character in literature or a real person whose determination led to great accomplishments

Share your responses with a partner. Discuss the traits that the hero in each example demonstrates. Then, decide which attributes you think truly define a hero.

As you talk, you may discover you have very different perspectives about heroism and heroes. Work to understand each other's ideas by posing meaningful questions and answering thoughtfully. Pause periodically to summarize ways in which you agree and disagree. Consider whether your partner's ideas help you to see the topic in new ways. Finally, gather your ideas into a brief report and share it with the class.

Connecting to the Literature Each reading in this unit will give you additional insight into the Big Question.

PHLit
Online!
www.PHLitOnline.com

- Big Question video
- Illustrated vocabulary words
- Interactive vocabulary games
- BQ Tunes

Learning Big Question Vocabulary

Acquire and Use Academic Vocabulary Academic vocabulary is the language you encounter in textbooks and on standardized tests. Review the definitions of these academic vocabulary words.

character (kar´ ik tər) *n.* moral strength or discipline

conduct (kän´ dukt´) *n.* the way a person behaves

inherent (in hir´ ənt) *adj.* existing naturally in something

integrity (in teg´ rə tē) *n.* commitment to right conduct or justice; moral certainty

principles (prin´ sə pəls) *n.* rules for right conduct

resolute (rez´ ə lüt) *adj.* committed, determined, or firm

responsibility (ri spon´ sə bil´ ə tē) *n.* obligation or duty

Use these words as you complete Big Question activities in this unit that involve reading, writing, speaking, and listening.

Gather Vocabulary Knowledge Additional Big Question words are listed below. Categorize the words by deciding whether you know each one well, know it a little bit, or do not know it at all.

attributes	honor	sacrifice
courage	legendary	selflessness
determination	persevere	

Then, do the following:

1. Work with a partner to write each word on one side of an index card and its definition on the other side.

2. Verify each definition by looking the word up in a print or online dictionary and revising its meaning as needed.

3. Place the cards in a pile with the words facing up.

4. Take turns drawing a word card. Pronounce the word on the front of the card, and use it in a true or false statement about heroes or heroism. For example, *Mario was commended for his* selflessness *when he helped his grandfather to safety.* Invite your partner to explain whether the statement is true or false.

Common Core State Standards

Speaking and Listening

1. Initiate and participate effectively in a range of collaborative discussions with diverse partners on grades 9–10 topics, texts, and issues, building on others' ideas and expressing their own clearly and persuasively.

1.c. Propel conversations by posing and responding to questions that relate the current discussion to broader themes or larger ideas; actively incorporate others into the discussion; and clarify, verify, or challenge ideas and conclusions.

1.d. Respond thoughtfully to diverse perspectives, summarize points of agreement and disagreement, and, when warranted, qualify or justify their own views and understanding and make new connections in light of the evidence and reasoning presented.

Language

6. Acquire and use accurately general academic and domain-specific words and phrases, sufficient for reading, writing, speaking, and listening at the college and career readiness level; demonstrate independence in gathering vocabulary knowledge when considering a word or phrase important to comprehension or expression.

Elements of the Oral Tradition

In the **oral tradition,** storytellers pass along stories by word of mouth, preserving shared cultural **values.**

Long before the invention of writing and books, singers and storytellers recited the tales and lore of their cultures. Passed from one generation to the next, the poems and stories they told are referred to as the **oral tradition.** Through the oral tradition, the stories of different cultures have been preserved through the ages.

The oral tradition is a treasure trove of tragic, exciting, and funny stories. In their day, these stories also served as a powerful tool for education. By giving memorable, moving examples of heroes and monsters, of deeds both good and bad, the oral tradition helped a culture answer questions such as "What should I be like?" and "What should I do?"

Like other literature, the stories of the oral tradition express **themes**—insights about life and human nature. One important source of these themes is the **cultural experience** of the storytellers—their core values and concerns. At the same time, their stories express **universal themes,** or truths about life that are meaningful to people of all times and all places. Examples of universal themes include the virtues of courage and the dangers of greed.

In telling their tales, storytellers very often used **archetypes**—characters, situations, images, and symbols that recur in the narratives of all cultures. The chart below gives examples of archetypes.

Storytellers in the oral tradition explore **universal themes**— insights into life that recur throughout world literature. Often, they develop these themes using **archetypes.** The use of archetypal patterns likely made stories easier to remember and retell.

Examples of Archetypal Characters

- The **wise and virtuous ruler,** whose reign brings in a golden age, or time of peace and prosperity
- The **dreamer** or **transgressor,** a character who imagines new possibilities and defies danger to bring an important gift to society
- The **hero,** an unpromising youth who triumphs over stronger forces through cleverness or virtue and blossoms into a wise, strong, and courageous leader

Examples of Archetypal Patterns

- The struggle between the **protagonist,** or main character, and the **antagonist,** a person or force that opposes the protagonist
- A series of tests that a character must pass
- A quest or task that a character must complete
- Characters, events, or objects that come in threes
- A fair and just end that rewards good or punishes evil

Forms and Characteristics of the Oral Tradition

Generations of storytellers in the oral tradition developed narrative forms following the same basic patterns. These forms are found in many different cultures, and include myths, folk tales, legends, fairy tales, and epics.

Traditional stories in these forms do not express an individual author's **point of view,** or attitudes and beliefs about the world. (Indeed, historians have no way of identifying the original authors of most folk literature.) Instead, stories in these forms tend to express the shared **values,** or model behaviors and attitudes, cherished by the society from which they originated.

Despite that fact, individual storytellers did leave their marks on these tales. As the tales were retold and passed down, the storytellers sometimes changed narrative details, resulting in different versions of the same basic story. For example, stories about King Arthur have been retold throughout the ages, through various forms—poetry, song, and novel—and set in different places and time periods.

In This Section

Elements of the Oral Tradition

Analyzing Theme

Close Read: Determining Themes Across Cultures
- Model Text
- Practice Text

After You Read

 Common Core State Standards

RL.9-10.2, RL.9-10.6
[For the full wording of the standards, see the standards chart in the front of your textbook.]

Narrative Forms in the Oral Tradition

Form	Characteristics
Myths	• Explain the actions of gods and their interactions with humans • May explain the causes of natural phenomena or the origins of cultural traditions
Folk Tales	• Deal with heroic acts, adventures, magic, or romance; often concern the relationship between mortals and gods • Focus on human or animal heroes
Legends	• Are folk tales about larger-than-life heroes and events from the past • Often are based on historical fact, with factual details becoming exaggerated and fictionalized over time
Fairy Tales	• Are simple folk tales, usually told to entertain small children • Include magic or supernatural elements
Epics	• Are long narrative poems that use elevated language and extended, elaborate comparisons of unlike subjects called epic similes • Combine features of myths and legends • Describe the adventures of larger-than-life **epic heroes,** who are important to the history of their cultures • Often tell of the heroes' journeys or quests, on which the heroes are helped or hindered by gods and other supernatural creatures • Often begin with the poet's mention of the subject and a plea to a divine being for inspiration and guidance in the telling of the tale

Analyzing Theme

A literary work develops a **theme**, or central message or insight, which may be **universal** or **culturally specific**.

 **Common Core State Standards**

Reading Literature

2. Determine a theme or central idea of a text and analyze in detail its development over the course of the text, including how it emerges and is shaped and refined by specific details; provide an objective summary of the text.

6. Analyze a particular point of view or cultural experience reflected in a work of literature from outside the United States, drawing on a wide reading of world literature.

The **theme** of a work is the insight it conveys into life or human nature. To develop a theme, a story combines narrative elements, such as characters, setting, and plot, in ways that express an underlying meaning. Usually, the theme of a story is not directly stated, although a character may make statements that suggest it. Instead, the theme is usually implied, or indirectly expressed, by the arrangement of story elements.

Literary Elements The following literary elements often contribute to the development of theme:

- Characters—the people, animals, or creatures that take part in the action
- Setting—the time and place of a story
- Plot—the sequence of events in a story
- Conflict—the struggle between opposing forces that drives the plot
- Archetypes—patterns of story elements that recur across cultures and often have strong associations

Theme and Point of View An author's **point of view,** or perspective, consists of the author's thoughts and attitude about a topic. Point of view is often closely tied to theme. For example, if an author believes that society is too preoccupied with money, the author might convey themes about the dangers of losing touch with the natural world.

To recognize an author's point of view, focus on the way the author describes settings, situations, characters, and characters' actions. Pay close attention to the author's **diction,** or word choice, which can indicate positive or negative attitudes.

Development of Theme To understand how narrative elements can be used to develop a theme, consider the story outlined in the following example.

Story Element	Development of Theme
Characters: One brother is selfish. The other is generous.	This contrast between characters encourages you to focus on ideas of selfishness and generosity.
Conflict: The selfish brother is robbed, but none of his friends will help him because he is mean-spirited.	Selfishness is connected to a bad outcome—it deprives a person of the help of others. This connection refines the theme.
Plot: The kind brother lends the selfish brother the money he needs.	The contrast between selfishness and generosity is reinforced.
Character's Insight: The selfish brother thanks the kind brother and begs his forgiveness.	This insight further develops the idea that it is better to be generous than selfish.
Theme: It is better to be generous than selfish.	

While the example story does not state its theme directly, an alert reader will find the theme developed through the patterns and associations the story creates using literary elements.

Theme and Cultural Experience Point of view and theme are influenced by the author's **cultural experiences**—the events, beliefs, and values that shape the culture in which the author lives. Those cultural experiences may be reflected in the values and beliefs characters hold as well as in the practices and customs they follow.

In works from the oral tradition, readers often do not distinguish the teller's point of view from that of the culture as a whole. A work is taken to "speak for" its entire culture.

Universal and Culturally Specific Themes
While a given cultural experience may shape a work in important ways, the work may still convey a **universal theme**—an insight into life that recurs in the literature of various times and places. At the same time, a work may express themes that are **culturally specific;** they reflect the particular circumstances and beliefs of the author's culture. Consider the example of "Pandora's Box," a Greek myth. The work conveys both universal and culturally specific themes.

Pandora's Box	Universal Themes
When Zeus created Pandora, he bestowed many wonderful gifts on her, including a box that he told her never to open. However, among her other gifts was curiosity, which caused Pandora to open the box. When she did, all the previously unknown evils and horrors of the world escaped.	• Unbridled curiosity can lead to trouble. • We must follow the rules or deal with the consequences. **Culturally Specific Themes** • It is risky for mortals to ignore the gods. • The gods know what is best for mortals.

Shifting Points of View As stories were passed down through the oral tradition, story details changed as the point of view of the authors changed. Consider, for example, how a changing view of the world affected retellings of the traditional fairy tale "Snow White."

Example: Snow White
Because the Queen is jealous of her stepdaughter, the beautiful Snow White, she plots to kill her.

German Version: "Little Snow White"— retold by the Brothers Grimm in 1812, based on original Old World tales
Point of View: Reflects the cruel, chaotic, and violent medieval view of the world
Details: The Queen asks a huntsman to take Snow White into the woods, kill her, and bring back her liver and lungs, which are to be served for dinner. In the end, the Queen dances herself to death at Snow White's wedding in a pair of burning-hot iron shoes.

English Version: "Snow Drop"—retold by Edgar Taylor in 1823
Point of View: Reflects a softer, kinder view of the world
Details: The Queen asks a huntsman to take Snow Drop away but does not request proof of the girl's death. Snow Drop dies from eating a poisoned apple, but revives when the chunk of apple falls from her mouth. In the end, the Queen dies after choking with anger at Snow Drop's wedding.

Theme and Point of View in Nonfiction
Like works in the oral tradition, modern fiction expresses themes. In addition, some literary nonfiction may be said to have themes. For example, a writer may tell true stories of friendship that illustrate the central idea, or theme, that our friends know us better than we know ourselves. Literary nonfiction may also present an author's point of view explicitly, as when the writer argues a position, or implicitly, as when a true story suggests an author's beliefs and attitudes.

Close Read: Determining Themes Across Cultures

Themes in literature are developed through the patterning of story elements.

To identify themes along with different cultural experiences and points of view in literature, you need to analyze and draw conclusions from story elements. Use the tips in the chart to guide you (Note that many nonfiction works incorporate literary elements, and you may apply these strategies, as appropriate, to such works.)

Clues to Theme

Setting
The **setting**—the time and place of the story—may help to develop the theme in a number of ways. As you read, ask yourself

- How does setting shape the characters' choices? What problems arise there?
- What does the setting suggest about life? For example, is life in the setting a struggle? Is it stagnant? Is it superficial?

Characters
To determine theme, consider the qualities, interactions, and fates of characters. Ask yourself

- What are the characters like, as revealed by what they say, do, or think?
- How do the characters interact?
- What does the main character learn from, or how is he or she changed by, events?

Cultural Context and Point of View
The **cultural context** of a story, or the traditions, beliefs, and historical experiences of characters, can help shape its theme. Cultural context also helps shape the author's **point of view,** or attitudes and beliefs. Ask yourself

- Which clues indicate the author's or characters' cultural background?
- What values, customs, and beliefs do characters embrace or encounter?
- Which details suggest the author's point of view on a topic? What is this point of view?

Conflict and Plot
A plot is powered by a **conflict,** or struggle between opposing forces. To determine theme, consider the ideas emphasized by the plot. Ask yourself

- What conflict do the characters face?
- How is the conflict resolved?
- What insights do characters have, or what lessons does the resolution teach?

Statements and Observations
Sometimes, a work includes a statement by a character or by the narrator that suggests or illuminates the theme. As you read, ask yourself

- Which statements, if any, sum up and express a judgment about story events?
- Which statements, if any, express an insight about people or life based on story events?

Archetypal Elements
Archetypes are character types, plot patterns, images, and symbols that recur in the narratives of all cultures. Because they often have strong, constant meanings, they can serve as clues to theme. As you read, ask yourself

- Which character types and plot patterns, if any, have I encountered in other literature? Which of these are archetypes?
- What view of or lesson about life does each archetype suggest? (For example, the appearance of an archetypal hero suggests a theme of good triumphing over evil.)

Model

About the Text Britain began its official colonization of Nigeria in 1861, and it was only in 1960 that Nigeria achieved independence. Nigerian author Chinua (chin´ wä) Achebe (ä chā´ bā) grew up under British colonial rule. In his famous novel *Things Fall Apart* (1958), Achebe depicts the tragic consequences of British colonization for traditional Ibo tribal culture. This excerpt is from Chapter 1 of the book.

from *Things Fall Apart* by Chinua Achebe

Okonkwo was well known throughout the nine villages and even beyond. His fame rested on solid personal achievements. As a young man of eighteen he had brought honor to his village by throwing Amalinze the Cat. Amalinze was the great wrestler who for seven years was unbeaten, from Umuofia to Mbaino. He was called the Cat because his back would never touch the earth. It was this man that Okonkwo threw in a fight which the old men agreed was one of the fiercest since the founder of their town engaged a spirit of the wild for seven days and seven nights.

The drums beat and the flutes sang and the spectators held their breath. Amalinze was a wily craftsman, but Okonkwo was as slippery as a fish in water. Every nerve and every muscle stood out on their arms, on their backs and their thighs, and one almost heard them stretching to breaking point. In the end Okonkwo threw the Cat.

That was many years ago, twenty years or more, and during this time Okonkwo's fame had grown like a bush-fire in the *harmattan*[1]. He was tall and huge, and his bushy eyebrows and wide nose gave him a very severe look. He breathed heavily, and it was said that, when he slept, his wives and children in their houses could hear him breathe. When he walked, his heels hardly touched the ground and he seemed to walk on springs, as if he was going to pounce on somebody. And he did pounce on people quite often. He had a slight stammer and whenever he was angry and could not get his words out quickly enough, he would use his fists. He had no patience with unsuccessful men. He had had no patience with his father.

Unoka, for that was his father's name, had died ten years ago. In his day he was lazy and improvident and was quite incapable of thinking about tomorrow. If any money came his way, and it seldom did, he immediately bought gourds of palm-wine, called round his neighbors and made merry. He always said that

Characters Okonkwo is an archetypal hero, admired by his people for his strength and deeds. However, his "fierceness" and refusal to display weakness will prove to be his tragic flaw. Okonkwo's behavior and attitudes are keys to universal themes of status and self-worth.

Archetypal Elements The elders compare Okonkwo's fight to a fight in a legend. The founding of a village or city by a hero who vanquishes a monster is an archetypal plot pattern, as is the notion of a battle that lasts for days.

Statements and Observations The narrator contrasts Okonkwo's aggressive behavior with his father's laziness. These statements reveal one of the novel's culturally specific themes—the importance of status and ambition among the Ibo people.

---

1. harmattan (här mä tän´) *n.* a hot, dry, dusty wind that blows on the northwest Atlantic coast of Africa.

© EXEMPLAR TEXT

Model continued

whenever he saw a dead man's mouth he saw the folly of not eating what one had in one's lifetime. Unoka was, of course, a debtor, and he owed every neighbor some money, from a few cowries to quite substantial amounts.

He was tall but very thin and had a slight stoop. He wore a haggard and mournful look except when he was drinking or playing on his flute. He was very good on his flute, and his happiest moments were the two or three moons after the harvest when the village musicians brought down their instruments, hung above the fireplace. Unoka would play with them, his face beaming with blessedness and peace. Sometimes another village would ask Unoka's band and their dancing *egwugwu*[2] to come and stay with them and teach them their tunes. They would go to such hosts for as long as three or four markets, making music and feasting. Unoka loved the good fare and the good fellowship, and he loved this season of the year, when the rains had stopped and the sun rose every morning with dazzling beauty. And it was not too hot either, because the cold and dry harmattan wind was blowing down from the north. Some years the harmattan was very severe and a dense haze hung on the atmosphere. Old men and children would then sit round log fires, warming their bodies. Unoka loved it all, and he loved the first kites[3] that returned with the dry season, and the children who sang songs of welcome to them. He would remember his own childhood, how he had often wandered around looking for a kite sailing leisurely against the blue sky. As soon as he found one he would sing with his whole being, welcoming it back from its long, long journey, and asking it if it had brought home any lengths of cloth.

That was years ago, when he was young. Unoka, the grown-up, was a failure. He was poor and his wife and children had barely enough to eat. People laughed at him because he was a loafer, and they swore never to lend him any more money because he never paid back. But Unoka was such a man that he always succeeded in borrowing more, and piling up his debts.

One day a neighbor called Okoye came in to see him. He was reclining on a mud bed in his hut playing on the flute. He immediately rose and shook hands with Okoye, who then unrolled the goatskin which he carried under his arm, and sat down. Unoka went into an inner room and soon returned with a small wooden disc containing a kola nut[4], some alligator pepper and a lump of white chalk.

"I have kola," he announced when he sat down, and passed the disc over to his guest.

Cultural Context and Point of View Achebe wrote this novel to present Ibo society in all its complexity. He also wished to counter European stereotypes of Africans as "primitive" people. The details in this passage—the customs and traditions of the Ibo, their fellowship and appreciation of music, food, and nature—reveal Achebe's point of view as well as the cultural experience that shapes his themes.

Characters Unoka's weaknesses are directly described by the narrator. Achebe is setting up a further contrast between the father and son.

---

2. **egwugwu** (e gōō gōō) *n.* men disguised as spirits of revered ancestors who settle arguments among the people of the village.
3. **kites** (kits) *n.* birds of prey.
4. **kola nut** seed of the cola tree, containing caffeine; often served by the Ibo during prayer and other ceremonies.

"Thank you. He who brings kola brings life. But I think you ought to break it," replied Okoye, passing back the disc.

"No, it is for you, I think," and they argued like this for a few moments before Unoka accepted the honor of breaking the kola. Okoye, meanwhile, took the lump of chalk, drew some lines on the floor, and then painted his big toe.

As he broke the kola, Unoka prayed to their ancestors for life and health, and for protection against their enemies. When they had eaten they talked about many things: about the heavy rains which were drowning the yams, about the next ancestral feast and about the impending war with the village of Mbaino. Unoka was never happy when it came to wars. He was in fact a coward and could not bear the sight of blood. And so he changed the subject and talked about music, and his face beamed. He could hear in his mind's ear the blood-stirring and intricate rhythms of the *ekwe*[5] and the *udu*[6] and the *ogene*[7], and he could hear his own flute weaving in and out of them, decorating them with a colorful and plaintive tune. The total effect was gay and brisk, but if one picked out the flute as it went up and down and then broke up into short snatches, one saw that there was sorrow and grief there.

Point of View Unoka's thoughts about music hint at Achebe's point of view: There is sorrow and grief as well as joy in tribal life.

Okoye was also a musician. He played on the *ogene*. But he was not a failure like Unoka. He had a large barn full of yams and he had three wives. And now he was going to take the Idemili title, the third highest in the land. It was a very expensive ceremony and he was gathering all his resources together. That was in fact the reason why he had come to see Unoka. He cleared his throat and began:

"Thank you for the kola. You may have heard of the title I intend to take shortly."

Having spoken plainly so far, Okoye said the next half a dozen sentences in proverbs. Among the Ibo the art of conversation is regarded very highly, and proverbs are the palm-oil with which words are eaten. Okoye was a great talker and he spoke for a long time, skirting round the subject and then hitting it finally. In short, he was asking Unoka to return the two hundred cowries he had borrowed from him more than two years before. As soon as Unoka understood what his friend was driving at, he burst out laughing. He laughed loud and long and his voice rang out clear as the *ogene*, and tears stood in his eyes. His visitor was amazed, and sat speechless. . . .

Conflict Here, Achebe begins to set up yet another contrast: Okoye is everything that Unoka is not. Okoye is successful and wealthy, whereas Unoka is regarded as a failure. This passage hints at conflict to come between Unoka and Okoye.

---

5. *ekwe* (ek′ wā′) slit-drum; an Ibo drum made from a tree trunk.
6. *udu* Ibo drum made of pottery, used to produce bass sounds.
7. *ogene* Ibo bell-like metal percussion instrument.

Theme In the contrast between Okonkwo and his father, and between the father and Okoye, Achebe introduces themes of status and ambition. In his descriptions of Ibo culture, he introduces the theme of tradition. By comparing Okonkwo to folkloric heroes, he ensures that the reader will see in Okonkwo's story a message about the fate of traditional ways.

Independent Practice

About the Text In this selection, John Phillip Santos (b. 1957) uses stories and memories of lost objects—from a Christmas card list to old photographs—as a means of exploring questions of remembrance and identity. As he relates anecdotes of his family's history, he also probes his reactions to these stories as messages from the past.

from *Places Left Unfinished at the Time of Creation* by John Phillip Santos

. . . The past can be difficult to conjure again when so little has been left behind. A few photographs, a golden medal, a pair of eyeglasses as delicate as eggshells, an old Bible, a letter or two. Some families in Mexico have troves of their ancestors' belongings, from pottery of the ancients and exquisite paintings of Mexico City in the eighteenth century to helmets and shields of the Spaniards, and even hundred-year-old parrots and maguey plants[1] that have been handed down, from the great-grandparents who first tended them.

By comparison, the Santos are traveling light through time. In my family, virtually nothing has been handed down, not because there was nothing to give, but after leaving Mexico to come to Texas—so many loved ones left behind, cherished places and things abandoned—the antepasados[2] ceased to regard anything as a keepsake. Everything was given away. Or they may have secretly clung so closely to their treasured objects that they were never passed on.

Then they were lost.

My mother's mother, Leandra Lopez, whom we called simply "Grandmother," sat in her cluttered dark house on West Russell Street like an aged Tejana[3] sphinx during the last ten years of her life. Through the year, she filed away embossed death notices and patron saint prayer cards of departed family and friends in the black leather address book I consulted to write out her Christmas cards every year. In early December, I would sit down with her and first cross out the entries for all those who had "passed onward," as she used to say. By each name in the book, she had already scratched a cross with thick black pencil lines.

Memo Montalvo from Hebbronville, Texas. According to Grandmother, a good man. He had married a not-very-pretty cousin from Laredo.

Efraín Vela from Mier, Tamaulipas. Son of a cousin on her father's side whom she never spoke to. Supposedly, he was the keeper of the family coat of arms, awarded to the family by the Viceroy of Nueva España himself. What would happen to it now?

Cultural Context How does the use of these words help establish the author's cultural background? In what way are they related to themes of memory and identity?

Conflict What conflict does this sentence suggest? What theme might the conflict help to develop?

---

1. **maguey** (mag´ wā´) **plants** *n.* fleshy-leaved plants common to Mexico, Central America, and the southwestern U.S.; used for making rope and tequila.
2. **antepasados** (än tä pä sä´ dōs) *n.* Spanish for "forebears, ancestors."
3. **Tejana** (tā hä´ nä) *adj.* Spanish for "Texan female."

Socorro Mendiola, from Alice, Texas. She and Grandmother had taught school together in a one-room schoolhouse in Cotulla in 1910. Then Socorro became a Franciscan nun, breaking the heart of Grandmother's cousin, Emeterio Vela, whom, she noted with a sigh, had died just last year.

And every year, by the degrees of each ended life, as the world grew older, our addressing marathons grew shorter—though Grandmother would change the subject if I pointed out this mortal ratio.

Inside her rolltop writing desk, she kept a mysterious wooden polygonal[4] star that had a different swatch of old Mexican fabrics glued on each facet. The multicolored curiosity smelled like Mexico, all cumin, wild honey, and smoky rose, and when you shook it, a small solitary object rattled inside. A stone? A marble? A gem? To me, it seemed like some magician's puzzle, and locked inside were all of the secrets of old Mexico.

During one of our annual Christmas-card sessions, I asked her if I could have that star, instead of the customary reward of a box of animal crackers and five dollars in change, which she laboriously fished out of her zippered, yellowing plastic coin purse. Grandmother was almost completely blind by then, so I put her hand to the last of the Hallmark Christmas cards in the place for her to sign her name. She slowly scratched out Leandra Vela Lopez, and told me no, I could not have the star.

I never saw it again.

My uncle, Lico Lopez, her son, ferreted out the past as a passionate genealogist who used research, fantasy, and spells of breathless diabetic madness to craft his ancestral charts of the Lopez and Vela families. Some are elaborate discs, in which each outward concentric ring represents a new generation. In these, as you delve closer to the center, you also go deeper into the past. In others, quickly dashed off as notes to himself, ragged trees and jagged lines are drawn between names like Evaristo, Viviano, Blas, and Hermenegilda. In one, going back to 1763, the capstone slot contains the cryptic entry,

"King of Spain,"

from whom, presumably, he believed we were descended. Subtle faculties and proclivities[5] were passed, speechlessly, through the flesh of successive generations. The ghosts of Spanish royalty mingled with Indios, Negros, and people from every part of the world—in Uncle Lico's secret genealogy of

---

Statements and Observations Why do you think Santos makes this observation about the shorter length of his Christmas-card-addressing sessions with his grandmother? How does this observation relate to the theme of identity?

Conflict What conflict is heightened by Grandmother's refusal to give Santos the wooden star? What connection might her refusal have to the theme?

---

4. **polygonal** (pə lig´ ə nəl) *adj.* many-sided.
5. **proclivities** (prō kliv´ ə tēz) *n.* natural or habitual inclinations.

Practice continued

Characters How is Uncle Lico similar to the archetypal dreamer of the folk tradition? How does his behavior contribute to the theme of identity?

Conflict What happened to Madrina's trunkful of photographs? How does this event reinforce the author's message?

Mexico. Yet, despite the uninterest and ridicule of many, he managed to recover numerous family names and stories.

Lico knew I had some of the same magnetic attraction to the past that fueled his manic genealogies, as if the molecules of our bodies were polarized in a way that drew us both back in time, back, inexorably, toward the ancestors. Before he died, suddenly, in San Antonio, of a heart attack, he sent me all of the notes and charts accumulated in his forty years of digging in the family root cellars. He also gave me a receipt, dated May 25, 1928, laminated and mounted on wood, from my grandfather's grocery store, Leonides Lopez Groceries, in Cotulla, Texas. In my grandfather's filigreed wrought iron pencil script, it details a sale on that day of *harina* (flour), *azúcar* (sugar), *fideos* (vermicelli), *manteca* (lard), *papas* (potatoes), and other assorted dry goods, for a total of $5.05.

A relic like this is the exception, though. A trunkful of the Santos family photographs disappeared when Madrina moved out of the old house on Cincinnati Street. She swears she remembers seeing it fall off the truck near the corner of Zarzamora Street, where La Poblanita bakery was located. It was a pine box the size of a shipping trunk, stuffed with heirloom photographs. She can't remember why she said nothing at the time. It fell off a truck onto the dusty streets of old San Antonio de Bejar one day and was left behind, abandoned, lost.

In one photo that survived it is 1960, and the whole Santos tribe is standing on the porch of my grandmother's house, in early evening shadows. It must have been Easter because my many cousins and I are in church clothes, standing in the yard around the trunk of a great sycamore tree. My aunts and uncles are there, partly old Mexican, partly new American, looking handsome, hopeful, proud of the brood standing in front of them. In the very middle of the scene, *las Ancianas*, Grandmother Santos, whom we called "Uela," short for *abuela*, and Madrina, her sister, are standing regally in a perfect moment, radiating the indelible light of Mexico. On the porch, Mother and an aunt have my newborn twin brothers, George and Charles, wrapped in blankets in their arms. My father looks serious, with a distant gaze, in a dark suit and silky tie. To one side, standing apart from us, is one of my eldest cousins, René, who would be killed in Vietnam just seven years later.

These are the memento mori[6] of the Santos. There are a few photographs, rosary chains of half-remembered stories, carried out of another time by the old Mexicans I grew up with. In dreams, the ancestors who have passed on visit with me, in this world, and in a world that lies perhaps within, amidst, and still beyond this world—a mystical limbo dimension that the descendants of the Aztecs call *el Inframundo*. In the *Inframundo*, all that has been forgotten still

---

6. **memento mori** (mə men´ tō mōr´ ē) *n.* reminders of death.

lives. Nothing is lost. All remembrance is redeemed from oblivion.

These ancestors, living and dead, have asked me the questions they were once asked: Where did our forebears come from and what have we amounted to in this world? Where have we come to in the span of all time, and where are we headed, like an arrow shot long ago into infinite empty space? What messages and markings of the ancient past do we carry in these handed-down bodies we live in today?

With these questions swirling inside me, I have rediscovered some stories of the family past in the landscapes of Texas and Mexico, in the timeless language of stone, river, wind, and trees. Tío Abrín, twin brother to my great-grandfather Jacobo, was a master of making charcoal. He lived in the hill country, where the cedars needed to make charcoal were planted a century ago to supply the industry. Today, long after he worked there, walking in that central Texas landscape crowded with deep green cedar, I feel old Abrán's presence, like the whisper of a tale still waiting to be told, wondering whether my intuition and the family's history are implicitly intertwined. Even if everything else had been lost— photographs, stories, rumors, and suspicions—if nothing at all from the past remained for us, the land remains, as the original book of the family.

It was always meant to be handed down. . . .

Once they arrived in Texas during the revolution, maybe the Santos and Garcia families simply wanted to forget their past in Mexico—the dusty streets, broken-down houses, and hunger. They wanted to burn away the memory of when the families came north across the Rio Grande. Northern Mexico became one of the most violent and chaotic battlefields of *la Revolución* of 1910, a revolution that was to last eleven years. But for the first years, the revolution was only distant thunder, more of a concern to Mexicans well to the south of Coahuila in states such as Guerrero, Puebla, and Mexico City. The family's flight from Coahuila was in 1914, the year Pancho Villa, along with a myriad of other revolutionary bands, rose up to occupy the bare constellation of towns across the parched high Norteño desert where they had made their homes. San Antonio provided them a convenient escape from the fighting, and—despite other intentions—a shelter for memory, instead of its negation.

For my cousins, as for my brothers and me, the homes of *las Viejitas*[7] were sanctuaries where Coahuila was still alive, and places where the inhibitions and proprieties of the Gringo world of San Antonio, Texas, outside did not apply. Those were days when the taco and the tamal[8] were stigmatized in public, and Spanish was seldom heard on downtown streets. The old tíos[9] had to speak

Statements and Observations Earlier, the author says that virtually all of the objects of his family's past were lost. Now he says, "Nothing is lost." How can both ideas be true, and what does this contradiction reveal about the theme of identity?

Setting What does Santos mean by "the timeless language of stone, river, wind, and trees"? How does this description of setting relate to the theme of identity?

Cultural Context How did the events described affect the Santos family? Why do you think this historical reference is important for the author to include?

---

7. **las Viejitas** (läs bē̃´ ā hē´ täs) *n.* Spanish for "little old ladies." Santos is using this as a term of endearment for his elderly women relatives.
8. **tamal** (tä´ mäl) *n.* tamale, a steamed corn husk filled with meat and cornmeal.
9. **tíos** (tī´ ōs) *n.* Spanish for "uncles."

Practice continued

English, often haltingly, to get along in the working world. Most of *las Viejitas*, staying in their homes, spoke only Spanish, or at least pretended not to speak English. When Uela spoke Spanish, her sentences moved in one steady arc, like a bow across a violin, and her words were delicately pronounced, so that you could hear every tinkle of an old chandelier, every gust of a Coahuila wind falling to a hush, and the grain of a rustling squash blossom.

The migrations continued through the century. In the 1960s, my parents moved us from one of the old neighborhoods of the city to a new suburb at the city's northwestern edge, in order to get us into the better public schools in San Antonio. We were the first Mexicans in the neighborhood, in a two-floor house with a two-car garage, a built-in dishwasher, central air-conditioning, and intercom consoles in every room. We spoke English to each other, and Spanish to the old ones in the family. When the mariachis played in our backyard, the rapid plucking of the bajo sexto[10] and the shimmering trumpet lines echoed off the neighbors' houses and drew them out to listen. Out there in that virgin neighborhood, it always felt as if we were closer to the iridescent Texas sky, stripped of the protective canopy of sycamore, wisteria, china berry, and live oak that arched over so many of the streets of our old, secret Mexican city, San Antonio de Bejar.

That old San Antonio was part of the hoary earth of the ancestors. Out there in the suburb at the edge of the city, following the early Gemini and Apollo space missions, I read books about space and prepared for the day in the future, which would undoubtedly come, when I would leave this planet in a rocket of my own.

Today, in New York City, I live in a world *las Viejitas* never visited, very far from the land they knew well. I have been to places they never imagined, like England, Europe, Turkey, Peru, and the Sudan. Yet, wherever I go, there is a ribbon of primordial Mexican night, the color of obsidian,[11] snaking in a dream through the skies high over my head. Sometimes it is easily visible to me, like a burning galaxy, sometimes it is not. Sometimes it drizzles a fine rain of voices, images, and stories. And *las Viejitas* are here now, too, as they have always been, invisible yet abiding. They are keeping a vigil over the stories they told to me as if they are a *compromiso*, a promise that has been handed on. I have always felt connected, oriented, and imparted to by them, but unsure how I fit into a story that was never meant to be told.

Setting How does the author use the setting to emphasize the idea that integrating into American society can involve the loss of family culture and traditions?

Point of View Compare Santos's relation to his family's past with a storyteller's relation to the oral tradition. What is Santos's point of view toward his family history?

Theme Draw a conclusion about the theme of the selection, and explain how Santos develops it. Support your answer by citing details about his use of literary elements, including setting, plot, and character.

---

10. **bajo sexto** (bä´ hō seks´ tō) *n.* Spanish for "six-string bass."
11. **obsidian** (əb sid´ ē ən) *n.* dark or black volcanic glass.

from **Places Left Unfinished at the Time of Creation**

1. Key Ideas and Details Summarize: Write an **objective summary** of Santos's account of his family. Remember that an objective summary should not include your personal reaction to the selection and should include only the most important ideas and details.

2. Key Ideas and Details (a) According to Santos, why does the Santos family move to San Antonio? **(b) Analyze Cause and Effect:** Why might the circumstances of their move have affected their desire to remember the past?

3. Key Ideas and Details (a) Interpret: What does Santos mean when he says his family is "traveling light through time"? **(b) Generalize:** Do you think "traveling light" is common or unusual among families today? Explain.

4. Key Ideas and Details (a) Compare and Contrast: In what specific ways is Santos's life different from the lives of his Mexican ancestors? **(b) Analyze:** How does Santos maintain a connection to his family's past?

5. Craft and Structure (a) Analyze: How does Santos make the description of his Grandmother's star vivid and real for readers? **(b) Draw Conclusions:** What associations does the star have for Santos?

6. Craft and Structure Evaluate: What role does the oral tradition play in helping Santos understand his family's past?

7. Integration of Knowledge and Ideas (a) Using a chart like the one shown, identify passages containing cultural details that help the Santos family maintain its identity over time.

Passage	Cultural Detail	Why It Is Important

(b) Collaborate: Combine your findings with those of a classmate. Eliminate duplications and rewrite the list in order of importance. **(c) Interpret:** Discuss the values each item represents to the Santos family.

ⓒ Leveled Texts

Build your skills and improve your comprehension of myths with texts of increasing complexity.

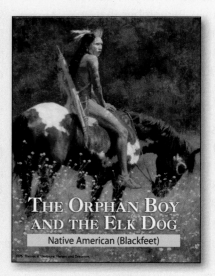

Read **"Prometheus and the First People"** to discover what ancient Greeks believed and valued.

Read **"The Orphan Boy and the Elk Dog"** to find out how the Blackfeet acquired horses.

ⓒ Common Core State Standards

Meet these standards with either **"Prometheus and the First People"** (p. 1066) or **"The Orphan Boy and the Elk Dog"** (p. 1076).

Reading Literature
6. Analyze a particular point of view or cultural experience reflected in a work of literature from outside the United States, drawing on a wide reading of world literature. *(Reading Skill: Analyze Cultural Context)*
7. Analyze the representation of a subject or a key scene in two different artistic mediums, including what is emphasized or absent in each treatment. *(Analyze Representations)*

Spiral Review: RL.9-10.2

Writing
3.a. Engage and orient the reader by setting out a problem, situation, or observation, establishing one or multiple point(s) of view, and introducing a narrator and/

or characters; create a smooth progression of experiences or events. **3.b.** Use narrative techniques, such as dialogue, pacing, description, reflection, and multiple plot lines, to develop experiences, events, and/or characters. *(Writing: Myth)*

Speaking and Listening
6. Adapt speech to a variety of contexts and tasks, demonstrating command of formal English when indicated or appropriate. *(Speaking and Listening: Retelling)*

Language
1.b. Use various types of phrases and clauses to convey specific meanings and add variety and interest to writing or presentations. *(Conventions: Simple and Compound Sentences)*

Literary Analysis: Myths

Myths are stories that are part of the oral tradition: Before being written down, they were told and retold from one generation to the next. Myths reflect the cultures of the people who originated and shared them.

- Some myths explain a natural phenomenon or a specific custom by describing its **origins,** or how it came to be. These myths reveal the beliefs of ancient cultures.
- Myths include characters with exceptional characteristics such as strength, bravery, or wisdom. These traits emphasize qualities that the culture admired or feared.
- Some myths tell of a **quest,** or search, for knowledge or a valued object. These myths reveal what was important to the culture.
- Other myths tell of a **transgression,** or the violation of a rule. By example, these myths teach the values of the culture.

Reading Skill: Analyze Cultural Context

The cultural context of any literary work refers to the set of values, beliefs, customs, traditions, and shared experiences that define a society. To understand a myth, **analyze cultural context,** or determine ways in which the myth reflects the perspectives of those who told it. Before you read, **generate questions** about the cultural context. Ask yourself one question about each element shown in the chart.

Using the Strategy: Cultural Context Chart

Use a **cultural context chart** to record the details in the myth that help you answer your questions.

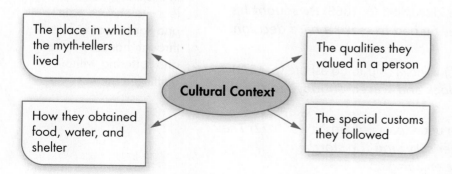

The place in which the myth-tellers lived

The qualities they valued in a person

Cultural Context

How they obtained food, water, and shelter

The special customs they followed

Can anyone be a *hero?*

Writing About the Big Question

In "Prometheus and the First People," a character helps others, even though his actions endanger his own life. Use these sentence starters to develop your ideas about the Big Question:

One should always act with **honor** and **responsibility** because _____.

Hope and **integrity** can help you **persevere** in difficult situations because _____.

While You Read Look for examples of characters, whether gods or human beings, whose actions help others. Decide which characters act most heroically.

Vocabulary

Read each word and its definition. Decide whether you know the word well, know it a little bit, or do not know it at all. After you read, see how your knowledge of each word has increased.

- **toil** (toil) *n.* hard, tiring work (p. 1067) *After much sweat and toil, I finally finished building the wall.* toil *v.* toiler *n.*

- **heedless** (hēd´ lis) *adj.* careless; thoughtless (p. 1067) *His heedless remark was hurtful.* heed *v.* heedlessly *adv.* heedlessness *n.*

- **inhabit** (in hab´ it) *v.* live in (p. 1067) *Many birds inhabit our yard because it has lots of trees.* inhabitable *adj.* inhabitation *n.* habitat *n.*

- **counsel** (koun´ səl) *n.* advice; discussion (p. 1069) *He sought his brother's counsel whenever he had to make a hard decision.* counsel *v.* counselor *n.*

- **disembarked** (dis´ im bärkt´) *v.* left a ship to go ashore (p. 1071) *They disembarked at the dock and waved goodbye to the ship's crew.* disembarkation *n.* embark *v.*

- **endure** (en door´) *v.* hold up under pain or hardship (p. 1072) *They could endure anything after surviving the storm.* endurable *adj.* endurably *adv.* enduring *adj.*

Word Study

The **Latin root -dur-** means "hard" or "to last."

In this story, humans learn to **endure** pain and sorrow, or to last through hardship and suffering without quitting.

Meet
The Ancient Greeks and
Olivia E. Coolidge (1908–2006)

Author of the retelling of
PROMETHEUS AND THE FIRST PEOPLE

Thousands of years ago in Greece, the Mycenaeans (mī´ sə nē´ ənz) told stories of a great sea god. Their civilization collapsed around 1200 B.C., but settlers from the north, the Dorians, blended the old myths with their own stories. Classical Greek mythology was born.

The ancient Greeks represented the Olympic gods as having human qualities. Just as the typical Greek household was dominated by the father, so Zeus dominates the Olympic gods.

Retelling the Tale Greek myths were a favorite of **Olivia E. Coolidge,** who retells the myth of Prometheus. Born in London, England, Coolidge studied Latin, Greek, and philosophy.

DID YOU KNOW?
Many traditions of Western civilization, including democracy, science, and philosophy, began with the ancient Greeks.

BACKGROUND FOR THE MYTH

The Greek Gods

Many of the characters in "Prometheus and the First People" are Olympians, the family of gods and goddesses ruled by Zeus and his wife Hera. Each god and goddess governs an aspect of nature or human life. For example, Ares (er´ ēz´) is the god of war.

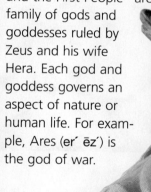

PROMETHEUS AND THE FIRST PEOPLE

OLIVIA E. COOLIDGE

Humanity's Beginnings

The Greeks have several stories about how man came to be. One declares that he was created in the age of Kronos,[1] or Saturn, who ruled before Zeus [zoos]. At that time, the legend says, there was no sorrow, toil, sickness, or age. Men lived their lives in plenty and died as though they went to sleep. They tilled[2] no ground, built no cities, killed no living thing, and among them war was unknown. The earth brought forth strawberries, cherries, and ears of wheat for them. Even on the bramble bushes grew berries good to eat. Milk and sweet nectar flowed in rivers for men to drink, and honey dripped from hollow trees. Men lived in caves and thickets, needing little shelter, for the season was always spring.

Another legend declares that Zeus conceived of animals first and he entrusted their creation to Prometheus [prō mē′ thē əs] and Epimetheus [ep ə mē′ thē əs], his brother. First, Epimetheus undertook to order all things, but he was a heedless person and soon got into trouble. Finally he was forced to appeal to Prometheus.

"What have you done?" asked Prometheus.

"Down on the earth," answered his brother, "there is a green, grassy clearing, ringed by tall oak trees and shaded by steep slopes from all but the midday sun. There I sat and the animals came to me, while I gave to each the gifts which should be his from this time forward. Air I gave to the birds, seas to the fishes, land to four-footed creatures and the creeping insects, and to some, like the moles, I gave burrows beneath the earth."

"That was well done," answered Prometheus. "What else did you do?"

"Strength," said Epimetheus, "I gave to lions and tigers, and the fierce animals of the woods. Size I gave to others like the great whales of the sea. The deer I made swift and timid, and the insects I made tiny that they might escape from sight. I gave warm fur to the great bears and the little squirrels, keen eyes and sharp talons[3] to the birds of prey, tusks to the elephant, hide to the wild boar, sweet songs and bright feathers to the birds. To each I gave some special excellence, that whether large or small, kind or terrible, each might live in his own place, find food, escape enemies, and enjoy the wide world which is his to inhabit."

"All this is very good," said his brother, Prometheus. "You have done well. Wherein lies your trouble?"

---

1. **Kronos** (krō′ nəs) son of the sky and the earth; father of Zeus.
2. **tilled** v. cultivated; plowed or hoed.
3. **talons** (tal′ ənz) n. claws (of birds of prey).

◀ **Analyze Representations**
Compare and contrast this painting of Prometheus with his portrayal in the myth. **[Compare and Contrast]**

Vocabulary
toil (toil) n. hard, tiring work
heedless (hēd′ lis) adj. careless; thoughtless
inhabit (in hab′ it) v. live in

Literary Analysis
Myths Which details show you that this myth will explain the origins of something?

Reading Skill
Analyze Cultural Context What question does this paragraph suggest to you about the region where the Greeks lived?

Reading Check

What task does Zeus give to Prometheus and his brother?

Culture Connection

The Twelve Olympian Gods

The ancient Greeks worshiped a family of gods said to have their home on Mount Olympus:

Zeus (zo͞os) ruler of the gods

Hera (hir´ə) queen of the gods; goddess of marriage

Aphrodite (af´rə dīt´ē) goddess of love and beauty

Apollo (ə päl´ō) god of music, poetry, and light

Ares (er´ ēz´) god of war

Artemis (är´ tə mis) goddess of the moon, wild animals, and hunting

Athene (ə thē´ nē) goddess of wisdom

Demeter (di mēt´ ər) goddess of grain and agriculture

Hephaestus (hē fes´ təs) god of fire; blacksmith of the gods

Hermes (hur´ mēz´) messenger of the gods; god of business, science, and speech

Hestia (hes´ tē ə) goddess of the hearth

Poseidon (pō sī´ dən) god of earthquakes, the sea, and horses

Connect to the Literature

According to this myth, what is the relationship between the gods and humans like?

"Because I did not think it out beforehand," said the heedless brother sadly, "I did not count how many animals there were to be before I started giving. Now when I have given all, there comes one last animal for whom I have neither skill nor shape, nor any place to dwell in. Everything has been given already."

"What is this animal," said Prometheus, "who has been forgotten?"

"His name," said Epimetheus, "is Man."

Thus it was that the future of man was left to Prometheus, who was forced to make man different from all other creatures. Therefore he gave him the shape of the gods themselves and the privilege of walking upright as they do. He gave him no special home, but made him ruler over the whole earth, and over the sea and air. Finally, he gave him no special strength or swiftness, but stole a spark from heaven and lighted a heavenly fire within his mind which should teach him to understand, to count, to speak, to remember. Man learned from it how to build cities, tame animals, raise crops, build boats, and do all the things that animals cannot. Prometheus also kindled fire on earth that man might smelt[4] metals and make tools. In fact, from this heavenly fire of Prometheus all man's greatness comes.

Before this time fire was a divine thing and belonged only to the gods. It was one of their greatest treasures, and Zeus would never have given Prometheus permission to use it in the creation of man. Therefore when Prometheus stole it, Zeus was furious indeed. He chained Prometheus to a great, lofty rock, where the sun scorched him by day and the cruel frost tortured him by night. Not content with that, he sent an eagle to tear him, so that, though he could not die, he lived in agony. For many centuries Prometheus hung in torment, but he was wiser than Zeus, and by reason of a secret he had, he forced Zeus in later ages to set him free. By then, also, Zeus had learned that there is more in ruling than power and cruelty. Thus, the two at last were friends. ●

---

4. smelt *v.* purify metal by melting it.

The Coming of Evil

After the punishment of Prometheus, Zeus planned to take his revenge on man. He could not recall the gift of fire, since it had been given by one of the immortals,[5] but he was not content that man should possess this treasure in peace and become perhaps as great as were the gods themselves. He therefore took counsel with the other gods, and together they made for man a woman. All the gods gave gifts to this new creation. Aphrodite [af´ rə dīt´ ē] gave her fresh beauty like the spring itself. The goddess Athene [ə thē´ nē] dressed her and put on her a garland of flowers and green leaves. She had also a golden diadem[6] beautifully decorated with figures of animals. In her heart Hermes [hʉr´ mēz´] put cunning, deceit, and curiosity. She was named Pandora [pan dôr´ ə], which means All-Gifted, since each of the gods had given her something. The last gift was a chest in which there was supposed to be great treasure, but which Pandora was instructed never to open. Then Hermes, the Messenger, took the girl and brought her to Epimetheus.

Epimetheus had been warned by his brother to receive no gifts from Zeus, but he was a heedless person, as ever, and Pandora was very lovely. He accepted her, therefore, and for a while they lived together in happiness, for Pandora besides her beauty had been given both wit and charm. Eventually, however, her curiosity got the better of her, and she determined to see for herself what treasure it was that the gods had given her. One day when she was alone, she went over to the corner where her chest lay and cautiously lifted the lid for a peep. The lid flew up out of her hands and knocked her aside, while before her frightened eyes dreadful, shadowy shapes flew out of the box in an endless stream. There were hunger, disease, war, greed, anger, jealousy, toil, and all the griefs and hardships to which man from that day has been subject. Each was terrible in appearance, and as it passed, Pandora saw something of the misery that her thoughtless action had brought on her descendants. At last the stream slackened,[7] and Pandora, who had been paralyzed with fear and horror, found strength to shut her box. The only thing left in it now, however, was the one good gift the gods had put in among so many evil ones. This was hope, and since that time the hope that is in man's heart is the only thing which has made him able to bear the sorrows that Pandora brought upon him.

---

5. **immortals** (i môrt´ 'lz) *n.* those who do not die.
6. **diadem** (dī´ ə dem´) *n.* crown.
7. **slackened** (slak´ ənd) *v.* diminished; became less active.

Vocabulary
counsel (koun´ səl)
n. advice; discussion

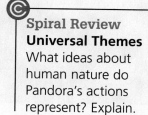

Spiral Review
Universal Themes
What ideas about human nature do Pandora's actions represent? Explain.

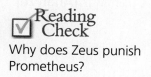
Reading Check
Why does Zeus punish Prometheus?

▲ **Analyze Representations**
Which details in this painting echo details in the text of the myth? What details in the myth are not represented in the painting? **[Analyze]**

The Great Flood

When evil first came among mankind, people became very wicked. War, robbery, treachery, and murder prevailed throughout the world. Even the worship of the gods, the laws of truth and honor, reverence[8] for parents and brotherly love were neglected.

Finally, Zeus determined to destroy the race of men altogether, and the other gods agreed. All the winds were therefore shut up in a cave except the South Wind, the wet one. He raced over the earth with water streaming from his beard and long, white hair. Clouds gathered around his head, and dew dripped from his wings and the ends of his garments. With him went Iris, the rainbow goddess,

---

8. **reverence** (rev´ ə rəns) *n.* feeling or display of great respect.

while below Poseidon [pō sī´ dən] smote the earth with his trident until it shook and gaped open, so that the waters of the sea rushed up over the land.

Fields and farmhouses were buried. Fish swam in the tops of the trees. Sea beasts were quietly feeding where flocks and herds had grazed before. On the surface of the water, boars, stags, lions, and tigers struggled desperately to keep afloat. Wolves swam in the midst of flocks of sheep, but the sheep were not frightened by them, and the wolves never thought of their natural prey. Each fought for his own life and forgot the others. Over them wheeled countless birds, winging far and wide in the hope of finding something to rest upon. Eventually they too fell into the water and were drowned.

All over the water were men in small boats or makeshift rafts. Some even had oars which they tried to use, but the waters were fierce and stormy, and there was nowhere to go. In time all were drowned, until at last there was no one left but an old man and his wife, Deucalion [doo kāl´ ē ən] and Pyrrha [pir´ ə]. These two people had lived in truth and justice, unlike the rest of mankind. They had been warned of the coming of the flood and had built a boat and stocked it. For nine days and nights they floated until Zeus took pity on them and they came to the top of Mount Parnassus, the sacred home of the Muses.[9] There they found land and **disembarked** to wait while the gods recalled the water they had unloosed.

When the waters fell, Deucalion and Pyrrha looked over the land, despairing. Mud and sea slime covered the earth; all living things had been swept away. Slowly and sadly they made their way down the mountain until they came to a temple where there had been an oracle.[10] Black seaweed dripped from the pillars now, and the mud was over all. Nevertheless the two knelt down and kissed the temple steps while Deucalion prayed to the goddess to tell them what they should do. All men were dead but themselves, and they were old. It was impossible that they should have children to people the earth again. Out of the temple a great voice was heard speaking strange words.

"Depart," it said, "with veiled heads and loosened robes, and throw behind you as you go the bones of your mother."

Pyrrha was in despair when she heard this saying. "The bones of our mother!" she cried. "How can we tell now where they lie? Even

Vocabulary
disembarked (dis´ im bärkt´) *v.* left a ship to go ashore

Reading Check

Why does Zeus punish man?

---

9. **Muses** (myoo´ əz) *n.* nine goddesses who rule over literature and the arts and sciences.
10. **oracle** (ôr´ ə kəl) *n.* person who, when consulted on a matter, is said to reveal the will of the gods.

if we knew, we could never do such a dreadful thing as to disturb their resting place and scatter them over the earth like an armful of stones."

"Stones!" said Deucalion quickly. "That must be what the goddess means. After all Earth is our mother, and the other thing is too horrible for us to suppose that a goddess would ever command it."

Accordingly both picked up armfuls of stones, and as they went away from the temple with faces veiled, they cast the stones behind them. From each of those Deucalion cast sprang up a man, and from Pyrrha's stones sprang women. Thus the earth was repeopled, and in the course of time it brought forth again animals from itself, and all was as before. Only from that time men have been less sensitive and have found it easier to endure toil, and sorrow, and pain, since now they are descended from stones.

Critical Thinking

Cite textual evidence to support your responses.

1. **Key Ideas and Details** **(a)** What problem does Epimetheus face when it is humanity's turn to receive a gift? **(b) Contrast:** Contrast the gifts Prometheus gives humanity with the gifts Epimetheus gives the animals. **(c) Evaluate:** Which gift is most valuable? Why?

2. **Key Ideas and Details** **(a)** Which of Prometheus' actions angers Zeus? **(b) Infer:** Why does it anger him?

3. **Key Ideas and Details** **Analyze Cause and Effect:** What changes does Pandora bring to the world by opening the box?

4. **Integration of Knowledge and Ideas** Which characters in these three myths make heroic efforts during trying circumstances? Explain their acts of heroism. *[Connect to the Big Question: Can anyone be a hero?]*

Literary Analysis: Myths

© 1. **Craft and Structure** Identify which characteristics of **myths** are found in the story. Support your choices with text evidence.

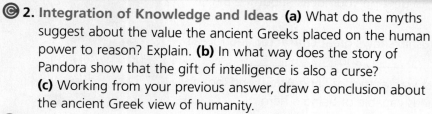

What the Story Explains	Exceptional or Fantastic Characters	Quest	Transgression

PROMETHEUS AND THE FIRST PEOPLE
OLIVIA E. COOLIDGE

© 2. **Integration of Knowledge and Ideas** **(a)** What do the myths suggest about the value the ancient Greeks placed on the human power to reason? Explain. **(b)** In what way does the story of Pandora show that the gift of intelligence is also a curse? **(c)** Working from your previous answer, draw a conclusion about the ancient Greek view of humanity.

© 3. **Integration of Knowledge and Ideas** **(a)** Why does Zeus save Deucalion and Pyrrha? **(b)** Draw a conclusion about ancient Greek values from their story.

Reading Skill: Analyze Cultural Context

4. **(a)** Give two examples of questions you might ask to **analyze the cultural context** of the myth. **(b)** Explain what answers the myth suggests, and support your answer with details from the text.

Vocabulary

© **Acquisition and Use** Copy each of the following word pairs. Write *S* for **synonyms** or *A* for **antonyms.** Explain each of your choices.

1. toil, work
2. heedless, cautious
3. counsel, recommendation
4. disembarked, boarded
5. inhabit, abandon
6. endure, tolerate

Word Study Use the context of the sentences and what you know about the **Latin root -dur-** to explain your answer to each question.

1. Will a *durable* pair of jeans easily tear?
2. Does training for a marathon help to build up one's *endurance*?

Word Study

The **Latin root -dur-** means "hard" or "to last."

Apply It Explain how the root -dur- contributes to the meanings of these words. Consult a dictionary if necessary.
duration
duress
obdurate

Can anyone be a *hero?*

Writing About the Big Question

In "The Orphan Boy and the Elk Dog," a young man's bravery plays an important role in his quest to help his tribe and discover his own self worth. Use this sentence starter to develop your ideas about the Big Question.

To **persevere** in times of hardship shows great **character** and reveals **attributes** such as _____ , and _____ .

While You Read Analyze the characteristics of Long Arrow and look for evidence to help you decide if he is capable of being a hero.

THE ORPHAN BOY
AND THE ELK DOG
Native American (Blackfeet)

Vocabulary

Read each word and its definition. Decide whether you know the word well, know it a little bit, or do not know it at all. After you read, see how your knowledge of each word has increased.

- **refuse** (ref´ yo͞os) *n.* waste; trash (p. 1077) *We filled three trash cans in the park with <u>refuse</u> from the picnic.*

- **surpassed** (sər past´) *v.* went beyond; excelled (p. 1079) *Her score was so high, it <u>surpassed</u> even her own expectations.* *surpassable adj.*

- **emanating** (em´ ə nāt´ iŋ) *v.* coming forth, as from a source (p. 1082) *We were curious about the light <u>emanating</u> from the basement window of the abandoned house. emanation n.*

- **relish** (rel´ ish) *n.* enjoyment (p. 1082) *Her vivid gestures show that she talks with <u>relish</u>. relish v.*

- **stifle** (stī´ fəl) *v.* smother; hold back (p. 1084) *She grew bored and could not <u>stifle</u> a yawn. stifling adj. stiflingly adv.*

- **humble** (hum´ bəl) *adj.* showing an awareness of one's short-comings; modest (p. 1085) *She is <u>humble</u> and will not boast about her award. humbleness n. humbly adv.*

Word Study

The Latin root **-fus-** means "to pour."

In this story, a character is forced to survive on **refuse** material, or trash, that has been rejected and poured into the garbage.

Creators of
THE ORPHAN BOY AND THE ELK DOG

The Blackfeet are one of the many Native American nations that have lived on the Great Plains of North America. At one time, most Plains Indians were farmers who lived in one place, grew their own food, and sometimes hunted buffalo on foot. Then, in the 1600s, many tribes captured and tamed wild horses.

New Way of Life In time, the Blackfeet became skillful riders, and horses transformed their way of life. A mounted hunter could search for game more efficiently. Hunting replaced farming, and the tribes followed the buffalo herds.

Today, the Blackfeet live on reservations in Montana and in Canada. Myths like "The Orphan Boy and the Elk Dog" reflect the importance of the horse in early Blackfeet culture.

BACKGROUND FOR THE MYTH

Horses in America

"The Orphan Boy and the Elk Dog" explains the origin of an important part of the North American Blackfeet culture—horses. Horses did not always exist in North America. Spanish explorer Hernando Cortés brought the first horses to Mexico in 1519, and they quickly spread northward. By the 1600s, many Native American tribes had captured and tamed wild horses.

DID YOU KNOW?

The name "Blackfeet" is a reference to the dark moccasins worn by early Blackfeet people.

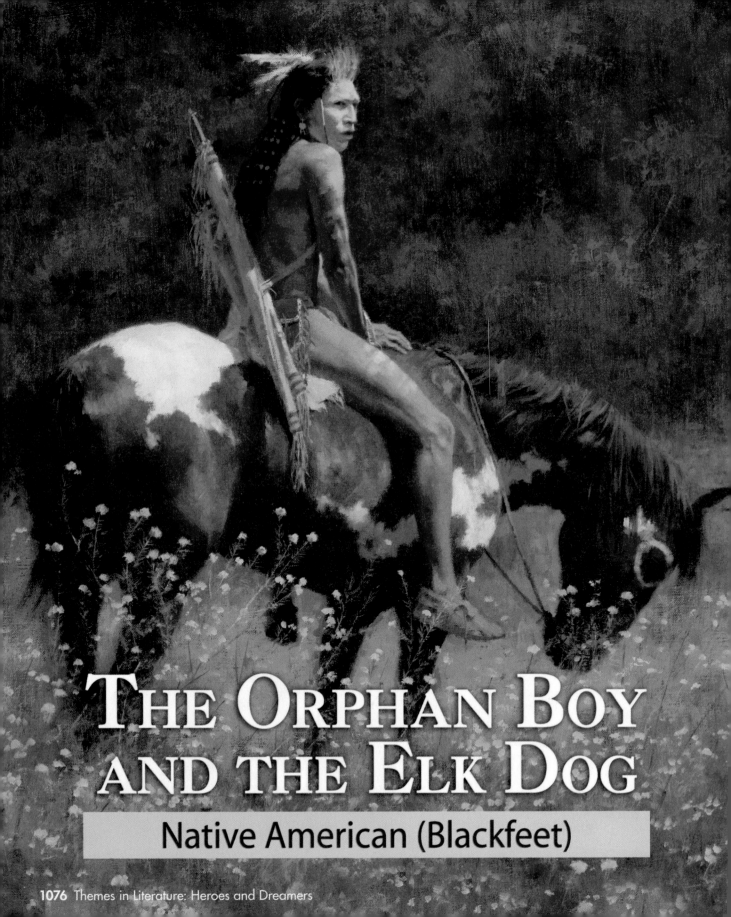

THE ORPHAN BOY
AND THE ELK DOG

Native American (Blackfeet)

In the days when people had only dogs to carry their bundles, two orphan children, a boy and his sister, were having a hard time. The boy was deaf, and because he could not understand what people said, they thought him foolish and dull-witted. Even his relatives wanted nothing to do with him. The name he had been given at birth, while his parents still lived, was Long Arrow. Now he was like a beaten, mangy dog, the kind who hungrily roams outside a camp, circling it from afar, smelling the good meat boiling in the kettles but never coming close for fear of being kicked. Only his sister, who was bright and beautiful, loved him.

Then the sister was adopted by a family from another camp, people who were attracted by her good looks and pleasing ways. Though they wanted her for a daughter, they certainly did not want the awkward, stupid boy. And so they took away the only person who cared about him, and the orphan boy was left to fend for himself. He lived on scraps thrown to the dogs and things he found on the refuse heaps. He dressed in remnants of skins and frayed robes discarded by the poorest people. At night he bedded down in a grass-lined dugout, like an animal in its den.

Eventually the game was hunted out near the camp that the boy regarded as his, and the people decided to move. The lodges were taken down, belongings were packed into rawhide bags and put on dog travois,[1] and the village departed. "Stay here," they told the boy. "We don't want your kind coming with us."

For two or three days the boy fed on scraps the people had left behind, but he knew he would starve if he stayed. He had to join his people, whether they liked it or not. He followed their tracks, frantic that he would lose them, and crying at the same time. Soon the sweat was running down his skinny body. As he was stumbling, running, panting, something suddenly snapped in his left ear with a sound like a small crack, and a wormlike substance came out of that ear. All at once on his left side he could hear birdsongs for the first time. He took this wormlike thing in his left hand and hurried on. Then there was a snap in his right ear and a wormlike thing came out of it, and on his right side he could hear the rushing waters of a stream. His hearing was restored! And it was razor-sharp—he could make out the rustling of a tiny mouse in dry leaves a good distance away. The orphan boy laughed and was happy for the first time in his life. With renewed courage he followed the trail his people had made.

In the meantime the village had settled into its new place. Men were already out hunting. Thus the boy came upon Good Running,

---

1. **travois** (trə voi´) sled with two poles and a net or platform in between, pulled along the ground by a person or an animal.

The Orphan Boy and the Elk Dog **1077**

◄ **Critical Viewing**
Use the selection title and this painting to predict what this story is about. **[Predict]**

Reading Skill
Analyze Cultural Context What questions about Blackfeet culture does the first paragraph suggest?

Vocabulary
refuse (ref´ yo͞os) *n.* waste; trash

Reading Skill
Analyze Cultural Context In this paragraph, what do you learn about Blackfeet life?

Reading Check
What difficulties does Long Arrow face?

a kindly old chief, butchering a fat buffalo cow he had just killed. When the chief saw the boy, he said to himself, "Here comes that poor good-for-nothing boy. It was wrong to abandon him." To the boy Good Running said "Rest here, grandson, you're sweaty and covered with dust. Here, have some tripe."[2]

The boy wolfed down the meat. He was not used to hearing and talking yet, but his eyes were alert and Good Running also noticed a change in his manner. "This boy," the chief said to himself, "is neither stupid nor crazy." He gave the orphan a piece of the hump meat, then a piece of liver, then a piece of raw kidney, and at last the very best kind of meat—a slice of tongue. The more the old man looked at the boy, the more he liked him. On the spur of the moment he said, "Grandson, I'm going to adopt you; there's a place for you in my tipi. And I'm going to make you into a good hunter and warrior." The boy wept, this time for joy. Good Running said, "They called you a stupid, crazy boy, but now that I think of it, the name you were given at birth is Long Arrow. I'll see that people call you by your right name. Now come along."

The chief's wife was not pleased. "Why do you put this burden on me," she said, "bringing into our lodge this good-for-nothing, this slow-witted crazy boy? Maybe you're a little slow-witted and crazy yourself!"

---

2. tripe (trīp) *n.* walls of the stomach of a buffalo or other grazing animal, used as food.

"Woman, keep talking like that and I'll beat you! This boy isn't slow or crazy; he's a good boy, and I have taken him for my grandson. Look—he's barefooted. Hurry up, and make a pair of moccasins for him, and if you don't do it well I'll take a stick to you."

Good Running's wife grumbled but did as she was told. Her husband was a kind man, but when aroused, his anger was great.

So a new life began for Long Arrow. He had to learn to speak and to understand well, and to catch up on all the things a boy should know. He was a fast learner and soon surpassed other boys his age in knowledge and skills. At last even Good Running's wife accepted him. ●

He grew up into a fine young hunter, tall and good-looking in the quilled buckskin outfit the chief's wife made for him. He helped his grandfather in everything and became a staff for Good Running to lean on. But he was lonely, for most people in the camp could not forget that Long Arrow had once been an outcast. "Grandfather," he said one day, "I want to do something to make you proud and show people that you were wise to adopt me. What can I do?"

Good Running answered, "Someday you will be a chief and do great things."

"But what's a great thing I could do now, Grandfather?"

The chief thought for a long time. "Maybe I shouldn't tell you this," he said. "I love you and don't want to lose you. But on winter nights, men talk of powerful spirit people living at the bottom of a faraway lake. Down in that lake the spirit people keep mystery animals who do their work for them. These animals are larger than a great elk, but they carry the burdens of the spirit people like dogs. So they're called Pono-Kamita—Elk Dogs. They are said to be swift, strong, gentle, and beautiful beyond imagination. Every fourth generation, one of our young warriors has gone to find these spirit folk and bring back an Elk Dog for us. But none of our brave young men has ever returned."

"Grandfather, I'm not afraid. I'll go and find the Elk Dog."

"Grandson, first learn to be a man. Learn the right prayers and ceremonies. Be brave. Be generous and open-handed. Pity the old and the fatherless, and let the holy men of the tribe find a medicine[3] for you which will protect you on your dangerous journey. We will begin by purifying you in the sweat bath."

So Long Arrow was purified with the white steam of the sweat lodge. He was taught how to use the pipe, and how to pray to the Great Mystery Power. The tribe's holy men gave him a medicine and made for him a shield with designs on it to ward off danger.

---

3. **medicine** in Native American culture, an object, a ceremony, a song, and so on with religious or magical power.

Vocabulary
surpassed (sər past') *v.* went beyond; excelled

Literary Analysis
Myths What mythical qualities do the Elk Dogs have?

Reading
Check
Identify two ways Long Arrow's life has improved.

Literary Analysis
Myths What quest does Long Arrow undertake?

Then one morning, without telling anybody, Good Running loaded his best travois dog with all the things Long Arrow would need for traveling. The chief gave him his medicine, his shield, and his own fine bow and, just as the sun came up, went with his grandson to the edge of the camp to purify him with sweet-smelling cedar smoke. Long Arrow left unheard and unseen by anyone else. After a while some people noticed that he was gone, but no one except his grandfather knew where and for what purpose.

Following Good Running's advice, Long Arrow wandered southward. On the fourth day of his journey he came to a small pond, where a strange man was standing as if waiting for him. "Why have you come here?" the stranger asked.

"I have come to find the mysterious Elk Dog."

"Ah, there I cannot help you," said the man, who was the spirit of the pond. "But if you travel further south, four-times-four days, you might chance upon a bigger lake and there meet one of my uncles. Possibly he might talk to you; then again, he might not. That's all I can tell you."

▼ **Critical Viewing**
Judging from this picture, why would having a means of transportation be important to the people living in this type of landscape?

Long Arrow thanked the man, who went down to the bottom of the pond, where he lived.

Long Arrow wandered on, walking for long hours and taking little time for rest. Through deep canyons and over high mountains he went, wearing out his moccasins and enduring cold and heat, hunger and thirst.

Finally Long Arrow approached a big lake surrounded by steep pine-covered hills. There he came face to face with a tall man, fierce and scowling and twice the height of most humans. This stranger carried a long lance with a heavy spearpoint made of shining flint. "Young one," he growled, "why did you come here?"

"I came to find the mysterious Elk Dog."

The stranger, who was the spirit of the lake, stuck his face right into Long Arrow's and shook his mighty lance. "Little one, aren't you afraid of me?" he snarled.

"No, I am not," answered Long Arrow, smiling.

The tall spirit man gave a hideous grin, which was his way of being friendly. "I like small humans who aren't afraid," he said, "but I can't help you. Perhaps our grandfather will take the trouble to listen to you. More likely he won't. Walk south for four-times-four days, and maybe you'll find him. But probably you won't." With that the tall spirit turned his back on Long Arrow and went to the bottom of the lake, where he lived.

Long Arrow walked on for another four-times-four days, sleeping and resting little. By now he staggered and stumbled in his weakness, and his dog was not much better off. At last he came to the biggest lake he had ever seen, surrounded by towering snow-capped peaks and waterfalls of ice. This time there was nobody to receive him. As a matter of fact, there seemed to be no living thing around. "This must be the Great Mystery Lake," thought Long Arrow. Exhausted, he fell down upon the shortgrass meadow by the lake, fell down among the wild flowers, and went to sleep with his tired dog curled up at his feet. •

When Long Arrow awoke, the sun was already high. He opened his eyes and saw a beautiful child standing before him, a boy in a dazzling white buckskin robe decorated with porcupine quills of many colors. The boy said, "We have been expecting you for a long time. My grandfather invites you to his lodge. Follow me."

Telling his dog to wait, Long Arrow took his medicine shield and his grandfather's bow and went with the wonderful child.

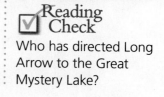
The Orphan Boy and the Elk Dog **1081**

They came to the edge of the lake. The spirit boy pointed to the water and said, "My grandfather's lodge is down there. Come." The child turned himself into a kingfisher[4] and dove straight to the bottom.

Afraid, Long Arrow thought, "How can I follow him and not be drowned?" But then he said to himself, "I knew all the time that this would not be easy. In setting out to find the Elk Dog, I already threw my life away." And he boldly jumped into the water. To his surprise, he found it did not make him wet, that it parted before him, that he could breathe and see. He touched the lake's sandy bottom. It sloped down, down toward a center point.

Long Arrow descended this slope until he came to a small flat valley. In the middle of it stood a large tipi of tanned buffalo hide. The images of two strange animals were drawn on it in sacred vermilion[5] paint. A kingfisher perched high on the top of the tipi flew down and turned again into the beautiful boy, who said, "Welcome. Enter my grandfather's lodge."

Long Arrow followed the spirit boy inside. In the back at the seat of honor sat a black-robed old man with flowing white hair and such power emanating from him that Long Arrow felt himself in the presence of a truly Great One. The holy man welcomed Long Arrow and offered him food. The man's wife came in bringing dishes of buffalo hump, liver, tongues, delicious chunks of deer meat, the roasted flesh of strange, tasty water birds, and meat pounded together with berries, chokecherries, and kidney fat. Famished after his long journey, Long Arrow ate with relish. Yet he still looked around to admire the furnishings of the tipi, the painted inner curtain, the many medicine shields, wonderfully wrought weapons, shirts and robes decorated with porcupine quills in rainbow colors, beautifully painted rawhide containers filled with wonderful things, and much else that dazzled him.

After Long Arrow had stilled his hunger, the old spirit chief filled the pipe and passed it to his guest. They smoked, praying silently. After a while the old man said, "Some came before you from time to time, but they were always afraid of the deep water, and so they went away with empty hands. But you, grandson, were brave enough to plunge in, and therefore you are chosen to receive a wonderful gift to carry back to your people. Now, go outside with my grandson."

The beautiful boy took Long Arrow to a meadow on which some strange animals, unlike any the young man had ever seen, were galloping and gamboling, neighing and nickering. They were truly

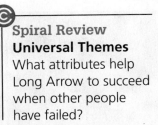
---

4. **kingfisher** n. type of water bird that dives for its food.
5. **vermilion** (vər mil´ yən) n. bright red.

wonderful to look at, with their glossy coats fine as a maiden's hair, their long manes and tails streaming in the wind. Now rearing, now nuzzling, they looked at Long Arrow with gentle eyes which belied their fiery appearance.

"At last," thought Long Arrow, "here they are before my own eyes, the Pono-Kamita, the Elk Dogs!" ●

"Watch me," said the mystery boy, "so that you learn to do what I am doing." Gracefully and without effort, the boy swung himself onto the back of a jet-black Elk Dog with a high, arched neck. Larger than any elk Long Arrow had ever come across, the animal carried the boy all over the meadow swiftly as the wind. Then the boy returned, jumped off his mount, and said, "Now you try it." A little timidly Long Arrow climbed up on the beautiful Elk Dog's back. Seemingly regarding him as feather-light, it took off like a flying arrow. The young man felt himself soaring through the air as a bird does, and experienced a happiness greater even than the joy he had felt when Good Running had adopted him as a grandson.

When they had finished riding the Elk Dogs, the spirit boy said to Long Arrow, "Young hunter from the land above the waters, I want you to have what you have come for. Listen to me. You may have noticed that my grandfather wears a black medicine robe as long as a woman's dress, and that he is always trying to hide his feet. Try to get a glimpse of them, for if you do, he can refuse you nothing. He will then tell you to ask him for a gift, and you must ask for these three things: his rainbow-colored quilled belt, his black medicine robe, and a herd of these animals which you seem to like."

"At last," thought Long Arrow, "here they are before my own eyes, the Pono-Kamita, the Elk Dogs!"

☑ **Reading Check**

What creatures does Long Arrow find in the spirit chief's lake?

▲ Critical Viewing
Based on this paint-
ing, what qualities of
horses might impress
someone who has never
seen one before?

Vocabulary
stifle (stī´ fəl) v.
smother; hold back

Long Arrow thanked him and vowed to follow his advice. For
four days the young man stayed in the spirit chief's lodge, where
he ate well and often went out riding on the Elk Dogs. But try as
he would, he could never get a look at the old man's feet. The spirit
chief always kept them carefully covered. Then on the morning of
the fourth day, the old one was walking out of the tipi when his
medicine robe caught in the entrance flap. As the robe opened,
Long Arrow caught a glimpse of a leg and one foot. He was awed to
see that it was not a human limb at all, but the glossy leg and firm
hoof of an Elk Dog! He could not stifle a cry of surprise, and the old
man looked over his shoulder and saw that his leg and hoof were
exposed. The chief seemed a little embarrassed, but shrugged and
said, "I tried to hide this, but you must have been fated to see it.
Look, both of my feet are those of an Elk Dog. You may as well ask
me for a gift. Don't be timid; tell me what you want."

Long Arrow spoke boldly: "I want three things: your belt of
rainbow colors, your black medicine robe, and your herd of Elk
Dogs."

"Well, so you're really not timid at all!" said the old man. "You ask for a lot, and I'll give it to you, except that you cannot have all my Elk Dogs; I'll give you half of them. Now I must tell you that my black medicine robe and my many-colored belt have Elk Dog magic in them. Always wear the robe when you try to catch Elk Dogs; then they can't get away from you. On quiet nights, if you listen closely to the belt, you will hear the Elk Dog dance song and Elk Dog prayers. You must learn them. And I will give you one more magic gift: this long rope woven from the hair of a white buffalo bull. With it you will never fail to catch whichever Elk Dog you want."

The spirit chief presented him with the gifts and said, "Now you must leave. At first the Elk Dogs will not follow you. Keep the medicine robe and the magic belt on at all times, and walk for four days toward the north. Never look back—always look to the north. On the fourth day the Elk Dogs will come up beside you on the left. Still don't look back. But after they have overtaken you, catch one with the rope of white buffalo hair and ride him home. Don't lose the black robe, or you will lose the Elk Dogs and never catch them again."

Long Arrow listened carefully so that he would remember. Then the old spirit chief had his wife make up a big pack of food, almost too heavy for Long Arrow to carry, and the young man took leave of his generous spirit host. The mysterious boy once again turned himself into a kingfisher and led Long Arrow to the surface of the lake, where his faithful dog greeted him joyfully. Long Arrow fed the dog, put his pack of food on the travois, and started walking north.

On the fourth day the Elk Dogs came up on his left side, as the spirit chief had foretold. Long Arrow snared the black one with the arched neck to ride, and he caught another to carry the pack of food. They galloped swiftly on, the dog barking at the big Elk Dogs' heels.

When Long Arrow arrived at last in his village, the people were afraid and hid. They did not recognize him astride his beautiful Elk Dog but took him for a monster, half man and half animal. Long Arrow kept calling, "Grandfather Good Running, it's your grandson. I've come back bringing Elk Dogs!"

Recognizing the voice, Good Running came out of hiding and wept for joy, because he had given Long Arrow up for lost. Then all the others emerged from their hiding places to admire the wonderful new animals.

Long Arrow said, "My grandfather and grandmother who adopted me, I can never repay you for your kindness. Accept these wonderful Elk Dogs as my gift. Now we no longer need to be humble footsloggers, because these animals will carry us swiftly everywhere we want to go. Now buffalo hunting will be easy. Now our tipis will be larger, our possessions will be greater, because

The Orphan Boy and the Elk Dog **1085**

an Elk Dog travois can carry a load ten times bigger than that of a dog. Take them, my grandparents. I shall keep for myself only this black male and this black female, which will grow into a fine herd."

"You have indeed done something great, grandson," said Good Running, and he spoke true. The people became the bold riders of the Plains and soon could hardly imagine how they had existed without these wonderful animals.

After some time Good Running, rich and honored by all, said to Long Arrow, "Grandson, lead us to the Great Mystery Lake so we can camp by its shores. Let's visit the spirit chief and the wondrous boy; maybe they will give us more of their power and magic gifts."

Long Arrow led the people southward and again found the Great Mystery Lake. But the waters would no longer part for him, nor would any of the kingfishers they saw turn into a boy. Nor, gazing down into the crystal-clear water, could they discover people, Elk Dogs, or a tipi. There was nothing in the lake but a few fish.

Literary Analysis
Myths What does this myth explain?

Critical Thinking

Cite textual evidence to support your responses.

1. **Key Ideas and Details** **(a)** Why do the villagers shun Long Arrow at the beginning of the story? **(b) Analyze:** What does this behavior suggest about the villagers?

2. **Key Ideas and Details** **(a)** What reason does Long Arrow give for asking Good Running for a "great" thing to do? **(b) Infer:** What does his reason show about Long Arrow's feelings for Good Running?

3. **Key Ideas and Details** **(a) Summarize:** List three obstacles Long Arrow faces on his journey. **(b) Analyze:** Explain how he overcomes each one.

4. **Integration of Knowledge and Ideas** **(a) Interpret:** What lesson does this myth teach about helping others? **(b) Discuss:** Share and discuss responses with a partner. Work together to formulate a response that presents both of your opinions. Share your ideas with the class.

5. **Integration of Knowledge and Ideas** **(a)** Identify two reasons to explain why Long Arrow seems an unlikely hero at the beginning of the story. **(b)** What heroic traits does Long Arrow display later in the story? *[Connect to the Big Question: Can anyone be a hero?]*

Literary Analysis: Myths

© **1. Craft and Structure** Identify which characteristics of **myths** are found in the story. Support your choices with text evidence.

What the Story Explains	Exceptional or Fantastic Characters	Quest	Transgression

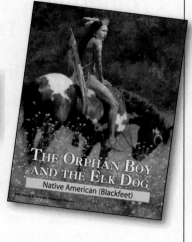

© **2. Key Ideas and Details (a)** What qualities help Long Arrow overcome the obstacles he faces on his quest? Support your answer with details from the text. **(b)** Working from your answer, draw a conclusion about the qualities the Blackfeet valued in a person.

© **3. Key Ideas and Details (a)** What advice does Good Running give Long Arrow before his journey? **(b)** Draw a conclusion about the customs and beliefs of the Blackfeet based on this advice.

Reading Skill: Analyze Cultural Context

4. (a) Give two examples of questions you might ask to **analyze the cultural context** of the myth. **(b)** Explain the answers that the myth suggests, and provide details from the text.

Vocabulary

© **Acquisition and Use** Copy each of the following word pairs. Write *S* for **synonyms** or *A* for **antonyms.** Explain each of your choices.

1. surpassed, failed

2. emanating, absorbing

3. relish, pleasure

4. stifle, conceal

5. refuse, rubbish

6. humble, arrogant

Word Study Use the context of the sentences and what you know about the **Latin root -fus-** to explain your answer to each question.

1. Is *diffuse* flooding usually concentrated in one spot?

2. Would you feel appreciated if you received *effusive* praise?

Word Study

The **Latin root -fus-** means "to pour."

Apply It Explain how the root *-fus-* contributes to the meanings of these words. Consult a dictionary if necessary.

infusion
profuse
suffuse

Integrated Language Skills

Prometheus and the First People • The Orphan Boy and the Elk Dog

Conventions: Simple and Compound Sentences

A **clause** is a group of words with a subject and a verb. An **independent clause** is a clause that can stand on its own as a sentence. Clauses form different types of sentences.

- A **simple sentence** consists of a single independent clause.

- A **compound sentence** contains two or more independent clauses linked by a semicolon or coordinating conjunction, such as *and, but, or, for, nor, so,* or *yet.*

In the following examples, subjects are underlined once and verbs are underlined twice.

Simple Sentence: The <u>myth</u> of Prometheus <u>explains</u> the early origins of fire.

Compound Sentence: <u>Myths</u> <u>explain</u> the world; <u>legends</u> <u>record</u> great deeds.

Compound Sentence: <u>You</u> can <u>compare</u> the Greek myths and the Native American myths, but <u>they</u> <u>come</u> from different cultures.

Practice A Underline the subjects and circle the verbs in each sentence. Then, tell whether the sentence is a simple or a compound sentence.

1. Epimetheus gave gifts to all the animals.

2. Prometheus stole fire from the gods; the gods were not happy.

3. Pandora was beautiful and curious.

4. A great flood covered the earth, but two people remained alive.

Ⓒ **Reading Application** In "Prometheus and the First People," find an example of a simple sentence and an example of a compound sentence.

Practice B Identify each of the following sentences as *simple* or *compound*. Rewrite each compound sentence as two or more simple sentences.

1. People treated Long Arrow cruelly.

2. Good Running was kind, and he adopted Long Arrow.

3. Elk Dogs are swift, beautiful, and mysterious.

4. Spirit people kept the Elk Dogs; the animals worked hard.

Ⓒ **Writing Application** Write two simple sentences about the painting on page 1076. Then, combine the two sentences into a compound sentence.

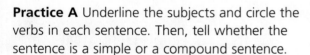

PH WRITING COACH | Further instruction and practice are available in *Prentice Hall Writing Coach*.

Writing

Common Core State Standards

L.9-10.1.b; W.9-10.3.a, W.9-10.3.b; SL.9-10.6
[For the full wording of the standards, see page 1062.]

Narrative Text In a small group, write a contemporary **myth.** You may write about the origin of some aspect of human life, such as how gossip or forgiveness entered the world, *or* you may describe the origin of some feature of your everyday world, such as television, computers, or automobiles. Follow these steps:

- Agree on a topic that group members find interesting.

- Make a plan for writing that addresses your purpose, identifies characters and a logical sequence, and sets a time frame for completion.

- Have one member write an opening sentence.

- With your planned sequence in mind, each group member should take a turn writing a paragraph that logically follows from the one before. Writers should develop the action with dialogue, pacing, and description.

- As a group, review the story as it progresses, and make any revisions agreed upon by the group members.

Present your myth to the class.

Grammar Application Make sure your myth contains a variety of correctly structured sentences, including simple and compound sentences.

Writing Workshop: *Work in Progress*

Prewriting for a Technical Document Make a list of tasks that you do every day. Select one of the tasks and list the basic steps that go into the task. Save your Task List in your writing portfolio.

Use this prewriting activity to prepare for the **Writing Workshop** on page 1146.

Speaking and Listening

Presentation of Ideas Locate another Greek myth about the gods and humans *or* another Native American myth that explains the origin of an animal. Present your own **retelling** of the myth to your class. Do the following:

- Engage your audience with an exciting introduction to the story.

- Present the sequence of events in a logical order.

- Accurately and vividly describe important scenes, action, and characters, using sensory details whenever possible.

- Vary the pitch and tone of your voice to reflect the action and mood of the story.

- Include a conclusion that helps listeners understand the lesson.

Afterward, have classmates summarize your retelling. Then, lead a discussion in which you compare and contrast the myth to either story.

PHLit Online!
www.PHLitOnline.com
- Interactive graphic organizers
- Grammar tutorial
- Interactive journals

ⓒ Leveled Texts

Build your skills and improve your comprehension of epics with texts of increasing complexity.

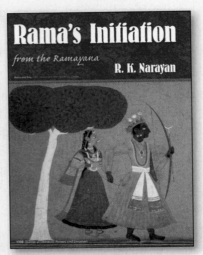

Read the excerpt from **Sundiata: An Epic of Old Mali** to find out how a boy who is the subject of ridicule defends his mother's honor.

Read **"Rama's Initiation"** from the **Ramayana** to learn how a young man accepts his destiny by going on a perilous journey.

ⓒ Common Core State Standards

Meet these standards with either the excerpt from **Sundiata: An Epic of Old Mali** (p. 1094) or **"Rama's Initiation"** (p. 1108).

Reading Literature
6. Analyze a particular point of view or cultural experience reflected in a work of literature from outside the United States, drawing on a wide reading of world literature. (*Reading Skill: Analyze Cultural Context*)

Writing
2. Write informative/explanatory texts to examine and convey complex ideas, concepts, and information clearly and accurately through the effective selection, organization, and analysis of content. **2.b.** Develop the topic with well-chosen, relevant, and sufficient facts, extended definitions, concrete details, quotations, or other information and examples appropriate to the audience's knowledge of the topic. **6.** Use technology to produce, publish, and update individual or shared writing products. (*Writing: Newspaper Report*)

Speaking and Listening
1. Initiate and participate effectively in a range of collaborative discussions with diverse partners on *grades 9–10 topics, texts, and issues,* building on others' ideas and expressing their own clearly and persuasively. (*Speaking and Listening: Improvised Dialogue*)

Language
1.b. Use various types of phrases and clauses to convey specific meanings and add variety and interest to writing or presentations. (*Conventions: Complex and Compound-Complex Sentences*)

Literary Analysis: Epic and Epic Hero

An **epic** is an extended narrative poem about the deeds of heroes. The typical **epic hero** is a warrior, and his character may be based on a historic or a legendary figure. In a number of epics, the hero strives to win immortality or undying fame through great deeds, especially in combat. The typical epic hero has the following characteristics:

- He has a high position in society and the virtues of a warrior, such as strength, courage, and perseverance.
- He defends his family's honor, and he behaves ethically—fighting evil and striving for justice.
- He may be marked by the gods or by fate and so may benefit from special blessings or suffer from special burdens.

An epic often reflects the culture that created it, celebrating that culture's values and reinforcing its ideals.

Reading Skill: Analyze Cultural Context

To understand an epic, **analyze cultural context,** or determine ways in which the epic reflects the ideas and values of the historical period and the culture in which it was composed. You can **acquire background knowledge** about the culture in these ways:

- Read text features, such as introductory sections and footnotes, and examine artwork and photos, noting how they add to your understanding of the culture or text.
- Draw conclusions from the details in the selection.

Using the Strategy: Cultural Context Chart

As you read, take notes on a **cultural context chart** like the one shown.

Background	Support
At age twelve, boys in this culture are initiated as full members of the tribe.	Footnote 3
Men in this culture are free to express their emotions.	The two friends cry when they part.

Can anyone be a *hero?*

Writing About the Big Question

In the excerpt from *Sundiata: An Epic of Old Mali*, a young man's determination allows him to overcome his infirmity and regain his family's honor. Use this sentence starter to develop your ideas about the Big Question.

Showing **determination** and **courage** in the face of adversity is heroic because _____.

While You Read Look for examples of behavior that made Mari Djata an unlikely hero.

Vocabulary

Read each word and its definition. Decide whether you know the word well, know it a little bit, or do not know it at all. After you read, see how your knowledge of each word has increased.

- **fathom** (fath´ əm) *v.* understand thoroughly (p. 1095) *I cannot fathom why he behaved so strangely.* fathomable *adj.*

- **innuendo** (in´ yōō en´ dō) *n.* indirect insult or accusation; insinuation (p. 1096) *She will not accuse him directly, but her innuendo let him know she suspects him.*

- **estranged** (e strānjd´) *adj.* kept apart; in the condition of having had affection turn into indifference or hostility (p. 1096) *The two friends became estranged after an especially bitter quarrel.* estrange *v.* estrangement *n.*

- **derisively** (di rī´ siv lē) *adv.* in a mocking and ridiculing manner (p. 1100) *He commented derisively on our poster which hurt ourfeelings.* derision *n.* derisive *adj.*

- **affront** (ə frunt´) *n.* open insult (p. 1100) *Their nasty laughter was an affront to her pride.* affront *v.*

- **efface** (ə fās´) *v.* rub or blot out (p. 1102) *In order to efface the memory of that day, we never spoke of it again.* effaced *v.* effacement *n.*

Word Study

The **Latin suffix** *-ive* means "belonging to" or "quality of."

In this story, a character chuckles **derisively**, or in a manner filled with scorn and ridicule.

Retellers of
Sundiata
AN EPIC OF OLD MALI

BACKGROUND FOR THE EPIC

A Great Leader

Sundiata tells the tale of Mari (or Sogolon) Djata, also known as Sundiata. Nearly 1,000 years ago, a warrior named Sumanguru took control of the area around Mali in West Africa and oppressed its Malinke people. A hero arose to unite the people, defeat Sumanguru, and usher in a period of peace. That hero was Sundiata.

Sundiata's people, the Malinke, are one of the Mande peoples of West Africa. Mande society is divided into different classes of people, from nobles to commoners. In his day, Sundiata's people traded in gold. After his victory over Sumanguru, Sundiata conquered neighboring lands and built an extensive kingdom known as the Mali empire.

The Griot Tradition Sundiata's achievements were celebrated over the centuries by West African oral historians known as griots (grē´ ōz). The twentieth-century griot Mamadou Kouyaté (mä´ mä dōō kōō ya´ tā) continued this tradition. "I derive my knowledge from my father, Djeli Kedian, who also got it from his father," Kouyaté explained. "History holds no mystery for us." The scholar **D. T. Niane** (nī´ yan) wrote an account of Sundiata based on Kouyaté's retellings.

Did You Know?
Kouyaté belongs to the same clan as the kings of Old Mali.

from Sundiata
AN EPIC OF OLD MALI

D. T. NIANE

▲ **Critical Viewing**
Contrast this depiction of Mari (or Sogolon) Djata with the child described in the opening paragraphs. **[Contrast]**

CHARACTERS IN SUNDIATA

Balla Fasséké (bä´ lä fä sä´ kä): Griot and counselor of Sundiata

Boukari (boo kä´ rē): Son of the king and Namandjé, one of his wives; also called Manding (män´ diŋ) Boukari

Dankaran Touman (dän´ kä rän too´ män): Son of the king and his first wife, Sassouma, who is also called Sassouma Bérété

Djamarou (jä mä´ roo): Daughter of Sogolon and the king; sister of Sundiata and Kolonkan

Farakourou (fä rä koo´ roo): Master of the forges

Gnankouman Doua (nän koo´ män doo´ ə): The king's griot; also called, simply, Doua

Kolonkan (kō lōn´ kən): Sundiata's eldest sister

Namandjé (nä män´ jē): One of the king's wives

Naré Maghan (nä´ rä mäg´ hän): Sundiata's father; the king of Mali before Sundiata

Nounfaïri (noon´ fä ē´ rē): Soothsayer and smith; father of Farakourou

Sassouma Bérété (sä soo´ mä be´ re te): The king's first wife

Sogolon (sô gô lōn´): Sundiata's mother; also called Sogolon Kedjou (kā´ joo)

Sundiata (soon dyä´ tä): Legendary king of Mali; referred to as Djata (dyä´ tä) and Sogolon Djata ("son of Sogolon"), and Mari (mä´ rē) Djata.

CHILDHOOD

God has his mysteries which none can fathom. You, perhaps, will be a king. You can do nothing about it. You, on the other hand, will be unlucky, but you can do nothing about that either. Each man finds his way already marked out for him and he can change nothing of it.

Sogolon's son had a slow and difficult childhood. At the age of three he still crawled along on all-fours while children of the same age were already walking. He had nothing of the great beauty of his father Naré Maghan. He had a head so big that he seemed unable to support it; he also had large eyes which would open wide whenever anyone entered his mother's house. He was taciturn[1] and used to spend the whole day just sitting in the middle of the house. Whenever his mother went out he would crawl on all-fours to rummage about in the calabashes[2] in search of food, for he was very greedy.

Vocabulary
fathom (fath´ əm) v. understand thoroughly

Reading Check

Why is Mari (or Sogolon) Djata's childhood difficult?

---

1. taciturn (tas´ ə turn´) *adj.* almost always silent; not liking to talk.
2. calabashes (kal´ ə bash´ əz) *n.* dried, hollow shells of gourds (squashlike fruits), used as bowls, cups, and so on.

Reading Skill
Analyze Cultural Context What detail does the background information in footnote 2 help you understand?

Malicious tongues began to blab. What three-year-old has not yet taken his first steps? What three-year-old is not the despair of his parents through his whims and shifts of mood? What three-year-old is not the joy of his circle through his backwardness in talking? Sogolon Djata (for it was thus that they called him, prefixing his mother's name to his), Sogolon Djata, then, was very different from others of his own age. He spoke little and his severe face never relaxed into a smile. You would have thought that he was already thinking, and what amused children of his age bored him. Often Sogolon would make some of them come to him to keep him company. These children were already walking and she hoped that Djata, seeing his companions walking, would be tempted to do likewise. But nothing came of it. Besides, Sogolon Djata would brain the poor little things with his already strong arms and none of them would come near him any more.

The king's first wife was the first to rejoice at Sogolon Djata's infirmity. Her own son, Dankaran Touman, was already eleven. He was a fine and lively boy, who spent the day running about the village with those of his own age. He had even begun his initiation in the bush.[3] The king had had a bow made for him and he used to go behind the town to practice archery with his companions. Sassouma was quite happy and snapped her fingers at Sogolon, whose child was still crawling on the ground. Whenever the latter happened to pass by her house, she would say, "Come, my son, walk, jump, leap about. The jinn didn't promise you anything out of the ordinary,[4] but I prefer a son who walks on his two legs to a lion that crawls on the ground." She spoke thus whenever Sogolon went by her door. The innuendo would go straight home and then she would burst into laughter, that diabolical laughter which a jealous woman knows how to use so well.

Her son's infirmity weighed heavily upon Sogolon Kedjou; she had resorted to all her talent as a sorceress to give strength to her son's legs, but the rarest herbs had been useless. The king himself lost hope.

How impatient man is! Naré Maghan became imperceptibly estranged but Gnankouman Doua never ceased reminding him of the hunter's words. Sogolon became pregnant again. The king hoped for a son, but it was a daughter called Kolonkan. She

Literary Analysis
Epic and Epic Hero In what two ways is Mari (or Sogolon) Djata set apart from other children?

Vocabulary
innuendo (in´ yoo en´ dō) *n.* indirect insult or accusation; insinuation

estranged (e strānjd´) *adj.* kept apart; in the condition of having had affection turn into indifference or hostility

3. **initiation in the bush** education in tribal lore given to twelve-year-old West African boys so they can become full members of the tribe.
4. **The jinn . . . ordinary** Jinn are supernatural beings said to influence human affairs. They promised that the son of Sogolon would make Mali a great empire.

resembled her mother and had nothing of her father's beauty. The disheartened king debarred Sogolon from his house and she lived in semi-disgrace for a while. Naré Maghan married the daughter of one of his allies, the king of the Kamaras. She was called Namandjé and her beauty was legendary. A year later she brought a boy into the world. When the king consulted soothsayers[5] on the destiny of this son he received the reply that Namandjé's child would be the right hand of some mighty king. The king gave the newly-born the name of Boukari. He was to be called Manding Boukari or Manding Bory later on.

Naré Maghan was very perplexed. Could it be that the stiff-jointed son of Sogolon was the one the hunter soothsayer had foretold?

"The Almighty has his mysteries," Gnankouman Doua would say and, taking up the hunter's words, added, "The silk-cotton tree emerges from a tiny seed."

One day Naré Maghan came along to the house of Nounfaïri, the blacksmith seer of Niani. He was an old, blind man. He received the king in the anteroom which served as his workshop. To the king's question he replied, "When the seed germinates growth is not always easy; great trees grow slowly but they plunge their roots deep into the ground."

"But has the seed really germinated?" said the king.

"Of course," replied the blind seer. "Only the growth is not as quick as you would like it; how impatient man is."

This interview and Doua's confidence gave the king some assurance. To the great displeasure of Sassouma Bérété the king restored Sogolon to favor and soon another daughter was born to her. She was given the name of Djamarou.

However, all Niani talked of nothing else but the stiff-legged son of Sogolon. He was now seven and he still crawled to get about. In spite of all the king's affection, Sogolon was in despair. Naré Maghan aged and he felt his time coming to an end. Dankaran Touman, the son of Sassouma Bérété, was now a fine youth.

One day Naré Maghan made Mari Djata come to him and he spoke to the child as one speaks to an adult. "Mari Djata, I am growing old and soon I shall be no more among you, but before death takes me off I am going to give you the present each king gives his successor. In Mali every prince has his own griot. Doua's father was my father's griot, Doua is mine and the son of Doua, Balla Fasséké here, will be your griot. Be inseparable friends from

What three-year-old has not yet taken his first steps?

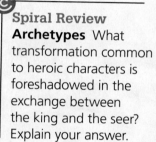

Spiral Review
Archetypes What transformation common to heroic characters is foreshadowed in the exchange between the king and the seer? Explain your answer.

Reading Skill
Analyze Cultural Context What does the background information on page 1093 suggest about how powerful Mari Djata will one day become?

Reading Check
What advice does the blind seer give to the king?

---

5. **soothsayers** (sooth′ sā′ ərz) *n.* people who profess to foretell the future.

this day forward. From his mouth you will hear the history of your ancestors, you will learn the art of governing Mali according to the principles which our ancestors have bequeathed to us. I have served my term and done my duty too. I have done everything which a king of Mali ought to do. I am handing an enlarged kingdom over to you and I leave you sure allies. May your destiny be accomplished, but never forget that Niani is your capital and Mali the cradle of your ancestors."

The child, as if he had understood the whole meaning of the king's words, beckoned Balla Fasséké to approach. He made room for him on the hide he was sitting on and then said, "Balla, you will be my griot."

"Yes, son of Sogolon, if it pleases God," replied Balla Fasséké.

The king and Doua exchanged glances that radiated confidence.

◀ **Critical Viewing**
What relationship in the epic might this picture illustrate? Explain. **[Connect]**

THE LION'S AWAKENING

A short while after this interview between Naré Maghan and his son the king died.

Sogolon's son was no more than seven years old. The council of elders met in the king's palace. It was no use Doua's defending the king's will which reserved the throne for Mari Djata, for the council took no account of Naré Maghan's wish. With the help of Sassouma Bérété's intrigues, Dankaran Touman was proclaimed king and a regency council[6] was formed in which the queen mother was all-powerful. A short time after, Doua died.

As men have short memories, Sogolon's son was spoken of with nothing but irony and scorn. People had seen one-eyed kings, one-armed kings, and lame kings, but a stiff-legged king had never been heard tell of. No matter how great the destiny promised for Mari Djata might be, the throne could not be given to someone who had no power in his legs; if the jinn loved him, let them begin by giving him the use of his legs. Such were the remarks that Sogolon heard every day. The queen mother, Sassouma Bérété, was the source of all this gossip.

Having become all-powerful, Sassouma Bérété persecuted Sogolon because the late Naré Maghan had preferred her. She banished Sogolon and her son to a back yard of the palace. Mari

Reading Skill
Analyze Cultural Context What do the details here indicate about the way in which West African society was ruled?

Reading Check

After the king's death, who takes power in the kingdom?

---

6. **regency** (rē´ jən sē) **council** group that rules instead of the king or queen when the king or queen is still a child or is otherwise incapable of ruling.

Literary Analysis
Epic and Epic Hero In what way is the honor of Mari Djata's family threatened?

Vocabulary
derisively (di rī´siv lē) *adv.* in a mocking and ridiculing manner

affront (ə frunt´) *n.* open insult

Djata's mother now occupied an old hut which had served as a lumber-room of Sassouma's.

The wicked queen mother allowed free passage to all those inquisitive people who wanted to see the child that still crawled at the age of seven. Nearly all the inhabitants of Niani filed into the palace and the poor Sogolon wept to see herself thus given over to public ridicule. Mari Djata took on a ferocious look in front of the crowd of sightseers. Sogolon found a little consolation only in the love of her eldest daughter, Kolonkan. She was four and she could walk. She seemed to understand all her mother's miseries and already she helped her with the housework. Sometimes, when Sogolon was attending to the chores, it was she who stayed beside her sister Djamarou, quite small as yet.

Sogolon Kedjou and her children lived on the queen mother's leftovers, but she kept a little garden in the open ground behind the village. It was there that she passed her brightest moments looking after her onions and gnougous.[7] One day she happened to be short of condiments and went to the queen mother to beg a little baobab leaf.[8]

"Look you," said the malicious Sassouma, "I have a calabash full. Help yourself, you poor woman. As for me, my son knew how to walk at seven and it was he who went and picked these baobab leaves. Take them then, since your son is unequal to mine." Then she laughed derisively with that fierce laughter which cuts through your flesh and penetrates right to the bone.

Sogolon Kedjou was dumbfounded. She had never imagined that hate could be so strong in a human being. With a lump in her throat she left Sassouma's. Outside her hut Mari Djata, sitting on his useless legs, was blandly eating out of a calabash. Unable to contain herself any longer, Sogolon burst into sobs and seizing a piece of wood, hit her son.

"Oh son of misfortune, will you never walk? Through your fault I have just suffered the greatest affront of my life! What have I done, God, for you to punish me in this way?"

Mari Djata seized the piece of wood and, looking at his mother, said, "Mother, what's the matter?"

"Shut up, nothing can ever wash me clean of this insult."

"But what then?"

"Sassouma has just humiliated me over a matter of a baobab leaf. At your age her own son could walk and used to bring his mother baobab leaves."

---

7. **gnougous** (noo´ gooz´) *n.* root vegetables.
8. **baobab** (bā´ ō bab´) **leaf** The baobab is a thick-trunked tree; its leaves are used to flavor foods.

"Cheer up, Mother, cheer up."

"No. It's too much. I can't."

"Very well then, I am going to walk today," said Mari Djata. "Go and tell my father's smiths to make me the heaviest possible iron rod. Mother, do you want just the leaves of the baobab or would you rather I brought you the whole tree?"

"Ah, my son, to wipe out this insult I want the tree and its roots at my feet outside my hut."

Balla Fasséké, who was present, ran to the master smith, Farakourou, to order an iron rod.

Sogolon had sat down in front of her hut. She was weeping softly and holding her head between her two hands. Mari Djata went calmly back to his calabash of rice and began eating again as if nothing had happened. From time to time he looked up discreetly at his mother who was murmuring in a low voice, "I want the whole tree, in front of my hut, the whole tree."

All of a sudden a voice burst into laughter behind the hut. It was the wicked Sassouma telling one of her serving women about the scene of humiliation and she was laughing loudly so that Sogolon could hear. Sogolon fled into the hut and hid her face under the blankets so as not to have before her eyes this heedless boy, who was more preoccupied with eating than with anything else. With her head buried in the bedclothes Sogolon wept and her body shook violently. Her daughter, Sogolon Djamarou, had come and sat down beside her and she said, "Mother, Mother, don't cry. Why are you crying?"

Mari Djata had finished eating and, dragging himself along on his legs, he came and sat under the wall of the hut for the sun was scorching. What was he thinking about? He alone knew.

The royal forges were situated outside the walls and over a hundred smiths worked there. The bows, spears, arrows and shields of Niani's warriors came from there. When Balla Fasséké came to order the iron rod, Farakourou said to him, "The great day has arrived then?"

"Yes. Today is a day like any other, but it will see what no other day has seen."

▼ Critical Viewing
Why might Mari Djata have difficulty gathering leaves from a baobab tree like this one? **[Analyze]**

Reading Check
What incident provokes Mari Djata to order an iron bar?

from Sundiata: An Epic of Old Mali **1101**

Reading Skill
Analyze Cultural Context What do these details suggest about the role of blacksmiths and warriors in West African culture?

Vocabulary
efface (ə fās′) *v.* rub or blot out

The master of the forges, Farakourou, was the son of the old Nounfaïri, and he was a soothsayer like his father. In his workshops there was an enormous iron bar wrought by his father, Nounfaïri. Everybody wondered what this bar was destined to be used for. Farakourou called six of his apprentices and told them to carry the iron bar to Sogolon's house.

When the smiths put the gigantic iron bar down in front of the hut the noise was so frightening that Sogolon, who was lying down, jumped up with a start. Then Balla Fasséké, son of Gnankouman Doua, spoke.

"Here is the great day, Mari Djata. I am speaking to you, Maghan, son of Sogolon. The waters of the Niger can efface the stain from the body, but they cannot wipe out an insult. Arise, young lion, roar, and may the bush know that from henceforth it has a master."

The apprentice smiths were still there, Sogolon had come out and everyone was watching Mari Djata. He crept on all-fours and came to the iron bar. Supporting himself on his knees and one hand, with the other hand he picked up the iron bar without any effort and stood it up vertically. Now he was resting on nothing but his knees and held the bar with both his hands. A deathly silence had gripped all those present. Sogolon Djata closed his eyes, held tight, the muscles in his arms tensed. With a violent jerk he threw his weight on to it and his knees left the ground. Sogolon Kedjou was all eyes and watched her son's legs which were trembling as though from an electric shock. Djata was sweating and the sweat ran from his brow. In a great effort he straightened up and was on his feet at one go—but the great bar of iron was twisted and had taken the form of a bow!

Then Balla Fasséké sang out the "Hymn to the Bow," striking up with his powerful voice:

"Take your bow, Simbon,
Take your bow and let us go.
Take your bow, Sogolon Djata."

When Sogolon saw her son standing she stood dumb for a moment, then suddenly she sang these words of thanks to God, who had given her son the use of his legs:

"Oh day, what a beautiful day,
Oh day, day of joy;
Allah[9] Almighty, you never created a finer day.
So my son is going to walk!"

---

9. **Allah** (al´ ə) Muslim name for God.

Literary Analysis
Epic and Epic Hero
What qualities of an epic hero does Mari Djata display here?

Reading Check
What causes both Mari Djata's mother and his griot to sing?

LITERATURE IN CONTEXT

Culture Connection

Griot: The Mind of the People

In West Africa, the griot (pronounced "gree-oh") was the storyteller and historian of the village. The griot memorized the births, deaths, marriages, hunts, and wars of the people and its ancestors. Sometimes speaking or singing for days, the griot recited these events as stories, often to musical accompaniment. To the Mandinka, the griot was the "mind" of the people, an oral library of history and culture.

Many griots use talking drums, like this one, as they tell their stories.

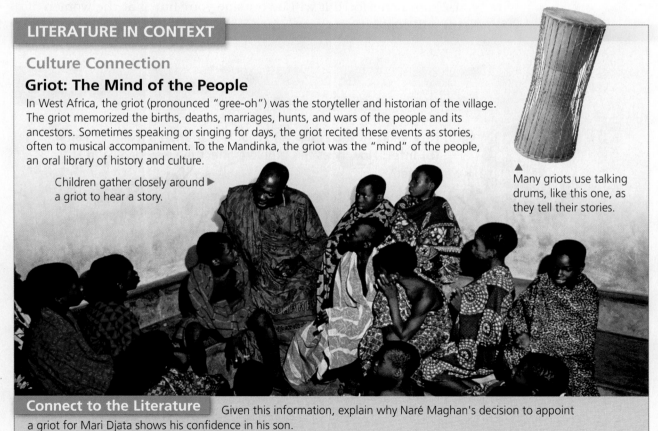

◄ Children gather closely around a griot to hear a story.

Connect to the Literature Given this information, explain why Naré Maghan's decision to appoint a griot for Mari Djata shows his confidence in his son.

from Sundiata: An Epic of Old Mali **1103**

Standing in the position of a soldier at ease, Sogolon Djata, supported by his enormous rod, was sweating great beads of sweat. Balla Fasséké's song had alerted the whole palace and people came running from all over to see what had happened, and each stood bewildered before Sogolon's son. The queen mother had rushed there and when she saw Mari Djata standing up she trembled from head to foot. After recovering his breath Sogolon's son dropped the bar and the crowd stood to one side. His first steps were those of a giant. Balla Fasséké fell into step and pointing his finger at Djata, he cried:

"Room, room, make room!
The lion has walked;
Hide antelopes,
Get out of his way."

Behind Niani there was a young baobab tree and it was there that the children of the town came to pick leaves for their mothers. With all his might the son of Sogolon tore up the tree and put it on his shoulders and went back to his mother. He threw the tree in front of the hut and said, "Mother, here are some baobab leaves for you. From henceforth it will be outside your hut that the women of Niani will come to stock up."

Reading Skill
Analyze Cultural Context What do the images in the griot's song indicate about the region in which the Malinke live?

Critical Thinking

Cite textual evidence to support your responses.

© 1. **Key Ideas and Details (a)** What is Mari Djata's main difficulty? **(b) Infer:** How does this problem affect the way people treat his mother?

© 2. **Key Ideas and Details (a)** What does the king specify as his wish for Mari Djata? **(b) Analyze Cause and Effect:** How do the soothsayers' predictions help prompt the king's wishes?

© 3. **Key Ideas and Details (a)** After the king's death, where does Sassouma Bérété force Sogolon and Mari Djata to live? **(b) Infer:** Why does Sassouma Bérété treat Mari Djata and Sogolon as she does?

© 4. **Integration of Knowledge and Ideas (a)** What event finally prompts Mari Djata to transcend his own problems for the sake of his mother? **(b)** Why would his actions be considered "heroic"? *[Connect to the Big Question: Can anyone be a hero?]*

Literary Analysis: Epic and Epic Hero

1. Key Ideas and Details Explain two ways in which the challenges Mari Djata faces differ from other **epic** struggles.

2. Key Ideas and Details Using the following chart, give examples of the qualities of an **epic hero** that Mari Djata possesses.

Noble Birth	Warrior Virtues	Acts Honorably	Chosen by the Gods or Fate

3. Integration of Knowledge and Ideas What values or beliefs are conveyed in this tale? Support your response with details from the text.

Reading Skill: Analyze Cultural Context

4. (a) List three things that you learned about West African culture from the features that appear before the selection and from the footnotes. **(b)** Explain how knowing the **cultural context** in which the *Sundiata* was written helped you to understand it.

Vocabulary

Acquisition and Use Use a word from the vocabulary list on page 1092 to write a sentence about each of the following situations.

1. ceasing to socialize with a group of friends

2. confusion about a friend's buying a python as a pet

3. an exchange of snide remarks

4. an effort to harm someone's reputation

5. to laughingly make fun of someone

6. attempt to wipe away graffiti

Word Study Use the context of the sentences and what you know about the **Latin suffix -*ive*** to explain your answer to each question.

1. Is someone who is *combative* usually the peacemaker?

2. If a plant is *native* to North America, did it come from overseas?

Word Study

The **Latin suffix -*ive*** means "belonging to" or "quality of."

Apply It Explain how the suffix -*ive* contributes to the meanings of these words. Consult a dictionary if necessary.
elusive
persuasive
restorative

Can anyone be a *hero?*

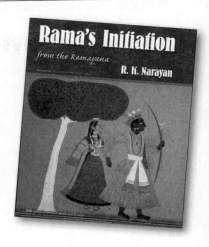

Writing About the Big Question

In "Rama's Initiation," a young boy discovers the importance of bravery and strength as he becomes a hero in a fight against evil. Use these sentence starters to develop your ideas about the Big Question.

Being able to **sacrifice** something important to you for the greater good can be considered heroic because _____.

Having **courage** and faith in oneself can help a person accomplish a difficult task such as _____.

While You Read Look for the challenges Rama faces on his journey and decide what role faith plays in his growth.

Vocabulary

Read each word and its definition. Decide whether you know the word well, know it a little bit, or do not know it at all. After you read, see how your knowledge of each word has increased.

- **renounced** (ri nounst´) *v.* to have given up formally (p. 1110) *We renounced our claim to the prize because we did not follow the rules of the contest.* renouncement *n.*

- **decrepitude** (dē krep´ ə tood´) *n.* feebleness; condition of being worn out by age or illness (p. 1110) *His love for the ratty old chair blinded him to its extreme decrepitude.* decrepit *adj.*

- **secular** (sek´ yə lər) *adj.* of wordly, as opposed to religious, matters (p. 1112) *The singer sang both religious and secular songs.* secularism *n.*

- **exuberance** (eg zoo´ bər əns) *n.* good health and high spirits (p. 1114) *Her exuberance was apparent in the way she laughed and danced.* exuberant *adj.* exuberantly *adv.*

- **adversaries** (ad´ vər ser´ ēz) *n.* opponents (p. 1116) *Our adversaries attacked us.* adversarial *adj.* adversary *n.*

- **esoteric** (es´ ə ter´ ik) *adj.* beyond the understanding or knowledge of most people (p. 1116) *Since Quantum Mechanics is esoteric, the class sizes are often small.* esoterically *adv.*

Word Study

The **Latin suffix** *-tude* means "condition of" or "quality of."

In this story, a character is not affected by **decrepitude,** or the condition of being worn out by age or illness.

Reteller of

Rama's Initiation
from the Ramayana

The foundations of Hindu culture were laid around 1500 B.C., when a warrior people, the Aryans, invaded northern India. The Aryans enforced the caste system, in which society is rigidly divided into castes, or groups, each with its own occupation and duties. The caste system supports Hindu emphasis on righteous behavior and spiritual self-improvement.

From Poet-Sage to Modern Novelist The earliest surviving version of Rama's story, credited to the poet-sage Valmiki, dates to perhaps 300 B.C. Among the story's most recent retellers is Indian novelist **R. K. Narayan.** According to Narayan, "All imaginative writing in India has had its origin in . . . the 10,000-year-old epics of India."

Did You Know?

To this day, Hindus take Rama as their model for conduct.

BACKGROUND FOR THE EPIC

Hinduism

The *Ramayana*, the great Hindu epic telling of Prince Rama, is one of the sacred books of Hinduism, the major religion of India. Hinduism involves a belief in many gods, each representing an aspect of life and nature. The most important gods are Brahma, the creator; Vishnu, the preserver; and Siva, the destroyer.

Rama's Initiation

from the Ramayana

R. K. Narayan

Rama and Sita, 1740. Victoria and Albert Museum, London.

Steeped in the Hindu religion of India, the **Ramayana** is the story of Prince Rama (rä′ mə), son of King Dasaratha (dä sä rä′ tä). With the guidance of several Hindu sages, or wise men, Rama confronts and overcomes many obstacles, including a test of strength to win his wife Sita. Just as he is about to inherit his throne, he is banished and spends fourteen years in exile before returning to his kingdom. Through the challenges he meets, he reaches a spiritual and moral state so perfect that many associate him with Krishna, the incarnation, or embodiment, of the Hindu god Vishnu (vēsh′ nōō).

This excerpt tells of adventures from Rama's childhood that occur before his fourteen-year banishment. Even as boys, he and his brother Lakshmana (läks mä′nä) show extraordinary strength and skill.

The new assembly hall, Dasaratha's latest pride, was crowded all day with visiting dignitaries, royal emissaries, and citizens coming in with representations or appeals for justice. The King was always accessible, and fulfilled his duties as the ruler of Kosala without grudging the hours spent in public service.

◀ **Critical Viewing**
What details in this painting indicate that Rama is an epic hero? **[Analyze]**

Reading Skill
Analyze Cultural Context What background information on page 1107 helps explain the king's treatment of the sage?

Vocabulary
renounced (ri nounst´) *v.* to have given up formally

decrepitude (dē krep´ ə tood´) *n.* feebleness; condition of being worn out by age or illness

Literary Analysis
Epic and Epic Hero What typical epic conflict does the sage describe here?

On a certain afternoon, messengers at the gate came running in to announce, "Sage Viswamithra" [vish wä´ mē trä]. When the message was relayed to the King, he got up and hurried forward to receive the visitor. Viswamithra, once a king, a conqueror, and a dreaded name until he renounced his kingly role and chose to become a sage (which he accomplished through severe austerities[1]), combined in himself the sage's eminence and the king's authority and was quick tempered and positive. Dasaratha led him to a proper seat and said, "This is a day of glory for us; your gracious presence is most welcome. You must have come from afar. Would you first rest?"

"No need," the sage replied simply. He had complete mastery over his bodily needs through inner discipline and austerities, and was above the effects of heat, cold, hunger, fatigue, and even decrepitude. The King later asked politely, "Is there anything I can do?" Viswamithra looked steadily at the King and answered, "Yes. I am here to ask of you a favor. I wish to perform, before the next full moon, a *yagna*[2] at Sidhasrama [sēd häs rä´ mä]. Doubtless you know where it is?"

"I have passed that sacred ground beyond the Ganges many times."

The sage interrupted. "But there are creatures hovering about waiting to disturb every holy undertaking there, who must be overcome in the same manner as one has to conquer the five-fold evils[3] within before one can realize holiness. Those evil creatures are endowed with immeasurable powers of destruction. But it is our duty to pursue our aims undeterred. The yagna I propose to perform will strengthen the beneficial forces of this world, and please the gods above."

"It is my duty to protect your sublime[4] effort. Tell me when, and I will be there."

The sage said, "No need to disturb your august self. Send your son Rama with me, and he will help me. He can."

"Rama!" cried the King, surprised, "When I am here to serve you."

Viswamithra's temper was already stirring. "I know your greatness," he said, cutting the King short. "But I want Rama to go with me. If you are not willing, you may say so."

The air became suddenly tense. The assembly, the ministers and officials, watched in solemn silence. The King looked miserable. "Rama is still a child, still learning the arts and practicing the use of arms." His sentences never seemed to conclude, but trailed away

---

1. **austerities** (ô ster´ ə tēz) *n.* acts or habits of self-denial.
2. **yagna** (yäg nä´) *n.* Sanskrit term for sacrifice.
3. **five-fold evils** In Hindu belief, the five evils are lust, anger, miserliness, egoism, and envy.
4. **sublime** (sə blīm´) *adj.* noble; grand.

as he tried to explain. "He is a boy, a child, he is too young and tender to contend with demons."

"But I know Rama," was all that Viswamithra said in reply.

"I can send you an army, or myself lead an army to guard your performance. What can a stripling[5] like Rama do against those terrible forces . . . ? I will help you just as I helped Indra[6] once when he was harassed and deprived of his kingdom."

Viswamithra ignored his speech and rose to leave. "If you cannot send Rama, I need none else." He started to move down the passage.

The King was too stricken to move. When Viswamithra had gone half way, he realized that the visitor was leaving unceremoniously and was not even shown the courtesy of being escorted to the door. Vasishtha [vä sē′ shtä], the King's priest and

Literary Analysis
Epic and Epic Hero
In what way is Rama singled out as an epic hero?

Reading Check

What does Viswamithra ask of the king?

---

5. **stripling** (strip′ liŋ) *n.* young boy passing into manhood.
6. **Indra** (in′ drə) Hindu god associated with rain and thunderbolts.

guide, whispered to Dasaratha, "Follow him and call him back," and hurried forward even before the King could grasp what he was saying. He almost ran as Viswamithra had reached the end of the hall and, blocking his way, said, "The King is coming; please don't go. He did not mean . . ."

A wry smile played on Viswamithra's face as he said without any trace of bitterness, "Why are you or anyone agitated? I came here for a purpose; it has failed: no reason to prolong my stay."

"Oh, eminent one, you were yourself a king once."

Vocabulary
secular (sek´ yə lər) *adj.* of worldly, as opposed to religious, matters

"What has that to do with us now?" asked Viswamithra, rather irked, since he hated all reference to his secular past and wanted always to be known as a Brahma Rishi.[7]

Vasishtha answered mildly, "Only to remind you of an ordinary man's feelings, especially a man like Dasaratha who had been childless and had to pray hard for an issue . . ."

"Well, it may be so, great one; I still say that I came on a mission and wish to leave, since it has failed."

"It has not failed," said Vasishtha, and just then the King came up to join them in the passage; the assembly was on its feet.

Dasaratha made a deep obeisance and said, "Come back to your seat, Your Holiness."

"For what purpose, Your Majesty?" Viswamithra asked.

"Easier to talk seated . . ."

"I don't believe in any talk," said Viswamithra; but Vasishtha pleaded with him until he returned to his seat.

When they were all seated again, Vasishtha addressed the King: "There must be a divine purpose working through this seer, who may know but will not explain. It is a privilege that Rama's help should be sought. Do not bar his way. Let him go with the sage."

"When, oh when?" the King asked anxiously.

"Now," said Viswamithra. The King looked woebegone and desperate, and the sage relented enough to utter a word of comfort. "You cannot count on the physical proximity of someone you love, all the time. A seed that sprouts at the foot of its parent tree remains stunted until it is transplanted. Rama will be in my care, and he will be quite well. But ultimately, he will leave me too. Every human being, when the time comes, has to depart and seek his fulfillment in his own way."

"Sidhasrama is far away . . .?" began the King.

"I'll ease his path for him, no need for a chariot to take us there," said Viswamithra, reading his mind.

---

7. **Brahma Rishi** (brä´ mä ri´ shē) enlightened wise person.

"Rama has never been separated from his brother Lakshmana. May he also go with him?" pleaded the King, and he looked relieved when he heard Viswamithra say, "Yes, I will look after both, though their mission will be to look after me. Let them get ready to follow me; let them select their favorite weapons and prepare to leave."

Dasaratha, with the look of one delivering hostages into the hand of an enemy, turned to his minister and said, "Fetch my sons." •

Following the footsteps of their master like his shadows, Rama and Lakshmana went past the limits of the city and reached the Sarayu River, which bounded the capital on the north. When night fell, they rested at a wooded grove and at dawn crossed the river. When the sun came over the mountain peak, they reached a pleasant grove over which hung, like a canopy, fragrant smoke from numerous sacrificial fires. Viswamithra explained to Rama, "This is where God Shiva[8] meditated once upon a time and reduced

to ashes the god of love when he attempted to spoil his meditation. From time immemorial saints praying to Shiva come here to perform their sacrifices, and the pall of smoke you notice is from their sacrificial fires."

A group of hermits emerged from their seclusion, received Viswamithra, and invited him and his two disciples to stay with them for the night. Viswamithra resumed his journey at dawn and reached a desert region at midday. The mere expression "desert" hardly conveys the absolute aridity of this land. Under a relentless sun, all vegetation had dried and turned to dust, stone and rock crumbled into powdery sand, which lay in vast dunes, stretching away to the horizon. Here every inch was scorched and dry and hot beyond imagination. The ground was cracked and split, exposing enormous fissures everywhere. The distinction between dawn, noon, and evening did not exist here, as the sun seemed to stay overhead and burn the earth without moving. Bleached bones

Reading Skill
Analyze Cultural Context What background information helps explain details in this paragraph?

Reading Check

Whom does the king send to accompany Rama and Viswamithra?

---

8. **Shiva** (shē´ və) Hindu god of destruction and reproduction; along with Vishnu and Brahma, one of the three most important gods in Hinduism.

lay where animals had perished, including those of monstrous serpents with jaws open in deadly thirst; into these enormous jaws had rushed (says the poet) elephants desperately seeking shade, all dead and fossilized, the serpent and the elephant alike. Heat haze rose and singed the very heavens. While traversing this ground, Viswamithra noticed the bewilderment and distress on the faces of the young men, and transmitted to them mentally two mantras[9] (called "Bala" and "Adi-Bala"). When they meditated on and recited these incantations, the arid atmosphere was transformed for the rest of their passage and they felt as if they were wading through a cool stream with a southern summer breeze blowing in their faces. Rama, ever curious to know the country he was passing through, asked, "Why is this land so terrible? Why does it seem accursed?"

"You will learn the answer if you listen to this story—of a woman fierce, ruthless, eating and digesting all living creatures, possessing the strength of a thousand mad elephants." ●

▲ **Critical Viewing**
Based on this painting, what traits does Rama possess? **[Infer]**

Vocabulary
exuberance (eg zoo ´bər əns) *n.* good health and high spirits

Thataka's Story

The woman I speak of was the daughter of Suketha [soo kā´ tä] a *yaksha*,[10] a demigod of great valor, might, and purity. She was beautiful and full of wild energy. When she grew up she was married to a chieftain named Sunda. Two sons were born to them—Mareecha [mä´ rē chä] and Subahu [sä bä´ hoo]—who were endowed with enormous supernatural powers in addition to physical strength; and in their conceit and exuberance they laid waste their surroundings. Their father, delighted at their pranks and infected by their mood, joined in their activities. He pulled out ancient trees by their roots and flung them about, and he slaughtered all

---

9. mantras (man´ trəz) *n.* sacred syllables or hymns chanted in prayer.
10. yaksha Sanskrit term for a good nature spirit.

creatures that came his way. This depredation came to the notice of the great savant[11] Agasthya [ä gus tē yä´] (the diminutive[12] saint who once, when certain demoniac beings hid themselves at the bottom of the sea and Indra appealed for his help to track them, had sipped off the waters of the ocean). Agasthya had his hermitage in this forest, and when he noticed the destruction around, he cursed the perpetrator of this deed and Sunda fell dead. When his wife learned of his death, she and her sons stormed in, roaring revenge on the saint. He met their challenge by cursing them. "Since you are destroyers of life, may you become *asuras*[13] and dwell in the nether worlds." (Till now they had been demigods. Now they were degraded to demonhood.) The three at once underwent a transformation; their features and stature became forbidding, and their natures changed to match. The sons left to seek the company of superdemons. The mother was left alone and lives on here, breathing fire and wishing everything ill. Nothing flourishes here; only heat and sand remain. She is a scorcher. She carries a trident with spikes; a cobra entwined on her arm is her armlet. The name of this fearsome creature is Thataka [tä tä´ kä]. Just as the presence of a little *loba* (meanness) dries up and disfigures a whole human personality, so does the presence of this monster turn into desert a region which was once fertile. In her restlessness she constantly harasses the hermits at their prayers; she gobbles up anything that moves and sends it down her entrails.

Touching the bow slung on his shoulder, Rama asked, "Where is she to be found?"

Before Viswamithra could answer, she arrived, the ground rocking under her feet and a storm preceding her. She loomed over them with her eyes spitting fire, her fangs bared, her lips parted revealing a cavernous mouth; and her brows twitching in rage. She raised her trident and roared, "In this my kingdom, I have crushed out the minutest womb of life and you have been sent down so that I may not remain hungry."

Rama hesitated; for all her evil, she was still a woman. How could he kill her? Reading his thoughts, Viswamithra said, "You shall not consider her a woman at all. Such a monster must receive no consideration. Her strength, ruthlessness, appearance, rule her out of that category. Formerly God Vishnu himself killed Kyathi [kyä´ tē], the wife of Brigu [brë´ go͞o], who harbored the *asuras* fleeing his wrath, when she refused to yield them. Mandorai, [mänd rä´ ē] a woman bent upon destroying all the worlds, was vanquished by

---

Literary Analysis
Epic and Epic Hero
Why is Thataka a suitable opponent for an epic hero?

Reading Skill
Analyze Cultural Context What do the details in this paragraph suggest about the place of women in Hindu culture?

Reading Check
Why does nothing grow in the land where Thataka lives?

---

11. savant (sə vänt´) *n.* learned person.
12. diminutive (də min´ yo͞o tiv) *adj.* much smaller than ordinary or average.
13. asuras (ä so͞o´ räz) in Hindu belief, group of demons at war with gods and human beings.

Indra and he earned the gratitude of humanity. These are but two instances. A woman of demoniac tendencies loses all consideration to be treated as a woman. This Thataka is more dreadful than Yama, the god of death, who takes a life only when the time is ripe. But this monster, at the very scent of a living creature, craves to kill and eat. Do not picture her as a woman at all. You must rid this world of her. It is your duty."

Rama said, "I will carry out your wish."

Thataka threw her three-pronged spear at Rama. As it came flaming, Rama strung his bow and sent an arrow which broke it into fragments. Next she raised a hail of stones under which to crush her adversaries. Rama sent up his arrows, which shielded them from the attack. Finally Rama's arrow pierced her throat and ended her career; thereby also inaugurating Rama's life's mission of destroying evil and demonry in this world. The gods assembled in the sky and expressed their joy and relief and enjoined Viswamithra, "Oh, adept and master of weapons, impart without any reserve all your knowledge and powers to this lad. He is a savior." Viswamithra obeyed this injunction and taught Rama all the esoteric techniques in weaponry. Thereafter the presiding deities of various weapons, *asthras* [äs′ träz], appeared before Rama submissively and declared, "Now we are yours: command us night or day."

Critical Thinking

Cite textual evidence to support your responses.

1. **Key Ideas and Details (a)** What favor does Viswamithra ask of King Dasaratha? **(b) Hypothesize:** Why does he want Rama, rather than the king, to perform the favor?

2. **Key Ideas and Details (a)** List three details describing the region through which Rama, Lakshmana, and Viswamithra pass.
   (b) Analyze: How does the land seem different to Rama and Lakshmana when they use Viswamithra's mantras?
   (c) Draw Conclusions: What does this episode suggest about the sage's power?

3. **Key Ideas and Details (a)** Summarize the outcome of Rama's first battle. **(b) Interpret:** This part of the epic is called "Rama's Initiation." Into what activity or way of life is he initiated?

4. **Integration of Knowledge and Ideas (a)** What role does faith have in the creation of a hero? **(b)** Identify two people in the story who had to have faith in order for Rama to succeed, and explain why that faith was important. *[Connect to the Big Question: Can anyone be a hero?]*

After You Read

Literary Analysis: Epic and Epic Hero

© **1. Key Ideas and Details (a)** What is the goal of the sage's **epic** journey? **(b)** What is Rama's goal in accompanying the sage? **(c)** Compare and contrast these goals with the goals of heroes who fight for honor or glory.

© **2. Key Ideas and Details** Using the following chart, give examples of the qualities of an **epic hero** that Rama possesses.

Noble Birth	Warrior Virtues	Acts Honorably	Chosen by the Gods or Fate

© **3. Integration of Knowledge and Ideas (a)** Why does Rama hesitate before fighting Thataka? **(b)** Does his hesitation suit the character of an epic hero? Explain.

Reading Skill: Analyze Cultural Context

4. (a) List three things that you learned about Hindu culture from the features that appear before the selection. **(b)** Explain how knowing the **cultural context** in which the *Ramayana* was written helped you to understand it.

Vocabulary

© **Acquisition and Use** Write a sentence about each of the following situations by using a word from page 1106.

1. a building with peeling paint, a sagging door, and a broken fence

2. a successful lawyer who is also very spiritual

3. a scientist's most difficult theory

4. a girl who is excited about winning a soccer game

5. someone who is concerned about his opponents in an election

6. a leader who leaves her political party

Word Study Use the context of the sentences and what you know about the **Latin suffix -*tude*** to explain your answer to each question.

1. Is there a large crowd if a *multitude* of fans greet the author?

2. If you like *solitude*, would you like reading in a deserted library?

Word Study

The **Latin suffix -*tude*** means "condition of" or "quality of."

Apply It Explain how the suffix -*tude* contributes to the meanings of these words. Consult a dictionary if necessary.
aptitude
fortitude
latitude

Integrated Language Skills

from **Sundiata: An Epic of Old Mali** • **Rama's Initiation** from the **Ramayana**

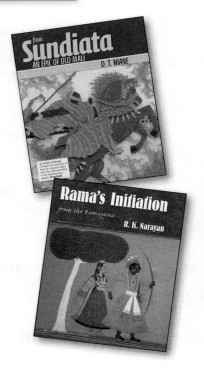

Conventions: Complex and Compound-Complex Sentences

- An **independent clause** contains a subject and verb and can stand alone as a complete sentence.

- A **subordinate clause** has a subject and verb but cannot stand alone as a complete sentence. It includes a subordinating conjunction such as *while, although, when, after* or *because.*

A **complex sentence** contains one independent clause and one or more subordinate clauses. **Compound-complex sentences** contain as least one subordinate clause and at least two independent clauses.

In these examples, the independent clauses are underlined once and the subordinate clauses are underlined twice.

Complex: After reading about knights, Don Quixote became a knight.

Complex: Sancho Panza was a simple peasant, although Don Quixote called Panza his squire.

Compound-complex: When Cervantes wrote about Don Quixote, the age of knighthood was over, and Spain had become a power.

Practice A Identify each sentence as complex or compound-complex. Indicate which clauses are independent and which are subordinate.

1. Although he was born to a king, Mari Djata had a difficult childhood, which made his mother sad.

2. When the king was about to die, he called Mari Djata to him, and he spoke as if the child were an adult.

3. When Mari Djata could not walk, his mother was worried, and her enemies were cruel.

© **Reading Application** In the excerpt from *Sundiata: An Epic of Old Mali*, find an example of a complex and a compound-complex sentence.

Practice B Use each phrase below and create either a complex or compound-complex sentence. You may add words to the phrase if necessary.

1. the boy was chosen for a journey (complex)

2. the sage became angry at the king (compound-complex)

3. the king was protective of his two sons (complex)

4. who went on to become a hero (compound-complex)

© **Writing Application** Write a simple sentence about the painting on page 1111. Add a subordinate clause to make it a complex sentence. Then, add another independent clause to make it a compound-complex sentence.

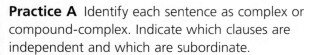

PH **WRITING COACH** | Further instruction and practice are available in *Prentice Hall Writing Coach.*

Writing

Informative Text The main characters in these two stories perform heroic feats. Write a **newspaper report** on the events at the end of the selection you read. First, take notes in which you identify main characters and outline key story events. As you draft, include the following elements:

- a catchy headline, subheadings, or illustrations
- concise information on *who, what, where, when, how,* and *why*
- believable quotations from participants and onlookers
- comments on the significance of the events

After finishing your draft, use a computer's publishing software or a graphic program to design your report. Choose readable headline and text fonts and set the news report in a double-column layout.

Grammar Application Use a variety of correctly structured sentence types in your report, including complex and compound-complex.

Writing Workshop: *Work in Progress*

Prewriting for a Technical Document Use the Task List from your writing portfolio to create an outline. Fill in and briefly describe additional steps that are necessary to accomplish the task. Save the outline in your writing portfolio.

Common Core State Standards

L.9-10.1.b; W.9-10.2, W.9-10.2.b, W.9-10.6; SL.9-10.1
[For the full wording of the standards, see page 1090.]

Use this prewriting activity to prepare for the **Writing Workshop** on page 1146.

Speaking and Listening

Comprehension and Collaboration With two classmates, present an **improvised dialogue** about one of the following situations:

- A queen of Mali, her son, a rival queen, and a sage discuss an insult the rival queen delivered to the queen.
- An Indian king, his son, and a sage consult about venturing forth against the demons of the world.

Apply what you have learned about West African or Hindu culture, and be sure that characters speak in a manner suited to their positions.

- As your group brainstorms for ideas, have one group member take notes. Then, use these notes to draft your dialogue.
- Take ten minutes to prepare and ten minutes for the presentation.
- When presenting, make eye contact with the audience and vary your speaking volume to emphasize key words.

PHLit Online!
www.PHLitOnline.com
- Interactive graphic organizers
- Grammar tutorial
- Interactive journals

Test Practice: Reading

Analyze Cultural Context

Fiction Selection

Directions: *Read the selection. Then, answer the questions.*

Logane lifted the small torch. Darkness surrounded him ahead and behind the small circle of light as he crawled through the damp cave. At last he reached the open cavern. The dim lamplight revealed paintings on the walls—horses, bison, woolly mammoths: the spirits of animals hunted by Logane's people. The flickering flame made the animals seem to move. Logane paused, overwhelmed by the power of the spirits. At last, he removed the stone pots from his skin bag. Each pot contained a different color—black, red, yellow—mixed with animal fat. Logane touched the paint with his brushes, twigs whose ends had been pounded to fine threads. Hunters of Logane's clan were getting ready for the great hunt before the long winter. Logane had to renew the herds through his painting. Only that would ensure success in the hunt.

1. Which of the following questions is answered in this passage?

   A. Where and when did Logane's people live?
   B. What was an important source of food for Logane's community?
   C. What gods did Logane's community worship?
   D. How competitive were the members of Logane's community?

2. The details in this passage suggest that, in this culture, cave paintings are considered—

   A. necessary for survival because they lead to a successful hunt.
   B. a historical record of the accomplishments of the community.
   C. valuable ways to teach young people myths and legends.
   D. important for their beauty alone.

3. What does the passage show about cultural practices of Logane's people?

   A. They lived deep inside caves.
   B. They painted animals for enjoyment.
   C. They hunted in caves.
   D. They believed in animal spirits.

4. Which statement *best* portrays the life of Logane's people?

   A. They were prehistoric hunters.
   B. They were highly skilled artists.
   C. They were brave explorers.
   D. They were shy cave dwellers.

Writing for Assessment

Based on the details in this passage, make a list of three values you believe are important in this culture. Write a paragraph in which you explain how you reached your conclusions.

Nonfiction Selection

Directions: *Read the selection. Then, answer the questions.*

The prehistoric people called "Cro-Magnon" were the first known people to practice art. Cro-Magnons were early modern humans who lived in caves and rock shelters throughout Spain and France from 35,000 years ago to about 10,000 years ago. Many of the rock shelters and caves show signs of habitation over long periods of time. Cro-Magnon people carved and sculpted figures of animals as well as humans. The Cro-Magnons also created beautiful cave paintings of animals, which probably related to their ritual beliefs and practices. Cro-Magnon art is highly sophisticated, showing that they were not amateurs but had long been experimenting with creating art in various mediums. They decorated their weapons and tools as well.

1. Which question about Cro-Magnon culture is *not* answered by this passage?

   A. Who created art before the Cro-Magnons did?

   B. Where did Cro-Magnons live?

   C. Why did Cro-Magnons decorate their weapons and tools?

   D. What types of art did Cro-Magnons create?

2. Based on this passage, what could you conclude about the lifestyle of Cro-Magnons?

   A. They had enough surplus food and time to create art.

   B. They were all highly skilled hunters.

   C. They were primitive people who feared animals.

   D. They appreciated music.

3. Cro-Magnons lived in Europe for about 25,000 years. Based on this and other details in the passage, what do you think this indicates about their culture?

   A. Their culture was the only one in Europe at the time.

   B. Cro-Magnon culture was constantly changing.

   C. Cro-Magnon culture was relatively stable over a long period of time.

   D. They were bloodthirsty, powerful, and able to drive out other culture groups.

4. Based on this passage, one can infer that the Cro-Magnon people—

   A. believed animals were for food only.

   B. placed a high value on animals.

   C. worshiped animals as gods.

   D. used animals for food and clothing.

Writing for Assessment

Connecting Across Texts

What details in the second passage might lead you to conclude that Logane is one of the Cro-Magnon people? Write a detailed paragraph in which you support your answer.

www.PHLitOnline.com
- Online practice
- Instant feedback

Reading for Information

Analyzing Expository Texts

Interview

Public Document

© Common Core State Standards

Reading Informational Text
5. Analyze in detail how an author's ideas or claims are developed and refined by particular sentences, paragraphs, or larger portions of a text.

Language
4.b. Identify and correctly use patterns of word changes that indicate different meanings or parts of speech.
6. Acquire and use accurately general academic and domain-specific words and phrases sufficient for reading, writing, speaking, and listening at the college and career readiness level; demonstrate independence in gathering vocabulary knowledge when considering a word or phrase important to comprehension or expression.

Writing
2.e. Establish and maintain a formal style and objective tone while attending to the norms and conventions of the discipline in which they are writing.
4. Produce clear and coherent writing in which the development, organization, and style are appropriate to task, purpose, and audience. *(Timed Writing)*

Reading Skill: Generate Questions

To better understand the ideas and claims in informational texts, read actively and engage with the text by **generating questions.** First, preview the text to get a general overview of its content. Formulate questions about the claims and ideas you observe. As you read more closely, look for answers to those questions. Notice where you find the answers and whether the author has devoted specific paragraphs or sections to the development of certain ideas. Evaluate the logic of that organization and note whether you have additional questions about the issues presented in the text. Use a chart like this one to help you generate questions.

What I Know	What I Learned	Relevant Questions
You need a high school diploma to become a firefighter.	A college degree is required for some firefighting positions.	What additional education and training is necessary to advance in a firefighting career?

Content-Area Vocabulary

These words appear in the selections that follow. You may also encounter them in other content-area texts.

- **paramedic** (par´ ə med´ ik) *n.* person who gives medical treatment at the scene of an emergency

- **hydraulic** (hī drô´ lik) *adj.* operated by the pressure of water or other liquids in motion

- **simulates** (sim´ yoo lāts) *v.* acts like, looks like; imitates

Careers in Science

Interviews with science professionals

Interview

Features:

- background information about the guest
- a discussion between a host and a guest
- a series of questions and answers
- text written for a general or specific audience

Firefighter

The Science Teacher focuses on success stories this month and Denise Dierich has one of her own. With an innate interest in the dynamic nature of life, Denise forged a unique career path. From biochemistry and teaching, to firefighting and paramedics, her love of learning constantly yields new challenges and rewards as she provides a vital service to her community.

This section might lead you to generate questions about the lives of firefighters working 24-hour shifts: *How many days a week do they work? Can they rest while on duty?*

1. What inspired you to become involved in your career endeavors?

Growing up in Alaska, I appreciated the value of understanding the biological world. Later, in high school, a biology teacher extended this interest through various field trips and lab demonstrations—science became more than just words in a book. As an undergraduate, I was drawn to biochemistry because it offered explanations of natural phenomena and how organisms work. (Denise has a bachelor's degree in biochemistry from University of California, Santa Cruz, as well as a secondary teaching credential in biology and chemistry.) Although the science itself was fascinating, I found the lab work to be tedious so I pursued a career in science education, which was anything but boring. Just as teaching is service-oriented, so is being a firefighter. I left teaching to become a firefighter because it also incorporates many of my ambitions and interests and provides the opportunity to help people and communities.

As I worked on aid calls (when a fire engine accompanies a paramedic unit), I realized I could apply my science background and enthusiasm for learning by becoming a paramedic.

2. Please describe a typical day at work.

We work 24-hour shifts. The day starts with an informal report from the previous crew involving issues with equipment and potential problems. Rig checks are performed to ensure the apparatus is in proper working order (i.e., fuel, fluids, equipment, gear, and lights). Next, our captain assigns training and duties for the day, which consist of hose evolutions, emergency medical technician practice scenarios, pump operation, and hydraulic system exercises, for example. Continual training is essential; because the job is so multifaceted, skills and knowledge must be constantly reinforced. Training may be interrupted if there is a call, which could be a medical or fire emergency, a motor vehicle accident, a fire alarm, a hazardous spill, or a public assist request. We respond to a variety of situations. Each day, and every call, is different.

3. How do you use your science background in the fire service?

The problem-solving skills developed through my science education have been very beneficial in my career as a firefighter. No fire or aid call is the same; we have to constantly evaluate situations and react appropriately. My background in biochemistry and study skills acquired through college science classes have been instrumental in preparing for the academic portion of the paramedic program—a commitment that involves several courses and certification tests.

When previewing, you might scan this bold-face question and want to find out what kind of science background could be used in the fire service. When reading, you would discover the answer.

4. What advice would you give to an interested high school student?

The more education obtained, the better—it will only help a career in the fire service. The only specific requirement for eligibility is a high school diploma; however, a bachelor's degree shows self-discipline and the ability to complete tasks. Firefighting has become a very popular and competitive field—600 people tested for five openings in our last round.

For some areas of advancement, a bachelor's degree is required (for example, a college degree is needed to become a battalion chief). Also, most firefighting tests include a fitness component, which can be quite demanding.

Investigate the possibilities for a ride-along with local fire departments. Many firefighters and paramedics allow civilians to ride a medic unit or engine for part of a day. Consider joining a volunteer fire department; they will provide training and valuable experience. Some volunteer districts even provide housing at the station and help finance college tuitions.

When reading, you might note that you'd like to research the fitness component of the firefighting test: *What is involved? Why is it considered demanding?*

5. Is there anything else you would like to share?

One of the things I like best about this job is that, like science, it is dynamic. There are always new things to learn. The best preparation is to enjoy learning. Firefighting is an honorable field that is respected by the community, and I enjoy the camaraderie and teamwork that are essential to the job.

Features:

- information published for the benefit of the public
- the name of a government depart-ment prominently displayed to show it is an official document
- current and updated content
- text written for a specific audience

CITY OF PERRY FIRE DEPARTMENT

THE GEORGIA CERTIFIED FIREFIGHTERS PHYSICAL AGILITY TEST

The following series of tasks comprise the approved physical agility test as specified in OCGA 25-4-8(a) (5). All of the nine tasks must be completed in seven minutes or less.

This note might prompt you to question how many times applicants may retake the test if they fail initially.

━ TASKS ━

1. STAIR CLIMB

The candidate, given a rolled 50-foot section of 2½" diameter hose and a multistory structure, shall carry the hose up one flight of stairs to the second floor and then raise a 2½" hose through the upstairs window using a utility rope. This exercise simulates the fire ground operation of carrying a section of fire hose to an upper level of a structure.

2. LADDER EXTENSION

The candidate, given a 24-foot aluminum extension ladder in a securely supported vertical position, must extend the fly section of the ladder to the top rung. The candidate must then lower the fly section in a con-trolled fashion to the starting position. This exercise simulates the fire ground operation of extending and lowering the fly section of a ground ladder as to reach an upper story of a structure.

3. HOSE ADVANCE

The candidate, given a charged (75 PSI nozzle pressure) 150-foot 1½" or 1¾" hoseline, shall pick up the nozzle and advance the pressurized hoseline for a distance of 100 feet. After reaching the destination, the candidate shall lay the hose on the ground and use a hose clamp, approximately 5 feet from the nozzle, to secure the hose. This exercise simulates the fire ground operation of advancing a charged hoseline to a fire.

4. BOX FAN CARRY

The candidate, given a gas generated box fan, shall use proper lifting techniques, and carry the box fan for a distance of 50 feet. After reaching the destination, the candidate shall set the box fan on the ground. This exercise simulates carrying bulky objects on the fire scene, to and from the structure.

5. UPPER SLED HIT

The candidate, given a 12-pound sledgehammer, shall hit an object placed on top of the sled for a distance of 2 feet. The candidate then shall go to the other side of the sled and hit the same object in the opposite direction 2 feet. This exercise simulates using tools on the fire ground in a standing position using upper torso strength.

6. CONE COURSE

The candidate shall walk through a cone course that is approximately 50 feet in length.

> Most items in the list include an explanation that answers questions about the purpose of each task.

7. VENTILATION EXERCISE

Given a fire department axe and standing on level ground with a target (such as a wooden pallet) placed on the ground in front of them, the candidate must strike the target with the axe 20 times. The axe must be brought completely over the shoulder to simulate a chopping motion as if cutting a ventilation hole.

8. LADDER REMOVAL/REPLACEMENT

The candidate, given a 14-foot roof ladder placed in a horizontal position at a height of 5 feet and with the ladder rungs in a vertical position, shall lift the ladder from its support and place it on the ground then pick it up and return it to its original position. This exercise simulates the fire ground operation of removing from and replacing a ladder on its mounting bracket on the fire apparatus.

9. RESCUE DRAG

The candidate, given a 165-pound dummy on a level paved surface, shall drag the dummy a distance of 50 feet. This exercise simulates the fire ground operation of an emergency removal from a hazardous area of a team member or victim who may be rendered incapacitated.

Expository Texts

1. Key Ideas and Details **(a)** Make a list of **questions** you generated after previewing the interview and public document. List at least three questions for each text. **(b)** Identify the answers you found for each question, and explain where in each text you found them. **(c)** Explain how the ideas are organized in each text.

Content-Area Vocabulary

2. (a) Using the base word *simulate,* explain how the addition of the suffix *-tion* alters the word's meaning and part of speech. **(b)** Do the same for the suffix *-or.* **(c)** Use the base word and the newly created words in separate sentences that show their meanings.

⏱ Timed Writing

Explanatory Text: Letter

> **Format and Audience**
> The prompt directs you to write a formal letter. Format your letter correctly, and use appropriately formal language and tone.

Write a formal letter to a firefighter in which you request additional information about firefighting as a career. In your letter, cite specific passages from the interview and public document, and ask questions based on those passages.
(35 minutes)

> **Academic Vocabulary**
> When you *cite* a passage, you refer to it as an example.

5-Minute Planner

Complete these steps before you begin to write:

1. Read the prompt carefully, noting highlighted key words.

2. Review the interview and public document to identify aspects of firefighting that interest you. Make a list of questions that are not answered in either of the texts. **TIP** To help organize your notes, create a two-column chart. List your questions in the left column of the chart. In the right column, list the passages that deal with the topics of your questions.

3. Decide how you will structure your letter. For example, you might include a brief introductory paragraph in which you explain that you are researching firefighting as a career and are requesting information on the subject. Make your request using a friendly but formal tone.

4. Prepare a quick outline, based on the structure you have chosen for your letter. Then, refer to your outline and your notes as you write.

Comparing Archetypal Narrative Patterns

Archetypal narrative patterns are storytelling structures found in the literature of cultures around the world. These patterns often appear in stories from the oral tradition, such as folk tales, fairy tales, and myths. Like familiar routines, patterns make the stories easier to remember and retell. Common archetypal narrative patterns include the following:

- a series of tests that a character must pass
- a quest or task a character must perform
- secondary characters that guide and help the hero or heroine
- characters, events, or objects that come in threes
- a greedy, cruel, or jealous relative who behaves unfairly
- a hero who triumphs over stronger forces through cleverness or virtue
- a just end that rewards good or punishes evil

These narrative patterns may seem very familiar to you. Although they originate in folk literature, archetypal structures continue to shape modern stories in all genres. Movies, television shows, and video games are often built on such archetypes. Some psychological theories hold that the existence of archetypal patterns in literature from every era and culture shows essential truths about how human beings understand and process information.

As you read the selections, analyze the narrative patterns in each story using a chart like the one shown.

Story Detail	Archetypal Pattern
three sisters	characters that come in threes
help from the birds	

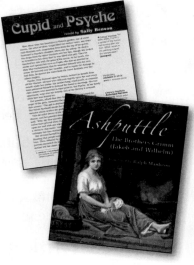

Common Core State Standards

Reading Literature

2. Determine a theme or central idea of a text and analyze in detail its development over the course of the text, including how it emerges and is shaped and refined by specific details; provide an objective summary of the text.

5. Analyze how an author's choices concerning how to structure a text, order events within in it, and manipulate time create such effects as mystery, tension, or surprise.

Writing

2. Write informative/explanatory texts to examine and convey complex ideas, concepts, and information clearly and accurately through the effective selection, organization, and analysis of content.

2.c. Use appropriate and varied transitions to link the major sections of the text, create cohesion, and clarify the relationships among complex ideas and concepts. *(Timed Writing)*

PHLit Online!
www.PHLitOnline.com

- Vocabulary flashcards
- Interactive journals
- More about the authors
- Selection audio
- Interactive graphic organizers

Can anyone be a *hero?*

Writing About the Big Question

In both "Cupid and Psyche" and "Ashputtle," the main characters face unusual obstacles. As you read the selections, you can decide if their actions in the face of these challenges are heroic. Use this sentence starter to develop your ideas about the Big Question.

In the face of an unusual obstacle, a true hero would show **attributes** such as _____ and _____.

Meet the Authors

Lucius Apuleius (ca. A.D. 124–170)
Sally Benson (1900–1972)
Retellers of "Cupid and Psyche"

Although the tale of Cupid and Psyche goes back to Greek mythology, the best-known version is in the *Metamorphoses* by the ancient Roman writer Lucius Apuleius (lōō′ shəs ap′ yōō lē′ əs). This work is often considered the world's first novel.

A Modern Reteller Sally Benson won fame with her short stories. Her collection *Meet Me in St. Louis,* based on her own Missouri childhood, was adapted as a movie musical.

Jakob Grimm (1785–1863)
Wilhelm Grimm (1786–1859)
Retellers of "Ashputtle"

Born in the German state of Hesse, Jakob and Wilhelm Grimm grew up in poverty after their father died. Although both studied law, they were most interested in language and literature. Eventually both brothers found work as librarians.

A National Literature The brothers began collecting tales that people told in Hesse and neighboring places. They also wrote books on literature, and Jakob made contributions to linguistics. Today, they are most remembered for the folktales they preserved, including "Rumpelstiltskin" and "Snow White."

Cupid

There once lived a king and queen who had three daughters. The two elder daughters were beautiful, but the youngest daughter, Psyche,[1] was the loveliest maiden in the whole world. The fame of her beauty was so great that strangers from neighboring countries came in crowds to admire her, paying her the homage which is only due Venus[2] herself. In fact, Venus found her altars deserted, as men turned their devotion to the exquisite young girl. People sang her praises as she walked the streets, and strewed chaplets and flowers before her.

This adulation infuriated Venus. Shaking her silken locks in indignation, she exclaimed, "Am I then to be eclipsed by a mortal girl? In vain did that royal shepherd whose judgment was approved by Jupiter himself give me the palm of beauty over my illustrious rivals, Minerva and Juno.[3] I will give this Psyche cause to repent of so unlawful a beauty."

She complained to her son, Cupid, and led him to the land where Psyche lived, so that he could see for himself the insults the girl unconsciously heaped upon his mother. "My dear son," said Venus, "punish that beauty. Give thy mother a revenge as sweet as her injuries are great. Infuse into the bosom of that haughty girl a passion for some low, mean, unworthy being, so that she may reap a shame as great as her present joy and triumph."

---

1. **Psyche** (sī´ kē) a beautiful princess in Roman mythology.
2. **Venus** (vē´ nəs) the Roman goddess of love and beauty.
3. **royal shepherd. . . Minerva** (mi nur´ və) **and Juno** (jōō´ nō) In Greek and Roman mythology, Paris, a prince who lived as a shepherd, was called to judge who was most beautiful of three goddesses: Juno, queen of the gods; Minerva, goddess of wisdom; or Venus, goddess of love.

Now, there were two fountains in Venus's garden, one of sweet waters, the other of bitter. Cupid filled two amber vases, one from each fountain and, suspending them from the top of his quiver, hastened to Psyche's chamber, where she lay asleep. He shed a few drops from the bitter fountain over her lips, though she looked so beautiful in her sleep that he was filled with pity. Then he touched her side with the point of his arrow. At the touch, she awoke and opened her eyes on Cupid, who was so startled by their blue enchantment that he wounded himself with his own arrow. He hovered over her, invisible, and to repair the damage he had done, he poured the water from the sweet fountain over her silken ringlets.

Psyche, thus frowned upon by Venus, derived no benefit from all her charms. All eyes were still cast eagerly upon her and every mouth spoke her praise, but neither king, royal youth, or common man presented himself to demand her hand in marriage. Her two elder sisters were married to royal princes, but Psyche, in her lonely apartment, wept over her beauty, sick of the flattery it aroused, while love was denied her.

Her parents, afraid that they had unwittingly incurred the anger of the gods, consulted the oracle of Apollo,[4] and received this answer: "The girl is destined for the bride of no mortal lover. Her future husband awaits her on the top of the mountain. He is a monster whom neither the gods nor men can resist."

This dreadful decree of the oracle filled all the people with dismay, and her parents abandoned themselves to grief. But Psyche said, "Why, my dear parents, do you now lament me? You should rather have grieved when the people showered undeserved honors upon me and with one voice called me 'Venus.' I now perceive I am a victim to that name. I submit. Lead me to that rock to which my unhappy fate has destined me."

She dressed herself in gorgeous robes, and her beauty was so dazzling that people turned away as it was more than they could bear. Then, followed by wailing and lamenting crowds, she and her parents ascended the mountain. On the summit, her father and mother left her alone, and returned home in tears.

---

4. **oracle** (ôr´ ə kəl) **of Apollo** (ə päl´ ō) Apollo was the Greek and Roman god of light, music, and medicine. An oracle was a person who revealed the will of the gods in answer to people's questions.

◀ **Critical Viewing** For some artists, Psyche is a symbol of the human soul striving after wisdom. Which details in this painting support this interpretation? **[Interpret]**

Literary Analysis
Archetypal Narrative Patterns Which archetypal pattern does the fact that there are three sisters illustrate?

Vocabulary
adulation (a´ jσō lā´ shən) *n.* excessive praise

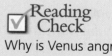
Reading
Check
Why is Venus angry with Psyche?

While Psyche stood on the ridge of the mountain, panting with fear and sobbing aloud, the gentle Zephyrus[5] raised her from the earth and bore her with an easy motion into a flowery dale. There she lay down on a grassy bank and fell asleep. She awoke refreshed, and saw near by a pleasant grove of tall and stately trees. She entered it, and discovered a fountain sending forth clear and crystal waters, and near it stood a magnificent palace that was too stupendous to have been the work of mortal hands. Drawn by admiration and wonder, she walked through the huge doors. Inside, golden pillars supported the vaulted roof, and the walls were hung with delightful paintings. She wandered through the empty rooms marveling at what she saw, when suddenly a voice addressed her. "Sovereign lady," it said, "all that you see is yours. We whose voices you hear are your servants and shall obey all your commands with the utmost care and diligence. Retire, therefore, to your chamber and repose on your bed of down, and when you see fit, repair to the bath. Supper awaits you in the adjoining alcove when it pleases you to take your seat there."

Psyche listened with amazement, and, going to her room, she lay down and rested. Then, after a refreshing bath, she went to the alcove, where a table wheeled itself into the room without any visible aid. It was covered with the finest delicacies and the most wonderful wines. There even was music from invisible performers.

She had not yet seen her destined husband. He came only in the hours of darkness and fled before dawn, but his accents were full of love and inspired a like passion in her. She often begged him to stay and let her behold him, but he would not consent. On the contrary, he charged her to make no attempt to see him, for it was his pleasure, for the best of reasons, to remain concealed. "Why should you wish to behold me?" he asked. "Have you any doubt of my love? If you saw me, perhaps you would fear me, perhaps adore me. But all I ask of you is to love me. I would rather have you love me as an equal than adore me as a god."

This reasoning satisfied Psyche for a time and she lived quite happily alone in the huge palace. But at length she thought of her

---

5. Zephyrus (zef´ ə rəs) in Greek mythology, god of the west wind.

parents who were in ignorance of her fate, and of her sisters with whom she wished to share the delights of her new home. These thoughts preyed on her mind and made her think of her splendid mansion as a prison. When her husband came one night, she told him of her distress, and at last drew from him an unwilling consent that her sisters should be brought to see her.

So, calling Zephyrus, she told him of her husband's command, and he soon brought them across the mountain down to their sister's valley. They embraced her, and Psyche's eyes filled with tears of joy. "Come," she said, "enter my house and refresh yourselves." Taking them by their hands, she led them into her golden palace and committed them to the care of her numerous train[6] of attendant voices, to refresh themselves in her baths and at her table, and to show them all her treasures. The sight of all these splendid things filled her sisters with envy, and they resented the thought that she possessed such splendor which far exceeded anything they owned.

They asked her numberless questions, and begged her to tell them what sort of person her husband was. Psyche replied that he was a beautiful youth who generally spent the daytime in hunting upon the mountains. The sisters, not satisfied with this reply, soon made her confess that she had never seen him. They then proceeded to fill her bosom with dire suspicions. "Call to mind," they said, "the Pythian oracle[7] that declared that you were destined to marry a direful and tremendous monster. The inhabitants of this valley say that your husband is a terrible and monstrous serpent, who nourishes you for a while with dainties that he may by and by devour you. Take our advice. Provide yourself with a lamp and a sharp knife. Put them in concealment so that your husband may not discover them, and when he is sound asleep, slip out of bed, bring forth your lamp and see for yourself whether what they say is true or not. If it is, hesitate not to cut off the monster's head, and thereby recover your liberty."

Psyche resisted these persuasions as well as she could, but they did not fail to have their effect on her mind, and when her sisters were gone, their words and her own curiosity were too strong for her to resist. She prepared her lamp and a sharp knife, and hid them out of sight of her husband. When he had fallen into his first sleep, she silently arose, and uncovering her lamp beheld him. He lay there, the most beautiful and charming of the gods, with his golden ringlets wandering over his snowy neck and crimson cheek. On his shoulders were two dewy wings, whiter than snow, with shining feathers.

---

6. **train** (trān) *n.* group of followers, such as servants.
7. **Pythian** (pith´ ē ǝn) **oracle** oracle of Apollo, called Pythian after Python, the monstrous snake that Apollo killed.

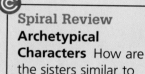

Spiral Review
Archetypical Characters How are the sisters similar to other antagonists found in literature?

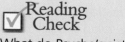

Reading Check

What do Psyche's sisters persuade her to do?

As she leaned over with the lamp to have a closer view of his face, a drop of burning oil fell on his shoulder, and made him wince with pain. He opened his eyes and fixed them full upon her. Then, without saying a word, he spread his white wings and flew out of the window. Psyche cried out and tried to follow him, falling from the window to the ground. Cupid, beholding her as she lay in the dust, stopped his flight for an instant and said, "O foolish Psyche! Is it thus you repay my love? After having disobeyed my mother's commands and made you my wife, will you think me a monster and cut off my head? But go. Return to your sisters whose advice you seem to think better than mine. I inflict no other punishment on you than to leave you forever. Love cannot dwell with suspicion."

He soared into the air, leaving poor Psyche prostrate on the ground.

When she recovered some degree of composure, she looked around her. The palace and gardens had vanished, and she found herself in an open field not far from the city where her sisters dwelt. She went to them and told them the whole story of her misfortune, at which, pretending to grieve, they inwardly rejoiced. "For now," they said, "he will perhaps choose one of us." With this idea, without saying a word of her intentions, each of them rose early the next morning and ascended the mountain and, having reached the top, called upon Zephyrus to receive her and bear her to his lord. Then, leaping into space, and not being sustained by Zephyrus, they fell down the precipice and were dashed to pieces.

Psyche, meanwhile, wandered day and night, without food or rest, in search of her husband. One day, seeing a lofty mountain in the distance, she sighed and said to herself, "Perhaps my love, my lord, inhabits there."

On the mountain top was a temple and she no sooner entered it than she saw heaps of corn, some in loose ears and some in sheaves,[8] with mingled ears of barley. Scattered about lay sickles and rakes, and all the instruments of harvest, without order, as if thrown carelessly out of the weary reapers' hands in the sultry hours of the day.

Psyche put an end to this unseemly confusion by separating and sorting everything to its proper place and kind, believing that she ought to neglect none of the gods, but endeavor by her piety to engage them all in her behalf. The holy Ceres,[9] whose temple it was, finding her so religiously employed, spoke to her, "O Psyche, truly worthy of our pity, though I cannot shield you from the frowns of Venus, yet I can teach you how to best allay her displeasure. Go then, and voluntarily surrender yourself to her, and try by modesty and submission to win her forgiveness, and perhaps her favor will restore you to the husband you have lost."

Literary Analysis
Archetypal Narrative Patterns In what other stories have you encountered a mysterious building like the palace?

Vocabulary
allay (a lā´) v. relieve; lessen; calm

---

8. **sheaves** (shēvz) n. bundles of stalks of grain.
9. **Ceres** (sir´ ēz´) Roman goddess of farming.

Psyche obeyed the commands of Ceres and journeyed to the temple of Venus. Venus received her in a fury of anger. "Most undutiful and faithless of servants," she said, "do you at last remember that you really have a mistress? Or have you come to see your sick husband, yet laid up with the wound given him by his loving wife? You are so ill-favored and disagreeable that the only way you can merit your lover must be by dint of industry and diligence. I will make trial of your housewifery."

She ordered Psyche to be led to the storehouse of her temple, where a great quantity of wheat, barley, millet, beans and lentils, which was used as food for her pigeons, lay scattered about the floors. Then Venus said, "Take and separate all these grains into their proper parcels, and see that you get it done before evening."

Psyche, in consternation over the enormous task, sat stupid and silent. While she sat despairing, Cupid stirred up the little ant, a native of the fields, to take compassion on her. The leader of the ant-hill, followed by whole hosts of his six-legged subjects, went to work and sorted each grain to its parcel. And when all was done, the ants vanished out of sight.

At twilight, Venus returned from the banquet of the gods, crowned with roses. Seeing the task done, she exclaimed, "This is no work of yours, wicked one, but his, whom to your own and his misfortune you have enticed." So saying, she threw her a piece of black bread for her supper and went away.

Next morning Venus ordered Psyche to be called and said to her, "Behold yonder grove which stretches along the margin of the water. There you will find sheep feeding without a shepherd, with gold-shining fleeces on their backs. Go, fetch me a sample of that precious wool from every one of their fleeces."

Psyche obediently went to the river side, prepared to do her best to execute the command. But the river god inspired the reeds with harmonious murmurs, which seemed to say, "O maiden, severely tried, tempt not the dangerous flood, nor venture among formidable rams on the other side, for as long as they are under the influence of the rising sun they burn with a cruel rage to destroy mortals with their sharp horns or rude teeth. But when the noontide sun has driven the cattle to the shade, and the serene spirit of the flood has lulled them to rest, you may then cross in safety, and you will find the woolly gold sticking to the bushes and the trunks of the trees."

She followed the compassionate river god's instructions and soon returned to Venus with her arms full of the golden fleece. Venus, in a rage, cried, "I know very well it is by none of your own doings that you have succeeded in this task. And I am not satisfied yet that you have any capacity to make yourself useful. But I have another task for you. Here, take this box, and go your way to the infernal shade

Reading Check
What does Cupid do after Psyche exposes his identity?

and give this box to Proserpina[10] and say, 'My mistress, Venus, desires you to send her a little of your beauty, for in tending her sick son, she has lost some of her own.' Be not too long on your errand, for I must paint myself with it to appear at the circle of gods and goddesses this evening."

Psyche was now sure that her destruction was at hand, being obliged to go with her own feet down to the deathly regions of Erebus.[11] So as not to delay, she went to the highest tower prepared to hurl herself headlong from it down to the shades below. But a voice from the tower said to her, "Why, poor unlucky girl, dost thou design to put an end to thy days in so dreadful a manner? And what cowardice makes thee sink under this last danger who hast been so miraculously supported in all thy former perils?"

Then the voice told her how she might reach the realms of Pluto[12] by way of a certain cave, and how to avoid the perils of the road, how to pass by Cerberus,[13] the three-headed dog, and prevail on Charon,[14] the ferryman, to take her across the black river and bring her back again. And the voice added, "When Proserpina has given you the box filled with her beauty, of all things this is chiefly to be observed by you, that you never once open or look into the box, nor allow your curiosity to pry into the treasure of the beauty of the goddesses."

Psyche, encouraged by this advice, obeyed in all things, and traveled to the kingdom of Pluto. She was admitted to the palace of Proserpina, and without accepting the delicate seat or delicious banquet that was offered her, but content with coarse bread for her food, she delivered her message from Venus. Presently the box was returned to her, shut, and filled with the precious commodity. She returned the way she came, happy to see the light of day once more.

Having got so far successfully through her dangerous task, a desire seized her to examine the contents of the box. "What," she said to herself, "shall I, the carrier of this divine beauty, not take the least bit to put on my cheeks to appear to more advantage in the eyes of my beloved husband!" She carefully opened the box, and found nothing there of any beauty at all, but an infernal and truly Stygian[15] sleep, which, being set free from its prison, took possession of her. She fell down in the road, unconscious, without sense or motion.

---

10. **infernal shade . . . Proserpina** (prō sur´ pi nə) In Greek and Roman mythology, the dead inhabit an "infernal shade," or dark region under the earth. Proserpina, daughter of Ceres, is the wife of Pluto, the god who rules this region.

11. **Erebus** (er´ ə bəs) in Greek mythology, the place under the earth through which the dead pass before entering the underworld.

12. **Pluto** (plōōt´ ō) Roman god of the underworld.

13. **Cerberus** (sur´ bər əs) in Greek and Roman mythology, the three-headed dog guarding the entrance to the underworld.

14. **Charon** (ker´ ən) in Greek mythology, the ferryman who carried the dead over the river Styx into the underworld.

15. **Stygian** (stij´ ē ən) *adj.* of the river Styx, a mythological river crossed by the dead on their way to the underworld.

Cupid had recovered from his wound and was no longer able to bear the absence of his beloved Psyche. He slipped through the smallest crack in the window of his chamber and flew to the spot where Psyche lay. He gathered up the sleep from her body and closed it again in the box. Then he waked Psyche with a light touch from one of his arrows.

"Again," he said, "hast thou almost perished by the same curiosity. But now perform exactly the task imposed on you by my mother, and I will take care of the rest."

Swift as lightning, he left the earth and penetrated the heights of heaven. Here he presented himself before Jupiter with his supplication. The god lent a favoring ear, and pleaded the cause of the lovers so earnestly with Venus that he won her consent. Then he sent Mercury to bring Psyche up to the heavenly assemblage, and when she arrived, he handed her a cup of ambrosia[16] and said, "Drink this, Psyche, and be immortal. Nor shall Cupid ever break away from the knot in which he is tied, but these nuptials[17] shall be perpetual."

Psyche became at last united to Cupid forever.

---

16. **ambrosia** (am brō′ zhə) *n.* food of the gods.
17. **nuptials** (nup′ shəlz) *n.* wedding.

Critical Thinking

Cite textual evidence to support your responses.

1. **Key Ideas and Details (a)** What reason does Venus give for sending Cupid to Psyche? **(b) Compare and Contrast:** Compare her plan with its actual outcome.

2. **Key Ideas and Details (a) Summarize:** What tasks does Venus require Psyche to perform? **(b) Connect:** In the third task, in what way does Psyche repeat her earlier mistake with Cupid?

3. **Key Ideas and Details (a) Interpret:** What does Cupid mean when he says, "Love cannot dwell with suspicion"? **(b) Draw Conclusions:** What lesson does the story suggest about love? Explain.

4. **Integration of Knowledge and Ideas** Do you think that Psyche could be considered a hero? If your answer is *yes,* explain in what way you think she is heroic. If your answer is *no,* what do you think she could have done differently that would have made her a hero? *[Connect to the Big Question: Can anyone be a hero?]*

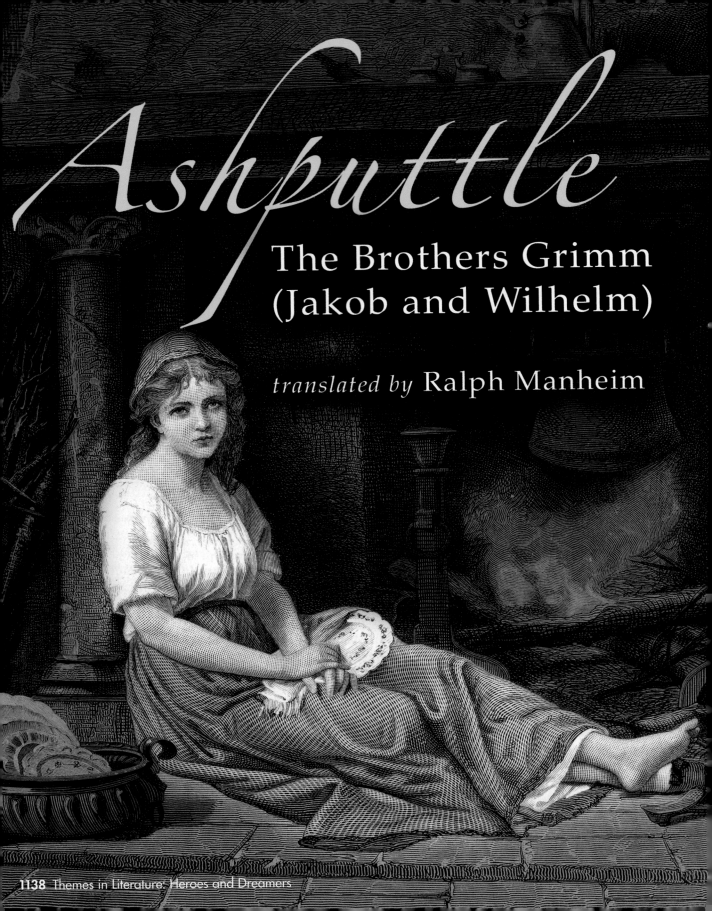

Ashputtle

The Brothers Grimm
(Jakob and Wilhelm)

translated by Ralph Manheim

A rich man's wife fell sick and, feeling that her end was near, she called her only daughter to her bedside and said: "Dear child, be good and say your prayers; God will help you, and I shall look down on you from heaven and always be with you." With that she closed her eyes and died. Every day the little girl went out to her mother's grave and wept, and she went on being good and saying her prayers. When winter came, the snow spread a white cloth over the grave, and when spring took it off, the man remarried.

His new wife brought two daughters into the house. Their faces were beautiful and lily-white, but their hearts were ugly and black. That was the beginning of a bad time for the poor stepchild. "Why should this silly goose sit in the parlor[1] with us?" they said. "People who want to eat bread must earn it. Get into the kitchen where you belong!" They took away her fine clothes and gave her an old gray dress and wooden shoes to wear. "Look at the haughty princess in her finery!" they cried and, laughing, led her to the kitchen. From then on she had to do all the work, getting up before daybreak, carrying water, lighting fires, cooking and washing. In addition the sisters did everything they could to plague her. They jeered at her and poured peas and lentils[2] into the ashes, so that she had to sit there picking them out. At night, when she was tired out with work, she had no bed to sleep in but had to lie in the ashes by the hearth. And they took to calling her Ashputtle because she always looked dusty and dirty.

One day when her father was going to the fair, he asked his two stepdaughters what he should bring them. "Beautiful dresses," said one. "Diamonds and pearls," said the other. "And you, Ashputtle. What would you like?" "Father," she said, "break off the first branch that brushes against your hat on your way home, and bring it to me." So he bought beautiful dresses, diamonds and pearls for his two stepdaughters, and on the way home, as he was riding through a copse,[3] a hazel branch brushed against him and knocked off his hat. So he broke off the branch and took it home with him. When he got home, he gave the stepdaughters what they had asked for, and gave Ashputtle the branch. After thanking him, she went to her mother's grave and planted the hazel sprig over it and cried so hard that her tears fell on the sprig and watered it. It grew and became a beautiful tree. Three times a day Ashputtle went and sat under it and wept and prayed. Each time a little white bird came and perched on the tree, and when Ashputtle made a wish the little bird threw down what she had wished for.

Now it so happened that the king arranged for a celebration. It was to go on for three days and all the beautiful girls in the

---

1. **parlor** (pär´ lər) n. room set aside for entertaining guests; living room.
2. **lentils** (lent´ 'lz) n. pea-like, edible seeds of the lentil, a plant in the pea family.
3. **copse** (käps) n. group of small trees growing thickly together.

◄ **Critical Viewing**
Based on this illustration, predict what Ashputtle's personality will be like in the story. **[Predict]**

Vocabulary
plague (pläg) v. pester; harass; torment
jeered (jird) v. made fun of

Literary Analysis
Archetypal Narrative Patterns What other stories do you know that feature a heroine faced with cruel relatives?

Reading Check

Describe the way that Ashputtle's stepsisters treat her.

kingdom were invited, in order that his son might choose a bride. When the two stepsisters heard they had been asked, they were delighted. They called Ashputtle and said: "Comb our hair, brush our shoes, and fasten our buckles. We're going to the wedding at the king's palace." Ashputtle obeyed, but she wept, for she too would have liked to go dancing, and she begged her stepmother to let her go. "You little sloven!"[4] said the stepmother. "How can you go to a wedding when you're all dusty and dirty? How can you go dancing when you have neither dress nor shoes?" But when Ashputtle begged and begged, the stepmother finally said: "Here, I've dumped a bowlful of lentils in the ashes. If you can pick them out in two hours, you may go." The girl went out the back door to the garden and cried out: "O tame little doves, O turtledoves, and all the birds under heaven, come and help me put

> the good ones in the pot,
> the bad ones in your crop."[5]

Two little white doves came flying through the kitchen window, and then came the turtledoves, and finally all the birds under heaven came flapping and fluttering and settled down by the ashes. The doves nodded their little heads and started in, peck peck peck peck, and all the others started in, peck peck peck peck, and they sorted out all the good lentils and put them in the bowl. Hardly an hour had passed before they finished and flew away. Then the girl brought the bowl to her stepmother, and she was happy, for she thought she'd be allowed to go to the wedding. But the stepmother said: "No, Ashputtle. You have nothing to wear and you don't know how to dance; the people would only laugh at you." When Ashputtle began to cry, the stepmother said: "If you can pick two bowlfuls of lentils out of the ashes in an hour, you may come." And she thought: "She'll never be able to do it." When she had dumped the two bowlfuls of lentils in the ashes, Ashputtle went out the back door to the garden and cried out: "O tame little doves, O turtledoves, and all the birds under heaven, come and help me put

> the good ones in the pot,
> the bad ones in your crop."

Then two little white doves came flying through the kitchen window, and then came the turtledoves, and finally all the birds under heaven came flapping and fluttering and settled down by the ashes. The doves nodded their little heads and started in, peck peck peck peck, and all the others started in, peck peck peck peck, and they sorted out all the good lentils and put them in the bowls.

Literary Analysis
Archetypal Narrative Patterns What task does Ashputtle's step-mother set for her?

Literary Analysis
Archetypal Narrative Patterns What does the fact that the birds help her suggest about Ashputtle's character?

---

4. **sloven** (sluv´ ən) *n.* dirty or untidy person.
5. **crop** (kräp) *n.* part of a bird's throat in which it stores food.

Before half an hour had passed, they had finished and they all flew away. Then the girl brought the bowls to her stepmother, and she was happy, for she thought she'd be allowed to go to the wedding. But her stepmother said: "It's no use. You can't come, because you have nothing to wear and you don't know how to dance. We'd only be ashamed of you." Then she turned her back and hurried away with her two proud daughters.

When they had all gone out, Ashputtle went to her mother's grave. She stood under the hazel tree and cried:

> "Shake your branches, little tree,
> Throw gold and silver down on me."

Whereupon the bird tossed down a gold and silver dress and slippers embroidered with silk and silver. Ashputtle slipped into the dress as fast as she could and went to the wedding. Her sisters and stepmother didn't recognize her. She was so beautiful in her golden dress that they thought she must be the daughter of some foreign king. They never dreamed it could be Ashputtle, for they thought she was sitting at home in her filthy rags, picking lentils out of the ashes. The king's son came up to her, took her by the hand and danced with her. He wouldn't dance with anyone else and he never let go her hand. When someone else asked for a dance, he said: "She is my partner."

She danced until evening, and then she wanted to go home. The king's son said: "I'll go with you, I'll see you home," for he wanted to find out whom the beautiful girl belonged to. But she got away from him and slipped into the dovecote.[6] The king's son waited until her father arrived, and told him the strange girl had slipped into the dovecote. The old man thought: "Could it be Ashputtle?" and he sent for an ax and a pick and broke into the dovecote, but there was no one inside. When they went indoors, Ashputtle was lying in the ashes in her filthy clothes and a dim oil lamp was burning on the chimney piece, for Ashputtle had slipped out the back end of the dovecote and run to the hazel tree. There she had taken off her fine clothes and put them on the grave, and the bird had taken them away. Then she had put her gray dress on again, crept into the kitchen and lain down in the ashes.

Next day when the festivities started in again and her parents and stepsisters had gone, Ashputtle went to the hazel tree and said:

---

6. **dovecote** (duv´ kōt´) *n.* small house with compartments for nesting birds.

▲ **Critical Viewing**
Name another fairy tale that this picture might illustrate. Explain. **[Connect]**

Reading Check

How does it come about that Ashputtle is able to attend the wedding?

> *"Shake your branches, little tree,*
> *Throw gold and silver down on me."*

Whereupon the bird threw down a dress that was even more dazzling than the first one. And when she appeared at the wedding, everyone marveled at her beauty. The king's son was waiting for her. He took her by the hand and danced with no one but her. When others came and asked her for a dance, he said: "She is my partner." When evening came, she said she was going home. The king's son followed her, wishing to see which house she went into, but she ran away and disappeared into the garden behind the house, where there was a big beautiful tree with the most wonderful pears growing on it. She climbed among the branches as nimbly as a squirrel and the king's son didn't know what had become of her. He waited until her father arrived and said to him: "The strange girl has got away from me and I think she has climbed up in the pear tree." Her father thought: "Could it be Ashputtle?" He sent for an ax and chopped the tree down, but there was no one in it. When they went into the kitchen, Ashputtle was lying there in the ashes as usual, for she had jumped down on the other side of the tree, brought her fine clothes back to the bird in the hazel tree, and put on her filthy gray dress.

On the third day, after her parents and sisters had gone, Ashputtle went back to her mother's grave and said to the tree:

> *"Shake your branches, little tree,*
> *Throw gold and silver down on me."*

Whereupon the bird threw down a dress that was more radiant than either of the others, and the slippers were all gold. When she appeared at the wedding, the people were too amazed to speak. The king's son danced with no one but her, and when someone else asked her for a dance, he said: "She is my partner."

When evening came, Ashputtle wanted to go home, and the king's son said he'd go with her, but she slipped away so quickly that he couldn't follow. But he had thought up a trick. He had arranged to have the whole staircase brushed with pitch,[7] and as she was running down it the pitch pulled her left slipper off. The king's son picked it up, and it was tiny and delicate and all gold. Next morning he went to the father and said: "No girl shall be my wife but the one this golden shoe fits." The sisters were overjoyed,

Spiral Review
Univeral Theme
What universal theme is suggested by Ashputtle's daring return to the wedding?

> *He took her by the hand and danced with no one but her.*

---

7. pitch (pich) *n.* sticky substance used for waterproofing.

for they had beautiful feet. The eldest took the shoe to her room to try it on and her mother went with her. But the shoe was too small and she couldn't get her big toe in. So her mother handed her a knife and said: "Cut your toe off. Once you're queen you won't have to walk any more." The girl cut her toe off, forced her foot into the shoe, gritted her teeth against the pain, and went out to the king's son. He accepted her as his bride-to-be, lifted her up on his horse, and rode away with her. But they had to pass the grave. The two doves were sitting in the hazel tree and they cried out:

> "Roocoo, roocoo,
> There's blood in the shoe.
> The foot's too long, the foot's too wide,
> That's not the proper bride."

He looked down at her foot and saw the blood spurting. At that he turned his horse around and took the false bride home again. "No," he said, "this isn't the right girl; let her sister try the shoe on." The sister went to her room and managed to get her toes into the shoe, but her heel was too big. So her mother handed her a knife and said: "Cut off a chunk of your heel. Once you're queen you won't have to walk any more." The girl cut off a chunk of her heel, forced her foot into the shoe, gritted her teeth against the pain, and went out to the king's son. He accepted her as his bride-to-be, lifted her up on his horse, and rode away with her. As they passed the hazel tree, the two doves were sitting there, and they cried out:

> "Roocoo, roocoo,
> There's blood in the shoe.
> The foot's too long, the foot's too wide,
> That's not the proper bride."

He looked down at her foot and saw that blood was spurting from her shoe and staining her white stocking all red. He turned his horse around and took the false bride home again. "This isn't the right girl, either," he said. "Haven't you got another daughter?" "No," said the man, "there's only a puny little kitchen drudge[8] that my dead wife left me. She couldn't possibly be the bride." "Send her up," said the king's son, but the mother said: "Oh no, she's much too dirty to be seen." But he insisted and they had to call her. First she washed her face and hands, and when they were clean, she went upstairs and curtseyed to the king's son. He handed her the golden slipper and sat down on a footstool, took her foot out of her heavy wooden shoe, and put it into the slipper. It fitted perfectly.

---

8. **drudge** (druj) *n.* person whose job consists of hard, unpleasant work.

Literary Analysis
Archetypal Narrative Patterns How does the number of dances Ashputtle attends reflect an archetypal narrative element?

Reading Check
How does the prince propose to find the woman he wishes to marry?

And when she stood up and the king's son looked into her face, he recognized the beautiful girl he had danced with and cried out: "This is my true bride!" The stepmother and the two sisters went pale with fear and rage. But he lifted Ashputtle up on his horse and rode away with her. As they passed the hazel tree, the two white doves called out:

> "Roocoo, roocoo,
> No blood in the shoe.
> Her foot is neither long nor wide,
> This one is the proper bride."

Then they flew down and alighted on Ashputtle's shoulders, one on the right and one on the left, and there they sat.

On the day of Ashputtle's wedding, the two stepsisters came and tried to ingratiate themselves and share in her happiness. On the way to church the elder was on the right side of the bridal couple and the younger on the left. The doves came along and pecked out one of the elder sister's eyes and one of the younger sister's eyes. Afterward, on the way out, the elder was on the left side and the younger on the right, and the doves pecked out both the remaining eyes. So both sisters were punished with blindness to the end of their days for being so wicked and false.

Literary Analysis
Archetypal Narrative Patterns Which events show that evil is punished in the story?

Critical Thinking

Cite textual evidence to support your responses.

1. **Key Ideas and Details (a)** What does Ashputtle do with her father's gift? **(b) Infer:** What do her actions suggest about her character? **(c) Contrast:** Contrast Ashputtle with her stepmother and stepsisters.

2. **Key Ideas and Details (a)** What type of help does Ashputtle receive? **(b) Connect:** What lesson about life is suggested by the fact that a person like Ashputtle receives this help?

3. **Key Ideas and Details (a) Support:** In what way do the schemes of the stepmother and stepsisters lead to their punishment? **(b) Connect:** In what way do these events support the lesson of "Ashputtle"?

4. **Integration of Knowledge and Ideas** Do you think that Ashputtle is in some way a hero? If your answer is *yes,* explain in what way you think she is heroic. If your answer is *no,* what do you think she could have done differently that would have made her a hero? *[Connect to the Big Question: Can anyone be a hero?]*

Comparing Archetypal Narrative Patterns

Ⓒ **1. Craft and Structure** Identify the **archetypal narrative patterns** in "Cupid and Psyche" and "Ashputtle."

Heroine	Powerful Older Woman	Ideal Lover	Rivals for Love	Supernatural Assistance

Ⓒ **2. Craft and Structure** Compare the tasks that Psyche must perform with the tasks that Ashputtle must perform. Consider each of these structural elements: **(a)** the number of tasks; **(b)** who assigns the task and why; **(c)** the difficulty of the task; and **(d)** by what means the character completes the task.

Ⓒ **3. Integration of Knowledge and Ideas** Explain how your comparison of the tasks shows that the stories follow archetypal narrative patterns.

🕐 Timed Writing

Explanatory Text: Essay

In an essay, compare and contrast the central female characters of Psyche and Ashputtle in these two tales. Decide whether each heroine is simply an archetypal character or has a unique personality, as well. (40 minutes)

5-Minute Planner

1. Read the prompt carefully and completely.

2. Use these questions to help you analyze the characters:

   • What is the same and what is different about each character's situation in life?

   • How does each character respond to her situation? What qualities do these responses reveal?

   • How does each character react to the forces that help or hinder her?

3. As you draft your essay, remember to include transitions to connect your ideas and clarify meaning. Words and phrases like *by contrast, on the other hand,* and *alternatively* show contrast, while *similarly, likewise,* and *in addition to* suggest similarities.

Writing Workshop

 **Common Core State Standards**

Write an Explanatory Text

Exposition: Technical Document

Defining the Form A **technical document** provides information and instruction on how to perform an action. You might use elements of a technical document when assembling a product, such as a bike, or when following a recipe.

Assignment Write a technical document that explains a process to readers. For example, you may explain how to build a kite, how to follow the rules of baseball, or how to read a bus schedule. Include these elements:

- ✓ instructions that are presented *clearly* and *logically*
- ✓ *scenarios*, *definitions*, and *examples* to help understanding
- ✓ *discussion of problems or misunderstandings* readers may have
- ✓ accurate use of *technical terms*
- ✓ error-free grammar, with a focus on *correcting sentence fragments and run-on sentences*

To preview the criteria on which your technical document may be judged, see the rubric on page 1151.

 Writing Workshop: *Work in Progress*

Review the work you did on pages 1089 and 1119.

Prewriting/Planning Strategy

Consider your audience. Think about your audience—the people who will be reading your technical document. Include a level of detail in your writing that addresses these questions:

- **How much does my audience know about this topic?** Do they need a lot of background, or just a little? Will they need definitions of any special terms I use?

- **What is the age of my audience?** Do I need to use simple vocabulary and sentence structure for children, or can I use a style appropriate for people my age or older?

- **What skills might my audience have**? Do they have the basic skills needed to perform the action I am describing?

Writing

2. Write informative/explanatory texts to examine and convey complex ideas, concepts, and information clearly and accurately through the effective selection, organization, and analysis of content.

2.a. Introduce a topic; organize complex ideas, concepts, and information to make important connections and distinctions; include formatting, graphics, and multimedia when useful to aiding comprehension.

2.b. Develop the topic with well-chosen, relevant, and sufficient facts or other information and examples appropriate to the audience's knowledge of the topic.

2.d. Use precise language and domain-specific vocabulary to manage the complexity of the topic.

Explaining the Process

Organization is the order in which you present your directions or process in your technical document. Technical writers should use a type of organization that clearly explains what to do and how to do it. Technical writing not only presents the "how-to" but the "how to prepare" and "what happens if." For example, a manual explaining how to assemble a bicycle includes the tools that will be needed, the step-by-step instructions, and the troubleshooting guide to use if something is not working properly.

Use a timeline to organize details. A logical organization for a technical document is chronological order. Because one step usually affects the following steps, explaining the steps in time order will help readers follow the logical sequence. Organize the steps you wish to explain by creating a timeline. Leave wide spaces between steps so you can add sub-steps as needed. Look at this example:

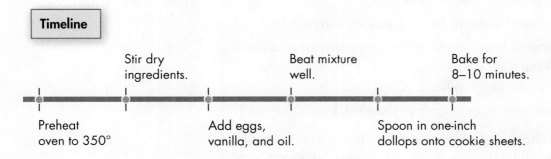

Timeline

Stir dry ingredients.　　Beat mixture well.　　Bake for 8–10 minutes.

Preheat oven to 350°　　Add eggs, vanilla, and oil.　　Spoon in one-inch dollops onto cookie sheets.

Add a glossary of technical terms. To address the needs of readers who may be unfamiliar with the process you are describing, include a glossary defining technical terms and phrases. For example, for a manual about conducting meetings, you might define *adjournment, agenda, making a motion, tabling an issue, voice vote*, and so on. In most cases, glossaries appear at the end of a document.

Drafting Strategies

Write a strong introduction. Begin with an image or an idea that leads your reader into the document. Look through your prewriting notes to find details that remind you why you enjoy the activity, why it is important, or why you decided to write about it. The details that grabbed your interest may spark your audience's interest as well. Use one of these ideas to make your first sentence sell the process or product.

Provide elaboration. As your writing takes shape, you may find that some sections need more detail. Through elaboration—the adding of details—you can help readers understand exactly what is required at each step. Look for places where adding details will clarify your meaning. As you draft, answer the following questions about the process you are describing.

- How much?
- Why?
- For how long?
- How?
- In what order?
- What will it look like?

Use definitions, scenarios, and examples. Use a variety of methods to help your readers understand your instructions.

- Define all technical terms, or create a glossary and refer readers to it.
- Describe scenarios to aid understanding, especially when discussing troubleshooting.
- Use examples when appropriate.
- Include visuals, graphs, or diagrams as needed, labeling key parts.

Use clear transitions. Make sure readers can follow the order of instructions by using precise transitional words and phrases. For example, indicate sequence with words and phrases like *at first, secondly,* and *initially.* Indicate finality with words like *finally, lastly,* and *in the end.*

Revising Strategies

Revise for organization. Reread your draft. If you use a step-by-step organization, clearly explain each step in the order it is to be completed. Make sure the subjects you discuss are in a logical place. For example, if you are describing the process of conducting a meeting, instructions for preparing an agenda should go near the beginning of the document.

Revise for clarification. Review your document, underlining information that needs further explanation or words that need to be defined.

Revising to Correct Fragments and Run-on Sentences

Fragments and run-on sentences can make your writing confusing and difficult for readers to understand.

Identifying and Correcting Fragments and Run-ons A complete sentence contains a subject and a verb and expresses a complete thought.

Fragment A fragment is a group of words that does not express a complete thought but is punctuated as if it were a sentence. To correct fragments, combine them with nearby sentences or add words to complete the sentence.

> **Fragments:** She felt relieved. *After passing the test.*
>
> **Combined:** *After passing the test,* she felt relieved.

Run-on A *run-on* is two or more complete sentences that are not properly joined or separated.

> **Fused:** They hiked quickly they stopped to eat lunch.
>
> **Comma splice:** They hiked quickly, they stopped to eat lunch.

Correcting a Run-on Sentence

Run-on: They wandered through the store they bought a novel.

Use a period to separate a run-on into two sentences. Begin each with a capital letter.	They wandered through the store. They bought a novel.
Use a comma and a coordinating conjunction, such as *and, but, or, for,* or *nor,* to combine two related independent clauses.	They wandered through the store, and they bought a novel.

PH | **WRITING COACH**

Further instruction and practice are available in *Prentice Hall Writing Coach.*

Fixing Errors Use the following steps to correct fragments and run-ons.

1. Decide if a problematic sentence is a fragment or a run-on.

2. If it is a fragment, add information to make a complete thought or combine the fragment with another sentence.

3. If it is a run-on, split it into two sentences. You might also add a comma and a conjunction to make it a correct single sentence.

Grammar in Your Writing

Review the sentences in your draft to find fragments and run-ons. Neatly correct any errors using the strategies that have been presented.

Student Model: Amanda Scarcella, San Diego, CA

Common Core
State Standards

Language
2.c. Spell correctly.

How to Run a Meeting

A successful meeting is important to groups and organizations because it helps people to set goals and stay on track. Meetings are the best way to formulate ideas and collaborate with others. To have a successful meeting there are general guidelines that should be followed.

> The first paragraph provides an introduction and overview of the steps that follow.

Basic Steps To A Successful Meeting:

Agenda:
- This document consists of the date and topics of the meeting being held.
- The topics being presented on the agenda should be numbered and titled.
- Each topic should be given a specific amount of time, to keep the meeting moving.
- A leader should make and share copies of agenda with every person attending the meeting.

> Here, Amanda provides concise information on how to prepare an agenda.

Leaders:
- Select a speaker to oversee and run the meeting in an orderly and timely way.
- Choose a person to take notes on discussions and decisions.

Guidelines:
- Establish guidelines about how the meeting will be run, and decide what will and will not happen during the meeting.
- Reinforce the practice of being respectful while others are talking.
- Encourage group members to be open to the voices and opinions of others.

Preparing:
- Everyone who attends a meeting should be prepared. It is important that group members and guests have a general idea of what decisions will be discussed.
- Provide materials such as paper and pens for the people attending the meeting.
- Group leaders should be organized and ready. For example, they might bring extra copies of the agenda and other important documents.

> Notice that Amanda has chosen to organize the technical document by subject—leaders; guidelines; and preparing, for example.

Trouble-shooting:
- To be sure that decisions and action steps are clear, the note-taker should distribute notes before the next meeting, and group members should read and correct them if necessary.
- While an agenda is useful, people should realize that a meeting may not follow it exactly if an urgent matter arises. In this case, the leader should keep the group informed about why the order of discussion may change.
- It is a good rule to end meetings on time even if agenda is not finished. This is respectful to the people who attended. Be polite and thank everyone for coming.

> Amanda provides a troubleshooting section to address possible misunderstandings.

Following these basic steps will result in a successful meeting—people will feel positive about their participation and the meeting will be efficient.

Editing and Proofreading

Check your draft for errors in grammar, spelling, and punctuation.

Focus on spelling. Look for homophone errors, such as *who's* and *whose* or *their, there,* and *they're.* Review word formation rules, like those that cover adding prefixes and suffixes. Know the words that give you trouble, and check to be sure you have spelled them correctly.

Publishing and Presenting

Consider one of the following ways to share your writing:

Create a podcast. Podcasts are recordings that can be distributed through the Internet and downloaded as MP3 files. Find information on the Internet on how to create a podcast of your manual. If possible, complete the procedure and make your podcast available to your class or school.

Present your manual to a school club or organization. Share your manual with a club or student organization to which you belong. Discuss the procedures in your manual with the club members, and request their feedback.

Reflecting on Your Writing

Writer's Journal Jot down your answers to this question:

How did writing about the task you chose help you understand it better?

Rubric for Self-Assessment

Find evidence in your writing to address each category. Then, use the rating scale to grade your work.

Spiral Review

Earlier in this unit you learned about **simple and compound sentences** (p. 1088) and **complex and compound-complex sentences** (p. 1118). Review your technical document to make sure you have correctly used a variety of sentence structures.

Criteria	Rating Scale
	not very ⟶ very
Focus: How clear and accurate are your instructions?	1 2 3 4 5
Organization: How logically and correctly are your procedures conveyed?	1 2 3 4 5
Support/Elaboration: How clear are your scenarios and examples? How clearly do you explain possible problems and misunderstandings readers may have?	1 2 3 4 5
Style: How well do you avoid fragments and run-ons?	1 2 3 4 5
Conventions: How correct is your grammar and spelling?	1 2 3 4 5

Leveled Texts

Build your skills and improve your comprehension of legends with texts of increasing complexity.

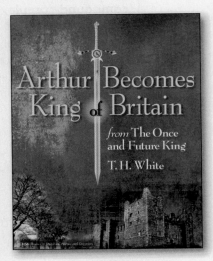

Read **"Arthur Becomes King of Britain"** to find out how a legendary king is revealed.

Read **"Morte d'Arthur"** to learn about the death and legacy of King Arthur.

Common Core State Standards

Meet these standards with **"Arthur Becomes King of Britain"** (p. 1156) or **"Morte d'Arthur"** (p. 1174).

Reading Literature

6. Analyze a particular point of view or cultural experience reflected in a work of literature from outside the United States, drawing on a wide reading of world literature. *(Literary Analysis: Legends and Legendary Heroes; Reading Skill: Compare Worldviews)*

7. Analyze the representation of a subject or a key scene in two different artistic mediums, including what is emphasized or absent in each treatment. *(Analyze Representations; Research and Technology: Influences Chart)*

9. Analyze how an author draws on and transforms source material in a specific work. *(Reading Skill: Compare Worldviews)*

Writing

2.b. Develop the topic with well-chosen, relevant, and sufficient facts, extended definitions, concrete details,

quotations, or other information and examples appropriate to the audience's knowledge of the topic. **2.e.** Establish and maintain a formal style and objective tone while attending to the norms and conventions of the discipline in which they are writing. *(Writing: Script)*

Speaking and Listening

4. Present information, findings, and supporting evidence clearly, concisely, and logically. *(Research and Technology: Influences Chart)*

Language

2. Demonstrate command of the conventions of standard English capitalization, punctuation, and spelling when writing. *(Conventions: Commas and Dashes)*

4. a. Use context as a clue to the meaning of a word or phrase. *(Vocabulary: Word Study)*

Literary Analysis: Legends and Legendary Heroes

Legends are popular stories about the past that have been handed down for generations. Because they are shared over time, many legends gradually change and form the foundations of other stories. Legends share the following characteristics:

- A focus on the life and adventures of **legendary heroes,** or characters who are human yet "larger than life"
- A deep concern with right and wrong
- Support for feelings of national pride

Legends help shape a people's cultural identity and reflect the values of a community or nation.

Reading Skill: Compare Worldviews

A **worldview** consists of values and beliefs held by a culture. When a writer retells a legend, the retelling may reflect two worldviews—that of the writer and that of the original tale. To understand a retelling, **compare and contrast** worldviews.

- **Identify details** that indicate characters' beliefs and their reasons for acting or feeling as they do. Then, identify details suggesting the writer's attitudes.
- Think about ways in which these worldviews are alike and different.
- **Draw a conclusion** about the values and basic beliefs of the different characters and of the writer. What **theme,** or insight about life, is revealed?

Using the Strategy: Worldview Diagram

As you read, record details on a **worldview diagram** to help draw conclusions.

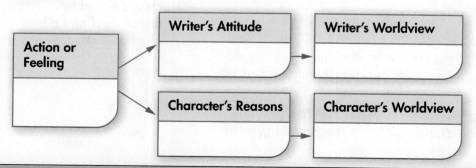

Can anyone be a *hero?*

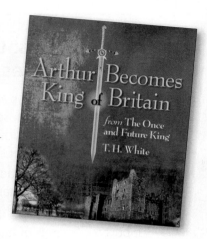

Writing About the Big Question

In "Arthur Becomes King of Britain," a nation must mourn a lost king and look toward its next leader. Use these sentence starters to develop your ideas about the Big Question.

An example of how a person's **character** can reflect the values of his or her culture is _____.

An official leader such as a king or president should be heroic because _____.

While You Read Notice the way people treat the character called "the Wart." Look for clues that reveal the facets of Wart's personality that might reveal his potential for leadership and heroism.

Vocabulary

Read each word and its definition. Decide whether you know the word well, know it a little bit, or do not know it at all. After you read, see how your knowledge of each word has increased.

- **stickler** (stik´ lər) *n.* person who insists on strict obedience to rules or standards (p. 1158) *She is a stickler for perfect grammar.*

- **petulantly** (pech´ ə lənt lē) *adv.* in a manner that expresses impatience or irritation, especially over a minor matter (p. 1158) *The child petulantly refuses to let anyone tie her shoes. petulance n. petulant adj.*

- **skeptically** (skep´ ti kəl lē) *adv.* with doubt; questioningly (p. 1160) *She shook her head as she listened skeptically to his questionable explanation. skeptic n. skeptical adj. skepticism n.*

- **surmise** (sər mīz´) *n.* guess; idea based on evidence that is not conclusive (p. 1161) *His surmise about how I felt was wrong. surmise v.*

- **sumptuous** (sump´ choo əs) *adj.* costly; lavish (p. 1162) *The dollhouse was sumptuous, filled with designer furniture and silk curtains. sumptuously adv. sumptuousness n.*

- **desolate** (des´ ə lit) *adj.* empty; solitary (p. 1163) *The desolate farmhouse was the only thing visible on the prairie. desolated v. desolation n.*

Word Study

The **Latin suffix -*ate*** means "characterized by" or "showing."

In this story, the landscape is described as being **desolate,** characterized by barren land and a lack of inhabitants.

Meet
T. H. White
(1906–1964)

Author of
Arthur Becomes King of Britain

Terence Hanbury White is widely known for his tales of Britain's national hero, King Arthur, but he was not born in England. He was born in India when it was still a British colony. White was educated at Cambridge University in England, where he received first-class honors in English.

Finding a Passion After school, White went to work as a teacher. When his autobiographical work *England Have My Bones* met with success, the thirty-year-old White became a full-time writer. The four-part novel *The Once and Future King,* a retelling of the King Arthur legends, is White's most famous work.

DID YOU KNOW?

White's version of the Arthur legends has inspired movies as well as the musical *Camelot* (1960).

BACKGROUND FOR THE LEGEND
Legends of King Arthur

Tales of King Arthur, legendary ruler of Britain, and of the knights of his Round Table have been retold for centuries. Sir Thomas Malory wrote the first English prose version of the legends, *Le Morte d'Arthur,* in 1470. In "Arthur Becomes King of Britain," an excerpt from his series *The Once and Future King,* T. H. White modernizes Malory's version of the legends.

Arthur Becomes King of Britain

from The Once and Future King

T. H. White

K
ing Pellinore arrived for the important weekend in a high state of flurry.

"I say," he exclaimed, "do you know? Have you heard? Is it a secret, what?"

"Is what a secret, what?" they asked him.

"Why, the King," cried his majesty. "You know, about the King?"

"What's the matter with the King?" inquired Sir Ector. "You don't say he's comin' down to hunt with those darned hounds of his or anythin' like that?"

"He's dead," cried King Pellinore tragically. "He's dead, poor fellah, and can't hunt any more."

Sir Grummore stood up respectfully and took off his cap of maintenance.

"The King is dead," he said. "Long live the King."

Everybody else felt they ought to stand up too, and the boys' nurse burst into tears.

"There, there," she sobbed. "His loyal highness dead and gone, and him such a respectful gentleman. Many's the illuminated picture I've cut out of him, from the Illustrated Missals,[1] aye, and stuck up over the mantel. From the time when he was in swaddling bands,[2] right through them world towers till he was a-visiting the dispersed areas as the world's Prince Charming, there wasn't a picture of 'im but I had it out, aye, and give 'im a last thought o' nights."

"Compose yourself, Nannie," said Sir Ector.

"It is solemn, isn't it?" said King Pellinore, "what? Uther the Conqueror, 1066 to 1216."

---

1. **Missals** (mis´ əlz) *n.* books produced by the Roman Catholic Church for solemn religious purposes.
2. **swaddling** (swäd´´liŋ) **bands** in former times, long, narrow bands of cloth wrapped around a newborn baby.

◀ **Critical Viewing**
What does the ornamented hilt of this sword indicate about a knight's attitude toward his weapons? **[Infer]**

Reading Skill
Compare Worldviews
Which details in the nurse's speech reflect a modern outlook? Which details reflect medieval life?

☑ **Reading Check**
What news does King Pellinore bring?

Vocabulary
stickler (stik´ lər) *n.* person who insists on strict obedience to rules or standards

petulantly (pech´ ə lənt lē) *adv.* in a manner that expresses impatience or irritation, especially over a minor matter

"A solemn moment," said Sir Grummore. "The King is dead. Long live the King."

"We ought to pull down the curtains," said Kay, who was always a stickler for good form, "or half-mast[3] the banners."

"That's right," said Sir Ector. "Somebody go and tell the sergeant-at-arms."

It was obviously the Wart's[4] duty to execute this command, for he was now the junior nobleman present, so he ran out cheerfully to find the sergeant. Soon those who were left in the solar[5] could hear a voice crying out, "Nah then, one-two, special mourning fer 'is lite majesty, lower awai on the command Two!" and then the flapping of all the standards, banners, pennons, pennoncells, banderolls, guidons, streamers and cognizances[6] which made gay the snowy turrets of the Forest Sauvage.

"How did you hear?" asked Sir Ector.

"I was pricking through the purlieus[7] of the forest after that Beast, you know, when I met with a solemn friar of orders gray, and he told me. It's the very latest news."

"Poor old Pendragon," said Sir Ector.

"The King is dead," said Sir Grummore solemnly. "Long live the King."

"It is all very well for you to keep on mentioning that, my dear Grummore," exclaimed King Pellinore petulantly, "but who is this King, what, that is to live so long, what, accordin' to you?"

"Well, his heir," said Sir Grummore, rather taken aback.

"Our blessed monarch," said the Nurse tearfully, "never had no hair. Anybody that studied the loyal family knowed that."

"Good gracious!" exclaimed Sir Ector. "But he must have had a next-of-kin?"

"That's just it," cried King Pellinore in high excitement. "That's the excitin' part of it, what? No hair and no next of skin, and who's to succeed to the throne? That's what my friar was so excited about, what, and why he was asking who could succeed to what, what? What?"

"Do you mean to tell me," exclaimed Sir Grummore indignantly, "that there ain't no King of Gramarye?"

"Not a scrap of one," cried King Pellinore, feeling important. "And there have been signs and wonders of no mean might."

"I think it's a scandal," said Sir Grummore. "God knows what the dear old country is comin' to. Due to these lollards and communists, no doubt."

Literary Analysis
Legends and Legendary Heroes
Why is humor like this surprising in a retelling of a legend?

---

3. **half-mast** *v.* lower a flag halfway down a pole as a sign of mourning.
4. **the Wart** nickname for Arthur.
5. **solar** (sō´ lər) *n.* sun room.
6. **standards . . . cognizances** (käg´ nə zən´ səz) banners or flags.
7. **purlieus** (pʉrl´ yōōz´) *n.* outlying part of a forest, in which forest laws were not enforced.

"What sort of signs and wonders?" asked Sir Ector.

"Well, there has appeared a sort of sword in a stone, what, in a sort of a church. Not in the church, if you see what I mean, and not in the stone, but that sort of thing, what, like you might say."

"I don't know what the Church is coming to," said Sir Grummore.

"It's in an anvil,"[8] explained the King.

"The Church?"

"No, the sword."

"But I thought you said the sword was in the stone?"

"No," said King Pellinore. "The stone is outside the church."

"Look here, Pellinore," said Sir Ector. "You have a bit of a rest, old boy, and start again. Here, drink up this horn of mead[9] and take it easy."

"The sword," said King Pellinore, "is stuck through an anvil which stands on a stone. It goes right through the anvil and into the stone. The anvil is stuck to the stone. The stone stands outside a church. Give me some more mead."

"I don't think that's much of a wonder," remarked Sir Grummore. "What I wonder at is that they should allow such things to happen. But you can't tell nowadays, what with all these Saxon agitators."[10]

"My dear fellah," cried Pellinore, getting excited again, "it's not where the stone is, what, that I'm trying to tell you, but what is written on it, what, where it is."

"What?"

"Why, on its pommel."[11]

"Come on, Pellinore," said Sir Ector. "You just sit quite still with your face to the wall for a minute, and then tell us what you are talkin' about. Take it easy, old boy. No need for hurryin'. You sit still and look at the wall, there's a good chap, and talk as slow as you can."

"There are words written on this sword in this stone outside this church," cried King Pellinore piteously, "and these words are as follows. Oh, do try to listen to me, you two, instead of interruptin' all the time about nothin', for it makes a man's head go ever so."

"What are these words?" asked Kay.

"These words say this," said King Pellinore, "so far as I can understand from that old friar of orders gray."

"Go on, do," said Kay, for the King had come to a halt.

Reading Check

Why is there no new king once the King is dead?

---

8. **anvil** (an´ vəl) *n.* iron or steel block on which a blacksmith rests metal to hammer it into shape.

9. **mead** (mēd) *n.* drink made of fermented honey and water.

10. **Saxon** (sak´ sən) *agitators* (aj´ i tāt´ ərz) The Saxons were Germanic people who conquered parts of England in ancient times. Agitators are those who stir up people for a cause.

11. **pommel** (päm´ əl) *n.* knob at the end of the hilt of some swords.

Arthur Becomes King of Britain **1159**

Literary Analysis
Legends and Legendary Heroes
Why is the formal sound of the words on the stone suitable to a legend?

Vocabulary
skeptically (skep´ ti kəl lē) *adv.* with doubt; questioningly

Reading Skill
Compare Worldviews
How do these details about the choosing of the next king suggest a belief in mysterious powers guiding human affairs?

Reading Skill
Compare Worldviews
What modern values are reflected in Kay's request?

"Go on," said Sir Ector, "what do these words on this sword in this anvil in this stone outside this church, say?"

"Some red propaganda, no doubt," remarked Sir Grummore.

King Pellinore closed his eyes tight, extended his arms in both directions, and announced in capital letters, "Whoso Pulleth Out This Sword of this Stone and Anvil, is Rightwise King Born of All England."

"Who said that?" asked Sir Grummore.

"But the sword said it, like I tell you."

"Talkative weapon," remarked Sir Grummore skeptically.

"It was written on it," cried the King angrily. "Written on it in letters of gold."

"Why didn't you pull it out then?" asked Sir Grummore.

"But I tell you that I wasn't there. All this that I am telling you was told to me by that friar I was telling you of, like I tell you."

"Has this sword with this inscription been pulled out?" inquired Sir Ector.

"No," whispered King Pellinore dramatically. "That's where the whole excitement comes in. They can't pull this sword out at all, although they have all been tryin' like fun, and so they have had to proclaim a tournament all over England, for New Year's Day, so that the man who comes to the tournament and pulls out the sword can be King of all England forever, what, I say?"

"Oh, father," cried Kay. "The man who pulls the sword out of the stone will be the King of England. Can't we go to the tournament, father, and have a shot?"

"Couldn't think of it," said Sir Ector.

"Long way to London," said Sir Grummore, shaking his head.

"My father went there once," said King Pellinore.

Kay said, "Oh, surely we could go? When I am knighted I shall have to go to a tournament somewhere, and this one happens at just the right date. All the best people will be there, and we should see the famous knights and great kings. It does not matter about the sword, of course, but think of the tournament, probably the greatest there has ever been in Gramarye, and all the things we should see and do. Dear father, let me go to this tourney, if you love me, so that I may bear away the prize of all, in my maiden fight."

"But, Kay," said Sir Ector, "I have never been to London."

"All the more reason to go. I believe that anybody who does not go for a tournament like this will be proving that he has no noble blood in his veins. Think what people will say about us, if we do not go and have a shot at that sword. They will say that Sir Ector's family was too vulgar and knew it had no chance."

"We all know the family has no chance," said Sir Ector, "that is, for the sword."

"Lot of people in London," remarked Sir Grummore, with a wild surmise. "So they say."

He took a deep breath and goggled at his host with eyes like marbles.

"And shops," added King Pellinore suddenly, also beginning to breathe heavily.

"Dang it!" cried Sir Ector, bumping his horn mug on the table so that it spilled. "Let's all go to London, then, and see the new King!"

They rose up as one man.

"Why shouldn't I be as good a man as my father?" exclaimed King Pellinore.

"Dash it all," cried Sir Grummore. "After all, it is the capital!"

"Hurray!" shouted Kay.

"Lord have mercy," said the nurse.

At this moment the Wart came in with Merlyn, and everybody was too excited to notice that, if he had not been grown up now, he would have been on the verge of tears.

"Oh, Wart," cried Kay, forgetting for the moment that he was only addressing his squire, and slipping back into the familiarity of their boyhood. "What do you think? We are all going to London for a great tournament on New Year's Day!"

"Are we?"

"Yes, and you will carry my shield and spears for the jousts, and I shall win the palm[12] of everybody and be a great knight!"

"Well, I am glad we are going," said the Wart, "for Merlyn is leaving us too."

"Oh, we shan't need Merlyn."

"He is leaving us," repeated the Wart.

"Leavin' us?" asked Sir Ector. "I thought it was we that were leavin'?"

"He is going away from the Forest Sauvage."

Sir Ector said, "Come now, Merlyn, what's all this about? I don't understand all this a bit."

▲ **Analyze Representations**
Which details from the story does this illustration capture, and which does it change or omit altogether? **[Analyze]**

Vocabulary
surmise (sər mīz′) *n.* guess; idea based on evidence that is not conclusive

Reading Check

What is written on the sword?

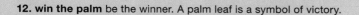

12. **win the palm** be the winner. A palm leaf is a symbol of victory.

History Connection

Tournaments

The first tournaments were held in France in the 1100s. Groups of knights would split into two sides and fight each other. Death and injury often resulted. In the 1200s, the real battles were replaced with mock ones called *jousts*. In a joust, two horsemen would charge at each other with blunt weapons. Each would try to knock the other from his horse. Jousting tournaments were social gatherings attended by ladies and common people as well as by knights.

Connect to the Literature

In light of these facts, should Kay be nervous about his first jousting tournament? Explain.

Vocabulary
sumptuous (sump′ choo əs) *adj.* costly; lavish

"I have come to say Goodbye, Sir Ector," said the old magician. "Tomorrow my pupil Kay will be knighted, and the next week my other pupil will go away as his squire. I have outlived my usefulness here, and it is time to go."

"Now, now, don't say that," said Sir Ector. "I think you're a jolly useful chap whatever happens. You just stay and teach me, or be the librarian or something. Don't you leave an old man alone, after the children have flown."

"We shall all meet again," said Merlyn. "There is no cause to be sad."

"Don't go," said Kay.

"I must go," replied their tutor. "We have had a good time while we were young, but it is in the nature of Time to fly. There are many things in other parts of the kingdom which I ought to be attending to just now, and it is a specially busy time for me. Come, Archimedes,[13] say Goodbye to the company."

"Goodbye," said Archimedes tenderly to the Wart.

"Goodbye," said the Wart without looking up at all.

"But you can't go," cried Sir Ector, "not without a month's notice."

"Can't I?" replied Merlyn, taking up the position always used by philosophers who propose to dematerialize. He stood on his toes, while Archimedes held tight to his shoulder—began to spin on them slowly like a top—spun faster and faster till he was only a blur of grayish light—and in a few seconds there was no one there at all.

"Goodbye, Wart," cried two faint voices outside the solar window.

"Goodbye," said the Wart for the last time—and the poor fellow went quickly out of the room. ●

The knighting took place in a whirl of preparations. Kay's sumptuous bath had to be set up in the box room, between two towel-horses and an old box of selected games which contained a wornout straw dart-board—it was called fléchette in those days—because all the other rooms were full of packing. The nurse spent the whole time constructing new warm pants for everybody, on the principle that the climate of any place outside the Forest Sauvage must be treacherous to the extreme, and, as for the sergeant, he polished all the armor till it was quite brittle and sharpened the swords till they were almost worn away.

---

13. Archimedes (är′ kə mē′ dēz′) Merlin's owl, who is able to talk.

At last it was time to set out.

Perhaps, if you happen not to have lived in the Old England of the twelfth century, or whenever it was, and in a remote castle on the borders of the Marches at that, you will find it difficult to imagine the wonders of their journey.

The road, or track, ran most of the time along the high ridges of the hills or downs, and they could look down on either side of them upon the desolate marshes where the snowy reeds sighed, and the ice crackled, and the duck in the red sunsets quacked loud on the winter air. The whole country was like that. Perhaps there would be a moory marsh on one side of the ridge, and a forest of a hundred thousand acres on the other, with all the great branches weighted in white. They could sometimes see a wisp of smoke among the trees, or a huddle of buildings far out among the impassable reeds, and twice they came to quite respectable towns which had several inns to boast of, but on the whole it was an England without civilization. The better roads were cleared of cover for a bow-shot on either side of them, lest the traveler should be slain by hidden thieves.

They slept where they could, sometimes in the hut of some cottager who was prepared to welcome them, sometimes in the castle of a brother knight who invited them to refresh themselves, sometimes in the firelight and fleas of a dirty little hovel with a bush tied to a pole outside it—this was the signboard used at that time by inns—and once or twice on the open ground, all huddled together for warmth between their grazing chargers. Wherever they went and wherever they slept, the east wind whistled in the reeds, and the geese went over high in the starlight, honking at the stars.

London was full to the brim. If Sir Ector had not been lucky enough to own a little land in Pie Street, on which there stood a respectable inn, they would have been hard put to it to find a lodging. But he did own it, and as a matter of fact drew most of his dividends from that source, so they were able to get three beds between the five of them. They thought themselves fortunate.

On the first day of the tournament, Sir Kay managed to get them on the way to the lists at least an hour before the jousts could possibly begin. He had lain awake all night, imagining how he was going to beat the best barons in England, and he had not been able to eat his breakfast. Now he rode at the front of the cavalcade, with pale cheeks, and Wart wished there was something he could do to calm him down.

Reading Skill
Compare Worldviews
How does this section connect past and present views of the world?

Vocabulary
desolate (des´ ə lit)
adj. empty; solitary

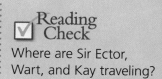

Reading Check
Where are Sir Ector, Wart, and Kay traveling?

For country people, who only knew the dismantled tilting ground[14] of Sir Ector's castle, the scene which met their eyes was ravishing. It was a huge green pit in the earth, about as big as the arena at a football match. It lay ten feet lower than the surrounding country, with sloping banks, and the snow had been swept off it. It had been kept warm with straw, which had been cleared off that morning, and now the close-worn grass sparkled green in the white landscape. Round the arena there was a world of color so dazzling and moving and twinkling as to make one blink one's eyes. The wooden grandstands were painted in scarlet and white. The silk pavilions of famous people, pitched on every side, were azure and green and saffron and checkered. The pennons and pennoncells which floated everywhere in the sharp wind were flapping with every color of the rainbow, as they strained and slapped at their flagpoles, and the barrier down the middle of the arena itself was done in chessboard squares of black and white. Most of the combatants and their friends had not yet arrived, but one could see from those few who had come how the very people would turn the scene into a bank of flowers, and how the armor would flash, and the scalloped sleeves of the heralds jig in the wind, as they raised their brazen trumpets to their lips to shake the fleecy clouds of winter with joyances[15] and fanfares.

"Good heavens!" cried Sir Kay. "I have left my sword at home."

"Can't joust without a sword," said Sir Grummore. "Quite irregular."

"Better go and fetch it," said Sir Ector. "You have time."

"My squire will do," said Sir Kay. "What an awful mistake to make! Here, squire, ride hard back to the inn and fetch my sword. You shall have a shilling[16] if you fetch it in time."

The Wart went as pale as Sir Kay was, and looked as if he were going to strike him. Then he said, "It shall be done, master," and turned his ambling palfrey[17] against the stream of newcomers. He began to push his way toward their hostelry[18] as best he might.

"To offer me money!" cried the Wart to himself. "To look down at this beastly little donkey-affair off his great charger and to call me Squire! Oh, Merlyn, give me patience with the brute, and stop me from throwing his filthy shilling in his face."

When he got to the inn it was closed. Everybody had thronged to see the famous tournament, and the entire household had followed after the mob. Those were lawless days and it was not safe to leave your house—or even to go to sleep in it—unless you were certain

---

14. **tilting ground** ground on which a joust takes place.
15. **joyances** (joi´ əns iz) n. old word meaning "rejoicing."
16. **shilling** (shil´ iŋ) n. British silver coin.
17. **palfrey** (pôl´ frē) n. old term for a saddle horse, especially one for women.
18. **hostelry** (häs´ təl rē) n. inn.

◄ **Critical Viewing**
Contrast the idea of knighthood conveyed by this illustration with the concerns of Pellinore and Kay. **[Contrast]**

Literary Analysis
Legends and Legendary Heroes
What does Wart's reaction have in common with the reaction a legendary hero would have in these circumstances?

Reading Check
How does Kay feel on the morning of his first tournament?

that it was impregnable.[19] The wooden shutters bolted over the downstairs windows were two inches thick, and the doors were double-barred.

"Now what do I do," asked the Wart, "to earn my shilling?"

He looked ruefully at the blind little inn, and began to laugh.

"Poor Kay," he said. "All that shilling stuff was only because he was scared and miserable, and now he has good cause to be. Well, he shall have a sword of some sort if I have to break into the Tower of London.

"How does one get hold of a sword?" he continued. "Where can I steal one? Could I waylay some knight, even if I am mounted on an ambling pad, and take his weapons by force? There must be some swordsmith or armorer in a great town like this, whose shop would be still open."

He turned his mount and cantered off along the street. There was a quiet churchyard at the end of it, with a kind of square in front of the church door. In the middle of the square there was a heavy stone with an anvil on it, and a fine new sword was stuck through the anvil.

"Well," said the Wart, "I suppose it is some sort of war memorial, but it will have to do. I am sure nobody would grudge Kay a war memorial, if they knew his desperate straits."

He tied his reins round a post of the lych gate,[20] strode up the gravel path, and took hold of the sword.

"Come, sword," he said. "I must cry your mercy and take you for a better cause.

"This is extraordinary," said the Wart. "I feel strange when I have hold of this sword, and I notice everything much more clearly. Look at the beautiful gargoyles[21] of the church, and of the monastery which it belongs to. See how splendidly all the famous banners in the aisle are waving. How nobly that yew[22] holds up the red flakes of its timbers to worship God. How clean the snow is. I can smell something like fetherfew and sweet briar—and is it music that I hear?"

It was music, whether of pan-pipes or of recorders, and the light in the churchyard was so clear, without being dazzling, that one could have picked a pin out twenty yards away.

"There is something in this place," said the Wart. "There are people. Oh, people, what do you want?"

Nobody answered him, but the music was loud and the light beautiful.

---

19. **impregnable** (im preg´ nə bəl) *adj.* not capable of being captured or entered by force.
20. **lych** (lich) **gate** roofed gate at the entrance to a churchyard.
21. **gargoyles** (gär´ goilz´) *n.* grotesque sculptures of animals or fantastic creatures decorating a building.
22. **yew** (yo͞o) *n.* type of evergreen tree with red cones.

"People," cried the Wart, "I must take this sword. It is not for me, but for Kay. I will bring it back."

There was still no answer, and Wart turned back to the anvil. He saw the golden letters, which he did not read, and the jewels on the pommel, flashing in the lovely light.

"Come, sword," said the Wart.

He took hold of the handles with both hands, and strained against the stone. There was a melodious consort[23] on the recorders, but nothing moved.

The Wart let go of the handles, when they were beginning to bite into the palms of his hands, and stepped back, seeing stars.

"It is well fixed," he said.

He took hold of it again and pulled with all his might. The music played more strongly, and the light all about the churchyard glowed like amethysts; but the sword still stuck.

"Oh, Merlyn," cried the Wart, "help me to get this weapon."

There was a kind of rushing noise, and a long chord played along with it. All round the churchyard there were hundreds of old friends. They rose over the church wall all together, like the Punch-and-Judy[24] ghosts of remembered days, and there were badgers and nightingales and vulgar crows and hares and wild geese and falcons and fishes and dogs and dainty unicorns and solitary wasps and corkindrills and hedgehogs and griffins and the thousand other animals he had met. They loomed round the church wall, the lovers and helpers of the Wart, and they all spoke solemnly in turn. Some of them had come from the banners in the

Literary Analysis

Legends and Legendary Heroes
How does the mysterious music here add to the legendary quality of events?

 Reading Check
Where does Wart find a sword for Kay?

---

23. **consort** (kän´ sôrt´) *n.* piece of music composed for a small group.
24. **Punch-and-Judy** puppets of the quarrelsome Punch and his wife, Judy, who fight constantly in a comical way.

Reading Skill
Compare Worldviews
Which details in this
paragraph suggest the
worldview of
legendary times?

church, where they were painted in heraldry, some from the waters
and the sky and the fields about—but all, down to the smallest
shrew mouse, had come to help on account of love. Wart felt his
power grow.

"Put your back into it," said a luce (or pike) off one of the heraldic
banners, "as you once did when I was going to snap you up.
Remember that power springs from the nape of the neck."

"What about those forearms," asked a badger gravely, "that are
held together by a chest? Come along, my dear embryo,[25] and find
your tool."

A merlin sitting at the top of the yew tree cried out, "Now then,
Captain Wart, what is the first law of the foot? I thought I once
heard something about never letting go."

"Don't work like a stalling woodpecker," urged a tawny owl
affectionately. "Keep up a steady effort, my duck, and you will have
it yet."

A white-front said. "Now, Wart, if you were once able to fly the
great North Sea, surely you can coordinate a few little wing-muscles
here and there? Fold your powers together, with the spirit of your
mind, and it will come out like butter. Come along, Homo sapiens,[26]
for all we humble friends of yours are waiting here to cheer."

The Wart walked up to the great sword for the third time. He
put out his right hand softly and drew it out as gently as from a
scabbard.

Literary Analysis
**Legends and
Legendary Heroes**
How does this event
mark Wart as a legend-
ary hero?

There was a lot of cheering, a noise like a hurdy-gurdy[27] which
went on and on. In the middle of this noise, after a long time, he
saw Kay and gave him the sword. The people at the tournament
were making a frightful row.

"But this is not my sword," said Sir Kay.

"It was the only one I could get," said the Wart. "The inn was
locked."

"It is a nice-looking sword. Where did you get it?"

"I found it stuck in a stone, outside a church."

Sir Kay had been watching the tilting nervously, waiting for his
turn. He had not paid much attention to his squire.

"That is a funny place to find one," he said.

"Yes, it was stuck through an anvil."

"What?" cried Sir Kay, suddenly rounding upon him. "Did you
just say this sword was stuck in a stone?"

Literary Analysis
**Legends and
Legendary Heroes**
Contrast Wart's everyday
language with the
significance of the
event he describes.

---

25. **embryo** (em′ brē ō′) *n.* anything in an early stage of development.
26. **Homo sapiens** (hō′ mō sā′ pē enz′) scientific name for human beings.
27. **hurdy-gurdy** (hʉr′ dē gʉr′ dē) *n.* musical instrument played by turning a crank.

"It was," said the Wart. "It was a sort of war memorial."

Sir Kay stared at him for several seconds in amazement, opened his mouth, shut it again, licked his lips, then turned his back and plunged through the crowd. He was looking for Sir Ector, and the Wart followed after him.

"Father," cried Sir Kay, "come here a moment."

"Yes, my boy," said Sir Ector. "Splendid falls these professional chaps do manage. Why, what's the matter, Kay? You look as white as a sheet."

"Do you remember that sword which the King of England would pull out?"

"Yes."

"Well, here it is. I have it. It is in my hand. I pulled it out."

Sir Ector did not say anything silly. He looked at Kay and he looked at the Wart. Then he stared at Kay again, long and lovingly, and said, "We will go back to the church."

"Now then, Kay," he said, when they were at the church door. He looked at his firstborn kindly, but straight between the eyes. "Here is the stone, and you have the sword. It will make you the King of England. You are my son that I am proud of, and always will be, whatever you do. Will you promise me that you took it out by your own might?"

Kay looked at his father. He also looked at the Wart and at the sword.

Then he handed the sword to the Wart quite quietly.

He said, "I am a liar. Wart pulled it out."

As far as the Wart was concerned, there was a time after this in which Sir Ector kept telling him to put the sword back into the stone—which he did—and in which Sir Ector and Kay then vainly tried to take it out. The Wart took it out for them, and stuck it back again once or twice. After this, there was another time which was more painful.

He saw that his dear guardian was looking quite old and powerless, and that he was kneeling down with difficulty on a gouty[28] knee.

"Sir," said Sir Ector, without looking up, although he was speaking to his own boy.

"Please do not do this, father," said the Wart, kneeling down also. "Let me help you up, Sir Ector, because you are making me unhappy."

"Nay, nay, my lord," said Sir Ector, with some very feeble old tears. "I was never your father nor of your blood, but I wote[29] well ye

---

28. **gouty** (gout´ ē) *adj.* having gout, a disease causing swelling and severe pain in the joints.
29. **wote** (wōt) *v.* old word meaning "know."

Reading Skill
Compare Worldviews
What details of the conversation between Sir Ector and Kay reflect both modern and medieval values?

Spiral Review
Archetype Based on this scene, how is Kay both like and unlike an archetypal relative?

Reading Check
What does Sir Kay tell his father about the sword?

Literary Analysis
**Legends and
Legendary Heroes**
How does the change
in the style of words Sir
Ector uses emphasize the
legendary importance of
the event?

are of an higher blood than I wend[30] ye were."

"Plenty of people have told me you are not my father," said the
Wart, "but it does not matter a bit."

"Sir," said Sir Ector humbly, "will ye be my good and gracious lord
when ye are King?"

"Don't!" said the Wart.

"Sir," said Sir Ector, "I will ask no more of you but that you will
make my son, your foster-brother, Sir Kay, seneschal[31] of all your
lands?"

Kay was kneeling down too, and it was more than the Wart could
bear.

"Oh, do stop," he cried. "Of course he can be seneschal, if I have
got to be this King, and, oh, father, don't kneel down like that,
because it breaks my heart. Please get up, Sir Ector, and don't
make everything so horrible. Oh, dear, oh, dear, I wish I had never
seen that filthy sword at all."

And the Wart also burst into tears.

---

30. **wend** (wend) *v.* thought (past tense of *ween*, an old word meaning "think").
31. **seneschal** (sen´ ə shəl) *n.* steward, or manager, in the house of a medieval noble.

Critical Thinking

1. **Key Ideas and Details (a)** How is the new king of England to be
chosen? **(b) Draw Conclusions:** What does this method suggest
about the reason men become kings in the world of the story?

2. **Key Ideas and Details (a)** What does Kay ask Wart to do when
Kay discovers his sword is missing? **(b) Analyze:** Describe the
reactions Wart has to Kay's request. **(c) Contrast:** Based on this
incident, contrast the characters of Wart and Kay.

3. **Key Ideas and Details (a)** Who or what offers advice to Wart as
he attempts to pull the sword from the stone? **(b) Interpret:** How
does this episode add to the sense of the importance of Wart's
action?

4. **Integration of Knowledge and Ideas (a)** Which characters
treat Wart differently at the end of the story? Why? **(b)** How do
the responses of others help define the role of a hero?
[Connect to the Big Question: Can anyone be a hero?]

*Cite textual
evidence to
support your
responses.*

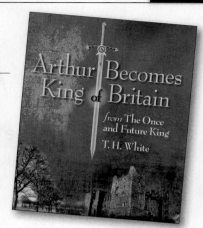

Literary Analysis: Legends and Legendary Heroes

1. Craft and Structure Which features of **legends** are present in this excerpt? Gather examples from the text.

Life Story of Legendary Hero	Concern With Right and Wrong	Reflections of National Pride

2. Integration of Knowledge and Ideas What point about heroes might the author be making by mixing ordinary and legendary characteristics in Wart? Explain.

Reading Skill: Compare Worldviews

3. (a) Based on King Pellinore's tales of "signs and wonders," draw a conclusion about his basic beliefs. **(b)** Describe Sir Grummore's reaction to the report. **(c) Compare and contrast** Pellinore's and Grummore's **worldviews.**

4. (a) Find three examples in which characters speak casually or in slang about legendary events. **(b)** What might these examples suggest about the difference between the author's worldview and the worldview of those who originally told the legend of Arthur?

Vocabulary

Acquisition and Use Answer each question. Explain your responses.

1. Will a *stickler* for cleanliness complain when you spill milk?

2. If you want to impress someone, should you behave *petulantly*?

3. Is it fair to jail a person based on a neighbor's *surmise*?

4. Will a trusting person respond *skeptically* to a friend's excuse?

5. Would a *sumptuous* house have silk pillows and velvet drapes?

6. Is a *desolate* road a convenient place to get a flat tire?

Word Study Use the context of the sentences and what you know about the **Latin suffix -ate** to explain your answer to each question.

1. Would a *moderate* climate generally have very high temperatures?

2. Is an *articulate* person likely to be troubled by speaking in public?

Word Study

The **Latin suffix -ate** means "characterized by" or "showing."

Apply It Explain how the suffix -ate contributes to the meanings of these words. Consult a dictionary if necessary.

collegiate
delicate
desperate

 **Can anyone be a *hero?***

Morte d'Arthur
Alfred, Lord Tennyson

Writing About the Big Question

In "Morte d'Arthur," a poet shows the human, flawed side of a legendary hero who is facing death. Use this sentence starter to develop your ideas about the Big Question.

A reader can more easily identify with a **legendary** hero who displays **attributes** such as _____ than one who demonstrates _____.

While You Read Look for examples of Arthur's and Sir Bedivere's behavior that show them not just as heroes, but as humans with flaws.

Vocabulary

Read each word and its definition. Decide whether you know the word well, know it a little bit, or do not know it at all. After you read, see how your knowledge of each word has increased.

- **disparagement** (di spar´ ij mənt) *n.* comments expressing a low opinion of or lack of respect for (p. 1176) *The critic's* <u>*disparagement*</u> *of her painting upset her.* disparage *v.* disparagingly *adv.*

- **bore** (bôr) *v.* carried (p. 1176) *We* <u>*bore*</u> *the injured player to the sidelines on a stretcher.* bear *v.*

- **reverence** (rev´ ə rəns) *n.* a feeling of deep respect, love, or awe (p. 1179) *The queen's subjects showed* <u>*reverence*</u> *toward her by bowing.* reverent *adj.* reverently *adv.* revere *v.*

- **brandished** (bran´ disht) *v.* showed, waved, or shook in a threatening or triumphant manner (p. 1180) *As he ran home, he* <u>*brandished*</u> *his excellent report card.*

- **wistfully** (wist´ fəl lē) *adv.* showing vague yearnings (p. 1181) *She looked* <u>*wistfully*</u> *at her old house, remembering the time she had lived there.* wistful *adj.* wistfulness *n.*

- **languid** (laŋ´ gwid) *adj.* without energy (p. 1181) *His* <u>*languid*</u> *arms dangled by his side.* languidly *adv.* languidness *n.* languish *v.*

Word Study

The **Latin suffix -ment** means "act" or "state of." It often indicates a noun.

In this poem, the speaker shows his **disparagement,** or state of disappointment or disregard for the work he is about to read.

Meet
Alfred, Lord Tennyson
(1809–1892)

Author of
Morte d'Arthur

Alfred, Lord Tennyson was born in eastern Lincolnshire in England. His work was immensely popular during his lifetime and won him the friendship of Queen Victoria. In 1850, Tennyson was appointed poet laureate of England.

A Life's Work It took Tennyson more than forty years to complete *The Idylls of the King*, his epic retelling of the King Arthur legends. By conjuring up a golden Arthurian age—and the problems that doomed it—Tennyson expressed the questions people of his own time had about life.

DID YOU KNOW?
Tennyson was known as "the poet of the people."

BACKGROUND FOR THE LEGEND
Legends of King Arthur

The figure of King Arthur, the legendary ruler of England, may be based on a historical Welsh ruler who resisted Germanic invaders of Britain in the 500s. The first English prose version of the legends, *Le Morte d'Arthur,* was written around 1470 by Sir Thomas Malory. In "Morte d'Arthur," Alfred, Lord Tennyson adapts the tale of Arthur's passing.

Morte d'Arthur

Alfred, Lord Tennyson

The Epic

At Francis Allen's on the Christmas eve—
The game of forfeits[1] done—the girls all kissed
Beneath the sacred bush and passed away—
The parson Holmes, the poet Everard Hall,
5 The host, and I sat round the wassail bowl,[2]
Then halfway ebbed; and there we held a talk,
How all the old honor had from Christmas gone,
Or gone or dwindled down to some odd games
In some odd nooks like this; till I, tired out
10 With cutting eights[3] that day upon the pond,
Where, three times slipping from the outer edge,
I bumped the ice into three several stars,
Fell in a doze; and half-awake I heard
The parson taking wide and wider sweeps,
15 Now harping on the church commissioners,
Now hawking at geology and schism;[4]
Until I woke, and found him settled down
Upon the general decay of faith
Right through the world: "at home was little left,
20 And none abroad; there was no anchor, none,
To hold by." Francis, laughing, clapped his hand
On Everard's shoulder, with "I hold by him."
"And I," quoth Everard, "by the wassail-bowl."
"Why yes," I said, "we knew your gift that way
25 At college; but another which you had—
I mean of verse (for so we held it then)—
What came of that?" "You know," said Frank, "he burnt
His epic, his King Arthur, some twelve books"—
And then to me demanding why: "O, sir,
30 He thought that nothing new was said, or else
Something so said 'twas nothing—that a truth
Looks freshest in the fashion of the day;
God knows; he has a mint of reasons; ask.
It pleased *me* well enough." "Nay, nay," said Hall,

---

1. **forfeits** (fôr´ fits) *n.* game in which something is taken away as a penalty for making
   a mistake.
2. **wassail** (wäs´ əl) **bowl** *n.* punch bowl.
3. **cutting eights** ice-skating in such a way that the skates cut figure eights in the ice.
4. **schism** (siz´ əm) *n.* division within an organization, especially
   a church, because of a difference of opinion.

◀ **Analyze Representations**
Analyze similarities and differences in how this painting and the poem depict the scene of Arthur's death. **[Analyze]**

Reading Skill Compare Worldviews
What do lines 13–21 show about people's worldview in the poet's time?

Reading Check
What has Everard written?

35 "Why take the style of those heroic times?
For nature brings not back the mastodon,
Nor we those times; and why should any man
Remodel models? these twelve books of mine
Were faint Homeric echoes,[5] nothing-worth,

40 Mere chaff and draff, much better burnt." "But I,"
Said Francis, "picked the eleventh from this hearth,
And have it; keep a thing, its use will come.
I hoard it as a sugarplum for Holmes."
He laughed, and I, though sleepy, like a horse

45 That hears the corn-bin open, pricked my ears;
For I remembered Everard's college fame
When we were freshmen. Then at my request
He brought it; and the poet, little urged,
But with some prelude of disparagement,

50 Read, mouthing out his hollow o's and a's,
Deep-chested music, and to this result. ●

Morte d'Arthur

So all day long the noise of battle rolled
Among the mountains by the winter sea,
Until King Arthur's table, man by man,

55 Had fallen in Lyonnesse[6] about their lord,
King Arthur; then, because his wound was deep,
The bold Sir Bedivere uplifted him,
Sir Bedivere, the last of all his knights,
And bore him to a chapel nigh the field,

60 A broken chancel[7] with a broken cross,
That stood on a dark strait of barren land.
On one side lay the ocean, and on one
Lay a great water, and the moon was full.
        Then spake King Arthur to Sir Bedivere:

65 "The sequel of today unsolders[8] all
The goodliest fellowship of famous knights
Whereof this world holds record. Such a sleep
They sleep—the men I loved. I think that we

Vocabulary
disparagement (di spar′ ij mənt) *n.* comments expressing a low opinion of or lack of respect for
bore (bôr) *v.* carried

---

5. **Homeric** (hō mer′ ik) **echoes** imitations of the Greek poet Homer (of the eighth century B.C.).
6. **Lyonnesse** (lī ə nes′) *n.* legendary country off the southwestern coast of England, supposed to have sunk beneath the sea.
7. **chancel** (chan′ səl) *n.* part of a church around the altar.
8. **unsolders** (un säd′ ərz) *v.* separates.

Shall never more, at any future time,
70 Delight our souls with talk of knightly
     deeds,
Walking about the gardens and the halls
Of Camelot, as in the days that were.
I perish by this people which I made—
Though Merlin[9] sware that I should come
     again
75 To rule once more—but let what will be be,
I am so deeply smitten through the helm
That without help I cannot last till morn.
Thou therefore take my brand Excalibur,
Which was my pride; for thou rememberest
     how
80 In those old days, one summer noon, an
     arm
Rose up from out the bosom of the lake,
Clothed in white samite,[10] mystic,
     wonderful,
Holding the sword—and how I rowed
     across
And took it, and have worn it, like a king;
85 And, wheresoever I am sung or told
In aftertime, this also shall be known.
But now delay not; take Excalibur,
And fling him far into the middle mere;[11]
Watch what thou seest, and lightly[12] bring me word."
90   To him replied the bold Sir Bedivere:
"It is not meet,[13] Sir King, to leave thee thus,
Aidless, alone, and smitten through the helm.
A little thing may harm a wounded man.
Yet I thy hest will all perform at full,[14]
95 Watch what I see, and lightly bring thee word."
          So saying, from the ruined shrine he stepped
And in the moon athwart the place of tombs,
Where lay the mighty bones of ancient men,
Old knights, and over them the sea wind sang

How Sir Bedivere Cast the Sword Excalibur Into the Water,
Aubrey Beardsley. Houghton Library, Harvard University.

Reading Skill
Compare Worldviews
What does Sir Bedivere's response show about the importance of obedience in Arthurian times?

Reading Check
What does Arthur ask Bedivere to do?

---

  9. Merlin sorcerer who advised King Arthur.
10. samite (sam´ ĭt) *n.* heavy silk fabric worn in the Middle Ages.
11. mere (mir) *n.* old or poetic word for "lake."
12. lightly *adv.* old or poetic word for "quickly."
13. meet *adj.* old or poetic word for "proper."
14. I thy hest will all perform at full I will carry out your order completely.

▶ **Critical Viewing**
Judging from the manuscript on page 1179, were the Arthur stories told only in England? Explain. **[Draw Conclusions]**

100 Shrill, chill, with flakes of foam. He, stepping down
By zigzag paths and juts of pointed rock,
Came on the shining levels of the lake.
    There drew he forth the brand Excalibur,
And o'er him, drawing it, the winter moon,
105 Brightening the skirts of a long cloud, ran forth
And sparkled keen with frost against the hilt;
For all the haft twinkled with diamond sparks,
Myriads of topaz-lights, and jacinth-work[15]
Of subtlest jewelry. He gazed so long
110 That both his eyes were dazzled, as he stood,
This way and that dividing the swift mind,
In act to throw; but at the last it seemed
Better to leave Excalibur concealed
There in the many-knotted water flags,[16]
115 That whistled stiff and dry about the marge.[17]
So strode he back slow to the wounded king.
    Then spake King Arthur to Sir Bedivere:
"Hast thou performed my mission which I gave?
What is it thou hast seen, or what hast heard?"
120   And answer made the bold Sir Bedivere:
"I heard the ripple washing in the reeds,
And the wild water lapping on the crag."
    To whom replied King Arthur, faint and pale:
"Thou hast betrayed thy nature and thy name,
125 Not rendering[18] true answer, as beseemed
Thy fealty,[19] nor like a noble knight;
For surer sign had followed, either hand,
Or voice, or else a motion of the mere.
This is a shameful thing for men to lie.
130 Yet now, I charge thee, quickly go again
As thou art lief and dear, and do the thing
I bade thee, watch, and lightly bring me word."
    Then went Sir Bedivere the second time
Across the ridge, and paced beside the mere,
135 Counting the dewy pebbles, fixed in thought;
But when he saw the wonder of the hilt,
How curiously and strangely chased,[20] he smote

Reading Skill
Compare Worldviews
To what values does Arthur appeal in lines 124–126?

---

15. topaz-lights, and jacinth-work yellow and reddish-orange jewels.
16. water flags marsh plants.
17. marge (märj) *n.* margin; edge.
18. rendering (ren´ dər iŋ) *v.* giving.
19. beseemed (bē sēm´ əd) / **Thy fealty** (fē´ əl tē) was suitable to the loyalty you owe your lord.
20. chased *adj.* decorated by engraving or embossing.

His palms together, and he cried aloud:

"And if indeed I cast the brand away;
140 Surely a precious thing, one worthy note,
Should thus be lost forever from the earth,
Which might have pleased the eyes of many men.
What good should follow this, if this were done?
What harm, undone? deep harm to disobey,
145 Seeing obedience is the bond of rule.
Were it well to obey then, if a king demand
An act unprofitable, against himself?
The king is sick, and knows not what he does.
What record, or what relic of my lord
150 Should be to aftertime, but empty breath
And rumors of a doubt? But were this kept,
Stored in some treasure-house of mighty kings,
Some one might show it at a joust of arms,
Saying, 'King Arthur's sword, Excalibur,
155 Wrought by the lonely maiden of the lake;
Nine years she wrought it, sitting in the deeps
Upon the hidden bases of the hills.'
So might some old man speak in the aftertime
To all the people, winning reverence;
160 But now much honor and much fame were lost."

So spake he, clouded with his own conceit,
And hid Excalibur the second time,
And so strode back slow to the wounded king.

Then spoke King Arthur, breathing heavily:
165 "What is it thou hast seen, or what hast heard?"

And answer made the bold Sir Bedivere:
"I heard the water lapping on the crag,
And the long ripple washing in the reeds."

To whom replied King Arthur, much in wrath:
170 "Ah, miserable and unkind, untrue,
Unknightly, traitor-hearted! Woe is me!
Authority forgets a dying king,
Laid widowed of the power in his eye
That bowed the will. I see thee what thou art,
175 For thou, the latest-left of all my knights,
In whom should meet the offices[21] of all,
Thou wouldst betray me for the precious hilt;
Either from lust of gold, or like a girl

---

21. **offices** *n.* duties.

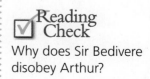

Vocabulary
reverence (rev´ ə rəns)
n. a feeling of deep
respect, love, or awe

Reading
Check

Why does Sir Bedivere
disobey Arthur?

Morte d'Arthur **1179**

▶ **Critical Viewing**
Which details in the painting on page 1181 contrast Arthur's warrior life with the civilized life he fought to protect?
[Contrast]

Spiral Review
Archetype What archetypal pattern occurs in lines 184–192?

Vocabulary
brandished (bran´ disht)
v. showed, waved, or shook in a threatening or triumphant manner

Valuing the giddy pleasure of the eyes.
180 Yet, for a man may fail in duty twice,
And the third time may prosper, get thee hence;
But, if thou spare to fling Excalibur,
I will arise and slay thee with my hands."
Then quickly rose Sir Bedivere, and ran,
185 And, leaping down the ridges lightly, plunged
Among the bulrush beds,²² and clutched the sword,
And strongly wheeled and threw it. The great brand
Made lightnings in the splendor of the moon,
And flashing round and round, and whirled in an arch,
190 Shot like a streamer of the northern morn,²³
Seen where the moving isles of winter shock²⁴
By night, with noises of the northern sea.
So flashed and fell the brand Excalibur;
But ere he dipped the surface, rose an arm
195 Clothed in white samite, mystic, wonderful,
And caught him by the hilt, and brandished him
Three times, and drew him under in the mere.
And lightly went the other to the king.
Then spoke King Arthur, drawing thicker breath:
200 "Now see I by thine eyes that this is done.
Speak out; what is it thou hast heard, or seen?"
And answer made the bold Sir Bedivere:
"Sir King, I closed mine eyelids, lest the gems
Should blind my purpose, for I never saw,
205 Nor shall see, here or elsewhere, till I die,
Not though I live three lives of mortal men,
So great a miracle as yonder hilt.
Then with both hands I flung him, wheeling him;
But when I looked again, behold an arm,
210 Clothed in white samite, mystic, wonderful,
That caught him by the hilt, and brandished him
Three times, and drew him under in the mere."
And answer made King Arthur, breathing hard:
"My end draws nigh; 'tis time that I were gone.
215 Make broad thy shoulders to receive my weight,
And bear me to the margin; yet I fear
My wound hath taken cold, and I shall die."
So saying, from the pavement he half rose,

---

22. bulrush (bŏŏl´ rush´) **beds** growth of marsh plants.
23. a streamer of the northern morn northern lights; the aurora borealis.
24. the moving isles of winter shock icebergs crash.

Slowly, with pain, reclining on his arm,
220 And looking *wistfully* with wide blue eyes
As in a picture. Him Sir Bedivere
Remorsefully regarded through his tears,
And would have spoken, but he found not words,
Then took with care, and kneeling on one knee,
225 O'er both his shoulders drew the *languid* hands,
And rising bore him through the place of tombs.
　　　But, as he walked, King Arthur panted hard,
Like one that feels a nightmare on his bed
When all the house is mute. So sighed the king,
230 Muttering and murmuring at his ear, "Quick,
　　quick!
I fear it is too late, and I shall die."
But the other swiftly strode from ridge to ridge,
Clothed with his breath, and looking, as he walked,
Larger than human on the frozen hills.
235 He heard the deep behind him, and a cry
Before. His own thought drove him like a goad.[25]
Dry clashed his harness[26] in the icy caves
And barren chasms, and all to left and right
The bare black cliff clanged round him, as he based
240 His feet on juts of slippery crag that rang
Sharp-smitten with the dint of armèd heels—
And on a sudden, lo! the level lake,
And the long glories of the winter moon.
　　　Then saw they how there hove a dusky barge,
245 Dark as a funeral scarf from stem to stern,
Beneath them; and descending they were ware
That all the decks were dense with stately forms
Black-stoled, black-hooded, like a dream—by these
Three queens with crowns of gold—and from them rose
250 A cry that shivered to the tingling stars,
And, as it were one voice, an agony
Of lamentation, like a wind that shrills
All night in a waste land, where no one comes,
Or hath come, since the making of the world.
255　　　Then murmured Arthur, "Place me in the barge,"
And to the barge they came. There those three queens
Put forth their hands, and took the king, and wept.

The **Dream of Arthur in Avalon** (detail), Sir Edward Burne-Jones. The Museo de Arte de Ponce. The Luis A. Ferré Foundation Inc. Ponce, Puerto Rico.

---

25. goad (gōd) *n.* sharp-pointed stick used to drive oxen.
26. harness (här′ nis) *n.* armor.

Vocabulary
wistfully (wist′ fəl lē)
adv. showing vague
yearnings
languid (laŋ′ gwid)
adj. without energy

Literary Analysis
Legends and
Legendary Heroes
Why is the arrival of the
mysterious barge appro-
priate to the death of a
legendary hero?

Reading
Check
What does Sir Bedivere
do on his third visit to
the shore?

Reading Skill
Compare Worldviews
How does the arrival of the three queens reflect a belief in supernatural forces or mystical events?

But she that rose the tallest of them all
And fairest laid his head upon her lap,
260 And loosed the shattered casque, and chafed his hands,
And called him by his name, complaining loud,
And dropping bitter tears against his brow
Striped with dark blood; for all his face was white
And colorless, and like the withered moon
265 Smote by the fresh beam of the springing east;
And all his greaves and cuisses dashed with drops
Of onset; and the light and lustrous curls—
That made his forehead like a rising sun
High from the dais-throne—were parched with dust;
270 Or, clotted into points and hanging loose,
Mixed with the knightly growth that fringed his lips.
So like a shattered column lay the king;
Not like that Arthur who, with lance in rest,
From spur to plume a star of tournament,
275 Shot through the lists at Camelot, and charged
Before the eyes of ladies and of kings.
            Then loudly cried the bold Sir Bedivere:
"Ah! my Lord Arthur, whither shall I go?
Where shall I hide my forehead and my eyes?
280 For now I see the true old times are dead,
When every morning brought a noble chance,
And every chance brought out a noble knight.
Such times have been not since the light that led
The holy Elders with the gift of myrrh.[27]
285 But now the whole ROUND TABLE is dissolved
Which was an image of the mighty world;
And I, the last, go forth companionless,
And the days darken round me, and the years,
Among new men, strange faces, other minds."

Literary Analysis
Legends and Legendary Heroes
Which ideas in Bedivere's speech encourage English national pride?

290 And slowly answered Arthur from the barge:
"The old order changeth, yielding place to new,
And God fulfills himself in many ways,
Lest one good custom should corrupt the world.
Comfort thyself: what comfort is in me?
295 I have lived my life, and that which I have done
May He within himself make pure! but thou,
If thou shouldst never see my face again,

Reading Skill
Compare Worldviews
What is the main difference between Bedivere's and Arthur's view of the world?

---

27. **the light . . . of myrrh** (mur) star that guided the three kings ("the holy Elders") with their gifts of myrrh (a gum from plants, used to make incense and perfume), to Bethlehem at the birth of Jesus.

Pray for my soul. More things are wrought by prayer
Than this world dreams of. Wherefore, let thy voice
300 Rise like a fountain for me night and day.
For what are men better than sheep or goats
That nourish a blind life within the brain,
If, knowing God, they lift not hands of prayer
Both for themselves and those who call them friend?
305 For so the whole round earth is every way
Bound by gold chains about the feet of God.
But now farewell. I am going a long way
With these thou seest—if indeed I go—
For all my mind is clouded with a doubt—
310 To the island-valley of Avilion;[28]
Where falls not hail, or rain, or any snow,
Nor ever wind blows loudly, but it lies
Deep-meadowed, happy, fair with orchard lawns
And bowery[29] hollows crowned with summer sea,
315 Where I will heal me of my grievous wound."

    So said he, and the barge with oar and sail
Moved from the brink, like some full-breasted swan
that, fluting a wild carol ere her death,
Ruffles her pure cold plume, takes the flood
320 With swarthy webs. Long stood Sir Bedivere
Revolving many memories, till the hull
Looked one black dot against the verge of dawn,
And on the mere the wailing died away. •

    Here ended Hall, and our last light, that long
325 Had winked and threatened darkness, flared and fell;
At which the parson, sent to sleep with sound,
And waked with silence, grunted "Good!" but we
Sat rapt: it was the tone with which he read—
Perhaps some modern touches here and there
330 Redeemed it from the charge of nothingness—
Or else we loved the man, and prized his work;
I know not; but we sitting, as I said,
The cock crew loud, as at that time of year
The lusty bird takes every hour for dawn.
335 Then Francis, muttering, like a man ill-used,
    "There now—that's nothing!" drew a little back,

▲ Critical Viewing
What important quali-
ties of a knight does
this drawing depict?
[Interpret]

Reading
Check
Who comes to take
Arthur away?

---

28. **island-valley of Avilion** According to ancient British myth, heroes were taken after death
   to the island paradise of Avalon, called "Avilion" here.
29. **bowery** (bou´ ər ē) *adj.* enclosed by overhanging boughs of trees or by vines.

And drove his heel into the smoldered log,
That sent a blast of sparkles up the flue.
And so to bed, where yet in sleep I seemed
340 To sail with Arthur under looming shores,
Point after point; till on to dawn, when dreams
Begin to feel the truth and stir of day,
To me, methought, who waited with the crowd,
There came a bark that, blowing forward, bore
345 King Arthur; like a modern gentleman
Of stateliest port;[30] and all the people cried,
"Arthur is come again: he cannot die."
Then those that stood upon the hills behind
Repeated—"Come again, and thrice as fair";
350 And, further inland, voices echoed—"Come
With all good things, and war shall be no more."
At this a hundred bells began to peal,
That with the sound I woke, and heard indeed
The clear church bells ring in the Christmas morn.

30. Of stateliest port who carried himself in a most majestic or dignified manner.

Literary Analysis
Legends and
Legendary Heroes
In what way do lines
344–351 suggest that
faith and the opportunity
for noble action might
return in modern times,
as strong as in the Arthur
legend?

Critical Thinking

1. **Key Ideas and Details** **(a)** What occasion is celebrated at the opening of the poem? **(b) Interpret:** What complaint does the parson make on this occasion?

2. **Key Ideas and Details** **(a)** In Everard's poem, what has happened to Arthur and his knights? **(b) Interpret:** When Bedivere says that "the true old times are dead," what does he imply will vanish from the world?

3. **Key Ideas and Details** **(a)** What does Arthur specifically request of Bedivere? **(b) Interpret:** Why does Bedivere fear that if he obeys Arthur's request, "much honor and much fame were lost"? **(c) Connect:** What attitude toward the past do Bedivere and the parson share?

4. **Key Ideas and Details** **(a)** What attitude toward heroes and honor do the men at the beginning of the poem have? **(b)** Do their opinions change by the end of the poem? Explain. *[Connect to the Big Question: Can anyone be a hero?]*

Literary Analysis: Legends and Legendary Heroes

1. Craft and Structure Which features of **legends** are present in this poem? Gather examples from the selection.

Life Story of Legendary Hero	Concern With Right and Wrong	Reflections of National Pride

2. Key Ideas and Details In what way does the end of the poem suggest that King Arthur still unites the people of England, past and present?

Reading Skill: Compare Worldviews

3. Arthur says, "The old order changeth, yielding place to new." **(a)** Describe the "old order" of Arthur's reign, using details from the poem. **(b)** What do the parson's complaints show about the "new order" of modern times? **(c) Compare and contrast** the parson's **worldview** with the worldview of the old order.

4. In the narrator's dream, the people cry, "Arthur is come again: he cannot die." Based on this dream, explain what basic values or beliefs Tennyson might hold.

Vocabulary

Acquisition and Use Answer each question. Explain your responses.

1. Are football players noted for their *languid* movements?

2. Should you make a *disparagement* about a friend's clothes?

3. Why scold a child who *brandished* a pair of scissors while running?

4. If you *bore* a heavy backpack up a mountain, did you push it?

5. Would dedicating a memorial to a soldier be a sign of *reverence*?

6. Why might you sigh *wistfully* while looking through old photos?

Word Study Use the context of the sentences and what you know about the **Latin suffix -ment** to explain your answer to each question.

1. If you were upset with your grades, would you feel *contentment*?

2. Does a receipt of purchase show your *entitlement* to that object?

Word Study

The **Latin suffix -ment** means "act" or "state of."

Apply It Explain how the suffix -ment contributes to the meanings of these words. Consult a dictionary if necessary.

atonement
embodiment
government

Morte d'Arthur

Alfred, Lord Tennyson

Integrated Language Skills

Arthur Becomes King of Britain • Morte d'Arthur

Conventions: Commas and Dashes

Commas are used to separate or join similar sentence elements and to show the relationship between ideas. **Dashes** are used to create longer, more emphatic pauses than commas.

- Use commas to separate three or more words or phrases in a series.
- Use a comma and a coordinating conjunction (*and, but, or, nor, for, so,* and *yet*) to link two independent clauses in a compound sentence.
- Use commas to set off introductory, parenthetical, and nonessential words, phrases, and clauses.
- Use dashes to indicate an abrupt change of thought, a dramatic interrupting idea, or a summary statement.

> **COMMAS:** The king, **who ruled for a long time,** was very wise.
>
> **DASHES:** The legend—**and there are some outlandish versions of the story**—has endured for many years.

Practice A Insert dashes or commas where necessary in the following sentences.

1. Wart is thoughtful kind and diligent.
2. Merlin who has been Wart's tutor disappears into thin air.
3. Sir Kay takes Wart to London only to treat him meanly.
4. Wart returns to the inn riding on his little donkey to fetch Kay's sword.

Practice B Rewrite the following sentences, correcting any errors with commas or dashes. If no corrections are necessary, write *correct.*

1. Finally—Sir Bedivere throws the sword into the lake.
2. Arthur is wounded and he prepares to die.
3. Three magnificent queens—weeping bitter tears—tended to the king.
4. The narrator who finally fell asleep, dreamed of a heroic future.

© **Reading Application** Find an example of commas and an example of dashes in "Arthur Becomes King of Britain." Explain why the punctuation marks were used in each case.

© **Writing Application** Write a brief paragraph about the painting on page 1181. Use commas and dashes to set off pieces of information where appropriate.

PH **WRITING COACH** | Further instruction and practice are available in *Prentice Hall Writing Coach.*

Writing

Ⓒ Informative Text In the fictional world where the Arthurian legend takes place, the discovery that Wart will be king of England and the death of King Arthur are two big news stories. Write a brief **script** for a television news report on one of these stories. Follow these tips:

- First, provide sufficient facts, including *who* is involved, *what* happened, and *where, when, why,* and *how* it happened.

- Outline the various perspectives you will offer. For example, you might open with a news anchor and conclude with a discussion among commentators.

- As you draft, clearly identify each speaker and describe the visuals you would incorporate.

- Revise, making sure the tone of your report is objective.

Grammar Application Make sure you have correctly punctuated your script, using commas and dashes appropriately.

Writing Workshop: *Work in Progress*

Prewriting for a Comparison-and-Contrast Essay For a comparison-and-contrast essay you may write, choose two literary works. Freewrite about each piece for two to four minutes. Then, circle similar ideas and underline different ideas. Save these Freewrites in your writing portfolio.

Research and Technology

Ⓒ Build and Present Knowledge The legend of King Arthur has inspired many interpretations in art and film. Look at the illustration on page 1161. Then, watch a movie based on the legends of King Arthur. Fill out a two-column **"influences" chart** that reflects the choices the artist and the director make in each medium for the scene depicting Arthur pulling the sword from the stone. Follow these steps to complete your chart:

- Analyze choices the artist might make to represent the scene in a particular way, such as how young or old to make Arthur appear. Analyze choices the director might make in the film version, such as which camera angles to use and which characters to include in the scene.

- Note similarities and differences between the illustration and the film.

- In one column, note details that tell how the artist represents the scene.

- In the other column, note details that tell how the director represents the scene.

Present your findings to the class.

Ⓒ Common Core State Standards

L.9-10.2, L.9-10.4.a; W.9-10.2.b, W.9-10.2.e; SL.9-10.4

[For the full wording of the standards, see page 1152.]

Use this prewriting activity to prepare for the **Writing Workshop** on page 1242.

from **A Connecticut Yankee in King Arthur's Court** •
from **Don Quixote**

© Leveled Texts

Build your skills and improve your comprehension of parodies with texts
of increasing complexity.

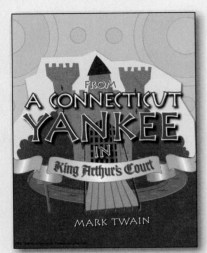

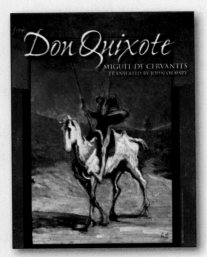

Read the excerpt from **A
Connecticut Yankee in King
Arthur's Court** to find out
how a reluctant time traveler
gets in and out of trouble.

Read the excerpt from **Don
Quixote** to find out what
happens when a well-meaning
gentleman decides to become
a legendary hero.

© Common Core State Standards

Meet these standards with the excerpt from **A Connecticut Yankee in King Arthur's Court**
(p. 1192) or the excerpt from **Don Quixote** (p. 1208).

Reading Literature
1. Cite strong and thorough textual evidence to support
analysis of what the text says explicitly as well as
inferences drawn from the text. *(Reading Skill: Compare
Worldviews)*
Spiral Review: RL.9-10.2
Writing
3. Write narratives to develop real or imagined experiences
or events using effective technique, well-chosen details,
and well-structured event sequences. **3.b.** Use narrative
techniques, such as dialogue, pacing, description,
reflection, and multiple plot lines, to develop experiences,
events, and/or characters. *(Writing: Parody)*

7. Conduct short as well as more sustained research
projects to answer a question or solve a problem; narrow
or broaden the inquiry when appropriate; synthesize
multiple sources on the subject, demonstrating
understanding of the subject under investigation.
(Research and Technology: Biographical Brochure)
Language
2. Demonstrate command of the conventions of standard
English capitalization, punctuation, and spelling when
writing. **2.a.** Use a semicolon to link two or more closely
related independent clauses. **2.b.** Use a colon to introduce
a list or quotation. *(Conventions: Semicolons, Colons, and
Ellipsis Points)*

Literary Analysis: Parody

A **parody** is a humorous work in which the author imitates the style or ideas of other works in an exaggerated or a ridiculous way. For example, the following passage parodies the style, conflict, and characters typically found in sports stories:

> John was tense as he flipped the final peanut into the air. Then, he exploded into action. In one flawless move, he snapped his head back, and the peanut dropped neatly into his mouth.

Although parodies are humorous, they often have a deeper purpose: to convey a **theme** or insight about life. Parodies point out the faulty attitudes, ideals, and values of past and current society. As you read a parody, look for language and story elements that exaggerate and mock ideas from other literary works.

Reading Skill: Compare Worldviews

A serious work of literature reflects the writer's **worldview,** or basic beliefs and values. Very often, those beliefs and values stem directly from the time period and culture of the work's author. In a parody, another writer may portray the original author's worldview as faulty or an illusion and therefore open to ridicule. Usually, such criticism is not explicitly stated, but is woven into the fabric of the parody itself.

As you read, **compare and contrast** illusion and reality in the narrative as shown in the different characters' beliefs and actions.

Using the Strategy: Worldview Diagram

Record textual evidence from the selections on a **worldview diagram** like this one.

Character 1

Actions:
Draws sword
Beliefs: The thing is a dragon.
Attitudes: Fear

Beliefs:
There is a large, powerful thing present.

Actions:
Tries to calm Character 1
Beliefs: The thing is a train.
Attitudes: Amusement

Character 2

PHLit
Online!
www.PHLitOnline.com

Hear It!
• Selection summary audio
• Selection audio

See It!
• Get Connected video
• Background video
• More about the author
• Vocabulary flashcards

Do It!
• Interactive journals
• Interactive graphic organizers
• Self-test
• Internet activity
• Grammar tutorial
• Interactive vocabulary games

Can anyone be a *hero?*

Writing About the Big Question

In the excerpt from *A Connecticut Yankee in King Arthur's Court,* a man's resourcefulness and ingenuity help him out in a "unique" circumstance. Use this sentence starter to develop your ideas about the Big Question.

When faced with seemingly insurmountable obstacles, a person with **determination** can **persevere** because _____.

While You Read Look for positive and negative points in the man's plan for escape. Decide if any of his actions are heroic.

Vocabulary

Read each word and its definition. Decide whether you know the word well, know it a little bit, or do not know it at all. After you read, see how your knowledge of each word has increased.

- **plight** (plīt) *n.* a distressing situation (p. 1193) *The plight of the cat was eased when we rescued her from the tree.*

- **contrive** (kən trīv´) *v.* bring about; manage (p. 1195) *We must contrive a plan to get everyone home in time for the surprise party.* contrivance *n.* contriver *n.*

- **rudiments** (rōō´ də mənts) *n.* basics; slight beginning (p. 1195) *First graders learn only the rudiments of arithmetic.* rudimental *adj.* rudimentary *adj.*

- **calamity** (kə lam´ ə tē) *n.* terrible misfortune; disaster (p. 1196) *The powerful hurricane was a great calamity.* calamitous *adj.*

- **multitudes** (mul´ tə tōōdz) *n.* crowds; large number of people or things (p. 1199) *Outside the stadium, multitudes of excited fans swarmed.* multitudinous *adj.*

- **conspicuous** (kən spik´ yōō əs) *adj.* easy to see (p. 1199) *We were conspicuous in our bright clothes when everyone else wore black.* conspicuously *adv.* conspicuousness *n.*

Word Study

The Latin **prefix** *multi-* means "many" or "much."

In this story, **multitudes**, or a crowd of many people, fill the court of the castle.

Author of
A CONNECTICUT YANKEE IN KING ARTHUR'S COURT

Samuel Clemens, who later won fame as Mark Twain, grew up in the small Mississippi River port of Hannibal, Missouri. He left school early to learn the printing trade and later found work as a steamboat pilot. After the Civil War, he headed west, hunting for silver in Nevada and gold in California while writing accounts of his travels.

A Connecticut Writer In 1870, Twain married Olivia Langdon and began to raise a family. Settling in Hartford, Connecticut, he penned his popular boyhood tale *The Adventures of Tom Sawyer* and a string of other bestsellers.

DID YOU KNOW?

Twain took his pen name from a riverboat cry, "Mark twain!," meaning the water was deep enough for safe passage.

BACKGROUND FOR THE PARODY

Yankees and Knights

The days of King Arthur are typically depicted as a time of great deeds and noble characters. Twain paints a different picture of this time. Hank Morgan, the hero of Twain's *A Connecticut Yankee in King Arthur's Court,* is a nineteenth-century "Yankee," or New Englander. Hank has all the shrewdness often associated with New Englanders. His ingenuity is tested, though, in King Arthur's court.

FROM A CONNECTICUT YANKEE IN King Arthur's Court

MARK TWAIN

The practical Hank Morgan is manager of an arms factory in Connecticut in 1879. One day, in a fight with an employee named Hercules, he is knocked unconscious. Awakening in a strange place, he finds himself the prisoner of a knight in armor, Sir Kay. On their way to King Arthur's court, Hank meets Clarence, a friendly young page. Hank is unsure of where he is, and he is astonished when Clarence tells him that it is June 19 in the year 528. Hank knows that a solar eclipse occurred at noon on June 21 in the year 528 but that no eclipse is predicted for his own year. If an eclipse occurs, he reasons, it will confirm that he has traveled in time. In the meantime, he is taken to a dungeon to await execution.

CHAPTER V—AN INSPIRATION

I was so tired that even my fears were not able to keep me awake long.

When I next came to myself, I seemed to have been asleep a very long time. My first thought was, "Well, what an astonishing dream I've had! I reckon I've waked only just in time to keep from being hanged or drowned or burned or something. . . . I'll nap again till the whistle blows, and then I'll go down to the arms factory and have it out with Hercules."

But just then I heard the harsh music of rusty chains and bolts, a light flashed in my eyes, and that butterfly,[1] Clarence, stood before me! I gasped with surprise; my breath almost got away from me.

"What!" I said, "you here yet? Go along with the rest of the dream! scatter!"

But he only laughed, in his light-hearted way, and fell to making fun of my sorry plight.

"All right," I said resignedly, "let the dream go on; I'm in no hurry."

"Prithee[2] what dream?"

"What dream? Why, the dream that I am in Arthur's court—a person who never existed; and that I am talking to you, who are nothing but a work of the imagination."

"Oh, la, indeed! and is it a dream that you're to be burned tomorrow? Ho-Ho—answer me that!"

The shock that went through me was distressing. I now began to reason that my situation was in the last degree serious, dream or

---

1. **butterfly** *n.* sociable, lighthearted person.
2. **Prithee** (prith´ ē) *interjection* old term for "please."

◀ **Critical Viewing** Based on this illustration, predict whether this selection will be serious or humorous. Explain your reasoning. **[Predict]**

Vocabulary
plight (plīt) *n.* a distressing situation

Reading Skill
Compare Worldviews
What illusion does Hank think he has? What illusion does Clarence think Hank has?

Reading Check
What danger is Hank facing?

no dream; for I knew by past experience of the lifelike intensity of dreams, that to be burned to death, even in a dream, would be very far from being a jest, and was a thing to be avoided, by any means, fair or foul, that I could contrive. So I said beseechingly:

"Ah, Clarence, good boy, only friend I've got—for you *are* my friend, aren't you?—don't fail me; help me to devise some way of escaping from this place!"

"Now do but hear thyself! Escape? Why, man, the corridors are in guard and keep of men-at-arms."

"No doubt, no doubt. But how many, Clarence? Not many, I hope?"

"Full a score.[3] One may not hope to escape." After a pause—hesitatingly: "and there be other reasons—and weightier."

"Other ones? What are they?"

"Well, they say—oh, but I daren't, indeed and indeed, I daren't!"

"Why, poor lad, what is the matter? Why do you blench? Why do you tremble so?"

"Oh, in sooth, there is need! I do want to tell you, but—"

"Come, come, be brave, be a man—speak out, there's a good lad!"

He hesitated, pulled one way by desire, the other way by fear; then he stole to the door and peeped out, listening; and finally crept close to me and put his mouth to my ear and told me his fearful news in a whisper, and with all the cowering apprehension of one who was venturing upon awful ground and speaking of things whose very mention might be freighted with death.

"Merlin, in his malice, has woven a spell about this dungeon, and there bides not the man in these kingdoms that would be desperate enough to essay to cross its lines with you! Now God pity me, I have told it! Ah, be kind to me, be merciful to a poor boy who means thee well; for an thou betray me I am lost!"

I laughed the only really refreshing laugh I had had for some time; and shouted:

"Merlin has wrought a spell! *Merlin,* forsooth! That cheap old humbug,[4] that maundering old ass? Bosh, pure bosh, the silliest bosh in the world! Why, it does seem to me that of all the childish, idiotic, chuckleheaded, chicken-livered superstitions that ev—oh, [curse] Merlin!"

But Clarence had slumped to his knees before I had half finished, and he was like to go out of his mind with fright.

"Oh, beware! These are awful words! Any moment these walls may crumble upon us if you say such things. Oh, call them back before it is too late!" ●

Literary Analysis
Parody Which phrases in Clarence's speech imitate the style of tales of knights?

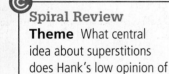

Spiral Review
Theme What central idea about superstitions does Hank's low opinion of Merlin suggest?

---

3. **a score** twenty.
4. **humbug** *n.* con artist; impostor; one who misrepresents himself or herself in order to take advantage of others.

Now this strange exhibition gave me a good idea and set me to thinking. If everybody about here was so honestly and sincerely afraid of Merlin's pretended magic as Clarence was, certainly a superior man like me ought to be shrewd enough to contrive some way to take advantage of such a state of things. I went on thinking, and worked out a plan. Then I said:

"Get up. Pull yourself together; look me in the eye. Do you know why I laughed?"

"No—but for our blessed Lady's sake, do it no more."

"Well, I'll tell you why I laughed. Because I'm a magician myself."

"Thou!" The boy recoiled a step, and caught his breath, for the thing hit him rather sudden; but the aspect which he took on was very, very respectful. I took quick note of that; it indicated that a humbug didn't need to have a reputation in this asylum; people stood ready to take him at his word, without that. I resumed.

"I've known Merlin seven hundred years, and he—"

"Seven hun—"

"Don't interrupt me. He has died and come alive again thirteen times, and traveled under a new name every time: Smith, Jones, Robinson, Jackson, Peters, Haskins, Merlin—a new alias every time he turns up. I knew him in Egypt three hundred years ago; I knew him in India five hundred years ago—he is always blethering around in my way, everywhere I go; he makes me tired. He don't amount to shucks, as a magician; knows some of the old common tricks, but has never got beyond the rudiments, and never will. He is well enough for the provinces[5]—one-night stands and that sort of thing, you know—but dear me, *he* oughtn't to set up for an expert—anyway not where there's a real artist. Now look here, Clarence, I am going to stand your friend, right along, and in return you must be mine. I want

---

5. **for the provinces** (präv´ ins iz) for unsophisticated audiences in places far from a big city.

Vocabulary
contrive (kən trīv´) *v.* bring about; manage

Vocabulary
rudiments (r̅o̅o̅´ də mənts) *n.* basics; slight beginning

☑ Reading Check
What does Hank claim to be?

Literary Analysis
Parody Which phrases
in Hank's speech are
humorously out of step
with traditional ideas of a
mighty sorcerer?

Vocabulary
calamity (kə lam´
ə tē) *n.* terrible mis-
fortune; disaster

Reading Skill
Compare Worldviews
What do Hank's
thoughts reveal about
his worldview? What do
they suggest about the
worldview of Clarence
and others of his time?

you to do me a favor. I want you to get word to the king that I am
a magician myself—and the Supreme Grand High-yu-Muckamuck
and head of the tribe, at that; and I want him to be made to
understand that I am just quietly arranging a little calamity here
that will make the fur fly in these realms if Sir Kay's project is
carried out and any harm comes to me. Will you get that to the
king for me?"

The poor boy was in such a state that he could hardly answer
me. It was pitiful to see a creature so terrified, so unnerved, so
demoralized. But he promised everything; and on my side he made
me promise over and over again that I would remain his friend, and
never turn against him or cast any enchantments upon him. Then
he worked his way out, staying himself with his hand along the
wall, like a sick person.

Presently this thought occurred to me: how heedless I have been!
When the boy gets calm, he will wonder why a great magician like
me should have begged a boy like him to help me get out of this
place; he will put this and that together, and will see that I am a
humbug.

I worried over that heedless blunder for an hour, and called
myself a great many hard names, meantime. But finally it occurred
to me all of a sudden that these animals didn't reason; that *they*
never put this and that together; that all their talk showed that
they didn't know a discrepancy when they saw it. I was at rest,
then.

But as soon as one is at rest, in this world, off he goes on
something else to worry about. It occured to me that I had made
another blunder: I had sent the boy off to alarm his betters with
a threat—I intending to invent a calamity at my leisure; now the
people who are the readiest and eagerest and willingest to swallow
miracles are the very ones who are hungriest to see you perform
them; suppose I should be called on for a sample? Suppose I should
be asked to name my calamity? Yes, I had made a blunder; I ought
to have invented my calamity first. "What shall I do? what can I say,
to gain a little time?" I was in trouble again; in the deepest kind of
trouble: . . . "There's a footstep!—they're coming. If I had only just a
moment to think. . . . Good, I've got it. I'm all right."

You see, it was the eclipse. It came into my mind, in the nick
of time, how Columbus, or Cortez, or one of those people, played
an eclipse as a saving trump once, on some savages, and I saw
my chance. I could play it myself, now; and it wouldn't be any
plagiarism, either, because I should get it in nearly a thousand
years ahead of those parties.

Clarence came in, subdued, distressed, and said:

"I hasted the message to our liege the king, and straightway he had me to his presence. He was frighted even to the marrow, and was minded to give order for your instant enlargement,[6] and that you be clothed in fine raiment and lodged as befitted one so great; but then came Merlin and spoiled all; for he persuaded the king that you are mad, and know not whereof you speak; and said your threat is but foolishness and idle vaporing. They disputed long, but in the end, Merlin, scoffing, said, 'Wherefore hath he not *named* his brave calamity? Verily it is because he cannot.' This thrust did in a most sudden sort close the king's mouth, and he could offer naught to turn the argument; and so, reluctant, and full loth to do you the discourtesy, he yet prayeth you to consider his perplexed case, as noting how the matter stands, and name the calamity—if so be you have determined the nature of it and the time of its coming. Oh, prithee delay not; to delay at such a time were to double and treble the perils that already compass thee about. Oh, be thou wise—name the calamity!"

I allowed silence to accumulate while I got my impressiveness together, and then said:

"How long have I been shut up in this hole?"

"Ye were shut up when yesterday was well spent. It is nine of the morning now."

"No! Then I have slept well, sure enough. Nine in the morning now! And yet it is the very complexion of midnight, to a shade. This is the 20th, then?"

"The 20th—yes."

"And I am to be burned alive to-morrow." The boy shuddered.

"At what hour?"

"At high noon."

"Now then, I will tell you what to say." I paused, and stood over that cowering lad a whole minute in awful silence; then, in a voice deep, measured, charged with doom, I began, and rose by dramatically graded stages to my colossal climax, which I delivered in as sublime and noble a way as ever I did such a thing in my life: "Go back and tell the king that at that hour I will smother the whole world in the dead blackness of midnight; I will blot out the sun, and he shall never shine again; the fruits of the earth shall rot for lack of light and warmth, and the peoples of the earth shall famish and die, to the last man!"

I had to carry the boy out myself, he sunk into such a collapse. I handed him over to the soldiers, and went back. •

---

6. **enlargement** *n.* old term for "release."

Literary Analysis
Parody Given the nature of the argument Clarence describes, why does the formality of his language seem exaggerated?

Reading
Check

How do the king and Merlin respond to Hank's threat of a "calamity"?

CHAPTER VI—THE ECLIPSE

In the stillness and the darkness, realization soon began to supplement knowledge. The mere knowledge of a fact is pale; but when you come to *realize* your fact, it takes on color. It is all the difference between hearing of a man being stabbed to the heart, and seeing it done. In the stillness and the darkness, the knowledge that I was in deadly danger took to itself deeper and deeper meaning all the time; a something which was realization crept inch by inch through my veins and turned me cold.

But it is a blessed provision of nature that at times like these, as soon as a man's mercury[7] has got down to a certain point there comes a revulsion, and he rallies. Hope springs up, and cheerfulness along with it, and then he is in good shape to do something for himself, if anything can be done. When my rally came, it came with a bound. I said to myself that my eclipse would be sure to save me, and make me the greatest man in the kingdom besides; and straightway my mercury went up to the top of the tube, and my solicitudes all vanished. I was as happy a man as there was in the world. I was even impatient for tomorrow to come, I so wanted to gather in that great triumph and be the center of all of the nation's wonder and reverence. Besides, in a business way it would be the making of me; I knew that.

Meantime there was one thing which had got pushed into the background of my mind. That was the half-conviction that when the nature of my proposed calamity should be reported to those superstitious people, it would have such an effect that they would want to compromise. So, by and by when I heard footsteps coming, that thought was recalled to me, and I said to myself, "As sure as anything, it's the compromise. Well, if it is good, all right, I will accept; but if it isn't, I mean to stand my ground and play my hand for all it is worth."

The door opened, and some men-at-arms appeared. The leader said:

"The stake is ready. Come!"

The stake! The strength went out of me, and I almost fell down. It is hard to get one's breath at such a time, such lumps come into one's throat, and such gaspings; but as soon as I could speak, I said:

"But this is a mistake—the execution is tomorrow."

"Order changed; been set forward a day. Haste thee!"

I was lost. There was no help for me. I was dazed, stupefied; I had

Reading Skill
Compare Worldviews
What does Hank indicate about his values in the last sentence of this paragraph?

Reading Skill
Compare Worldviews
What reasoning does Hank follow to determine that he will not succeed in creating his illusion?

---

7. **mercury** referring to the liquid metal used in a thermometer; the mercury rises and falls in the thermometer with the temperature.

Science Connection

Eclipses

An eclipse occurs when one heavenly body blocks our view of another. In a lunar eclipse, the earth comes between the sun and the moon, casting its shadow on the moon. In a solar eclipse, the moon comes between the Earth and the sun, blocking our view of the sun. In a famous incident to which Twain refers, Christopher Columbus, who knew that a lunar eclipse was to occur on February 29, 1504, won the cooperation of natives on Jamaica by predicting that the moon would change color and lose its light.

In a solar eclipse, the moon's shadow falls on Earth, turning day into night.

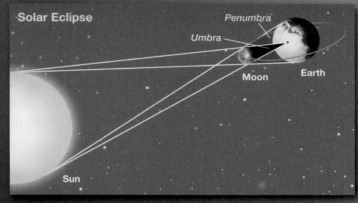

Solar Eclipse

Penumbra

Umbra

Moon   Earth

Sun

Connect to the Literature

How might a solar eclipse affect people, like those in this story, who lack a scientific understanding of the solar system?

no command over myself; I only wandered purposelessly about, like one out of his mind; so the soldiers took hold of me, and pulled me along with them, out of the cell and along the maze of underground corridors, and finally into the fierce glare of daylight and the upper world. As we stepped into the vast inclosed court of the castle I got a shock; for the first thing I saw was the stake, standing in the center, and near it the piled fagots[8] and a monk. On all four sides of the court the seated multitudes rose rank above rank, forming sloping terraces that were rich with color. The king and the queen sat in their thrones, the most conspicuous figures there, of course.

To note all this, occupied but a second. The next second Clarence had slipped from some place of concealment and was pouring news into my ear, his eyes beaming with triumph and gladness. He said:

"'Tis through *me* the change was wrought! And main hard have I worked to do it, too. But when I revealed to them the calamity in store, and saw how mighty was the terror it did engender, then saw I also that this was the time to strike! Wherefore I diligently

---

8. fagots (fag´ əts) *n.* bundles of sticks used as fuel.

Vocabulary
multitudes (mul´ tə tōōdz´) *n.* crowds; large number of people or things

conspicuous (kən spik´ yōō əs) *adj.* easy to see

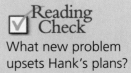
Reading Check

What new problem upsets Hank's plans?

from A Connecticut Yankee in King Arthur's Court **1199**

Literary Analysis
Parody In what way is Clarence's scheming a parody of Hank's?

pretended, unto this and that and the other one, that your power against the sun could not reach its full until the morrow; and so if any would save the sun and the world, you must be slain today, while your enchantments are but in the weaving and lack potency. Odsbodikins, it was but a dull lie, a most indifferent invention, but you should have seen them seize it and swallow it, in the frenzy of their fright, as it were salvation sent from heaven; and all the while was I laughing in my sleeve the one moment, to see them so cheaply deceived, and glorifying God the next, that He was content to let the meanest[9] of His creatures be His instrument to the saving of thy life. Ah, how happy has the matter sped! You will not need to do the sun a *real* hurt—ah, forget not that, on your soul forget it not! Only make a little darkness—only the littlest little darkness, mind, and cease with that. It will be sufficient. They will see that I spoke falsely—being ignorant, as they will fancy—and with the falling of the first shadow of that darkness you shall see them go mad with fear; and they will set you free and make you great! Go to thy triumph, now! But remember—ah, good friend, I implore thee remember my supplication, and do the blessed sun no hurt. For *my* sake, thy true friend."

I choked out some words through my grief and misery; as much as to say I would spare the sun; for which the lad's eyes paid me back with such deep and loving gratitude that I had not the heart to tell him his good-hearted foolishness had ruined me and sent me to my death. •

As the soldiers assisted me across the court the stillness was so profound that if I had been blindfold I should have supposed I was in a solitude instead of walled in by four thousand people. There was not a movement perceptible in those masses of humanity; they were as rigid as stone images, and as pale; and dread sat upon every countenance. This hush continued while I was being chained to the stake; it still continued while the fagots were carefully and tediously piled about my ankles, my knees, my thighs, my body. Then there was a pause, and a deeper hush, if possible, and a man knelt down at my feet with a blazing torch; the multitude strained forward, gazing, and parting slightly from their seats without knowing it; the monk raised his hands above my head, and his eyes toward the blue sky, and began some words in Latin; in this attitude he droned on and on, a little while, and then stopped. I waited two or three moments; then looked up; he was standing there petrified. With a common impulse the multitude rose slowly up and stared into the sky. I followed their eyes; as sure as guns,

---

9. meanest *adj.* lowest; least significant.

there was my eclipse beginning! The life went boiling through my veins; I was a new man! The rim of black spread slowly into the sun's disk, my heart beat higher and higher, and still the assemblage and the priest stared into the sky, motionless. I knew that this gaze would be turned upon me, next. When it was, I was ready. I was in one of the most grand attitudes I ever struck, with my arm stretched up pointing to the sun. It was a noble effect. You could see the shudder sweep the mass like a wave. Two shouts rang out, one close upon the heels of the other:

"Apply the torch!"

"I forbid it!"

The one was from Merlin, the other from the king. Merlin started from his place—to apply the torch himself, I judged. I said:

"Stay where you are. If any man moves—even the king— before I give him leave, I will blast him with thunder, I will consume him with lightnings!"

The multitude sank meekly into their seats, and I was just expecting they would. Merlin hesitated a moment or two, and I was on pins and needles that

◄ **Critical Viewing**
How do the emotions expressed in this illustration compare to those expressed by the king in the story? **[Compare and Contrast]**

Reading Check
What surprising event occurs just before Hank is about to be executed?

little while. Then he sat down, and I took a good breath; for I knew I was master of the situation now. The king said:

"Be merciful, fair sir, and essay no further in this perilous matter, lest disaster follow. It was reported to us that your powers could not attain unto their full strength until the morrow; but—"

"Your Majesty thinks the report may have been a lie? It *was* a lie."

That made an immense effect; up went appealing hands everywhere, and the king was assailed with a storm of supplications that I might be bought off at any price, and the calamity stayed.

The king was eager to comply. He said:

"Name any terms, reverend sir, even to the halving of my kingdom; but banish this calamity, spare the sun!"

My fortune was made, I would have taken him up in a minute, but I couldn't stop an eclipse; the thing was out of the question. So I asked time to consider. The king said:

"How long—ah, how long, good sir? Be merciful; look, it groweth darker, moment by moment. Prithee how long?"

"Not long. Half an hour—maybe an hour."

There were a thousand pathetic protests, but I couldn't shorten up any, for I couldn't remember how long a total eclipse lasts. I was in a puzzled condition, anyway, and wanted to think. Something was wrong about that eclipse, and the fact was very unsettling. If this wasn't the one I was after, how was I to tell whether this was the sixth century, or nothing but a dream? Dear me, if I could only prove it was the latter! Here was a glad new hope. If the boy was right about the date, and this was surely the 20th, it *wasn't* the sixth century. I reached for the monk's sleeve, in considerable

"HOW LONG—AH, HOW LONG, GOOD SIR? BE MERCIFUL; LOOK, IT GROWETH DARKER, MOMENT BY MOMENT. PRITHEE HOW LONG?"

excitement, and asked him what day of the month it was.

Hang him, he said it was the *twenty-first*! It made me turn cold to hear him. I begged him not to make any mistake about it; but he was sure; he knew it was the 21st. So, that feather-headed boy had botched things again! The time of the day was right for the eclipse; I had seen that for myself, in the beginning, by the dial[10] that was near by. Yes, I *was* in King Arthur's court, and I might as well make the most of it I could.

The darkness was steadily growing, the people becoming more and more distressed. I now said:

"I have reflected, Sir King. For a lesson, I will let this darkness proceed, and spread night in the world; but whether I blot out the sun for good, or restore it shall rest with you. These are the terms, to wit: You shall remain king over all your dominions, and receive all the glories and honors that belong to the kingship; but you shall appoint me your perpetual minister and executive, and give me for my services one per cent. of such actual increase of revenue[11] over and above its present amount as I may succeed in creating for the state. If I can't live on that, I sha'n't ask anybody to give me a lift. Is it satisfactory?"

There was a prodigious roar of applause, and out of the midst of it the king's voice rose, saying:

"Away with his bonds, and set him free! and do him homage, high and low, rich and poor, for he is become the king's right hand, is clothed with power and authority, and his seat is upon the highest step of the throne! Now sweep away this creeping night, and bring the light and cheer again, that all the world may bless thee."

But I said:

"That a common man should be shamed before the world, is nothing; but it were dishonor to the *king* if any that saw his minister naked should not also see him delivered from his shame. If I might ask that my clothes be brought again—"

"They are not meet," the king broke in. "Fetch raiment of another sort; clothe him like a prince!"

My idea worked. I wanted to keep things as they were till the eclipse was total, otherwise they would be trying again to get me to dismiss the darkness, and of course I couldn't do it. Sending for the clothes gained some delay, but not enough. So I had to make another excuse. I said it would be but natural if the king should change his mind and repent to some extent of what he had done under excitement; therefore I would let the darkness grow awhile,

---

10. **dial** *n.* sundial, or device used to measure time by the position of the sun in the sky.
11. **revenue** (rev´ ə noo´) *n.* money taken in by a government in the form of taxes, fees, and penalties.

Reading Skill
Compare Worldviews
What are the differing ways in which Hank and the crowd interpret the eclipse?

Literary Analysis
Parody What two types of language does Hank mix together in this speech? Explain.

Literary Analysis
Parody Which elements of the situation make the king's solemn words into a parody?

Reading Check
What does Hank ask for in return for bringing back the sun?

and if at the end of a reasonable time the king had kept his mind the same, the darkness should be dismissed. Neither the king nor anybody else was satisfied with that arrangement, but I had to stick to my point.

It grew darker and darker and blacker and blacker, while I struggled with those awkward sixth-century clothes. It got to be pitch-dark, at last, and the multitude groaned with horror to feel the cold uncanny night breezes fan through the place and see the stars come out and twinkle in the sky. At last the eclipse was total, and I was very glad of it, but everybody else was in misery; which was quite natural. I said:

"The king, by his silence, still stands to the terms." Then I lifted up my hand—stood just so a moment—then I said, with the most awful solemnity: "Let the enchantment dissolve and pass harmless away!"

There was no response, for a moment, in that deep darkness and that graveyard hush. But when the silver rim of the sun pushed itself out, a moment or two later, the assemblage broke loose with a vast shout and came pouring down like a deluge to smother me with blessings and gratitude.

And Clarence was not the last of the wash, to be sure.

Critical Thinking

Cite textual evidence to support your responses.

1. **Key Ideas and Details** **(a)** What threat does Hank face? **(b) Infer:** Why does he think he may be dreaming?

2. **Key Ideas and Details** **(a)** What does Clarence say Merlin has woven? **(b) Analyze:** What story about himself does this information prompt Hank to tell?

3. **Key Ideas and Details** **(a) Interpret:** What does the deal Hank strikes with King Arthur show about his character? **(b) Make a Judgment:** Is Hank's manipulation of Clarence and the king justified? Why or why not?

4. **Integration of Knowledge and Ideas** **(a)** List two reasons why Hank could continue to be successful as a "hero" in King Arthur's court. **(b)** List two reasons why Hank might not be successful. *[Connect to the Big Question: Can anyone be a hero?]*

Literary Analysis: Parody

© 1. Craft and Structure (a) Identify the main personality traits of Clarence, Merlin, and King Arthur. **(b)** Which traits would the characters in the King Arthur legends probably not display? Explain.

© 2. Craft and Structure Using a chart like the one shown, give examples of ways in which Hank is a **parody** of a heroic figure.

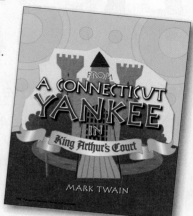

Arthurian Hero	Hank Morgan
1. wins with great strength or supernatural power 2. desires glory 3. serves his king out of loyalty 4. other _____	1. 2. 3. 4.

© 3. Key Ideas and Details What attitudes, values, or beliefs of Twain's are suggested in this parody?

Reading Skill: Compare Worldviews

4. (a) Compare and contrast two of Hank's and Clarence's reactions to danger. **(b)** What does the contrast suggest about common illusions in Arthur's day?

Vocabulary

© Acquisition and Use Replace the italicized word in each sentence with its **antonym,** or word of opposite meaning, from the list on page 1190. Then, explain which version of the sentence works better.

1. To master the *subtleties* of the saxophone, take advanced lessons.

2. The entire nation mourned his *success*.

3. The band was successful, so *handfuls* of people came to the show.

4. She is concerned about the *benefits* of stray dogs and cats.

5. She needed to *destroy* a way to win the election.

6. The bland color of his outfit makes him *unnoticeable*.

Word Study Use the context of the sentences and what you know about the **Latin prefix *multi-*** to explain your answer to each question.

1. Is a *multilingual* teacher limited to speaking only in English?

2. If a person is good at *multitasking*, can he or she do several things at once?

Word Study

The **Latin prefix *multi-*** means "many" or "much."

Apply It Explain how the prefix *multi-* contributes to the meanings of these words. Consult a dictionary if necessary.

multicultural

multipurpose

multisyllabic

THE BIG

Can anyone be a *hero?*

Writing About the Big Question

In the excerpt from *Don Quixote,* a gentleman sets out to become a hero. Use these sentence starters to develop your ideas about the Big Question.

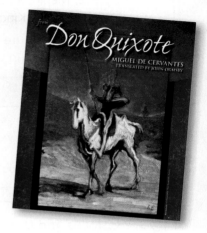

Someone dreaming about being a **legendary** hero might imagine that it is important to _____. However, the most useful **attributes** for a hero in real life are _____.

While You Read Examine Don Quixote's actions and ideas to discover what he thinks a hero should do.

Vocabulary

Read each word and its definition. Decide whether you know the word well, know it a little bit, or do not know it at all. After you read, see how your knowledge of each word has increased.

- **lucidity** (lōō sid´ ə tē) *n.* clarity; quality of being readily understood (p. 1209) *We built the model well because of the lucidity of the instructions in the manual. lucid adj. lucidly adv.*

- **affable** (af´ ə bəl) *adj.* pleasant; friendly (p. 1210) *Because she was so affable, she had many friends. affability n. affably adv.*

- **ingenuity** (in´ jə nōō´ ə tē) *n.* cleverness (p. 1211) *His ingenuity was apparent when he mended the chair with only tape and string. genius n. ingenious adj.*

- **sonorous** (sə nôr´ əs) *adj.* having a rich or impressive sound (p. 1212) *His sonorous voice echoed across the room. sonority n. sonorously adv.*

- **veracious** (və rā´ shəs) *adj.* truthful; honest (p. 1212) *Her veracious account of the accident left no doubt as to who was at fault. verify v. veracity n.*

- **extolled** (ek stōld´) *adj.* praised (p. 1213) *The joys of country living are often extolled. extol v. extoller n.*

Word Study

The **Latin prefix ex-** means "up" or "out."

In this story, a character thinks his accomplishments have not been adequately **extolled,** or praised highly enough.

Meet
Miguel de Cervantes
(1547–1616)

Author of
Don Quixote

Born near Madrid, Spain, Miguel de Cervantes (mē gel´ də sər vän´ tēz) joined the army as a young man. Returning to Spain from a war, he was captured by pirates, who enslaved him for five years. Even after returning home, Cervantes's troubles were not over: Financial problems eventually led to fines and imprisonment.

A Change of Fortune Cervantes's luck changed when he published his novel *Don Quixote* (dän´ kē hōt´ ē). Although the book did not make him rich, it did ease his debts and win him fame. Cervantes is widely regarded as Spain's greatest writer.

BACKGROUND FOR THE PARODY
The Age of Chivalry

The days of knights were long gone when Miguel de Cervantes wrote *Don Quixote*, his parody of medieval romance—tales of knightly adventure. In these stories, knights live by the code of chivalry, rules for conduct that stress courage and courtesy.

> ### DID YOU KNOW?
> Tradition has it that Cervantes wrote at least part of *Don Quixote* while he was in prison.

Don Quixote, Pablo Picasso, Bridgeman Art Library, London/New York, ©2004 Estate of Pablo Picasso/Artists Rights Society (ARS), New York

from

Don Quixote

MIGUEL DE CERVANTES
TRANSLATED BY JOHN ORMSBY

CHAPTER I

*W*hich Treats of the Character and Pursuits of the Famous Gentleman Don Quixote[1] of La Mancha[2]

In a village of La Mancha, which I prefer to leave unnamed, there lived not long ago one of those gentlemen that keep a lance in the lance-rack, an old shield, a lean hack, and a greyhound for hunting. A stew of rather more beef than mutton, hash on most nights, bacon and eggs on Saturdays, lentils on Fridays, and a pigeon or so extra on Sundays consumed three quarters of his income. The rest went for a coat of fine cloth and velvet breeches and shoes to match for holidays, while on weekdays he cut a fine figure in his best homespun. He had in his house a housekeeper past forty, a niece under twenty, and a lad for the field and marketplace, who saddled the hack as well as handled the pruning knife. The age of this gentleman of ours was bordering on fifty. He was of a hardy constitution, spare, gaunt-featured, a very early riser, and fond of hunting. Some say that his surname was Quixada or Quesada (for there is no unanimity among those who write on the subject), although reasonable conjectures tend to show that he was called Quexana. But this scarcely affects our story; it will be enough not to stray a hair's breadth from the truth in telling it.

You must know that the above-named gentleman devoted his leisure (which was mostly all the year round) to reading books of chivalry—and with such ardor and avidity that he almost entirely abandoned the chase and even the management of his property. To such a pitch did his eagerness and infatuation go that he sold many an acre of tillage land to buy books of chivalry to read, bringing home all he could find.

But there were none he liked so well as those written by the famous Feliciano de Silva, for their lucidity of style and complicated conceits[3] were as pearls in his sight, particularly when in his reading he came upon outpourings of adulation[4] and courtly challenges. There he often found passages like *"the reason of the unreason with which my reason is afflicted so weakens my reason that with reason I complain of your beauty"*; or again, *"the high heavens, that of your divinity divinely fortify you with the stars, render you deserving of the desert your greatness deserves."*

Over this sort of folderol[5] the poor gentleman lost his wits, and he used to lie awake striving to understand it and worm

---

1. **Don Quixote** (dän´ kē hōt´ ē).
2. **La Mancha** province (region) in south-central Spain.
3. **conceits** (kən sēts´) *n.* elaborate comparisons or metaphors.
4. **adulation** (a´ jōō lā´ shən) *n.* intense or excessive praise or admiration.
5. **folderol** (fäl´ də räl´) *n.* mere nonsense.

Literary Analysis
Parody Which details in this paragraph make the formal-sounding chapter title seem ridiculous?

Vocabulary
lucidity (lōō sid´ ə tē) *n.* clarity; quality of being readily understood

Literary Analysis
Parody What qualities of the language of heroic tales are mocked in the quotations in this paragraph?

Reading Check

To what activity does Quixada devote most of his time?

▲ **Critical Viewing**
What feelings or ideas might Don Quixote associate with this image? Explain. **[Connect]**

out its meaning; though Aristotle[6] himself could have made out or extracted nothing, had he come back to life for that special purpose. He was rather uneasy about the wounds which Don Belianís gave and received, because it seemed to him that, however skilled the surgeons who had cured him, he must have had his face and body covered all over with seams and scars. He commended, however, the author's way of ending his book, with a promise to go on with that interminable adventure, and many a time he felt the urge to take up his pen and finish it just as its author had promised. He would no doubt have done so, and succeeded with it too, had he not been occupied with greater and more absorbing thoughts.

Many an argument did he have with the priest of his village (a learned man, and a graduate of Sigüenza[7]) as to which had been the better knight, Palmerín of England or Amadís of Gaul. Master Nicolás, the village barber, however, used to say that neither of them came up to the Knight of Phœbus, and that if there was any that could compare with *him* it was Don Galaor, the brother of Amadís of Gaul, because he had a spirit equal to every occasion, and was no wishy-washy knight or a crybaby like his brother, while in valor he was not a whit behind him.

In short, he became so absorbed in his books that he spent his nights from sunset to sunrise, and his days from dawn to dark, poring over them; and what with little sleep and much reading his brain shriveled up and he lost his wits. His imagination was stuffed with all he read in his books about enchantments, quarrels, battles, challenges, wounds, wooings, loves, agonies, and all sorts of impossible nonsense. It became so firmly planted in his mind that the whole fabric of invention and fancy he read about was true, that to him no history in the world was better substantiated. He used to say the Cid Ruy Díaz[8] was a very good knight but that he was not to be compared with the Knight of the Burning Sword who with one backstroke cut in half two fierce and monstrous giants. He thought more of Bernardo del Carpio because at Roncesvalles he slew Roland in spite of enchantments, availing himself of Hercules' trick when he strangled Antæus the son of Terra in his arms. He approved highly of the giant Morgante, because, although of the giant breed which is always arrogant and ill-mannered, he alone was **affable** and well-bred. But above all he admired Reinaldos of

Ⓒ **Spiral Review**
Theme What central idea about reading is expressed in this paragraph?

Reading Skill
Compare Worldviews
Why might Don Quixote's illusion be so appealing to him?

Vocabulary
affable (af´ə bəl) *adj.* pleasant; friendly

---

6. **Aristotle** (ar´ is tät´´l) ancient Greek thinker and scientist.
7. **Siguenza** (sē gwän´ sä) one of a group of "minor universities" granting degrees that were often laughed at by Spanish humorists.
8. **Cid Ruy Díaz** (sēd rōō´ ē dē´ äs) famous Spanish soldier Ruy Díaz de Vivar; called "the Cid," a derivation of the Arabic word for "lord."

Montalbán, especially when he saw him sallying forth from his castle and robbing everyone he met, and when beyond the seas he stole that image of Mohammed which, as his history says, was entirely of gold. To have a bout of kicking at that traitor of a Ganelon he would have given his housekeeper, and his niece into the bargain.

In a word, his wits being quite gone, he hit upon the strangest notion that every madman in this world hit upon. He fancied it was right and requisite, no less for his own greater renown than in the service of his country, that he should make a knight-errant of himself, roaming the world over in full armor and on horseback in quest of adventures. He would put into practice all that he had read of as being the usual practices of knights-errant: righting every kind of wrong, and exposing himself to peril and danger from which he would emerge to reap eternal fame and glory. Already the poor man saw himself crowned by the might of his arm Emperor of Trebizond[9] at least. And so, carried away by the intense enjoyment he found in these pleasant fancies, he began at once to put his scheme into execution. •

The first thing he did was to clean up some armor that had belonged to his ancestors and had for ages been lying forgotten in a corner, covered with rust and mildew. He scoured and polished it as best he could, but the one great defect he saw in it was that it had no closed helmet, nothing but a simple morion.[10] This deficiency, however, his ingenuity made good, for he contrived a kind of half-helmet of

---

9. **Trebizond** (treb´ i zänd´) in medieval times, a Greek empire off the southeast coast of the Black Sea.
10. **morion** (mōr´ ē än´) *n.* old-fashioned soldier's helmet with a brim, covering the top part of the head.

▲ **Critical Viewing**
In this illustration, what elements convey Don Quixote's condition? **[Analyze]**

Vocabulary
ingenuity (in´ jə nōō´ ə tē) *n.* cleverness

Reading Check
What effect does Don Quixote's reading have on his mind?

from Don Quixote **1211**

Reading Skill
Compare Worldviews
How does the narrator's view of the helmet differ from Don Quixote's?

Literary Analysis
Parody How does the contrast between the "lofty, sonorous name" and the horse's actual qualities add to the parody?

Vocabulary
sonorous (sə nôr´ əs)
adj. having a rich or impressive sound
veracious (və rā´ shəs)
adj. truthful; honest

pasteboard which, fitted on to the morion, looked like a whole one. It is true that, in order to see if it was strong and fit to withstand a cut, he drew his sword and gave it a couple of slashes, the first of which undid in an instant what had taken him a week to do. The ease with which he had knocked it to pieces disconcerted him somewhat, and to guard against the danger he set to work again, fixing bars of iron on the inside until he was satisfied with its strength. Then, not caring to try any more experiments with it, he accepted and commissioned it as a helmet of the most perfect construction.

He next proceeded to inspect his nag, which, with its cracked hoofs and more blemishes than the steed of Gonela, that "*tantum pellis et ossa fuit,*"[11] surpassed in his eyes the Bucephalus of Alexanderia or the Babieca of the Cid.[12] Four days were spent in thinking what name to give him, because (as he said to himself) it was not right that a horse belonging to a knight so famous, and one with such merits of its own, should be without some distinctive name. He strove to find something that would indicate what it had been before belonging to a knight-errant, and what it had now become. It was only reasonable that it should be given a new name to match the new career adopted by its master, and that the name should be a distinguished and full-sounding one, befitting the new order and calling it was about to follow. And so, after having composed, struck out, rejected, added to, unmade, and remade a multitude of names out of his memory and fancy, he decided upon calling it Rocinante. To his thinking this was a lofty, sonorous name that nevertheless indicated what the hack's[13] status had been before it became what now it was, the first and foremost of all the hacks in the world.

Having got a name for his horse so much to his taste, he was anxious to get one for himself, and he spent eight days more pondering over this point. At last he made up his mind to call himself Don Quixote—which, as stated above, led the authors of this veracious history to infer that his name quite assuredly must have been Quixada, and not Quesada as others would have it. It occurred to him, however, that the valiant Amadís was not content to call himself Amadís and nothing more but added the name of his kingdom and country to make it famous and called himself Amadís of Gaul. So he, like a good knight, resolved to add on the name of his own region and style himself Don Quixote of La Mancha. He believed that this accurately described his origin and country, and

---

11. "***tantum pellis et ossa fuit***" (tän´ tum pel´ is et äs´ ə foo´ it) "creature made of skin and bones" (Latin).
12. **Bucephalus** (byoo sef´ ə ləs) **of Alexander or the Babieca** (bäb ē ā´ kä) **of the Cid** Bucephalus was Alexander the Great's war horse; Babieca was the Cid's war horse.
13. **hack's** An old, worn-out horse.

that he did it honor by taking its name for his own.

So then, his armor being furbished, his morion turned into a helmet, his hack christened, and he himself confirmed, he came to the conclusion that nothing more was needed now but to look for a lady to be in love with, for a knight-errant without love was like a tree without leaves or fruit, or a body without a soul.

"If, for my sins, or by my good fortune," he said to himself, "I come across some giant hereabouts, a common occurrence with knights-errant, and knock him to the ground in one onslaught, or cleave him asunder at the waist, or, in short, vanquish and subdue him, will it not be well to have someone I may send him to as a present, that he may come in and fall on his knees before my sweet lady, and in a humble, submissive voice say, 'I am the giant Caraculiambro, lord of the island of Malindrania, vanquished in single combat by the never sufficiently *extolled* knight Don Quixote of La Mancha, who has commanded me to present myself before your grace, that your highness may dispose of me at your pleasure'?"

Oh, how our good gentleman enjoyed the delivery of this speech, especially when he had thought of someone to call his lady! There was, so the story goes, in a village near his own a very good-looking farm-girl with whom he had been at one time in love, though, so far as is known, she never knew it nor gave a thought to the matter. Her name was Aldonza Lorenzo, and upon her he thought fit to confer the title of Lady of his Thoughts. Searching for a name not too remote from her own, yet which would aim at and bring to mind that of a princess and great lady, he decided upon calling her Dulcinea del Toboso, since she was a native of El Toboso. To his way of thinking, the name was musical, uncommon, and significant, like all those he had bestowed upon himself and his belongings. ●

Don Quixote, Pablo Picasso. Bridgeman Art Library, London/New York. © 2004 Estate of Pablo Picasso/Artists Rights Society, (ARS), New York.

▲ **Critical Viewing**
In this painting, how does the physical contrast between Sancho Panza and Don Quixote reflect different views of the world? **[Connect]**

Vocabulary
extolled (ek stōld´)
adj. praised

Reading Check
What three steps has Don Quixote taken to transform himself into a knight?

CHAPTER VIII

Of the Good Fortune Which the Valiant Don Quixote Had in the Terrible and Undreamed-of Adventure of the Windmills, With Other Occurrences Worthy to Be Fitly Recorded

At this point they came in sight of thirty or forty windmills that are on that plain.

"Fortune," said Don Quixote to his squire, as soon as he had seen them, "is arranging matters for us better than we could have hoped. Look there, friend Sancho Panza,[14] where thirty or more monstrous giants rise up, all of whom I mean to engage in battle and slay, and with whose spoils we shall begin to make our fortunes. For this is righteous warfare, and it is God's good service to sweep so evil a breed from off the face of the earth."

"What giants?" said Sancho Panza.

"Those you see there," answered his master, "with the long arms, and some have them nearly two leagues[15] long."

"Look, your worship," said Sancho. "What we see there are not giants but windmills, and what seem to be their arms are the vanes that turned by the wind make the millstone go."

"It is easy to see," replied Don Quixote, "that you are not used to this business of adventures. Those are giants, and if you are afraid, away with you out of here and betake yourself to prayer, while I engage them in fierce and unequal combat."

So saying, he gave the spur to his steed Rocinante, heedless of the cries his squire Sancho sent after him, warning him that most certainly they were windmills and not giants he was going to attack. He, however, was so positive they were giants that he neither heard the cries of Sancho, nor perceived, near as he was, what they were.

"Fly not, cowards and vile beings," he shouted, "for a single knight attacks you."

A slight breeze at this moment sprang up, and the great vanes began to move.

"Though ye flourish more arms than the giant Briareus, ye have to reckon with me!" exclaimed Don Quixote, when he saw this.

So saying, he commended himself with all his heart to his lady Dulcinea, imploring her to support him in such a peril. With lance braced and covered by his shield, he charged at Rocinante's fullest gallop and attacked the first mill that stood in front of him. But as he drove his lance-point into the sail, the wind whirled it around with

Reading Skill
Compare Worldviews
What different ideas about the windmills do Sancho Panza and Don Quixote have?

---

14. Sancho Panza a simple countryman whom Don Quixote takes as his squire. In contrast to Don Quixote, Panza is practical and has common sense.

15. leagues (lēgz) *n.* A league is a distance of about three miles in English-speaking countries.

such force that it shivered the lance to pieces. It swept away with it horse and rider, and they were sent rolling over the plain, in sad condition indeed.

Sancho hastened to his assistance as fast as the animal could go. When he came up he found Don Quixote unable to move, with such an impact had Rocinante fallen with him.

"God bless me!" said Sancho. "Did I not tell your worship to watch what you were doing, because they were only windmills? No one could have made any mistake about it unless he had something of the same kind in his head."

"Silence, friend Sancho," replied Don Quixote. "The fortunes of war more than any other are liable to frequent fluctuations. Moreover I think, and it is the truth, that that same sage Frestón who carried off my study and books, has turned these giants into mills in order to rob me of the glory of vanquishing them, such is the enmity he bears me. But in the end his wicked arts will avail but little against my good sword."

"God's will be done," said Sancho Panza, and helping him to rise got him up again on Rocinante, whose shoulder was half dislocated. Then, discussing the adventure, they followed the road to Puerto Lápice, for there, said Don Quixote, they could not fail to find adventures in abundance and variety, as it was a well-traveled thoroughfare. For all that, he was much grieved at the loss of his lance, and said so to his squire.

"I remember having read," he added, "how a Spanish knight, Diego Pérez de Vargas by name, having broken his sword in battle, tore from an oak a ponderous bough or branch. With it he did such things that day, and pounded so many Moors, that he got the surname of Machuca, and he and his descendants from that day forth were called Vargas y Machuca. I mention this because from the first oak I see I mean to tear such a branch, large and stout. I am determined and resolved to do such deeds with it that you may deem yourself very fortunate in being found worthy to see them and be an eyewitness of things that will scarcely be believed."

"Be that as God wills," said Sancho, "I believe it all as your worship says it. But straighten yourself a little, for you seem to be leaning to one side, maybe from the shaking you got when you fell."

▲ **Critical Viewing**
Which details in this painting capture the humor of Don Quixote's "battle" with the windmills? **[Analyze]**

Literary Analysis
Parody How does the contrast between Don Quixote's ridiculous defeat and these brave words contribute to the humor in this parody?

Reading Check
Which "enemy" does Don Quixote decide to battle?

"That is the truth," said Don Quixote, "and if I make no complaint of the pain it is because knights-errant are not permitted to complain of any wound, even though their bowels be coming out through it."

"If so," said Sancho, "I have nothing to say. But God knows I would rather your worship complained when anything ailed you. For my part, I confess I must complain however small the ache may be, unless this rule about not complaining applies to the squires of knights-errant also."

Don Quixote could not help laughing at his squire's simplicity, and assured him he might complain whenever and however he chose, just as he liked. So far he had never read of anything to the contrary in the order of knighthood.

Sancho reminded him it was dinner time, to which his master answered that he wanted nothing himself just then, but that Sancho might eat when he had a mind. With this permission Sancho settled himself as comfortably as he could on his beast, and taking out of the saddlebags what he had stowed away in them, he jogged along behind his master munching slowly. From time to time he took a pull at the wineskin with all the enjoyment that the thirstiest tavernkeeper in Málaga might have envied. And while he went on in this way, between gulps, he never gave a thought to any of the promises his master had made him, nor did he rate it as hardship but rather as recreation going in quest of adventures, however dangerous they might be.

Reading Skill
Compare Worldviews
What contrasting views of bodily comfort do Don Quixote and Sancho Panza have?

Critical Thinking

Cite textual evidence to support your responses.

© **1. Key Ideas and Details (a)** What does Don Quixote spend most of his time doing before he decides to become a knight? **(b) Analyze Cause and Effect:** In what way does this activity bring about his decision?

© **2. Key Ideas and Details (a)** Why does Don Quixote attack the windmills? **(b) Connect:** How does he explain his failure to conquer them? **(c) Hypothesize:** What would happen to his dreams of knightly adventure if he admitted the truth about the windmills?

© **3. Key Ideas and Details Speculate:** Why do you think Sancho agrees to go adventuring with Don Quixote?

© **4. Integration of Knowledge and Ideas (a)** Do you think Don Quixote displays heroic qualities? Explain. **(b)** What are the advantages and dangers of Don Quixote's illusion of being a legendary hero? *[Connect to the Big Question: Can anyone be a hero?]*

Literary Analysis: Parody

1. Craft and Structure In what way is Don Quixote's adventure with the windmills a **parody** of an episode in a romance or legend?

2. Craft and Structure Using a chart like the one shown, give examples of specific ways in which Don Quixote parodies a heroic knight.

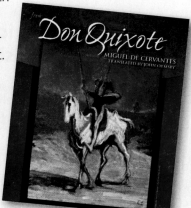

Legendary Knight	Don Quixote
1. wears shining armour	1.
2. rides a great steed	2.
3. pledges love to a lady	3.
4. conquers giants	4.
5. other _____	5.

3. Integration of Knowledge and Ideas What attitudes, values, or beliefs of Cervantes' are suggested in this parody?

Reading Skill: Compare Worldviews

4. (a) Compare and contrast Don Quixote's responses with Sancho Panza's in two situations. **(b)** In what way do these contrasts emphasize the fact that Don Quixote's beliefs are illusions?

Vocabulary

Acquisition and Use Replace the italicized word in each sentence with its **antonym,** or word of opposite meaning, from the list on page 1206. Then, explain which version of the sentence works better.

1. The *vagueness* of his idea convinced other scientists to accept it.

2. The speaker's *squeaky* voice soothed his listeners.

3. I knew we had similar tastes when she *criticized* my favorite poet.

4. Everyone liked her because of her *unpleasant* personality.

5. Her clear and original science project showcased her *inability*.

6. She was *dishonest* to a fault and always said what she meant.

Word Study Use the context of the sentences and what you know about the **Latin prefix ex-** to explain your answer to each question.

1. If you *excavate* a hole, are you filling it in?

2. If a store charges *exorbitant* prices, are its prices normal?

Word Study

The **Latin prefix ex-** means "up" or "out."

Apply It Explain how the prefix ex- contributes to the meanings of these words. Consult a dictionary if necessary.

excel

exalt

expansion

Integrated Language Skills

from A Connecticut Yankee in King Arthur's Court • *from* Don Quixote

Conventions: Semicolons, Colons, and Ellipsis Points

Semicolons, colons, and **ellipsis points** are three forms of punctuation that suggest pauses in a sentence.

Use a **semicolon** to join independent clauses not already joined by a coordinating conjunction (*and, but, or, nor, for, so,* and *yet*). Use semicolons to separate items in a series when one or more of the items includes a comma or the word "and."

• **Example:** Ivan devised a plan; he was confident of success.

A **colon** directs the reader's attention to the text that follows it. Use a colon to introduce a list, a quotation, or an example.

• **Example:** The list contained only a few items: milk, soap, and eggs.

The three spaced periods that form **ellipsis points** represent a gap or a pause in a sentence. Ellipsis points may also show that something has been omitted.

• **Example:** As I read about Don Quixote, I counted the imaginary giants, "One, two, three . . . "

Practice A Copy each of the following sentences, adding semicolons, colons, or ellipsis points where necessary.

1. Hank was a manager in a factory he did not believe in time travel.

2. Clarence had many good qualities loyalty, honesty, and courage.

3. Hank was sure all was well until he saw the stake and wood for the fire.

© Reading Application Find an example of a semicolon, a colon, and ellipsis points in *A Connecticut Yankee in King Arthur's Court.*

Practice B Rewrite the following sentences, correcting any errors by inserting or deleting semicolons, colons, or ellipsis points. If no corrections are necessary, write "correct."

1. Don Quixote collected the necessary items; armor, a helmet, his sword, and a horse.

2. They decided to: fight a great foe . . . windmills.

3. Don Quixote conquers the windmills; although Sancho does not help him.

© Writing Application Write three sentences about the painting on page 1211. Use a semicolon, a colon, or ellipsis points in each sentence.

PH WRITING COACH Further instruction and practice are available in *Prentice Hall Writing Coach.*

Writing

Narrative Text Write a **parody** in which a twenty-first-century time traveler lands in King Arthur's world *or* a parody in which Don Quixote takes on a twenty-first-century challenge. Follow these tips:

- Choose a situation that causes problems for your time traveler or that Don Quixote might misunderstand. Outline the events of your story.

- Decide on your story's narrator and his or her attitudes about the story's characters and events.

- Clearly depict both the reality of what is happening and the illusions in the characters' minds. Write interior monologues expressing the characters' feelings and opinions. Use dialogue to depict interactions with other characters.

- Add details in longer sentences to slow the story's pace and introduce characters or settings. Use short sentences and punchy language to speed the pace and add excitement.

- Exaggerate to convey the humor of the events and characters' reactions.

Grammar Application Make sure you have properly used semicolons, colons, and ellipsis points in your parody.

Writing Workshop: *Work in Progress*

Prewriting for a Comparison-and-Contrast Essay Use the Freewrites from your writing portfolio to develop a **Venn diagram** of similarities and differences. List similarities in the left oval and differences in the right oval. Write points that apply to both literary works in the overlapping oval. Save the Venn Diagram in your writing portfolio.

Research and Technology

Build and Present Knowledge Working with a group, create a **biographical brochure** on Mark Twain or Miguel de Cervantes. Brainstorm several research questions to guide your work. Then, use biographical dictionaries, the Internet, the library, and other reliable sources to find answers to your research questions.

- Include the key details of the author's life, along with a timeline of the author's life and works.

- Use publishing software to design and publish your document.

- Apply design principles when setting margins, tabs, spacing, or columns. Select a readable font.

- Incorporate drawings and graphics into your finished work.

**Common Core
State Standards**

L.9-10.2, L.9-10.2.a,
L.9-10.2.b; W.9-10.3,
W.9-10.3.b, W.9-10.7
[For the full wording of the standards, see page 1188.]

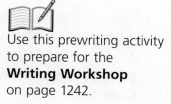

Use this prewriting activity to prepare for the **Writing Workshop** on page 1242.

Test Practice: Reading

Compare Worldviews

Fiction Selection

Directions: *Read the selection. Then, answer the questions.*

Alex and Randy stepped through the broad wooden doors into a thick forest. Alex gasped. A moment ago they had been in a museum. Alex turned around, but the doors had disappeared. "Cool," said Randy casually. Alex had promised Randy he would see the dinosaur exhibit, but this must be real. Alex could feel the fear crawling up his back. Just then, a deep roar shook the ground. "Very cool," said Randy with a big grin.

"Randy, this isn't funny! Where are we?"

"We're in a museum! Think rationally! This is an exhibit." said Randy.

"No. We must have gone back in time or something. The doors have disappeared! I can hear a dinosaur! We've got to get out of here!" cried Alex.

Randy laughed. "You always jump to conclusions!" He pushed a button set into a nearby tree trunk. The screen of trees slid back, revealing the doors. "See?" Randy said. "*I* read the brochure. It's just an illusion!"

1. Which of the following *best* describes Randy's reaction to the exhibit?

    A. He jokes that it is cool.
    B. He believes it is boring.
    C. He thinks it is scary.
    D. He wonders if he is lost.

2. What *best* describes the difference between Alex's and Randy's worldview?

    A. Alex jumps to unrealistic conclusions; Randy believes in thinking rationally.
    B. Alex is always fearful and afraid; Randy reads instructions carefully.
    C. Alex believes in having fun; Randy believes in being cautious.
    D. Alex believes in dinosaurs; Randy believes dinosaurs are imaginary creatures.

3. At the exhibit Alex is under the impression that he has—

    A. traveled to the future.
    B. frightened Randy with a trick.
    C. entered the ancient world of dinosaurs.
    D. discovered a new exhibit at the museum.

4. Alex could have avoided this misconception by—

    A. entering the exhibit later.
    B. playing a different trick on Randy.
    C. learning more about dinosaurs.
    D. reading the museum's brochure.

Writing for Assessment

In a brief paragraph, describe how Randy and Alex's different worldviews influenced their reactions after they entered the exhibit Support your response with details.

Nonfiction Selection

Directions: *Read the selection. Then, answer the questions.*

Long before scientists knew about the existence of dinosaurs, ancient people knew about dinosaur bones. Many legends surrounded the fossils of dinosaurs and other prehistoric beasts. The ancient Chinese believed that these fossils were "dragon bones" and "dragon teeth" and ground them up for use as medicines. Dinosaur fossils may have been the basis for ancient Greek myths about the griffin, a mythic creature that looked like a lion but had wings and a beak. Greek historian Herodotus wrote about griffins from Central Asia, where the skeleton of a dinosaur the size of a lion with a beak and frilled neck fringe was found.

Even as recently as the 17th century, dinosaur bones were misunderstood. Robert Plot, a chemist, discovered a huge dinosaur fossil in England in 1676. He identified it as the leg bone of a giant human and published a drawing of it in his book on natural history. Though views of dinosaur bones have changed over the years, people have always found them fascinating.

1. According to this passage, the ancient Chinese believed that—

   A. dragons had ruled the earth.
   B. fossils they found had medicinal powers.
   C. giant humans lived in ancient Greece.
   D. ancient bones came from the gods.

2. According to both the ancient Chinese and the ancient Greek worldviews,—

   A. dangerous, gigantic flying monsters had once lived on Earth.
   B. griffins originated in Asia.
   C. ancient bones had medicinal properties.
   D. dinosaur bones were proof that strange creatures had existed.

3. What did Robert Plot's view of fossils have in common with the view of scientists today?

   A. a belief that fossils should be studied
   B. a desire to display fossils in museums
   C. a concern about preserving fossils
   D. a fear that fossils belong to giant humans

4. People from all times in history have found dinosaur bones to be—

   A. signs that dragons exist.
   B. useful as medicine.
   C. very interesting.
   D. worthless.

Writing for Assessment

Connecting Across Texts

Imagine a conversation in which Alex and Randy describe their view of dinosaur bones to a person from ancient China. Write a ten-line script in which you reveal each person's worldview. Use details from both selections.

PHLit Online!
www.PHLitOnline.com
- Online practice
- Instant feedback

Reading for Information

Analyzing Argumentative Texts

Book Review

Movie Review

**Common Core
State Standards**

Reading Informational Text
8. Delineate and evaluate the argument and specific claims in a text, assessing whether the reasoning is valid and the evidence is relevant and sufficient; identify false statements and fallacious reasoning.

Language
4. Determine or clarify the meaning of unknown and multiple-meaning words or phrases based on *grades 9–10 reading and content,* choosing flexibly from a range of strategies.
6. Acquire and use accurately general academic and domain-specific words and phrases, sufficient for reading, writing, speaking, and listening at the college and career readiness level; demonstrate independence in gathering vocabulary knowledge when considering a word or phrase important to comprehension or expression.

Reading Skill: Critique Generalizations and Evidence

When reading a review, **evaluate the credibility of the author's argument** by critiquing, or judging, generalizations. Generalizations are broad statements that apply to many specific cases. To be valid, generalizations must be supported by precise and relevant evidence. Poorly supported claims may lead you to conclude that an author's overall argument is not valid or reliable. Use a chart like this one to keep track of your evaluations.

What does the author say?	How does the author support this claim?	Are the author's generalizations credible?

Content-Area Vocabulary

These words appear in the selections that follow. You may also encounter them in other content-area texts.

- **distinctive** (dis tingk´ tiv) *adj.* clearly showing a difference from others; special

- **vignettes** (vin yets´) *n.* brief literary descriptions or sketches

- **melodrama** (mel´ ō drä´ mə) *n.* movie or play in which emotions and conflicts are exaggerated and characters are stereotypes

Mothers and Daughters

A dazzling first novel illuminates two generations of Chinese-American life.

Reviewed by **MICHAEL DORRIS**, *An author whose new book,* The Broken Cord, *will be published this summer.*
Copyright Chicago Tribune Co.
Mar 12, 1989

The Joy Luck Club by Amy Tan, Putnam, 277 pages, $18.95

Features:

- a summary of the work
- background information about the writer
- quotations or excerpts from the book
- the reviewer's analysis and evaluation of the work
- text written for a general audience

> The review begins by stating the reviewer's opinion. In a credible review, the following paragraphs will offer sufficient evidence to support this opinion.

> The reviewer offers details as evidence that his opinion is valid.

The Joy Luck Club is that rare, mesmerizing novel one always seeks but seldom finds. Tracing the poignant destinies of two generations of tough, intelligent women, each gorgeously written page welcomes the reader and leads to an enlightenment that, like all true wisdom, sometimes brings pleasure and sometimes sadness.

The book's four aging mothers, born in a pre-World War II China just embarked on a major cultural transition, are migrants who interpret life through the vivid eyes of their youth, through the experience and example of their own mothers. Their four daughters, first-generation Californians, stand at the midpoint of a seesaw. If they inch in one direction, they are traditional Chinese; if they inch in the other, they are Americans. Theirs is an ongoing quest for balance between the past and the future.

To tell this complex story, Amy Tan, a writer of dazzling talent, has created an intricate tapestry of a book—one tale woven into the other, a panorama of **distinctive** voices that call out to each other over time.

Tan's characters, regardless of their cultural orientation or age, speak with authority and authenticity. The details of their lives, unfamiliar to most American readers, are rendered with such conviction that almost immediately their rules seem to become the adages and admonitions with which we ourselves grew up. From the mainland China of the '30s and '40s to the San Francisco Bay area of today, the settings are so beautifully visualized that when we finish *The Joy Luck Club* we know the right bakeries in which to shop for dim sum and the best park in which to watch the old men play chess, and we have glimpsed the hidden meaning of carved jade.

The book opens and closes with the voice of Jing-mei "June" Woo, whose mother, Suyuan, had decades before, in a war-torn refugee center in interior China, initiated the Joy Luck Club.

"My idea," Suyuan confides, "was to have a gathering of four women, one for each corner of my mah jong table." She invited An-mei Hsu, Lindo Jong, and Ying-Ying, who was later to marry an American named St. Clair, to join her. They were a disparate group, uprooted from different regions and economic strata, but had in common their youth and their "wishful faces," their anxiety and their loneliness. Each week one of the women hosted a party, served special though simple delicacies and defied the depression their precarious circumstances might dictate.

"What was worse, we asked among ourselves," Suyuan says. "To sit and wait for our own deaths with proper somber faces? Or to choose our own happiness?

"So we decided to hold parties and pretend each week had become the new year. . . . We feasted, we laughed, we played games, lost and won, we told the best stories. And each week, we could hope to be lucky. That was our only joy. And that's how we came to call our little parties Joy Luck."

The Club, and the friendships it reflects, endured. It expanded to include the women's spouses; it became the clearing house for news about their children. Eventually all money won or lost was shared in common, an emergency bank on which any member could draw. Joy Luck remains their stable center despite the turbulence of immigration and social change; and when Suyuan dies, June is invited to take her mother's place ("on the East, where things begin") at the mah jong table.

It seems at first an uncomfortable and artificial wedding of generations grown apart, until, at the conclusion of the first evening's session, the existence of June's two half-sisters—lost as infants and believed dead—is revealed. June is instructed to go to Shanghai, meet her siblings and answer their inevitable questions.

> The reviewer provides quotations, excerpts, and details from the book as evidence for his opinion.

"'See my sisters and tell them about my mother?' June says, nodding. 'What will I say? What can I tell them about my mother? I don't know anything. She was my mother.'

'Not know your mother?' cries Auntie An-mei with disbelief. 'How can you say? Your mother is in your bones!'

'Tell them stories of your family here. How she became success,' offers Auntie Lin.

'Tell them stories she told you, lessons she taught, what you know about her mind that has become your mind,' says Auntie Ying. 'Your mother very smart lady.'"

There follows a litany of specific suggestions of what to convey: Suyuan's kindness, her intelligence, her hopes, the good food she knew how to cook. Finally June understands.

"They are frightened. In me, they see their own daughters, just as ignorant, just as unmindful of all the truths and hopes they have brought to America. They see daughters who grow impatient when their mothers talk in Chinese, who think they are stupid when they explain things in fractured English. They see that joy and luck do not mean the same to their daughters, that to these closed American-born minds "joy luck" is not a word, it does not exist. They see daughters who will bear grandchildren grown without any connecting hope passed from generation to generation."

"I will tell them everything," June says simply, and the aunties look at her with "doubtful faces."

They need not have worried. Not only does June fulfill her promise, but also, before she deplanes at the Shanghai airport, eight lives have been meticulously revealed. In exquisite passages, each of the senior women reflects on the formative events in her past; then, in counterpoint, each of their daughters—June, Rose, Waverly and Lena—examines her own path to maturity.

It is a large cast for a first novelist to direct, and *The Joy Luck Club* is an ambitious book. But Tan performs the miracle of making every character, even the minor and disagreeable ones, ultimately sympathetic. We understand their obsessions, the sources of their weaknesses and strengths, the quiet love or desperate fear that underpins their sacrifices. Elements of Chinese-American culture that often have often been distorted or ignorantly stereotyped are here illuminated, burnished, made fresh.

Literature is writing that makes a difference, that alters the way we understand the world and ourselves. By that standard, *The Joy Luck Club* is the real thing. Without a hint of polemic, the book leaves the reader changed, more

> Here, the reviewer makes a generalization about literature and offers no evidence to support it.

cognizant of subtleties, anxious to explore the confusions of any parent's motivation, any child's rebellion. Tan succeeds not only in her careful language, not only in the vista she opens before us, but also in the heart with which she invests this generous book. *The Joy Luck Club* is well-named; it is a pure joy to read.

THE JOY LUCK CLUB

A Film Review by JAMES BERARDINELLI

- Rating: 3 stars (out of 4 stars)
- United States, 1993
- U.S. Release Date: 9/24/93 (limited); 10/1/93 (general)
- Running Length: 2:19
- MPAA Classification: R
- Theatrical Aspect Ratio: 1.85:1

CAST: Ming-Na Wen, Tamlyn Tomita, Lauren Tom, Rosalind Chao, Kieu Chinh, Tsai Chin, France Nuyen, Lisa Lu

DIRECTOR: Wayne Wang

PRODUCERS: Wayne Wang, Amy Tan, Ronald Bass, and Patrick Markey

SCREENPLAY: Amy Tan and Ronald Bass based on the novel by Amy Tan

CINEMATOGRAPHY: Amir M. Mokri

MUSIC: Rachel Portman

U.S. DISTRIBUTOR: Hollywood Pictures

In English and Chinese with English subtitles

> The review begins with a summary of the plot and a description of the characters in the movie. This information will help the reader understand how the reviewer arrived at his opinion.

THE JOY LUCK CLUB, as stated in the movie's opening narrative, is a collection of four aging Chinese women bound together more by hope than joy or luck. The four women—Suyuan (Kieu Chinh), Lindo (Tsai Chin), Ying Ying (France Nuyen), and An Mei (Lisa Lu)—came to America many years ago to escape China's feudal society for the promise of the United States' democracy. Now, however, Suyuan has died and the three surviving members of the club invite her daughter June (Ming-Na Wen) to take her place. June belongs to the "new" generation, those of Chinese heritage who grew up speaking English and learning American customs. Also of roughly the same age are Waverly (Tamlyn Tomita), Lindo's daughter; Lena (Lauren Tom), Ying Ying's daughter; and Rose (Rosalind Chao), An Mei's daughter. *The Joy Luck Club* tells of the varied difficulties and tragedies involved in these mother/daughter relationships.

Features:

- information about the film, including release date, running time, and cast
- a summary of the plot
- evaluations of the actors' performances
- text written for a general audience

The reviewer quotes one of the film's writers about the structure of the movie. This evidence helps support the reviewer's opinion.

Co-writer Ronald Bass (who, along with Amy Tan, adapted from Tan's novel) says that there are sixteen separate stories in *The Joy Luck Club*. Since I didn't count, I can't verify this statement, but it sounds about right. Taken as a whole, these **vignettes** combine to lend greater meaning to the whole. *The Joy Luck Club* is the sum total of its parts with common themes giving solid grounding and greater resonance to the overall film. As Bass comments, "I saw all the mothers' and daughters' stories as facets of the same experience. Put together, they formed a mosaic. That's the genius of the book, and if we cut it down to just a couple of stories it would be like any other movie."

The stories are not related in such a manner as to seem pared down or truncated, nor is their presentation confusing, thanks to a cleverly-orchestrated framing scene with the principal characters gathered together. However, it is apparent that a lot more could have been told, and we're left wondering about all that we didn't get to see. The characters are mostly well-developed, but it's tantalizing to consider how much fuller some of them could have been with a different plot structure.

Here the reviewer makes generalizations about the dialogue and story and does not offer any specific evidence as support.

The Joy Luck Club is clearly—perhaps too clearly—an adaptation of a book. The dialogue is often too poetic to be real, and the story too clearly plotted to be acceptable as anything more than an imperfect reflection of the world we live in. The line between drama and **melodrama** is a fine one, and, while *The Joy Luck Club* most often successfully navigates the tightrope, there are times when it slips and comes across as heavy-handed. This film is no stranger to moments of manipulation.

The characters are *The Joy Luck Club's* real strength. Many are played by more than one actor (as children then adults, for example), but all transitions are smooth and seamless. It's as easy to accept both a little girl and the beautiful, sophisticated-looking Tamlyn Tomita as Waverly, and that's because the characters transcend the performers portraying them.

It's fascinating and satisfying the way the diverse threads are knitted together into a single tapestry. *The Joy Luck Club's* message is one of hope—that catharsis and emotional fulfillment often come through tragedy. Sure, a lot of bad things happen during the course of this film, but at the end, the tears are of happiness and new beginnings, not loss.

Comparing Argumentative Texts

1. Craft and Structure (a) In what ways is the **evidence** that supports the **generalizations** of the book review similar to the evidence that supports the generalizations of the movie review? **(b)** In what ways is the evidence different?

Content-Area Vocabulary

2. (a) Review the definitions of the words *distinctive, vignettes,* and *melodrama,* noting how the words can be applied to discussions of literature or movies.

(b) Use the words in a brief paragraph about a movie you have seen or a book you have read.

Timed Writing

Argumentative Text: Essay

> **Format**
> The prompt directs you to write an essay. Therefore, be sure your response includes an introduction, several supporting paragraphs, and a conclusion.

Write an essay in which you evaluate the credibility of each reviewer's arguments and opinions. Critique the evidence in each review, and decide whether it is sufficient to support the writer's generalizations. Then, decide which review you judge to be more credible, and explain your choice. Use details from the text to support your ideas. (40 minutes)

> **Academic Vocabulary**
> When you *critique* something, you make judgments about its strengths and weaknesses.

5-Minute Planner

Complete these steps before you begin to write:

1. Read the prompt carefully. Pay special attention to key words and phrases that are highlighted in color. Note that the prompt directs you to **evaluate the credibility** of the arguments, **critique** evidence, and decide which review is more credible.

2. Skim the reviews to find generalizations and the evidence used to support them. Make notes about your observations.

3. Review your notes and consider whether the evidence sufficiently supports the generalizations and the author's opinions.

4. Decide which review you find to be more credible.

5. Use your notes to create a rough outline for your essay. Then, refer to your notes and outline as you write.

Comparing Literary Works

Comparing Themes and Worldviews

The **theme** of a literary work is the central message or idea about life that it conveys. Many themes are universal, appearing in the literature of different time periods and places. The struggle between good and evil, for example, is a universal theme. The theme of a literary work often reflects the author's worldview—basic beliefs that shape the author's outlook. A writer's worldview is influenced by the time and place in which he or she lives.

For example, in past eras many writers portrayed a well-ordered world in which every event happens for a reason, and true heroes defend the innocent. Such writers might have shown good people being rewarded while bad people are punished. By contrast, many modern writers depict a chaotic or an indifferent world filled with ordinary, limited people. Modern writers may show good people triumphing over terrible odds, or they may show bad people succeeding. When compared with traditional works, the thematic insights in modern literature usually reflect a worldview in which justice is uncertain and order is not always restored.

Moral Dilemma and Theme Writers often convey a literary work's theme by confronting characters with moral dilemmas. A **moral dilemma** is a situation in which potential actions conflict with the character's idea of right and wrong. Like themes, the moral dilemmas characters face reflect the time and place in which the writer lives.

Both "Damon and Pythias," an ancient legend, and "Two Friends," a more modern short story, center on the theme of friendship. Each involves characters who face moral dilemmas that test the bonds of friendship. Yet each work is filtered through a different cultural worldview. As you read, identify the central message expressed in each story. Then, use a chart like the one shown to compare and contrast differences in the **themes** and **moral dilemmas** each work presents.

Common Core State Standards

Reading Literature
6. Analyze a particular point of view or cultural experience reflected in a work of literature from outside the United States, drawing on a wide reading of world literature.

Writing
2. Write informative/explanatory texts to examine and convey complex ideas, concepts, and information clearly and accurately through the effective selection, organization, and an analysis of content.
2.b. Develop the topic with well-chosen, relevant, and sufficient facts, extended definitions, concrete details, quotations, or other information and examples appropriate to the audience's knowledge of the topic. *(Timed Writing)*

	Time Period, Country, and Culture	Theme	Moral Dilemma
Damon and Pythias			
Two Friends			

www.PHLitOnline.com

- Vocabulary flashcards
- Interactive journals
- More about the authors
- Selection audio
- Interactive graphic organizers

Can anyone be a *hero?*

Writing About the Big Question

In both "Damon and Pythias" and "Two Friends," the loyalty between two men is put to an extreme test. Such a test might bring out the hero in a person, but it also raises more questions. Can anyone who faces life's tests with strength and courage be a hero? Use this sentence starter to develop your ideas.

The best way to discover a person's true **character** is _____.

Meet the Authors

Ancient Greek Legends and Their Retellers

Like other legends, "Damon and Pythias" exaggerates the characteristics of people to provide examples of the best—and the worst—conduct. In this way, a legend serves as a cultural how-to manual, showing people which virtues they should honor and cultivate.

Retelling the Tales Over the centuries, the legend of Damon and Pythias has been retold and adapted in many forms, including plays. William F. Russell, a recent reteller of this and many other myths and legends, is also the author of a widely read newspaper column on education.

Guy de Maupassant (1850–1893)
Author of "Two Friends"

In his short stories, Guy de Maupassant often focuses on the environment in which his characters live. The outcome of events in his work is determined by forces beyond a character's control, such as family history, social circumstances, and the character's basic disposition. His stories provide a fascinating record of nineteenth-century life.

A Productive Life Maupassant seemed destined for success. A gifted writer born into an aristocratic family, he won the attention of famous authors while he was still a young man. He soon became famous in his own right. Unfortunately, his career was cut short by illness. Maupassant died while still in his early forties. Yet, he left a fortune to every future reader: 300 short stories.

DAMON
AND
PYTHIAS

retold by **William F. Russell, Ed.D.**

Literary Analysis
Theme and Worldview
What subject or theme is suggested in the first paragraph of the story?

Damon [dā′ mən] and Pythias [pith′ ē əs] were two noble young men who lived on the island of Sicily in a city called Syracuse. They were such close companions and were so devoted to each other that all the people of the city admired them as the highest examples of true friendship. Each trusted the other so completely that nobody could ever have persuaded one that the other had been unfaithful or dishonest, even if that had been the case.

Now it happened that Syracuse was, at that time, ruled by a famous tyrant named Dionysius [dī′ ə nis′ ē əs],[1] who had gained the throne for himself through treachery, and who from then on flaunted his power by behaving cruelly to his own subjects and to all strangers and enemies who were so unfortunate as to fall into his clutches. This tyrant, Dionysius, was so unjustly cruel that once, when he awoke from a restless sleep during which he dreamt that a certain man in the town had attempted to kill him, he immediately had that man put to death.

It happened that Pythias had, quite unjustly, been accused by Dionysius of trying to overthrow him, and for this supposed crime of treason Pythias was sentenced by the king to die. Try as he might, Pythias could not prove his innocence to the king's satisfaction, and so, all hope now lost, the noble youth asked only for a few days' freedom so that he could settle his business affairs and see to it that his relatives would be cared for after he was executed. Dionysius, the hardhearted tyrant, however, would not believe Pythias' promise to return and would not allow him to leave unless he left behind him a hostage, someone who would be put to death in his place if he should fail to return within the stated time.

Vocabulary
dire (dīr) *adj.* calling for quick action

Pythias immediately thought of his friend Damon, and he unhesitatingly sent for him in this hour of dire necessity, never thinking for a moment that his trusty companion would refuse his request. Nor did he, for Damon hastened straightaway to the palace—much to the amazement of King Dionysius—and gladly

---

1. Dionysius Dionysius the Elder (ca. 430 B.C.–367 B.C.), ruler of ancient Syracuse.

offered to be held hostage for his friend, in spite of the dangerous condition that had been attached to this favor. Therefore, Pythias was permitted to settle his earthly affairs before departing to the Land of the Shades,[2] while Damon remained behind in the dungeon, the captive of the tyrant Dionysius.

After Pythias had been released, Dionysius asked Damon if he did not feel afraid, for Pythias might very well take advantage of the opportunity he had been given and simply not return at all, and then he, Damon, would be executed in his place. But Damon replied at once with a willing smile: "There is no need for me to feel afraid, O King, since I have perfect faith in the word of my true friend, and I know that he will certainly return before the appointed time— unless, of course, he dies or is held captive by some evil force. Even so, even should the noble Pythias be captured and held against his will, it would be an honor for me to die in his place."

Such devotion and perfect faith as this was unheard of to the friendless tyrant; still, though he could not help admiring the true nobility of his captive, he nevertheless determined that Damon should certainly be put to death should Pythias not return by the appointed time.

And, as the Fates would have it, by a strange turn of events, Pythias *was* detained far longer in his task than he had imagined. Though he never for a single minute intended to evade the sentence of death to which he had been so unjustly committed, Pythias met with several accidents and unavoidable delays. Now his time was running out and he had yet to overcome the many impediments that had been placed in his path. At last he succeeded in clearing away all the hindrances, and he sped back the many miles to the palace of the king, his heart almost bursting with grief and fear that he might arrive too late.

Meanwhile, when the last day of the allotted time arrived, Dionysius commanded that the place of execution should be readied at once, since he was still ruthlessly determined that if one of his victims escaped him, the other should not. And so, entering the chamber in which Damon was confined, he began to utter words of sarcastic pity for the "foolish faith," as he termed it, that the young man of Syracuse had in his friend.

In reply, however, Damon merely smiled, since, in spite of the fact that the eleventh hour had already arrived, he still believed that his lifelong companion would not fail him. Even when, a short time later, he was actually led out to the site of his execution, his serenity remained the same.

2. **Land of the Shades** in Greek mythology, place where people go when they die.

▲ **Critical Viewing** As he appears on this coin, does Dionysius seem to have the characteristics of the man in the legend? Explain. **[Interpret]**

Vocabulary
serenity (sə ren′ ə tē) *n.* state of calm or peace

Reading
Check
What does Damon agree to do for his friend Pythias?

Great excitement stirred the crowd that had gathered to witness the execution, for all the people had heard of the bargain that had been struck between the two friends. There was much sobbing and cries of sympathy were heard all around as the captive was brought out, though he himself somehow retained complete composure even at this moment of darkest danger.

Presently the excitement grew more intense still as a swift runner could be seen approaching the palace courtyard at an astonishing speed, and wild shrieks of relief and joy went up as Pythias, breathless and exhausted, rushed headlong through the crowd and flung himself into the arms of his beloved friend, sobbing with relief that he had, by the grace of the gods, arrived in time to save Damon's life.

This final exhibition of devoted love and faithfulness was more than even the stony heart of Dionysius, the tyrant, could resist. As the throng of spectators melted into tears at the companions' embrace, the king approached the pair and declared that Pythias was hereby pardoned and his death sentence canceled. In addition, he begged the pair to allow him to become their friend, to try to be as much a friend to them both as they had shown each other to be.

Thus did the two friends of Syracuse, by the faithful love they bore to each other, conquer the hard heart of a tyrant king, and in the annals of true friendship there are no more honored names than those of Damon and Pythias—for no person can do more than be willing to lay down his life for the sake of his friend.

Literary Analysis
Theme and Worldview
What details here show the belief that good people are rewarded?

Critical Thinking

Cite textual evidence to support your responses.

1. **Key Ideas and Details (a)** What does Damon risk for Pythias? **(b) Interpret:** What does his decision show you about their friendship?

2. **Key Ideas and Details (a) Infer:** Why is Damon patient and not fearful as he waits for Pythias? **(b) Take a Position:** Could a friendship like the one between Damon and Pythias exist today? Why or why not?

3. **Key Ideas and Details (a)** What changes Dionysius' mind about executing one of the young men? **(b) Infer:** What does this ending suggest about the world view of the ancient Greeks? Explain.

4. **Integration of Knowledge and Ideas (a)** Who do you think was more of a hero—Damon or Pythias? Explain. **(b)** Does Dionysius' decision to spare both men make him a hero? Why or why not? *[Connect to the Big Question: Can anyone be a hero?]*

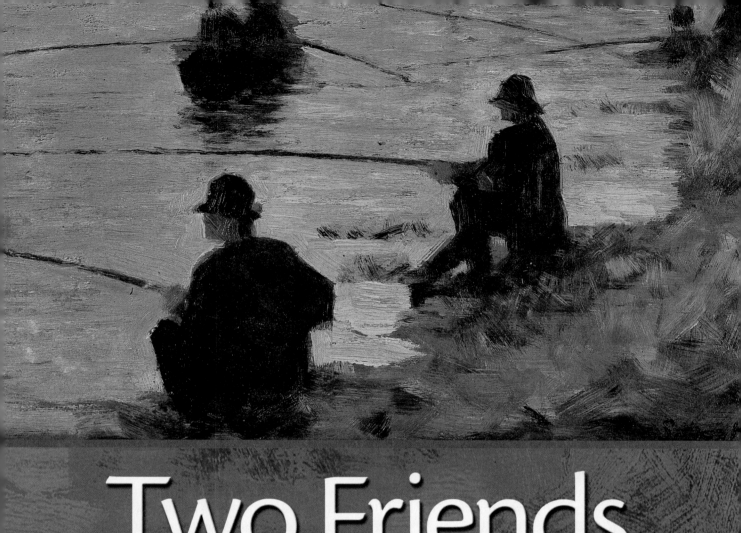

Two Friends

Guy de Maupassant

translated by Gordon R. Silber

The following story is set during the Franco-Prussian War, a conflict between France and Germany that began on July 19, 1870. The Germans won a series of victories, one of which ended in the capture of the French leader, Napoleon III. On September 19, 1870, the German army established a blockade around Paris. Movement in and out of the city was severely restricted. Led by a provisional government and plagued by famine and hopelessness, Paris managed to hold out until January 28, 1871, when the city surrendered. As Maupassant's story begins, the city is on the verge of surrender.

▲ **Critical Viewing**
What insight into friend-ship does this painting convey? **[Interpret]**

P aris was blockaded, starved, in its death agony. Sparrows were becoming scarcer and scarcer on the rooftops and the sewers were being depopulated. One ate whatever one could get.

As he was strolling sadly along the outer boulevard one bright January morning, his hands in his trousers pockets and his stomach empty, M.[1] Morissot [mô rē sō′], watchmaker by trade but local militiaman for the time being, stopped short before a fellow militiaman whom he recognized as a friend. It was M. Sauvage [sō väzh′], a riverside acquaintance.

Every Sunday, before the war, Morissot left at dawn, a bamboo pole in his hand, a tin box on his back. He would take the Argenteuil [ȧr zhän të′y′] railroad, get off at Colombes, and walk to Marante Island. As soon as he arrived at this ideal spot he would start to fish; he fished until nightfall.

Every Sunday he would meet a stout, jovial little man, M. Sauvage, a haberdasher[2] in Rue Notre-Dame-de-Lorette, another ardent fisherman. Often they spent half a day side by side, line in hand and feet dangling above the current. Inevitably they had struck up a friendship.

Some days they did not speak. Sometimes they did; but they understood one another admirably without saying anything because they had similar tastes and responded to their surroundings in exactly the same way.

On a spring morning, toward ten o'clock, when the young sun was drawing up from the tranquil stream wisps of haze which floated off in the direction of the current and was pouring down its vernal warmth on the backs of the two fanatical anglers,[3] Morissot would sometimes say to his neighbor, "Nice, isn't it?" and M. Sauvage would answer, "There's nothing like it." And that was enough for them to understand and appreciate each other.

On an autumn afternoon, when the sky, reddened by the setting sun, cast reflections of its scarlet clouds on the water, made the whole river crimson, lighted up the horizon, made the two friends look as ruddy as fire, and gilded the trees which were already brown and beginning to tremble with a wintery shiver, M. Sauvage would look at Morissot with a smile and say, "Fine sight!" And Morissot, awed, would answer, "It's better than the city, isn't it?" without taking his eyes from his float.

As soon as they recognized one another they shook hands energetically, touched at meeting under such changed circumstances. M. Sauvage, with a sigh, grumbled, "What goings-on!"

Vocabulary
ardent (är′ dənt) *adj.* intensely enthusiastic or devoted

Literary Analysis
Theme and Worldview
What idea about friendship does this paragraph suggest?

---

1. **M.** abbreviation for Monsieur (mə syʉr′), "Mister" or "Sir" in French.
2. **haberdasher** (hab′ ər dash′ ər) *n.* person in the business of selling men's clothing.
3. **anglers** (aŋ′ glərz) *n.* people who fish with hook and line.

Morissot groaned dismally, "And what weather! This is the first fine day of the year."

The sky was, in fact, blue and brilliant.

They started to walk side by side, absent-minded and sad. Morissot went on, "And fishing! Ah! Nothing but a pleasant memory."

"When'll we get back to it?" asked M. Sauvage.

They went into a little café and had an absinthe,[4] then resumed their stroll along the sidewalks.

Morissot stopped suddenly, "How about another, eh?" M. Sauvage agreed, "If you want." And they entered another wine shop.

On leaving they felt giddy, muddled, as one does after drinking on an empty stomach. It was mild. A caressing breeze touched their faces.

The warm air completed what the absinthe had begun. M. Sauvage stopped. "Suppose we went?"

"Went where?"

"Fishing, of course."

"But where?"

"Why, on our island. The French outposts are near Colombes. I know Colonel Dumoulin; they'll let us pass without any trouble."

---

4. **absinthe** (ab´ sinth´) *n.* type of liqueur.

▲ **Critical Viewing**
What does this painting suggest about the pace of life in the French countryside? Explain. **[Interpret]**

Reading Check

What pleasure do M. Morissot and M. Sauvage share?

Morissot trembled with eagerness: "Done! I'm with you." And they went off to get their tackle.

An hour later they were walking side by side on the highway. They reached the villa which the Colonel occupied. He smiled at their request and gave his consent to their whim. They started off again, armed with a pass.

Soon they passed the outposts, went through the abandoned village of Colombes, and reached the edge of the little vineyards which slope toward the Seine. It was about eleven.

Opposite, the village of Argenteuil seemed dead. The heights of Orgemont and Sannois dominated the whole countryside. The broad plain which stretches as far as Nanterre was empty, absolutely empty, with its bare cherry trees and its colorless fields.

Pointing up to the heights, M. Sauvage murmured, "The Prussians are up there!" And a feeling of uneasiness paralyzed the two friends as they faced this deserted region.

"The Prussians!" They had never seen any, but for months they had felt their presence—around Paris, ruining France, pillaging, massacring, starving the country, invisible and all-powerful. And a kind of superstitious terror was superimposed on the hatred which they felt for this unknown and victorious people.

Morissot stammered, "Say, suppose we met some of them?"

His Parisian jauntiness coming to the surface in spite of everything, M. Sauvage answered, "We'll offer them some fish."

But they hesitated to venture into the country, frightened by the silence all about them.

Finally M. Sauvage pulled himself together: "Come on! On our way! But let's go carefully." And they climbed over into a vineyard, bent double, crawling, taking advantage of the vines to conceal themselves, watching, listening.

A stretch of bare ground had to be crossed to reach the edge of the river. They began to run, and when they reached the bank they plunged down among the dry reeds.

Morissot glued his ear to the ground and listened for sounds of anyone walking in the vicinity. He heard nothing. They were indeed alone, all alone.

Reassured, they started to fish.

Opposite them Marante Island, deserted, hid them from the other bank. The little building which had housed a restaurant was shut up and looked as if it had been abandoned for years.

M. Sauvage caught the first gudgeon.[5] Morissot got the second, and from then on they pulled in their lines every minute or two with a silvery little fish squirming on the end, a truly miraculous draught.

Literary Analysis
Theme and Worldview
Which details here show that the men are not exceptional heroes?

---

5. **gudgeon** (guj´ ən) *n.* small European freshwater fish.

Skillfully they slipped the fish into a sack made of fine net which they had hung in the water at their feet. And happiness pervaded their whole being, the happiness which seizes upon you when you regain a cherished pleasure of which you have long been deprived.

The good sun was pouring down its warmth on their backs. They heard nothing more; they no longer thought about anything at all; they forgot about the rest of the world—they were fishing!

But suddenly a dull sound which seemed to come from underground made the earth tremble. The cannon were beginning.

Morissot turned and saw, over the bank to the left, the great silhouette of Mount Valérien wearing a white plume on its brow, powdersmoke which it had just spit out.

And almost at once a second puff of smoke rolled from the summit, and a few seconds after the roar still another explosion was heard.

Then more followed, and time after time the mountain belched forth death-dealing breath, breathed out milky-white vapor which rose slowly in the calm sky and formed a cloud above the summit.

M. Sauvage shrugged his shoulders. "There they go again," he said.

As he sat anxiously watching his float bob up and down, Morissot was suddenly seized by the wrath which a peace-loving man will feel toward madmen who fight, and grumbled, "Folks sure are stupid to kill one another like that."

M. Sauvage answered, "They're worse than animals."

And Morissot, who had just pulled in a bleak,[6] went on, "And to think that it will always be like this as long as there are governments."

M. Sauvage stopped him: "The Republic[7] wouldn't have declared war—"

Morissot interrupted: "Under kings you have war abroad; under the Republic you have war at home."

And they started a leisurely discussion, unraveling great political problems with the sane reasonableness of easygoing, limited individuals, and found themselves in agreement on the point that men would never be free. And Mount Valérien thundered

They heard nothing more; they no longer thought about anything at all; they forgot about the rest of the world—they were fishing!

Literary Analysis
Theme and Worldview
What goals or ideals do the men seem to have?

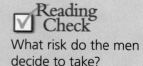

Reading Check

What risk do the men decide to take?

---

6. **bleak** *n.* small European freshwater fish with silvery scales.
7. **The Republic** the temporary republican government that assumed control of France when Napoleon III was captured by the Prussians.

unceasingly, demolishing French homes with its cannon, crushing out lives, putting an end to the dreams which many had dreamt, the joys which many had been waiting for, the happiness which many had hoped for, planting in wives' hearts, in maidens' hearts, in mothers' hearts, over there, in other lands, sufferings which would never end.

"That's life for you," opined M. Sauvage.

"You'd better say 'That's death for you,'" laughed Morissot.

But they shuddered in terror when they realized that someone had just come up behind them, and looking around they saw four men standing almost at their elbows, four tall men, armed and bearded, dressed like liveried[8] servants, with flat caps on their heads, pointing rifles at them.

The two fish lines dropped from their hands and floated off down stream.

In a few seconds they were seized, trussed up,[9] carried off, thrown into a rowboat and taken over to the island.

And behind the building which they had thought deserted they saw a score of German soldiers.

A kind of hairy giant who was seated astride a chair smoking a porcelain pipe asked them in excellent French: "Well, gentlemen, have you had good fishing?"

Then a soldier put down at the officer's feet the sack full of fish which he had carefully brought along. The Prussian smiled: "Aha! I see that it didn't go badly. But we have to talk about another little matter. Listen to me and don't get excited.

"As far as I am concerned, you are two spies sent to keep an eye on me. I catch you and I shoot you. You were pretending to fish in order to conceal your business. You have fallen into my hands, so much the worse for you. War is like that.

▼ **Critical Viewing**
What does this officer's posture suggest about his attitude and training? Explain. **[Interpret]**

---

8. **liveried** (liv´ ər ēd) *adj.* uniformed
9. **trussed up** tied up.

"But—since you came out past the outposts you have, of course, the password to return. Tell me that password and I will pardon you."

The two friends, side by side, pale, kept silent. A slight nervous trembling shook their hands.

The officer went on: "No one will ever know. You will go back placidly. The secret will disappear with you. If you refuse, it is immediate death. Choose."

They stood motionless, mouths shut.

The Prussian quietly went on, stretching out his hand toward the stream: "Remember that within five minutes you will be at the bottom of that river. Within five minutes! You have relatives, of course?"

Mount Valérien kept thundering.

The two fishermen stood silent. The German gave orders in his own language. Then he moved his chair so as not to be near the prisoners and twelve men took their places, twenty paces distant, rifles grounded.

The officer went on: "I give you one minute, not two seconds more."

Then he rose suddenly, approached the two Frenchmen, took Morissot by the arm, dragged him aside, whispered to him, "Quick, the password? Your friend won't know. I'll pretend to relent."

Morissot answered not a word.

The Prussian drew M. Sauvage aside and put the same question.

M. Sauvage did not answer.

They stood side by side again.

And the officer began to give commands. The soldiers raised their rifles.

Then Morissot's glance happened to fall on the sack full of gudgeons which was lying on the grass a few steps away.

A ray of sunshine made the little heap of still squirming fish gleam. And he almost weakened. In spite of his efforts his eyes filled with tears.

He stammered, "Farewell, Monsieur Sauvage."

M. Sauvage answered, "Farewell, Monsieur Morissot."

They shook hands, trembling from head to foot with a shudder which they could not control.

The officer shouted, "Fire!"

The twelve shots rang out together.

M. Sauvage fell straight forward, like a log. Morissot, who was taller, tottered, half turned, and fell crosswise on top of his comrade, face up, as the blood spurted from his torn shirt.

The German gave more orders.

Vocabulary
relent (ri lent´) *v.* to become less strong or intense

Literary Analysis
Theme and Worldview
Which actions show the heroism of M. Morissot and M. Sauvage?

Reading Check

What does the German officer order the men to do?

His men scattered, then returned with rope and stones which they tied to the dead men's feet. They carried them to the bank.

Mount Valérien continued to roar, its summit hidden now in a mountainous cloud of smoke.

Two soldiers took Morissot by the head and the feet, two others seized M. Sauvage. They swung the bodies for a moment then let go. They described an arc and plunged into the river feet first, for the weights made them seem to be standing upright.

There was a splash, the water trembled, then grew calm, while tiny wavelets spread to both shores.

A little blood remained on the surface.

The officer, still calm, said in a low voice: "Now the fish will have their turn."

And he went back to the house.

And all at once he caught sight of the sack of gudgeons in the grass. He picked it up, looked at it, smiled, shouted, "Wilhelm!"

A soldier in a white apron ran out. And the Prussian threw him the catch of the two and said: "Fry these little animals right away while they are still alive. They will be delicious."

Then he lighted his pipe again.

Literary Analysis
Theme and Worldview
What details of this ending emphasize the injustice of the heroes' fate?

Critical Thinking

Cite textual evidence to support your responses.

1. **Key Ideas and Details (a)** Before the siege, what did Morissot and Sauvage do together on Sundays? **(b) Analyze Cause and Effect:** Why does the situation in Paris force them to change their habits?

2. **Key Ideas and Details (a) Analyze Cause and Effect:** What circumstances lead the two friends to risk going outside town? **(b) Support:** Identify two details that show the pleasure the two experience when fishing. **(c) Interpret:** What aspects of life does fishing represent for them?

3. **Key Ideas and Details (a) Analyze:** Use details from the story to describe the friendship of the two men. **(b) Draw Conclusions:** What role does friendship play in the decision each man makes in the ending?

4. **Integration of Knowledge and Ideas (a)** Do M. Morissot and M. Sauvage fit your image of stereotypical heroes? Why or why not? **(b)** Do you believe that situations make heroes, or do you think some people are naturally heroic? Explain your answer. *[Connect to the Big Question: Can anyone be a hero?]*

Comparing Theme and Worldview

1. Craft and Structure (a) Analyze each story by completing a chart like the one shown.

Friends	Powerful Person	Test of Loyalty	Result of Test

(b) Use your chart to draw a conclusion about the theme of each story. **(c)** Compare and contrast differences in these similar themes that express the worldviews of different eras.

2. Key Ideas and Details What is the relationship between loyalty and power in each story?

3. Integration of Knowledge and Ideas (a) Describe the moral dilemma Damon and Pythias each face. **(b)** What moral dilemma is developed in "Two Friends"? **(c)** Analyze the differences in the moral dilemmas in these works of fiction.

4. Integration of Knowledge and Ideas (a) How does the perception of heroism in the legend differ from the perception of heroism in the story? **(b)** Which work makes heroism seem most "heroic"? Explain.

⏱ Timed Writing

Explanatory Text: Essay

Write an essay comparing the themes and moral dilemmas in "Damon and Pythias" and "Two Friends." In your essay, state which writer's views most strongly resemble your own. **(30 minutes)**

5-Minute Planner

1. Read the prompt carefully and completely.

2. Use these questions to get started:

- How are the themes of the stories similar? How are they different?
- What do the moral dilemmas in the stories have in common? How do they differ?
- How does each story's theme and moral dilemma reflect a particular worldview?
- Which work's worldview is closer to your own perspective? Why?

3. Reread the prompt, and then draft your essay.

Writing Workshop

Write an Informative Text

Exposition: Comparison-and-Contrast Essay

Defining the Form A **comparison-and-contrast** essay explores the similarities and differences between or among two or more topics, thus bringing the topics into clearer focus. You might use elements of the comparison-and-contrast essay in profiles of historical figures, reviews of literature or performances, or descriptive essays.

Assignment Write a comparison-and-contrast essay about two literary characters, two concepts, or two events. Include these elements:

✓ a clear *thesis statement* that reveals your purpose for writing

✓ *supporting evidence*, including facts and examples that show similarities and differences between the two subjects

✓ a clear and logical *organizational pattern*

✓ *transitions* that show clear relationships between ideas

✓ error-free grammar and *varied sentence structure and length*

To preview the criteria on which your comparison-and-contrast essay may be judged, see the rubric on page 1249.

 Writing Workshop: *Work in Progress*

Review the work you did on pages 1187 and 1219.

WRITE GUY
Jeff Anderson, M.Ed.

What Do You Notice?

Contrasting

Read the following sentence from Maya Angelou's "Occupation: Conductorette" several times.

Downtown San Francisco became alien and cold, and the streets I had loved in a personal familiarity were unknown lanes that twisted with malicious intent.

With a partner, discuss what you notice about this sentence. Consider how Angelou has contrasted her different perceptions of San Francisco. Work to find ways to incorporate contrasts like these in your comparison-and-contrast essay.

 **Common Core State Standards**

Writing

2.a. Introduce a topic; organize complex ideas, concepts, and information to make important connections and distinctions; include formatting, graphics, and multimedia when useful to aiding comprehension.

2.b. Develop the topic with well-chosen, relevant, and sufficient facts, extended definitions, concrete details, quotations, or other information and examples appropriate to the audience's knowledge of the topic.

Prewriting/Planning Strategies

Your comparison-and-contrast essay should explore subjects that share traits but are significantly different. Use these strategies to find a topic:

List related topics. Think of a broad subject area, such as music, sports, or fictional characters. Then, list specific items. For example, you might list favorite athletes or unusual places. Look for similarities—and differences—between two or more items on your list. Choose one set as your subject.

Fill in a sentence frame. Find at least three ways to complete a sentence frame. Then, choose your best idea to explore in your essay.

Sample Sentence Frame

I often confuse _____ and _____ because they are both _____. However, they are also different because of _____ and _____.

Consider your purpose. The comparisons and contrasts you explore should fulfill a larger purpose or idea, such as one of the following:

- **To persuade**—You believe one of your subjects is better than the other and you want to convince your readers to share your opinion.

- **To reflect**—Both subjects are meaningful to you, but in different ways, and you want to explore why this is the case.

- **To describe**—The similarities and differences in your subjects are very striking and you want to portray them.

Evaluate your topic. Be sure your topics offer enough interesting similarities and differences. To evaluate your topic choices, use a Venn diagram like the one shown.

Going to a Movie Theater
- big screen
- live audience (comedies are funnier)
- see the movie sooner

- same movie
- same running time

- home comfort
- convenience
- no audience noise
- see the movie later

Watching a Streaming Video

Conduct research. Consider conducting research to further explore your analysis. For example, after creating a Venn diagram, a writer might read movie industry journals to find the average time between a movie's release into theaters and its release as streaming video.

Formulate a thesis statement. Write a *thesis statement* that incorporates a sense of your larger purpose. You will include this thesis statement in your introduction.

PHLit Online!
www.PHLitOnline.com
- Author video: Writing Process
- Author video: Rewards of Writing

Drafting Strategies

Choose an organization. Most comparison-and-contrast essays are organized in one of two ways. In **subject-by-subject organization,** you analyze all of the features of one subject and then all the features of the second subject. In **point-by-point organization,** you discuss one point about both subjects and then move on to a second point. Select an organizational structure that best suits your subjects.

Use your thesis statement and purpose. Include your thesis in your introduction. Check that the ideas you include in each body paragraph connect directly to your thesis statement and purpose. Restate or reevaluate your thesis statement in a strong and memorable concluding section.

Support opinions. Using a wide variety of evidence can make your ideas more convincing and add interest to your essay.

- **Examples:** Illustrations help clarify similarities and differences.
- **Facts:** Evidence helps readers understand each subject.
- **Quotations:** The exact words of experts add authority.

Use transitions. Help readers follow the logic of your comparisons and contrasts by using effective transitions to show the relationships between ideas. These transitional words and phrases are especially useful:

similarly	*on the other hand*	*conversely*	*however*
although	*nevertheless*	*in contrast*	*whereas*

**Common Core
State Standards**

Writing

2.b. Develop the topic with well-chosen, relevant, and sufficient facts, extended definitions, concrete details, quotations, or other information and examples appropriate to the audience's knowledge of the topic.

2.c. Use appropriate and varied transitions to link the major sections of the text, create cohesion, and clarify the relationships among complex ideas and concepts.

2.e. Provide a concluding statement or section that follows from and supports the information or explanation presented.

Types of Organization

Subject-by-Subject	Point-by-Point
Subject A	Point A
• Point 1	• Subject 1
• Point 2	• Subject 2
Subject B	Point B
• Point 1	• Subject 1
• Point 2	• Subject 2

Model: Using Transitions to Clarify Connections

If you have to choose one sport in which to participate, the three most popular are basketball, soccer, and volleyball. All are fast-moving sports that require being in good physical condition, a commitment of time and energy, and an ability to think and react quickly.

Despite the similarities in the physical demands they make, each sport has its own special requirements.

The writer uses a transitional phrase to signal a shift from comparison to contrast.

Writers on Writing

John Phillip Santos On Making Comparisons

John Phillip Santos is the author of *Places Left Unfinished at the Time of Creation* (p. 1055).

In the following passage from my book, I wanted to find a way to illuminate the history of Mexican Americans by comparing and contrasting my family's name—Santos—with its literal meaning in Spanish and earlier versions of the name that had been used in the past.

"You're part of a long tradition of writers."
—John Philip Santos

Professional Model:

from *Places Left Unfinished at the Time of Creation*

It is ~~It's~~ a common name my family carries, ~~through a skyful of generations~~ out of our Mexican past. It is a name that invokes the saints and embroiders daily prayers of Latinos in North and South America. The old ones in the family say the name was once *de Los Santos*. "From the saints." But no one remembers when or why it was shortened. There were Santos in San Antonio two hundred years ago. In the records for the year 1793 at the Mission San Antonio de Valero, which later became the Alamo, you find the names of Manuel and Jorge de Los Santos, referred to as "Indios," but it's not clear whether they are our ancestors.

It sometimes seems as if Mexicans are to forgetting what the Jews are to remembering. We have made selective forgetting a sacramental obligation. Leave it all in the past, all that you were, and all that you could not be. There is pain enough in the present to go around. Some memories cannot not be abandoned. Let the past reclaim all the rest forever, and let stories come to their fitting end.

In this early section of the book, by asking readers to move between English and Spanish, I am slowly preparing them for the mix of the two languages that I use in telling the story to come.

By adding this passage, I was able to establish the broader historical background of our Mexican families from San Antonio. This allowed me to compare our experience to the storied legacy of Jewish people.

After comparing traditions of remembering and forgetting to a sacramental obligation, I wanted the rest of the paragraph to have a chant-like quality. The final sentences are short, written with short words, making the passage seem solemn and ceremonial.

Revising Strategies

Revise to balance your organization. An effective comparison-and-contrast essay provides a thorough analysis of each subject being compared. Follow these steps to check the balance of your coverage:

- First, use one color to highlight places where you discuss one subject. Use another color to highlight places where you discuss a different subject. Use other colors for any additional subjects.

- Next, review your highlighted draft to determine whether you have addressed each subject equally. Add details to support under-developed subjects.

Revise for precision. When you compare and contrast, you discuss subjects that share many traits. To clearly distinguish one from the other, use words that are specific and precise.

Vague: The effects used in the first *Star Wars* movies were *good*, but today's computerized images *are also good*.

Specific: The effects used in the first *Star Wars* movies were *convincing*, but today's computerized images *are truly lifelike*.

Peer Review

Ask a partner to read your essay and evaluate how well you have presented details about your subjects of comparison. Discuss whether or not you need to provide additional support for either subject. Consider developing an idea further or adding details to provide more thorough comparisons and contrasts.

Common Core State Standards

Writing

2.d. Use precise language and domain-specific vocabulary to manage the complexity of the topic.

Language

1. Demonstrate command of the conventions of standard English grammar and usage when writing or speaking.

3. Apply knowledge of language to understand how language functions in different contexts, to make effective choices for meaning or style, and to comprehend more fully when reading or listening.

Model: Revising to Create Balance

Basketball requires the ability to turn, pivot, start, and stop suddenly. It also requires the ability to instantaneously read and react to the opponents' moves. Soccer requires the ability to predict the ball's movement, be aware of the location of team members, and quickly intervene in plays. Volleyball also requires quick reflexes. Players must be prepared to make snap judgments about whether a ball is going out of bounds or requires a return.

> The writer adds information about her third topic to create a better balance.

Revising to Vary Sentence Structure and Length

A sequence of too many sentences of the same length and structure can be monotonous. Vary sentence lengths, sentence beginnings, and subject-verb order to create an engaging flow in your writing.

Vary sentence length. The constant use of short sentences can make your writing seem undeveloped and choppy. Work to identify whether you have too many short sentences in sequence and combine some to create a better flow. Reserve a short, punchy sentence for an idea you want to emphasize.

Choppy: I like lakes more than the ocean. It is easier to swim. You can fish. You can water ski. Lakes are nice at all times of day. They are pretty in all weather. I feel at home on a lake.

Flowing: I like lakes more than the ocean because it is easier to swim, fish, and water ski. Lakes are beautiful at all times of day and in all weather. I feel at home on a lake.

Vary sentence beginnings. Avoid using the same parts of speech to start a series of sentences. Vary your sentence beginnings by using different parts of speech, phrases, and clauses.

Adjective: *Blue* skies always remind her of home.
Prepositional phrase: *Until then,* she was not sure she would make friends at her new school.
Adverb clause: *Wherever she went,* she still thought about the people she had left.
Gerund phrase: *Spending lunchtime alone* was most distressing to her.

PH | WRITING COACH

Further instruction and practice are available in *Prentice Hall Writing Coach*.

You can also vary subject-verb order to add interest. Create variety in your sentences by reversing the usual subject-verb order.

Original: The statue stood outside the theater.

Inverted: Outside the theater stood the statue.

Grammar in Your Writing

Review three body paragraphs of your draft, highlighting sequences of sentences that have similar length and structure. Add variety to your sentences by changing sentence lengths, altering sentence beginnings, or inverting subject-verb order.

You've Got Mail

Personal communications have gone through a major evolution in modern times. The letter gave way to the telephone call, and now they have both been overwhelmed in popularity by e-mail. While the three modes of communication have a lot in common, there are differences that let each stand out on its own.

Letters, phone calls, and e-mail are similar because they all involve personal communication. They allow people to share ideas and feelings with other people. Communicators do not have to be face to face; they can be across the world and get the same points across. Letter writers, phone callers, and e-mailers are generally not limited by time either. They can create and share their communications round the clock.

Despite their similarities, letters, phone calls, and e-mail communicate differently. Letters convey a personal touch and make recipients especially happy when received. They can be saved, to be reread (often over and over) at a later time. Unlike a letter, e-mail is usually more spontaneous and less likely to be reread. Phone call messages quickly fade. Of all three modes, letters take the longest time between the sender and the receiver. If time is important, letters are probably the worst format to use.

E-mail is seldom personal. It is more convenient than "snail mail," though. You never have to move away from your computer. Plus, you can edit without cross-outs. Once you send an e-mail, it is delivered instantly. This speed has its disadvantages. Because people create e-mails with such haste, they often do not stop to think carefully about what they want to say—or correct grammar or spelling mistakes—before they click an e-mail on its way.

A phone call is extremely personal, and it shows that you have set aside time for the other person. You are able to hear the tone of voice and expression of the other person. Phone calls may be expensive, temporary, and time-sensitive—unlike a letter or an e-mail, which a recipient can read when he or she has the time. Another problem with the phone is that once you say something, you cannot take it back, in contrast to the way you can edit writing.

There is a time and a place for all three types of communication. People are often so busy that they have time only for e-mail, but maybe people should set aside some time to write a letter or call a friend.

In her introduction, Amanda identifies the subjects she will compare.

In this paragraph, Amanda discusses the similarities that the three formats share.

In the third, fourth, and fifth paragraphs, Amanda addresses the unique qualities of each form.

Transitions help clarify the contrasts between subjects.

Editing and Proofreading

Review your draft to correct errors in grammar, spelling, and punctuation.

Focus on transitional words. Double-check the meanings of the transitional words you have used, and make sure they are punctuated correctly. If you start a sentence with a coordinating conjunction, such as *however* or *nevertheless*, follow it with a comma.

Publishing and Presenting

Consider one of the following ways to share your writing:

Present a shared reading. With a partner, deliver an oral presentation of your essay. First, present to a small group. Read the paragraphs that discuss one subject, while your partner reads the paragraphs that discuss the other subject. Ask for listeners' comments to improve your presentation before sharing it with another group.

Create a class book. Compile a collection of comparison-and-contrast essays. Devise a title that reflects the content of the collection and place the finished book in your classroom or school library.

Reflecting on Your Writing

Writer's Journal Jot down your answers to this question:

How did comparing and contrasting your subjects help you understand them?

Rubric for Self-Assessment

Find evidence in your writing to address each category. Then, use the rating scale to grade your work.

Spiral Review

Earlier in this unit, you learned about **commas and dashes** (p. 1186) and **semicolons, colons, and ellipsis points** (p. 1218). Check your essay to be sure that you have used these punctuation marks correctly.

PH WRITING COACH

Further instruction and practice are available in *Prentice Hall Writing Coach*.

Criteria	Rating Scale
	not very very
Focus: How clear is your purpose and thesis?	1 2 3 4 5
Organization: How effectively does your organization show comparisons and contrasts?	1 2 3 4 5
Support/Elaboration: How varied and convincing is your evidence?	1 2 3 4 5
Style: How well do you use transitions to connect ideas?	1 2 3 4 5
Conventions: How correct is your grammar? How consistently and well do you vary sentence lengths and structures?	1 2 3 4 5

Vocabulary Workshop

Idioms, Jargon, and Technical Terms

**Common Core
State Standards**

Language

4.d. Verify the preliminary determination of the meaning of a word or phrase.

5. Demonstrate understanding of figurative language, word relationships, and nuances in word meanings.

Words have *literal meanings,* which are the denotative or actual meanings of the words. Many words and phrases in English also have a figurative meaning. *Figurative language* is language that is not meant to be understood literally. **Idioms** are expressions that are characteristic of a language, region, community, or class of people. They cannot be understood literally. Many dictionaries list idioms with the entry for the main word in the phrase. Look at these examples of idioms:

Idiom	Meaning
It *beats me.*	I don't know.
Let's *call it a day.*	Let's stop working for today.
Amy should *brush up on* her Spanish.	Amy should refresh her knowledge of Spanish.
The thief tried to *cover her tracks.*	The thief tried to hide what she had done.

Technical terms are the words used by people in specific fields to describe their activities. The words themselves may be familiar, but they have specialized meanings in a particular profession. Examples from the field of theater include *stage left, curtain time, fly space,* and *apron.* Technical terms help those with knowledge of the field communicate effectively.

Jargon, like technical terminology, is the specialized language used in a specific field. However, when jargon is used with people outside the field, it results in confusion. Try to figure out what this means: *When you get the proof, stet the correx.* It means that the corrections should not be made on a page printout. In most writing, jargon should generally be avoided.

Practice A Identify the jargon in each sentence. Then, rewrite the sentence using more understandable language. Use a dictionary if necessary.

1. Bringing up that topic will have a negative impact on our relationship.
2. The real estate agent flipped the property.
3. The business owner said it was necessary to downsize.

4. Occasioned by an increase in the number of the involuntarily undomiciled, the city council opened new shelter units.

5. We will hold the decision in abeyance until we have heard from all members of the council.

Practice B Identify the idiom in each sentence and write a definition for each. If you are unsure of the meaning of the word or phrase, check the definition in a dictionary.

1. Let's fan out and try to find Sarah's lost earring.

2. I think you had better be quiet, if you catch my drift.

3. The sound of nails on a chalkboard drove her up the wall.

4. I'll go on record in support of the new proposal.

5. George left no stone unturned as he searched for his car keys.

6. Jordan's little sister is a pain in the neck.

7. They were taken to the principal's office and given the third degree.

8. Your mother started tearing her hair out when you didn't answer your cell phone.

9. Three hundred people in the box factory got the axe.

10. The district will break ground on the new high school tomorrow.

Activity Prepare five note cards like this one. Write each of the following words and its definition on a card. Look the word up in a dictionary and find a technical meaning for the word. Write the field it comes from and the technical meaning on the card.

case   strike   term   pitch   pin

Word:
Definition:
Field:
Technical Definition:

Comprehension and Collaboration

Working with one or two classmates, research a profession and the jargon typically used in that field. For example, you might interview a sports coach to learn jargon associated with gymnastics or swimming. Compile a glossary and share your findings with classmates.

Communications Workshop

Comparing Media Coverage

The same event can be described in varying ways. The rising number of media sources presents a challenge: People must analyze coverage to fully understand issues and events. The following techniques will help you assess presentations in different formats and media and compare the delivery of information.

Learn the Skills

Choose two different reports of the same event. Consider print, television, and Web sources.

Evaluate each report separately.

- **Determine purpose.** Is the report attempting to inform, persuade, or entertain? The presentation should be appropiate to the purpose.

- **Consider background.** Does the reporter have an agenda—a particular viewpoint or opinion to support? Knowing the background of the person or group structuring the information allows you to actively listen for *propaganda,* or one-sided and false information, and *bias,* or a prejudiced view of an issue.

- **Recognize facts and opinions.** Are the items presented as facts verifiable? Are facts accompanied by music or images that add an emotional dimension? Does the reporter add comments that are not facts of the story?

- **Actively listen and watch.** Is the language factual and objective, or emotional and subjective? Is the pacing of speech designed to elicit an emotional response from the audience?

Compare the reports. After you evaluate the reports separately, compare them.

- **Focus on emphasis.** Note the facts that each report highlights. Which points are omitted from one, but not the other? Which report contains more opinions? Compare the items that each reporter chose to emphasize.

- **Analyze the techniques.** Compare the techniques each presentation uses to convey information. Note the use of music, pictures, and colors that might evoke emotional responses from the audience. Compare how each report uses language and pacing to convey a specific tone or attitude.

- **Evaluate the reports.** After you have compared the two reports, write a statement explaining which one is more factual and objective.

Common Core State Standards

Reading Informational Text

7. Analyze various accounts of a subject told in different mediums, determining which details are emphasized in each account.

Speaking and Listening

4. Present information, findings, and supporting evidence clearly, concisely, and logically such that listeners can follow the line of reasoning and the organization, development, substance, and style are appropriate to purpose, audience, and task.

Practice the Skills

Ⓒ Presentation of Knowledge and Ideas Use what you've learned in this workshop to complete the following activity.

ACTIVITY: Compare Coverage of the Same Event

Evaluate the same event as presented in two different mediums, such as in print, online, or on radio or television. Work with a partner to present a brief report comparing the treatments in both examples of coverage. Answer the following questions in your report:

- What event is being covered?
- Have I summarized the content in both mediums?
- How are the examples similar or different?
- What role, if any, do the presenter's perceptions or opinions play in influencing the audience?
- How do formality and tone differ between the two treatments?
- Have I presented my ideas clearly and logically?

Use the Presentation Checklist to analyze classmates' presentations.

Presentation Checklist

Presentation Content
Does the presentation meet all the requirements of the activity?
Check all that apply.

- ☐ accurately and thoroughly summarized the content in both mediums
- ☐ used relevant and appropriate examples to compare the coverage in both mediums
- ☐ analyzed each writer's individual perceptions and biases
- ☐ noted differences in formality and tone between the mediums
- ☐ presented ideas clearly and in a logical order

Presentation Delivery
Did the speaker make an effective presentation?
Check all that apply.

- ☐ presented information in a logical, easy-to-follow sequence
- ☐ spoke clearly and at an appropriate pace
- ☐ maintained eye contact with the audience
- ☐ provided clear answers to audience questions

Cumulative Review

I. Reading Literature

Common Core
State Standards

RL.9-10.1, RL.9-10.2, RL.9-10.3,
RL.9-10.5; L.9-10.4.a
[For the full wording of the standards,
see the standards chart in the front of
your textbook.]

Directions: *Read the passage. Then, answer each question that follows.*

Jane Babbitt and the Cordless Phone

Everyone from Pennsbury, Pennsylvania, has heard stories of Jane Babbitt. Some say that Jane saved the school music program by making instruments for all the students. Others say that mighty Jane single-handedly defeated the Brookline High School basketball team by playing all positions when the rest of the team was ill. I do not know about those stories, but I do know that Jane invented the cordless phone.

Jane's best friend, Molly Kubrick, had fifty brothers and sisters. Imagine trying to have a private conversation with one hundred prying sibling ears around you! Molly grew more frustrated every day. When Jane saw how annoyed her best friend was, she knew she had to help.

One day after school, Jane went over to Molly's house to have a look at her phone. "Listen, phone," she said to the black phone connected to the wall, "Molly's got to be able to have private conversations. Your cord will just have to stretch." Apparently, even Molly's phone had heard about Jane. The phone resolved to let its cord stretch as far as possible.

Molly took the phone off the receiver and left the house. "Hi, Molly!" her sister Veronica yelled from the yard. "Who are you calling?" Molly kept walking down the street. She got the to end of the block.

"Hi, Molly!" shouted her brothers Rich and Eddie. "Are you calling your boyfriend?" She rolled her eyes and kept going. The cord stretched and stretched. Molly had to walk all the way to the other side of town before she was finally free of the eyes of her many brothers and sisters.

She looked down at the phone. The cord had snapped along the way. Molly's eyes filled with tears. Suddenly, she heard Jane come up behind her. "Did you make your call?" Jane said <u>affably,</u> with a smile.

"I can't. The phone is broken," Molly said sadly.

"No way. This phone will still work. Right, phone?" said Jane to the phone. Suddenly, Molly heard the dial tone. She started to dial and made her first private call.

I lived across the street at the time, and saw Molly make her call. That's how I know we all have Jane to thank for the cordless phone.

1. This selection shares all of the following characteristics with **myths** except—

   A. it includes a character with exceptional skills.
   B. it explains how something originated.
   C. it has a protagonist.
   D. it explains the actions of the gods.

2. Which statement characterizes Molly's **worldview?**

   A. Share everything with your family.
   B. Forgive and forget.
   C. Do not trust your friends too much.
   D. Everyone deserves to have some privacy.

3. What does the first paragraph tell you about the **cultural context** of this selection?

   A. The selection is set in modern times.
   B. The selection is set in the Midwest.
   C. The telephone has just been invented.
   D. It is unusual for females to attend school.

4. In what way is Jane similar to an **epic hero?**

   A. Her story has been passed down for hundreds of years.
   B. She goes on a long journey to foreign lands.
   C. She struggles against the gods.
   D. Her amazing skills make her larger-than-life.

5. Which of these **narrative patterns** does this selection follow?

   A. Someone has a need, and a hero helps that person.
   B. A hero desires power and uses others to get it.
   C. A protagonist struggles with an antagonist, and the antagonist triumphs.
   D. Someone challenges a hero to a duel, and the hero accepts.

6. **Vocabulary** What is the *best* definition for the underlined word *affably?*

   A. angrily   **B.** cheerfully
   C. wisely   **D.** sadly

7. Why does the author include the detail that Molly has fifty siblings?

   A. to convince the reader that gigantic families are beneficial for everyone
   B. to confuse the reader with extra information
   C. to prove that Molly complains too much
   D. to emphasize Molly's difficulties in finding privacy in a humorous way

8. What does the author say to suggest that Jane is a **legendary hero** in her community?

   A. The author saw Molly make her phone call.
   B. The author claims that Jane defeated a basketball team without anyone else's help.
   C. The author states that everyone in the community knows about Jane's adventures.
   D. The author went to high school with Jane.

9. This story fits the characteristics of a **folk tale** because—

   A. it describes human deeds.
   B. no gods appear in the story.
   C. it expresses values.
   D. All of the above.

 Timed Writing

10. **Identify** one **universal theme** in this selection. In a paragraph, **explain** how this theme is developed. **Support** your answer with details from the selection.

GO ON

II. Reading Informational Text

Directions: *Read the passage. Then, answer each question that follows.*

 **Common Core State Standards**

RI.9-10.2, RI.9-10.5; L.9-10.1.b, L.9-10.2.b, L.9-10.4.a
[For the full wording of the standards, see the standards chart in the front of your textbook.]

The Fire Makers

The use and production of fire is one of humanity's most distinctive traits. As long as 1.5 million years ago, one of our earliest ancestors—*Homo erectus*—may have been using fire. U.S. and South African researchers have found evidence of burnt bones in South Africa. Using a method called "electron spin resonance," the scientists have determined that the bones had been heated to high temperatures, leading them to believe that the bones were burnt in a hearth fire. According to Dr. Anne Skinner, "These bones could have been burnt in a forest fire or brush fire, but that's generally a low temperature flame. These had been heated to a very high temperature."

There is little evidence that to tell us exactly when humans learned this skill. Scientists have determined that prehistoric people commonly used caves as shelters and have found the remains of communal campfires. These sites include bones of extinct animals such as cave bears and saber-toothed tigers, indicating these sites are very old. *Using* fire, however, is not *making* fire, and whether the fires were created or were "stolen" from natural brush fires remains uncertain. Because carrying fire can be hazardous and fires can easily go out, though, it seems likely that <u>nomadic</u> hunter-gatherers must have learned to make fires themselves, as they did not remain in one place. Additionally, being without fire in Ice Age Europe would almost certainly have meant death; people would have had to know how to create their own fires to survive.

1. If you wanted to learn more about how *Homo erectus* lived, which of the following questions would *not* help to guide your research?

　A. What other creatures existed 1.5 million years ago?

　B. What did *Homo erectus* look like?

　C. What foods did *Homo erectus* eat?

　D. How does electron spin resonance work?

2. Which claim about fire is most strongly supported in this passage?

　A. Fire originated in South Africa.

　B. Ancient hunter-gatherers could create fire.

　C. *Homo erectus* used fire.

　D. European Ice Age hunters did not use fire.

3. Vocabulary What is the *best* definition of the underlined word *nomadic*?

　A. ancient

　B. related to hunting

　C. wandering

　D. pre-human

4. Which detail provides support for the writer's claim that ancient people in South Africa used fire?

　A. Prehistoric people commonly used fire.

　B. Scientists determined that the bones had been burnt in hearth fires.

　C. Scientists used "electron spin resonance."

　D. Nomadic people worried about fire.

III. Writing and Language Conventions

Directions: *Read the passage. Then, answer each question that follows.*

Guidelines for Volunteer Counselors

(1) All children will be pre-registered. (2) When they arrive at the facility, escort them directly to Room 12B. (3) Check tags against the master list. (4) First, make sure each child has a name tag. (5) Once you organize the children, bring them to the buses. (6) List of activities to conduct while on the bus. (7) When you arrive at the site park, rangers will have lighted the campfire. (8) Adult counselors will be present to conduct activities singing songs, learning rhymes, and playing games. (9) Your job is to see that no child wanders away from the site or gets too near the fire. (10) At end of event, help children reboard the bus; check name tags against the list. (11) Arrive at the facility. (12) Make sure each parent signs his or her child out of camp. (13) You'll have a total blast!

1. Which revision should be made to this passage to improve its **organization**?

  A. Switch sentences 3 and 4.
  B. Delete sentence 1.
  C. Switch sentences 1 and 2.
  D. Delete sentence 3.

2. Which sentence should be deleted to maintain a consistent professional **tone?**

  A. sentence 1
  B. sentence 3
  C. sentence 9
  D. sentence 13

3. What is the *best* way to correct the **fragment** in sentence 6?

  A. Add "You will have a" to the beginning.
  B. Change "to conduct" to "conducting."
  C. Delete "on the."
  D. Combine sentences 6 and 7.

4. Where should a **colon** be added in sentence 8?

  A. after "counselors"
  B. after "activities"
  C. after "rhymes"
  D. Leave as is.

5. In what way should sentence 10 be revised?

  A. Replace the semicolon with the word "so."
  B. Replace the semicolon with the word "and."
  C. Add another semicolon after "event."
  D. Leave as is.

6. What is the *best* way to combine sentences 11 and 12 into a single **complex sentence?**

  A. After you arrive at the facility, make sure each parent signs his or her child out of camp.
  B. Arrive back at the facility and make sure each parent signs his or her child out of camp.
  C. Make sure that each parent signs his or her child out of camp, but you can only do that after you arrive back.
  D. Arrive back, find parent, and sign child out.

Performance Tasks

Directions: *Follow the instructions to complete the tasks below as required by your teacher.*

As you work on each task, incorporate both general academic vocabulary and literary terms you learned in this unit.

Common Core
State Standards

RL.9-10.2, RL.9-10.3, RL.9-10.5, RL.9-10.6, RL.9-10.9; W.9-10.9.a; SL.9-10.4; L.9-10.1, L.9-10.2

[For the full wording of the standards, see the standards chart in the front of your textbook.]

Writing

Task 1: Literature [RL.9-10.6; W.9-10.9.a]
Analyze Cultural Context

Write an essay in which you analyze how cultural experience is reflected in a work of world literature.

- Select a story from this unit that represents the ideas and values of a culture other than your own.

- Locate specific details that reveal the work's cultural context, and analyze what you can infer about the culture from these details. Remember that cultural context includes customs, beliefs, attitudes, values, and traditions, as well as time and place.

- Discuss the ways in which the culture is reflected in the story. You might include characters, plot, conflict, setting, or theme in your discussion.

- Provide a conclusion that follows from and supports your points.

Task 2: Literature [RL.9-10.2; W.9-10.9.a]
Analyze Theme

Write an essay in which you trace the development of a universal theme through culturally specific details.

- Select a work from this unit with a strong cultural context that expresses a universal theme. State the universal theme.

- Trace the development of the universal theme through specific cultural details. Refer to story details that describe the time, place, social structure, beliefs, conflicts, and lifestyle.

- Draw a conclusion about whether or not the cultural context of the work alters the theme in any way.

- Use a variety of sentence structures in your writing. Throughout your essay, apply the conventions of standard English grammar and usage.

Task 3: Literature [RL.9-10.5; W.9-10.9.a]
Analyze Archetypal Narrative Patterns

Write an essay in which you compare the use of archetypal narrative patterns in two works from this unit.

- Select two works from this unit that contain similar archetypal narrative structures, such as quests, patterns of threes, tests or trials, transgressions, or just endings. Identify the narrative structures you will be comparing, and provide enough information about each pattern so that readers can easily understand your points.

- Evaluate the function of the archetypal narrative structures in each work. For example, you might compare how the narrative structures create effects such as suspense or mystery and how they help to convey meaning.

- Make inferences about the cultures in which the stories originated based on the particular way in which archetypal patterns are used.

- Support your ideas with details from the texts.

- Correctly apply the conventions of standard English grammar and usage in your writing.

Speaking and Listening

© Task 4: Literature [RL.9-10.3; SL.9-10.4]
Compare Heroic Characters

Prepare and deliver an oral presentation in which you compare two heroes and their significance.

- Select two heroes from works of different genres in this unit.

- Describe each hero, using details from the text. Include physical attributes, personality traits, and motivations, as well as strengths and weaknesses. If the hero fits into the category of legendary or epic hero, explain the ways in which he or she exhibits the qualities of that character type.

- Determine whether the hero changes at all over the course of the work and, if so, in what way. Describe the main conflicts that each hero faces.

- Make inferences about what each hero's qualities reveal about the culture.

- In your conclusion, present a generalization about the relationship between heroes and the cultures that create them.

- Present your ideas and evidence clearly, logically, and concisely so that listeners can follow your reasoning.

© Task 5: Literature [RL.9-10.9; SL.9-10.4]
Analyze Authors' Interpretations of Source Material

Direct a small-group discussion exploring the ways in which authors draw on and transform elements of older works.

- Refer to the three works in this unit by Tennyson, White, and Twain that are based on Arthurian legend.
- Note key differences in the author's perspective and the author's purpose in each work.
- Analyze the way in which each author furthers his purpose by drawing on Arthurian legend.
- Prepare a list of questions for discussion based on your comparative analysis. Make sure you have enough commentary ready to keep a discussion going.

- Actively involve all members of the group into the discussion. In a collegial manner, clarify, challenge, or verify statements when needed. Refer to the texts for support.
- Conclude your discussion with a review of the main points that were made.

© Task 6: Literature [RL.9-10.6; SL.9-10.4]
Compare Genres

Prepare and deliver a speech in which you compare myth, epic, and legend—genres that have their roots in the oral tradition.

- Define *myth, epic,* and *legend.* To provide examples and evidence, focus on one example of each genre from this unit.

- Discuss some of the similarities of the genres, including the ways in which a sense of the oral tradition continues in each of the examples you have chosen.

- Explain any significant differences among the genres.

- Examine ways in which each genre communicates cultural information.

- Draw a conclusion about the lasting power of myth, legend, and epic.

- Speak expressively, establish eye contact, and use appropriate volume as you present your speech.

Can anyone be a hero?
At the beginning of Unit 6, you participated in a discussion of the Big Question. Now that you have completed the unit, write a response to the question. Discuss how your initial ideas have changed or been reinforced. Support your response with at least one example from literature and one example from an additional subject area or your own life. Use Big Question vocabulary words (see p. 1047) in your response.

Featured Titles

In this unit, you have read a wide variety of thematically related literary works. Continue to explore thematic connections in literature. Select works that you enjoy, but challenge yourself to explore new writers and works of increasing depth and complexity. The titles suggested below will help you get started.

Literature

Candide
by Voltaire   EXEMPLAR TEXT

In this **novel** and political satire, the agreeable Candide is expelled from his home after kissing the baron's daughter and spends his life trying to reunite with her. Along the way, Voltaire pokes fun at political and religious figures, philosophers, adventure and romance tales, and a whole host of other targets. While the novel was initially banned due to its sharp religious and political satire, Voltaire arranged for it to be published secretly. It quickly became an underground hit that was read eagerly throughout Europe.

The Once and Future King
by T. H. White
Ace, 1987

Escape into the legendary world of Camelot, where chivalry defines the age. This **novel** describes in vivid detail the rise of King Arthur, his idealistic kingdom, and its eventual collapse.

The Norton Anthology of African American Literature
Edited by Henry Louis Gates, Jr., and Nellie Y. McKay

W.W. Norton and Company, 1996   EXEMPLAR TEXT

This extraordinary **anthology** includes poems, spirituals, short stories, jazz and hip hop music, excerpts from novels and autobiographies, and more by important and gifted African American artists. It includes "Yet Do I Marvel" by Countee Cullen.

The Metamorphosis
by Franz Kafka   EXEMPLAR TEXT

As this **novella** begins, Gregor Samsa wakes up to discover that he has been transformed into a giant insect. Gregor has to work through feelings of fear and alienation, as well as more practical matters—such as how to turn over—in this darkly comic story.

Informational Texts

Early Irish Myths and Sagas
Translated by Jeffrey Gantz

Capturing a mystical world of battle and beauty, these ancient **myths** and **sagas** provide a glimpse into the mind and soul of the Celtic world. First written down around the eighth century, these tales are far older, having been transmitted orally from generation to generation centuries before that time.

Son of the Morning Star: Custer and the Little Bighorn
by Evan S. Connell   EXEMPLAR TEXT

This **nonfiction** book gives a compelling and comprehensive history of the Battle of the Little Bighorn, focusing on Custer, who was a commander of the U.S. 7th Cavalry Regiment, and Crazy Horse and others, who led the combined forces of the Lakota Sioux and Northern Cheyenne nations.

A Sacred Union of Citizens: George Washington's Farewell Address and the American Character
by Matthew Spalding and Patrick J. Garrity
Rowman and Littlefield, 1998   EXEMPLAR TEXT

This **nonfiction** book, part biography and part history, tells the story of Washington's life and his efforts to establish the new republic. It includes the full text of his farewell speech, still quoted today by historians and politicians to warn against entangling America's foreign policy goals with the ambitions of other nations.

Preparing to Read Complex Texts

Attentive Reading As you read literature on your own, bring your imagination and questions to the text. The questions shown below and others that you ask as you read will help you learn and enjoy literature even more.

Common Core State Standards

Reading Literature/Informational Text 10. By the end of Grade 10, read and comprehend literature, including stories, dramas, poems, and literary nonfiction at the high end of the grades 9–10 text complexity band independently and proficiently.

When reading texts from the oral tradition, ask yourself...

- What type of text is this? For example, is it an epic, a myth, a tale, or a legend? What types of characters, events, and ideas do I expect to find in this text?
- From what culture does this text come? What do I know about that culture?
- Does my knowledge of the culture lead me to expect certain qualities in this text? If so, what are my expectations?
- Does the text meet my expectations? Why or why not?
- What elements of the culture do I see in the text? For example, do I notice beliefs, foods, or settings that have meaning for the people of this culture?
- Does the text express a moral or theme that has meaning for modern readers? Why or why not?

© Key Ideas and Details

- Is this text a retelling by a modern author? If so, does the author change the text for modern readers?
- How do I think the text on the page is different from the text when it was originally related, sung, or performed? Which parts of the text might a performer have exaggerated or altered?
- Does the text include characters and tell a story? If so, are the characters and plot interesting?
- What do I notice about the language, including descriptions and dialogue? How does the language compare to that of modern texts?
- Does the text include symbols? If so, do they have special meanings in the original culture of the text? Do they also have meanings in modern life?
- Does the text include patterns of events or repetitions of statements or images? If so, which ones? What is the effect?

© Craft and Structure

- How does this text round out the picture of the culture I might get from a nonfiction source, such as an encyclopedia entry?
- Does this text express universal ideas or values—those that are common to people in many different cultures and time periods?
- Does this text seem like others I have read or heard? Why or why not?
- Do I know of any modern versions of this text? How are they similar to or different from this one?
- If I were researching this culture for a report, would I include passages from this text? If so, what would those passages show?
- Do I enjoy reading this text and others like it? Why or why not?

© Integration of Ideas

Resources

Vocabulary Handbook **R1**
    Glossary R1
    Spanish Glossary R8

Literary Handbook **R15**
    Literary Terms R15
    Tips for Discussing Literature R25
    Literary Criticism R27
    Literary Movements R28
    Tips for Improving Reading Fluency R29

Writing Handbook **R31**
    Types of Writing R31
    Writing Friendly Letters R33
    Writing Business Letters R34
    Writing a Résumé R35
    Citing Sources and Preparing Manuscript R36
    Guide to Rubrics R38

Twenty-First Century Skills **R42**

Rules of Debate **R48**

Grammar, Usage, and Mechanics Handbook **R50**

Index **R57**
    Index of Skills R57
    Index of Features R71
    Index of Authors and Titles R74

Acknowledgments (continued) **R76**

Credits **R80**

Glossary

Big Question vocabulary appears in **blue type**. High-utility Academic Vocabulary is <u>underlined</u>.

A

abruptly (uh BRUHPT lee) *adv.* happening suddenly; unexpectedly

abysmal (uh BIHZ muhl) *adj.* immeasurably deep; terrible

accomplices (uh KOM plihs uhz) *n.* people who help another person commit a crime

adamant (AD uh mant) *adj.* not giving in; unyielding; firm

<u>adapt</u> (uh DAPT) *v.* change or adjust

adept (uh DEHPT) *adj.* expert; highly skilled

adulation (aj uh LAY shuhn) *n.* high or excessive praise; intense admiration

adversaries (AD vuhr sehr eez) *n.* opponents

adversity (ad VUR suh tee) *n.* state of difficulty or misfortune

affable (AF uh buhl) *adj.* pleasant; friendly

affront (uh FRUHNT) *n.* open insult

aggregate (AG ruh giht) *n.* a group of distinct things gathered into a whole; a sum

aggrieved (uh GREEVD) *adj.* wronged; suffering grief or injury

allay (uh LAY) *v.* relieve; lessen; calm

alleviate (uh LEE vee ayt) *v.* to lighten; relieve

amenable (uh MEE nuh buhl) *adj.* responsive; open

amiably (AY mee uh blee) *adv.* in a cheerful, friendly way

anguish (ANG gwihsh) *n.* extreme suffering, as from grief or pain

<u>anticipate</u> (an TIHS uh payt) *v.* look forward to

apathy (AP uh thee) *n.* lack of interest or emotion

apprehension (ap rih HEHN shuhn) *n.* anxious feeling; fear

arable (AR uh buhl) *adj.* suitable for growing crops

ardent (AHR duhnt) *adj.* intensely enthusiastic; devoted

aspirations (as puh RAY shuhnz) *n.* strong ambitions

assuage (uh SWAYJ) *v.* lessen (pain or distress); satisfy (thirst or hunger)

attributes (AT rihb yoots) *n.* characteristics of a person or thing

audaciously (aw DAY shuhs lee) *adv.* in a bold manner

augmented (awg MEHNT ihd) *adj.* made greater; enhanced

august (aw GUHST) *adj.* impressive; majestic

<u>awareness</u> (uh WAIR nuhs) *n.* having knowledge

B

<u>background</u> (BAK grownd) *n.* conditions that surround or come before something

<u>bias</u> (BY uhs) *n.* point of view one has before the facts are known

blemished (BLEHM ihsht) *adj.* damaged; spoiled

bore (bohr) *v.* carried

brandished (BRAN dihsht) *v.* showed, waved, or shook in a threatening or triumphant manner

brazen (BRAY zuhn) *adj.* shameless; bold

buffer (BUHF uhr) *v.* lessen a shock; cushion

C

cajoling (kuh JOHL ihng) *n.* coaxing with flattery

calamity (kuh LAM uh tee) *n.* terrible misfortune; disaster

candid (KAN dihd) *adj.* honest; direct

canopied (KAN uh peed) *adj.* covered by a cloth suspended from poles or a framework

catalyst (KAT uh lihst) *n.* person or thing that triggers an event or action

cessation (seh SAY shuhn) *n.* halt; stopping

change (chaynj) *v.* become different; transform

<u>character</u> (KAR ihk tuhr) *n.* moral strength; self-discipline

chastisement (chas TYZ muhnt) *n.* severe criticism; punishment

choleric (KOL uhr ihk) *adj.* quick tempered; inclined to anger

circuit (SUR kiht) *n.* act of going around something; route

clenching (KLEHNCH ihng) *v.* closing; holding tightly

clustering (KLUHS tuhr ihng) *adj.* gathering; forming in a group

commemorates (kuh MEHM uh rayts) *v.* honors a memory

commences (kuh MEHNS ez) *v.* begins

commiserate (kuh MIHZ uh rayt) *v.* sympathize with; show sorrow for

<u>comprehend</u> (kom prih HEHND) *v.* grasp mentally; understand

compromise (KOM pruh myz) *n.* agreement where both sides give something up

compulsory (kuhm PUHL suhr ee) *adj.* required; mandatory

comrade (KOM rad) *n.* close companion; friend

concession (kuhn SEHSH uhn) *n.* act of granting or giving; allowance

concrete (KON kreet) *adj.* something specific or tangible

condemn (kuhn DEHM) *v.* disapprove of; pass unfavorable judgment on

condemned (kuhn DEHMD) *v.* declared to be guilty of wrongdoings; convicted

conduct (KON duhkt) *n.* the way a person acts; behavior

configuration (kuhn FIHG yuh RAY shuhn) *n.* arrangement of parts; pattern

confirm (kuhn FURM) *v.* establish the truth or correctness of something

confounded (kon FOWND ihd) *adj.* made to feel confused

confrontation (kon fruhn TAY shuhn) *n.* clashing of forces or ideas

confusion (kuhn FYOO zhuhn) *n.* state of disorder or distraction

conjured (KON juhrd) *v.* performed tricks in which things seem to appear, disappear, or change as if by magic

connection (kuh NEHK shuhn) *n.* relationship between things

consigned (kuhn SYND) *v.* handed over; gave up or delivered

conspicuous (kuhn SPIHK yu uhs) *adj.* easy to see

constricting (kuhn STRIHKT ihng) *adj.* preventing freedom of movement; limiting

contempt (kuhn TEHMPT) *n.* scorn; the attitude of someone who looks down on something or someone else

contested (KON tehst uhd) *v.* tried to disprove or invalidate something; disputed

context (KON tehkst) *n.* environment or situation in which something is found

context (KON tehkst) *n.* circumstances that form the setting of an event

contrive (kuhn TRYV) *v.* to bring about; manage

convalesce (kon vuh LEHS) *v.* to regain strength and health

converge (kuhn VURJ) *v.* to come together

convey (kuhn VAY) *v.* communicate or make known

convoluted (kon vuh LOOT uhd) *adj.* twisted in a complicated way

counsel (KOWN suhl) *n.* advice; discussion

countenance (KOWN tuh nuhns) *n.* face; the look of a face, showing a person's nature

courage (KUR ihj) *n.* willingness to deal with something dangerous

credulity (kruh DOO luh tee) *n.* tendency to believe too readily

customarily (kuhs tuh MEHR ih lee) *adv.* usually; by habit or tradition

D

debate (dih BAYT) *v.* argue or discuss

debut (day BYOO) *n.* first public appearance

decorum (dih KAWR uhm) *n.* behavior that is polite and is correct for an occasion

decrepitude (dih KREHP uh tood) *n.* feebleness; condition of being worn out by age or illness

deference (DEHF uhr uhns) *n.* a yielding to the ideas, wishes, and so on of another

deficiency (dih FIHSH uhn see) *n.* lack of something essential

deflects (dih FLEHKTS) *v.* wards off; turns aside

deftness (dehft nehs) *n.* skillfulness

defunct (dih FUHNGKT) *adj.* no longer in use or existence; dead

dejectedly (dih JEHK tihd lee) *adv.* in a depressed way

delusion (dih LOO zhuhn) *n.* an erroneous belief that is held despite evidence to the contrary

demeanor (dih MEE nuhr) *n.* way of conducting oneself; behavior

derisively (dih RY sihv lee) *adv.* in a mocking and ridiculing manner

derived (dih RYVD) *v.* reached by reasoning

desolate (DEHS uh liht) *adj.* empty; solitary

destitute (DEHS tuh toot) *adj.* lacking the basic necessities of life; poverty-stricken

determination (dih TUR muh NAY shuhn) *n.* firmness of purpose

detestable (dee TEHS tuh buhl) *adj.* deserving hate or scorn; offensive

dexterous (DEHKS tuhr uhs) *adj.* having or showing mental or physical skill

differentiate (dihf uh REHN shee ayt) *v.* distinguish between

dignity (DIHG nuh tee) *n.* quality of deserving respect and honor; self-respect

dilapidated (duh LAP uh dayt ihd) *adj.* shabby; broken down

diligence (DIHL uh juhns) *n.* constant, careful effort

dimpled (DIHM puhld) *adj.* marked with small hollows or indentations

dingy (DIHN jee) *adj.* dirty-looking; shabby

dire (dyr) *adj.* urgent; terrible; calling for quick action

discern (duh ZURN) *v.* tell the difference between two or more things; perceive

disconsolate (dihs KON suh liht) *adj.* so unhappy that nothing brings comfort; miserable

discord (DIHS kawrd) *n.* conflict; disagreement

discourse (DIHS kawrs) *v.* speak (on a topic) formally and at length

discourse (DIHS kawrs) *n.* ongoing communication of ideas and information

disdain (dihs DAYN) *n.* disgust for something or someone; scorn

disembarked (DIHS ehm BAHRKT) *v.* left a ship to go ashore

disparagement (dihs PAR ihj muhnt) *n.* comments expressing a low opinion of or lack of respect for

disreputable (dihs REHP yuh tuh buhl) *adj.* not respectable; having or deserving a bad reputation

dissent (dih SEHNT) *n.* refusal to accept a common belief or opinion; disagreement

distinct (dihs TIHNGKT) *adj.* clearly different; separate

distortion (dihs TAWR shuhn) *n.* anything that shows something in an untrue way

dogged (DAWG ihd) *adj.* stubborn

E

earnest (UR nihst) *adj.* serious and intense; not joking

eased (eezd) *v.* freed from pain or trouble; lessened

ebony (EHB uh nee) *adj.* black

edict (EE dihkt) *n.* public order; decree

edifying (EHD uh fy ihng) *adj.* instructive in such a way as to improve morally or intellectually

efface (uh FAYS) *v.* rub or blot out

elude (ih LOOD) *v.* avoid; escape by quickness or cleverness

elusive (ih LOO sihv) *adj.* hard to grasp mentally

emanating (EHM uh nayt ihng) *v.* coming forth, as from a source

embodied (ehm BOD eed) *v.* gave form to; made concrete

emigrants (EHM uh gruhnts) *n.* people who leave their country or region to settle elsewhere

emotion (ih MOH shuhn) *n.* strong feeling, such as love

empathy (EHM puh thee) *n.* sharing in another person's feelings

encroaching (ehn KROHCH ihng) *adj.* intruding on, especially in a gradual way

endeavored (ehn DEHV uhrd) *v.* tried to achieve a set goal

endure (ehn DUR) *v.* hold up under pain or hardship

engaging (ehn GAYJ ihng) *adj.* attractive; pleasant

enlighten (ehn LY tuhn) *v.* make clear through knowledge

enthralls (ehn THRAWLZ) *v.* captivates; fascinates

entreated (ehn TREET uhd) *v.* begged; pleaded with

ephemeral (ih FEHM uhr uhl) *adj.* short-lived

equilibrium (ee kwuh LIHB ree uhm) *n.* a state of balance

esoteric (ehs uh TEHR ihk) *adj.* beyond the understanding or knowledge of most people

estranged (ehs TRAYNJD) *adj.* kept apart; in the condition of having had affection turn into indifference or hostility

eternal (ih TUR nuhl) *adj.* without beginning or end; everlasting

evaluate (ih VAL yoo ayt) *v.* determine the worth of something

evidence (EHV uh duhns) *n.* information that indicates whether something is true or valid

evoking (ih VOHK ihng) *v.* to draw forth emotions or responses

evolve (ih VOLV) *v.* develop through gradual changes

exorbitant (ehg ZAWR buh tuhnt) *adj.* going beyond what is reasonable; excessive

expectations (ehks pehk TAY shuhnz) *n.* something looked forward to

explanation (ehks pluh NAY shuhn) *n.* clarifying statement

expound (ehk SPOWND) *v.* explain in detail

extolled (ehk STOHLD) *adj.* praised

extricating (EHKS truh kayt ihng) *n.* setting free; removing from a difficult situation

exuberance (ehg ZOO buhr uhns) *n.* good health and high spirits

F

falteringly (FAWL tuhr ihng lee) *adv.* spoken hesitatingly or with a wavering voice

fate (fayt) *n.* destiny; what happens to a person or thing; final outcome

fathom (FATH uhm) *v.* understand thoroughly

fawned (fawnd) *v.* flattered; act with excessive concern for the wishes and moods of another, as a servant might

flourishes (FLUR ihsh uhz) *v.* grows vigorously; thrives

fluttered (FLUHT uhrd) *v.* flapped or vibrated rapidly

foe (foh) *n.* enemy

forbore (fawr BAWR) *v.* prevented oneself from doing something; refrained from

foreboding (fawr BOHD ihng) *n.* a feeling that something bad will happen; premonition

formidable (FAWR muh duh buhl) *adj.* causing fear or dread

fraud (frawd) *n.* deceit; trickery

furtively (FUR tihv lee) *adj.* secretively; sneakily; stealthily

futile (FYOO tuhl) *adj.* not successful; useless

G

gauge (gayj) *v.* measure the size, amount, extent, or capacity of

grave (grayv) *adj.* very serious and worrying

grimacing (GRIHM ihs ihng) *v.* making a twisted face showing disgust or pain

growth (grohth) *n.* the process of developing

H

haphazardly (hap HAZ uhrd lee) *adv.* in an unplanned or a disorganized way

haste (hayst) *n.* quickness of motion; rapidity

heedless (HEED lihs) *adj.* careless; thoughtless

history (HIHS tuhr ee) *n.* account of what has happened

honor (ON uhr) *n.* strong sense of right and wrong

humble (HUHM buhl) *adj.* showing an awareness of one's shortcomings; modest

hypocrisy (hih POK ruh see) *n.* the act of saying one thing but doing another

I

idealistic (y dee uh LIHS tihk) *adj.* representing things as they should be rather than how they are

identity (y DEHN tuh tee) *n.* qualities of a person that make up who they are

idle (Y duhl) *adj.* useless; not busy

ignorance (IHG nuhr uhns) *n.* lack of knowledge or education

immaterial (ihm uh TIHR ee uhl) *adj.* not consisting of matter

imminent (IHM uh nuhnt) *adj.* about to happen

impeded (ihm PEED uhd) *v.* blocked; obstructed

impediments (ihm PEHD uh muhnts) *n.* things that slow something or someone down or that get in the way; barriers

impending (ihm PEHN dihng) *adj.* about to happen

imperceptibly (ihm puhr SEHP tuh blee) *adv.* so slowly or slightly as to be barely noticeable

imperiously (ihm PIHR ee uhs lee) *adv.* arrogantly

impervious (ihm PUR vee uhs) *adj.* not affected by (used with to)

impetuosity (ihm pehch oo OS uh tee) *n.* quality of acting suddenly, with great force and little thought; rashness

impression (ihm PREHSH uhn) *n.* an effect produced on the mind

improbable (ihm PROB uh buhl) *adj.* not likely to happen or be true

inaudibly (ihn AW duh blee) *adv.* in a way that cannot be heard

incessant (ihn SEHS uhnt) *adj.* not stopping; constant

incredulity (ihn kruh DOO luh tee) *n.* unwillingness to believe

indigence (IHN duh juhns) *n.* poverty

indignant (ihn DIHG nuhnt) *adj.* feeling anger, especially at injustice

indignation (IHN dihg NAY shuhn) *n.* anger that is a reaction to injustice or meanness

individual (ihn duh VIHJ oo uhl) *adj.* relating to a single person or thing

indulgence (ihn DUHL juhns) *n.* leniency; readiness to tolerate or forgive bad behavior

inexorably (ihn EHK suhr uh blee) *adv.* without the possibility of being delayed or stopped; unalterable

infinite (IHN fuh niht) *adj.* beyond measure or comprehension; endless

infirm (ihn FURM) *adj.* weak; feeble

infirmity (ihn FUR muh tee) *n.* weakness; physical defect

influence (IHN floo uhns) *n.* the power of people to change others

ingenuity (ihn juh NOO uh tee) *n.* cleverness

ingratiating (ihn GRAY shee ayt ihng) *adj.* acting in a way intended to win someone's favor

inhabit (ihn HAB iht) *v.* live in

inherent (ihn HIHR uhnt) *adj.* existing naturally in something

inheritance (ihn HEHR uh tuhns) *n.* gift handed down to a later generation in a family

innuendo (ihn yoo EHN doh) *n.* indirect insult or accusation; insinuation

insight (ihn syt) *n.* clear idea of the nature of things

instinct (IHN stihngkt) *n.* an inborn pattern of behavior, as opposed to a learned skill

insurrection (ihn suh REHK shuhn) *n.* rebellion

integrity (ihn TEHG ruh tee) *n.* willingness to stand by moral principles

interact (ihn tuhr AKT) *v.* relate to one another; affect another

interminable (ihn TUR muh nuh buhl) *adj.* seemingly endless

interpretation (ihn tur pruh TAY shuhn) *n.* explanation of the meaning of something

interred (ihn TURD) *v.* buried (said of a dead body)

intertidal (ihn tuhr TY duhl) *adj.* pertaining to a shore zone bounded by the levels of low and high tide

intervened (ihn tuhr VEEND) *v.* came between

intrigues (ihn TREEGZ) *n.* plots; schemes

irascible (ih RAS uh buhl) *adj.* irritable

irreproachable (ihr ih PROH chuh buhl) *adj.* above criticism

irretrievable (IHR ih TREE vuh buhl) *adj.* impossible to regain or recover

isolation (y suh LAY shuhn) *n.* being alone or set apart

itinerary (y TIHN uh rehr ee) *n.* route; travel plan

J

jauntiness (JAWN tee nuhs) *n.* carefree, easy attitude

jeered (jihrd) *v.* made fun of; mocked; taunted

jurisdiction (jur ihs DIHK shuhn) *n.* sphere of authority or power

K

keenest (KEEN uhst) *adj.* sharpest; most cutting

knowledge (NOL ihj) *n.* awareness and understanding of information

L

lacquered (LAK uhrd) *adj.* covered in tough, sticky varnish

lamentation (lam uhn TAY shuhn) *n.* act of crying out in grief; wailing; weeping

language (LANG gwihj) *n.* system used for expressing or communicating; word choice

languid (LANG gwihd) *adj.* without energy

lavished (LAV ihsht) *v.* gave with extreme generosity

lease (lees) *n.* contract by which something is rented for a specified period of time; rental

legacies (LEHG uh seez) *n.* money, property, or position left in a will to someone

legendary (LEHJ uhn DEHR ee) *adj.* extraordinary; memorable

livid (LIHV ihd) *adj.* discolored, as by a bruise; red with anger

lofty (LAWF tee) *adj.* elevated in rank or character; noble

looming (LOOM ihng) *adj.* appearing unclearly but in a threatening form; threatening to occur

lowly (LOH lee) *adj.* humble; of low rank

lucidity (loo SIHD uh tee) *n.* quality of being readily understood

lucrative (LOO kruh tihv) *adj.* producing wealth; profitable

lunar (LOO nuhr) *adj.* of the moon

M

maligned (muh LYND) *adj.* spoken ill of

manifestations (man uh fehs TAY shuhnz) *n.* appearances; forms

manipulate (muh NIHP yuh layt) *v.* control by use of influence, often in an unfair way

manipulated (muh NIHP yuh layt uhd) *v.* managed or controlled through clever moves

marginal (MAHR juh nuhl) *adj.* at, on, or near the edge

meager (MEE guhr) *adj.* of poor quality or small amount

meaning (MEE nihng) *n.* significance of something

meditates (MEHD uh tayts) *v.* thinks deeply

melancholy (MEHL uhn kol ee) *adj.* sad and depressed

millennial (muh LEHN ee uhl) *adj.* of 1,000 years

mirth (murth) *n.* joyfulness; merriment

misconstrued (mihs kuhn STROOD) *v.* misinterpreted

misinterpret (mihs ihn TUR priht) *v.* not understand correctly

modified (MOD uh fyd) *v.* changed; altered slightly

monotonously (muh NOT uh nuhs lee) *adv.* in a dull, unvarying way

motive (MOH tihv) *n.* something that causes a person to act in a certain way

multitudes (MUHL tuh toodz) *n.* large number of people or things

mutable (MYOO tuh buhl) *adj.* changeable

N

negotiate (nih GOH shee ayt) *v.* bargain with the hope of reaching an agreement

nevertheless (nehv uhr thuh LEHS) *adv.* in spite of that; however

nimbly (NIHM buh lee) *adv.* in a quick, easy, light way; with agility

nomadic (noh MAD ihk) *adj.* moving from place to place; without a permanent home

nonchalantly (NON shuh luhnt lee) *adv.* casually; indifferently

O

objective (uhb JEHK tihv) *adj.* not dependent on another's point of view

oblivious (uh BLIHV ee uhs) *adj.* unaware

obscured (uhb SKYURD) *v.* made dark; blocked from view; hid

oppose (uh POHZ) *v.* to set against; disagree with

oppressive (uh PREHS ihv) *adj.* causing great discomfort; distressing

oratory (AWR uh tawr ee) *n.* act of public speaking; strategies used in such speaking

overcome (oh vuhr KUHM) *v.* to master or prevail over

P

pallor (PAL uhr) *n.* lack of color; unnatural paleness

paradox (PAR uh doks) *n.* a statement or situation that seems contradictory

paranoia (par uh NOY uh) *n.* mental disorder characterized by delusions

perception (puhr SEHP shuhn) *n.* the way one understands the world through the senses

perpetually (puhr PEHCH oo uhl ee) *adv.* continuing forever; constantly

persevere (PUR suh VIHR) *v.* continue despite opposition; persist

perspective (puhr SPEHK tihv) *n.* the way one sees things; viewpoint

petulantly (PEHCH uh luhnt lee) *adv.* in a manner that expresses impatience or irritation

piety (PY uh tee) *n.* loyalty and devotion to family, the divine, or some other object of respect

piqued (peekt) *adj.* annoyed or upset

plague (playg) *v.* pester; harass; torment

plausibility (PLAW zuh BIHL uh tee) *n.* believability; seeming truth

plight (plyt) *n.* distressing situation

poignant (POY nuhnt) *adj.* emotionally moving; piercing

portentous (pawr TEHN tuhs) *adj.* ominous; giving signs of evil to come

presume (prih ZOOM) *v.* rely too much on; take advantage of

presumptuous (prih ZUHMP choo uhs) *adj.* overstepping appropriate bounds; too bold

pretense (prih TEHNS) *n.* a pretending; a false show of something

principles (PRIHN suh puhlz) *n.* rules for right conduct; basics

prodigious (pruh DIHJ uhs) *adj.* of great size or power

profuse (pruh FYOOS) *adj.* giving or pouring forth freely, often to excess; plentiful

progress (PROG rehs) *n.* development; improvement

prostrate (PROS trayt) *adj.* lying flat

prudent (PROO duhnt) *adj.* exercising sound judgment; cautious

purified (PYUR uh fyd) *v.* rid of impurities or pollution; made pure

Q

quench (kwehnch) *v.* satisfy; to fulfill the needs or desires of something

question (KWEHS chuhn) *v.* express uncertainty about; ask

R

radical (RAD uh kuhl) *adj.* extreme change

rash (rash) *adj.* too hasty in speech or action; reckless

rave (rayv) *v.* to talk incoherently or wildly

reality (ree AL uh tee) *n.* quality of being true to life

reapers (REE puhrz) *n.* people who gather or harvest grain

reciprocity (rehs uh PROS uh tee) *n.* relations of exchange; interdependence

reconciliation (rehk uhn sihl ee AY shuhn) *n.* restoring friendship and harmony

reflect (rih FLEHKT) *v.* think seriously about something

refuse (REHF yoos) *n.* waste; trash

rejoiced (rih JOYST) *v.* showed happiness

rejuvenation (rih joo vuh NAY shuhn) *n.* making new, youthful, or energetic again; revitalization

relent (rih LEHNT) *v.* become less strong, severe, or intense; ease up

relish (REHL ihsh) *n.* enjoyment

renounced (rih NOWNST) *v.* gave up formally

repertoire (REHP uhr twahr) *n.* stock of works, such as songs, that a performer is prepared to present

replenished (rih PLEHN ihsht) *v.* made complete or full again

replication (rehp luh KAY shuhn) *n.* duplicate; reproduction

resolute (REHZ uh loot) *adj.* showing a fixed purpose

resolution (rehz uh LOO shuhn) *n.* strong determination; a plan or decision

resolve (rih ZOLV) *v.* reach a conclusion or decision

respond (rih SPOND) *v.* answer

responsibility (rih spon suh BIHL uh tee) *n.* having to answer to someone or something else; being accountable for success or failure

reveling (REHV uhl ihng) *v.* taking great pleasure; celebrating

reverence (REHV uhr uhns) *n.* a feeling of deep respect, love, or awe

revise (rih VYZ) *v.* reconsider; modify

rudiments (ROO duh muhnts) *n.* basics; slight beginnings

S

sacrifice (SAK ruh fys) *v.* give up

sated (SAYT uhd) *adj.* satisfied; provided with more than enough

scrutinized (SKROO tuh nyzd) *v.* examined carefully

secular (SEHK yuh luhr) *adj.* of worldly, as opposed to religious, matters

self-expression (sehlf ehk SPREHSH uhn) *n.* sharing one's personality or emotions

selflessness (SEHLF lihs nuhs) *n.* being devoted to others' interests rather than one's own

self-sufficiency (sehlf suh FIHSH uhn see) *n.* independence

sententiously (sehn TEHN shuhs lee) *adv.* in a way that shows excessive fondness for wise sayings; in lecturing tones

serenity (suh REHN uh tee) *n.* state of calm or peace

servile (SUR vuhl) *adj.* slavelike; humbly submissive to authority

silhouette (sihl oo EHT) *n.* outline drawing filled in with a solid color

simulating (SIHM yuh layt ihng) *v.* giving the appearance of

skeptically (SKEHP tuh kuhl ee) *adv.* with doubt; questioningly

slumbering (SLUHM buhr ihng) *adj.* sleeping

sonorous (suh NAWR uhs) *adj.* having a rich or impressive sound

spare (spair) *adj.* lean; thin

spectacle (SPEHK tuh kuhl) *n.* strange or remarkable sight

squalid (SKWOL ihd) *adj.* foul; unclean

staidness (STAYD nuhs) *n.* state of being settled; calm

stance (stans) *n.* the way one stands, especially the placement of the feet

stark (stahrk) *adj.* bare; harsh

staunch (stawnch) *adj.* steadfast; loyal

steady (STEHD ee) *adj.* firm; sure in movement

stereotype (STEHR ee uh typ) *n.* overly broad and often incorrect notion of a group

stickler (STIHK luhr) *n.* person who insists on strict obedience to rules or standards

stifle (STY fuhl) *v.* smother; hold back

stipulates (STIHP yuh layts) *v.* includes specifically as part of an agreement

strife (stryf) *n.* struggle; conflict

struggle (STRUHG uhl) *v.* face difficulty

subdued (suhb DOOD) *adj.* quiet; lacking energy

subjective (suhb JEHK tihv) *adj.* based on or influenced by a person's feelings or point of view

subordinate (suh BAWR duh niht) *adj.* below another in importance or rank

subtle (SUH tuhl) *adj.* fine; delicate

subversion (suhb VUR zhuhn) *n.* activity meant to overthrow something established; rebellion

successive (suhk SEHS ihv) *adj.* following one after another in sequence

succinct (suhk SIHNGKT) *adj.* clearly and briefly stated

sullen (SUHL uhn) *adj.* gloomy and showing resentment

sumptuous (SUHMP choo uhs) *adj.* costly; lavish

supercilious (soo puhr SIHL ee uhs) *adj.* expressing an attitude of superiority; contemptuous

surmise (suhr MYZ) *n.* guess; idea based on evidence that is not conclusive

surpassed (suhr PAST) *v.* went beyond; excelled

T

tactile (TAK tuhl) *adj.* related to the sense of touch

tangible (TAN juh buhl) *adj.* able to be touched; actual

temperate (TEHM puhr iht) *adj.* mild; kept within limits

tempering (TEHM puhr ihng) *n.* changing to make more suitable, usually by mixing with something

tentative (TEHN tuh tihv) *adj.* hesitant; not confident

tenuous (TEHN yoo uhs) *adj.* not strong

threshold (THREHSH ohld) *n.* the bottom of a doorway; entrance or a point of beginning

titanic (ty TAN ihk) *adj.* powerful; of great size

toil (toyl) *n.* hard, tiring work

trace (trays) *n.* tiny amount; hint

transcends (tran SEHNDZ) *v.* goes beyond the limits of; exceeds

tremulous (TREHM yuh luhs) *adj.* trembling; quivering

tumult (TOO muhlt) *n.* noisy commotion

twinges (TWIHNJ uhz) *n.* sharp, sudden pains, either physical or mental

U

ulterior (uhl TIHR ee uhr) *adj.* further; beyond what is openly stated or implied

uncertainty (uhn SUR tuhn tee) *n.* inability to be sure

understanding (uhn duhr STAN dihng) *n.* power to comprehend and discern

unify (YOO nuh fy) *v.* combine into one

universal (yoo nuh VUR suhl) *adj.* existing in all things

unorthodox (uhn AWR thuh doks) *adj.* not typical; breaking with tradition

unwieldy (uhn WEEL dee) *adj.* hard to manage because of shape or weight; awkward

V

vagaries (vuh GAIR eez) *n.* erratic or unpredictable actions; whims

venerable (VEHN uhr uh buhl) *adj.* worthy of respect because of age or character

venturing (VEHN chuhr ihng) *v.* attempting to do something that involves taking risks

veracious (vuh RAY shuhs) *adj.* truthful; honest

verbal (VUR buhl) *adj.* relating to words

verified (VEHR uh fyd) *v.* proved to be true

verify (VEHR uh fy) *v.* prove that something is true

vile (vyl) *adj.* evil; low; extremely disgusting

W

waver (WAY vuhr) *v.* show indecision; fluctuate

wistfully (WIHST fuhl ee) *adv.* showing vague yearnings

wither (WIHTH uhr) *v.* dry up; shrivel from loss of moisture

wrathfully (RATH fuhl ee) *adv.* with intense anger

Spanish Glossary

El vocabulario de Gran Pregunta aparece en **azul**. El Vocabulario Academico de alta utilidad esta <u>subraydo</u>.

A

abruptly / abruptamente *adv.* que sucede de repente; inesperadamente

abysmal / abismal *adj.* inmensamente malo o extremo; terrible

accomplices / cómplices *s.* personas que ayudan a otros a cometer un crimen

adamant / obstinado *adj.* que no cede; inflexible; firme

<u>**adapt / adaptar**</u> *v.* cambiar o ajustar

adept / adepto *adj.* experto; altamente calificado

adulation / adulación *s.* grandes o excesivos elogios; intensa admiración

adversaries / adversarios *s.* opositores

adversity / adversidad *s.* estado de dificultad o infortunio

affable / afable *adj.* agradable; amistoso

affront / afrenta *s.* insulto abierto

aggregate / agregado *s.* grupo de cosas concretas que unidas forman un todo; una suma

aggrieved / agraviado *adj.* que sufre perjuicio; afligido o herido

allay / aliviar *v.* mitigar; reducir; calmar

alleviate / mitigar *v.* aliviar; aliviar

amenable / receptivo *adj.* sensible; abierto

amiably / amigablemente *adv.* de manera jovial y amistosa

anguish / angustia *s.* sufrimiento extremo, como de pena o dolor

<u>**anticipate / anticipar**</u> *v.* aguardar con interés

apathy / apatía *s.* falta de interés o sentimiento

apprehension / aprensión *s.* sentimiento ansioso; temor

arable / arable *adj.* apto para cultivar cosechas

ardent / ferviente *adj.* intensamente entusiasta; devoto

aspirations / aspiraciones *s.* ambiciones fuertes

assuage / aplacar *v.* aminorar (dolor o aflicción); satisfacer (sed o hambre)

attributes / atributos *s.* características de una persona o cosa

audaciously / audazmente *adv.* de manera intrépida

augmented / aumentado *adj.* hecho más grande; realzado

august / augusto *adj.* impresionante; majestuoso

<u>**awareness / conciencia**</u> *s.* tener conocimiento

B

<u>**background / antecedentes**</u> *s.* condiciones que rodean o preceden a algo

<u>**bias / prejuicio**</u> *s.* el punto de vista que uno tiene antes de conocer los hechos

blemished / manchado *adj.* dañado; estropeado

bore / portó *v.* cargó

brandished / blandió *v.* mostró, esgrimió o batió de manera amenazante o triunfante

brazen / descarado *adj.* sin vergüenza; audaz

buffer / amortiguar *v.* aminorar un golpe; suavizar

C

cajoling / lisonjeo *s.* persuasión de alguien con lisonjas

calamity / calamidad *s.* desgracia terrible; desastre

candid / candoroso *adj.* franco; directo

canopied / entoldado *adj.* cubierto por una tela suspendida de postes o una estructura

catalyst / catalizador *s.* persona o cosa que desata un evento o acción

cessation / cesación *s.* detención; alto

change / cambiar *v.* convertirse en algo distinto; transformar

<u>**character / temperamento**</u> *s.* fortaleza moral; autodisciplina

chastisement / castigo *s.* crítica severa; corrección

choleric / colérico *adj.* malgeniado; irascible

circuit / circuito *s.* acción de girar alrededor de algo; ruta

clenching / apretar *v.* cerrar; agarrar firmemente

clustering / amontonado *adj.* reunido; formado en un grupo

commemorates / conmemora *v.* honra la memoria de

commences / comienza *v.* inicia

commiserate / compadecer *v.* apiadarse de; tener lástima por

<u>**comprehend / comprender**</u> *v.* captar mentalmente; entender

compromise / acuerdo *s.* convenio donde ambas partes ceden algo

compulsory / obligatorio *adj.* requerido; exigido

comrade / camarada *s.* compañero cercano; amigo

concession / concesión *s.* acción de otorgar o dar; indulgencia

concrete / concreto *adj.* algo específico o tangible

condemn / condenar *v.* desaprobar de; emitir un juicio desfavorable sobre

condemned / condenado *v.* que ha sido declarado culpable de fechorías; sentenciado por un juez

conduct / conducta *s.* la forma de actuar de una persona; comportamiento

configuration / configuración *s.* disposición de partes; patrón

confirm / confirmar *v.* establecer la verdad o precisión de algo

confounded / aturdido *adj.* sentirse confundido

confrontation / confrontación *s.* choque de fuerzas o ideas

confusion / confusión *s.* estado de desorden o distracción

conjured / invocado *v.* llamado como por acto de magia

connection / conexión *s.* relación entre cosas

consigned / consignado *v.* entregado; cedido o entregado

conspicuous / conspicuo *adj.* fácil de ver

constricting / restrictivo *adj.* que evita la libertad de movimiento; limitante

contempt / desprecio *s.* desdén; la actitud de alguien que tiene a menos a algo o a alguien

contested / disputó *v.* que intentó refutar o invalidar algo; impugnó

context / contexto *s.* circunstancias que crean el entorno de un evento

context / contexto *s.* entorno o situación en la que algo se encuentra

contrive / ingeniar *v.* procurar hacer; lograr

convalesce / convalecer *v.* recuperar fuerza y salud

converge / converger *v.* unirse

convey / transmitir *v.* comunicar o dar a conocer

convoluted / intrincado *adj.* retorcido de manera complicada

counsel / consejo *s.* orientación; discusión

countenance / semblante *s.* rostro; la expresión de una cara que muestra la naturaleza de una persona

courage / valor *s.* la voluntad de lidiar con algo peligroso

credulity / credulidad *s.* tendencia a creer con demasiada facilidad

customarily / habitualmente *adv.* comúnmente; por hábito o tradición

D

debate / debatir *v.* argumentar o discutir

debut / debut *s.* primera aparición pública

decorum / decoro *s.* comportamiento cortés y apropiado para cierta ocasión

decrepitude / decrepitud *s.* debilidad; condición de estar desgastado por edad o enfermedad

deference / deferencia *s.* el ceder a las ideas, deseos, etc. de otra persona

deficiency / deficiencia *s.* falta de algo esencial

deflects / desvía *v.* que detiene algo; que rechaza algo

deftness / habilidad *s.* destreza

defunct / difunto *adj.* que ya no está en uso o existencia; muerto

dejectedly / abatidamente *adv.* estar desalentado; de forma deprimida

delusion / ilusión *s.* una creencia errónea que se mantiene a pesar de haber evidencia en contra

demeanor / comportamiento *s.* manera de comportarse; conducta

derisively / burlonamente *adv.* de manera irónica y ridiculizante

derived / derivado *v.* que se obtuvo mediante razonamiento

desolate / desolado *adj.* vacío; solitario

destitute / indigente *adj.* carente de las necesidades básicas de la vida; de gran pobreza

determination / determinación *s.* firmeza de propósito

dexterous / diestro *adj.* tener o mostrar destreza mental o física; experto

differentiate / diferenciar *v.* distinguir entre

dignity / dignidad *s.* cualidad de merecer respeto y honor; respeto de sí mismo

dilapidated / dilapidado *adj.* estado ruinoso; raído

diligence / diligencia *s.* esfuerzo constante y esmerado

dimpled / con hoyuelos *adj.* marcado con pequeños hoyos o hendiduras

dingy / manchado *adj.* de aspecto sucio; deslustrado

dire / abrumador *adj.* urgente; terrible; que exige una acción rápida

discern / discernir *v.* distinguir la diferencia entre dos o más cosas; percibir

disconsolate / desconsolado *adj.* tan infeliz que nada le reconforta; miserable

discord / discordia *s.* conflicto; desacuerdo

discourse / discurso *s.* comunicación continua de ideas e información

discourse / disertar *v.* hablar (sobre un tema) formal y detalladamente

disdain / desdeño *s.* disgusto por alguien o algo; desprecio

disembarked / desembarcó *v.* abandonó un buque para ir a tierra

disparagement / menosprecio *s.* comentarios que expresan una mala opinión o falta de respeto por alguien

disreputable / desacreditado *adj.* no respetable; que tiene o merece mala reputación

dissent / desacuerdo *s.* renuencia a aceptar una creencia u opinión común; desavenencia

distinct / distinto *adj.* claramente diferente; separado

distortion / distorsión *s.* cualquier cosa que muestra algo de manera engañosa

dogged / obstinado *adj.* terco

E

earnest / formal *adj.* serio e intenso; sin bromear

eased / alivió *v.* liberó de dolor o dificultad; alivianó

ebony / ébano *adj.* de color negro

edict / edicto *s.* mandato público; decreto

edifying / edificante *adj.* algo educativo que permite que la persona mejore moral o intelectualmente

efface / tachar *v.* borrar o suprimir

elude / eludir *v.* evitar; escapar con celeridad o astucia

elusive / elusivo *adj.* difícil de comprender

emanating / emanar *v.* brotar hacia afuera, como de una fuente

embodied / materializó *v.* dio forma a; concretó

emigrants / emigrantes *s.* personas que abandonan su país o región para establecerse en otro lugar

emotion / emoción *s.* sentimiento fuerte, como el amor

empathy / empatía *s.* compartir los sentimientos de otra persona

encroaching / invadir *adj.* cometer una intrusión, especialmente de manera gradual

endeavored / se esforzó por *v.* trató de alcanzar una meta fijada

endure / soportar *v.* aguantar con dolor o penuria

engaging / cautivador *adj.* atractivo; agradable

enlighten / ilustrar *v.* aclarar algo mediante el conocimiento

enthralls / encantar *v.* que cautiva; fascina

entreated / suplicó *v.* imploró; rogó

ephemeral / efímero *adj.* pasajero

equilibrium / equilibrio *s.* estado de balance

esoteric / esotérico *adj.* más allá de la comprensión o conocimiento de la mayoría de las personas

estranged / apartado *adj.* que se mantiene separado; condición en la que el afecto se torna en indiferencia u hostilidad

eternal / eterno *adj.* sin principio ni fin; sempiterno

evaluate / evaluar *v.* determinar el valor de algo

evidence / evidencia *s.* información que indica si algo es veraz o válido

evoking / evocar *v.* hacer salir las emociones o reacciones

evolve / evolucionar *v.* desarrollarse a través de cambios graduales

exorbitant / exorbitante *adj.* más allá de lo razonable; excesivo

expectations / expectativas *s.* algo que se aguarda con interés

explanation / explicación *s.* declaración aclaratoria

expound / enunciar *v.* explicar en detalle

extolled / elogiado *adj.* alabado

extricating / liberar *v.* dejar libre; sacar de una situación difícil

exuberance / exuberancia *s.* buena salud; vivacidad

F

falteringly / titubeante *adv.* dicho con titubeo o con voz trémula

fate / sino *s.* destino; lo que le sucede a una persona o cosa; resultado final

fathom / desentrañar *v.* comprender a fondo

fawned / aduló *v.* lisonjeó; actuó con preocupación excesiva por los deseos y antojos de otro, como lo haría un sirviente

flourishes / florece *v.* que crece vigorosamente; que prospera

fluttered / revoloteó *v.* agitó o vibró rápidamente

foe / adversario *s.* enemigo

forbore / abstuvo *v.* que desistió de realizar algo; que renunció a algo

foreboding / presentimiento *s.* una sensación de que algo malo ocurrirá; premonición

formidable / temible *adj.* que causa temor o pánico

fraud / fraude *s.* engaño; embuste

futile / fútil *adj.* ineficaz; inútil

G

gauge / aforar *v.* medir el tamaño, cantidad, alcance o capacidad de algo

grave / grave *adj.* que requiere de consideración seria; importante e inquietante

grimacing / haciendo muecas *v.* haciendo un gesto que muestre disgusto o dolor

growth / crecimiento *s.* el proceso del desarrollo

H

haphazardly / al azar *adv.* de manera no planeada o desorganizada

haste / apuro *s.* con rapidez de movimiento; prisa

heedless / desatento *adj.* descuidado; imprudente

history / historia *s.* relato de lo que ha pasado

honor / honor *s.* fuerte sentido del bien y del mal

humble / humilde *adj.* que muestra estar consciente de sus propios defectos; modesto

hypocrisy / hipocresía *s.* fingir ser o sentir lo que uno no es o siente

I

idealistic / idealista *adj.* que representa las cosas como deberían ser en lugar de como son en realidad

identity / identidad *s.* cualidades de una persona que representan lo que es

idle / ocioso *adj.* inútil; desocupado

ignorance / ignorancia *s.* falta de conocimiento o educación

immaterial / inmaterial *adj.* que no consiste de materia

imminent / inminente *adj.* a punto de suceder

impeded / impidió *v.* bloqueó; obstruyó

impediments / impedimentos *s.* cosas que retrasan a alguien o a algo, o que obstaculizan; barreras

impending / inminente *adj.* a punto de suceder

imperceptibly / imperceptiblemente *adv.* tan lento o leve que casi no se nota

imperiously / imperiosamente *adv.* arrogantemente

impervious / impenetrable *adj.* que no lo afecta algo

impetuosity / impetuosidad *s.* calidad de actuar repentinamente, con gran fuerza y poca consideración; temeridad

impression / impresión *s.* efecto que se produce sobre la mente

improbable / improbable *adj.* que no es factible que suceda o sea verdad

inaudibly / inaudiblemente *adv.* de forma que no se pueda oír

incessant / incesante *adj.* que no se detiene; constante

incredulity / incredulidad *s.* renuencia a creer

indigence / indigencia *s.* pobreza

indignant / indignado *adj.* que siente ira, especialmente por una injusticia

indignation / indignación *s.* ira en reacción a la injusticia o mezquindad

individual / individual *adj.* relativo a una sola persona o cosa

indulgence / indulgencia *s.* lenidad; estar dispuesto a tolerar o perdonar la mala conducta

inexorably / inexorablemente *adv.* sin la posibilidad de que lo atrasen o detengan; inalterable

infinite / infinito *adj.* más allá de medida o comprensión; interminable

infirm / enfermo *adj.* débil; endeble

infirmity / enfermedad *s.* debilidad; defecto físico

influence / influencia *s.* el poder de las personas para cambiar a otras

ingenuity / ingenio *s.* inventiva

ingratiating / congraciado *adj.* que actúa de cierta manera para ganarse el favor de alguien

inhabit / habitar *v.* residir en

inherent / inherente *adj.* que existe naturalmente en algo

inheritance / herencia *s.* dote que es pasada a la siguiente generación de una familia

innuendo / alusión *s.* insulto o acusación indirecta; insinuación

insight / discernimiento *s.* idea clara de la naturaleza de las cosas

instinct / instinto *s.* un patrón innato de comportamiento, en contraposición a una destreza aprendida

insurrection / insurrección *s.* rebelión

integrity / integridad *s.* voluntad para cumplir con los principios morales

interact / interactuar *v.* relacionarse entre sí, afectar a otro

interminable / interminable *adj.* que parece no tener fin

interpretation / interpretación *s.* explicación del significado de algo

interred / sepultó *v.* enterró (dícese de un cuerpo)

intertidal / entre marea alta y baja *adj.* característico de una zona litoral sujeta a los niveles de mareas alta y baja

intervened / intervino *v.* se interpuso entre

intrigues / intrigas *s.* tramas; maquinaciones

irascible / irascible *adj.* irritable

irreproachable / irreprochable *adj.* por encima de la crítica

irretrievable / irrecuperable *adj.* imposible de alcanzar de nuevo o recobrar

isolation / aislamiento *s.* estar solo o aislado

itinerary / itinerario *s.* ruta; plan de viaje

J

jauntiness / garbo *s.* actitud libre y desenvuelta

jeered / burló *v.* escarneció; mofó; ridiculizó

jurisdiction / jurisdicción *s.* esfera de autoridad o poder

K

keenest / más agudo *adj.* el más penetrante; cortante

knowledge / conocimiento *s.* conciencia y comprensión de información

L

lacquered / laqueado *adj.* cubierto con un barniz resistente y pegajoso

lamentation / lamento *s.* acto de vociferar con aflicción; gemido; llanto

language / lenguaje *s.* sistema usado para expresarse o comunicar; escogencia de palabras

languid / lánguido *adj.* falto de energía

lavished / derrochó *v.* dio con extrema generosidad

lease / arrendamiento *s.* contrato mediante el cual algo es alquilado por un plazo determinado de tiempo; alquiler

legacies / legados *s.* dinero, propiedades o posición que se deja a alguien en un testamento

legendary / legendario *adj.* extraordinario; memorable

livid / lívido *adj.* pálido, como por haber sufrido una herida; enrojecido por la ira

lofty / eminente *adj.* elevado en rango o temperamento; noble

looming / que aparece *adj.* que se asoma en forma vaga, indistinta, pero amenazante; que amenaza con ocurrir

lowly / inferior *adj.* humilde; de baja posición

lucidity / lucidez *s.* cualidad de ser fácilmente entendido

lucrative / lucrativo *adj.* que produce riqueza; rentable

lunar / lunar *adj.* de la luna

M

maligned / difamado *adj.* que se habló mal de

manifestations / manifestaciones *s.* apariciones; formas

manipulate / manipular *v.* controlar mediante el uso de influencia, a menudo de forma injusta

manipulated / manipuló *v.* que manejó o controló mediante jugadas astutas

marginal / marginal *adj.* en o cerca del borde

meager / escaso *adj.* de mala calidad o poca cantidad

meaning / significado *s.* el sentido de algo

meditates / medita *v.* que piensa profundamente

melancholy / melancólico *adj.* triste y deprimido

millennial / milenario *adj.* de 1.000 años

mirth / regocijo *s.* alegría; júbilo

misconstrued / malinterpretó *v.* entendió mal

misinterpret / malinterpretar *v.* no entender correctamente

modified / modificó *v.* cambió; alteró ligeramente

monotonously / monótonamente *adv.* de forma aburrida e invariable

motive / motivo *s.* lo que causa que una persona actúe de cierta manera

multitudes / multitudes *s.* gran cantidad de personas o cosas

mutable / mutable *adj.* cambiable

N

negotiate / negociar *v.* pactar con la esperanza de llegar a un acuerdo

nevertheless / sin embargo *adv.* a pesar de eso; no obstante

nimbly / ágilmente *adv.* de forma rápida, fácil y liviana; con agilidad

nomadic / nómada *adj.* que se traslada de un lugar a otro; sin hogar permanente

nonchalantly / indiferentemente *adv.* casualmente; imperturbablemente

O

objective / objetivo *adj.* que no está sujeto al punto de vista de otro

oblivious / olvidadizo *adj.* absorto

obscured / oscureció *v.* hizo oscuro; obstruyó la vista; escondió

oppose / oponer *v.* ponerse en contra; estar en desacuerdo con

oppressive / opresivo *adj.* que causa gran incomodidad; angustiante

oratory / oratoria *s.* acto de hablar en público; estrategias usadas en disertaciones

overcome / vencer *v.* conquistar o prevalecer sobre

P

pallor / palor *s.* carencia de color; palidez poco natural

paradox / paradoja *s.* declaración o situación que parece contradictoria

paranoia / paranoia *s.* trastorno mental que se caracteriza por delirios

perception / percepción *s.* la forma en que uno entiende el mundo a través de los sentidos

perpetually / perpetuamente *adv.* que continua para siempre; constantemente

persevere / perseverar *v.* continuar a pesar de la oposición; persistir

perspective / perspectiva *s.* la forma en que uno ve las cosas; punto de vista

petulantly / petulantemente *adv.* de forma que expresa impaciencia o irritación

piety / piedad *s.* lealtad y devoción hacia la familia, lo divino o algún otro objeto de respeto

piqued / molesto *adj.* enojado o irritado

plague / importunar *v.* molestar; fastidiar; atormentar

plausibility / admisibilidad *s.* credibilidad; verdad aparente

plight / aprieto *s.* situación difícil

poignant / conmovedor *adj.* que afecta emocionalmente; desgarrador

portentous / portentoso *adj.* ominoso; que da señales de cosas nefastas por venir

presume / presumir *v.* depender demasiado de; abusar de

presumptuous / descarado *adj.* que traspasa los límites de lo correcto; demasiado imprudente

pretense / pretensión *s.* jactancia; simulación fingida de algo

principles / principios *s.* reglas para una conducta correcta; normas

prodigious / prodigioso *adj.* de gran tamaño o poder

profuse / profuso *adj.* dar o vaciar libremente, a menudo en exceso; abundante

progress / progreso *s.* desarrollo; mejoras

prostrate / postrado *adj.* yacer tendido

prudent / prudente *adj.* practicar un razonamiento acertado; cauteloso

purified / purificó *v.* libró de impurezas o contaminación; hizo puro

Q

quench / aplacar *v.* satisfacer; llenar las necesidades o deseos de algo

question / preguntar *v.* expresar incertidumbre sobre algo; formular una pregunta

R

radical / radical *adj.* cambio extremo

rash / imprudente *adj.* demasiado apresurado en el dicho o en el hecho; precipitado

rave / desvariar v. hablar incoherentemente o decir disparates

reality / realidad s. calidad de ser conforme a la verdad

reapers / segadores s. personas que recogen o cosechan los granos

reciprocity / reciprocidad s. relaciones de intercambio; interdependencia

reconciliation / reconciliación s. reestablecer la amistad y la armonía

reflect / reflexionar v. pensar seriamente sobre algo

refuse / desechos s. desperdicios; basura

rejoiced / regocijó v. mostró alegría

rejuvenation / rejuvenecimiento s. hacer nuevo, más joven o energético una vez más; revitalización

relent / ceder v. volverse menos fuerte, severo o intenso; ablandarse

relish / deleite s. goce

renounced / renunció v. se rindió formalmente

repertoire / repertorio s. lista de obras, por ejemplo, canciones que un artista está preparado para presentar

replenished / reabasteció v. completó o llenó de nuevo

replication / réplica s. duplicado; reproducción

resolute / resuelto adj. que muestra un propósito fijo

resolution / resolución s. fuerte determinación; plan o decisión firme

resolve / resolver v. llegar a una conclusión o decisión

respond / responder v. contestar

responsibility / responsabilidad s. tener que responder ante alguien o algo; rendir cuentas por el éxito o el fracaso

reveling / deleitarse v. disfrutar; celebrar

reverence / reverencia s. un sentimiento de profundo respeto, amor o admiración

revise / revisar v. reconsiderar; modificar

rudiments / rudimentos s. fundamentos; inicios modestos

S

sacrifice / sacrificar v. ceder

sated / saciado adj. satisfecho; provisto con más que suficiente

scrutinized / escudriñó v. examinó detenidamente

secular / seglar adj. relativo a asuntos mundanos, en comparación con religiosos

self-expression / expresión del carácter propio s. compartir con otros la personalidad o las emociones

selflessness / desprendimiento s. tener devoción por los intereses de los demás por encima de los propios

self-sufficiency / autosuficiencia s. independencia

sententiously / sentenciosamente adv. que muestra un gusto excesivo por los proverbios; en tono de disertación

serenity / serenidad s. estado de calma o paz

servile / servil adj. semejante a un esclavo; humildemente sumiso a la autoridad

silhouette / silueta s. dibujo de un perfil relleno con un color sólido

simulating / simular v. dar la apariencia de

skeptically / escépticamente adv. con duda; interrogativamente

slumbering / soñoliento adj. adormecido

sonorous / sonoro adj. tener un sonido rico o impresionante

spare / frugal adj. enjuto; descarnado

spectacle / espectáculo s. presenciar algo extraño o extraordinario

squalid / escuálido adj. impuro; sucio

staidness / sobriedad s. estado de estar tranquilo; sosegado

stance / postura s. la forma en que uno se para, especialmente en cuanto a la colocación de los pies

stark / desolado adj. desierto; severo

staunch / firme adj. constante; leal

steady / estable adj. firme; de movimiento seguro

stereotype / estereotipo s. noción de un grupo que es demasiado amplia y a menudo incorrecta

stickler / rigorista s. persona que insiste en la obediencia estricta a las reglas o normas

stifle / sofocar v. asfixiar; reprimir

stipulates / estipula v. que incluye específicamente como parte de un acuerdo

strife / refriega s. lucha; conflicto

struggle / luchar v. enfrentar dificultades

subdued / alicaído adj. quieto; que le falta energía

subjective / subjetivo adj. basado en o influenciado por los sentimientos o punto de vista de una persona

subordinate / subordinado adj. inferior a otro en importancia o rango

subtile / sutil adj. fino; delicado

subversion / subversión s. actividad con intención de derrocar algo establecido; rebelión

successive / sucesivo adj. que uno le sigue al otro en secuencia

succinct / sucinto adj. expresado clara y brevemente

sullen / taciturno adj. adusto y que muestra resentimiento

sumptuous / suntuoso adj. costoso; espléndido

supercilious / altanero adj. que muestra una actitud de superioridad; desdeñoso

surmise / suposición s. conjetura; idea basada en evidencia que no es concluyente

surpassed / sobrepasó v. que fue más allá; superó

T

tactile / táctil adj. relativo al sentido del tacto

tangible / tangible *adj.* capaz de ser tocado; real

temperate / temperado *adj.* moderado; que se mantiene dentro de los límites

tempering / temperar *s.* cambiar para hacer más apto, generalmente al mezclarlo con otra cosa

tentative / tentativo *adj.* vacilante; incierto

tenuous / tenue *adj.* sin fuerza

threshold / umbral *s.* la parte inferior de un portal; entrada o punto de inicio

titanic / titánico *adj.* poderoso; de gran tamaño

toil / labor *s.* trabajo arduo y cansado

trace / trazo *s.* pequeña cantidad; pizca

transcends / trasciende *v.* que va más allá de los límites de; excede

tremulous / trémulo *adj.* tembloroso; que se estremece

tumult / tumulto *s.* conmoción ruidosa

twinges / punzadas *s.* dolores agudos y repentinos, ya sea físicos o mentales

U

ulterior / ulterior *adj.* subsecuente; más allá de lo que está abiertamente expresado o implícito

uncertainty / incertidumbre *s.* incapacidad de estar seguro

understanding / entendimiento *s.* poder de comprender y discernir

unify / unificar *v.* combinar en uno solo

universal / universal *adj.* que existe en todas las cosas

unorthodox / no ortodoxo *adj.* atípico; que rompe con la tradición

unwieldy / abultado *adj.* difícil de manejar debido a su forma o peso; incómodo

V

vagaries / caprichos *s.* acciones erráticas o impredecibles; antojos

venerable / venerable *adj.* digno de respeto debido a edad o posición

venturing / atreverse *v.* tomar el riesgo de

veracious / veraz *adj.* verdadero; honesto

verbal / verbal *adj.* relativo a las palabras

verified / verificó *v.* demostró que es cierto

verify / verificar *v.* probar que algo es cierto

vile / vil *adj.* malo; bajo; extremadamente detestable

W

waver / vacilar *v.* mostrar indecisión; titubear

wistfully / anhelantemente *adv.* mostrando vagos deseos

wither / marchitar *v.* secar; que se encoge por falta de humedad

wrathfully / coléricamente *adv.* con intenso enojo

Literary Terms

ACT See *Drama.*

ALLEGORY An *allegory* is a story or tale with two or more levels of meaning—a literal level and one or more symbolic levels. The events, setting, and characters in an allegory are symbols for ideas and qualities.

ALLITERATION *Alliteration* is the repetition of initial consonant sounds. Writers use alliteration to give emphasis to words, to imitate sounds, and to create musical effects. In the following line from Theodore Roethke's "The Waking" (p. 685), there is alliteration of the *f* sound:

I *f*eel my *f*ate in what I cannot *f*ear.

ALLUSION An *allusion* is a reference to a well-known person, place, event, literary work, or work of art. The title of the story "By the Waters of Babylon" (p. 314) is an allusion to the Bible's Psalm 137, in which the Hebrew people lament their exile in Babylon. It begins, "By the rivers of Babylon, there we sat down, yea, we wept. . . ."

ANALOGY An *analogy* makes a comparison between two or more things that are similar in some ways but otherwise unalike.

ANECDOTE An anecdote is a brief story told to entertain or to make a point. In the excerpt from "The Way to Rainy Mountain" (p. 595), N. Scott Momaday tells anecdotes about his grandmother to reveal her character and provide a glimpse into a vanishing way of life.

See also *Narrative.*

ANTAGONIST An *antagonist* is a character or force in conflict with a main character, or protagonist.

ANTICLIMAX Some stories end in an *anticlimax.* Like a climax, an *anticlimax* is the turning point in a story. However, an anticlimax is always a letdown. It is the point at which you learn that the story will not turn out in a way that truly resolves the problem or satisfies the reader.

ARCHETYPE An *archetype* is a type of character, detail, image, or situation that appears in literature throughout history. Some critics believe that archetypes reveal deep truths about human experience.

ARGUMENT See *Persuasion.*

ASIDE An *aside* is a short speech delivered by a character in a play in order to express his or her thoughts and feelings. Traditionally, the aside is directed to the audience and is presumed not to be heard by the other characters.

ASSONANCE *Assonance* is the repetition of vowel sounds followed by different consonants in two or more stressed syllables. Assonance is found in this phrase from Elizabeth Bishop's "The Fish" (p. 650): "frayed and wavering."

ATMOSPHERE See *Mood.*

AUTOBIOGRAPHICAL ESSAY See *Essay.*

AUTOBIOGRAPHY An *autobiography* is a form of nonfiction in which a writer tells his or her own life story. An autobiography may tell about the person's whole life or only a part of it. An example of an autobiography is Erik Weihenmayer's *Touch the Top of the World* (p. 449).

See also *Biography* and *Nonfiction.*

BALLAD A *ballad* is a songlike poem that tells a story, often one dealing with adventure and romance. Most ballads are written in four- to six-line stanzas and have regular rhythms and rhyme schemes. A ballad often features a *refrain*—a regularly repeated line or group of lines.

See also *Oral Tradition.*

BIOGRAPHY A *biography* is a form of nonfiction in which a writer tells the life story of another person. Biographies have been written about many famous people, historical and contemporary, but they can also be written about "ordinary" people.

See also *Autobiography* and *Nonfiction.*

BLANK VERSE *Blank verse* is poetry written in unrhymed iambic pentameter lines. This verse form was widely used by William Shakespeare.

CHARACTER A *character* is a person or an animal who takes part in the action of a literary work. The main character, or protagonist, is the most important character in a story. In Chinua Achebe's story "Civil Peace" (p. 358), Jonathan Iwegbu is the protagonist. This character often changes in some important way as a result of the story's events.

Characters are sometimes classified as round or flat, dynamic or static. A *round character* shows many different traits—faults as well as virtues. A *flat character* shows only one trait. A *dynamic character* develops and grows during the course of the story; a **static character** does not change.

See also **Characterization** and **Motivation.**

CHARACTERIZATION **Characterization** is the act of creating and developing a character. In direct characterization, the author directly states a character's traits. For example, in "The Masque of the Red Death" (p. 372), Poe directly characterizes Prince Prospero: "But the Prince Prospero was happy and dauntless and sagacious."

In indirect characterization, an author gives clues about a character by describing what a character looks like, does, and says, as well as how other characters react to him or her. It is up to the reader to draw conclusions about the character based on this indirect information.

The most effective indirect characterizations usually result from showing characters acting or speaking.

See also **Character.**

CLIMAX The **climax** of a story, novel, or play is the high point of interest or suspense. The events that make up the rising action lead up to the climax. The events that make up the falling action follow the climax.

See also **Conflict, Plot,** and **Anticlimax.**

COMEDY A **comedy** is a literary work, especially a play, that has a happy ending. Comedies often show ordinary characters in conflict with society. These conflicts are introduced through misunderstandings, deceptions, and concealed identities. When the conflict is resolved, the result is the correction of moral faults or social wrongs. Types of comedy include *romantic comedy,* which involves problems among lovers, and the *comedy of manners,* which satirically challenges the social customs of a sophisticated society. Comedy is often contrasted with tragedy, in which the protagonist meets an unfortunate end.

COMIC RELIEF **Comic relief** is a technique that is used to interrupt a serious part of a literary work by introducing a humorous character or situation.

CONFLICT A **conflict** is a struggle between opposing forces. Characters in conflict form the basis of stories, novels, and plays.

There are two kinds of conflict: external and internal. In an *external conflict,* the main character struggles against an outside force. This force may be another character, as in "Civil Peace" (p. 358), in which Jonathan Iwegbu struggles with the leader of the thieves. The outside force could also

be the standards or expectations of a group, such as the oppression and censorship that Juan struggles against in "The Censors" (p. 410). The outside force may be nature itself, as when Erik Weihenmayer struggles to climb Mt. Everest in *Touch the Top of the World* (p. 449).

An *internal conflict* involves a character in conflict with himself or herself. In *Julius Caesar* (p. 892), Brutus experiences an internal conflict when trying to decide whether to assassinate Caesar.

See also **Plot.**

CONNOTATION The **connotation** of a word is the set of ideas associated with it in addition to its explicit meaning.

See also **Denotation.**

CONSONANCE **Consonance** is the repetition of final consonant sounds in stressed syllables with different vowel sounds, as in *hat* and *sit.*

CONTEMPORARY INTERPRETATION A **contemporary interpretation** is a literary work of today that responds to and sheds new light on a well-known, earlier work of literature. Such an interpretation may refer to any aspect of the older work, including plot, characters, settings, imagery, language, and theme. T. H. White's *The Once and Future King* (p. 1156) provides a modern version of the legend of King Arthur.

COUPLET A **couplet** is a pair of rhyming lines, usually of the same length and meter. In the following couplet from Sonnet 29 by William Shakespeare, the speaker comforts himself with the thought of his love:

> For thy sweet love remember'd such wealth brings
> That then I scorn to change my state with kings.

See also **Stanza.**

DENOTATION The **denotation** of a word is its dictionary meaning, independent of other associations that the word may have. The denotation of the word *lake,* for example, is "an inland body of water." "Vacation spot" and "place where the fishing is good" are connotations of the word *lake.*

See also **Connotation.**

DESCRIPTION A **description** is a portrait in words of a person, place, or object. Descriptive writing uses sensory details, those that appeal to the senses: sight, hearing, taste, smell, and touch. Description can be found in all types of writing. Anita Desai's "Games at Twilight" (p. 138) has vivid descriptive passages.

DESCRIPTIVE ESSAY See *Essay.*

DIALECT *Dialect* is a special form of a language, spoken by people in a particular region or group. It may involve changes to the pronunciation, vocabulary, and sentence structure of the standard form of the language. Rudyard Kipling's "Danny Deever" (p. 652) is a poem written in the Cockney dialect of English, used by working-class Londoners.

DIALOGUE A *dialogue* is a conversation between characters that may reveal their traits and advance the action of a narrative. In fiction or nonfiction, quotation marks indicate a speaker's exact words, and a new paragraph usually indicates a change of speaker. Following is an exchange between two characters in "The Monkey's Paw". (p. 32):

> "*What's that?*" cried the old woman, starting up.
> "A rat," said the old man in shaking tones—"a rat. It passed me on the stairs."

Quotation marks are not used in *script*, the printed copy of a play. Instead, the dialogue follows the name of the speaker, as in this example from *Julius Caesar* (p. 892):

> **PORTIA.** Is Caesar yet gone to the Capitol?

DICTION *Diction* refers to an author's choice of words, especially with regard to range of vocabulary, use of slang and colloquial language, and level of formality. This sentence from "The Masque of the Red Death" (p. 372) is an example of formal diction containing many words derived from Latin: "This was an extensive and magnificent structure, the creation of the prince's own eccentric yet august taste."

See also *Connotation* and *Denotation.*

DIRECT CHARACTERIZATION
See *Characterization.*

DRAMA A *drama* is a story written to be performed by actors. The script of a drama is made up of *dialogue*—the words the actors say—and *stage directions,* which are descriptions of how and where action happens.

The drama's *setting* is the time and place in which the action occurs. It is indicated by one or more sets, including furniture and backdrops, that suggest interior or exterior scenes. *Props* are objects, such as a sword or a cup of tea, that are used onstage.

At the beginning of most plays, a brief *exposition* gives the audience some background information about the characters and the situation. Just as in a story or novel, the plot of a drama is built around characters in conflict.

Dramas are divided into large units called *acts,* which are divided into smaller units called *scenes.* A long play may include many sets that change with the scenes, or it may indicate a change of scene with lighting. *Julius Caesar* (p. 892) is a play in five acts.

See also *Dialogue, Genre, Stage Directions,* and *Tragedy.*

DRAMATIC IRONY See *Irony.*

DRAMATIC MONOLOGUE A *dramatic monologue* is a poem in which a character reveals himself or herself by speaking to a silent listener or thinking aloud.

DRAMATIC POETRY *Dramatic poetry* is poetry that utilizes the techniques of drama. The dialogue between the bride and the bridegroom at the end of "The Bridegroom" (p. 642) is an example.

END RHYME See *Rhyme.*

EPIC An *epic* is a long narrative poem about the deeds of gods or heroes. *Sundiata: An Epic of Old Mali* (p. 1094) and the *Ramayana* (p. 1108) are examples of the genre.

An epic is elevated in style and usually follows certain patterns. In Greek epics and in the epics modeled after them, the poet begins by announcing the subject and asking a Muse—one of the nine goddesses of the arts, literature, and sciences—to help.

An *epic hero* is the larger-than-life central character in an epic. Through behavior and deeds, the epic hero displays qualities that are valued by the society in which the epic originated.

See also *Epic Simile* and *Narrative Poem.*

EPIC SIMILE An *epic simile,* also called *Homeric simile,* is an elaborate comparison of unlike subjects. In this example from the *Odyssey,* Homer compares the bodies of men killed by Odysseus to a fisherman's catch heaped up on the shore:

> Think of a catch that fishermen haul in to a
>   half-moon bay
> in a fine-meshed net from the whitecaps of the sea:
> how all are poured out on the sand, in throes
>   for the salt sea,
> twitching their cold lives away in Helios' fiery air:
> so lay the suitors heaped on one another.

See also *Figurative Language* and *Simile.*

EPIPHANY An *epiphany* is a character's sudden flash of insight into a conflict or situation. At the end of the poem "The Fish" (p. 650), the speaker has an epiphany that causes her to release the fish.

ESSAY An **essay** is a short nonfiction work about a particular subject. While classification is difficult, five types of essays are sometimes identified.

A *descriptive essay* seeks to convey an impression about a person, place, or object.

An *expository essay* gives information, discusses ideas, or explains a process. In "The Spider and the Wasp"(p. 464), Alexander Petrunkevitch compares and contrasts the two creatures mentioned in the title.

A *narrative essay* tells a true story. In "The Dog That Bit People" (p. 525), James Thurber tells the story of a troublesome pet. An *autobiographical essay* is a narrative essay in which the writer tells a story from his or her own life.

A *persuasive essay* tries to convince readers to do something or to accept the writer's point of view. In "Keep Memory Alive" (p. 542), Elie Wiesel argues the importance of speaking out against evil.

See also **Description, Exposition, Genre, Narration, Nonfiction,** and **Persuasion.**

EXPOSITION **Exposition** is writing or speech that explains a process or presents information. In the plot of a story or drama, the exposition is the part of the work that introduces the characters, the setting, and the basic situation.

See also **Plot.**

EXPOSITORY ESSAY See **Essay.**

EXTENDED METAPHOR In an **extended metaphor,** as in regular metaphor, a writer speaks or writes of a subject as though it were something else. An extended metaphor sustains the comparison for several lines or for an entire poem. In *Julius Caesar* (p. 892), Brutus uses an extended metaphor in Act II, Scene i, lines 21–27, when he speaks of "ambition's ladder."

See also **Figurative Language** and **Metaphor.**

FALLING ACTION See **Plot.**

FANTASY A **fantasy** is a work of highly imaginative writing that contains elements not found in real life. Examples of fantasy include stories that involve supernatural elements, such as fairy tales, and stories that deal with imaginary places and creatures.

See also **Science Fiction.**

FICTION **Fiction** is prose writing that tells about imaginary characters and events. The term is usually used for novels and short stories, but it also applies to dramas and narrative poetry. Some writers rely on their imaginations alone to create their works of fiction. Others base their fiction on actual events and people, to which they add invented characters, dialogue, and plot situations.

See also **Genre, Narrative,** and **Nonfiction.**

FIGURATIVE LANGUAGE **Figurative language** is writing or speech not meant to be interpreted literally. It is often used to create vivid impressions by setting up comparisons between dissimilar things.

Some frequently used figures of speech are **metaphors, similes,** and **personifications.**

See also **Literal Language.**

FLASHBACK A **flashback** is a means by which authors present material that occurred earlier than the present time of the narrative. Authors may include this material in the form of a characters' memories, dreams, or accounts of past events, or they may simply shift their narrative back to the earlier time.

FOIL A **foil** is a character who provides a contrast to another character. In *Julius Caesar* (p. 892), the impetuous and resentful Cassius is a foil for the cooler and more rational Brutus.

FOOT See **Meter.**

FORESHADOWING **Foreshadowing** is the use in a literary work of clues that suggest events that have yet to occur. This technique helps to create suspense, keeping readers wondering about what will happen next.

FREE VERSE **Free verse** is poetry not written in a regular pattern of meter or rhyme. Cornelius Eady's "The Poetic Interpretation of the Twist" (p. 633) is an example.

GENRE A **genre** is a category or form of literature. Literature is commonly divided into three major types of writing: poetry, prose, and drama. For each type, there are several distinct genres, as follows:

1. Poetry: Lyric Poetry, Concrete Poetry, Dramatic Poetry, Narrative Poetry, and Epic Poetry
2. Prose: Fiction (Novels and Short Stories) and Nonfiction (Biography, Autobiography, Letters, Essays, and Reports)
3. Drama: Serious Drama and Tragedy, Comic Drama, Melodrama, and Farce

See also **Drama, Poetry,** and **Prose.**

HAIKU The **haiku** is a three-line verse form. The first and third lines of a haiku each have five syllables. The second line has seven syllables. A haiku seeks to convey a single vivid emotion by means of images from nature.

HOMERIC SIMILE See *Epic Simile.*

HYPERBOLE A *hyperbole* is a deliberate exaggeration or overstatement. In Mark Twain's "The Notorious Jumping Frog of Calaveras County," the claim that Jim Smiley would follow a bug as far as Mexico to win a bet is a hyperbole. As this example shows, hyperboles are often used for comic effect.

IAMB See *Meter.*

IDIOM An *idiom* or *idiomatic expression* is an expression that is characteristic of a language, region, community or class of people. Idiomatic expressions mean something more than or different from the meaning of the words making them up. Following is an example of an idiom from T. H. White's *The Once and Future King* (p. 1156): "Think what people will say about us, if we do not go and *have a shot at that sword.*"

See also *Dialect.*

IMAGE An *image* is a word or phrase that appeals to one or more of the five senses—sight, hearing, touch, taste, or smell. Writers use images to re-create sensory experiences in words.

See also *Description.*

IMAGERY *Imagery* is the descriptive or figurative language used in literature to create word pictures for the reader. These pictures, or images, are created by details of sight, sound, taste, touch, smell, or movement.

INDIRECT CHARACTERIZATION
See *Characterization.*

INTERNAL RHYME See *Rhyme.*

IRONY *Irony* is the general term for literary techniques that portray differences between appearance and reality, or expectation and result. In *verbal irony,* words are used to suggest the opposite of what is meant. In *dramatic irony,* there is a contradiction between what a character thinks and what the reader or audience knows to be true. In *irony of situation,* an event occurs that directly contradicts the expectations of the characters, the reader, or the audience.

LITERAL LANGUAGE *Literal language* uses words in their ordinary senses. It is the opposite of *figurative language.* If you tell someone standing on a diving board

to jump in, you speak literally. If you tell someone on the street to "go jump in a lake," you are speaking figuratively. See also *Figurative Language.*

LYRIC POEM A *lyric poem* is a poem written in highly musical language that expresses the thoughts, observations, and feelings of a single speaker.

MAIN CHARACTER See *Character.*

METAPHOR A *metaphor* is a figure of speech in which one thing is spoken of as though it were something else. Unlike a simile, which compares two things using *like* or *as,* a metaphor implies a comparison between them. In "A Tree Telling of Orpheus" (p. 659), the speaker is a tree and describes music as if it were water: "my roots felt music moisten them."

See also *Extended Metaphor* and *Figurative Language.*

METER The *meter* of a poem is its rhythmical pattern. This pattern is determined by the number and arrangements of stressed syllables, or beats, in each line. To describe the meter of a poem, you must scan its lines. Scanning involves marking the stressed and unstressed syllables, as shown with the following two lines from *Julius Caesar* (p. 892):

> Wĕ bóth hăve féd ăs wéll, ănd wé căn bóth
>
> Eñdúre thĕ wíntĕr's cóld ăs wéll ăs hé . . .

As you can see, each stressed syllable is marked with a slanted line (´) and each unstressed syllable with a horseshoe symbol (˘). The stressed and unstressed syllables are then divided by vertical lines (|) into groups called *feet.* The following types of feet are common in English poetry:

1. *Iamb:* a foot with one unstressed syllable followed by a stressed syllable, as in the word "again"

2. *Trochee:* a foot with one stressed syllable followed by an unstressed syllable, as in the word "wonder"

3. *Anapest:* a foot with two unstressed syllables followed by one strong stress, as in the phrase "on the beach"

4. *Dactyl:* a foot with one strong stress followed by two unstressed syllables, as in the word "wonderful"

5. *Spondee:* a foot with two strong stresses, as in the word "spacewalk"

Depending on the type of foot that is most common in them, lines of poetry are described as *iambic, trochaic, anapestic,* and so forth.

Lines are also described in terms of the number of feet that occur in them, as follows:

1. *Monometer:* verse written in one-foot lines
   All things
   Must pass
   Away.

2. *Dimeter:* verse written in two-foot lines
   Thomas | Jefferson
   What do | you say
   Under the | gravestone
   Hidden | away?
   —Rosemary and Stephen Vincent Benét,
   "Thomas Jefferson, 1743–1826"

3. *Trimeter:* verse written in three-foot lines
   I know | not whom | I meet
   I know | not where | I go.

4. *Tetrameter:* verse written in four-foot lines

5. *Pentameter:* verse written in five-foot lines

6. *Hexameter:* verse written in six-foot lines

7. *Heptameter:* verse written in seven-foot lines

Blank verse, used by Shakespeare in *Julius Caesar* (p. 892), is poetry written in unrhymed iambic pentameter.

Free verse, used by Cornelius Eady in "The Poetic Interpretation of the Twist" (p. 633), is poetry that does not follow a regular pattern of meter and rhyme.

MONOLOGUE A *monologue* in a play is a long speech by one character that, unlike a *soliloquy*, is addressed to another character or characters. An example from Shakespeare's *Julius Caesar* (p. 892) is the famous speech by Antony to the Roman people in Act III, Scene ii. It begins, "Friends, Romans, countrymen, lend me your ears. . . ." (line 74).

See also **Soliloquy.**

MOOD *Mood,* or *atmosphere,* is the feeling created in the reader by a literary work or passage. The mood is often suggested by descriptive details. Often the mood can be described in a single word, such as lighthearted, frightening, or despairing. Notice how this passage from Edgar Allan Poe's "The Masque of the Red Death" (p. 372) contributes to an eerie, fearful mood:

> And now was acknowledged the presence of the Red Death. He had come like a thief in the night. And one by one dropped the revelers in the blood-bedewed halls of their revel, and died each in the despairing posture of his fall.

See also **Tone.**

MORAL A *moral* is a lesson taught by a literary work, especially a fable—many fables, for example, have a stated moral at the end. It is customary, however, to discuss contemporary works in terms of the themes they explore, rather than a moral that they teach.

MOTIVATION *Motivation* is a reason that explains or partially explains why a character thinks, feels, acts, or behaves in a certain way. Motivation results from a combination of the character's personality and the situation he or she must deal with. In *Antigone* (p. 814), the protagonist is motivated by loyalty to her dead brother and reverence for the laws of the gods.

See also **Character** and **Characterization.**

MYTH A *myth* is a *fictional* tale that describes the actions of gods and heroes or explains the causes of natural phenomena. Unlike legends, myths emphasize supernatural rather than historical elements. Many cultures have collections of myths, and the most familiar in the Western world are those of the ancient Greeks and Romans. "Prometheus and the First People" (p. 1066) is a retelling of a famous ancient Greek myth.

See also **Oral Tradition.**

NARRATION *Narration* is writing that tells a story. The act of telling a story in speech is also called narration. Novels and short stories are fictional narratives. Nonfiction works—such as news stories, biographies, and autobiographies—are also narratives. A narrative poem tells a story in verse.

See also **Anecdote, Essay, Narrative Poem, Nonfiction, Novel,** and **Short Story.**

NARRATIVE A *narrative* is a story told in fiction, nonfiction, poetry, or drama.

See also **Narration.**

NARRATIVE ESSAY See **Essay.**

NARRATIVE POEM A *narrative poem* is one that tells a story. Alexander Pushkin's "The Bridegroom" (p. 642) is a narrative poem that tells how Natasha, a merchant's daughter, outwits a thief and murderer.

See also **Dramatic Poetry, Epic,** and **Narration.**

NARRATOR A *narrator* is a speaker or character who tells a story. The writer's choice of narrator determines the story's *point of view*, or the perspective from which the story is told. By using a consistent point of view, a writer controls the amount and type of information revealed to the reader.

When a character in the story tells the story, that character is a *first-person narrator*. This narrator may be a major character, a minor character, or just a witness. Readers see only what this character sees, hear only what he or she hears, and so on. Stephen Vincent Benét's "By the Waters of Babylon" (p. 314) is told by a first-person narrator. Viewing unfolding events from this character's perspective, the reader shares in his discoveries and feels more suspense than another point of view would provide.

When a voice outside the story narrates, the story has a *third-person narrator*. An *omniscient*, or all-knowing, third-person narrator can tell readers what any character thinks and feels. For example, in "The Monkey's Paw" (p. 32), we know the thoughts of the father, the wife, and the son. A *limited third-person narrator* sees the world through one character's eyes and reveals only that character's thoughts. In Jack Finney's "Contents of the Dead Man's Pocket" (p. 118), the narrator reveals only Tom's thoughts and feelings.

See also *Speaker.*

NONFICTION *Nonfiction* is prose writing that presents and explains ideas or that tells about real people, places, ideas, or events. To be classified as nonfiction, a work must be true. Dorothy West's "The Sun Parlor" (p. 490) is a true account of events related to a particular room in a house.

See also *Autobiography, Biography,* and *Essay.*

NOVEL A *novel* is a long work of fiction. It has a plot that explores characters in conflict. A novel may also have one or more subplots, or minor stories, and several themes.

OCTAVE See *Stanza.*

ONOMATOPOEIA *Onomatopoeia* is the use of words that imitate sounds. *Whirr, thud, sizzle,* and *hiss* are typical examples. Writers can deliberately choose words that contribute to a desired sound effect.

ORAL TRADITION The *oral tradition* is the retelling of songs, stories, and poems passed orally, or by spoken word, from generation to generation. Many folk songs, ballads, fairy tales, legends, and myths originated in the oral tradition.

See also *Myth.*

OXYMORON An *oxymoron* is a combination of words that contradict each other. Examples are "deafening silence," "honest thief," "wise fool," and "bittersweet." This device is effective when the apparent contradiction reveals a deeper truth.

PARADOX A *paradox* is a statement that seems contradictory but that actually may express a deeper truth. Because a paradox is surprising, it catches the reader's attention.

PARALLELISM See *Rhetorical Devices.*

PERSONIFICATION *Personification* is a type of figurative language in which a nonhuman subject is given human characteristics. Denise Levertov personifies a tree in her poem "A Tree Telling of Orpheus" (p. 659). In fact, the tree is the speaker in this poem: "I listened, and language came into my roots . . ."

See also *Figurative Language.*

PERSUASION *Persuasion* is writing or speech that attempts to convince the reader to adopt a particular opinion or course of action.

An *argument* is a logical way of presenting a belief, conclusion, or stance. A good argument is supported with reasoning and evidence.

PERSUASIVE ESSAY See *Essay.*

PLOT *Plot* is the sequence of events in a literary work. In most novels, dramas, short stories, and narrative poems, the plot involves both characters and a central conflict. The plot usually begins with an **exposition** that introduces the setting, the characters, and the basic situation. This is followed by the *inciting incident*, which introduces the central conflict. The conflict then increases during the *development* until it reaches a high point of interest or suspense, the **climax.** All the events leading up to the climax make up the *rising action.* The climax is followed by the *falling action*, which leads to the *denouement*, or *resolution*, in which the conflict is resolved and in which a general insight may be conveyed.

POETRY *Poetry* is one of the three major types of literature, the others being prose and drama. Most poems make use of highly concise, musical, and emotionally charged language. Many also make use of imagery, figurative language, and special devices of sound such as rhyme. Poems are often divided into lines and stanzas and often employ regular rhythmical patterns, or meters. Poetry that does not follow a regular metrical pattern is called **free verse.**

See also **Genre.**

POINT OF VIEW See **Narrator.**

PROSE **Prose** is the ordinary form of written language. Most writing that is not poetry, drama, or song is considered prose. Prose is one of the major categories of literature and occurs in two forms: fiction and nonfiction.

See also **Fiction, Genre,** and **Nonfiction.**

PROTAGONIST The **protagonist** is the main character in a literary work.

See also **Antagonist** and **Character.**

PUN A **pun** is a play on words involving a word with two or more different meanings or two words that sound alike but have different meanings. In *Julius Caesar* (p. 892), there is a pun on the phrase *mend you* (Act I, Scene i, lines 17–18): "yet if you be out [angry], sir, I can mend you." The speaker is a cobbler and by *mend you* he means both "mend your shoes" and "improve your disposition."

QUATRAIN A **quatrain** is a stanza, or section, of a poem made up of four lines, usually with a definite rhythm and rhyme scheme.

REPETITION **Repetition** is the use of any element of language—a sound, a word, a phrase, a clause, or a sentence—more than once.

Poets use many kinds of repetition. **Alliteration, assonance, consonance, rhyme,** and **rhythm** are repetitions of certain sounds and sound patterns. A *refrain* is a repeated line or group of lines. In both prose and poetry, repetition is used for musical effects and for emphasis.

See also **Alliteration, Assonance, Consonance, Rhyme,** and **Rhythm.**

RESOLUTION See **Plot.**

RHETORICAL DEVICES **Rhetorical devices** are special patterns of words and ideas that create emphasis and stir emotion, especially in speeches or other oral presentations. *Parallelism,* for example, is the repetition of a grammatical structure in order to create a rhythm and make words more memorable. In "Keep Memory Alive" (p. 548), Elie Wiesel uses parallelism: "Neutrality helps the oppressor, never the victim. Silence encourages the tormentor, never the tormented."

Other common rhetorical devices include *restatement,* expressing the same idea in different words, and *rhetorical questions,* questions with obvious answers.

RHYME **Rhyme** is the repetition of sounds at the ends of words. *End rhyme* occurs when the rhyming words come at the ends of lines, as in "The Desired Swan Song" by Samuel Taylor Coleridge:

> Swans sing before they die—'twere no bad thing
> Should certain persons die before they sing.

Internal rhyme occurs when one of the rhyming words appears within a line, as in these lines from "The Waking" (p. 685):

> God bless the Ground! I shall walk softly *there,*
> And learn by going *where* I have to go.

Exact rhyme involves the repetition of the same final vowel and consonant sounds in words like *ball* and *hall. Slant rhyme* involves the repetition of words that sound alike but do not rhyme exactly, like *grove* and *love.*

See also **Repetition** and **Rhyme Scheme.**

RHYME SCHEME A **rhyme scheme** is a regular pattern of rhyming words in a poem. The rhyme scheme of a poem is indicated by using different letters of the alphabet for each new rhyme. In an *aabb* stanza, for example, line 1 rhymes with line 2 and line 3 rhymes with line 4. "Meeting at Night" (p. 744) uses an *abccba* rhyme scheme in each of its two stanzas:

The gray sea and the long black land;	a
And the yellow half-moon large and low;	b
And the startled little waves that leap	c
In fiery ringlets from their sleep,	c
As I gain the cove with pushing prow,	b
And quench its speed i' the slushy sand.	a

Many poems use the same pattern of rhymes, though not the same rhymes, in each stanza.

See also **Rhyme.**

RHYTHM **Rhythm** is the pattern of *beats,* or *stresses,* in spoken or written language. Some poems follow a very specific pattern, or meter, whereas prose and free verse may use the natural rhythms of everyday speech.

See also **Meter.**

RISING ACTION See **Plot.**

ROUND CHARACTER See **Character.**

SATIRE A *satire* is a literary work that ridicules the foolishness and faults of individuals, an institution, society, or even humanity in general.

SCENE See *Drama.*

SCIENCE FICTION *Science fiction* is writing that tells about imaginary events involving science or technology. Many science-fiction stories are set in the future. C. J. Cherryh's science-fiction story "The Threads of Time" (p. 229) plays with the dimension of time.

See also *Fantasy.*

SENSORY LANGUAGE *Sensory language* is writing or speech that appeals to one or more of the senses.

See also *Image.*

SESTET See *Stanza.*

SET See *Drama.*

SETTING The *setting* of a literary work is the time and place of the action. Time can include not only the historical period—past, present, or future—but also a specific year, season, or time of day. Place may involve not only the geographical place—a region, country, state, or town—but also the social, economic, or cultural environment.

In some stories, setting serves merely as a backdrop for action, a context in which the characters move and speak. In others, however, setting is a crucial element.

See also *Mood.*

SHORT STORY A *short story* is a brief work of fiction. In most short stories, one main character faces a conflict that is resolved in the plot of the story. Great craftsmanship must go into the writing of a good story, for it has to accomplish its purpose in relatively few words.

See also *Fiction* and *Genre.*

SIMILE A *simile* is a figure of speech in which the words like or as are used to compare two apparently dissimilar items. The comparison, however, surprises the reader into a fresh perception by finding an unexpected likeness. In "The Guitar" (p. 648), for example, García Lorca says that the guitar "weeps monotonously / As weeps the water, / As weeps the wind / Over snow."

SOLILOQUY A *soliloquy* is a long speech expressing the thoughts of a character alone on stage. In William Shakespeare's *Julius Caesar* (p. 892), Brutus delivers a soliloquy in which he confirms and justifies his participation in the plot to assassinate Caesar (Act II, Scene i, lines 10–34): "It must be by his death . . ."

See also *Monologue.*

SONNET A *sonnet* is a fourteen-line lyric poem, usually written in rhymed iambic pentameter. The *English,* or *Shakespearean,* sonnet consists of three quatrains (four-line stanzas) and a couplet (two lines), usually rhyming *abab cdcd efef gg.* The couplet usually comments on the ideas contained in the preceding twelve lines. The sonnet is usually not printed with the stanzas divided, but a reader can see distinct ideas in each. (See Sonnet 18 by William Shakespeare on page 686.)

The *Italian,* or *Petrarchan,* sonnet consists of an octave (eight-line stanza) and a sestet (six-line stanza). Often, the octave rhymes *abbaabba* and the sestet rhymes *cdecde.* The octave states a theme or asks a question. The sestet comments on the theme or answers the question.

See also *Lyric Poem; Meter;* and *Stanza.*

SPEAKER The *speaker* is the imaginary voice assumed by the writer of a poem. In many poems, the speaker is not identified by name. When reading a poem, remember that the speaker within the poem may be a person, an animal, a thing, or an abstraction. The speaker in the following stanza by Emily Dickinson is a person who has died:

> Because I could not stop for Death—
> He kindly stopped for me—
> The Carriage held but just Ourselves—
> And Immortality.

STAGE DIRECTIONS *Stage directions* are notes included in a drama to describe how the work is to be performed or staged. These instructions are printed in italics and are not spoken aloud. They are used to describe sets, lighting, sound effects, and the appearance, personalities, and movements of characters.

See also *Drama.*

STANZA A *stanza* is a repeated grouping of two or more lines in a poem that often share a pattern of rhythm and rhyme. Stanzas are sometimes named according to the number of lines they have—for example, a *couplet,* two lines; a *quatrain,* four lines; a *sestet,* six lines; and an *octave,* eight lines.

See also *Sonnet.*

STATIC CHARACTER See *Character.*

STYLE *Style* refers to an author's unique way of writing. Elements determining style include diction; tone; characteristic use of figurative language, dialect, or rhythmic devices; and typical grammatical structures and patterns.

See also *Diction* and *Tone.*

SURPRISE ENDING A *surprise ending* is a conclusion that violates the expectations of the reader but in a way that is both logical and believable.

O. Henry's "One Thousand Dollars" (p. 308) and Saki's "The Open Window" (p. 195) have surprise endings. Both authors were masters of this form.

SYMBOL A *symbol* is a character, place, thing or event that stands for something else, often an abstract idea. For example, a flag is a piece of cloth, but it also represents the idea of a country. Writers sometimes use conventional symbols like flags. Frequently, however, they create symbols of their own through emphasis or repetition. In "The Garden of Stubborn Cats" (p. 384), for example, the cats come to symbolize nature's stubborn resistance to human development.

THEME A *theme* is a central message or insight into life revealed through a literary work.

The theme of a literary work may be stated directly or implied. When the theme of a work is implied, readers think about what the work suggests about people or life.

Archetypal themes are those that occur in folklore and literature across the world and throughout history. The hero who makes civilization possible, the theme of "Prometheus and the First People" (p. 1066), is an example of an archetypal theme.

TONE The *tone* of a literary work is the writer's attitude toward his or her audience and subject. The tone can often be described by a single adjective, such as *formal* or *informal, serious* or *playful, bitter* or *ironic.* When Valenzuela discusses the fate of Juan in "The Censors" (p. 410), she uses an ironic tone: ". . . another victim of his devotion to his work."

See also *Mood.*

TRAGEDY A *tragedy* is a work of literature, especially a play, that tells of a catastrophe, a disaster or great misfortune, for the main character. In ancient Greek drama, the main character was always a significant person—a king or a hero—and the cause of the tragedy was often a tragic flaw, or weakness, in his or her character. In modern drama, the main character can be an ordinary person, and the cause of the tragedy can be some evil in society itself. Tragedy not only arouses fear and pity in the audience, but also, in some cases, conveys a sense of the grandeur and nobility of the human spirit.

Shakespeare's *Julius Caesar* (p. 892) is a tragedy. Brutus suffers from the tragic flaw of blindness to reality and people's motives. His noble-mindedness is almost a form of arrogance. This flaw ultimately leads to his death.

See also *Drama.*

UNDERSTATEMENT An *understatement* is a figure of speech in which the stated meaning is purposely less than (or "under") what is really meant. It is the opposite of *hyperbole,* which is a deliberate exaggeration.

UNIVERSAL THEME A *universal theme* is a message about life that can be understood by most cultures. Many folk tales and examples of classic literature address universal themes such as the importance of courage, the effects of honesty, or the danger of greed.

VERBAL IRONY See *Irony.*

VILLANELLE A *villanelle* is a nineteen-line lyric poem written in five three-line stanzas and ending in a four-line stanza. It uses two rhymes and repeats two refrain lines that appear initially in the first and third lines of the first stanza. These lines then appear alternately as the third line of subsequent three-line stanzas and, finally, as the last two lines of the poem. Theodore Roethke's "The Waking" (p. 684) is a villanelle.

VOICE *Voice* is a writer's distinctive "sound" or way of "speaking" on the page. It is related to such elements as word choice, sentence structure, and tone. It is similar to an individual's speech style and can be described in the same way—fast, slow, blunt, meandering, breathless, and so on.

Voice resembles *style,* an author's typical way of writing, but style usually refers to a quality that can be found throughout an author's body of work, while an author's voice may sometimes vary from work to work.

See also *Style.*

Tips for Discussing Literature

As you read and study literature, discussion with other readers can help you understand, enjoy, and develop interpretations of what you read. Use the following tips to practice good speaking and listening skills while participating in group discussions of literature.

- ## Understand the purpose of your discussion

  When you discuss literature, your purpose is to broaden your understanding and appreciation of a work by testing your own ideas and hearing the ideas of others. Stay focused on the literature you are discussing and keep your comments relevant to that literature. Starting with one focus question will help to keep your discussion on track.

- ## Communicate effectively

  Effective communication requires thinking before speaking. Plan the points that you want to make and decide how you will express them. Organize these points in logical order and cite details from the work to support your ideas. Jot down informal notes to help keep your ideas focused.

  Remember to speak clearly, pronouncing words slowly and carefully so that others can understand your points. Also, keep in mind that some literature touches readers deeply—be aware of the possibility of counterproductive emotional responses and work to control them. Negative emotional responses can also be conveyed through body language, so work to demonstrate respect in your demeanor as well as in your words.

- ## Encourage everyone to participate

  While some people are comfortable participating in discussions, others are less eager to speak up in groups. However, everyone should work to contribute thoughts and ideas. To encourage the entire group's participation, try the following strategies:

  - If you enjoy speaking, avoid monopolizing the conversation. After sharing your ideas, encourage others to share theirs.
  - Try different roles. For example, have everyone take turns being the facilitator or host of the discussion.
  - Use a prop, such as a book or gavel. Pass the prop around the group, allowing whomever is holding the prop to have the floor.

- ## Make relevant contributions

  Especially when responding to a short story, a poem, or a novel, avoid simply summarizing the plot. Instead, consider *what* you think might happen next, *why* events take place as they do, or *how* a writer provokes a response in you. Let your ideas inspire deeper thought or discussion about the literature.

- ## Consider other ideas and interpretations

  A work of literature can generate a wide variety of responses in different readers— and that can make your discussions exciting. Be open to the idea that many interpretations can be valid. To support your own ideas, point to the events, descriptions, characters, or other literary elements in the work that produced your interpretation. To consider someone else's ideas, decide whether details in the work support the interpretation he or she presents. Be sure to convey your criticism of the ideas of others in a respectful and supportive manner.

• Ask questions and extend the contributions of others

Get in the habit of asking questions to help you clarify your understanding of another reader's ideas. You can also use questions to call attention to possible areas of confusion, to points that are open to debate, or to errors.

In addition, offer elaboration of the points that others make by providing examples and illustrations. To move a discussion forward, pause occasionally to summarize and evaluate tentative conclusions reached by the group members. Then, continue the discussion with a fresh understanding of the material and ideas you have already covered.

• Manage differing opinions and views

Each participant brings his or her own personality, experiences, ideas, cultural background, likes and dislikes to the experience of reading, making disagreement almost inevitable. As differences arise, be sensitive to each individual's point of view. Do not personalize disagreements, but keep them focused on the literature or ideas under discussion.

When you meet with a group to discuss literature, use a chart like the one shown to analyze the discussion.

Work Being Discussed:	
Focus Question:	
Your Response:	Another Student's Response:
Supporting Evidence:	Supporting Evidence:
One New Idea That You Considered About the Work During the Discussion:	

Literary Criticism

Criticism is writing that explores the meaning and techniques of literary works, usually in order to evaluate them. Writing criticism can help you think through your experience of a work of literature and can also help others deepen their own understanding. All literary criticism shares similar goals:

- **Making Connections** within or between works, or between a work of literature and its context
- **Making Distinctions** or showing differences between elements of a single work or aspects of two or more works
- **Achieving Insights** that were not apparent from a superficial reading
- **Making a Judgment** about the quality or value of a literary work

Critics use various **theories of literary criticism** to understand, appreciate, and evaluate literature. Some theories focus on the context of the work while others focus on the work itself. Sometimes critics combine one or more theories. These charts show a few examples of the many theories of criticism:

Focus on Contexts	
Human Experience	**Mythic Criticism** Explores universal situations, characters, and symbols called archetypes as they appear in a literary work
Culture and History	**Historical Criticism** Analyzes how circumstances or ideas of an era influence a work
Author's Life	**Biographical Criticism** Explains how the author's life sheds light on the work

Focus on the Work Itself
Formal Criticism Shows how the work reflects characteristics of the genre, or literary type, to which it belongs

Examples of Literary Theories in Action

- **Mythic Criticism:** discussing how the Greek myth "Prometheus and the First People," p. 1066, reveals Prometheus as an archetypal character
- **Historical Criticism:** showing how William Shakespeare was influenced by Elizabethan concepts of nature and politics in *Julius Caesar*, p. 892
- **Biographical Criticism:** showing how James Thurber's family relationships influenced the theme of "The Dog That Bit People," p. 525
- **Formal Criticism:** analyzing how "Contents of the Dead Man's Pocket," p. 118, combines short-story elements like plot, suspense, setting, character, and theme

Literary Movements

Our literary heritage has been shaped by a number of *literary movements,* directions in literature characterized by shared assumptions, beliefs, and practices. This chart shows, in chronological order, some important literary movements. While these movements developed at particular historical moments, all of them may still influence individual writers working today.

Movement	Beliefs and Practices	Examples
Classicism Europe during the Renaissance (c. 1300–1650)	• Looks to classical literature of ancient Greece and Rome as models • Values logic, clarity, balance, and restraint • Prefers "ordered" nature of parks and gardens	the clarity and restraint of Robert Frost's verse ("Mowing," p. 658)
Romanticism Europe during the late 1700s and the early 1800s	• Rebels against Classicism • Values imagination and emotion • Focuses on everyday life	the celebration of the natural world in Rachel Carson's writings ("The Marginal World," p. 156)
Realism Europe and America from the mid-1800s to the 1890s	• Rebels against Romanticism's search for the ideal • Focuses on everyday life	the faithful rendering of Russian life in Anton Chekhov's fiction ("A Problem," p. 256)
Naturalism Europe and America during the late 1800s and early 1900s	• Assumes people cannot choose their fate but are shaped by psychological and social forces • Views society as a competitive jungle	the indifference to human life that characters show in Guy de Maupassant's fiction ("Two Friends," p. 1233)
Modernism Worldwide between 1890 and 1945	• In response to WWI, questions human reason • Focuses on studies of the unconscious and the art of primitive peoples • Experiments with language and form	the experiments with free verse in Carl Sandburg's poetry ("Jazz Fantasia," p. 739)
Post-Modernism Worldwide after 1945; still prevalent today	• Believes works of art comment on themselves • Finds inspiration in information technology	the self-consciousness about tradition in John Phillip Santos's nonfiction (from *Places Left Unfinished at the Time of Creation,* p. 1053)

Tips for Improving Reading Fluency

When you were younger, you learned to read. Then, you read to expand your experiences or for pure enjoyment. Now, you are expected to read to learn. As you progress in school, you are given more and more material to read. The tips on these pages will help you improve your reading fluency, or your ability to read easily, smoothly, and expressively.

Keeping Your Concentration

One common problem that readers face is the loss of concentration. When you are reading an assignment, you might find yourself rereading the same sentence several times without really understanding it. The first step in changing this behavior is to notice that you do it. Becoming an active, aware reader will help you get the most from your assignments. Practice using these strategies:

- Cover what you have already read with a note card as you go along. Then, you will not be able to reread without noticing that you are doing it.
- Set a purpose for reading beyond just completing the assignment. Then, read actively by pausing to ask yourself questions about the material as you read.
- Use the Reading Strategy instruction and notes that appear with each selection in this textbook.
- Stop reading after a specified period of time (for example, 5 minutes) and summarize what you have read. To help you with this strategy, use the Reading Check questions that appear with each selection in this textbook. Reread to find any answers you do not know.

Reading Phrases

Fluent readers read phrases rather than individual words. Reading this way will speed up your reading and improve your comprehension. Here are some useful ideas:

- Experts recommend rereading as a strategy to increase fluency. Choose a passage of text that is neither too hard nor too easy. Read the same passage aloud several times until you can read it smoothly. When you can read the passage fluently, pick another passage and keep practicing.
- Read aloud into a tape recorder. Then, listen to the recording, noting your accuracy, pacing, and expression. You can also read aloud and share feedback with a partner.
- Use the *Prentice Hall Listening to Literature* audiotapes or CDs to hear the selections read aloud. Read along silently in your textbook, noticing how the reader uses his or her voice and emphasizes certain words and phrases.

Understanding Key Vocabulary

If you do not understand some of the words in an assignment, you may miss out on important concepts. Therefore, it is helpful to keep a dictionary nearby when you are reading. Follow these steps:

- Before you begin reading, scan the text for unfamiliar words or terms. Find out what those words mean before you begin reading.
- Use context—the surrounding words, phrases, and sentences—to help you determine the meanings of unfamiliar words.
- If you are unable to understand the meaning through context, refer to the dictionary.

Paying Attention to Punctuation

When you read, pay attention to punctuation. Commas, periods, exclamation points, semicolons, and colons tell you when to pause or stop. They also indicate relationships between groups of words. When you recognize these relationships, you will read with greater understanding and expression. Look at the chart below.

Punctuation Mark	Meaning
comma	brief pause
period	pause at the end of a thought
exclamation point	pause that indicates emphasis
semicolon	pause between related but distinct thoughts
colon	pause before giving explanation or examples

Using the Reading Fluency Checklist

Use the checklist below each time you read a selection in this textbook. In your Language Arts journal or notebook, note which skills you need to work on and chart your progress each week.

Reading Fluency Checklist
❑ Preview the text to check for difficult or unfamiliar words.
❑ Practice reading aloud.
❑ Read according to punctuation.
❑ Break down long sentences into the subject and its meaning.
❑ Read groups of words for meaning rather than reading single words.
❑ Read with expression (change your tone of voice to add meaning to the word).

Reading is a skill that can be improved with practice. The key to improving your fluency is to read. The more you read, the better your reading will become.

Types of Writing

Good writing can be a powerful tool used for many purposes. Writing can allow you to defend something you believe in or show how much you know about a subject. Writing can also help you share what you have experienced, imagined, thought, and felt. The three main types of writing are argument, informative/explanatory, and narrative.

Argument

When you think of the word *argument*, you might think of a disagreement between two people, but an argument is more than that. An argument is a logical way of presenting a belief, conclusion, or stance. A good argument is supported with reasoning and evidence.

Argument writing can be used for many purposes, such as to change a reader's point of view or opinion or to bring about an action or a response from a reader.

There are three main purposes for writing a formal argument:

- to change the reader's mind
- to convince the reader to accept what is written
- to motivate the reader to take action, based on what is written

The following are some types of argument writing:

Advertisements An advertisement is a planned communication meant to be seen, heard, or read. It attempts to persuade an audience to buy a product or service, accept an idea, or support a cause. Advertisements may appear in printed or broadcast form.

Several common types of advertisements are public-service announcements, billboards, merchandise ads, service ads, and political campaign literature.

Persuasive Essay A persuasive essay presents a position on an issue, urges readers to accept that position, and may encourage a specific action. An effective persuasive essay

- Explores an issue of importance to the writer
- Addresses an issue that is arguable
- Uses facts, examples, statistics, or personal experiences to support a position
- Tries to influence the audience through appeals to the readers' knowledge, experiences, or emotions
- Uses clear organization to present a logical argument

Forms of persuasion include editorials, position papers, persuasive speeches, grant proposals, advertisements, and debates.

Informative/Explanatory

Informative/explanatory writing should rely on facts to inform or explain. Informative/explanatory writing serves some closely related purposes: to increase readers' knowledge of a subject, to help readers better understand a procedure or process, or to provide readers with an enhanced comprehension of a concept. It should also feature a clear introduction, body, and conclusion. The following are some examples of informative/explanatory writing:

Cause-and-Effect Essay A cause-and-effect essay examines the relationship between events, explaining how one event or situation causes another. A successful cause-and-effect essay includes

- A discussion of a cause, event, or condition that produces a specific result
- An explanation of an effect, outcome, or result
- Evidence and examples to support the relationship between cause and effect
- A logical organization that makes the explanation clear

Comparison-and-Contrast Essay A comparison-and-contrast essay analyzes the similarities and differences between or among two or more things. An effective comparison-and-contrast essay

- Identifies a purpose for comparison and contrast
- Identifies similarities and differences between or among two or more things, people, places, or ideas
- Gives factual details about the subjects
- Uses an organizational plan suited to the topic and purpose

Descriptive Writing Descriptive writing creates a vivid picture of a person, place, thing, or event. Most descriptive writing includes

- Sensory details—sights, sounds, smells, tastes, and physical sensations
- Vivid, precise language
- Figurative language or comparisons
- Adjectives and adverbs that paint a word picture
- An organization suited to the subject

Types of descriptive writing include descriptions of ideas, observations, travel brochures, physical descriptions, functional descriptions, remembrances, and character sketches.

Problem-and-Solution Essay A problem-and-solution essay describes a problem and offers one or more solutions to it. It describes a clear set of steps to achieve a result. An effective problem-and-solution essay includes

- A clear statement of the problem, with its causes and effects summarized for the reader
- The most important aspects of the problem
- A proposal of at least one realistic solution
- Facts, statistics, data, or expert testimony to support the solution
- A clear organization that makes the relationship between problem and solution obvious

Research Writing Research writing is based on information gathered from outside sources. A research paper—a focused study of a topic—helps writers explore and connect ideas, make discoveries, and share their findings with an audience. An effective research paper

- Focuses on a specific, narrow topic, which is usually summarized in a thesis statement
- Presents relevant information from a wide variety of sources
- Uses a clear organization that includes an introduction, body, and conclusion
- Includes a bibliography or works-cited list that identifies the sources from which the information was drawn

Other types of writing that depend on accurate and insightful research include multimedia presentations, statistical reports, annotated bibliographies, and experiment journals.

Workplace Writing Workplace writing is probably the format you will use most after you finish school. In general, workplace writing is fact-based and meant to communicate specific information in a structured format. Effective workplace writing

- Communicates information concisely
- Includes details that provide necessary information and anticipate potential questions
- Is error-free and neatly presented

Common types of workplace writing include business letters, memorandums, résumés, forms, and applications.

Narrative

Narrative writing conveys experience, either real or imaginary, and uses time to provide structure. It can be used to inform, instruct, persuade, or entertain. Whenever writers tell a story, they are using narrative writing. Most types of narrative writing share certain elements, such as characters, a setting, a sequence of events, and, often, a theme. The following are some types of narration:

Autobiographical Writing Autobiographical writing tells a true story about an important period, experience, or relationship in the writer's life. Effective autobiographical writing includes

- A series of events that involve the writer as the main character
- Details, thoughts, feelings, and insights from the writer's perspective
- A conflict or an event that affects the writer
- A logical organization that tells the story clearly
- Insights that the writer gained from the experience

Types of autobiographical writing include autobiographical sketches, personal narratives, reflective essays, eyewitness accounts, and memoirs.

Short Story A short story is a brief, creative narrative. Most short stories include

- Details that establish the setting in time and place
- A main character who undergoes a change or learns something during the course of the story
- A conflict or a problem to be introduced, developed, and resolved
- A plot, the series of events that make up the action of the story
- A theme or message about life

Types of short stories include realistic stories, fantasies, historical narratives, mysteries, thrillers, science-fiction stories, and adventure stories.

Writing Friendly Letters

Writing Friendly Letters

A friendly letter is an informal letter to a friend, a family member, or anyone with whom the writer wants to communicate in a personal way. Most friendly letters are made up of five parts:

✔ the heading

✔ the salutation, or greeting

✔ the body

✔ the closing

✔ the signature

The purpose of a friendly letter is often one of the following:

✔ to share personal news and feelings

✔ to send or to answer an invitation

✔ to express thanks

Model Friendly Letter

In this friendly letter, Betsy thanks her grandparents for a birthday present and gives them some news about her life.

11 Old Farm Road
Topsham, Maine 04011

April 14, 20—

Dear Grandma and Grandpa,

Thank you for the sweater you sent me for my birthday. It fits perfectly, and I love the color. I wore my new sweater to the carnival at school last weekend and got lots of compliments.

The weather here has been cool but sunny. Mom thinks that "real" spring will never come. I can't wait until it's warm enough to go swimming.

School is going fairly well. I really like my Social Studies class. We are learning about the U.S. Constitution, and I think it's very interesting. Maybe I will be a lawyer when I grow up.

When are you coming out to visit us? We haven't seen you since Thanksgiving. You can stay in my room when you come. I'll be happy to sleep on the couch. (The TV is in that room!!)

Well, thanks again and hope all is well with you.

Love,

Betsy

The **heading** includes the writer's address and the date on which he or she wrote the letter.

The **body** is the main part of the letter and contains the basic message.

Some common **closings** for personal letters include "Best wishes," "Love," "Sincerely," and "Yours truly."

Writing Business Letters

Formatting Business Letters

Business letters follow one of several acceptable formats. In **block format,** each part of the letter begins at the left margin. A double space is used between paragraphs. In **modified block format,** some parts of the letter are indented to the center of the page. No matter which format is used, all letters in business format have a heading, an inside address, a salutation, or greeting, a body, a closing, and a signature. These parts are shown and annotated on the model business letter below, formatted in modified block style.

Model Business Letter

In this letter, Yolanda Dodson uses modified block format to request information.

Students for a Cleaner Planet
c/o Memorial High School
333 Veteran's Drive
Denver, CO 80211

January 25, 20—

Steven Wilson, Director
Resource Recovery Really Works
300 Oak Street
Denver, CO 80216

Dear Mr. Wilson:

Memorial High School would like to start a branch of your successful recycling program. We share your commitment to reclaiming as much reusable material as we can. Because your program has been successful in other neighborhoods, we're sure that it can work in our community. Our school includes grades 9–12 and has about 800 students.

Would you send us some information about your community recycling program? For example, we need to know what materials can be recycled and how we can implement the program.

At least fifty students have already expressed an interest in getting involved, so I know we'll have the people power to make the program work. Please help us get started.

Thank you in advance for your time and consideration.

Sincerely,

Yolanda Dodson

Yolanda Dodson

The **heading** shows the writer's address and organization (if any), and the date.

The **inside address** indicates where the letter will be sent.

A **salutation** is punctuated by a colon. When the specific addressee is not known, use a general greeting such as "To whom it may concern:"

The **body** of the letter states the writer's purpose.

The **closing** "Sincerely" is common, but "Yours truly" or "Respectfully yours" are also acceptable. To end the letter, the writer types her name and provides a **signature.**

Writing a Résumé

Writing a Résumé

A résumé summarizes your educational background, work experiences, relevant skills, and other employment qualifications. It also tells potential employers how to contact you. An effective résumé presents the applicant's name, address, and phone number. It follows an accepted résumé organization, using labels and headings to guide readers.

A résumé should outline the applicant's educational background, life experiences, and related qualifications using precise and active language.

Model Résumé

With this résumé, James, a college student, hopes to find a full-time job.

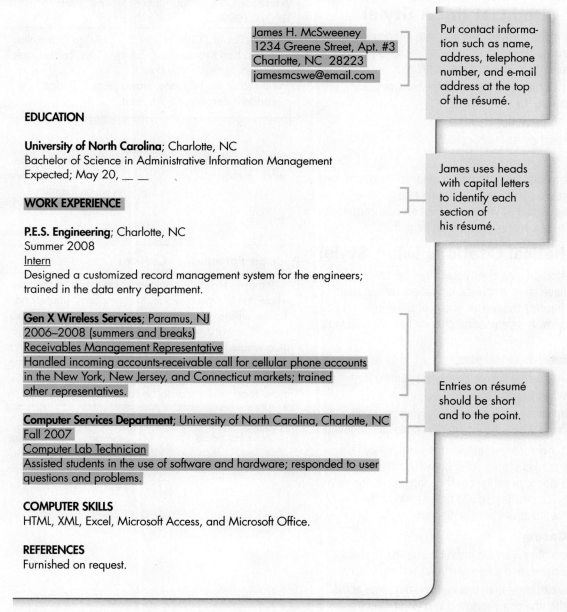

James H. McSweeney
1234 Greene Street, Apt. #3
Charlotte, NC 28223
jamesmcswe@email.com

> Put contact information such as name, address, telephone number, and e-mail address at the top of the résumé.

EDUCATION

University of North Carolina; Charlotte, NC
Bachelor of Science in Administrative Information Management
Expected; May 20, __ __

> James uses heads with capital letters to identify each section of his résumé.

WORK EXPERIENCE

P.E.S. Engineering; Charlotte, NC
Summer 2008
Intern
Designed a customized record management system for the engineers; trained in the data entry department.

Gen X Wireless Services; Paramus, NJ
2006–2008 (summers and breaks)
Receivables Management Representative
Handled incoming accounts-receivable call for cellular phone accounts in the New York, New Jersey, and Connecticut markets; trained other representatives.

> Entries on résumé should be short and to the point.

Computer Services Department; University of North Carolina, Charlotte, NC
Fall 2007
Computer Lab Technician
Assisted students in the use of software and hardware; responded to user questions and problems.

COMPUTER SKILLS
HTML, XML, Excel, Microsoft Access, and Microsoft Office.

REFERENCES
Furnished on request.

Citing Sources and Preparing Manuscript

In research writing, cite your sources. In the body of your paper, provide a footnote, an endnote, or a parenthetical citation, identifying the sources of facts, opinions, or quotations. At the end of your paper, provide a bibliography or a works-cited list, a list of all the sources you cite. Follow an established format, such as Modern Language Association (MLA) Style.

Works-Cited List (MLA Style)

A works-cited list must contain accurate information sufficient to enable a reader to locate each source you cite. The basic components of an entry are as follows:

- Name of the author, editor, translator, or group responsible for the work
- Title of the work
- Place and date of publication
- Publisher

For print materials, the information required for a citation generally appears on the copyright and title pages of a work. For the format of works-cited list entries, consult the examples at right and in the chart on page R37.

Parenthetical Citations (MLA Style)

A parenthetical citation briefly identifies the source from which you have taken a specific quotation, factual claim, or opinion. It refers the reader to one of the entries on your works-cited list. A parenthetical citation has the following features:

- It appears in parentheses.
- It identifies the source by the last name of the author, editor, or translator.
- It gives a page reference, identifying the page of the source on which the information cited can be found.

Punctuation A parenthetical citation generally falls outside a closing quotation mark but within the final punctuation of a clause or sentence. For a long quotation set off from the rest of your text, place the citation at the end of the excerpt without any punctuation following.

Special Cases

- If the author is an organization, use the organization's name, in a shortened version if necessary.
- If you cite more than one work by the same author, add the title or a shortened version of the title.

Sample Works-Cited Lists (MLA 7th Edition)

Carwardine, Mark, Erich Hoyt, R. Ewan Fordyce, and Peter Gill. *The Nature Company Guides: Whales, Dolphins, and Porpoises.* New York: Time-Life, 1998. Print.

"Discovering Whales." *Whales on the Net.* 1998. Whales in Danger Information Service. Web. 18 Oct. 1999.

Neruda, Pablo. "Ode to Spring." *Odes to Opposites.* Trans. Ken Krabbenhoft. Ed. and illus. Ferris Cook. Boston: Little, 1995. Print.

The Saga of the Volsungs. Trans. Jesse L. Byock. London: Penguin, 1990. Print.

> List an anonymous work by title.

> List both the title of the work and the collection in which it is found.

Sample Parenthetical Citations

It makes sense that baleen whales such as the blue whale, the bowhead whale, the humpback whale, and the sei whale (to name just a few) grow to immense sizes (Carwardine, Hoyt, and Fordyce 19–21). The blue whale has grooves running from under its chin to partway along the length of its underbelly. As in some other whales, these grooves expand and allow even more food and water to be taken in (Ellis 18–21).

> Author's last name

> Page numbers where information can be found

MLA Style for Listing Sources

Book with one author	Pyles, Thomas. *The Origins and Development of the English Language.* 2nd ed. New York: Harcourt, 1971. Print.
Book with two or three authors	McCrum, Robert, William Cran, and Robert MacNeil. *The Story of English.* New York: Penguin, 1987. Print.
Book with an editor	Truth, Sojourner. *Narrative of Sojourner Truth.* Ed. Margaret Washington. New York: Vintage, 1993. Print.
Book with more than three authors or editors	Donald, Robert B., et al. *Writing Clear Essays.* Upper Saddle River: Prentice, 1996. Print.
Single work in an anthology	Hawthorne, Nathaniel. "Young Goodman Brown." *Literature: An Introduction to Reading and Writing.* Ed. Edgar V. Roberts and H. E. Jacobs. Upper Saddle River: Prentice, 1998. 376–385. Print. [Indicate pages for the entire selection.]
Introduction to a work in a published edition	Washington, Margaret. Introduction. *Narrative of Sojourner Truth.* By Sojourner Truth. Ed. Washington. New York: Vintage, 1993. v–xi. Print.
Signed article from an encyclopedia	Askeland, Donald R. "Welding." *World Book Encyclopedia.* 1991 ed. Print.
Signed article in a weekly magazine	Wallace, Charles. "A Vodacious Deal." *Time* 14 Feb. 2000: 63. Print.
Signed article in a monthly magazine	Gustaitis, Joseph. "The Sticky History of Chewing Gum." *American History* Oct. 1998: 30–38. Print.
Newspaper	Thurow, Roger. "South Africans Who Fought for Sanctions Now Scrap for Investors." *Wall Street Journal* 11 Feb. 2000: A1+. Print. [For a multipage article that does not appear on consecutive pages, write only the first page number on which it appears, followed by the plus sign.]
Unsigned editorial or story	"Selective Silence." Editorial. *Wall Street Journal* 11 Feb. 2000: A14. Print. [If the editorial or story is signed, begin with the author's name.]
Signed pamphlet or brochure	[Treat the pamphlet as though it were a book.]
Work from a library subscription service	Ertman, Earl L. "Nefertiti's Eyes." *Archaeology* Mar.–Apr. 2008: 28–32. *Kids Search.* EBSCO. New York Public Library. Web. 18 June 2008 [Indicate the date you accessed the information.]
Filmstrips, slide programs, videocassettes, DVDs, and other audiovisual media	*The Diary of Anne Frank.* Dir. George Stevens. Perf. Millie Perkins, Shelley Winters, Joseph Schildkraut, Lou Jacobi, and Richard Beymer. 1959. Twentieth Century Fox, 2004. DVD.
CD-ROM (with multiple publishers)	Simms, James, ed. *Romeo and Juliet.* By William Shakespeare. Oxford: Attica Cybernetics; London: BBC Education; London: Harper, 1995. CD-ROM.
Radio or television program transcript	"Washington's Crossing of the Delaware." *Weekend Edition Sunday.* Natl. Public Radio. WNYC, New York. 23 Dec. 2003. Television transcript.
Internet Web page	"Fun Facts About Gum." NACGM site. 1999. National Association of Chewing Gum Manufacturers. Web. 19 Dec. 1999 [Indicate the date you accessed the information.]
Personal interview	Smith, Jane. Personal interview. 10 Feb. 2000.

All examples follow the style given in the *MLA Handbook for Writers of Research Papers,* seventh edition, by Joseph Gibaldi.

Guide to Rubrics

What is a rubric?

A rubric is a tool, often in the form of a chart or a grid, that helps you assess your work. Rubrics are particularly helpful for writing and speaking assignments.

To help you or others assess, or evaluate, your work, a rubric offers several specific criteria to be applied to your work. Then, the rubric helps you or an evaluator indicate your range of success or failure according to those specific criteria. Rubrics are often used to evaluate writing for standardized tests.

Using a rubric will save you time, focus your learning, and improve the work you do. When you know what the rubric will be before you begin writing a persuasive essay, for example, you will be aware as you write of specific criteria that are important in that kind of an essay. As you evaluate the essay before giving it to your teacher, you will focus on the specific areas that your teacher wants you to master—or on areas that you know present challenges for you. Instead of searching through your work randomly for any way to improve it or correct its errors, you will have a clear and helpful focus on specific criteria.

How are rubrics constructed?

Rubrics can be constructed in several different ways.

- Your teacher may assign a rubric for a specific assignment.
- Your teacher may direct you to a rubric in your textbook.
- Your teacher and your class may construct a rubric for a particular assignment together.
- You and your classmates may construct a rubric together.
- You may create your own rubric with criteria you want to evaluate in your work.

How will a rubric help me?

A rubric will help you assess your work on a scale. Scales vary from rubric to rubric but usually range from 6 to 1, 5 to 1, or 4 to 1, with 6, 5, or 4 being the highest score and 1 being the lowest. If someone else is using the rubric to assess your work, the rubric will give your evaluator a clear range within which to place your work. If you are using the rubric yourself, it will help you make improvements to your work.

What are the types of rubrics?

- A holistic rubric has general criteria that can apply to a variety of assignments. See p. R-40 for an example of a holistic rubric.
- An analytic rubric is specific to a particular assignment. The criteria for evaluation address the specific issues important in that assignment. See p. R-39 for examples of analytic rubrics.

Sample Analytic Rubrics

Rubric With a 4-point Scale

The following analytic rubric is an example of a rubric to assess a persuasive essay. It will help you evaluate focus, organization, support/elaboration, and style/convention.

	Focus	Organization	Support/Elaboration	Style/Convention
4	Demonstrates highly effective word choice; clearly focused on task.	Uses clear, consistent organizational strategy.	Provides convincing, well-elaborated reasons to support the position.	Incorporates transitions; includes very few mechanical errors.
3	Demonstrates good word choice; stays focused on persuasive task.	Uses clear organizational strategy with occasional inconsistencies.	Provides two or more moderately elaborated reasons to support the position.	Incorporates some transitions; includes few mechanical errors.
2	Shows some good word choices; minimally stays focused on persuasive task.	Uses inconsistent organizational strategy; presentation is not logical.	Provides several reasons, but few are elaborated; only one elaborated reason.	Incorporates few transitions; includes many mechanical errors.
1	Shows lack of attention to persuasive task.	Demonstrates lack of organizational strategy.	Provides no specific reasons or does not elaborate.	Does not connect ideas; includes many mechanical errors.

Rubric With a 6-point Scale

The following analytic rubric is an example of a rubric to assess a persuasive essay. It will help you evaluate presentation, position, evidence, and arguments.

	Presentation	Position	Evidence	Arguments
6	Essay clearly and effectively addresses an issue with more than one side.	Essay clearly states a supportable position on the issue.	All evidence is logically organized, well presented, and supports the position.	All reader concerns and counterarguments are effectively addressed.
5	Most of essay addresses an issue that has more than one side.	Essay clearly states a position on the issue.	Most evidence is logically organized, well presented, and supports the position.	Most reader concerns and counterarguments are effectively addressed.
4	Essay adequately addresses issue that has more than one side.	Essay adequately states a position on the issue.	Many parts of evidence support the position; some evidence is out of order.	Many reader concerns and counterarguments are adequately addressed.
3	Essay addresses issue with two sides but does not present second side clearly.	Essay states a position on the issue, but the position is difficult to support.	Some evidence supports the position, but some evidence is out of order.	Some reader concerns and counterarguments are addressed.
2	Essay addresses issue with two sides but does not present second side.	Essay states a position on the issue, but the position is not supportable.	Not much evidence supports the position, and what is included is out of order.	A few reader concerns and counterarguments are addressed.
1	Essay does not address issue with more than one side.	Essay does not state a position on the issue.	No evidence supports the position.	No reader concerns or counterarguments are addressed.

Sample Holistic Rubric

Holistic rubrics such as this one are sometimes used to assess writing assignments on standardized tests. Notice that the criteria for evaluation are focus, organization, support, and use of conventions.

Points	Criteria
6 Points	• The writing is strongly focused and shows fresh insight into the writing task. • The writing is marked by a sense of completeness and coherence and is organized with a logical progression of ideas. • A main idea is fully developed, and support is specific and substantial. • A mature command of the language is evident, and the writing may employ characteristic creative writing strategies. • Sentence structure is varied, and writing is free of all but purposefully used fragments. • Virtually no errors in writing conventions appear.
5 Points	• The writing is clearly focused on the task. • The writing is well organized and has a logical progression of ideas, though there may be occasional lapses. • A main idea is well developed and supported with relevant detail. • Sentence structure is varied, and the writing is free of fragments, except when used purposefully. • Writing conventions are followed correctly.
4 Points	• The writing is clearly focused on the task, but extraneous material may intrude at times. • Clear organizational pattern is present, though lapses may occur. • A main idea is adequately supported, but development may be uneven. • Sentence structure is generally fragment free but shows little variation. • Writing conventions are generally followed correctly.
3 Points	• Writing is generally focused on the task, but extraneous material may intrude at times. • An organizational pattern is evident, but writing may lack a logical progression of ideas. • Support for the main idea is generally present but is sometimes illogical. • Sentence structure is generally free of fragments, but there is almost no variation. • The work generally demonstrates a knowledge of writing conventions, with occasional misspellings.
2 Points	• The writing is related to the task but generally lacks focus. • There is little evidence of organizational pattern, and there is little sense of cohesion. • Support for the main idea is generally inadequate, illogical, or absent. • Sentence structure is unvaried, and serious errors may occur. • Errors in writing conventions and spellings are frequent.
1 Point	• The writing may have little connection to the task and is generally unfocused. • There has been little attempt at organization or development. • The paper seems fragmented, with no clear main idea. • Sentence structure is unvaried, and serious errors appear. • Poor word choice and poor command of the language obscure meaning. • Errors in writing conventions and spelling are frequent.
Unscorable	The paper is considered unscorable if: • The response is unrelated to the task or is simply a rewording of the prompt. • The response has been copied from a published work. • The student did not write a response. • The response is illegible. • The words in the response are arranged with no meaning. • There is an insufficient amount of writing to score.

Student Model

Persuasive Writing

This persuasive letter, which would receive a top score according to a persuasive rubric, is a response to the following writing prompt, or assignment:

With the increased use of technology in the workplace, the skills that high-school graduates must possess have changed. Write a letter to your principal advocating new technology courses that could give high-school graduates a competitive edge.

Dear Principal:

I am writing to alert you to an urgent need in our school's curriculum. We need computer graphics courses!

Although you would have to find funds to buy the equipment, I've concluded that setting up this course would well be worth it. By adding this course, you would be adding many high paying career options for students. Computer graphics is a type of art, and businesses all around us involve art in some form. You see computer graphics in commercials, movies, news broadcasts, weather broadcasts, architectural design, and business presentations. Workers with computer graphics skills are well paid because they are in such high demand.

You may argue that the school already has computer science classes. Good point! I'm in a computer science class and it is mainly programming. Once we did have an assignment to design a graphic of a pumpkin. You wouldn't believe how much coding it takes to get a simple, animated drawing. In order to get a really creative image with definite lines, shading, lifelike colors, and texture, you need to use computer graphics software designed especially for that purpose. With software, you can make images that move and talk smoothly and environments with realistic colors and lighting. This is the same graphics software that businesses use for commercials, movies, and brochures. Students should be learning how to use this software.

Most important, computer graphics is a subject area that allows students to express their creativity. Adding a computer graphics course would have a positive effect on students. Course participants would enjoy doing their assignments, so they would earn good grades and turn in creative work. The energy and enthusiasm they would bring to their projects would catch the attention of the community at large. As a result, they would make the school and the principal look good.

As you can see, adding a computer graphics course could be a very profitable idea for you, the students, and the community. You would be ensuring the success of the students who desire an art or computer career. You would be opening hundreds of different career pathways. Wouldn't it be great to know you were the reason for these students' success? Thanks for your time and consideration.

Sincerely,
Dawn Witherspoon

The letter begins with an engaging introduction that clearly states the persuasive focus.

The author effectively counters an opposing argument to increase the persuasive power of her own argument.

A positive argument that is well supported enhances the letter's persuasive appeal.

21st-Century Skills

New technology has created many new ways to communicate. Today, it is easy to contribute information to the Internet and send a variety of messages to friends far and near. You can also share your ideas through photos, illustrations, video, and sound recordings. *21st Century Skills* gives you an overview of some ways you can use today's technology to create, share, and find information. Here are the topics you will find in this section.

✔ Blogs   ✔ Social Networking   ✔ Widgets & Feeds

✔ Multimedia Elements   ✔ Podcasts   ✔ Wikis

BLOGS

A **blog** is a common form of online writing. The word *blog* is a contraction of *Web log*. Most blogs include a series of entries known as *posts*. The posts appear in a single column and are displayed in reverse chronological order. That means that the most recent post is at the top of the page. As you scroll down, you will find earlier posts.

Blogs have become increasingly popular. Researchers estimate that 75,000 new blogs are launched every day. Blog authors are often called *bloggers*. They can use their personal sites to share ideas, songs, videos, photos, and other media. People who read blogs can often post their responses with a comments feature found in each new post.

Because blogs are designed so that they are easy to update, bloggers can post new messages as often as they like, often daily. For some people blogs become a public journal or diary, in which they share their thoughts about daily events.

Types of Blogs

Not all blogs are the same. Many blogs have a single author, but others are group projects. These are some common types of blog:

✔ Personal blogs often have a general focus. Bloggers post their thoughts on any topic they find interesting in their daily lives.

✔ Topical blogs focus on a specific theme, such as movie reviews, political news, class assignments, or health-care opportunities.

Web Safety

Always be aware that information you post on the Internet can be read by everyone with access to that page. Once you post a picture or text, it can be saved on someone else's computer, even if you later remove it.

Using the Internet safely means keeping personal information personal. Never include your address (e-mail or real), last name, or telephone numbers. Avoid mentioning places you can be frequently found. Never give out passwords you use to access other Web sites and do not respond to e-mails from people you do not know.

Anatomy of a Blog

Here are some of the features you can include in a blog.

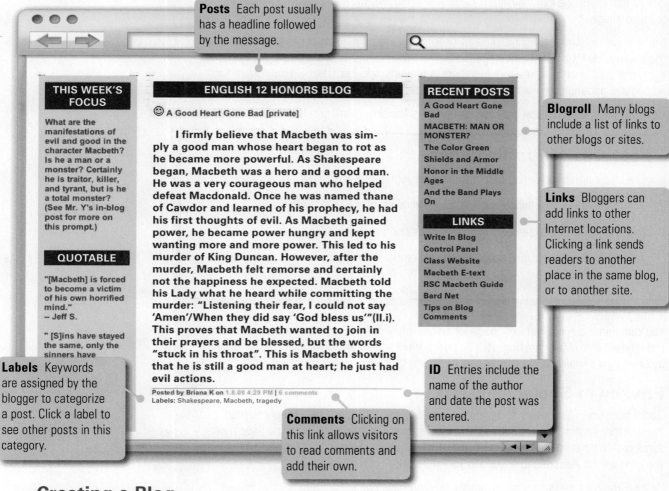

Posts Each post usually has a headline followed by the message.

THIS WEEK'S FOCUS

What are the manifestations of evil and good in the character Macbeth? Is he a man or a monster? Certainly he is traitor, killer, and tyrant, but is he a total monster? (See Mr. Y's in-blog post for more on this prompt.)

QUOTABLE

"[Macbeth] is forced to become a victim of his own horrified mind."
-- Jeff S.

" [S]ins have stayed the same, only the sinners have

ENGLISH 12 HONORS BLOG

☺ A Good Heart Gone Bad [private]

I firmly believe that Macbeth was simply a good man whose heart began to rot as he became more powerful. As Shakespeare began, Macbeth was a hero and a good man. He was a very courageous man who helped defeat Macdonald. Once he was named thane of Cawdor and learned of his prophecy, he had his first thoughts of evil. As Macbeth gained power, he became power hungry and kept wanting more and more power. This led to his murder of King Duncan. However, after the murder, Macbeth felt remorse and certainly not the happiness he expected. Macbeth told his Lady what he heard while committing the murder: "Listening their fear, I could not say 'Amen'/When they did say 'God bless us'"(II.i). This proves that Macbeth wanted to join in their prayers and be blessed, but the words "stuck in his throat". This is Macbeth showing that he is still a good man at heart; he just had evil actions.

Posted by Briana K on 1.8.08 4:29 PM | 6 comments
Labels: Shakespeare, Macbeth, tragedy

RECENT POSTS

A Good Heart Gone Bad
MACBETH: MAN OR MONSTER?
The Color Green
Shields and Armor
Honor in the Middle Ages
And the Band Plays On

LINKS

Write In Blog
Control Panel
Class Website
Macbeth E-text
RSC Macbeth Guide
Bard Net
Tips on Blog Comments

Blogroll Many blogs include a list of links to other blogs or sites.

Links Bloggers can add links to other Internet locations. Clicking a link sends readers to another place in the same blog, or to another site.

Labels Keywords are assigned by the blogger to categorize a post. Click a label to see other posts in this category.

Comments Clicking on this link allows visitors to read comments and add their own.

ID Entries include the name of the author and date the post was entered.

Creating a Blog

Keep these hints and strategies in mind to help you create an interesting and fair blog:

- ✔ Focus each blog entry on a single topic.

- ✔ Vary the length of your posts. Sometimes, all you need is a line or two to share a quick thought. Other posts will be much longer.

- ✔ Choose font colors and styles that can be read easily.

- ✔ Many people scan blogs rather than read them closely. You can make your main ideas pop out by using clear or clever headlines and boldfacing key terms.

- ✔ Give credit to other people's work and ideas. State the names of people whose ideas you are quoting or add a link to take readers to that person's blog or site.

- ✔ If you post comments, try to make them brief and polite.

SOCIAL NETWORKING

Social networking means any interaction between members of an online community. People can exchange many different kinds of information, from text and voice messages to video images.

Many social network communities allow users to create permanent pages that describe themselves. Users create home pages to express themselves, share ideas about their lives, and post messages to other members in the network. Each user is responsible for adding and updating the content on his or her profile page.

Here are some features you are likely to find on a social network profile:

Features of Profile Pages

- A biographical description, including photographs and artwork.

- Lists of favorite things, such as books, movies, music, and fashions.

- Playable media elements such as videos and sound recordings.

- Message boards, or "walls" in which members of the community can exchange messages.

You can create a social network page for an individual or a group, such as a school or special interest club. Many hosting sites do not charge to register, so you can also have fun by creating a page for a pet or a fictional character.

Privacy in Social Networks

Social networks allow users to decide how open their profiles will be. Be sure to read introductory information carefully before you register at a new site. Once you have a personal profile page, monitor your privacy settings regularly. Remember that any information you post will be available to anyone in your network.

Users often post messages anonymously or using false names, or *pseudonyms*. People can also post using someone else's name. Judge all information on the net critically. Do not assume that you know who posted some information simply because you recognize the name of the post author. The rapid speed of communication on the Internet can make it easy to jump to conclusions—be careful to avoid this trap.

Tips for Sending Effective Messages

Technology makes it easy to share ideas quickly, but writing for the Internet poses some special challenges, as well. The writing style for blogs and social networks is often very conversational. In blog posts and comments, instant messages, and e-mails, writers often express themselves very quickly, using relaxed language, short sentences, and abbreviations. However, in a conversation, we get a lot of information from a speaker's tone of voice and body language. On the Internet, those clues are missing. As a result, Internet writers often use italics or bracketed labels to indicate emotions. Another alternative is using emoticons—strings of characters that give visual clues to indicate emotion:

:-) smile (happy)	:-(frown (unhappy)	;-) wink (light sarcasm)

Use these strategies to communicate effectively when using technology:

✔ Reread your messages. Before you click *Send,* read your message through and make sure that your tone will be clear to the reader.

✔ Do not jump to conclusions—ask for clarification first. Make sure you really understand what someone is saying before you respond.

✔ Use abbreviations your reader will understand.

WIDGETS & FEEDS

A **widget** is a small application that performs a specific task. You might find widgets that give weather predictions, offer dictionary definitions or translations, provide entertainment such as games, or present a daily word, photograph, or quotation.

A **feed** is a special kind of widget. It displays headlines taken from the latest content on a specific media source. Clicking on the headline will take you to the full article.

Many social network communities and other Web sites allow you to personalize your home page by adding widgets and feeds.

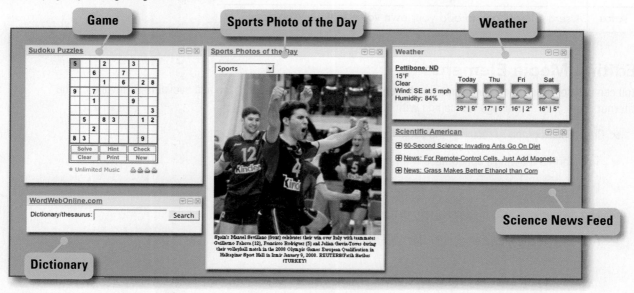

MULTIMEDIA ELEMENTS

One of the great advantages of communicating on the Internet is that you are not limited to using text only. When you create a Web profile or blog, you can share your ideas using a wide variety of media. In addition to widgets and feeds (see page R45), these media elements can make your Internet communication more entertaining and useful.

Graphics	
Photographs	You can post photos taken by digital cameras.
Illustrations	Artwork can be created using computer software. You can also use a scanner to post a digital image of a drawing or sketch.
Charts, Graphs, and Maps	Charts and graphs can make statistical information clear. Use spreadsheet software to create these elements. Use Internet sites to find maps of specific places.

Video	
Live Action	Digital video can be recorded by a camera or recorded from another media source.
Animation	Animated videos can also be created using software.

Sound	
Music	Many social network communities make it easy to share your favorite music with people who visit your page.
Voice	Use a microphone to add your own voice to your Web page.

Editing Media Elements

You can use software to customize media elements. Open source software is free and available to anyone on the Internet. Here are some things you can do with software:

✔ Crop a photograph to focus on the subject or brighten an image that is too dark.

✔ Transform a drawing's appearance from flat to three-dimensional.

✔ Insert a "You Are Here" arrow on a map.

✔ Edit a video or sound file to shorten its running time.

✔ Add background music or sound effects to a video.

PODCASTS

A **podcast** is a digital audio or video recording of a program that is made available on the Internet. Users can replay the podcast on a computer, or download it and replay it on a personal audio player. You might think of podcasts as radio or television programs that you create yourself. They can be embedded on a Web site or fed to a Web page through a podcast widget.

Creating an Effective Podcast

To make a podcast, you will need a recording device, such as a microphone or digital video camera, as well as editing software. Open source editing software is widely available and free of charge. Most audio podcasts are converted into the MP3 format. Here are some tips for creating a podcast that is clear and entertaining:

- ✔ Listen to several podcasts by different authors to get a feeling for the medium. Make a list of features and styles you like and also those you want to avoid.

- ✔ Test your microphone to find the best recording distance. Stand close enough to the microphone so that your voice sounds full, but not so close that you create an echo.

- ✔ Create an outline that shows your estimated timing for each element.

- ✔ Be prepared before you record. Rehearse, but do not create a script. Podcasts are best when they have a natural, easy flow.

- ✔ Talk directly to your listeners. Slow down enough so they can understand you.

- ✔ Use software to edit your podcast before publishing it. You can edit out mistakes or add additional elements.

WIKIS

A **wiki** is a collaborative Web site that lets visitors create, add, remove, and edit content. The term comes from the Hawaiian phrase *wiki wiki,* which means "quick." Web users at a wiki are both the readers and the writers of the site. Some wikis are open to contributions from anyone. Others require visitors to register before they can edit the content.

All of the text in these collaborative Web sites was written by people who use the site. Articles are constantly changing, as visitors find and correct errors and improve texts.

Wikis have both advantages and disadvantages as sources of information. They are valuable open forums for the exchange of ideas. The unique collaborative writing process allows entries to change over time. However, entries can also be modified incorrectly. Careless or malicious users can delete good content and add inappropriate or inaccurate information.

You can change the information on a wiki, but be sure your information is correct and clear before you add it. Wikis keep track of all changes, so your work will be recorded and can be evaluated by other users.

Rules of Debate

A **debate** is a structured contest based on a formal discussion of opinion. In essence, it is a battle of intellect and verbal skill. The goal is mastering the art of persuasion. Who can best express, argue, and support opinions on a given topic? Who can best refute an argument, showing that the opponent's points are invalid? Which team, in the end, can convince the judges that their argument is the most sound?

Teams

A **formal debate** is conducted with two teams—an Affirmation team and a Negative team. As the names suggest, the Affirmation team is responsible for presenting the "pro" side of an issue, while the Negative team presents the "con" side of the issue. Each team has a main purpose and will offer both constructive and rebuttal speeches, practicing the art of persuasion and debate.

Affirmation team The Affirmation team as a whole carries the burden of proof for the debate. They must prove there is a problem. To do so, they need to cite credible sources, include relevant details, and present and support valid points. Each team member has a specific job. The first speaker has the most responsibility. He or she must

- define the issue or problem

- introduce the team line—a one-line summary of the team's position on the issue

- identify the point of the argument each speaker will discuss

The remaining team members have the job of presenting and supporting the main points of the argument.

Negative team Though the Negative team does not carry the burden of proof, the team must show that there is no problem or that the Affirmation team's solutions are invalid. Though their purpose is to rebut an argument, the rebuttal technique calls for a formation of their own argument. They must argue against the Affirmation team. To construct their argument, they must use—like the Affirmation team—credible sources, relevant details, and valid points. They should incorporate any available statistics, pertinent facts, or applicable testimonies to bolster their argument. Even though the first speaker of the Affirmation team lays out each point of the argument, the Negative team speakers cannot address points that have not been thoroughly discussed by an Affirmation team member.

Structure

Just like most other contests, debates have a set structure. Debates are divided into halves. The first half begins with the constructive speeches from both teams, which last ten minutes each.

After the first half, there is a short intermission. Then, the second half begins with the Negative team. This half is reserved for the rebuttal speeches, which last five minutes each and include rebuttals and refutations. This is each team's chance to rebuild their arguments that the other team broke down (rebuttal), and put forth evidence to show the other team is wrong (refutation). Although the Negative team begins the argument in the second half, every debate begins and ends with the Affirmation team.

Structure of Debate

1st Half: Constructive Speeches (10 minutes each)	2nd Half: Rebuttal Speeches (5 minutes each)
1st Affirmative Team Speaker	1st Negative Team Speaker
1st Negative Team Speaker	1st Affirmative Team Speaker
2nd Affirmative Team Speaker	2nd Negative Team Speaker
2nd Negative Team Speaker	2nd Affirmative Team Speaker
3rd Affirmative Team Speaker	3rd Negative Team Speaker
3rd Negative Team Speaker	3rd Affirmative Team Speaker

Speeches—Content, Organization, and Delivery

Debate speeches are the result of practicing the art of persuasion. To be effective, speakers must include pertinent content, use clear and logical organization, and have a powerful delivery. These combined elements make a strong speech.

Content Debates often focus on concrete issues that can be proved or disproved. The basis for a debate speech is its content. The Affirmation team should first determine their position. They should be sure to include any facts and/or statistics that concretely support the argument. Speech writers should cite specific instances and occurrences that solidify their position. Writers might also include testimonies or ideas from professionals. Finally, the Affirmation team needs to propose possible solutions to the problem or issue and examine the costs and effects of those solutions.

Though the Negative team does not have to state a position—their position is automatically the opposing position—they still need to include facts, statistics, testimony, and descriptions of specific instances or occurrences to make their counterpoints. They need to analyze the Affirmation team's proposed solutions and explain why they will not work. In essence, the Negative team must construct an argument around the Affirmation team's argument.

Organization Debate speeches are organized like other speeches and essays. They should have an introduction, transitions, body, and conclusion. The speeches should have clear main points and supporting details for those points. Because a debate is a structured discussion, there will be a specific order of points and the speakers who present them must be identified. Speakers can use note cards to help them stick to the planned organization, but they should only use brief notes, never reading directly from the cards.

Delivery The manner in which a speech is delivered can make or break the argument. The impression the speaker makes on the audience, including the judges, is key. To make a good impression, the speaker must present the material with confidence. He or she can portray confidence by forming a connection with the audience through eye contact, glancing away only briefly to consult notes. A speaker should focus on his or her voice, varying the tone, volume, and pace appropriately. Body movements should not include fidgeting or nervous movement. They should only be used if they are deliberate and help express or underscore a point. Finally, speakers should be concise, focusing on vivid and clear word choice and using words that emphasize the point.

Scoring

Debates are scored much like other contests. Each side is judged on the content and delivery of their speeches. Judges contemplate different elements of content and delivery in order to determine the number of points to give each team. They might ask themselves the questions in the chart below in order to determine the score.

Finally, judges look at the observation of debate etiquette. Speakers are expected to be mature and respectful of their opponents. Speakers should never attack an opponent, but instead should attack the argument. Judges will deduct points for personal attacks.

Scoring Criteria

Content	Delivery
Were arguments convincing?	Were speakers able to speak extemporaneously?
Were arguments supported with credible, valid and relevant reasons?	Were body movements deliberate and effective?
Were refutations and rebuttals effective?	Did speakers make a connection with the audience?
Were speakers confident and knowledgeable?	Did speakers stay within their time limits?

Grammar, Usage, and Mechanics Handbook

Parts of Speech

Nouns A **noun** is the name of a person, place, or thing. A **common noun** names any one of a class of people, places, or things. A **proper noun** names a specific person, place, or thing.

Common Noun	Proper Noun
city	Washington, D.C.

Pronouns A **pronoun** is a word that stands for a noun or for a word that takes the place of a noun.

A **personal pronoun** refers to (1) the person speaking, (2) the person spoken to, or (3) the person, place, or thing spoken about.

	Singular	Plural
First Person	I, me, my, mine	we, us, our, ours
Second Person	you, your, yours	you, your, yours
Third Person	he, him, his, she, her, hers, it, its	they, them, their, theirs

Antecedents are nouns (or words that take the place of nouns) for which pronouns stand. In the following sentence, the pronoun *it* stands for the noun *Florida.*

Florida is popular because it has a warm climate.

A **reflexive pronoun** ends in *-self* or *-selves* and adds information to a sentence by pointing back to a noun or a pronoun earlier in the sentence.

"If you were honest folk *yourselves* you wouldn't let a thief go free."

— Leo Tolstoy, p. 338

An **intensive pronoun** ends in *-self* or *-selves* and simply adds emphasis to a noun or a pronoun in the same sentence.

After a time, I *myself* was allowed to go into the dead houses and search for metal.

— Stephen Vincent Benét, p. 314

A **demonstrative pronoun** directs attention to a specific person, place, or thing.

this   these   that   those

These are the juiciest pears I have ever tasted.

A **relative pronoun** begins a subordinate clause and connects it to another idea in the sentence.

The poet *who* wrote "Fear" is Gabriela Mistral.

An **interrogative pronoun** is used to begin a question. The five interrogative pronouns are *what, which, who, whom,* and *whose.*

An **indefinite pronoun** refers to a person, place, or thing, often without specifying which one.

all   anyone   each   everyone   few   one   someone

And then, for a moment, *all* is still, . . .

— Edgar Allan Poe, p. 372

Verbs A **verb** is a word that expresses time while showing an action, a condition, or the fact that something exists.

An **action verb** indicates the action of someone or something.

An action verb is **transitive** if it directs action toward someone or something named in the same sentence.

He *dusted* his hands, muttering.

— Jack Finney, p. 118

An action verb is **intransitive** if it does not direct action toward something or someone named in the same sentence.

I *smiled* and looked up at the crew . . .

— Lynne Cox, p. 62

A **linking verb** is a verb that connects the subject of a sentence with a noun or a pronoun that renames or describes the subject. The noun, pronoun, or phrase acting as a noun that renames the subject is called a **predicate nominative.**

Romance at short notice was her specialty.

— Saki, p. 195

A **helping verb** is a verb that can be added to another verb to make a verb phrase.

Nor *did* I suspect that these experiences could be part of a novel's meaning.

Adjectives An **adjective** describes a noun or a pronoun or gives a noun or a pronoun a more specific meaning. Adjectives answer these questions:

What kind?	*blue* lamp, *large* tree
Which one?	*this* table, *those* books
How many?	*five* stars, *several* buses
How much?	*less* money, *enough* votes

The articles *the, a,* and *an* are adjectives. *An* is used before a word beginning with a vowel sound.

A noun may sometimes be used as an adjective.

diamond necklace   *summer* vacation

Adverbs An **adverb** modifies a verb, an adjective, or another adverb. Adverbs answer the questions *where, when, in what way,* or *to what extent.*

He could stand *there.* (modifies verb *stand*)

He was *blissfully* happy. (modifies adjective *happy*)

It ended *too* soon. (modifies adverb *soon*)

Prepositions A **preposition** relates a noun or a pronoun that appears with it to another word in the sentence.

before the end   *near* me   *inside* our fence

Conjunctions A **conjunction** connects words or groups of words.

A **coordinating conjunction** connects similar kinds or groups of words.

    mother *and* father   simple *yet* stylish

Correlative conjunctions are used in pairs to connect similar words or groups of words.

    both Sue *and* Meg   *neither* he *nor* I

A **subordinating conjunction** connects two complete ideas by placing one idea below the other in rank or importance.

    You would know him *if* you saw him.

Sentences, Phrases, and Clauses

Sentences A **sentence** is a group of words with a subject and a predicate. Together, these parts express a complete thought.

A **fragment** is a group of words that does not express a complete thought.

The Four Structures of Sentences There are two kinds of clauses: independent and subordinate. An independent clause can stand by itself as a sentence; a subordinate clause cannot. These can be used to form four basic sentence structures: *simple, compound, complex,* and *compound-complex.*

A **simple sentence** consists of a single independent clause.

A **compound sentence** consists of two or more independent clauses.

The clauses in a compound sentence can be joined by a comma and a coordinating conjunction *(and, but, for, nor, or, so, yet)* or by a semicolon (;).

A **complex sentence** consists of one independent clause and one or more subordinate clauses.

The independent clause in a complex sentence is often called the *main clause* to distinguish it from the subordinate clause or clauses.

A **compound-complex sentence** consists of two or more independent clauses and one or more subordinate clauses.

Phrases A **phrase** is a group of words, without a subject and a verb, that functions in a sentence as one part of speech.

A **prepositional phrase** is a group of words that includes a preposition and a noun or a pronoun that is the object of the preposition.

    outside my window   below the counter

An **adjective phrase** is a prepositional phrase that modifies a noun or a pronoun by telling *what kind* or *which one.*

    The wooden gates *of that lane* stood open.

An **adverb phrase** is a prepositional phrase that modifies a verb, an adjective, or an adverb by pointing out *where, when, in what way,* or *to what extent.*

    On a sudden impulse, he got to his feet. . . .

                — Jack Finney, p. 118

An **appositive phrase** is a noun or a pronoun with modifiers, placed next to a noun or a pronoun to identify it or add information and details.

    M. Morissot, watchmaker by trade but local militiaman for the time being, stopped short. . . .

          — Guy de Maupassant, p. 1233

A **participial phrase** is a participle with its modifiers or complements. The entire phrase acts as an adjective.

    Choosing such a tide, I hoped for a glimpse of the pool.

              — Rachel Carson, p. 156

A **gerund** is a form of a verb that is used as a noun. It ends in *-ing.* A **gerund phrase** is a gerund with modifiers or a complement, all acting together as a noun.

    . . . *moving along the ledge* was quite as easy as he had thought it would be.

              — Jack Finney, p. 118

An **infinitive** is the form of a verb using to. It acts as a noun, adjective, or adverb. An **infinitive phrase** is an infinitive with modifiers, complements, or a subject, all acting together as a single part of speech.

    To be dead, and never again behold my city!

              —Dreams, p. 676

Clauses A **clause** is a group of words with a subject and a verb.

An **independent clause** has a subject and a verb and can stand by itself as a complete sentence.

A **subordinate clause** has a subject and a verb but cannot stand by itself as a complete sentence; it can only be part of a sentence.

An **adjective clause** is a subordinate clause that modifies a noun or a pronoun by telling *what kind* or *which one.*

    The people *who read the book* loved it.

An **adverb clause** modifies a verb, an adjective, an adverb, or a verbal by telling *where, when, in what way, to what extent, under what condition,* or *why.*

    They read it as soon *as it was published.*

A **noun clause** is a subordinate clause that acts as a noun.

    Whoever reads it is overcome with joy.

Parallelism **Parallelism** is the placement of equal ideas in words, phrases, or clauses of similar type.

Parallel Words: The camp has excellent facilities for *riding*, *hiking*, and *swimming*.

Parallel Phrases: Jennings had gone to the country *to rest*, *to think*, and *to catch a few fish*.

Parallel Clauses: A news story should tell *what happened*, *when it happened*, and *who was involved*.

Verb Usage

The Four Principal Parts of Verbs A verb has four **principal parts:** the *present*, the *present participle*, the *past*, and the *past participle*.

Regular verbs form the past and past participle by adding *-ed* to the present form.

Present: walk
Present Participle: (am) walking
Past: walked
Past Participle: (have) walked

The past and past participle of an **irregular verb** are not formed by adding *-ed* or *-d* to the present form. Irregular verbs form the past and past participle by changing form. Whenever you are in doubt about the principal parts of an irregular verb, use a dictionary to check them.

Present: go
Present Participle: (am) going
Past: went
Past Participle: (have) gone

Pronoun Usage

Pronoun Case The **case** of a pronoun is the form it takes to show its use in a sentence. There are three pronoun cases: *nominative*, *objective*, and *possessive*.

The **nominative case** is used to rename the subject of the sentence. The nominative case pronouns are *I, you, he, she, it, we, you, they*.

As the subject: *She* is brave
Renaming the subject: The leader is *she*.

The **objective case** is used as the direct object, indirect object, or object of the preposition. The objective case pronouns are *me, you, him, her, it, us, you, them*.

As a direct object: Tom called *me*.
As an indirect object: My friend gave *me* advice.
As an object of preposition: The coach gave pointers to *me*.

The **possessive case** is used to show ownership. The possessive pronouns are *my, your, his, her, its, our, their, mine, yours, his, hers, its, ours, theirs*.

Agreement

Subject and Verb Agreement To make a subject and verb agree, make sure that both are singular or both are plural.

Many *storms are* the cause of beach erosion.

In the case of a plural and a singular subject joined by *or* or *nor*, choose the form of the verb that agrees with the closer of the two.

Either the *cats* or the *dog is* hungry.
Neither *Angie* nor *her sisters were* present.

Pronoun-Antecedent Agreement Pronouns must agree with their antecedents in number and gender. Use singular pronouns with singular antecedents and plural pronouns with plural antecedents. Many errors in pronoun-antecedent agreement occur when a plural pronoun is used to refer to a singular antecedent for which the gender is not specified.

Incorrect: Everyone did their best.
Correct: Everyone did his or her best.

The following indefinite pronouns are singular: *anybody, anyone, each, either, everybody, everyone, neither, nobody, no one, one, somebody, someone*.

The following indefinite pronouns are plural: *both, few, many, several*.

The following indefinite pronouns may be either singular or plural: *all, any, most, none, some*. Treat these pronouns as singular when the antecedent is singular.

All of the <u>gold</u> is gone, and we do not know who took *it*.

Treat these pronouns as plural when the antecedent is plural.

Most of my <u>friends</u> are going, and *they* will have a good time.

Using Modifiers

Degrees of Comparison Most adjectives and adverbs have three different forms to show degrees of comparison—the *positive*, the *comparative*, the *superlative*.

Use *-er* or *more* to form the comparative degree and *-est* or *most* to form the superlative degree of most one- and two-syllable modifiers.

Use *more* and *most* to form the comparative and superlative degrees of all modifiers with three or more syllables.

The irregular comparative and superlative forms of certain adjectives and adverbs must be memorized.

The form of some irregular modifiers differs only in the positive degree. The modifiers *bad, badly,* and *ill,* for example, all have the same basic form in the comparative and superlative degrees (*worse, worst*).

Capitalization and Punctuation

Capitalization Capitalize the first word of a sentence and also the first word in a quotation if the quotation is a complete sentence.

> "No matter," he concluded, "I'll go toward the
> rising sun." — Leo Tolstoy, p. 338

Capitalize all proper nouns and adjectives.

> W. W. Jacobs   Flanders Fields   African writers

Capitalize a person's title when it is followed by the person's name or when it is used in direct address.

> Reverend Tallboys   Mrs. Prothero   "Hello, Major."

Capitalize titles showing family relationships when they refer to a specific person and are used with a name or as a name.

> Aunt Mae   Let's ask Grandmother.   *but*   his father

Capitalize the first word and all other key words in the titles of books, periodicals, poems, stories, plays, paintings, and other works of art.

> *Lord of the Flies*   "Spring and All"

End Marks Use a **period** to end a declarative sentence, an imperative sentence, an indirect question, and most abbreviations.

> The class will meet at noon.

Use a **question mark** to end a direct question, an incomplete question, or a statement that is intended as a question.

> Did you prepare your assignment?

Use an **exclamation mark** after a statement showing strong emotion, an urgent imperative sentence, or an interjection expressing strong emotion.

> Wait until you hear the news!

Commas Use a **comma** before the coordinating conjunction to separate two independent clauses in a compound sentence.

> His arms had begun to tremble from the steady strain
> of clinging to this narrow perch, and he did not know
> what to do now. . . . — Jack Finney, p. 118

Use commas to separate three or more words, phrases, or clauses in a series.

> . . . he produced about fifteen hundred *drawings,*
> *prints, pastels,* and *oil paintings* with ballet themes.
> — Richard Mühlberger, p. 568

Use commas to separate adjectives of equal rank. Do not use commas to separate adjectives that must stay in a specific order.

> With *pink, dimpled* knees, Henri, not yet a year old,
> sprawls on the lap of his nurse. . . .
> [In Degas's painting], the *creamy white* tones of the
> passengers stand out.
> — Richard Mühlberger, p. 568

Use a comma after an introductory word, phrase, or clause.

> When Marian Anderson again returned to America,
> she was a seasoned artist.
> — Langston Hughes, p. 98

Use commas to set off parenthetical and nonessential expressions.

> Now, *yes, now,* it was about to set!
> — Leo Tolstoy, p. 338

Use commas with places, dates, and titles.

> Poe was raised in Richmond, Virginia.
> August 4, 2026
> Alfred, Lord Tennyson

Use a comma to indicate the words left out of an elliptical sentence, to set off a direct quotation, and to prevent a sentence from being misunderstood.

> Vincent Canby writes for *The New York Times;*
> Roger Ebert, for the *Chicago Sun Times.*

Semicolons Use a **semicolon** to join independent clauses that are not already joined by a conjunction.

> They could find no buffalo; they had to hang an old
> hide from the sacred tree.
> — N. Scott Momaday, p. 595

Use a semicolon to join independent clauses separated by either a conjunctive adverb or a transitional expression.

> James Thurber wrote many books; moreover, he was
> a cartoonist and a journalist.

Use semicolons to avoid confusion when independent clauses or items in a series already contain commas.

> Thurber is remembered for his character Walter
> Mitty; for his cartoons, many of which illustrated his
> books; and for his terrifically funny essays.

Colons Use a **colon** in order to introduce a list of items following an independent clause.

> The authors we are reading include a number of
> poets: Robert Frost, Octavio Paz, and Emily Dickinson.

Use a colon to introduce a formal quotation.

> The next day Howard Taubman wrote enthusiastically
> in The New York Times: "Marian Anderson has
> returned to her native land one of the great singers
> of our time. . . ."
> — Langston Hughes, p. 98

Quotation Marks A **direct quotation** represents a person's exact speech or thoughts and is enclosed in quotation marks.

> "Clara, my mind is made up."

An **indirect quotation** is a restatement or paraphrase of what a person said or thought and does not require quotation marks.

> The cops suggested that it might be a good idea to tie the dog up, but mother said that it mortified him to be tied up. . . .   — James Thurber, p. 525

Always place a comma or a period inside the final quotation mark.

> "Eh, you're a stranger," she said. "I thought so."
> — Josephina Niggli, p. 272

Place a question mark or an exclamation mark inside the final quotation mark if the end mark is part of the quotation; if it is not part of the quotation, place it outside the final quotation mark.

> He asked, "Which poetry do you like best?"
> Have you ever read the poem "Africa"?

Use single quotation marks for a quotation within a quotation.

Use quotation marks around the titles of short written works, episodes in a series, songs, and titles of works mentioned as parts of a collection.

> "Making a Fist"   "These Are Days"

Underline or italicize titles of longer works, such as plays, movies, or novels.

Dashes   Use **dashes** to indicate an abrupt change of thought, a dramatic interrupting idea, or a summary statement.

> It made her so mad to see Muggs lying there, oblivious of the mice—they came running up to her—that she slapped him and he slashed at her, but didn't make it.   — James Thurber, p. 525

Parentheses   Use **parentheses** to set off asides and explanations only when the material is not essential or when it consists of one or more sentences.

> When I finished (What a lot of facts I found out!), I turned in my report.

Hyphens   Use a **hyphen** with certain numbers, after certain prefixes, with two or more words used as one word, and with a compound modifier coming before a noun.

> fifty-two   greenish-blue water

Apostrophes   Add an **apostrophe** and s to show the possessive case of most singular nouns.

> Prospero's castle   the playwright's craft

Add an apostrophe to show the possessive case of plural nouns ending in -s and -es.

> the sailors' ships   the babies' mothers

Add an apostrophe and -s to show the possessive case of plural nouns that do not end in -s or -es.

> the children's games   the people's friend

Use an apostrophe in a contraction to indicate the position of the missing letter or letters.

> I *didn't* love any one of you more than any other.
> — William Melvin Kelley, p. 242

Glossary of Common Usage

among, between: *Among* is usually used with three or more items. *Between* is generally used with only two items.

> *Among* the poems we read this year, Eve Merriam's "Metaphor" was my favorite.
> "Like the Sun" tells of the conflict *between* telling the truth and telling white lies.

around: In formal writing, *around* should not be used to mean *approximately* or *about*. These usages are allowable, however, in informal writing or in colloquial dialogue.

> *Romeo and Juliet* had its first performance in *approximately* 1595.
> Shakespeare was *about* thirty when he wrote it.

as, because, like, as to: The word *as* has several meanings and can function as several parts of speech. To avoid confusion, use *because* rather than *as* when you want to indicate cause and effect.

> *Because* Cyril was interested in African American poetry, he wrote his report on Langston Hughes.

Do not use the preposition *like* to introduce a clause that requires the conjunction *as*.

> James Thurber conversed as he wrote—wittily.

The use of *as to* for *about* is awkward and should be avoided.

> Rosa has a theory *about* Edgar Allan Poe's style.

beside, besides: *Beside* is a preposition meaning "at the side of" or "close to." Do not confuse *beside* with *besides*, which means "in addition to." *Besides* can be a preposition or an adverb.

> As the men cross the lawn and approach the open window, a brown spaniel trots *beside* them.
> There are many other Indian oral epics *besides* the *Ramayana*.

can, may: The verb *can* generally refers to the ability to do something. The verb *may* generally refers to permission to do something.

> Dylan Thomas describes his childhood Christmases so vividly that most readers can visualize the scenes.
> Creon's edict states that no one may bury Polyneices.

different from, different than: The preferred usage is *different from*.

> The structure and rhyme scheme of a Shakespearean sonnet are *different from* the organization of a Petrarchan sonnet.

farther, further: Use *farther* when you refer to distance. Use *further* when you mean "to a greater degree" or "additional."

> The *farther* the ants travel, the more ominous and destructive they seem.

> The storm in Act I of *The Tragedy of Julius Caesar further* hints at the ominous deeds to come.

fewer, less: Use *fewer* for things that can be counted. Use *less* for amounts or quantities that cannot be counted.

> Poetry often uses *fewer* words than prose to convey ideas and images.

> It takes *less* time to perform a Greek tragedy than to perform a Shakespearean play.

good, well: Use the adjective *good* after linking verbs such as *feel, look, smell, taste,* and *seem.* Use *well* whenever you need an adverb or as an adjective describing health.

> Caesar remarks that Cassius does not look *good*; on the contrary, his appearance is "lean."

> Twain wrote especially *well* when he described eccentric characters.

hopefully: Do not attach this adverb to a sentence loosely, as in "*Hopefully*, the rain will stop by noon." Rewrite the sentence so that *hopefully* modifies a specific verb. Other possible ways of revising such sentences include using the adjective *hopeful* or a phrase such as *everyone hopes that.*

> Dr. Martin Luther King, Jr., wrote and spoke *hopefully* about his dream of racial harmony.

> Mr. White was *hopeful* that the monkey's paw would bring him good fortune.

> *Everyone hopes that* the class production of *Antigone* will be a big success.

its, it's: Do not confuse the possessive pronoun its with the contraction *it's*, used in place of "it is" or "it has."

> In *its* very first lines, "The Stolen Child" establishes an eerie mood.

> In "The Street of the Cañon," Pepe Gonzalez knows that *it's* dangerous to attend the party.

just, only: When you use *just* as an adverb meaning "no more than," be sure you place it directly before the word it logically modifies. Likewise, be sure you place *only* before the word it logically modifies.

> *Just* one wish changed the Whites' lives forever.

> A short story can usually develop *only* a few characters, whereas a novel can include many.

kind of, sort of: In formal writing, you should not use these colloquial expressions. Instead, use a word such as *rather* or *somewhat.*

> Poe portrays Prince Prospero as *rather* arrogant.

> The tone of the biography is *somewhat* harsh.

lay, lie: Do not confuse these verbs. *Lay* is a transitive verb meaning "to set or put something down." Its principal parts are *lay, laying, laid, laid. Lie* is an intransitive verb meaning "to recline." Its principal parts are *lie, lying, lay, lain.*

> They laid the monkey's paw on the table for a while before anyone dared to pick it up.

> La Belle Dame sans Merci enchants the knight as he *lies* in her "elfin grot."

leave, let: Be careful not to confuse these verbs. *Leave* means "to go away" or "to allow to remain." *Let* means "to permit."

> Threatening Antigone not to disobey his orders, Creon angrily *leaves* the stage.

> Creon did not want to *let* Antigone bury her brother.

raise, rise: *Raise* is a transitive verb that usually takes a direct object. *Rise* is an intransitive verb and never takes a direct object.

> In his speech, Antony unexpectedly *raises* the subject of Caesar's will.

> When the Cabuliwallah comes to call, Mini *rises* from her chair and runs to greet him.

set, sit: Do not confuse these verbs. *Set* is a transitive verb meaning "to put (something) in a certain place." Its principal parts are *set, setting, set, set. Sit* is an intransitive verb meaning "to be seated." Its principal parts are *sit, sitting, sat, sat.*

> Antigone's conduct *sets* a high standard for us.

> Jerry's mother *sits* in her beach chair while Jerry swims in the ocean.

so, so that: Be careful not to use the coordinating conjunction *so* when your context requires *so that. So* means "accordingly" or "with the result that" and expresses a cause-and-effect relationship. *So that* expresses purpose—what someone intends to achieve.

> He wanted to do well on the test, *so* he read *The Tragedy of Julius Caesar* again.

> Antony uses eloquent rhetoric to stir up the people *so that* they will rebel.

than, then: The conjunction *than* is used to connect the two parts of a comparison. Do not confuse *than* with the adverb *then*, which usually refers to time.

> I enjoyed "The Marginal World" more *than* "Flood."

Marian Anderson gave a triumphant singing recital in New York that evening, and she *then* embarked on a coast-to-coast American tour.

that, which, who: Use the relative pronoun *that* to refer to things. Use *which* only for things and *who* only for people.

The poem *that* Cheryl liked the most was "The street."

Haiku, *which* consists of only seventeen syllables, is often built around one or two vivid images.

The assassin *who* strikes Caesar first is Casca.

unique: Because *unique* means "one of a kind," you should not use it carelessly to mean "interesting" or "unusual." Avoid such illogical expressions as "most unique," "very unique," and "extremely unique."

Emily Dickinson's bold experiments with form make her *unique* in the history of nineteenth-century American poetry.

when, where: Do not directly follow a linking verb with *when* or *where*. Be careful not to use *where* when your context requires *that*.

Faulty: The exposition is *when* an author provides the reader with important background information.

Revised: In the exposition, an author provides the reader with important background information.

Faulty: Madras, India, is *where* R. K. Narayan was born.

Revised: R. K. Narayan was born in Madras, India.

Faulty: We read *where* the prizes were worth hundreds of dollars.

Revised: We read *that* the prizes were worth hundreds of dollars.

Index of Skills

Boldface numbers indicate pages where terms are defined.

Literary Analysis

Action, rising/falling, **29**, 43, 55, 109, 887

Actions and events
drama, **796**, 798, 802, 804

Acts, **792**, 887

Address, **445**

Advertisement, R31

Allegory, **369**, 381, 397, **R15**

Alliteration, **629, 733**, 741, 747, **R15**

Allusion, **R15**

Analogy, **20**, 447, **715, R15**

Analytic essay, **557**, 561, 565, 569, 573

Analytic response to literature, **768**

Anapest, **628**

Ancient Greek theater, 884

Anecdote, **20, R15**
article, 23

Antagonist, **224, 794**, 1048, **R15**
drama, **794, 811**, 815, 816, 820, 822, 826, 827, 830, 831, 833

Anticlimax, **R15**

Archetypal elements, **1048**
oral tradition, 1052

Archetypal narrative patterns, **1128**, 1131, 1132, 1134, 1136, 1139, 1140, 1143, 1144, 1145

Archetype, **1048, 1052, R15**

Arguments, lxviii, lxix, 182, 268, 295, 408, 512, 532, 534, 604, 606, 608, 614, 616, 617, 618, 620
elements, lxiv
persuasive essay, **445**
rhetorical devices and persuasive techniques, lxvi
types of, R31

Aside, **793, 939**, 963, **R15**

Assonance, **629, 733**, 741, 747, **R15**

Author's point of view/perspective, **59**, 63, 64, 65, 67, 69, 71, 72, 74, 75, 80, 85, **444**, 448, 1049, 1050, 1052

Author's purpose, **7, 444**
comparison, **584**, 587, 588, 589, 590, 593, 594, 597, 598, 600, 601, 602, 603
nonfiction, **7, 153**, 158, 160, 164, 165, 168, 171, 176, 177, **444**, 1243
style and, **96**

Autobiographical essay, **R15**

Autobiographical narrative, **108**, R32

Autobiography, **5, R15**

Ballad, **631, R15**

Bandwagon/anti-bandwagon approach, **lxvi**

Bibliography, **1026**

Biographies, **5, R15**

Blank verse, **915**, 917, 919, 924, 927, 935, 937, **R15**

Catastrophe, **887**

Cause-and-effect essay, **200**, 202, R31

Cause-and-effect organization, **446, 578**

Central idea, 4, **7, 444**, 448
essay, 22, 455, 459

Character development, **228, 239**, 253, 265

Characterization, 4, 226, 794, **795, R16**
direct/indirect, **226**
short story, **226**, 228, **239**, 244, 245, 248, 251, 253, 258, 260, 262, 264, 265

Characters, **8, 226**, 1052, **R15**
complex, 794, 795
drama, 792, 794, 796, 798, 799, 800, 801, 804, 805, **887**
fiction, 4, 6, **8**
motivation, **226, 228**
mythical, **1063**, 1073, 1087
novel, 11, 12, 13, 14, 15, 16, 17
oral tradition, 1050, 1052, 1053, 1054, 1058
round/flat/static/dynamic, **794**
short story, 224, **226, 228**, 230, 233, 234, 236, **239**, 253, 265
types, 226, 228

Character's motivation, 226, 228, 792, **794, 1014**, 1017, 1019
short story, 230, 235

Chorus, **793**

Chorus, Greek, 810A

Chronological organization, 109, 202, 227, 446, **578, 710**, 880, **1023**

Claim (assertion), lxiv

Climax, 224, **225, R16**
drama, 792, **793, 794, 887**
plot, **29**, 43, 55, **109**, 224

Comedy, **793, R16**

Comic relief, **887, R16**

Comparison-and-contrast essay, **1242**, R31

Comparison-and-contrast organization, **446, 578, 1023**

Complex character
drama, 794, 795

Conflict, 8, 1052, **R16**
book, 1055
Can progress be made without conflict? **222**, 428
drama, 792, **794**, 796, 798, 800, 803, 805, 887, **965**, 976, 977, 981, 983
fiction, 4, 8, **29, 115**, 119, 121, 125, 128, 130, 133, 135, 140, 144, 146, 149
novel, 12, 13, 16, 18, 19
oral tradition, 1050, 1052, 1056, 1057, 1058
short story, 224, **228**, 229, 230, 231, 232, 233, 235

Conflict chart, 115

Connotation, 608, 709, **630, 778, R16**

Consonance, **629, 733**, 741, 747, **R16**

Contemporary interpretations, **R16**

Context clues, **614**

Couplet, 629, 631, **671**, 681, 689, **R16**

Craft and structure, **27, 237**, 459, 637, 1061

Crisis, **887**

Cultural context, 1052
oral tradition, **1048**, 1049, **1051**, 1052, 1054, 1056, 1059

Culturally specific theme, **868**, 877

Dactyl, **628**

Denotation, **630**, 709, **778, R16**

Description, **446, R16**
nonfiction, 153, 1243
setting, **269**, 281, 293

Descriptive essay, **445, 708, R17**

Descriptive writing, **708**, R31–R32

Dialect, **R17**

Dialogue, 226, **792, R17**
drama, **792, 793**, 795, 796, 797, 799, 800, 801, 803, **939, R17**
short story, 226, **239**, 253, 265

Diction, **1050, R17**
  expository essay, **461,** 471, 483
  short story, **408,** 419
  style and, **96**
  theme and, 758

Diction and tone chart, 461

Direct characterization, **226, 795**

Dithyrambs, 810A

Drama, **792, R17**
  acts and scenes, **792**
  dramatic speech, 795, 796
  elements/types, **792,** 793
  forms of, **793**
  Greek, **810A–810D**
  structure, **793**

Dramatic effect, **792**

Dramatic poetry, **631, R17**

Dramatic speeches, **939,** 941, 947,
  948, 949, 950, 952, 953, 955,
  961, 963

Dynamic characters
  short story, 230, 233, 234, 236

Elegy, **631**

Emotional appeal, **lxvi**

Endorsement, **lxvi**

Enjambment, **628**

Entertainment as purpose, 153

Epic, **631, 1049, 1091,** 1096, 1100, 1103,
  1105, 1110, 1111, 1115, 1117, **R17**

Epic hero, 1049, **1091,** 1096, 1100, 1103,
  1105, 1110, 1111, 1115, 1117

Epic poem, **631**

Epic simile, **R17**

Epiphany, **R17**

Essays, **5, 444, R18**
  analytic/interpretive, **557,** 561, 565,
  569, 573
  cause-and-effect, **200,** R31
  comparison-and-contrast, **1242,** R31
  descriptive, **441, 708**
  elements, **444**
  expository, **441, 461,** 465, 469, 471,
  480, 483
  humorous, **518**
  narrative, **441**
  persuasive, **441, 604,** R31
  problem-and-solution, **420,** R32
  reflective, **441 487,** 492, 496, 497,
  502, 503, 505, 507, **878**
  structure, 444, 448
  support, types of, **446**
  types, 445

Etymology, **430**

Examples, **20,** 446
  article, 23, 24
  essay, 22

Expert opinion, **20, 446**
  essay, 22

Explanatory writing
  types of, R31–R32

Exposition, **R18**
  drama, **793,** 887
  plot, **29,** 43, 55, **109**

Expository essay, **444, 445, 461,** 465,
  469, 471, 480, 483, **R18**

Extemporaneous speech, **445**

Extended metaphor, **R18**

External conflict, 4, **224, 794**

Facts, **20, 446**
  article, 24
  essay, 21

Falling action, **793**

Fairy tales, **1049**

Fate, **837,** 859

Feet, **628**

Fiction, **4, R18**
  elements/types, **4, 5**
  theme in, **6,** 8, **224**
  See also Short stories

Figurative language, **447,** 448, **630,** 632,
  R18
  descriptive essay, 452, 708
  meanings, **1252**
  poetry, **630,** 632, 633, 634, 635, 636,
  637, **639, 715,** 722, 723, 726, 729
  speech, 449

Figures of speech, 447, **715**

Flashbacks, **29, 109, 226,** 227, 330, **R18**

Flaw, tragic, **837,** 859, **887,** 913,
  985, 1001

Foil, **985, R18**

Folk literature. *See* Oral tradition

Folk tales, **1049**

Foreshadowing, **29,** 43, 55, **R18**

Formal verse, **631**

Free verse, **629, 631, R19**

Functional texts, **5**

General-to-specific organization, **710**

Genre, **225, R19**

Greek tragedies, **810A–810D, 837,** 840,
  841, 843, 846, 851, 856, 859

Grounds (evidence), lxiv

Haiku, **631, R19**

Heroes, 887
  Can anyone be a hero?, **1046,** 1250
  epic, **1091,** 1096, 1100, 1103, 1105,
  1110, 1111, 1115, 1117
  legendary, **1153,** 1158, 1160, 1165, 1167,
  1168, 1170, 1171, 1181, 1184, 1185
  oral tradition, 1048
  tragic, **887, 985,** 988, 990, 992, 994,
  995, 997, 1001

Historical characters, **887**

Historical context, **335,**

Historical fiction, **225**

Hubris, 810A

Humorous essay, **518**

Humorous fiction, **225**

Humorous writing, **518,** 521, 523, 524,
  526, 529, 530, 531

Hyperbole, **lxvi, 518,** 531, **630, R19**

Iamb, 628, 672, **915, R19**

Iambic pentameter, **628, 672, 915,** 937

Idioms, **1252, R19**

Imagery, 447, **R19**
  poetry, 639, 655, 667, **715**

Images, **R19**

Implied themes, **6**

Indirect characterization, **226, 795**

Information as purpose, 153

Informative writing
  types of, R31–R32

Integration of knowledge and ideas, **27,**
  237, 459, 637, 1061

Internal conflict, 4, **224, 794,** 887

Interpreting themes, **6**

Interpretive essay, **557,** 561, 565, 569, 573

Irony, **188,** 192, 194, 197, 199, **227, 306,**
  R19

Jargon, **1252**

Journal, **5**

Justification, lxiv

Key ideas and details, **27, 237,** 459, 637,
  1061

Lecture, **445**

Legendary heroes, **1153,** 1158, 1160, 1165,
  1167, 1168, 1170, 1171, 1181, 1182, 1184,
  1185

Legends, **1049,** 1165, 1167, 1168, 1170,
  1171, 1181, 1182, 1184, 1185

List, 446, **578**

Literal language, 632 **R19**

Literary nonfiction, **5**

Loaded language, **lxvi**

Lyric poetry **631, 639,** 643, 647, 649, 651, 655, 659, 660, 662, 663, 664, 665, 667, **R19**

Memoir, **5**

Metaphors, **lxvi, R19**
    essay, **447,** 708, **880**
    poetry, **630, 715,** 723, 729

Meter, **628,** 632, 671, **R19**
    poetry, 634, 636

Methods of development, **448**
    essay, 454, 456
    speech, 449, 450

Monologue, **793, 939,** 963, **R20**

Mood, **224, 700,** 707, **R20**

Moral, **R20**

Motivation, **R20**

Multiple themes, **6**

Myths, **1049, 1063,** 1067, 1072, 1073, 1079, 1080, 1086, 1087, **R20**

Mythology, 810A

Narration, 4, **R20**

Narrative effects
    short story, **228,** 230, 231, 232, 235, 236

Narrative essay, **445, R20**

Narrative poetry, **631, 639,** 667, **R20**

Narrative writing
    types of, R32

Narrator, 4, **226,** 793, **R21**
    naïve first-person, **306**

Newsletter, **5**

Nonfiction, **4, R21**
    central ideas in, **7**
    elements, **4,** 27
    literary, **5**
    purposes, 153, 1243
    types, 5

Novellas, **5**

Novels, **5, R21**

Objective Summary, **lvi, lvii,** 27, 237, 459, 460, 620, 637, 807, 1061

Observations, **8, 20**
    novel, 11
    oral tradition, 1052, 1053, 1057, 1059

Ode, 631

Omniscient/limited point of view, **306**

One-act plays, **793**

Online reference sources, **5**

Onomatopoeia, **629, 733,** 741, 747, **R21**

Oral tradition, **1048, R21**
    archetypes, **1048**
    elements of, **1048**
    forms and characteristics of, 1049
    themes, **1050,** 1051, 1052

Order of importance, 202, **578,** 880, **1023**

Organization
    essay, 202, **710,** 444, **446,** 448, 451, 452, 455, 880, **1244**
    informational text, **578**
    narrative, 109
    research report, **1023**
    technical document, **1147,** 1148

Origins, myth, **1063,** 1073, 1087

Oxymoron, **R21**

Pacing, **227**

Paradox, **188,** 192, 194, 197, 199, **R21**

Parallel plots, **227**

Parallelism, **lxvi,** 447, **539,** 545, 553, **609, R21**

Parody, **225, 1189,** 1194, 1196, 1197, 1200, 1203, 1205, 1209, 1212, 1215, 1217

Part-to-whole organization, **1023**

Pentameter, **672, 915,** 937, **R21**

Persona, **408**

Personal narrative, **5**

Personal observations, **20**
    article, 23, 25, 26
    essay, 21

Personification, **R21**
    essay, 447, 708, **880**
    poetry, **630, 715,** 723, 729

Perspective, author's, **59,** 63, 64, 65, 67, 69, 71, 72, 74, 75, 80, 85

Persuasion, 153, 1243, **R21**

Persuasive appeals, **557,** 565, 573

Persuasive essay, **444, 604, R21,** R31

Persuasive speech, **539,** 545, 553

Persuasive writing, **539,** 543, 545, 549, 553

Petrarchan sonnet, **631, 687**

Philosophical assumption, **335,** 355, 365

"Plain folks" appeal, **lxvi**

Plays. *See* Drama

Playwright, **792**

Plot, 224, 1052, **R21**
    drama, **792, 793, 887**
    elements, **29, 109,** 224
    fiction, 4, 8, 33, 35, 37, 38, 40, 42, 43, 49, 51, 54, 55
    novel, 12, 13, 16, 18, 19
    oral tradition, 1050, 1052
    parallel, **227**
    short story, 224, 227, 228, 229, 230, 231, 232, 233, 235, 237

Plot diagram, 29, 109, 887

Poetic form chart, 672

Poetic forms, **671,** 681, 689

Poetry, **628, R22**
    elements and characteristics, **628**
    types, **631**

Point-by-point organization, **1244**

Point of view, 1051, **R22**
    essay, 444, 458
    fiction/nonfiction, 4, **110**
    first-person, 4
    literary nonfiction, 448
    oral tradition, 1048, 1050, 1052, 1054, 1055, 1060
    short story, **306,** 309, 310, 312, 313, 315, 316, 317, 318, 320, 322, 323, 324, 325, 326, 327
    speech, 449
    third-person, 4
    See also Author's point of view/ perspective

Presentation, **445**

Problem-and-solution essay, **420, 446,** R32

Props, **792**

Prose, **R22**

Protagonist, **224,** 1048, **R22**
    drama, 793, **794, 811,** 815, 816, 820, 822, 826, 827, 830, 831, 833

Pun, **R22**

Purpose. *See* Author's purpose

Pyrrhus, **628**

Quatrains, **671,** 681, 689, **R22**

Quest, **1063,** 1073, 1087

Realistic fiction, **225**

Reality and truth, 208

Reasons, **446**

Reflective essay, **445, 487,** 492, 496, 497, 502, 503, 505, 507, **878**

Repetition, **lxvi,** 447, **R22**
    nonfiction, 447, **539,** 545, 553

Report, **5**

Research writing, **1020,** R32

Resolution, **224, R22**
    conflict and, 115, 135, 149, 792
    plot, **6, 29,** 55, 109, 224, **793**

Restatement, **447**

Rhetoric, **444**

Rhetorical devices, **447**, 448, **539**, 545, 553, **R22**
  essay, 457
  speech, 450

Rhetorical questions, **lxvi, 447, 539**, 545, 553

Rhyme, **629**, 632, 671, **R22**
  poetry, 633

Rhyme scheme, **629**, 671, 672, **R22**

Rhyming couplet, **629**

Rhythm, 632, **R23**
  poetry, 634, 636

Rising action, **793**

Satire, **518**, 531, **R23**

Satyr play, 810A

Scanning, **628**

Scenes, **792, 794**

Science fiction, **225, R23**

Screenplay, **793**

Script, 792, **794**

Sensory language, 630, 639, 655, 667, **R23**

Sermon, **445**

Sets, **792, 794, R23**

Setting, **8**, 1052, **R23**
  fiction, 4, **8**
  novel, 9, 10, 14
  oral tradition, 1052, 1059, 1060
  short story, 224, **227**, 228, 229, 231, **269**, 273, 278, 281, 287, 288, 293

Setting chart, 269

Shakespearean sonnet, **631, 671**, 677, 687

Shakespearean theater, 884

Shakespeare's tragedies, **887**, 897, 900, 902, 909, 913

Short story, **5, 224, R23**
  analyzing, 227
  characterization, 228
  elements of, **224, 228**
  genre, 225
  structure, 225, 227, 228

Similes, **lxvi, 447, 630**, 708, **715**, 723, 729, **880, R23**

Slogans/saws, **539**, 545, 553

Soliloquy, **793, 939**, 963, **985, R23**

Sonnet, **631, 671**, 677, 681, 687, 689, **R23**

Sound devices, **lxvi, 629**, 632, **733**, 737, 741, 744, 747
  poetry, 633, 636, 637

Spatial organization, **446, 578, 710**

Speaker in poetry, **630, 639**, 643, 647, 649, 651, 655, 659, 660, 662, 663, 664, 665, 667, **R23**

Speculative fiction, **225**

Speeches
  dramatic, **795, 939**, 941, 947, 948, 949, 950, 952, 953, 955, 961, 963
  elements, **444**
  extemporaneous, **445**
  humorous, **518**
  persuasive, **444, 445, 539**, 545, 553
  types, 445

Spondee, **628**

Stage, Shakespearean, **884**

Stage directions, **792**, 795, 796, **R23**
  drama, 797, 801, 802, 804, 805

Stanza, **628, R23**

Statements, **8**
  novel, 9, 11, 13
  oral tradition, 1052, 1053, 1057, 1059

Statistics, **446**

Structure, **444**
  drama, **792**, 793
  Greek tragedy, 810C–810D
  poetry, **628**
  short story, **225, 227**

Style, **444, R24**
  comparison, **96**, 99, 100, 103, 104, 106, 107

Subject-by-subject organization, **1244**

Subplots, **5**

Summary, **811**

Supporting roles, **887**

Surprise ending, **R24**

Symbol, **8**, 369, 381, 397, **630, R24**
  novel, 9, 17

Symbol diagram, 369

Symbolism, **369**, 380, 381, 385, 389, 392, 397

Syntax, **96**

Talk, **445**

Tanka, **671**, 680, 681, 688, 689

Technical document, **1146**

Technical terms, **1252**

Teleplay, **793**

Test Practice, 214, 434, 618, 782, 1038, 1256

Testimony, **lxvi**

Tetralogy, 810A

Theater
  ancient Greek, 808
  Shakespearean, 884

Theme, 4, **6, 224, R24**
  comparison, **758**, 762, 763, 764, 767
  drama, 792, 795, **796, 837**, 859
  fiction, 4, **6**, 8
  implied, **6**
  novel, 9, 19
  oral tradition, 1048, **1050, 1051**, 1055, 1060
  short story, **224, 335**, 339, 341, 342, 344, 351, 353, 355, 359, 365
  universal, **868, 877, 1048**, 1228
  universal/culturally specific, **868**, 871, 872, 873, 875, 876, 877, **1051**
  worldviews and, **1228**, 1230, 1232, 1234, 1236, 1237, 1239, 1240, 1241

Thesis, 7, 20, **153**, 165, 177

Title, **8**, 20
  essay, 21
  novel, 10

Tone, **444, 447**, 448, **R24**
  essay, 453, 454, 456
  fiction/nonfiction, **408**, 411, 412, 413, 415, 417, 419
  nonfiction, **444, 447, 448, 461**, 471, 483
  optimistic/pessimistic, **424**
  poetry, **630**, 632, 634, 635, 636, **700**, 702, 703, 705, 706, 707
  speech, 450

Topic sentence, **7, 20**
  essay, 21

Tragedy, **793, R24**
  Greek, **810A–810D, 837**, 840, 841, 843, 846, 851, 856, 859
  Shakespeare's, **887**, 897, 900, 902, 909, 913

Tragic flaw, **793, 837**, 859, **887**, 913, **985**, 1001

Tragic heroes
  drama, **793**
  Shakespeare's, **887, 985**, 988, 990, 992, 994, 995, 997, 1001

Transgression, **1063**, 1073, 1087

Trochee, **628**

Truth and reality, 208

Understatement, **518**, 531, **R24**

Universal themes, **1048**, 1051, **R24**
  drama, **868**, 877
  worldviews and, 1228

Verse drama, 810B

Villanelle, **672**, 679, 681, 685, 689, **R24**

Voice, **408,** 419, **533,** 630, **R24**

Word choice, **447**
  drama, 795
  essay, 453, 454, 456
  nonfiction, 448
  speech, 450

Workplace writing, R32

Works-Cited List, **1026**

Worldview, theme and, **1228,** 1230, 1232, 1234, 1236, 1237, 1239, 1240, 1241

Reading

Reading for Information

Atlas, 752, **753,** 757

Book review, 1222, **1223,** 1227

Complex texts, lviii–lxiii

Course catalog, 578, **581,** 583

Drama reviews, 864, **865, 866,** 867

Feature article, 90, **91,** 95

Interview, 1122, **1123,** 1127

Job application, 1008, **1009,** 1013

Magazine article, 752, **755,** 757

Movie review, 1222, **1225,** 1227

News release, 298, **303,** 305

Newsletter, 90, **93,** 95

Newspaper editorial, 402, **403,** 407

Primary source, 182, **185,** 187, 402, **405,** 407

Public document, 1008, **1011,** 1013

Research source, 578, **579,** 583

Signs, 694, **695,** 699

Technical article, 298, **299,** 305

Technical directions, 512, **513,** 517

Test Practice, 216, 436, 620, 784, 1040, 1258

User's guide, 512, **515,** 517

Web site, 182, **183,** 187, 694, **697,** 699

Reading Skills

Analysis, extend ideas through, 298

Archetypal narrative patterns, compare, **1128,** 1145

Author's purpose
  compare, **584,** 603
  make predictions, **694,** 699

Background knowledge, acquire, **1091,** 1105, 1117

Cause and effect, analyze
  reflect on key details, **115,** 120, 122, 125, 126, 128, 131, 132, 135, 141, 147, 149
  reread, **153,** 159, 162, 165, 168, 173, 175, 177
  Test Practice, 180

Character chart, use, 985

Characters
  compare/contrast, **985,** 987, 990, 998, 1001
  relate to own experience, **239,** 253, 265

Characters' motivations, compare, **1014,** 1019

Close reading, lx–lxi
  drama, 796
  fiction, 8
  nonfiction, 448
  oral tradition, 1052
  poetry, 632
  short story, **228**

Conclusions, draw
  to compare worldviews, **1153,** 1171, 1185
  identify patterns, **369,** 373, 374, 377, 381, 386, 390, 394, 397
  recognize key details, **335,** 342, 343, 347, 348, 352, 355, 361, 365
  Test Practice, 400

Credibility, analyze, **182,** 187, **1222,** 1227

Cultural context, analyze
  acquire background knowledge, **1091,** 1096, 1097, 1099, 1102, 1104, 1105, 1110, 1113, 1115, 1117
  generate questions, **1063,** 1067, 1073, 1077, 1082, 1085, 1087
  Test Practice, 1120

Cultural context chart, use, 1063, 1091

Details, analyze
  ask questions, **487,** 497, 507
  summarize, **461,** 471, 483

Details, identify
  analyze cause and effect, **115,** 135, 149
  compare worldviews, **1153,** 1171, 1185
  draw conclusions, **335,** 355, 365
  paraphrase to, **402,** 407

Elaboration and evaluation, extend ideas through, 298

Events
  determine sequence, 153
  relate to own experience, **239,** 253, 265

Evidence, evaluate, **1222,** 1227

Fact
  distinguish opinion and, **557,** 565, 573
  make generalizations, **752,** 757

Fact and opinion chart, use, 557

Generalizations
  critique, **1222,** 1227
  make, synthesize to, **752,** 757

Glosses, consult, **887,** 913

Humorous writing, compare, **518,** 531

Ideas
  analyze texts to extend, **298,** 305
  paraphrase to connect, **402,** 407
  synthesize and connect, **864,** 867

Illusion and reality, compare/contrast, **1189,** 1205, 1217

Imagery
  analyze, **939,** 945, 946, 948, 950, 956, 957, 959, 960, 962, 963
  picture, **715,** 723, 729

Imagery chart, use, 939

Inference chart, use, 239, 281, 965

Inferences, make
  read on, **269,** 273, 277, 280, 281, 286, 291, 293
  relate characters/events to own experience, **239,** 244, 250, 253, 259, 262, 265
  Test Practice, 296

Irony and paradox, compare, **188,** 199

Key details diagram, use, 335

Main idea
  ask questions, **487,** 492, 494, 497, 502, 504, 507
  paraphrase to determine, **402,** 407
  summarize, **461,** 466, 470, 471, 477, 479, 483
  Test Practice, 510

Main ideas and supporting details chart, use, 487

Mood, compare tone and, **700,** 707

Notes, take to summarize, **837**

Opinion and fact, distinguish, **557,** 562, 565, 573

Paradox and irony, compare, **188,** 199

Paraphrase
  break down long sentences, **733,** 739, 741, 745, 747
  to connect ideas, **402,** 407
  picture imagery, **715,** 718, 723, 728, 729
  Shakespearean drama, **915,** 920, 924, 928, 929, 932, 937
  Test Practice, 407, 750

Paraphrase chart, use, 715, 733, 915

Patterns
  compare archetypal, **1128,** 1145
  recognize, **335, 369,** 381, 397

Persuasive appeals, evaluate
   distinguish between fact/opinion, **557,** 562, 565, 573
   evaluate arguments/techniques, **539,** 545, 552, 553
   Test Practice, 576

Persuasive appeals chart, use, 539

Points of view, compare, **306,** 327

Prediction chart, use, 59

Predictions, make
   about purpose, **694,** 699
   ask questions, **59,** 63, 65, 68, 72, 75, 82, 85
   Test Practice, 88
   use prior knowledge, **29,** 36, 39, 43, 48, 52, 55

Preview to read fluently, **673,** 681, 689

Prior knowledge, use, **29,** 43, 55

Punctuation
   paraphrase using, 915
   read fluently according to, 673

Purpose. *See* Author's purpose

Questions, ask/generate, lxii–lxiii
   analyzing cultural context, **1063,** 1073, 1087
   analyzing main idea, **487,** 497, 507
   craft and structure, lxii
   extending ideas, 298
   integration of knowledge and ideas, lxii
   key ideas and details, lxii
   making predictions, **59**
   reading for information, **1122,** 1127

Read aloud, **639,** 655, 667

Read between the lines, **965,** 970, 971, 975, 978, 979, 981, 983

Read fluently
   adjust reading rate, **639,** 644, 650, 653, 655, 665, 667
   preview, **673,** 679, 681, 689
   Test Practice, 692

Read on to support/modify inference, **269,** 281, 293

Reading rate, adjust, **639,** 655, 667

Reading rate chart, use, 639, 655, 667

Reread to analyze cause and effect, **153**

Retell, pause to, **811**

Scan/skim to analyze text structures, **578,** 583

Sentences, break down long, **733,** 741, 747

Sequence, examine, 153, **512,** 517

Sequence of events chart, use, 153

Shakespearean drama
   analyze imagery, **939,** 945, 946, 948, 950, 956, 957, 959, 960, 962, 963
   compare/contrast characters, **985,** 987, 990, 998, 1001
   paraphrase, **915,** 920, 924, 928, 929, 932, 937
   read between the lines, **965,** 970, 971, 975, 978, 979, 981, 983
   Test Practice, 1006
   use text aids, **887,** 894, 897, 902, 904, 907, 910, 913

Sources, evaluate, **182,** 187

Structure and format, analyze
   to predict purpose, **694,** 699
   scan and skim, **578,** 583
   use text features, **90,** 95, **1008,** 1013

Style, compare, **96,** 107

Subject and verb, identify/reorder, 915

Summarize
   main idea/supporting details, **461,** 471, 483
   retell, **811,** 816, 818, 820, 822, 825, 829, 832, 833
   take notes, **837,** 840, 845, 855, 859
   Test Practice, 862

Summary chart, use, 811, 837

Synthesize
   and connect ideas, **864,** 867
   to make generalizations, **752,** 757

Technical directions, follow/critique, **512,** 517

Text aids, use, **887,** 894, 897, 902, 904, 907, 910, 913

Texts, analyze to extend ideas, **298,** 305

Themes, compare, **758,** 767
   universal/culturally specific, **868,** 877
   worldviews and, **1228,** 1241

Tone
   compare, **408,** 419
   compare mood and, **700,** 707
   listen for, 639

Workplace documents, analyze, 1008, 1013

Worldview diagram, use, 1153, 1189

Worldviews, compare
   compare/contrast illusion and reality, **1189,** 1193, 1196, 1198, 1203, 1205, 1210, 1212, 1214, 1216, 1217
   identify details/draw conclusion, **1153,** 1157, 1160, 1163, 1166, 1168, 1169, 1171, 1175, 1177, 1178, 1182, 1185
   Test Practice, 1220
   themes and, **1228,** 1241

Writer's argument, evaluate, **539,** 545, 553

Vocabulary

Big Question/Academic Vocabulary, 3, 223, 443, 627, 791, 1047

Building speaking vocabulary, l

Domain-specific academic vocabulary, l, liii–liv

General academic vocabulary, l–lii

Increasing word knowledge, lv

Grammar, Usage, and Mechanics

Absolute phrases, **1002**

Absolutes, **1002**

Active voice, **398**

Adjective clauses, **860**

Adjective phrases, **730**

Adjectives, **R50**
   absolute, **1002**
   begin sentence with, 1247
   degrees, **574,** 608
   predicate, **508,** 535

Adverb clauses, **860, 1027,** 1247

Adverb phrases, **730**

Adverbs, **554, R50**

Apostrophes, 111, **R54**

Capitalization, 1031, **R53**

Clauses, **R51**
   adverb, **1027,** 1247
   independent/subordinate, **860, 1088, 1118**
   prepositional phrase vs., 773

Colons, **1218, R53**

Commas, 711, 883, 1027, **1186,** 1249, **R53**

Common usage, **R54**

Comparatives, 608, **R52**

Complex sentence, **1118**

Compound-complex sentence, **1118**

Compound sentence, **1088**

Conjunctions, **1027,** 1249, **R51**

Coordinating conjunctions, 1249

Dashes, **1186, R54**

Direct objects, **484, 690**

Ellipsis points, **1218**

End marks, **R53**

Fragments, **1149**

Gerund phrases, **834, 881**

Gerunds, **834**

Hyphens, **R54**

Independent clauses, **860, 1027, 1088, 1118**

Indirect objects, **484**

Infinitive phrases, **748, 881**

Infinitives, **748**

Language Conventions:
    Test Practice, 218, 438, 622, 786, 1042, 1260
    Writer's Toolbox, 111, 331, 425, 773

Nominatives, predicate **508,** 535

Noun clauses, **860**

Nouns, **R50**
    abstract/concrete, **86**
    common/proper, **56**
    possessive, **111**

Objects
    compound, 535
    direct/indirect, **484, 690**
    of the preposition, **668**

Parallelism, 609, **R52**

Parentheses, **R54**

Participial phrases, **834, 881**

Participles, **834**

Passive voice, **398**

Phrases, **R51**
    absolute, **1002**
    infinitive, **748**
    participial/gerund, **834**
    prepositional, **668, 711, 730,** 773, 1247
    verbal, **881**

Predicate adjectives, **508,** 535

Predicate nominatives, **508,** 535

Prepositional phrases, **668, 711, 730,** 773, 1247

Prepositions, **668, R50**

Principal parts of verbs, **R52**

Pronoun-antecedent agreement, **205, R50**

Pronoun case, **R52**

Pronouns, **R50**
    indefinite, **425**
    personal, **150**
    relative, **178**

Punctuation, **R53**
    citations, 1031
    clauses, 1027
    commas, 883
    dialogue, 113
    prepositional phrases, 711
    transitional words, 1249
    types, **1186, 1218**

Quotation marks, 113, **R53**

Run-on sentences, **1149**

Semicolons, **1218**

Sentences, **R51**
    combine, 535, 881, 1027

complete, 333
complex/compound-complex, **1118**
fragment/run-on, **1149**
simple/compound, **1088**
vary length/structure, 110, 711, 1247

Simple sentence, **1088**

Spelling
    citations, 1031
    endings, 775
    homophones, 713, 1151
    silent vowels, 611
    words with double letters, 333

Subject complements, **508**

Subject-verb agreement, **425, R52**

Subordinate clauses, **860, 1027, 1118**

Subordinating conjunctions, **1027**

Superlatives, 608

Transitional words, 1249

Usage problems, common, 207, **773, R52**

Verbal phrases, **881**

Verbs, **R50**
    action/linking, **366,** 608
    direct objects and, 690
    irregular, **294**
    principal parts of regular, **266**
    tenses, **331**

Voice
    active/passive, **398**
    finding, **533**

Vocabulary Practice

Analogies
    choose word to make, 565, 573, 767, 963, 1019
    complete, relate, 43, 55

Antonyms
    choose best, use in sentence, 165, 177
    explain, use in sentence, 545, 553
    identify, explain, 1073, 1087
    replace words with, explain, 355, 365, 913, 1205, 1217

Examples, give/explain, 1241

Oxymoron, identify/explain, 741, 747

Questions, answer
    explain response, 135, 149, 327, 1171, 1185
    explain word meaning, 253, 265, 471, 483

Sentences
    complete for sense, explain, 531
    explain if true or false, 1145
    explain sense, revise for sense, 75, 85
    rewrite, explain word choice, 419
    write, explain word choice, 1001
    write about person, 707
    write about situation, 655, 667, 1105, 1117

write new with same meaning, 497, 507
write using word pairs, 199, 603, 723, 729, 877

Statement, match with word/explain, 281, 293

Synonyms
    choose word that is not, explain, 381, 397
    explain, use in sentence, 545, 553
    identify, explain, 937, 1073, 1087
    replace word with, use in sentence, 859

Test Practice, 217, 437, 621, 785, 1041, 1259

Words
    define/write paragraph, 983
    identify one that does not belong, explain, 107, 681, 689, 833

Word Choice: Writer's Toolbox, 205, 709

Word Origins/Meanings

Borrowed and foreign words, 1034

Connotation and denotation, 608, 709, 778

Dictionary, use, 210, 614

Idioms, jargon, and technical terms, 1252

Multiple meanings, words with, 614

Prefixes:
    com-, 356, 365
    dis-, 336, 355
    em-, 558, 565
    en-, 914, 937
    ex-, 1206, 1217
    fore-, 640, 655
    im-, 566, 573
    inter-, 154, 165
    multi-, 1190, 1205
    ob-, 166, 177
    para-, 498, 507
    pro-, 60, 75
    re-, 656, 667
    suc-/sub-, 488, 497
    super-, 76, 85

Roots:
    -cred-, 30, 43
    -dict-, 812, 833
    -dur-, 1064, 1073
    -fer-, 838, 859
    -fig-, 472, 483
    -fus-, 1074, 1087
    -jur-, 546, 553
    -lun-, 674, 681
    -scend-, 540, 545
    -spect-, 938, 963
    -strict-, 44, 55
    -stru-, 984, 1001
    -sum-, 964, 983
    -tact-/-tang-, 462, 471
    -temp-, 682, 689
    -ven-, 136, 149
    -ver-, 116, 135

Suffixes:
  -*able*, 254, 265
  -*ary*, 724, 729
  -*ate*, 1154, 1171
  -*ence*, 240, 253
  -*ial*, 742, 747
  -*ic*, 282, 293
  -*id*, 382, 397
  -*ile*, 888, 913
  -*ity*, 270, 281
  -*ive*, 1092, 1105
  -*ment*, 1172, 1185
  -*or*, 734, 741
  -*ous*, 716, 723
  -*tion*, 370, 381
  -*tude*, 1106, 1117
Thesaurus, use, 210
Workshop, 210, 430, 614, 778, 1034, 1252

Writing

Writing Applications

Analytical response to literature
  Professional Model (Eady), 771
  Student Model, 774
  Work in Progress, 731, 749
  Writing Workshop, 768

Anecdote, 151

Argument, lxviii, lxix, 268, 295, 408, 512, 532, 634, 604, 606, 608, 614, 616, 617, 618

Autobiographical narrative
  Student Model, 112
  Work in Progress, 57, 87
  Writing Workshop, 108

Book review, 295

Business letter, 485

Cause-and-effect essay
  Professional Model (Vreeland), 203
  Student Model, 204, 205
  Work in Progress, 151, 179
  Writing Workshop, 200

Character analysis, 367

Comparison-and-contrast essay
  archetypal narrative patterns, 1145
  authors' purposes, 603
  characters' motivations, 1019
  humorous writing, 531
  irony and paradox, 199
  points of view, 327
  Professional Model (Santos), 1245
  Student Model, 1248
  styles, 107
  theme, 767
  theme and worldview, 1241
  tone, 419
  tone and mood, 707

universal and culturally specific themes, 877
  Work in Progress, 1187, 1219
  Writing Workshop, 1242

Critical essay, 731

Critique, 575

Description, 87

Descriptive essay
  Student Model, 712
  Work in Progress, 669, 691
  Writing Workshop, 708

Editorial, 1003

Essay
  analyze mood, 707
  explore conflict, 835

Letter
  to author, 555
  business, 485
  friendly, 295

Letter to the editor
  Student Model, 536
  Work in Progress, 485, 509
  Writing Workshop, 532

Lyric poem, 669

Memoir, 509

Myth, 1089

Narrative, 399

Newspaper report, 1119

Obituary, 1003

Objective Summary, lvi, lvii

Parody, 1219

Persuasive essay
  Professional Model (Weihenmayer), 607
  Student Model, 610
  Work in Progress, 555, 575
  Writing Workshop, 604

Poem, 749

Problem-and-solution essay
  Professional Model (Cherryh), 423
  Student Model, 422, 424, 426
  Work in Progress, 367, 399
  Writing Workshop, 420

Proposal, 179

Reflective essay
  on character's fate, 861
  Student Model, 882
  Work in Progress, 835, 861
  Writing Workshop, 878

Research report
  Professional Model (Hwang), 1024
  Student Model, 1028

Work in Progress, 1003
  Writing Workshop, 1020

Response to Big Question, 209, 429, 613, 777, 1033, 1251

Retellings, 267

Script for television news report, 1187

Sentence starters
  Can anyone be a hero?, 1064, 1074, 1092, 1106, 1129, 1154, 1172, 1190, 1206, 1229
  Can progress be make without conflict?, 240, 254, 270, 282, 307, 336, 356, 370, 382, 409
  Does all communication serve a positive purpose?, 640, 656, 674, 682, 701, 716, 724, 734, 742, 759
  Is there a difference between reality and truth?, 30, 44, 60, 76, 97, 116, 136, 154, 166, 189
  To what extent does experience determine what we perceive?, 812, 838, 869, 888, 1015
  What kind of knowledge changes our lives?, 462, 472, 488, 498, 519, 540, 546, 558, 566, 585

Sequel, 57

Short story
  Student Model, 332
  Work in Progress, 267, 295
  Writing Workshop, 328

Technical document
  Student Model, 1150
  Work in Progress, 1089, 1119
  Writing Workshop, 1146

Writing for Assessment.
  See **TEST PRACTICE**

Writing Strategies

Prewriting:

Arguments, list, 605

Audience, consider, 421, 533, 769, 1146

Bias, evaluate, 1022

Brainstorm, 201, 605, 835

Cause-and-effect chart, create, 201

Character cards, create, 108

Character chart, create, 328

Character descriptions, create, 267

Characters
  gather details, 328
  identify/list traits, 367
  identify main, 1119
  identify perspective, 267
  imagine, 329
  review details, 1003

Chronological order, use, 109

Conflict chart, create, 295

Connotation, consider, 709

Consequences, list/explain, 1003

Counterarguments, identify, 605

Criteria, decide/follow, 731

Denotation, consider, 709

Details
    choose, 109
    gather, 328, 708, 1146
    list concise, 1147
    record sensory, 669, 709, 878
    review, 1003
    skim for/write down, 769

Dictionary, use, 731

Emotions, jot down, 749

Event notes, create, 835

Events
    list main, 267
    outline, 1119, 1219
    think about/consider significance, 879, 1119

Evidence, gather, 575

Fact and opinion, evaluate, 1022

Figurative language
    develop, 708
    evaluate, 731
    list examples, 669

Freewrite, 605, 1187

Group discussion, hold, 769

Ideas
    develop story, 329
    find effective/refine, 879
    focus on strong, 691
    reread for, 179

Imagery, chart ideas, 669

Images
    choose appropriate, 709
    describe, 731
    focus on strong, 691

Imagination, use, 329

Index cards, write details on/organize, 769

Issues, list/look at both sides, 532, 605

Issues list, create, 485, 509

Lessons learned, consider, 879

Lists, make, 201, 1022, 1147, 1243

Magazine articles, scan, 201

Main idea list, create, 509

Media sources, browse, 421

Message, identify/explain, 835

Mood, determine, 87, 749

Newspapers, scan, 201, 532

Note cards, create, 1022

Notebooks, scan, 1021

Notes
    organize, 1022
    review, 1021
    take, 1003, 1119, 1187

Opinions
    evaluate, 1022
    note differing, 532, 605

Organization chart, create, 669

Outline, create
    for descriptive essay, 691
    for story, 57, 1119, 1219
    for technical document, 1119

Paraphrase, 731, 1022

Past, think about, 879

Periodicals, review, 1021

Phrases, choose effective, 533

Place list, develop, 57, 87

Plan, devise, 109, 1089

Plot, imagine, 329

Plot diagram, use, 57, 109, 267

Point to make, decide, 109

Prior knowledge, use, 87, 879

Pro-and-con chart, use, 605

Problem
    define, 367
    evaluate solutions, 421

Problem/solution web, use, 367, 399

Process, explain, 1147

Purpose, determine, 1003, 1089, 1243

Questions
    answer, 749, 861
    ask, 201, 769
    list, 151, 179, 731, 1022

Quotations, record, 769, 1022

Research, conduct, 605, 1243

Research plan, develop, 1021

Sensory details, gather, 669, 709, 878

Sentence frame, fill in, 1243

Sequence of events, plan, 1089

Setting, imagine, 329

Setting cards, create, 108

Solution chart, use, 421

Solutions
    evaluate, 421
    identify/clarify, 379, 399

Source cards, create, 1022

Sources, primary/secondary
    document, 1022
    go back to, 769
    list, 151
    scan/review, 1021
    use variety, 1022

Story map, use, 267

Strengths/weaknesses, identify, 367

Task list, create, 1089

Technical terms, identify, 1147

Television, watch to find topic, 532

Thesis statement, formulate, 1021, 1243

Time frame, plan, 1089

Tone, consider, 533

Topic
    evaluate, 1243
    find/choose, 201, 532, 605, 769, 1003, 1021, 1089, 1243
    narrow, 201, 421, 605

Topic defense list, create, 575

Topic list, create/prioritize, 555

Universal themes, use, 329

Validity, evaluate, 1022

Venn diagram, use, 1219, 1243

Voice
    find appropriate, 533
    personalize, 709

"Why" questions, ask, 151, 179, 201

Word choice, consider, 533, 709, 1147

Working thesis statement, start with, 1021

Drafting:

Action, pace, 109, 151

Adjectives, use vivid, 399

Allusion, add, 669

Analysis, clarify, 202

Anecdotes, include, 606

Arguments
    evaluate/emphasize strongest, 606
    exclude irrelevant, 295

Audience
    consider, 202, 606
    use language for, 295, 422, 485, 555

Bias, anticipate, 1003

Block format, use, 534

Case studies, include, 606

Characters, express point of view, 267, 1219

Chronological order, use, 202, 880, 1023

Climax, delay, 330

Comments, add, 1119

Comparison-and-contrast organization, use, 1023

Concerns, anticipate, 1003

Conclusion, evaluate evidence, 575

Conflict, resolve with irony, 151

Connections, make, 1244

Consequences, explain, 1003

Controlling idea, present, 710

Counterarguments, deflect, 1003

Definitions, use, 1148

Details
include relevant, 835
include to set up outcome, 151
link to main idea, 367
organize, 1148
use descriptive, 57
use sensory, 87, 509
use to construct unified picture, 1003
use to develop ideas, 710

Dialogue, use, 110

Eady, Cornelius on writing poetry about music, 771

Emotions
appeal to, 534
express characters', 1219

Essay map, create, 422

Events, link symbol to, 399

Evidence
discuss/evaluate, 575
offer, 606

Exaggeration, use, 1219

Examples, use, 835, 1148, 1244

Facts
document source, 1023
stick to, 422
support with, 606, 1244

Flashbacks, use, 57, 330

Foreshadowing, use, 57

Format, use proper, 534

Graphic aids, use, 1023

Headline, use catchy, 1119

Hints, include, 151

Hwang, David Henry on using research, 1024

Ideas
connect, 367
fully develop, 710
present controlling, 710

support with quotations, 731, 861
synthesize, 1023

Illusion and reality, depict, 1219

Imagery, use effective, 880

Information, add relevant, 295, 399, 1119

Language
use appropriate, 295, 485, 555
use formal/informal, 422
use strong/precise, 770

Language techniques
explain, 731
use, 749

Logic, appeal to, 534

Main idea
link details to, 367
present/develop, 710, 861

Metaphor, use, 880

Modified block format, use, 534

Monologues, create interior, 110, 1219

Note cards, make/organize, 606

Opinions
express characters', 1219
give reasons/summarize, 1003
include expert, 606
state/support, 295, 861, 1244

Order of importance, use, 202, 880, 1023

Organization, choose
to compare and contrast, 1244
for description, 710
for narrative, 109
for obituary, 1003
for research report, 1023
for response, 770
for technical document, 1147, 1148
use logical, 202, 835, 861, 880

Outline, create, 422, 1187

Pacing, keep in mind, 109, 151, 330

Parallelism, use, 534

Paraphrase, 770, 1023

Part-to-whole order, use, 1023

Personification, use, 880

Perspectives, outline, 1187

Persuasive techniques, use, 534

Plot diagram, make, 330

Point-by-point organization, use, 1244

Point of view, use character's, 267, 1219

Purpose, use/check, 1244

Quotations
identify source, 606
include believable, 1119
support with, 731, 861, 1244
use direct, 1023
use exact, 770

Reality and illusion, depict, 1219

Response, organize, 770

Rhetorical devices, use, 534, 555

Santos, John Phillip on making comparisons, 1245

Scenarios, describe, 1148

Sensory details, use, 87, 509

Sentences
add to deflect counterargument, 1003
take turns writing, 1089

Sequential organization, use, 1148

Simile, use, 880

Sound devices, use, 749

Sources
identify, 606
use/credit, 1023

Speaker, identify, 1187

Statistics, include, 606

Subject-by-subject organization, use, 1148, 1244

Summaries, use, 770, 1023

Support, provide convincing, 606, 1244

Technical terms, define, 1148

Text, use information from, 770

Thesis statement
refine, 1023
use/restate, 1244
write, 770

Tone, use appropriate, 57, 485, 1187

Transitions, use, 202, 367, 1244

Visual aids, use, 1023

Visuals, describe, 1187

Weihenmayer, Erik on persuasive techniques, 607

Word choice, consider, 87, 509, 691

Word order, invert normal, 691

Revising:

Action verbs, use, 608

Active voice, use, 330

Arguments, test support, 608

Balance, check/create, 1246

Bibliography, create, 1026

Characters, use dialogue to develop, 330

Cherryh, C. J. on revising to tighten sentences, 423

Clarification, underline information needing, 1148

Coherence, strengthen, 1025

Color, use to check balance, 1246

Comparatives/superlatives, use, 608

Computer software, use, 1119

Conciseness, omit/replace words for, 1025

Connotations, be aware of, 608

Description, frame, 710

Details
    add supporting, 330, 608, 710, 1246
    color-code related, 204
    cut unrelated, 772

Dialogue, use, 330

Effectiveness, assess, 424

Evidence, support with, 534, 608

Feedback, get, 151

Focus, strengthen, 204

Formality, create appropriate, 533

Graphics program, use, 1119

Group review, conduct, 1089

Ideas, cut repeated, 772

Inconsistencies, cut out, 772

Insight, clarify, 110

Main ideas
    evaluate support, 534, 608
    strengthen coherence, 1025

MLA style, use, 1026

Organization
    balance, 1246
    check for logical, 1025, 1148

Parallelism, identify/fix errors, 609

Passive voice, replace, 330

Peer review, use, 204, 424, 608, 772, 1025, 1246

Plagiarism, avoid, 1025

Point of view, evaluate, 267

Possessive nouns, fix, 111

Precision, improve, 1246

Prepositional phrases, use, 711, 1247

Print work, cite sources, 1026

Pronoun-antecedent agreement, fix, 205

Questions, ask, 424

Read aloud, 669, 691, 711, 749

Repetition, look for, 204

Sensory details, add, 330

Sentences
    combine with adverb clauses, 1027
    combine with verbal phrases, 881
    correct fragment/run-on, 1149
    cut/rewrite for unity, 880
    fix choppy, 535
    strengthen focus, 204
    vary length/structure, 110, 711, 1247

Sources, cite, 1025, 1026

Style, evaluate, 424

Subject-verb agreement, fix, 425

Subject-verb order, vary, 1247

Support, evaluate, 534, 608

Thesis statement, strengthen coherence, 1025

Tone, evaluate, 424

Topic sentence, add, 204, 608

Unity, cut/rewrite sentences, 880

Usage problems, fix, 773

Verb tenses, fix, 331

Voice, use active, 330

Vreeland, Susan on showing causes and effects, 203

Web sites, cite sources, 1026

Word choice, fix, 424, 608, 710, 772, 880, 1246

Works-Cited List, create, 1026

Writing, cut excess, 772

Editing/Proofreading:

Accuracy, focus on, 537, 1031

Citations, focus on accuracy, 1031

Commas, check, 883

Dialogue, punctuate, 113

Homophones, spell, 713, 1151

Mnemonic devices, make up, 611

Punctuation, focus on, 113, 883, 1249

Quotation marks, check, 113

References, focus on clear, 427

Sentences, focus on complete, 333

Spelling, focus on, 333, 611, 713, 775, 1151

Transitional words, focus on, 1249

Usage errors, focus on, 207

Word formation rules, review, 1151

Words, check commonly confused, 207

Publishing/Presenting:

Anthology, compile, 333

Audience, publish for, 611

Book club, present to, 775

Class book, create, 1249

Class presentation, give, 207

Discussion, launch, 427

Display, organize, 713

Dramatic reading, give, 333

E-mail, use, 207

Essay, submit, 427

Internet, publish on, 883, 1031

Letter, submit, 537

Manual, present, 1151

Multimedia presentation, share, 1031

Narrative, illustrate, 113

Narrative presentation, deliver, 113

Online review, publish, 775

Podcast, create, 1151

Reading
    give, 333, 883
    prepare oral, 713
    present shared, 1249

Speaker's corner, hold, 537

Speech, deliver, 611

Reflecting on Writing (Writer's Journal):

Analytic response, 775

Autobiographical narrative, 113

Cause-and-effect essay, 207

Comparison-and-contrast essay, 1249

Descriptive essay, 713

Letter to the editor, 537

Persuasive essay, 611

Problem-and-solution essay, 427

Reflective essay, 883

Research report, 1031

Short story, 333

Technical document, 1151

Rubric for Self-Assessment:

Analytic response, 775

Autobiographical narrative, 113

Cause-and-effect essay, 207

Comparison-and-contrast essay, 1249

Descriptive essay, 713

Letter to the editor, 537

Persuasive essay, 611

Problem-and-solution essay, 427

Reflective essay, 883

Research report, 1031

Short story, 333

Technical document, 1151

Professional Models:

Analytic response (Eady), 771

Cause-and-effect essay (Vreeland), 203

Comparison-and-contrast essay (Santos), 1245

Persuasive essay (Weihenmayer), 607

Problem-and-solution essay (Cherryh), 423

Research report (Hwang), 1024

Student Models:

Analytic response, 774

Autobiographical narrative, 112

Cause-and-effect essay, 204, 206

Comparison-and-contrast essay, 1248

Descriptive essay, 712

Letter to the editor, 536

Persuasive essay, 610

Problem-and-solution essay, 422, 424, 426

Reflective essay, 882

Research report, 1028

Short story, 332

Technical document, 1150

Writer's Toolbox:

Conventions, 111, 331, 425, 773

Ideas, 329, 879

Organization, 109, 1147

Sentence fluency, 535, 609, 711, 881,
1027, 1149, 1247

Voice, 533

Word choice, 205, 709

More Skills

Critical Thinking

Analyze, 74, 103, 106, 292, 313, 364, 396,
413, 470, 482, 496, 530, 552, 572, 594,
654, 666, 688, 706, 722, 746, 763, 832,
858, 936, 962, 1086, 1116, 1170, 1204,
1240

Analyze cause and effect, 74, 84, 134,
176, 354, 482, 594, 706, 722, 858,
1000, 1072, 1104, 1216, 1240

Apply, 148, 354, 482, 552, 703, 722, 728

Apply to Big Question, 208, 428, 612, 776,
1032, 1250

Assess, 936

Classify, 470

Compare and contrast, 54, 134, 164, 198,
252, 264, 313, 470, 482, 496, 506, 564,
832, 982, 1018, 1137

Connect, 134, 176, 194, 198, 252, 364,
418, 496, 506, 524, 552, 572, 602, 654,
688, 746, 763, 766, 858, 876, 982,
1000, 1072, 1137, 1144, 1184, 1216

Contrast, 42, 380, 654, 680, 740, 858,
1072, 1144, 1170

Deduce, 763

Discuss, 42, 54, 134, 176, 292, 354, 396,
572, 982, 1000, 1086

Draw conclusions, 27, 84, 106, 134, 148,
194, 313, 326, 413, 544, 594, 602, 703,
722, 740, 876, 1000, 1072, 1116, 1137,
1170, 1240

Evaluate, 27, 74, 134, 252, 264, 326, 380,
396, 418, 572, 680, 740, 936, 982, 1072

Extend, 544, 564, 572, 728

Generalize, 706

Hypothesize, 252, 274, 280, 354, 722, 912,
1116, 1216

Infer, 42, 54, 103, 134, 148, 164, 194, 264,
280, 292, 313, 326, 364, 380, 396, 413,
418, 496, 524, 530, 564, 666, 680, 688,
706, 740, 746, 763, 766, 832, 876, 912,
936, 962, 982, 1000, 1018, 1072, 1086,
1104, 1144, 1204, 1232

Interpret, 27, 54, 84, 106, 148, 164, 176,
198, 292, 313, 354, 380, 418, 496, 506,
524, 544, 552, 564, 602, 666, 680, 688,
728, 740, 763, 766, 832, 912, 936, 1018,
1086, 1116, 1137, 1170, 1184, 1204,
1232, 1240

Make a judgment, 292, 470, 728, 858,
876, 962, 982, 1000, 1018, 1204

Reflect, 292

Relate, 264

Respond, 42, 54, 74, 84, 103, 106, 134,
148, 164, 176, 194, 198, 252, 264, 280,
292, 313, 326, 354, 364, 380, 396, 413,
418, 470, 482, 496, 506, 524, 530, 544,
552, 564, 572, 594, 602, 654, 666, 680,
688, 703, 706, 722, 728, 740, 746, 763,
766, 832, 858, 876, 912, 936, 962, 982,
1000, 1018, 1072, 1086, 1104, 1116,
1137, 1144, 1170, 1184, 1204, 1216,
1232, 1240

Speculate, 74, 134, 176, 198, 252, 326,
766, 1216

Summarize, 54, 74, 103, 176, 252, 280,
354, 396, 413, 706, 962, 1018, 1086,
1116, 1137

Support, 27, 194, 198, 530, 602, 1144,
1240

Synthesize, 106, 326, 666

Take a position, 264, 396, 1232

Critical Viewing

Analyze, 525, 648, 651, 663, 727, 739, 817,
839, 842, 922, 944, 999, 1067, 1070,
1078, 1101, 1109, 1132, 1211, 1215

Apply, 765

Assess, 570

Compare and contrast, 260, 277, 286, 324,
375, 395, 528, 592, 660, 744, 746, 885,
1201

Connect, 66, 73, 120, 174, 247, 360, 379,
412, 469, 491, 493, 494, 501, 504, 548,
551, 598, 599, 677, 685, 687, 704, 809,
824, 894, 951, 966, 986, 993, 1099,
1141, 1210, 1213

Contrast, 145, 146, 906, 958, 1094, 1165,
1180

Draw conclusions, 158, 193, 1178

Evaluate, 854

Hypothesize, 943, 974

Infer, 49, 80, 272, 309, 316, 319,
320, 340, 600, 823, 849, 896, 899,
1114, 1157

Integrate vocabulary, 658

Interpret, 102, 120, 161, 345, 346, 377,
387, 476, 642, 646, 679, 702,
737, 821, 828, 846, 911,
916, 926, 955, 969, 973, 982, 1017,
1131, 1161, 1183, 1231, 1233, 1235,
1238

Make a judgment, 522, 738

Predict, 98, 118, 243, 257, 285, 289, 815,
871, 1077, 1139, 1175, 1193

Preview, 410, 520

Relate, 124, 156

Speculate, 143, 416, 596, 808, 874, 933

Support, 34, 101, 480, 569

Synthesize, 852

Listening and Speaking

Activities:

Debate, 555, 777

Dialogue, improvised, 1119

Discussion, poetry reading, 691

Group discussion
Big Question, 209, 429
poetry reading, 691
theme, 367

Group screening, 1004

Humorous persuasive speech, 485

Interpretation, oral, 669, 778

Interview, 57, 1251

Media coverage, compare, 1252

Media presentations, analyze, 210

Mock trial, 861

Multimedia presentation of research report, 1034

Persuasive speech, 614

Problem-solving group, 151

Reading
dramatic, 1004
oral, 295

Recollection, oral, 509

Report, oral, 835

Retelling, 1089

Speech
Big Question, 613, 1033
persuasive, 485, 614
view and evaluate, 430

Steps/Tips:

Accuracy, consider, 432

Action, pace, 1089

Anecdotes, use, 555

Arguments
assess, 432
present/support, 861

Audience
assess impact on, 691
meet interests/address concerns, 485

Background, evaluate, 1254

Backup plan, make, 1036

Bias, consider, 212

Body language, use effective, 780

Clarification, ask for, 151

Comments, summarize/evaluate, 151

Communication skills, evaluate, 432

Conclusion
formulate, 151, 1089
prepare engaging, 613
summarize points, 555, 616

Content
evaluate, 212, 432
lan, 616
prepare, 780, 1036

Cultural assumptions, avoid, 212

Delivery, prepare, 616, 780, 1036

Details
include sensory, 509, 1089
note, 209, 1033

Dictionary, use, 295, 835

Director's influence, identify/discuss, 1004

Electronic media, use variety, 1036

Emphasis, compare, 1254

Equipment, choose/check, 1036

Events, order, 1089

Evidence, provide, 555

Eye contact, make, 616, 780, 835, 1119

Fact/opinion, evaluate, 1254

Feedback, revise based on, 509

Feedback Form, use, 212, 780, 1036

Figurative language, use, 485

Gestures, use, 295

Ideas
accurately/coherently convey, 835
advance judgment, 780
express/add to/challenge, 367
organize, 780
support, 151, 780

Illegal statements, look out for, 212

Images, include, 509, 1036

Importance, explain, 1089

Inconsistencies or ambiguities, consider, 212

Internet resources, use, 835

Introduction, present engaging, 555, 613, 616

Knowledge, demonstrate, 57

Language
be alert to charged/manipulative, 212
choose effective, 485
evaluate/compare, 1254
evaluate level, 432
use appropriate, 57, 1119

Listen actively, 1254

Logic, consider, 432

Main points
clarify, 835
jot down/reinforce, 613
summarize, 151

Media Coverage checklist, use, 1254

Mood, pace to reflect, 1089

Narration, pace to reflect action/mood, 1089

Nonverbal communication, evaluate, 432

Note cards, use, 209, 613, 780, 1033, 1251

Notes, take, 57, 151, 1004, 1119

Opinion, support, 616

Organization, choose logical, 616, 861, 1089

Pacing
evaluate/compare, 1254
use to reflect action/mood, 1089

Perspectives, include shifting, 509

Point of view
establish, 509
present/support, 367, 777, 780

Practice, conduct, 295, 616, 669, 1004, 1036, 1251

Presentation, evaluate, 212

Problem, identify, 151

Purpose
evaluate, 1254
identify, 432

Questions
ask/answer, 151, 669, 691, 780, 1251
respond appropriately, 57

Quotations, add, 555

Reader's script, prepare, 616

Relationship, establish, 509

Relevance, consider, 212

Reports, evaluate/compare, 1254

Responses
clarify/illustrate/expand on, 367
prepare, 555

Revised version, present, 509

Rhetorical devices, use, 616, 861

Sensory details, include, 509, 1089

Speech evaluation checklist, use, 432

Stereotypes, be aware of, 212

Strategies, discuss, 151

Style, evaluate, 432

Summarize, 151

Techniques, compare, 1254

Thesaurus, use, 835

Thesis, formulate clear, 485

Tone, vary, 295, 780, 1004

Voice, use effectively, 780, 1004

Word choice, evaluate, 432

Word origins, research, 835

Media Literacy

Camera shots and angles, lxx

Focus and framing, lxxii

Lighting and shadow, lxxii

Persuasive techniques, lxxiv

Special effects, lxxi

Special techniques, lxxiii

Text and graphics, lxxv

Research and Technology

Activities:

Advertising poster, 1005

Biographical brochure, 1219

Bulletin board display on Vreeland, 27

Cover letter and résumé, 575

Daily observation journal, 87

Film "influences" chart, 1187

Literary history report, 731

Multimedia presentation, 1005

Report
  on sources, 267

Research summary, 399

Spreadsheet, 179

Visual arts presentation, 749

Women's history report, 1005

Steps/Tips:

Accuracy, evaluate, 267, 731

Action verbs, use, 575

Biographical dictionary, use, 1219

Chart, create, 87

Comments, ask for, 399

Complexities, identify, 267

Computer software, use, 87, 179, 1005, 1219

Data, review, 179

Design principles, use appropriate, 575, 1219

Details, include, 179, 1219

Director's influence, discuss/chart, 1187

Discrepancies, identify, 267

Expectations, anticipate/address, 399

Format, find/follow suitable, 575

Graph, create, 87

Ideas, jot down, 267

Information
  add interesting, 1005
  choose significant/integrate, 731
  order, 1005

Internet resources, use, 399, 731, 1005, 1219

Library resources, use, 399, 731, 1005, 1219

Misunderstandings, anticipate/address, 399

Opinions, jot down, 267

Paraphrase, 1005

Proofread carefully, 575

Props, use, 749

Questions, address, 267, 399

Quotations, add, 27

Reliability, evaluate, 267, 731

Sources
  document, 1005
  use variety/evaluate, 267, 731

Summary, write/share, 87

Technical terms, explain, 399

Text features, identify/evaluate, 267

Visual aids, use, 749, 1005

Test Practice

Reading for Information

Comparing, 95, 187, 305, 407, 517, 583, 699, 757, 867, 1013, 1127, 1227

Reading, 216, 436, 620, 784, 1040, 1258

Literary Skills, 214, 434, 618, 782, 1038, 1256

Reading Skills, 88, 180, 296, 400, 510, 576, 692, 750, 862, 1006, 1120, 1220

Vocabulary Skills, 217, 437, 621, 785, 1041, 1259

Writing and Language Conventions, 218, 438, 622, 786, 1042, 1260

Writing for Assessment:

Connecting Across Texts, 89, 181, 297, 401, 511, 577, 693, 751, 863, 1121, 1221

Drama, 862, 1007, 1039, 1043

Fiction/nonfiction, 88, 180, 215, 219

Nonfiction, 510, 576, 619, 623

Poetry, 692, 750, 783, 787

Short story, 296, 400, 435, 439

Themes in oral tradition, 1120, 1220, 1257, 1261

Timed, 95, 187, 305, 407, 517, 583, 699, 757, 867, 1013, 1127, 1227

Index of Features

Boldface numbers indicate pages where terms are defined.

Assessment Workshops

Cumulative Review, 212, 432, 616, 780, 1036, 1254

Performance Tasks, 216, 436, 620, 784, 1040, 1258

Background

Age of Chivalry, The, 1207
Age of Discovery, The, 167
Allusion, 642, 659
Ancient Greece, 808
Ancient Greek Theater, 810
Ancient Rome, 889
Atomic Age, The, 283
Battlegrounds of Flanders, 738
Before Computers, 117
Black Death, The, 371
British View of India, The, 31
Celebrities, 704
Censorship in Argentina, 410
Circus Families, 45
Cold-Water Swimming, 61
Coming to America, 559
Courtship and Marriage in Old Mexico, 271
Degas and Impressionism, 567
Dialect, 241, 653, 658
Elizabethan England, 884
Elizabethan Theater, 886A
Enemy of the People, An, 870
Family Feud, 813
Franco-Prussian War, 1233
Great Leader, A, 1093
Greek Gods, The, 1065
Hinduism, 1107
Holocaust, The, 541
Horses in America, 1075
India's Hot Season, 137
Instinct vs. Intelligence, 463
Japanese Americans, 587
Julius Caesar, 889

Jobs and World War II, 77
Kiowa, 595
Landless in Russia, 337
Legends of King Arthur, 1155, 1173
Libraries, 499
Marcovaldo, 383
Marian Anderson, 98
Misty Poets, The, 765
Money Lending, 255
Navigation, 473
Nigerian Civil War, The, 357
Parlors and Sun Parlors, 489
Raisin in the Sun, A, 1017
Shakespearean Theater, The, 884, 889, 891
Sonnets, 677, 687
Tides, 155
Writer in Exile, A, 547
Yankees and Knights, 1191

Big Question, The

Can anyone be a hero? 1048, 1049
Independent Reading, 1255
Reading for Information, 1124, 1126, 1224, 1226
Themes, 1072, 1086, 1104, 1116, 1137, 1144, 1170, 1184, 1204, 1216, 1232, 1240
Writing About, 1064, 1074, 1092, 1106, 1129, 1154, 1172, 1190, 1206, 1229, 1251

Can progress be made without conflict? 222, 223
Independent Reading, 433
Reading for Information, 302, 304, 404, 406
Short Stories, 252, 264, 280, 292, 313, 326, 354, 364, 380, 396, 413, 418
Writing About, 240, 254, 270, 282, 307, 336, 356, 370, 382, 409, 429

Does all communication serve a positive purpose? 626, 627
Independent Reading, 781
Reading for Information, 696, 698, 754, 756
Poetry, 654, 666, 680, 688, 703, 706, 722, 728, 740, 746, 763, 766

Writing About, 640, 656, 674, 682, 701, 716, 724, 734, 742, 759, 777

Is there a difference between reality and truth? 2, 3
Fiction/Nonfiction, 42, 54, 74, 84, 103, 106, 134, 148, 164, 176, 194, 198
Independent Reading, 213
Reading for Information, 92, 94, 184, 186
Writing About, 30, 44, 60, 76, 97, 116, 136, 154, 166, 189, 209

To what extent does experience determine what we perceive?, 790, 791
Drama, 832, 858, 876, 912, 936, 962, 982, 1000, 1018
Independent Reading, 1037
Reading for Information, 866, 1008, 1012
Writing About, 812, 838, 869, 888, 1015, 1033

What kind of knowledge changes our lives? 442, 443
Independent Reading, 617
Reading for Information, 514, 516, 580, 582
Nonfiction, 470, 482, 496, 506, 524, 530, 544, 552, 564, 572, 594, 602
Writing About, 462, 472, 488, 498, 519, 540, 546, 558, 566, 585, 613

Communications Workshop

Analyzing Media Messages, 210
Comparing Media Coverage, 1252
Delivering a Multimedia Presentation, 1034
Delivering a Persuasive Speech, 614
Delivering an Oral Interpretation of a Literary Work, 778
Viewing and Evaluating a Speech, 430

Comparing Literary Works

Archetypal Narrative Patterns, 1128, 1145
Author's Purpose, 584, 603
Character Motivation, 1014, 1019
Humorous Writing, 518, 531
Irony and Paradox, 188, 199

Points of View, 306, 327

Style, 96, 107

Theme, 758, 767

Themes and Worldviews, 1228, 1241

Tone in Fiction and Nonfiction, 408, 419

Tone and Mood, 700, 707

Universal and Culturally Specific
  Themes, 868, 877

Extended Study

Antigone, 808

Tragedy of Julius Caesar, The, 884

Independent Reading

Can anyone be a hero? 1260

Can progress be made without conflict?
  438

Does all communication serve a positive
  purpose? 786

Is there a difference between reality and
  truth? 218

To what extent does experience determine what we perceive? 1042

What kind of knowledge changes our
  lives? 622

Reading for Information

Atlas, 753

Book Review, 1223

Course Catalog, 581

Drama Review, 865, 866

Feature Article, 91

Interview, 1123

Job Application, 1009

Magazine Article, 755

Movie Review, 1225

News Release, 303

Newsletter, 93

Newspaper Editorial, 403

Newspaper Features, 91

Primary Source, 182, 405

Public Document, 1011, 1125

Research Source, 578

Signs, 694

Technical Article, 298

Technical Directions, 512

User's Guide, 512

Web Site, 182, 694

Literary Analysis Workshop

Drama, 792–807

Essays and Speeches, 444–459

Fiction and Nonfiction, 4–27

Poetry, 628–637

Short Stories, 224–237

Themes in Literature: Heroes and
  Dreamers, 1048–1061

Literature in Context

Architecture Connection

Architectural Features, 388

Culture Connection

Ancient Greek Funeral Rites, 844
Griot: The Mind of the People, 1103
Mexican American Pride, 503
Roman Augurs, 928
Traditional Great Plains Culture, 1081
Twelve Olympian Gods, The, 1068

Geography Connection

Antarctica: The Coldest Place on
Earth, 69
Nigerian Civil War, 362

History Connection

American Revolution, The, 563
Babylonian Captivity, The, 321
Emancipation of the Serfs, The, 350
Encyclopedias and the Enlightenment,
26
Great Migration, The, 249
Roman Forum, The, 942
Roman Senate, The, 930
Roman Society, 900
Roman Triumphs, 991
San Francisco and the Gold Rushes, 83
Tournaments, 1162
Voyages of Captain James Cook, The, 175

Humanities Connection

Greek Chorus, 830
Stoicism, 976

Language Connection

Archaic Word Forms, 918
Spanish Vocabulary, 274

Science Connection

Eclipses, 1199
Longitude and Latitude, 478
Physics, 129
Studying Animal Behavior, 468

World Events Connection

Repression in the Soviet Union, 550

Vocabulary Workshop

Borrowed and Foreign Words, 1032

Connotation and Denotation, 776

Idioms, Jargon, and Technical Terms, 1250

Using a Dictionary and Thesaurus, 208

Word Origins, 428

Words With Multiple Meanings, 612

Writing Workshop: Work in Progress

Argumentative Text: Analytic Response to Literature

Prewriting, 731, 749
Writing, 768

Argumentative Text: Letter to the Editor

Prewriting, 485, 509
Writing, 532

Argumentative Text: Persuasive Essay

Prewriting, 555, 575
Writing, 604

Explanatory Text: Cause-and-Effect Essay

Prewriting, 151, 179
Writing, 200

Explanatory Text: Descriptive Essay

Prewriting, 669, 691
Writing, 708

Explanatory Text: Technical Document

Prewriting, 1089, 1119
Writing, 1146

Informative Text: Comparison-and-Contrast Essay

Prewriting, 1187, 1219
Writing, 1242

Informative Text: Problem-and-Solution Essay

Prewriting, 367, 399
Writing, 420

Informative Text: Research Report

Prewriting, 1003
Writing, 1020

Narrative Text: Autobiographical Narrative

Prewriting, 57, 87
Writing, 108

Narrative Text: Reflective Essay

Prewriting, 835, 861
Writing, 878

Narrative Text: Short Story

Prewriting, 267, 295
Writing, 328

Index of Authors and Titles

Notes: Page numbers in *italics* refer to biographical information; Nonfiction and informational text appears in red.

A

Achebe, Chinua, *357,* 358, 1053
Address to Students at Moscow State University, 449
All, 764
Also All, 765
American Idea, The, 560
Anaya, Rudolfo A., *499,* 500
Ancient Greek Theater, 810A
Angelou, Maya, *77,* 78
Antigone
    Part 1, 814
    Part 2, 839
    reviews, 865, 866
Apuleius, Lucius, *1129,* 1130
Artful Research, 23
Arthur Becomes King of Britain, 1156
Ashputtle, 1138
Atoms for Peace, from, lxi

B

Baca, Jimmy Santiago, 633
Bean Eaters, The, 703
Bei Dao, *759,* 764
Benét, Stephen Vincent, *307,* 314
Benson, Sally, *1129,* 1130
Bishop, Elizabeth, *641,* 650
Blackfeet, The, *1075,* 1076
Bradbury, Ray, 9, *283,* 284
Bridegroom, The, 642
Brooks, Gwendolyn, *701,* 703
Browning, Robert, *743,* 744
Burreson, Jay, *167,* 168
By the Waters of Babylon, 314

C

Calvino, Italo, *383,* 384
Cannon, Annie J., lxiii
Carson, Rachel, *155,* 156
Censors, The, 410
Cervantes, Miguel de, *1207,* 1208
Chekhov, Anton, *255,* 256
Cherryh, C. J., 231, 423
Circumference, from, lxiii
Cisneros, Sandra, *97,* 104

Civil Peace, 358
Classifying the Stars, from, lxiii
clustering clouds..., *The,* 680
Connecticut Yankee in King Arthur's Court, from, A, 1192
Conscientious Objector, 726
Contents of the Dead Man's Pocket, 118
Coolidge, Olivia E., *1065,* 1066
Cox, Lynne, *61,* 62
Cupid and Psyche, retelling, 1130

D

Damon and Pythias, retelling, 1230
Danny Deever, 652
Desai, Anita, *137,* 138
Desert Exile: The Uprooting of a Japanese-American Family, from, 586
Dickinson, Emily, *717,* 718, *725,* 728
Do Not Go Gentle Into That Good Night, 678
Dog That Bit People, The, 525
Doll House, from A, 797
Don Quixote, from, 1208
Dorris, Michael, 1223
Douglas, Ann, 91
Duty, Honor, Country, from, lxvii

E

Eady, Cornelius, 634, 636, 771
Early Autumn, 229
Eco, Umberto, *701,* 704
Egyptology Resources, 183
Eisenhower, Dwight D., lxi
Empty Dance Shoes, The, 636
Enemy of the People, from An, 870
Erdrich, Louise, *45,* 46
Everest, from Touch the Top of the World, 452

F

Fahrenheit 451, from, 9
Fear, 702
Feel the City's Pulse?, 91
Finney, Jack, *117,* 118
Fish, The, 650
Friedman, Renée, 185
Frost, Robert, *657,* 658

G

Games at Twilight, 138
García Lorca, Federico, *641,* 648
Garden of Stubborn Cats, The, 384
Glory, 720
Grimm, Jakob and Wilhelm, *1129,* 1138
Guitar, The, 648

H

Hansberry, Lorraine, *1015,* 1016
Henry, O., *307,* 308
Hill, Thomas A., 579
History of the Guitar, The, 579
Hold Fast Your Dreams—and Trust Your Mistakes, 760
How Much Land Does a Man Need?, 338
How to React to Familiar Faces, 704
Hughes, Langston, *97,* 98, 229, *735,* 736
Hwang, David Henry, 1024

I

I Am Offering This Poem, 633
I Know Why the Caged Bird Sings, from, 78
Ibsen, Henrik, 797, *869,* 870
Inaugural Address, from, lix
In Commemoration: One Million Volumes, from, 500
In Flanders Fields, 738
Interactive Dig, 185

J

Jacobs, W. W., *31,* 32
Jakuren, Priest, *683,* 688
Jazz Fantasia, 739
Joel, Billy, *759,* 760
Johnson, James Weldon, *675,* 677

K

Keep Memory Alive, 542
Kelley, William Melvin, *241,* 242
Kipling, Rudyard, *641,* 652
Komachi, Ono, *683,* 688
Komunyakaa, Yusef, *717,* 720
Kraken, The, 745

L

Le Couteur, Penny, *167*, 168
Leader in the Mirror, The, 414
Leap, The, 46
Levertov, Denise, *657*, 659
Like the Sun, 190
Longitude, from, 474
Lorca, Federico García, 648

M

Magdalena Looking, 10
Making a Fist, 664
Making History With Vitamin C, 168
Marginal World, The, 156
Marian Anderson, Famous Concert Singer, 98
Masque of the Red Death, The, 372
Maupassant, Guy de, *1229*, 1233
MacArthur, Douglas, lxvii
McCrae, John, *735*, 738
Meeting at Night, 744
Merriam, Eve, *717*, 722
Metaphor, 722
Mielcarek, Marco, 405
Millay, Edna St. Vincent, *725*, 726
Mistral, Gabriela, *701*, 702
Momaday, N. Scott, *585*, 595
Monkey's Paw, The, 32
Mora, Pat, *409*, 414
Morte d'Arthur, 1174
Mowing, 658
Mühlberger, Richard, *567*, 568
Munro, H. H. *See* Saki
My City, 676

N

Narayan, R. K., *189*, 190, *1107*, 1108
Niane, D. T., *1093*, 1094
Nicastro, Nicholas, lxiii
Niggli, Josephina, *271*, 272
Nobel Lecture, from, 548
Nye, Naomi Shihab, *657*, 664

O

Occupation: Conductorette, 78
Once and Future King, from *The*, 1156
One cannot ask loneliness..., 688
One Thousand Dollars, 308
Open Window, The, 195
Orphan Boy and the Elk Dog, The, 1076

P

Petrunkevitch, Alexander, *463*, 464
Places Left Unfinished at the Time of Creation, from, 1056, 1245
Poe, Edgar Allan, *371*, 372
Poetic Interpretation of the Twist, The, 634
Pride, 727
Problem, A, 256
Prometheus and the First People, retelling, 1066
Pushkin, Alexander, *641*, 642

Q

Quilt of a Country, from *A*, 21
Quindlen, Anna, 21

R

Raisin in the Sun, from *A*, 1016
Rama's Initiation, from the *Ramayana*, 1108
Ravikovitch, Dahlia, *725*, 727
Reagan, Ronald, 449
Reapers, 746
Roethke, Theodore, *683*, 684
Roosevelt, Theodore, lix
Russell, William F., *1229*, 1230

S

Saki, *189*, 195
Sandburg, Carl, *735*, 739
Santos, John Phillip, *1049*, *1056*, 1245
Shakespeare, William, *683*, 687, *890*, 892
Shakespearean Theater, The, 884
Shu Ting, *759*, 765
Sobel, Dava, *473*, 474
Solzhenitsyn, Alexander, *547*, 548
Sonnet 18, 687
Sophocles, *813*, 814
Spider and the Wasp, The, 464
Spring and All, 665
Stearns, Rich, lxv
Street of the Cañon, The, 272
Strudwick, Nigel, 183
Sun Parlor, The, 490
Sundiata: An Epic of Old Mali, from, 1094
Swimming to Antarctica, from, *62*

T

Tell all the Truth but tell it slant—, 728
Tennyson, Lord Alfred, *743*, 745, *1173*, 1174
Tepeyac, 104
Thank Heaven for Little Girls, from, lxv

There Will Come Soft Rains, 284
Things Fall Apart, from, 1053
Thomas, Dylan, *675*, 679
Threads of Time, The, 231
Thurber, James, *519*, 525
Tibet Through the Red Box, from, 799
Toast to the Oldest Inhabitant: The Weather of New England, A, 520
Tolstoy, Leo, *337*, 338
Toomer, Jean, *743*, 746
Toshiyori, Minamoto no, *675*, 680
Touch the Top of the World, from, 452
Tragedy of Julius Caesar, The
   Act I, 892
   Act II, 916
   Act III, 940
   Act IV, 966
   Act V, 986
Tree Telling of Orpheus, A, 659
Tsurayuki, Ki no, *675*, 680
Twain, Mark, *519*, 520, *1191*, 1192
Two Friends, 1233

U

Uchida, Yoshiko, *585*, 586

V

Valenzuela, Luisa, *409*, 410
Visit to Grandmother, A, 242
Voices from the Wall, 405
Vreeland, Susan, *5*, 10, 22, 203

W

Waking, The, 684
Was it that I went to sleep..., 688
Way to Rainy Mountain, from *The*, 595
Weary Blues, The, 736
Weihenmayer, Erik, 452
West, Dorothy, *489*, 490
What Makes a Degas a Degas? 568
When I went to visit..., 680
White, T. H., *1155*, 1156
White, Theodore H., *559*, 560
Wiesel, Elie, *541*, 542
Williams, William Carlos, *657*, 665
Wind—tapped like a tired Man, The, 718

Acknowledgments

Dr. Renee Friedman "Archaeology's Interactive Dig - Narmer's Temple: Week 1" by Renee Friedman from *http://www.archaeology.org* Copyright © 2003 Archaeological Institute of America. Used by permission.

Garmin International, Inc. "GPS Quick Start Guide" from *www.garmin.com*. Copyright © 2004 Garmin Ltd. or its subsidiaries. Used by permission.

Sanford J. Greenburger Associates "The Threads of Time" by C.J. Cherryh from *The Collected Short Fiction of C.J. Cherryh*. First Printing, February 2004. All rights reserved. Used by permission.

Grove/Atlantic, Inc. "Tanka: The Clustering Clouds" from *Anthology of Japanese Literature* by Minamoto no Toshiyori, translated by Donald Keene. Copyright © 1965 by Grove Atlantic, Inc. Used by permission.

Harcourt, Inc. "The Garden of Stubborn Cats" by Italo Calvino from *Marcovaldo of the Seasons in the City*, copyright © 1963 by Giulio Einaudi editore s.p.a., Torino. English translation by William Weaver copyright © 1983 by Harcourt, Inc. and Martin Secker & Warburg, Ltd. "How to React to Familiar Faces" from *How to Travel with a Salmon & Other Essays* by Umberto Eco, copyright © Gruppo Editoriale Fabbri, Bompiani, Sonzogno, Etas S.p.A., English translation by William Weaver copyright © 1994 by Harcourt, Inc. "Jazz Fantasia" by Carl Sandburg from *Smoke and Steel*. Copyright © 1920 by Harcourt, Inc. and renewed 1948 by Carl Sandburg. "Antigone" by Sophocles from *Sophocles: The Oedipus Cycle, An English Version*. The Oedipus Cycle: An English Version by Dudley Fitts and Robert Fitzgerald, copyright © 1939 by Harcourt Inc., and renewed 1967 by Dudley Fitts and Robert Fitzgerald. This material may not be reproduced in any form or by any means without the prior written permission of the publisher. **CAUTION:** All rights, including professional, amateur, motion picture, recitation, lecturing, performance, public reading, radio broadcasting, and television are strictly reserved. Inquiries of all rights should be addressed to Harcourt, Inc., Permissions Dept., Orlando, FL 32887. Used by permission of the publisher.

Harper's Magazine "The Leap" by Louise Erdrich from *Harper's Magazine*. Copyright © 1990 by Harper's Magazine Foundation. Used from the March issue by special permission.

Harvard Observatory "Classifying the Stars" by Annie J. Cannon from *The University of Stars*. Cambridge, Mass.: Harvard Observatory, 1926.

Harvard University Press "Tell all the Truth but tell it slant (#1129)", "The Wind-tapped like a tired man (#436)" by Emily Dickinson from *The Poems of Emily Dickinson*, Thomas H. Johnson, ed., Cambridge, Mass.: The Belknap Press of Harvard University Press, Copyright © 1951, 1955, 1979, 1983 by the President and Fellows of Harvard College. Used by permission of the publishers and the Trustees of Amherst College. Copyright © 1951, 1955, byt the President and Fellows of Harvard College. © Copyright 1914, 1914, 1918, 1919, 1924, 1929, 1930, 1932, 1935, 1937, 1942 by Martha Dickinson Bianchi.

Healdsburg Jazz Festival "Healdsburg Jazz Festival Winter 2007 Newsletter" from *www.healdsburgjazzfestival.org*. Used by permission.

Thomas A. Hill "The History of the Guitar" by Thomas A. Hill from *The Guitar: An Introduction of the Instrument*. Copyright © 1973 by Thomas A. Hill. All rights reserved. Used with permission of Thomas A. Hill.

Hispanic Society of America "The Guitar" by Federico García Lorca from *Translations From Hispanic Poets*. Copyright 1938 by The Hispanic Society of America. Used with permission of the Hispanic Society of America.

The Barbara Hogenson Agency, Inc. "The Dog That Bit People" by James Thurber from *My Life and Hard Times*. Copyright © 1933, 1961 by James Thurber. Used by arrangement with Rosemary Thurber and The Barbara Hogenson Agency. All rights reserved.

Houghton Mifflin Company, Inc. "The Marginal World" from *The Edge of the Sea* by Rachel Carson. Copyright © 1955 by Rachel L. Carson, renewed 1983 by Roger Christie. "Prometheus and the First People" (originally titled "The Creation of Man" and "The Coming of Evil") from *Greek Myths* by Olivia E. Coolidge. Copyright © 1949 by Olivia E. Coolidge; copyright renewed © 1977 by Olivia E. Coolidge. Adapted by permission of Houghton Mifflin Company. Text © 1949 by Olivia E. Coolidge. Used by permission of Houghton Mifflin Co. All rights reserved.

David Henry Hwang From "Tibet Through the Red Box" from Act II by David Henry Hwang. Used by permission.

The Jazz Society of Pensacola "The Jazz Society of Pensacola, March 2007 Newsletter" by Andrew R. Metzger from *http://www.jazzpensacola.com*. Copyright © 2001 Jazz Society of Pensacola. Used by permission.

Johnson & Alcock Ltd., London "The Bridegroom" by Alexander Pushkin from *The Bronze Horseman and Other Poems*, Secker & Warburg, 1982. Translation © D.M. Thomas. Used by permission of Johnson and Alcock Ltd., London.

Johnson Outdoors Inc. "Compass Directions and Warranty" by Staff from *www.silvacompass.com* Copyright 2002 Johnson Outdoors Inc. All rights reserved. Used by permission.

Alfred A. Knopf, Inc. From "Swimming to Antarctica: Tales of a Long-Distance Swimmer" by Lynne Cox. Copyright © 2004 by Lynne Cox. "The Weary Blues" by Langston Hughes from *Selected Poems of Langston Hughes*, copyright © 1994 by The Estate of Langston Hughes. Copyright © 1926 Alfred A. Knopf, Inc., Renewed 1954 Estate of Langston Hughes. Used by permission of Alfred A. Knopf, a division of Random House, Inc. All rights reserved.

Little, Brown & Company, Inc. "Theseus" from *Mythology* by Edith Hamilton. Copyright © 1942 by Edith Hamilton. Copyright © renewed 1969 by Dorian Fielding Reid and Doris Fielding Reid. By permission of Little, Brown, and Co., Inc.

Liveright Publishing Corporation "Reapers" by Jean Toomer from *Cane*. Copyright 1923 by Boni & Liveright, renewed 1951 by Jean Toomer. Used by permission of Liveright Publishing Corporation.

Los Angeles Public Library "Los Angeles Public Library: Borrower Services" from *http://www.lapl.org*. Used by permission of the City of Los Angeles.

The Jennifer Lyons Literary Agency, LLC "Fear" by Gabriela Mistral from *Selected Poems of Gabriela Mistral*, translated by Doris Dana. Copyright 1961, 1964, 1970, 1971 by Doris Dana. Used by permission.

Marco Mielcarek "Voices from the Wall: Ich bin ein Berliner" by Marco Mielcarek. Used by permission.

Random House Children's Books "Ashputtle" by Jakob and Wilhelm Grimm translated by Ralph Manheim from *Grimm's Tales for Young and Old: The Complete Stories*, copyright © 1977 by Ralph Manheim. Translation copyright © 1977 by Ralph Manheim. All rights reserved. Used by permission of Random House Children's Books, a division of Random House, Inc.

Marian Reiner, Literary Agent "Metaphor" by Eve Merriam from *It Doesn't Always Have to Rhyme*. Copyright © 1964, 1970, 1973, 1986 by Eve Merriam. Used by permission of Marian Reiner.

Rogers, Coleridge and White, Ltd. "Games at Twilight" by Anita Desai from *Games at Twilight and Other Stories*. Copyright © 1978 by Anita Desai. Used by permission of the author c/o Rogers, Coleridge & White Ltd., 20 Powis Mews, London W11 1JN.

Heyden White Rostow "The American Idea" by Theodore H. White from *The New York Times Magazine, July 6, 1986*. Copyright © 1986 by Theodore H. White. Copyright © 1986 by The New York Times Company. All rights reserved. Used by permission.

St. Martin's Press "Circumference: Eratosthenos and the Ancient Quest to Measure the Globe" by Nicholas Nicastro from *The Astrolabe*. St. Martin's Press, 2008.

Scientific American "The Spider and the Wasp" by Alexander Petrunkevitch from *Scientific American, August, 1952*. Copyright © 1952 by Scientific American, Inc. Used by permission.

The Sheep Meadow Press "Pride" by Dahlia Ravikovitch translated by Chana Bloch and Ariel Bloch from *The Window*. Copyright © 1987 by Chana Bloch. All rights reserved. Used by permission.

Signet Classic *A Doll's House* by Henrik Ibsen from Act I. New York: Signet Classics, 2006. (1879)

Elyse Sommer "A Curtain Up Review: Antigone As Acted and Played by the Three Fates on the Way to Becoming the Three Graces". Review by Elyse Sommer in www.curtainup.com, the online theater magazine. Copyright 2004, Elyse Sommer. Used by permission.

Sonoma County "The County of Sonoma Volunteer Application" from *http://www.sonoma-county.org*. Used by permission.

Talkin' Broadway "Antigone (Theatre Review)" by Matthew Murray from www.talkinbroadway.com. Used by permission.

Jeremy P. Tarcher/Putnam "Making History with Vitamin C (originally titled: Ascorbic Acid)" by Penny Le Couteur and Jay Burreson from *Napoleon's Buttons: How 17 Molecules Changed History*. Copyright © 2003 by Micron Geological Ltd. and Jay Burreson. All rights reserved.

Anthony Thwaite "Tanka: "Was it that I went to sleep"" by Ono no Komachi translated and co-edited by Geoffrey Bownas and Anthony Thwaite from *The Penguin Book of Japanese Verse*. "When I went to visit" by Ki no Tsurayuki translated by Bownas & Thwaite from *The Penguin Book of Japanese Verse*. "One cannot ask loneliness" by Priest Jakuren translated by Bownas & Thwaite from *The Penguin Book of Japanese Verse*. Penguin Books copyright © 1964, revised edition 1998. Translation copyright © Geoffrey Bownas and Anthony Thwaite, 1964, 1998. Used by permission.

UCLA Office of Media Relations "Strong Earth Tides Can Trigger Earthquakes" from *http://www.newsroom.ucla.edu/*. Courtesy of UCLA. Used by permission.

David Unger "The Censors" by Luisa Valenzuela translated by Hortense Carpentier from *Open Door: Stories*. Copyright © translation by David Unger. Used by permission.

University of North Carolina Press The Street of the Canon" by Josefina Niggli from *Mexican Village*. Copyright © 1945 by the University of North Carolina Press, renewed 1972 by Josefina Niggli. Used by permission of the publisher.

U.S. News & World Report Will All the Blue Men End Up in Timbuktu?" by Stefan Lovgren from *US News and World Report, December 7, 1998*. Copyright © 1998 U.S. News & World Report, L.P. All rights reserved. Used by permission.

Viking Penguin, Inc. "Like the Sun" by R.K. Narayan, from *Under the Banyan Tree*. Copyright © 1985 by R. K. Narayan. "My City" by James Weldon Johnson from *Saint Peter Relates an Incident*. Copyright © 1935 by James Weldon John, © renewed 1963 by Grace Nail Johnson. All rights reserved. From "What Makes a Degas a Degas?" by Richard Muhlberger. Published by The Metropolitan Museum of Art, New York, and Viking, a Division of Penguin Putnam Books for Young Readers, copyright © 1993 by The Metropolitan Museum of Art. "What Makes a Degas a Degas?" is a registered trademark of The Metropolitan Museum of Art. All rights reserved.

Susan Vreeland "Artful Research" by Susan Vreeland from *The Writer, January 2002*. Copyright © 2001. "Magdalena Looking" by Susan Vreeland from *Girl in Hacinth Blue*. Copyright © 1999 by Susan Vreeland. Available in hardback: MacAdam-Cage; paperback: Penguin. Used with permission.

W. W. Norton & Company, Inc. "Don Quixote", excerpt from *Don Quixote: A Norton Critical Edition: The Ormsby Translation, Revised*, by Miguel de Cervantes, edited by Joseph Jones and Kenneth Douglas. Copyright © 1981 by W.W. Norton & Company, Inc. Used by permission of W.W. Norton & Company, Inc.

Walker Publishing Company "Imaginary Lines" by Dava Sobel from *Longitude: The True Story of a Lone Genius Who Solved the Greatest Scientific Problem of His Time*. Copyright © Dava Sobel, 1995. All rights reserved. Used by permission.

Wallace Literary Agency, Inc. "Rama's Initiation" from *The Ramayana* by R.K. Narayan. Published by Penguin Books. Copyright © 1972 by R.K. Narayanan. Used by permission of the Wallace Literary Agency, Inc.

Wesleyan University Press "Glory" by Yusef Komunyakaa from *Magic City* (Wesleyan University Press, 1992) Copyright © 1992 by Yusef Komunyakaa and used by permission of Wesleyan University Press.

World Vision Magazine "Thank Heaven for Little Girls" by Rich Stearns from *World Vision Magazine*, Spring 2007. Used by permission.

The Wylie Agency, Inc. "The Garden of Stubborn Cats" by Italo Calvino from *Marcovaldo or the Seasons in the City*. Copyright © 1963 by Guilio Einaudi editore s.p.a., used with the permission of the Wylie Agency Inc. English translation copyright © 1983 by Harcourt Brace Jovanovich, Inc. and Martin Secker & Warburg Limited.

Note: Every effort has been made to locate the copyright owner of material reproduced on this component. Omissions brought to our attention will be corrected in subsequent editions.

Credits

Photo Credits

viii–ix: © James O'Mara/Taxi/Getty Images; x–xi: © James O'Mara/Taxi/ Getty Images; xii–xiii: Flying Colours Ltd./Digital Vision/Getty Images, Inc.; xiv–xv: Flying Colours Ltd./Digital Vision/Getty Images, Inc.; xx–xxi: © Neil Brennan/Canopy Illustration/Veer; xxii–xxiii: © Neil Brennan/Canopy Illustration/Veer; xxiv–xxv: Ron Sanford/CORBIS; xxvi–xxvii: Ron Sanford/ CORBIS; xxviii–xxix: Masterfile; xxx–xxxi: Masterfile; xlviii: Kompaniets Taras/Shutterstock; Gr10 U1 1: © James O'Mara/Taxi/Getty Images; 2: © Alexandra Day/CORBIS; 3: StockTrek/Getty Images; 5: Brand X Pictures/ Getty Images; 6: *Speed Bump* © 2003 Dave Coverly. Reprinted with the permission of Dave Coverly and the Cartoonist Group. All rights reserved; 7: © Bob Krist/CORBIS; 9: *Detail of Head of a Young Woman*, Jan Vermeer, Francis G. Mayer/CORBIS; 10: Corel Professional Photos CD-ROM™; 12: *The Allegory of the Art of Painting*, c. 1670, Jan Vermeer, Kunsthistorisches Museum, Vienna/CORBIS; 15: Corel Professional Photos CD-ROM™; 16: Corel Professional Photos CD-ROM™; 21: t. Getty Images; 21: t. © Dorling Kindersley; 21: t. © Dorling Kindersley; 21: m. © Dorling Kindersley; 23: b. Courtesy of Susan Vreeland; 24: t. Images.com/CORBIS; 26: b. Hulton Archive/Getty Images Inc.; 26: bl. © Dorling Kindersley; 26: bm. Erich Lessing/Art Resource, NY; 26: br. Giraudon//The Bridgeman Art Library, London/New York; 26: br. Corel Professional Photos CD-ROM™; 26: b. © Dorling Kindersley; 31: b. © Alen MacWeeney/CORBIS; 31: tr. © Bettmann/CORBIS; 32: © Alen MacWeeney/CORBIS; 32: m. © Sebastian Derungs/Reuters/Reuters/CORBIS; 33: istockphoto.com; 34: Frederick Ayer III / Photo Researchers, Inc.; 35: © Gregg Roth/Gregg Roth Studios/Sculpture by Andrew Leman; 36–37: border. © Alen MacWeeney/CORBIS; 37: Pamela Hodson/istockphoto.com; 38–39: border. © Alen MacWeeney/CORBIS; 40: istockphoto.com; 40–41: border. © Alen MacWeeney/CORBIS; 42: border. © Alen MacWeeney/CORBIS; 42: tl. istockphoto.com/Nathan Cox; 45: © Thomas Victor; 61: t. AP/Wide World Photos; 61: b. © Fergus Greer/Fergus Greer Studio; 62: © Patrik Giardino/CORBIS; 64: © bülent gültek/istockpho-to.com; 66–67: © Patrik Giardino/CORBIS; 68: © Ty Milford/Aurora/Getty Images; 69: Galen Rowell/CORBIS; 70: Geoff Renner/Robert Harding World Imagery; 78–79: © Kit Kittle/CORBIS; 72: © bülent gültek/istockphoto.com; 73: © Keren Su/Digital Vision /Getty Images; 77: Mansell/Mansell/Time & Life Pictures/Getty Images; 77: tl. Getty Images; 80: Courtesy of the Market Street Railway, San Francisco; 80–81: © Bettmann/CORBIS; 82: Slim Aarons/Hulton Archive/Getty Images; 92: Maps.com; 97: mr. CORBIS; 97: bl. AP/Wide World Photos; 98: © Bettmann/CORBIS; 101: AP/Wide World Photos; 102: Department of the Interior; 104–105: Gina Martin/National Geographic/Getty Images; 105: br. Linda Whitwam/Dorling Kindersley/ Getty Images; 106: © Macduff Everton/CORBIS; 137: t. Colin McPherson/ CORBIS; 137: b. Nancy Sheehan/PhotoEdit; 138: bl. © Kamal Kishore/ Reuters/CORBIS; 138–139: istockphoto.com; 141: © ADNAN ABIDI/Reuters/ CORBIS; 142: © Photographer: Paul Butchard | Agency: Dreamstime.com; 143: Royalty-Free/CORBIS; 145: Chase Swift/CORBIS; 146–147: Nancy Sheehan/PhotoEdit; 155: Photofest; 155: b. © Peter Adams/JAI/CORBIS; 156–157: © Atlantide Phototravel/CORBIS; 158–159: © Brandon D. Cole/ CORBIS; 161: © George D. Lepp/CORBIS; 162: © Riccardo Spila/Grand Tour/ CORBIS; 163: © Arthur Morris/CORBIS; 163: ml. Courtesy of Jay Burreson; 167: tl. Courtesy Penny Le Couteur; 167: tl. RF © Slavoljub Pantelic/istock-photo.com; 168: tl. RF © Slavoljub Pantelic/istockphoto.com; 168: tl. istock-photo.com; 169: *As for Resolution* (oil on canvas), Brooks, Robin /Private Collection, /The Bridgeman Art Library International; 170: b. © Mike Kowalski/Illustration Works/CORBIS; 170: bl. © Stefano Bianchetti/CORBIS; 172: FoodCollection/Superstock; 174: t. James Cook (1728–79) from *Gallery of Portraits*, published 1833 (engraving) (later colouration), English School, (19th century) /Private Collection, Ken Welsh /The Bridgeman Art Library International; 176: Steve Gorton © Dorling Kindersley; 183: t. Barnabas Kindersley/© Dorling Kindersley; 183: b. Corel Professional Photos CD-ROM™; 184: Barnabas Kindersley/© Dorling Kindersley; 186: tl. © courtesy of the Hierakonpolis Expedition - Renee Friedman; 186: tr.

istockphoto.com; 186: m. Ivor Kerslake/The British Museum/© Dorling Kindersley; 186: b. © courtesy of the Hierakonpolis Expedition - Renee Friedman; 189: t. AP/Wide World Photos; 189: b. The Granger Collection, New York; 190: istockphoto.com; 191: istockphoto.com; 192: © John Foxx/ Stockbyte/Getty Images; 193: © John Reader/Time Life Pictures/Getty Images; 194: © John Foxx /Stockbyte/Getty Images; 195: *Through a Window*, 1922, Farmer, Walter (1887–1947) /Private Collection/The Bridgeman Art Library International; 196: © Christie's Images; 198: THOMAS D. MCAVOY/Time & Life Pictures/Getty Images; 200: David Young-Wolff/PhotoEdit Inc.; 203: Prentice Hall; 208: © Alexandra Day/ CORBIS; 210: © Bonnie Kamin/PhotoEdit Inc.; 218 (CL) © Associated Press, (BCR) © Classic Image/Alamy Images, (TR) Getty Images; Gr10 U2 220–221: Flying Colours Ltd./Digital Vision/Getty Images, Inc.; 222: © Stefano Bianchetti/CORBIS; 223: © Bettmann/CORBIS; 225: Mark Shaver/images. com; 226: © The New Yorker Collection 1999 David Sipress from cartoon-bank.com. All Rights Reserved.; 227: © Jim West/Photo Edit; 241: t. Carl Van Vechten, photographer, Permission Van Vechten Trust; 241: b. *Young Man in Blue Suit*, Alice Kent Stoddard /SuperStock; 242: Smithsonian American Art Museum, Washington, D.C. /Art Resource, NY; 245: *Young Man in Blue Suit*, Alice Kent Stoddard /SuperStock; 246: *Haystack*, 1938 (tempera with oil glaze on linen on panel), Benton, Thomas Hart (1889–1975) /Museum of Fine Arts, Houston, Texas, USA, © DACS /Gift of Mr. Frank J. Hevrdejs /The Bridgeman Art Library International; 249: Stock Montage, Inc.; 255: t. © Bettmann/CORBIS; 255: b. © José Fuste Raga/Age Fotostock; 256: Private Collection, Roy Miles Fine Paintings /The Bridgeman Art Library; 258: Lebrecht Music & Arts; 261: *Candelabra*, 2003 (oil on canvas), Ireland, William (Contemporary Artist) /Private Collection, /The Bridgeman Art Library International; 263: © SuperStock, Inc. / SuperStock; 271: *Reina Xochtl* (gouache on newspaper) by Alfredo Ramos Martinez (1872–1946); 272: *Dance in Tehuantepec*, 1935, Diego Rivera, Los Angeles Museum of Art, Gift of Mr. and Mrs. Milton W. Lipper, from the Milton W. Lipper Estate. Photograph ©2003 Museum Associates/LACMA. ©Banco de Mexico Diego Rivera and Frida Kahlo Museums Trust Av. Cinco de Mayo No. 2, Col. Centro, Del. Cuauhtemoc 06059, Mexico, D.F. Reproduction authorized by the Instituto Nacional de Belles Artes y Literatura; 275: Images.com/CORBIS; 277: John Newcomb/SuperStock; 279: *Reina Xochtl* (gouache on newspaper) by Alfredo Ramos Martinez (1872–1946); 283: t. Thomas Victor; 283: *The Body of a House #5 of 8.* © Robert Beckmann 1993, oil on canvas, 69" x 96 1/2". Collection; Nevada Museum of Art, Reno. Photo by Tony Scodwell; 285: *The Body of a House #1 of 8.* © Robert Beckmann 1993, oil on canvas, 69" x 96 1/2". Collection; Nevada Museum of Art, Reno. Photo by Tony Scodwell; 286: *The Body of a House #2 of 8.* © Robert Beckmann 1993, oil on canvas, 69" x 96 1/2". Collection; Nevada Museum of Art, Reno. Photo by Tony Scodwell; 289: *The Body of a House #4 of 8.* © Robert Beckmann 1993, oil on canvas, 69" x 96 1/2". Collection; Nevada Museum of Art, Reno. Photo by Tony Scodwell; 291: *The Body of a House #5 of 8.* © Robert Beckmann 1993, oil on canvas, 69" x 96 1/2". Collection; Nevada Museum of Art, Reno. Photo by Tony Scodwell; 299: tl. W. Kenneth Hamblin; 299: tr. PhotoDisc, Inc./ Getty Images; 299: b. W. Kenneth Hamblin; 299: bkgrnd. istockphoto.com; 300: istockphoto.com; 307: t. © Bettmann/CORBIS; 307: b. AP/Wide World Photos; 308: CORBIS; 312: Don Mason/CORBIS; 314–315: © David Tipling / Alamy; 317: *Sydney Harbour Bridge*, 1995 (oil on canvas), Blackall, Ted (Contemporary Artist) /Private Collection, /The Bridgeman Art Library International; 318: © Marshall Arisman; 320: © Marshall Arisman; 322: © Christel Tranberg/Getty Images; 324: *Tudor City at night, Overlooking East River*, 1998 (oil on canvas), Gibbs, Nicholas (Contemporary Artist) /Private Collection, /The Bridgeman Art Library International; 337: t. L. N. Tolstoi, I. E. Repin, Sovfoto/Eastfoto; 337: b. Scala /Art Resource, NY; 338: Corel Professional Photos CD-ROM™; 340: *The Toast*, G.K. Totybadse, Scala/Art Resource, NY; 342: Tate, London /Art Resource, NY; 345: Scala /Art Resource, NY; 346: Scala /Art Resource, NY; 350: © Bettmann/CORBIS; 353: © SuperStock, Inc. /SuperStock; 357: AP/Wide World Photos;

357: Campbell William/CORBIS; 358: Betty Press/Woodfin Camp & Associates; 360: © John Curtis Photography; 363: Corel Professional Photos CD-ROM™; 371: t. © Bettmann/CORBIS; 371: b. © Stefan Grambart; 372: © Stefan Grambart; 375: © Stefan Grambart; 376: © Stefan Grambart; 379: © Stefan Grambart; 380: © Stefan Grambart; 383: t. © Ulf Andersen/Getty Images; 383: b. istockphoto.com; 384: Frank Siteman/Stock, Boston; 386: Jane Burton © Dorling Kindersley; 387: M.C. Escher's *Relativity*. Copyright © 2004 The M.C. Escher Company-Baarn-Holland. All rights reserved.; 389: ©Russell Illig/PhotoDisc/Getty Images; 392: istockphoto. com; 395: Ingram Publishing /SuperStock; 396: istockphoto.com; 403: David Turnley/CORBIS; 404: Alexandra Avakian/Getty Images; 405: AP/Wide World Photos; 406: © Bernard Bisson & Thierry Orban/Sygma/CORBIS; 405–406: istockphoto.com; 409: t. Diaz-Piferrer; 409: b. Cheron Bayna; 410: © Smithsonian American Art Museum, Washington, D.C./Art Resource; 411: *Man Writing*, 2004 (oil on canvas) by Ruth Addinall (Contemporary Artist), Private Collection/The Bridgeman Art Library; 412: © Patti Mollica / SuperStock; 414: bkgrnd. istockphoto.com; 414: bkgrnd. istockphoto.com; 414: m. istockphoto.com; 414: r. istockphoto.com; 414: tl. istockphoto.com; 414: tr. istockphoto.com; 416: © Bob Daemmrich; 416–417: © Felicia Martinez /Photo Edit; 420: Will Hart/PhotoEdit Inc.; 423: Prentice Hall; 430: © Mike Booth /Alamy; 438 (CL) © Stock Montage/SuperStock; **Gr10 U3** 442: © Ian Shaw /Alamy; 443: © JAUBERT BERNARD /Alamy; 445: © Images.com/CORBIS; 446: PEANUTS © United Feature Syndicate, Inc.; 447: © Michael Newman /Photo Edit; 449: Getty Images; 450–451: Courtesy of Didrik Johnck; 453: Courtesy of Didrik Johnck; 454: Courtesy of Didrik Johnck; 456: Courtesy of Didrik Johnck; 463: Time Life Pictures/Getty Images; 463: Brian P. Kenney/Animals Animals; 464: Brian P. Kenney/Animals Animals; 465: © Minden Pictures, Inc.; 467: © Dorling Kindersley; 468: Getty Images; 469: © OSF/M. Fogden/Animals Animals; 470: © Geoff Dann/Dorling Kindersley; 473: t. AP/Wide World Photos; 473: b. istockphoto.com; 474–475: © Mike Agliolo/CORBIS; 475: istockphoto.com; 476: Les Stone/CORBIS; 479: *As for Resolution* (oil on canvas), Brooks, Robin (Contemporary Artist) / Private Collection, /The Bridgeman Art Library International; 480: *Portrait of George III in his Coronation Robes* (1738–1820), © 1760 (oil on canvas), Ramsay, Allan (1713–1784) /Private Collection, /The Bridgeman Art Library International; 481: l. The Bridgeman Art Library, London/New York; 481: r. The Bridgeman Art Library, London/New York; 482: istockphoto.com; 489: AP/Wide World Photos; 490: © Connie Hayes /Images.com; 493: © Colin Bootman/Bridgeman Art Library/Getty Images; 495: © Connie Hayes / Images.com; 499: Courtesy of the author; 500: © Alberto Ruggieri/ Illustration Works/CORBIS; 503: l. Vic Bider/PhotoEdit; 503: r. Michael Newman/PhotoEdit; 504: © Paul Vismara /Images.com; 515: Nick Koudis/ Getty Images; 516: Nick Koudis/Getty Images; 519: t. Courtesy of the Library of Congress; 519: b. © Bettmann/CORBIS; 520: istockphoto.com; 521: l. istockphoto.com; 521: m. istockphoto.com; 521: r. istockphoto.com; 522: istockphoto.com; 525: *My Life and Hard Times* Copyright ©1933 by James Thurber. Copyright © renewed 1961 by James Thurber. Reprinted by arrangement with Rosemary A. Thurber and The Barbara Hogenson Agency.; 528: *My Life and Hard Times* Copyright ©1933 by James Thurber. Copyright © renewed 1961 by James Thurber. Reprinted by arrangement with Rosemary A. Thurber and The Barbara Hogenson Agency.; 541: © Bettmann/CORBIS; 542: © Bettmann/CORBIS; 543: © CORBIS; 544: © Alain Nogues/CORBIS SYGMA; 547: t. © Lesegretain/CORBIS Sygma; 547: b. Jacques Langevin/CORBIS SYGMA; 548: t. Jacques Langevin/CORBIS SYGMA; 548: bl. Penguin Signet Classics; 548: br. © Bettmann/CORBIS; 550: t. Dean Conger/CORBIS; 550: b. Private Collection/The Bridgeman Art Library, London/New York; 551: Hulton Archive/Getty Images Inc.; 559: t. Carl Mydans/Time Life Pictures/Getty Images; 559: b. istockphoto.com; 560: istockphoto.com; 561: istockphoto.com; 562: © SuperStock, Inc. / SuperStock; 563: l. *Thomas Jefferson* (1743–1826) (colour litho), Peale, Rembrandt (1778–1860) /Private Collection, Peter Newark American Pictures / The Bridgeman Art Library International; 563: r. *John Adams* (oil on canvas), Otis, Bass (1784–1861) (attr.to) /© Collection of the New-York Historical Society, USA, /The Bridgeman Art Library International; 568: Image copyright © The Metropolitan Museum of Art /Art Resource, NY; 571: Photograph © 2008 Museum of Fine Arts, Boston. All Rights Reserved.; 572: *Self Portrait* (oil on canvas), Degas, Edgar (1834–1917) / Private Collection, /The Bridgeman Art Library International; 581: t. Ted Foxx/Alamy; 581: b. David McNew/Getty Images; 582: Ted Foxx/Alamy; 585: Thomas Victor; 586: © Bettmann/CORBIS; 586–587: istockphoto.com; 588–589: istockphoto.com; 589: © CORBIS; 590–591: istockphoto.com; 591: © Zen Shui /SuperStock; 592: © Seattle Post-Intelligencer Collection; Museum of History and Industry /CORBIS; 592–593: border. istockphoto. com; 593: © Bettmann/CORBIS; 594: istockphoto.com; 595: © Stapleton Collection/CORBIS; 596: © CORBIS; 599: © Joseph Sohm; *Visions of America*/CORBIS; 600: © Lindsay Hebberd/CORBIS; 604: Jose Luis Palaez, Inc./CORBIS; 607: Prentice Hall; 612: © Ian Shaw /Alamy; 614: © Myrleen Ferguson Cate /Photo Edit; **Gr10 U4** 624–625: © Neil Brennan/Canopy Illustration/Veer; 626: ©Spencer Grant /Photo Edit; 626: istockphoto.com; 627: © wsr /Alamy; 630: CALVIN AND HOBBES © 1999 Watterson. Reprinted with permission of UNIVERSAL PRESS SYNDICATE. All rights reserved.; 631: © David Young-Wolff /Photo Edit; 633: t. © Hulton-Deutsch Collection/CORBIS; 633: b. © Hulton-Deutsch Collection/CORBIS; 634: © Bettmann/CORBIS; 641: t. The Granger Collection, New York; 641: mt. AP/Wide World Photos; 641: mb. Art Resource, NY; 641: b. Courtesy of the Library of Congress; 642: *The Lights of Marriage*, (detail) Marc Chagall, Kunsthaus, Zurich, ©1998 Artists Rights Society (ARS), New York/ADAGP, Paris; 645: Giraudon /Art Resource, NY; 646: Smithsonian Banque d'Images, ADAGP / Art Resource, NY; 648: *The Old Guitarist*, 1903, Pablo Picasso, Spanish, 1881–1973, oil on panel 122.9 x 82.6 cm, Helen Birch Bartlett Memorial Collection, 1926.253. Reproduction, The Art Institute of Chicago, © 2004 Estate of Pablo Picasso/Artists Rights Society (ARS), New York; 650: *The Black Carp* (woodblock print), Harunobu, Gakutei (fl. 1818–30) /Private Collection, Photo © Held Collection /The Bridgeman Art Library International; 650–651: © Micha Pawlitzki/zefa/CORBIS; 652: © Bettmann/CORBIS; 654: *The Royal Fusiliers*, 1876 (w/c on paper), Simkin, Richard (1840–1926) /Private Collection, © Malcolm Innes Gallery, London, UK / The Bridgeman Art Library International; 657: b. National Portrait Gallery, Smithsonian Institution /Art Resource, NY; 657: ml. AP/Wide World Photos; 657: ml. Photo by James Evans; 657: t. Time Life Pictures/Getty Images; 658: *Haymaking*, 1898, Alfred Glendenning, Tate Gallery, London/ Art Resource, NY; 659: *The Oak of Flagey, called Vercingetorix*, Courbet, Gustave (1819–1877) /Pennsylvania Academy of the Fine Arts, Philadelphia, USA, /The Bridgeman Art Library International; 660: Attic red-figure hydria, decorated with a scene of the Thracian bard Thamyris being deprived of sight and voice, from the Group of Polygnotus, from Greece, c. 440–420 B.C. (ceramic), / © Ashmolean Museum, University of Oxford, UK, /The Bridgeman Art Library International; 661: *Reconstruction of the Queen's Lyre,* from Ur, c. 2600–2400 B.C., Mesopotamian /British Museum, London, UK, /The Bridgeman Art Library International; 662: © Stefan Klein/istockphoto.com; 663: Corel Professional Photos CD-ROM™; 664: Kamil Vojnar; 665: © Catherine Hazard /SuperStock; 675: t. The Granger Collection, New York; 675: mt. *Dylan Thomas* (1914–1953), c. 1937–1938 (oil on canvas), John, Augustus Edwin (1878–1961)/© National Museum and Gallery of Wales, Cardiff/www.bridgeman.co.uk; 675: mb. Minamoto Toshiyori, Heibonsha/Pacific Press Service; 675: b. Kino Tsurayuki, Heibonsha/Pacific Press Service; 676: © Patti Mollica /SuperStock; 678: *Old Man in Sorrow (On the Threshold of Eternity)* 1890 (oil on canvas), Gogh, Vincent van (1853–1890) /Rijksmuseum Kroller-Muller, Otterlo, Netherlands, /The Bridgeman Art Library International; 680: © Christie's Images; 683: t. Bentley Historical Library; 683: mt. SuperStock; 683: mb. Jakuren Houshi, Heibonsha/Pacific Press Service; 683: b. Onono-komachi, Heibonsha/Pacific Press Service; 684: *Cumberland Hills*, 1948 (oil on board), Nicholson, Winifred (1893–1981) /Arts Council Collection, Hayward Gallery, London, UK, /The Bridgeman Art Library International; 686: Frances Howard, Isaac Oliver, Victoria and Albert Museum/Art Resource, NY; 686: border. Lisa Thornberg /istockphoto.com; 688: *View of the Summer Palace,* Peking (colour on silk), Chinese School /Bibliotheque Nationale, Paris, France, /The Bridgeman Art Library International; 695: © Michael Freeman/CORBIS; 696: © Michael Freeman/CORBIS; 697: Tetra Images/Getty Images; 701: t. © Bettmann/CORBIS; 701: m. © Bettmann/CORBIS; 701: b. J. P. Gauthier/Globe Photos; 702: © Christie's Images /

Staff Credits

The people who made up the Pearson Prentice Hall Literature team—representing design, editorial, editorial services, education technology, manufacturing and inventory planning, market research, marketing services, planning and budgeting, product planning, production services, project office, publishing processes, and rights and permissions—are listed below. Boldface type denotes the core team members.

Tobey Antao, Margaret Antonini, Rosalyn Arcilla, Penny Baker, James Ryan Bannon, Stephan Barth, **Tricia Battipede,** Krista Baudo, Rachel Beckman, Julie Berger, Lawrence Berkowitz, Melissa Biezin, **Suzanne Biron,** Rick Blount, **Marcela Boos, Betsy Bostwick,** Kay Bosworth, Jeff Bradley, Andrea Brescia, Susan Brorein, Lois Brown, **Pam Carey,** Lisa Carrillo, **Geoffrey Cassar,** Patty Cavuoto, Doria Ceraso, Jennifer Ciccone, Jaime Cohen, Rebecca Cottingham, Joe Cucchiara, Jason Cuoco, **Alan Dalgleish, Karen Edmonds, Irene Ehrmann,** Stephen Eldridge, Amy Fleming, Dorothea Fox, Steve Frankel, Cindy Frederick, Philip Fried, Diane Fristachi, Phillip Gagler, **Pamela Gallo,** Husain Gatlin, **Elaine Goldman,** Elizabeth Good, John Guild, Phil Hadad, Patricia Hade, Monduane Harris, Brian Hawkes, Jennifer B. Heart, Martha Heller, John Hill, Beth Hyslip, Mary Jean Jones, Grace Kang, Nathan Kinney, Roxanne Knoll, **Kate Krimsky,** Monisha Kumar, Jill Kushner, Sue Langan, Melisa Leong, Susan Levine, Dave Liston, **Mary Luthi, George Lychock, Gregory Lynch, Joan Mazzeo, Sandra McGloster,** Eve Melnechuk, Kathleen Mercandetti, Salita Metha, Artur Mkrtchyan, Karyn Mueller, Alison Muff, Christine Mulcahy, Kenneth Myett, Elizabeth Nemeth, Stefano Nese, Carrie O'Connor, April Okano, Kim Ortell, Sonia Pap, Raymond Parenteau, Dominique Pickens, Linda Punskovsky, **Sheila Ramsay,** Maureen Raymond, Mairead Reddin, **Erin Rehill-Seker, Renée Roberts, Laura Ross,** Bryan Salacki, Sharon Schultz, Jennifer Serra, **Melissa Shustyk,** Rose Sievers, Christy Singer, Yvonne Stecky, **Cynthia Summers,** Steve Thomas, Merle Uuesoo, Roberta Warshaw, Patricia Williams, Daniela Velez

Additional Credits

Lydie Bemba, Victoria Blades, Denise Data, Rachel Drice, Eleanor Kostyk, Jill Little, Loraine Machlin, Evan Marx, Marilyn McCarthy, Patrick O'Keefe, Shelia M. Smith, Lucia Tirondola, Laura Vivenzio, Linda Waldman, Angel Weyant